PRAISE FOR THE ULTIMATE SCHOLARSHIP BOOK BY GEN AND KELLY TANABE

"Upbeat, well-organized and engaging, this comprehensive tool is an exceptional investment for the college-bound."
—PUBLISHERS WEEKLY

"Gen and Kelly Tanabe are by far the best experts on winning scholarships. Not only will their books help you find scholarships that you qualify for, they will show you how to win them. Soon after applying the strategies in their book, I won a $1,000 scholarship. I couldn't have done it without them. The Tanabes can help you win scholarships too!"
—DOUG WONG, UNIVERSITY OF CALIFORNIA, SAN DIEGO

"A present for anxious parents."
—THE HONOLULU ADVERTISER

"Upbeat tone and clear, practical advice."
—BOOK NEWS

"Unlike other authors, the Tanabes use their experiences and those of other students to guide high school and college students and their parents through the scholarship and financial aid process."
—PALO ALTO DAILY NEWS

"If the Tanabes could earn over $100,000 in scholarships and graduate from an Ivy League institution owing nothing, others can, too."
—STAR-BULLETIN

"This is a helpful, well-organized guide. A good resource for all students."
—KLIATT

"A common sense approach to scholarship searches. The Ultimate Scholarship Book gives a down to earth step by step method of finding, applying for and winning scholarships. The scholarship list has many opportunities for students to showcase their talents for financial reward."
—LYNDA MCGEE, COLLEGE COUNSELOR, DOWNTOWN MAGNETS HIGH SCHOOL, LOS ANGELES

"This guide (has) ... practical tips on where to find scholarships; how to write effective applications, resumes and winning essays; and how to get glowing recommendations and ace scholarship interviews."
—C.E. KING, IOWA STATE UNIVERSITY, CHOICE MAGAZINE

"Getting into college is only half of the game. How to pay for it offers the second big challenge. Whether they qualify for financial need or are just looking for ways to help their parents with this heavy burden, all students will profit from The Ultimate Scholarship Book which both outlines the process of finding financial help for college as well as it provides an extensive and up to date list of current scholarship sources.

"Take these important tips from two experienced writers who are nationally recognized for their expertise on all facets of the college application process. Both members of this impressive husband and wife team paid for their Harvard educations by following the precepts which they share with you now in this easy to read guidebook."
—DAVID MILLER, DIRECTOR OF COLLEGE COUNSELING, STEVENSON SCHOOL, PEBBLE BEACH, CALIFORNIA

Dedication

To our families for shaping who we are.

To Harvard for four of the best years of our lives.

To the many students and friends who made this book possible by sharing their scholarship experiences, secrets, successes and failures.

To all the students and parents who understand that paying for college is a challenging but worthwhile endeavor.

The Ultimate Scholarship Book 2026

Billions of Dollars in Scholarships, Grants and Prizes

Gen and Kelly Tanabe

Winners of over $100,000 in college scholarships and award-winning authors of *Get Free Cash for College* and *How to Write a Winning Scholarship Essay*

- Comprehensive scholarship directory to over 1.5 million awards worth more than $2 billion
- Scholarships for high school and college students of every background, talent and achievement level
- Easy to use indexes to quickly find the best matching scholarships

The Ultimate Scholarship Book 2026: Billions of Dollars in Scholarships, Grants and Prizes

By Gen and Kelly Tanabe

Published by SuperCollege
2713 Newlands Avenue
Belmont, CA 94002
650-395-9655
editor@supercollege.com
www.supercollege.com

Copyright © 2025 by SuperCollege

All rights reserved. No part of this book may be reproduced, stored in a retrieval system, or transmitted, in any form or by any means, electronic, mechanical, photocopying, recording, or otherwise, without the written permission of SuperCollege. This book is protected under International and Pan-American Copyright Conventions.

Credits: Cover: Monica Thomas, www.tlcgraphics.com. Cover photograph: ©iStockphoto.com/Bubaone. Layout: The Roberts Group, www.editorialservice.com. Back cover photograph: Alvin Gee, www.alvingee.com.

Scholarship Data: The scholarship data in this book is copyrighted by SuperCollege. © 2025. All rights reserved. Corrections may be sent to editor@supercollege.com.

Trademarks: All brand names, product names and services used in this book are trademarks, registered trademarks or tradenames of their respective holders. SuperCollege is not associated with any college, university, product, service or vendor.

Disclaimers: The authors and publisher have used their best efforts in preparing this book. It is intended to provide helpful and informative material on the subject matter. Some narratives and names have been modified for illustrative purposes. SuperCollege and the authors make no representations or warranties with respect to the accuracy or completeness of the contents of the book and specifically disclaim any implied warranties or merchantability or fitness for a particular purpose. There are no warranties which extend beyond the descriptions contained in this paragraph. The accuracy and completeness of the information provided herein and the opinions stated herein are not guaranteed or warranted to produce any particular results. It is sold with the understanding that neither the publisher nor the authors are engaged in rendering legal, accounting or other professional services. If legal advice or other expert assistance is required, the services of a competent professional person should be sought. SuperCollege and the authors specifically disclaim any responsibility for any liability, loss or risk, personal or otherwise, which is incurred as a consequence, directly or indirectly, of the use and application of any of the contents of this book.

The Ultimate Scholarship Book is the #1 bestselling scholarship guide based on Nielsen/BookScan sales data of the 2025 editions of comparable titles.

Special Sales: For information on using SuperCollege books in the classroom or special prices for bulk quantities, please contact our Special Sales Department at sales@supercollege.com.

ISBN-13: 978-1-61760-191-0
ISBN-10: 1-61760-191-8

Manufactured in the United States of America
10 9 8 7 6 5 4 3 2 1

Library of Congress ISSN (International Standard Serial Number)
The ultimate scholarship book
ISSN 2644-0555

CONTENTS

1	How to Use the Ultimate Scholarship Book	7
2	Where to Find the Best Scholarships	17
3	How to Win the Scholarships You Find	31
4	How to Write a Winning Scholarship Essay	43
5	The Scholarship Resume	59
6	Getting Great Recommendations	65
7	Ace the Scholarship Interview	73
8	Final Thoughts	87
9	The Ultimate Scholarship Directory	91
10	Scholarship Indexes	551

How to Use the Ultimate Scholarship Book

chapter 1

A Scholarship Book That's Better Than a Website

Is it crazy to say that a bound stack of paper and glue is superior to the high speed bits and bytes of a scholarship website? Absolutely not! Because it is true.

Let us explain.

Unless you're starting out, you've probably used a scholarship website. Typically you fill out a profile questionnaire to provide information about yourself before hitting the "search" button. So far, this seems much easier than using a book.

Until you get your results.

No matter what website you use, there will be an unusually large number of scholarships that aren't good matches. After reading the eligibility requirements, you will discover that only a small handful are worth your time to apply.

You've just discovered the first major weakness of every scholarship website: your life (background, experiences, goals, talents, awards, interests and accomplishments) cannot be defined or summarized by a computer-generated questionnaire.

Your Life is MORE Than a 30-Question Profile

The simple truth is that no computer can match you to scholarships as well as you can. You are a complex individual with a variety of passions, interests and goals. Nothing—person or machine—knows you better than you know yourself.

And think about that profile form. That's the only information the computer has about you. But what if you don't know all the answers? Are you really set on becoming an orthopedic surgeon, or did that just sound cool? Even worse, you are limited by the choices provided on that profile questionnaire. Imagine that you wrote a poem that was published in your town's community newspaper. Should you select "poet" as a future career? Will that trigger a great poetry scholarship? Or maybe under hobbies, you should select "writing and journalism"? Of course, that might trigger a flood of journalism scholarships that wouldn't apply to you. Or maybe, even though your school doesn't have a poetry club, you should still tell the computer that you are a member of one in order to trick it into showing you a sweet poetry award?

Do you see where we're going?

The very fact that you need to give the computer information about yourself while only using the choices the computer provides, without any clue about how those answers will affect your results, almost guarantees that you are going to miss out on some good scholarships. How do you know that because you answered a single question in the way that you did, that you are not missing out on some fantastic scholarship opportunities?

The answer is, you don't.

About Your Authors

What makes us qualified to write *The Ultimate Scholarship Book*? Primarily it's because at one time we were exactly where you are now. We needed money to pay for college, and scholarships turned out to be our only answer. Not only did we do pretty well (winning more than $100,000 in free cash for college) but since then, we've continued to help thousands of students do the same.

Here's our story:

Kelly grew up in Los Angeles and when she got accepted to Harvard (which costs about $83,000 per year!), her family just didn't have the money to pay for it. Gen grew up in Hawaii and faced a similar financial crunch when he got into Harvard. In fact, his father even tried to bribe him to attend his state university by offering him a new car if he would give up his idea of attending the ivy-league college. Even considering the cost of a brand new car, it would have been cheaper for Gen's family to make car payments than pay Harvard tuition!

Since we both had our hearts set on attending a very expensive college that our families could not afford, we had little choice but to become fanatics about applying for scholarships. While we made a lot of beginner mistakes and it was by no means a quick or easy process, we were ultimately successful in winning more than $100,000 in scholarships. It was only because of this money that we were able to attend Harvard and were both able to graduate from college debt free.

As you may have guessed by now, we met while at college. We were actually next door neighbors in the dorm, and we were married a few years after we graduated from Harvard.

Chapter 1:
How to Use the Ultimate Scholarship Book

Knowing first-hand how hard it can be for families to pay for college, we decided to share what we had learned as a result of our own pursuits to find funds for tuition. Our first books were about how to win scholarships and get financial aid. In fact, you can find *1001 Ways to Pay for College* and *How to Write a Winning Scholarship Essay* in bookstores. But despite the success of these books, we found that whenever we spoke to groups of students or parents, the number one question they asked was, "Do you know of scholarships for such-and-such a student?"

At the same time, we were also noticing a growing dissatisfaction from students who only relied on websites for scholarship information. This was somewhat of a mystery to us since we knew of thousands of great scholarships that were available. Why weren't these awards being found? Why wasn't every student applying for these scholarships?

All of this led to our decision to build our own database of scholarships and publish the results in *The Ultimate Scholarship Book*. We have a team of researchers who help us investigate scholarships, verify awards and ensure that the scholarships that make it into the book are the best and most up-to-date possible.

So that's our story and why we feel so passionate about what we write in this book. It's not just a collection of words on paper; it's really the collective experience and intelligence of our own quest for scholarships along with thousands of hours of research by our scholarship staff.

How This Book Overcomes the Disadvantages of Websites

A book has certain advantages over websites; for example, a book can work for you without the necessity of input. In many ways, a book is more flexible than a computer site because you are not penalized for not having an answer to a specific question that is worded in a narrow and inflexible way. Likewise, you are not forced to fit yourself into a predetermined, inflexible category. A book also lets you do the matching, a tool which we have found to be far better than outsourcing that work to some machine.

The Ultimate Scholarship Book is designed to be browsed. Spend an hour with this book and you will be able to evaluate hundreds of scholarships quickly and efficiently. By scanning the descriptions, you (not some computer) can decide if you have the right combination of background, interests or skills to qualify. By seeing all of the possibilities, you remain in control of how you prioritize which awards are right for you.

Now it is true that this is a slower process than using a website. But the trade-off is that it is far more accurate, and accuracy is what it's all about. You're not trying to find hundreds of awards that you may or may not win. Who has time to apply for that many scholarships anyway?! Your goal is to find the best awards that you have highest chances of winning. So while you'll invest more time in the finding of scholarships by using a book, we guarantee that the payoff (which in this case is literally thousands of extra dollars in scholarships) will be worth it.

If the time aspect of using a book versus a website still bothers you, here's one more thought. You can use books practically anywhere—especially when you have downtime. In other words, you can transform the natural wasted time during your day into highly productive scholarship time.

A Dirty Secret of Websites: They're Out-of-Date

It's natural to assume that anything online is more current than something printed on paper. But is this really true? Use a few scholarship websites and you'll soon realize that many are horribly out of date. Does it make you angry? Do you want to demand a refund? Of course not! Most scholarship websites are free services! Now it is true that many so-called "free" websites do actually make money by reselling your information; and once they get this from your profile form, you are of little value to the site. This is very annoying. However, we digress. Our point is that as a free service, there is really very little incentive for the website to maintain a high level of accuracy in their data. You really do get what you pay for with most scholarship websites!

It's a lot different with a book. There are two strong incentives that ensure the data in this book is up-to-date and accurate. The first is that we know once we commit something to paper, it's permanent. That creates a very strong desire to get it right the first time. This degree of permanence—the finality of words on paper—is a huge responsibility for us. Once the book goes to press, it is very difficult and expensive to update a mistake. The second powerful incentive is that you're paying hard earned money for this book! It's not free. Because of this, you expect to receive only the best product. If we don't deliver, we'll hear from you!

Together, these two incentives guarantee that each award in this book has been checked and re-checked. We have a small army of researchers whose only job is to verify each award in the book before it goes to press. We also send out communication twice a year to every scholarship listed to ask the providers themselves to verify and update their information. The end result is that this book is extremely accurate and up-to-date.

We also never keep this book in print for longer than a year—which is what we have found to be the typical time in which scholarships change. So as long as you are buying this book new, you are guaranteed to have the latest information possible.

Given how diligent and thorough our researchers are and the rigorous process we apply to every award we publish, we would happily pit this book against any website!

Another Dirty Secret of Websites: They Don't Actually List Millions of Awards

Here's a controversial statement: Websites often claim to list millions of awards worth billions of dollars, but the truth is that these numbers are just marketing hype. To arrive at these numbers, the websites use the most liberal definitions possible. For example, the Coca-Cola Foundation awards $3.55 million per year to 1,400 students. So the website counts their single listing of the Coca-Cola Foundation Scholarship as being 1,400 awards valued at $3.55 million. Or consider that the Jack Kent Cooke Foundation awards about 100 scholarships for up to $55,000 each. The total value of $5.5 million is added to the website's sum even though you can only win up to $55,000 of this amount. The results are highly inflated numbers.

Now before we claim the high road in this debate, we have to admit that we do the exact same thing! Take a look at the front cover of this book. Our numbers are just as impressive as many scholarship websites. But unlike the websites, we don't hide reality. All you need to do is pick up our book and see how thick it is to know how many awards we have inside. But you can't do this with a website. There is no way to know (and the website will never tell you) how many actual awards they have. They want you to think that they have millions when in reality they often contain no more—and often much less—than what you'll find in this book!

The Bottom Line: Books Can Beat Websites

It should be obvious by now that we are just a little bothered when we hear that websites—just because they are online—are superior to books.

It's just not true.

This is not to say that websites don't have any value. They absolutely do and inside this book, we list a number of websites that we think are worth your time. However, you need to understand that you must go beyond websites if you hope to find the best scholarships. In fact, you need to go beyond books too! The entire next chapter is dedicated to places in which to find scholarships other than books and websites. We highly recommend that you explore all these sources in order to find the best scholarships for you.

Chapter 1:
How to Use the Ultimate Scholarship Book

> **Why Choose *This* Book?**
>
> We know that there are other books that provide directories of scholarships, so why choose this one?
> - Discover the best scholarships for you with awards in the humanities, academics, public service, extracurricular activities, talents, athletics, religion, ethnicity, social science and science based on career goals and more.
> - Find scholarships that are not based on grades.
> - Get all the information you need in one place with the application details, eligibility requirements, deadlines, contact information and website addresses.
> - Find scholarships you can use at any college.
> - Avoid wasting money on scholarship competitions that require a fee to enter.
> - Save time and find the best scholarships that fit you with the easy-to-use indexes.
> - Access the most up-to-date information that has been checked and double-checked.
> - Learn not only how to find scholarships but how to win them! Get insider advice from judges and scholarship winners.

Common Scholarship Myths Busted

Now that we've cleared up some of the misconceptions about books and websites, let's debunk some of the common scholarship myths. We hate these myths because not only are they untrue, but they often prevent students from applying for scholarships.

Myth: You need to be financially destitute to be eligible to apply for scholarships.

Busted: While it is true that financial need is a consideration for some scholarships, the definition of "need" varies considerably. Given the cost of a college education, many families who consider themselves to be "middle class" actually qualify for some need-based scholarships. In addition, there are many scholarships where financial need is not even a factor. These "merit-based" scholarships are based on achievements, skills, career goals, family background and a host of other considerations that have nothing to do with a family's financial situation. You could actually be the son or daughter of Bill Gates and still win a "merit-based" scholarship.

Myth: You can only win scholarships as a high school senior.

Busted: It is never too early or too late to apply for scholarships. There are awards for students as young as seventh grade. If you win, the money is usually held in an account until it is time for you to actually go to college. But even if there are not as many awards for younger students as there are for seniors, it doesn't mean it's not important to look. Finding awards that you can apply for next year or even two years from now is a huge advantage. Keep a list of these awards since you are going to be super busy as a senior (think college apps and AP classes!) and you are going to be so thankful when you can just refer to your file of previously found awards and don't have to spend time searching. At the same time, you also don't want to stop applying for scholarships after you graduate from high school. There are many awards for college students. Once you are in college, you should continue to apply for scholarships, especially those geared toward specific majors and careers.

Myth: Only star athletes get college scholarships.

Busted: While star running backs receiving full-tuition scholarships are often what make the news, the majority of scholarships awarded by colleges are not for athletics. As you will see in this book, there are literally thousands of scholarships for those of us who don't know the difference between a touchdown and a touchback. Even if you are an athlete, you might also be surprised to know that many colleges give scholarships to student athletes who may not be destined to become the next Steph Curry. The needs of a college's athletic program depend on the level of their competition. You may find that at one college your soccer skill wouldn't earn you a place on the team as a bench warmer; but at another school, you might not only be a starter but also earn a half-tuition scholarship.

Myth: You need straight A's to win money for college.

Busted: While straight A's certainly don't hurt, most students mistakenly assume that grades are the primary determinate for selecting scholarship winners. This is just not true. Most scholarships are based on criteria other than grades and reward specific skills or talents such as linguistic, athletic or artistic ability. Even for scholarships in which grades are considered, GPAs are often not the most important factor. What's more relevant is that you best match the qualities the scholarship committee seeks. Don't let the lack of a perfect transcript prevent you from applying for scholarships.

Myth: You should get involved in as many extracurricular activities as possible to win a scholarship.

Busted: Scholarship competitions are not pie eating contests where you win through volume. They are more like baking contests in which you create an exquisite dessert with an appearance and flavor that matches the tastes of the judges. Scholarships are won by quality, not quantity. Scholarship judges are looking for students who have made quality contributions. For example, for a public service scholarship, the judges would be more impressed if you organized a school-wide volunteer day than if you were a member of 20 volunteer organizations but did little to distinguish yourself in any one of them.

Myth: If you qualify for financial aid, you don't need to apply for scholarships.

Busted: Financial aid and scholarships are not mutually exclusive but complimentary. You need to do both—apply for financial aid and scholarships—at the same time! Relying only on financial aid is dangerous. First, financial aid is "need based" which means if you're a middle or upper middle class family, you may not receive any free money (i.e. grants) but only student loans which you need to pay back. Even if you do qualify for grants, it may not be enough. The maximum Pell Grant, for example, is $7,395 per year, which is still far short of what tuition plus room and board costs at most schools. While financial aid is important, we consider scholarships to be far superior. With few, if any, strings attached, scholarships represent free cash that does not have to be paid back and which you can use at almost any school. Best of all, you can win scholarships regardless of your family's income!

Myth: You should apply to every scholarship that you find.

Busted: When you turn 35, you technically are eligible to run for President of the United States. This hardly means you should start packing your bags for the White House. Let's apply that same logic to scholarships. Just because you are technically eligible for a scholarship does not mean you should start filling out the paperwork for it. Why? You have a limited amount of time to spend on scholarship applications. It is necessary to allocate your time to those that you have the best chance of winning. You may find that you are eligible for 500 scholarships. Unless you're willing to make applying to scholarships your full-time avocation, it's unlikely that you can apply for more than several dozen awards. Thus, you need to be selective about which scholarships fit you the best. One caveat: This does not mean that you should only apply to two or three scholarships. You should still apply to as many scholarships as you can—just make sure you have them prioritized.

How a Solid Scholarship Strategy Helps Win You Money

Back in high school, Kelly applied for a scholarship from her father's employer. She was confident she would win since academically she had both high grades and test scores—which she diligently listed on the application. After turning in her application, she eagerly waited for the check to arrive. But the check never came. In fact, when Kelly found out who did win, she was surprised to learn that he had lower grades and lower test scores. What happened? How did this guy win instead of Kelly?

The answer was that Kelly relied solely on grades and test scores to win while the other applicant clearly used the entire application to stand out. That was when Kelly learned the importance of having a strategy.

So what does it take to win a scholarship?

The answer is that scholarship winners are not superstars. Rather, they are the students who have prepared—those young men and women that have invested the time to create applications that highlight their strengths. It's really sad to see students who don't apply for scholarships because they mistakenly assume that they don't have a chance to win.

Unlike a lottery, scholarships are not based on luck. To win scholarships, you need to show the scholarship judges how you fit the award. Often this is through the scholarship application, essay and interview. In fact, almost all scholarship competitions come down to one key factor—how well you can show that you fit the purpose of the scholarship. In this respect, you have power over the outcome. Through what you choose to highlight (and ignore) in the scholarship application, you are able to construct a case for why you deserve to win.

In the following chapters we will lay out what we found to be the keys to a winning strategy. Now turn the page and let's get started!

Where to Find the Best Scholarships

chapter 2

Scholarships Beyond this Book

We know you bought this book because it's the largest and most up-to-date directory of scholarships available. However, we do want to show you how to find even more scholarships above and beyond the ones listed in this book.

We learned how to find scholarships through trial and often painful error. For example, when we first started to search for scholarships, we spent a lot of time tracking down scholarships that we later discovered were listed in our high school counseling office. But we did learn from each mistake and slowly developed an efficient strategy for finding scholarships.

Our approach to finding scholarships consists of two important steps. First, you must create a list of as many scholarships as possible that fit you. Second, once you have a big list of scholarships, prioritize the awards. Here is where you will do some detective work that will show you which scholarships are worth your time to fill out.

By following this two-step approach, you will end up with a prioritized list of scholarships that are closely matched to your background and achievements. So, even before you fill out a single scholarship application form, you will have greatly improved your chances of winning. Plus, you saved time by not wasting energy on awards that you won't win.

Start Your Scholarship Search in Your Own Backyard

When we began looking for scholarships, we made what is perhaps the biggest mistake of the novice scholarship hunter—we started by looking as far away as possible. We were mesmerized by the big prizes of the large (and often well-publicized) national awards. We thought, "If I won just one of these national scholarship competitions, I'd be set and could end my search." This turned out to be a big mistake and an even bigger time-waster. It seemed that everyone and his brother, sister and cousin were also applying to these competitions. The Coca-Cola scholarship competition, for example, receives more than 100,000 applications each year.

It turned out that the last place we looked for scholarships was our most lucrative source. Best of all, this place turned out to be in our own backyard!

What are backyard scholarships and where do you find them? Think about all the civic groups, clubs, businesses, churches and organizations in your community. Each of these is a potential source for scholarships. (If you are already in college, you have two communities: your hometown and the city in which you go to school.) Since these awards are usually only available to students in your community, the competition is a lot less fierce.

You may be thinking, "What good is a $500 Lions Club scholarship when my college costs 35 grand a year?" It's true that local scholarships don't award the huge prizes that some of the national competitions do. You already know that we won over $100,000 in scholarships. What we haven't told you is that the majority of this money came from local scholarships! We literally won $500 here and $1,500 there. By the time we graduated from Harvard and added up all the awards, it turned out to be a huge amount. Plus, some of the local scholarships that we won were "renewable," which meant that we received that money each year we were in college. So a $500 renewable scholarship was really worth $2,000 over four years.

If you still can't get excited because these local awards seem small compared to the cost of tuition, try this exercise: Take the amount of the award and divide it by the time you invested in the application. For the $500 Lions Club award, let's say that you spent one hour each night for three days to complete the application and write the essay. Take $500 and divide it by three hours. That works out to a little over $166 per hour. (Now imagine that the award was for $1,000 instead. That would make it $333 per hour!) Not bad by any measure. If you can find a job that pays you more than $166 an hour, then take it and forget applying to scholarships. If not, get back to applying for scholarships—even the little ones!

Let's get specific and look at all of the places in your backyard to find scholarships.

✓ High school counselor or college financial aid officer

If you are a high school student, start with your counselor. Ask if he or she has a list of scholarship opportunities. Most counselors have a list of local scholarships. It's helpful if before your meeting, you prepare information about your family's financial background as well as special interests or talents you have that would make you eligible for scholarships. Don't forget that your own high school will have a variety of scholarships from such places as the parent-teacher organization, alumni group and athletic booster clubs.

If you are a college student, make an appointment with your school's financial aid office. Before the appointment, think about what interests and talents you have and what field you may want to enter after graduation. Take a copy of your Free Application for Federal Student Aid (FAFSA) as background (https://studentaid.gov). Mention any special circumstances about your family's financial situation. Ask the financial aid officer for recommendations of scholarships offered by the college or by community organizations.

Also, if you have already declared a major, check with the department's administrative assistant or chair for any awards that you might be eligible to win.

It's important whenever you speak to a counselor (either in high school or college) that you inquire about any scholarships that require nomination. Often these scholarships are easier to win since the applicant pool is smaller. You have nothing to lose by asking, and if anything, it shows how serious you are about financing your education.

High school websites

You may not visit your school's website daily, but when you are looking for scholarships, it pays to search the site for lists of scholarships. Most high schools post scholarship opportunities for students on their websites. (You may have to dig down a few levels to find this list.)

Other high school websites

If your school does not post scholarship opportunities, surf over to the websites of other high schools in the area. You'll find that many offer a wealth of scholarship resources.

Nearby colleges

While your college has great scholarship resources, wouldn't it be great if you had double or triple these resources? You can. Simply seek the resources of other local colleges. Ask permission first, but you'll find that most neighboring schools are more than willing to help you. If you are in high school, nothing prevents you from visiting a local college and asking for scholarship information. Because you are a prospective student, the college will often be happy to provide whatever assistance it can.

Student clubs and organizations

Here's a reason to enjoy your extracurricular activities even more. One benefit of participating may be a scholarship sponsored by the organization. Inquire with the officers or advisors of the organization about scholarship funds. Bands, newspapers, academic clubs, athletic organizations and service organizations often have scholarships that are awarded to outstanding members. If the organization has a national parent organization (e.g. National Honor Society) visit the national organization website. There are often awards that are given by the parent organization for members of local chapters.

Community organizations

Maybe you've wondered why community organizations have so many breakfast fundraisers—one reason is that some provide money for scholarships. You usually don't have to be a member of these organizations to apply. In fact, many community groups sponsor scholarships that are open to all students who live in the area. As we have mentioned, college students really have two communities: their hometown and where they go to college. Don't neglect either of these places.

How do you find these organizations? Many local government websites list them. Visit the websites for your town, city and state. Also visit or call your community association or center. You can search online to look up organizations and a calendar of annual events that are sponsored by various civic groups. Finally, don't forget to pay a visit to the public library and ask the reference librarian for help. Here is a brief list of some of the more common civic groups to track down:

- Altrusa
- American Legion and American Legion Auxiliary
- American Red Cross
- Association of Junior Leagues International
- Boys and Girls Clubs
- Circle K
- Civitan
- Elks Club
- Lions Club
- 4-H Clubs
- Fraternal Order of Eagles
- Friends of the Library
- Kiwanis International
- Knights of Columbus
- National Exchange Club
- National Grange
- Optimist International
- Performing Arts Center
- Rotary Club
- Rotaract and Interact
- Ruritan
- Scouts and Girl Scouts
- Sertoma International
- Soroptimist International of the Americas

- U.S. Jaycees
- USA Freedom Corps
- Veterans of Foreign Wars
- YMCA and YWCA
- Zonta International

 Local businesses

Businesses like to return some of their profits to employees and students in the community. Many offer scholarships as a way to reward students who both study and work. Ask your manager if your employer has a scholarship fund and how you can apply. Some companies—particularly large conglomerates that have offices, distributorships or factories in your community—offer scholarships that all students in the community are eligible to win. Check with the chamber of commerce for a list of the largest companies in the area. You can call the public relations or community outreach department in these companies to inquire about any scholarship opportunities. Visit the large department and chain stores in the area and ask the store manager or customer service manager about scholarships.

 Parents' employer

Your parents may hate their jobs, but they'll love the fact that many companies award scholarships to the children of employees as a benefit. They should speak with someone in the human resources department or with their direct managers about scholarships and other educational programs offered by their company.

 Parents' or grandparents' military service

If your parents or grandparents served in the U.S. Armed Forces, you may qualify for a scholarship from a military association. Each branch of the service and even specific divisions within each branch have associations. Speak with your parents and grandparents about their military service and see if they belong to or know of these military associations.

 Your employer

Flipping burgers may have an up side. Even if you work only part-time, you may qualify for an educational scholarship given by your employer. For example, McDonald's offers the Archways to Opportunity tuition assistance to reward the accomplishments of its student-employees. If you have a full- or part-time job, ask your employer about scholarships.

 Parents' union

Don't know if your parents are in a union? Ask and find out. Some unions sponsor scholarships for the children of their members. Ask your parents to speak with the union officers about scholarships and other educational programs sponsored by their union.

Interest clubs

Performing arts centers, city orchestras, equestrian associations and amateur sports leagues are just a few of the many special interest clubs that may offer scholarships. While some limit their awards to members, many simply look for students who are interested in what they support. A city performing arts center, for example, may offer an award for a talented performing artist in the community.

 ### Professional sports teams

They may not have won a World Series since the 1950s, but don't discount them as a viable scholarship source. Many local professional athletic teams offer community awards (and not necessarily for athletes) as a way to contribute to the cities in which they are based.

 ### Church or religious organizations

Religious organizations may provide scholarships for members. If you or your parents are members of a religious organization, check with the leaders to see if a scholarship is offered.

 ### Local government

Some cities and counties provide scholarships specifically designated for local students. Often, local city council members and state representatives sponsor a scholarship fund. Even if you didn't vote for them, call their offices and ask if they offer a scholarship.

 ### Local newspaper

Local newspapers often print announcements about students who win scholarships. Keep a record of the scholarships featured or go to the library or look online at back issues of the newspaper. Check last year's spring issues (between March and June) for announcements of scholarship recipients. Contact the sponsoring organizations to see if you're eligible to enter the next competition.

Is There a Magic Number of Scholarships?

We often are asked, "How many scholarships should I apply to?" The truth is that there is no magic number of scholarships for which you should apply. But you should avoid the extremes. Don't select only a couple of scholarships with the intention of spending countless hours crafting the perfect application. While it is true that to win you need to turn in quality applications, there is also a certain amount of subjective decision making. So even with the perfect application, you may not win. This means that you need to apply to more than a few scholarships. On the other hand, don't apply for 75 awards, sending in the same application to each. You'll just waste your time. You need to strike a balance between quantity and quality.

Searching Beyond Your Backyard

Once you have exhausted the opportunities in the community, it is time to broaden your search. Although the applicant pool is often larger with national awards, you shouldn't rule them out. Because many national award programs have marketing budgets, finding these awards may actually be easier than local awards. Most national awards will be advertised and the following places will help you track them down:

Internet

Forget the time-wasting social networks, and let's use the Internet for something productive. We recommend that you use as many online scholarship databases as possible as long as they are free. There are enough quality free databases that you should not have to pay for any online search. Here are a few we recommend:

- SuperCollege (www.supercollege.com)
- Verified Scholarships (www.verifiedscholarships.com)
- moolahSPOT (www.moolahspot.com)
- Sallie Mae (www.salliemae.com/scholarships)
- FastWeb (www.fastweb.com)
- CollegeXpress (www.collegexpress.com)
- The College Board (www.collegeboard.org)
- Scholarships.com (www.scholarships.com)
- CareerOneStop (https://www.careeronestop.org)

Just remember that while many online databases claim to have billions of dollars in scholarships listed, they represent only a tiny fraction of what is available. We have personally used nearly every free scholarship database on the Internet and know from experience that none of them (including our own at www.supercollege.com) lists every scholarship that you might win. Think of these databases as starting points, and remember that they are not the only places to find awards.

Professional associations

There is an association for every profession you can imagine. Whether you want to be a doctor, teacher or helicopter pilot, there are professional organizations that exist not only to advance the profession, but also to encourage students to enter that field by awarding grants and scholarships.

To find these associations, contact people who are already in the profession. If you think you want to become a computer programmer, ask computer programmers about the associations to which they belong. Also look at the trade magazines that exist for the profession since they have advertisements for various professional organizations.

Another way to find associations is through books like *The Encyclopedia of Associations*. This multi-volume set found at most college libraries lists nearly every professional association in the United States. Once you find these associations, contact them or visit their websites to see if they offer scholarships.

Professional associations often provide scholarships for upper-level college students, graduate school or advanced training. But even high school students who know what they want to do after college can find money from associations.

 Big business

If you've never received a personal "thank you" from large companies like Coca-Cola, Tylenol or Microsoft, here it is. A lot of these have charitable foundations that award scholarships. Companies give these awards to give something back to the community (and the positive PR sure doesn't hurt either). When you visit company websites, look for links to their foundations, which often manage the scholarship programs.

Many companies offer similar types of scholarships. What if you're a student film maker? Think about all the companies that make money or sell products to you from cameras to editing software to tripods. Are you into industrial music? What special equipment or instruments do you use? Consider the companies that will benefit from more people using their products and services. Some companies also offer awards to attract future employees. For example, Microsoft, the software company, sponsors a scholarship program for student programmers. Be sure to investigate companies that employ people in your field of study—especially if it is highly competitive—to see if they offer scholarships.

 Colleges

You may think that checks only travel from your pocket to your college to pay for tuition. But colleges actually give a lot of money to students. Some of this money comes from the college itself while other money is from generous donations of alumni. Every college administers a number of scholarships, some based on financial need and some based on merit. What many students don't know is that often a student's application for admission is also used by the college to determine if he or she may win a scholarship. This is one reason it is worth the submission of any optional essay suggested on a college application. Even if the essay does not impact your admission, it could be used to award you some scholarship dollars.

Chapter 2:
Where to Find the Best Scholarships

Don't Look for Scholarships Alone

One of the biggest mistakes we made when looking for scholarships was that we did so alone. Maybe we didn't want to share what we found with our friends and thereby increase competition, or perhaps we just didn't see the benefits of working in groups. Whatever the reason, it probably cost us a ton of money.

Since then we've met thousands of students who have won scholarships. Of these the most successful are those who did not look for scholarships alone. In fact, they made it the biggest group project imaginable.

Take for example the three guys we met in Los Angeles. Essentially, all three young men are going to college for free because they were able to win way more money than they could ever use! How did they do it? They formed a "scholarship group". Every Saturday morning they met at Starbucks and one of their parents agreed to pick up the tab for Frappuccinos. The only rule was that each had to bring at least two new scholarships. What happened was that one guy might find an award that was not right for him but was perfect for someone else in the group. This sharing of information was a tremendous advantage over laboring individually and literally tripled their chances of finding scholarships.

Another benefit was that working in a group kept these guys motivated. There certainly must have been weeks when searches were fruitless and the scholarship pickings were slim. The guys might have been tempted to give up, but being in a group brings with it a sense of responsibility not to disappoint the other members of the unit. Searching for scholarships alone is very difficult and it's so easy to just quit. But when you work in a group, you keep one another motivated and you have a natural support base that keeps you going when you feel like quitting.

So did these guys increase the competition by sharing scholarships? In some cases they did. But this was far outweighed by the sheer number of scholarships that they found collectively that they never would have found working alone.

As a general rule, students who worked with others discovered that by sharing the awards they found and pooling their resources, they were able to find more scholarships in less time than they would have found individually. The end result was that these students had more scholarships to apply to and more time to focus on their applications. Hence, they won more money.

Let this be a lesson to all of us. Look around you and find others who are also hunting for scholarships. Convince them that the way to really win lots of free money for college is to work in groups.

Prioritize the Scholarships You Find

Until now, we have focused on where to find scholarships. If you invest time exploring these areas, you should have a fairly long list of potential scholarships. It may be tempting to start cranking out applications. We actually have a name for the methodology used by students that apply to anything and everything they find—it's called the "shotgun" approach and it never works. Just because you find an award for which you qualify does not mean that you should immediately apply. You want to focus your energies (and limited time) only on those awards that you have the best chance of winning.

It would save a lot of time if you knew beforehand which scholarships you'd win and which you wouldn't. With this information, you'd only spend time applying for the scholarships that you knew would result in cash in your pocket. While there is no way to be 100 percent certain that you'll win any scholarship, you can do some research and make an educated guess.

Here are the steps you should take with each scholarship to determine if you have a reasonable chance of winning it. By prioritizing your list based on these criteria, you'll be able to focus time on awards that you have the best odds of winning while not wasting time on the ones where being a match is a long shot.

Step 1   Learn the Purpose

Nobody, and we mean nobody, gives away money without a reason. Every sponsor of a scholarship has a concrete reason for giving away their hard-earned cash to students like you. For example, a teachers' organization might award a scholarship to encourage students to enter the teaching profession. An environmental group might sponsor a scholarship with the purpose of promoting environmental awareness, or it might reward students who have done environmental work in school. A local bank might give money to a student who has done a great deal of public service as a way to give back to the community in which it does business.

Your job is to uncover the purpose of every scholarship on your list. If you're lucky, it will be stated in the description of the award. Look at the eligibility requirements to see what kind of questions the scholarship sponsors are asking. Is there a GPA requirement? If there is and it's relatively high, academic achievement is probably important. If the GPA requirement is low, then grades are probably not important. Does the application ask for a list of extracurricular activities? If so, they are probably a significant part of the selection criteria. Do you need to submit an essay on a specific topic or a project to demonstrate proficiency in a field of study? All these requirements are clues about what the scholarship judges think will (and won't) be important.

For example, the sole purpose of a public service scholarship may be to reward a student's philanthropic acts. If that is the case, the application will most likely be focused on descriptions of a student's selfless deeds. On the other hand, a scholarship given by a major corporation may be based on a combination of grades, leadership and character.

If you cannot determine the purpose of the scholarship by reading its description and eligibility requirements, then you need to look for the purpose of the group that sponsors the award. For example, even if the scholarship description does not directly state it, you can be sure that an award given by an organization that is composed of local physicians will probably prefer that the winner have a connection with medicine or an intention to enter the medical field.

The membership of the organization can be a big clue. Just as your friends are a reflection of who you are, most clubs and organizations want to reach students who are similar to their membership. If you don't know much about the organization, contact them to learn background information regarding the history, purpose or contributions of the group. Visit the organization's website. Read their brochures or publications. The more you know about why the organization is giving the award, the better you'll understand how you may or may not fit.

Somewhere on your list of potential scholarships, note in a few words its purpose. You'll be using this information in the next step which is to determine if you can make a case that you are the type of person the scholarship committee is looking for.

Beware of Scholarship Scams

While the great majority of scholarship providers and services have philanthropic intentions, not all do. There are some scholarship services and even scholarships themselves that you need to avoid. According to the Federal Trade Commission, in one year there were more than 175,000 cases reported of scholarship scams, costing consumers $22 million. And this is a low estimate since most scholarship scams go unreported!

While we were fortunate to have not been victims of a scholarship scam, we have to admit that the offers we received were tempting. We both received letters in high school and college from companies that promised to help us find and win "unclaimed" scholarships. The pitch was tempting: There is money out there that no one is claiming. All we needed to do was purchase their service to get a list of these awards. Had we done so, we would have been $400 poorer and certainly none the richer. In this chapter, we will describe some of the common scams that you may encounter. You must avoid these offers, no matter how glamorous they seem.

The key to avoiding a scholarship scam is to understand the motivation of the people behind these scams. Those who operate financial aid rip-offs know that paying for college is something that makes you extremely nervous. They also know that most people don't have extensive experience when it comes to scholarships and may therefore believe that there are such things as "hidden" or "unclaimed" scholarships. These charlatans take advantage of your fears and discomfort by offering an easy answer with a price tag that seems small compared to the promised benefits. Be aware that you are

Chapter 2:
Where to Find the Best Scholarships

> vulnerable to these kinds of inducements. Think about it this way. If you have a weakness for buying clothes, you need to be extra vigilant when you are at the shopping mall. Similarly, because you need money for college, you are more susceptible to tempting scholarship offers. Acknowledging that these fears make you a target of scam artists is the first step to spotting their traps.

Step 2 Think Like a Judge

Once you know the purpose of the scholarship, you need to see if you are a match for the organization that sponsors it. At this point students often make one of two mistakes. Either they 1) overestimate how well they fit the purpose or, more commonly, 2) underestimate their qualifications and don't apply. After working with thousands of students, we have learned that students more often underestimate their abilities than overestimate. Try to be realistic, but also don't sell yourself short. Remember that scholarship judges are not looking for the perfect match. There are a lot of factors that will influence their decision, and many of these things—like personality, character and motivation—are difficult to measure.

Let's look at an example. If you are your school's star journalist, naturally you should apply for journalism scholarships. But if all you have done is write a single letter to the editor, then spend your time applying to scholarships that better match what you have accomplished. You can still apply for a journalism scholarship, especially if you only recently realized that you want to become a journalist, but you will be at a disadvantage compared to the other applicants and therefore should prioritize this award below other awards on your to-do list.

As you go through your list of scholarships, move to the bottom those which are the weakest matches to the goal of the scholarships. Make those awards that fit you best your highest priority. These are the ones that you want to focus on first.

Step 3 Take a Reality Check

Scholarship deadlines are not like tax deadlines, where there is a single day when all forms are due. The deadlines for scholarships vary. Be aware of these crucial dates. Unless you plan carefully, you may miss out on a scholarship simply because you don't have the time to create a decent application. Sandwiched among studying, sleeping and everything else in your busy life, there is limited time to spend on applying for scholarships. If you find a great scholarship that is due next week but requires a yet to-be-written original composition that would take a month, you should probably pass on the competition. If you know that, given the amount of time available, you won't be able to do an acceptable job, it's better to pass and move on to awards in which you have the time to put together a winning application. Remember too that you may be able to apply for the award next year.

Review Your List Daily

After you prioritize your scholarships with the ones you feel fit you best at the top of the list, push yourself to apply to as many as you can, working from top to bottom. You probably won't get to the end. This is okay since you have the least chance of winning the awards at the bottom anyway. By prioritizing and working methodically down your list, you will have hedged your bets by making sure that your first applications are for the scholarships that you have the best chance of winning while also not limiting yourself to only a handful of awards.

How to Win the Scholarships You Find

Chapter 3

Attacking the Scholarship Application

At first glance, scholarship applications look easy—most are only a single page in length. Piece of cake, right? Don't let their diminutive size fool you. The application is a vital part of winning any scholarship. Scholarship judges must sift through hundreds or even thousands of applications, and the application form is what they use to determine which applicants continue to the next stage. It's crucial that you ace your application to make this first cut.

In this chapter, we'll look at strategies you can use to transform an ordinary scholarship application form into a screaming testament of why you deserve to win free cash for college.

Five Steps to Crafting a Winning Application

Step 1 Strategically Choose What to List

Imagine that you need to give a speech to two groups of people. Without knowing who your audience is, you would have a difficult time composing a speech that would appeal to them, right? It would make a huge difference if one were a group of mathematicians and the other a group of fashion designers. To grab the attention of each of these audiences, you'd need to adjust your speech accordingly. References to mathematical theorems would hardly go over well with the designers, just as the mathematicians probably couldn't care less about how black the "new" black really is.

In much the same way, you need to decide what to highlight on your scholarship application based on the purpose of the award. When you know what the scholarship judges are looking for, it makes it easier to decide what to include or omit. As we mentioned earlier, organizations don't give away scholarships and expect nothing in return. Behind their philanthropic motives lies an ulterior motive—to promote their organization's purpose. If you prioritized your list of scholarships correctly, you've already uncovered the purpose for each award. Now look at all your activities, interests, hobbies and achievements. Ask yourself which ones fit the purpose of each award and would make a positive impression on the scholarship judges.

Let's imagine that you are applying for an award given by an organization of professional journalists. In visiting their website, you learn that print and broadcast journalists join this group because they are passionate about the profession of journalism and want to encourage public awareness about the importance of a free press. Immediately, you know that you need to highlight those experiences that demonstrate your zeal for journalism and, if applicable, your belief in the value of a free press.

Among your activities and accomplishments are the following:

- Soccer team captain
- Vice President of the Writers' Club
- Key Club treasurer
- Columnist for your high school newspaper
- English essay contest winner
- Summer job working at a pet store
- Summer internship at a radio station

As you look at this list, you can eliminate some activities outright. Your involvement on the soccer team, with the Key Club, and your job at the pet store are not relevant and don't show how you fit with the purpose of the scholarship.

However, even looking at what's left, you still have to decide which ones to list first. As you think about the purpose of the scholarship, you remember that in the Writers' Club you participated in a workshop that helped a local elementary school start its own newspaper. Since this achievement almost perfectly matches the mission of our hypothetical journalism organization, use your limited space in the application to list it first and to add an explanation.

You might write something like this:

```
Writers' Club, Vice President, organized "Writing Counts"
workshop at Whitman Elementary School, which resulted in the
launch of the school's first student-run newspaper.
```

Think of the impact this would have on the scholarship judges. "Look here, Mark!" one journalist on the judging committee would say. "This student does what we do! Definitely someone we should interview!"

When choosing accomplishments to list, don't be afraid to eliminate any that don't fit—even good ones. You have limited space in which to cram a lot of information. As you fill out the application, you may find that you are trying to squeeze in too many details or simply too many things. You need to be ruthless in trimming down what you submit to the judges. Make sure to include the accomplishments that *best fit* the purpose of the award.

At the same time you are picking which things to include in your application, be sure to also be aware of what might be offensive to the organization's members. Just imagine what would happen if you thoughtlessly mentioned that you were the author of an economics project entitled "How Labor Unions Make the U.S. Unable to Compete and Lower Our Standard of Living" to judges who are members of the International Brotherhood of Teamsters.

Clearly you can't use the same list of activities and accomplishments for every scholarship. You must take the time to craft a unique list that matches what each of the scholarships is intended to reward.

> **Create a Timeline**
>
> Every scholarship has a deadline. Even though you have created a prioritized list of awards, you need also be aware of the deadlines. In fact, the due date for an award may also influence how you prioritize it. It's also helpful to set yourself deadlines and create a schedule for applying. Set deadlines for when you will have the application forms completed, essays written and any required recommendations submitted. Post this schedule where you can see it every day. We also recommend that you share it with your parents. Moms and dads are great at nagging (we mean reminding) you to meet deadlines, so you might as well use their nagging (we mean motivating) skills to your advantage.

Step 2   List Important Accomplishments First

In movies, the most dare-devilish car chase, the most harrowing showdown and the most poignant romantic revelations are usually saved until the end. While this works for Hollywood, it does not for scholarship applications. Since scholarship judges review so many applications and the space on the form is limited, you must learn to highlight your most impressive points first.

If you have listed four extracurricular activities, assume that some judges won't read beyond the first two. This doesn't mean that all judges will be this rushed, but there are always some who are. It's extremely important that you prioritize the information that you present and rank your accomplishments according to the following criteria—which should not come as too much of a surprise.

Fit: The most important factor in ordering your achievements is how they fit with the purpose of the scholarship. This is, after all, why these kind people want to hand you some free dough. Emphasize accomplishments that match the purpose of the scholarship. If you are applying for an award that rewards athleticism, stress how well you've done in a particular sport before listing your volunteer activities.

Scope: Next prioritize your accomplishments by their scope, or how much of an impact they have made. How many people have been affected by your work? To what extent has your accomplishment affected your community? Did your contribution produce measurable results? In simple terms, put the big stuff before the small stuff.

Uniqueness: Since your application will be compared to those of perhaps thousands of others, include accomplishments that are uncommon. Give priority to those that are unique or difficult to win. Being on your school's honor roll is certainly an achievement, but it is an honor that many others have received. Try to select honors that fewer students have received—you want to stand out in order to be selected.

Timeliness: This is the least-important criterion, but if you get stuck and aren't sure how to arrange some of your accomplishments, put the more recent achievements first. Having won an election in the past year is more relevant than having won one three years ago. Some students ask us if they should list junior high or even elementary school achievements. Generally, stick to accomplishments from high school if you're a high school student and to college if you're a college student. An exception is if your accomplishment is extremely impressive and relevant—such as publishing your own book in the eighth grade. Of course, if you run out of recent achievements and there is still space on the form, go ahead and reach back to the past—but try to limit yourself to only one or two items.

You want your application to be as unforgettable as the best Hollywood movies. The only difference between your work and Spielberg's—besides the millions of dollars—is that you need to place the grand finale first.

You Can Recycle Your Applications

The first scholarship for which you apply will take the most time. But with each application you complete, it will get easier. This is because for each successive application, you can draw on the materials you developed for the previous one. To complete your first application, you need to think about your activities and recall achievements that you have forgotten. If there is an essay component, you will need to find a topic and craft an articulate essay. When you work on your second application, you can benefit from the work you've already done for the first. As you're building your timeline, look for scholarships in which you can recycle information from one application to another. Recycling will save you time. In addition, you can improve on your work each time that you use it. For example, the second time you answer a question about your plans after graduation, you can craft your response more effectively than the first. As you recycle information, don't just reuse it—improve it!

Step 3 Spin Your Application to Impress the Judges

Politicians are notorious for telling voters what they want to hear. Good politicians never lie, but they do put a flattering "spin" on their words depending on whom they're addressing. While you must never lie on your application forms, you do want to present yourself in the best possible way so that you appeal to your audience. In other words, employ a little spin.

We know that some politicians have a difficult time distinguishing between lying and spinning. You shouldn't. Let's say you are applying for a scholarship that rewards students who are interested in promoting literacy. You have been a volunteer at your local library where, aside from typical page duties each week, you also read stories to a dozen children for story time. Here are three ways you could describe this activity on your application:

Non-spin description:
```
Library volunteer.
```

Lie:
```
Library reading program founder. Started a national program
that reaches thousands of children every day to promote
literacy.
```

Spin:
```
Library volunteer. Promoted literacy among children through
weekly after-school reading program at public library.
```

At one extreme, you can see that a lie exaggerates well beyond the truth. At the other extreme, the non-spin description is not very impressive because it does not explain how the activity relates to the purpose of the scholarship. The spin version is just right. It does not stretch the truth, but it does make clear how this activity fits within the context of the purpose of the scholarship. It focuses on what is important to the judges while at the same time, it ignores other aspects of your job that are not relevant—such as shelving books.

To take this example one step further, let's say that now you are applying for a scholarship that rewards student leaders. One of your other responsibilities as a library volunteer is to maintain the schedule for volunteers and help with the recruitment of new volunteers. Your description for this scholarship might read something like this:

```
Library volunteer. In charge of volunteer schedule and re-
cruitment of new members.
```

Notice how you have "spun" your activity so that it highlights a different aspect of what you did and better shows the judges how you fit their criteria. In the application, you should use the opportunity to spin your accomplishments to match the purpose of the award.

To be able to spin effectively, you need to know your audience. When you prioritized your scholarships earlier, you should have discovered the purpose of each scholarship. Remember that in most cases the scholarship judges want to give their money to students who are the best reflections of themselves. For example, the Future Teachers of America judges will want to fund students who seem the most committed to pursuing a teaching career. The American Congress of Surveying and Mapping judges, on the other hand, want to award their money to students who have the strongest interest in cartography.

Step 4 Write to Impress

The inspiring words of Martin Luther King Jr.'s "I Have a Dream" speech were punctuated with his dramatic, emotion-filled voice, hopeful expression and confident presence. His delivery would not have been as forceful had he spoken in a drab, monotone, with hands stuffed into his pockets and eyes lowered to avoid contact with the audience. Nor would his dramatic presentation have been as effective had his message been unimportant. The lesson? Both content and delivery count. While you don't have the opportunity for person-to-person delivery with your scholarship applications, you can and should present information in a compelling way. Here are some time-tested writing strategies for creating a positive impression through your applications:

Showcase Your Smarts. There's a reason why your parents wanted you to study and do well in school. In addition to the correlation between studying and success in college, almost all scholarship judges (even those of athletic awards) are impressed by academic achievement. College is, after all, about learning (at least that's what you want your parents to believe).

As you are completing your applications, keep in mind that while you may be applying for a public service scholarship, you should also include at least one academic achievement. For example, it does not hurt to list on an athletic scholarship form that you also came in second place at the science fair. This should not be the first thing you list, but it should be included somewhere to show the committee that you have brains in addition to brawn.

Extracurricular Activities and Hobbies Show Your Passion. If your only activity were studying, your life would be severely lacking in excitement. Scholarship organizers recognize this and thus the criteria for many scholarships include extracurricular activities or hobbies. Scholarship committees want evidence that you do more than read textbooks, take exams and watch Youtube. They want to know that you have other interests. This makes you a more well-rounded person.

As always, when completing your applications, select extracurricular activities and hobbies that fit with the scholarship's mission. If you are applying for a music scholarship, describe how you've been involved in your school's orchestra or how you've taken violin lessons. By showing that you not only have taken classes in music theory but have also been involved with music outside of your studies, the scholarship committee will get a more complete picture of your love for music. Remember to use your activities and hobbies to illustrate your passion for a subject.

Leadership Is Always Better Than Membership. If you've ever tried to motivate a group of peers to do anything (without taking the easy way out—bribery) you know that it takes courage, intelligence and creativity to be a leader. Because of this, many scholarships give extra points to reward leadership. Scholarship judges want to know that the dollars will be awarded to someone who will not only make a difference in the future but who will also be a leader and motivate others to do the same. Think of it this way: If you were a successful businessperson trying to encourage entrepreneurship, wouldn't you want to give your money to a young person who is not only an entrepreneur but who also motivates others to become entrepreneurs?

- Describing leadership in your activities or hobbies will also help set you apart from the other applicants. Many students are involved with environmental groups, but what if you are the only one to actually help increase recycling on your campus? Wouldn't that make your application a standout?

To show scholarship judges that you are a leader, list any activities in which you took responsibility for a specific project. Use action verbs when describing your work:

- Organized band fundraiser to purchase new instruments
- Led a weeklong nature tour in Yosemite Valley
- Founded first website to list volunteer activities
- Directed independent musical performance

Remember that you don't need to be an elected officer to be a leader. Many students have organized special projects, led teams or helped run events. Even if you didn't have an official title, you can include these experiences. Here's an example:

```
Environmental Action Committee Member. Spearheaded subcom-
mittee on reducing waste and increasing recycling on campus.
```

When describing your leadership, include both formal and informal ways you have led groups. This shows the scholarship committee that you are a worthy investment.

Honors and Awards Validate Your Strengths. There's a reason why all trophies are gold and gaudy. They shout to the world in a deafening roar, "Yes, this glittery gold miniature figure means I am the best!" For applications that ask for your honors and awards, impart some of that victorious roar and attitude. In no way are we recommending that you ship your golden statuettes off with your applications. We are saying that you should highlight honors and awards in a way that gets the scholarship committee to pay attention to your application. What makes an award impressive is scope. Not a minty mouthwash, scope in this case is the impact and influence of the award. You worked for the award and earned every golden inch of it. Show the committee that they don't just hand these statuettes out to anybody. One way to do this is to point out how many awards are given:

```
English Achievement Award. Presented to two outstanding juniors each year.
```

By itself, the English Achievement Award does not tell the scholarship committee very much. Maybe half the people in your class were given the award. By revealing the scope of the award (particularly if it was given to only a few) it becomes much more impressive.

In competitions that reach beyond your school, it is important to qualify your awards. For example, while everyone at your school may know that the Left Brain Achievement Award is given to creative art students, the rest of the world does not.

Don't write:
```
Left Brain Achievement Award.
```

Do write:
```
Left Brain Achievement Award. Recognized as an outstanding creative talent in art as conferred upon by vote of art department faculty.
```

You've worked hard to earn the honors and awards that you have received, and you should not hesitate to use them in your applications to help you win scholarships.

Know when to leave a space blank. An official mom rule from childhood is this: "If you don't have anything nice to say, don't say it." While this is a good lesson on self-restraint, it does not always hold true for scholarship applications. In general, it is not a good idea to leave any area blank. You don't need to fill the entire space, but you should make an effort to list something in every section. However, before you try to explain how the handmade certificate that your mom presented you for being Offspring of the Year qualifies as an "award," realize that there are limits. If you've never held a job, don't list anything under work experience. If, however, you painted your grandmother's house one summer and got paid for it, you might consider listing it if you don't have any other options.

Perfect every sentence. Succinct and terse, scholarship application forms bear the well-earned reputation for having less space than you need. Often offering only a page or less, scholarship and award forms leave little room for much more than just the facts. As you are completing your applications, remember to abbreviate where appropriate and keep your sentences short. Often judges are scanning the application form. If they want an essay, they will ask for one. However, you do not want to take instructions so literally that you miss their intent. For instance, if the instructions say to list your awards, don't feel like you can't add explanation if you need to. And, as always, be selective in what you list. If you have three great awards, it is better to use your space to list those three with short explanations rather than cram in all 15 awards that you've won in your life. (No argument can be made for the timeliness of your Perfect Attendance Award from kindergarten.) You are trying to present the most relevant information that shows the scholarship judges why you deserve their money. Use the space to explain how each award, job or activity relates to the scholarship.

Also, feel free to interpret some instructions. Work experience does not have to be limited to traditional jobs. Maybe you started your own freelance design business or cut lawns on the weekends—those count! The same goes for leadership positions. Who said that leadership has to be an elected position within an organization? Just be sure to explain the entry if the relationship is not totally clear. Here's an example:

```
Volunteer Wilderness Guide. Led clients through seven-day
trek in Catskills. Responsible for all aspects of the trip
including group safety.
```

Always remember that the application is you. A scholarship application is more than just a form. In the eyes of the scholarship judges, it is *you*. It may not be fair, but in many cases the application is the only thing that the judges will have as a measurement standard. The last thing you want to be is a dry list of academic and extracurricular achievements. You are a living, breathing person. Throughout the application, take every opportunity—no matter how small—to show the judges who you really are. Use descriptions and vocabulary that reveal your passion and commitment. Always remember that the application is a reflection of you.

Step 5 Separate Yourself from the Competition

Think of the scholarship competition as a reverse police lineup where you want to stand out and be picked by the people behind the one-way mirror. You want the judge to say without hesitation, "That's the one!" The only way this will happen is if your application is noticed and doesn't get lost in the stack. One of the best ways to accomplish this is to know what you're up against—in other words, think about who else will be in the lineup with you.

Try to anticipate your competition—even if it's just an educated guess. Depending on to whom the scholarship is offered, you may have a limited or broad pool of competitors. If the award is confined to your school, you may know everyone who will enter on a first-name basis. If it's national, all you may know is that all the applicants have a similar interest in a broad field. For a medical scholarship, for instance, the applicants might be students interested in becoming doctors or nurses. More important than the scope of the competition is the type of students who will apply. One of the biggest challenges in any competition is to break away from the pack. If 500 pre-med students are applying for a $10,000 scholarship from a medical association, you need to make sure that your application stands out from those of the 499 other applicants. If you are lucky, you may have done something that few have done. (Inventing a new vaccine in your spare time would certainly set you apart!) Unfortunately, most of us will have to distinguish ourselves in more subtle ways, such as through the explanation of our activities and accomplishments.

Say you are applying for a scholarship given by a national medical association that seeks to promote the medical sciences. It just so happens that you are considering a pre-med major and you have interned at a local hospital. If you hadn't read this book, you might have listed under activities something like this entry:

```
Summer Internship at Beth Israel Children's Hospital.
```

But you did read this book! So you know that this is a great activity to elaborate on since it demonstrates your commitment to medicine and shows that you truly are interested in entering the medical field. You also know that you need to stand out from the competition; and as great as this activity is, you know that a lot of other applicants also will have volunteered at hospitals. So instead of simply listing the internship, you add detail to make the experience more unique. You could write it this way:

```
Summer Internship at Beth Israel Children's Hospital; assisted with clinical trial of new allergy medication.
```

This description is much more unique and memorable. By providing details, you can illustrate to the judges how your volunteer work is different from that of other students. Remember that you can add short descriptions in most applications even if the instructions do not explicitly ask for them.

If you can anticipate who your competition will be and what they might write in their applications, you will be able to find a way to go one step further to distinguish yourself from the crowd. Even the simple act of adding a one-sentence description to an activity can make the difference between standing out or being overlooked.

Now that you know the five steps to insure that your application is a winner, here is our Top Ten list of application form do's and don'ts which will serve as a final reminder of how to create that stunning application!

Be a Neat and Detail Freak

You may have dirty laundry strewn across your room and a pile of papers large enough to be classified as its own life form, but you don't want the scholarship judges to know that. When it comes to applications, neatness and attention to detail do count. We would not ordinarily be neatness zealots—we admit to having our own mountains of life-imbibed papers—but submitting an application with misspellings, missing words or grammatical errors will severely diminish your message. Think how much less impressive the Mona Lisa would be if da Vinci had painted it on a dirty old bed sheet. You may have the most incredible thoughts to convey in your applications, but if your form is filled with errors, none of it will matter. In a sea of hundreds and even thousands of other applications, you don't want yours to be penalized by sloppy presentation.

Top Ten Application Do's and Don'ts

With money on the table, it's much better to learn from others' successes and mistakes before you risk your own fortunes. From interviews with students and scholarship judges and firsthand experience reviewing scholarship applications, we've developed our Top Ten list of scholarship application do's and don'ts. Let's shed the negative energy first and start with the don'ts.

Don'ts

1. DON'T prioritize quantity over quality. It's not the quantity of your accomplishments that is important. It's the quality of your contributions.

2. DON'T stretch the truth. Tall tales are prohibited.

3. DON'T squeeze to the point of illegibility. Scholarship applications afford minimal space. It's impossible to fit in everything that you want to say. Don't try by sacrificing legibility.

4. DON'T write when you have nothing to say. If you don't have something meaningful to present, leave it blank.

5. DON'T forget to edit and proofread.

6. DON'T procrastinate. Don't think you can finish your applications the night before they're due.

7. DON'T settle for less than perfect. You can have imperfections. Just don't let the selection committee know.

8. DON'T miss deadlines. No matter the reason, if you miss the deadline, you won't win the scholarship.

9. DON'T turn in incomplete applications. Make sure your application is finished before sending it.

10. DON'T underestimate what you can convey. Scholarship applications may appear to be short and simple. Don't undervalue them. In a small space, you can create a powerful story of why you should win.

And now the good stuff.

Do's

1. DO understand the scholarship's mission. Know why they're giving out the dough.
2. DO remember who your audience is. You need to address animal rights activists and retired dentists differently.
3. DO show how you fit with the scholarship's mission. You're not going to win unless you have what the selection committee wants.
4. DO be proud of your accomplishments. Don't be afraid to brag.
5. DO focus on leadership and contributions. Make your contributions known.
6. DO make your application stand out.
7. DO practice to make sure everything fits. Make practice copies of the original form before you begin filling it out. Then use your spare copies for trial and error. If you apply electronically, edit so everything fits.
8. DO get editors. They'll help you create the best, error-free applications you can.
9. DO include a resume. Whether they ask for it or not, make sure you include a tailored scholarship resume. See the next chapter for how to create a great resume.
10. DO take photos of or download your finished applications for reference. Save them for next year when you do this all over again.

Double Check Your App

Once you've completed your applications, check and double-check for accuracy. Look at every line and every question to make sure you've filled out all the information that is requested on the form. Make sure you have someone else take a look at your application. A second set of eyes may catch mistakes that you invariably will miss. Remember that presentation affects how scholarship judges view applications. You want to convey that you are serious about winning the scholarship by submitting an application that is complete and error-free.

Finally, before submitting your application, save or print a copy. If for some reason your application form is lost, you have a copy to resend. Plus, by saving this year's applications, you have recycling possibilities (especially the essays: you'll see what we mean in Chapter 4!) and a great starting place for next year's scholarships.

How to Write a Winning Scholarship Essay

chapter 4

The Essay Can Make or Break Your Chances of Winning

Here's a situation repeated a million times each year. A student receives a scholarship application and quickly glances over the form. It looks pretty straightforward, so it's tossed into the "to do" pile. The day before it's due, the student finally gets around to filling it out. Breezing through the application form, the student is about to celebrate finishing when he or she encounters the final requirement. It reads as follows:

```
In 1894 Donald VonLudwig came to America with 10 cents in
his pocket and within a decade built an empire. Write an
800-word essay on how you would incorporate the lessons
of VonLudwig's success into your life.
```

Uh, oh. Life just got harder. Meet the dreaded scholarship essay. The hypothetical student described above—the one we are poking fun at—was one of us! After a few experiences like this one, (which were usually accompanied by all night writing sessions), we learned to work on the essay first and never underestimate how much time it requires.

For most scholarship competitions, it is the essay that will make or break your chances of winning. Why? Because the essay offers you the best chance to show the scholarship judges why you deserve to win. While your application form will get you to the semifinals, it is the essay that will carry you into the winner's circle.

Since the essay is so important, you must not assume that you can crank out a quality essay the night before it's due. A quality essay will take both time and effort. In this chapter we will take you step by step through the process of crafting a winning essay—don't worry, it's easier than you may have imagined. Plus, you will read examples of essays that won thousands of dollars in scholarships. From these, you can see firsthand how the strategies presented in this chapter are actually put to use in real life.

All Essays Ask the Same Underlying Question

Regardless of the specific wording, the underlying question for almost all essay questions is the same: "Why do you deserve to win?" (Your answer should *not* be, "Because I need the money!")

Think about these questions: The Future Teachers of America scholarship asks you to write about the "future of education". The Veterans of Foreign Wars asks you to define "patriotism". The National Sculpture Society asks you to "describe your extracurricular passions". Believe it or not, all these seemingly different questions are asking for the same answer: Why do you deserve to win our money?

Your answers to each must address this underlying question. When writing the Future Teachers of America essay, you can discuss the general state of education and quote a few facts and figures, but you'd better be sure to include how you personally fit into the future of education. If you are planning to be a teacher, you might elaborate on how you will contribute to shaping students' lives. Similarly use the topic of patriotism to impress the VFW judges with not only what you perceive patriotism to be but also how you have actually acted upon those beliefs. And if you answer the National Sculpture Society question with an essay on how much you love to play the guitar, then you really don't deserve to win!

Six Steps to Writing a Winning Scholarship Essay

By now you should be tired of hearing us repeat our mantra of knowing the purpose of the scholarship. You have used this to guide your selection of those scholarships you are most likely to win and how to complete the application form for them. It shouldn't surprise you that you must also use it to guide your essay. Remember, when you are writing about why you deserve to win, the answer and all the examples that you use should show how you fulfill that mission of the scholarship. With this in mind, let's begin our six steps to writing a winning scholarship essay.

Step 1 Find the Right Topic and Approach

You will encounter two types of essay questions. The first asks you to write about a specific topic. For example, "Why is it important to protect our natural environment?" The second type of question gives you a very broad topic such as, "Tell us about yourself." In the first case you don't need to think about a topic, but you do need to develop an approach to answering the question. In the latter you need to come up with both a topic and an approach. Let's look at how this is done, starting with the more difficult task of finding a topic.

Finding a Topic

Let's imagine that you are applying for a scholarship that presents an essay question so broad that you can essentially choose your own topic. To get the ideas flowing, you should use that idea-generating technique you learned in fifth grade—brainstorming. Take out a notebook or start a new electronic file and just start listing possible topics and themes. Ask yourself questions like these:

- What was a significant event in my life?
- What teacher, relative or friend has influenced who I am?
- What have I learned from my experiences?
- What are my goals for the future?
- Where will I be ten years from now?
- What motivates me to achieve my goals?

When brainstorming, don't be critical of the topics you unearth—just let the creativity flow. Ask parents and friends for suggestions.

Once you have a list of topics, you can start to eliminate those that don't help you answer the question of why you deserve to win. For example, if you apply to a scholarship that rewards public service, you would not want to write about the time you got lost in the woods for three days and had to survive on a single candy bar and wild roots. While that might make an interesting and exciting essay, it does not show the scholarship judges why you are the epitome of public service. This topic, however, may come in handy when you need to write an essay for a scholarship based on character or leadership or why you love Snickers bars.

After you whittle down your list to a few topics that will help show why you deserve to win this particular scholarship, then choose the topic that is the most interesting to you or that you care about the most. It seems self-evident, but surprisingly many students do not select topics that excite them. Why is it important to pick a topic that you are passionate about? Because if you truly like your topic, you will write a better essay. In fact, your enthusiasm and excitement will naturally permeate your writing, which will make it interesting and memorable. It's so much easier to stay motivated writing about something you enjoy rather than something you find boring.

How to Develop a Unique Approach

Whether you have to think of a topic yourself or one is given to you, the next task is to figure out how you are going to approach it. For any given topic there are probably a hundred ways you could address the subject matter in an essay. Most topics are also way too large to completely cover in an 800- to 1,000-word essay, so you are going to have to narrow it down and only share a small part of the larger story. All this involves coming up with an approach to what you will present in your essay—an approach that must convince the judges that you deserve to win their money.

Chapter 4:
How to Write a Winning Scholarship Essay

Let's take a look at writing about the traumatic experience of being lost in the woods for three days. You choose this topic since the scholarship wants to reward students with strong character and leadership and this is an experience that you believe shows both. But how do you write about it? If you just retell the story of the ordeal, it will not help the judges see why such an experience reveals the quality of your character or leadership. You need to dig deeper and think about how this experience revealed your strengths. To do this, ask yourself questions like these:

- What does this topic reveal about me?
- How has my life been changed by this experience?
- Why did I do what I did?
- What is the lesson that I learned from this experience?
- What aspect of this topic is most important to making my point?

In thinking about your experience alone in the woods, you may realize that on the second day you came close to breaking down and losing all hope of being rescued. This was the critical point where you had to make a decision to give up or push forward. You decide to focus your essay only on this small sliver of time, what went through your mind and how you decided that you were not going to give up. The details of how you got lost and of your eventual rescue would be unimportant and may be mentioned in only a sentence or two. Focusing your essay on just the second day—and more particularly on how you were able to conquer your fears and not lose hope—would clearly demonstrate to the judges that even under extreme pressure, your true character was revealed. Since you also need to address the leadership aspect, you decide to focus on how you took charge of your fears on the second day. To do this, your essay will describe specific actions you took to lead yourself successfully through this ordeal.

Finding the right approach is just as important as finding the right topic. This is especially true if you answer a question that provides a specific topic. With every scholarship applicant writing about the same topic, you need to be sure that your approach persuasively shows the judges why you deserve to win more than anyone else.

Step 2   Share a Slice of Life

Now that you have a topic and an idea for your approach, you need to decide how you are going to convey your message on paper. Keep in mind that scholarship judges are going to read hundreds if not thousands of essays. Often the essays will be on similar topics, particularly if the topic was given in the scholarship application. Therefore, you need to make sure that your writing is original. The best way to do this is to share a "slice of your life" in the essay.

Imagine that you are writing about your summer trip to Europe. Travel is a very common topic. If you decide to write about how your trip made you realize people from around the world are really quite similar, then you run the real risk of sounding just like every other travel essay. The same would be true for writing about sports. If you tell the story of how your team rallied and came from behind to win the game, you can be sure that it will sound like many other essays about sports. To make sure your essay is original, you need to share a "slice of life." Find one incident that happened during your travels or pick one particular moment in the game and use that to make your point. By focusing on a single day, hour or moment, you greatly reduce your chances of having an essay that sounds like everyone else's. Plus, essays that share a slice of life are usually a lot more interesting and memorable.

Let's look at an example. What if you choose to write about how your mom has been your role model? Moms are one of the most popular role models for essays (and they should be, considering the pain of childbirth). How do you make your mom distinct from all the other applicants writing about their moms? Go ahead and take a moment to think about your mom. Be very specific. Can you find one character trait or incident that really influenced you? Let's say your mom has an obsession with collecting porcelain figurines and this passion led to you becoming interested in collecting baseball cards. Because of this, you are now considering a career in sports management. Now we have something! Imagine that first day when you realized how much your mom loved collecting figurines. Maybe you even bought her one as a present and now she cherishes it above all others. Perhaps it was that moment that jump-started your love for baseball cards, which has now developed into a full blown obsession with sports to the point that you intend to make it a career. You've just succeeded in turning a very popular topic—Mom—into an entirely original essay by finding that slice of life. No two people share the exact same slice of life, so by finding one to share, you are almost always guaranteed to have an original essay.

Want another example? Let's set the stage. Imagine that you are applying to a scholarship for students who major in psychology. The question posed on the application is this: "Tell us about an influential person who inspired you to pursue psychology." As you brainstorm, you list the authors of books you've read and some professors whose classes you have enjoyed. But how many students will be writing about these same people? You could even wager money that every other essay will be about Freud!

As you brainstorm, you recall the worst fight you have ever had with your best friend Susan. As you think about this fight that nearly destroyed a 10-year friendship, you realize that it was one of the first times you applied classroom knowledge to a real life experience. In analyzing the fight, you realize that those psychology principles you studied have practical applications beyond the textbook. So for your essay you decide to write about the fight and how it made you even more committed than ever to become a psychology major.

You don't have to look far to find originality. We all have experiences that are unique to us. Even common experiences can be made original, depending on how you approach them. So don't exclude a topic just because it is common. By spending some time thinking about how you will write about it, you may be surprised at how original it could be.

Step 3   Stop Thinking, Start Writing

The most challenging part of writing a scholarship essay is getting started. Our advice: Just start writing. The first words you put down on paper may not be brilliant, but don't worry. You can always return to edit your work. It's easier to edit words you've already written than words that don't exist.

Do you think you have a bad case of writer's block? If so, the cure may surprise you. The best cure for writer's block is to just start writing!

We all have different writing styles, but certain points should be kept in mind as you are writing something that is focused on winning over a scholarship committee. Think about these things as you craft that winning essay:

Write for the Scholarship Judges. Let's pretend you're a stand-up comedian who has two performances booked: one at the trendiest club in town where all cool college students congregate and the other at a retirement home. As a skilled comedian, you would prepare different material aimed at the different audiences. The college crowd would be able to relate to jokes about relationships and dating, while your jokes about dentures and arthritis would probably—and this is a hunch—go over better with the senior citizens. The same goes for writing your essays. Since many are given by specialized organizations or for specific purposes, you need to write an essay that is appropriate for the audience. Think about who is going to read your essay. Is your audience natural science professors, circus performers or used car salesmen? Write your essay so it appeals to that audience. This should guide not only your selection of topics but also your word choice, language and tone.

Be Yourself. While you want to present yourself in a way that attracts the attention of the scholarship judges, you don't want to portray yourself as someone you are not. It's okay to present selected highlights from your life that fit with the award, but it's not ethical to exaggerate or outright lie. If you apply for a scholarship to promote the protection of animals, don't write about your deep compassion for helping animals when you've never ventured closer than 10 feet to one because of your allergies. Feel comfortable about everything you write, and don't go overboard trying to mold yourself into being the student you think the scholarship judges want to read about. If you've done your job of picking scholarships that match you best, you already know that you are a good fit. Your task in the essay is to demonstrate this to the judges.

Personalize Your Essay. Think of the scholarship judges as an audience that has come to see your Broadway show. You are the star. To keep them satisfied, give them what they want. In other words, the scholarship judges want to know about your life and experiences. When you write your essay, write about what has happened to you personally or about how you personally have been affected by something. If you are writing about drug abuse for an essay about a problem that faces college students today, do more than recite the latest national drug use statistics and the benefits of drug rehabilitation programs. Otherwise, your essay may be informative, but it won't be interesting. Instead, write about how a friend nearly overdosed on drugs, how others tried to pressure you into trying drugs or about your volunteer work at a rehabilitation clinic. Instantly, your essay will be more interesting and memorable. Plus, the judges really do want to learn more about you, and the only way for them to do this is if you share something about yourself in your essay.

Make Sure You Have a Point. Try this exercise: See if you can encapsulate the point of your essay into a single sentence. If you can't, you don't have a main point. So, you'd better get one! You may think this is obvious, but many students' essays don't have a main point. Use that most basic lesson from Composition 101: Have a thesis statement that states the main point of your essay. Let's say you are writing about growing up in the country. You might structure your essay around the idea that growing up in the country gave you a strong work ethic. This is the essay's main point. You can describe all the flat land and brush you like, but unless these descriptions help to support your point, you don't have a quality essay.

Support Your Statement. Once you put your main point out there, you can't abandon it. Like a baby learning to walk, you have to support your thesis statement because it can't stand on its own. This means you have to provide reasons why your statement is true. You can do this by giving detailed and vivid examples from your personal experiences and accomplishments.

Use Examples and Illustrations. When a reader can visualize what you are writing, it helps to make an impression. Anecdotes and stories accomplish this very effectively. Examples and illustrations also make your ideas clearer. If you want to be a doctor, explain how you became interested in becoming one. You might describe the impact of getting a stethoscope from your father when you were a child. Or maybe you can write about your first day volunteering at the hospital. Examples help readers picture what you are saying and even relate to your experiences. The scholarship judge may have never volunteered at a hospital; but by reading your example, that judge can easily understand how such an experience could be so influential. The one danger of examples is that you need to be sure to keep them concise. It is often too easy to write a long and detailed example when only a few sentences are sufficient. Remember, in an example you are not retelling an entire story but just pulling out a few highlights to illustrate the point you are trying to make.

Show Activity. If you were forced to sit in an empty room with nothing but a bare wall to stare at, you would probably get bored pretty quickly. The same goes for an essay. Don't force the scholarship judges to read an essay that does nothing. Your essay needs activity and movement to bring it to life. This may consist of dialogue, action, stories and thoughts. The last thing you want to do is bore your readers. With action, you won't have to worry about that!

Chapter 4: How to Write a Winning Scholarship Essay

Highlight Your Growth. You may not have grown an inch since seventh grade, but scholarship judges will look for your growth in other ways. They want to see evidence of emotional and intellectual growth, what your strengths are and how you have developed them. Strengths may include—but certainly aren't limited to—mastery of an academic course, musical talent, a desire to help others, athletic ability, leadership of a group and more. Overcoming adversity or facing a challenge may also demonstrate your growth.

Be Positive. You don't need to break out the pompoms and do a cheer, but you need to convey a positive attitude in your essay. Scholarship committees want to see optimism, excitement and confidence. They prefer not to read essays that are overly pessimistic, antagonistic or critical. This doesn't mean that you have to put a happy spin on every word written or that you can't write about a serious topic or problem. For example, if you were a judge reading the following essays about the very serious topic of teen pregnancy, to which author's education fund would you rather make a contribution?

Thesis 1:
```
We could reduce the number of pregnant teens if we shifted
our efforts away from scare tactics to providing responsible
sex education combined with frank discussions regarding the
responsibilities of caring for a child.
```

Thesis 2:
```
Teen pregnancy is incurable. Teenagers will always act ir-
responsibly and it would be futile for us to believe that we
can control this behavior.
```

Scholarship committees favor authors who not only recognize problems but also present potential solutions. Leave being pessimistic to adults. You are young, with your entire future ahead of you. Your optimism is what makes you so exciting and why organizations want to give you money to pursue your passion for changing the world. Don't shy away from this opportunity.

Be Concise. The scholarship essay may not have the strict limits of a college admission essay, but that does not give you a license to be verbose. Keep your essay tight, focused and within the recommended length of the scholarship guidelines. If no parameters are given, one or two pages should suffice. You certainly want the readers to get through the entirety of your masterpiece. Remember that most scholarship selection committees are composed of volunteers who are under no obligation to read your entire essay. Make your main points quickly and keep your essay as brief and to the point as possible.

Step 4 Don't Neglect Your Introduction and Conclusion

Studies have found that the most important parts of a speech are the first and last minutes. In between, listeners fade in and out rather than constantly pay attention. It is the introduction and conclusion that leave a lasting impact. This holds true for scholarship essays as well. You need to have a memorable introduction and conclusion. If you don't, the readers may not make it past your introductory paragraph or they may discount your quality essay after reading a lackluster ending. Spend extra time making sure these two parts deliver the message you want. Here are some tips to create knockout introductions and conclusions:

For Introductions

Create action or movement. Think of the introduction as the high-speed car chase at the beginning of a movie that catches the audience's attention.

Pose a question. Questions draw the readers' attention for two reasons. First, they think about how they would answer the query as you have posed it. Second, they are curious to see how you will answer or present solutions to the question in your essay.

Describe. If you can create a vivid image for readers, they will be more likely to want to read on.

For Conclusions

Be thoughtful. Your conclusion should make the second most powerful statement in your essay because this is what your readers will remember. (The most powerful statement should be in your introduction.)

Leave a parting thought. The scholarship committee members have already read your essay (we hope), so you don't need to rehash what you have already said. It's okay to summarize in one sentence, but you want to do more than just "wrap it up". You have one final opportunity to make an impression, so add a parting thought. This should be one last observation or idea that ties into the main point of your essay.

Don't be too quick to end. Too many students tack on a meaningless conclusion or even worse, don't have one at all. Have a decent conclusion that goes with the rest of your essay. Never end your essay with the two words, "The End."

Step 5 Find Editors

Despite what you may think, you're not infallible. Stop gasping—it's true. This means it's important to get someone else to edit your work. Roommates, friends, family members, teachers, professors or advisors make great editors. When you get another person to read your essay, he or she will find errors that eluded you, as well as parts that are unclear to someone reading your essay for the first time. Ask your editors to make sure your ideas are clear, that you answer the question

Chapter 4:
How to Write a Winning Scholarship Essay

appropriately and that your essay is interesting. Take their suggestions seriously. The more input you get from others and the more times you rewrite your work, the better.

You want your essay to be like silk—smooth and elegant. When you read your work, make sure the connections between ideas are logical and the flow of your writing is understandable. (This is where editors can be extremely helpful.) Also check that you have not included any unnecessary details that might obscure the main point of your essay. Be careful to include any information that is vital to your thesis. Your goal is to produce an essay with clear points and supporting examples that logically flow together.

You also want to make sure that your spelling and grammar are perfect. Again, the best way to do this is to have someone else read your work. If you don't have time to ask someone, then do it yourself—but do it carefully. Read your essay at least once with the sole purpose of looking for spelling and grammatical mistakes. (Your computer's spell check is not 100 percent reliable and won't catch when you accidentally describe how you bake bread with one cup of "flower" instead of "flour.") Try reading your work out loud to listen for grammatical mistakes.

Step 6　Recycle Your Essays

This has no relation to aluminum cans or newspapers. In this case recycling means reusing essays you have written for college applications, classes or even other scholarships. Because colleges and scholarship committees usually ask very broad questions, this is generally doable and saves you a tremendous amount of time. Later in this chapter you will read an example essay. You may be surprised to learn that the author recycled her essay with minimal changes to answer such differing questions as these: "Tell us about one of your dreams," "What is something you believe in strongly?" and "What past experience continues to influence you today?"

However, be careful not to recycle an essay when it just doesn't fit. It's better to spend the extra time to write an appropriate essay than to submit one that doesn't match the scholarship or answer the question.

Seven Sins of the Scholarship Essay

Instead of writing an essay, one student placed the sheet of paper on the floor and tap danced on it. She then wrote that she hoped the scuff marks on the paper were evidence of her enthusiasm. In the judges' eyes, this was a silly stunt and, of course, her application was sent to the rejection pile. While you may not make such an egregious error, there are common mistakes that you need to avoid. Most of these lessons were learned the hard way—through actual experience.

1. DON'T Write a Sob Story

Everyone who applies for a scholarship needs money. Many have overcome obstacles and personal hardships. However, few scholarships are designed to reward students based on the "quantity" of hardships. Scholarship judges are not looking to give their money to those who have suffered the most. On the contrary, they want to give money to students who came up with a plan to succeed despite an obstacle. Therefore, if you are writing about the hardships you have faced, be sure that you spend as much time, if not more, describing how you have overcome or plan to rise above those challenges.

2. DON'T Use the Shotgun Approach

A common mistake is to write one essay and submit it without any changes to dozens of scholarships—hoping that maybe one will be a winner. While we do recommend that you recycle your essays, you should not just copy your essays and blast them out to every scholarship committee. This simply does not work. Unless the scholarships have identical questions, missions and goals, your essay cannot be reused verbatim. Spend the time to craft an essay for each scholarship, and you will win more than if you write just one and blindly send it off to many awards.

3. DON'T Be Afraid to Get Words on Paper

One common cause of writer's block is the fear of beginning. When you sit down to write, don't be afraid to write a draft, or even ideas for a draft, that are not perfect. You will have time to revise your work. What you want to do is get words on paper. They can be wonderfully intelligent words or they can be vague concepts. The point is that you should just write. Too many students wait until the last minute and get stuck at the starting line.

4. DON'T Try to Be Someone Else

Since you want to be the one the scholarship judges are seeking to reward with money, you need to highlight achievements and strengths that match the criteria of the scholarship. But you don't want to lie about yourself or try to be someone you are not. Besides being dishonest, the scholarship judges will probably pick up on your affectation and hold it against you.

5. DON'T Try to Impress with Feats of Literary Gymnastics

You won't get any bonus points for overusing clichés, quotes or words you don't understand. Too many students think that quotes and clichés will impress scholarship judges; but unless they are used sparingly and appropriately, they will win you no favors. (Remember that quotes and clichés are not your words and are therefore not original.) The same goes for overusing the thesaurus. Do experiment with words that are less familiar to you, but do not make the thesaurus your co-author. It's better to use simple words correctly than to make blunders with complicated ones.

6. DON'T Stray Too Far from the Topic

A mistake that many students make is that they don't actually answer the question. This is especially true with recycled essays. Make sure that your essays, whether written from scratch or recycled from others, address the question asked.

7. DON'T Write Your Stats

A common mistake is to repeat your statistics from your application form. Often these essays begin with "My name is" and go on to list classes, GPAs and extracurricular activities. All this information is found in your application. On top of that, it's boring. If you are going to write about a class or activity, make it interesting by focusing on a specific class or activity.

Example Winning Scholarship Essays

It's one thing to study the theory behind the pheromones of love, but it is entirely a different thing to experience the euphoria, quickened heartbeat and walking-on-clouds feeling that goes with love. In a similar way, you have seen the theory behind writing a powerful scholarship essay. It is now time to see this theory in action.

The following two essays were written by students who won scholarships. In each essay you will see how winning principles are put to use. The results are essays that inspire, provoke and most important, win money. As with any example essay, please remember that this is not necessarily the way your essay should be written. Use these sample essays as illustrations of how a good essay might look. Your essay will naturally be different and unique to your own style and personality.

Winning Essay: My Two Dads

This essay was written by Gregory James Yee, a graduate of Whitney High School in Cerritos, California. Although Gregory is a student at Stanford University, he wrote this essay as part of his application to the University of Southern California. Besides garnering an acceptance to USC, this essay also earned him a $7,500 per year Trustee Scholarship. Remember that many colleges use your college application to automatically consider you for scholarships they offer.

The topic of the essay is Gregory's musical talent, which was discovered early in his life. At the age of two, he could hum *The Star-Spangled Banner* in perfect rhythm and pitch; and at age four, he began piano lessons. Throughout his 15 years of lessons, he won numerous awards, including the Raissa Tselentis Award given to one student nationwide for outstanding performance in the Advanced Bach category of the National Guild Audition. He is also a composer.

My Two Dads

I have two fathers. My first and biological father is the one who taught me how to drive a car, throw a baseball and find the area under a curve using integral calculus, among the innumerable other common duties of a good dad. He has been there for me through the ups of my successful piano career and the downs of my first breakup, and has always offered his insightful hand of guidance. My second father is who I connect with on a different level; he is the only person I know who thinks like I do. My second dad is my music composition teacher, Tony Fox, and he shares the one passion that has been a part of my life since the age of two: music.

Tony is a hardworking professor who can spend hours illustrating the meaning of a particular chord in a famous classical composition or ease an extraordinarily stressful situation with his colorful wit. He may appear intimidating to a new student at USC as the Assistant Band Director, but once someone mentions music, there is no one more adept, more creative or more dedicated to making music for the world to hear than Tony.

Tony has touched my life in a way few people have experienced. At my lessons with him, I bring compositions I am in the progress of perfecting, and with a few words of his guidance, I can almost see the changes needed before he mentions them. Almost instantly after I ask a question — such as which chord progression works best at a certain point in the music or why a certain counter melody sounds so beautiful—we agree on what is best for the music. It is almost as if we know what the other is thinking and merely state aloud our thoughts just in case one or the other is caught off guard. It is truly rare to find two people who agree with each other on what it is exactly that makes compositions aesthetically pleasing. Last year when I was working on a composition, I ran into a discouraging roadblock that could have delayed my progress significantly. No one in my family and none of my friends could help.

However, as soon as I shared the piece with Tony, he made some suggestions and together we made the necessary amendments to the music. The result was a finished project, a beautiful mosaic of our collective design, and it was debuted last year by my high school wind ensemble. When I first heard my music performed, I thought back to the hours I had spent tinkering at my piano and Tony's thoughtful guidance. This is how Tony and I relate. It's a common frequency upon which the most advanced radio cannot even begin to comprehend.

Tony has filled in areas of my life where few people, including my real father, could understand. He is the teacher of lessons big and small, from looking into the eyes of those whose hands I shake to recognizing that time is the most valuable gift one can give or receive. Whereas many of my peers have only one father, I have been fortunate enough to have two of them.

Why This Essay Won

An accomplished musician like Gregory could have written an essay that was simply a retelling of all the musical awards he had won. Instead, Gregory gives insight into what music means to him and takes us into his mind to see the creative and learning process at work. Writing about what he goes through to create a composition allows even those of us who are tone deaf to experience vicariously what it is like to create music.

Notice how Gregory uses powerful imagery to show us how he interacts with his music teacher and overcomes difficulties while composing. Gregory also subtly includes some of his most important musical accomplishments. Although he

Chapter 4:
How to Write a Winning Scholarship Essay

listed many of his awards in his application, this essay takes us beyond those achievements and really lets us see the wonderful person behind those awards.

Winning Essay: Leadership

Donald H. Matsuda, Jr. is the kind of person who doesn't just act. He inspires others to act as well. In his application for the Truman Scholarship, Donald shared how he directed community leaders and health professionals to start a series of health insurance drives. This is one of the essays that he wrote to become one of 80 Truman Scholars in the country.

From Sacramento and a graduate of Stanford University, Donald also founded the San Mateo Children's Health Insurance Program, directed the United Students for Veterans' Health and founded the Nepal Pediatric Clinical Internship.

Leadership

A few years ago, I saw a shocking headline on the front page of the New York Times that read: "Forty-Four Million Americans Without Health Insurance." Upon reading the article, I was stunned to discover that one-third of these uninsured Americans were children. Such figures made it clear to me that work needed to be done to remedy this problem, and I was ready to take action.

At this time, I was working at the Health for All Clinic as a public health and community outreach intern, and I decided to approach the director about this problem. He clearly agreed that immediate action needed to be taken to control the growing numbers of America's uninsured. However, he admitted that the clinic did not have the time, energy or the funds to invest in such an ambitious endeavor. I was not discouraged by his response. Instead, I saw this challenge as an opportunity to gain firsthand experience as a change agent in the field of public policy.

After completing extensive research, I discovered a unique program called Healthy Families. The ultimate goal of this government program is to provide low-cost insurance coverage to children who do not qualify for traditional insurance plans. I decided to develop my own project from scratch, proposing to launch a sustainable series of Healthy Families insurance drives at the Health for All Clinic. I applied for funding through the Haas Center for Public Service Fellowship program, and the clinic director signed on as my community partner for the project.

During the next six months, I worked very closely with the clinic staff to organize and plan this series of insurance drives. I recruited various ethnic community leaders and healthcare professionals to help generate support for the program and assembled several advertising campaigns in the surrounding communities. The clinic director and I also developed a workshop on immigrant health to attract more diverse populations to our insurance drives. After holding three Healthy Families drives, the clinic managed to sign up over 150 children for this program. The director was elated by this turnout and established an entire Healthy Families division to build upon the success of this project. Upon completion of this project, I started directing other insurance drives with the hope of improving the health and well-being of America's children.

Why This Essay Won
Donald's essay only scratches the surface of his accomplishments, which is exactly how it should be. Instead of listing every leadership role he has ever had, Donald explains how he created a health care program in his community. He begins with his motivation for starting the program and then recounts the initial skepticism that he faced when he first proposed the idea. Donald's essay describes the various difficulties and ultimate success of his project.

Notice that Donald does not describe a typical leadership role, one in which he was elected as a leader. This is an excellent example of how you can take a project in which you played a significant role and show how it demonstrates your leadership abilities. Remember, leadership is not just an elected position.

Where to Find More Winning Scholarship Essays
We believe that reading real essays is the best way for you to really see what works, and these essays are certainly a start. Unfortunately, we could not include more than two examples in this book. If you want more scholarship essay examples, take a look at our book, *How to Write a Winning Scholarship Essay*. In it you will find 30 additional winning essays from students who tested the waters of many topics and wrote in a variety of styles. Also, take a look at our website, SuperCollege (www.supercollege.com), where we post additional example essays. We think you'll be inspired.

The Scholarship Resume

Chapter 5

Write Your Own One-Page Autobiography

If you want to say that your life is a book, then be ready to follow with the analogy that your scholarship resume is the *CliffsNotes* summary. A scholarship resume is your opportunity to tout your greatest achievements and life's accomplishments. The only catch is that you are limited to one page. Some scholarship committees require resumes as a part of the application process so that they can use them to get a quick overview of your achievements. Others don't, but including a resume will always enhance your application.

A scholarship resume is not the same as one that you would use to get a job. It's unlikely that your work experience (if you have any) will be the focus. However, the principles and format are the same. A good resume that scores you a job shows employers that you have the right combination of work experience and skills to be their next hire. Similarly, your scholarship resume should show the committee why you are the most qualified student to win their award.

Think of the scholarship resume as a "cheat sheet" that you give to the judges. By looking at your resume, the judges get a quick overview of your achievements and interests. The resume is not an exhaustive list of everything you have done. It rather highlights and summarizes the most impressive and relevant achievements.

To make sure that it really focuses on the crème de la crème, your resume should fit on a single sheet of paper. This is sometimes harder than it sounds.

Here is the information you need for a scholarship resume:

- **Contact information:** Your vital statistics, including name, address, phone number and email.

- **Education:** Schools you've attended beginning with high school, expected or actual graduation dates.

- **Academic achievements:** Relevant coursework, awards and honors received.

- **Extracurricular experience.** Relevant extracurricular activities, locations and dates of participation, job titles, responsibilities and accomplishments.

- **Work experience:** Where and when you've worked, job titles, responsibilities and accomplishments on the job.

- **Skills and interests:** Additional relevant technical, lingual or other skills or talents that do not fit in the categories above.

Don't worry if your resume presents the same information that's in the application form. Some judges will read only the application or your resume, so it's important your key points are in both. However, in the resume, try to expand on areas that you were not able to cover fully in the application.

Example Resume that Worked

There are many good ways to format a resume. Most important, your resume should be easy to skim and be organized in a logical manner. Here is an example of a well-written scholarship resume. Remember that there are other equally good formats in which to present this information.

Melissa Lee
1000 University Drive
San Francisco, CA 94134
(415) 555-5555
melissa@email.com

Education
University of San Francisco; San Francisco, CA
B.A. candidate in sociology. Expected graduation in 2030. Honor roll.

Lowell High School; San Francisco, CA
Graduated in 2026 with highest honors. Principal's Honor Roll, 4 years.

Activities and Awards
SF Educational Project; San Francisco, CA
Program Assistant. Recruited and trained 120 students for various community service projects in semester-long program. Managed and evaluated student journals, lesson plans and program participation. 2024-present.

Lowell High School Newspaper; San Francisco, CA
Editor-In-Chief. Recruited and managed staff of 50. Oversaw all editorial and business functions. Newspaper was a finalist for the prestigious Examiner Award for excellence in student journalism. 2022-2026.

Evangelical Church; San Francisco, CA
Teacher. Prepared and taught weekly lessons for third grade Sunday School class. Received dedication to service award from congregation. 2022-2026.

Asian Dance Troupe; San Francisco, CA
Member. Performed at community functions and special events. 2024-present.

Employment
Palo Alto Daily News; Palo Alto, CA
Editorial Assistant. Researched and wrote eight feature articles on such topics as education reform, teen suicide and summer fashion. Led series of teen-reader response panels. Summer 2026.

Russian Hill Public Library; San Francisco, CA
Library Page. Received "Page of the Month" Award for outstanding performance. Summers 2024-2025.

Interests
Fluent in Mandarin and HTML. Interests include journal writing, creative writing, photography, swimming and aerobics.

Chapter 5:
The Scholarship Resume

- Some points to note about this resume:

- Notice how this resume is concise and very easy to read. By limiting herself to a single page, Melissa makes sure that even if you just scan her resume, you will pick up her key strengths.

- See how each description includes examples of leadership as well as awards or special recognition.

- Melissa conveys the impact of her work by pointing out concrete results (which you should also do on the application form).

- Notice how her description of summer jobs highlights some of her key accomplishments.

- The final section adds a nice balance by describing some of her other hobbies and interests.

Elements of a Powerful Resume

Your resume should be descriptive enough for the judges to understand each item but not so wordy that they can't find what they need. It should be neatly organized and easy to follow. Having reviewed hundreds of resumes, here are some simple strategies that we've developed to help you:

Include only the important information. Remember to incorporate only the most relevant items and use what you know about the scholarship organization to guide how you prioritize what you share in your resume. Only include things that support your fit with the scholarship's mission. For each piece of information, ask yourself these two questions: Will including this aid the selection committee in seeing that I am a match for the award? Is this information necessary to convince them that I should receive the award?

Focus on responsibilities and achievements. In describing your experiences in work and activities, focus on the responsibilities you held and highlight measurable or unique successes such as starting a project, reaching goals or implementing one of your ideas. For example, if you were the treasurer of the Literary Club, you would want to include that you were responsible for managing a $10,000 annual budget.

Demonstrate in your resume how you showed leadership. Leadership could include leading a project or team, instructing others or mentoring your peers. What's more important than your title or where you worked is the quality of your involvement. Explaining your successes and your role as a leader will provide concrete evidence of your contribution.

Be proud. Your resume is your time to shine. Don't be afraid to draw attention to all that you've accomplished. If you played a key role in a project, say so. If you exceeded your goals, advertise it. No one else is going to do your bragging for you.

Use action verbs. When you are describing your achievements, use action verbs such as these: founded, organized, achieved, created, developed, directed and (our personal favorite) initiated.

Don't tell tall stories. On the flip side of being proud is being untruthful. It's important that you describe yourself in the most glowing way possible, but stay connected with the truth. If you developed a new filing system at your job, don't claim that you single-handedly led a corporate revolution. With your complete scholarship application, selection committees can see through a resume that is exaggerated and doesn't match the rest of the application, essay and recommendations.

Get editors. After the hundredth time reading your resume, you'll probably not notice an error that someone reading it for the first time will catch. Get others to read and edit your resume. Editors can let you know if something doesn't make sense, offer you alternative wording and help correct your boo-boos. Some good choices for editors may be teachers or professors, work supervisors or parents. Work supervisors may be especially helpful since part of their job is to review resumes of job applicants. Your school may also offer resume help in the counseling department or career services office.

Avoid creating an eye test. In trying to squeeze all the information onto a single page, don't make your font size so small that the words are illegible. Try to leave space between paragraphs. The judges may have tired, weary eyes from reading all those applications. Don't strain them even more.

Strive for perfection. It's a given that your resume should be error-free. There's no excuse for mistakes on a one-page document that is meant to exemplify your life's work.

Include Your Resume in Every Application

Once you have a resume, include it with every scholarship application. In addition, you should also give it to your recommenders so that they have a "cheat sheet" that highlights your accomplishments when it comes time to write those letters of recommendations. They will no doubt want to mention some of your successes to make their letters on point and personal. Remember, your resume is *you*!

Getting Great Recommendations

Chapter 6

Letters of Recommendation Count

If you need a reason to kiss up to your teachers or professors, here's one: recommendations. Scholarships sometime require that you submit recommendations from teachers, professors, school administrators, employers or others who can vouch for your accomplishments. Scholarship judges use these testaments to get another perspective of your character and accomplishments. Viewed together with your application and essay, the recommendation helps the judges get a more complete picture of who you are. Plus, it's always impressive when someone else extols your virtues.

Many students believe that they have no control over the recommendation part of their application. This isn't true. You actually can have a lot of input regarding the letters that your recommenders write. In this chapter we will explore several ways—all perfectly ethical—to ensure that you get great recommendations.

A recommendation is an important opportunity for someone else to tell scholarship judges why you deserve to win. You may assume that because others do the actual writing, recommendations are completely out of your control. Banish that thought. The secret is to not only pick the right people but to also provide them with all of the information they need to turn out a great letter of recommendation. Many applicants overlook this fact. But not you, right? Armed with superb recommendations, your scholarship application is sure to rise to the top.

Find People to Say Nice Things about You

Your first task is to find recommenders. Unfortunately, Mom, Dad and anyone else related to you is excluded. So, how do you get those recommendations without familial ties to sing your praises?

First, think about all the people in your life who can speak meaningfully about you and your accomplishments. Your list may include teachers, professors, advisors, school administrators, employers, religious leaders, coaches or leaders of organizations and activities in which you are involved. While some scholarships require recommendations from specific people (like a teacher or professor), most are pretty liberal and allow you to select anyone who knows you.

Second, once you have a list of potential recommenders, analyze which of these people could present information about you that best matches the goals of the scholarships.

If you apply for an academic scholarship, you'll want at least one teacher or professor to write a recommendation. If you apply for an athletic scholarship, a coach would be a good choice. Select people who are able to write about the things that are most important to the scholarship judges. A good exercise is to imagine what your potential recommender would write and whether or not this would enhance your case for winning the scholarship.

After considering these two questions, you should be left with only a few people from which to choose. If you can't decide between two equally qualified people, choose the one who knows you the best as a person. For example, if you got A's in three classes and are trying to decide which professor to ask for a recommendation, pick the one who can write *more* than a testament to your academic ability. This is important because a recommendation that contains comments on your character is extremely memorable. Maybe one of the professors knows you well enough to include a few sentences on your drive to succeed or your family background. Ideally, your recommender is able to describe not only your performance in the classroom but also the values and character traits that make you special.

Give Your Recommender the Chance to Say "No"

Once you've selected those you'd like to write your recommendations, ask them to do so—early. A general rule is to allow at least three weeks before the recommendation is due. Explain that you are applying for scholarships and are required to submit recommendations from people who know you and who can comment on some of your achievements.

It's important to ask the person a question like this: "Do you feel comfortable writing a recommendation letter for me?" This allows the person the opportunity to decline your request if he or she doesn't feel comfortable or doesn't have the time. If you get a negative or hesitant response, don't assume that it's because he or she has a low opinion of you. It could simply be that the person doesn't know you well enough or is too busy to write a thoughtful recommendation. It's much better to have the recommender decline to write a letter than to get one that is rushed or not entirely positive. In most cases, however, potential recommenders are flattered and happy to oblige.

Don't Play the Name Game

From being recognized by strangers to getting preferential reservations at the hottest restaurants, there are a lot of perks to being famous. You might think that this special treatment carries over to recommendations, and that scholarship judges will be star-struck by a letter from someone with a fancy title. However, don't assume that just because you ask someone well known to write your recommendations that you are a shoo-in for the scholarship. In fact, you might be surprised to learn that doing so could actually hurt your chances of winning.

So the question is this: "Should I try to find someone famous to write a letter of recommendation for me?" The answer comes down to the principles outlined above. How well does the person know you, and can he or she write about you in a way that presents you as a viable candidate for the scholarship? If the answer is "yes," then by all means ask the person to help you. However, if you don't know the person very well or if what he or she will write could lack a connection to the qualities that the scholarship committee is looking for, it's better to forgo the value of high name recognition and ask someone who can address what's most important in a letter of recommendation.

For example, if you work as a summer intern for your state senator, you may think that a letter from such a political luminary would give your application the star power to set it apart from others with recommendations from mere mortals. However, if you spent more time photocopying or stuffing envelopes than you did developing keen political strategies, and you saw the senator as many times as you have fingers on your left hand, chances are that he or she would have very few meaningful things to say about your performance. "A skilled photocopier" and "brewed a mean cup of coffee" are not compliments you want sent to the scholarship judges.

If you ask someone well known to write your recommendations, make sure that he or she really knows you and can speak about your accomplishments personally and meaningfully. The quality of what is said in the recommendations is much more important than whose signature is at the bottom of the page.

Do the Grunt Work for Your Recommenders

Once you've selected your recommenders, give them everything they need to get the job done. Since they are doing you a favor, make the process as easy as possible for them. This is also where you can most influence what they write and actually direct what accomplishments they highlight. But before we delve into the specifics, here is an overview of what you need to provide each recommender:

Cover letter: This describes the scholarships you are applying for. In the letter, you should list deadlines and give the recommenders direct guidance on what to write. More on this in a bit.

Resume: A resume provides a quick overview of your most important achievements in an easy to follow one-page format. It is also what your recommenders will use as they cite your important achievements.

Chapter 6:
Getting Great Recommendations

Recommendation form: Some scholarships provide an actual form that your recommenders need to complete either electronically or on paper. Fill in the parts that you can, such as your name and address.

Pre-addressed, stamped envelopes: Read the application materials to find out if you need to submit your recommendations separately or with the rest of your application. For letters that are to be mailed separately, provide your recommenders with envelopes that are stamped and have the scholarship's mailing address on them. If you are supposed to submit the letters with your application, provide your recommenders with envelopes on which you have written your name. Many recommenders prefer to write letters that are confidential and that you don't get to read. Once you have everything, place it in a folder or envelope and label it with your recommender's name.

Give Your Recommenders a Script

Because you know yourself better than anyone else, you would probably receive the best recommendations if you sat down and wrote them yourself. Unfortunately, this practice is frowned upon by scholarship judges. Short of writing your own recommendations, you can influence how they turn out by providing your recommenders with detailed descriptions of your accomplishments that can help them decide which aspects of you to highlight in their letters. This is best done through the cover letter that you send to the prospective recommender.

Your cover letter provides your recommenders with all the information that they need to write your recommendations, including details about the scholarships and suggestions for what you'd like the recommendations to address. Since the cover letter also includes other essentials like deadlines, mailing or submitting instructions and a thank you, you will not sound as if you are giving orders but rather that you are providing helpful assistance. In fact, your recommenders will appreciate your reminding them what's important and what they should include.

Here are the elements to include in your cover letter:

Details on the scholarships: List the scholarships for which you will use their letters. Give a brief one-paragraph description of the mission of each of the awards and what qualities the scholarship committee seeks. This information will help your recommenders understand which of your qualities are important to convey and who will read the letters.

How you fit the scholarship: This is the most important part of your cover letter because it's your chance to remind your recommenders of your accomplishments and to offer suggestions for what to write. Make sure that you highlight how you match the goals of the scholarships. For example, if you are applying for a scholarship for future teachers, include information about your student teaching experience and the coursework you've taken in education. Leave out the fact that you were on the tennis team.

Deadlines: Inform your recommenders of how long they have to compose the letters. If time permits, ask them to mail the letters a week before the actual deadlines.

What to do with the letters when they're done: Give your recommenders instructions about what to do with the completed letters. You may want to offer to pick them up, or you might explain that you have included addressed, stamped envelopes so that the letters can be mailed. If the letters are to be submitted electronically, provide these details.

Thank you: Recommendations may take several hours to complete, and your recommenders are very busy people. Don't forget to say thank you in advance for writing you a great letter of recommendation.

To illustrate the power of a good cover letter, read the example on the following page as if you were a recommender. Remember that this is only one example and your cover letter will naturally be different. However, regardless of your individual writing style, your cover letter should include the same points as the following example.

Chapter 6:
Getting Great Recommendations

Some notes about this cover letter:

- Beth describes each scholarship she is applying for, its goal and deadline, and why she feels she is a match for the award.
- The heart of the cover letter is here, where Beth gives a quick summary of information she suggests her professor include in the letter.
- Beth provides instructions about what to do with the letters when completed.
- This is a well-written cover letter that is brief and easy to understand.

Dear Dr. Louis,

Thank you again for writing my scholarship recommendations. I want to do my best to be competitive for these awards. They are very important for my family as they will help me to pay for my education. Here are the scholarships I am applying for:

SuperCollege.com Scholarship Deadline: July 31
This is a national scholarship based on academic and non-academic achievement, including extracurricular activities and honors. I believe I'm a match for this scholarship because of my commitment to academics (I currently have a 3.85 grade point average) and because of the volunteer work I do with the Youth Literacy Project and the PLUS program.

Quill & Scroll Scholarship Deadline: April 20
This scholarship is for students who want to pursue a career in journalism. As you know, I am an editor for our school newspaper, contributing a column each week on issues that affect our student body. Journalism is the field I want to enter after graduation.

Community Scholarship Deadline: May 5
This scholarship is for students who have given back to their communities through public service. I have always been committed to public service. Outside of class, I not only formed the Youth Literacy Project but have also volunteered with the PLUS program.

To help you with your recommendation, I've enclosed a resume. Also, here are some highlights of specific accomplishments that I was hoping you might comment on in your letter:

* The essay I wrote for your class that won the Young Hemingway competition
* How I formed the Youth Literacy Project with you as the project's advisor
* My three years of volunteer work with the PLUS program
* The weekly column I've written for the newspaper on school issues

After you've finished, please return the recommendations to me in the envelopes I've enclosed. If you have any questions, please feel free to contact me at 555-5555. Again, thank you very much for taking the time to help me.

Sincerely,

Beth

Don't Let Your Recommenders Miss Deadlines

All recommenders have one thing in common: Too much to do and not enough time. It's important that you check with your recommender a couple of weeks before the letters are due. You need to monitor the progress of your recommendations. You may find that they're complete and already in the mail. A more common discovery is that they won't have been touched. Be polite yet diligent when you ask about the progress. It's crucial that you work with your recommenders to get the letters in on time.

The "You Can't Spell Success Without U" Mug

You now have everything you need to receive stellar recommendations. It's important to remember that even if it is a part of their job description, your recommenders are spending their time to help you. Remember this as you ask others to write recommendation letters and be sure to let them know that you appreciate their efforts.

Sometimes, a thank you gift is appropriate. Every time my (Kelly) mother wants to say thank you to a friend or acquaintance, she writes a note and gives a small token gift. My favorite is the "You Can't Spell Success Without U" mug because of its campy play on words.

Whether or not you select an equally campy token of appreciation, it's important that you thank your recommenders. After all, they are dedicating their free time to help you win funds for college.

Ace the Scholarship Interview

Chapter 7

The Face-to-Face Encounter

A judge for the Rotary scholarship shared with us the following true story. For the last phase of the scholarship competition for his region, the finalists met with the selection committee for an interview. The interview was very important and was the final step in determining who would win the $25,000 scholarship.

One finalist was an Ivy League student who flew across the country for the interview. Within the first five minutes, it was painfully clear to all the judges that the applicant didn't have the foggiest idea what the Rotary Club stood for. It's as if the applicant thought that his resume and Ivy League pedigree would make him a winner. As you can guess, this applicant had a very disappointing flight back to his college. Lesson number one for the scholarship interview: At the very least, know what the organization stands for.

Many students dread the interview. If your heart beats faster or your palms moisten when you think about the prospect of sitting face to face with the judges, you are not alone. While the other parts of the scholarship application take time and effort, they can be done in the privacy of your home. Interviews, on the other hand, require interaction with—gasp—a real live human.

The good news is that the interview is usually the final step in the scholarship application process and if you make it that far, you're a serious contender. In this chapter, we show you what most scholarship committees are looking for and how you should prepare to deliver a winning interview. We also show you how to make the most of your nervousness and how to turn it into an asset rather than a liability.

There are two secrets for doing well in scholarship interviews. The first is this: Remind yourself over and over again that scholarship interviewers are real people. Repeat it until you believe it. As such, your goal is to have as normal a conversation as possible, despite the fact that thousands of dollars may hang in the balance. It's essential that you treat interviewers as real people, interact with them and ask them questions.

The second secret is just as important: The best way to have successful interviews is to train for them. The more you practice interviewing, the more comfortable you'll be during the real thing. Don't worry—we'll tell you what kinds of questions to expect and how to perfect your answers.

Why Human Interaction Is Necessary

The first step to delivering a knockout interview is to understand why some scholarships require interviews in the first place. With the popularity of technology like e-mail and text messaging, there seems to be less need for human interaction. (Believe it or not, there was a time when telephones were answered by a person instead of a maze of touchtone options.)

For some scholarship committees, a few pieces of paper with scores and autobiographical writing are not enough to get a full picture of who the applicants really are. They are giving away a lot of cash and the judges are responsible for making sure they are giving it to the most deserving students possible.

Scholarship judges use interviews as a way to learn how you compare in person versus on paper. Having been on both sides of the interview table, we can attest to the fact that the person you expect based on the written application is not always the person you meet at the interview. It's important to know that the purpose of interviews is not to interrogate you, but rather for the scholarship committee to get to know you better and probe deeper into the reason that you deserve their money.

Interviewers Are Real People Too

If you've ever met someone famous, you've probably realized that while celebrities' faces may grace the covers of magazines and they have houses big enough to merit their own ZIP code, they eat, drink and sleep and have likes and dislikes just like other people. The same thing holds true for interviewers.

Interviewers can be high-profile professors or high-powered businesspeople, but they are all passionate about some topics and bored with others. They enjoy speaking about themselves and getting to know more about you. Acknowledging this will help keep your nerves under control. Throughout the interview, remind yourself that your interviewer is human, and strive to make the interview a conversation, not an interrogation.

Interview Homework

You'd never walk into a test and expect to do well without studying the material. The same is true for interviews. Don't attempt them without doing your homework. There is basic information you need to know before starting your interviews so that you appear informed and knowledgeable. It's not difficult information to obtain, and it goes a long way in demonstrating that you care enough about winning to have put in some effort. Here are some things you should know before any interview:

Purpose of the scholarship: What is the organization hoping to accomplish by awarding the scholarship? Whether it's promoting students to enter a certain career area, encouraging a hobby or interest or rewarding students for leadership, every scholarship has a mission.

Criteria for selecting the winner: From the scholarship materials, you can get information about what the judges are hoping to find in a winner. From the kinds of information they request in the application to the topic of the essay question, each piece is a clue about what is important to the judges. Scholarships can be based on academic achievement, nonacademic achievement or leadership, to name a few criteria. Understand what kind of student the organization is seeking and stress that side of yourself during the interview.

Background of the awarding organization: Do a little digging on the organization itself. Check out its website or publications. Attend a meeting or speak with someone who's a member. From this detective work, you will get a better idea of who the organization's members are and what they are trying to achieve. It can also be a great topic of conversation during the interview.

Background of your interviewer: If possible, find out as much as you can about who will be interviewing you. In many cases, you may know little more than their names and occupations, but if you can, find out more. You already have one piece of important information about your interviewers: You know that they are passionate about the organization and its mission. They wouldn't be volunteering their time to conduct interviews if they weren't.

Use Your Detective Work to Create an Advantage

Once you've done your detective work on the above topics, it's time to use the information you've uncovered. For example, if you are in front of a group of doctors and they ask you about your activities, you would be better off discussing your work at the local hospital than your success on the baseball diamond. As much as possible, focus the conversation on areas where your activities, goals, interests and achievements match the goal of the awarding organization. By discussing what matters most to the scholarship judges, you will insure that this will be a memorable conversation—one that will set you apart from the other applicants that are interviewed.

By knowing something about your interviewers beforehand, you can think of topics and questions that will be interesting to them. Most interviewers allow some time for you to ask questions. Here again your detective work will come in handy since you can ask them about their background or the history of the organization. By asking intelligent questions (i.e. not the ones that can be answered by simply reading the group's mission statement) you will demonstrate that you've done your homework.

You'll also give interviewers something interesting to talk about—either themselves or their organization. The more information you can get before the

Chapter 7:
Ace the Scholarship Interview

interview, the better you will perform. Having this background material will also allow you to answer unexpected questions better and come up with thoughtful questions for the judges if you are put on the spot.

You Are Not the Center of the Universe

Despite what Mom or Dad says, the Earth revolves around the sun, not you. It helps to remember this in your interviews. Your life may be the most interesting ever lived, but this is still no excuse for speaking only about yourself for the duration of the interview.

The secret to successful interviews is simply this: They should be *interactive*. The surest way to bore your interviewers is to spend the entire time speaking only about yourself. You may have had the unfortunate experience of being on the receiving end of a conversation like this if you have a friend who speaks nonstop about herself and who never seems to be interested in your life or what you have to say. Don't you just hate this kind of conversation? So will your scholarship interviewers.

To prevent a self-centered monologue, constantly look for ways to interact with your interviewers. In addition to answering questions, ask some yourself. Ask about their experiences in school or with the organization. Inquire about their thoughts on some of the questions they pose to you. Take time to learn about your interviewers' experiences and perspectives.

Also, speak about topics that interest your interviewers. You can tell which topics intrigue them by their reactions and body language. From the detective work you've done, you also have an idea of what they are passionate about.

Try to make your interviews a two-way conversation instead of a one-way monologue. Engage your interviewers and keep them interested. If you do this, they will remember your interview as a great conversation and you as a wonderful, intelligent person deserving of their award.

Look and Sound the Part

Studies on the effectiveness of speeches have shown that how you sound and how you look when you present your material is more important than what you actually say. From that, we can learn that it is positively essential that you make a good visual presentation. Here are some tips to make sure that you look and sound your best, an important complement to what you actually say to the judges:

Dress appropriately: A backward-turned baseball cap and baggy jeans slung down to your thighs may be standard fare for the mall (at least they were last season), but they are not appropriate for interviews.

You probably don't have to wear a suit unless you find out through your research that the organization is very conservative, but you should dress appropriately. No-no's include the following: hats, bare midriffs, short skirts or shorts and iron-free wrinkles. Think about covering obtrusive tattoos or removing extra ear/nose/tongue/eyebrow rings. Don't dress so formally that you feel uncomfortable, but dress nicely. It may not seem fair, but your dress will affect the impression you make and influence the decision of the judges. Save making a statement of your individuality for a time when money is not in question.

Sit up straight: During interviews, do not slouch. Sitting up straight conveys confidence, leadership and intelligence. It communicates that you are interested in the conversation. Plus, it makes you look taller.

Speak in a positive tone of voice: One thing that keeps interviewers engaged is your tone. Make sure to speak in a positive one. This will not only maintain your interviewers' interest but will also suggest that you have an optimistic outlook. Of course, don't try so hard that you sound fake.

Don't be monotonous: If you've ever had a teacher or professor who speaks at the same rate and tone without variation, you know that this is the surest reason for a nap. Don't give your interviewers heavy eyelids. Record yourself and pay attention to your tone of voice. There should be natural variation in your timbre.

Speak at a natural pace: If you're like most people, the more nervous you are, the faster you speak. Be aware of this so that you don't speed talk through your interview.

Make natural gestures: Let your hands and face convey action and emotions. Use them as tools to illustrate anecdotes and punctuate important points.

Make eye contact: Eye contact engages interviewers and conveys self-assurance and honesty. If it is a group interview, make eye contact with all your interviewers—don't just focus on one. Maintaining good eye contact can be difficult, but just imagine little dollar signs in your interviewers' eyes and you shouldn't have any trouble. Ka-ching!

Smile: There's nothing more depressing than having a conversation with someone who never smiles. Don't smile nonstop, but show some teeth at least once in a while. If you use these tips, you will have a flawless look and sound to match what you're saying. All these attributes together create a powerful portrait of who you are. Unfortunately, not all these things come naturally, and you'll need to practice so that they can become unconscious actions.

The Practice Interview

One of the best ways to prepare for an interview is to do a dress rehearsal. This allows you to run through answering questions you might be asked and to practice honing your interview skills, including demeanor and style. You will feel more comfortable when it comes time for the actual interview. If anything will help you deliver a winning interview, it's practice. It may be difficult, but force yourself to set aside some time to run through a practice session at least once. Here's how:

Find a mock interviewer. Bribe or coerce a friend or family member to be your mock interviewer. Parents or teachers often make the best interviewers because they are closest in age and perspective to most actual scholarship interviewers.

Prep your mock interviewer. Share with your interviewer highlights from this chapter such as the purpose of scholarship interviews, what skills you want to practice and typical interview questions, which are described in the next section. If you're having trouble with eye contact, for example, ask them to take special notice of where you are looking when you speak and to make suggestions for correcting this.

Video yourself. Use your phone to video yourself so that you can review your mock interview afterward. Position it behind your interviewer so you can observe how you appear from their perspective.

Do the dress rehearsal. Grab two chairs and go for it. Answer questions and interact with your mock interviewer as if you were at the real thing. Get feedback. After you are finished, get constructive criticism from your mock interviewer. Find out what you did well and what you need to work on. What were the best parts of the interview? Which of your answers were strong, and which were weak? When did you capture or lose your mock interviewer's attention? Was your conversation one-way or two-way?

Review the video. Evaluate your performance. If you can, watch or listen to the video with your mock interviewer so you can get additional feedback. Listen carefully to how you answer questions so you can improve on them. Pay attention to your tone of voice. Watch your body language to see what you are unconsciously communicating.

Do it again. If you have the time and your mock interviewer has the energy or you can find another mock interviewer, do a second interview. If you can't find anyone, do it solo. Practice your answers, and focus on making some of the weaker ones more interesting. The bottom line is the more you practice, the better you'll do.

How to Answer to the Most Common Interview Questions

The best way to ace an exam would be to know the questions beforehand. The same is true for interview questions. From interviewing dozens of judges and applicants as well as having judged dozens of scholarship competitions ourselves, we've developed a list of commonly asked questions along with suggestions for answering them. This list is by no means comprehensive. There is no way to predict every question you will be asked, and in your actual interviews, the questions may not be worded in exactly the same way. However, the answer that interviewers are seeking is often the same.

Before your interviews, take the time to review this list. Add more questions particular to the specific scholarship to which you are applying. Practice answering these questions to yourself and in your mock interviews with friends and family. You will find that the answers you prepare to these questions will be invaluable during your real interviews. Even though the questions you are asked may be different, the thought that you put in now will help you formulate better answers. To the interviewer, you will sound incredibly articulate and thoughtful. Let's take a look at those questions.

Why did you choose your major?

- For major-based scholarships and even for general scholarships, interviewers want to know what motivated you to select the major, and they want a sense of how dedicated you are to that area of study. Make sure you have reasons for your decision. Keep in mind that an anecdote will provide color to your answer.

- If you are still in high school, you will probably be asked about your intended major. Make sure you have reasons for considering this major.

Why do you want to enter this career field?

- For scholarships that promote a specific career field, interviewers want to know your inspiration for entering the field and how committed you are to it. You will need to articulate the reasons and experiences that prompted your interest in this career and also anything you have done to prepare yourself for associated studies in this area.

- Be prepared to discuss your plans for after graduation, i.e. how will you use your education in the field you have chosen. You may be asked what kind of job you plan to have and why you would like it.

- Know something about the news in the field associated with the scholarship. For example, if you are applying for an information technology award, read up on the trends in the IT industry. There may be some major changes occurring that you will be asked to comment on.

What are your plans after graduation?

- You are not expected to know precisely what you'll do after graduation, but you need to be able to respond to this common question. Speak about what you are thinking about doing once you have that diploma in hand. The more specific you can be, the better.

- Provide reasons for your plans. Explain the process in which you developed your plans and what your motivation is.

- It's okay to discuss a couple of possible paths you may take, but don't bring up six very different options. Even if you are deciding among investment banking, the Peace Corps, banana farming and seminary, don't say so. The interviewer will think that you don't have a clear direction of what you want to do. This may very well be true, but it's not something you want to share. Select the one or two possible paths that you are most likely to take.

Why do you think you should win this scholarship?

- Focus your answer on characteristics and achievements that match the mission of the scholarship. For example, if the scholarship is for biology majors, discuss your accomplishments in the field of biology. Your answer may include personal qualities as well as specific accomplishments.

- Be confident but not arrogant. For this type of question, be careful about balancing pride and modesty in your answer. You want to be confident enough to have reasons why you should win the scholarship, but you don't want to sound overly boastful. To avoid sounding pompous, don't say that you are better than all the other applicants or put down your competition. Instead, focus on your strengths independent of the other people who are applying.

- Have three reasons. Three is the magic number that is not too many or too few. To answer this question just right, offer three explanations for why you fulfill the mission of the scholarship.

Tell me about times when you've been a leader.

- Interviewers ask this type of question (although sometimes worded a little differently) to gauge your leadership ability and your accomplishments as a leader. They want to award scholarships to students who will be leaders in the future. When you answer, try to discuss leadership you've shown that matches what the scholarship is meant to achieve.

- Don't just rattle off the leadership positions you've held. Instead, give qualitative descriptions of what you accomplished as a leader. Did your group meet its goals? Did you start something new? How did you shape the morale of the group you led? For this kind of question, anecdotes and short stories are a good way to illustrate how you've been effective.

- Remember that leadership doesn't have to be a formally elected position. You can describe how you've informally led a special project or group. You could even define how you are a leader among your siblings.

- Be prepared to discuss what kind of leader you are. Your interviewer may ask about your approach to leadership or your philosophy on being a good leader. Have examples ready that show how you like to lead. For example, do you lead by example? Do you focus on motivating others and getting their buy-in?

What are your strengths? Weaknesses?

- As you are applying for jobs, you will answer this question more times than you will shake hands. It is a common job interview question that you may also get asked in scholarship interviews. Be prepared with three strengths and three weaknesses. Be honest about your weaknesses.

- Your strengths should match the mission of the scholarship and should highlight skills and accomplishments that match the characteristics the judges are seeking.

- You should be able to put a positive spin on your weaknesses. (And you'd better say you have some!) For example, your perfectionism could make you frustrated when things don't go the way you plan but could also make you a very motivated person. Your love of sports could detract from your studies but could provide a needed break and be representative of your belief in balance for your life. Just make sure that the spin you put on your weakness is appropriate and that your weakness is really a weakness.

Where do you see yourself ten years from now?

- We know that nobody knows exactly what he or she is going to be doing in ten years. The interviewers don't need specific details. They just want a general idea of what your long-term goals are and what you aspire to become. If you have several possibilities, at least one should be in line with the goals of the scholarship.

- Try to be as specific as possible without sounding unrealistic. For example, you can say that you would like to be working at a high-tech company in marketing, but leave out that you plan to have a daughter Sawyer, son Parker and dog Skip. Too much detail will make your dreams sound too naive.

Tell me about yourself. Or, is there anything you want to add?

- The most difficult questions are often the most open-ended. You have the freedom to say anything. For these kinds of questions, go back to the mission of the scholarship and shape your answer to reflect the characteristics that the judges are seeking in the winner. Practice answering this question several times because it is the one that stumps applicants the most.

- Have three things to say about yourself that match the goal of the scholarship. For example, you could discuss three personal traits you have, such as motivation, leadership skills and interpersonal skills. Or, you could discuss three skills applicable to academics, such as analytical skills, problem-solving skills and your love of a good challenge.

- The alternative, "Is there anything you want to add?" is typically asked at the end of the interview. In this case, make your response brief but meaningful. Highlight the most important thing you want your interviewer to remember.

Other Questions

In addition to these, here are some more common questions:

- What do you think you personally can contribute to this field?
- How do you plan to use what you have studied after graduation?
- Do you plan to continue your studies in graduate school?
- What do you want to specifically focus on within this field of study?
- Do you plan to do a thesis or senior project?
- Who are your role models in the field?
- What do you see as the future of this field?
- How do you see yourself growing in your career?
- What can you add to this field?
- What do you think are the most challenging aspects of this field?
- What is your ideal job after graduating from college?
- Tell me about a time that you overcame adversity.
- What are your opinions about (fill in political or field-related issue)?
- Tell me about your family.
- What do you hope to gain from college?
- Who is a role model for you?
- What is your favorite book? Why?
- What is the most challenging thing you have done?

Remember that with all these questions your goal is to demonstrate that you are the best fit for the scholarship. Be sure to practice these with your mock interviewer. The more comfortable and confident you feel answering these questions, the better you'll do in your interviews.

Questions for the Questioner

There is a huge difference between an interview and an interrogation. In an interview, you also ask questions. Make certain that your interview does not become an interrogation. Ask questions yourself throughout the conversation. Remember that you want to keep the conversation two-way.

Toward the end of your interview, you will probably have the opportunity to ask additional questions. Take this opportunity. If you don't ask any questions, it will appear that you are uninterested in the conversation or haven't put much thought into your interview. Take time before the interview to develop a list of questions you may want to ask. Of course you don't have to ask all your questions, but you need to be prepared to ask a few.

To get you started, we've developed some suggestions. Adapt these questions to the specific scholarship you are applying for and personalize them.

- How did you get involved with this organization?
- How did you enter this field? What was your motivation?
- Who do you see as your mentors in this field?
- What do you think are the most exciting things about your career?
- What advice do you have for someone starting out?
- What do you see as the greatest challenges for this field?
- What do you think will be the greatest advancements in ten years?
- What effect do you think technology will have on this field?
- I read that there is a (insert trend) in this field. What do you think?

The best questions are those that come from your detective work. Let's say that in researching an organization you discover that they recently launched a new program to research a cure for diabetes. Inquiring about this new program would be a perfect question to ask. It not only shows that you have done your homework, but it is also a subject about which the organization is deeply concerned.

Use Time to Your Advantage

The best time to ask Mom or Dad for something is when they're in a good mood. It's all about timing. Timing is also important in interviews. If you have more than one scholarship interview, time them strategically. Schedule less important and less demanding interviews first. This will allow you the opportunity to practice before your more difficult interviews. You will improve your skills as you do more interviews. It makes sense to hone your skills on the less important ones first.

If you are one of a series of applicants who will be interviewed, choose the order that fits you best. If you like to get things over with, try to be interviewed in the beginning. If you need more time to prepare yourself mentally, select a time near the end. We recommend that you don't choose to go first because the judges will use your interview as a benchmark for the rest. They may not recognize you as the best applicant even though it turns out to be true.

The Long-Distance Interview

If you've ever been in a long-distance relationship, you know there's a reason why most don't last. You simply can't communicate over the telephone in the same way you can in person. Scholarship interviews are the same. You may find that an interview will not be face to face but over the telephone instead. If this happens, here are some strategies to help bridge the distance:

Find a quiet place to do the interview where you won't be interrupted. You need to be able to give your full attention to the conversation you are having.

Know who's on the other end of the line. You may interview with a panel of people. Write down each of their names and positions when they first introduce themselves to you. They will be impressed when you are able to respond to them individually and thank each of them by name.

Use notes from your practice interviews. One of the advantages of doing an interview over the telephone is that you can refer to notes without your interviewers knowing. Take advantage of this.

Look and sound like you would in person. Pretend that your interviewers are in the room with you, and use the same gestures and facial expressions that you would if you were meeting in person. It may sound strange, but your interviewers will actually be able to hear through your voice when you are smiling, when you are paying attention and when you are enthusiastic about what you're saying. Don't do your interview lying down in your bed or slouched back in a recliner.

Don't use an unreliable phone. Speaker phones often echo and pick up distracting surrounding noise. If you use a cell phone, make sure you have good reception and a charged battery.

Turn off call waiting. Nothing is more annoying than hearing the call waiting beep while you are trying to focus and deliver an important thought. (And, this may sound obvious, but never take a second call.) Use the techniques of regular interviews. You'd be surprised how much is translated over the telephone. Don't neglect good speaking and delivery points just because the interviewers can't see you!

Secrets to the Group Interview

So it's you on one side of the table and a panel of six on the other side. It's certainly not the most natural way to have a conversation. How do you stay calm when you are interviewed by a council of judges?

Think of the group as individuals. Instead of thinking it's you versus the team, think of each of the interviewers as an individual. Try to connect with each person separately.

Try to get everyone's name if you can. Have a piece of paper handy that you can use to jot down everyone's name and role so that you can refer to them in the conversation. You want to be able to target your answers to each of the constituents. If you are interviewing with a panel of employees from a company and you know that Ms. Sweeny works in accounting while Mr. Duff works in human resources, you can speak about your analytical skills to appeal to Ms. Sweeny and your people skills to appeal to Mr. Duff.

Make eye contact. Look into the eyes of each of the panelists. Don't stare, but show them that you are confident. Be careful not to focus on only one member of the group.

Respect the hierarchy. You may find that there is a leader in the group like the scholarship chair or the CEO of the company. Pay a little more attention to stroke the ego of the person or persons in charge. They are used to it, they expect it and a little kissing up never hurt anyone.

Include everyone. In any group situation, there are usually one or two more vocal members who take the lead. Don't focus all your attention only on the loud ones. Spread your attention among the panelists as evenly as possible.

The Disaster Interview

Even if you do your interview homework and diligently practice mock interviewing, you may still find that you and your interviewer(s) just don't connect or that you just don't seem to have the right answers. For students who spend some time preparing, this is a very rare occurrence. Interviewers are not trying to trick you or make you feel bad. They are simply trying to find out more about you and your fit with the award. Still, if you think that you've bombed, here are some things to keep in mind:

Avoid should have, would have, could have. Don't replay the interview in your head again and again, thinking of all the things you should have said. It's too easy to look back and have the best answers. Instead, use what you've learned to avoid making the same mistakes in your next interview.

There are no right answers. Remember that in reality there really are no right answers. Your answers may not have been perfect, but that doesn't mean that they were wrong. There are countless ways to answer the same question.

The toughest judge is you. Realize that you are your own greatest critic. While you may think that you completely bombed an interview, your interviewer will most likely not have as harsh an opinion.

The Post-Interview

After you complete your interviews, follow up with a thank you note. Remember that interviewers are typically volunteers and have made the time to meet with you. If you feel that there is very important information that you forgot to share in your interview, mention it briefly in your thank you note. If not, a simple note will suffice. You will leave a polite, lasting impression on your interviewer(s).

Final Thoughts

Chapter 8

How to Keep the Money You Win

When you learn to skydive, your first lesson does not start with jumping out of an airplane. First you go through training in which you learn techniques and safety measures—on the ground. Only after practicing on the ground can you take to the sky. In your scholarship education, you have just completed the ground training and are ready to take the plunge. As you move from the *strategies* for applying for scholarships to actually *applying* for them, we have a few words of advice on how to keep the dollars you earn and how to stay motivated.

Let's jump ahead to after you win a cache of scholarship dollars. It would be nice once the scholarship checks were written if you could run off for that well-deserved trip to the Bahamas. Alas, there are restrictions on how you can spend the cash and how you must maintain your scholarship. (Besides, everyone knows that Hawaii is the place to go.) Here are some tips to keep in mind:

Get to know your scholarship and financial aid administrators. These people will be able to answer questions about your award and make sure you are spending it in the way that you should.

Give the scholarship committee members proof if they want it. Some awards require that you provide proof of enrollment or transcripts. Send the committee whatever they need.

Be aware of your award's requirements and what happens if something changes. How long does the award last? What happens if you take a leave of absence, study part time, study abroad, transfer schools or quit your studies? College is full of possibilities! Do you have to maintain a minimum grade point average or take courses in a certain field?

87

Know if there are special requirements for athletic scholarships. If you've won an athletic scholarship, you are most likely required to play the sport. (You didn't get that full ride scholarship for nothing!) Understand the implications of what would happen if you were not able to play because of circumstances such as an injury or not meeting academic requirements.

Find out if the award is a cash cow (renewable). If an award is renewable, you are eligible to get it every year that you are in school. If so, find out what you need to do, and when you need to do it, to renew your scholarship. Some awards just require a copy of your transcript, while others require you to submit an entirely new application.

Understand restrictions for spending the dough. Some awards are limited to tuition. Others can be used for books, travel or even living expenses. Some provide the money directly to your school; others provide a check made out to you. Be aware of what you can spend the money on and what sort of records you need to keep.

Learn the tax implications of your award. Speak with the award administrator or your pals at the IRS (www.irs.gov or 800-829-1040). Be aware of requirements after you graduate. Some awards such as ROTC scholarships require employment after graduation. Because these arrangements can drastically affect your future, learn about the requirements now.

Keep the awarding organization up to date on your progress as a student. Write the organization a thank you note, and keep them updated on your progress at the end of the year. This is not only good manners, but it will also help ensure that the award is around in the future.

Parting Words

I (Gen) remember when I won the Sterling Scholarship, one of the highest honors for students in Hawaii. The awards ceremony was televised live throughout the state. For weeks before submitting my application, I prepared for the competition, compiling a 50-page application book, practicing for the eight hours of interviews and enlisting the help of no less than three teachers from my high school. Even though the scholarship was only $1,000, my parents still keep the trophy on display and share with unwitting visitors the videotape of my triumph. I realize now that I was able to put in such extensive effort because of my outlook on the award. I knew whether I won or lost, I would gain the experience of building a portfolio, becoming a skilled interviewee, working closely with my teachers and meeting some incredible students.

While scholarships are primarily a source of funding for your education, approach them in the same way you do your favorite sport or hobby. I also played for my school's tennis team—and lost just about every match. Yet, I continued because I enjoyed the sport and found the skills a challenge. If you approach your scholarships in this manner, you'll probably win more of them and have fun in the process. Treat them like a chore, and you'll hate every minute, neglecting to put in the effort required to win.

The bottom line is that if you are going to take the time to apply, you should take the time to win. The secrets, tips and strategies in this book will put you within striking distance. Follow them and you'll win more and more often. This book is unique in that it really is two books in one. Now that you know how to win, it's time to begin finding scholarships to put these strategies to use. The second half of this book is a complete listing of scholarships and awards and is indexed by various criteria so you can quickly find those that match your interests and qualifications. And, because we know you just can't get enough of us, we also encourage you to visit our website, SuperCollege.com, for the most up-to-date information on scholarships and financial aid.

We both wish you the best of luck.

A SPECIAL REQUEST

As you jump headlong into the wonderful world of scholarships, we have a special request. We would love to hear about your experiences with scholarships and how this book has helped you. Please send us a note after you've finished raking in your free cash for college.

Gen and Kelly Tanabe
c/o SuperCollege
2713 Newlands Avenue
Belmont, CA 94002

Onward! Flip the page and start finding scholarships. It's time to put all the strategies and tips you've just learned to work for you!

The Ultimate Scholarship Directory

Now it's time to put into action all that you learned in the first half of the book. We've done the hard work of scouring the country to find the best scholarships that you can win. We've made a special effort to select awards with broad eligibility requirements, which means you'll find plenty of scholarships that fit your background, goals and interests.

Before you jump into the directory, spend a few moments to learn how the scholarships are organized so you don't miss out on any awards for which you might be a good fit.

To help find the awards that match you best, we've conveniently organized our directory of scholarships into eight major categories.

Below is the complete list of categories and descriptions of the types of awards you'll find in each one. Remember to also use the various indexes in the back of the book to help you zero in on more scholarships.

General
This section lists scholarships that have the broadest eligibility requirements. Included are awards based on **academics**, **leadership** and **community service** to name a few. While some of the scholarships have GPA requirements, you'll be surprised at how many are not based on grades. Some are even awarded by random drawing.

Humanities / Arts
This section includes awards for students interested in **English** and **writing** as well as **foreign language** and **area studies**. It also includes all of the **visual and performing arts** such as **dancing**, **singing**, **acting**, **music**, **drawing**, **painting**, **sculpture**, **photography** and **graphic art**.

Social Sciences

This section deals with the study of the human aspects of the world. Often called the "soft sciences" it includes:

- Anthropology
- Accounting / Finance
- Archaeology
- Business Management
- Communications
- Criminology
- Economics
- Education / Teaching
- Geography
- History
- Hospitality / Travel
- International Relations
- Journalism / Broadcasting
- Law / Legal Studies
- Marketing / Sales
- Political Science
- Psychology
- Public Administration / Social Work
- Sociology
- Urban Studies

Sciences

Typically known as the "hard sciences," this category includes:

- Aerospace / Aviation
- Agriculture / Horticulture / Animals
- Anatomy
- Architecture
- Astronomy
- Biological Sciences / Life Sciences
- Biochemistry
- Chemistry
- Computer and Information Science
- Dentistry
- Earth and Planetary Sciences
- Ecology
- Engineering
- Forestry / Wildlife
- Geology
- Health Professions / Medicine
- Mathematics
- Neuroscience
- Nursing
- Oceanography
- Paleontology

- Pathology
- Pharmacology
- Physics
- Zoology

State of Residence

Here's your opportunity to get something back from your (or your parents') state tax dollars. Every state offers scholarships and grants for their residents. Some states even offer awards to out-of-state students who study in their states. Be sure to look at both your home state as well as any of the states you are planning to go to college in to find the most awards.

Membership

Many large **companies**, **unions**, **organizations** and **religious organizations** give awards to their members. If you or your parents are members of any of the groups in this category, you may qualify for a scholarship.

Ethnicity /Race/Gender/Family Situation/Sexual Orientation

There are a lot of awards for members of minority and nonminority ethnic groups, women and students with unique family situations.

Disability / Illness

This section has awards for students with physical, hearing, vision, mental and learning disabilities. It also includes awards for students who have been afflicted with certain illnesses.

"Take Off the Blinders" to Find the Most Scholarships

Now that you know the categories, the best way to find scholarships is to jump right in and head to the sections that fit you best.

Do you remember when your elementary school teacher used to say, "Take off the mental blinders"? Ours did to encourage us to think broadly. In the same way, we want to encourage you to "take off the scholarship blinders" and not think about yourself too narrowly. Consider your accomplishments, activities, goals and background as broadly as possible. Look through some of the categories even if you don't immediately see a fit. You might discover that you actually fit one of the leadership scholarships even if you haven't held a formal leadership position. Or you may find an award in the sciences category in a field that you love but never realized was a science.

Don't be afraid to be forward-thinking. Write down any scholarships that fit, even if you have to wait a year to apply. The awards we have selected are from the larger organizations and businesses, so you can be certain that they are going to be around for a long time.

We are really excited that you can now put everything that you learned to good use to help you find and win some free cash for college.

Happy scholarship hunting!

The Ultimate Scholarship Book 2026
Scholarship Directory (General Awards)

GENERAL

[1] • $1,000 All Star Verified Scholarship

Verified Scholarships
2713 Newlands Avenue, Belmont, CA 94002
Email: admin@verifiedscholarships.com
https://www.verifiedscholarships.com/scholarship-program/
Purpose: This scholarship is to help students pay for college and it may be used to pay for tuition or any related fees such as room and board.
Eligibility: Applicants must be high school, college, graduate, or adult students or parents of high school and college students. Applicants must complete the application form and answer in 450 characters or less the question: "What is the best or worst part about finding or applying to scholarships?"
Target applicant(s): Junior high students or younger. High school students. College students. Adult students.
Amount: $1,000.
Number of awards: 3.
Deadline: March 30, August 31, December 31.
How to apply: Applications are available online.
Exclusive: Visit www.UltimateScholarshipBook.com and enter code VE126 for updates on this award.

[2] • $1,000 College JumpStart Gratitude Scholarship

College JumpStart Scholarship Fund
https://www.jumpstart-scholarship.net/application-us
Purpose: To support students who share thanks for someone who has done something kind for them.
Eligibility: Applicants must be 10th, 11th or 12th grade high school, college or adult students. Applicants may study any major and attend any college in the U.S. Applicants must be legal residents of the U.S. and complete the online application form including the required personal statement. The award may be used for tuition, room and board, books or any related educational expense.
Target applicant(s): High school students. College students. Adult students.
Amount: $1,000.
Number of awards: 4.
Deadline: June 30.
How to apply: Applications are available online.
Exclusive: Visit www.UltimateScholarshipBook.com and enter code CO226 for updates on this award.

[3] • $1,000 College JumpStart Love of Learning Scholarship

College JumpStart Scholarship Fund
https://www.jumpstart-scholarship.net/application-us
Purpose: To recognize students who are committed to using education to better their life and that of their family and/or community.
Eligibility: Applicants must be 10th, 11th or 12th grade high school, college or adult students. Applicants may study any major and attend any college in the U.S. Applicants must be legal residents of the U.S. and complete the online application form including the required personal statement. The award may be used for tuition, room and board, books or any related educational expense.
Target applicant(s): High school students. College students. Adult students.
Amount: $1,000.
Number of awards: 4.
Deadline: December 31.
How to apply: Applications are available online.
Exclusive: Visit www.UltimateScholarshipBook.com and enter code CO326 for updates on this award.

[4] • $1,000 College JumpStart Pay It Forward Scholarship

College JumpStart Scholarship Fund
https://www.jumpstart-scholarship.net/application-us
Purpose: To support students who share a time that they have paid it forward.
Eligibility: Applicants must be 10th, 11th or 12th grade high school, college or adult students. Applicants may study any major and attend any college in the U.S. Applicants must be legal residents of the U.S. and complete the online application form including the required personal statement. The award may be used for tuition, room and board, books or any related educational expense.
Target applicant(s): High school students. College students. Adult students.
Amount: $1,000.
Number of awards: 4.
Deadline: September 30.
How to apply: Applications are available online.
Exclusive: Visit www.UltimateScholarshipBook.com and enter code CO426 for updates on this award.

[5] • $1,000 College JumpStart Show Grit Scholarship

College JumpStart Scholarship Fund
https://www.jumpstart-scholarship.net/application-us
Purpose: To reward students who demonstrate grit and who continue to push themselves in spite of obstacles or challenges.
Eligibility: Applicants must be 10th, 11th or 12th grade high school, college or adult students. Applicants may study any major and attend any college in the U.S. Applicants must be legal residents of the U.S. and complete the online application form including the required personal statement. The award may be used for tuition, room and board, books or any related educational expense.
Target applicant(s): High school students. College students. Adult students.
Amount: $1,000.
Number of awards: 4.
Deadline: March 31.
How to apply: Applications are available online.
Exclusive: Visit www.UltimateScholarshipBook.com and enter code CO526 for updates on this award.

[6] • $1,000 GK Tanabe Student Scholarship

Gen and Kelly Tanabe Scholarship Program
Email: info@gkscholarship.com
https://www.gkscholarship.com
Purpose: To assist high school, college and graduate school students with educational expenses.
Eligibility: Applicants must be 9th-12th grade high school students, college students or graduate school students who are U.S. residents. Students may study any major and attend any college in the U.S.

Target applicant(s): High school students. College students. Adult students.
Amount: $1,000.
Number of awards: 2.
Deadline: July 31, December 31.
How to apply: Applications are available online.
Exclusive: Visit www.UltimateScholarshipBook.com and enter code GE626 for updates on this award.

[7] • $1,000 Moolahspot Scholarship

MoolahSPOT
http://www.moolahspot.com/scholarship/
Purpose: To help students pay for college or graduate school.
Eligibility: Students must be at least 16 years or older and plan to attend or currently attend college or graduate school. Applicants may study any major or plan to enter any career field at any accredited college or graduate school. A short personal statement is required.
Target applicant(s): High school students. College students. Adult students.
Amount: $1,000.
Number of awards: 3.
Deadline: April 30, August 31, December 31.
How to apply: Applications are only available online.
Exclusive: Visit www.UltimateScholarshipBook.com and enter code MO726 for updates on this award.

[8] • $1,000 Scholarship Detective Scholarship

Scholarship Detective
https://www.scholarshipdetective.com/scholarship/
Purpose: To help college and adult students pay for college or graduate school.
Eligibility: Applicants must be high school, college or graduate students (including adult students) who are U.S. citizens or permanent residents. Students may study any major. The funds may be used to attend an accredited U.S. institution for undergraduate or graduate education.
Target applicant(s): High school students. College students. Adult students.
Amount: $1,000.
Number of awards: 3.
Deadline: May 31, August 31, December 31.
How to apply: Applications are available online.
Exclusive: Visit www.UltimateScholarshipBook.com and enter code SC826 for updates on this award.

[9] • 1 for 2 Education Foundation Scholarship

1 For 2 Education Foundation
4337 East Grand River Road, Suite 198, Howell, MI 48843
Phone: 810-908-6295
Email: 1for2foundation@gmail.com
https://www.1for2edu.com/scholarship/
Purpose: To support highly motivated students who agree to "pay it forward."
Eligibility: Applicants must be enrolling as full-time students at an accredited four-year college or university and maintain a 3.0 GPA. Recipients agree to provide scholarships in the future. The scholarship may close earlier than the deadline, once 250 completed applications are received.
Target applicant(s): High school students. College students. Graduate school students. Adult students.
Minimum GPA: 3.7
Amount: Up to $20,000.
Number of awards: Up to 2.
Deadline: February 1.
How to apply: Applications are available online.
Exclusive: Visit www.UltimateScholarshipBook.com and enter code 1 926 for updates on this award.

[10] • 100th Infantry Battalion Memorial Scholarship Fund

Hawaii Community Foundation - Scholarships
827 Fort Street Mall, Honolulu, HI 96813
Phone: 888-731-3863
Email: scholarships@hcf-hawaii.org
https://www.hawaiicommunityfoundation.org/
Purpose: To support students who promote the legacy of the 100th Infantry Battalion of World War II.
Eligibility: Applicants must be full-time undergraduate or graduate students at a two- or four-year college or university. They must be a direct descendant of a 100th Infantry Battalion World War II veteran and demonstrate excellence in academics and community service. A minimum 3.0 GPA is required. Students do not need to be a Hawaii resident.
Target applicant(s): High school students. College students. Graduate school students. Adult students.
Minimum GPA: 3.0
Amount: Varies.
Number of awards: Varies.
Deadline: January 31.
How to apply: Applications are available online. An application form, transcript and two letters of recommendation are required.
Exclusive: Visit www.UltimateScholarshipBook.com and enter code HA1026 for updates on this award.

[11] • 1Dental Scholarship

1Dental.com
5535 Airport Freeway, Haltom City, TX 76117
Phone: 800-372-7615
Email: scholarships@1dental.com
http://www.1dental.com/scholarship/
Purpose: To support students in higher education.
Eligibility: Applicants must be currently enrolled high school seniors, college or graduate school students who are also U.S. citizens. Applicants must answer a 30-question survey.
Target applicant(s): High school students. College students. Graduate school students. Adult students.
Amount: $500.
Number of awards: 1.
Deadline: May 31.
How to apply: Apply by submitting the essay by email along with your full name, address, phone number, name of high school or college you are attending, school address, current GPA and grade level.
Exclusive: Visit www.UltimateScholarshipBook.com and enter code 1D1126 for updates on this award.

The Ultimate Scholarship Book 2026
Scholarship Directory (General Awards)

[12] • 1st Marine Division Association Scholarship
1st Marine Division Association Inc.
P.O. Box 9000, Box #902, Oceanside, CA 92051
Phone: 760-763-3268
Email: june.oldbreed@fmda.us
https://www.oldbreedscholarshipfund.com/apply
Purpose: To provide financial aid to undergraduate students who are the dependents of deceased or disabled veterans of the 1st Marine Division.
Eligibility: Applicants must be dependents of honorably discharged veterans of the 1st Marine Division or units attached to or supporting the Division who are now deceased or totally and permanently disabled for any reason. Applicants must attend an accredited university as full-time undergraduate students.
Target applicant(s): College students. Adult students.
Amount: Up to $2,500.
Number of awards: Varies.
Scholarship may be renewable.
Deadline: Varies.
How to apply: Applications are available online.
Exclusive: Visit www.UltimateScholarshipBook.com and enter code 1S1226 for updates on this award.

[13] • 25th Infantry Division Association Educational Scholarship
25th Infantry Division Association (TIDA)
P.O. Box 7, Flourtown, PA 19031-0007
http://www.25thida.org
Purpose: To aid in the education of the members of the 25th Infantry Division Association or the children and grandchildren of active and former members of the association.
Eligibility: Applicants must be high school seniors who are the child or grandchild of an active association member, the child of a former member who died during combat with the Division or an active member who will be discharged before the end of the award year. Applicants must be entering a four-year college or university as a freshman. Selection is based on future plans, school activities, interests, financial status and academic achievement.
Target applicant(s): High school students.
Amount: Up to $1,500.
Number of awards: Varies.
Deadline: March 15.
How to apply: Applications are available throughout the year in Tropic Lightning Flashes, the quarterly newsletter of the 25th Infantry Division Association.
Exclusive: Visit www.UltimateScholarshipBook.com and enter code 251326 for updates on this award.

[14] • A+A Altruism + All Good Deeds Scholarship
National Parent Volunteer Association
1875 Mission Street Suite 103-133, San Francisco, CA 94103
Email: programs@parent-volunteer.org
https://www.parent-volunteer.org/scholarships
Purpose: To support students who participate in volunteer work and community service.
Eligibility: Applicants must be currently enrolled or plan to be enrolled full-time in an accredited U.S. college or university. Students must be a high school junior or senior, undergraduate student or graduate student and have a minimum 2.5 GPA. Recipients must provide an official transcript confirming their reported GPA and proof of enrollment.
Target applicant(s): High school students. College students. Graduate school students. Adult students.
Amount: $1,000.
Number of awards: Varies.
Deadline: May 31.
How to apply: Applications are available online.
Exclusive: Visit www.UltimateScholarshipBook.com and enter code NA1426 for updates on this award.

[15] • Aaliyah Lee Scholarship
National Parent Volunteer Association
1875 Mission Street Suite 103-133, San Francisco, CA 94103
Email: programs@parent-volunteer.org
https://www.parent-volunteer.org/scholarships
Purpose: To support students who value education and to honor the memory of Aaliyah Lee.
Eligibility: Applicants must be currently enrolled or plan to be enrolled full-time in an accredited U.S. college or university. Students must be a high school junior or senior, undergraduate student or graduate student and have a minimum 2.5 GPA. Recipients must provide an official transcript confirming their reported GPA and proof of enrollment.
Target applicant(s): High school students. College students. Graduate school students. Adult students.
Amount: $1,000.
Number of awards: Varies.
Deadline: November 30.
How to apply: Applications are available online.
Exclusive: Visit www.UltimateScholarshipBook.com and enter code NA1526 for updates on this award.

[16] • AAU Karate Scholarship
AAU National Headquarters
c/o AAU Karate Scholarship, P.O. Box 22409, Lake Buena Vista, FL 32830
Phone: 407-828-3704
Email: jennifer@aausports.org
https://aaukarate.org/page.php?page_id=105811
Purpose: To reward a young man or woman who participated in AAU Karate for no less than four years.
Eligibility: Applicants must be enrolled in an accredited college or university or plan to attend an accredited college or university in the fall.
Target applicant(s): High school students. College students. Adult students.
Amount: $1,000.
Number of awards: 2.
Deadline: May 19.
How to apply: Applications are available online. An application form, an essay, a letter of recommendation and transcripts are required.
Exclusive: Visit www.UltimateScholarshipBook.com and enter code AA1626 for updates on this award.

[17] • AAUS Student Scholarships
American Academy of Underwater Sciences
P.O. Box 9067, Mobile, AL 36691-9067
Phone: 251-591-3775
Email: aausfoundation@gmail.com
https://www.aausfoundation.org/

Purpose: To support students involved in collegiate research in which diving is a principal research tool.
Eligibility: Applicants must be a current member of AAUS and attending an undergraduate or a graduate level program. Selection is based on the project proposal submitted by the applicant. The proposal must describe the benefits of the project and how the funds will be used.
Target applicant(s): College students. Graduate school students. Adult students.
Amount: Up to $3,000.
Number of awards: Varies.
Deadline: June 30.
How to apply: Applications are available online and include a written project proposal and at least one letter of recommendation.
Exclusive: Visit www.UltimateScholarshipBook.com and enter code AM1726 for updates on this award.

---

[18] • Abacus Life Scholarship
Abacus Life
2101 Park Center Drive, Suite 170, Orlando, FL 32835
Phone: 800-561-4148
Email: scholarships@abacuslife.com
https://abacuslifesettlements.com/abacus-scholarship/
Purpose: To reward students who express a superior amount of involvement in, and care for, their communities.
Eligibility: Applicants must be full-time or part-time students at an accredited four-year college or university in the United States. Students must submit a video on a provided prompt along with a current college transcript. Selection is based on creativity and showing a superior involvement in what makes you unique.
Target applicant(s): High school students. College students. Graduate school students. Adult students.
Amount: $1,000.
Number of awards: 1.
Deadline: January 6.
How to apply: Applications are available online.
Exclusive: Visit www.UltimateScholarshipBook.com and enter code AB1826 for updates on this award.

---

[19] • ACJA/Lambda Alpha Epsilon Scholarship
American Criminal Justice Association
Interim National Office, 3211 Fitzgerald Dr, Montgomery, TX 77356
Phone: 402-414-2520
https://www.acjalae.com/scholarships.html
Purpose: To assist criminal justice students.
Eligibility: Applicants must be undergraduate or graduate students who are studying criminal justice. Students must be ACJA/LAE members, but they may submit a membership form at the time of application. Applicants must have completed at least two semesters or three quarters of their education while earning at least a 3.0 GPA. Applicants must submit transcripts, letters of enrollment and goals statements.
Target applicant(s): High school students. College students. Graduate school students. Adult students.
Minimum GPA: 3.0
Amount: $200-$800.
Number of awards: 3.
Deadline: January 31.
How to apply: Applications are available online and by written request.
Exclusive: Visit www.UltimateScholarshipBook.com and enter code AM1926 for updates on this award.

---

[20] • Act of Kindness Scholarship
National Parent Volunteer Association
1875 Mission Street Suite 103-133, San Francisco, CA 94103
Email: programs@parent-volunteer.org
https://www.parent-volunteer.org/scholarships
Purpose: To support students who are committed to helping others in their schools or communities.
Eligibility: Applicants must be currently enrolled or plan to be enrolled full-time in an accredited U.S. college or university. Students must be a high school junior or senior, undergraduate student or graduate student and have a minimum 2.5 GPA. Recipients must provide an official transcript confirming their reported GPA and proof of enrollment.
Target applicant(s): High school students. College students. Graduate school students. Adult students.
Amount: $1,000.
Number of awards: Varies.
Deadline: February 28.
How to apply: Applications are available online.
Exclusive: Visit www.UltimateScholarshipBook.com and enter code NA2026 for updates on this award.

---

[21] • Adult Learner Scholarship from Study.com
Study.com
100 View Street, Suite 202, Mountain View, CA 94041
https://study.com/resources/student-scholarships
Purpose: To support adult students.
Eligibility: Applicants must be adult learners, accepted by or enrolled in a college or university within the United States and planning on continuing the next year. Students must have a minimum of 30 semester or 45 quarter hours to complete.
Target applicant(s): Adult students.
Amount: $1,000.
Number of awards: 1.
Deadline: November 1.
How to apply: Applications are available online.
Exclusive: Visit www.UltimateScholarshipBook.com and enter code ST2126 for updates on this award.

---

[22] • Adult Skills Education Award
Imagine America Foundation
12001 Sunrise Valley Drive, Suite 203, Reston, VA 20191
Phone: 571-267-3010
Email: Leed@imagine-america.org
https://www.imagine-america.org/students/scholarships-education/
Purpose: To support adult learners with tuition assistance and college scholarships to career colleges.
Eligibility: Applicants must be U.S. citizens or permanent residents enrolling in a participating career college. Applicants must also either have a high school diploma, GED or pass an Ability to Benefit test. The minimum age requirement for application is 19. Applicants must also complete the NCCT Educational Success Potential Assessment. Selection is based on the overall strength of the application.
Target applicant(s): Adult students.
Amount: $1,000.
Number of awards: Varies.
Deadline: December 31.
How to apply: Applications are available online.
Exclusive: Visit www.UltimateScholarshipBook.com and enter code IM2226 for updates on this award.

The Ultimate Scholarship Book 2026
Scholarship Directory (General Awards)

[23] • AFCEA ROTC Scholarships
Armed Forces Communications and Electronics Association (AFCEA)
4114 Legato Road, Suite 1000, Fairfax, VA 22033
Phone: 703-631-6149
http://www.afcea.org
Purpose: To assist ROTC sophomores or juniors who are majoring in aerospace engineering, electronics, computer science, computer engineering, physics or mathematics.
Eligibility: Applicants must major in electrical or aerospace engineering, electronics, computer science, computer engineering, physics or mathematics at an accredited U.S. four-year college or university. Applicants must also be enrolled full-time as college sophomores or juniors and be nominated by professors of military science, naval science or aerospace studies. Applicants must be U.S. citizens enrolled in ROTC, have good moral character, demonstrate academic excellence and the potential to serve as an officer in the U.S. Armed Forces and have financial need.
Target applicant(s): College students. Adult students.
Minimum GPA: 3.0
Amount: $2,000-$3,000.
Number of awards: Varies.
Deadline: January 1.
How to apply: Applications are available online.
Exclusive: Visit www.UltimateScholarshipBook.com and enter code AR2326 for updates on this award.

[24] • AFSA National Essay Contest
American Foreign Service Association (AFSA)
2101 East Street NW, Washington, DC 20037
Phone: 202-944-5504
Email: dec@afsa.org
http://www.afsa.org/afsa-scholarships
Purpose: To support students interested in writing an essay on foreign service.
Eligibility: Applicants must be U.S. Citizens, high school students and have parents who are not members of the Foreign Service. Students must attend a public, private, parochial school, home school or participate in a high school correspondence program in any of the 50 states, the District of Columbia or U.S. territories or must be U.S. citizens attending schools overseas. The current award is $2,500 to the student and an all-expenses paid trip to Washington, DC, for the winner and parents.
Target applicant(s): High school students.
Amount: $2,500.
Number of awards: 1.
Deadline: April 1.
How to apply: The registration form is available online. Applicants must write a no more than 1,250-word essay on the topic provided.
Exclusive: Visit www.UltimateScholarshipBook.com and enter code AM2426 for updates on this award.

[25] • Ag Day Essay Contest
Agriculture Council of America
11020 King Street, Suite 205, Overland Park, KS 66210
Phone: 913-491-1895
Email: jenam@nama.org
https://www.agday.org/essay-contest
Purpose: To support agricultural awareness while encouraging students to pursue higher education.
Eligibility: Applicants must be in 9th to 12th grade during the current school year and be a U.S. citizen. The contest requires an essay or video response to the given prompt on the website.
Target applicant(s): High school students.
Amount: $1,000.
Number of awards: 2.
Deadline: February 9.
How to apply: Applications are available online.
Exclusive: Visit www.UltimateScholarshipBook.com and enter code AG2526 for updates on this award.

[26] • Agota M. Bardos Award
Bardos Foundation
Email: contact@bardos.foundation
https://www.bardos.foundation/
Purpose: To reward students who are refugees and first-generation immigrants.
Eligibility: Applicants must be immigrants currently residing in the U.S. who have financial need. Students must be in their final year of high school or enrolled in an undergraduate degree program within the past six months. Applicants must have demonstrated their commitment to visual arts or music, academic rigor and community or family service.
Target applicant(s): High school students. College students. Adult students.
Amount: $1,000.
Number of awards: 4.
Deadline: May 1.
How to apply: Applications are available online.
Exclusive: Visit www.UltimateScholarshipBook.com and enter code BA2626 for updates on this award.

[27] • AHHS Foundation Scholarship
American Hackney Horse Society
4059 Iron Works Parkway A-3, Lexington, KY 40511-8462
Phone: 859-255-8694
Email: ahhscsl@qx.net
http://hackneysociety.com/
Purpose: To aid incoming college freshmen who promote the Hackney industry.
Eligibility: The applicant must be a high school senior or recent graduate. Selection is based on academic achievement, financial need, community service, involvement with Hackney Horses and the letters of recommendation.
Target applicant(s): High school students.
Amount: $2,500.
Number of awards: Varies.
Deadline: July 15.
How to apply: Applications are available online and include a personal essay, an official transcript and three letters of recommendation. A personal interview may also be required.
Exclusive: Visit www.UltimateScholarshipBook.com and enter code AM2726 for updates on this award.

[28] • AIFS Green Ambassador Scholarship
American Institute for Foreign Study
AIFS Abroad, 1 High Ridge Park, Stamford, CT 06905
Phone: 800-727-2437
Email: AIFSAbroad@aifs.com
https://www.aifsabroad.com/scholarships.asp

Purpose: To support students who plan to pursue higher education.
Eligibility: Applicants must be AIFS Abroad study abroad and/or intern students. Students must demonstrate a strong commitment to environmental sustainability.
Target applicant(s): High school students. College students. Adult students.
Amount: $300-$500.
Number of awards: Varies.
Deadline: April 15 for fall; October 1 for spring.
How to apply: Applications are available online.
Exclusive: Visit www.UltimateScholarshipBook.com and enter code AM2826 for updates on this award.

[29] • Air Force ROTC ASCP

Air Force Reserve Officer Training Corps
HQ AFROTC/DOR, 60 West Maxwell Boulevard, Maxwell AFB, AL 36112-6501
Phone: 866-423-7682
https://www.afrotc.com/
Purpose: To allow active duty Air Force personnel to earn a commission while completing their bachelor's degree.
Eligibility: Applicants must be active-duty Air Force personnel who are U.S. citizens under the age of 31, with the exception of nurses, who must be under the age of 42. They must also meet all testing and waiver requirements and be recommended by their commanding officer. Applicants must have at least 24 hours of graded college course work with at least a 3.0 cumulative GPA and have a minimum ACT composite score of 26 or an SAT combined Reading and Math score of 1180 or an AFOQT Academic Aptitude score of 55.
Target applicant(s): High school students. College students. Adult students.
Minimum GPA: 3.0
Amount: Up to $18,000 plus textbook allowance and stipend.
Number of awards: Varies.
Scholarship may be renewable.
Deadline: October 15.
How to apply: Application details are available online.
Exclusive: Visit www.UltimateScholarshipBook.com and enter code AI2926 for updates on this award.

[30] • Air Force ROTC High School Scholarship Program

Air Force Reserve Officer Training Corps
HQ AFROTC/DOR, 60 West Maxwell Boulevard, Maxwell AFB, AL 36112-6501
Phone: 866-423-7682
https://www.afrotc.com/
Purpose: To help students with financial need who are also interested in joining the Air Force in order to pay for college.
Eligibility: Applicants must pass the physical fitness assessment and demonstrate academic achievement or outstanding leadership skills. There are three types of awards: one that pays full tuition, most fees and a book allowance, one that pays tuition and fees up to $18,000 and a book allowance and one that pays the equivalent of in-state tuition and a book allowance. In return for the scholarship, recipients must serve in the Air Force. Applicants must have minimum ACT score of 24 or minimum SAT score of 1100. GPA minimum requirement is 3.0.
Target applicant(s): High school students.
Minimum GPA: 3.0
Amount: Up to full tuition plus fees, books and stipend.
Number of awards: Varies.
Scholarship may be renewable.
Deadline: December 31.
How to apply: Applications are available online.
Exclusive: Visit www.UltimateScholarshipBook.com and enter code AI3026 for updates on this award.

[31] • Air Force ROTC In-College Program

Air Force Reserve Officer Training Corps
HQ AFROTC/DOR, 60 West Maxwell Boulevard, Maxwell AFB, AL 36112-6501
Phone: 866-423-7682
https://www.afrotc.com/
Purpose: To promote the Air Force ROTC program.
Eligibility: Applicants must be U.S. citizens who have passed the Air Force Officer Qualifying Test, the Air Force ROTC Physical Fitness Test and a Department of Defense medical examination. Students must also be college freshmen or sophomores and have a GPA of 2.5 or higher.
Target applicant(s): College students. Adult students.
Minimum GPA: 2.5
Amount: Varies.
Number of awards: Varies.
Scholarship may be renewable.
Deadline: January 11.
How to apply: Applications are available from your school's Air Force ROTC detachment.
Exclusive: Visit www.UltimateScholarshipBook.com and enter code AI3126 for updates on this award.

[32] • Air Force ROTC Professional Officer Course- Early Release Program

Air Force Reserve Officer Training Corps
HQ AFROTC/DOR, 60 West Maxwell Boulevard, Maxwell AFB, AL 36112-6501
Phone: 866-423-7682
https://www.afrotc.com/
Purpose: To allow active duty Air Force personnel the opportunity for early release in order to complete their bachelor's degrees.
Eligibility: Applicants must be active-duty Air Force personnel who are U.S. citizens under the age of 31, with the exception of nurses, who must be under the age of 42. They must also meet all testing and waiver requirements, be recommended by their commanding officer and not be within one year of receiving their degree.
Target applicant(s): College students. Adult students.
Minimum GPA: 2.5
Amount: Varies.
Number of awards: Varies.
Scholarship may be renewable.
Deadline: Contact the sponsor to confirm the deadline.
How to apply: Application details are available online.
Exclusive: Visit www.UltimateScholarshipBook.com and enter code AI3226 for updates on this award.

[33] • Air Force ROTC SOAR Program

Air Force Reserve Officer Training Corps
HQ AFROTC/DOR, 60 West Maxwell Boulevard, Maxwell AFB, AL 36112-6501
Phone: 866-423-7682
https://www.afrotc.com/

The Ultimate Scholarship Book 2026
Scholarship Directory (General Awards)

Purpose: To give active duty Air Force personnel the opportunity to earn their commissions while completing their bachelor's degrees.
Eligibility: Applicants must be active-duty Air Force personnel who are U.S. citizens under the age of 31, with the exception of nurses, who must be under the age of 47. They must also meet all testing and waiver requirements and be recommended by their commanding officer. Students must have at least 24 hours of graded college course work with at least a 3.0 cumulative GPA and have a minimum ACT composite score of 25 or an SAT combined Reading and Math score of 1180 or an AFOQT Academic Aptitude score of 55.
Target applicant(s): College students. Adult students.
Minimum GPA: 3.0
Amount: Up to $18,000 plus textbook allowance and stipend.
Number of awards: Varies.
Scholarship may be renewable.
Deadline: October 15.
How to apply: Application details are available online.
Exclusive: Visit www.UltimateScholarshipBook.com and enter code AI3326 for updates on this award.

[34] • Airmen Memorial Foundation Scholarship Program
Air Force Sergeants Association
5211 Auth Road, Suitland, MD 20746
Phone: 301-899-3500
Email: staff@hqafsa.org
http://www.hqafsa.org
Purpose: To assist dependents of Air Force enlisted personnel in obtaining higher education.
Eligibility: Applicants must be dependents of Air Force enlisted personnel who are attending high school or college. They must have a GPA of 3.5 or higher and be accepted to the college of their choice.
Target applicant(s): High school students. College students.
Minimum GPA: 3.5
Amount: $1,000 to $5,000.
Number of awards: Varies.
Deadline: March 31.
How to apply: Applications are available online.
Exclusive: Visit www.UltimateScholarshipBook.com and enter code AI3426 for updates on this award.

[35] • Akash Kuruvilla Memorial Scholarship
Akash Kuruvilla Memorial Scholarship Fund Inc.
P.O. Box 140900, Gainesville, FL 32614
Email: akmsfinfo@gmail.com
https://www.akmscholarship.com
Purpose: To continue the legacy of Akash Jacob Kuruvilla.
Eligibility: Applicants must be entering or current full-time college students at an accredited U.S. four-year college or university. They must demonstrate academic achievement, leadership, integrity and excellence in diversity. Selection is based on character, financial need and the applicant's potential to impact his or her community.
Target applicant(s): High school students. College students. Adult students.
Amount: $1,000.
Number of awards: 2.
Deadline: June 28.
How to apply: Applications are available online. An application form, essay, personal statement, recommendation letter and resume are required.

Exclusive: Visit www.UltimateScholarshipBook.com and enter code AK3526 for updates on this award.

[36] • All-American Scholars (Cheerleading)
Pop Warner Little Scholars Inc.
P.O. Box 307, Langhorne, PA 19047
https://www.popwarner.com/Default.aspx?tabid=1404834
Purpose: To recognize Pop Warner participants for their academic accomplishments.
Eligibility: Applicant must be a participant in the Pop Warner program as a cheerleader, be in grade 5 or higher and maintain a 96 percent grade point average or higher. Selection will be based on academic achievement and additional non-sport related activities and achievements.
Target applicant(s): Junior high students or younger. High school students.
Minimum GPA: 3.8
Amount: Varies.
Number of awards: Varies.
Deadline: October 15.
How to apply: Applications are available online.
Exclusive: Visit www.UltimateScholarshipBook.com and enter code PO3626 for updates on this award.

[37] • All-American Scholars (Football)
Pop Warner Little Scholars Inc.
P.O. Box 307, Langhorne, PA 19047
https://www.popwarner.com/Default.aspx?tabid=1404834
Purpose: To recognize Pop Warner participants for their academic accomplishments.
Eligibility: Applicants must be a participant in the Pop Warner program as a football player, be in grade 5 or higher and maintain a 96 percent grade point average or higher. Selection will be based on academic achievement and additional non-sport related activities and achievements.
Target applicant(s): Junior high students or younger. High school students.
Minimum GPA: 3.8
Amount: Varies.
Number of awards: Varies.
Deadline: October 15.
How to apply: Applications are available online.
Exclusive: Visit www.UltimateScholarshipBook.com and enter code PO3726 for updates on this award.

[38] • Alpha Kappa Alpha Financial Need Scholars
Alpha Kappa Alpha Educational Advancement Foundation Inc.
5656 S. Stony Island Avenue, Chicago, IL 60637
Phone: 800-653-6528
Email: akaeaf@akaeaf.net
https://akaeaf.org/scholarships
Purpose: To assist undergraduate and graduate students who have overcome hardship to achieve educational goals.
Eligibility: Applicants must be studying full-time at the sophomore level or higher at an accredited institution and have a GPA of 2.5 or higher. Students must also demonstrate leadership, volunteer, civic or academic service. The program is open to students without regard to sex, race, creed, color, ethnicity, religion, sexual orientation or disability. Students do not need to be members of Alpha Kappa Alpha.
Target applicant(s): College students. Graduate school students. Adult students.
Minimum GPA: 2.5

Amount: Varies.
Number of awards: Varies.
Deadline: April 15 (Undergrads); August 15 (Grad).
How to apply: Applications are available online. An application form, personal statement and three letters of recommendation are required.
Exclusive: Visit www.UltimateScholarshipBook.com and enter code AL3826 for updates on this award.

[39] • America's 911 Foundation Scholarship
America's 911 Foundation Inc.
13630 Barnhouse Place, Leesburg, VA 20176
Phone: 703-771-0118
Email: info@americas911foundation.org
http://www.americas911foundation.org
Purpose: To support students who are children of a first responder.
Eligibility: Applicants must be a child of an active duty or volunteer first responder. Students must be accepted to a college or university.
Target applicant(s): High school students. College students. Graduate school students. Adult students.
Amount: $2,000.
Number of awards: 17.
Deadline: March 10.
How to apply: Applications are available online.
Exclusive: Visit www.UltimateScholarshipBook.com and enter code AM3926 for updates on this award.

[40] • American Bar Association Law Day Art Contest
American Bar Association (ABA) Law Day
321 North Clark Street, Chicago, IL 60654
Phone: 312-988-5000
https://www.americanbar.org/groups/public_education/law-day/
Purpose: To encourage students to learn about the legal system.
Eligibility: Applicants must be high school students in grades 9-12 or the equivalent within the United States. Students must create an art piece representing the theme for Law Day.
Target applicant(s): High school students.
Amount: Up to $100.
Number of awards: 2.
Deadline: April 14.
How to apply: Applications are available online.
Exclusive: Visit www.UltimateScholarshipBook.com and enter code AM4026 for updates on this award.

[41] • American Legion Baseball Scholarship
American Legion Baseball
700 N. Pennsylvania Street, P.O. Box 1055, Indianapolis, IN 46206
Phone: 317-630-1203
Email: baseball@legion.org
https://www.legion.org/scholarships
Purpose: To award scholarships to members of American Legion-affiliated baseball teams.
Eligibility: Applicants must have graduated high school and be nominated by a head coach or team manager. One player per department (state) will be selected. Nominations should be sent to the local Department Headquarters. Scholarships may be used to further education at any accredited college, university or other institution of higher education.
Target applicant(s): High school students. College students. Adult students.
Amount: $22,000-$25,000.
Number of awards: 9.
Deadline: June 1.
How to apply: Applications are available online.
Exclusive: Visit www.UltimateScholarshipBook.com and enter code AM4126 for updates on this award.

[42] • American Legion Legacy Scholarships
American Legion
700 North Pennsylvania Street, P.O. Box 1055, Indianapolis, IN 46206
Phone: 317-630-1202
https://www.legion.org/scholarships
Purpose: To support the children of deceased U.S. military personnel.
Eligibility: Applicants must be the children or adopted children of a parent who was in the U.S. military and died in active duty on or after September 11, 2001. Students must be high school seniors or high school graduates pursuing or planning to pursue undergraduate study in the U.S.
Target applicant(s): High school students. College students. Adult students.
Amount: Up to $20,000.
Number of awards: Varies.
Deadline: March 27.
How to apply: Applications are available online.
Exclusive: Visit www.UltimateScholarshipBook.com and enter code AM4226 for updates on this award.

[43] • Americanism Essay Contest
Fleet Reserve Association (FRA)
FRA Scholarship Administrator, 125 N. West Street, Alexandria, VA 22314
Phone: 800-372-1924
Email: fra@fra.org
https://www.fra.org/essay
Purpose: To recognize outstanding student essayists.
Eligibility: Applicants must be in grades 7 through 12 and must be sponsored by a Fleet Reserve Association (FRA) branch or Ladies Auxiliary unit. They must submit an essay on a sponsor-determined topic. Selection is based on the overall strength of the essay.
Target applicant(s): Junior high students or younger. High school students.
Amount: $500-$1,500.
Number of awards: Varies.
Deadline: December 1.
How to apply: Entry instructions are available online - look under "events and programs" link. An essay and cover sheet are required.
Exclusive: Visit www.UltimateScholarshipBook.com and enter code FL4326 for updates on this award.

[44] • Americorps National Civilian Community Corps
AmeriCorps
250 E Street, SW, Washington, DC 20525
Phone: 202-606-5000
Email: questions@americorps.org
http://www.americorps.gov

Purpose: To strengthen communities and develop leaders through community service.
Eligibility: Applicants must be U.S. citizens who are between 18 and 26 years of age. Recipients must live on one of five AmeriCorps campuses in Denver, Colorado; Sacramento, California; Baltimore, Maryland; Vinton, Iowa or Vicksburg, Mississippi. Applicants must commit to 10 months of service on projects in areas such as education, public safety, the environment and other unmet needs. The projects are located within the region of one of the four campuses.
Target applicant(s): High school students. College students. Graduate school students. Adult students.
Amount: $5,775.
Number of awards: Varies.
Deadline: January 4.
How to apply: Applications are available online.
Exclusive: Visit www.UltimateScholarshipBook.com and enter code AM4426 for updates on this award.

[45] • Americorps Vista

AmeriCorps
250 E Street, SW, Washington, DC 20525
Phone: 202-606-5000
Email: questions@americorps.org
http://www.americorps.gov
Purpose: To provide education assistance in exchange for community service.
Eligibility: Applicants must be United States citizens who are at least 18 years of age. They must be available to serve full-time for one year at a nonprofit organization or local government agency with an objective that may include to fight illiteracy, improve health services, create businesses or strengthen community groups.
Target applicant(s): High school students. College students. Graduate school students. Adult students.
Amount: Varies.
Number of awards: Varies.
Deadline: Contact the sponsor to confirm the deadline.
How to apply: Applications are available online.
Exclusive: Visit www.UltimateScholarshipBook.com and enter code AM4526 for updates on this award.

[46] • AMVETS Children/Grandchildren Scholarships

AMVETS National Headquarters
4647 Forbes Boulevard, Lanham, MD 20706-4380
Phone: 877-726-8387
Email: thilton@amvets.org
http://www.amvets.org
Purpose: To provide education assistance for graduating JROTC cadets.
Eligibility: Applicants must be high school seniors with a minimum GPA of 3.0 or documented extenuating circumstances. They must be United States citizens and children or grandchildren of U.S. veterans. They must show academic potential and financial need.
Target applicant(s): High school students.
Minimum GPA: 3.0
Amount: $1,000-$4,000.
Number of awards: 4.
Deadline: April 30.
How to apply: Applications are available online.
Exclusive: Visit www.UltimateScholarshipBook.com and enter code AM4626 for updates on this award.

[47] • AMVETS National Scholarships for Veterans

AMVETS National Headquarters
4647 Forbes Boulevard, Lanham, MD 20706-4380
Phone: 877-726-8387
Email: thilton@amvets.org
http://www.amvets.org
Purpose: To provide financial assistance for veterans.
Eligibility: Applicants must be United States citizens and veterans who demonstrate financial need. They must have been honorably discharged or be on active duty and eligible for release. They must agree to allow AMVET to publicize their award if selected.
Target applicant(s): College students. Adult students.
Amount: $1,000-$12,000.
Number of awards: Varies.
Deadline: April 30.
How to apply: Applications are available online.
Exclusive: Visit www.UltimateScholarshipBook.com and enter code AM4726 for updates on this award.

[48] • Anchor Scholarship Foundation Scholarship

Anchor Scholarship Foundation
138 South Rosemont Road, Suite 10206, Virginia Beach, VA 23452
Phone: 757-671-3200
Email: ScholarshipAdmin@AnchorScholarship.com
https://anchorscholarship.org
Purpose: To assist the dependents of current and former members of the Naval Surface Forces, Atlantic and Naval Surface Forces, Pacific.
Eligibility: Applicants must be high school seniors or college students planning to attend or currently attending an accredited, two- or four-year college or university full-time pursuing a first associates, BA or BS degree or Industry Certification in the United States. Applicants must also be dependents of service members who are on active duty or retired and have served a minimum of six years in a unit under the administrative control of Commander, Naval Surface Forces, U.S. Atlantic Fleet or U.S. Pacific Fleet. Applicants must be the dependent child or spouse of a U.S. Navy sailor (active, retired, honorably discharged) now referred to as sponsor. The award is based on academics, extracurricular activities, character, all-around ability and financial need.
Target applicant(s): High school students. College students. Adult students.
Amount: Up to $10,000.
Number of awards: Varies.
Deadline: March 1.
How to apply: Applications are available online.
Exclusive: Visit www.UltimateScholarshipBook.com and enter code AN4826 for updates on this award.

[49] • Armed Services YMCA Annual Essay Contest

Armed Services YMCA
7405 Alban Station Court, Suite B215, Springfield, VA 22150-2318
Phone: 703-313-9600
Email: essaycontest@asymca.org
http://www.asymca.org

Purpose: To promote reading among children of service members and civilian Department of Defense employees.
Eligibility: Applicants must be K-12 students who are children of active duty or Reserve/Guard military personnel. Entrants up to eighth grade should write an essay of 300 words or less. High school entrants should write an essay of 500 words or less.
Target applicant(s): Junior high students or younger. High school students.
Amount: Varies.
Number of awards: Varies.
Deadline: April 30.
How to apply: Applications are available online.
Exclusive: Visit www.UltimateScholarshipBook.com and enter code AR4926 for updates on this award.

[50] • Army Emergency Relief's MG James Ursano Scholarship Program
Army Emergency Relief (AER)
200 Stovall Street Room 5S33, Alexandria, VA 22332
Phone: 703-428-0035
Email: education@aerhq.org
https://www.armyemergencyrelief.org/scholarships/
Purpose: To assist the children of Army families with their undergraduate education, vocational training and service academy education.
Eligibility: Applicants must be dependent children of Army soldiers who are unmarried and under the age of 22. Students must also be registered with the Defense Eligibility Enrollment Reporting System, have a minimum 2.0 GPA and be enrolled and accepted or pending acceptance as full-time students in post-secondary educational institutions. Awards are based primarily on financial need.
Target applicant(s): High school students. College students.
Minimum GPA: 2.0
Amount: Varies.
Number of awards: Varies.
Scholarship may be renewable.
Deadline: April 1.
How to apply: Applications are available online and by mail.
Exclusive: Visit www.UltimateScholarshipBook.com and enter code AR5026 for updates on this award.

[51] • Army Engineer Memorial Awards
Army Engineer Spouses' Club
P.O. Box 6332, Alexandria, VA 22306-6332
Email: aema@armyengineerspouses.org
https://www.armyengineerspouses.org/
Purpose: To support students who have a parent or legal guardian who is a member of the U.S. Army Engineers.
Eligibility: Applicants must be high school seniors who are U.S. citizens. Students must have a sponsor, parent or legal guardian who is a member of the Army Engineer Spouses club and U.S. Army Engineer (active duty, reserve/national guard, retired or deceased) or current Department of the Army employee of the United States Army Corps of Engineers.
Target applicant(s): High school students.
Amount: Varies.
Number of awards: Varies.
Deadline: February 28.
How to apply: Applications are available online.
Exclusive: Visit www.UltimateScholarshipBook.com and enter code AR5126 for updates on this award.

[52] • Army Nurse Corps Association Scholarships
Army Nurse Corps Association (ANCA)
Scholarship Program, P.O. Box 458, Lisbon, MD 21765
Phone: 210-650-3534
Email: education@e-anca.org
http://e-anca.org/Scholarships
Purpose: To support nursing and nurse anesthesia students who are or plan to become affiliated with the U.S. Army.
Eligibility: Applicants must be enrolled in a bachelor's or graduate degree program in nursing or nurse anesthesia. They must be in the U.S. Army, planning to enter the U.S. Army or be the parent, spouse or child of a U.S. Army officer. They cannot already be receiving funding from any source that is associated with the U.S. Army. Selection is based on the overall strength of the application.
Target applicant(s): College students. Graduate school students. Adult students.
Amount: $3,000.
Number of awards: Varies.
Deadline: March 31.
How to apply: Applications are available online. An application form, personal statement, endorsement from student's academic dean, official transcript and military service documents (if applicable) are required.
Exclusive: Visit www.UltimateScholarshipBook.com and enter code AR5226 for updates on this award.

[53] • Army ROTC Advanced Course
U.S. Army
Human Resources Command, 1600 Spearhead Division Avenue, Department #410, Fort Knox, KY 40122-5401
Phone: 888-276-9472
Email: askhrc.army@us.army.mil
https://www.goarmy.com
Purpose: To prepare ROTC members for service as officers.
Eligibility: Applicants must be rising college juniors who have completed the ROTC Basic Course or Leader's Training Course and have made a commitment to serve as an officer in the Army after they graduate. Students must take an ROTC class or lab each semester of their final two years of school and attend a summer leadership camp.
Target applicant(s): College students. Adult students.
Amount: Varies.
Number of awards: Varies.
Scholarship may be renewable.
Deadline: Contact the sponsor to confirm the deadline.
How to apply: Applications are available from your school's military science department.
Exclusive: Visit www.UltimateScholarshipBook.com and enter code U.5326 for updates on this award.

[54] • Army ROTC Four-Year Scholarship Program
Army Headquarters
U.S. Army Cadet Command, 55 Patch Road, Fort Monroe, VA 23651
Phone: 502-624-6998
Email: usarmy.knox.usacc.mbx.train2lead@army.mil
https://www.goarmy.com/rotc/scholarships.html
Purpose: To bolster the ranks of the Army, Army Reserve and Army National Guard by providing monetary assistance to eligible student candidates.
Eligibility: Applicants must be U.S. citizens and high school seniors, graduates or college freshmen with at least four years of college remaining

The Ultimate Scholarship Book 2026
Scholarship Directory (General Awards)

who wish to attend one of 600 colleges and earn a commission. Recipients must serve in the Army for four to eight years after graduation.
Target applicant(s): High school students.
Minimum GPA: 2.5
Amount: Up to full tuition.
Number of awards: Varies.
Scholarship may be renewable.
Deadline: October 9; January 15; March 11.
How to apply: Applications are available online.
Exclusive: Visit www.UltimateScholarshipBook.com and enter code AR5426 for updates on this award.

[55] • Army ROTC Green To Gold Scholarship Program
Army Headquarters
U.S. Army Cadet Command, 55 Patch Road, Fort Monroe, VA 23651
Phone: 502-624-6998
Email: usarmy.knox.usacc.mbx.train2lead@army.mil
https://www.goarmy.com/rotc/scholarships.html
Purpose: To provide scholarship funds for Army enlisted soldiers.
Eligibility: Applicants must be active duty enlisted members of the Army who wish to complete their baccalaureate degree requirements and obtain a commission. Recipients are required to serve in the U.S. Army. Applicants must also meet numerous U.S. Army related requirements, be a high school graduate or equivalent, have a minimum GPA of 2.5 (high school or college) and be a U.S. citizen under age 31.
Target applicant(s): High school students. College students. Adult students.
Minimum GPA: 2.5
Amount: Varies.
Number of awards: Varies.
Deadline: Last Friday of November.
How to apply: Applications are available online.
Exclusive: Visit www.UltimateScholarshipBook.com and enter code AR5526 for updates on this award.

[56] • AU Student Contest
Americans United for Separation of Church and State
1310 L Street NW, Suite 200, Washington, DC 20005
Phone: 202-466-3234
Email: johnson@au.org
https://www.au.org/studentcontest/#
Purpose: To emphasize the importance of religious freedom and the separation of church and state.
Eligibility: Applicants must be current high school students and undergraduate students attending any two- or four-year college or university including trade and technical schools. Students must live in the United States including the fifty states, the District of Columbia and the U.S. territories. Applicants can submit an essay or video reflecting on why religious freedom and church-state separation are important to them and their communities.
Target applicant(s): High school students. College students. Adult students.
Amount: Up to $1,500.
Number of awards: 15.
Deadline: October 31.
How to apply: Applications are available online.
Exclusive: Visit www.UltimateScholarshipBook.com and enter code AM5626 for updates on this award.

[57] • Babe Ruth League Scholarships
Babe Ruth League Inc.
1770 Brunswick Avenue, P.O. Box 5000, Trenton, NJ 08638
Phone: 800-880-3142
https://www.baberuthleague.org/scholarships/babe-ruth-league-scholarship.aspx
Purpose: To provide educational assistance to players in the Babe Ruth Baseball and Softball divisions.
Eligibility: Applicants must be members or former members of the Babe Ruth Baseball or Softball leagues. They must be graduating high school seniors or enrolled college students. A short essay, copy of high school transcript and a letter of recommendation are required.
Target applicant(s): High school students. College students. Adult students.
Amount: Varies.
Number of awards: Varies.
Deadline: June 30.
How to apply: Applications are available online.
Exclusive: Visit www.UltimateScholarshipBook.com and enter code BA5726 for updates on this award.

[58] • Banana George Blair Ambassador Scholarship
USA Water Ski and Wake Sports Foundation
6039 Cypress Gardens Boulevard, Suite 481, Winter Haven, FL 33884
Phone: 863-324-2472
Email: info@waterskihalloffame.com
https://www.usa-wwf.org/ourscholarships
Purpose: To help current active members of USA Water Ski pursue their educational goals.
Eligibility: Applicants must be student-athletes enrolled in a college or university on a full-time basis. Students must be U.S. citizens and members of USA Water Ski and Wake Sports. This scholarship is open to all water sports disciplines.
Target applicant(s): High school students. College students. Adult students.
Amount: $2,200.
Number of awards: 1.
Scholarship may be renewable.
Deadline: April 1.
How to apply: Applications are available online.
Exclusive: Visit www.UltimateScholarshipBook.com and enter code US5826 for updates on this award.

[59] • Barbizon's College Tuition Scholarship
Barbizon International
4950 West Kennedy Boulevard, Suite 200, Tampa, FL 33609
Phone: 888-999-9404
Email: barbizon@barbizonmodeling.com
https://www.barbizonmodeling.com/scholarships/
Purpose: To support students who wish to continue their education.
Eligibility: Applicants must be legal U.S. residents who are planning to attend an accredited college or university. Students must fill out an entry form for the sweepstakes and must be accepted at an accredited college or university within three years of graduation.
Target applicant(s): High school students.
Amount: Up to $100,000.
Number of awards: 1.
Deadline: December 31.
How to apply: Applications are available online.

Exclusive: Visit www.UltimateScholarshipBook.com and enter code BA5926 for updates on this award.

[60] • Be the Boss Scholarship
GoSkills
555 Bryant Street, #901, Palo Alto, CA 94301
Phone: 650-822-7732
Email: support@goskills.com
https://www.goskills.com/Scholarship
Purpose: To encourage women to start their own online business.
Eligibility: Applicants must be female high school or college students interested in starting their own online business. Students must submit their business plan to apply.
Target applicant(s): High school students. College students. Adult students.
Amount: $2,000.
Number of awards: 2.
Scholarship may be renewable.
Deadline: March 15 (Spring); September 15 (Fall).
How to apply: Applications are available online.
Exclusive: Visit www.UltimateScholarshipBook.com and enter code GO6026 for updates on this award.

[61] • Beyond the Boroughs Scholarship
Beyond the Boroughs
30 East 125th Street, Suite 242, New York, NY 10035
Phone: 914-458-2926
Email: ray@beyondtheboroughs.org
http://www.beyondtheboroughs.org
Purpose: To support students with financial need in pursuing a bachelor's degree.
Eligibility: Applicants must be accepted to an accredited four-year college. A minimum GPA of 2.5 is required. Selection is primarily based on demonstration of financial need, academic achievement, work history and extracurricular involvement.
Target applicant(s): High school students. College students. Adult students.
Minimum GPA: 2.5
Amount: Up to $20,000.
Number of awards: Varies.
Scholarship may be renewable.
Deadline: March 15.
How to apply: Applications are available online.
Exclusive: Visit www.UltimateScholarshipBook.com and enter code BE6126 for updates on this award.

[62] • Big Al Wagner Western Region Scholarship
USA Water Ski and Wake Sports Foundation
6039 Cypress Gardens Boulevard, Suite 481, Winter Haven, FL 33884
Phone: 863-324-2472
Email: info@waterskihalloffame.com
https://www.usa-wwf.org/ourscholarships
Purpose: To help current active members of USA Water Ski pursue their educational goals.
Eligibility: Applicants must be U.S. citizens and be incoming freshmen, sophomores, juniors or seniors at a two-year or four-year accredited college and enrolled full-time. Students must remain enrolled full-time at their chosen college during the year of receipt of the scholarship. Applicants must be members of USA Water Ski and Wake Sports, be students who are AWSA Western Region Skiers and be qualified for the Western Regional Water Ski Tournament.
Target applicant(s): High school students. College students. Adult students.
Amount: $1,500.
Number of awards: 1.
Scholarship may be renewable.
Deadline: April 1.
How to apply: Applications are available online.
Exclusive: Visit www.UltimateScholarshipBook.com and enter code US6226 for updates on this award.

[63] • BMTX Financial Empowerment Scholarship
BM Technologies Inc.
P.O. Box 278, Maple Shade, NJ 08052
Email: scholarship@bmtx.com
https://www.bmtx.com/scholarship
Purpose: To support student financial literacy.
Eligibility: Applicants must be undergraduate or graduate level students, U.S. citizens, and have a minimum 3.0 GPA. Students must submit a creative video explaining the importance of financial literacy in both their lives and their career. Special consideration is given to applicants who are actively promoting financial literacy within their community.
Target applicant(s): College students. Graduate school students. Adult students.
Minimum GPA: 3.0
Amount: $1,500.
Number of awards: 1.
Deadline: July 12.
How to apply: Applications are available online and must include an official transcript (high school or college) and the essay.
Exclusive: Visit www.UltimateScholarshipBook.com and enter code BM6326 for updates on this award.

[64] • Bob Warnicke Scholarship
Bob Warnicke Memorial Scholarship Fund
USA BMX/BMX Canada, 490 N. Lansing Avenue East, Tulsa, OK 74120
Phone: 480-961-1903
Email: programs@usabmxfoundation.org
http://www.usabmx.com
Purpose: To help students who have participated in BMX racing events.
Eligibility: Applicants must be members, have a current NBL competition license or official's license and have participated in BMX racing events for at least a year. Students must also be high school graduates and plan to or currently attend a postsecondary institution full- or part-time.
Target applicant(s): High school students. College students. Adult students.
Amount: $500-$3,000.
Number of awards: 51.
Deadline: January 22.
How to apply: Applications are available online, by mail or by phone.
Exclusive: Visit www.UltimateScholarshipBook.com and enter code BO6426 for updates on this award.

[65] • Bonner Scholars Program
Bonner Foundation
10 Mercer Street, Princeton, NJ 08540
Phone: 609-924-6663
Email: info@bonner.org

The Ultimate Scholarship Book 2026
Scholarship Directory (General Awards)

http://www.bonner.org/apply
Purpose: To award four-year community service scholarships to students planning to attend one of 75 participating colleges.
Eligibility: Students must complete annual service requirements as stipulated by the organization. Awards are geared toward students demonstrating significant financial need. Scholarship recipients are named Bonner Scholars.
Target applicant(s): High school students.
Amount: Varies.
Number of awards: Varies.
Deadline: Contact the sponsor to confirm the deadline.
How to apply: Contact the admission office at each participating school to request an application.
Exclusive: Visit www.UltimateScholarshipBook.com and enter code BO6526 for updates on this award.

[66] • Boomer Benefits Scholarship
Boomer Benefits
2601 Meacham Boulevard Suite 500, Fort Worth, TX 76137
Phone: 817-249-8600
http://boomerbenefits.com
Purpose: To support adult students who are at least 50 years of age in returning to school to complete their degree.
Eligibility: Applicants must be enrolled in an undergraduate or graduate degree program at an accredited educational institution. A minimum GPA of 3.0 is required. Selection is primarily based on demonstration of academic achievement and community service.
Target applicant(s): Adult students.
Minimum GPA: 3.0
Amount: $2,500.
Number of awards: 1.
Deadline: August 27.
How to apply: Applications are available online.
Exclusive: Visit www.UltimateScholarshipBook.com and enter code BO6626 for updates on this award.

[67] • Bright!Tax Global Scholar Initiative
Bright!Tax
244 Fifth Avenue, New York, NY 10001
Phone: 212-465-2528
Email: inquiries@brighttax.com
https://brighttax.com/scholarships/
Purpose: To support students wishing to study abroad.
Eligibility: Applicants must be U.S. citizens who want to study abroad for at least one full semester at an accredited institution. Selection is based on academic and extracurricular achievement, community involvement, future ambitions and financial need.
Target applicant(s): High school students. College students. Graduate school students. Adult students.
Amount: $1,000.
Number of awards: Minimum of 2.
Deadline: June 1; November 1.
How to apply: Applications are available online.
Exclusive: Visit www.UltimateScholarshipBook.com and enter code BR6726 for updates on this award.

[68] • Brown Hudner Navy Scholarship
Brown Hudner Navy Scholarship Foundation
909 North Washington Street, Suite 400, Alexandria, VA 22314
Phone: 571-386-2642
Email: scholarship@brownhudner.org
https://www.brownhudner.org/
Purpose: To support students who are the children of Navy sailors.
Eligibility: Applicants must be children of active duty, reserve, honorably discharged or fallen Sailors. Students must be planning to pursue a degree in science, technology, engineering, mathematics (STEM) or health science and have a minimum 2.0 GPA. Applicants must demonstrate financial need.
Target applicant(s): High school students. College students. Adult students.
Minimum GPA: 2.0
Amount: Varies.
Number of awards: Varies.
Deadline: March 1.
How to apply: Applications are available online.
Exclusive: Visit www.UltimateScholarshipBook.com and enter code BR6826 for updates on this award.

[69] • Building Bridges Scholarship
National Parent Volunteer Association
1875 Mission Street Suite 103-133, San Francisco, CA 94103
Email: programs@parent-volunteer.org
https://www.parent-volunteer.org/scholarships
Purpose: To assist students who are involved in their communities.
Eligibility: Applicants must be currently enrolled or plan to be enrolled full-time in an accredited U.S. college or university. Students must be a high school junior or senior, undergraduate student or graduate student and have a minimum 2.5 GPA. Recipients must provide an official transcript confirming their reported GPA and proof of enrollment.
Target applicant(s): High school students. College students. Graduate school students. Adult students.
Amount: $1,000.
Number of awards: Varies.
Deadline: September 30.
How to apply: Applications are available online.
Exclusive: Visit www.UltimateScholarshipBook.com and enter code NA6926 for updates on this award.

[70] • Burger King Scholars Program
Burger King Scholars Program
Scholarship America, One Scholarship Way, St. Peter, MN 56082
Phone: 305-378-3000
Email: burgerkingscholars@scholarshipamerica.org
https://www.burgerkingfoundation.org/programs/burger-king-sm-scholars
Purpose: To provide financial assistance for high school seniors who have part-time jobs.
Eligibility: Applicants must be graduating high school seniors (U.S. and Puerto Rico), graduating from grade 12 (Canada) or graduating from home school education in the U.S., Puerto Rico or Canada and must reside in the U.S., Canada or Puerto Rico. Students must also have a minimum 2.5 GPA and plan to enroll full-time in an accredited two- or four-year college, university or vocational/technical school by the fall term of the graduating year. Applicants do NOT need to work at Burger King, but Burger King employees are eligible. Consideration will be given to each applicant's academic record and participation in school and community activities.

Target applicant(s): High school students.
Minimum GPA: 2.5
Amount: Up to $60,000.
Number of awards: Varies.
Deadline: December 16.
How to apply: Applications are available online and may only be completed online.
Exclusive: Visit www.UltimateScholarshipBook.com and enter code BU7026 for updates on this award.

[71] • C.I.P. Scholarship

College Is Power
1025 Alameda de las Pulgas #215, Belmont, CA 94002
http://collegeispower.com/scholarship.cfm
Purpose: To assist adult students age 17 and over with college expenses.
Eligibility: Applicants must be adult students currently attending or planning to attend a two-year or four-year college or university within the next 12 months. Students must be 17 years or older and U.S. citizens or permanent residents. The award may be used for full- or part-time study at either on-campus or online schools.
Target applicant(s): High school students. College students. Adult students.
Amount: $1,000.
Number of awards: 3.
Deadline: May 31, August 31, December 31.
How to apply: Applications are available online.
Exclusive: Visit www.UltimateScholarshipBook.com and enter code CO7126 for updates on this award.

[72] • Capt. James J. Regan Scholarship

Explorers Learning for Life
1325 West Walnut Hill Lane, P.O. Box 152225, Irving, TX 75015-2225
Phone: 972-580-2433
Email: exploring@lflmail.org
http://www.exploring.org/scholarships/
Purpose: To support students who are Law Enforcement Explorers.
Eligibility: Students must be at least in their senior year of high school or in an accredited college program. Applicants must submit three letters of recommendation and an essay.
Target applicant(s): High school students. College students. Adult students.
Amount: $2,500.
Number of awards: 1.
Deadline: March 31.
How to apply: Applications are available online.
Exclusive: Visit www.UltimateScholarshipBook.com and enter code EX7226 for updates on this award.

[73] • Captain Caliendo College Assistance Fund

U.S. Coast Guard Chief Petty Officers Association
CCCAF Scholarship Committee, 5520-G Hempstead Way, Springfield, VA 22151-4009
Phone: 703-941-0395
Email: cgcpoa@aol.com
https://uscgcpoa.org
Purpose: To provide financial assistance for children of CPOA/CGEA members.
Eligibility: Applicants must be dependents of a living or deceased USCG CPOA/CGEA member who are under the age of 24 as of March 1 of the award year. The age limit does not apply to disabled children. Proof of acceptance or enrollment in an institution of higher learning is required.
Target applicant(s): High school students. College students.
Amount: $1,000-$5,000.
Number of awards: 3.
Deadline: April 1.
How to apply: Applications are available online. An essay not exceeding 500 words is required.
Exclusive: Visit www.UltimateScholarshipBook.com and enter code U.7326 for updates on this award.

[74] • CareerFitter Scholarship

CareerFitter.com
P.O. Box 124, Pisgah Forest, NC 28768
https://www.careerfitter.com/scholarship
Purpose: To support students in pursuing their college educations.
Eligibility: Applicants must be planning to enroll or already enrolled in an accredited college or graduate school program. Students are encouraged to take a career test on Career Fitter's website and include the results on their application. Selection is based on the overall strength of the application.
Target applicant(s): High school students. College students. Graduate school students. Adult students.
Minimum GPA: 2.4
Amount: $1,000.
Number of awards: 1.
Scholarship may be renewable.
Deadline: January 31.
How to apply: Applications must be completed online.
Exclusive: Visit www.UltimateScholarshipBook.com and enter code CA7426 for updates on this award.

[75] • Carolyn Hines Memorial Scholarship Program

Civilian Marksmanship Program
P.O. Box 576, Port Clinton, OH 43452
Phone: 419-635-2141
Email: kwilliams@thecmp.org
https://thecmp.org/youth/cmp-scholarship-program/
Purpose: To aid students who have participated in marksmanship competitions with their higher education costs.
Eligibility: Applicants must be U.S. Citizens, represent good moral character, have a 3.0 or higher GPA and participate in rifle or pistol marksmanship competitions. Selection is based on academic achievement, a letter of recommendation and a personal letter to the committee explaining how the scholarship will help you to reach your goals and marksmanship participation and success.
Target applicant(s): High school students.
Minimum GPA: 3.0
Amount: $20,000.
Number of awards: 4.
Deadline: March 31.
How to apply: Applications are available online and must include the letter to the committee, one letter of recommendation, a transcript and documentation of marksmanship activity.
Exclusive: Visit www.UltimateScholarshipBook.com and enter code CI7526 for updates on this award.

The Ultimate Scholarship Book 2026
Scholarship Directory (General Awards)

[76] • Carson Scholars
Carson Scholars Fund
305 W Chesapeake Avenue, Suite 310, Towson, MD 21204
Phone: 877-773-7236
Email: katie@carsonscholars.org
http://carsonscholars.org/scholarships/
Purpose: To recognize students who demonstrate academic excellence and commitment to the community.
Eligibility: Applicants must be nominated by their school. They must be in grades 4 through 11 and have a GPA of 3.75 or higher in English, reading, language arts, math, science, social studies and foreign language. They must have participated in some form of voluntary community service beyond what is required by their school. Scholarship recipients must attend a four-year college or university upon graduation to receive funds.
Target applicant(s): Junior high students or younger. High school students.
Minimum GPA: 3.75
Amount: $1,000.
Number of awards: Varies.
Deadline: December 18.
How to apply: Applications are available from the schools of those nominated. Only one student per school may be nominated.
Exclusive: Visit www.UltimateScholarshipBook.com and enter code CA7626 for updates on this award.

[77] • Cashtelligent Financial Literacy Scholarship
Cashtelligent
https://www.cashtelligent.com/scholarship/
Purpose: This scholarship is designed to encourage students to increase their financial literacy skills and adopt positive habits for managing their personal finances both in college and beyond.
Eligibility: Applicants must be high school or college students, graduate school students, adult students or parents of a student enrolled or planning to enroll in any accredited college in the U.S. There are no requirements for field of study.
Target applicant(s): High school students. College students. Graduate school students. Adult students.
Amount: $1,000.
Number of awards: 4.
Deadline: March 31, June 30, September 30, December 31.
How to apply: Applications are available online.
Exclusive: Visit www.UltimateScholarshipBook.com and enter code CA7726 for updates on this award.

[78] • CCA Christian Cheer Nationals
Christian Cheerleaders of America
P.O. Box 49, Bethania, NC 27010
Phone: 877-243-3722
Email: info@cheercca.com
http://www.cheercca.com
Purpose: To support cheerleaders who participate in cheer through Christian Cheerleaders of America.
Eligibility: Applicants must be a junior or senior in high school, participate in Christian Cheerleaders of America and be nominated by the cheer coach. The student should have a 3.0 GPA or higher. Selection is based on academic achievement and Christian service.
Target applicant(s): High school students.
Minimum GPA: 3.0
Amount: Varies.
Number of awards: Varies.
Deadline: March 2.
How to apply: Nomination forms are available online.
Exclusive: Visit www.UltimateScholarshipBook.com and enter code CH7826 for updates on this award.

[79] • Challenge Scholarship
National Strength and Conditioning Association (NSCA) Foundation
1885 Bob Johnson Drive, Colorado Springs, CO 80906
Phone: 800-815-6826
Email: Foundation@nsca.com
http://www.nsca.com/foundation/
Purpose: To support NSCA members pursuing studies related to strength and conditioning.
Eligibility: Applicants must be NSCA members for one year before applying and be pursuing careers in strength and conditioning. Students must submit an essay detailing their course of study, career goals and financial need. Applications are evaluated based on grades, courses, experience, honors, recommendations and involvement in the community and with NSCA.
Target applicant(s): High school students. College students. Graduate school students. Adult students.
Amount: $2,000.
Number of awards: Varies.
Deadline: October 15.
How to apply: Applications are available with membership.
Exclusive: Visit www.UltimateScholarshipBook.com and enter code NA7926 for updates on this award.

[80] • Chief Master Sergeants of the Air Force Scholarships
Air Force Sergeants Association
5211 Auth Road, Suitland, MD 20746
Phone: 301-899-3500
Email: staff@hqafsa.org
http://www.hqafsa.org
Purpose: To provide financial assistance to the families of Air Force enlistees.
Eligibility: Applicants must be dependents of enlisted Air Force members, either on active duty or retired. They must meet the eligibility requirements and participate in the Airmen Memorial Foundation Scholarship Program. An unweighted GPA of 3.5 or higher is required. Extenuating circumstances are considered.
Target applicant(s): High school students. College students. Adult students.
Minimum GPA: 3.5
Amount: Varies.
Number of awards: Varies.
Deadline: March 31.
How to apply: Applications are available online.
Exclusive: Visit www.UltimateScholarshipBook.com and enter code AI8026 for updates on this award.

[81] • Chief Petty Officer Scholarship Fund
Chief Petty Officer Scholarship Fund
328 Office Square Lane, Suite 101A, Virginia Beach, VA 23462
Phone: 757-233-9136
Email: cposfboard@cposf.org

http://www.cposf.org
Purpose: To aid the families of Chief Petty Officers of the U.S. Navy.
Eligibility: Applicants must be spouses or children of active, retired, honorably discharged or deceased or reserve Chief, Senior Chief or Master Chief Petty Officers of the U.S. Navy. They must be high school graduates or have earned a GED and plan to attend a college, university or post-secondary vocational institution to earn an AA, BA or BS degree. Current college students may also apply. Selection criteria include scholastic proficiency, character and all-around ability.
Target applicant(s): High school students. College students. Adult students.
Amount: Varies.
Number of awards: Varies.
Deadline: April 1.
How to apply: Applications are available online. An application form, three letters of recommendation, a copy of your dependents ID card and a personal statement are required.
Exclusive: Visit www.UltimateScholarshipBook.com and enter code CH8126 for updates on this award.

[82] • Children of Warriors National Presidents' Scholarship

American Legion Auxiliary
3450 Founders Road, Indianapolis, IN 46268
Phone: 317-569-4500
Email: alahq@alaforveterans.org
https://www.legion-aux.org/scholarships
Purpose: To award scholarships to children, grandchildren and great-grandchildren of veterans who served in the Armed Forces.
Eligibility: Applicants must be the children, grandchildren or great-grandchildren of veterans who served in the Armed Forces for membership in The American Legion, be high school seniors and complete 50 hours of community service. Selection is based on character, application/essay, scholastic achievement, leadership and financial need.
Target applicant(s): High school students.
Amount: $5,000.
Number of awards: 15.
Deadline: March 1.
How to apply: Applications are available online. Applicants should submit applications, four recommendation letters, essays, proof of volunteering, transcripts, ACT or SAT scores and parent's or grandparent's military service description.
Exclusive: Visit www.UltimateScholarshipBook.com and enter code AM8226 for updates on this award.

[83] • Chinese American Citizens Alliance Essay Contest

Chinese American Citizens Alliance
1044 Stockton Street, San Francisco, CA 94108
Phone: 415-829-9332
Email: info@cacanational.org
http://www.cacanational.org
Purpose: To provide a forum for expression for future leaders of the United States.
Eligibility: Applicants must be high school students in grades 9 through 12. Students do NOT need to be Chinese Americans. They must write a 500-word essay on a topic chosen by the Chinese American Citizens Alliance. The essay must be written on a given date at the student's local lodge or other designated location.
Target applicant(s): High school students.
Amount: Up to $1,000.
Number of awards: 13.
Deadline: March 2.
How to apply: Applications are available online. An application form and essay are required.
Exclusive: Visit www.UltimateScholarshipBook.com and enter code CH8326 for updates on this award.

[84] • Christophers Video Contest for College Students

Christophers
5 Hanover Square, 22nd Floor, New York, NY 10004
Phone: 212-759-4050
Email: youth@christophers.org
https://www.christophers.org/video-contest-for-college-students
Purpose: To support college students who believe in The Christophers' mission that any one person can make a difference.
Eligibility: Applicants must be current undergraduate or graduate level college students and U.S. citizens. Selection is based on the video submitted and how well it depicts the theme of "One Person Can Make a Difference."
Target applicant(s): College students. Graduate school students. Adult students.
Amount: $100-$2,000.
Number of awards: 3.
Deadline: February 16.
How to apply: Applications are available online. Students must also submit a video of five minutes or less communicating the theme.
Exclusive: Visit www.UltimateScholarshipBook.com and enter code CH8426 for updates on this award.

[85] • CIA Undergraduate Scholarship Program

Central Intelligence Agency
Office of Public Affairs, Washington, DC 20505
Phone: 703-482-0623
https://www.cia.gov/careers/student-programs/
Purpose: To encourage students to pursue careers with the CIA.
Eligibility: Applicants must be high school seniors or college freshmen or sophomores. High school students must have an SAT score of 1000 or higher or an ACT score of 21 or higher, while all applicants must have a GPA of at least 3.0. Applicants must demonstrate financial need, defined as a gross annual household income ceiling up to $120,000. They must meet all criteria for regular CIA employees, including security checks and medical examinations. Applicants must commit to a work experience each summer during college and agree to CIA employment for 1.5 times the length of their CIA-sponsored scholarship.
Target applicant(s): High school students. College students. Adult students.
Minimum GPA: 3.0
Amount: Varies.
Number of awards: Varies.
Scholarship may be renewable.
Deadline: June 30.
How to apply: Applications are available online. A resume, SAT/ACT scores, family income information, copy of FAFSA or Student Aid Report, transcript and two letters of recommendation are required.
Exclusive: Visit www.UltimateScholarshipBook.com and enter code CE8526 for updates on this award.

The Ultimate Scholarship Book 2026
Scholarship Directory (General Awards)

[86] • CJ Pony Parts Scholarship Video Contest

CJ Pony Parts
7461 Allentown Boulevard, Harrisburg, PA 17112
Phone: 800-888-6473
https://www.cjponyparts.com
Purpose: To support graduating seniors and undergraduate students in pursuing post-secondary education.
Eligibility: Applicants must be U.S. residents who will be enrolling in classes for the upcoming semester. Students must submit a video addressing an automotive related topic. Selection is based on the overall strength of the submission.
Target applicant(s): High school students. College students. Adult students.
Amount: $500.
Number of awards: 2.
Deadline: April 15 (Spring); October 15 (Fall).
How to apply: Applications are available online.
Exclusive: Visit www.UltimateScholarshipBook.com and enter code CJ8626 for updates on this award.

[87] • Clubs of America Scholarship Award for Career Success

Clubs of America
484 Wegner Road, Lakemoor, IL 60051
Phone: 800-800-9122
Email: scholarship@greatclubs.com
https://www.greatclubs.com/scholarship/
Purpose: To support undergraduate students in funding their education.
Eligibility: Applicants must be enrolled at an accredited U.S. educational institution. A minimum GPA of 3.0 is required. Students must submit an essay explaining their career goals. Selection is based on the overall strength of the submission.
Target applicant(s): College students. Adult students.
Minimum GPA: 3.0
Amount: $1,000.
Number of awards: 1.
Deadline: August 31.
How to apply: Applications are available online.
Exclusive: Visit www.UltimateScholarshipBook.com and enter code CL8726 for updates on this award.

[88] • Coast Guard College Student Pre-Commissioning Initiative

U.S. Coast Guard
2703 Martin Luther King Jr. Avenue SE, Washington, DC 20593-7000
Phone: 877-663-8724
http://www.gocoastguard.com
Purpose: To train future Coast Guard officers for success.
Eligibility: Applicants must be between 19 and 27 years of age and be college sophomores or juniors with at least 60 credits completed toward their degrees. They must be enrolled in a four-year degree program at a Coast Guard-approved institution with at least a 25 percent minority population. Students must be U.S. citizens, have a 2.5 or higher GPA and meet all physical requirements of the Coast Guard. Applicants must have a minimum score of 1100 on the SAT, 23 on the ACT or 109 on the ASVAB.
Target applicant(s): College students. Adult students.
Minimum GPA: 2.5
Amount: Tuition plus salary.
Number of awards: Varies.
Scholarship may be renewable.
Deadline: Contact the sponsor to confirm the deadline.
How to apply: Applications are available online. An application form, physical exam results, immunization record, copy of Social Security card and driver's license, transcript, test results, proof of enrollment and tuition statement are required.
Exclusive: Visit www.UltimateScholarshipBook.com and enter code U.8826 for updates on this award.

[89] • Coast Guard Foundation Scholarship Fund

Coast Guard Foundation
394 Taugwonk Road, Stonington, CT 06378
Phone: 860-535-0786
Email: info@cgfdn.org
http://www.coastguardfoundation.org
Purpose: To provide financial assistance to children of Coast Guard members.
Eligibility: Applicants must be unmarried dependent children of U.S. Coast Guard members, living, retired or deceased or Coast Guard reservists on extended active duty. They must be high school seniors or full-time undergraduate students in a four-year program or vocational/technical program. They must be under 23 years old.
Target applicant(s): High school students. College students.
Amount: $2,000 to $5,000.
Number of awards: Varies.
Scholarship may be renewable.
Deadline: March 15.
How to apply: Applications are available online.
Exclusive: Visit www.UltimateScholarshipBook.com and enter code CO8926 for updates on this award.

[90] • Coca-Cola Community College Academic Team

Coca-Cola Scholars Foundation
P.O. Box 442, Atlanta, GA 30301
Phone: 800-306-2653
Email: Scholars@coca-cola.com
http://www.coca-colascholarsfoundation.org/apply/
Purpose: To assist community college students with college expenses.
Eligibility: Applicants must be enrolled in community college, have a minimum GPA of 3.5 on a four-point scale and be on track to earn an associate's or bachelor's degree. Students attending community college in the U.S. do NOT need to be members of Phi Theta Kappa. Fifty students will win a $1,500 scholarship, fifty students will win a $1,250 scholarship and fifty students will win a $1,000 scholarship.
Target applicant(s): College students. Adult students.
Minimum GPA: 3.5
Amount: $1,000-$1,500.
Number of awards: 150.
Deadline: December 1.
How to apply: Applications are available online. Nomination from the designated nominator at your school is required. A list of nominators is available at http://www.ptk.org.
Exclusive: Visit www.UltimateScholarshipBook.com and enter code CO9026 for updates on this award.

[91] • Coca-Cola Scholars Program

Coca-Cola Scholars Foundation
P.O. Box 442, Atlanta, GA 30301
Phone: 800-306-2653
Email: Scholars@coca-cola.com
http://www.coca-colascholarsfoundation.org/apply/
Purpose: Begun in 1986 to celebrate the Coca-Cola Centennial, the program is designed to contribute to the nation's future and to assist a wide range of students.
Eligibility: Applicants must be high school seniors in the U.S., be U.S. citizens, nationals or permanent residents and must use the awards at an accredited U.S. college or university. Selection is based on the transcript, school profile, school and non-school related clubs and organizations, honors and awards and volunteer service. The application period typically reopens on August 1 of each year.
Target applicant(s): High school students.
Amount: $20,000.
Number of awards: 150.
Scholarship may be renewable.
Deadline: October 2.
How to apply: Applications are available online.
Exclusive: Visit www.UltimateScholarshipBook.com and enter code CO9126 for updates on this award.

[92] • College Prep Scholarship for High School Juniors

QuestBridge
120 Hawthorne Avenue, Suite 103, Palo Alto, CA 94301
Phone: 888-275-2054
Email: questions@questbridge.org
http://www.questbridge.org
Purpose: To equip outstanding low-income high school juniors with the knowledge necessary to compete for admission to leading colleges.
Eligibility: Applicants must be high school juniors who have a strong academic record and an annual household income of less than $65,000. Many past award recipients have also been part of the first generation in their family to attend college. Scholarships are open to all qualified students, regardless of race or ethnicity.
Target applicant(s): High school students.
Amount: Varies.
Number of awards: Varies.
Deadline: March 22.
How to apply: Applications are available on the QuestBridge website in February. An application form, transcript and one teacher recommendation are required.
Exclusive: Visit www.UltimateScholarshipBook.com and enter code QU9226 for updates on this award.

[93] • Collegiate Championship Award Program

U.S. Figure Skating
20 First Street, Colorado Springs, CO 80906
Phone: 719-635-5200
Email: info@usfigureskating.org
https://www.usfigureskating.org/skate/scholarships-and-funding
Purpose: To aid eligible collegiate figure skaters with their college tuition.
Eligibility: The award is presented to the senior ladies champion and senior men's champion at the U.S. Collegiate Figure Skating Championships.
Target applicant(s): College students. Adult students.
Amount: $5,000.
Number of awards: 2.
Deadline: July 1.
How to apply: The award is presented at the U.S. Collegiate Figure Skating Championships.
Exclusive: Visit www.UltimateScholarshipBook.com and enter code U.9326 for updates on this award.

[94] • Completing the Dream Scholarship

Sallie Mae Completing the Dream Scholarship
https://www.tmcf.org/students-alumni/scholarship/tmcf-sallie-mae-fund-completing-the-dream-gap-scholarship/
Purpose: To support students who wish to continue their education into college.
Eligibility: Applicants must be citizens or permanent residents of the United States or United States territories. Students must be current college students in the final year of study with financial need from minority or other historically underserved communities.
Target applicant(s): College students. Adult students.
Minimum GPA: 3.0
Amount: Up to $2,500.
Number of awards: Up to 260.
Deadline: June 28.
How to apply: Applications are available online.
Exclusive: Visit www.UltimateScholarshipBook.com and enter code SA9426 for updates on this award.

[95] • Congress Bundestag Youth Exchange Program

Congress Bundestag Youth Exchange Program
Cultural Vistas, 233 Broadway, 21st Floor, New York, NY 20279
Phone: 212-497-3572
Email: cbyx@culturalvistas.org
http://www.usagermanyscholarship.org
Purpose: To aid high school students who wish to study abroad in Germany.
Eligibility: Applicants must be U.S. citizens or permanent residents and be current high school students who will be between the ages of 15 and 18 at the beginning of the exchange program. They must have a GPA of 3.0 or higher on a four-point scale. Previous knowledge of the German language is not required. Selection is based on academic achievement, written and oral communication skills and temperamental suitability for adjusting to different cultures.
Target applicant(s): High school students.
Minimum GPA: 3.0
Amount: Full Tuition.
Number of awards: Varies.
Deadline: November 1.
How to apply: Applications are available online. An application form and supporting materials are required.
Exclusive: Visit www.UltimateScholarshipBook.com and enter code CO9526 for updates on this award.

[96] • Congressional Medal of Honor Society Scholarships

Congressional Medal of Honor Society
40 Patriots Point Road, Mount Pleasant, SC 29464
Phone: 843-884-8862
Email: medalhq@earthlink.net
http://www.cmohs.org

Purpose: To provide education assistance to children of Congressional Medal of Honor recipients.
Eligibility: Applicants must be ROTC undergraduate students of the Air Force, Army, Navy or Marine Corps and must demonstrate leadership and a commitment to serve in the United States Armed Forces. Applicants must also be enrolled as sophomores or juniors. Applicants must have a minimum 3.5 GPA.
Target applicant(s): College students. Adult students.
Minimum GPA: 3.5
Amount: Varies.
Number of awards: Varies.
Deadline: Contact the sponsor to confirm the deadline.
How to apply: Applications are available from the Congressional Medal of Honor Society.
Exclusive: Visit www.UltimateScholarshipBook.com and enter code CO9626 for updates on this award.

[97] • Coolidge Scholarship

Calvin Coolidge Memorial Foundation Inc.
P.O. Box 97, Plymouth, VT 05056
Phone: 802-672-3389
Email: coolidgescholars@coolidgefoundation.org
https://coolidgescholars.org/
Purpose: To reward high school juniors who have achieved academic excellence and have an interest in public policy.
Eligibility: Applicants must be U.S. citizens planning on enrolling full-time in an accredited U.S. college or university. Students must apply during their junior year in high school. Selection is based on academic excellence, interest in public policy and appreciation for Coolidge values and demonstrated humility and leadership.
Target applicant(s): High school students.
Amount: Full tuition.
Number of awards: 2.
Deadline: December 11.
How to apply: Applications are available online through the website and include an essay, a transcript, a resume and two letters of recommendation.
Exclusive: Visit www.UltimateScholarshipBook.com and enter code CA9726 for updates on this award.

[98] • Corporate Culture Scholarship

Investor's Podcast
Email: contact@theinvestorspodcast.com
https://www.theinvestorspodcast.com/corporate-culture/
Purpose: To encourage awareness of sustainable profitability.
Eligibility: Applicants must be current undergraduate or graduate students enrolled at any North American university. Students must write an essay relating to corporate culture and their ideal workplace culture.
Target applicant(s): College students. Graduate school students. Adult students.
Amount: $1,000.
Number of awards: 1.
Deadline: Contact the sponsor to confirm the deadline.
How to apply: Applications are available online.
Exclusive: Visit www.UltimateScholarshipBook.com and enter code IN9826 for updates on this award.

[99] • Corporate Office Interiors Scholarship Contest

Corporate Office Interiors
2831 East Oakland Park Boulevard, Ft. Lauderdale, FL 33306
Phone: 954-784-7778
Email: info@corporateofficeint.com
https://www.corporateofficeint.com/blog/Corporate-Office-Interiors-Scholarship-Contest/
Purpose: To support students who write about office furniture and cubicles.
Eligibility: Applicants must currently be enrolled in a high school, college, university or trade school in the U.S. or Canada. Students must write and submit an essay about a given topic related to office furniture and cubicles.
Target applicant(s): Junior high students or younger. High school students. College students. Adult students.
Amount: $1,000.
Number of awards: Varies.
Deadline: June 15.
How to apply: Applications are available online.
Exclusive: Visit www.UltimateScholarshipBook.com and enter code CO9926 for updates on this award.

[100] • Courage to Grow Scholarship

Courage to Grow Scholarship
P.O. Box 2507, Chelan, WA 98816
Phone: 509-731-3056
Email: support@couragetogrowscholarship.com
http://www.couragetogrowscholarship.com
Purpose: To assist high school and college students.
Eligibility: Applicants must be high school juniors and seniors or college students with a minimum GPA of 2.5 and must also be U.S. citizens.
Target applicant(s): High school students. College students. Adult students.
Minimum GPA: 2.5
Amount: $500.
Number of awards: 1 per month.
Deadline: October 31.
How to apply: Applications are available online.
Exclusive: Visit www.UltimateScholarshipBook.com and enter code CO10026 for updates on this award.

[101] • CPI Highest Point Hunt Seat Rider

College Preparatory Invitational
P.O. Box 566357, Miami, FL 33256-6357
Phone: 786-369-9040
Email: info@collegeprepinvitational.com
http://www.collegeprepinvitational.com
Purpose: To support young riders and promote higher education as a foundation to future success.
Eligibility: Applicants must attend the College Preparatory Invitational and be students in grades 8 through 12. The scholarship is awarded to the rider with the highest point score.
Target applicant(s): Junior high students or younger. High school students.
Amount: $500.
Number of awards: 1.
Deadline: March 8.
How to apply: Applications are available online.
Exclusive: Visit www.UltimateScholarshipBook.com and enter code CO10126 for updates on this award.

[102] • Craig Dickinson Memorial Scholarship
Home Education Recognition Organization Inc. (HERO)
820 North Fig Tree Lane, Plantation, FL 33317
Email: help@heroscholarship.org
https://www.heroscholarship.org/
Purpose: To support homeschooled students who have excelled in their chosen path of education.
Eligibility: Applicants must be graduating seniors who were home educated for at least the last two years. Students must graduate and begin an educational program at a college or university. Selection will be based on the application, references, autobiography, homeschool transcript and selected test scores if applicable.
Target applicant(s): High school students.
Amount: $1,000.
Number of awards: 1.
Deadline: March 1.
How to apply: Applications are available online.
Exclusive: Visit www.UltimateScholarshipBook.com and enter code HO10226 for updates on this award.

[103] • Create Real Impact Contest
Impact Teen Drivers
Attn.: Create Real Impact Contest, P.O. Box 161209, Sacramento, CA 95816
Phone: 916-733-7432
Email: info@impactteendrivers.org
https://createrealimpact.com/
Purpose: To raise awareness of the dangers of distracted driving and poor decision making.
Eligibility: Applicants must be legal U.S. residents who are between the ages of 14 and 22. They must be enrolled full-time at an accredited secondary or post-secondary school. They must submit an original, creative project that offers a solution to the problem of distracted driving. Selection is based on project concept, message effectiveness and creativity.
Target applicant(s): High school students. College students. Graduate school students.
Amount: $250 - $10,000.
Number of awards: 8.
Deadline: April 25.
How to apply: Contest entry instructions are available online. A creative project is required.
Exclusive: Visit www.UltimateScholarshipBook.com and enter code IM10326 for updates on this award.

[104] • Create-a-Greeting-Card Scholarship
Gallery Collection
Prudent Publishing, 65 Challenger Road, P.O. Box 150, Ridgefield Park, NJ 07660
Phone: 800-950-7064
Email: service@gallerycollection.com
https://www.gallerycollection.com/greeting-cards-scholarship.htm
Purpose: To reward high school, college, university and homeschooled students who enter a contest to create a Christmas card, holiday card, birthday card or all-occasion greeting card.
Eligibility: Applicants must be U.S. citizens or legal residents who are at least 14 years old. The submission must include original artwork or photographs. Selection is based on the overall quality of the submission including creativity, uniqueness and suitability.
Target applicant(s): High school students. College students. Adult students.
Amount: $10,000.
Number of awards: 1.
Deadline: March 1.
How to apply: Online entry is required.
Exclusive: Visit www.UltimateScholarshipBook.com and enter code GA10426 for updates on this award.

[105] • Crossword Hobbyist Crossword Scholarship
Crossword Hobbyist
Email: scholarship@crosswordhobbyist.com
https://blog.crosswordhobbyist.com/crossword-hobbyist-crossword-scholarship/
Purpose: To support students who are pursuing a higher education.
Eligibility: Applicants must be current or incoming undergraduate students who will be enrolled for the upcoming fall semester. Students must create a newspaper-style crossword puzzle on a topic they are passionate about. Friends or family members of committee members are not allowed to apply for this scholarship.
Target applicant(s): High school students. College students. Adult students.
Amount: $1,000.
Number of awards: 1.
Deadline: May 3.
How to apply: Applications are available online.
Exclusive: Visit www.UltimateScholarshipBook.com and enter code CR10526 for updates on this award.

[106] • Curt Greene Memorial Scholarship
Harness Horse Youth Foundation
16575 Carey Road, Westfield, IN 46074
Phone: 317-867-5877
Email: ellen@hhyf.org
http://www.hhyf.org
Purpose: To support students who are interested in harness racing.
Eligibility: Students must demonstrate financial need, and must be enrolled or planning to enroll full-time (minimum of 12 credit hours) in an undergraduate program. Applicants must submit an essay and two letters of reference.
Target applicant(s): High school students. College students.
Minimum GPA: 2.5
Amount: $2,500.
Number of awards: Varies.
Deadline: June 1.
How to apply: Applications are available online.
Exclusive: Visit www.UltimateScholarshipBook.com and enter code HA10626 for updates on this award.

[107] • Curwen-Guidry-Blackburn Scholarship Fund
Southern Bowling Congress
9817 Miller Road, Sherwood, AR 72120
Phone: 501-425-2299
Email: dclements858@sbcglobal.net
http://www.southernbowlingcongress.org/scholarship.html
Purpose: To aid any senior youth bowler in Southern Bowling Congress member states in their education.
Eligibility: Students must be high school seniors and currently bowling in a USBC Certified Youth League. Students must reside in a Southern

The Ultimate Scholarship Book 2026
Scholarship Directory (General Awards)

Bowling Congress member state which includes Alabama, Arkansas, Florida, Georgia, Kentucky, Louisiana, Mississippi, Tennessee and Texas. Applicants must have bowled in a USBC Certified Youth League three of four years in high school and have bowled 75 percent of the league schedule. Students must have a minimum grade point average of 2.5 on a 4.0 scale and achieved an ACT composite score of 20 or SAT composite score of 1410.
Target applicant(s): High school students.
Minimum GPA: 2.5
Amount: $750.
Number of awards: 16.
Deadline: March 15.
How to apply: Applications are available online. An application form, official high school grade and credits transcript with a minimum of six semesters of information that includes ACT and/or SAT scores and a personal letter of recommendation from high school principal or counselor are required.
Exclusive: Visit www.UltimateScholarshipBook.com and enter code SO10726 for updates on this award.

[108] • Daedalian Foundation Scholarship Program
Daedalian Foundation
P.O. Box 249, Randolph AFB, TX 78148
Phone: 210-945-2111
Email: info@daedalians.org
http://daedalians.org/programs/scholarships/
Purpose: To aid undergraduates who are studying to become military pilots.
Eligibility: Applicants must be rising or current undergraduates attending a four-year institution and must have a demonstrated interest in pursuing a career in military aviation. Selection is based on the overall strength of the application.
Target applicant(s): High school students. College students. Adult students.
Amount: Varies.
Number of awards: Varies.
Scholarship may be renewable.
Deadline: June 1.
How to apply: Applications are available online. An application form and applicant photo are required.
Exclusive: Visit www.UltimateScholarshipBook.com and enter code DA10826 for updates on this award.

[109] • Daughters of the Cincinnati Scholarship
Daughters of the Cincinnati
National Headquarters, 271 Madison Avenue, Suite 1408, New York, NY 10016
Phone: 212-991-9945
Email: scholarships@daughters1894.org
http://daughters1894.org/
Purpose: To support daughters of Armed Services commissioned officers.
Eligibility: Applicants must be daughters of career officers in the United States Army, Navy, Air Force, Coast Guard or Marine Corps (active, retired or deceased). Daughters of reserve officers or enlisted personnel cannot apply. Applicants must also be high school seniors.
Target applicant(s): High school students.
Amount: $16,000-$20,000 paid over four years.
Number of awards: Varies.
Scholarship may be renewable.
Deadline: February 15.
How to apply: More details are available by contacting the organization. An essay, a secondary school report, a letter of recommendation and a Student Aid Report are required.
Exclusive: Visit www.UltimateScholarshipBook.com and enter code DA10926 for updates on this award.

[110] • Davidson Fellows Scholarships
Davidson Institute for Talent Development
9665 Gateway Drive, Suite B, Reno, NV 89521
Phone: 775-852-3483
Email: DavidsonFellows@davidsongifted.org
http://www.davidsongifted.org/
Purpose: To reward young people for their works in mathematics, science, technology, music, literature, philosophy or "outside the box."
Eligibility: Applicants must be 18 or younger and be able to attend the awards reception in Washington, DC. In addition to the monetary award, the institute will pay for travel and lodging expenses. Three nominator forms, three copies of a 15-minute DVD and additional materials are required.
Target applicant(s): Junior high students or younger. High school students.
Amount: $10,000-$50,000.
Number of awards: Varies.
Deadline: February 14.
How to apply: Applications are available online.
Exclusive: Visit www.UltimateScholarshipBook.com and enter code DA11026 for updates on this award.

[111] • Davis-Putter Scholarship Fund
Davis-Putter Scholarship Fund
P.O. Box 7307, New York, NY 10116
Email: information@davisputter.org
http://www.davisputter.org
Purpose: To assist students who are both academically capable and who aid the progressive movement for peace and justice both on campus and in their communities.
Eligibility: Applicants must be undergraduate or graduate students who participate in the progressive movement, acting in the interests of issues such as expansion of civil rights and international solidarity, among others. Applicants must also have demonstrated financial need as well as a solid academic record.
Target applicant(s): College students. Graduate school students. Adult students.
Amount: Up to $15,000.
Number of awards: Varies.
Deadline: April 1.
How to apply: Applications are available online.
Exclusive: Visit www.UltimateScholarshipBook.com and enter code DA11126 for updates on this award.

[112] • Delete Cyberbullying Beyond School Walls Scholarship
Delete Cyberbullying
Email: help@endcyberbullying.net
https://www.endcyberbullying.net/scholarship
Purpose: To get students committed to the cause of deleting cyberbullying both inside and outside of school.
Eligibility: Applicants must be attending or planning to attend an accredited U.S. college or university for undergraduate or graduate studies. Applicants must also be a high school (9th to 12th grade), college

or graduate student or a student planning to enter college. Selection is based on the written statement and focused on creativity, content and commitment to the cause of deleting cyberbullying.
Target applicant(s): High school students. College students. Graduate school students. Adult students.
Amount: $1,000.
Number of awards: 3.
Deadline: October 31.
How to apply: Applications are available online.
Exclusive: Visit www.UltimateScholarshipBook.com and enter code DE11226 for updates on this award.

[113] • Delete Cyberbullying Mental Health Awareness Scholarship
Delete Cyberbullying
Email: help@endcyberbullying.net
https://www.endcyberbullying.net/scholarship
Purpose: To support students who understand cyberbullying's impact on mental health.
Eligibility: Applicants must be attending or planning to attend an accredited U.S. college or university for undergraduate or graduate studies. Applicants must also be a high school (9th to 12th grade), college or graduate student or a student planning to enter college. Selection is based on the written statement and focused on creativity, content and commitment to the cause of deleting cyberbullying.
Target applicant(s): High school students. College students. Graduate school students. Adult students.
Amount: $1,000.
Number of awards: 3.
Deadline: June 30.
How to apply: Applications are available online.
Exclusive: Visit www.UltimateScholarshipBook.com and enter code DE11326 for updates on this award.

[114] • Delete Cyberbullying Social Media Scholarship
Delete Cyberbullying
Email: help@endcyberbullying.net
https://www.endcyberbullying.net/scholarship
Purpose: To get students committed to the cause of deleting cyberbullying in social media.
Eligibility: Applicants must be attending or planning to attend an accredited U.S. college or university for undergraduate or graduate studies. Applicants must also be a high school (9th to 12th grade), college or graduate student or a student planning to enter college. Selection is based on the written statement and focused on creativity, content and commitment to the cause of deleting cyberbullying.
Target applicant(s): High school students. College students. Graduate school students. Adult students.
Amount: $1,000.
Number of awards: 3.
Deadline: February 28.
How to apply: Applications are available online. An application form and an essay are required.
Exclusive: Visit www.UltimateScholarshipBook.com and enter code DE11426 for updates on this award.

[115] • Dell Scholars Program
Michael and Susan Dell Foundation
P.O. Box 163867, Austin, TX 78716
Phone: 512-329-0799
Email: apply@dellscholars.org
https://www.dellscholars.org/scholarship/
Purpose: To support underprivileged high school seniors.
Eligibility: Students must be participants in an approved college readiness program, and they must have at least a 2.4 GPA. Applicants must be planning to enroll full-time in a bachelor's degree program in the fall directly after graduation. Students must also be U.S. citizens or permanent residents and demonstrate financial need. Selection is based on "individual determination to succeed," future goals, hardships that have been overcome, self-motivation and financial need.
Target applicant(s): High school students.
Minimum GPA: 2.4
Amount: $20,000.
Number of awards: 500.
Scholarship may be renewable.
Deadline: December 1.
How to apply: Applications are available online. An online application is required.
Exclusive: Visit www.UltimateScholarshipBook.com and enter code MI11526 for updates on this award.

[116] • Delta Theta Chi Sorority National Memorial Scholarship
Delta Theta Chi Sorority
Attn: Cindi Cook, 2614 S. Lulu, Wichita, KS 67216
https://www.deltathetachi.com
Purpose: To support the pursuit of higher education.
Eligibility: Applicants must provide transcripts for the past four years. Students graduating high school or current undergraduate freshmen must provide official documentation of grade point average, SAT and/or ACT scores. Applicants must complete application in full, including the essay, and provide at least one letter of reference.
Target applicant(s): High school students. College students. Adult students.
Amount: $1,600.
Number of awards: 3.
Deadline: February 1.
How to apply: Applications are available online.
Exclusive: Visit www.UltimateScholarshipBook.com and enter code DE11626 for updates on this award.

[117] • Denes I. Bardos Award
Bardos Foundation
Email: contact@bardos.foundation
https://www.bardos.foundation/
Purpose: To reward students who are refugees and first-generation immigrants.
Eligibility: Applicants must be immigrants currently residing in the U.S. who have financial need. Students must be in their final year of high school or enrolled in an undergraduate degree program within the past six months. Applicants must have demonstrated their commitment to innovation, academic rigor and community or family service.
Target applicant(s): High school students. College students. Adult students.
Amount: $1,000.
Number of awards: 4.

The Ultimate Scholarship Book 2026
Scholarship Directory (General Awards)

Deadline: May 1.
How to apply: Applications are available online.
Exclusive: Visit www.UltimateScholarshipBook.com and enter code BA11726 for updates on this award.

[118] • Digital Privacy Scholarship
Digital Responsibility
3101 Ocean Park Boulevard, Suite 100-485, Santa Monica, CA 90405
Email: mjefferson@digitalresponsibility.org
https://www.digitalresponsibility.org/scholarships
Purpose: To help students understand why it's important to be cautious about what they post on the Internet.
Eligibility: Applicants must be a high school freshman, sophomore, junior or senior or a current or entering college or graduate school student of any level. Home-schooled students are also eligible. There is no age limit. Students must also be a U.S. citizen or legal resident.
Target applicant(s): High school students. College students. Graduate school students. Adult students.
Amount: $1,000.
Number of awards: 1.
Deadline: June 30.
How to apply: Applications are available online.
Exclusive: Visit www.UltimateScholarshipBook.com and enter code DI11826 for updates on this award.

[119] • Dinah Shore Scholarship
Ladies Professional Golf Association
100 International Golf Drive, Daytona Beach, FL 32124-1092
Phone: 386-274-6200
Email: info@lpgafoundation.org
http://www.lpga.com/lpga-foundation/scholarships
Purpose: To honor the late Dinah Shore.
Eligibility: Applicants must be female high school seniors who have been accepted into a full-time course of study at an accredited U.S. institution of higher learning. They must have played golf regularly for the past two years but not played on a competitive collegiate golf team. A minimum GPA of 3.2 is required.
Target applicant(s): High school students.
Minimum GPA: 3.2
Amount: $2,500.
Number of awards: 2.
Deadline: January 31.
How to apply: Applications are available online.
Exclusive: Visit www.UltimateScholarshipBook.com and enter code LA11926 for updates on this award.

[120] • Dixie Boys Baseball Scholarship Program
Dixie Boys Baseball
P.O. Box 8263, Dothan, AL 36304
Phone: 334-793-3331
Email: jjones29@sw.rr.com
https://www.dbbusa.org/
Purpose: To help high school seniors who have participated in a franchised Dixie Boys Baseball Inc. program.
Eligibility: Applicants must plan to pursue undergraduate studies at a college or university. An application, financial statement, two recommendation letters, proof of baseball participation, transcript and essay are required. Selection is based on class rankings, strong school and community leadership and financial need. Programs are in Alabama, Arkansas, Florida, Georgia, Louisiana, Mississippi, North Carolina, South Carolina, Tennessee, Texas and Virginia.
Target applicant(s): High school students.
Amount: $1,250.
Number of awards: 11.
Deadline: April 1.
How to apply: Applications are available online.
Exclusive: Visit www.UltimateScholarshipBook.com and enter code DI12026 for updates on this award.

[121] • Dixie Softball Scholarships
Dixie Softball Inc.
Doug Garrett, Chairman, Dixie Softball Scholarship Committee, 106 Woodlake Drive, Pineville, LA 71360
Phone: 318-451-4344
Email: dayprodoug@suddenlink.net
https://www.dixiegirlsoftball.org
Purpose: To support Dixie softball participants as they seek to further their education beyond high school.
Eligibility: Applicants must be female Dixie Softball participants, be high school seniors and have played softball for at least two seasons. Selection is based on financial need, academic achievement and future goals.
Target applicant(s): High school students.
Amount: $1,500.
Number of awards: 8.
Deadline: February 1.
How to apply: Applications are available online and must include the following: copy of most recent tax return, letter from parent or guardian explaining financial need, verification letter from Dixie Softball league official, photo and personal letter describing goals, activities and achievements.
Exclusive: Visit www.UltimateScholarshipBook.com and enter code DI12126 for updates on this award.

[122] • Dixie Youth Scholarship Program
Dixie Youth Baseball Inc.
Johnny Berthelot, Chairman Scholarship Committee, 110 South Bolivar Street, Suite 207, Marshall, TX 75670
Phone: 903-927-2255
Email: dyb@dixie.org
http://youth.dixie.org
Purpose: To help high school seniors who have participated in a franchised Dixie Youth Baseball league.
Eligibility: Applicants must have been registered on a Dixie Youth Baseball team participating in a franchised Dixie Youth Baseball Inc. league prior to reaching age thirteen. Selection is based on financial need, scholastic record and citizenship. Programs are located in Alabama, Arkansas, Florida, Georgia, Louisiana, Mississippi, North Carolina, South Carolina, Tennessee, Texas and Virginia.
Target applicant(s): High school students.
Amount: $2,000.
Number of awards: Varies.
Deadline: March 1.
How to apply: Contact your local league officials or a district, state or national director for an application, and applications are also available online.
Exclusive: Visit www.UltimateScholarshipBook.com and enter code DI12226 for updates on this award.

[123] • Dizzy Dean Scholarship
Dizzy Dean Baseball Inc.
2470 Highway 51 South, Hernando, MS 38632
Phone: 662-429-7790
Email: dphil10513@aol.com
http://dizzydeanbbinc.org/
Purpose: To aid members of the Dizzy Dean Baseball/Softball program in pursuing their college education.
Eligibility: Applicants must have played on a Dizzy Dean Baseball/Softball program for four years. Students must also be graduating seniors and be able to provide a high school transcript, copy of diploma and a copy of parent/guardian prior years' federal income tax form.
Target applicant(s): High school students.
Amount: Varies.
Number of awards: Varies.
Scholarship may be renewable.
Deadline: June 15.
How to apply: Applications are available online.
Exclusive: Visit www.UltimateScholarshipBook.com and enter code DI12326 for updates on this award.

[124] • Dollars for Scholars Scholarship
Citizens' Scholarship Foundation of America
One Scholarship Way, St. Peter, MN 56082
Phone: 800-537-4180
Email: dollarsforscholars@scholarshipamerica.org
http://www.scholarshipamerica.org
Purpose: To encourage students to aim for and achieve loftier educational goals.
Eligibility: Applicants must be members of a local Dollars for Scholars chapter. There are more than 1,200 Dollars for Scholars chapters that award more than $29 million in awards each year.
Target applicant(s): High school students.
Amount: Varies.
Number of awards: Varies.
Deadline: Contact the sponsor to confirm the deadline.
How to apply: Contact your local Dollars for Scholars chapter for more information. A list of chapters is available online.
Exclusive: Visit www.UltimateScholarshipBook.com and enter code CI12426 for updates on this award.

[125] • Dolphin Scholarships
Dolphin Scholarship Foundation
4966 Euclid Road, Suite 109, Virginia Beach, VA 23462
Phone: 757-671-3200
Email: scholars@dolphinscholarship.org
http://www.dolphinscholarship.org
Purpose: To assist the children of members of the Navy Submarine Force and other Navy submarine support personnel.
Eligibility: Applicants must be the unmarried children or stepchildren of navy submariners or navy members who have served in submarine support activities and must be under 24 years old at the time of the application deadline. The parents must have been part of the Submarine Force for at least eight years, have served in submarine support activities for at least 10 years or died on active duty while in the Submarine Force. The children of submariners who served less than the required number of years due to injury or illness occurring in the line of duty may also be eligible. Applicants must also be high school seniors or college students planning to attend or currently attending an accredited four-year college, working for a bachelor's degree.
Target applicant(s): High school students. College students.
Amount: Up to $4,000 per year.
Number of awards: 25-30.
Scholarship may be renewable.
Deadline: March 15.
How to apply: Applications are available online.
Exclusive: Visit www.UltimateScholarshipBook.com and enter code DO12526 for updates on this award.

[126] • Don't Text and Drive Scholarship
Digital Responsibility
3101 Ocean Park Boulevard, Suite 100-485, Santa Monica, CA 90405
Email: mjefferson@digitalresponsibility.org
https://www.digitalresponsibility.org/scholarships
Purpose: To help students understand the risks of texting while driving.
Eligibility: Applicants must be a high school freshman, sophomore, junior or senior or a current or entering college or graduate school student of any level. Home-schooled students are also eligible. There is no age limit. Students must also be a U.S. citizen or legal resident.
Target applicant(s): High school students. College students. Graduate school students. Adult students.
Amount: $1,000.
Number of awards: 1.
Deadline: September 30.
How to apply: Applications are available online.
Exclusive: Visit www.UltimateScholarshipBook.com and enter code DI12626 for updates on this award.

[127] • DoSomething Monthly Scholarships
Do Something (Scholarships)
19 West 21st Street, Floor 8, New York, NY 10010
Phone: 212-254-2390
Email: scholarships@dosomething.org
https://www.dosomething.org/us/about/easy-scholarships
Purpose: To assist students who participate in a social issue campaign.
Eligibility: Applicants must be age 25 or younger and be U.S. or Canadian citizens. There is a new scholarship each month. Selection is based on a random drawing of all students who participate in the campaign.
Target applicant(s): Junior high students or younger. High school students. College students. Graduate school students.
Amount: Varies.
Number of awards: Varies.
Deadline: Monthly.
How to apply: Applications are available online.
Exclusive: Visit www.UltimateScholarshipBook.com and enter code DO12726 for updates on this award.

[128] • Dr. James Earl Kennamer Scholarship
National Wild Turkey Federation (NWTF)
770 Augusta Road, Edgefield, SC 29824-0530
Phone: 800-843-6983
Email: scholarshipinfo@nwtf.net
https://www.nwtf.org/
Purpose: To support those students committed to conservation and preserving our hunting heritage.
Eligibility: Applicants must be a senior, have a 3.0 or higher GPA, plan to attend an institution of higher education after high school, be a member of the National Wild Turkey Federation and actively participate in hunting sports. Selection is based on scholastic achievement, leadership abilities, community service and commitment to conservation.

Target applicant(s): High school students.
Minimum GPA: 3.0
Amount: $250-$10,000.
Number of awards: Varies.
Deadline: December 31.
How to apply: Applications are available online and require a personal essay and three letters of reference.
Exclusive: Visit www.UltimateScholarshipBook.com and enter code NA12826 for updates on this award.

[129] • Dwight F. Davis Memorial Scholarship
United States Tennis Association Foundation
70 W. Red Oak Lane, White Plains, NY 10604
Phone: 914-696-7223
Email: foundation@usta.com
http://www.ustafoundation.com/
Purpose: To support youth tennis players who represent the sport with distinction.
Eligibility: Applicants must be high school seniors who have participated in an organized youth tennis program. Students must excel in academics, have participated in extracurricular activities and have participated in various community service projects.
Target applicant(s): High school students.
Amount: $10,000.
Number of awards: 2.
Scholarship may be renewable.
Deadline: May 15.
How to apply: Applications are available online.
Exclusive: Visit www.UltimateScholarshipBook.com and enter code UN12926 for updates on this award.

[130] • Dwight Mosley Scholarship Award
United States Tennis Association Foundation
70 W. Red Oak Lane, White Plains, NY 10604
Phone: 914-696-7223
Email: foundation@usta.com
http://www.ustafoundation.com/
Purpose: To support youth tennis players of ethnically diverse backgrounds who have excelled both on and off the court.
Eligibility: Applicants must be USTA ranked high school seniors who are of an ethnically diverse background and who have participated extensively in an organized youth community tennis program. Selection is based on academic excellence and exemplary sportsmanship on and off the court.
Target applicant(s): High school students.
Amount: $10,000.
Number of awards: 2.
Scholarship may be renewable.
Deadline: May 15.
How to apply: Applications are available online.
Exclusive: Visit www.UltimateScholarshipBook.com and enter code UN13026 for updates on this award.

[131] • E-waste Scholarship
Digital Responsibility
3101 Ocean Park Boulevard, Suite 100-485, Santa Monica, CA 90405
Email: mjefferson@digitalresponsibility.org
https://www.digitalresponsibility.org/scholarships
Purpose: To help students understand the impact of e-waste and what can be done to reduce e-waste.
Eligibility: Applicants must be high school, college, graduate or homeschooled students. There is no age limit. Students must also be U.S. citizens or legal residents. A 140-character message about e-waste is required to apply. The top 10 applications will be selected as finalists; finalists will be asked to write a full length 500- to 1,000-word essay about e-waste. Only online applications are accepted.
Target applicant(s): High school students. College students. Graduate school students. Adult students.
Amount: $1,000.
Number of awards: 1.
Deadline: April 30.
How to apply: Applications are available online.
Exclusive: Visit www.UltimateScholarshipBook.com and enter code DI13126 for updates on this award.

[132] • Earl Anthony Memorial Scholarships
United States Bowling Congress
IBC Youth Headquarters, 621 Six Flags Drive, Arlington, TX 76011
Phone: 800-514-2695
Email: contactus@ibcyouth.com
https://www.bowl.com/scholarships/
Purpose: To recognize USBC members for community involvement and academic achievement.
Eligibility: Applicants must be USBC members in good standing who are high school seniors or current college students. They must have a GPA of 3.0 or higher. Community involvement, academic achievement and financial need are considered.
Target applicant(s): High school students. College students. Adult students.
Minimum GPA: 3.0
Amount: $5,000.
Number of awards: 5.
Deadline: December 1.
How to apply: Applications are available online.
Exclusive: Visit www.UltimateScholarshipBook.com and enter code UN13226 for updates on this award.

[133] • Eco-Warrior Scholarship
HeySunday
2810 N Church Street, Unit 35267, Wilmington, 19 DE
https://heysunday.com
Purpose: To support students who have an interest in the environment.
Eligibility: Applicants must be high school seniors, undergraduate or graduate students. Students must have demonstrated interest and involvement in environmental sustainability initiatives. Applicants must be U.S. citizens or permanent legal residents.
Target applicant(s): High school students. College students. Graduate school students. Adult students.
Amount: $1,000.
Number of awards: Varies.
Deadline: December 1.
How to apply: Applications are available online.

Exclusive: Visit www.UltimateScholarshipBook.com and enter code HE13326 for updates on this award.

[134] • Edith Nourse Rogers STEM Scholarship
United States Department of Veterans Affairs
810 Vermont Avenue NW, Washington, DC 20420
https://www.va.gov/education/other-va-education-benefits/
Purpose: To support GI Bill students.
Eligibility: Applicants must be enrolled in an undergraduate STEM degree or qualifying dual-degree program that requires at least 120 standard semester credit hours (or 180 quarter credit hours) to complete and have completed at least 60 standard credit hours (or 90 quarter credit hours) toward their degree. Students must be enrolled in a qualifying undergraduate STEM degree program. Applicants must have six months or less of their Post-9/11 GI Bill (or Fry Scholarship) benefits.
Target applicant(s): College students. Adult students.
Amount: Up to $30,000.
Number of awards: Varies.
Deadline: Varies.
How to apply: Applications are available online.
Exclusive: Visit www.UltimateScholarshipBook.com and enter code UN13426 for updates on this award.

[135] • Education Accessibility Scholarship
Connecticut Trial Firm LLC
437 Naubuc Avenue, Suite 107, Glastonbury, CT 06033
Phone: 860-471-8333
Email: info@cttrialfirm.com
https://cttrialfirm.com/education-accessibility-scholarship/
Purpose: To encourage students who are the first in their family to attend college.
Eligibility: Applicants must be currently enrolled with the intent to complete either a two-year, four-year or graduate program at any junior college, community college, paralegal program, college or university in the United States. Students must be the first in their family to attend a four-year college or university and have a minimum 3.0 GPA. An essay submission on a provided topic is required.
Target applicant(s): High school students. College students. Graduate school students. Adult students.
Minimum GPA: 3.0
Amount: $1,000.
Number of awards: 1.
Deadline: December 31.
How to apply: Applications are available online.
Exclusive: Visit www.UltimateScholarshipBook.com and enter code CO13526 for updates on this award.

[136] • Educational Advancement Foundation Merit Scholarship
Alpha Kappa Alpha Educational Advancement Foundation Inc.
5656 S. Stony Island Avenue, Chicago, IL 60637
Phone: 800-653-6528
Email: akaeaf@akaeaf.net
https://akaeaf.org/scholarships
Purpose: To support academically talented students.
Eligibility: Applicants must be full-time college students at the sophomore level or higher, including graduate students, at an accredited school. They must have a GPA of at least 3.0 and demonstrate community involvement and service. The program is open to students without regard to sex, race, creed, color, ethnicity, religion, sexual orientation or disability. Students do NOT need to be members of Alpha Kappa Alpha.
Target applicant(s): College students. Graduate school students. Adult students.
Minimum GPA: 3.0
Amount: Varies.
Number of awards: Varies.
Deadline: April 15 (undergraduates) and August 15 (graduates).
How to apply: Applications are available online. An application form, personal statement and three letters of recommendation are required.
Exclusive: Visit www.UltimateScholarshipBook.com and enter code AL13626 for updates on this award.

[137] • EOD Warrior Foundation Scholarship
EOD Warrior Foundation
716 Crestview Avenue, Niceville, FL 32578
Phone: 850-729-2401
Email: info@eodwarriorfoundation.org
https://eodwarriorfoundation.org/scholarship-program/
Purpose: To support those connected to Explosive Ordnance Disposal (EOD) technicians.
Eligibility: Applicants must be accepted or enrolled as full-time undergraduates in a U.S. accredited two-year, four-year or vocational school. Students must also be the family member of an active duty, guard/reserve, retired or deceased EOD technician. The award is based on academic achievement, community involvement and financial need. Applicants should submit the Free Application for Federal Student Aid form.
Target applicant(s): High school students. College students. Adult students.
Amount: Varies.
Number of awards: Varies.
Deadline: February 24.
How to apply: Applications are available online.
Exclusive: Visit www.UltimateScholarshipBook.com and enter code EO13726 for updates on this award.

[138] • Eon Essay Contest
Eon Essay Contest LLC
Players Philanthropy Fund, 1122 Kenilworth Drive, Suite 201, Towson, MD 21204
Email: info@eonessaycontest.com
https://www.eonessaycontest.com/
Purpose: To support students who are interested in raising awareness about the importance of avoiding existential risks.
Eligibility: Applicants must be legal residents of the 50 United States or the District of Columbia, Canada (excluding the province of Quebec) or the United Kingdom. Students must be at least 13 years of age but no older than 24 years of age. Applicants must be enrolled as a full-time or part-time student in a public school, private school, registered homeschool or a legally recognized educational institution. An essay is required to be submitted after the student has read "The Precipice."
Target applicant(s): Junior high students or younger. High school students. College students. Graduate school students.
Amount: Up to $15,000.
Number of awards: 10.
Deadline: June 15.
How to apply: Applications are available online.
Exclusive: Visit www.UltimateScholarshipBook.com and enter code EO13826 for updates on this award.

The Ultimate Scholarship Book 2026
Scholarship Directory (General Awards)

[139] • Equitable Excellence Scholarship
Equitable Holdings Inc.
1290 Avenue of the Americas, New York, NY 10104
https://equitable.com/foundation/equitable-excellence-scholarship
Purpose: To provide financial assistance to ambitious students.
Eligibility: Applicants must be U.S. citizens or legal residents who are current high school seniors and are planning to enroll full-time in an accredited college or university in the fall following their graduation. They must show ambition and drive evidenced by outstanding achievement in school, community or workplace activities. A recommendation from an unrelated adult who can vouch for the student's achievement is required.
Target applicant(s): High school students.
Amount: $5,000.
Number of awards: 100.
Deadline: December 18.
How to apply: Applications are available online.
Exclusive: Visit www.UltimateScholarshipBook.com and enter code EQ13926 for updates on this award.

[140] • Ethnic Minority and Women's Enhancement Scholarship
National Collegiate Athletic Association
700 W. Washington Street, P.O. Box 6222, Indianapolis, IN 46206
Phone: 317-917-6222
Email: lthomas@ncaa.org
http://www.ncaa.org/about/resources/ncaa-scholarships-and-grants
Purpose: To assist minority and female students in intercollegiate athletics with graduate scholarships.
Eligibility: Applicants must be seeking admission or have been accepted into a sports administration or program that will help the applicant obtain a career in intercollegiate athletics.
Target applicant(s): College students. Adult students.
Minimum GPA: 3.2
Amount: $10,000.
Number of awards: 26.
Deadline: February 1.
How to apply: Application details are available online.
Exclusive: Visit www.UltimateScholarshipBook.com and enter code NA14026 for updates on this award.

[141] • Eve Kraft Education and College Scholarship
United States Tennis Association Foundation
70 W. Red Oak Lane, White Plains, NY 10604
Phone: 914-696-7223
Email: foundation@usta.com
http://www.ustafoundation.com/
Purpose: To support youth tennis participants who have come from an economically disadvantaged community.
Eligibility: Applicants must be high school seniors who have participated in an organized youth tennis program and who reside in an economically disadvantaged community. Selection is based on academic excellence and community service.
Target applicant(s): High school students.
Amount: $2,500.
Number of awards: 2.
Deadline: May 15.
How to apply: Applications are available online.
Exclusive: Visit www.UltimateScholarshipBook.com and enter code UN14126 for updates on this award.

[142] • Families of Freedom Scholarship Fund
Families of Freedom c/o Scholarship America
One Scholarship Way, P.O. Box 297, St. Peter, MN 56082
Phone: 877-862-0136
Email: info@familiesoffreedom.org
https://www.familiesoffreedom.org/students-families/families-of-freedom-fund/
Purpose: To support dependents of victims of the 9/11 attacks.
Eligibility: Applicants must be dependent children, spouses or domestic partners of 9/11 victims. Children of victims must enroll in a postsecondary program by age 24 and must continue studies uninterrupted after their 24th birthday to continue to receive assistance. Financial need is required.
Target applicant(s): High school students. College students. Graduate school students. Adult students.
Amount: Varies.
Number of awards: Varies.
Scholarship may be renewable.
Deadline: October 1.
How to apply: Applications are available online. An application form, copy of most recent tax return, transcript and copy of school billing statement are required.
Exclusive: Visit www.UltimateScholarshipBook.com and enter code FA14226 for updates on this award.

[143] • First Cavalry Division Foundation Scholarship
Foundation of the First Cavalry Division Association
Alumni Of The First Team, 302 North Main Street, Copperas Cove, TX 76522
Phone: 254-547-6537
Email: firstcav@1cda.org
http://www.1cda.org
Purpose: To assist the children of First Cavalry troopers who have become disabled or who died while serving in the Division.
Eligibility: Applicants must be First Cavalry Division troopers who have become totally disabled while serving in the division or active duty members, their spouses or children. Applicants may also be the spouses or children of First Cavalry Division troopers who have died while serving in the division.
Target applicant(s): High school students. College students. Adult students.
Amount: $1,200.
Number of awards: Varies.
Deadline: July 31.
How to apply: Applications are available by request.
Exclusive: Visit www.UltimateScholarshipBook.com and enter code FO14326 for updates on this award.

[144] • FMAA Scholarship Program
Flag Manufacturers Association of America
Hope Silverman, 994 Old Eagle School Road, Suite 1019, Wayne, PA 19087-1866
Phone: 610-971-4850
Email: hope@mmco1.com
https://fmaa-usa.com/Scholarship.php
Purpose: To support students who create a video on the United States flag.

Eligibility: Applicants must create a video essay discussing a given topic related to the United States flag. Students must post their one and a half to two minute video online.
Target applicant(s): High school students. College students. Graduate school students. Adult students.
Amount: Up to $2,000.
Number of awards: Varies.
Deadline: June 14.
How to apply: Applications are available online.
Exclusive: Visit www.UltimateScholarshipBook.com and enter code FL14426 for updates on this award.

[145] • FMC Skaters Scholarship
Facility Management Corporation (FMC) Ice Sports
100 Schoosett Street, Building 3, Pembroke, MA 02359
Phone: 888-747-5283
Email: customercare@fmcicesports.com
http://www.fmcicesports.com
Purpose: To support ice sport participants and recreational ice skaters seeking to further their education beyond high school.
Eligibility: Applicants must be New England residents, seniors in high school and skate at an FMC arena. Selection is based on academic achievement, extracurricular activities, community service and accomplishments and leadership on the ice.
Target applicant(s): High school students.
Amount: Varies.
Number of awards: Varies.
Deadline: May 1.
How to apply: Applications are available online. Along with the application form, students must submit a high school transcript, one letter of recommendation, a student resume and a personal essay.
Exclusive: Visit www.UltimateScholarshipBook.com and enter code FA14526 for updates on this award.

[146] • Folds of Honor Higher Education Scholarship
Folds of Honor
5800 N. Patriot Drive, Owasso, OK 74055
Phone: 918-274-4700
Email: scholarships@foldsofhonor.org
https://foldsofhonor.org/scholarships/
Purpose: To support spouses and children of American military service members pursuing higher education.
Eligibility: Applicants must be spouses or children of U.S. service members who were killed in action, lost a limb, died while on active duty or who have at least a 10 percent combined service-connected evaluation. Students must be currently attending or recently accepted into an accredited degree program or vocation program.
Target applicant(s): High school students. College students. Adult students.
Amount: $5,000.
Number of awards: Varies.
Deadline: March 31.
How to apply: Applications are available online.
Exclusive: Visit www.UltimateScholarshipBook.com and enter code FO14626 for updates on this award.

[147] • Foreclosure Scholarship Program
Foreclosure.com
1825 NW Corporate Boulevard, Suite 110, Boca Raton, FL 33431
Phone: 561-988-9669 x 7387
Email: scholarship@foreclosure.com
http://www.foreclosure.com/scholarship/
Purpose: To support current undergraduate college students who are interested in addressing critical issues facing the nation, namely issues involving real estate/housing.
Eligibility: Applicants must be U.S. citizens 13 years of age or older who are currently enrolled as undergraduate college students. They must write an essay between 800 and 2,000 words providing creative solutions to a given topic involving critical issues facing the nation centered around real estate/housing. Selection is based on the overall strength of the essay and application.
Target applicant(s): College students. Adult students.
Amount: $1,000-$4,000.
Number of awards: 3.
Deadline: December 15.
How to apply: Applications are available online. An application form and essay are required.
Exclusive: Visit www.UltimateScholarshipBook.com and enter code FO14726 for updates on this award.

[148] • Fraternal Order of Eagles Memorial Foundation
Fraternal Order of Eagles
1623 Gateway Circle S., Grove City, OH 43123
Phone: 614-883-2200
Email: help@foe.com
http://www.foe.com
Purpose: To provide financial support for post-secondary education to the children of Eagles.
Eligibility: Applicants must be the children of Eagles who lost their lives while serving in the military or in the commission of their daily employment. Applicants must have a 2.0 minimum GPA, be under the age of 25, unmarried and non-self supporting.
Target applicant(s): High school students. College students. Graduate school students.
Minimum GPA: 2.0
Amount: Varies.
Number of awards: Varies.
Scholarship may be renewable.
Deadline: Contact the sponsor to confirm the deadline.
How to apply: Eligible juniors in high school will be sent a form requesting post high school plans, and eligible seniors will be mailed the scholarship application form.
Exclusive: Visit www.UltimateScholarshipBook.com and enter code FR14826 for updates on this award.

[149] • Fulbright Grants
U.S. Department of State
Office of Academic Exchange Programs, Bureau of Educational and Cultural Affairs, U.S. Department of State, SA-44, 301 4th Street SW, Room 234, Washington, DC 20547
Phone: 202-632-3238
Email: fulbright@state.gov
https://us.fulbrightonline.org/
Purpose: To increase the understanding between the people of the United States and the people of other countries.

Eligibility: Applicants must be graduating college seniors, graduate students, young professionals and artists. Funds are generally used to support students in university teaching, advanced research, graduate study or teaching in elementary and secondary schools.
Target applicant(s): College students. Graduate school students. Adult students.
Amount: Varies.
Number of awards: Varies.
Deadline: October 10.
How to apply: Applications are available online.
Exclusive: Visit www.UltimateScholarshipBook.com and enter code U.14926 for updates on this award.

[150] • Future Without Speciesism Cash Award
People for the Ethical Treatment of Animals (PETA)
501 Front Street, Norfolk, VA 23510
Phone: 757-622-PETA
Email: 757-622-0457
https://www.peta.org/features/future-without-speciesism-competition/
Purpose: To support students who develop an idea to help animals.
Eligibility: Applicants must develop a game-changing idea for an invention that the student can develop into a specific action plan or design to replace animal use. Students must identify an area where animals are still exploited and create a potentially patentable, original idea or prototype that allows for their replacement. Applicants' inventions must be marketable as a viable alternative to the methods they seek to replace.
Target applicant(s): High school students. College students. Graduate school students. Adult students.
Amount: $1,000 to $10,000.
Number of awards: Varies.
Deadline: Varies.
How to apply: Applications are available online.
Exclusive: Visit www.UltimateScholarshipBook.com and enter code PE15026 for updates on this award.

[151] • GE-Reagan Foundation Scholarship Program
Ronald Reagan Presidential Foundation
40 Presidential Drive, Simi Valley, CA 93065
Phone: 844-402-0354
Email: ge-reagan@scholarshipamerica.org
https://www.reaganfoundation.org/education/
Purpose: To reward students who demonstrate leadership, drive, integrity and citizenship.
Eligibility: Applicants must be high school seniors and pursue a bachelor's degree at an accredited U.S. college or university the following fall. Students must demonstrate strong academic performance (3.0 or greater GPA or equivalent), demonstrate financial need and be a U.S. citizen. Funds may be used for student tuition and room and board.
Target applicant(s): High school students.
Minimum GPA: 3.0
Amount: Up to $40,000.
Number of awards: Varies.
Scholarship may be renewable.
Deadline: January 4.
How to apply: Applications are available online. The competition will close earlier than the deadline once 25,000 applications are received.
Exclusive: Visit www.UltimateScholarshipBook.com and enter code RO15126 for updates on this award.

[152] • Gene Carte Student Paper Competition
American Society of Criminology Gene Carte Student Paper Competition
Daniel Ragan, Department of Sociology, University of New Mexico, 1915 Roma N.E., Suite 1103, MSCO5 3080, Albuquerque, NM 87131
Phone: 602-543-6601
Email: dragan@unm.edu
http://www.asc41.com
Purpose: To recognize outstanding student works in criminology.
Eligibility: Applicants must be full-time undergraduate or graduate students. The writing competition requires applicants to write on a topic directly related to criminology and must be accompanied by a letter signed by the dean or department chair. Other paper formatting requirements are listed on the website. The first place winner also receives a travel award.
Target applicant(s): College students. Graduate school students. Adult students.
Amount: $200-$500.
Number of awards: Up to 3.
Deadline: April 15.
How to apply: There is no application form. Paper must be mailed in. The paper specifications are on the website.
Exclusive: Visit www.UltimateScholarshipBook.com and enter code AM15226 for updates on this award.

[153] • General Henry H. Arnold Education Grant Program
Air Force Aid Society Inc.
P.O. Box 2208, Arlington, VA 22202
Phone: 703-972-2650
Email: ed@afas-hq.org
https://www.afas.org/how-we-help/education-support/
Purpose: To help Air Force family members realize their academic goals.
Eligibility: Applicants must be the dependent sons and daughters of Air Force members, spouses of active duty members or surviving spouses of Air Force members who died while on active duty or in retired status. They must also be high school seniors or college students enrolled or accepted as full-time undergraduates for the following school year and maintain a minimum 2.0 GPA.
Target applicant(s): High school students. College students.
Minimum GPA: 2.0
Amount: $500-$2,000.
Number of awards: Varies.
Scholarship may be renewable.
Deadline: April 30.
How to apply: Applications are available online.
Exclusive: Visit www.UltimateScholarshipBook.com and enter code AI15326 for updates on this award.

[154] • George Montgomery/NRA Youth Wildlife Art Contest
National Rifle Association
11250 Waples Mill Road, Fairfax, VA 22030
Phone: 800-672-3888
Email: grantprogram@nrahq.org
https://awards.nra.org/scholarships/

Purpose: To support young artists and encourage awareness of local game birds and animals.
Eligibility: Applicants must be in grades 1 through 12 and submit an original artwork depicting any North American game bird or animal that may be legally hunted or trapped. NRA membership is not required. Art is divided into categories based on grade level and is judged on effort, creativity, anatomical accuracy and composition.
Target applicant(s): Junior high students or younger. High school students.
Amount: Up to $1,000.
Number of awards: Varies.
Deadline: October 31.
How to apply: Application information is available online. A statement of authenticity signed by a parent, guardian or teacher must be submitted along with the artwork.
Exclusive: Visit www.UltimateScholarshipBook.com and enter code NA15426 for updates on this award.

[155] • George S. and Stella M. Knight Essay Contest

National Society, Sons of the American Revolution
809 West Main Street, Louisville, KY 40202
Phone: 502-589-1776
Email: coggins.sar@gmail.com
https://www.sar.org/education/
Purpose: To reward students who have written outstanding essays on the American Revolution, the U.S. Constitution or the Declaration of Independence.
Eligibility: Applicants must be U.S. citizens or legal residents. Students must be high school sophomores, juniors or seniors. Applicants must submit an 800- to 1,200-word essay on some topic that is related to the Declaration of Independence, the American Revolution or the U.S. Constitution. Selection is based on the overall strength of the essay.
Target applicant(s): High school students.
Amount: $500-$3,000.
Number of awards: 4.
Deadline: February 15.
How to apply: Applications are available online.
Exclusive: Visit www.UltimateScholarshipBook.com and enter code NA15526 for updates on this award.

[156] • Gift for Life Scholarships

United States Bowling Congress
IBC Youth Headquarters, 621 Six Flags Drive, Arlington, TX 76011
Phone: 800-514-2695
Email: contactus@ibcyouth.com
https://www.bowl.com/scholarships/
Purpose: To provide financial assistance to high school students with financial need.
Eligibility: Applicants must be USBC Youth members who are current high school students in grades 9-12. They must have a GPA of 2.5 or higher and demonstrate financial need. Two awards each year are reserved for children of fire department, emergency rescue or police personnel. Candidates may win once per year up until graduation.
Target applicant(s): High school students.
Minimum GPA: 2.5
Amount: $1,000.
Number of awards: 6.
Deadline: December 1.
How to apply: Applications are available online.
Exclusive: Visit www.UltimateScholarshipBook.com and enter code UN15626 for updates on this award.

[157] • Global Citizen Scholarship

EF Educational Tours
EF Center Boston, Two Education Circle, Cambridge, MA 02141
Phone: 800-665-5364
Email: EF.Global.Citizen@ef.com
http://www.eftours.com
Purpose: To help students reflect on their place in the world through writing and then have a chance to experience it first-hand.
Eligibility: Applicants must be U.S. residents who are currently enrolled in a tour with EF educational tours and must create a video on a topic related to global citizenship. Up to 100 scholarship recipients will receive $1,000 towards their current EF educational tour.
Target applicant(s): High school students.
Amount: $1,000.
Number of awards: 100.
Deadline: August 15; November 15; February 15; May 15.
How to apply: Applications are available online on the EF Tours Facebook page.
Exclusive: Visit www.UltimateScholarshipBook.com and enter code EF15726 for updates on this award.

[158] • Gloria Barron Prize for Young Heroes

Barron Prize
P.O. Box 1470, Boulder, CO 80306
Email: admin@barronprize.org
http://www.barronprize.org
Purpose: To reward young people who have organized and led extraordinary service projects.
Eligibility: Applicants must be residents of the U.S. or Canada between the ages of 8 and 18. Students must be currently working on a service project or have completed a service project within the past year. Selection is primarily based on demonstration of generosity, tenacity and positive impact on the world.
Target applicant(s): Junior high students or younger. High school students.
Amount: $10,000.
Number of awards: 25.
Deadline: April 15.
How to apply: Applications are available online.
Exclusive: Visit www.UltimateScholarshipBook.com and enter code BA15826 for updates on this award.

[159] • GMR Transcription Academic Scholarship

GMR Transcription Services
2552 Walnut Avenue, Suite 110, Tustin, CA 92780
Phone: 714-202-9653
https://www.gmrtranscription.com/scholarship/scholarshiphome
Purpose: To help students offset the costs of continuing education.
Eligibility: Applicants must be enrolled as full-time students at an accredited college or university. Students must have a minimum 3.0 grade point average. Applicants must submit essays and complete a qualification quiz.
Target applicant(s): College students. Adult students.
Minimum GPA: 3.0
Amount: $500.
Number of awards: 2.
Deadline: June 15 and December 15.

How to apply: Applications are available online.
Exclusive: Visit www.UltimateScholarshipBook.com and enter code GM15926 for updates on this award.

[160] • GNC Nutritional Research Grant
National Strength and Conditioning Association (NSCA) Foundation
1885 Bob Johnson Drive, Colorado Springs, CO 80906
Phone: 800-815-6826
Email: Foundation@nsca.com
http://www.nsca.com/foundation/
Purpose: To fund nutrition-based research.
Eligibility: Applicants must be graduate students and be NSCA members for one year before applying and pursuing careers in strength and conditioning. Students must also plan a research project that falls within the mission of the NSCA and submit a proposal describing the rationale, purpose and methods of the planned research. Applications are evaluated based on grades, courses, experience, honors, recommendations and involvement in the community and with NSCA.
Target applicant(s): College students. Graduate school students. Adult students.
Amount: Up to $10,000.
Number of awards: Up to 2.
Deadline: February 15.
How to apply: Applications are available with membership.
Exclusive: Visit www.UltimateScholarshipBook.com and enter code NA16026 for updates on this award.

[161] • Go City Education Scholarship
Go City
https://gocity.com/en/education-scholarship
Purpose: To support students who write about travel destinations.
Eligibility: Applicants must be enrolled at a UK or U.S. university. Students must either be citizens, permanent residents or currently studying in the UK or in the US on a student visa. Applicants must pick one Go City destination and tell what attractions they think should be added to the passes and why, using no more than 280 characters.
Target applicant(s): Junior high students or younger.
Amount: $4,000.
Number of awards: Varies.
Deadline: November 9.
How to apply: Applications are available online.
Exclusive: Visit www.UltimateScholarshipBook.com and enter code GO16126 for updates on this award.

[162] • Golden Door Scholars
Golden Door Scholars
1423 Red Ventures Drive, Fort Mill, SC 29707
Email: info@goldendoorscholars.org
https://www.goldendoorscholars.org/
Purpose: To assist DACA students pursuing higher education.
Eligibility: Applicants must be approved DACA students with strong academic records who are enrolling in an undergraduate program or who are current high school seniors or undergraduate students. Students pursuing engineering, computer science, technology or math are given preference.
Target applicant(s): High school students. College students. Adult students.
Amount: Varies.
Number of awards: Varies.
Deadline: October 1.

How to apply: Applications are available online.
Exclusive: Visit www.UltimateScholarshipBook.com and enter code GO16226 for updates on this award.

[163] • Google SVA Scholarship
Student Veterans of America
1625 K Street North West, Suite 320, Washington, DC 20006
Phone: 202-223-4710
http://studentveterans.org/programs/scholarships
Purpose: To support students who are veterans and are pursuing a degree in computer science.
Eligibility: Applicants must be veterans who are currently enrolled as a full-time undergraduate or graduate student at a four-year university. Students must exhibit a strong academic performance and be pursuing a degree in either computer science or computer engineering. Applicants must currently be in good standing with their military branch or have an honorable discharge.
Target applicant(s): College students. Graduate school students. Adult students.
Amount: $10,000.
Number of awards: 8.
Deadline: May 15.
How to apply: Applications are available online.
Exclusive: Visit www.UltimateScholarshipBook.com and enter code ST16326 for updates on this award.

[164] • Graduate Research Grant – Master and Doctoral
National Strength and Conditioning Association (NSCA) Foundation
1885 Bob Johnson Drive, Colorado Springs, CO 80906
Phone: 800-815-6826
Email: Foundation@nsca.com
http://www.nsca.com/foundation/
Purpose: To support research in strength and conditioning.
Eligibility: Applicants must be master's or doctoral students and submit a proposal for a research project in the field of strength and conditioning that fulfills the mission of the NSCA. Students must be NSCA members for one year before applying and pursuing careers in strength and conditioning. Applications are evaluated based on grades, courses, experience, honors, recommendations and involvement in the community and with NSCA.
Target applicant(s): Graduate school students. Adult students.
Amount: Up to $15,000.
Number of awards: Varies.
Deadline: February 15.
How to apply: Applications are available with membership.
Exclusive: Visit www.UltimateScholarshipBook.com and enter code NA16426 for updates on this award.

[165] • H and P Veterans Helping Veterans Scholarship
Hill & Ponton
605 E. Robinson Street, Suite 635, Orlando, FL 32801
https://www.hillandponton.com/veterans-scholarship/
Purpose: To support veterans pursuing post-secondary education.
Eligibility: Applicants must be veterans of the U.S. armed forces. Students must plan to use their education to help fellow veterans. Applicants must complete a statement explaining how their education will be used to assist veterans.
Target applicant(s): College students. Adult students.

Amount: $1,000.
Number of awards: 4.
Deadline: November 1; May 1.
How to apply: Applications are available online.
Exclusive: Visit www.UltimateScholarshipBook.com and enter code HI16526 for updates on this award.

[166] • H. U. Lee Scholarship
H.U. Lee Memorial Foundation
1800 Riverfront Drive, Little Rock, AR 72202
Phone: 501-568-2821 x2263
Email: hulf@ataonline.com
https://www.huleefoundation.org/scholarship-requirements
Purpose: To support the advancement of discipline, respect and courtesy through Taekwondo.
Eligibility: Applicants must be current high school seniors graduating from an accredited high school with a minimum 3.0 GPA. Students must have received a letter of acceptance from an accredited U.S. college for full-time study beginning no later than September 30. Applicants must have a minimum combined score of 1200 on the SAT and/or 27 on the ACT, must have registered with Selective Service if required and have no convictions of drug possession or distribution.
Target applicant(s): High school students.
Minimum GPA: 3.0
Amount: Varies.
Number of awards: Varies.
Deadline: February 15.
How to apply: Applications are available through the student's instructor. An application form, a sealed copy of high school transcripts with the signature of the school's director of admissions across the sealed envelope, two recommendation letters and an essay are required.
Exclusive: Visit www.UltimateScholarshipBook.com and enter code H.16626 for updates on this award.

[167] • Hagan Scholarship
Hagan Scholarship Foundation
P.O. Box 1225, Columbia, MO 65205
Email: scholarships@hsfmo.org
https://haganscholarships.org
Purpose: To help high-achieving, dedicated students who live in smaller counties.
Eligibility: Applicants must be U.S. citizens and be graduating seniors from a public, private or charter high school with a 3.5 GPA or higher and a household income of $100,000 or less. Students must be enrolling in a four-year college or university the first semester following high school graduation. Applicants must work 240 hours in the year prior to the start of each academic year.
Target applicant(s): High school students.
Minimum GPA: 3.5
Amount: $7,500.
Number of awards: 1000.
Scholarship may be renewable.
Deadline: Fall-December 1; Spring-March 1.
How to apply: Applications are available online.
Exclusive: Visit www.UltimateScholarshipBook.com and enter code HA16726 for updates on this award.

[168] • Hamilton Award
Alexander Hamilton Scholars
P.O. Box 81047, Seattle, WA 98108
Phone: 206-774-0764
Email: program@hamiltonscholars.org
http://www.hamiltonscholars.org
Purpose: To reward the academic, personal, service and entrepreneurial accomplishments of students.
Eligibility: Applicants must be high-achieving, service-focused high school juniors with grit, perseverance and demonstrated need. Students must be committed to participating in a rigorous five-year curriculum designed to provide a comprehensive network of support and practical guidance to Alexander Hamilton Scholars as they transition from high school to college and college to career.
Target applicant(s): High school students.
Amount: $1,000.
Number of awards: 40.
Deadline: January 31.
How to apply: Applications are available online.
Exclusive: Visit www.UltimateScholarshipBook.com and enter code AL16826 for updates on this award.

[169] • Hanscom Air Force Base Spouses' Club Scholarship
Hanscom Officers' Spouses' Club
75 Grenier Street, Unit 8888, Hanscom AFB, MA 01731
Phone: 781-538-5361
Email: scholarship@hanscomsc.org
https://hanscomsc.org/scholarships.html
Purpose: To aid dependents of past and present members of the military.
Eligibility: Applicants must be children or spouses of retired, deceased or current active duty members of any branch of the military. They must hold a valid military ID card. Children of military members must be high school seniors.
Target applicant(s): High school students. College students. Adult students.
Amount: Varies.
Number of awards: Varies.
Deadline: March 13.
How to apply: Applications are available online. An application form and copy of military ID are required.
Exclusive: Visit www.UltimateScholarshipBook.com and enter code HA16926 for updates on this award.

[170] • HD Hogan Rodeo Scholarship
HD Hogan Memorial Rodeo Scholarship Fund
407 S. X Road, Aurora, NE 68818
Email: beabullfighter@hotmail.com
https://www.hdhoganfoundation.org
Purpose: To aid students in continuing their education and their rodeo careers in college.
Eligibility: Applicants must be a current high school senior and current rodeo participant. Selection is based solely on the essay about what being an American means to you and also what the sport of rodeo means to you.
Target applicant(s): High school students.
Amount: Varies.
Number of awards: Varies.
Deadline: December 1.
How to apply: Applications are in the form of the essay that must be mailed.

The Ultimate Scholarship Book 2026
Scholarship Directory (General Awards)

Exclusive: Visit www.UltimateScholarshipBook.com and enter code HD17026 for updates on this award.

[171] • Heisman High School Scholarship
Acceptance Insurance Company
111 Broadway, Suite 103A, New York, NY 10006
Phone: 800-205-6367
Email: heismanscholarship@scholarshipamerica.org
https://heismanscholarship.com/
Purpose: To reward high school seniors who are outstanding scholar-athletes.
Eligibility: Applicants must participate or have participated in grades 9, 10 or 11 in at least one of the sports recognized by the International Olympic Committee in the Summer and Winter Olympic Games, the Paralympic Games or the National Federation of State High School Association. Students must have a minimum 3.0 GPA, be a leader in school and their community and serve as a role model for underclassmen.
Target applicant(s): High school students.
Minimum GPA: 3.0
Amount: Up to $10,000.
Number of awards: 100.
Deadline: October 17.
How to apply: Applications are available online.
Exclusive: Visit www.UltimateScholarshipBook.com and enter code AC17126 for updates on this award.

[172] • Helen Gee Chin Scholarship Foundation Scholarship
Helen Gee Chin Scholarship Foundation
66 Winchester Street, Newton Highlands, MA 02461
Phone: 617-527-8890
Email: hgc@calvinchin.com
http://www.hgcscholarshipfoundation.org
Purpose: To promote academic achievement and inspire individuals to become students of the Chinese martial arts.
Eligibility: Applicants must be a U.S. citizen, plan to attend an accredited U.S. four year college or university as a full-time student for the entire academic year and have a B GPA. Applicants must have studied for at least five years one or more of the Chinese martial arts including Kung Fu, Wu Shu or Tai Chi. Selection is based on achievement in academics and martial arts, recommendations, work experience, educational and career goals and leadership in school and community activities.
Target applicant(s): High school students. College students. Adult students.
Minimum GPA: 3.0
Amount: $3,000.
Number of awards: At least 2.
Deadline: June 15.
How to apply: Applications are available online. An application form, an essay, official transcripts covering the previous two years, a recommendation letter from current or most recent Sifu and a recommendation letter from a teacher, counselor or advisor are required.
Exclusive: Visit www.UltimateScholarshipBook.com and enter code HE17226 for updates on this award.

[173] • High School Scholarship
National Strength and Conditioning Association (NSCA) Foundation
1885 Bob Johnson Drive, Colorado Springs, CO 80906
Phone: 800-815-6826
Email: Foundation@nsca.com
http://www.nsca.com/foundation/
Purpose: To support high school students entering the strength and conditioning field.
Eligibility: Applicants must be high school seniors planning to graduate with a degree related to strength and conditioning with a current 3.0 GPA. Students must be NSCA members, although applicants may enroll at the time of application, and pursuing a career in strength and conditioning. Applications are evaluated based on grades, courses, experience, honors, recommendations and involvement in the community and with NSCA.
Target applicant(s): High school students.
Minimum GPA: 3.0
Amount: $2,000.
Number of awards: Varies.
Deadline: October 15.
How to apply: Applications are available by contacting the organization.
Exclusive: Visit www.UltimateScholarshipBook.com and enter code NA17326 for updates on this award.

[174] • Horatio Alger National Scholarship Program
Horatio Alger Association
Attn.: Scholarship Department, 99 Canal Center Plaza, Suite 320, Alexandria, VA 22314
Phone: 703-684-9444
Email: association@horatioalger.org
https://scholars.horatioalger.org/
Purpose: To assist students who are committed to pursuing a bachelor's degree and have demonstrated integrity, financial need, academic achievement and community involvement.
Eligibility: Applicants must be a high school junior, have at least a 2.0 GPA, be in need of financial aid ($55,000 or less adjusted gross income per family is preferred) and be involved in extracurricular and community activities. Students applying from Louisiana, Montana and Idaho have additional state specific requirements.
Target applicant(s): High school students.
Minimum GPA: 2.0
Amount: Up to $25,000.
Number of awards: 500.
Deadline: March 15.
How to apply: Applications are available online.
Exclusive: Visit www.UltimateScholarshipBook.com and enter code HO17426 for updates on this award.

[175] • Humane Studies Fellowship: Flexible Support for PhD Students
Institute for Humane Studies at George Mason University
3434 Washington Boulevard, Vernon Smith Hall, 1st Floor, Arlington, VA 22201
Phone: 800-697-8799
Email: Funding@TheIHS.org
https://theihs.org/funding/humane-studies-fellowship/
Purpose: To encourage master's and PhD students who have not advanced to candidacy.
Eligibility: Applicants must be full-time students in an MA or PhD program. Students at any university and international students are eligible to apply. Priority is given to applicants at top research institutions. Previous applicants and winners are welcome to apply. Prior participation in IHS programs is not required.
Target applicant(s): Graduate school students. Adult students.
Amount: Up to $5,000.

Number of awards: Varies.
Deadline: April 1; August 1; December 1.
How to apply: Applications are available online.
Exclusive: Visit www.UltimateScholarshipBook.com and enter code IN17526 for updates on this award.

[176] • Humane Studies Fellowship: Graduate Sabbatical Grants

Institute for Humane Studies at George Mason University
3434 Washington Boulevard, Vernon Smith Hall, 1st Floor, Arlington, VA 22201
Phone: 800-697-8799
Email: Funding@TheIHS.org
https://theihs.org/funding/humane-studies-fellowship/
Purpose: To support PhD candidates by buying out teaching or research responsibilities for a semester so that they may develop dissertation chapters or other work into publishable paper drafts.
Eligibility: Applicants must have published previously or have an article currently under review and be enrolled as full-time PhD students who have advanced to candidacy. Students at any university as well as international students are eligible to apply. Priority is given to applicants at top research institutions. Previous applicants and winners are welcome to apply and prior participation in IHS programs is not required.
Target applicant(s): Graduate school students. Adult students.
Amount: Up to $15,000.
Number of awards: Varies.
Scholarship may be renewable.
Deadline: Applications are reviewed on a rolling basis.
How to apply: Applications are available online. There is a $25 application fee that is waived by applying by January 5.
Exclusive: Visit www.UltimateScholarshipBook.com and enter code IN17626 for updates on this award.

[177] • IAPMO Essay Scholarship Contest

International Association of Plumbing and Mechanical Officials (IAPMO)
4755 E. Philadelphia Street, Ontario, CA 91761
Phone: 909-472-4100
Email: essay@iwsh.org
https://www.iwsh.org/hidden/iwsh-essay-scholarship-contest/
Purpose: To share the "importance the plumbing and mechanical industry plays in our everyday lives."
Eligibility: Applicants must be current high school seniors or enrolled or accepted as full-time students in an accredited technical school, community college, trade school, four-year accredited college or university or an apprentice program.
Target applicant(s): High school students. College students. Adult students.
Amount: $1,000-$2,000.
Number of awards: 4.
Deadline: April 30.
How to apply: Applications are available online. An essay of 800 to 1,600 words on the topic provided is required.
Exclusive: Visit www.UltimateScholarshipBook.com and enter code IN17726 for updates on this award.

[178] • IEA Founders College Scholarship Awards

Interscholastic Equestrian Association
467 Main Street, Melrose, MA 02176
Phone: 877-743-3432
Email: info@rideiea.org
https://www.rideiea.org/opportunities/for-riders/
Purpose: To recognize the top participants in the Interscholastic Equestrian Association's National Final Competitions.
Eligibility: Students must be a high school senior, compete in either the IEA Hunt Seat National Finals or the IEA Western National Finals and place in the top two in their category.
Target applicant(s): High school students.
Amount: Up to $1,100.
Number of awards: Varies.
Deadline: Contact the sponsor to confirm the deadline.
How to apply: Participant must qualify during their IEA Zone Final Competition.
Exclusive: Visit www.UltimateScholarshipBook.com and enter code IN17826 for updates on this award.

[179] • IEA Zone Specific Scholarships

Interscholastic Equestrian Association
467 Main Street, Melrose, MA 02176
Phone: 877-743-3432
Email: info@rideiea.org
https://www.rideiea.org/opportunities/for-riders/
Purpose: To support high school seniors in each Interscholastic Equestrian Association zone as they further their education beyond high school.
Eligibility: Students must be active participants in an IEA zone, display outstanding sportsmanship, maintain academic excellence and portray an overall role model to the IEA membership. Each zone has varied selection criteria.
Target applicant(s): High school students.
Amount: Varies.
Number of awards: Varies.
Deadline: August 15.
How to apply: All zone applications are available online. Most zones require letters of recommendation, high school transcript and an essay.
Exclusive: Visit www.UltimateScholarshipBook.com and enter code IN17926 for updates on this award.

[180] • Ike Foundation Scholarship

Ike Foundation
348 Palatine Road, Elmer, NJ 08318
Phone: 856-466-7798
Email: theikefoundation@gmail.com
https://theikefoundation.org
Purpose: To support students involved in the sport of fishing.
Eligibility: Applicants must be U.S. citizens or permanent residents and high school seniors who are planning to enroll full-time in a two- or four-year institution. Students must have a minimum GPA of 3.2 and demonstrate an interest in fishing and/or conservation. Applicants must submit an original essay along with their application materials.
Target applicant(s): High school students.
Minimum GPA: 3.2
Amount: Up to $2,000.
Number of awards: 5.
Deadline: April 1.

The Ultimate Scholarship Book 2026
Scholarship Directory (General Awards)

How to apply: Applications are available online.
Exclusive: Visit www.UltimateScholarshipBook.com and enter code IK18026 for updates on this award.

[181] • In the Driver's Seat
DMVEdu.org
64 Shattuck Square, Suite 285, Berkeley, CA 94704
https://www.dmvedu.org/scholarship/
Purpose: To reward students who are safe drivers.
Eligibility: Applicants must be currently enrolled as a full-time student in high school or college. Students must write an essay using the given prompts.
Target applicant(s): High school students. College students. Adult students.
Amount: $500.
Number of awards: 6.
Deadline: November 30.
How to apply: Applications are available online.
Exclusive: Visit www.UltimateScholarshipBook.com and enter code DM18126 for updates on this award.

[182] • Individual Scholarship Program
International Surfing Association
5580 La Jolla Boulevard, #145, La Jolla, CA 92037
Phone: 858-551-8580
Email: info@isasurf.org
https://www.isasurf.org/development-programs/isa-scholarship/
Purpose: To aid student surfers who plan to pursue higher education after high school.
Eligibility: Applicants must be U18 junior surfers. Selection is based on financial need and the ability of the applicant to represent themselves as a positive role model both within the sport of surfing and at school.
Target applicant(s): Junior high students or younger. High school students.
Amount: Up to $1,000.
Number of awards: Varies.
Deadline: January 15.
How to apply: Applications are available online and must include the following: a recent report card, one letter of recommendation, a personal essay, a budget plan and four photos (family, school, surfing and headshot).
Exclusive: Visit www.UltimateScholarshipBook.com and enter code IN18226 for updates on this award.

[183] • Industrial Metal Service Scholarship
Industrial Metal Service
260 Phelan Avenue, San Jose, CA 95112
Phone: 408-294-2334
Email: metalsales@industrialmetalservice.com
https://industrialmetalservice.com/scholarship/
Purpose: To support students who write an essay on an environment-related topic.
Eligibility: Applicants must be undergraduates currently enrolled full-time in accredited universities within the U.S. and high school seniors who have been accepted into a university program. Students must be legal residents of the U.S. or holders of a valid student visa and be 18 years old or older. Applicants must write an essay on one of the environment-related topics provided.
Target applicant(s): High school students. College students. Adult students.
Amount: $500.
Number of awards: 1.
Deadline: December 27.
How to apply: Applications are available online.
Exclusive: Visit www.UltimateScholarshipBook.com and enter code IN18326 for updates on this award.

[184] • International College Counselors Scholarship
International College Counselors
3107 Stirling Road, Suite 208, Ft. Lauderdale, FL 33312
Phone: 954-414-9986
Email: info@internationalcollegecounselors.com
https://iccscholarship.com/
Purpose: To increase awareness of the value of higher education.
Eligibility: Applicants must be current high school freshmen, sophomores or juniors attending a high school or who are home-schooled. Students must write an essay on the topic, "The transition from middle school to high school is oftentimes filled with anxiety, frustration, and isolation. What advice would you give middle school students on smoothly transitioning to high school?" Selection is based on content, originality, clarity, insight and writing quality.
Target applicant(s): High school students.
Amount: $250.
Number of awards: 2.
Deadline: April 17.
How to apply: Applications are available online.
Exclusive: Visit www.UltimateScholarshipBook.com and enter code IN18426 for updates on this award.

[185] • Iowa Student Loan Midwest Senior Scholarship
Iowa Student Loan Education Lending
6805 Vista Drive, West Des Moines, IA 50266
Phone: 855-811-9849
Email: scholarship@studentloan.org
https://www.iowastudentloan.org/scholarships/
Purpose: To help students with expenses related to their pursuit of post-secondary education.
Eligibility: Applicants must be high school seniors who are at least 13 years of age. Students must be a permanent resident of and enrolled in a high school located in one of the following states: Illinois, Nebraska, South Dakota, Wisconsin, Missouri or Minnesota and who will attend an eligible U.S. college. Selection is based on a random drawing.
Target applicant(s): High school students.
Amount: $1,000.
Number of awards: 10.
Deadline: April 30.
How to apply: Application information is available online. Two online financial literacy tutorials, an online financial literacy assessment and a short essay are required.
Exclusive: Visit www.UltimateScholarshipBook.com and enter code IO18526 for updates on this award.

[186] • ISIA Education Foundation Scholarship

Ice Skating Institute of America (ISIA) Education Foundation
6000 Custer Road, Building 9, Plano, TX 75023
Phone: 972-735-8800
Email: ISI@skateisi.org
https://www.skateisi.org
Purpose: To encourage skaters to make athletic and educational achievements.
Eligibility: Applicants must have completed at least three years of high school with a minimum 3.0 GPA during the last two years and enroll as full-time undergraduate students. Applicants must also have been members of the Ice Skating Institute (ISI), have participated in the ISI Recreational Skater Program for at least four years and have completed 120 hours of volunteer service. Applicants must also submit two evaluation forms and an essay of 500 words or less explaining why they should receive the award.
Target applicant(s): High school students. College students. Adult students.
Minimum GPA: 3.0
Amount: $4,000.
Number of awards: Varies.
Deadline: March 1.
How to apply: Applications are available online.
Exclusive: Visit www.UltimateScholarshipBook.com and enter code IC18626 for updates on this award.

[187] • Jack Kent Cooke Foundation College Scholarship Program

Jack Kent Cooke Foundation
44325 Woodridge Parkway, Lansdowne, VA 20176
Phone: 800-941-3300
Email: scholarships@jkcf.org
http://www.jkcf.org
Purpose: To assist high school seniors with financial need.
Eligibility: Applicants must plan to graduate from a U.S. high school in the spring and plan to enroll in an accredited four-year college beginning in the fall following application. Students must have a minimum 3.5 GPA and have standardized test scores in the top 15 percent: SAT combined critical reading and math score of 1200 or above and/or ACT composite score of 26 or above. Applicants must also demonstrate significant unmet financial need. Family incomes up to $95,000 are considered.
Target applicant(s): High school students.
Minimum GPA: 3.5
Amount: Up to $55,000 per year for four years.
Number of awards: Up to 40.
Scholarship may be renewable.
Deadline: November 14.
How to apply: Applications are available online.
Exclusive: Visit www.UltimateScholarshipBook.com and enter code JA18726 for updates on this award.

[188] • James M. and Virginia M. Smyth Scholarship

Community Foundation for Greater Atlanta Inc.
50 Hurt Plaza, Suite 449, Atlanta, GA 30303
Phone: 404-688-5525
Email: info@cfgreateratlanta.org
https://cfgreateratlanta.org/scholarships/
Purpose: To support students who are pursuing undergraduate degrees.
Eligibility: Students must have at least a 3.0 GPA, and they must have community service experience. Applicants must plan to obtain a degree in the arts and sciences, music, ministry or human services. Preference will be given to students from the following states: Missouri, Mississippi, Georgia, Illinois, Oklahoma, Texas and Tennessee. Applicants must demonstrate financial need. Adult students may also apply.
Target applicant(s): High school students. College students. Adult students.
Minimum GPA: 3.0
Amount: $2,000.
Number of awards: 12-15.
Scholarship may be renewable.
Deadline: February 15.
How to apply: Applications are available online.
Exclusive: Visit www.UltimateScholarshipBook.com and enter code CO18826 for updates on this award.

[189] • Jane Austen Society of North America Essay Contest

Jane Austen Society of North America
Phone: 206-739-6225
Email: essay-contest@jasna.org
http://www.jasna.org
Purpose: To encourage students who write about family relationships.
Eligibility: Applicants must be high school students, college or university students enrolled in at least six credit hours of course work or graduate students enrolled in at least three credit hours of graduate course work. An essay submission on a provided prompt is required. Membership in The Jane Austen Society of North America is not required to enter the contest.
Target applicant(s): High school students. College students. Graduate school students. Adult students.
Amount: $250-$1,000.
Number of awards: 3.
Deadline: June 1.
How to apply: Applications are available online.
Exclusive: Visit www.UltimateScholarshipBook.com and enter code JA18926 for updates on this award.

[190] • John F. Duffy Scholarship/Grant Program

California Peace Officers' Memorial Foundation
1700 I Street, Suite 100, Sacramento, CA 95811
Email: cpomf@camemorial.org
http://www.camemorial.org
Purpose: To provide financial assistance to survivors of California peace officers who have died in the line of duty.
Eligibility: Applicants must be spouses, children, stepchildren or adopted children of peace officers who died in the line of duty and are enrolled on the California memorial monument. They must carry no less than six units per quarter or eight units per semester at an accredited college or university, and they must maintain a 2.0 or higher GPA.
Target applicant(s): High school students. College students. Graduate school students. Adult students.
Minimum GPA: 2.0
Amount: Up to $5,000.
Number of awards: Varies.
Deadline: June 1.
How to apply: Applications are available online.
Exclusive: Visit www.UltimateScholarshipBook.com and enter code CA19026 for updates on this award.

The Ultimate Scholarship Book 2026
Scholarship Directory (General Awards)

[191] • John J. Smith Graduate School Scholarship
National Intercollegiate Rodeo Association
2033 Walla Walla Avenue, Walla Walla, WA 99362
Phone: 509-529-4402
Email: rodeo@collegerodeo.com
http://www.collegerodeo.com/
Purpose: To support students who have participated in the National Intercollegiate Rodeo Association as they continue on into graduate level coursework.
Eligibility: Applicants must be current graduate level college students or be entering into a graduate program and be current NIRA members.
Target applicant(s): College students. Graduate school students. Adult students.
Amount: $2,000.
Number of awards: 1.
Deadline: May 20.
How to apply: Applications are available online. The following are to be included with the application: cover letter, proof of acceptance into a graduate level program, an official college transcript and two letters of recommendation.
Exclusive: Visit www.UltimateScholarshipBook.com and enter code NA19126 for updates on this award.

[192] • John S. Linakis Scholarship
American Institute for Foreign Study
AIFS Abroad, 1 High Ridge Park, Stamford, CT 06905
Phone: 800-727-2437
Email: AIFSAbroad@aifs.com
https://www.aifsabroad.com/scholarships.asp
Purpose: To provide students with challenging educational programs in culturally diverse locations around the world.
Eligibility: Applicants must be AIFS students with limited financial resources who also demonstrate an interest in and commitment to social justice. Students must complete scholarship and program applications or before the deadline date and this must be postmarked or sent via email before the deadline date.
Target applicant(s): High school students. College students. Adult students.
Amount: $5,000.
Number of awards: 1.
Deadline: April 15 for fall; October 7 for spring.
How to apply: Applications are available online.
Exclusive: Visit www.UltimateScholarshipBook.com and enter code AM19226 for updates on this award.

[193] • Jon C. Ladda Memorial Foundation Scholarship
Jon C. Ladda Memorial Foundation
P.O. Box 55, Unionville, CT 06085
Email: info@jonladda.org
http://www.jonladda.org
Purpose: To provide financial assistance to children of Naval Academy graduates and Navy members who have died or become disabled while on active duty.
Eligibility: Applicants must be children of United States Naval Academy graduates or Navy members who served in the submarine service. The Navy member or Academy graduate must have died on active duty or have 100 percent disability and be medically retired. Applicants must also be accepted and enroll in an accredited institution of higher learning.
Target applicant(s): High school students. College students. Adult students.
Amount: Varies.
Number of awards: Varies.
Scholarship may be renewable.
Deadline: March 15.
How to apply: Applications are available by mail.
Exclusive: Visit www.UltimateScholarshipBook.com and enter code JO19326 for updates on this award.

[194] • Jonathan Jasper Wright Award
National Association of Blacks in Criminal Justice
1801 Fayetteville Street, 106 Whiting Criminal Justice Building, P.O. Box 20011-C, Durham, NC 27707
Phone: 919-683-1801
Email: Office@NABCJ.org
https://nabcj.org/
Purpose: To reward regional and national leadership in the field of criminal justice.
Eligibility: Award recipients will be involved in affecting policy change. The nominator should be a member of NABCJ.
Target applicant(s): College students. Graduate school students. Adult students.
Amount: Varies.
Number of awards: 1.
Deadline: March 15.
How to apply: Nomination applications are available online.
Exclusive: Visit www.UltimateScholarshipBook.com and enter code NA19426 for updates on this award.

[195] • Joseph P. and Helen T. Cribbins Scholarship
Association of the United States Army
2425 Wilson Boulevard, Arlington, VA 22201
Phone: 703-841-4300
Email: Membersupport@ausa.org
https://www.ausa.org/resources/scholarships
Purpose: To aid U.S. Army soldiers who are studying engineering or a related subject.
Eligibility: Applicants must be active duty or honorably discharged enlisted soldiers in the U.S. Army or one of its affiliate entities (Army Reserve, National Guard, etc.). They must be accepted or enrolled at an accredited college or university and majoring in or planning to major in engineering or a related subject. Selection is based on the overall strength of the application.
Target applicant(s): High school students. College students. Adult students.
Amount: $10,000.
Number of awards: 2.
Deadline: May 31.
How to apply: Applications are available online. An application form, two recommendation letters, an applicant autobiography, an official transcript, a course of study outline, certificates of completion for other training courses (if applicable) and a copy of form DD-214 (for discharged soldiers) are required.
Exclusive: Visit www.UltimateScholarshipBook.com and enter code AS19526 for updates on this award.

[196] • Judith Haupt Member's Child Scholarship
Navy Wives Clubs of America (NWCA)
P.O. Box 54022, NSA Mid-South, Millington, TN 38053-6022
Phone: 866-511-6922
Email: scholarships@navywivesclubsofamerica.org
https://navywivesclubsofamerica.org
Purpose: To aid college students who are the adult children of members of the Navy Wives Clubs of America (NWCA).
Eligibility: Applicants must be unmarried college students who are the adult children of NWCA members. They cannot be carrying a military ID card and must have been accepted into a college no later than the application due date. Selection is based on academic merit and financial need.
Target applicant(s): High school students. College students. Adult students.
Amount: $1,000 to $1,500.
Number of awards: 1.
Deadline: March 31.
How to apply: Applications are available online. An application form and an official transcript are required.
Exclusive: Visit www.UltimateScholarshipBook.com and enter code NA19626 for updates on this award.

[197] • Justin Dignam Memorial Scholarship
USA Water Polo Inc.
6 Morgan, Suite 150, Irvine, CA 92618
Phone: 714-500-5445
Email: epadilla@usawaterpolo.org
https://usawaterpolo.org/sports/2022/5/18/justin-dignam-memorial-fund-scholarship.aspx
Purpose: To support high school students who are members of USA Water Polo.
Eligibility: Applicants must be high school student athletes in grades 9-12. Students must be current USA Water Polo members in good standing. A video submission on a provided prompt is required.
Target applicant(s): High school students.
Amount: $500.
Number of awards: 2.
Deadline: September 30.
How to apply: Applications are available online.
Exclusive: Visit www.UltimateScholarshipBook.com and enter code US19726 for updates on this award.

[198] • Kathern F. Gruber Scholarship Program
Blinded Veterans Association (BVA)
P.O. Box 90770, Washington, DC 20090
Phone: 800-669-7079
Email: bva@bva.org
http://www.bva.org
Purpose: To assist the spouses, children and grandchildren of blinded veterans with their higher-learning goals.
Eligibility: Applicants must be the spouses, children or grandchildren of a blind veteran and be accepted or enrolled at an accredited, higher learning institution.
Target applicant(s): High school students. College students. Graduate school students. Adult students.
Amount: $2,000.
Number of awards: 6.
Deadline: April 30.
How to apply: Contact the BVA for application materials.
Exclusive: Visit www.UltimateScholarshipBook.com and enter code BL19826 for updates on this award.

[199] • Kemper Human Rights Education Foundation
Kemper Human Rights Education Foundation
184 Fillow Street, Norwalk, CT 06850
Phone: 646-400-2406
Email: kemperhumanrights@gmail.com
https://khref.org/this-years-question/
Purpose: To reward students who advocate for human rights.
Eligibility: Applicants must be high school students who have demonstrated an interest in human rights and progress. They must also write and submit an essay about a given topic related to human rights.
Target applicant(s): Junior high students or younger. High school students.
Amount: $1,000-$4,000.
Number of awards: Varies.
Deadline: December 10.
How to apply: Applications are available online.
Exclusive: Visit www.UltimateScholarshipBook.com and enter code KE19926 for updates on this award.

[200] • Kevin Higgins College Scholarship
US Rugby Foundation
2131 Pan American Plaza, San Diego, CA 92101
Phone: 619-233-0765
Email: bvizard@usrugbyfoundation.com
https://www.usrugbyfoundation.org/
Purpose: To support those high school rugby players who plan on continuing to play rugby at the collegiate level.
Eligibility: Applicants must be a U.S. high school senior rugby player, have a 2.5 or better GPA and plan to continue playing rugby at the collegiate level. Selection is based on character recommendations, community service, rugby potential and the personal statement. Financial need will be considered.
Target applicant(s): High school students.
Minimum GPA: 2.5
Amount: $1,000.
Number of awards: Up to 10.
Deadline: August 31.
How to apply: Applications are available online and should include an official transcript, at least one letter of recommendation, a rugby resume, a copy of the previous year's taxes and the personal statement.
Exclusive: Visit www.UltimateScholarshipBook.com and enter code US20026 for updates on this award.

[201] • La Fra Scholarship
Ladies Auxiliary of the Fleet Reserve Association
LA FRA National Scholarship Chairman, Kelly Pena RPWC, P.O. Box 9572, San Jose, CA 95157
Phone: 408-642-7722
Email: penakelly66@gmail.com
https://la-fra.org
Purpose: To support the female descendants of sea personnel.
Eligibility: Students must have a father or grandfather who was in the Marine Corps, Coast Guard, Navy, Fleet Reserve, Coast Guard Reserve or Fleet Marine Corps Reserve.
Target applicant(s): High school students. College students. Graduate school students. Adult students.

The Ultimate Scholarship Book 2026
Scholarship Directory (General Awards)

Amount: Varies.
Number of awards: Varies.
Deadline: April 15.
How to apply: Applications are available online.
Exclusive: Visit www.UltimateScholarshipBook.com and enter code LA20126 for updates on this award.

[202] • LA Tutors Innovation in Education Scholarship
LA Tutors
9454 Wilshire Boulevard, Suite 600, Beverly Hills, CA 90212
Phone: 424-335-0067
Email: contact@latutors123.com
https://www.latutors123.com/scholarship/
Purpose: To reward innovation.
Eligibility: Applicants must be a high school or college student within the U.S. or Canada. A minimum 3.0 GPA is required. Students must be a citizen of, permanent resident of or hold a valid student visa in the U.S. or Canada. Applicants will have designed an innovative project that makes a difference in the lives of others. The project can include a website, series of blogs, an app, fundraising event, etc. An essay describing the goal of the project and providing supporting documentation is required. The contest is monthly.
Target applicant(s): High school students. College students. Adult students.
Minimum GPA: 3.0
Amount: $500.
Number of awards: 12.
Deadline: 20th of each month.
How to apply: Applications are available online.
Exclusive: Visit www.UltimateScholarshipBook.com and enter code LA20226 for updates on this award.

[203] • Leadership Essay Contest
United States Naval Institute (USNI)
291 Wood Road, Annapolis, MD 21402
Phone: 410-268-6110
Email: customer@usni.org
https://www.usni.org/essay-contests
Purpose: To promote awareness of sea services.
Eligibility: Applicants must be junior officers, O-4 and below from the U.S. Navy, Marine Corps or Coast Guard. Students must write an essay discussing leadership.
Target applicant(s): Adult students.
Amount: $1,500-$5,000.
Number of awards: 3.
Deadline: November 30.
How to apply: Applications are available online.
Exclusive: Visit www.UltimateScholarshipBook.com and enter code UN20326 for updates on this award.

[204] • Life Lessons Scholarship Program
Life and Health Insurance Foundation for Education
1655 N. Fort Myer Drive, Suite 610, Arlington, VA 22209
Phone: 202-464-5000
Email: info@lifehappens.org
http://www.lifehappens.org
Purpose: To support students who have been affected financially and emotionally by the death of a parent.
Eligibility: Applicants must submit either a 500-word essay or a three-minute video describing the impact of losing a parent at a young age. The grand prize winner of the video contest is selected by an online public vote.
Target applicant(s): High school students. College students. Graduate school students.
Amount: Varies.
Number of awards: Varies.
Deadline: March 1.
How to apply: Applications are available online.
Exclusive: Visit www.UltimateScholarshipBook.com and enter code LI20426 for updates on this award.

[205] • Live Mas Scholarship
Taco Bell Foundation
Email: info@livemasscholarship.com
http://www.livemasscholarship.com
Purpose: To assist innovative and creative students who submit a two-minute video.
Eligibility: Applicants must be a legal resident of the United States and at least 16 years of age and no older than 26 years of age. Applicants must be on track to apply for or currently enrolled in accredited post-high school/post-secondary educational programs. Applicants must create and submit a video (two minutes or less in length) that answers the scholarship question.
Target applicant(s): High school students. College students. Adult students.
Amount: $5,000-$25,000.
Number of awards: 100.
Deadline: January 4.
How to apply: Applications are available online.
Exclusive: Visit www.UltimateScholarshipBook.com and enter code TA20526 for updates on this award.

[206] • Lou Manzione Scholarship
Atlantic Amateur Hockey Association
Attn.: Tom Koester, President, P.O. Box 213, Lafayette Hill, PA 19444
Email: info@atlantic-district.org
https://www.atlantic-district.org/scholarships
Purpose: To aid hockey students who are planning to continue their education beyond high school.
Eligibility: Applicants must be a high school senior in New Jersey, Pennsylvania or Delaware and registered with USA Hockey. Selection is based on the personal essay, scholastic achievement, the coach and teacher recommendations and extracurricular activities.
Target applicant(s): High school students.
Amount: $1,000.
Number of awards: 2.
Deadline: April 1.
How to apply: Applications are available online.
Exclusive: Visit www.UltimateScholarshipBook.com and enter code AT20626 for updates on this award.

[207] • LULAC National Scholastic Achievement Awards
League of United Latin American Citizens
1133 19th Street NW, Suite 1000, Washington, DC 20036
Phone: 202-835-9646
Email: scholarships@lnesc.org
https://www.lnesc.org

Purpose: To aid students of all ethnic backgrounds attending colleges, universities and graduate schools.
Eligibility: Applicants do not need to be Hispanic or Latino to apply. Applicants must have applied to or be enrolled in a college, university or graduate school and be U.S. citizens or legal residents. Students must also have a minimum 3.5 GPA. Eligible candidates cannot be related to scholarship committee members, the Council President or contributors to the Council funds. Since applications must be sent from local LULAC Councils, students without LULAC Councils in their states are ineligible.
Target applicant(s): High school students. College students. Graduate school students. Adult students.
Minimum GPA: 3.5
Amount: $2,000.
Number of awards: Varies.
Deadline: March 31.
How to apply: Applications are available online.
Exclusive: Visit www.UltimateScholarshipBook.com and enter code LE20726 for updates on this award.

[208] • Marian Wood Baird College Scholarship
United States Tennis Association Foundation
70 W. Red Oak Lane, White Plains, NY 10604
Phone: 914-696-7223
Email: foundation@usta.com
http://www.ustafoundation.com/
Purpose: To support youth tennis players who have excelled both on and off the court.
Eligibility: Applicants must be high school seniors who have participated extensively in an organized community tennis program. Students must also excel academically, demonstrate leadership skills and exemplify good sportsmanship both on and off the court.
Target applicant(s): High school students.
Amount: Up to $15,000.
Number of awards: 1.
Scholarship may be renewable.
Deadline: May 15.
How to apply: Applications are available online.
Exclusive: Visit www.UltimateScholarshipBook.com and enter code UN20826 for updates on this award.

[209] • Marine Corps League Scholarships
Marine Corps League
P.O. Box 3070, Merrifield, VA 22116
Phone: 800-625-1775
https://www.mcleaguelibrary.org
Purpose: To provide educational opportunities to spouses and descendants of Marine Corps League members.
Eligibility: Applicants must be Marine Corp League or Auxiliary members in good standing, their spouses or their descendants, children of Marines who died in the line of duty or honorably discharged Marines who need rehabilitation training that is not being subsidized by government programs.
Target applicant(s): High school students. College students. Adult students.
Minimum GPA: 3.0
Amount: Varies.
Number of awards: Varies.
Scholarship may be renewable.
Deadline: July 21.
How to apply: Applications are available online.
Exclusive: Visit www.UltimateScholarshipBook.com and enter code MA20926 for updates on this award.

[210] • Marine Corps Scholarship Foundation Scholarship
Marine Corps Scholarship Foundation
909 North Washington Street, Suite 400, Alexandria, VA 22314
Phone: 703-549-0060
Email: Scholarship@mcsf.org
https://www.mcsf.org
Purpose: To provide financial assistance to sons and daughters of U.S. Marines and children of former Marines in their pursuit of higher education.
Eligibility: Applicants must be children or grandchildren of one of the following: an active duty or reserve U. S. Marine, a U.S. Marine who has received an Honorable Discharge, Medical Discharge or was killed while serving in the U.S. Marine Corps, an active duty or reserve U.S. Navy Corpsman who is serving, or has served, with the U.S. Marine Corps, U.S. Navy Chaplain or Religious Programs Specialist who is/was attached to a U.S. Marine Corps unit or who was killed while serving with a U.S. Marine Corps unit or a U.S. Navy Corpsman who has served with the U.S. Marine Corps and has received an Honorable Discharge, Medical Discharge or was killed while serving in the U.S. Navy. Applicants can also be grandchildren of one of the following: A U.S. Marine who served with the 4th Marine Division during World War II and is/was a member of their association, a U.S. Marine who served with the 6th Marine Division during World War II and is/was a member of their association or a U.S. Marine who served in the 531 Gray Ghost Squadron and is/was a member of their association. Applicants must be either high school graduates or undergraduate students. There is a family income limit.
Target applicant(s): High school students. College students. Adult students.
Minimum GPA: 2.0
Amount: Up to $10,000.
Number of awards: Varies.
Scholarship may be renewable.
Deadline: March 1.
How to apply: Applications are available online.
Exclusive: Visit www.UltimateScholarshipBook.com and enter code MA21026 for updates on this award.

[211] • Markley Scholarship
National Association for Campus Activities
13 Harbison Way, Columbia, SC 29212
Phone: 803-732-6222
Email: info@naca.org
https://www.naca.org/resources/scholarships-grants/scholarships.html
Purpose: To support undergraduate and graduate students who have made exceptional contributions in the field of student activities. The focus is on involvement with NACA Central, along with contributions to other activities-based organizations.
Eligibility: Applicants must attend a college/university in the former NACA South Central Region (AR, LA, NM, OK, TX); must be enrolled as juniors, seniors or graduate students at a four-year institution or as sophomores at a two-year institution and must have a minimum 2.5 GPA.
Target applicant(s): College students. Graduate school students. Adult students.
Minimum GPA: 2.5
Amount: $500.
Number of awards: Up to 2.
Deadline: November 30.

How to apply: Applications are available online. Only electronic applications and supporting documents submitted through the online scholarship application will be accepted.
Exclusive: Visit www.UltimateScholarshipBook.com and enter code NA21126 for updates on this award.

[212] • Marsh Scholarship Fund
Eastern Surfing Association
P.O. Box 4736, Ocean City, MD 21843
Phone: 302-988-1953
Email: scholastics@surfesa.org
https://surfesa.org/scholarship/
Purpose: To assist Eastern Surfing Association (ESA) student surfers.
Eligibility: Applicants must be current ESA members. Transcripts, a recommendation letter, purpose letters and applications are required. The award is based on academics and citizenship, not athletic ability.
Target applicant(s): High school students. College students. Graduate school students. Adult students.
Amount: Varies.
Number of awards: Varies.
Deadline: July 1.
How to apply: Applications are available online and by email.
Exclusive: Visit www.UltimateScholarshipBook.com and enter code EA21226 for updates on this award.

[213] • Marshall Memorial Fellowship
German Marshall Fund of the United States
1744 R Street NW, Washington, DC 20009
Phone: 202-683-2650
Email: info@gmfus.org
https://www.gmfus.org/leadership-development/fellowships
Purpose: To provide fellowships for future community leaders to travel in Europe and to explore its societies, institutions and people.
Eligibility: Applicants must be nominated by a recognized leader in their communities or professional fields. They must be between 28 and 40 years of age and demonstrate achievement within their profession, civic involvement and leadership. They must be U.S. citizens or permanent residents or be permanent citizens of one of the 38 countries listed on the scholarship page. European applicants will visit the United States for their fellowship opportunities. Candidates should have little or no previous experience traveling through Europe. Fellows visit five or six cities and meet with policy makers, business professionals and other community leaders.
Target applicant(s): College students. Graduate school students. Adult students.
Amount: Varies.
Number of awards: 24 to 27.
Deadline: November 1.
How to apply: Applications are available online.
Exclusive: Visit www.UltimateScholarshipBook.com and enter code GE21326 for updates on this award.

[214] • Marshall Scholar
Marshall Aid Commemoration Commission
Email: info@marshallscholarship.org
http://www.marshallscholarship.org
Purpose: Established in 1953 and financed by the British government, the scholarships are designed to bring academically distinguished Americans to study in the United Kingdom to increase understanding and appreciation of the British society and academic values.
Eligibility: Applicants must be U.S. citizens who expect to earn a degree from an accredited four-year college or university in the U.K. with a minimum 3.7 GPA. Students may apply in one of eight regions in the U.S.
Target applicant(s): College students. Graduate school students. Adult students.
Minimum GPA: 3.7
Amount: Varies.
Number of awards: Up to 40.
Deadline: September 26.
How to apply: Contact your regional center at the address listed on the website.
Exclusive: Visit www.UltimateScholarshipBook.com and enter code MA21426 for updates on this award.

[215] • Mary Church Terrell Award
National Association of Blacks in Criminal Justice
1801 Fayetteville Street, 106 Whiting Criminal Justice Building, P.O. Box 20011-C, Durham, NC 27707
Phone: 919-683-1801
Email: Office@NABCJ.org
https://nabcj.org/
Purpose: To reward activism for positive change in criminal justice on city and state levels.
Eligibility: The nominator should be a member of NABCJ. This award is given to an individual who has initiated relationships with churches, courts, councils and assemblies.
Target applicant(s): High school students. College students. Adult students.
Amount: Varies.
Number of awards: Varies.
Deadline: March 15.
How to apply: Nomination applications are available online.
Exclusive: Visit www.UltimateScholarshipBook.com and enter code NA21526 for updates on this award.

[216] • Mary Paolozzi Member's Scholarship
Navy Wives Clubs of America (NWCA)
P.O. Box 54022, NSA Mid-South, Millington, TN 38053-6022
Phone: 866-511-6922
Email: scholarships@navywivesclubsofamerica.org
https://navywivesclubsofamerica.org
Purpose: To aid students who are members of the Navy Wives Clubs of America (NWCA).
Eligibility: Applicants must have been accepted into a college no later than the application due date. Selection is based on academic merit and financial need.
Target applicant(s): High school students. College students. Graduate school students. Adult students.
Amount: $1,000 to $1,500.
Number of awards: 1.
Deadline: March 31.
How to apply: Applications are available online. An application form, official transcript and tax form copies are required.
Exclusive: Visit www.UltimateScholarshipBook.com and enter code NA21626 for updates on this award.

[217] • Mason Lighthouse Scholarship
Home Education Recognition Organization Inc. (HERO)
820 North Fig Tree Lane, Plantation, FL 33317
Email: help@heroscholarship.org
https://www.heroscholarship.org/
Purpose: To support homeschooled students interested in community service.
Eligibility: Applicants must be graduating high school seniors who have been homeschooled for the last four years of high school. Students must graduate and begin an educational program in a trade school, college or university or enter a missions program. Selection will be based on the application, service experience, references, homeschool transcript and autobiography.
Target applicant(s): High school students.
Amount: $1,000.
Number of awards: 1.
Deadline: March 1.
How to apply: Applications are available online.
Exclusive: Visit www.UltimateScholarshipBook.com and enter code HO21726 for updates on this award.

[218] • Medgar Evers Award
National Association of Blacks in Criminal Justice
1801 Fayetteville Street, 106 Whiting Criminal Justice Building, P.O. Box 20011-C, Durham, NC 27707
Phone: 919-683-1801
Email: Office@NABCJ.org
https://nabcj.org/
Purpose: To reward efforts to ensure that all people, including those in institutions, receive equal justice under the law.
Eligibility: This award honors the slain civil rights leader. The nominator should be a member of NABCJ.
Target applicant(s): College students. Graduate school students. Adult students.
Amount: Varies.
Number of awards: 1.
Deadline: March 15.
How to apply: Nomination applications are available online.
Exclusive: Visit www.UltimateScholarshipBook.com and enter code NA21826 for updates on this award.

[219] • Memorial Fund Scholarships
U.S. Figure Skating
20 First Street, Colorado Springs, CO 80906
Phone: 719-635-5200
Email: info@usfigureskating.org
https://www.usfigureskating.org/skate/scholarships-and-funding
Purpose: To support students who have a continuing interest in figure skating.
Eligibility: Applicants must be pursuing a college degree, be a current member of U.S. Figure Skating, have competed at the sectional level, be participating in volunteer work in skating if no longer skating and have a 3.0 or higher GPA. Selection is based on financial need, academic success and continuing participation in competitive figure skating or U.S. Figure Skating.
Target applicant(s): High school students. College students. Adult students.
Minimum GPA: 3.0
Amount: Varies.
Number of awards: Varies.
Deadline: August 31.
How to apply: Applications are available online.
Exclusive: Visit www.UltimateScholarshipBook.com and enter code U.21926 for updates on this award.

[220] • Memorial Scholarship Fund
Third Marine Division Association
Patrick J. Conroy, Secretary MSF, P.O. Box 2296, Stow, OH 44224
Phone: 352-726-2767
Email: scholarship@caltrap.org
http://www.caltrap.com
Purpose: To assist veterans and their families.
Eligibility: Applicants must be the children of Marines (Corpsman or other) who served with the Third Marine Division or in support of the Division at any time and who have been members of the Third Marine Division Association for at least two years. Applicants must be 16-23 and unmarried dependents. Applicants must attend school in the U.S. or Canada. Applicants must have and maintain a minimum 2.5 GPA.
Target applicant(s): High school students. College students.
Minimum GPA: 2.5
Amount: Varies.
Number of awards: Varies.
Scholarship may be renewable.
Deadline: May 13.
How to apply: Applications are available by written request after September 1.
Exclusive: Visit www.UltimateScholarshipBook.com and enter code TH22026 for updates on this award.

[221] • Mensa Foundation Scholarship Program
Mensa Education and Research Foundation
1315 Brookside Drive, Hurst, TX 76053
Phone: 817-607-5577
Email: info@mensafoundation.org
http://www.mensafoundation.org
Purpose: To support students seeking higher education.
Eligibility: Applicants do not need to be members of Mensa. They must be enrolled in a degree program at an accredited U.S. college or university in the academic year after application. They must write an essay explaining career, academic or vocational goals.
Target applicant(s): High school students. College students. Adult students.
Amount: $2,500.
Number of awards: Varies.
Deadline: January 15.
How to apply: Applications are available online in September.
Exclusive: Visit www.UltimateScholarshipBook.com and enter code ME22126 for updates on this award.

[222] • Metro Youth Football Association Scholarship
Metro Youth Football Association
P.O. Box 2171, Cedar Rapids, IA 52406
Phone: 319-393-8696
Email: info@metroyouthfootball.com
http://www.metroyouthfootball.com/scholarship
Purpose: To aid college-bound Metro Youth Tackle Football participants.
Eligibility: Applicants must be graduating high school seniors. They must be current or former Metro Youth Tackle Football (MYTF) participants. They must be current high school football players who have a GPA of 2.5

The Ultimate Scholarship Book 2026
Scholarship Directory (General Awards)

or higher and have plans to pursue post-secondary education. Selection is based on good citizenship, character and leadership potential.
Target applicant(s): High school students.
Minimum GPA: 2.5
Amount: $1,000-$1,500.
Number of awards: 5.
Deadline: August 16.
How to apply: Applications are available online. An application form, essay and one recommendation letter are required.
Exclusive: Visit www.UltimateScholarshipBook.com and enter code ME22226 for updates on this award.

[223] • Mike and Gail Donley Spouse Scholarship
Air Force Association
1501 Lee Highway, Arlington, VA 22209
Phone: 800-727-3337
Email: lcross@afa.org
https://www.afa.org
Purpose: To aid U.S. Air Force spouses who wish to pursue undergraduate and graduate degrees.
Eligibility: Applicants must be the spouses of active duty members of the U.S. Air Force, Air National Guard or Air Force Reserve. They must be accepted or enrolled at an accredited college or university and have a minimum GPA of 3.5. Applicants who are themselves Air Force members or in ROTC are not eligible. Selection is based on the overall strength of the application.
Target applicant(s): High school students. College students. Graduate school students. Adult students.
Minimum GPA: 3.5
Amount: $2,500.
Number of awards: 14.
Deadline: April 30.
How to apply: Applications are available online. An application form, official transcript, personal essay, applicant photo, proof of college acceptance (rising freshmen only) and two letters of recommendation are required.
Exclusive: Visit www.UltimateScholarshipBook.com and enter code AI22326 for updates on this award.

[224] • Military Award Program (MAP)
Imagine America Foundation
12001 Sunrise Valley Drive, Suite 203, Reston, VA 20191
Phone: 571-267-3010
Email: Leed@imagine-america.org
https://www.imagine-america.org/students/scholarships-education/
Purpose: To help those who have served in the military with their education and make the transition from military to civilian life.
Eligibility: Applicants must be enrolling in a participating college and be active duty, reservists, honorably discharged or retired veterans of the U.S. military. They must be likely to enroll in and successfully complete their postsecondary education and may not be a previous recipient of any other Imagine America Foundation scholarships/awards. Applicants must also have financial need.
Target applicant(s): College students. Adult students.
Amount: $1,000.
Number of awards: Varies.
Deadline: Contact the sponsor to confirm the deadline.
How to apply: Applications are available online.
Exclusive: Visit www.UltimateScholarshipBook.com and enter code IM22426 for updates on this award.

[225] • Military Family Support Trust Scholarships
Military Family Support Trust
1010 American Eagle Boulevard, Box 400, Sun City Center, FL 33573
Phone: 813-634-4675
Email: president@mfst.us
https://www.milfamilysupport.org/marketing-services
Purpose: To provide financial assistance to children and grandchildren of military members E-5 and above and others who have served their country.
Eligibility: Applicants must be children or grandchildren of current or former military members, federal employees of GS-7 or higher equivalent officer grade, foreign services officers (FSO-8 and below) and honorably discharged or retired foreign military officers of Allied Nations living in the U.S. The applicant must be a high school senior who has been recommended by his or her principal, have financial need and demonstrate leadership skills. The minimum GPA required is 3.0. The award is renewable for four years.
Target applicant(s): High school students.
Minimum GPA: 3.0
Amount: $2,000-$12,000.
Number of awards: Varies.
Scholarship may be renewable.
Deadline: February 1.
How to apply: Applications are available online.
Exclusive: Visit www.UltimateScholarshipBook.com and enter code MI22526 for updates on this award.

[226] • Mometrix College Scholarship
Mometrix Test Preparation
3827 Phelan #179, Beaumont, TX 77707
Phone: 800-673-8175
https://www.mometrix.com/scholarships/
Purpose: To support graduating seniors or students already enrolled in an accredited college or university.
Eligibility: Applicants must submit a 2,000 character (about 400 words) or less essay based on their test preparation practices. First, second and third place prizes are awarded.
Target applicant(s): High school students. College students. Adult students.
Amount: Up to $1,000.
Number of awards: 3.
Deadline: May 24.
How to apply: Applications are available online.
Exclusive: Visit www.UltimateScholarshipBook.com and enter code MO22626 for updates on this award.

[227] • Montgomery GI Bill – Active Duty
Department of Veterans Affairs
Phone: 800-698-2411
https://www.va.gov/education/
Purpose: To provide educational benefits to veterans.
Eligibility: Applicants must have an Honorable Discharge and high school diploma and meet other service requirements. The bill provides up to 36 months of educational benefits to veterans for college, technical or vocational courses, correspondence courses, apprenticeship/job training or flight training, high-tech training, licensing and certification tests, entrepreneurship training and certain entrance examinations. In most cases the award must be used within 10 years of being discharged.
Target applicant(s): College students. Graduate school students. Adult students.
Amount: Varies.

Number of awards: Varies.
Deadline: Contact the sponsor to confirm the deadline.
How to apply: Applications are available online.
Exclusive: Visit www.UltimateScholarshipBook.com and enter code DE22726 for updates on this award.

[228] • Montgomery GI Bill - Selected Reserve
Department of Veterans Affairs
Phone: 800-698-2411
https://www.va.gov/education/
Purpose: To support members of the United States military Selected Reserve.
Eligibility: Applicants must have a six-year commitment to the Selected Reserve signed after June 30, 1985. The Selected Reserve includes the Army Reserve, Navy Reserve, Air Force Reserve, Marine Corps Reserve and Coast Guard Reserve and the Army National Guard and the Air National Guard. Applicants must have completed basic military training, meet the requirements to receive a high school diploma or equivalency certificate and may use the funds for degree programs, certificate or correspondence courses, cooperative training, independent study programs, apprenticeship/on-the-job training and vocational flight training programs.
Target applicant(s): High school students. College students. Graduate school students. Adult students.
Amount: Varies.
Number of awards: Varies.
Scholarship may be renewable.
Deadline: Contact the sponsor to confirm the deadline.
How to apply: Applications are available online.
Exclusive: Visit www.UltimateScholarshipBook.com and enter code DE22826 for updates on this award.

[229] • Montgomery GI Bill Tuition Assistance Top-Up
Department of Veterans Affairs
Phone: 800-698-2411
https://www.va.gov/education/
Purpose: To support students who are receiving tuition assistance from the military that doesn't cover the full cost of courses.
Eligibility: Applicants must be eligible for MGIB-Active Duty benefits, and they must have served on active duty in the United States military for at least two years.
Target applicant(s): College students. Graduate school students. Adult students.
Amount: Varies.
Number of awards: Varies.
Scholarship may be renewable.
Deadline: Contact the sponsor to confirm the deadline.
How to apply: Applications are available online. Contact your education services officer or education counselor for more information.
Exclusive: Visit www.UltimateScholarshipBook.com and enter code DE22926 for updates on this award.

[230] • Most Valuable Student Scholarships
Elks National Foundation Headquarters
2750 North Lakeview Avenue, Chicago, IL 60614
Phone: 773-755-4732
Email: scholarship@elks.org
https://www.elks.org/scholars/
Purpose: To support high school seniors who have demonstrated scholarship, leadership and financial need.
Eligibility: Applicants must be graduating high school seniors who are U.S. citizens and who plan to pursue a four-year degree on a full-time basis at a U.S. college or university. Male and female students compete separately.
Target applicant(s): High school students.
Amount: $1,000-$7,500.
Number of awards: Varies.
Scholarship may be renewable.
Deadline: November 12.
How to apply: Contact the scholarship chairman of your local Lodge or the Elks association of your state.
Exclusive: Visit www.UltimateScholarshipBook.com and enter code EL23026 for updates on this award.

[231] • NABF Scholarship Program
National Amateur Baseball Federation
Awards Committee Chairman, P.O. Box 705, Bowie, MD 20718
Phone: 301-464-5460
Email: nabf1914@aol.com
http://www.nabf.com/scholarships
Purpose: To support students who have been involved with the federation.
Eligibility: Applicants must be enrolled in an accredited college or university, must have participated in a federation event and must be sponsored by a member association. Selection is based on grades, financial need and previous awards.
Target applicant(s): High school students. College students. Adult students.
Amount: Varies.
Number of awards: Varies.
Deadline: Contact the sponsor to confirm the deadline.
How to apply: Applications are available online.
Exclusive: Visit www.UltimateScholarshipBook.com and enter code NA23126 for updates on this award.

[232] • NACOP Scholarship
National Association of Chiefs of Police
NACOP Scholarship Program, 6350 Horizon Drive, Titusville, FL 32780
Phone: 321-264-0911
Email: kimc@aphf.org
http://www.nacoponline.org
Purpose: To recognize law enforcement individuals.
Eligibility: Applicants must be disabled officers wishing to retrain through education or the collegebound children of a disabled officer. Students must maintain a 2.0 GPA and be enrolled in a minimum of six credit hours.
Target applicant(s): High school students. College students. Adult students.
Minimum GPA: 2.0
Amount: $500.
Number of awards: Varies.
Deadline: Varies.
How to apply: Applications are available by written request.
Exclusive: Visit www.UltimateScholarshipBook.com and enter code NA23226 for updates on this award.

[233] • NATA Scholarship

National Athletic Trainers' Association
National Athletic Trainer's Association Research and Education Foundation Inc., 2952 Stemmons Freeway, Dallas, TX 75247
Phone: 214-637-6282
Email: barbaran@nata.org
http://www.nata.org
Purpose: To encourage study among athletic trainers.
Eligibility: Applicants must be at least a junior in college and scholarships are available for undergraduate, master's and doctoral levels. Students must have a minimum 3.2 GPA and be sponsored by a certified athletic trainer and be a member of the NATA. There is an earlier deadline to start the application online.
Target applicant(s): College students. Graduate school students. Adult students.
Minimum GPA: 3.2
Amount: $2,300.
Number of awards: Varies.
Deadline: January 15.
How to apply: Applications are available online.
Exclusive: Visit www.UltimateScholarshipBook.com and enter code NA23326 for updates on this award.

[234] • National College Match Program

QuestBridge
120 Hawthorne Avenue, Suite 103, Palo Alto, CA 94301
Phone: 888-275-2054
Email: questions@questbridge.org
http://www.questbridge.org
Purpose: To connect outstanding low-income high school seniors with admission and full four-year scholarships to some of the nation's most selective colleges.
Eligibility: Applicants must have demonstrated academic excellence in the face of economic obstacles. Students of all races and ethnicities are encouraged to apply. Many past award recipients have been among the first generation in their families to attend college.
Target applicant(s): High school students.
Amount: Full tuition plus room and board.
Number of awards: Varies.
Scholarship may be renewable.
Deadline: September 26.
How to apply: Applications are available on the QuestBridge website in August of each year. An application form, two teacher recommendations, one counselor recommendation (Secondary School Report), a transcript and SAT and/or ACT score reports are required.
Exclusive: Visit www.UltimateScholarshipBook.com and enter code QU23426 for updates on this award.

[235] • National Intercollegiate Rodeo Foundation Scholarship

National Intercollegiate Rodeo Association
2033 Walla Walla Avenue, Walla Walla, WA 99362
Phone: 509-529-4402
Email: rodeo@collegerodeo.com
http://www.collegerodeo.com/
Purpose: To support student members of NIRA.
Eligibility: Applicants must be current college students, have at least a 3.0 GPA and be state financial assistance qualified or show evidence of financial need. Selection is based on academic achievement, financial need and the essay.
Target applicant(s): College students. Adult students.
Minimum GPA: 3.0
Amount: $1,500.
Number of awards: 1.
Deadline: May 19.
How to apply: Applications are available online and must be submitted with an official transcript, financial verification and at least one but no more than three letters of recommendation and an essay.
Exclusive: Visit www.UltimateScholarshipBook.com and enter code NA23526 for updates on this award.

[236] • National Marbles Tournament Scholarship

National Marbles Tournament
Matt Corley, 10908 Bornedale Drive, Hyattsville, MD 20783
Phone: 301-801-0795
Email: matt.corley@nationalmarblestournament.org
https://www.nationalmarblestournament.org/
Purpose: To assist "mibsters," or marble shooters.
Eligibility: Applicants must win first place in a local marble tournament and then compete in the National Marbles Tournament held each summer in New Jersey. Students must be between 7 and 14 years old.
Target applicant(s): Junior high students or younger. High school students.
Amount: Varies.
Number of awards: Varies.
Deadline: Contact the sponsor to confirm the deadline.
How to apply: Information on the tournament is available online.
Exclusive: Visit www.UltimateScholarshipBook.com and enter code NA23626 for updates on this award.

[237] • National Merit Scholarship Program and National Achievement Scholarship Program

National Merit Scholarship Corporation
1560 Sherman Avenue, Suite 200, Evanston, IL 60201-4897
Phone: 847-866-5100
https://www.nationalmerit.org
Purpose: To provide scholarships through a merit-based academic competition.
Eligibility: Applicants must be enrolled full-time in high school, progressing normally toward completion and planning to enter college no later than the fall following completion of high school, be U.S. citizens or permanent legal residents in the process of becoming U.S. citizens and take the PSAT/NMSQT no later than the 11th grade. Participation in the program is based on performance on the exam.
Target applicant(s): High school students.
Amount: $2,500.
Number of awards: Varies.
Scholarship may be renewable.
Deadline: October 11.
How to apply: Application is made by taking the PSAT/NMSQT test.
Exclusive: Visit www.UltimateScholarshipBook.com and enter code NA23726 for updates on this award.

[238] • National Oratorical Contest

American Legion
Attn.: Americanism and Children and Youth Division, P.O. Box 1055, Indianapolis, IN 46206
Phone: 317-630-1249
Email: acy@legion.org
http://www.legion.org
Purpose: To reward students for their knowledge of government and oral presentation skills.
Eligibility: Applicants must be high school students under the age of 20 who are U.S. citizens or legal residents. Students first give an oration within their state and winners compete at the national level. The oration must be related to the Constitution of the United States focusing on the duties and obligations citizens have to the government. It must be in English and be between eight and ten minutes. There is also an assigned topic which is posted on the website, and it should be between three and five minutes.
Target applicant(s): High school students.
Amount: $2,500-$25,000.
Number of awards: Varies.
Deadline: Contact the sponsor to confirm the deadline.
How to apply: Applications are available from your local American Legion post or state headquarters. Deadlines for local competitions are set by the local Posts.
Exclusive: Visit www.UltimateScholarshipBook.com and enter code AM23826 for updates on this award.

[239] • National Scholarship Program

National Scholastic Surfing Association
P.O. Box 495, Huntington Beach, CA 92648
Phone: 714-906-7423
Email: jaragon@nssa.org
http://www.nssa.org
Purpose: To assist NSSA members in their pursuit of post-high school education.
Eligibility: Applicants must be competitive student NSSA members and have a minimum 3.0 GPA in the current school year. Scholastic achievement, leadership, service, career goals and recommendations are considered.
Target applicant(s): High school students. College students. Adult students.
Minimum GPA: 3.0
Amount: Varies.
Number of awards: Varies.
Deadline: Contact the sponsor to confirm the deadline.
How to apply: Applications are available with organization membership.
Exclusive: Visit www.UltimateScholarshipBook.com and enter code NA23926 for updates on this award.

[240] • National Sportsmanship Award

Interscholastic Equestrian Association
467 Main Street, Melrose, MA 02176
Phone: 877-743-3432
Email: info@rideiea.org
https://www.rideiea.org/opportunities/for-riders/
Purpose: To help riders pursue a college education.
Eligibility: Students must earn a Sportsmanship Award at a local, regional or zone IEA competition during the school year and maintain a 3.0 GPA. Selection is based on academic achievement, extracurricular involvement, equestrian participation and characteristics that portray good sportsmanship and a role model.
Target applicant(s): Junior high students or younger. High school students.
Minimum GPA: 3.0
Amount: Up to $500.
Number of awards: 8.
Deadline: May 6.
How to apply: Riders who have earned a Sportsmanship Award at a lower level will be given an application for the national award. The application includes a 250-word essay, personal resume, copy of official transcript and three letters of recommendation.
Exclusive: Visit www.UltimateScholarshipBook.com and enter code IN24026 for updates on this award.

[241] • National Table Tennis Scholarship

National College Table Tennis Association
154 Mill Run Lane, Saint Peters, MO 63376-7106
Phone: 800-581-6770
Email: info@nctta.org
http://nctta.org/scholarship/
Purpose: To support table tennis athletes by providing financial support for their higher education expenses.
Eligibility: Applicants must be attending or plan on attending an active NCTTA school and plan on being active on the collegiate team. Students must be full time and have at least a 2.0 GPA. Selection is based on table tennis skill, academic achievement, financial need and a personal essay. The essay should explain your involvement and contributions to the sport of table tennis.
Target applicant(s): High school students. College students. Adult students.
Minimum GPA: 2.0
Amount: $800-$1,200.
Number of awards: Varies.
Deadline: May 15.
How to apply: Applications are available online and must include an official transcript.
Exclusive: Visit www.UltimateScholarshipBook.com and enter code NA24126 for updates on this award.

[242] • Naval Enlisted Reserve Association Scholarships

Naval Enlisted Reserve Association
6703 Farragut Avenue, Falls Church, VA 22042-2189
Phone: 800-776-9020
Email: members@nera.org
https://www.nera.org
Purpose: To recognize the service and sacrifices made by Navy, Marine and Coast Guard members, retirees and their families.
Eligibility: Applicants must be members of the Naval Enlisted Reserve Association in good standing or their spouses, children or grandchildren. Children and grandchildren of members must be single and under 23 years of age on the application deadline. Applicants must be graduating high school seniors or students who are already pursuing an undergraduate degree.
Target applicant(s): High school students. College students. Adult students.
Amount: $1,000-$2,000.
Number of awards: 5.
Deadline: July 19.
How to apply: Applications are available online.
Exclusive: Visit www.UltimateScholarshipBook.com and enter code NA24226 for updates on this award.

[243] • Naval Helicopter Association Scholarship
Naval Helicopter Association
P.O. Box 180578, Coronado, CA 92178-0578
Phone: 619-435-7139
Email: nhascholars@hotmail.com
http://www.nhascholarshipfund.org
Purpose: To assist those who wish to pursue educational goals.
Eligibility: Applicants must be members of or dependents of members of the association or have an affiliation with naval aviation. Students may pursue undergraduate degrees in any field.
Target applicant(s): High school students. College students. Adult students.
Amount: $2,000-$3,000.
Number of awards: Varies.
Deadline: January 31.
How to apply: Applications are available by mail.
Exclusive: Visit www.UltimateScholarshipBook.com and enter code NA24326 for updates on this award.

[244] • Naval Intelligence Essay Contest
United States Naval Institute (USNI)
291 Wood Road, Annapolis, MD 21402
Phone: 410-268-6110
Email: customer@usni.org
https://www.usni.org/essay-contests
Purpose: To promote sea services.
Eligibility: Applicants must be active duty military, reservists, veterans, government civilian personnel or civilians. Students must write an essay discussing the history of Naval Intelligence and how lessons from the past can be applied to today.
Target applicant(s): College students. Adult students.
Amount: $1,500-$5,000.
Number of awards: 3.
Deadline: July 31.
How to apply: Applications are available online.
Exclusive: Visit www.UltimateScholarshipBook.com and enter code UN24426 for updates on this award.

[245] • Navin Narayan College Scholarship
American Red Cross Youth
2025 E Street NW, Washington, DC 20006
Phone: 202-303-4498
Email: syyin.nyc@gmail.com
https://www.redcross.org/red-cross-youth/opportunities/scholarships-and-awards/navin-narayan-college-scholarship.html
Purpose: The scholarship is named after Navin Narayan, a former youth volunteer with the Red Cross who died from cancer at the age of 23. In his honor, the Red Cross awards this scholarship to youth volunteers who have made significant humanitarian contributions to the organization and who have also achieved academic excellence in high school.
Eligibility: Applicants must plan to attend a four-year college or university and have volunteered a minimum of two years with the Red Cross.
Target applicant(s): High school students.
Amount: $1,000.
Number of awards: 1.
Deadline: March 27.
How to apply: Application forms are available online.
Exclusive: Visit www.UltimateScholarshipBook.com and enter code AM24526 for updates on this award.

[246] • Navy College Fund
U.S. Navy Personnel
5720 Integrity Drive, Millington, TN 38055
Phone: 866-827-5672
Email: bupers_webmaster@navy.mil
https://www.navy.com/
Purpose: To encourage entry into the Navy for recruits who have skills and specialties for which there is a critical shortage.
Eligibility: Applicants must be Navy recruits who are qualified for training in selected Navy ratings as non-prior service enlistees and agree to serve on active duty for at least three years. They must have graduated from high school, be 17 to 35 years old, agree to a pay reduction and receive an "Honorable" Character of Service.
Target applicant(s): High school students. College students. Adult students.
Amount: Varies.
Number of awards: Varies.
Scholarship may be renewable.
Deadline: Contact the sponsor to confirm the deadline.
How to apply: Applications are available from Navy recruiters.
Exclusive: Visit www.UltimateScholarshipBook.com and enter code U.24626 for updates on this award.

[247] • Navy Supply Corps Foundation Scholarship
Navy Supply Corps Foundation Inc.
2061 Experiment Station Road, Suite 301, PMB 423, Watkinsville, GA 30677
Phone: 706-354-4111
Email: foundation@usnscf.com
https://www.usnscf.com
Purpose: To provide financial aid for undergraduate studies to spouses and children of Navy Supply Corps Officers and supply enlisted rating.
Eligibility: Applicants must be a spouse, child or grandchild of a living or deceased regular, retired, reserve or prior service Navy Supply Corps officer or a spouse or child of an Active or Retired (Navy) Enlisted with supply enlisted rating (e.g., AK, SK, MS/CS, SH, DK, LI, PC, LS). Awards are based on character, leadership, academic performance, hardship and financial need.
Target applicant(s): High school students. College students. Adult students.
Amount: Up to $10,000.
Number of awards: Varies.
Deadline: March 15.
How to apply: Applications are available online.
Exclusive: Visit www.UltimateScholarshipBook.com and enter code NA24726 for updates on this award.

[248] • Navy-Marine Corps ROTC College Program
U.S. Navy Naval Reserve Officers Training Corps (NROTC)
Naval Service Training Command Officer Development, NAS Great Lakes, 2601A Paul Jones Street, Great Lakes, IL 60088-2845
Phone: 800-628-7682
Email: grlk_nrotc.scholarship@navy.mil
https://www.netc.navy.mil/NSTC/NROTC/
Purpose: To provide education opportunities for NROTC students.
Eligibility: Applicants must be accepted to or attending a college with an NROTC program. They must complete naval science and other specified university courses and attend a summer training session. Scholarships are available for two or four years, depending on time of application.
Target applicant(s): College students. Adult students.

Amount: Up to full tuition plus stipend and allowance.
Number of awards: Varies.
Scholarship may be renewable.
Deadline: January 31.
How to apply: Applications are available online.
Exclusive: Visit www.UltimateScholarshipBook.com and enter code U.24826 for updates on this award.

[249] • Navy-Marine Corps ROTC Four-Year Scholarships

U.S. Navy Naval Reserve Officers Training Corps (NROTC)
Naval Service Training Command Officer Development, NAS Great Lakes, 2601A Paul Jones Street, Great Lakes, IL 60088-2845
Phone: 800-628-7682
Email: grlk_nrotc.scholarship@navy.mil
https://www.netc.navy.mil/NSTC/NROTC/
Purpose: To provide education opportunities for ROTC members.
Eligibility: Applicants must plan to attend an eligible college or university. They must commit to eight years of military service, four of which must be on active duty. The scholarship pays full tuition and fees plus a stipend for textbooks.
Target applicant(s): High school students.
Amount: Tuition plus stipend.
Number of awards: Varies.
Scholarship may be renewable.
Deadline: January 31.
How to apply: Applications are available online.
Exclusive: Visit www.UltimateScholarshipBook.com and enter code U.24926 for updates on this award.

[250] • Navy-Marine Corps ROTC Two-Year Scholarships

U.S. Navy Naval Reserve Officers Training Corps (NROTC)
Naval Service Training Command Officer Development, NAS Great Lakes, 2601A Paul Jones Street, Great Lakes, IL 60088-2845
Phone: 800-628-7682
Email: grlk_nrotc.scholarship@navy.mil
https://www.netc.navy.mil/NSTC/NROTC/
Purpose: To provide education opportunities for NROTC students.
Eligibility: Applicants must be attending a college with an NROTC program as a freshman or sophomore. They must complete naval science and other specified university courses and attend a summer training session. They must also attend a Naval Science Institute program during the summer between their sophomore and junior years.
Target applicant(s): College students. Adult students.
Amount: Varies.
Number of awards: Varies.
Scholarship may be renewable.
Deadline: January 31.
How to apply: Applications are available online.
Exclusive: Visit www.UltimateScholarshipBook.com and enter code U.25026 for updates on this award.

[251] • Navy/Marine Corps/Coast Guard (NMCCG) Enlisted Dependent Spouse Scholarship

Navy Wives Clubs of America (NWCA)
P.O. Box 54022, NSA Mid-South, Millington, TN 38053-6022
Phone: 866-511-6922
Email: scholarships@navywivesclubsofamerica.org
https://navywivesclubsofamerica.org
Purpose: To provide financial assistance to spouses of certain military members.
Eligibility: Applicants must be spouses of enlisted Navy, Marine Corps or Coast Guard personnel. They must be accepted to an institution of higher learning by May 30 of the year of application.
Target applicant(s): High school students. College students. Graduate school students. Adult students.
Amount: Varies.
Number of awards: 2.
Deadline: March 31.
How to apply: Applications are available online. Financial information and a transcript are required.
Exclusive: Visit www.UltimateScholarshipBook.com and enter code NA25126 for updates on this award.

[252] • NCAA Division II Degree Completion Award Program

National Collegiate Athletic Association
700 W. Washington Street, P.O. Box 6222, Indianapolis, IN 46206
Phone: 317-917-6222
Email: lthomas@ncaa.org
http://www.ncaa.org/about/resources/ncaa-scholarships-and-grants
Purpose: To assist student-athletes who are no longer eligible for athletics-based aid.
Eligibility: Applicants must have exhausted athletics eligibility at an NCAA Division II school within the past calendar year. They must be within their first 10 semesters or 15 quarters of full-time attendance and must have received athletics-related aid from the institution. Applicants must be within 32 semester or 48 quarter hours of earning their first undergraduate degree and have a GPA of 2.5 or higher.
Target applicant(s): High school students. College students. Adult students.
Minimum GPA: 2.5
Amount: $7,000.
Number of awards: Varies.
Deadline: February 15.
How to apply: Applications are available online.
Exclusive: Visit www.UltimateScholarshipBook.com and enter code NA25226 for updates on this award.

[253] • NCAA Postgraduate Scholarship

National Collegiate Athletic Association
700 W. Washington Street, P.O. Box 6222, Indianapolis, IN 46206
Phone: 317-917-6222
Email: lthomas@ncaa.org
http://www.ncaa.org/about/resources/ncaa-scholarships-and-grants
Purpose: To reward student athletes who excel academically and athletically and are at least in their final year of intercollegiate athletics competition.
Eligibility: Student athletes must show achievement in their last year of varsity-level intercollegiate athletics at an NCAA school. Applicants must be nominated by the faculty athletic representative or athletic director and

be enrolling as a full- or part-time graduate student. Students must also have a minimum 3.2 GPA.
Target applicant(s): College students. Adult students.
Minimum GPA: 3.2
Amount: $10,000.
Number of awards: Up to 126.
Deadline: January 10 (fall); March 21 (winter); May 23 (spring).
How to apply: Applications are available online.
Exclusive: Visit www.UltimateScholarshipBook.com and enter code NA25326 for updates on this award.

[254] • Newman Civic Fellow Awards
Campus Compact
89 South Street, Boston, MA 02111
Phone: 617-357-1881
Email: campus@compact.org
http://www.compact.org
Purpose: To provide scholarships and opportunities for civic mentoring to students with financial need.
Eligibility: Emphasis is on students who have demonstrated leadership abilities and significant interest in civic responsibility. Students must attend one of the 1,000 Campus Compact member institutions and be nominated by the Campus Compact member president. Applicants must be sophomores or juniors at four-year colleges or must attend a two-year college.
Target applicant(s): College students. Graduate school students. Adult students.
Amount: Varies.
Number of awards: Varies.
Deadline: March 1.
How to apply: Nominations must be made by the Campus Compact member president.
Exclusive: Visit www.UltimateScholarshipBook.com and enter code CA25426 for updates on this award.

[255] • Next Gen Scholars Award
Navy Exchange
3280 Virginia Beach Boulevard, Virginia Beach, VA 23452-5724
Phone: 800-628-3924
https://www.mynavyexchange.com/
Purpose: To assist children of active-duty Navy members in paying for their college educations.
Eligibility: Applicants must be full-time students in first through 12th grade who are dependents of active-duty military members, reservists or retirees and have a B or higher grade point average.
Target applicant(s): Junior high students or younger. High school students.
Minimum GPA: 3.0
Amount: $500-$2,500.
Number of awards: 4.
Deadline: May 31; August 31; November 30; February 28.
How to apply: Applications are available from the Navy Exchange.
Exclusive: Visit www.UltimateScholarshipBook.com and enter code NA25526 for updates on this award.

[256] • NFAA Scholarship Program
National Field Archery Association
800 Archery Lane, Yankton, SD 57078
Phone: 605-260-9279
Email: info@nfaausa.com
https://nfaausa.com/about/scholarship-opportunities
Purpose: To help those students who have participated in National Field Archery Association events continue their education beyond high school.
Eligibility: Applicants must be high school sophomores, juniors or seniors. Applicants must also be current members of NFAA or the NAA/USA Archery. Students must have a minimum GPA of 3.0. Selection is based on academic achievements, level of participation in NFAA and USAT rankings.
Target applicant(s): High school students.
Minimum GPA: 3.0
Amount: $1,000.
Number of awards: Varies.
Deadline: April 30.
How to apply: Applications are available online.
Exclusive: Visit www.UltimateScholarshipBook.com and enter code NA25626 for updates on this award.

[257] • Nicholas Virgilio Haiku and Senryu Contest
Haiku Society of America
NVHA Haiku Contest, c/o George Vallianos, 16 Sandringham Terrace, Cherry Hill, NJ 08003
http://www.hsa-haiku.org/hsa-contests.htm
Purpose: To reward students for excellent haiku poetry.
Eligibility: Applicants must be in grades 7 through 12. Students must submit up to three original, previously unpublished haiku. Selection is based on the overall strength of the submission.
Target applicant(s): Junior high students or younger. High school students.
Amount: $150-$250.
Number of awards: 6.
Deadline: February 15.
How to apply: Applications are available online.
Exclusive: Visit www.UltimateScholarshipBook.com and enter code HA25726 for updates on this award.

[258] • Non Commissioned Officers Association Scholarships
Non Commissioned Officers Association
9330 Corporate Drive, Suite 708, Selma, TX 78154
Phone: 800-662-2620
Email: tkish@ncoausa.org
http://www.ncoausa.org
Purpose: The scholarships are given to help the children and spouses of members of the Non Commissioned Officers Association.
Eligibility: Students must be children or spouses of members of the Non Commissioned Officers Association. Children must be under 25 to receive the scholarship.
Target applicant(s): High school students. College students. Adult students.
Amount: $900.
Number of awards: Varies.
Scholarship may be renewable.
Deadline: March 31.
How to apply: Applications are available online.

Exclusive: Visit www.UltimateScholarshipBook.com and enter code NO25826 for updates on this award.

[259] • NROTC Nurse Corps Scholarship

U.S. Navy Naval Reserve Officers Training Corps (NROTC)
Naval Service Training Command Officer Development, NAS Great Lakes, 2601A Paul Jones Street, Great Lakes, IL 60088-2845
Phone: 800-628-7682
Email: grlk_nrotc.scholarship@navy.mil
https://www.netc.navy.mil/NSTC/NROTC/
Purpose: To aid students who are planning to pursue nursing degrees at an NROTC college or university.
Eligibility: Applicants must be in the second semester of their junior year of high school. They must plan to attend an NROTC college or university that offers the bachelor's degree in nursing. They must be in the top 10 percent of their class or have a combined critical reading and math SAT score of 1080 or higher or have a combined English and math ACT score of 43 or higher. Selection is based on the overall strength of the application.
Target applicant(s): High school students.
Amount: Varies.
Number of awards: Varies.
Scholarship may be renewable.
Deadline: February 15.
How to apply: Applications are available online. An application form, official transcript, standardized test scores and three references are required.
Exclusive: Visit www.UltimateScholarshipBook.com and enter code U.25926 for updates on this award.

[260] • NROTC Scholarship Program

Naval Service Training Command Officer Development
NS Great Lakes, 2601A Paul Jones St, Great Lakes, IL 60088-2845
Phone: 800-NAV-ROTC
Email: grlk_nrotc.scholarship@navy.mil
http://www.nrotc.navy.mil
Purpose: To prepare young men and women for leadership roles in the Navy and Marine Corps.
Eligibility: Applicants must be U.S. citizens who are at least 17 years old as of September 1 of their first year of college, no older than 23 on June 30 of that first year and must be younger than 27 at the time of anticipated graduation. Students must attend an NROTC college and have no moral or personal convictions against military service. Those interested in the Navy program, including Nurse-option, must have an SAT critical reading score of 530 and a math score of 520 or an ACT score of 22 in English and 22 in math. For the Marine Corps option, students must have an SAT composite score of 1000 or an ACT composite score of 22. Applicants must also meet all Navy or Marine Corps physical standards.
Target applicant(s): High school students. College students.
Amount: Full tuition and fees, books, uniforms and monthly stipend.
Number of awards: Varies.
Scholarship may be renewable.
Deadline: February 15.
How to apply: Applications are available online. Contact information for regional offices is available online.
Exclusive: Visit www.UltimateScholarshipBook.com and enter code NA26026 for updates on this award.

[261] • NSCA Scholarship

National Sporting Clays Association
5931 Roft Road, San Antonio, TX 78253
Phone: 800-877-5338
http://nssa-nsca.org
Purpose: To aid high school senior sporting clay participants to reach their career goals by helping to fund their college expenses.
Eligibility: Applicants must be high school seniors, have at least a minimum 2.5 GPA, be NSCA participants and plan to attend a four-year degree program in college. Selection is based on scholarship, citizenship and NSCA participation.
Target applicant(s): High school students.
Minimum GPA: 2.5
Amount: $5,000.
Number of awards: 4.
Scholarship may be renewable.
Deadline: March 1.
How to apply: Applications are available online and must include an essay, one letter of recommendation, a transcript and a copy of shooting history and accomplishments.
Exclusive: Visit www.UltimateScholarshipBook.com and enter code NA26126 for updates on this award.

[262] • Odenza Marketing Group Scholarship

Odenza Vacations
4664 Lougheed Highway, Suite 230, Burnaby, BC V5C5T5
Phone: 877-297-2661
http://www.odenzascholarships.com
Purpose: To aid current and future college students who are between the ages of 16 and 25.
Eligibility: Applicants must be U.S. or Canadian citizens who have at least one full year of college study remaining. They must have a GPA of 2.5 or higher. Selection is based on the overall strength of the essays submitted.
Target applicant(s): High school students. College students. Graduate school students.
Minimum GPA: 2.5
Amount: $500.
Number of awards: Varies.
Deadline: November 15.
How to apply: Applications are available online. An application form and two essays are required.
Exclusive: Visit www.UltimateScholarshipBook.com and enter code OD26226 for updates on this award.

[263] • Oleg Fastovsky Outstanding Citizenship Scholarship

Maryland Criminal Defense Group
Oleg Fastovsky Attorney at Law, 5072 Dorsey Hall Drive, Suite 202B, Ellicott City, MD 21042
Phone: 410-650-4358
Email: info@mdcriminalattorney.net
https://mdcriminalattorney.net
Purpose: To help students pursue higher education.
Eligibility: Applicants must be enrolling in an accredited post-secondary program, including community college, undergraduate and graduate programs. Students must have a minimum GPA of 3.0 and submit an essay pertaining to the given prompt.
Target applicant(s): High school students. College students. Adult students.
Minimum GPA: 3.0
Amount: $1,000.
Number of awards: 1.
Deadline: September 30.
How to apply: Applications are available online.

The Ultimate Scholarship Book 2026
Scholarship Directory (General Awards)

Exclusive: Visit www.UltimateScholarshipBook.com and enter code MA26326 for updates on this award.

[264] • Pacific Academy Foundation Scholarship
Pacific Academy Foundation
4947 Alton Parkway, Irvine, CA 92604
Phone: 949-398-5288
Email: info@PacificAcademyFoundation.org
https://www.pacificacademyfoundation.org/get-sponsored
Purpose: To help students who exhibit talent in arts or sports.
Eligibility: Applicants must be between 7 and 24 years old and exhibit talent in arts or sports and a passion for excellence in their academic pursuits. Students must have received at least one award as a top-three finalist at the state or international level. Applicants must demonstrate financial need, as defined by their family's inability to support the applicant's talent without financial assistance or the family's income must not exceed 4x the poverty level and must provide the most recent tax return.
Target applicant(s): Junior high students or younger. High school students. College students. Graduate school students.
Amount: Up to $5,000.
Number of awards: Varies.
Deadline: March 31.
How to apply: Applications are available online.
Exclusive: Visit www.UltimateScholarshipBook.com and enter code PA26426 for updates on this award.

[265] • Paul and Daisy Soros Fellowships for New Americans
Paul and Daisy Soros
224 W. 57th Street, New York, NY 10019
Phone: 212-547-6926
Email: pdsoros_fellows@sorosny.org
http://www.pdsoros.org
Purpose: Named after Hungarian immigrants, the Paul and Daisy Soros Fellowships are designed to assist the graduate studies of immigrant children.
Eligibility: Applicants must be immigrants who are resident aliens, have been naturalized or are the children of two parents who have been naturalized. The potential winner of a fellowship must already have a bachelor's degree or be a college senior and must not be over the age of 30 by the application deadline.
Target applicant(s): College students. Graduate school students. Adult students.
Amount: Up to $90,000 over 2 years.
Number of awards: 30.
Scholarship may be renewable.
Deadline: October 26.
How to apply: Applications are available online and should be submitted online.
Exclusive: Visit www.UltimateScholarshipBook.com and enter code PA26526 for updates on this award.

[266] • Pauline Langkamp Memorial Scholarship
Navy Wives Clubs of America (NWCA)
P.O. Box 54022, NSA Mid-South, Millington, TN 38053-6022
Phone: 866-511-6922
Email: scholarships@navywivesclubsofamerica.org
https://navywivesclubsofamerica.org
Purpose: To aid college students who are the adult children of members of the Navy Wives Clubs of America (NWCA).
Eligibility: Applicants must be the child of an NWCA member. They must not be carrying a military ID card and must be enrolled or planning to enroll at an accredited postsecondary institution. High school seniors must have been accepted into a college or university no later than the application due date. Selection is based on academic merit and financial need.
Target applicant(s): High school students. College students. Adult students.
Amount: $1,000 to $1,500.
Number of awards: 1.
Deadline: March 31.
How to apply: Applications are available online. An application form and an official transcript are required.
Exclusive: Visit www.UltimateScholarshipBook.com and enter code NA26626 for updates on this award.

[267] • Pedro Zamora Young Leaders Scholarship
National AIDS Memorial
870 Market Street, Suite 965, San Francisco, CA 94102
Phone: 415-765-0446
Email: mkennedy@aidsmemorial.org
https://www.aidsmemorial.org/
Purpose: To support students with a commitment to ending HIV/AIDS.
Eligibility: Applicants must complete the application with a personal statement and a written essay describing their service or leadership in the fight against HIV/AIDS. Students must provide a letter of recommendation and transcripts demonstrating a minimum grade point average of 2.5.
Target applicant(s): High school students. College students. Adult students.
Minimum GPA: 2.5
Amount: $5,000.
Number of awards: 10.
Deadline: July 16.
How to apply: Applications are available online.
Exclusive: Visit www.UltimateScholarshipBook.com and enter code NA26726 for updates on this award.

[268] • PGA WORKS John and Tamara Lundgren Scholars Program
PGA WORKS Golf Management University Scholarship Program
Scholarship America, One Scholarship Way, Saint Peter, MN 56082
Phone: 507-931-1682
Email: pgaworks@scholarshipamerica.org
https://learnmore.scholarsapply.org/pgaworks/
Purpose: To support students pursuing a PGA Golf Management University Program degree.
Eligibility: Applicants must be high school seniors, have graduated high school or be a current undergraduate level student. Students must attend a PGA Golf Management University listed on the sponsor's website and enroll in full-time undergraduate study. Applicants must be pursuing a PGA Golf Management University Program degree and plan to pursue a PGA of America membership.
Target applicant(s): High school students. College students. Adult students.
Amount: $8,000.
Number of awards: 11.
Deadline: February 6.

How to apply: Applications are available online.
Exclusive: Visit www.UltimateScholarshipBook.com and enter code PG26826 for updates on this award.

[269] • Pilot International Scholarship
Pilot International Foundation
102 Preston Court, Macon, GA 31210
Phone: 478-477-1208
Email: piffscholarships@pilothq.org
https://www.pilotinternational.org/grants-and-scholarships/
Purpose: To support students who are preparing for a career that focuses on caring for others.
Eligibility: Applicants must be an undergraduate student and pursuing a career that focuses on helping others.
Target applicant(s): College students. Adult students.
Amount: Up to $1,500.
Number of awards: Varies.
Scholarship may be renewable.
Deadline: March 14.
How to apply: Applications are available online.
Exclusive: Visit www.UltimateScholarshipBook.com and enter code PI26926 for updates on this award.

[270] • Pilot Pen G2 Overachievers Student Grant
Pilot Pen
3855 Regent Boulevard, Jacksonville, FL 32224
Phone: 904-645-9999
https://powertothepen.com/g2overachievers/
Purpose: To support students involved in community and public service.
Eligibility: Applicants must be ages 13 to 19 years old. Students must demonstrate exceptional academics and a dedication to serving others and must write an essay describing how they are working to help others outside of the classroom.
Target applicant(s): Junior high students or younger. High school students.
Amount: $15,000.
Number of awards: 1.
Deadline: December 15.
How to apply: Applications are available online.
Exclusive: Visit www.UltimateScholarshipBook.com and enter code PI27026 for updates on this award.

[271] • Play! Pokemon Scholarship
Pokemon Company International
601 108th Avenue N.E., Bellevue, WA 98004
http://www.pokemon.com/us/play-pokemon/about/
Purpose: To reward students who are successful at playing Pokemon.
Eligibility: Applicants must participate in the Pokemon Championship series and be a finalist.
Target applicant(s): Junior high students or younger. High school students. College students. Adult students.
Amount: Varies.
Number of awards: Varies.
Deadline: Monthly.
How to apply: Applications are in the form of entries into the Pokemon Championship series and Pokemon World Series.
Exclusive: Visit www.UltimateScholarshipBook.com and enter code PO27126 for updates on this award.

[272] • Pony Alumni Scholarship
Pony Baseball/Softball
1951 Pony Place, P.O. Box 225, Washington, PA 15301
Phone: 724-225-1060
Email: info@pony.org
http://www.pony.org
Purpose: To support those students who have played on a Pony League, Colt League and/or Palomino League team for at least two years as they continue their education beyond high school.
Eligibility: Applicants must have played on one of the leagues for at least two years prior to submitting the application. Applicants must be a senior in high school and submit the application prior to May 1 of their senior year.
Target applicant(s): High school students.
Amount: Varies.
Number of awards: 8.
Deadline: May 1.
How to apply: Applications are available online. The application consists of the application form as well as sending in a school and community activities form, an essay on the supplied topic, a secondary school transcript, test results from the ACT, SAT or TOEFL, a copy of a letter of acceptance to the college, a notarized letter confirming participation in an affiliated league and two letters of recommendation.
Exclusive: Visit www.UltimateScholarshipBook.com and enter code PO27226 for updates on this award.

[273] • Project Yellow Light/Hunter Garner Scholarship
Project Yellow Light
Hunter Garner Scholarship, One Shockoe Plaza, Richmond, VA 23219-4132
Phone: 804-698-8203
Email: julie.garner@martinagency.com
http://www.projectyellowlight.com
Purpose: To encourage students interested in safe driving.
Eligibility: Applicants must be high school juniors or seniors between the ages of 14 and 20 or full-time undergraduate college students between the ages of 15 and 25. Students must submit a video ad, design for a billboard ad or radio spot to encourage safe driving.
Target applicant(s): High school students. College students.
Amount: Up to $8,000.
Number of awards: 6.
Deadline: March 1 (Billboard) or April 1 (Radio and Video).
How to apply: Applications are available online.
Exclusive: Visit www.UltimateScholarshipBook.com and enter code PR27326 for updates on this award.

[274] • Prudential Emerging Visionaries
Prudential Financial and Ashoka
Prudential Financial Inc., 751 Broad Street, Newark, NJ 07102
Phone: 973-802-4568
Email: EmergingVisionaries@ashoka.org
https://www.prudential.com/links/about/emergingvisionaries

Purpose: To support young people for their innovative solutions to financial and societal challenges facing their communities.
Eligibility: Applicants must be individuals between the ages of 14-18 and a legal resident of the U.S. or Puerto Rico. Participants must have started a project to solve a financial or societal challenge in their community before June 1 of the application year.
Target applicant(s): Junior high students or younger. High school students.
Amount: Up to $15,000.
Number of awards: 25.
Deadline: November 2.
How to apply: Applications are available online.
Exclusive: Visit www.UltimateScholarshipBook.com and enter code PR27426 for updates on this award.

[275] • Pulse of Perseverance Scholarship
Pulse of Perseverance
, Chicago, IL
Email: help@pulseofp3.org
https://www.pulseofp3.org/scholarship-info-and-winner
Purpose: To support students who are making a difference in their community.
Eligibility: Applicants must read the book, "Pulse of Perseverance: Three Black Doctors on Their Journey to Success" and submit a 250-word essay focusing on how they are making a difference in their community and why they believe they have the pulse of perseverance. Students must provide proof of current enrollment and submit a short video on why they possess the pulse of perseverance and what the scholarship will mean to them.
Target applicant(s): Junior high students or younger. High school students. College students. Adult students.
Amount: $1,000.
Number of awards: Varies.
Deadline: First of every month.
How to apply: Applications are available online.
Exclusive: Visit www.UltimateScholarshipBook.com and enter code PU27526 for updates on this award.

[276] • Race Entry Student Scholarship
Race Entry LLC
105 S State Street #617, Orem, UT 84058
Phone: 801-851-5520
https://www.raceentry.com/race-to-inspire-scholarship
Purpose: To support runners in pursuing post-secondary education.
Eligibility: Applicants must be enrolled at an accredited U.S. educational institution in the fall of the year in which the award is granted. Students must submit an essay explaining what inspires them to run. Selection is based on the overall strength of the submission.
Target applicant(s): High school students. College students. Adult students.
Amount: $500.
Number of awards: 1.
Deadline: August 15.
How to apply: Applications are available online.
Exclusive: Visit www.UltimateScholarshipBook.com and enter code RA27626 for updates on this award.

[277] • Rawhide Scholarship
National Intercollegiate Rodeo Association
2033 Walla Walla Avenue, Walla Walla, WA 99362
Phone: 509-529-4402
Email: rodeo@collegerodeo.com
http://www.collegerodeo.com/
Purpose: To aid students who exemplify the Rodeo Athletes on Wellness (Rawhide) principles.
Eligibility: Students must be current NIRA members, be college undergraduates and be academically eligible. Selection is based on the applicant's representation of the principles of positive choices, commitment to personal fitness, balance between rodeo and other commitments and having academic and career goals. Applicants should be involved in community service, have been in leadership roles and have a dedication to rodeo.
Target applicant(s): College students. Adult students.
Amount: $500.
Number of awards: Varies.
Deadline: May 19.
How to apply: Applications are available online.
Exclusive: Visit www.UltimateScholarshipBook.com and enter code NA27726 for updates on this award.

[278] • RealtyHop Scholarship
RealtyHop
355 Madison Avenue, 4th Floor, New York, NY 10017
https://www.realtyhop.com/resources/scholarship
Purpose: To support students who demonstrate ambition, diligence, leadership and an entrepreneurial spirit.
Eligibility: Applicants must be graduating high school seniors or currently enrolled undergraduates seeking a bachelor's or associate's degree. Students must submit their application including an essay via their school email address.
Target applicant(s): High school students. College students. Adult students.
Amount: $1,000.
Number of awards: 2.
Deadline: April 30 and August 31.
How to apply: Applications are available online.
Exclusive: Visit www.UltimateScholarshipBook.com and enter code RE27826 for updates on this award.

[279] • RentHop's College and University Scholarship
RentHop
32 West 40th Street, New York, NY 10018
Phone: 913-982-6682
Email: college-scholarship@renthrop.com
https://www.renthop.com/resources/college-scholarship
Purpose: To support undergraduate students who display ambition, diligence, leadership and an entrepreneurial spirit as they pursue their college education.
Eligibility: Applicants must be a graduating high school senior or an undergraduate pursuing a bachelor's or an associate's degree. Students will need to submit a 500-word essay on the topic provided.
Target applicant(s): High school students. College students. Adult students.
Amount: $1,000.
Number of awards: 2.
Deadline: April 30 and August 31.

How to apply: An application consists of the essay being emailed to RentHop via a school email address. If the applicant doesn't have a school email address, proof of enrollment will need to be provided.
Exclusive: Visit www.UltimateScholarshipBook.com and enter code RE27926 for updates on this award.

[280] • Return 2 College Scholarship
R2C Scholarship Program
Email: info@return2college.com
http://www.return2college.com/awardprogram.cfm
Purpose: To provide financial assistance for college and adult students with college or graduate school expenses.
Eligibility: Applicants must be college or adult students currently attending or planning to attend a two-year or four-year college or graduate school within the next 12 months. Students must be 17 years or older and U.S. citizens or permanent residents. The award may be used for full- or part-time study at either on-campus or online schools.
Target applicant(s): High school students. College students. Adult students.
Amount: $1,000.
Number of awards: 3.
Deadline: January 31, April 30, September 30.
How to apply: Applications are available online.
Exclusive: Visit www.UltimateScholarshipBook.com and enter code R228026 for updates on this award.

[281] • Rhodes Scholar
Rhodes Scholarship Trust
Attn.: Elliot F. Gerson, 8229 Boone Boulevard, Suite 240, Vienna, VA 22182
Phone: 703-821-5960
Email: amsec@rhodesscholar.org
http://www.rhodesscholar.org
Purpose: To recognize the qualities of young people who will contribute to the "world's fight."
Eligibility: Applicants must be U.S. citizens between the ages of 18 and 24 and have a bachelor's degree at the time of the award. The awards provide for two to three years of study at the University of Oxford including educational costs and other expenses. Selection is extremely competitive and is based on literary and scholastic achievements, athletic achievement and character.
Target applicant(s): College students.
Amount: Full tuition plus stipend.
Number of awards: 32.
Deadline: October 4.
How to apply: Applications are available online.
Exclusive: Visit www.UltimateScholarshipBook.com and enter code RH28126 for updates on this award.

[282] • Richard Avila Scholarship
USA Water Ski and Wake Sports Foundation
6039 Cypress Gardens Boulevard, Suite 481, Winter Haven, FL 33884
Phone: 863-324-2472
Email: info@waterskihalloffame.com
https://www.usa-wwf.org/ourscholarships
Purpose: To help current active members of USA Water Ski pursue their educational goals.
Eligibility: Applicants must be student athletes who preferably compete in National Water Ski Racing Association (NWSRA) events or athletes who demonstrate strong athletic abilities, strong academic standings and are involved in good community service projects in the Western region of USA-WSWS. Students must be U.S. citizens and be incoming freshmen, sophomores, juniors or seniors at a two-year or four-year accredited college and enrolled full-time. Applicants must be members of USA Water Ski and Wake Sports.
Target applicant(s): High school students. College students. Adult students.
Amount: $2,500.
Number of awards: 1.
Scholarship may be renewable.
Deadline: April 1.
How to apply: Applications are available online.
Exclusive: Visit www.UltimateScholarshipBook.com and enter code US28226 for updates on this award.

[283] • Roller Skating Foundation Scholarship, High School Student Category
Roller Skating Foundation
Attn.: Scholarship, 6905 Corporate Drive, Indianapolis, IN 46278
Phone: 317-347-2626
Email: foundation@rollerskating.com
https://www.rollerskating.com/scholarships.html
Purpose: To aid college-bound high school seniors.
Eligibility: Applicants must be high school seniors who plan to enroll at an accredited college or university in the fall following high school graduation. They must have a GPA of 3.4 or higher on a four-point scale and must be the child of an owner or employee of an RSA skating center or RSA affiliated member. They must have composite standardized test scores that are in the 85th percentile or higher. Selection is based on the overall strength of the application.
Target applicant(s): High school students.
Minimum GPA: 3.4
Amount: $1,000-$3,000.
Number of awards: 3.
Deadline: March 31.
How to apply: Applications are available online. An application form, transcript, personal essay, three recommendation letters and income tax information are required.
Exclusive: Visit www.UltimateScholarshipBook.com and enter code RO28326 for updates on this award.

[284] • Rosalind P. Walter College Scholarship
United States Tennis Association Foundation
70 W. Red Oak Lane, White Plains, NY 10604
Phone: 914-696-7223
Email: foundation@usta.com
http://www.ustafoundation.com/
Purpose: To support young tennis participants who believe in always putting forth a best effort and giving back to the community.
Eligibility: Applicants must be high school seniors who have participated in an organized youth tennis program. Selection is based on high academic achievement, good character and community involvement.
Target applicant(s): High school students.
Amount: $10,000.
Number of awards: 2.
Scholarship may be renewable.
Deadline: May 15.
How to apply: Applications are available online.
Exclusive: Visit www.UltimateScholarshipBook.com and enter code UN28426 for updates on this award.

[285] • Rover Sitter Scholarship
A Place for Rover Inc.
2101 4th Avenue #400, Seattle, WA 98121
https://www.rover.com/college-scholarship/
Purpose: To support students who are pet sitters.
Eligibility: Applicants must be residents of the United States at least 18 years of age and be existing pet care providers on Rover.com. Applicants must be graduating high school seniors with a minimum grade point average of 3.0 or current undergraduate or graduate students with a 3.0 or better grade point average.
Target applicant(s): High school students. College students. Graduate school students. Adult students.
Minimum GPA: 3.0
Amount: $2,500.
Number of awards: 1.
Deadline: May 1.
How to apply: Applications are available online.
Exclusive: Visit www.UltimateScholarshipBook.com and enter code A28526 for updates on this award.

[286] • Rubincam Youth Writing Competition
National Genealogical Society
3108 Columbia Pike Suite 300, Arlington, VA 22204
Phone: (703) 525-0050
http://www.ngsgenealogy.org
Purpose: To support students who are interested in genealogy.
Eligibility: Applicants must be high school students in grades 9 to 12 or middle school students in grades 6 to 8. This award is eligible worldwide.
Target applicant(s): Junior high students or younger. High school students.
Amount: $500.
Number of awards: 1.
Deadline: December 15.
How to apply: Applications are available online.
Exclusive: Visit www.UltimateScholarshipBook.com and enter code NA28626 for updates on this award.

[287] • Russel R. Taylor Foundation Scholarship
American Institute for Foreign Study
AIFS Abroad, 1 High Ridge Park, Stamford, CT 06905
Phone: 800-727-2437
Email: AIFSAbroad@aifs.com
https://www.aifsabroad.com/scholarships.asp
Purpose: To provide students with challenging educational programs in culturally diverse locations around the world.
Eligibility: Applicants must be study abroad students who have demonstrated academic excellence and who have significant financial need. Students must have a minimum 3.5 GPA and must send completed applications via email on or before the application deadline.
Target applicant(s): High school students. College students. Adult students.
Minimum GPA: 3.5
Amount: Varies.
Number of awards: 1.
Deadline: April 15 for fall; October 7 for spring.
How to apply: Applications are available online.
Exclusive: Visit www.UltimateScholarshipBook.com and enter code AM28726 for updates on this award.

[288] • Sallie Mae Bridging the Dream Scholarship
Sallie Mae Bridging the Dream Scholarship
https://www.salliemae.com/about/scholarship-opportunities/
Purpose: To assist students who belong to a diverse community.
Eligibility: Applicants must be currently enrolled as high school seniors and plan to attend college full-time at a two-year institution, four-year institution or vocational/technical certification program. Students must have a 2.75 minimum GPA, be U.S. citizens or legal permanent residents and be Pell Grant eligible. Students must be diverse candidates. Diverse includes but is not limited to gender, disability, race, ethnicity or belonging to an underserved community.
Target applicant(s): High school students.
Minimum GPA: 2.75
Amount: $2,500.
Number of awards: 260.
Deadline: June 28.
How to apply: Applications are available online.
Exclusive: Visit www.UltimateScholarshipBook.com and enter code SA28826 for updates on this award.

[289] • Samuel Huntington Public Service Award
Samuel Huntington Fund
Attn: Amy Stacy, National Grid, 40 Sylvan Road, Waltham, MA 02451
Phone: 508-389-2000
Email: amy.stacy@nationalgrid.com
https://www.samuelhuntingtonaward.org/
Purpose: To assist students who wish to perform one year of humanitarian service immediately upon graduation.
Eligibility: Applicants must be graduating college seniors, and must intend to perform one year of public service in the U.S. or abroad. The service may be individual work or through charitable, religious, educational, governmental or other public service organizations.
Target applicant(s): College students. Adult students.
Amount: Up to $30,000.
Number of awards: Varies.
Deadline: January 12.
How to apply: Applications are available online.
Exclusive: Visit www.UltimateScholarshipBook.com and enter code SA28926 for updates on this award.

[290] • Sandra Hancock Scholarship
Home Education Recognition Organization Inc. (HERO)
820 North Fig Tree Lane, Plantation, FL 33317
Email: help@heroscholarship.org
https://www.heroscholarship.org/
Purpose: To support homeschooled students with their pursuit of higher education.
Eligibility: Applicants must be graduating seniors who were homeschooled through four years of high school. This scholarship is given to the applicant whose bio in the H.E.R.O. scholarship application best exemplifies the benefits of home education.
Target applicant(s): High school students.
Amount: $500.
Number of awards: 1.
Deadline: March 1.
How to apply: Applications are available online.
Exclusive: Visit www.UltimateScholarshipBook.com and enter code HO29026 for updates on this award.

[291] • Sarah Josephine Langstaff Memorial Scholarship

Daughters of the British Empire in the USA
Email: scholarship@dbenational.org
https://www.dbenational.org/scholarship
Purpose: To support female students with British or Commonwealth of Nations ancestry.
Eligibility: Applicants must be female students, at least 18 years of age and residents of the United States with British or Commonwealth of Nations ancestry. Students must be currently enrolled full-time at an accredited two- or four-year college or university and have a minimum 3.0 GPA. An essay submission and transcript are required.
Target applicant(s): College students. Adult students.
Minimum GPA: 3.0
Amount: $500-$1,000.
Number of awards: Up to 12.
Deadline: November 1.
How to apply: Applications are available online.
Exclusive: Visit www.UltimateScholarshipBook.com and enter code DA29126 for updates on this award.

[292] • SASS Scholarship Foundation Scholarships

Single Action Shooting Society (SASS)
215 Cowboy Way, Edgewood, NM 87015
Phone: 505-843-1320
Email: misty@sassnet.com
http://www.sassscholarship.org/
Purpose: To support students who have participated in SASS by helping with higher education costs.
Eligibility: Applicants must be a high school senior or college undergraduate, have at least a 2.0 GPA and have been active in SASS for at least one year. Selection is based on academic achievement, leadership, character, extracurricular activities and commitment to cowboy action shooting.
Target applicant(s): High school students. College students. Adult students.
Minimum GPA: 2.0
Amount: $500-$3,000.
Number of awards: Varies.
Scholarship may be renewable.
Deadline: May 1.
How to apply: Applications are available online and must also include an official transcript, an essay on the provided topic, five letters of recommendation, a personal statement of goals and a photo of the applicant in full cowboy attire.
Exclusive: Visit www.UltimateScholarshipBook.com and enter code SI29226 for updates on this award.

[293] • Scholars Helping Collars Scholarship

Pet Lifestyle and You (P.L.A.Y.)
246 2nd Street, Unit A, San Francisco, CA 94105
Phone: 855-300-7529
https://www.petplay.com/pages/scholarship
Purpose: To reward graduating seniors with a passion for animal welfare.
Eligibility: Applicants must have a history of volunteer work to help animals in need. Students must submit an essay about how that volunteer work has impacted their lives and the importance of animal welfare. Selection is based on the overall strength of the submission.
Target applicant(s): High school students.
Amount: $200 up to $1,500.
Number of awards: 1.
Deadline: February 26.
How to apply: Applications are available online.
Exclusive: Visit www.UltimateScholarshipBook.com and enter code PE29326 for updates on this award.

[294] • Scholarship America Dream Award

Scholarship America Dream Award
One Scholarship Way, Saint Peter, MN 56082
Phone: 507-931-1682
Email: dreamaward@scholarshipamerica.org
https://learnmore.scholarsapply.org/dreamaward/
Purpose: To assist students in their second year or higher of post-secondary education.
Eligibility: Applicants must be U.S. citizens or permanent or legal residents who received a high school diploma from a U.S. school. Students must be planning to complete a minimum of one full year of post-secondary education and be planning to enroll as full-time undergraduates at the sophomore level or higher for the coming academic year. Applicants must have a grade point average of 3.0 or better.
Target applicant(s): College students. Adult students.
Minimum GPA: 3.0
Amount: $5,000-$15,000.
Number of awards: Varies.
Scholarship may be renewable.
Deadline: December 6.
How to apply: Applications are available online.
Exclusive: Visit www.UltimateScholarshipBook.com and enter code SC29426 for updates on this award.

[295] • Scholarships for Military Children

Defense Commissary Agency (DeCA)
1300 E Avenue, Fort Lee, VA 23801-1800
Phone: 804-734-8000
Email: militaryscholar@scholarshipmanagers.com
http://www.militaryscholar.org
Purpose: To provide educational opportunities for children of military personnel.
Eligibility: Applicants must be unmarried dependents under the age of 21 (23 if full-time students) of active duty, reserve, retired or deceased members of the military. They must be enrolled in the Defense Enrollment Eligibility Reporting System database. Applicants must be enrolled or plan to enroll in a full-time undergraduate degree-seeking program and have a minimum GPA of 3.0. Community or junior college students must be in a program that will allow transfer directly into a four-year program. Applicants also must not be accepted to a U.S. Military Academy or be the recipients of full scholarships at any accredited institution.
Target applicant(s): High school students. College students.
Minimum GPA: 3.0
Amount: $2,000.
Number of awards: 500.
Deadline: February 14.
How to apply: Applications are available online or from military commissaries.
Exclusive: Visit www.UltimateScholarshipBook.com and enter code DE29526 for updates on this award.

[296] • Scholarships for Student Leaders
National Association for Campus Activities
13 Harbison Way, Columbia, SC 29212
Phone: 803-732-6222
Email: info@naca.org
https://www.naca.org/resources/scholarships-grants/scholarships.html
Purpose: The NACA foundation is committed to developing professionals in the field of campus activities.
Eligibility: Applicants must be current undergraduate students who hold a significant campus leadership position, have made significant contributions to their campus communities and have demonstrated leadership skills and abilities.
Target applicant(s): College students. Adult students.
Amount: Varies.
Number of awards: Varies.
Deadline: November 30.
How to apply: Applications are available online.
Exclusive: Visit www.UltimateScholarshipBook.com and enter code NA29626 for updates on this award.

[297] • Scholastic Honors Team
U.S. Figure Skating
20 First Street, Colorado Springs, CO 80906
Phone: 719-635-5200
Email: info@usfigureskating.org
https://www.usfigureskating.org/skate/scholarships-and-funding
Purpose: To support high school U.S. Figure Skating members who are distinguished in both figure skating and high school academics.
Eligibility: Students must be current members of U.S. Figure Skating, entering the junior or senior year of high school, have at least a 3.4 minimum GPA and have competed in a U.S. Figure Skating qualifying competition. Selection is based on academic performance and honors, community and extracurricular involvement, skating achievements and the essay.
Target applicant(s): High school students.
Minimum GPA: 3.4
Amount: $2,500.
Number of awards: Varies.
Deadline: September 15.
How to apply: Applications are available online and must include a high school transcript, SAT/ACT results, photo and essay.
Exclusive: Visit www.UltimateScholarshipBook.com and enter code U.29726 for updates on this award.

[298] • Scott Hamilton Skaters Education Fund
U.S. Figure Skating
20 First Street, Colorado Springs, CO 80906
Phone: 719-635-5200
Email: info@usfigureskating.org
https://www.usfigureskating.org/skate/scholarships-and-funding
Purpose: To assist amateur and professional skaters seeking a college education.
Eligibility: Applicants must be a high school senior or college undergraduate and have competed in a U.S. Figure Skating qualifying competition. Synchronized skating is not eligible. Selection is based on academic success, honors, demonstrated leadership in extracurricular activities, work experience, goals and the essay.
Target applicant(s): High school students. College students. Adult students.
Amount: $4,000-$8,000.
Number of awards: Varies.
Deadline: February 17.
How to apply: Applications are available online and include an official transcript, competition documentation and an IRS 1040 tax form for the past two years.
Exclusive: Visit www.UltimateScholarshipBook.com and enter code U.29826 for updates on this award.

[299] • Seabee Memorial Scholarship
Seabee Memorial Scholarship Association
P.O. Box 391, Springfield, VA 22150
Phone: 703-690-7672
Email: smsa@seabee.org
http://www.seabee.org
Purpose: To provide scholarships for the children of Seabees, both past and present, active, reserve or retired.
Eligibility: Applicants must be sons, daughters, step-children or grandchildren of Regular, Reserve, Retired or deceased officers or enlisted members who have served or are now serving with the Naval Construction Force or Naval Civil Engineer Corps, or who have served but have been honorably discharged. Applicants must be a senior in high school or a high school graduate. Selection is based on scholastic record, citizenship, financial need and leadership. Scholarships are for undergraduate degree programs only.
Target applicant(s): High school students. College students. Adult students.
Amount: Varies.
Number of awards: Varies.
Deadline: April 15.
How to apply: Applications are available online or by written request.
Exclusive: Visit www.UltimateScholarshipBook.com and enter code SE29926 for updates on this award.

[300] • Shari Simon Greenberg Community Scholarship
Simon Youth Foundation
225 W. Washington Street, Indianapolis, IN 46204
Phone: 800-509-3676
Email: syf@simon.com
https://syf.org
Purpose: To assist promising students who live in communities with Simon properties.
Eligibility: Applicants must be high school seniors who plan to attend an accredited two- or four-year college, university or technical/vocational school full-time. Scholarships are awarded without regard to race, color, creed, religion, gender, disability or national origin, and recipients are selected on the basis of financial need, academic record, potential to succeed, participation in school and community activities, honors, work experience, a statement of career and educational goals and an outside appraisal. Awards are given at every Simon mall in the U.S.
Target applicant(s): High school students.
Amount: $1,500.
Number of awards: Varies.
Deadline: February 16.
How to apply: Applications are available online. Only the first 3,000 applications that the organization receives are considered.
Exclusive: Visit www.UltimateScholarshipBook.com and enter code SI30026 for updates on this award.

[301] • Sheryl A. Horak Memorial Scholarship
Explorers Learning for Life
1325 West Walnut Hill Lane, P.O. Box 152225, Irving, TX 75015-2225
Phone: 972-580-2433
Email: exploring@lflmail.org
http://www.exploring.org/scholarships/
Purpose: To support students who are pursuing careers in law enforcement.
Eligibility: Students must be in their senior year of high school, and they must be members of a Law Enforcement Explorer post. Applicants must submit three letters of recommendation and an essay.
Target applicant(s): High school students.
Amount: $1,000.
Number of awards: 1.
Deadline: March 31.
How to apply: Applications are available online.
Exclusive: Visit www.UltimateScholarshipBook.com and enter code EX30126 for updates on this award.

[302] • Sir Cyril Taylor Legacy Scholarship
American Institute for Foreign Study
AIFS Abroad, 1 High Ridge Park, Stamford, CT 06905
Phone: 800-727-2437
Email: AIFSAbroad@aifs.com
https://www.aifsabroad.com/scholarships.asp
Purpose: To provide students with challenging educational programs in culturally diverse locations around the world.
Eligibility: Applicants must be students who demonstrate high academic achievements and articulate their objectives in a required essay. Students must meet the minimum requirements for the program to which they are applying and have a minimum 3.0 GPA.
Target applicant(s): High school students. College students. Adult students.
Minimum GPA: 3.0
Amount: $1,000.
Number of awards: 1.
Deadline: April 15 for fall; October 7 for spring.
How to apply: Applications are available online.
Exclusive: Visit www.UltimateScholarshipBook.com and enter code AM30226 for updates on this award.

[303] • Sloane Stephens Doc and Glo Scholarship
Bold.org Sloane Stephens Doc & Glo Scholarship
133 Kearny, Suite 400, San Francisco, CA 94108
Email: contact@bold.org
https://bold.org/scholarships/sloane-stephens/
Purpose: To support students in paying for their education and following their dreams.
Eligibility: Applicants must be current high school seniors or undergraduate students. Students must have a minimum 2.5 GPA. An essay is required on a provided prompt.
Target applicant(s): High school students. College students. Adult students.
Minimum GPA: 2.5
Amount: Varies.
Number of awards: 6.
Deadline: Aug 2.
How to apply: Applications are available online.
Exclusive: Visit www.UltimateScholarshipBook.com and enter code BO30326 for updates on this award.

[304] • Sodexo Stephen J. Brady STOP Hunger Scholarship
Sodexo Foundation
9801 Washingtonian Boulevard, Gaithersburg, MD 20878
Phone: 800-763-3946
Email: stophunger@sodexofoundation.org
http://us.stop-hunger.org/home/grants.html
Purpose: To aid students who have been active in the movement to eradicate hunger.
Eligibility: Applicants must be U.S. citizens or permanent residents. They must be students in kindergarten through graduate school who are enrolled at an accredited U.S. institution. They must have been active in at least one unpaid volunteer effort to end hunger during the past 12 months. Sodexo employees and previous recipients of this award are ineligible. Selection is based on the overall strength of the application.
Target applicant(s): Junior high students or younger. High school students. College students. Graduate school students.
Amount: $7,500.
Number of awards: Varies.
Deadline: December 5.
How to apply: Applications are available online. An application form and supporting materials are required.
Exclusive: Visit www.UltimateScholarshipBook.com and enter code SO30426 for updates on this award.

[305] • Soliant's Sunrise Scholarship
Soliant Consulting
Phone: 800-528-0170
Email: scholarship@soliantconsulting.com
https://www.soliantconsulting.com/community-service/sunrise-scholarship/
Purpose: To reward students who understand how businesses can be both philanthropic and profitable.
Eligibility: Applicants must be incoming freshmen or current undergraduate students at an accredited two-year or four-year college or university in the United States. A minimum 3.0 GPA is required. Students will need to submit a 500-word essay on the provided topic.
Target applicant(s): High school students. College students. Adult students.
Minimum GPA: 3.0
Amount: $1,000.
Number of awards: 1.
Deadline: April 30.
How to apply: Applications are available online.
Exclusive: Visit www.UltimateScholarshipBook.com and enter code SO30526 for updates on this award.

[306] • Sons of Union Veterans of the Civil War Scholarships
Sons of Union Veterans of the Civil War
Executive Director David W. Demmy, Sr., 1 Lincoln Circle at Reservoir Park, Suite 240 (National Civil War Museum), Harrisburg, PA 17103-2411
Email: execdir@suvcw.org
http://www.suvcw.org
Purpose: To assist students connected with the Sons of Union Veterans of the Civil War in obtaining higher education.
Eligibility: Male applicants must be members or associates of the Sons of Union Veterans of the Civil War. Female applicants must be daughters or granddaughters of members or associates and must be current members

of the Women's Relief Corps, Ladies of the Grand Army of the Republic, Daughters of Union Veterans of the Civil War 1861-1865 or Auxiliary to the Sons of Union Veterans of the Civil War. All applicants must rank in the upper quarter of their graduating class, have a record of school and community service and provide three letters of recommendation.
Target applicant(s): High school students. College students. Adult students.
Amount: $2,500.
Number of awards: 2.
Deadline: March 31.
How to apply: Applications are available online.
Exclusive: Visit www.UltimateScholarshipBook.com and enter code SO30626 for updates on this award.

[307] • Southern Region/Elmer Stailing Scholarship
USA Water Ski and Wake Sports Foundation
6039 Cypress Gardens Boulevard, Suite 481, Winter Haven, FL 33884
Phone: 863-324-2472
Email: info@waterskihalloffame.com
https://www.usa-wwf.org/ourscholarships
Purpose: To support current active members of USA Water Ski in their educational goals.
Eligibility: Applicants must be U.S. citizens and be incoming freshmen, sophomores, juniors or seniors at an accredited two-year or four-year college. Applicants must continue to be enrolled full-time at their college during the year of receipt of the scholarship. Selection is based on the applicant's academic achievement, work record, need and school and community activities as well as their contributions to the sport of water skiing.
Target applicant(s): College students. Adult students.
Amount: $2,000.
Number of awards: 1.
Deadline: April 1.
How to apply: Applications are available online. An application form, 500-word essay and two recommendation letters are required.
Exclusive: Visit www.UltimateScholarshipBook.com and enter code US30726 for updates on this award.

[308] • Spirit of Giving Scholarship
Wine Country Gift Baskets
Phone: 800-394-0394
Email: scholarship@winecountrygiftbaskets.com
https://www.winecountrygiftbaskets.com/information/scholarship.asp
Purpose: To encourage acts of kindness, service and giving.
Eligibility: Applicants must be high school seniors or currently enrolled students in an accredited U.S. certificate program, college, trade school or university who will be attending the program in the following year. Students must submit an essay relating to giving and service to others.
Target applicant(s): High school students. College students. Adult students.
Amount: $1,000.
Number of awards: 3.
Deadline: July 31.
How to apply: Applications are available online.
Exclusive: Visit www.UltimateScholarshipBook.com and enter code WI30826 for updates on this award.

[309] • Stamps Scholars
Stamps Family Charitable Foundation Inc.
P.O. Box 98374, Atlanta, GA 30359-2074
Email: info@stampsfoundation.org
https://www.stampsfoundation.org/
Purpose: To support students pursuing higher education with their related expenses.
Eligibility: Applicants must be currently enrolled high school seniors, undergraduates or graduate students attending an accredited college or university. Selection is based on the overall strength of the application as well as the following: academic achievement, leadership ability, integrity, perseverance, extracurricular activities and community involvement.
Target applicant(s): High school students. College students. Graduate school students. Adult students.
Amount: Varies.
Number of awards: Varies.
Deadline: Contact the sponsor to confirm the deadline.
How to apply: Applications are available online. An application form, official transcripts and SAT and/or ACT scores are required.
Exclusive: Visit www.UltimateScholarshipBook.com and enter code ST30926 for updates on this award.

[310] • Steps For Change Scholarship
Wealth By Health Steps For Change Foundation
5419 Hollywood Boulevard, Suite B, Los Angeles, CA 90027
Phone: 888-996-9985
Email: scholarships@wealthbyhealth.org
https://www.wealthbyhealth.org/scholarship-programs
Purpose: To support students who have financial need or are from disadvantaged backgrounds and demonstrate their drive to succeed.
Eligibility: Applicants must be current high school seniors expecting to graduate and in the process of applying to, or having been accepted to, a college or university. Students must have a household income of less than $55,000 and a minimum 3.5 cumulative GPA. A one-minute video submission on a provided topic is required.
Target applicant(s): High school students.
Minimum GPA: 3.5
Amount: $2,000.
Number of awards: 3.
Deadline: May 3.
How to apply: Applications are available online.
Exclusive: Visit www.UltimateScholarshipBook.com and enter code WE31026 for updates on this award.

[311] • Stokes Educational Scholarship Program
National Security Agency (NSA)
Attn.: MB3, Stokes Program, 9800 Savage Road, Suite 6272, Ft. George G. Meade, MD 20755-6000
Phone: 301-688-6311
Email: help@intelligencecareers.gov
https://www.intelligencecareers.gov/nsa/students-and-internships
Purpose: To recruit those with skills useful to the NSA, especially minority high school students.
Eligibility: Students must be seniors at the time of application, be U.S. citizens, have a 3.0 GPA, have a minimum ACT score of 25 or a minimum SAT score of 1200 and demonstrate leadership skills. Applicants must be planning to major in computer science or computer/electrical engineering.
Target applicant(s): High school students.
Minimum GPA: 3.0
Amount: Up to $30,000.

Number of awards: Varies.
Scholarship may be renewable.
Deadline: October 31.
How to apply: Applications are available online.
Exclusive: Visit www.UltimateScholarshipBook.com and enter code NA31126 for updates on this award.

[312] • Stossel in the Classroom Essay Contest
Stossel in the Classroom
20 Rope Lane, Levittown, NY 11756
Phone: 516-731-3047
Email: RJSchimenz@stosselintheclassroom.org
https://stosselintheclassroom.org/student-contests/
Purpose: To support students who write about the benefits of hashtags, the betterment of life or liberty.
Eligibility: Applicants must be between the ages of 10-18 and reside in North America or Hawaii. An essay on a provided topic is required to be submitted. Essay submissions may be submitted by students, their parents or teachers.
Target applicant(s): Junior high students or younger. High school students.
Amount: Up to $2,500.
Number of awards: 51.
Deadline: March 22.
How to apply: Applications are available online.
Exclusive: Visit www.UltimateScholarshipBook.com and enter code ST31226 for updates on this award.

[313] • Stossel in the Classroom Video Contest
Stossel in the Classroom
20 Rope Lane, Levittown, NY 11756
Phone: 516-731-3047
Email: RJSchimenz@stosselintheclassroom.org
https://stosselintheclassroom.org/student-contests/
Purpose: To reward students who are interested in the benefits of hashtags, the betterment of life or liberty.
Eligibility: Applicants must be between the ages of 10-23 and reside in North America or Hawaii. A video submission on a provided topic is required. The video may be submitted by the students, their parents or teachers.
Target applicant(s): Junior high students or younger. High school students. College students.
Amount: Up to $2,500.
Number of awards: 16.
Deadline: March 22.
How to apply: Applications are available online.
Exclusive: Visit www.UltimateScholarshipBook.com and enter code ST31326 for updates on this award.

[314] • Stuck at Prom Scholarship
Henkel Consumer Adhesives
32150 Just Imagine Drive, Avon, OH 44011-1355
http://stuckatprom.com/
Purpose: To reward students for their creativity with duct tape.
Eligibility: Applicants must attend a high school prom as a couple in the spring wearing the most original attire that they make from duct tape. Both members of the couple do not have to attend the same school. Photographs of past winners are available on the website.
Target applicant(s): High school students.
Amount: $1,000-$15,000.
Number of awards: 13.
Deadline: June 5.
How to apply: Applications are available online. Contact information, release form and prom picture are required.
Exclusive: Visit www.UltimateScholarshipBook.com and enter code HE31426 for updates on this award.

[315] • Student Activist Awards
Freedom from Religion Foundation
P.O. Box 750, Madison, WI 53701
Phone: 608-256-8900
Email: info@ffrf.org
https://ffrf.org/outreach/awards
Purpose: To assist high school and college student activists.
Eligibility: Selection is based on activism for free thought or separation of church and state.
Target applicant(s): High school students. College students. Adult students.
Amount: $1,000.
Number of awards: Varies.
Deadline: Contact the sponsor to confirm the deadline.
How to apply: Contact the organization for more information.
Exclusive: Visit www.UltimateScholarshipBook.com and enter code FR31526 for updates on this award.

[316] • Student Paper Competition
American Criminal Justice Association
Interim National Office, 3211 Fitzgerald Dr, Montgomery, TX 77356
Phone: 402-414-2520
https://www.acjalae.com/scholarships.html
Purpose: To encourage scholarship in criminal justice students.
Eligibility: Applicants must be student members (undergraduate or graduate) of the American Criminal Justice Association-Lambda Alpha Epsilon and submit an original paper on criminology, law enforcement, juvenile justice, courts, corrections, prevention, planning and evaluation or career development and education in the field of criminal justice. Students may apply for membership along with their paper submission. Applicants should submit applications and three copies of the paper.
Target applicant(s): College students. Graduate school students. Adult students.
Amount: $100-$200.
Number of awards: 9.
Deadline: January 31.
How to apply: Applications are available by contacting the Executive Secretary.
Exclusive: Visit www.UltimateScholarshipBook.com and enter code AM31626 for updates on this award.

[317] • Student Video Contest
World of 7 Billion
2120 L Street NW, Suite 500, Washington, DC 20037
Phone: 800-767-1956
https://www.worldof7billion.org

The Ultimate Scholarship Book 2026
Scholarship Directory (General Awards)

Purpose: To support students who are interested in global challenges.
Eligibility: Applicants must be in grades 6-12 and students may be located anywhere in the world. Students must submit a 60-second video about human population growth and how it affects climate change, ocean health or rapid urbanization and at least one sustainable solution must be mentioned.
Target applicant(s): Junior high students or younger. High school students.
Amount: $300-$1,200.
Number of awards: 5.
Deadline: March 5.
How to apply: Applications are available online.
Exclusive: Visit www.UltimateScholarshipBook.com and enter code WO31726 for updates on this award.

[318] • Student View Scholarship
Student Insights
136 Justice Drive, Valencia, PA 16059
Phone: 724-612-3685
Email: jbecker@studentinsights.com
http://studentinsights.com
Purpose: To support graduating high school seniors regardless of academic achievement or need.
Eligibility: Applicants must complete an online survey and then they will be entered into a random drawing for an award.
Target applicant(s): High school students.
Amount: Up to $10,000.
Number of awards: 8.
Deadline: April 23.
How to apply: Applications are available online.
Exclusive: Visit www.UltimateScholarshipBook.com and enter code ST31826 for updates on this award.

[319] • StudentCam Competition
C-SPAN
Phone: 800-523-7586
Email: educate@c-span.org
http://www.studentcam.org
Purpose: To reward students interested in government and societal issues.
Eligibility: Applicants must be either middle school or high school students in the United States, U.S. territories or the District of Columbia. Students must follow rules for the documentary competition. Applicants' entries must reflect the current theme.
Target applicant(s): Junior high students or younger. High school students.
Amount: Varies.
Number of awards: 150.
Deadline: January 19.
How to apply: Applications are available online.
Exclusive: Visit www.UltimateScholarshipBook.com and enter code C-31926 for updates on this award.

[320] • Study.com College Scholarship for Homeschool Students
Study.com
100 View Street, Suite 202, Mountain View, CA 94041
https://study.com/resources/student-scholarships
Purpose: To support homeschool students who plan to pursue higher education.
Eligibility: Applicants must be homeschooled. Students must be enrolled (or accepted) in an accredited college or university within the United States and plan on continuing next year. Applicants must consent to provide a digital photograph of themselves and a quote for display on Study.com if the selection committee notified them as the award winner.
Target applicant(s): High school students. College students. Adult students.
Amount: $1,000.
Number of awards: 1.
Deadline: November 1.
How to apply: Applications are available online.
Exclusive: Visit www.UltimateScholarshipBook.com and enter code ST32026 for updates on this award.

[321] • Study.com Community College Student Scholarship
Study.com
100 View Street, Suite 202, Mountain View, CA 94041
https://study.com/resources/student-scholarships
Purpose: To support community college students.
Eligibility: Applicants must be students pursuing an associate's or bachelor's degree from a community college. Students must be enrolled (or accepted) in an accredited college or university within the United States and planning on continuing the next year.
Target applicant(s): College students. Adult students.
Amount: $1,000.
Number of awards: 1.
Deadline: November 1.
How to apply: Applications are available online.
Exclusive: Visit www.UltimateScholarshipBook.com and enter code ST32126 for updates on this award.

[322] • Study.com Online Graduate Degree Scholarship
Study.com
100 View Street, Suite 202, Mountain View, CA 94041
https://study.com/resources/student-scholarships
Purpose: To support graduate students who plan to pursue higher education online.
Eligibility: Applicants must be pursuing a master's degree in a distance learning program. Students must be enrolled (or accepted) in an accredited college or university within the United States and plan on continuing next year.
Target applicant(s): College students. Graduate school students. Adult students.
Amount: $1,000.
Number of awards: 1.
Deadline: November 1.
How to apply: Applications are available online.
Exclusive: Visit www.UltimateScholarshipBook.com and enter code ST32226 for updates on this award.

[323] • Study.com Online Undergraduate Degree Scholarship

Study.com
100 View Street, Suite 202, Mountain View, CA 94041
https://study.com/resources/student-scholarships
Purpose: To support students who plan to pursue higher education online.
Eligibility: Applicants must be attending an online undergraduate degree program in any field. Students must be enrolled (or accepted) in an accredited college or university within the United States and plan on continuing next year.
Target applicant(s): College students. Adult students.
Amount: $1,000.
Number of awards: 1.
Deadline: November 1.
How to apply: Applications are available online.
Exclusive: Visit www.UltimateScholarshipBook.com and enter code ST32326 for updates on this award.

[324] • Study.com Scholarship for Children of First Responders

Study.com
100 View Street, Suite 202, Mountain View, CA 94041
https://study.com/resources/student-scholarships
Purpose: To support the children of first responders who plan to pursue higher education.
Eligibility: Applicants must be children of first responders. Students must be enrolled (or accepted) in an accredited college or university within the United States and plan on continuing next year. Applicants must consent to provide a digital photograph of themselves and a quote for display on Study.com if the selection committee notified them as the award winner.
Target applicant(s): High school students. College students. Graduate school students. Adult students.
Amount: $1,000.
Number of awards: 1.
Deadline: November 1.
How to apply: Applications are available online.
Exclusive: Visit www.UltimateScholarshipBook.com and enter code ST32426 for updates on this award.

[325] • Study.com Scholarship for Military Members and Veterans

Study.com
100 View Street, Suite 202, Mountain View, CA 94041
https://study.com/resources/student-scholarships
Purpose: To support students who plan to pursue higher education.
Eligibility: Applicants must be current or former members of the United States military. Students must be enrolled (or accepted) in an accredited college or university within the United States and plan on continuing next year.
Target applicant(s): College students. Graduate school students. Adult students.
Amount: $1,000.
Number of awards: 1.
Deadline: November 1.
How to apply: Applications are available online.
Exclusive: Visit www.UltimateScholarshipBook.com and enter code ST32526 for updates on this award.

[326] • Study.com Scholarship for Military Spouses and Children

Study.com
100 View Street, Suite 202, Mountain View, CA 94041
https://study.com/resources/student-scholarships
Purpose: To support students who are military spouses or children.
Eligibility: Applicants must be spouses or children of a member of the U.S. military. Students must be enrolled (or accepted) in an accredited college or university within the United States and planning on continuing the next year.
Target applicant(s): College students. Graduate school students. Adult students.
Amount: $1,000.
Number of awards: 1.
Deadline: November 1.
How to apply: Applications are available online.
Exclusive: Visit www.UltimateScholarshipBook.com and enter code ST32626 for updates on this award.

[327] • Study.com Scholarship for Nontraditional Students

Study.com
100 View Street, Suite 202, Mountain View, CA 94041
https://study.com/resources/student-scholarships
Purpose: To support nontraditional students.
Eligibility: Applicants must be nontraditional students, accepted by or enrolled in a college or university within the United States and planning on continuing the next year. Students must have a minimum of 30 semester or 45 quarter hours to complete.
Target applicant(s): Adult students.
Amount: $1,000.
Number of awards: 1.
Deadline: November 1.
How to apply: Applications are available online.
Exclusive: Visit www.UltimateScholarshipBook.com and enter code ST32726 for updates on this award.

[328] • Study.com Scholarship for Transfer Students

Study.com
100 View Street, Suite 202, Mountain View, CA 94041
https://study.com/resources/student-scholarships
Purpose: To support transfer students.
Eligibility: Applicants must be enrolled (or accepted) in an accredited college or university within the United States and planning on continuing next year. Students must have a minimum of 30 semester hours or 44 quarter hours to complete.
Target applicant(s): College students. Adult students.
Amount: $1,000.
Number of awards: 1.
Deadline: May 31.
How to apply: Applications are available online.
Exclusive: Visit www.UltimateScholarshipBook.com and enter code ST32826 for updates on this award.

The Ultimate Scholarship Book 2026
Scholarship Directory (General Awards)

[329] • Subic Bay-Cubi Point Scholarship
Navy League Foundation
2300 Wilson Boulevard, Suite 200, Arlington, VA 22201-5424
Phone: 800-356-5760
Email: scholarships@navyleague.org
https://www.navyleague.org/programs/scholarships/
Purpose: To support students who are either dependents or direct descendants of a member of the U.S. Marine Corps, U.S. Navy or U.S.-Flag Merchant Marines or who are active members of the U.S. Naval Sea Cadet Corps.
Eligibility: Applicants must be enrolled at an accredited institution of higher education. Only dependents or direct descendants of a member of the U.S. Marine Corps, U.S. Navy or U.S.-Flag Merchant Marines or who are active members of the U.S. Naval Sea Cadet Corps are eligible to apply. Selection is based on the overall strength of the application.
Target applicant(s): High school students. College students. Adult students.
Amount: $10,000.
Number of awards: 2.
Deadline: March 15.
How to apply: Applications are available online.
Exclusive: Visit www.UltimateScholarshipBook.com and enter code NA32926 for updates on this award.

[330] • SuperCollege Scholarship
SuperCollege.com
Scholarship Dept. 673, 2713 Newlands Avenue, Belmont, CA 94002
Email: supercollege@supercollege.com
https://www.supercollege.com/scholarship/
Purpose: SuperCollege donates a percentage of the proceeds from the sales of its books to award scholarships to high school, college, graduate and adult students.
Eligibility: Applicants must be high school students, college undergraduates, graduate students or adult students residing in the U.S. and attending or planning to attend any accredited college or university within the next 12 months. The scholarship may be used to pay for tuition, books, room and board, computers or any education-related expenses.
Target applicant(s): High school students. College students. Adult students.
Amount: $1,000.
Number of awards: 12.
Deadline: Monthly.
How to apply: Applications are available online.
Exclusive: Visit www.UltimateScholarshipBook.com and enter code SU33026 for updates on this award.

[331] • Supplemental Education Grant (SEG)
Coast Guard Mutual Assistance (CGMA)
4200 Wilson Boulevard, Coast Guard Stop 7180, Arlington, VA 20598-7180
Phone: 202-493-6621
Email: CGMA@cgmahq.org
https://www.cgmahq.org/programs/education.html
Purpose: To encourage students who are pursuing education to prepare them for their future career.
Eligibility: Applicants must be Coast Guard members applying for themselves or their dependents. Students must be either enrolled in a college or university undergraduate or graduate program, pursuing a multi-course VoTech program approved by the Department of Veteran Affairs or Department of Education that would prepare them for their career, pursuing a GED or completing a correspondence course for a college, university or VoTech program.
Target applicant(s): College students. Adult students.
Amount: $750 per calendar year.
Number of awards: Varies.
Scholarship may be renewable.
Deadline: Contact the sponsor to confirm the deadline.
How to apply: Applications are available online.
Exclusive: Visit www.UltimateScholarshipBook.com and enter code CO33126 for updates on this award.

[332] • Sweet Karen Alumni Scholarship
Harness Horse Youth Foundation
16575 Carey Road, Westfield, IN 46074
Phone: 317-867-5877
Email: ellen@hhyf.org
http://www.hhyf.org
Purpose: To help students interested in harness horses with their higher education expenses.
Eligibility: Applicants must be at least a high school senior and be planning to enroll as a full-time student or enrolled as a full-time undergraduate student at their selected college, university or trade school. Students must have participated in a Harness Horse Youth Foundation program to include the following events: Harness Racing Youth League event, Family Weekend and/or Leadership Program from 1999 to present.
Target applicant(s): High school students. College students.
Amount: Up to $1,000.
Number of awards: Varies.
Deadline: June 1.
How to apply: Applications are available online. An application form, financial information and an essay are required.
Exclusive: Visit www.UltimateScholarshipBook.com and enter code HA33226 for updates on this award.

[333] • Tailhook Educational Foundation Scholarship
Tailhook Association
The Tailhook Educational Foundation, 9696 Businesspark Avenue, San Diego, CA 92131-1643
Phone: 800-269-8267
Email: thookassn@aol.com
https://www.tailhook.net/
Purpose: To assist the members of and the children of the members of the United States Navy carrier aviation.
Eligibility: Applicants must be high school graduates who are accepted at an undergraduate institution and are the natural or adopted children of current or former Naval Aviators, Naval Flight Officers or Naval Aircrewmen. Applicants may also be individuals or children of individuals who are serving or have served on board a U.S. Navy Aircraft Carrier in the ship's company or the air wing. Educational and extracurricular achievements, merit and citizenship will be considered.
Target applicant(s): High school students. College students. Adult students.
Amount: $3,500-$15,000.
Number of awards: Varies.
Deadline: March 1.
How to apply: Applications are available online.
Exclusive: Visit www.UltimateScholarshipBook.com and enter code TA33326 for updates on this award.

[334] • Tampa Bay Buccaneers Foundation Girls in Football Scholarship

Tampa Bay Buccaneers Foundation
Girls in Football Scholarship, Scholarship America, One Scholarship Way, Saint Peter, MN 56082
Phone: 507-931-1682
Email: buccaneersgirlsinfootball@scholarshipamerica.org
https://learnmore.scholarsapply.org/buccaneersgirlsinfootball/
Purpose: To support female high school seniors who participate in a form of football.
Eligibility: Applicants must be female high school seniors participating in a form of football (touch, flag, tackle, etc.) planning to enroll in full-time undergraduate study at an accredited four-year college or university. Students must have a minimum 3.0 GPA and plan to use their college education and experience to make an impact in the sports industry. An essay on a provided prompt is required to be submitted.
Target applicant(s): High school students.
Minimum GPA: 3.0
Amount: $5,000.
Number of awards: 4.
Deadline: April 19.
How to apply: Applications are available online.
Exclusive: Visit www.UltimateScholarshipBook.com and enter code TA33426 for updates on this award.

[335] • Tattoo Journal Ink Scholarship

Tattoo-Journal.com
Email: finaid@tatoojournal.com
https://tattoo-journal.com/tattoo-journal-ink-scholarship/
Purpose: To encourage students who have the drive and ambition to succeed.
Eligibility: Applicants must be enrolled as undergraduate or graduate students. A 1,000- to 1,500-word essay on a provided prompt is required.
Target applicant(s): College students. Graduate school students. Adult students.
Amount: $700-$1,800.
Number of awards: 3.
Deadline: September 30.
How to apply: Applications are available online.
Exclusive: Visit www.UltimateScholarshipBook.com and enter code TA33526 for updates on this award.

[336] • Technology Addiction Awareness Scholarship

Digital Responsibility
3101 Ocean Park Boulevard, Suite 100-485, Santa Monica, CA 90405
Email: mjefferson@digitalresponsibility.org
https://www.digitalresponsibility.org/scholarships
Purpose: To help students understand the negative effects of too much screen time.
Eligibility: Applicant must be a high school, college, graduate or home schooled student who is a U.S. citizen or legal resident. A 140-character message about technology addiction is required to apply. The top 10 applications will be selected as finalists; finalists will be asked to write a full length 500- to 1,000-word essay about technology addiction. Only online applications are accepted.
Target applicant(s): High school students. College students. Graduate school students. Adult students.
Amount: $1,000.
Number of awards: 1.
Deadline: January 30.
How to apply: Applications are available online.
Exclusive: Visit www.UltimateScholarshipBook.com and enter code DI33626 for updates on this award.

[337] • Telluride Association Summer Seminars (TASS)

Telluride Association
217 West Avenue, Ithaca, NY 14850
Phone: 607-273-5011
Email: tasp-queries@tellurideassociation.org
https://www.tellurideassociation.org/our-programs/high-school-students/
Purpose: Summer program to provide high school students with a college-level, intellectually enriching experience.
Eligibility: Applicants must be sophomores to high school juniors. The association seeks applicants from a variety of socio-economic backgrounds and provides for their tuition and room and board during summer programs in New York and Michigan. Students are invited to apply either by receiving a score on the PSAT/NMSQT that is usually in the top 1 percent or by nomination by a teacher or counselor.
Target applicant(s): High school students.
Amount: Summer program tuition and fees.
Number of awards: Varies.
Deadline: December 3.
How to apply: Applications are sent to nominated students.
Exclusive: Visit www.UltimateScholarshipBook.com and enter code TE33726 for updates on this award.

[338] • Thiel Fellowship Grant

Thiel Fellowship
https://thielfellowship.org/
Purpose: To support students who plan to pursue higher education.
Eligibility: Applicants must be young people who dropped out of school and want to build new things instead of sitting in a classroom. Students must be 22 years old or younger. Applicants must drop out to accept the fellowship once selected. The funds may be used to repay student loans.
Target applicant(s): College students. Graduate school students.
Amount: $100,000.
Number of awards: 20 and 30.
Deadline: Open.
How to apply: Applications are available online.
Exclusive: Visit www.UltimateScholarshipBook.com and enter code TH33826 for updates on this award.

[339] • Think For Yourself College Scholarship Essay Contest

Let Grow
228 Park Avenue South, Suite 77212, New York, NY 10003
Email: info@letgrow.org
https://letgrow.org/program/think-for-yourself-scholarship/
Purpose: To reward high school students who value free speech.
Eligibility: Applicants must be at least 13 years of age and legal residents of the United States. Students must be currently in middle or high school. An essay submission on a provided prompt is required.

Target applicant(s): Junior high students or younger. High school students.
Amount: Up to $8,000.
Number of awards: 4.
Deadline: April 30.
How to apply: Applications are available online.
Exclusive: Visit www.UltimateScholarshipBook.com and enter code LE33926 for updates on this award.

[340] • Tim Olson Memorial Scholarship

USA Water Ski and Wake Sports Foundation
6039 Cypress Gardens Boulevard, Suite 481, Winter Haven, FL 33884
Phone: 863-324-2472
Email: info@waterskihalloffame.com
https://www.usa-wwf.org/ourscholarships
Purpose: To aid current active members of USA Water Ski with the continuing pursuit of their educational goals.
Eligibility: Applicants must be U.S. citizens and be incoming freshmen, sophomores, juniors or seniors at a two-year or four-year accredited college and enrolled full-time. Students must remain enrolled full-time at their chosen college during the year of receipt of the scholarship. Applicants must be a member of USA Water Ski and Wake Sports. Selection is based on the applicant's academic achievement record, need, community and school activities and work record as well as their contributions to the sport of water skiing.
Target applicant(s): College students. Adult students.
Amount: $1,500.
Number of awards: 1.
Deadline: April 1.
How to apply: Applications are available online. An application form, two letters of recommendation and a 500-word essay are required.
Exclusive: Visit www.UltimateScholarshipBook.com and enter code US34026 for updates on this award.

[341] • Trapshooting Hall of Fame College Scholarships

Trapshooting Hall of Fame
P.O. Box 281, Vandalia, OH 45377
Phone: 937-660-5663
Email: SpartaStaff@TrapHOF.org
http://www.traphof.org/Hall-Info/Scholarship-Information/
Purpose: To support high school seniors who have participated in trapshooting.
Eligibility: Applicants must be high school seniors and members of the Amateur Trapshooting Association. Selection is based on an essay explaining the need for the scholarship, prior shooting experience and accomplishments.
Target applicant(s): High school students.
Amount: Up to $5,000.
Number of awards: 7.
Deadline: July 1.
How to apply: Applications are available online and must include the essay, one letter of recommendation and a listing of your shooting history and accomplishments.
Exclusive: Visit www.UltimateScholarshipBook.com and enter code TR34126 for updates on this award.

[342] • Truman Scholar

Truman Scholarship Foundation
712 Jackson Place NW, Washington, DC 20006
Phone: 202-395-4831
Email: office@truman.gov
http://www.truman.gov
Purpose: To provide college junior leaders who plan to pursue careers in government, non-profits, education or other public service with financial support for graduate study and leadership training.
Eligibility: Applicants must be juniors, attending an accredited U.S. college or university and be nominated by the institution. Students may not apply directly. Applicants must be U.S. citizens or U.S. nationals, complete an application and write a policy recommendation.
Target applicant(s): College students. Adult students.
Amount: Up to $30,000.
Number of awards: 55-65.
Deadline: February 6.
How to apply: See your school's Truman Faculty Representative or contact the foundation.
Exclusive: Visit www.UltimateScholarshipBook.com and enter code TR34226 for updates on this award.

[343] • Truth Change Maker Awards

Truth Initiative
900 G Street, NW, Washington, DC 20001
Phone: 202-454-5555
Email: vacosta@truthinitiative.org
https://www.thetruth.com/
Purpose: To encourage students advocating for change.
Eligibility: Applicants must be 13-25 years old, reside in the United States and attend a higher education institution or trade school.
Target applicant(s): High school students. College students. Graduate school students. Adult students.
Amount: Up to $5,000.
Number of awards: 5.
Deadline: February 1.
How to apply: Applications are available online.
Exclusive: Visit www.UltimateScholarshipBook.com and enter code TR34326 for updates on this award.

[344] • U.S. Bank Scholarship Program

U.S. Bank
c/o U.S. Bank Office of Corporate Citizenship, 1420 Kettner Boulevard, 7th Floor, San Diego, CA 92101
Phone: 800-242-1200
https://www.usbank.com/financialiq/manage-your-household/student-center/enter-to-win-the-student-union-scholarship.html
Purpose: To support graduating high school seniors who plan to attend college.
Eligibility: Applicants must be high school seniors who plan to attend or current college freshmen, sophomores or juniors attending full-time at an accredited two- or four-year college and be U.S. citizens or permanent residents. Recipients are selected through a random drawing.
Target applicant(s): High school students. College students. Adult students.
Amount: $20,000.
Number of awards: Varies.

Deadline: October 30.
How to apply: Applications are only available online.
Exclusive: Visit www.UltimateScholarshipBook.com and enter code U.34426 for updates on this award.

[345] • U.S. JCI Senate Scholarship Grants
US JCI Senate Foundation
387 Sunset, Lawton, OK 73507
Email: scholarship@usjcisenate.org
http://www.usjcisenate.org
Purpose: To support high school students who wish to further their education.
Eligibility: Applicants must be high school seniors and U.S. citizens who are graduating from a U.S. accredited high school or state approved home school or GED program. Winners must attend college full-time to receive funds. Applications are judged at the state level.
Target applicant(s): High school students.
Amount: $1,500.
Number of awards: Varies.
Deadline: January 17.
How to apply: Applications are available from your school's guidance office.
Exclusive: Visit www.UltimateScholarshipBook.com and enter code US34526 for updates on this award.

[346] • U.S. Western Digital STEM Scholarship
U.S. Western Digital STEM Scholarship
7900 International Drive, Suite 500, Minneapolis, MN 55425
Phone: 800-537-4180
Email: westerndigital-stem@scholarshipamerica.org
https://scholarshipamerica.org/students/browse-scholarships/
Purpose: To assist students who have demonstrated interest in the pursuit of a STEM degree.
Eligibility: Applicants must be current full-time undergraduate students attending a two-year community college in the United States. Students must be planning to transfer to full-time enrollment at an accredited four-year college or university in the U.S. Applicants must demonstrate financial need or hardship. Students must be pursuing a Bachelor of Science degree in the field of engineering, mathematics or science excluding agricultural, health and other life sciences. Applicants must have a minimum 2.7 GPA. Students who have received two Western Digital Scholarships in the past are ineligible.
Target applicant(s): College students. Adult students.
Minimum GPA: 2.7
Amount: $5,000.
Number of awards: Up to 55.
Scholarship may be renewable.
Deadline: April 1.
How to apply: Applications are available online.
Exclusive: Visit www.UltimateScholarshipBook.com and enter code U.34626 for updates on this award.

[347] • UDT-SEAL Scholarship
Naval Special Warfare Foundation
1619 D Street, Virginia Beach, VA 23459
Phone: 757-363-7490
Email: info@udtseal.org
https://www.navysealfoundation.org/
Purpose: To assist the dependents of UDT-SEAL Association members.
Eligibility: Students must be single dependents of a UDT-SEAL Association member who has served in or is serving in the U.S. Armed Forces and the Naval Special Warfare community. Members must have paid UDT-SEAL Association dues for the last four consecutive years. Selection is based on academic achievement, a written essay and extracurricular involvement.
Target applicant(s): High school students. College students.
Amount: Varies.
Number of awards: Varies.
Deadline: February 16.
How to apply: Applications are available by contacting the NWSF.
Exclusive: Visit www.UltimateScholarshipBook.com and enter code NA34726 for updates on this award.

[348] • Unboxing Your Life Video Scholarship
Sttark
2 Task Industrial Court, Greenville, SC 29607
Phone: 877-277-4682
Email: marketing@sttark.com
https://www.sttark.com/scholarship/labels-scholarship
Purpose: To reward young creatives and innovators.
Eligibility: Applicants must be U.S. high school seniors, undergraduates or graduate students. Students must provide proof of college acceptance or a current transcript. Applicants must create a five-minute unboxing video of their life that showcases their originality and unique personality.
Target applicant(s): High school students. College students. Graduate school students. Adult students.
Amount: $3,000.
Number of awards: 1.
Deadline: March 1.
How to apply: Applications are available online.
Exclusive: Visit www.UltimateScholarshipBook.com and enter code ST34826 for updates on this award.

[349] • Undergraduate Transfer Scholarship
Jack Kent Cooke Foundation Undergraduate Transfer Scholarship
44325 Woodridge Parkway, Lansdowne, VA 20176
Phone: 800-941-3300
Email: scholarships@jkcf.org
http://www.jkcf.org
Purpose: To help community college students transfer to and attend four-year universities.
Eligibility: Applicants must be a current student at an accredited U.S. community college or two-year institution with sophomore status by December 31 of the application year or a recent graduate. Students must plan to enroll full time in a baccalaureate program at an accredited college or university in the following fall and have a cumulative undergraduate grade point average of 3.5 or better on a 4.0 scale. Applicants must also demonstrate significant unmet financial need. Family income of up to $95,000 will be considered. However, the majority of scholarship recipients will be eligible to receive a Pell grant.
Target applicant(s): College students. Adult students.
Minimum GPA: 3.5
Amount: Up to $55,000.
Number of awards: About 85.
Scholarship may be renewable.
Deadline: January 9.
How to apply: Applications are available online.
Exclusive: Visit www.UltimateScholarshipBook.com and enter code JA34926 for updates on this award.

The Ultimate Scholarship Book 2026
Scholarship Directory (General Awards)

[350] • United Daughters of the Confederacy Scholarships
United Daughters of the Confederacy
328 North Boulevard, Richmond, VA 23220
Phone: 804-355-1636
Email: hqudc@rcn.com
http://www.hqudc.org
Purpose: To support the descendants of Confederates.
Eligibility: Applicants must be lineal descendants of Confederates or other eligible descendants and have a minimum 3.0 GPA.
Target applicant(s): High school students. College students. Graduate school students. Adult students.
Minimum GPA: 3.0
Amount: Varies.
Number of awards: Varies.
Scholarship may be renewable.
Deadline: April 15.
How to apply: Contact any Division Second Vice President as listed on the website.
Exclusive: Visit www.UltimateScholarshipBook.com and enter code UN35026 for updates on this award.

[351] • United States Hispanic Leadership Institute Denny's Hungry for Education
United States Hispanic Leadership Institute Denny's Hunger for Education
Email: hungryforeducation@dennys.com
https://www.dennyshungryforeducation.com/
Purpose: To support students who have ideas for fighting childhood hunger.
Eligibility: Applicants must be high school seniors or college students, be citizens of the United States or be living in the United States legally and have a 2.5 GPA. Students must write an essay as part of their application and have ideas on ending childhood hunger. Applicants may apply regardless or race or national origin.
Target applicant(s): High school students. College students. Adult students.
Minimum GPA: 2.5
Amount: Varies.
Number of awards: varies.
Deadline: December 11.
How to apply: Applications are available online.
Exclusive: Visit www.UltimateScholarshipBook.com and enter code UN35126 for updates on this award.

[352] • Urban Fellows Program
New York City Department of Personnel
1 Centre Street, Room 2425, New York, NY 10007
Phone: 212-386-0058
https://www.nyc.gov/site/dcas/employment/internship-and-fellowships-nyc-urban-fellows.page
Purpose: To support high-achieving students pursue government and public service.
Eligibility: Applicants must have received their bachelor's degree within the last two years. Students must commit full-time to the nine-month Fellowship and suspend any graduate study or outside work. Applicants must be eligible to work in the U.S.
Target applicant(s): College students. Graduate school students. Adult students.
Amount: $31,563.
Number of awards: Varies.
Deadline: January 13.
How to apply: Applications are available online.
Exclusive: Visit www.UltimateScholarshipBook.com and enter code NE35226 for updates on this award.

[353] • USA Roller Sports Scholarship Fund
USA Roller Sports
Educational Scholarship Fund, 4730 South Street, Lincoln, NE 68506
Phone: 402-483-7551
Email: Foundation@USARollerSports.org
https://www.usarollersports.org/usars-resources/grants-and-scholarships
Purpose: To support U.S. Roller Sports athletes in paying for educational costs to prepare for their careers.
Eligibility: Applicants must be U.S. citizens or legal residents as well as current USARS members who have held membership for a minimum of three years. Applicants must also have participated in USARS Sanctioned National Championships. Students must be at least 17 years of age and in their final year of high school or must be high school graduates. A minimum GPA in the final year of high school of 3.0 is required. Eligible applicants must be currently enrolled or plan to enroll in a college or trade school seeking a degree or certificate and be of good academic standing. Selection is based on membership status, eligibility to compete, academic achievement and financial need.
Target applicant(s): High school students. College students. Adult students.
Minimum GPA: 3.0
Amount: $1,000-$2,000.
Number of awards: 3.
Deadline: October 31.
How to apply: Applications are available online.
Exclusive: Visit www.UltimateScholarshipBook.com and enter code US35326 for updates on this award.

[354] • USA Water Ski and Wake Sports Foundation Scholarships
USA Water Ski and Wake Sports Foundation
6039 Cypress Gardens Boulevard, Suite 481, Winter Haven, FL 33884
Phone: 863-324-2472
Email: info@waterskihalloffame.com
https://www.usa-wwf.org/ourscholarships
Purpose: To support those involved in USA Water Ski.
Eligibility: Applicants must be full-time undergraduates at a two- or four-year college as incoming freshmen to incoming seniors. Applicants must also be active members of a USA Water Ski division: AWSA-ABC-AKA-WSDA-NSSA-NCWSA-NCWSRA-USAWB-HYD. Students should submit an application, two reference letters, an essay and a transcript.
Target applicant(s): High school students. College students. Adult students.
Amount: $1,000-$5,000.
Number of awards: Varies.
Scholarship may be renewable.
Deadline: April 1.
How to apply: Applications are available online.
Exclusive: Visit www.UltimateScholarshipBook.com and enter code US35426 for updates on this award.

[355] • USAR Scholarship

USA Racquetball
2812 West Colorado Avenue, Suite 200, Colorado Springs, CO 80904-2906
Phone: 719-635-5396
Email: Peggine@usra.org
http://www.teamusa.org/USA-Racquetball
Purpose: To support USAR members who are aspiring collegiate athletes.
Eligibility: Applicants must be current USAR members and be graduating high school seniors or college undergraduates.
Target applicant(s): High school students. College students. Adult students.
Amount: Varies.
Number of awards: Varies.
Deadline: January 4.
How to apply: Applications are available online.
Exclusive: Visit www.UltimateScholarshipBook.com and enter code US35526 for updates on this award.

[356] • USBC Alberta E. Crowe Star of Tomorrow

United States Bowling Congress
IBC Youth Headquarters, 621 Six Flags Drive, Arlington, TX 76011
Phone: 800-514-2695
Email: contactus@ibcyouth.com
https://www.bowl.com/scholarships/
Purpose: To recognize star qualities in female students in high school or college who are competitive bowlers.
Eligibility: Applicants must be female high school seniors or college students 22 years of age or younger and USBC members who compete in certified events. They must hold an average of 175 or higher and must not have competed in professional tournaments except for Pro-AM's. They must also have a GPA of 2.5 or higher.
Target applicant(s): High school students. College students.
Minimum GPA: 2.5
Amount: $6,000.
Number of awards: 1.
Deadline: December 1.
How to apply: Applications are available online.
Exclusive: Visit www.UltimateScholarshipBook.com and enter code UN35626 for updates on this award.

[357] • USBC Annual Zeb Scholarship

United States Bowling Congress
IBC Youth Headquarters, 621 Six Flags Drive, Arlington, TX 76011
Phone: 800-514-2695
Email: contactus@ibcyouth.com
https://www.bowl.com/scholarships/
Purpose: To reward USBC Youth members with high academic achievement who have participated in community service.
Eligibility: Applicants must be high school juniors or seniors who are USBC Youth members in good standing. They must have a GPA of 2.0 or higher and must not have competed in any professional bowling tournament except for Pro-Am's.
Target applicant(s): High school students.
Minimum GPA: 2.0
Amount: $2,500 plus travel.
Number of awards: 1.
Deadline: December 1.
How to apply: Applications are available online.
Exclusive: Visit www.UltimateScholarshipBook.com and enter code UN35726 for updates on this award.

[358] • USBC Chuck Hall Star of Tomorrow

United States Bowling Congress
IBC Youth Headquarters, 621 Six Flags Drive, Arlington, TX 76011
Phone: 800-514-2695
Email: contactus@ibcyouth.com
https://www.bowl.com/scholarships/
Purpose: To recognize star qualities in male high school and college students who are competitive bowlers.
Eligibility: Applicants must be United States Bowling Congress members who compete in certified events and are high school seniors or college students with a GPA of 3.0 or higher. They must not have competed in a professional bowling tournament except for Pro-AM's.
Target applicant(s): High school students. College students. Adult students.
Minimum GPA: 3.0
Amount: $6,000.
Number of awards: 1.
Scholarship may be renewable.
Deadline: December 1.
How to apply: Applications are available online.
Exclusive: Visit www.UltimateScholarshipBook.com and enter code UN35826 for updates on this award.

[359] • USBC Youth Ambassador of the Year

United States Bowling Congress
IBC Youth Headquarters, 621 Six Flags Drive, Arlington, TX 76011
Phone: 800-514-2695
Email: contactus@ibcyouth.com
https://www.bowl.com/scholarships/
Purpose: To recognize contributions to the sport of bowling, academic achievement and community service.
Eligibility: Students must be USBC Youth members who will be 18 years of age or older by August 1 of the year of their selection. They must also be high school seniors and be nominated by a USBC member. The award is given to one male and one female student each year.
Target applicant(s): High school students.
Amount: $1,500.
Number of awards: 2.
Deadline: December 1.
How to apply: Applications are available online.
Exclusive: Visit www.UltimateScholarshipBook.com and enter code UN35926 for updates on this award.

[360] • USMA Metric Scholarship Award

U.S. Metric Association
P.O. Box 471, Windsor, CO 80550
Phone: 779-537-5611
https://usma.org/metric-awards
Purpose: To support students who help promote metric awareness and usage.
Eligibility: Applicants must be high school seniors who plan to enter college in the fall after graduation. Selection is based on involvement in promoting metric awareness and usage in the U.S. An additional award is available to a non-student.

The Ultimate Scholarship Book 2026
Scholarship Directory (General Awards)

Target applicant(s): High school students.
Amount: $250-$2,500.
Number of awards: Varies.
Deadline: March 31.
How to apply: Applications are available online.
Exclusive: Visit www.UltimateScholarshipBook.com and enter code U.36026 for updates on this award.

[361] • VA Essay Scholarship
VA Mortgage Center
2101 Chapel Plaza Court, Suite 107, Columbia, MO 65203
Phone: 800-405-6682
https://www.enhancelives.com/
Purpose: To reward students who are members of the military community as they pursue a college education.
Eligibility: Students must be a surviving spouse or child of a deceased veteran from the U.S. military, and be currently enrolled or planning to enroll in a college or university by the spring semester of the following school year. Students must also be comfortable sharing personal stories and aspirations with the Veteran's United Foundation and willing and able to provide requested documentation in a timely manner.
Target applicant(s): College students. Adult students.
Amount: $20,000.
Number of awards: Up to 5.
Deadline: March 31.
How to apply: Applications are available online.
Exclusive: Visit www.UltimateScholarshipBook.com and enter code VA36126 for updates on this award.

[362] • Veterans Caucus Scholarship
Veterans Caucus of the American Academy of Physician Assistants
P.O. Box 362, Hull, PA 02045
Email: mmckinnon@veteranscaucus.org
https://www.veteranscaucus.org
Purpose: To aid U.S. military veterans who are enrolled in a physician assistant training program.
Eligibility: Applicants must be U.S. military veterans. They must be enrolled in an accredited physician assistant (PA) training program. Selection is based on the overall strength of the application.
Target applicant(s): College students. Graduate school students. Adult students.
Amount: Varies.
Number of awards: 11.
Deadline: March 31.
How to apply: Applications are available online. An application form and personal statement are required.
Exclusive: Visit www.UltimateScholarshipBook.com and enter code VE36226 for updates on this award.

[363] • Voice of Democracy Audio Essay Contests
Veterans of Foreign Wars
406 West 34th Street, Kansas City, MO 64111
Phone: 816-968-1117
Email: kharmer@vfw.org
https://www.vfw.org/community/youth-and-education
Purpose: To encourage patriotism with students creating audio essays expressing their opinion on a patriotic theme.
Eligibility: Applicants must submit a three- to five-minute audio essay focused on a yearly theme. Students must be in the 9th to 12th grade in a public, private or parochial high school, home study program or overseas U.S. military school. Foreign exchange students are not eligible for the contest, and students who are age 20 or older also may not enter. Previous first place winners on the state level are ineligible.
Target applicant(s): High school students.
Amount: $1,000-$35,000.
Number of awards: Varies.
Deadline: October 31.
How to apply: Applications are available online but must be submitted to a local VFW post.
Exclusive: Visit www.UltimateScholarshipBook.com and enter code VE36326 for updates on this award.

[364] • Voyager Scholarship, The Obama-Chesky Scholarship for Public Service
Voyager Scholarship, The Obama-Chesky Scholarship for Public Service
Scholarship America, One Scholarship Way, Saint Peter, MN 56082
Phone: 800-537-4180
Email: obama-chesky-scholarship@scholarshipamerica.org
https://www.obama.org/voyager-scholarship/
Purpose: To support students who are the next generation of leaders ready to bridge divides and create meaningful change.
Eligibility: Applicants must be entering their junior year of college in the United States with demonstrated financial need and be U.S. citizens, permanent residents or DACA recipients. Students must plan to enroll in full-time undergraduate study at an accredited four-year college or university in the United States and have a minimum 3.0 GPA. Applicants must have demonstrated a commitment to public service and plan to pursue a future career in public service.
Target applicant(s): College students. Adult students.
Minimum GPA: 3.0
Amount: Up to $25,000.
Number of awards: 100.
Deadline: March 27.
How to apply: Applications are available online.
Exclusive: Visit www.UltimateScholarshipBook.com and enter code VO36426 for updates on this award.

[365] • VRG Scholarship
Vegetarian Resource Group
P.O. Box 1463, Baltimore, MD 21203
Phone: 410-366-8343
Email: vrg@vrg.org
https://www.vrg.org/student/scholar.htm
Purpose: To reward high school seniors who promote vegetarianism.
Eligibility: Applicants must be graduating U.S. high school students who have promoted vegetarianism in their schools or communities. Vegetarians do not eat meat, fish or fowl. The award is based on compassion, courage and commitment to promoting a "peaceful world through a vegetarian diet or lifestyle." Applicants should submit transcripts and at least three recommendations.
Target applicant(s): High school students.
Amount: $5,000-$10,000.
Number of awards: 3.
Deadline: February 20.
How to apply: Applications are available online, by mail, by phone or by email. A typed document containing the application's information will be accepted.

Exclusive: Visit www.UltimateScholarshipBook.com and enter code VE36526 for updates on this award.

[366] • W. H. Howie McClennan Scholarship
International Association of Fire Fighters
1750 New York Avenue, NW, Washington, DC 20006
Phone: 202-737-8484
Email: scholarships@iaff.org
http://www.iaff.org
Purpose: To provide scholarships for the children of firefighters who died in the line of duty.
Eligibility: Applicants must be the children (natural or legally-adopted) of firefighters who died in the line of duty. Applicant's parent must have been a member in good standing of the International Association of Fire Fighters, AFL-CIO/CLC at time of death. Selection is based on financial need, academic record and promise.
Target applicant(s): High school students. College students. Adult students.
Amount: $2,500.
Number of awards: 1.
Scholarship may be renewable.
Deadline: February 1.
How to apply: Applications are available by written request.
Exclusive: Visit www.UltimateScholarshipBook.com and enter code IN36626 for updates on this award.

[367] • Wade Trophy
Women's Basketball Coaches Association
4646 Lawrenceville Highway, Lilburn, GA 30047
Phone: 770-279-8027
Email: dtrujillo@wbca.org
https://wbca.org/recognize/player-awards
Purpose: To recognize the best women's college basketball player in the country who exceeds expectations on and off the court.
Eligibility: Applicants must be academically eligible NCAA Division I players and members of the WBCA NCAA Division I Coaches' All-American Team. Eligibility is limited to sophomore, junior and senior players.
Target applicant(s): College students. Adult students.
Amount: Varies.
Number of awards: Varies.
Deadline: Contact the sponsor to confirm the deadline.
How to apply: There is no formal application process. Eligible applicants are selected by the Wade Trophy Committee at the beginning of the basketball season.
Exclusive: Visit www.UltimateScholarshipBook.com and enter code WO36726 for updates on this award.

[368] • Waggle Human-Pet Bond Scholarship Opportunity
Waggle
https://www.waggle.org/waggle-scholarship
Purpose: To support students who are pet guardians.
Eligibility: Applicants must reside in the United States or Canada. Students must be enrolled in a full-time college or university program. Applicants must be pet guardians and must not work for Waggle or be related to somebody who does.
Target applicant(s): College students. Adult students.
Amount: $1,000.
Number of awards: Varies.
Deadline: November 1.
How to apply: Applications are available online.
Exclusive: Visit www.UltimateScholarshipBook.com and enter code WA36826 for updates on this award.

[369] • Walter Byers Graduate Scholarship
National Collegiate Athletic Association
700 W. Washington Street, P.O. Box 6222, Indianapolis, IN 46206
Phone: 317-917-6222
Email: lthomas@ncaa.org
http://www.ncaa.org/about/resources/ncaa-scholarships-and-grants
Purpose: To encourage academic excellence of student athletes by recognizing outstanding academic achievement and success in postgraduate studies.
Eligibility: Applicants must have a cumulative GPA of 3.5 or higher in their undergraduate work and have competed in intercollegiate athletics at an NCAA member institution as a member of a varsity team. Applicants should be a graduating senior or be enrolled in graduate studies. If not already in a graduate program, the applicant should have the intent of pursuing a graduate degree within five years at a properly accredited, nonprofit educational institution. Scholarship funds can also apply to a professional degree program at an accredited law school, medical school or the equivalent. Applicants must be able to demonstrate that athletic participation and community service have guided them to build superior character and leadership as well as helping to influence personal and intellectual growth.
Target applicant(s): College students. Graduate school students. Adult students.
Minimum GPA: 3.5
Amount: $24,000.
Number of awards: 2.
Scholarship may be renewable.
Deadline: January 10.
How to apply: Applicants must be nominated by a faculty athletics representative using the online application form. Applications also include a personal essay detailing future personal and academic goals. Included with the packet is a listing of involvement in activities and honors, as well as four recommendations.
Exclusive: Visit www.UltimateScholarshipBook.com and enter code NA36926 for updates on this award.

[370] • Watson Travel Fellowship
Thomas J. Watson Fellowship
11 Park Place, Suite 1503, New York, NY 10007
Phone: 212-245-8859
Email: tjw@watsonfellowship.org
http://watson.foundation/fellowships/tj
Purpose: To award one-year grants for independent study and travel outside the U.S. to graduating college seniors.
Eligibility: Only graduating seniors from the participating colleges are eligible to apply. A list of these colleges is available online. Applicants must first be nominated by their college or university. An interview with a representative will follow. Recipients must graduate before the fellowship can begin.
Target applicant(s): College students. Adult students.
Amount: Up to $36,000.

Number of awards: Varies.
Deadline: Contact campus advisor about deadlines.
How to apply: Interested students should contact their local Watson liaison to begin the application process. Once nominated, applicants must complete an online application form, project proposal and personal statement. A photo, transcripts and letters of recommendation are also required.
Exclusive: Visit www.UltimateScholarshipBook.com and enter code TH37026 for updates on this award.

[371] • WBCA Coaches' All-America
Women's Basketball Coaches Association
4646 Lawrenceville Highway, Lilburn, GA 30047
Phone: 770-279-8027
Email: dtrujillo@wbca.org
https://wbca.org/recognize/player-awards
Purpose: To recognize the 10 best women's or girl's basketball players at the NCAA Division I, NCAA Division II, NCAA Division III, NAIA, Junior/Community College and high school levels.
Eligibility: Applicants at the collegiate level must be eligible college women's basketball players whose coaches are members of the WBCA. Applicants at the high school level must be seniors. Selection at all levels is based on current season statistics and achievements, impact on the team, team success, sportsmanship and academic eligibility.
Target applicant(s): High school students. College students. Adult students.
Amount: Varies.
Number of awards: 10.
Deadline: Contact the sponsor to confirm the deadline.
How to apply: Applicants must be nominated using the online nomination form.
Exclusive: Visit www.UltimateScholarshipBook.com and enter code WO37126 for updates on this award.

[372] • We The Future Contest
Constituting America
P.O. Box 1988, Colleyville, TX 76034
Phone: 888-937-0917
Email: constitutingamerica@yahoo.com
https://constitutingamerica.org/enter/
Purpose: To encourage students who are learning about the importance of the U.S. Constitution.
Eligibility: Applicants must be U.S. citizens or legal residents and middle, high school or college students. Students must submit an entry in one of the following categories: essay, song, entrepreneurial plan, short film, PSA, STEM or speech - all with the theme of the U.S. Constitution.
Target applicant(s): Junior high students or younger. High school students. College students. Adult students.
Amount: Up to $5,000.
Number of awards: Varies.
Deadline: May 31.
How to apply: Applications are available online.
Exclusive: Visit www.UltimateScholarshipBook.com and enter code CO37226 for updates on this award.

[373] • Wells Fargo Veterans Scholarship Program
Wells Fargo Veterans Scholarship Program, Scholarship America
One Scholarship Way, Saint Peter, MN 56082
Phone: 800-537-4180
Email: wellsfargoveterans@scholarshipamerica.org
https://learnmore.scholarsapply.org/wellsfargoveterans/
Purpose: To reward those who have served in the United States military.
Eligibility: Applicants must be honorably-discharged veterans or spouses of disabled veterans who have graduated high school (or obtained a GED) and who have served in the U.S. military. Students must have at least a 2.0 GPA and plan to enroll full-time in an accredited two- or four-year college, university or vocational school the following fall. The award will increase with renewal to encourage completion of the program.
Target applicant(s): High school students. College students. Graduate school students. Adult students.
Minimum GPA: 2.0
Amount: Up to $5,000.
Number of awards: 35.
Scholarship may be renewable.
Deadline: April 10.
How to apply: Applications are available online.
Exclusive: Visit www.UltimateScholarshipBook.com and enter code WE37326 for updates on this award.

[374] • White House Fellows Program
White House
1600 Pennsylvania Avenue NW, Washington, DC 20500
Phone: 202-395-4522
Email: whitehousefellows@who.eop.gov
https://www.whitehouse.gov/get-involved/fellows/apply/
Purpose: To provide motivated students with first-hand experience working at high levels of federal government.
Eligibility: Applicants must be U.S. citizens who have completed their undergraduate education and demonstrate early professional achievement and evidence of leadership skills. Students must demonstrate commitment to public service and the ability to work as part of a team and provide three recommendations along with the application.
Target applicant(s): College students. Graduate school students. Adult students.
Amount: Varies.
Number of awards: Varies.
Deadline: January 3.
How to apply: Applications are available online.
Exclusive: Visit www.UltimateScholarshipBook.com and enter code WH37426 for updates on this award.

[375] • William J. Goaziou Scholarship
US Youth Soccer
9220 World Cup Way, Frisco, TX 75033
Phone: 800-476-2237
Email: jmagleby@usyouthsoccer.org
https://www.usyouthsoccer.org/players/scholarship/

Purpose: To aid high school senior soccer players who plan on continuing their education beyond high school.
Eligibility: Applicants must be high school seniors who have participated in a U.S. Youth Soccer program during the past two years. Students must have at least a 3.0 GPA. Selection is based on community service and the desire to give back to the game of soccer.
Target applicant(s): High school students.
Minimum GPA: 3.0
Amount: $1,250.
Number of awards: 2.
Deadline: April 16.
How to apply: Applications are available online and must also include an official transcript and two letters of recommendation.
Exclusive: Visit www.UltimateScholarshipBook.com and enter code US37526 for updates on this award.

[376] • William L. Hastie Award
National Association of Blacks in Criminal Justice
1801 Fayetteville Street, 106 Whiting Criminal Justice Building, P.O. Box 20011-C, Durham, NC 27707
Phone: 919-683-1801
Email: Office@NABCJ.org
https://nabcj.org/
Purpose: To reward demonstrations of national leadership in criminal justice and the pursuit of policy change within the field.
Eligibility: The award honors the first African American appointed to the bench in 1937 by President Franklin Roosevelt. The nominator should be a member of NABCJ.
Target applicant(s): High school students. College students. Adult students.
Amount: Varies.
Number of awards: 1.
Deadline: March 15.
How to apply: Nomination applications are available online.
Exclusive: Visit www.UltimateScholarshipBook.com and enter code NA37626 for updates on this award.

[377] • Women Divers Hall of Fame Scholarships and Grants
Women Divers Hall of Fame
43 Mackey Avenue, Port Washington, NY 10050
Email: scholarships@wdhof.org
https://www.wdhof.org/scholarships/sponsorship
Purpose: To support those of all ages who are pursuing careers involving diving.
Eligibility: Applicants must be interested in a career that involves diving. Several scholarships and grants are available, and each has various requirements. Not all are for women only.
Target applicant(s): Junior high students or younger. High school students. College students. Graduate school students. Adult students.
Amount: Up to $2,000.
Number of awards: Varies.
Deadline: November 15; January 15.
How to apply: All applications are online and all require a resume, essay and two letters of recommendation.
Exclusive: Visit www.UltimateScholarshipBook.com and enter code WO37726 for updates on this award.

[378] • Women in STEM Scholarship
MPOWER Financing
1875 Connecticut Avenue NW, 10th Floor, Washington, DC 20009
Phone: 571-216-5235
Email: ashley@mpoewrfinancing.com
https://www.mpowerfinancing.com/scholarships/
Purpose: To help international and DACA female STEM majors.
Eligibility: Applicants must be new-entering female students who plan to pursue a STEM major and must be international or DACA students. Students must maintain satisfactory academic progress requirements for the yearly renewal of this scholarship.
Target applicant(s): College students. Adult students.
Amount: Varies.
Number of awards: Varies.
Scholarship may be renewable.
Deadline: December 31.
How to apply: Applications are available online.
Exclusive: Visit www.UltimateScholarshipBook.com and enter code MP37826 for updates on this award.

[379] • Women Marines Association Scholarship Program
Women Marines Association
Scholarships, Dottie Stover-Kendrick, P.O. Box 134, Stilwell, KS 66085
Phone: 888-525-1943
Email: scholarship@womenmarines.org
https://www.womenmarines.org/scholarships
Purpose: To aid Marines and their families.
Eligibility: Applicants must be sponsored by a Women Marines Association member. They must have served or be serving in the Marine Corps or Reserve, be a direct descendant, sibling or descendant of a sibling of a member of the Marines or have completed two years in a Marine JROTC program. A minimum GPA of 3.0 is required.
Target applicant(s): High school students. College students. Adult students.
Minimum GPA: 3.0
Amount: Up to $5,000.
Number of awards: Varies.
Deadline: March 31.
How to apply: Applications are available online. An application form, copy of sponsor's membership card, photo, three letters of recommendation, proof of Marine or ROTC status or relationship to a Marine and proof of draft registration (for males) are required.
Exclusive: Visit www.UltimateScholarshipBook.com and enter code WO37926 for updates on this award.

[380] • Women on Par Scholarship
LPGA Amateur Golf Association
1 Deuce Court, Daytona Beach, FL 32124
Phone: 386-236-5353
Email: womenonpar@LPGAAmateurs.com
https://lpgaamateurs.com/memberships/scholarship/
Purpose: To support non-traditional female students.
Eligibility: Applicants must be female, at least 30 years of age and a U.S. or Canadian citizen or legal resident of the U.S. or Canada. Students must be first-time applicants to school or returning to school after an absence to complete a degree and pursuing a technical/vocational, associate's or bachelor's degree. Deadline will be shortened if 200 applications are received before stated date.

The Ultimate Scholarship Book 2026
Scholarship Directory (General Awards)

Target applicant(s): High school students. College students. Adult students.
Amount: Up to $2,000.
Number of awards: 2.
Deadline: April 2.
How to apply: Applications are available online.
Exclusive: Visit www.UltimateScholarshipBook.com and enter code LP38026 for updates on this award.

[381] • Women's Army Corps Veterans Association Scholarship

Women's Army Corps Veterans Association
P.O. Box 5577, Fort McClellan, AL 36205
Email: wacva@cox.net
https://www.armywomen.org/pdf/_10ScholarApp.pdf
Purpose: To support relatives of army service women based upon academic achievement and leadership as revealed by co-curricular activities and community involvement.
Eligibility: Applicants must be the child, grandchild, niece or nephew of an Army Service Woman. Students must have a GPA of 3.5 or higher and show academic promise. Students must be graduating seniors and U.S. citizens.
Target applicant(s): High school students.
Minimum GPA: 3.5
Amount: $1,500.
Number of awards: Varies.
Deadline: February 2.
How to apply: Applications are available online.
Exclusive: Visit www.UltimateScholarshipBook.com and enter code WO38126 for updates on this award.

[382] • Women's Overseas Service League Scholarships for Women

Women's Overseas Service League
Scholarship Committee, P.O. Box 124, Cedar Knoll, NJ 07927-0124
http://wosl.org
Purpose: To assist women in the military and other public service careers.
Eligibility: Applicants must demonstrate a commitment to advancement in their careers and must have completed at least 12 semester or 18 quarter hours of study at an institution of higher learning and be working toward a degree. Students must agree to enroll for at least six semester or nine quarter hours each academic period. A GPA of 2.5 or higher is required.
Target applicant(s): College students. Adult students.
Minimum GPA: 2.5
Amount: $500-$1,000.
Number of awards: Varies.
Scholarship may be renewable.
Deadline: March 1.
How to apply: Applications are available online. An application form, statement of financial need, resume, three letters of reference, essay and transcript are required.
Exclusive: Visit www.UltimateScholarshipBook.com and enter code WO38226 for updates on this award.

[383] • Women's Western Golf Foundation Scholarship

Women's Western Golf Foundation
Mrs. Richard Willis, Scholarship Selection Director, 393 Ramsay Road, Deerfield, IL 60015
Phone: 608-274-0173
Email: dkdink@aol.com
https://www.wwga.org/womens-western-golf-foundation
Purpose: To support female students who are involved in golf.
Eligibility: Applicants must be in their senior year of high school. Students must demonstrate academic excellence, good character and financial need. Recipients must maintain a 3.0 GPA for award renewal.
Target applicant(s): High school students.
Minimum GPA: 3.5
Amount: $20,000.
Number of awards: 20.
Scholarship may be renewable.
Deadline: March 8.
How to apply: Applications are available by mail.
Exclusive: Visit www.UltimateScholarshipBook.com and enter code WO38326 for updates on this award.

[384] • Young Scholars Program

Jack Kent Cooke Foundation Young Scholars Program
301 ACT Drive, P.O. Box 4030, Iowa City, IA 52243
Phone: 800-941-3300
Email: scholarships@jkcf.org
http://www.jkcf.org
Purpose: To help high-achieving students with financial need and provide them with educational opportunities throughout high school.
Eligibility: Applicants must have financial need, be in the 7th grade and plan to attend high school in the United States. Academic achievement and intelligence are important, and students must display strong academic records, academic awards and honors and submit a strong letter of recommendation. A GPA of 3.65 is usually required, but exceptions are made for students with unique talents or learning differences. The award is also based on students' will to succeed, leadership and public service, critical thinking ability and participation in the arts and humanities. During two summers, recipients must participate in a Young Scholars Week and Young Scholars Reunion in Washington, DC.
Target applicant(s): Junior high students or younger.
Minimum GPA: 3.65
Amount: Varies.
Number of awards: 60.
Scholarship may be renewable.
Deadline: May 9.
How to apply: Applications are available online and at regional talent centers. An application form, parental release, financial and tax forms, school report, teacher recommendation, personal recommendation and survey form are required.
Exclusive: Visit www.UltimateScholarshipBook.com and enter code JA38426 for updates on this award.

[385] • Zale Parry Scholarship

Academy of Underwater Arts and Sciences
27 West Anapamu Street #317, Santa Barbara, CA 93101
Phone: 919-369-0583
https://www.auas-nogi.org/scholarships
Purpose: To support students pursuing a career in ocean exploration, diving equipment technology, hyperbaric research or marine conservation.

Eligibility: Applicants must be enrolled in undergraduate or graduate level studies and must be a certified diver. Selection is based on merit.
Target applicant(s): College students. Graduate school students. Adult students.
Amount: $6,000.
Number of awards: Varies.
Deadline: August 31.
How to apply: Applications are available online and must include two letters of reference, a resume and an essay.
Exclusive: Visit www.UltimateScholarshipBook.com and enter code AC38526 for updates on this award.

HUMANITIES / ARTS

[386] • ACES Education Fund Scholarship
ACES: The Society for Editing
180 S. Western Avenue #132, Carpentersville, IL 60110
Email: info@aceseditors.org
https://aceseditors.org/awards
Purpose: To support students pursuing a career in editing written materials.
Eligibility: Applicants must be currently enrolled juniors, seniors or graduate students seeking a degree at a college or university. Students must provide an academic resume along with three references. Applicants must write an original essay as well as sample headlines with the given prompts.
Target applicant(s): College students. Graduate school students. Adult students.
Amount: $1,500-$3,500.
Number of awards: 5.
Deadline: November 15.
How to apply: Applications are available online.
Exclusive: Visit www.UltimateScholarshipBook.com and enter code AC38626 for updates on this award.

[387] • ACES Scholarships
ACES: The Society for Editing
180 S. Western Avenue #132, Carpentersville, IL 60110
Email: info@aceseditors.org
https://aceseditors.org/awards
Purpose: To support students who are interested in copy editing.
Eligibility: Applicants must be college juniors, seniors or graduate students. Graduating students who will take full-time copy editing jobs or internships are eligible. They must demonstrate an interest in and aptitude for copy editing.
Target applicant(s): College students. Graduate school students. Adult students.
Amount: $1,500-$2,500.
Number of awards: 6.
Deadline: November 15.
How to apply: Applications are available online. An application form, list of course work related to copy editing, list of copy editing experience, two letters of recommendation, copies of 5 to 10 headlines written by the applicant and a copy of a story edited by the applicant are required.
Exclusive: Visit www.UltimateScholarshipBook.com and enter code AC38726 for updates on this award.

[388] • ACL/NJCL National Greek Examination Scholarship
American Classical League
Scholarship Awards, 860 NW Washington Boulevard, Suite A, Hamilton, OH 45013
Phone: 513-529-7741
Email: info@aclclassics.org
https://www.aclclassics.org/
Purpose: To support outstanding students of Greek.

Eligibility: Applicants must be high school seniors who have earned purple or blue ribbons in the upper level National Greek Exam. They must agree to earn six credits in Greek during their freshman year in college.
Target applicant(s): High school students.
Amount: $2,000.
Number of awards: 1.
Deadline: January 15.
How to apply: Applications are sent to teachers of eligible students by mail.
Exclusive: Visit www.UltimateScholarshipBook.com and enter code AM38826 for updates on this award.

[389] • ACL/NJCL National Latin Examination Scholarships
American Classical League
Scholarship Awards, 860 NW Washington Boulevard, Suite A, Hamilton, OH 45013
Phone: 513-529-7741
Email: info@aclclassics.org
https://www.aclclassics.org/
Purpose: To support outstanding students of Latin.
Eligibility: Applicants must be Latin students and gold medal winners in the National Latin Exam Awards. They must also be high school seniors and must agree to take at least one Latin or classical Greek course each semester of their first year of college.
Target applicant(s): High school students.
Amount: $2,000.
Number of awards: Varies.
Scholarship may be renewable.
Deadline: February 15; April 16.
How to apply: Applications are mailed to NLE gold medal winners who are high school seniors.
Exclusive: Visit www.UltimateScholarshipBook.com and enter code AM38926 for updates on this award.

[390] • Adobe Design Circle Scholarships
Adobe
Institute of International Education, 530 Bush Street, Suite 1000, San Francisco, CA 94108
Phone: 415-362-6520
https://www.adobe.com/
Purpose: To support young people in pursuing a degree in a creative field.
Eligibility: Applicants must enter product design or experience design-related careers (e.g. digital, web, UX/UI, interaction design or similar). Applications are encouraged from candidates including, but not limited to racial or ethnic minorities, females, those who identify as LGBTQ+, first-generation college students and students with disabilities.
Target applicant(s): High school students. College students. Adult students.
Amount: Up to $25,000.
Number of awards: 10.
Scholarship may be renewable.
Deadline: March 12.
How to apply: Applications are available online.
Exclusive: Visit www.UltimateScholarshipBook.com and enter code AD39026 for updates on this award.

[391] • AGL Over the Rainbow Scholarship
AGL Over the Rainbow Foundation
Phone: 470-241-8435
Email: scholarship@aglfoundation.org
https://aglfoundation.org/scholarship-application
Purpose: To help support the dreams of talented students across the nation.
Eligibility: Applicants must submit a short video (three minutes) or sample of their highlighted performances or artwork and a resume of their musical, theatre, art or chorus background. Students must submit up to three letters of reference from teachers or mentors. Applicants must provide a copy of the acceptance letter from the college they will be attending in the fall.
Target applicant(s): High school students. College students. Adult students.
Amount: $1,000.
Number of awards: Varies.
Deadline: May 15.
How to apply: Applications are available online.
Exclusive: Visit www.UltimateScholarshipBook.com and enter code AG39126 for updates on this award.

[392] • AIGA Worldstudio Scholarships
AIGA, The Professional Association for Design
222 Broadway, 19th Floor, New York, NY 10038
Email: scholarship@aiga.org
https://www.aiga.org/worldstudio-scholarship
Purpose: To support art and design students who need financial assistance.
Eligibility: Applicants must be full-time undergraduate or graduate students in fine arts, graphic design, illustration, interactive design or photography. They must have a GPA of at least 2.0 and demonstrate financial need. Applicants must be U.S. citizens or permanent residents. Minority and economically disadvantaged students will be given special consideration.
Target applicant(s): High school students. College students. Graduate school students. Adult students.
Minimum GPA: 2.0
Amount: $2,500-$5,000.
Number of awards: Varies.
Deadline: April 21.
How to apply: Applications are available online.
Exclusive: Visit www.UltimateScholarshipBook.com and enter code AI39226 for updates on this award.

[393] • Alexia Foundation Student Grants
Alexia Foundation
215 University Place, Syracuse, NY 13210
https://newhouse.syr.edu/centers/the-alexia/
Purpose: To support students in producing photojournalism projects that promote world peace and cultural understanding.
Eligibility: Applicants must be enrolled as full-time undergraduate or graduate students in an accredited college or university in the United States or abroad. Professional photographers are not eligible. Selection is based on photographic skill as well as the strength of the proposal.

Target applicant(s): College students. Graduate school students. Adult students.
Amount: Up to full tuition.
Number of awards: Varies.
Deadline: February 15.
How to apply: Application submission must be completed online. A synopsis, proposal, resume and digital portfolio are required.
Exclusive: Visit www.UltimateScholarshipBook.com and enter code AL39326 for updates on this award.

[394] • AMCA Music Scholarship
Associated Male Choruses of America
Weldon Wilson, Scholarship Chair, 5143 S. 40th Street, St. Cloud, MN 56301
Phone: 320-260-1081
Email: scholarships@amcofa-sing.org
http://www.amcofa-sing.org/scholarships.html
Purpose: To promote the study of chorus and music studies in college.
Eligibility: Applicants must be full-time students obtaining their bachelor's degree in a music-related field (with preference given to voice or choral concentrations) and be sponsored by a chorus of the Associated Male Choruses of America. Applicants must submit references and a personal letter.
Target applicant(s): College students. Adult students.
Amount: $1,000-$1,200.
Number of awards: Varies.
Deadline: March 1.
How to apply: Applications are available online or by contacting your local AMCA chorus.
Exclusive: Visit www.UltimateScholarshipBook.com and enter code AS39426 for updates on this award.

[395] • Amy Lowell Poetry Travelling Scholarship
Choate, Hall and Stewart
2 International Place, Boston, MA 02110
Phone: 617-248-4877
Email: amylowell@choate.com
https://www.amylowell.org
Purpose: To support travel abroad for American-born poets.
Eligibility: Applicants should submit applications, curriculum vitae and poetry samples. Recipients should not accept another scholarship during the scholarship year, must travel outside North America and should have three poems by the end of the scholarship year.
Target applicant(s): High school students. College students. Graduate school students. Adult students.
Amount: $54,000.
Number of awards: 1-2.
Deadline: October 15.
How to apply: Applications are available online.
Exclusive: Visit www.UltimateScholarshipBook.com and enter code CH39526 for updates on this award.

[396] • Anthem Essay Contest
Ayn Rand Institute
6 Hutton Centre Drive, Suite 600, Santa Ana, CA 92707
Phone: 949-222-6550
Email: essays@aynrand.org
https://aynrand.org/students/essay-contests/
Purpose: To honor high school students who distinguish themselves in their understanding of Ayn Rand's novel "Anthem."
Eligibility: Applicants must be enrolled as an eighth, ninth, tenth, eleventh or twelfth grade student (ages 13-18) at some point during the year in which the contest is being held. Students are permitted to submit one entry per year. Essays should be written in English only and should be no fewer than 600 and no more than 1,200 words in length, double-spaced. Winning essays must demonstrate an outstanding grasp of the philosophic meaning of "Anthem."
Target applicant(s): Junior high students or younger. High school students.
Amount: Up to $2,000.
Number of awards: 84.
Deadline: April 25.
How to apply: An essay is required for the contest. There is no application.
Exclusive: Visit www.UltimateScholarshipBook.com and enter code AY39626 for updates on this award.

[397] • ASCAP Foundation Morton Gould Young Composer Awards
ASCAP Foundation
250 West 57th Street, New York, NY 10107
Phone: 212-621-6219
https://www.ascapfoundation.org/programs-and-grants
Purpose: To encourage young composers early in their careers.
Eligibility: Applicants must be composers who have not turned 30 before February 1 of the current year. They must be U.S. citizens or permanent residents or enrolled students with a student visa. Applicants must submit an original composition.
Target applicant(s): Junior high students or younger. High school students. College students. Graduate school students. Adult students.
Amount: Varies.
Number of awards: Varies.
Deadline: February 9.
How to apply: Applications are available online.
Exclusive: Visit www.UltimateScholarshipBook.com and enter code AS39726 for updates on this award.

[398] • Atlas Shrugged Essay Contest
Ayn Rand Institute
6 Hutton Centre Drive, Suite 600, Santa Ana, CA 92707
Phone: 949-222-6550
Email: essays@aynrand.org
https://aynrand.org/students/essay-contests/
Purpose: To honor students who distinguish themselves in their understanding of Ayn Rand's novel "Atlas Shrugged."
Eligibility: Applicants must be high school seniors, college undergraduates or graduate students who submit an 800-1,600-word essay which will be judged on both style and content with an emphasis on writing that is clear, articulate and logically organized. Winning essays must demonstrate an outstanding grasp of the philosophic meaning of "Atlas Shrugged."
Target applicant(s): High school students. College students. Graduate school students. Adult students.
Amount: Up to $10,000.
Number of awards: 84.
Deadline: December 27.
How to apply: An essay is required for the contest. There is no application.
Exclusive: Visit www.UltimateScholarshipBook.com and enter code AY39826 for updates on this award.

The Ultimate Scholarship Book 2026
Scholarship Directory (Humanities / Arts)

[399] • Bill Gove Scholarship
National Speakers Association
NSA Foundation, National Press Building, 529 14th Street NW, Suite 1280, Washington, DC 20045
Phone: 480-968-2552
Email: nsafcares@nsafoundation.org
http://www.nsaspeaker.org/recognition/
Purpose: To encourage study in the field of professional speaking.
Eligibility: Applicants must be full-time students majoring or minoring in speech. Selection is based on application, essay, recommendation and college transcript.
Target applicant(s): College students. Graduate school students. Adult students.
Amount: $5,000.
Number of awards: Varies.
Deadline: April 28.
How to apply: Applications are available online or by written request.
Exclusive: Visit www.UltimateScholarshipBook.com and enter code NA39926 for updates on this award.

[400] • Bridging Scholarships for Study Abroad in Japan
American Association of Teachers of Japanese
Bridging Project Clearinghouse, Campus Box 366, 1424 Broadway, University of Colorado, Boulder, CO 80309-0366
Phone: 303-492-5487
Email: aatj@aatj.org
http://www.aatj.org/
Purpose: To assist students with travel and living expenses while studying in Japan.
Eligibility: Applicants must be undergraduates, U.S. citizens and be enrolled in a U.S. college. Study in Japan must be for at least three months and take place during the academic year (summer programs are not eligible). Students must submit a letter of recommendation and an essay on their interest in studying in Japan.
Target applicant(s): College students. Adult students.
Amount: $2,500-$4,500.
Number of awards: Varies.
Deadline: March 15.
How to apply: Applications are available online.
Exclusive: Visit www.UltimateScholarshipBook.com and enter code AM40026 for updates on this award.

[401] • CardsDirect Future Designer Scholarship
CardsDirect
12750 Merit Drive, Suite 900, Dallas, TX 75251
Phone: 866-700-5030
Email: scholarship@cardsdirect.com
https://www.cardsdirect.com/scholarship.aspx
Purpose: To support aspiring card designers.
Eligibility: Applicants must be at least 17 years old and accepted at or already enrolled in any accredited post-secondary institution as a full-time student. Students must submit an original design for a holiday card.
Target applicant(s): High school students. College students. Graduate school students. Adult students.
Amount: $1,000.
Number of awards: 1.
Scholarship may be renewable.
Deadline: May 1.
How to apply: Applications are available online.
Exclusive: Visit www.UltimateScholarshipBook.com and enter code CA40126 for updates on this award.

[402] • Career Center
Entertainment Community Fund Formerly The Actors Fund
729 Seventh Avenue, 10th Floor, New York, NY 10019
Phone: 800-221-7303
Email: info@entertainmentcommunity.org
https://entertainmentcommunity.org
Purpose: To assist members of the entertainment industry with finding sideline work and pursuing new careers.
Eligibility: Applicants must be members in good standing of an entertainment industry union and others who have earned $6,500 in each of three of the last five years or $5,000 in each of five of the last 10 years. Those who do not have earnings can substitute 12 weeks of documented industry work.
Target applicant(s): Junior high students or younger. High school students. College students. Graduate school students. Adult students.
Amount: Varies.
Number of awards: Varies.
Deadline: Contact the sponsor to confirm the deadline.
How to apply: Applicants must attend an Actors Work Program Orientation to learn more about the program.
Exclusive: Visit www.UltimateScholarshipBook.com and enter code EN40226 for updates on this award.

[403] • Career Transition for Dancers Undergraduate Studies Scholarship
Actors Fund - Career Transition for Dancers
729 Seventh Avenue, 10th Floor, New York, NY 10019
Phone: 212-221-7300
Email: pschwadron@actorsfund.org
https://entertainmentcommunity.org/services-and-programs/career-transition-dancers
Purpose: To provide educational grants for dancers seeking second careers.
Eligibility: Applicants must provide documentation of 70 weeks or more of paid employment as a dance performer in the U.S. over at least five years. For work not performed under union jurisdiction, applicants must also provide documentation of total gross earnings of at least $40,000. Choreographers and dance teachers are not eligible for this program.
Target applicant(s): College students. Graduate school students. Adult students.
Amount: $2,000.
Number of awards: Varies.
Deadline: June 15 and October 15.
How to apply: Applicants must call to confirm their eligibility.
Exclusive: Visit www.UltimateScholarshipBook.com and enter code AC40326 for updates on this award.

[404] • Carl A. Ross Student Paper Award
Appalachian Studies Association
Carl A. Ross Student Paper Award, Casey LaFrance, Chair of the Selection Committee, One John Marshall Drive, Huntington, WV 25755
Phone: 304-696-2904
Email: TC-Lafrance@wiu.edu
http://appalachianstudies.org/awards/
Purpose: To promote Appalachian studies.

Eligibility: Applicants must submit a 12- to 30-page research paper on an Appalachian studies topic. Selections will be made from two categories: middle/high school and undergraduate/graduate.
Target applicant(s): Junior high students or younger. High school students. College students. Graduate school students. Adult students.
Amount: $100.
Number of awards: 2.
Deadline: January 15.
How to apply: Submission of the research paper is the application.
Exclusive: Visit www.UltimateScholarshipBook.com and enter code AP40426 for updates on this award.

[405] • Cavett Robert Scholarship
National Speakers Association
NSA Foundation, National Press Building, 529 14th Street NW, Suite 1280, Washington, DC 20045
Phone: 480-968-2552
Email: nsafcares@nsafoundation.org
http://www.nsaspeaker.org/recognition/
Purpose: To encourage study in the field of professional speaking.
Eligibility: Applicants must be full-time students majoring or minoring in speech. Selection is based on application, essay, recommendation and college transcript.
Target applicant(s): College students. Graduate school students. Adult students.
Amount: $5,000.
Number of awards: Varies.
Deadline: April 28.
How to apply: Applications are available online or by written request.
Exclusive: Visit www.UltimateScholarshipBook.com and enter code NA40526 for updates on this award.

[406] • Children in Need Scholarship
Bronx Brothers
https://bronxbrothers.org/scholarships/
Purpose: To support students who plan to pursue higher education.
Eligibility: Applicants must create a one- to three-minute video on the topic provided relating to how the scholarship will benefit them and how they will contribute to the community in the future. Students may be between the ages of 7 and 29.
Target applicant(s): Junior high students or younger. High school students. College students. Graduate school students. Adult students.
Amount: $1,000.
Number of awards: 5-10.
Deadline: Varies.
How to apply: Applications are available online.
Exclusive: Visit www.UltimateScholarshipBook.com and enter code BR40626 for updates on this award.

[407] • Christopher L. Hunt Scholarship
Educational Theatre Association
4555 Lake Forest Drive, Suite 650, Cincinnati, OH 45242
Phone: 513-421-7055
Email: awards@schooltheatre.org
https://www.schooltheatre.org/
Purpose: To reward student achievement in theatre.
Eligibility: Applicants must be inducted Thespians who plan to use skills learned through theatre in a career focused on business or marketing.
Target applicant(s): High school students.
Amount: $1,000.
Number of awards: 1.
Deadline: April 1.
How to apply: Applications are available online.
Exclusive: Visit www.UltimateScholarshipBook.com and enter code ED40726 for updates on this award.

[408] • Clauder Competition Prize
Portland Stage Company
Attn.: Literary Manager, P.O. Box 1458, Portland, ME 04104
Phone: 207-774-1043
Email: clauder@portlandstage.org
https://www.portlandstage.org/
Purpose: To support playwrights.
Eligibility: Applicants must live or attend school in Connecticut, Maine, Massachusetts, New Hampshire, Rhode Island or Vermont. This requirement may be waived for playwrights who have previously lived in New England and produce material relevant to the area. They must submit a full-length play that is an original work and has not been produced or published.
Target applicant(s): High school students. College students. Graduate school students. Adult students.
Amount: Up to $3,000.
Number of awards: Varies.
Deadline: March 31.
How to apply: No application form is required.
Exclusive: Visit www.UltimateScholarshipBook.com and enter code PO40826 for updates on this award.

[409] • College Television Awards
Academy of Television Arts and Sciences Foundation
5220 Lankershim Boulevard, North Hollywood, CA 91601
Phone: 818-754-2800
Email: ctasupport@televisionacademy.com
http://www.emmys.org
Purpose: To reward college student film or video producers.
Eligibility: Applicants must produce an original film or video in one of the following categories: scripted series, commercial, PSA or promo, animation series, news and sports, nonfiction or reality series and Loreen Arbus Focus on Disability. Professionals may not be involved in the production of the piece, including producers, directors, camera operators, lighting or sound technicians and production managers. Applicants must also be full-time students who have produced their video for course credit at an American college or university during the current year.
Target applicant(s): College students. Graduate school students. Adult students.
Amount: Varies.
Number of awards: Varies.
Deadline: October 19.
How to apply: Applications are available online and are also sent to college film and television departments.
Exclusive: Visit www.UltimateScholarshipBook.com and enter code AC40926 for updates on this award.

Scholarship Directory (Humanities / Arts)

[410] • ConnectHER Film Festival
Harvard College Social Innovation Collaborative (SIC)
ConnectHER, 12301 Zeller Lane, Austin, TX 78753
Email: filmfest@connecther.org
https://connectherfilmfest.org/
Purpose: To support high school and undergraduate college students in bringing awareness to global women's issues through a film contest.
Eligibility: Applicants must be current high school or undergraduate college students 25 years of age or under and must not be a resident of Cuba, Iran, North Korea, Sudan or Syria. Applicants must create three- to five-minute short films that either raise awareness about current global issues affecting women or propose solutions to such challenges. Selection is based on the overall strength of the film.
Target applicant(s): High school students. College students.
Amount: Up to $5,000.
Number of awards: Varies.
Deadline: October 14.
How to apply: Film submissions should be made online. A submission form, short film and proof of enrollment are required.
Exclusive: Visit www.UltimateScholarshipBook.com and enter code HA41026 for updates on this award.

[411] • Council on International Educational Exchange (CIEE) Scholarships
Council on International Educational Exchange
600 Southborough Drive, Suite 104, Portland, ME 04106
Phone: 800-40-STUDY
Email: scholarships@ciee.org
http://www.ciee.org
Purpose: To make the study abroad program available to a wider audience and to provide assistance to CIEE Study Center (CSC) members who have demonstrated academic talent and financial need in order to study abroad.
Eligibility: Applicants must plan to participate in a CIEE study abroad program. Financial need is strongly considered along with other materials from the study abroad application. Other eligibility requirements vary according to the specific scholarship. If awarded a scholarship, applicants are required to submit a one-page essay on their experiences after returning.
Target applicant(s): College students. Adult students.
Amount: Varies.
Number of awards: Varies.
Deadline: April 1; October 15; March 7.
How to apply: Applications are available online.
Exclusive: Visit www.UltimateScholarshipBook.com and enter code CO41126 for updates on this award.

[412] • DAAD/AICGS Research Fellowship Program
American Institute for Contemporary German Studies - (AICGS)
1776 Massachusetts Avenue NW, Suite 600, Washington, DC 20036
Phone: 202-332-9312
Email: sdieper@aicgs.org
http://www.aicgs.org
Purpose: To bring scholars and specialists working on Germany, Europe and/or transatlantic relations to AICGS for research stays.
Eligibility: Applicants must have a Ph.D. or be enrolled in a Ph.D. program, hold German citizenship, be non-Germans who work/live permanently in Germany or work at one of the DAAD Centers around the globe. The grant provides a research stay of two to four months at AICGS.
Target applicant(s): Graduate school students. Adult students.
Amount: Up to $4,725 monthly stipend.
Number of awards: Varies.
Deadline: November 19.
How to apply: Apply via email to jwindell@aicgs.org.
Exclusive: Visit www.UltimateScholarshipBook.com and enter code AM41226 for updates on this award.

[413] • Disney Entertainment Writing Program
Disney/ABC Television Group
Talent Development and Diversity, 500 South Buena Vista Street, Burbank, CA 91521-4016
Email: abcwritingfellowship@disney.com
https://sites.disney.com/ctdi/
Purpose: To help writers develop skills for careers in television writing.
Eligibility: Applicants must be age 21 or older. They must be able to work in the U.S. legally. Professional writing experience is not necessary, but applicants must have strong spec script writing skills. Selection is based on the overall strength of the application.
Target applicant(s): College students. Graduate school students. Adult students.
Amount: $50,000.
Number of awards: Varies.
Deadline: June 7.
How to apply: Applications are available online. An application form and spec script samples are required.
Exclusive: Visit www.UltimateScholarshipBook.com and enter code DI41326 for updates on this award.

[414] • Diversity Achievement Scholarship
American Institute for Foreign Study
AIFS Abroad, 1 High Ridge Park, Stamford, CT 06905
Phone: 800-727-2437
Email: AIFSAbroad@aifs.com
https://www.aifsabroad.com/scholarships.asp
Purpose: To support students who are in the AIFS study abroad programs.
Eligibility: Students must demonstrate maturity, good character and high academic achievement. Applicants must be African American, Asian American, Hispanic, Native American or Pacific Islander college students. While there is no fee to apply for this scholarship, there is a $95 fee to apply for the AIFS study abroad program.
Target applicant(s): High school students. College students. Adult students.
Amount: $5,000.
Number of awards: 2.
Deadline: April 15 for fall; October 7 for spring.
How to apply: Applications are available online.
Exclusive: Visit www.UltimateScholarshipBook.com and enter code AM41426 for updates on this award.

[415] • Dolly Parton Songwriters Award
BMI Foundation Inc.
7 World Trade Center, 250 Greenwich Street, New York, NY 10007
Phone: 212-586-2000
Email: info@bmifoundation.org
http://www.bmifoundation.org
Purpose: To support student composers.
Eligibility: Applicants must be between the ages of 17 and 24 and residents of the U.S. or its territories. Students must submit only one application per BMI Foundation awards program, and they may not submit the same musical work to more than one program.
Target applicant(s): High school students. College students. Graduate school students.

Amount: $20,000.
Number of awards: 2.
Deadline: Varies.
How to apply: Applications are available online.
Exclusive: Visit www.UltimateScholarshipBook.com and enter code BM41526 for updates on this award.

[416] • Doodle for Google

Google Doodle for Google
1600 Amphitheatre Parkway, Mountain View, CA 94043
Phone: 650-253-0000
Email: doodle4google-team@google.com
http://www.google.com/doodle4google
Purpose: To encourage creativity in United States school students through a logo contest.
Eligibility: Participants must be elementary or secondary school students in the 50 U.S. states or the District of Columbia who have registered for the contest. They must be U.S. residents who have obtained parental consent to enter. Employees, interns, contractors and office-holders of Google Inc. and their immediate families are not eligible.
Target applicant(s): Junior high students or younger. High school students.
Amount: Up to $30,000.
Number of awards: Varies.
Deadline: March 14.
How to apply: Applications are available from participating schools.
Exclusive: Visit www.UltimateScholarshipBook.com and enter code GO41626 for updates on this award.

[417] • Dr. Kenny D. Hasija Scholarship

Educational Theatre Association
4555 Lake Forest Drive, Suite 650, Cincinnati, OH 45242
Phone: 513-421-7055
Email: awards@schooltheatre.org
https://www.schooltheatre.org/
Purpose: To reward student achievement in theatre.
Eligibility: Applicants must be inducted members of the International Thespian Society (Thespians) who are graduating seniors. Students must be planning on a career in any area of the theater, from performing to producing. Applicants must be from groups traditionally underrepresented in the theatre industry, such as those who are black, indigenous or people of color.
Target applicant(s): High school students.
Amount: $1,000.
Number of awards: 1.
Deadline: April 1.
How to apply: Applications are available online.
Exclusive: Visit www.UltimateScholarshipBook.com and enter code ED41726 for updates on this award.

[418] • Dumbarton Oaks Fellowships

Dumbarton Oaks
1703 32nd Street NW, Washington, DC 20007
Phone: 202-339-6413
Email: FellowshipPrograms@doaks.org
https://www.doaks.org/research/fellowships-and-awards
Purpose: To provide fellowships to scholars engaged in Byzantine studies, Pre-Columbian studies and garden and landscape studies.
Eligibility: Applicants must hold a doctorate (or appropriate final degree) or have established themselves in their field and wish to pursue their own research or expect to have the Ph.D. in hand prior to taking up residence at Dumbarton Oaks. The fellowships are in the following areas: Byzantine Studies (including related aspects of late Roman, early Christian, western medieval, Slavic and Near Eastern Studies), Pre-Columbian Studies (of Mexico, Central America and Andean South America) and garden and landscape studies. Fellowships are based on demonstrated scholarly ability and preparation (including knowledge of the required languages), interest and value of the study or project and its relevance to Dumbarton Oaks.
Target applicant(s): Graduate school students. Adult students.
Amount: Up to $35,000 plus allowance and health benefits.
Number of awards: Varies.
Deadline: November 1.
How to apply: Applicants must submit ten complete, collated sets of the application letter, proposal and personal and professional data. Applicants must also submit three recommendation letters.
Exclusive: Visit www.UltimateScholarshipBook.com and enter code DU41826 for updates on this award.

[419] • Educational Theatre Association Board of Directors Scholarship

Educational Theatre Association
4555 Lake Forest Drive, Suite 650, Cincinnati, OH 45242
Phone: 513-421-7055
Email: awards@schooltheatre.org
https://www.schooltheatre.org/
Purpose: To support student achievement in theatre.
Eligibility: Applicants must be undergraduate students currently enrolled full-time at an accredited college or university who are upcoming sophomores, juniors or seniors. Students must be alumni of the International Thespian Society and pursuing a career in theatre education.
Target applicant(s): College students. Adult students.
Amount: $1,000.
Number of awards: 1.
Deadline: April 1.
How to apply: Applications are available online.
Exclusive: Visit www.UltimateScholarshipBook.com and enter code ED41926 for updates on this award.

[420] • Expressions Challenge by Walgreens

Expressions Challenge by Walgreens
230 E. Ohio Street, Suite 406, Chicago, IL 60611
Phone: 312-943-3330
Email: ExpressionsChallenge@gmail.com
https://expressionschallenge.com/the-challenge/
Purpose: To help students who encounter many hurdles in life.
Eligibility: Applicants must be legal United States residents in all 50 states, the District of Columbia, Puerto Rico and the U.S. Virgin Islands who are between 13 and 18 years of age and currently enrolled in high school as of the entry date. Students must be able to use their creativity to share how they feel about what is happening in their world. Applicants must share their entries through spoken word, visual arts, media arts or creative writing.
Target applicant(s): Junior high students or younger. High school students.
Amount: $1,750-$2,000.
Number of awards: Total of 12.
Deadline: March 31.
How to apply: Applications are available online.
Exclusive: Visit www.UltimateScholarshipBook.com and enter code EX42026 for updates on this award.

[421] • Fashion Scholarship Fund Scholarships

Fashion Scholarship Fund
1501 Broadway, Suite 1810, New York, NY 10036
Phone: 212-278-0008
Email: hharrison@fashionscholarshipfund.org
http://www.ymafsf.org/
Purpose: To support students attending FSF member schools across the United States.
Eligibility: Applicants must attend Fashion Scholarship Fund member schools and universities and have a demonstrated interest in fashion. Applicants must also be enrolled as full-time, current college sophomores, juniors or seniors with an overall GPA of 3.0 or above. Selection is based on merit with consideration given to GPA, the quality of a case study project, job experience, community service, personal essay and interview.
Target applicant(s): College students. Adult students.
Minimum GPA: 3.0
Amount: $5,000.
Number of awards: About 100.
Deadline: October 14.
How to apply: Applications are available online. Application, case study project, transcript, personal essay and interview are required.
Exclusive: Visit www.UltimateScholarshipBook.com and enter code FA42126 for updates on this award.

[422] • Federal Junior Duck Stamp Program and Scholarship Competition

U.S. Fish and Wildlife Service Headquarters
U.S. Fish and Wildlife Service, 1849 C Street, NW, Washington, DC 20240
Phone: 800-344-9453
Email: Suzanne_Fellows@fws.gov
http://www.fws.gov/juniorduck
Purpose: To encourage students to paint waterfowl and learn about the importance of habitat and wildlife conservation.
Eligibility: Applicants must be in kindergarten to 12th grade and submit their artwork to their state or local department. Students must be U.S. citizens, resident aliens or nationals. The first place national winner has their art made into the next Federal Junior Duck Stamp and travels with a parent to the next First Day of Sale event for their stamp.
Target applicant(s): Junior high students or younger. High school students.
Amount: Varies.
Number of awards: Varies.
Deadline: March 15.
How to apply: Applications are available online.
Exclusive: Visit www.UltimateScholarshipBook.com and enter code U.42226 for updates on this award.

[423] • Fellowships for Regular Program in Greece

American School of Classical Studies at Athens
321 Wall Street, Princeton, NJ 08540
Phone: 609-683-0800
Email: ascsa@ascsa.org
https://www.ascsa.edu.gr/programs/regular-member-program
Purpose: The institution is devoted to allowing advanced graduate students enrolled in North American colleges and institutions to study the classics and related fields of language, literature, art, history, archaeology and philosophy of Greece and the Greek world.
Eligibility: Applicants must have completed at least one to two years of graduate study and must take exams in the ancient Greek language, history and either literature or art and archaeology. Students must be able to read French, German, ancient Greek and Latin with an ability to also read modern Greek and Italian considered helpful. Applicants must be graduate students who are preparing for an advanced degree in classical and ancient Mediterranean studies or a related field. The fellowships provide study in Athens or Greece for nine months and may not be used for costs at the student's home institution.
Target applicant(s): Graduate school students. Adult students.
Amount: $11,500 plus housing, board and fees.
Number of awards: Up to 12.
Deadline: January 15.
How to apply: Applications are available online.
Exclusive: Visit www.UltimateScholarshipBook.com and enter code AM42326 for updates on this award.

[424] • Fellowships/Grants to Study in Scandinavia

American-Scandinavian Foundation
58 Park Avenue, New York, NY 10016
Phone: 212-779-3587
Email: info@amscan.org
http://www.amscan.org
Purpose: To encourage research and creative-arts projects in Scandinavia.
Eligibility: Applicant must be a United States citizen or permanent resident who has completed their undergraduate education by the start of their project in Scandinavia. Applicant must have a well-defined research or study project that makes a stay in Scandinavia essential and should have some ability in the language of the host country. First priority will be given to an applicant who has not previously received an ASF award.
Target applicant(s): College students. Graduate school students. Adult students.
Amount: $5,000-$23,000.
Number of awards: Varies.
Scholarship may be renewable.
Deadline: November 1.
How to apply: Applications are available online and by written request.
Exclusive: Visit www.UltimateScholarshipBook.com and enter code AM42426 for updates on this award.

[425] • FFTA Scholarship Competition

Flexographic Technical Association
900 Marconi Avenue, Ronkonkoma, NY 11779
Phone: 631-737-6020
Email: education@flexography.org
https://www.flexography.org/honors-awards/scholarships/
Purpose: To advance the state of the flexographic industry.
Eligibility: Applicants must demonstrate interest in a career in flexography and must be high school seniors with plans to attend a post-secondary institution or be presently enrolled at a post-secondary institution offering a course of study in flexography. Applicants must exhibit exemplary performance in their studies, particularly in the area of graphic communications and must have a minimum 3.0 GPA.
Target applicant(s): High school students. College students. Adult students.

Minimum GPA: 3.0
Amount: $3,000.
Number of awards: Varies.
Scholarship may be renewable.
Deadline: April 1.
How to apply: Applications are available online.
Exclusive: Visit www.UltimateScholarshipBook.com and enter code FL42526 for updates on this award.

[426] • Finlandia Foundation National Student Scholarships Program
Finlandia Foundation
470 W. Walnut Street, Pasadena, CA 91103
Phone: 626-795-2081
Email: ffnoffice@mac.com
https://finlandiafoundation.org/programs/scholarship/
Purpose: To support undergraduate and graduate students in Finland and the United States for conducting studies or research related to Finnish culture and society.
Eligibility: Applicants must be full-time undergraduate or graduate students enrolled in a college or university in the U.S. or Finland and must plan research on Finnish culture in the U.S. They must be studying at the sophomore level or higher and have a minimum GPA of 3.0. Financial need, course of study and citizenship are considered in evaluating applications. Students may not receive funds for two consecutive years.
Target applicant(s): High school students. College students. Graduate school students. Adult students.
Minimum GPA: 3.0
Amount: $1,000-$3,000.
Number of awards: Varies.
Deadline: February 1.
How to apply: Applications are available online. Application form and cover letter are required.
Exclusive: Visit www.UltimateScholarshipBook.com and enter code FI42626 for updates on this award.

[427] • Frame My Future Scholarship Contest
Church Hill Classics
594 Pepper Street, Monroe, CT 06468
Phone: 800-477-9005
Email: info@diplomaframe.com
https://www.diplomaframe.com/contests
Purpose: To help success-driven students attain their higher education goals.
Eligibility: Applicants must be high school seniors or current college students who plan to enroll full-time for the following academic year. Students must be residents of the United States, including APO/FPO addresses but excluding Puerto Rico. Employees of Church Hill Classics and affiliated companies, their family members and individuals living in the same household are not eligible.
Target applicant(s): High school students. College students. Graduate school students. Adult students.
Amount: $2,000.
Number of awards: 5.
Deadline: March 15.
How to apply: Applications must be submitted online. An entry form and original piece of artwork are required.
Exclusive: Visit www.UltimateScholarshipBook.com and enter code CH42726 for updates on this award.

[428] • Future Theatre Educator Scholarship
Educational Theatre Association
4555 Lake Forest Drive, Suite 650, Cincinnati, OH 45242
Phone: 513-421-7055
Email: awards@schooltheatre.org
https://www.schooltheatre.org/
Purpose: To reward student achievement in theatre.
Eligibility: Applicants must be inducted Thespians who successfully demonstrate leadership abilities.
Target applicant(s): High school students.
Amount: $1,500.
Number of awards: 1.
Deadline: April 1.
How to apply: Applications are available online.
Exclusive: Visit www.UltimateScholarshipBook.com and enter code ED42826 for updates on this award.

[429] • Gilman International Scholarship
Institute of International Education Gilman Scholarship Program
1800 West Loop South, Suite 250, Houston, TX 77027
Phone: 832-369-3484
Email: gilman@iie.org
https://www.gilmanscholarship.org/
Purpose: To support students with financial need who are planning to study abroad.
Eligibility: Students must be recipients of a Pell Grant. They must be currently attending a two-year or four-year college in the United States. Recipients must study abroad for at least four weeks in any country excluding Cuba and the countries on the Travel Warning list.
Target applicant(s): High school students. College students. Adult students.
Amount: Up to $5,000.
Number of awards: Varies.
Deadline: March 7.
How to apply: Applications are available online.
Exclusive: Visit www.UltimateScholarshipBook.com and enter code IN42926 for updates on this award.

[430] • Glenn Miller Scholarship Competition
Glenn Miller Birthplace Society
122 W. Clark Street, P.O. Box 61, Clarinda, IA 51632
Phone: 712-542-2461
Email: gmbs@glennmiller.org
http://glennmiller.org
Purpose: To honor Glenn Miller by recognizing future musical leaders.
Eligibility: Applicants may apply as instrumentalists or vocalists. They must be high school seniors or college freshmen who plan to focus on music in their future lives. Applicants must submit an audition file in addition to an application form. High school seniors may reapply as college freshmen as long as they weren't first-place winners the previous year.
Target applicant(s): High school students. College students. Adult students.
Amount: $1,000-$3,000.
Number of awards: 6.
Deadline: April 12.
How to apply: Applications are available online.
Exclusive: Visit www.UltimateScholarshipBook.com and enter code GL43026 for updates on this award.

[431] • Great Khalid Performing Arts Scholarship
Great Khalid Foundation
7500 Viscount Boulevard, El Paso, TX 79925
Phone: 915-500-1000
Email: scholarships@thegreatkhalidfoundation.org
https://thegreatkhalidfoundation.org/performing-arts-scholarship
Purpose: To help students planning to pursue higher education in the performing arts field.
Eligibility: Applicants must be high school seniors pursuing higher education in a performing arts program. Students must be recognized for their academic achievements and artistic ability and have a minimum GPA of 3.5. Applicants must present their acceptance letter or letter of verification from a performing arts college or university program.
Target applicant(s): High school students. College students. Adult students.
Amount: $10,000.
Number of awards: Varies.
Deadline: April 15.
How to apply: Applications are available online.
Exclusive: Visit www.UltimateScholarshipBook.com and enter code GR43126 for updates on this award.

[432] • Hedy Lamarr Achievement Award for Emerging Leaders in Entertainment Technology
DEG: The Digital Entertainment Group
Attn.: Hedy Lamarr Achievement Award Judging Panel, 11963 San Vicente Boulevard, Suite 116, Los Angeles, CA 90049
Phone: 424-248-3809
Email: natalie@degonline.org
http://degonline.org/
Purpose: To support female college juniors who have shown exceptional promise in the fields of entertainment and technology.
Eligibility: Applicants must be female students in their junior year at an accredited institution in the United States who are pursuing a career in entertainment and technology. Students must be citizens of the United States and have a minimum 3.0 GPA.
Target applicant(s): College students. Adult students.
Minimum GPA: 3.0
Amount: $10,000.
Number of awards: 1.
Deadline: March 29.
How to apply: Applications are available online.
Exclusive: Visit www.UltimateScholarshipBook.com and enter code DE43226 for updates on this award.

[433] • Heinlein Society Scholarship Program
Heinlein Society
3553 Atlantic Avenue, Suite 341, Long Beach, CA 90807-5606
Email: scholarships@heinleinsociety.org
https://www.heinleinsociety.org/scholarship-program/
Purpose: To reward students who are attending a four-year college.
Eligibility: Applicants must be full-time undergraduate students at an accredited college. One scholarship is awarded to a woman majoring in engineering, math or physical sciences (physics/chemistry). Two scholarships are awarded to male or female students majoring in engineering, math or biological or physical sciences as well as science fiction as literature. Students must submit a 500- to 1,000-word essay on one of the topics listed on the website.
Target applicant(s): High school students. College students. Adult students.
Amount: $4,000.
Number of awards: 4.
Deadline: April 1.
How to apply: Applications are available online and must be submitted with a brief biography including future goals and the required essay.
Exclusive: Visit www.UltimateScholarshipBook.com and enter code HE43326 for updates on this award.

[434] • Herb Alpert Young Jazz Composer Awards
ASCAP Foundation
250 West 57th Street, New York, NY 10107
Phone: 212-621-6219
https://www.ascapfoundation.org/programs-and-grants
Purpose: To recognize the talent of young jazz composers.
Eligibility: Applicants must be under the age of 30 and U.S. citizens or permanent residents. They must submit one original composition, including a score and performance, if possible.
Target applicant(s): Junior high students or younger. High school students. College students. Graduate school students. Adult students.
Amount: Varies.
Number of awards: Varies.
Deadline: December 1.
How to apply: Applications are available online.
Exclusive: Visit www.UltimateScholarshipBook.com and enter code AS43426 for updates on this award.

[435] • Herblock Award for Editorial Cartoon
Scholastic Art and Writing Awards
557 Broadway, New York, NY 10012
Email: info@artandwriting.org
http://www.artandwriting.org/scholarships/
Purpose: To support students whose visual art offers commentary or criticism on current events, social events or political topics.
Eligibility: Applicants must be in grades 7-12 (ages 13 and up) and enter visual art offering commentary or criticism on current events, social events or political topics. Submissions can be drawings, illustrations, a series of artworks or animated short films.
Target applicant(s): Junior high students or younger. High school students.
Amount: $2,000.
Number of awards: 3.
Deadline: December 1.
How to apply: Applications are available online.
Exclusive: Visit www.UltimateScholarshipBook.com and enter code SC43526 for updates on this award.

[436] • IACI/NUIG Visiting Fellowship in Irish Studies
Irish-American Cultural Institute (IACI)
An Foras Cultuir Gael-Mheircheanach, 1 Lackawanna Place, Morristown, NJ 07960
Phone: 973-605-1991
Email: info@iaci-usa.org
http://www.iaci-usa.org
Purpose: To award fellowships to Irish studies scholars to spend one semester at the University of Ireland-Galway.
Eligibility: Applicants must be Irish studies scholars resident in the U.S. who wish to spend a semester (not less than four months) at National University of Ireland-Galway, and whose work relates to any aspect of Irish

Studies. Candidates must provide a description of how the fellowship will be used and a curriculum vitae with a list of publications.
Target applicant(s): Graduate school students. Adult students.
Amount: $4,000.
Number of awards: Varies.
Deadline: December 31.
How to apply: Application is available online.
Exclusive: Visit www.UltimateScholarshipBook.com and enter code IR43626 for updates on this award.

[437] • ICWA Fellowship Program
Institute of Current World Affairs
1779 Massachusetts Avenue NW, Suite 605, Washington, DC 20036
Phone: 202-364-4068
Email: apply@icwa.org
http://www.icwa.org
Purpose: To promote independent study abroad.
Eligibility: Applicants must be under the age of 36 and must have strong, credible ties to American society. They must have excellent written and spoken English-language skills and must have completed the current phase of their formal education. Applications will not be accepted from currently enrolled undergraduate students. Candidates must have the necessary language skills to allow to them to carry out their proposed projects and enough language proficiency for them to be able to function in the local language within a few months of arriving in the country. Selection is based on the overall strength of the application.
Target applicant(s): Graduate school students. Adult students.
Amount: Full Tuition.
Number of awards: Varies.
Deadline: May 31.
How to apply: Application instructions are available online.
Exclusive: Visit www.UltimateScholarshipBook.com and enter code IN43726 for updates on this award.

[438] • IDSA Undergraduate and Graduate Scholarships
Industrial Designers Society of America
555 Grove Street, Suite 200, Herndon, VA 20170
Phone: 703-707-6000
Email: idsa@idsa.org
http://www.idsa.org
Purpose: To help industrial design students in their final year of schooling.
Eligibility: Applicants must be full-time students enrolled in an IDSA-listed program in their next-to-last year of the program, have a minimum 3.0 GPA, be members of an IDSA Student Chapter and be U.S. citizens or residents. Applicants must submit a letter of intent, 20 visual examples of their work and a transcript. Awards are based solely on the excellence of the submitted works.
Target applicant(s): College students. Graduate school students. Adult students.
Minimum GPA: 3.0
Amount: Varies.
Number of awards: 1.
Deadline: May 17.
How to apply: Applications are available online.
Exclusive: Visit www.UltimateScholarshipBook.com and enter code IN43826 for updates on this award.

[439] • IFDA Leaders Commemorative Scholarship
International Furnishings and Design Association (IFDA)
7908 Lasley Forest Road, Lewisville, NC 27023-8244
Phone: 336-946-1011
Email: scholarships@ifdaef.org
https://ifda.com/educational-foundation/
Purpose: To aid interior design students.
Eligibility: Applicants must be full-time undergraduate students at an accredited U.S. postsecondary institution. They must be majoring in interior design or a closely-related design subject and have completed four design courses at the time of application. Preference will be given to students who demonstrate leadership and volunteer experience. Selection is based on the overall strength of the application.
Target applicant(s): College students. Adult students.
Amount: $3,000.
Number of awards: 1.
Deadline: March 31.
How to apply: Applications are available online. An application form, personal essay, one recommendation letter and design work examples are required.
Exclusive: Visit www.UltimateScholarshipBook.com and enter code IN43926 for updates on this award.

[440] • IFDA Student Member Scholarship
International Furnishings and Design Association (IFDA)
7908 Lasley Forest Road, Lewisville, NC 27023-8244
Phone: 336-946-1011
Email: scholarships@ifdaef.org
https://ifda.com/educational-foundation/
Purpose: To aid interior design students who are members of the International Furnishings and Design Association (IFDA).
Eligibility: Applicants must be full-time undergraduate students who are attending an accredited U.S. postsecondary institution. They must be majoring in interior design or a closely-related design subject and have completed a minimum of four design courses. Selection is based on the overall strength of the application.
Target applicant(s): College students. Adult students.
Amount: $2,000.
Number of awards: 1.
Deadline: March 31.
How to apply: Applications are available online. An application form, personal statement, two recommendation letters and design work examples are required.
Exclusive: Visit www.UltimateScholarshipBook.com and enter code IN44026 for updates on this award.

[441] • ILA Jeanne S. Chall Research Fellowship
International Literacy Association
The Jeanne S. Chall Research Fellowship, Division of Research and Policy, P.O. Box 8139, Newark, DE 19714-8139
Phone: 302-731-1600
Email: research@reading.org
https://www.literacyworldwide.org
Purpose: To support dissertation research in reading.
Eligibility: Applicants must be doctoral students planning or beginning their dissertation on one of the following topics in the field of reading: beginning reading, readability, reading difficulty, stages of reading development, the relation of vocabulary to reading and diagnosing and teaching adults with limited reading ability. Applicants must also be members of the International Literacy Association.

Target applicant(s): Graduate school students. Adult students.
Amount: $5,000.
Number of awards: 1.
Deadline: March 15.
How to apply: Applications are available online.
Exclusive: Visit www.UltimateScholarshipBook.com and enter code IN44126 for updates on this award.

[442] • Illustrators of the Future
L. Ron Hubbard's Writers of the Future Contest
7051 Hollywood Boulevard, Los Angeles, CA 90028
Phone: 323-466-3310
Email: contests@authorservicesinc.com
http://www.writersofthefuture.com
Purpose: To discover deserving amateur aspiring illustrators.
Eligibility: Applicants must not have published more than three black-and-white story illustrations or more than one color painting in national media. Applicants must also submit three original illustrations done in either color or black-and-white medium in three different themes.
Target applicant(s): High school students. College students. Graduate school students. Adult students.
Amount: $1,500-$5,000.
Number of awards: 3 each quarter and a grand prize awarded annually.
Deadline: December 31; March 31; June 30; September 30.
How to apply: There is no application form.
Exclusive: Visit www.UltimateScholarshipBook.com and enter code L.44226 for updates on this award.

[443] • International Trumpet Guild Conference Scholarship
International Trumpet Guild
P.O. Box 16207, Hattiesburg, MS 39404
Email: confscholarships@trumpetguild.org
http://www.trumpetguild.org
Purpose: To improve the artistic level of trumpet players.
Eligibility: Applicants must be students and record audition songs. There are different age group categories, and each category has its own performance requirements. Applicants must be ITG members.
Target applicant(s): Junior high students or younger. High school students. College students. Graduate school students.
Amount: Varies.
Number of awards: Varies.
Deadline: December 15.
How to apply: Applications are available online.
Exclusive: Visit www.UltimateScholarshipBook.com and enter code IN44326 for updates on this award.

[444] • Jack Kent Cooke Young Artist Award
From the Top
295 Huntington Avenue, Suite 201, Boston, MA 02115
Phone: 617-437-0707
https://www.fromthetop.org/apply/
Purpose: To reward classical instrumentalists, vocalists and composers who have not yet entered college for extraordinary musical accomplishment.
Eligibility: Applicants must have interest in performing on NPRs "From the Top." Selection is primarily based on demonstration of strong musical ability, unmet financial need and strength of character.
Target applicant(s): High school students.
Amount: Up to $10,000.

Number of awards: 20.
Deadline: April 15; September 2; November 15.
How to apply: Applications are available online.
Exclusive: Visit www.UltimateScholarshipBook.com and enter code FR44426 for updates on this award.

[445] • Jaime Guttenberg Dance Scholarship
Orange Ribbons for Jaime
5944 Coral Ridge Drive, Suite 301, Coral Springs, FL 33076
Phone: 561-750-1500
Email: info@orangeribbonsforjaime.org
https://orangeribbonsforjaime.org/scholarship/
Purpose: To support students with a focus on a career in dance.
Eligibility: Applicants must be applying to a traditional four-year university or performing arts specialty program with a focus on a career in dance. Students must have a minimum of three years in dance classes during high school and a background in community service/volunteerism during high school with a minimum of 100 hours of service. Applicants must have a minimum 3.5 GPA and submit an essay on a provided topic.
Target applicant(s): High school students.
Minimum GPA: 3.5
Amount: Varies.
Number of awards: Varies.
Deadline: March 31.
How to apply: Applications are available online.
Exclusive: Visit www.UltimateScholarshipBook.com and enter code OR44526 for updates on this award.

[446] • Joel Polsky Academic Achievement Award
American Society of Interior Designers (ASID) Educational Foundation Inc.
608 Massachusetts Avenue NE, Washington, DC 20002-6006
Phone: 202-546-3480
https://www.asid.org/resources/awards/scholarships-and-grants
Purpose: To recognize an interior design student's project.
Eligibility: Applicants must be undergraduate or graduate students in interior design and should submit entry forms and projects such as research papers or doctoral and master's theses that focus on interior design topics. The projects are judged on content, breadth of material, coverage of the topic, innovative subject matter, bibliography and references. The society may exhibit any entry for two years.
Target applicant(s): High school students. College students. Graduate school students. Adult students.
Amount: $5,000.
Number of awards: 1.
Deadline: April 15.
How to apply: Applications are available online.
Exclusive: Visit www.UltimateScholarshipBook.com and enter code AM44626 for updates on this award.

[447] • John F. and Anna Lee Stacey Scholarship Fund for Art Education

John F. and Anna Lee Stacey Scholarship Fund
1700 NE 63rd Street, Oklahoma City, OK 73111
Phone: 405-478-2250
Email: scholarship@nationalcowboymuseum.org
http://www.nationalcowboymuseum.org/education/staceyfund/
Purpose: To educate young men and women who aim to enter the art profession.
Eligibility: Applicants must be U.S. citizens between the ages of 18 and 35 who aim to make fine art their profession. The online application process will ask the applicant to outline their ambitions and plans and to upload no more than 6 examples of their paintings/drawings for judging. Letters of recommendation will be requested of finalists.
Target applicant(s): High school students. College students. Graduate school students. Adult students.
Amount: Up to $5,000.
Number of awards: Varies.
Deadline: February 1.
How to apply: Applications are available online.
Exclusive: Visit www.UltimateScholarshipBook.com and enter code JO44726 for updates on this award.

[448] • John Lennon Scholarship Competition

BMI Foundation Inc.
7 World Trade Center, 250 Greenwich Street, New York, NY 10007
Phone: 212-586-2000
Email: info@bmifoundation.org
http://www.bmifoundation.org
Purpose: Established in 1997 by Yoko Ono in conjunction with the BMI Foundation, the John Lennon Scholarship recognizes the talent of young songwriters.
Eligibility: Applicants must be age 17 to 24 and write an original song to be reviewed by a prestigious panel of judges. Entries are to be submitted by music schools, universities, youth orchestras and the Music Educators National Conference (MENC).
Target applicant(s): College students. Graduate school students.
Amount: Up to $20,000.
Number of awards: 3.
Deadline: February 15.
How to apply: Please see the website for a full list of eligible organizations that may submit entries.
Exclusive: Visit www.UltimateScholarshipBook.com and enter code BM44826 for updates on this award.

[449] • Julius and Esther Stulberg International String Competition

Julius and Esther Stulberg Competition Inc.
359 South Kalamazoo Mall, Suite 14, Kalamazoo, MI 49007
http://www.stulberg.org
Purpose: To support young instrumentalists.
Eligibility: Applicants must be students of violin, viola, cello or double bass, be 19 years of age or younger as of January 1 of the year of competition and perform a Bach piece and a solo for the competition, which is typically held in May.
Target applicant(s): Junior high students or younger. High school students.
Amount: Up to $6,000.
Number of awards: Varies.
Deadline: February 1.
How to apply: Applications are available online. An application form, proof of age and audition recording are required.
Exclusive: Visit www.UltimateScholarshipBook.com and enter code JU44926 for updates on this award.

[450] • Junior Fellowships

Dumbarton Oaks
1703 32nd Street NW, Washington, DC 20007
Phone: 202-339-6413
Email: FellowshipPrograms@doaks.org
https://www.doaks.org/research/fellowships-and-awards
Purpose: To provide fellowships to scholars engaged in Byzantine studies, Pre-Columbian studies and garden and landscape studies.
Eligibility: Applicants at the time of application should have fulfilled all preliminary requirements for a Ph.D. and be willing to work on a dissertation or final project at Dumbarton Oaks under the direction of a faculty member at their own university. The fellowships are in the following areas: Byzantine Studies (including related aspects of late Roman, early Christian, western medieval, Slavic and Near Eastern Studies), Pre-Columbian Studies (of Mexico, Central America and Andean South America) and garden and landscape studies. Fellowships are based on demonstrated scholarly ability and preparation of the candidate (including knowledge of the required languages) and value of the study or project and its relevance to Dumbarton Oaks.
Target applicant(s): Graduate school students. Adult students.
Amount: Up to $21,000.
Number of awards: Varies.
Deadline: November 1.
How to apply: Applicants must submit ten complete, collated sets of: application letter, proposal and personal and professional data. They must also submit an official transcript and three recommendation letters, with one from the faculty advisor.
Exclusive: Visit www.UltimateScholarshipBook.com and enter code DU45026 for updates on this award.

[451] • Language Grants

Blakemore Foundation
701 Fifth Avenue, Suite 4200, Seattle, WA 98104
Phone: 206-427-4838
Email: contactus@blakemorefoundation.org
http://www.blakemorefoundation.org
Purpose: To support students pursuing a professional, business, technical or academic career that involves the regular use of Chinese, Japanese, Korean, Thai, Vietnamese, Indonesian, Khmer or Burmese.
Eligibility: Applicants must be U.S. citizens or permanent residents of the United States at or near an advanced level in one of the languages listed above, having completed (at minimum) the equivalent of third-year college-level language classes. Students must have received (at minimum) a bachelor's degree.
Target applicant(s): College students. Graduate school students. Adult students.
Amount: Varies.
Number of awards: Varies.

The Ultimate Scholarship Book 2026
Scholarship Directory (Humanities / Arts)

Deadline: December 30.
How to apply: Applications are available online.
Exclusive: Visit www.UltimateScholarshipBook.com and enter code BL45126 for updates on this award.

[452] • Laura Ziegler Scholarship
National Sculpture Society
6 East 39th Street, Suite 903, New York, NY 10016
Phone: 212-764-5645
Email: nss1893@aol.com
http://www.nationalsculpture.org
Purpose: To award scholarships to students who are emerging sculptors.
Eligibility: Applicants must be citizens of or residents in the United States with a social security number. Students must submit images of six to twelve works of sculpture and a brief resume.
Target applicant(s): College students. Graduate school students. Adult students.
Amount: $200.
Number of awards: 1.
Deadline: May 13.
How to apply: Follow the application guidelines listed on the website.
Exclusive: Visit www.UltimateScholarshipBook.com and enter code NA45226 for updates on this award.

[453] • Legacy Scholarship for Undergraduates
American Society of Interior Designers (ASID) Educational Foundation Inc.
608 Massachusetts Avenue NE, Washington, DC 20002-6006
Phone: 202-546-3480
https://www.asid.org/resources/awards/scholarships-and-grants
Purpose: To support undergraduate students who are pursuing a degree in interior design.
Eligibility: Applicants must be enrolled in their junior or senior year of undergraduate study. Selection is primarily based on demonstration of academic performance and creative achievement. Students must submit a design portfolio, official transcripts, a letter of recommendation and a personal statement.
Target applicant(s): College students. Adult students.
Amount: $4,000.
Number of awards: 1.
Deadline: April 15.
How to apply: Applications are available online.
Exclusive: Visit www.UltimateScholarshipBook.com and enter code AM45326 for updates on this award.

[454] • Leiber and Stoller Scholarship for Songwriters
ASCAP Foundation
250 West 57th Street, New York, NY 10107
Phone: 212-621-6219
https://www.ascapfoundation.org/programs-and-grants
Purpose: To support students who plan to pursue higher education in the music field.
Eligibility: Applicants must be high school seniors who will enroll in a four-year college or university-level music program on a full-time basis. Students must be U.S. citizens, U.S. permanent residents or enrolled students with a valid and current U.S. student visa. Applicants must be musicians, songwriters, composers, lyricists, arrangers and who write original works and must not be currently signed to a major publishing, record or administrative deal.
Target applicant(s): High school students. College students. Adult students.
Amount: $10,000.
Number of awards: Varies.
Deadline: May 22.
How to apply: Applications are available online.
Exclusive: Visit www.UltimateScholarshipBook.com and enter code AS45426 for updates on this award.

[455] • Lions International Peace Poster Contest
Lions Club International
300 W. 22nd Street, Oak Brook, IL 60523-8842
Phone: 630-571-5466
Email: pr@lionsclubs.org
https://www.lionsclubs.org/en/start-our-approach/youth/peace-poster
Purpose: To award creative youngsters cash prizes for outstanding poster designs.
Eligibility: Students must be 11, 12 or 13 years old as of the deadline and must be sponsored by their local Lions club. Entries will be judged at the local, district, multiple district and international levels. Posters will be evaluated on originality, artistic merit and expression of the assigned theme.
Target applicant(s): Junior high students or younger.
Amount: $500-$5,000.
Number of awards: 24.
Deadline: November 15.
How to apply: Applications are available from your local Lion's Club.
Exclusive: Visit www.UltimateScholarshipBook.com and enter code LI45526 for updates on this award.

[456] • Lotte Lenya Competition
Kurt Weill Foundation for Music
7 East 20th Street, 3rd Floor, New York, NY 10003
Phone: 212-505-5240
Email: kwfinfo@kwf.org
http://www.kwf.org
Purpose: To recognize excellence in music theater performance.
Eligibility: Applicants must be between 19 and 32 years old and attend a regional competition, performing four selections. If contestants are unable to participate in any of the scheduled regional auditions, they may instead submit a DVD, which must contain all four of the required repertoire selections. Finalists will be chosen, based on vocal beauty and technique, interpretation, acting, repertoire variety and presence.
Target applicant(s): High school students. College students. Graduate school students. Adult students.
Amount: Up to $25,000 plus travel stipend.
Number of awards: Varies.
Deadline: January 24.
How to apply: Applications are available online.
Exclusive: Visit www.UltimateScholarshipBook.com and enter code KU45626 for updates on this award.

[457] • Luce/ACLS Dissertation Fellowships in American Art
American Council of Learned Societies (ACLS)
633 Third Avenue, New York, NY 10017-6795
Phone: 212-697-1505
Email: mgoldfeder@acls.org
https://www.acls.org/
Purpose: To support Ph.D. candidates working on art history dissertations.

Eligibility: Applicants must be Ph.D. candidates in an art history department in the U.S. who are working on dissertations about American visual arts history. All the Ph.D. requirements should be met except the dissertation before taking the fellowship. Applicants should submit an application, a proposal, a bibliography, illustrations (optional), a publications list (optional), three reference letters and an official transcript of graduate record. The fellowship lasts for a year.
Target applicant(s): Graduate school students. Adult students.
Amount: $38,000 plus up to $4,000 travel allowance.
Number of awards: Varies.
Deadline: October 25.
How to apply: Applications are available online.
Exclusive: Visit www.UltimateScholarshipBook.com and enter code AM45726 for updates on this award.

[458] • Marian A. Smith Costume Award
Southeastern Theatre Conference Inc.
1175 Revolution Mill Drive, Studio 14, Greensboro, NC 27405
Phone: 336-272-3645
Email: emilystrickland@sjrstate.edu
https://setc.org/scholarships/
Purpose: To support graduate students majoring in costume design and/or technology.
Eligibility: Applicants must be finished with their undergraduate degrees at an SETC region institution by the August prior to application. They must also be first-time as well as full-time attendees of a regionally accredited graduate school specializing in costume design and/or costume technology. Selection is based on the overall strength of the application and interview.
Target applicant(s): College students. Graduate school students. Adult students.
Amount: $1,500.
Number of awards: 1.
Deadline: April 15.
How to apply: Applications are available online. An application, personal letter, resume, ten samples of completed work, five references, transcripts and interview are required.
Exclusive: Visit www.UltimateScholarshipBook.com and enter code SO45826 for updates on this award.

[459] • Mary Bowman Arts in Activism Award
National AIDS Memorial
870 Market Street, Suite 965, San Francisco, CA 94102
Phone: 415-765-0446
Email: mkennedy@aidsmemorial.org
https://www.aidsmemorial.org/
Purpose: To support students with a passion for health who plan to pursue higher education.
Eligibility: Applicants must be graduating high school seniors or current undergraduates who are actively engaged in health and social justice issues. Students must provide samples of their activist art. Applicants must also write and submit an essay about a given topic related to Mary Bowman's life and work.
Target applicant(s): High school students. College students. Adult students.
Amount: $5,000.
Number of awards: Varies.
Deadline: July 15.
How to apply: Applications are available online.
Exclusive: Visit www.UltimateScholarshipBook.com and enter code NA45926 for updates on this award.

[460] • Michael J. Peitz Leadership Scholarship
Educational Theatre Association
4555 Lake Forest Drive, Suite 650, Cincinnati, OH 45242
Phone: 513-421-7055
Email: awards@schooltheatre.org
https://www.schooltheatre.org/
Purpose: To support student achievement in theatre.
Eligibility: Applicants must be an inducted Thespian of the International Thespian Society, the student honorary organization of the Educational Theatre Association, who successfully demonstrates leadership abilities.
Target applicant(s): High school students.
Amount: $1,500.
Number of awards: 1.
Deadline: April 1.
How to apply: Applications are available online.
Exclusive: Visit www.UltimateScholarshipBook.com and enter code ED46026 for updates on this award.

[461] • Nadia Christensen Prize
American-Scandinavian Foundation
58 Park Avenue, New York, NY 10016
Phone: 212-779-3587
Email: info@amscan.org
http://www.amscan.org
Purpose: To recognize individuals who translate Scandinavian writings.
Eligibility: Selection is based on the overall strength of the application.
Target applicant(s): Junior high students or younger. High school students. College students. Graduate school students. Adult students.
Amount: $2,500.
Number of awards: 1.
Deadline: September 1.
How to apply: Applications are available online. Applications must include one copy of the work that was translated in its original language, one copy of the English translation of the work, a CV containing contact information for the translator and a letter granting the translation to be entered in the competition and published.
Exclusive: Visit www.UltimateScholarshipBook.com and enter code AM46126 for updates on this award.

[462] • National High School Poetry Contest/Easterday Poetry Award
Live Poets Society
P.O. Box 8841, Turnersville, NJ 08012
Email: lpsnj@comcast.net
http://www.highschoolpoetrycontest.com
Purpose: To provide a venue for young poets to be recognized.
Eligibility: Applicants must be U.S. high school students. Submitted poems must be 20 lines or less, in English, unpublished and not simultaneously submitted to any other competition. Applicants may only submit one poem during any 90-day span and must include a self-addressed, stamped envelope with each mailed entry, or applicants may submit their poems online. Submissions are accepted year-round.
Target applicant(s): High school students.
Amount: $500.
Number of awards: Varies.
Deadline: March 31.
How to apply: There is no application form.
Exclusive: Visit www.UltimateScholarshipBook.com and enter code LI46226 for updates on this award.

[463] • National Junior Classical League (NJCL) Scholarships

National Junior Classical League
860 NW Washington Blvd Suite A, Hamilton, OH 45013
Email: administrator@njcl.org
http://www.njcl.org
Purpose: To support students studying the classics.
Eligibility: Applicants must be NJCL members in good standing, entering college the upcoming year and studying the classics. Special consideration is given to those planning to teach Latin, Greek or classical humanities. Selection is based on financial need, JCL service, academics and recommendations.
Target applicant(s): High school students.
Amount: Up to $2,500.
Number of awards: Varies.
Deadline: February 7.
How to apply: Applications are available online or by written request.
Exclusive: Visit www.UltimateScholarshipBook.com and enter code NA46326 for updates on this award.

[464] • National Latin Exam Scholarship

National Latin Exam
University of Mary Washington, 1301 College Avenue, Fredericksburg, VA 22401
Phone: 888-378-7721
Email: nle@umw.edu
http://www.nle.org
Purpose: To reward students for their Latin proficiency.
Eligibility: Applicants must be gold medal winners in Latin III-IV Prose, III-IV Poetry or Latin V-VI on the National Latin Exam. Applicants must be high school seniors who agree to take at least one Latin or classical Greek each semester during their first year of college. A translation course does not count.
Target applicant(s): High school students.
Amount: $2,000-$5,000.
Number of awards: Varies.
Scholarship may be renewable.
Deadline: February 15.
How to apply: Applications are mailed to eligible students. Renewal applications are available online.
Exclusive: Visit www.UltimateScholarshipBook.com and enter code NA46426 for updates on this award.

[465] • National Vocal Competition for Young Opera Singers

Loren L. Zachary Society for the Performing Arts
2250 Gloaming Way, Beverly Hills, CA 90210
Phone: 310-276-2731
Email: infoz@zacharysociety.org
http://www.zacharysociety.org
Purpose: To assist in the development of a professional operatic career.
Eligibility: Applicants must be 21-35 years old, reside in the U.S. or Canada and must be available for all phases of the competition.
Target applicant(s): College students. Graduate school students. Adult students.
Amount: $15,000 up to $18,000.
Number of awards: Varies.
Deadline: February 29 (New York); March 26 (Los Angeles).
How to apply: Applications are available online.
Exclusive: Visit www.UltimateScholarshipBook.com and enter code LO46526 for updates on this award.

[466] • New York Life Award

Scholastic Art and Writing Awards
557 Broadway, New York, NY 10012
Email: info@artandwriting.org
http://www.artandwriting.org/scholarships/
Purpose: To support students whose art or writing explores personal grief, loss and bereavement.
Eligibility: Applicants must be in grades 7-12 (ages 13 and up) and enter art or writing works exploring personal grief, loss and bereavement. Students may enter work in any of the 28 listed art and writing categories and must include a personal statement of 50 words or more on their work. State scholarships are also available to two students from each of the following states: Arizona, Louisiana, Michigan, Mississippi, Montana, New Jersey, and New Mexico, Ohio, and Tennessee.
Target applicant(s): Junior high students or younger. High school students.
Amount: $2,500.
Number of awards: 10 national scholarships.
Deadline: December 1.
How to apply: Applications are available online.
Exclusive: Visit www.UltimateScholarshipBook.com and enter code SC46626 for updates on this award.

[467] • NFMC Lynn Freeman Olson Composition Awards

National Federation of Music Clubs Olson Awards
National Federation of Music Clubs, 1646 W Smith Valley Road, Greenwood, IN 46142
Phone: 317-882-4003
Email: info@nfmc-music.org
http://www.nfmc-music.org/competitions-awards/
Purpose: To support student composers.
Eligibility: Applicants must be at least in grade 7 and no older than age 25. Students must be members of the National Federation of Music Clubs and must submit an original piano composition to be judged. This biennial award is given in odd-numbered years.
Target applicant(s): Junior high students or younger. High school students.
Amount: $750-$1,500.
Number of awards: Varies.
Deadline: March 1.
How to apply: Applications are available online.
Exclusive: Visit www.UltimateScholarshipBook.com and enter code NA46726 for updates on this award.

[468] • NFMC Wendell Irish Viola Award

National Federation of Music Clubs (AR)
Dr. George Keck, 2112 Hinson Road, Suite 23, Little Rock, AR 72212
Phone: 317-882-4003
Email: keckg@att.net
https://www.nfmc-music.org/competitions-awards/
Purpose: To recognize musically talented students.
Eligibility: Applicants must be between the ages of 12 and 18 and must be Individual Junior Special members or Active Junior Club members of the National Federation of Music Clubs. Applicants must enter in their state of residence by submitting a taped performance.

Target applicant(s): Junior high students or younger. High school students.
Amount: $500-$2,000.
Number of awards: Varies.
Deadline: March 1.
How to apply: Applications are available online.
Exclusive: Visit www.UltimateScholarshipBook.com and enter code NA46826 for updates on this award.

[469] • Ocean Awareness Contest
Bow Seat
Email: info@bowseat.org
https://bowseat.org/programs/ocean-awareness-contest/rules-eligibility/
Purpose: To help students pursuing higher education through ocean awareness.
Eligibility: Applicants must be students ages 11-18, enrolled in middle school or high school (or the homeschool equivalent) worldwide. Students must create an account and submit their work online. Works may be in art, poetry, prose, film, music or dance.
Target applicant(s): High school students.
Amount: $100-$1,000.
Number of awards: Varies.
Deadline: June 9.
How to apply: Applications are available online.
Exclusive: Visit www.UltimateScholarshipBook.com and enter code BO46926 for updates on this award.

[470] • Office Supply Scholarship
BulkOfficeSupply.com
1614 Hereford Road, Hewlett, NY 11557
Phone: 800-658-1488
Email: service@bulkofficesupply.com
http://www.bulkofficesupply.com/scholarships-in-new-york
Purpose: To support students pursuing teaching or art or who plan on owning their own business.
Eligibility: Applicants must be high school students or college freshmen or sophomores. Students must be pursing degree programs in teaching or art or must wish to own their own business. Applicants will need to submit a 500- to 600-word essay describing where they plan to or are currently attending school, their desired major, how the student developed an interest in teaching, art or owning their own business and how the scholarship would help them to reach their goals.
Target applicant(s): High school students. College students. Adult students.
Amount: $1,000.
Number of awards: 1.
Deadline: February 1.
How to apply: Applications are available online and must include the essay.
Exclusive: Visit www.UltimateScholarshipBook.com and enter code BU47026 for updates on this award.

[471] • Optimist International Essay Contest
Optimist International
4494 Lindell Boulevard, St. Louis, MO 63108
Phone: 314-371-6000
Email: programs@optimist.org
https://www.optimist.org/member/scholarships1.cfm
Purpose: To reward students based on their essay-writing skills.
Eligibility: Applicants must be under 19 years of age as of December 31 of the current school year and application must be made through a local Optimist Club. The essay topic changes each year. Applicants compete at the club, district and international level. District winners receive a $2,500 scholarship. Scoring is based on organization, vocabulary and style, grammar and punctuation, neatness and adherence to the contest rules. The club-level contests are held in early February but vary by club. The deadline for clubs to submit their winning essay to the district competition is February 28.
Target applicant(s): High school students.
Amount: $2,500.
Number of awards: Varies.
Deadline: Early February.
How to apply: Contact your local Optimist Club.
Exclusive: Visit www.UltimateScholarshipBook.com and enter code OP47126 for updates on this award.

[472] • Part-Time Student Scholarship
International Furnishings and Design Association (IFDA)
7908 Lasley Forest Road, Lewisville, NC 27023-8244
Phone: 336-946-1011
Email: scholarships@ifdaef.org
https://ifda.com/educational-foundation/
Purpose: To aid part-time students who are majoring in interior design.
Eligibility: Applicants must be undergraduate students at an accredited U.S. postsecondary institution. They must be majoring in interior design or a related design subject, have completed four design courses at the time of application and be attending school on a part-time basis. Selection is based on the overall strength of the application.
Target applicant(s): College students. Adult students.
Amount: $1,500.
Number of awards: 1.
Deadline: March 31.
How to apply: Applications are available online. An application form, one letter of recommendation, personal essay and design work examples are required.
Exclusive: Visit www.UltimateScholarshipBook.com and enter code IN47226 for updates on this award.

[473] • Patriot's Pen Youth Essay Contest
Veterans of Foreign Wars
406 West 34th Street, Kansas City, MO 64111
Phone: 816-968-1117
Email: kharmer@vfw.org
https://www.vfw.org/community/youth-and-education
Purpose: To give students in grades 6 through 8 an opportunity to write essays that express their views on democracy.
Eligibility: Applicants must be enrolled as a 6th, 7th or 8th grader in a public, private or parochial school in the U.S., its territories or possessions. Home-schooled students and dependents of U.S. military or civilian personnel in overseas schools may also apply. Foreign exchange students and former applicants who placed in the national finals are ineligible. Students must submit essays based on an annual theme to their local

VFW posts. If an essay is picked to advance, the entry is judged at the District (regional) level, then the Department (state) level and finally at the National level. Essays are judged 30 percent on knowledge of the theme, 35 percent on development of the theme and 35 percent on clarity.
Target applicant(s): Junior high students or younger.
Amount: Up to $5,000.
Number of awards: 54.
Deadline: October 31.
How to apply: Applications are available online or by contacting the local VFW office. Entries must be turned into the local VFW office. Contact information for these offices can be found online or by calling the VFW National Programs headquarters at 816-968-1117.
Exclusive: Visit www.UltimateScholarshipBook.com and enter code VE47326 for updates on this award.

[474] • Platt Family Scholarship Prize Essay Contest
Lincoln Forum
c/o Don McCue, Curator of the Lincoln Memorial Shrine, 125 West Vine Street, Redlands, CA 92373
Phone: 909-798-7632
Email: archives@akspl.org
https://www.thelincolnforum.org/
Purpose: To reward students who have written the best essays on a topic related to Abraham Lincoln.
Eligibility: Applicants must be full-time undergraduate students who are enrolled at a U.S. college or university during the spring term of the contest entry year. They must submit an essay on a sponsor-determined topic that is related to Abraham Lincoln. Selection is based on the overall strength of the essay.
Target applicant(s): College students. Adult students.
Amount: $500-$1,500.
Number of awards: 3.
Deadline: July 31.
How to apply: Entry instructions are available online. An essay is required.
Exclusive: Visit www.UltimateScholarshipBook.com and enter code LI47426 for updates on this award.

[475] • Playwright Discovery Award
John F. Kennedy Center for the Performing Arts
2700 F Street NW, Washington, DC 20566
Phone: 800-444-1324
Email: vsainfo@kennedy-center.org
https://www.kennedy-center.org/education/opportunities-for-artists/competitions-and-commissions/
Purpose: To award promising young writers scholarship funds and a chance to have one of their scripts professionally produced at the John F. Kennedy Center for the Performing Arts.
Eligibility: Applicants must be students in grades 6-12. Applicants are to create an original one-act script of less than 40 pages that documents the experience of living with a disability. Applicants must have a disability, or the script can be a collaboration of a group of up to 5 students with one student having a disability. Selected scripts will be performed for middle school, high school and adult audiences. First and second place winners will have their plays performed at the JFK Performing Arts Center.
Target applicant(s): Junior high students or younger. High school students.

Amount: Varies.
Number of awards: Varies.
Deadline: January 10.
How to apply: Applications are available online.
Exclusive: Visit www.UltimateScholarshipBook.com and enter code JO47526 for updates on this award.

[476] • Poster Contest for High School Students
Christophers
5 Hanover Square, 22nd Floor, New York, NY 10004
Phone: 212-759-4050
Email: youth@christophers.org
https://www.christophers.org/video-contest-for-college-students
Purpose: To reward students for interpreting a given theme through poster art.
Eligibility: Entrants must be high school students. Students must work individually to create posters of original content. Posters are judged by a panel based on overall impact, expression of the year's theme, artistic merit and originality.
Target applicant(s): High school students.
Amount: $100-$1,000.
Number of awards: Up to 8.
Deadline: February 16.
How to apply: Applications are available online.
Exclusive: Visit www.UltimateScholarshipBook.com and enter code CH47626 for updates on this award.

[477] • Princess Grace Awards
Princess Grace Awards
565 Fifth Avenue, 23rd Floor, New York, NY 10017
Phone: 212-317-1470
Email: grants@pgfusa.org
http://www.pgfusa.org/
Purpose: To assist emerging young artists in theater, dance and film to realize their career goals.
Eligibility: Applicants must submit an example of their work in the category in which they apply: theatre, dance, choreography, film or playwriting. Theatre and dance applicants require the sponsorship of a professional company or school, one nominee per institution. Awards are based on the artistic quality of the artist's work, potential for future excellence and activities. Applicants must be U.S. citizens and (except playwrights) must be nominated by a school department chair/dean or company artistic director. Awards must be completed in the United States.
Target applicant(s): High school students. College students. Adult students.
Amount: Up to $15,000.
Number of awards: Varies.
Deadline: February 15.
How to apply: Applications are available online.
Exclusive: Visit www.UltimateScholarshipBook.com and enter code PR47726 for updates on this award.

[478] • Print and Graphics Scholarship
Print and Graphics Scholarship Foundation
301 Brush Creek Rd, Warrendale, PA 15086
Phone: 412-259-1740
Email: pgsf@printing.org
https://pgsf.org/
Purpose: To provide financial assistance for postsecondary education to students interested in graphic communications careers.

Eligibility: Applicants must be high school seniors, high school graduates or college students enrolled in a two- or four-year college printing or graphics program. Applicants must be full-time students, be interested in a career in printing technology, printing management, publishing or graphic communications and able to maintain a 3.0 GPA.
Target applicant(s): High school students. College students. Adult students.
Minimum GPA: 3.0
Amount: $1,000-$5,000.
Number of awards: Varies.
Scholarship may be renewable.
Deadline: May 1.
How to apply: Applications are available online.
Exclusive: Visit www.UltimateScholarshipBook.com and enter code PR47826 for updates on this award.

[479] • Prize in Ethics Essay Contest
Elie Wiesel Foundation for Humanity
555 Madison Avenue, Floor 13, New York, NY 10022
Phone: 212-490-7788
Email: info@eliewieselfoundation.org
https://eliewieselfoundation.org/prize-in-ethics/
Purpose: To promote the thought and discussion of ethics and their place in education.
Eligibility: Applicants must be registered full-time juniors and seniors at accredited colleges and universities in the U.S. Students must write an essay dealing with ethics and have a faculty sponsor review their essay and sign the entry form.
Target applicant(s): College students. Adult students.
Amount: $1,000-$5,000.
Number of awards: 5.
Deadline: December 29.
How to apply: Applications are available online.
Exclusive: Visit www.UltimateScholarshipBook.com and enter code EL47926 for updates on this award.

[480] • Ruth Clark Furniture Design Scholarship
International Furnishings and Design Association (IFDA)
7908 Lasley Forest Road, Lewisville, NC 27023-8244
Phone: 336-946-1011
Email: scholarships@ifdaef.org
https://ifda.com/educational-foundation/
Purpose: To aid interior design students who have an interest in residential furniture design.
Eligibility: Applicants must be full-time undergraduate or graduate students who are majoring in interior design or a closely related subject. They must have a concentration in residential upholstered and/or wood furniture design. Selection is based on the overall strength of the application.
Target applicant(s): College students. Graduate school students. Adult students.
Amount: $4,000.
Number of awards: 1.
Deadline: March 31.
How to apply: Applications are available online. An application form, transcript, personal essay, five original furniture designs and one recommendation letter are required.
Exclusive: Visit www.UltimateScholarshipBook.com and enter code IN48026 for updates on this award.

[481] • Ruth Lilly and Dorothy Sargent Rosenberg Poetry Fellowship Program
Poetry Magazine
61 West Superior Street, Chicago, IL 60654
Phone: 312-787-7070
Email: info@poetryfoundation.org
https://www.poetryfoundation.org/foundation/awards
Purpose: To encourage the study of writing and poetry.
Eligibility: Applicants must be U.S. residents between the ages of 21 and 31. They must be currently enrolled undergraduate or graduate students majoring in English or creative writing.
Target applicant(s): College students. Graduate school students. Adult students.
Amount: $25,800.
Number of awards: 5.
Deadline: April 15.
How to apply: Applications are available online. An essay and a poetry submission are required.
Exclusive: Visit www.UltimateScholarshipBook.com and enter code PO48126 for updates on this award.

[482] • Sara Tucker Study Grant
Richard Tucker Music Foundation
1790 Broadway, Suite 715, New York, NY 10019
Phone: 212-757-2218
http://www.richardtucker.org
Purpose: To support students who are transitioning from school to a professional career in music.
Eligibility: Applicants must have recently completed a graduate degree program or work in a young artist or apprentice program at a regional company and be generally under 30 years of age. Students must have had various performing opportunities but not in major roles.
Target applicant(s): College students. Adult students.
Amount: $5,000.
Number of awards: 4.
Deadline: July 1.
How to apply: Applications are available online.
Exclusive: Visit www.UltimateScholarshipBook.com and enter code RI48226 for updates on this award.

[483] • Scholastic Art and Writing Portfolio Award
Scholastic Art and Writing Awards
557 Broadway, New York, NY 10012
Email: info@artandwriting.org
http://www.artandwriting.org/scholarships/
Purpose: To reward creative young writers and artists.
Eligibility: Applicants must be high school seniors in U.S. or Canadian schools. Students must submit a total of six art or writing works with accompanying artist and personal statements in one of 28 categories of art and writing.
Target applicant(s): High school students.
Amount: Up to $12,500.
Number of awards: 46.
Deadline: February 29.
How to apply: Applications are available online.
Exclusive: Visit www.UltimateScholarshipBook.com and enter code SC48326 for updates on this award.

[484] • Senior Fellowship Program
National Gallery of Art
2000B South Club Drive, Landover, MD 20785
Phone: 202-842-6482
Email: thecenter@nga.gov
https://www.nga.gov/research/casva/fellowships.html
Purpose: To award fellowships to scholars in the visual arts.
Eligibility: Applicants should have held the Ph.D. for five years or more or possess an equivalent record of professional accomplishment at the time of application. They must submit application forms, proposals, copies of publications and three letters of recommendation. Fellowships are for full-time research, and scholars are expected to reside in Washington and to participate in the activities of the Center. One Paul Mellon Fellowship, one Frese Senior Fellowship and four to six Ailsa Mellon Bruce and Samuel H. Kress Senior Fellowships will be awarded for the academic year. The Paul Mellon and Ailsa Mellon Bruce Senior Fellowships support research in the history, theory and criticism of the visual arts of any geographical area and of any period. The Samuel H. Kress Senior Fellowships support research on European art before the early nineteenth century. The Frese Senior Fellowship is for study in the history, theory and criticism of sculpture, prints and drawings or decorative arts of any geographical area and of any period. Applications are also accepted from scholars in other disciplines whose work is related.
Target applicant(s): Graduate school students. Adult students.
Amount: Up to $50,000.
Number of awards: 6-8.
Deadline: October 15.
How to apply: Applications are available online.
Exclusive: Visit www.UltimateScholarshipBook.com and enter code NA48426 for updates on this award.

[485] • State of the Arts Scholarship
Home Education Recognition Organization Inc. (HERO)
820 North Fig Tree Lane, Plantation, FL 33317
Email: help@heroscholarship.org
https://www.heroscholarship.org/
Purpose: To encourage homeschooled students interested in studying visual or performing arts.
Eligibility: Applicants must have been homeschooled through four years of high school and demonstrate significant experience in the arts. Students must graduate and begin an educational program in an art school, college or university. Selection will be based on the application, references, autobiography, homeschool transcript and artistic accomplishments to date plus a portfolio of 10 pages or less or a CD or DVD of 5 minutes or less.
Target applicant(s): High school students.
Amount: $1,000.
Number of awards: 1.
Deadline: March 1.
How to apply: Applications are available online.
Exclusive: Visit www.UltimateScholarshipBook.com and enter code HO48526 for updates on this award.

[486] • Stella Blum Research Grant
Costume Society of America (CSA)
P.O. Box 852, Columbus, GA 31902-0852
Phone: 800-272-9447
Email: national.office@costumesocietyamerica.com
http://www.costumesocietyamerica.com
Purpose: To support a CSA student member working in the field of North American costume.
Eligibility: Applicants must be accepted into an undergraduate or graduate degree program at an accredited university for the time during which the grant would apply, conduct a research project in the area of North American costume and be members of the Costume Society of America (CSA) in good standing. Applications are judged according to significance of topic, feasibility, time frame, methodology, bibliography, budget, applicants' qualifications and how the research might further the field of costumes.
Target applicant(s): College students. Graduate school students. Adult students.
Amount: $3,000 plus a travel component of up to $600 to attend the National Symposium.
Number of awards: 1.
Deadline: August 21.
How to apply: Applications are available by email or phone.
Exclusive: Visit www.UltimateScholarshipBook.com and enter code CO48626 for updates on this award.

[487] • Stillman Kelley/Thelma Byrum Awards
National Federation of Music Clubs Stillman-Kelley Award
Nathalie Steinbach, 15 Mount Vernon Avenue, Fredericksburg, VA 22405
Phone: 512-892-5633
http://www.nfmc-music.org
Purpose: To support young musicians and composers.
Eligibility: Applicants must be instrumentalists, must not reach their 19th birthday by March 1 and be members of the National Federation of Music Clubs. This award rotates by region with the Northeastern and Southeastern regions in even years and Central and Western regions in odd years.
Target applicant(s): High school students.
Amount: $250-$1,500.
Number of awards: 9.
Deadline: March 1.
How to apply: Applications are available online.
Exclusive: Visit www.UltimateScholarshipBook.com and enter code NA48726 for updates on this award.

[488] • Student Academy Awards Competition
Academy of Motion Picture Arts and Sciences
8949 Wilshire Boulevard, Beverly Hills, CA 90211
Phone: 310-247-3031
Email: sguthrie@oscars.org
http://www.oscars.org
Purpose: To support filmmakers with no previous professional experience.
Eligibility: Applicants must be full-time students at an accredited U.S. college, university, film school or art school. Films must be made as a part of a school curriculum in the categories of alternative, animation, documentary or narrative. Selection is based on originality, entertainment, production quality and resourcefulness. A film under 40 minutes is required.
Target applicant(s): College students. Graduate school students. Adult students.
Amount: Varies.
Number of awards: Varies.
Deadline: June 1.
How to apply: Applications are available online.
Exclusive: Visit www.UltimateScholarshipBook.com and enter code AC48826 for updates on this award.

[489] • Student Design Competition

International Housewares Association
6400 Shafer Court, Suite 650, Rosemont, IL 60018
Phone: 847-292-4200
http://www.housewares.org
Purpose: To honor and encourage young, up-and-coming designers to enter careers in the housewares industry.
Eligibility: Applicants must be enrolled as an undergraduate or graduate student at an IDSA-affiliated college or university.
Target applicant(s): College students. Graduate school students. Adult students.
Amount: $12,000.
Number of awards: Varies.
Deadline: December 13.
How to apply: Applications are available online.
Exclusive: Visit www.UltimateScholarshipBook.com and enter code IN48926 for updates on this award.

[490] • Student Translation Award

American Translators Association
225 Reinekers Lane, Suite 590, Alexandria, VA 22314
Phone: 703-683-6100
Email: ata@atanet.org
http://www.atanet.org
Purpose: To encourage translation projects by students.
Eligibility: Applicants must be graduate or undergraduate students or a group of students attending an accredited U.S. college or university. The project should have post-grant results such as a publication, conference presentation or teaching material. Computer-assisted translations, dissertations and theses are not eligible, and students who are already published translators are not eligible. Translations must be from a foreign language into English. Preference is given to students who have been or are currently enrolled in translator training programs. There is a limit of one entry per student. Applicants should submit entry forms, statements of purpose, letter of recommendation, translation sample with corresponding source-language text, proof of permission to publish from copyright holder and sample outline or other material demonstrating the nature of the work (if the project is not a translation).
Target applicant(s): High school students. College students. Graduate school students. Adult students.
Amount: $500 plus $500 for conference.
Number of awards: 1.
Deadline: July 31.
How to apply: Applications are available online.
Exclusive: Visit www.UltimateScholarshipBook.com and enter code AM49026 for updates on this award.

[491] • Study Abroad Europe Scholarship

Study Aboard Europe
111 East Mosholu Parkway Suite 3F, New York, NY 10467
Phone: 718-710-0498
Email: info@studyabroadineurope.com
https://www.studyabroadineurope.com/pages.aspx?id=20&t=Scholarship
Purpose: To assist students who wish to study abroad in one of Study Abroad Europe's programs.
Eligibility: Applicants must be U.S. college students with a minimum 3.0 GPA.
Target applicant(s): College students. Adult students.
Minimum GPA: 3.0
Amount: $500-$1,000.
Number of awards: Up to 150.
Deadline: March 1 (Summer); April 1 (Summer); June 1 (Fall); October (Spring).
How to apply: Applications are available online. An application form, a one-page essay and a letter of recommendation from a professor or an assistant professor are required.
Exclusive: Visit www.UltimateScholarshipBook.com and enter code ST49126 for updates on this award.

[492] • Taylor/Blakeslee University Fellowships

Council for the Advancement of Science Writing (CASW)
P.O. Box 910, Hedgesville, WV 25427
Phone: 304-754-6786
Email: diane@casw.edu
http://www.casw.org
Purpose: To help graduate students in science writing.
Eligibility: Applicants must be U.S. citizens who are enrolled in U.S. graduate-level science writing programs.
Target applicant(s): Graduate school students. Adult students.
Amount: $6,000.
Number of awards: Varies.
Deadline: March 18.
How to apply: Contact the organization for more information.
Exclusive: Visit www.UltimateScholarshipBook.com and enter code CO49226 for updates on this award.

[493] • The Fountainhead Essay Contest

Ayn Rand Institute
6 Hutton Centre Drive, Suite 600, Santa Ana, CA 92707
Email: essays@aynrand.org
https://www.aynrand.org/students/essay-contests
Purpose: To honor high school students who distinguish themselves in their understanding of Ayn Rand's novel "The Fountainhead."
Eligibility: Applicants must be high school juniors or seniors who submit an 800- to 1,600-word essay, which will be judged on both style and content with an emphasis on writing that is clear, articulate and logically organized. Winning essays must demonstrate an outstanding grasp of the philosophic meaning of "The Fountainhead."
Target applicant(s): High school students.
Amount: Up to $25,000.
Number of awards: 84.
Deadline: December 20.
How to apply: Applications are only accepted online.
Exclusive: Visit www.UltimateScholarshipBook.com and enter code AY49326 for updates on this award.

[494] • Thelma A. Robinson Award in Ballet

National Federation of Music Clubs (Coral Gables, FL)
Gay Dill, National Chairman, 814 South Second Street, Atwood, KS 67730
Phone: 330-638-4003
Email: gaydill@att.net
http://www.nfmc-music.org
Purpose: To support students who are ballet dancers.
Eligibility: Applicants must be between the ages of 13 and 19. There is no entry fee, but applicants must be members of the NFMC. The award is given during even-numbered years.
Target applicant(s): Junior high students or younger. High school students.
Amount: $2,500.
Number of awards: 1.
Deadline: February 1 in odd-numbered year.
How to apply: Applications are available online. The award is only open in even-numbered years.
Exclusive: Visit www.UltimateScholarshipBook.com and enter code NA49426 for updates on this award.

[495] • Translation Prize Competition

American-Scandinavian Foundation
58 Park Avenue, New York, NY 10016
Phone: 212-779-3587
Email: info@amscan.org
http://www.amscan.org
Purpose: To encourage the English translation of Nordic literature.
Eligibility: The American-Scandinavian Foundation annually awards the following three translation prizes for outstanding translations of poetry, fiction, drama, or literary prose written by a twentieth or twenty-first-century Nordic author: 1. The Nadia Christensen Prize includes a $2,500 award, publication of an excerpt in Scandinavian Review, and a commemorative bronze medallion. 2. The Leif and Inger Sjöberg Award, given to an individual whose literature translations from a Nordic language have not previously been published, includes a $2,000 award, publication of an excerpt in Scandinavian Review, and a commemorative bronze medallion. 3. The Wigeland Prize, given to the best translation from Norwegian by a resident of Norway, includes a $2,000 award, publication of an excerpt in Scandinavian Review, and a commemorative bronze medallion.
Target applicant(s): Junior high students or younger. High school students. College students. Graduate school students. Adult students.
Amount: Up to $2,500.
Number of awards: 3.
Scholarship may be renewable.
Deadline: September 1.
How to apply: There is no application form. Please see the website for submission details.
Exclusive: Visit www.UltimateScholarshipBook.com and enter code AM49526 for updates on this award.

[496] • Tricia LeVangie Green/Sustainable Design Scholarship

International Furnishings and Design Association (IFDA)
7908 Lasley Forest Road, Lewisville, NC 27023-8244
Phone: 336-946-1011
Email: scholarships@ifdaef.org
https://ifda.com/educational-foundation/
Purpose: To aid interior design students who have a demonstrated interest in the green movement.
Eligibility: Applicants must be undergraduate students who are enrolled in an interior design or related furnishings design degree program at a U.S. postsecondary institution and have completed four design courses at the time of application. They must have a demonstrated interest in the green movement as it pertains to eco-friendly design and sustainability. Selection is based on the overall strength of the application.
Target applicant(s): College students. Adult students.
Amount: $1,500.
Number of awards: 1.
Deadline: March 31.
How to apply: Applications are available online. An application form, transcript, personal essay, two design work examples and one recommendation letter are required.
Exclusive: Visit www.UltimateScholarshipBook.com and enter code IN49626 for updates on this award.

[497] • Ukulele Festival Hawaii's College Scholarship Program

Ukulele Festival Hawaii
Scholarship Committee, Ukulele Festival Hawaii, 3555 Harding Avenue, Suite 1, Honolulu, HI 96816
Phone: 808-732-3739
Email: info@ukulelefestivalhawaii.org
http://www.roysakuma.net/
Purpose: To support students who play the ukulele.
Eligibility: Applicants must be Hawaii high school seniors in good standing. They must plan to attend a four-year college or university in the fall following graduation.
Target applicant(s): High school students.
Amount: $2,000.
Number of awards: Varies.
Deadline: April 30.
How to apply: Applications are available from Roy Sakuma Productions. An application form is required.
Exclusive: Visit www.UltimateScholarshipBook.com and enter code UK49726 for updates on this award.

[498] • Undergraduate Scholarships

Sigma Alpha Iota Philanthropies
Director, Undergraduate Scholarships, One Tunnel Road, Asheville, NC 28805
Phone: 828-251-0606
Email: jkpete@cox.net
http://www.sai-national.org
Purpose: To assist members of the Sigma Alpha Iota organization who have demonstrated outstanding leadership abilities, musical talent and scholastic achievement.
Eligibility: Applicants must be active members for at least one year in the Sigma Alpha Iota organization, be in good standing and demonstrate financial need.
Target applicant(s): College students. Adult students.
Amount: $1,500-$2,000.
Number of awards: 22.
Deadline: March 15.
How to apply: Applications are available online.
Exclusive: Visit www.UltimateScholarshipBook.com and enter code SI49826 for updates on this award.

[499] • Vectorworks Design Scholarship

Nemetschek Vectorworks
7150 Riverwood Drive, Columbia, MD 21046
Phone: 410-290-5114
http://www.vectorworks.net
Purpose: To reward students for excellent design work.
Eligibility: Applicants must be pursuing an undergraduate or graduate degree in a design-related field at an accredited educational institution. Students must submit a design project. Submissions may be made by individual students or by groups of up to six students. Selection is primarily based on design quality, technology, originality and explanation of the design.
Target applicant(s): College students. Graduate school students. Adult students.
Amount: $10,000.
Number of awards: 10.
Deadline: July 31.
How to apply: Applications are available online.
Exclusive: Visit www.UltimateScholarshipBook.com and enter code NE49926 for updates on this award.

[500] • Vercille Voss IFDA Graduate Student Scholarship

International Furnishings and Design Association (IFDA)
7908 Lasley Forest Road, Lewisville, NC 27023-8244
Phone: 336-946-1011
Email: scholarships@ifdaef.org
https://ifda.com/educational-foundation/
Purpose: To aid interior design graduate students.
Eligibility: Applicants must be graduate students who are majoring in interior design or a closely related subject at a U.S. postsecondary institution. Selection is based on the overall strength of the application.
Target applicant(s): College students. Graduate school students. Adult students.
Amount: $2,000.
Number of awards: 1.
Deadline: March 31.
How to apply: Applications are available online. An application form, transcript, personal essay, two original design work examples, one recommendation letter and proof of graduate school acceptance (for entering students only) are required.
Exclusive: Visit www.UltimateScholarshipBook.com and enter code IN50026 for updates on this award.

[501] • Visiting Senior Fellowship Program

National Gallery of Art
2000B South Club Drive, Landover, MD 20785
Phone: 202-842-6482
Email: thecenter@nga.gov
https://www.nga.gov/research/casva/fellowships.html
Purpose: To award fellowships to scholars in visual arts.
Eligibility: Applicants must have held their Ph.D. for five years or possess an equivalent record of professional accomplishment at the time of application. Applications are considered for research in the history, theory and criticism of the visual arts of any geographical area and of any period. Applicants must submit application forms, proposals, copies of a publication and two letters of recommendation. Fellowships are for full-time research, and scholars are expected to reside in Washington and to participate in the activities of the Center. Applications are also accepted from scholars in other disciplines whose work is related. The Center awards up to twelve short-term Paul Mellon and Ailsa Mellon Bruce Visiting Senior Fellowships. The deadlines are March 21 for the fellowship from September to February and September 21 for March through August.
Target applicant(s): Graduate school students. Adult students.
Amount: $7,000-$12,500.
Number of awards: Varies.
Scholarship may be renewable.
Deadline: March 21.
How to apply: Applications are available online.
Exclusive: Visit www.UltimateScholarshipBook.com and enter code NA50126 for updates on this award.

[502] • VMSD Scholarship

Planning and Visual Education Partnership (PAVE)
8570 Stirling Road, Suite 102-227, Hollywood, FL 33024
Phone: 954-551-9144
Email: info@paveglobal.org
http://paveglobal.org
Purpose: To support students in educational programs preparing them for careers in the retail environment industry.
Eligibility: Applicants must be third- or fourth-year students or equivalent or enrolled in a program working toward a degree in interior design, retail design, hospitality design, visual merchandising, UX design, architecture, engineering or product design. Students must be located and studying in the United States with a minimum 3.0 GPA. An essay on a provided prompt and a project folio are required to be submitted.
Target applicant(s): College students. Adult students.
Amount: Up to $4,400.
Number of awards: 1.
Deadline: September 15.
How to apply: Applications are available online.
Exclusive: Visit www.UltimateScholarshipBook.com and enter code PL50226 for updates on this award.

[503] • Women Band Directors International College Scholarships

Women Band Directors International
Karen Williams, WBDI Scholarship Chair, 3994 White Oak Road, Waynesville, NC 28785
Email: agreen@lamar.k12.ga.us
http://www.womenbanddirectors.org
Purpose: To support future female band directors.
Eligibility: Applicants must be studying music education with the intention of becoming a band director.
Target applicant(s): College students. Graduate school students. Adult students.
Amount: Varies.
Number of awards: Varies.
Deadline: November 1.
How to apply: Applications are available online.
Exclusive: Visit www.UltimateScholarshipBook.com and enter code WO50326 for updates on this award.

Scholarship Directory (Humanities / Arts)

[504] • Wyland National Art Challenge
Wyland Foundation
6 Mason, Irvine, CA 92618
Email: artchallenge@wylandfoundation.org
https://wylandfoundation.org/programs/wyland-art-contests-for-kids/
Purpose: To encourage students with an interest in conservation and art.
Eligibility: Applicants must be students in grades kindergarten through twelve in a U.S. school. Students must participate in the painting of a 4x8 foot mural that addresses the theme of conservation.
Target applicant(s): Junior high students or younger. High school students.
Amount: $1,500.
Number of awards: 3.
Deadline: December 1.
How to apply: Applications are available online.
Exclusive: Visit www.UltimateScholarshipBook.com and enter code WY50426 for updates on this award.

[505] • You Can t Label People, but You Can Label Products Essay and Label Design Scholarship
Sttark
2 Task Industrial Court, Greenville, SC 29607
Phone: 877-277-4682
Email: marketing@sttark.com
https://www.sttark.com/scholarship/labels-scholarship
Purpose: To reward young creatives and innovators.
Eligibility: Applicants must be aspiring designers, manufacturers, engineers, artists, architects or any other type of innovator. Students must be U.S. citizens and current high school seniors, undergraduate students or graduate students. Applicants must write and submit about a given topic related to innovation.
Target applicant(s): High school students. College students. Graduate school students. Adult students.
Amount: $3,000.
Number of awards: 1.
Deadline: March 1.
How to apply: Applications are available online.
Exclusive: Visit www.UltimateScholarshipBook.com and enter code ST50526 for updates on this award.

[506] • Young American Creative Patriotic Art Contest
Ladies Auxiliary VFW
406 West 34th Street, 10th Floor, Kansas City, MO 64111
Phone: 816-561-8655
Email: info@vfwauxiliary.org
https://vfwauxiliary.org/scholarships/
Purpose: To encourage patriotic art.
Eligibility: Applicants must be high school students in the same state as the sponsoring Ladies Auxiliary. They must submit one piece of patriotic art on paper or canvas. Art must have been completed during the current school year and must be accompanied by a teacher's signature. Applicants must participate in a local Auxiliary competition before advancing to the national level.
Target applicant(s): High school students.
Amount: Up to $37,000.
Number of awards: Varies.
Deadline: March 31.
How to apply: Applications are available online.
Exclusive: Visit www.UltimateScholarshipBook.com and enter code LA50626 for updates on this award.

[507] • Young Filmmakers Contest
One Earth Film Festival
805 Lake Street, #177, Oak Park, IL 60301
Phone: 708-824-6201
https://www.oneearthfilmfest.org/contest-details/
Purpose: To support student filmmakers.
Eligibility: Applicants must be from grade three to college students and beyond and be age 25 or younger. Students create a film that is three to eight minutes long or an animated or stop-motion film that is at least 45 seconds long. The theme for the film can be climate, energy, food, transportation, waste, water or wildlife and ecosystems.
Target applicant(s): Junior high students or younger. High school students. College students. Graduate school students.
Amount: $100-$1,000.
Number of awards: Varies.
Deadline: May 25.
How to apply: Applications are available online.
Exclusive: Visit www.UltimateScholarshipBook.com and enter code ON50726 for updates on this award.

[508] • Zicklin Contracting Restoration Awareness Scholarship
Zicklin Contracting
967 Longfellow Avenue, Bronx, NY 10474
Phone: 718-550-2779
https://www.zicklincontracting.com/restoration-awarness-scholarship/
Purpose: To support students who write an essay or create a video on water or fire restoration.
Eligibility: Applicants must be high school seniors, undergraduates or graduate students in the U.S. and Canada. Students must enroll in a college or university for the upcoming academic year and submit an essay, video or infographic on given topics related to water or fire restoration.
Target applicant(s): Junior high students or younger. High school students. College students. Graduate school students. Adult students.
Amount: $1,000.
Number of awards: Varies.
Deadline: June 1.
How to apply: Applications are available online.
Exclusive: Visit www.UltimateScholarshipBook.com and enter code ZI50826 for updates on this award.

SOCIAL SCIENCES

[509] • A.J. Grisanti Memorial Scholarship
National Restaurant Association Educational Foundation
2055 L Street NW Suite 700, Washington, DC 20036
Phone: 800-765-2122
Email: scholars@naref.org
http://www.nraef.org
Purpose: To support students pursuing degrees in restaurant, food service or hospitality related fields.
Eligibility: Applicants must be enrolled or accepted as a full-time or part-time undergraduate students at an accredited post-secondary institution. Students must be majoring in an undergraduate level restaurant, foodservice or hospitality-related program.
Target applicant(s): High school students. College students. Adult students.
Amount: Varies.
Number of awards: 1.
Deadline: March 15.
How to apply: Applications are available online.
Exclusive: Visit www.UltimateScholarshipBook.com and enter code NA50926 for updates on this award.

[510] • AALL Educational Scholarships
American Association of Law Libraries
105 W. Adams, Suite 3300, Chicago, IL 60603
Email: scholarships@aall.org
https://www.aallnet.org/education-training/scholarships/
Purpose: To encourage students to pursue careers as law librarians.
Eligibility: There are six levels of awards: 1. Library Degree for Law School Graduates, awarded to a law school graduate with law library experience pursuing a degree at an accredited library school. 2. Library School Graduates Attending Law School, awarded to a library school graduate pursuing a degree at an accredited law school who has law library experience and no more than 36 semester credit hours left before obtaining the law degree. 3. Library Degree for Non-Law School Graduates, awarded to a college graduate with law library experience who is seeking a degree involving law librarianship courses at an accredited library school. 4. Library School Graduates Seeking A Non-Law Degree, awarded to library school graduates who are seeking degrees in fields other than law. 5. Law Librarians in Continuing Education Courses, awarded to law librarians with a degree from an accredited library or law school who are continuing their education. 6. Dual JD/MLIS Degree, awarded to college graduates working toward a dual degree in an accredited law school and library school. Preference is given to AALL members, but a non-member can apply. All applicants must intend to have careers as law librarians. There must be financial need for awards 1-4.
Target applicant(s): Graduate school students. Adult students.
Amount: Varies.
Number of awards: Varies.
Scholarship may be renewable.
Deadline: April 1.
How to apply: Applications are available online, by mail with a self-addressed, stamped envelope, by fax, by phone or by email.
Exclusive: Visit www.UltimateScholarshipBook.com and enter code AM51026 for updates on this award.

[511] • ABF Summer Undergraduate Research Fellowship Program
American Bar Foundation
750 North Lake Shore Drive, Floor 4, Chicago, IL 60611-4557
Phone: 312-988-6500
Email: americanbarfoundation.org
https://www.americanbarfoundation.org/program/abf-summer-undergraduate-research-fellowship-program/
Purpose: To help students who plan to pursue work in the field of law or social science.
Eligibility: Applicants must be currently enrolled at colleges and universities in the U.S. and pursuing work in law or social science. Students must have completed at least two years of their undergraduate program and not received a bachelor's degree by the time the fellowship begins. Applicants must be authorized to work in the U.S. for the duration of the fellowship.
Target applicant(s): College students. Adult students.
Amount: Varies.
Number of awards: Varies.
Deadline: January 31.
How to apply: Applications are available online.
Exclusive: Visit www.UltimateScholarshipBook.com and enter code AM51126 for updates on this award.

[512] • Academic Merit Scholarships
American Bus Association (ABA)
111 K Street NE, 9th Floor, Washington, DC 20002
Phone: 202-842-1645
Email: info@buses.org
https://www.buses.org/aba-foundation/scholarships/
Purpose: To help students who plan to pursue work in the transportation industry.
Eligibility: Applicants must be undergraduate or graduate students at an accredited university (four-year university or college or community college) and must have a minimum GPA of 3.4 on a 4.0 scale. Students must have a declared major or course of study relevant to the transportation, travel and tourism industry. Applicants must write and submit a short essay on how their major or course of study is relevant to the transportation, travel and tourism industries.
Target applicant(s): College students. Graduate school students. Adult students.
Minimum GPA: 3.4
Amount: $5,000.
Number of awards: 2.
Deadline: April 1.
How to apply: Applications are available online.
Exclusive: Visit www.UltimateScholarshipBook.com and enter code AM51226 for updates on this award.

[513] • Accounting and Financial Women's Alliance Foundation Scholarship
Accounting and Financial Women's Alliance
2365 Harrodsburg Road, Suite A325, Lexington, KY 40504
Phone: 859-219-3532
Email: foundation@AFWA.org
https://www.afwa.org/
Purpose: To support female students pursuing accounting or finance degrees.

Eligibility: Applicants must be females. Students must be undergraduates attending their third, fourth or fifth year or graduate students enrolled and pursuing degrees in accounting or finance.
Target applicant(s): College students. Graduate school students. Adult students.
Amount: Varies.
Number of awards: Varies.
Deadline: April 1.
How to apply: Applications are available online.
Exclusive: Visit www.UltimateScholarshipBook.com and enter code AC51326 for updates on this award.

[514] • ACLS Fellowships
American Council of Learned Societies (ACLS)
633 Third Avenue, New York, NY 10017-6795
Phone: 212-697-1505
Email: mgoldfeder@acls.org
https://www.acls.org/
Purpose: To support a scholar in the study of humanities.
Eligibility: Applicants must have a Ph.D. degree and at least a three year period since their last supported research. An application, a proposal, bibliography, publications list and two reference letters are required. The award levels are based on the position of the applicant: professor and equivalent, associate professor and equivalent and assistant professor and equivalent. The ACLS fellowships include ACLS/SSRC/NEH International and Area Studies Fellowships and ACLS/New York Public Library Fellowships.
Target applicant(s): Graduate school students. Adult students.
Amount: Up to $60,000.
Number of awards: Varies.
Deadline: September 28.
How to apply: Applications are available online.
Exclusive: Visit www.UltimateScholarshipBook.com and enter code AM51426 for updates on this award.

[515] • ACOR-CAORC Fellowship
American Center of Oriental Research (ACOR)
209 Commerce Street, Alexandria, VA 22314
Phone: 703-789-9231
Email: usa.office@acorjordan.org
https://acorjordan.org/fellowships-2/
Purpose: To assist master's and pre-doctoral students conducting research in Jordan.
Eligibility: Applicants must be U.S. citizen graduate students researching topics involving scholarship in Near Eastern studies. Recipients are required to engage in scholarly and cultural activities while residing at the American Center of Oriental Research (ACOR) in Jordan. The fellowships last from two to six months. The award includes room and board at ACOR, transportation, a stipend and research funds.
Target applicant(s): Graduate school students. Adult students.
Amount: $30,000.
Number of awards: Varies.
Deadline: February 15.
How to apply: Applications are available online.
Exclusive: Visit www.UltimateScholarshipBook.com and enter code AM51526 for updates on this award.

[516] • Adelle and Erwin Tomash Fellowship in the History of Information Processing
Charles Babbage Institute
Center for the History of Information Processing, 211 Andersen Library, University of Minnesota, 222 - 21st Avenue South, Minneapolis, MN 55455
Phone: 612-624-5050
Email: yostx003@tc.umn.edu
http://www.cbi.umn.edu
Purpose: To support a graduate student who is researching the history of computing.
Eligibility: Applicants must be graduate students who have completed all doctoral degree requirements except the research and writing of the dissertation. Students must submit a curriculum vitae and a five-page statement and justification of the research program. To be eligible, scholars will reside outside the Twin Cities metropolitan region.
Target applicant(s): Graduate school students. Adult students.
Amount: $14,000.
Number of awards: 1.
Deadline: January 15.
How to apply: Visit the website for more information.
Exclusive: Visit www.UltimateScholarshipBook.com and enter code CH51626 for updates on this award.

[517] • Adult Students in Scholastic Transition (ASIST)
Executive Women International (EWI)
1288 Summit Avenue Suite 107, #124, Oconomowoc, WI 53066
Phone: 262-269-5625
Email: ewi@ewiconnect.com
https://ewiconnect.com/page/scholarships
Purpose: To assist adult students who face major life transitions.
Eligibility: Applicants may be single parents, individuals just entering the workforce or displaced workers.
Target applicant(s): College students. Adult students.
Amount: $2,000-$10,000.
Number of awards: 13.
Deadline: Late March.
How to apply: Contact your local EWI chapter.
Exclusive: Visit www.UltimateScholarshipBook.com and enter code EX51726 for updates on this award.

[518] • AICPA Foundation Scholarship for Future CPAs
American Institute of Certified Public Accountants
220 Leigh Farm Road, Durham, NC 27707-8110
Phone: 919-402-4500
Email: scholarships@aicpa.org
https://www.aicpa.org
Purpose: To encourage accounting majors planning to become CPAs.
Eligibility: Applicants must be enrolled as full-time undergraduate or graduate level students pursuing a degree in accounting or an accounting-related major. Students must have completed at least 30 semester hours of college coursework, including at least six semester hours in accounting while maintaining an overall and major GPA of 3.0. Applicants must be U.S. citizens or permanent residents and planning to pursue CPA licensure.
Target applicant(s): College students. Graduate school students. Adult students.
Minimum GPA: 3.0

Amount: $3,000-$10,000.
Number of awards: 26.
Deadline: March 15.
How to apply: Applications are available online.
Exclusive: Visit www.UltimateScholarshipBook.com and enter code AM51826 for updates on this award.

[519] • AICPA Foundation Two-year Transfer Scholarship

American Institute of Certified Public Accountants
220 Leigh Farm Road, Durham, NC 27707-8110
Phone: 919-402-4500
Email: scholarships@aicpa.org
https://www.aicpa.org
Purpose: To support students transferring from a two-year college to a four-year institution to complete their degree in accounting or an accounting-related field.
Eligibility: Applicants must be currently completing courses at a two-year college/university planning to transfer with a declared intent to major in accounting or an accounting-related field at a four-year college/university and maintaining an overall and major GPA of 3.0. Students must be U.S. citizens or permanent residents and planning to pursue the CPA licensure.
Target applicant(s): College students. Adult students.
Minimum GPA: 3.0
Amount: $5,000.
Number of awards: 40.
Deadline: March 15.
How to apply: Applications are available online.
Exclusive: Visit www.UltimateScholarshipBook.com and enter code AM51926 for updates on this award.

[520] • AICPA John L. Carey Scholarship

American Institute of Certified Public Accountants
220 Leigh Farm Road, Durham, NC 27707-8110
Phone: 919-402-4500
Email: scholarships@aicpa.org
https://www.aicpa.org
Purpose: To support non-business related degree holders who are pursuing graduate studies in accounting.
Eligibility: Applicants must be full-time students who have obtained a liberal arts or other non-business undergraduate degree and have earned 12 credits or fewer in accounting or business. Applicants must be pursuing their CPA. Two essays are required.
Target applicant(s): Graduate school students. Adult students.
Amount: $5,000.
Number of awards: 8.
Deadline: March 15.
How to apply: Applications are available online.
Exclusive: Visit www.UltimateScholarshipBook.com and enter code AM52026 for updates on this award.

[521] • AIERF College Scholarship

Appraisal Institute Education Trust
200 W. Madison, Suite 1500, Chicago, IL 60606
Phone: 312-335-4133
Email: wwoodburn@appraisalinstitute.org
http://www.appraisalinstitute.org
Purpose: To support students concentrating in real estate appraisal, land economics, real estate or allied fields.
Eligibility: Applicants must be students majoring in real estate appraisal, land economics, real estate or allied fields. Students must have a strong academic record.
Target applicant(s): College students. Adult students.
Amount: $1,000.
Number of awards: Varies.
Deadline: April 1.
How to apply: Applications are available online.
Exclusive: Visit www.UltimateScholarshipBook.com and enter code AP52126 for updates on this award.

[522] • AIERF Graduate Scholarship

Appraisal Institute Education Trust
200 W. Madison, Suite 1500, Chicago, IL 60606
Phone: 312-335-4133
Email: wwoodburn@appraisalinstitute.org
http://www.appraisalinstitute.org
Purpose: To support students who are working on a college degree concentrating on real estate appraisal, land economics, real estate or allied fields.
Eligibility: Applicants must be students majoring in real estate appraisal, land economics, real estate or allied fields. Students must be master's or doctoral candidates. Applicants must be full- or part-time students at a U.S. degree granting college or university with a strong academic record.
Target applicant(s): Graduate school students. Adult students.
Amount: $2,000.
Number of awards: Varies.
Deadline: April 1.
How to apply: Applications are available online.
Exclusive: Visit www.UltimateScholarshipBook.com and enter code AP52226 for updates on this award.

[523] • Alice L. Haltom Educational Fund Scholarship

Alice L. Haltom Educational Fund
P.O. Box 70530, Houston, TX 77270
http://www.alhef.org/scholarship/
Purpose: To support students pursuing information and records management.
Eligibility: Applicants must be U.S. or Canadian citizens pursuing an education for a career in information and records management. Students must submit an essay, three letters of recommendation and transcripts along with their application.
Target applicant(s): College students. Graduate school students. Adult students.
Amount: $2,000.
Number of awards: Varies.
Deadline: May 1.
How to apply: Applications are available online.
Exclusive: Visit www.UltimateScholarshipBook.com and enter code AL52326 for updates on this award.

The Ultimate Scholarship Book 2026
Scholarship Directory (Social Sciences)

[524] • Allied Van Lines Scholarship
Allied Van Lines
One Parkview Plaza, Oakbrook Terrace, IL 60181
Phone: 800-689-8684
https://www.allied.com/scholarship
Purpose: To support students pursuing logistics and moving-related fields.
Eligibility: Applicants must be U.S. citizens or permanent residents enrolling as full-time students pursuing an undergraduate degree in logistics or related field. Students must provide transcripts, enrollment verification and an essay.
Target applicant(s): College students. Adult students.
Amount: $1,000.
Number of awards: 3.
Deadline: December 15.
How to apply: Applications are available online.
Exclusive: Visit www.UltimateScholarshipBook.com and enter code AL52426 for updates on this award.

[525] • Ally Financial Public Policy Scholars
Congressional Black Caucus Foundation
1720 Massachusetts Avenue NW, Washington, DC 20036
Phone: 202-263-2800
Email: info@cbcfinc.org
https://www.cbcfinc.org/scholarships/
Purpose: To support students who demonstrate leadership ability through exemplary community service and academic talent.
Eligibility: Applicants must be U.S. residents and full-time sophomores or juniors at an accredited college at the time of application. Students must demonstrate a commitment to the public policy profession. Applicants must exhibit leadership and be active within the community.
Target applicant(s): College students. Adult students.
Amount: Varies.
Number of awards: Varies.
Deadline: March 15.
How to apply: Applications are available online.
Exclusive: Visit www.UltimateScholarshipBook.com and enter code CO52526 for updates on this award.

[526] • Alpha Kappa Psi Scholarships
Alpha Kappa Psi Foundation
8001 East 196th Street, Noblesville, IN 46062
Phone: 317-872-1553
Email: mail@akpsi.org
https://akpsifoundation.org/grants-and-scholarships/foundationscholarships/
Purpose: To support students who are members of the Alpha Kappa Psi society.
Eligibility: Applicants must be initiated Alpha Kappa Psi students who are currently undergraduate or graduate students with at least a 2.75 GPA. Students must have a strong record of chapter or campus leadership.
Target applicant(s): College students. Graduate school students. Adult students.
Minimum GPA: 2.75
Amount: $500-$10,000.
Number of awards: Varies.
Deadline: February 28.
How to apply: Applications are available online.
Exclusive: Visit www.UltimateScholarshipBook.com and enter code AL52626 for updates on this award.

[527] • American Bar Association Law Student Writing Competition
American Bar Association
321 North Clark Street, Chicago, IL 60654
Phone: 312-988-5624
Email: abalsd@americanbar.org
https://www.americanbar.org/groups/diversity/diversity_pipeline/projects_initiatives/legal_opportunity_scholarship/
Purpose: To support and recognize achievement among law students.
Eligibility: The American Bar Association (ABA) sponsors a variety of essay and writing competitions for ABA student members. Applicants must write an article about antitrust and have it published in an ABA-accredited school's law review or journal. Law students currently enrolled or graduating can write eligible articles of general interest to the antitrust law community, such as Civil and Criminal Antitrust Law, Competition Policy, Consumer Protection and International Competition Law. Selection is based on the strength of the essay.
Target applicant(s): Graduate school students. Adult students.
Amount: $1,000- $2,500.
Number of awards: Varies.
Deadline: May 31.
How to apply: Applications are available online. Application requirements vary by competition.
Exclusive: Visit www.UltimateScholarshipBook.com and enter code AM52726 for updates on this award.

[528] • American Culinary Federation Scholarships
American Culinary Federation
6816 Southpoint Parkway Suite 400, Jacksonville, FL 32216
Phone: 904-824-4468
Email: scholarships@acfchefs.net
http://www.acfchefs.org
Purpose: To support high school and college students looking to further their education or compete in student culinary teams at ACF conferences.
Eligibility: Applicants must have a minimum GPA of 2.5, be graduating high school seniors and be accepted into an accredited college or university or be currently enrolled students in an accredited college or university. Applicants must also be planning to major in culinary or pastry arts or be ACF registered apprentices and have career aspirations of being a chef or pastry chef. Selection is based on GPA, participation in culinary competitions, volunteer activities, involvement in the ACF, essay and references.
Target applicant(s): High school students. College students. Adult students.
Minimum GPA: 2.5
Amount: $1,500-$2,500.
Number of awards: Varies.
Deadline: April 30; October 31.
How to apply: Applications are available online. An application form, essay and references are required.
Exclusive: Visit www.UltimateScholarshipBook.com and enter code AM52826 for updates on this award.

[529] • American Express Scholarship Competition
American Hotel and Lodging Educational Foundation (AHLEF)
1250 Eye Street, N.W. Suite 1100, Washington, DC 20005
Phone: 202-289-3180
Email: foundation@ahla.com
https://www.ahlafoundation.org/scholarships/
Purpose: To provide financial assistance to students pursuing a degree in hospitality management.
Eligibility: Applicants must be enrolled in an accredited undergraduate program resulting in a degree in hospitality management. Students or their parents must be employed in the lodging industry by an American Hotel and Lodging Association member facility.
Target applicant(s): College students. Adult students.
Amount: $500-$2,000.
Number of awards: Varies.
Deadline: March 15.
How to apply: Applications are available online.
Exclusive: Visit www.UltimateScholarshipBook.com and enter code AM52926 for updates on this award.

[530] • APF Dr. Christine Blasey Ford Grant
American Psychological Association
750 First Street NE, Washington, DC 20002-4242
Phone: 800-374-2721
https://www.apa.org/apf/funding/scholarships
Purpose: To assist early career psychologists and graduate students using psychology to solve important problems and improve people's lives.
Eligibility: Applicants must be graduate students or early career psychologists (doctoral-level psychologists who are no more than 10 years postdoctoral) who are affiliated with nonprofit charitable, educational and scientific institutions, or governmental entities operating exclusively for charitable and educational purposes. Students must have a demonstrated knowledge of trauma and trauma research, demonstrate competence and capacity to execute the proposed work and have IRB approval from the host institution before funding can be awarded if human participants are involved.
Target applicant(s): Graduate school students. Adult students.
Amount: Up to $1,900.
Number of awards: 1.
Deadline: February 15.
How to apply: Applications are available online.
Exclusive: Visit www.UltimateScholarshipBook.com and enter code AM53026 for updates on this award.

[531] • APF/COGDOP Graduate Student Scholarships
American Psychological Foundation
750 First Street NE, Washington, DC 20002-4242
Phone: 202-336-5843
Email: foundation@apa.org
https://www.apa.org/apf/funding/grants
Purpose: To assist graduate students of psychology with research costs associated with the master's thesis or doctoral dissertation.
Eligibility: Applicants must be graduate students enrolled in an interim master's program or doctoral program. Students currently enrolled in a terminal master's program must intend to enroll in a Ph.D. program. Applicants at any stage of graduate study are encouraged to apply and must be enrolled in the graduate program at the time grants are awarded.
Target applicant(s): Graduate school students. Adult students.
Amount: $2,000-$5,000.
Number of awards: 21.
Deadline: June 26.
How to apply: Applicants must be nominated.
Exclusive: Visit www.UltimateScholarshipBook.com and enter code AM53126 for updates on this award.

[532] • APF/Division 54 Lizette Peterson-Homer Injury Prevention Grant
American Psychological Association
750 First Street NE, Washington, DC 20002-4242
Phone: 800-374-2721
https://www.apa.org/apf/funding/scholarships
Purpose: To assist students using psychology to solve important problems and improve people's lives.
Eligibility: Applicants must be students and/or faculty at accredited universities who have demonstrated research competence and area commitment. Research should focus on the prevention of physical injury in children and adolescents.
Target applicant(s): High school students. College students. Adult students.
Amount: $5,000.
Number of awards: 1.
Deadline: October 16.
How to apply: Applications are available online.
Exclusive: Visit www.UltimateScholarshipBook.com and enter code AM53226 for updates on this award.

[533] • ARIT Fellowships for Research in Turkey
American Research Institute in Turkey (ARIT)
3260 South Street, Philadelphia, PA 19104-6324
Phone: 215-898-3474
Email: leinwand@sas.upenn.edu
https://aritweb.org/
Purpose: To support scholars in their research in Turkey.
Eligibility: Applicants must be scholars or advanced graduate students involved in research on ancient, medieval or modern times in Turkey, in any field of the humanities and social sciences. Student applicants must have completed all requirements for the doctorate except the dissertation before beginning any ARIT-sponsored research. Non-U.S. applicants must be connected to an educational institution in the U.S. or Canada. Applicants should submit applications, three letters of recommendation and graduate transcripts.
Target applicant(s): Graduate school students. Adult students.
Amount: Varies.
Number of awards: Varies.
Deadline: November 1.
How to apply: Applications are available online.
Exclusive: Visit www.UltimateScholarshipBook.com and enter code AM53326 for updates on this award.

[534] • ARRL Foundation General Fund Scholarship
American Radio Relay League Foundation
225 Main Street, Newington, CT 06111-1494
Phone: 860-594-0200
Email: foundation@arrl.org
https://www.arrl.org/scholarship-program
Purpose: To assist ham radio operators in furthering their educations.
Eligibility: Applicants must have any level of ham radio license.

The Ultimate Scholarship Book 2026
Scholarship Directory (Social Sciences)

Target applicant(s): High school students. College students. Graduate school students. Adult students.
Amount: $2,000.
Number of awards: Varies.
Deadline: January 10.
How to apply: Applications are available online. Completed applications must be submitted by mail.
Exclusive: Visit www.UltimateScholarshipBook.com and enter code AM53426 for updates on this award.

[535] • Asparagus Club, Thomas K. Zaucha Scholarship
National Grocers Association
1005 N. Glebe Road, Suite 250, Arlington, VA 22201
Phone: 225-387-6126
https://www.nationalgrocers.org/foundation/nga-foundation-scholarships/
Purpose: To support students pursuing degrees related to the grocery field.
Eligibility: Applicants must be rising sophomores through postgraduate students, have a minimum 2.5 GPA and be enrolled in a two- or four-year degree-granting institution. Students must major in business, food management, IT or another field related to a career in the grocery industry. Experience in the grocery industry is preferred but not required.
Target applicant(s): College students. Graduate school students. Adult students.
Minimum GPA: 2.5
Amount: $2,500.
Number of awards: Varies.
Deadline: April 15.
How to apply: Applications are available online.
Exclusive: Visit www.UltimateScholarshipBook.com and enter code NA53526 for updates on this award.

[536] • AWSCPA Scholarship
American Institute of Certified Public Accountants
220 Leigh Farm Road, Durham, NC 27707-8110
Phone: 919-402-4500
Email: scholarships@aicpa.org
https://www.aicpa.org
Purpose: To support female students majoring in accounting.
Eligibility: Applicants must be women enrolled as full-time undergraduate or graduate level students pursuing a degree in accounting or an accounting-related major. Students must have completed at least 30 semester hours of college coursework, including at least six semester hours in accounting while maintaining an overall and major GPA of 3.0. Applicants must be U.S. citizens or permanent residents and planning to pursue CPA licensure.
Target applicant(s): College students. Graduate school students. Adult students.
Minimum GPA: 3.0
Amount: $5,000.
Number of awards: 8.
Deadline: March 15.
How to apply: Applications are available online.
Exclusive: Visit www.UltimateScholarshipBook.com and enter code AM53626 for updates on this award.

[537] • BEA National Scholarships in Broadcasting
Broadcast Education Association
1771 N Street NW, Washington, DC 20036
Phone: 888-380-7222
Email: beainfo@beaweb.org
http://www.beaweb.org
Purpose: To honor broadcasters and the broadcast industry.
Eligibility: Applicants must be college juniors or seniors or graduate students at BEA member universities, students pursuing freshman and sophomore instruction only or students who have already completed BEA two-year programs at a four-year college.
Target applicant(s): High school students. College students. Graduate school students. Adult students.
Amount: $1,000 to $4,000.
Number of awards: 10.
Deadline: October 13.
How to apply: Applications are available online.
Exclusive: Visit www.UltimateScholarshipBook.com and enter code BR53726 for updates on this award.

[538] • Beauty Changes Lives Foundation Scholarships
Beauty Changes Lives
P.O. Box 7174, Rancho Santa Fe, CA 92067
Phone: 760-733-8383
Email: info@beautychangeslives.org
http://www.beautychangeslives.org
Purpose: To support licensed hairstylists in attending a member school of the American Association of Cosmetology Schools.
Eligibility: Applicants must be accepted or currently enrolled in a member school of the American Association of Cosmetology Schools. Selection is based on the overall strength of the application.
Target applicant(s): College students. Adult students.
Amount: Up to $20,000.
Number of awards: 38.
Deadline: December 15.
How to apply: Applications are available online.
Exclusive: Visit www.UltimateScholarshipBook.com and enter code BE53826 for updates on this award.

[539] • Begun Scholarship
California Library Association
248 E. Foothill Boulevard, Suite 101, Monrovia, CA 91016
Phone: 916-779-4573
Email: info@cla-net.org
https://www.cla-net.org
Purpose: To assist California library or information sciences graduate students at California schools.
Eligibility: Applicants must be California graduate students attending an American Library Association accredited school and have completed core coursework toward a master's of library and science or information studies degree. Recipients must also plan to become a children's or young adult librarian in a California public library and to join the California Library Association if not already a member.
Target applicant(s): Graduate school students. Adult students.
Minimum GPA: 3.0
Amount: $3,000.
Number of awards: 1.
Deadline: March 31.
How to apply: Applications are available online.

Exclusive: Visit www.UltimateScholarshipBook.com and enter code CA53926 for updates on this award.

[540] • Betsy Plank/PRSSA Scholarship
Public Relations Student Society of America
120 Wall Street, 21st Floor, New York, NY 10005-4024
Phone: 212-460-1474
Email: prssa@prsa.org
https://prssa.prsa.org/scholarships-and-awards/
Purpose: To assist public relations students.
Eligibility: Applicants must be PRSSA members enrolled in an undergraduate public relations program and be college juniors or seniors. Eligible students may be nominated from each PRSSA chapter. Selection is based on academic achievement, leadership, experience and commitment to public relations. Applicants need to include a 300-word statement of commitment to public relations.
Target applicant(s): College students. Adult students.
Amount: $1,000-$5,000.
Number of awards: 3.
Deadline: April 30.
How to apply: Applications are available online.
Exclusive: Visit www.UltimateScholarshipBook.com and enter code PU54026 for updates on this award.

[541] • Beverly Murphy MLA Scholarship for Underrepresented Students
Medical Library Association
225 West Wacker Drive, Suite 650, Chicago, IL 60606
Phone: 312-419-9094
Email: lopez@mail.mlahq.org
http://www.mlanet.org
Purpose: To aid minority students entering or currently attending graduate library school.
Eligibility: Applicants must be members of an underrepresented group, such as Black/African-American, Latin, Asian, Aboriginal, North American Indian or Alaskan Native, or Native Hawaiian or other Pacific Islander. Students must be entering or currently attending an ALA-accredited library school and be no more than halfway through the program. Applicants must also be citizens or permanent residents of the United States or Canada.
Target applicant(s): Graduate school students. Adult students.
Amount: Up to $5,000.
Number of awards: 1.
Deadline: November 15.
How to apply: Applications are available online.
Exclusive: Visit www.UltimateScholarshipBook.com and enter code ME54126 for updates on this award.

[542] • Bill, W2ONV and Ann Salerno Memorial Scholarship
American Radio Relay League Foundation
225 Main Street, Newington, CT 06111-1494
Phone: 860-594-0200
Email: foundation@arrl.org
https://www.arrl.org/scholarship-program
Purpose: To provide financial assistance to amateur radio operators with high academic achievement.
Eligibility: Applicants must hold an active Amateur Radio License of any class and attend an accredited four-year college or university. They must have a GPA of 3.7 or higher, and their household income may not exceed $100,000 per year. They must not have previously received the Salerno Scholarship.
Target applicant(s): High school students. College students. Adult students.
Minimum GPA: 3.7
Amount: $1,000.
Number of awards: 2.
Deadline: January 10.
How to apply: Applications are available online.
Exclusive: Visit www.UltimateScholarshipBook.com and enter code AM54226 for updates on this award.

[543] • Bob East Scholarship
National Press Photographers Foundation Bob East Scholarship
Chuck Fadely, The Miami Herald, One Herald Plaza, Miami, FL 33132
Phone: 305-376-2015
http://www.nppf.org
Purpose: To encourage newcomers in photojournalism.
Eligibility: Applicants must either be an undergraduate in the first three and one half years of college or be planning to pursue postgraduate work.
Target applicant(s): High school students. College students. Graduate school students. Adult students.
Amount: $2,000.
Number of awards: 1.
Deadline: February 9.
How to apply: Applications are available online.
Exclusive: Visit www.UltimateScholarshipBook.com and enter code NA54326 for updates on this award.

[544] • Bob Richardson Legacy Scholarship
National Grocers Association
1005 N. Glebe Road, Suite 250, Arlington, VA 22201
Phone: 225-387-6126
https://www.nationalgrocers.org/foundation/nga-foundation-scholarships/
Purpose: To support students pursuing a degree related to the grocery field.
Eligibility: Applicants must be rising sophomores through postgraduate students, have a minimum 2.5 GPA and be enrolled in a two- or four-year degree-granting institution. Students must major in business, food management, IT or another field related to a career in the grocery industry. Experience in the grocery industry is preferred but not required.
Target applicant(s): College students. Graduate school students. Adult students.
Minimum GPA: 2.5
Amount: $1,000.
Number of awards: 1.
Deadline: April 15.
How to apply: Applications are available online.

The Ultimate Scholarship Book 2026
Scholarship Directory (Social Sciences)

Exclusive: Visit www.UltimateScholarshipBook.com and enter code NA54426 for updates on this award.

[545] • Bodie McDowell Scholarship
Outdoor Writers Association of America
121 Hickory Street, Suite 1, Missoula, MT 59801
Phone: 406-728-7434
Email: krhoades@owaa.org
http://www.owaa.org
Purpose: To support students in outdoor communications fields.
Eligibility: Applicants must be students of outdoor communications fields including print, film, art or broadcasting and must be either undergraduate students entering their junior or senior year or graduate students.
Target applicant(s): College students. Graduate school students. Adult students.
Amount: $1,000-$5,000.
Number of awards: 3 or more.
Deadline: March 31.
How to apply: Applicants are available online.
Exclusive: Visit www.UltimateScholarshipBook.com and enter code OU54526 for updates on this award.

[546] • Boren Scholarships
National Security Education Program Initiative, Administered by the Institute of International Education
1400 K Street, NW, 7th Floor, Washington, DC 20005
Phone: 800-618-6737
Email: boren@iie.org
https://www.borenawards.org
Purpose: To reward students who desire to study abroad in preparation for a career in U.S. national security.
Eligibility: Applicants must be U.S. citizens and undergraduate matriculated students at an accredited U.S. institution who have chosen a proposed country of study.
Target applicant(s): College students. Adult students.
Amount: $8,000-$25,000.
Number of awards: Varies.
Deadline: January 31.
How to apply: Applications are available online.
Exclusive: Visit www.UltimateScholarshipBook.com and enter code NA54626 for updates on this award.

[547] • Bound to Stay Bound Books Scholarship
Association for Library Service to Children
225 North Michigan Avenue, Suite 1300, Chicago, IL 60601
Phone: 800-545-2433
Email: scholarships@ala.org
http://www.ala.org/alsc/awardsgrants
Purpose: To support students pursuing their MLS degrees.
Eligibility: Applicants must intend to pursue an MLS or advanced degree, plan to work in children's librarianship and be U.S. or Canadian citizens. Selection is based on academic excellence, leadership and a desire to work with children in any type of library.
Target applicant(s): College students. Graduate school students. Adult students.
Amount: $8,000.
Number of awards: 4.
Deadline: March 1.
How to apply: Applications are available online.
Exclusive: Visit www.UltimateScholarshipBook.com and enter code AS54726 for updates on this award.

[548] • BSA Research Fellowship
Bibliographical Society of America
P.O. Box 1537, Lenox Hill Station, New York, NY 10021
Phone: 212-452-2710
Email: bsafellowships@bibsocamer.org
https://bibsocamer.org/awards/fellowships/
Purpose: To provide financial assistance to those pursuing bibliographical studies.
Eligibility: Applicants must submit proposals for studying books as historical evidence or an examination of the history of book trades or publishing history.
Target applicant(s): College students. Graduate school students. Adult students.
Amount: $3,000-$6,000.
Number of awards: Varies.
Deadline: October 2.
How to apply: Applications are available online.
Exclusive: Visit www.UltimateScholarshipBook.com and enter code BI54826 for updates on this award.

[549] • Byron Hanke Fellowship
Foundation for Community Association Research
6402 Arlington Boulevard, Suite 500, Falls Church, VA 22042
Phone: 703-970-9220
Email: foundation@caionline.org
http://www.cairf.org
Purpose: To support graduate students who are working on topics related to community associations.
Eligibility: Applicants must be currently enrolled in an accredited master's, doctoral or law program in the U.S. or Canada. Students must submit a research paper on community associations. Selection is primarily based on demonstration of research and writing abilities, academic achievement and faculty recommendations.
Target applicant(s): Graduate school students. Adult students.
Amount: $5,000.
Number of awards: 1.
Deadline: May 1.
How to apply: Applications are available online.
Exclusive: Visit www.UltimateScholarshipBook.com and enter code FO54926 for updates on this award.

[550] • California - Hawaii Elks Association Vocational Grants
California-Hawaii Elks Association
5450 E. Lamona Avenue, Fresno, CA 93727-2224
Phone: 559-255-4531
Email: chea@chea-elks.org
https://chea-elks.org/youth-activities/scholarships
Purpose: To provide assistance to those pursuing vocational/technical education.
Eligibility: Applicants must be U.S. citizens and California or Hawaii residents. They must plan to pursue a vocational or technical course of study above and supplemental to high school or preparatory school. A high school diploma or equivalent is not required. Students planning to

transfer into a bachelor's degree program upon completion of vocational studies are not eligible.
Target applicant(s): High school students. College students. Adult students.
Amount: $500-$2,000.
Number of awards: Varies.
Scholarship may be renewable.
Deadline: March 15.
How to apply: Applications are available online.
Exclusive: Visit www.UltimateScholarshipBook.com and enter code CA55026 for updates on this award.

[551] • Caples Student Campaign of the Year Award
ASL Marketing
2 Dubon Court, Farmingdale, NY 11735
Phone: 516-248-6100
http://www.caples.org
Purpose: To support students who are interested in direct marketing.
Eligibility: Applicants can be from anywhere in the world and the award is based on the boldness of the concept, the logic of the execution and the overall strength of the outcome.
Target applicant(s): College students. Adult students.
Amount: Varies.
Number of awards: Varies.
Deadline: March 28.
How to apply: Applications are available online.
Exclusive: Visit www.UltimateScholarshipBook.com and enter code AS55126 for updates on this award.

[552] • CardRates.com Financial Futures Scholarship
CardRates.com
c/o Digital Brands Inc., 15 SE 1st Avenue, Suite B, Gainesville, FL 32601
http://www.cardrates.com/scholarship/
Purpose: To support students pursuing a career in the personal finance industry.
Eligibility: Applicants must be U.S. residents and current college students or graduating high school seniors enrolling in college. Students must be majoring in a field related to personal finance such as business, accounting, finance, mathematics or management and hold a minimum 3.5 GPA.
Target applicant(s): High school students. College students. Adult students.
Minimum GPA: 3.5
Amount: $1,000.
Number of awards: 1.
Deadline: July 31.
How to apply: Applications are available online.
Exclusive: Visit www.UltimateScholarshipBook.com and enter code CA55226 for updates on this award.

[553] • Carole J. Streeter, KB9JBR, Scholarship
American Radio Relay League Foundation
225 Main Street, Newington, CT 06111-1494
Phone: 860-594-0200
Email: foundation@arrl.org
https://www.arrl.org/scholarship-program
Purpose: To support students who are involved in amateur radio.
Eligibility: Applicants must have an amateur radio license of Technician Class or higher. Preference will be given to applicants with Morse Code proficiency and those studying health and healing arts.
Target applicant(s): High school students. College students. Adult students.
Amount: $1,000.
Number of awards: 1.
Deadline: January 10.
How to apply: Applications are available online.
Exclusive: Visit www.UltimateScholarshipBook.com and enter code AM55326 for updates on this award.

[554] • Carole Simpson Scholarship
Radio Television Digital News Association
529 14th Street NW, Suite 1240, Washington, DC 20045
Phone: 202-659-6510
Email: karenh@rtdna.org
http://www.rtdna.org
Purpose: To honor professional achievements in electronic journalism.
Eligibility: Applicants must be full-time college sophomores or higher with at least one full academic year remaining. Applicants may be enrolled in any major as long as their career intent is television or radio news. Applicants may only apply for one RTNDA scholarship. Preference is given to students of color.
Target applicant(s): College students. Adult students.
Amount: $2,000.
Number of awards: 1.
Deadline: January 11.
How to apply: Applications are available online.
Exclusive: Visit www.UltimateScholarshipBook.com and enter code RA55426 for updates on this award.

[555] • Charles Clarke Cordle Memorial Scholarship
American Radio Relay League Foundation
225 Main Street, Newington, CT 06111-1494
Phone: 860-594-0200
Email: foundation@arrl.org
https://www.arrl.org/scholarship-program
Purpose: To assist ham radio operators in furthering their educations.
Eligibility: Applicants must have any class of ham radio license, have a minimum 2.5 GPA and be residents of and attend school in Georgia or Alabama.
Target applicant(s): High school students. College students. Adult students.
Minimum GPA: 2.5
Amount: $1,000.
Number of awards: 1.
Deadline: January 10.
How to apply: Applications are available online but may not be completed electronically. All completed applications must be mailed.
Exclusive: Visit www.UltimateScholarshipBook.com and enter code AM55526 for updates on this award.

[556] • Charles N. Fisher Memorial Scholarship
American Radio Relay League Foundation
225 Main Street, Newington, CT 06111-1494
Phone: 860-594-0200
Email: foundation@arrl.org

The Ultimate Scholarship Book 2026
Scholarship Directory (Social Sciences)

https://www.arrl.org/scholarship-program
Purpose: To assist ham radio operators in furthering their educations.
Eligibility: Applicants must have any class of radio license, be residents of the ARRL Southwestern Division (Arizona, Los Angeles, Orange County, San Diego or Santa Barbara), attend a regionally-accredited college or university and study electronics, communications or a related field.
Target applicant(s): High school students. College students. Graduate school students. Adult students.
Amount: $1,000.
Number of awards: 1.
Deadline: January 10.
How to apply: Applications are available online. Completed applications must be submitted by mail, not electronically.
Exclusive: Visit www.UltimateScholarshipBook.com and enter code AM55626 for updates on this award.

[557] • Charlie and Becky Bray Legacy Scholarship
National Grocers Association
1005 N. Glebe Road, Suite 250, Arlington, VA 22201
Phone: 225-387-6126
https://www.nationalgrocers.org/foundation/nga-foundation-scholarships/
Purpose: To support students pursuing degrees related to the grocery field.
Eligibility: Applicants must be rising sophomores through postgraduate students, have a minimum 2.5 GPA and be enrolled in a two- or four-year degree-granting institution. Students must major in business, food management, IT or another field related to a career in the grocery industry. Experience in the grocery industry is preferred but not required.
Target applicant(s): College students. Graduate school students. Adult students.
Minimum GPA: 2.5
Amount: Varies.
Number of awards: 1.
Deadline: April 15.
How to apply: Applications are available online.
Exclusive: Visit www.UltimateScholarshipBook.com and enter code NA55726 for updates on this award.

[558] • Chester Burger Scholarship for Excellence in Public Relations
Public Relations Student Society of America
120 Wall Street, 21st Floor, New York, NY 10005-4024
Phone: 212-460-1474
Email: prssa@prsa.org
https://prssa.prsa.org/scholarships-and-awards/
Purpose: To encourage public relations and journalism graduate students to pursue careers in corporate public relations.
Eligibility: Applicants must be entering or current graduate students at a U.S. college or university majoring in journalism, public relations or a related field. Students must have an undergraduate GPA of 3.0 or higher and be interested in pursuing a career in corporate public relations. Selection is based on the overall strength of the application.
Target applicant(s): College students. Graduate school students. Adult students.
Minimum GPA: 3.0
Amount: $1,000.
Number of awards: 1.
Deadline: April 30.

How to apply: Applications are available online. An application form, resume, essay and two recommendation letters are required.
Exclusive: Visit www.UltimateScholarshipBook.com and enter code PU55826 for updates on this award.

[559] • CLA Scholarship For BIPOC Students in Memory of Edna Yelland
California Library Association
248 E. Foothill Boulevard, Suite 101, Monrovia, CA 91016
Phone: 916-779-4573
Email: info@cla-net.org
https://www.cla-net.org
Purpose: To assist minority California graduate students who are pursuing degrees in library or information science.
Eligibility: Applicants must be California residents, be American Indian, African American, Mexican American, Latino, Asian American, Pacific Islander or Filipino and be accepted into or enrolled in an American Library Association accredited state library school. The award is based on financial need, and an interview is required.
Target applicant(s): College students. Graduate school students. Adult students.
Amount: $2,500.
Number of awards: up to 3.
Deadline: March 17.
How to apply: Applications are available online.
Exclusive: Visit www.UltimateScholarshipBook.com and enter code CA55926 for updates on this award.

[560] • Clifford H. Ted Rees Jr. Scholarship
Air-Conditioning, Heating and Refrigeration Institute
Clifford H., 2111 Wilson Boulevard, Suite 500, Arlington, VA 22201
Phone: 703-524-8800
Email: ReesApplications@ahrinet.org
http://www.ahrinet.org
Purpose: To support students preparing for careers in heating, ventilation, air-conditioning and refrigeration (HVACR) technology.
Eligibility: Applicants must be U.S. citizens, nationals or resident aliens intending to become U.S. citizens. They must be enrolled in an accredited HVACR technician training program and have plans to become entry-level commercial refrigeration technicians, residential air-conditioning and heating technicians or light commercial air-conditioning and heating technicians after graduation. Selection is based on stated career goals and commitment to pursuing entry-level work in the HVACR field.
Target applicant(s): College students. Adult students.
Amount: Up to $2,000.
Number of awards: 15.
Deadline: June 1; October 1.
How to apply: Applications are available online. An application form, two recommendation letters, a personal statement and a copy of the alien registration card (if applicable) are required.
Exclusive: Visit www.UltimateScholarshipBook.com and enter code AI56026 for updates on this award.

[561] • College Photographer of the Year
National Press Photographers Foundation College Photographer of the Year
David Rees, CPOY Director, School of Journalism, The University of Missouri, 106 Lee Hills Hall, Columbus, MO 65211
Phone: 573-882-4442
Email: info@cpoy.org

https://cpoy.org
Purpose: To reward outstanding student work in photojournalism and provide a forum for student photographers to gauge their skills.
Eligibility: Applicants must be currently enrolled in a full-time four-year college or university, provide a portfolio and demonstrate financial need. Applicants can apply to as many NPPA scholarships as desired, but only one award will be granted to each winner.
Target applicant(s): High school students. College students. Graduate school students. Adult students.
Amount: Varies.
Number of awards: Varies.
Deadline: September 18.
How to apply: Applications are available by written or email request.
Exclusive: Visit www.UltimateScholarshipBook.com and enter code NA56126 for updates on this award.

[562] • CREW Network Foundation Scholarship
Commercial Real Estate Women (CREW) Network
1201 Wakarusa Drive, Suite D, Lawrence, KS 66049
Phone: 785-832-1808
https://crewnetwork.org/foundation/college-scholarships
Purpose: To support female students as they pursue university-level education that will lead to careers in commercial real estate.
Eligibility: Applicants must be females who are full-time juniors, seniors or graduate students enrolled at an accredited college or university. Students must be citizens of the United States or Canada and have a minimum 3.0 GPA. Applicants must be focusing their studies in one or more of CREW Network's qualified fields of commercial real estate.
Target applicant(s): College students. Graduate school students. Adult students.
Minimum GPA: 3.0
Amount: $5,000.
Number of awards: 30.
Deadline: April 15.
How to apply: Applications are available online.
Exclusive: Visit www.UltimateScholarshipBook.com and enter code CO56226 for updates on this award.

[563] • Darrel Hess Community College Geography Scholarship
Association of American Geographers (AAG) Hess Scholarship
1710 Sixteenth Street NW, Washington, DC 20009
Phone: 202-234-1450
Email: grantsawards@aag.org
http://www.aag.org/cs/grantsawards
Purpose: To support geography majors.
Eligibility: Applicants must be currently enrolled at a U.S. community college, junior college, city college or similar two-year educational institution, have completed at least two transfer courses in geography and plan to transfer to a four-year institution as a geography major. The award is based on academic excellence and promise. Applications, personal statements, two recommendation letters and transcripts are required.
Target applicant(s): College students. Adult students.
Amount: $1,500.
Number of awards: 2.
Deadline: May 10.
How to apply: Applications are available online.
Exclusive: Visit www.UltimateScholarshipBook.com and enter code AS56326 for updates on this award.

[564] • David H. and Beverly A. Barlow Grant
American Psychological Foundation
750 First Street NE, Washington, DC 20002-4242
Phone: 202-336-5843
Email: foundetion@apa.org
https://www.apa.org/apf/funding/grants
Purpose: To support graduate students and early career researchers in innovative basic and clinical research on anxiety and anxiety-related disorders.
Eligibility: Applicants must be graduate students or early career researchers no more than 10 years postdoctoral. Students must be affiliated with nonprofit charitable, educational and scientific institutions or governmental entities operating exclusively for charitable and educational purposes. Applicants must have a demonstrated knowledge of anxiety and anxiety research, either basic or clinical.
Target applicant(s): Graduate school students. Adult students.
Amount: Up to $8,000.
Number of awards: Varies.
Deadline: September 18.
How to apply: Applications are available online.
Exclusive: Visit www.UltimateScholarshipBook.com and enter code AM56426 for updates on this award.

[565] • Dayton Amateur Radio Association Scholarship
American Radio Relay League Foundation
225 Main Street, Newington, CT 06111-1494
Phone: 860-594-0200
Email: foundation@arrl.org
https://www.arrl.org/scholarship-program
Purpose: To provide financial assistance to students who are amateur radio operators.
Eligibility: Applicants must be accepted or enrolled at an accredited four-year institution of higher learning. They must possess an Amateur Radio License of any class.
Target applicant(s): High school students. College students. Adult students.
Amount: $2,000.
Number of awards: Varies.
Deadline: January 10.
How to apply: Applications are available online.
Exclusive: Visit www.UltimateScholarshipBook.com and enter code AM56526 for updates on this award.

[566] • DEWALT Trades Scholarship
Stanley Black and Decker
DEWALT Trades Scholarship, Scholarship America, One Scholarship Way, Saint Peter, MN 56082
Phone: 800-537-4180
Email: DEWALTtrade@scholarshipamerica.org
https://learnmore.scholarsapply.org/DEWALTtrade/
Purpose: To support students pursuing a trade degree or certificate.
Eligibility: Applicants must be current high school seniors or college undergraduate students planning to enroll or enrolled in full-time undergraduate study at an accredited two-year college or vocational-technical school for the entire upcoming academic year. Students must be majoring in a trade construction, industrial, motor/power sector, mechanics or technology degree/certificate with a minimum 2.0 GPA.
Target applicant(s): High school students. College students. Adult students.

Minimum GPA: 2.0
Amount: $5,000.
Number of awards: 40.
Deadline: January 17.
How to apply: Applications are available online.
Exclusive: Visit www.UltimateScholarshipBook.com and enter code ST56626 for updates on this award.

---

[567] • Distinguished Service Award for Students
Society for Technical Communication
Manager of the Distinguished Community Awards Committee, 9401 Lee Highway, Suite 300, Fairfax, VA 22031
Phone: 703-522-4114
Email: stc@stc.org
http://www.stc.org
Purpose: To assist students who are pursuing degrees in an area of technical communication.
Eligibility: Applicants must be full-time undergraduate or graduate students who have completed at least one year of post-secondary education and who have at least one full year of academic work remaining to complete their degree programs. Students must also be in the field of communication of information about technical subjects and be student members of the STC. Applicants must be nominated by student chapters.
Target applicant(s): College students. Graduate school students. Adult students.
Amount: Varies.
Number of awards: Varies.
Deadline: January 5.
How to apply: Applications are available online.
Exclusive: Visit www.UltimateScholarshipBook.com and enter code SO56726 for updates on this award.

---

[568] • Don Riebhoff Memorial Scholarship
American Radio Relay League Foundation
225 Main Street, Newington, CT 06111-1494
Phone: 860-594-0200
Email: foundation@arrl.org
https://www.arrl.org/scholarship-program
Purpose: To assist ham radio operators in furthering their educations.
Eligibility: Applicants must have at least a technician ham radio license, be undergraduate or graduate students in international studies at an accredited post-secondary institution and be members of ARRL.
Target applicant(s): High school students. College students. Graduate school students. Adult students.
Amount: $1,000.
Number of awards: 1.
Deadline: January 10.
How to apply: Applications are available online. Completed applications must be mailed in. They cannot be completed electronically.
Exclusive: Visit www.UltimateScholarshipBook.com and enter code AM56826 for updates on this award.

---

[569] • Dr. Jack G. Shaheen Media Scholarship
American-Arab Anti-Discrimination Committee
1705 DeSales Street NW, Suite 500, Washington, DC 20036
Phone: 202-244-2990
https://adc.org/mediascholarship/
Purpose: To reward Arab-American students who excel in media studies.
Eligibility: Applicants must be U.S. citizens of Arab heritage currently enrolled in college as an undergraduate junior or senior or as a graduate student. Students must be majoring in journalism, radio, television or film. Applicants must have a minimum GPA of 3.0 and provide academic transcripts, a one-page statement, two letters of recommendation and copies of their work.
Target applicant(s): College students. Graduate school students. Adult students.
Minimum GPA: 3.0
Amount: $2,500.
Number of awards: 1.
Deadline: April 12.
How to apply: Applications are available online.
Exclusive: Visit www.UltimateScholarshipBook.com and enter code AM56926 for updates on this award.

---

[570] • Dr. James L. Lawson Memorial Scholarship
American Radio Relay League Foundation
225 Main Street, Newington, CT 06111-1494
Phone: 860-594-0200
Email: foundation@arrl.org
https://www.arrl.org/scholarship-program
Purpose: To assist ham radio operators in furthering their educations.
Eligibility: Applicants must have at least a general ham radio license, be residents of and attend post-secondary institutions in the New England states (Connecticut, Maine, Massachusetts, New Hampshire, Rhode Island or Vermont) or New York state and be pursuing a bachelor's or graduate degree in electronics, communications or a related field.
Target applicant(s): High school students. College students. Graduate school students. Adult students.
Amount: $1,000.
Number of awards: 1.
Deadline: January 10.
How to apply: Applications are available online but cannot be completed electronically. All applications must be mailed.
Exclusive: Visit www.UltimateScholarshipBook.com and enter code AM57026 for updates on this award.

---

[571] • Dr. Robert Hawkins Memorial Scholarship
John Philip Sousa Foundation
196 East 650 North, West Lafayette, IN 47906
Phone: 617-529-9402
Email: treynold@worldpath.net
http://www.sousafoundation.net
Purpose: To support students pursuing a degree in instrumental music education.
Eligibility: Applicants must plan on attending a college or university in the United States and pursue a degree in instrumental music education. Students must complete the application in full including an essay statement, three letters of recommendation and a current transcript.
Target applicant(s): High school students. College students. Adult students.
Amount: $1,000.
Number of awards: 1.
Scholarship may be renewable.
Deadline: November 6.
How to apply: Applications are available online.
Exclusive: Visit www.UltimateScholarshipBook.com and enter code JO57126 for updates on this award.

[572] • Earl Warren Scholarship
NAACP Legal Defense and Educational Fund
40 Rector Street, 5th Floor, New York, NY 10006
Phone: 212-965-2200
https://www.naacpldf.org
Purpose: To reward promising law students who have potential for training as civil rights and public interest attorneys.
Eligibility: Applicants must be law students entering their first or second year of full-time legal study at an accredited law school. Students must show a strong commitment to racial justice and civil rights. Applicants must be U.S. citizens. Students must either be college graduates, enrolled in their final year of college or university or be a first-year law student. Applicants must have a strong record of academic achievement.
Target applicant(s): College students. Graduate school students. Adult students.
Amount: $15,000.
Number of awards: Varies.
Scholarship may be renewable.
Deadline: May 1.
How to apply: Applications are available online.
Exclusive: Visit www.UltimateScholarshipBook.com and enter code NA57226 for updates on this award.

[573] • Ecolab Scholarship Competition
American Hotel and Lodging Educational Foundation (AHLEF)
1250 Eye Street, N.W. Suite 1100, Washington, DC 20005
Phone: 202-289-3180
Email: foundation@ahla.com
https://www.ahlafoundation.org/scholarships/
Purpose: To provide scholarships for students who intend to earn a degree in hospitality management.
Eligibility: Applicants must be enrolled or intend to enroll full-time in a two- or four-year U.S. college or university.
Target applicant(s): High school students. College students. Adult students.
Amount: $1,000-$2,000.
Number of awards: Varies.
Deadline: March 15.
How to apply: Applications are available online.
Exclusive: Visit www.UltimateScholarshipBook.com and enter code AM57326 for updates on this award.

[574] • Ed Bradley Scholarship
Radio Television Digital News Association
529 14th Street NW, Suite 1240, Washington, DC 20045
Phone: 202-659-6510
Email: karenh@rtdna.org
http://www.rtdna.org
Purpose: To honor professional achievements in electronic journalism.
Eligibility: Applicants must be full-time college sophomores or higher with at least one full academic year remaining. Applicants may be enrolled in any major as long as their career intent is television or radio news. Applicants may only apply for one RTNDA scholarship.
Target applicant(s): College students. Adult students.
Amount: $10,000.
Number of awards: 1.
Deadline: January 11.
How to apply: Applications are available online.
Exclusive: Visit www.UltimateScholarshipBook.com and enter code RA57426 for updates on this award.

[575] • Edmond A. Metzger Scholarship
American Radio Relay League Foundation
225 Main Street, Newington, CT 06111-1494
Phone: 860-594-0200
Email: foundation@arrl.org
https://www.arrl.org/scholarship-program
Purpose: To assist ham radio operators in furthering their educations.
Eligibility: Applicants must have at least a novice ham radio license, be undergraduate or graduate students in electrical engineering, be residents of and attend schools in the ARRL Central Division (Illinois, Indiana or Wisconsin) and be members of ARRL.
Target applicant(s): College students. Graduate school students. Adult students.
Amount: $500.
Number of awards: 1.
Deadline: January 10.
How to apply: Applications are available online. Completed applications must be mailed in. They cannot be completed electronically.
Exclusive: Visit www.UltimateScholarshipBook.com and enter code AM57526 for updates on this award.

[576] • Educational Foundation Scholarship
International Society of Automation
67 T.W. Alexander Drive, P.O. Box 12277, Research Triangle Park, NC 27709
Phone: 919-549-8411
Email: info@isa.org
https://www.isa.org/students/scholarships/
Purpose: To support students interested in the fields of automation and control.
Eligibility: Applicants must be full-time students in a graduate, undergraduate or two-year degree program. Students must have a minimum GPA of 2.5 and be enrolled in a program in automation and control or another closely related field.
Target applicant(s): College students. Graduate school students. Adult students.
Minimum GPA: 2.5
Amount: Varies.
Number of awards: Varies.
Deadline: February 28.
How to apply: Applications are available online.
Exclusive: Visit www.UltimateScholarshipBook.com and enter code IN57626 for updates on this award.

[577] • EGIA Foundation Scholarship Program
EGIA Foundation
3800 Watt Avenue, Suite 105, Sacramento, CA 95821
Phone: 866-562-9060
Email: chanson@egiafoundation.org
https://egiafoundation.org/what-we-do/scholarships/
Purpose: To support students wishing to pursue a career in the HVACR industry.
Eligibility: Applicants must be a high school senior or adult student who is enrolled or planning to enroll at an accredited two-year college, vocational or technical school or other approved technical institute to pursue studies in HVACR. A minimum 2.0 GPA or higher is required.
Target applicant(s): High school students. College students. Graduate school students. Adult students.
Minimum GPA: 2.0
Amount: $2,500.

Number of awards: 20.
Deadline: May 31.
How to apply: Applications are available online.
Exclusive: Visit www.UltimateScholarshipBook.com and enter code EG57726 for updates on this award.

[578] • Executive Women International Scholarship Program

Executive Women International (EWI)
1288 Summit Avenue Suite 107, #124, Oconomowoc, WI 53066
Phone: 262-269-5625
Email: ewi@ewiconnect.com
https://ewiconnect.com/page/scholarships
Purpose: To assist high school students in achieving their higher education goals.
Eligibility: Applicants must be high school seniors who plan to pursue four-year degrees at accredited colleges or universities. Selection is based on application materials, communication skills, academic record, extracurricular activities and leadership.
Target applicant(s): High school students.
Amount: $1,000-$5,000.
Number of awards: Varies.
Deadline: March 31.
How to apply: Applications are available by request from the applicant's local Executive Women International chapter. An application form and supporting documents are required.
Exclusive: Visit www.UltimateScholarshipBook.com and enter code EX57826 for updates on this award.

[579] • FMS Solutions Holdings LLC Legacy Scholarship

National Grocers Association
1005 N. Glebe Road, Suite 250, Arlington, VA 22201
Phone: 225-387-6126
https://www.nationalgrocers.org/foundation/nga-foundation-scholarships/
Purpose: To support students pursuing education related to the grocery field.
Eligibility: Applicants must be rising sophomores through postgraduate students, have a minimum 2.5 GPA and be enrolled in a two- or four-year degree-granting institution. Students must major in business, food management, IT or another field related to a career in the grocery industry. Experience in the grocery industry is preferred but not required. Preference is given to children of state or local law enforcement officers.
Target applicant(s): College students. Graduate school students. Adult students.
Minimum GPA: 2.5
Amount: $1,500.
Number of awards: 1.
Deadline: April 15.
How to apply: Applications are available online.
Exclusive: Visit www.UltimateScholarshipBook.com and enter code NA57926 for updates on this award.

[580] • FOARE Scholarship Program

Foundation for Outdoor Advertising Research and Education (FOARE)
1850 M Street NW, Suite 1040, Washington, DC 20036
Phone: 202-364-7130
Email: tmfsmith@rcn.com
http://oaaa.org/AboutOAAA/FOARE/FOAREScholarshipProgram.aspx
Purpose: To support undergraduate and graduate students in pursuing a career in the outdoor advertising industry.
Eligibility: Applicants must be graduating seniors, undergraduate students or graduate students. Selection is primarily based on demonstration of financial need, career goals, academic achievement, community service and extracurricular involvement.
Target applicant(s): High school students. College students. Graduate school students. Adult students.
Amount: $5,000.
Number of awards: 10.
Deadline: June 10.
How to apply: Applications are available online.
Exclusive: Visit www.UltimateScholarshipBook.com and enter code FO58026 for updates on this award.

[581] • Francis X. Crowley Scholarship

New England Water Works Association
125 Hopping Brook Road, Holliston, MA 01746
Phone: 508-893-7979
Email: tmacelhaney@preloadinc.com
http://www.newwa.org
Purpose: To support civil engineering, environmental engineering and business management students.
Eligibility: Applicants must be New England Water Works Association student members. They must be enrolled in a postsecondary degree program in civil engineering, environmental engineering or business management. Selection is based on the overall strength of the application.
Target applicant(s): High school students. College students. Adult students.
Amount: $3,000.
Number of awards: 1.
Deadline: April 1.
How to apply: Applications are available online. An application form, a personal essay, an official transcript and one recommendation letter are required.
Exclusive: Visit www.UltimateScholarshipBook.com and enter code NE58126 for updates on this award.

[582] • Frank M. Coda Scholarship

American Society of Heating, Refrigerating and Air-Conditioning Engineers (ASHRAE)
Scholarship Administrator, ASHRAE Inc., 180 Technology Parkway, Peachtree Corners, GA 30092
Phone: 404-636-8400
Email: lbenedict@ashrae.org
https://www.ashrae.org/communities/student-zone/scholarships-and-grants
Purpose: To support undergraduate students who are preparing for careers in the heating, ventilation, air-conditioning and refrigeration industry.
Eligibility: Applicants must be current or entering full-time undergraduates enrolled in a bachelor's of science, bachelor's of engineering or pre-engineering degree program in preparation for a career in HVACR.

They must attend a school that has an ASHRAE student branch, is accredited by ABET or is accredited by a non-USA agency that has signed a Memorandum of Understanding with ABET or the Washington Accord. They must be in the top 30 percent of their class and must have a GPA of 3.0 or higher on a four-point scale. Selection is based on the overall strength of the application.
Target applicant(s): High school students. College students. Adult students.
Minimum GPA: 3.0
Amount: $5,000.
Number of awards: 1.
Deadline: December 1.
How to apply: Applications are available online. An application form, official college transcript (or proof of enrollment for rising freshmen) and two letters of reference are required.
Exclusive: Visit www.UltimateScholarshipBook.com and enter code AM58226 for updates on this award.

[583] • Fred R. McDaniel Memorial Scholarship
American Radio Relay League Foundation
225 Main Street, Newington, CT 06111-1494
Phone: 860-594-0200
Email: foundation@arrl.org
https://www.arrl.org/scholarship-program
Purpose: To assist ham radio operators in furthering their educations.
Eligibility: Applicants must have at least a general ham radio license, be residents of and attend a post-secondary institution in the FCC Fifth Call District (Texas, Oklahoma, Arkansas, Louisiana, Mississippi or New Mexico) and be studying for a bachelor's or graduate degree in electronics, communications or a related field. Preference is given to applicants with a 3.0 GPA or higher.
Target applicant(s): High school students. College students. Graduate school students. Adult students.
Minimum GPA: 3.0
Amount: $1,000.
Number of awards: 1.
Deadline: January 10.
How to apply: Applications are available online but must be sent in by mail.
Exclusive: Visit www.UltimateScholarshipBook.com and enter code AM58326 for updates on this award.

[584] • Frederic G. Melcher Scholarship
Association for Library Service to Children
225 North Michigan Avenue, Suite 1300, Chicago, IL 60601
Phone: 800-545-2433
Email: scholarships@ala.org
http://www.ala.org/alsc/awardsgrants
Purpose: To support students who want to become children's librarians.
Eligibility: Applicants must intend to pursue an MLS degree, plan to work in children's librarianship and be U.S. or Canadian citizens. Selection is based on academic excellence, leadership and desire to work with children in any type of library.
Target applicant(s): College students. Graduate school students. Adult students.
Amount: $8,000.
Number of awards: Up to 2.
Deadline: March 1.
How to apply: Applications are available online.
Exclusive: Visit www.UltimateScholarshipBook.com and enter code AS58426 for updates on this award.

[585] • FTEE Scholarship: Undergraduate Major in Technology and Engineering Education
International Technology and Engineering Educators Association
Foundation for Technology and Engineering Educators, 1908 Association Drive, Suite C, Reston, VA 20191
Phone: 703-860-2100
Email: iteea@iteea.org
https://www.iteea.org/awards-and-scholarships
Purpose: To support undergraduate students majoring in technology education teacher preparation.
Eligibility: Applicants must be members of ITEEA, be full-time undergraduate students and have a minimum 2.5 GPA.
Target applicant(s): College students. Adult students.
Minimum GPA: 2.5
Amount: $500.
Number of awards: 1.
Deadline: November 1.
How to apply: Application information is available online.
Exclusive: Visit www.UltimateScholarshipBook.com and enter code IN58526 for updates on this award.

[586] • Fund for American Studies Internships
Fund for American Studies
1621 New Hampshire Avenue NW, Washington, DC 20009
Phone: 202-986-0384
Email: info@TFAS.org
https://www.dcinternships.org/
Purpose: To provide scholarships for students attending one of the Fund's internship programs.
Eligibility: There are programs in comparative political and economic systems, political journalism, business and government, philanthropy and international institutes. Each program includes classes, an internship and special events. Students live in on-campus housing at George Washington University or in furnished apartments in the Capitol Hill neighborhood. Each student takes 3-9 credit hours in courses at George Mason University in addition to interning 30-35 hours per week. Summer and school-year programs are available.
Target applicant(s): College students. Adult students.
Amount: Varies.
Number of awards: Varies.
Deadline: March 12.
How to apply: Applications are available online.
Exclusive: Visit www.UltimateScholarshipBook.com and enter code FU58626 for updates on this award.

[587] • Future Counselors of America Scholarship
DatingAdvice.com
c/o Digital Brands Inc., 15 SE 1st Avenue, Suite B, Gainesville, FL 32601
https://www.datingadvice.com/scholarship
Purpose: To assist psychology students who are planning careers in relationship counseling or a related field.
Eligibility: Applicants must be U.S. undergraduate or graduate students majoring in psychology and must have a minimum 3.5 GPA. Students must write a 500- to 900-word essay on the topic of "The Psychology of Online Dating."

The Ultimate Scholarship Book 2026
Scholarship Directory (Social Sciences)

Target applicant(s): College students. Graduate school students. Adult students.
Minimum GPA: 3.5
Amount: $1,000.
Number of awards: 1.
Deadline: June 30.
How to apply: An official transcript and essay must be submitted by mail.
Exclusive: Visit www.UltimateScholarshipBook.com and enter code DA58726 for updates on this award.

[588] • Future Journalism Teacher Scholarship
Journalism Education Association Future Teacher Scholarship
105 Kedzie Hall, 828 Mid-Campus Drive South, Manhattan, KS 66506-1505
Phone: 785-532-5532
Email: staff@jea.org
http://jea.org/wp/scholarships/
Purpose: To support education majors who intend to teach scholastic journalism.
Eligibility: Applicants must be a college junior, senior or graduate student in a program designed to prepare him/her for teaching at the secondary level. Current secondary-school journalism teachers who are in a degree program to improve their journalism teaching skills are also eligible.
Target applicant(s): College students. Graduate school students. Adult students.
Amount: $1,000.
Number of awards: 2.
Deadline: July 16.
How to apply: Applications are available online.
Exclusive: Visit www.UltimateScholarshipBook.com and enter code JO58826 for updates on this award.

[589] • Gamma Theta Upsilon-Geographical Honor Society Scholarships
Gamma Theta Upsilon
Dr. Ryan Weichelt, 258 Phillips Hall, University of Wisconsin-Eau Claire Department of Geography and Anthropology, Eau Claire, WI 54702
Phone: 715-836-4426
Email: weicherd@uwec.edu
https://gammathetaupsilon.org/scholarships.html
Purpose: To support geography knowledge and awareness by awarding monetary assistance to college and graduate students.
Eligibility: Applicants must be initiated through a Gamma Theta Upsilon chapter.
Target applicant(s): College students. Graduate school students. Adult students.
Amount: $1,000.
Number of awards: 5.
Deadline: June 1.
How to apply: Applications are available online.
Exclusive: Visit www.UltimateScholarshipBook.com and enter code GA58926 for updates on this award.

[590] • Gary Yoshimura Scholarship
Public Relations Student Society of America
120 Wall Street, 21st Floor, New York, NY 10005-4024
Phone: 212-460-1474
Email: prssa@prsa.org
https://prssa.prsa.org/scholarships-and-awards/
Purpose: To assist public relations students.
Eligibility: Applicants must be PRSSA members with a minimum 3.0 GPA in the pursuit of higher education in the public relations field. Students must submit an essay on personal or professional challenges and a statement on financial need.
Target applicant(s): High school students. College students. Graduate school students. Adult students.
Minimum GPA: 3.0
Amount: $2,400.
Number of awards: 1.
Deadline: April 30.
How to apply: Applications are available online.
Exclusive: Visit www.UltimateScholarshipBook.com and enter code PU59026 for updates on this award.

[591] • George A. Strait Minority Scholarship
American Association of Law Libraries
105 W. Adams, Suite 3300, Chicago, IL 60603
Email: scholarships@aall.org
https://www.aallnet.org/education-training/scholarships/
Purpose: To encourage minorities to enter careers as law librarians.
Eligibility: Applicants must be a member of a minority group as defined by U.S. government rules, degree candidates in an accredited library or law school and intend to pursue a career as law librarians. Law library experience is preferred. Applicants must also have financial need and have at least one quarter or semester left after the scholarship is given.
Target applicant(s): Graduate school students. Adult students.
Amount: Varies.
Number of awards: Varies.
Scholarship may be renewable.
Deadline: April 1.
How to apply: Applications are available online, by mail with a self-addressed, stamped envelope, by fax, by phone or by email.
Exclusive: Visit www.UltimateScholarshipBook.com and enter code AM59126 for updates on this award.

[592] • Giles Sutherland Rich Memorial Scholarship
Federal Circuit Bar Association
1620 I Street NW, Suite 801, Washington, DC 20006
Phone: 202-466-3923
Email: fcbascholarships@fedcirbar.org
http://www.fedcirbar.org
Purpose: To support promising law students who demonstrate financial need.
Eligibility: Applicants must be undergraduate or graduate law students who demonstrate academic ability and financial need. They must submit a one-page statement describing their financial need, their interest in law and their qualifications for the award. Applicants must also submit a transcript and curriculum vitae.
Target applicant(s): College students. Graduate school students. Adult students.
Amount: $10,000.
Number of awards: 1.

Deadline: April 15.
How to apply: There is no application form.
Exclusive: Visit www.UltimateScholarshipBook.com and enter code FE59226 for updates on this award.

[593] • GoFoodservice Scholarship
GoFoodservice
11206 Ampere Court, Louisville, KY 40299
Phone: 800-550-0706
Email: support@gofoodservice.com
https://www.gofoodservice.com/scholarship
Purpose: To support the next generation of chefs and restaurant managers.
Eligibility: Applicants must be graduating high school seniors enrolling in post-secondary education or students already enrolled in a college or accredited institution. Students must be majoring in culinary arts or hospitality management and must submit an essay along with the application.
Target applicant(s): High school students. College students. Adult students.
Amount: $500.
Number of awards: 1.
Deadline: June 15.
How to apply: Applications are available online.
Exclusive: Visit www.UltimateScholarshipBook.com and enter code GO59326 for updates on this award.

[594] • Goldberg-Miller Public Finance Scholarship
Government Finance Officers Association
203 N. LaSalle Street, Suite 2700, Chicago, IL 60601
Phone: 312-977-9700
https://www.gfoa.org/available-scholarships
Purpose: To support graduate students pursuing a career in state/provincial or local government finance.
Eligibility: Applicants must be permanent residents of the U.S. or Canada. Students may not be previous winners of a Government Finance Officers Association (GFOA) scholarship.
Target applicant(s): Graduate school students. Adult students.
Amount: $25,000.
Number of awards: 1.
Deadline: December 29.
How to apply: Applications are available online.
Exclusive: Visit www.UltimateScholarshipBook.com and enter code GO59426 for updates on this award.

[595] • Graduate Scholarship Program
Central Intelligence Agency
Office of Public Affairs, Washington, DC 20505
Phone: 703-482-0623
https://www.cia.gov/careers/student-programs/
Purpose: To help students get exposed to intelligence challenges while performing meaningful work related to their graduate studies.
Eligibility: Applicants must be enrolled at an accredited college or university full-time and work during summer breaks at the agency. Students must have financial need as demonstrated by their adjusted gross annual household income (AGI). Applicants must have maintained a competitive GPA (minimum 3.0 on a 4.0 scale).
Target applicant(s): Graduate school students. Adult students.
Minimum GPA: 3.0.

Amount: Up to $18,000.
Number of awards: Varies.
Deadline: June 30.
How to apply: Applications are available online.
Exclusive: Visit www.UltimateScholarshipBook.com and enter code CE59526 for updates on this award.

[596] • Great Scholarship Program
Great Clips
4400 W. 78th Street, Suite 700, Minneapolis, MN 55435
Phone: 800-999-5959
https://jobs.greatclips.com/scholarship-application
Purpose: To support students who are pursuing a career in cosmetology.
Eligibility: Selection is based on the overall strength of the application.
Target applicant(s): High school students.
Amount: $250-$5,000.
Number of awards: Varies.
Deadline: March 1 (Spring) and September 1 (Fall).
How to apply: Applications are available online.
Exclusive: Visit www.UltimateScholarshipBook.com and enter code GR59626 for updates on this award.

[597] • Gwendolyn S. Cruzat MLA Scholarship
Medical Library Association
225 West Wacker Drive, Suite 650, Chicago, IL 60606
Phone: 312-419-9094
Email: lopez@mail.mlahq.org
http://www.mlanet.org
Purpose: To aid a student with finishing their education at an ALA-accredited library school.
Eligibility: Applicants must be either entering or less than half-way through an accredited graduate school program in a field relevant to library science and be U.S. or Canadian citizens or permanent residents.
Target applicant(s): Graduate school students. Adult students.
Amount: Up to $5,000.
Number of awards: 1.
Deadline: November 15.
How to apply: Applications are available online.
Exclusive: Visit www.UltimateScholarshipBook.com and enter code ME59726 for updates on this award.

[598] • Harrell Family Fellowship
American Center of Oriental Research (ACOR)
209 Commerce Street, Alexandria, VA 22314
Phone: 703-789-9231
Email: usa.office@acorjordan.org
https://acorjordan.org/fellowships-2/
Purpose: To assist a graduate student with expenses on an archaeological project in Jordan.
Eligibility: Applicants must be graduate students in a program approved by a recognized academic review body. The funds must be used for archaeological or related research.
Target applicant(s): Graduate school students. Adult students.
Amount: $2,500.
Number of awards: 1.
Deadline: February 15.
How to apply: Applications are available online.
Exclusive: Visit www.UltimateScholarshipBook.com and enter code AM59826 for updates on this award.

[599] • Harry A. Applegate Scholarship
DECA Inc.
1908 Association Drive, Reston, VA 20191
Phone: 703-860-5000
Email: scholarships@deca.org
http://www.deca.org/scholarships/
Purpose: To reward current active members of DECA, the high school division or the college division of DECA.
Eligibility: Applicants must plan to be full-time students at a two-year or four-year program in marketing, entrepreneurship or management. This award is based on merit, not financial need, but applicants may include financial need statements for review. Applicants should submit transcripts, test scores, a statement of club participation, proof of leadership outside DECA, three recommendation letters and proof of membership.
Target applicant(s): High school students. College students. Adult students.
Amount: Varies.
Number of awards: Varies.
Deadline: January 12.
How to apply: Applications are available online and should be submitted to state/provincial DECA advisors.
Exclusive: Visit www.UltimateScholarshipBook.com and enter code DE59926 for updates on this award.

[600] • Harry S. Truman Research Grant
Harry S. Truman Library Institute for National and International Affairs
Grants Administrator, 500 W. U.S. Highway 24, Independence, MO 64050
Phone: 816-268-8248
Email: sullivan.hstli@gmail.com
http://www.trumanlibraryinstitute.org/research-grants/
Purpose: To promote the Truman Library as a center for research.
Eligibility: Graduate students and post-doctoral scholars are most encouraged to apply, but others completing advanced research will be considered. Preference is given to research that has a high chance of being published or otherwise shared publicly. Applicants can receive up to two research grants in a five-year period. Grant winners must submit a report at the end of their studies.
Target applicant(s): Graduate school students. Adult students.
Amount: Up to $2,500.
Number of awards: Varies.
Deadline: April 1; October 15.
How to apply: Applications are available online.
Exclusive: Visit www.UltimateScholarshipBook.com and enter code HA60026 for updates on this award.

[601] • Henry Belin du Pont Dissertation Fellowship
Hagley Museum and Library
Center for the History of Business, Technology and Society, 298 Buck Road, Wilmington, DE 19807
Phone: 302-658-2400
Email: rhorowitz@hagley.org
https://www.hagley.org/research/grants-fellowships
Purpose: To provide four-month fellowships for doctoral students performing dissertation research.
Eligibility: Applicants must be doctoral students who have completed all course work and are performing dissertation research. Research topics should involve historical questions and should relate to the collections in the Hagley Library. Fellows will receive housing, office space, a computer and Internet access. A presentation is required at the end of the residence period.
Target applicant(s): Graduate school students. Adult students.
Amount: $6,500 plus housing.
Number of awards: Varies.
Deadline: November 15.
How to apply: Applications are available online. For more information contact Dr. Roger Horowitz at rhorowitz@hagley.org.
Exclusive: Visit www.UltimateScholarshipBook.com and enter code HA60126 for updates on this award.

[602] • Herbert Hoover Research Travel Grant Award
Hoover Presidential Foundation
P.O. Box 696, West Branch, IA 52358
Phone: 800-828-0475
Email: info@hooverpf.org
http://www.hooverpresidentialfoundation.org
Purpose: To provide financial aid to individuals to research at the Herbert Hoover Presidential Library in West Branch, Iowa.
Eligibility: Applicants must be current graduate students, post-doctoral scholars or independent researchers. Applicants must also ensure that the library's contents will meet their research needs before applying.
Target applicant(s): Graduate school students. Adult students.
Amount: $500-$2,000.
Number of awards: Varies.
Deadline: March 1.
How to apply: Applications are available online.
Exclusive: Visit www.UltimateScholarshipBook.com and enter code HO60226 for updates on this award.

[603] • Honorable William Conner Writing Competition
New York Intellectual Property Association (NYIPLA)
229 Seventh Street, Suite 202, Garden City, NY 11530
Phone: 201-461-6603
Email: admin@nyipla.org
https://www.nyipla.org/nyipla/ConnerWritingAwards.asp
Purpose: To recognize exceptionally written papers that are submitted by law students.
Eligibility: Applicants must be law school students currently enrolled in a J.D. or LL.M. program (day or evening) in an accredited law school in the United States. Entries must be directed to any of the following subject areas of intellectual property: patents, trademarks, copyrights, trade secrets, unfair trade practices, antitrust and data security/privacy issues. Entries must be submitted by email and will be judged on interest and suitability of topic, organization, legal analysis, writing and professionalism of the work product.
Target applicant(s): Graduate school students. Adult students.
Amount: Up to $1,500.
Number of awards: 2.
Deadline: February 25.
How to apply: Applications are available online.

Exclusive: Visit www.UltimateScholarshipBook.com and enter code NE60326 for updates on this award.

[604] • Horatio Alger Career and Technical Scholarship
Horatio Alger Association
Attn.: Scholarship Department, 99 Canal Center Plaza, Suite 320, Alexandria, VA 22314
Phone: 703-684-9444
Email: association@horatioalger.org
https://scholars.horatioalger.org/
Purpose: To support students who have overcome great obstacles.
Eligibility: Applicants must be U.S. citizens under the age of 30 who are enrolling in a career or technical program at an accredited non-profit institution. Students must demonstrate financial need and perseverance in overcoming adversity.
Target applicant(s): High school students. College students. Adult students.
Amount: $2,500.
Number of awards: 500.
Deadline: September 15.
How to apply: Applications are available online.
Exclusive: Visit www.UltimateScholarshipBook.com and enter code HO60426 for updates on this award.

[605] • Humane Studies Fellowship: Publication Accelerator Grants
Institute for Humane Studies at George Mason University
3434 Washington Boulevard, Vernon Smith Hall, 1st Floor, Arlington, VA 22201
Phone: 800-697-8799
Email: Funding@TheIHS.org
https://theihs.org/funding/humane-studies-fellowship/
Purpose: To support students with an established publishing record who commit to submitting an article to a leading publication outlet.
Eligibility: Applicants must be full-time students enrolled in an MA or PhD program. Students at any university and international students are eligible to apply. Previous applicants and winners are welcome to apply. Prior participation in IHS programs is not required. Priority is given to applicants at top research institutions.
Target applicant(s): Graduate school students. Adult students.
Amount: Up to $5,000.
Number of awards: Varies.
Deadline: Varies.
How to apply: Applications are available online.
Exclusive: Visit www.UltimateScholarshipBook.com and enter code IN60526 for updates on this award.

[606] • Huntington Fellowships
Huntington Library, Art Collections and Botanical Gardens
1151 Oxford Road, San Marino, CA 91108
Phone: 626-405-2194
Email: cpowell@huntington.org
http://www.huntington.org
Purpose: To provide fellowships to doctoral students and recipients in British and American history, literature, art history and the history of science and medicine.
Eligibility: Applicants must have a Ph.D. or equivalent or be doctoral candidates at the dissertation stage. Cover sheets, project descriptions, curriculum vitae and three letters of recommendation are required.
Target applicant(s): Graduate school students. Adult students.
Amount: $3,000.
Number of awards: More than 150.
Deadline: November 15.
How to apply: Application materials are described online.
Exclusive: Visit www.UltimateScholarshipBook.com and enter code HU60626 for updates on this award.

[607] • Huntington-British Academy Fellowships for Study in Great Britain
Huntington Library, Art Collections and Botanical Gardens
1151 Oxford Road, San Marino, CA 91108
Phone: 626-405-2194
Email: cpowell@huntington.org
http://www.huntington.org
Purpose: To offer scholars exchange fellowships to research British and American history, literature, art history and the history of science and medicine.
Eligibility: Applicants must have a Ph.D. or equivalent. Applicants must submit cover sheets, project descriptions, curriculum vitae and three letters of recommendation.
Target applicant(s): Graduate school students. Adult students.
Amount: Varies.
Number of awards: Varies.
Deadline: November 15.
How to apply: There is no application form, and application materials are described online.
Exclusive: Visit www.UltimateScholarshipBook.com and enter code HU60726 for updates on this award.

[608] • IFEC Scholarships Award
International Foodservice Editorial Council (IFEC)
P.O. Box 581, Pleasant Valley, NY 12569
Phone: 845-229-6973
Email: ifec@ifeconline.com
http://www.ifeconline.com
Purpose: To assist students interested in foodservice combined with communication arts.
Eligibility: Applicants must be enrolled at a post-secondary, degree-granting educational institution and must demonstrate training, skill and interest in the foodservice industry and communication arts. Eligible majors from foodservice and communications areas include culinary arts, hotel/restaurant/hospitality management, dietetics, nutrition, food science/technology, journalism, public relations, mass communication, English, broadcast journalism, marketing, photography, graphic arts and related studies.
Target applicant(s): College students. Graduate school students. Adult students.
Amount: $1,500-$6,000.
Number of awards: 6.
Deadline: March 15.
How to apply: Applications are available online.
Exclusive: Visit www.UltimateScholarshipBook.com and enter code IN60826 for updates on this award.

The Ultimate Scholarship Book 2026
Scholarship Directory (Social Sciences)

[609] • IFSEA Worthy Goal Scholarship
International Food Service Executives Association
4955 Miller Street, Suite 107, Wheat Ridge, CO 80033
Phone: 502-589-3602
https://www.ifsea.org
Purpose: To help students receive food service management training beyond the high school level.
Eligibility: Applicants must be enrolled or accepted at a college as a full-time student in a food service related major. Students must provide a financial statement, personal statement, list of work experience and professional activities, transcripts, recommendations and a statement describing how the scholarship would help them reach their goals.
Target applicant(s): High school students. College students. Graduate school students. Adult students.
Amount: $250-$2,500.
Number of awards: Varies.
Deadline: March 31.
How to apply: Applications are available online.
Exclusive: Visit www.UltimateScholarshipBook.com and enter code IN60926 for updates on this award.

[610] • IMA Memorial Education Fund Scholarship
Institute of Management Accountants (IMA)
10 Paragon Drive, Montvale, NJ 07645-1760
Phone: 800-638-4427
Email: students@imanet.org
https://www.imanet.org
Purpose: To support students in fields related to management accounting.
Eligibility: Applicants must be full- and part-time undergraduate and graduate students, be IMA student members and declare which four- or five-year management accounting, financial management or information technology-related program they plan to pursue as a career or list a related field. Candidates should submit applications, resumes, transcripts, two recommendations and statements. Advanced degree students must pass one part of the CMA/CFM certification.
Target applicant(s): College students. Graduate school students. Adult students.
Minimum GPA: 3.0
Amount: $5,000.
Number of awards: Varies.
Deadline: March 10.
How to apply: Applications are available online.
Exclusive: Visit www.UltimateScholarshipBook.com and enter code IN61026 for updates on this award.

[611] • Imagine America High School Scholarship Program
Imagine America Foundation
12001 Sunrise Valley Drive, Suite 203, Reston, VA 20191
Phone: 571-267-3010
Email: Leed@imagine-america.org
https://www.imagine-america.org/students/scholarships-education/
Purpose: To help high school seniors pursue a postsecondary career education.
Eligibility: Applicants must have a minimum 2.5 high school GPA, demonstrate financial need and have demonstrated community service during their senior year.
Target applicant(s): High school students.
Minimum GPA: 2.5
Amount: $1,000.
Number of awards: 5.
Deadline: December 31.
How to apply: Applications are available online.
Exclusive: Visit www.UltimateScholarshipBook.com and enter code IM61126 for updates on this award.

[612] • Incoming Freshman Scholarship
American Hotel and Lodging Educational Foundation (AHLEF)
1250 Eye Street, N.W. Suite 1100, Washington, DC 20005
Phone: 202-289-3180
Email: foundation@ahla.com
https://www.ahlafoundation.org/scholarships/
Purpose: To recognize high school students who are interested in hospitality-related programs.
Eligibility: Applicants must be graduating seniors with preference given to those who have completed the two-year Lodging Management Program (LMP) high school program. Students must be planning to attend a post-secondary institution, be U.S. citizens or permanent residents and have a minimum 2.0 GPA.
Target applicant(s): High school students.
Minimum GPA: 2.0
Amount: $2,000-$4,000.
Number of awards: Varies.
Deadline: March 15.
How to apply: Applications are available online.
Exclusive: Visit www.UltimateScholarshipBook.com and enter code AM61226 for updates on this award.

[613] • International Facility Management Association Foundation Scholarship Program
International Facility Management Association
800 Gessner Road, Suite 900, Houston, TX 77024-4257
Phone: 713-623-4362
Email: amy.arnold@ifma.org
http://foundation.ifma.org
Purpose: To support students currently enrolled in facility management or facility management-related programs.
Eligibility: Applicants must be college or graduate students and include a letter of professional intent, resume and letter of recommendation with application.
Target applicant(s): College students. Graduate school students. Adult students.
Minimum GPA: 3.2
Amount: $1,500-$10,000.
Number of awards: Varies.
Deadline: May 16.
How to apply: Applications are available online.
Exclusive: Visit www.UltimateScholarshipBook.com and enter code IN61326 for updates on this award.

[614] • International Technology Engineering Educators Association Scholarship – FTEE/Undergraduate
International Technology and Engineering Educators Association
Foundation for Technology and Engineering Educators, 1908 Association Drive, Suite C, Reston, VA 20191
Phone: 703-860-2100
Email: iteea@iteea.org
https://www.iteea.org/awards-and-scholarships

Purpose: To encourage students majoring in technology and engineering education teacher preparation.
Eligibility: Applicants must be members of the International Technology Education Association. Students must not be a senior by the application deadline. Applicants must be full-time undergraduate students majoring in technology and engineering education teacher preparation.
Target applicant(s): College students. Adult students.
Minimum GPA: 2.5
Amount: $500.
Number of awards: 1.
Deadline: November 1.
How to apply: Applications are available online.
Exclusive: Visit www.UltimateScholarshipBook.com and enter code IN61426 for updates on this award.

[615] • IRARC Memorial, Joseph P. Rubino, WA4MMD, Scholarship
American Radio Relay League Foundation
225 Main Street, Newington, CT 06111-1494
Phone: 860-594-0200
Email: foundation@arrl.org
https://www.arrl.org/scholarship-program
Purpose: To provide financial assistance to amateur radio operators who are seeking an undergraduate degree or electronic technician certification.
Eligibility: Applicants must hold an active Amateur Radio License in any class and be studying at an accredited institution. They must have a minimum GPA of 2.5. Preference is given to Florida residents, particularly those from Brevard County and those with need and lower GPAs.
Target applicant(s): High school students. College students. Adult students.
Minimum GPA: 2.5
Amount: $750.
Number of awards: Varies.
Deadline: January 10.
How to apply: Applications are available online.
Exclusive: Visit www.UltimateScholarshipBook.com and enter code AM61526 for updates on this award.

[616] • James A. Turner, Jr. Memorial Scholarship
American Welding Society Foundation
550 NW LeJeune Road, Miami, FL 33126
Phone: 800-443-9353
Email: info@aws.org
https://www.aws.org/foundation/page/scholarships
Purpose: To aid those interested in a management career in welding store operations or distributorship.
Eligibility: Applicants must be full-time students pursuing a four-year bachelor's of business degree, plan to enter management careers in welding store operations or distributorship, be high school graduates at least 18 years of age and be employed a minimum of 10 hours per week at a welding distributorship. Preference is given to members of the American Welding Society.
Target applicant(s): High school students. College students. Adult students.
Amount: $3,500.
Number of awards: 1.
Deadline: March 1.
How to apply: Applications are available online.
Exclusive: Visit www.UltimateScholarshipBook.com and enter code AM61626 for updates on this award.

[617] • James Beard Foundation Scholarship
James Beard Foundation Scholarship Program/ISTS
167 West 12th Street, New York, NY 10011
Phone: 212-627-2308
Email: scholarships@jamesbeard.org
https://www.jamesbeard.org/scholarships
Purpose: To support students pursuing a culinary education.
Eligibility: Applicants must be graduating high school seniors or graduates pursuing a culinary or food-focused program at an accredited institution.
Target applicant(s): High school students. College students. Graduate school students. Adult students.
Amount: Up to $20,000.
Number of awards: Up to 60.
Deadline: April 5.
How to apply: Applications are available online.
Exclusive: Visit www.UltimateScholarshipBook.com and enter code JA61726 for updates on this award.

[618] • Jane M. Klausman Women in Business Scholarship Fund
Zonta International
1211 West 22nd Street, Suite 900, Oak Brook, IL 60523
Phone: 630-928-1400
Email: zontaintl@zonta.org
https://www.zonta.org
Purpose: To help female business management majors overcome gender barriers.
Eligibility: Applicants must be women of any age pursuing a business or business-related program who demonstrate outstanding potential. Applicants must also have an outstanding academic record in their college career, and they must show intent to complete a business program.
Target applicant(s): College students. Graduate school students. Adult students.
Amount: $2,000-$8,000.
Number of awards: 38.
Deadline: Contact the sponsor to confirm the deadline.
How to apply: Applications are available online or from your local Zonta Club.
Exclusive: Visit www.UltimateScholarshipBook.com and enter code ZO61826 for updates on this award.

[619] • Jennifer C. Groot Fellowship
American Center of Oriental Research (ACOR)
209 Commerce Street, Alexandria, VA 22314
Phone: 703-789-9231
Email: usa.office@acorjordan.org
https://acorjordan.org/fellowships-2/
Purpose: To assist students with expenses on an archaeological project.
Eligibility: Applicants must be undergraduate or graduate students with little or no archaeological field experience and be U.S. or Canadian citizens. Recipients will travel to Jordan for the project.
Target applicant(s): High school students. College students. Graduate school students. Adult students.
Amount: $3,000.
Number of awards: 2.
Deadline: February 15.
How to apply: Applications are available online but must be submitted by mail.
Exclusive: Visit www.UltimateScholarshipBook.com and enter code AM61926 for updates on this award.

[620] • JFLF Awards Programs
James F. Lincoln Arc Welding Foundation
Secretary, P.O. Box 17188, Cleveland, OH 44117-9949
http://www.jflf.org
Purpose: To award prizes for arc welding projects made by the applicant or a group of applicants.
Eligibility: Projects may fit into one of the following categories: home, recreational or artistic equipment; shop tool, machine or mechanical device; a structure; agricultural equipment or a repair. Applicants must submit a paper about the creation of the project and be enrolled in a shop class. Applicants must also be enrolled in high school, adult evening classes, two-year/community college, vocational school, apprentice program, trade school, in-plant training or technical school and may not be college students enrolled in a bachelor's or master's program.
Target applicant(s): High school students. College students. Graduate school students. Adult students.
Amount: Varies.
Number of awards: 95.
Deadline: July 1.
How to apply: Applications are available online.
Exclusive: Visit www.UltimateScholarshipBook.com and enter code JA62026 for updates on this award.

[621] • Joe Francis Haircare Scholarship Program
Joe Francis Haircare Scholarship Foundation
8101 Homestead Avenue South, Cottage Grove, MN 55016
Phone: 651-769-1757
Email: contact@joefrancis.com
http://www.joefrancis.com
Purpose: To provide barber and cosmetology students with financial aid.
Eligibility: Applicants must be sponsored by one of the following: a fully accredited, recognized barber or cosmetology school, a licensed salon owner or manager, a full-service distributor or a member of the International Chain Association, Beauty and Barber Supply Institute, Cosmetology Advancement Foundation or National Cosmetology Association. Applicants must be actively enrolled in cosmetology school or planning to enroll during or after the award month of August. Judging is based on financial need, motivation and character.
Target applicant(s): High school students. College students. Adult students.
Amount: Up to $3,000.
Number of awards: Varies.
Deadline: June 1.
How to apply: Applications are available online.
Exclusive: Visit www.UltimateScholarshipBook.com and enter code JO62126 for updates on this award.

[622] • Joe Perdue Scholarship
Club Foundation
1733 King Street, Alexandria, VA 22314
Phone: 703-739-9500
Email: schaverr@clubfoundation.org
https://www.clubfoundation.org
Purpose: To support students pursuing careers in private club management.
Eligibility: Applicants must be pursuing managerial careers in the private club industry, have completed their freshman year of college, have a minimum 2.5 GPA and be enrolled full-time for the following year. An essay and letters of recommendation are also required.
Target applicant(s): College students. Adult students.
Minimum GPA: 2.5
Amount: $2,500.
Number of awards: Varies.
Deadline: June 1.
How to apply: Applications are available online.
Exclusive: Visit www.UltimateScholarshipBook.com and enter code CL62226 for updates on this award.

[623] • John Bayliss Radio Scholarship
John Bayliss Broadcast Foundation
171 17th Street, Pacific Grove, CA 93950
Phone: 212-424-6410
Email: cbutrum@baylissfoundation.org
http://www.beaweb.org/bayliss/radio.html
Purpose: This scholarship helps students who are pursuing careers in radio.
Eligibility: Applicants must be attending an institution of higher learning in the U.S., be entering their junior or senior year and have a GPA of 3.0 or higher. Students must be working toward a career in the radio industry. Preference is given to students with a history of radio-related activities and those pursuing careers in commercial radio.
Target applicant(s): College students. Adult students.
Minimum GPA: 3.0
Amount: $5,000.
Number of awards: Varies.
Deadline: Contact the sponsor to confirm the deadline.
How to apply: Applications are available online. An application form, resume, transcript, essay and three letters of recommendation are required.
Exclusive: Visit www.UltimateScholarshipBook.com and enter code JO62326 for updates on this award.

[624] • John D. Graham Scholarship
Public Relations Student Society of America
120 Wall Street, 21st Floor, New York, NY 10005-4024
Phone: 212-460-1474
Email: prssa@prsa.org
https://prssa.prsa.org/scholarships-and-awards/
Purpose: To aid journalism and public relations students.
Eligibility: Applicants must be rising undergraduate seniors who are enrolled in a journalism or public relations degree program. Selection is based on academic merit, leadership, writing ability, relevant work experience and stated career goals.
Target applicant(s): College students. Adult students.
Amount: $1,000-$3,000.
Number of awards: 3.
Deadline: April 30.
How to apply: Applications are available online. An application form, resume and one recommendation letter are required.
Exclusive: Visit www.UltimateScholarshipBook.com and enter code PU62426 for updates on this award.

[625] • John F. Kennedy Profile in Courage Essay Contest
John F. Kennedy Library Foundation
Columbia Point, Boston, MA 02125
Phone: 617-514-1649
Email: profiles@nara.gov
http://www.jfklibrary.org/Education/Profile-in-Courage-Essay-Contest.aspx

Purpose: To encourage students to research and write about politics and John F. Kennedy.
Eligibility: Applicants must be in grades 9 through 12 in public or private schools or be home-schooled and write an essay about the political courage of a U.S. elected official who served during or after 1917. Essays must have source citations. Applicants must register online before sending essays and have a nominating teacher review the essay. The winner and teacher will be invited to the Kennedy Library to accept the award, and the winner's teacher will receive a grant. Essays are judged on content (55 percent) and presentation (45 percent).
Target applicant(s): High school students.
Amount: $100-$10,000.
Number of awards: Up to 25.
Deadline: January 17.
How to apply: Applications are available online. A registration form and essay are required.
Exclusive: Visit www.UltimateScholarshipBook.com and enter code JO62526 for updates on this award.

[626] • Joseph S. Rumbaugh Historical Oration Contest

National Society, Sons of the American Revolution
809 West Main Street, Louisville, KY 40202
Phone: 502-589-1776
Email: coggins.sar@gmail.com
https://www.sar.org/education/
Purpose: To encourage students to learn more about the Revolutionary War and its impact on modern America.
Eligibility: Applicants must prepare a speech of five to six minutes on some aspect of the Revolutionary War. The contest is open to high school students at public, private and parochial high schools, as well as home-schooled students. Eligibility for the national contest is determined by contests on the state and local level.
Target applicant(s): High school students.
Amount: $200-$8,000.
Number of awards: Varies.
Deadline: May 15.
How to apply: Applications are available from local chapters of Sons of the American Revolution.
Exclusive: Visit www.UltimateScholarshipBook.com and enter code NA62626 for updates on this award.

[627] • Junior Fellowships

American Institute of Indian Studies
1130 E. 59th Street, Chicago, IL 60637
Phone: 773-702-8638
Email: aiis@uchicago.edu
http://www.indiastudies.org
Purpose: To support doctoral candidates at U.S. universities who wish to travel to India to conduct dissertation research on Indian aspects of their academic discipline.
Eligibility: Applicants must be doctoral candidates at a U.S. university. Junior fellows are affiliated with Indian universities and research mentors. Awards may last up to 11 months.
Target applicant(s): Graduate school students. Adult students.
Amount: Varies.
Number of awards: Varies.
Deadline: November 15.
How to apply: Applications are available by mail or email.
Exclusive: Visit www.UltimateScholarshipBook.com and enter code AM62726 for updates on this award.

[628] • K2TEO Martin J. Green, Sr. Memorial Scholarship

American Radio Relay League Foundation
225 Main Street, Newington, CT 06111-1494
Phone: 860-594-0200
Email: foundation@arrl.org
https://www.arrl.org/scholarship-program
Purpose: To provide financial assistance to students who are amateur radio operators.
Eligibility: Applicants must hold a general class or higher amateur radio license. Preference is given to students from ham families.
Target applicant(s): High school students. College students. Graduate school students. Adult students.
Amount: $1,000.
Number of awards: 1.
Deadline: January 10.
How to apply: Applications are available online.
Exclusive: Visit www.UltimateScholarshipBook.com and enter code AM62826 for updates on this award.

[629] • Kimberly-Clark Corporation Legacy Scholarship

National Grocers Association
1005 N. Glebe Road, Suite 250, Arlington, VA 22201
Phone: 225-387-6126
https://www.nationalgrocers.org/foundation/nga-foundation-scholarships/
Purpose: To support students pursuing a degree related to the grocery field.
Eligibility: Applicants must be rising sophomores through postgraduate students, have a minimum 2.5 GPA and be enrolled in a two- or four-year degree-granting institution. Students must major in business, food management, IT or another field related to a career in the grocery industry. Experience in the grocery industry is preferred but not required.
Target applicant(s): College students. Graduate school students. Adult students.
Minimum GPA: 2.5
Amount: $2,500.
Number of awards: 1.
Deadline: April 15.
How to apply: Applications are available online.
Exclusive: Visit www.UltimateScholarshipBook.com and enter code NA62926 for updates on this award.

[630] • Kit C. King Graduate Scholarship Fund

National Press Photographers Association Kit C. King Graduate Scholarship Fund
120 Hooper Street, Athens, GA 30602-3018
Phone: 706-542-2506
Email: jwbrown@nppf.org
http://nppf.org/nppf-scholarships-grants-and-awards/
Purpose: To support photojournalism students.
Eligibility: Applicants must provide a portfolio, be pursuing an advanced degree in journalism with an emphasis in photojournalism and demonstrate financial need. Applicants can apply to as many NPPA scholarships as desired, but only one award will be granted per winner.
Target applicant(s): Graduate school students. Adult students.
Amount: $2,000.

Number of awards: 1.
Deadline: February 9.
How to apply: Applications are available online.
Exclusive: Visit www.UltimateScholarshipBook.com and enter code NA63026 for updates on this award.

[631] • L. Phil and Alice J. Wicker Scholarship

American Radio Relay League Foundation
225 Main Street, Newington, CT 06111-1494
Phone: 860-594-0200
Email: foundation@arrl.org
https://www.arrl.org/scholarship-program
Purpose: To assist ham radio operators in furthering their educations.
Eligibility: Applicants must have at least a general ham radio license, be residents of and attending school in the ARRL Roanoke Division (North Carolina, South Carolina, Virginia, West Virginia) and be undergraduate or graduate students in electronics, communications or another related field.
Target applicant(s): High school students. College students. Graduate school students. Adult students.
Amount: $2,000.
Number of awards: 1.
Deadline: January 10.
How to apply: Applications are available online. Completed applications must be submitted by mail.
Exclusive: Visit www.UltimateScholarshipBook.com and enter code AM63126 for updates on this award.

[632] • L.B. Cebik, W4RNL and Jean Cebik, N4TZP Memorial Scholarship

American Radio Relay League Foundation
225 Main Street, Newington, CT 06111-1494
Phone: 860-594-0200
Email: foundation@arrl.org
https://www.arrl.org/scholarship-program
Purpose: To provide scholarship assistance to amateur radio operators.
Eligibility: Applicants must hold a Technician Class Amateur Radio License or higher, and they must be attending a four-year college or university.
Target applicant(s): High school students. College students. Adult students.
Amount: $5,000.
Number of awards: 1.
Deadline: January 10.
How to apply: Applications are available online.
Exclusive: Visit www.UltimateScholarshipBook.com and enter code AM63226 for updates on this award.

[633] • Laurels Fund Scholarship

Educational Foundation for Women in Accounting
136 South Keowee Street, Dayton, OH 45402-2241
Phone: 610-407-9229
Email: info@efwa.org
http://www.efwa.org
Purpose: To provide scholarships to women pursuing advanced degrees in accounting.
Eligibility: This award is available to women pursuing a Ph.D. in accounting. The awardees are selected based on scholarship, service and financial need. Applicants must have completed their comprehensive exams before the previous fall semester.
Target applicant(s): Graduate school students. Adult students.
Amount: Up to $5,000.
Number of awards: Varies.
Deadline: May 15.
How to apply: Applications are available online.
Exclusive: Visit www.UltimateScholarshipBook.com and enter code ED63326 for updates on this award.

[634] • Lawrence G. Foster Award for Excellence in Public Relations

Public Relations Student Society of America
120 Wall Street, 21st Floor, New York, NY 10005-4024
Phone: 212-460-1474
Email: prssa@prsa.org
https://prssa.prsa.org/scholarships-and-awards/
Purpose: To assist public relations students.
Eligibility: Applicants must be undergraduate students majoring in public relations who are committed to careers in public relations and must be PRSSA members. Students must submit an essay on what excellence in public relations is and how they plan to achieve excellence in their own careers.
Target applicant(s): High school students. College students. Adult students.
Amount: $1,500.
Number of awards: 1.
Deadline: April 30.
How to apply: Applications are available online.
Exclusive: Visit www.UltimateScholarshipBook.com and enter code PU63426 for updates on this award.

[635] • Learning and Leadership Grants

NEA Foundation
1201 16th Street NW, Washington, DC 20036
Phone: 202-822-7840
Email: NEAFoundation@nea.org
https://www.neafoundation.org
Purpose: To support public school teachers, public education support professionals and faculty or staff in public institutions of higher education in professional development experiences such as summer institutes or action research.
Eligibility: Applicants must be current public school teachers in grades K-12, public school education support professionals or faculty and staff at public higher education institutions. The professional development must improve practice, curriculum and student achievement. Funds may be used for fees, travel expenses, books or materials. There is also a grant for groups for $5,000.
Target applicant(s): Graduate school students. Adult students.
Amount: $1,500-$5,000.
Number of awards: Varies.
Deadline: May 1.
How to apply: Applications are available online. Applications may be submitted at any time and are reviewed three times each year on February 1, June 1 and October 15.
Exclusive: Visit www.UltimateScholarshipBook.com and enter code NE63526 for updates on this award.

[636] • Lee Thornton Scholarship
Radio Television Digital News Association
529 14th Street NW, Suite 1240, Washington, DC 20045
Phone: 202-659-6510
Email: karenh@rtdna.org
http://www.rtdna.org
Purpose: To support students pursuing careers in radio, television or digital journalism.
Eligibility: Applicants must be a sophomore, junior or senior at a college or university with preference given to students of the University of Maryland and Howard University. Students should be pursuing a degree in journalism, broadcasting or communications. Applicants must include URL links to three to five work samples.
Target applicant(s): College students. Adult students.
Amount: $2,000.
Number of awards: 1.
Deadline: January 11.
How to apply: Applications are available online.
Exclusive: Visit www.UltimateScholarshipBook.com and enter code RA63626 for updates on this award.

[637] • Legal Opportunity Scholarship Fund
American Bar Association
321 North Clark Street, Chicago, IL 60654
Phone: 312-988-5624
Email: abalsd@americanbar.org
https://www.americanbar.org/groups/diversity/diversity_pipeline/projects_initiatives/legal_opportunity_scholarship/
Purpose: To assist first-year law school students.
Eligibility: Applicants must be U.S. citizens or permanent residents. They must be entering the first year of law school during the year of application. They must have a cumulative undergraduate GPA of 2.5 or higher. Selection is based on the overall strength of the application.
Target applicant(s): College students. Graduate school students. Adult students.
Minimum GPA: 2.5
Amount: $15,000.
Number of awards: 10-20.
Scholarship may be renewable.
Deadline: April 15.
How to apply: Applications are available online. An application form, personal statement, two recommendation letters and a transcript are required.
Exclusive: Visit www.UltimateScholarshipBook.com and enter code AM63726 for updates on this award.

[638] • LexisNexis / John R. Johnson Memorial Scholarship Endowment
American Association of Law Libraries
105 W. Adams, Suite 3300, Chicago, IL 60603
Email: scholarships@aall.org
https://www.aallnet.org/education-training/scholarships/
Purpose: To encourage current and future law librarians in memory of John Johnson, a prominent law librarian.
Eligibility: Applicants who apply for any of the AALL Educational Scholarships become automatically eligible to receive this award. No separate application is necessary. Applicants must intend to have careers as law librarians. Preference is given to AALL members, but a non-member may apply.
Target applicant(s): Graduate school students. Adult students.
Amount: Varies.
Number of awards: Varies.
Scholarship may be renewable.
Deadline: April 1.
How to apply: Applications are available online, by mail with a self-addressed, stamped envelope, by fax, by phone or by email.
Exclusive: Visit www.UltimateScholarshipBook.com and enter code AM63826 for updates on this award.

[639] • LimNexus Scholarship
National Asian Pacific American Bar Association Law Foundation
P.O. Box 65081, Washington, DC 20035
https://www.napabalawfoundation.org/scholarships
Purpose: To support students who demonstrate a commitment to serving the Asian Pacific American community.
Eligibility: Applicants must be U.S. citizens or permanent residents who are enrolled in an accredited U.S. law school. Students must demonstrate academic achievement, leadership potential and commitment to serving or contributing to the Asian Pacific American community. Applicants must include an essay emphasizing experiences that illustrate their commitment to the APA community.
Target applicant(s): Graduate school students. Adult students.
Amount: $2,500.
Number of awards: 1.
Deadline: September 4.
How to apply: Applications are available online.
Exclusive: Visit www.UltimateScholarshipBook.com and enter code NA63926 for updates on this award.

[640] • Litherland/ITEEA Scholarship
International Technology and Engineering Educators Association
Foundation for Technology and Engineering Educators, 1908 Association Drive, Suite C, Reston, VA 20191
Phone: 703-860-2100
Email: iteea@iteea.org
https://www.iteea.org/awards-and-scholarships
Purpose: To provide scholarships for undergraduate students pursuing a career in teaching technology.
Eligibility: Applicants must be members of ITEEA and be full-time undergraduate students majoring in technology and engineering education teacher preparation. Students must also have a minimum 2.5 GPA.
Target applicant(s): College students. Adult students.
Minimum GPA: 2.5
Amount: $500.
Number of awards: 1.
Deadline: November 1.
How to apply: Application information is available online.
Exclusive: Visit www.UltimateScholarshipBook.com and enter code IN64026 for updates on this award.

[641] • Lockheed Martin Vocational Scholarship Program
Lockheed Martin Vocational Scholarship Program
Scholarship America, One Scholarship Way, Saint Peter, MN 56082
Phone: 507-931-0465
Email: lmvocational@scholarshipamerica.org

https://lockheedmartin.com/vocational
Purpose: To support students pursuing an associate's degree or vocational-technical certification.
Eligibility: Applicants must be high school seniors, high school graduates (or GED equivalent) or current undergraduates with less than a bachelor's degree. Students must be U.S. citizens who are planning to enroll at an accredited vocational technical school, trade school, two-year community or state college. Applicants must be studying one of the following fields or a related field: computer and information sciences, engineering, engineering technologies/technicians, mechanic and repair technologies or advanced manufacturing and production.
Target applicant(s): High school students. College students. Adult students.
Amount: $5,000.
Number of awards: 150.
Deadline: April 1.
How to apply: Applications are available online.
Exclusive: Visit www.UltimateScholarshipBook.com and enter code LO64126 for updates on this award.

[642] • Lou and Carole Prato Sports Reporting Scholarship

Radio Television Digital News Association
529 14th Street NW, Suite 1240, Washington, DC 20045
Phone: 202-659-6510
Email: karenh@rtdna.org
http://www.rtdna.org
Purpose: To provide monetary assistance to a student pursuing a career as a sports reporter for radio or television.
Eligibility: Applicants must be full-time college sophomores or higher with at least one full academic year remaining. Applicants may be enrolled in any major but must have a career goal of becoming a sports reporter for television or radio. Applicants may only apply for one RTNDA scholarship.
Target applicant(s): College students. Adult students.
Amount: $1,000.
Number of awards: 1.
Deadline: January 11.
How to apply: Applications are available online.
Exclusive: Visit www.UltimateScholarshipBook.com and enter code RA64226 for updates on this award.

[643] • Lou Hochberg Awards

Orgone Biophysical Research Laboratory
P.O. Box 1148, Ashland, OR 97520
Phone: 541-522-0118
Email: info@orgonelab.org
http://www.orgonelab.org/hochberg.htm
Purpose: The Orgone Biophysical Research Lab offers a number of awards to students, scholars and journalists through a program set up by Louis Hochberg, a social worker who was dedicated to the sociological discoveries of Wilhelm Reich.
Eligibility: The Lou Hochberg Awards are given to winning theses and dissertations, university and college essays, high school essays and published articles that focus on Reich's sociological work. There are categories for students, scholars or journalists beginning at high school age through adulthood. A suggested list of topics and a bibliography is available online.

Target applicant(s): High school students. College students. Graduate school students. Adult students.
Amount: $500-$1,500.
Number of awards: Varies.
Deadline: Contact the sponsor to confirm the deadline.
How to apply: Each award has a specific set of instructions for submitting a package for consideration. Guidelines are listed online.
Exclusive: Visit www.UltimateScholarshipBook.com and enter code OR64326 for updates on this award.

[644] • Maley/FTEE Teacher Professional Development Scholarship

International Technology and Engineering Educators Association
Foundation for Technology and Engineering Educators, 1908 Association Drive, Suite C, Reston, VA 20191
Phone: 703-860-2100
Email: iteea@iteea.org
https://www.iteea.org/awards-and-scholarships
Purpose: To support technology education teachers.
Eligibility: Applicants must be members of ITEEA and plan to pursue or continue graduate study. Candidates must provide their plans for graduate study, description of need, college transcript and three recommendation letters.
Target applicant(s): College students. Graduate school students. Adult students.
Amount: $500.
Number of awards: Varies.
Deadline: November 1.
How to apply: Application information is available online.
Exclusive: Visit www.UltimateScholarshipBook.com and enter code IN64426 for updates on this award.

[645] • Maple Flooring Manufacturers Association Scholarship

Maple Flooring Manufacturers Association
1425 Tri State Parkway, Suite 110, Gurnee, IL 60031
Phone: 888-480-9138
Email: mfma@maplefloor.org
https://www.maplefloor.org/Programs-Services/Scholarship-Program.aspx
Purpose: To support students pursuing a higher education at a secondary, advanced or trade school with a focus on the sports flooring business.
Eligibility: Applicants must be legal residents of the U.S. attending college in the United States. Students must write a 500-word essay and be studying in one of the following fields: architecture, athletic administration, athletics, boiler inspection training, biological conservation, bio-mechanical sciences, building construction, civil engineering, coaching, commercial driving schools, construction sciences or management, dance education, forest science, forestry studies, engineering technology, environmental resource management, exercise science, industrial technology schools, kinesiology, LEED training or certification, mechanic schools, mechanical drafting, machine technologies, natural resources/conservation, physical administration, physical education, physical rehabilitation or therapy, recreation and park administration, small engine repair schools, sports and fitness management, survey schools, trucking schools or wood sciences.
Target applicant(s): High school students. College students. Adult students.
Amount: $1,000.
Number of awards: 5.
Deadline: July 14.
How to apply: Applications are available online.

Exclusive: Visit www.UltimateScholarshipBook.com and enter code MA64526 for updates on this award.

[646] • Mary Lou Brown Scholarship
American Radio Relay League Foundation
225 Main Street, Newington, CT 06111-1494
Phone: 860-594-0200
Email: foundation@arrl.org
https://www.arrl.org/scholarship-program
Purpose: To assist ham radio operators with furthering their educations.
Eligibility: Applicants must have at least a general ham radio license, be residents of the ARRL Northwest Division (Alaska, Idaho, Montana, Oregon or Washington), be working for a bachelor's or graduate degree, have a minimum 3.0 GPA and have demonstrated interest in promoting the Amateur Radio Service.
Target applicant(s): High school students. College students. Graduate school students. Adult students.
Minimum GPA: 3.0
Amount: $2,500.
Number of awards: Varies.
Deadline: January 10.
How to apply: Applications are available online. Completed applications must be submitted by mail.
Exclusive: Visit www.UltimateScholarshipBook.com and enter code AM64626 for updates on this award.

[647] • Material Handling Education Foundation
Material Handling Industry
8720 Red Oak Boulevard, Suite 201, Charlotte, NC 28217
Phone: 704-676-1190
https://www.mhi.org/mhefi/scholarship
Purpose: To support students who plan to pursue higher education.
Eligibility: Applicants must be undergraduate students pursuing a career in material handling, logistics or supply chain and enrolled full-time at a qualified college or university in a target program in the U.S. accredited by the Council for Higher Education. Students must be enrolled full-time with a B grade point average or above in their major. Applicants must be enrolled in school for the entire academic year without interruption, barring illness, emergency or military service.
Target applicant(s): College students. Adult students.
Amount: $1,500 to $6,000.
Number of awards: Varies.
Deadline: January 31.
How to apply: Applications are available online.
Exclusive: Visit www.UltimateScholarshipBook.com and enter code MA64726 for updates on this award.

[648] • MBA Fellowship
Goldman Sachs
200 West Street, New York, NY 10282
Phone: 212-902-1000
http://www.goldmansachs.com/careers/students/programs/americas/mba-fellowship.html
Purpose: To recognize outstanding students.
Eligibility: Applicants must be first-year MBA students. Students must be seeking a summer associate position at Goldman Sachs. Applicants must be Black, Hispanic/Latino, Native American or women.
Target applicant(s): Graduate school students. Adult students.
Amount: $35,000.
Number of awards: Varies.

Deadline: Rolling basis starting August 15.
How to apply: Applications are available online.
Exclusive: Visit www.UltimateScholarshipBook.com and enter code GO64826 for updates on this award.

[649] • Media Fellows Program
Washington Media Scholars Foundation
815 Slaters Lane, Suite 201, Alexandria, VA 22314
Phone: 703-299-4399
Email: info@mediascholars.org
https://www.mediascholars.org/media-fellows/
Purpose: To aid students who plan to pursue careers in the field of public policy and advertising.
Eligibility: Applicants must be rising undergraduate juniors and seniors who are attending school full time. They must be degree-seeking students who are majoring in subjects that provide preparation for a career in strategic public policy research, planning, advertising or buying. Eligible majors include but are not limited to political science, mass communication, marketing and journalism. They must have a demonstrated interest in pursuing a career in the field of strategic media planning. They must have a major GPA of 3.0 or higher and must demonstrate financial need. Selection is based on the overall strength of the application.
Target applicant(s): College students. Adult students.
Amount: $1,000-$2,000.
Number of awards: 50.
Deadline: December 2.
How to apply: Applications are available online. An application form, essay and one recommendation letter are required.
Exclusive: Visit www.UltimateScholarshipBook.com and enter code WA64926 for updates on this award.

[650] • Memorial Classic Golf Tournament Scholarship
Funeral Service Foundation
13625 Bishop's Drive, Brookfield, WI 53005-6607
Phone: 877-402-5900
Email: info@funeralservicefoundation.org
https://www.funeralservicefoundation.org/academicscholarships/
Purpose: To help students continue their education in funeral service and mortuary science education.
Eligibility: Applicants must be enrolled full- or part-time in an American Board of Funeral Service Education accredited program. Selection is based on the overall strength of the application.
Target applicant(s): College students. Graduate school students. Adult students.
Minimum GPA: 2.0
Amount: $2,500-$5,000.
Number of awards: Varies.
Deadline: April 1; November 1.
How to apply: Applications are available online. An application form, essay, academic transcript and video submissions are required.
Exclusive: Visit www.UltimateScholarshipBook.com and enter code FU65026 for updates on this award.

[651] • Merchants Exchange of Portland Scholarship

Merchants Exchange of Portland Scholarship Fund
200 SW Market Street, Suite 190, Portland, OR 97201
Phone: 503-804-0633
http://www.pdxmex.com/scholarship
Purpose: To support students seeking a maritime field career.
Eligibility: Applicants must be current juniors or seniors at a four-year college or university, freshmen or sophomores in a two-year degree program, students in a U.S. Coast Guard-approved training program or graduate students in Maritime affairs or international trade. Students must have a minimum GPA of 2.5 and provide transcripts, essays and a letter of recommendation.
Target applicant(s): College students. Graduate school students. Adult students.
Minimum GPA: 2.5
Amount: $2,000.
Number of awards: 5.
Deadline: May 31.
How to apply: Applications are available online.
Exclusive: Visit www.UltimateScholarshipBook.com and enter code ME65126 for updates on this award.

[652] • Microsoft Office Specialist World Championship

Microsoft Office
1276 S. 820 E. Suite 200, American Fork, UT 84003
https://moschampionship.certiport.com/#about
Purpose: To support students who compete in Microsoft Office.
Eligibility: Applicants must be identified as winners in a qualifying round contest and must be 13-25 years old at the time of the qualifying exam. Students must be enrolled in an approved academic institution. Applicants must not be residents of Colorado or Maryland and must not be students at a school within the Chicago Public School District.
Target applicant(s): High school students. College students. Graduate school students.
Amount: $2,000-$8,000.
Number of awards: Varies.
Deadline: June 15.
How to apply: Applications are available online.
Exclusive: Visit www.UltimateScholarshipBook.com and enter code MI65226 for updates on this award.

[653] • Mildred C. Hanson SIOR Memorial Scholarship

Society of Industrial and Office REALTORS (SIOR) Foundation
1201 New York Avenue, NW, Suite 350, Washington, DC 20005
Phone: 202-449-8208
Email: cnowak@sior.com
https://siorfoundation.org/
Purpose: To support female students pursuing undergraduate degrees in real estate, business or finance.
Eligibility: Applicants must be females and citizens of the United States or Canada. Students must be accepted or enrolled in an accredited four-year college or university geographically located in the United States or Canada pursuing an undergraduate degree related to commercial real estate. Applicants must be rising juniors or above.
Target applicant(s): College students. Adult students.
Amount: $8,000.
Number of awards: 1.
Deadline: November 1.
How to apply: Applications are available online.
Exclusive: Visit www.UltimateScholarshipBook.com and enter code SO65326 for updates on this award.

[654] • Minorities and Women Educational Scholarship

Appraisal Institute Education Trust
200 W. Madison, Suite 1500, Chicago, IL 60606
Phone: 312-335-4133
Email: wwoodburn@appraisalinstitute.org
http://www.appraisalinstitute.org
Purpose: To assist minority and women college students in pursuing degrees in real estate appraisal or related fields.
Eligibility: Applicants must be women or American Indians, Alaska Natives, Asians, African Americans, Hispanics or Latinos, Native Hawaiians or other Pacific Islanders. Applicants must be full- or part-time students enrolled in real estate courses and working toward a degree, have a minimum 2.5 GPA and demonstrate financial need.
Target applicant(s): High school students. College students. Adult students.
Minimum GPA: 2.5
Amount: $1,000.
Number of awards: Varies.
Deadline: January 1; April 1; July 1 and October 1.
How to apply: Applications are available online.
Exclusive: Visit www.UltimateScholarshipBook.com and enter code AP65426 for updates on this award.

[655] • Minority Fellowship Program

American Sociological Association Minority Fellowship Program
1430 K Street NW, Suite 600, Washington, DC 20005
Phone: 202-383-9005
Email: minority.affairs@asanet.org
https://www.asanet.org/academic-professional-resources/asa-grants-and-fellowships/
Purpose: To provide pre-doctoral graduate education for sociology students.
Eligibility: Applicants must be enrolled in and have completed one full year in a Ph.D. program in Sociology. Students must be members of an underrepresented minority group in the U.S.: African American, Latino, Asian/Pacific Islander or American Indians/Alaska Natives. Applicants must also be U.S. citizens, non-citizen nationals of the U.S. or have been lawfully admitted to the U.S. for permanent residence. The fellowship is awarded for 12 months and typically renewable for up to three years in total. Tuition and fees are arranged with the home department. MFP Fellows are selected each year by the MFP Advisory Panel, a rotating, appointed group of senior scholars in sociology. Fellows can be involved in any area of sociological research, though particular MFP award lines devoted to drug abuse research may be possible contingent on funding.
Target applicant(s): Graduate school students. Adult students.
Amount: $20,000.
Number of awards: Varies.
Deadline: January 31.
How to apply: Applications are available online.
Exclusive: Visit www.UltimateScholarshipBook.com and enter code AM65526 for updates on this award.

[656] • Mondelez International Legacy Scholarship

National Grocers Association
1005 N. Glebe Road, Suite 250, Arlington, VA 22201
Phone: 225-387-6126
https://www.nationalgrocers.org/foundation/nga-foundation-scholarships/
Purpose: To support students pursuing education related to the grocery field.
Eligibility: Applicants must be rising sophomores through postgraduate students, have a minimum 2.5 GPA and be enrolled in a two- or four-year degree-granting institution. Students must major in business, food management, IT or another field related to a career in the grocery industry. Experience in the grocery industry is preferred but not required.
Target applicant(s): College students. Graduate school students. Adult students.
Minimum GPA: 2.5
Amount: $2,500.
Number of awards: 1.
Deadline: April 15.
How to apply: Applications are available online.
Exclusive: Visit www.UltimateScholarshipBook.com and enter code NA65626 for updates on this award.

[657] • Moody Research Grant

Lyndon B. Johnson Foundation
2313 Red River Street, Austin, TX 78705
Phone: 512-721-0263.
Email: grants@lbjfoundation.org
https://www.lbjlibrary.org/foundation/grants
Purpose: To assist with the travel and room-and-board expenses of those wishing to conduct research at the Lyndon B. Johnson Foundation Library.
Eligibility: Applicants must first contact the library to determine if their topic is appropriate for study at the facility. Applicants must also calculate the estimated amount of the grant before making a request.
Target applicant(s): College students. Adult students.
Amount: $600-$3,000.
Number of awards: Varies.
Deadline: September 15; March 15.
How to apply: Applications are available online.
Exclusive: Visit www.UltimateScholarshipBook.com and enter code LY65726 for updates on this award.

[658] • NACA Mid Atlantic Graduate Student Scholarship

National Association for Campus Activities
13 Harbison Way, Columbia, SC 29212
Phone: 803-732-6222
Email: info@naca.org
https://www.naca.org/resources/scholarships-grants/scholarships.html
Purpose: To provide assistance to graduate students who are attending a college or university on the East Coast.
Eligibility: Applicants must be enrolled in master's or doctorate degree programs in student personnel services or a related area. Applicants must be attending a graduate school in Washington, DC, Delaware, Maryland, New Jersey, New York or eastern Pennsylvania, be involved in campus activities and plan to pursue a career in campus activities.
Target applicant(s): Graduate school students. Adult students.
Amount: Varies.
Number of awards: Varies.
Deadline: March 31.
How to apply: Applications are available online.
Exclusive: Visit www.UltimateScholarshipBook.com and enter code NA65826 for updates on this award.

[659] • Nancy Curry Scholarship

School Nutrition Association
120 Waterfront Street, Suite 300, National Harbor, MD 20745
Phone: 301-686-3100
Email: servicecenter@schoolnutrition.org
https://schoolnutrition.org/Membership/AwardsScholarships/
Purpose: To support students wishing to enter the school foodservice industry.
Eligibility: Applicants must be School Nutrition Association members for at least one year and be enrolled in a school foodservice-related program at an educational institution. Children of SNA members are not eligible to apply. Applicants must be currently employed in school food service.
Target applicant(s): High school students. College students. Graduate school students. Adult students.
Amount: $500.
Number of awards: 1.
Deadline: March 30.
How to apply: Applications are available online.
Exclusive: Visit www.UltimateScholarshipBook.com and enter code SC65926 for updates on this award.

[660] • Nancy McManus Washington Internship Scholarships

Pi Sigma Alpha
1527 New Hampshire Avenue NW, Washington, DC 20036
Email: office@pisigmaalpha.org
https://pisigmaalpha.org
Purpose: To provide Pi Sigma Alpha members with scholarships to participate in summer or fall term internships in Washington, DC.
Eligibility: Applicants must belong to Pi Sigma Alpha and be nominated by their local chapter. The award is for a political science internship is based on academic achievement and service to the organization.
Target applicant(s): College students. Graduate school students. Adult students.
Amount: $2,000.
Number of awards: 5.
Deadline: May 1.
How to apply: Applications are available online.
Exclusive: Visit www.UltimateScholarshipBook.com and enter code PI66026 for updates on this award.

[661] • National Academic Scholarships
Association of Government Accountants (AGA)
2208 Mount Vernon Avenue, Alexandria, VA 22301-1314
Phone: 800-242-7211x309
Email: rortiz@agacgfm.org
http://www.agacgfm.org
Purpose: To support public financial management students.
Eligibility: Applicants for full-time or part-time scholarships must be an AGA member or family member (spouse, child or grandchild), and scholarships must be used for full-time or part-time undergraduate study in a financial management academic area such as accounting, auditing, budgeting, economics, finance, electronic data processing, information resources management or public administration. Essays and transcripts are required. There are two categories for high school students/graduates and undergraduates/graduates. The Academic Scholarships are based on academic achievement and the student's potential for making a contribution to public financial management. A reference letter from an AGA member and from another professional such as a professor, guidance counselor or employer is required. Applicants to the Community Service Scholarships do not have to be AGA members, must be pursuing a degree in a financial management academic discipline and must be actively involved in community service projects. The awards are based on community service and accomplishments. A letter of recommendation from a community service organization and from another professional are required.
Target applicant(s): High school students. College students. Graduate school students. Adult students.
Minimum GPA: 2.5
Amount: Up to $3,000.
Number of awards: Varies.
Deadline: June 11.
How to apply: Applications are available online.
Exclusive: Visit www.UltimateScholarshipBook.com and enter code AS66126 for updates on this award.

[662] • National Foundation Scholarships
Institute of Scrap Recycling Industries
1250 H Street, NW, Suite 400, Washington, DC 20006
Phone: 202-662-8500
Email: ngrant@isri.org
https://www.isri.org/membership/isri-chapters/paper-stock-industries-chapter/psi---scholarships
Purpose: To support students seeking a graduate degree in scrap processing or recycling.
Eligibility: Applicants must be pursuing a graduate level degree, be a U.S. citizen and have a minimum 2.5 GPA. The program is open to those seeking a graduate degree in a program that supports the scrap processing and recycling industry as a whole.
Target applicant(s): Graduate school students. Adult students.
Minimum GPA: 2.5
Amount: $5,000.
Number of awards: 1.
Deadline: March 15.
How to apply: Applications are available online.
Exclusive: Visit www.UltimateScholarshipBook.com and enter code IN66226 for updates on this award.

[663] • National History Day Contest
National History Day
4511 Knox Road, Suite 205, College Park, MD 20740
Phone: 301-314-9739
Email: info@nhd.org
http://www.nhd.org
Purpose: To reward students for their scholarship, initiative and cooperation.
Eligibility: Applicants must be in grades 6-12 and prepare throughout the school year history presentations based on an annual theme. Around February or March students compete in district History Day contests. District winners then prepare for the state contests, held usually in April or May. Those winners advance to the national contest held in June at the University of Maryland.
Target applicant(s): Junior high students or younger. High school students.
Amount: Varies.
Number of awards: Varies.
Deadline: May 14.
How to apply: Applications are available online.
Exclusive: Visit www.UltimateScholarshipBook.com and enter code NA66326 for updates on this award.

[664] • National Press Club Scholarship for Journalism Diversity
National Press Club
529 14th Street NW, 13th Floor, Washington, DC 20045
Phone: 202-662-7500
http://www.press.org
Purpose: To support promising future journalists.
Eligibility: Applicants must be high school seniors, have a GPA of 3.0 or higher and plan to enter college the year after graduation. Students must intend to become a journalist and bring diversity to U.S. journalism.
Target applicant(s): High school students.
Minimum GPA: 3.0
Amount: Up to $20,000.
Number of awards: 1.
Deadline: February 18.
How to apply: Applications are available online. An application form, essay, transcript, copy of FAFSA, letter of acceptance or proof of college application, three letters of recommendation and up to five work samples are required.
Exclusive: Visit www.UltimateScholarshipBook.com and enter code NA66426 for updates on this award.

[665] • National Scholarship Program
American Board of Funeral Service Education
Scholarship Committee, 992 Mantua Pike, Suite 108, Woodbury Heights, NJ 08097
Phone: 816-233-3747
Email: scholarships@abfse.org
http://www.abfse.org
Purpose: To assist students enrolled in funeral service or mortuary science programs.
Eligibility: Applicants must be undergraduate students who have completed at least one semester or quarter of study in funeral service or mortuary science education at an accredited school and have at least one term remaining in their study. Applicants must be U.S. citizens.
Target applicant(s): College students. Adult students.
Amount: $1,500-$2,500.

Number of awards: Varies.
Deadline: March 1; September 1.
How to apply: Applications are available online.
Exclusive: Visit www.UltimateScholarshipBook.com and enter code AM66526 for updates on this award.

[666] • National Washington Crossing Foundation Scholarship

Washington Crossing Foundation
P.O. Box 503, Levittown, PA 19058
Phone: 215-949-8841
Email: info@gwcf.org
http://www.gwcf.org
Purpose: To support students who are planning careers in government service.
Eligibility: Students must be in their senior year of high school. Applicants must submit an essay and a letter of recommendation.
Target applicant(s): High school students.
Amount: $500-$5,000.
Number of awards: 31.
Scholarship may be renewable.
Deadline: January 15.
How to apply: Applications are available online.
Exclusive: Visit www.UltimateScholarshipBook.com and enter code WA66626 for updates on this award.

[667] • NCRA A to Z Scholarship

National Court Reporters Association
12030 Sunrise Valley Drive, Suite 400, Reston, VA 20191
Phone: 800-272-6272
Email: schools@ncra.org
https://www.ncra.org/home/get-involved/foundation/foundation-programs/NCRF-scholarships-and-grants
Purpose: To support students who are enrolled in a court reporting program.
Eligibility: Applicants must have completed an NCRA A to Z Intro to Steno Machine Shorthand program and received an NCRA A to Z Certificate of Completion. Students must have attained an exemplary academic record and passed one skills test writing 60 to 100 words per minute.
Target applicant(s): College students. Adult students.
Amount: $750.
Number of awards: 15.
Deadline: September 1.
How to apply: Applications are available online.
Exclusive: Visit www.UltimateScholarshipBook.com and enter code NA66726 for updates on this award.

[668] • NCRA CASE Student Scholarship

National Court Reporters Association
12030 Sunrise Valley Drive, Suite 400, Reston, VA 20191
Phone: 800-272-6272
Email: schools@ncra.org
https://www.ncra.org/home/get-involved/foundation/foundation-programs/NCRF-scholarships-and-grants
Purpose: To support students from NCRA-approved reporter education programs.
Eligibility: Applicants must attend an NCRA-approved court reporting program and hold student membership in NCRA. Students must have attained an exemplary academic record and passed one skills test writing 140-180 words per minute.
Target applicant(s): College students. Adult students.
Amount: Up to $1,500.
Number of awards: 5.
Deadline: March 1.
How to apply: Applications are available online.
Exclusive: Visit www.UltimateScholarshipBook.com and enter code NA66826 for updates on this award.

[669] • NEA-Retired Jack Kinnaman Memorial Scholarship

National Education Association
Center for Governance, Attn.: The NEA-Retired Jack Kinnaman Memorial Scholarship, 1201 16th Street NW, Washington, DC 20036-3290
Phone: 202-833-4000
http://www.nea.org
Purpose: To honor the memory of NEA-retired vice president and former advisory council member Jack Kinnaman.
Eligibility: Applicants must be NEA student members, major in education and have a minimum 2.5 GPA. An essay describing activities in NEA, a brief paragraph describing financial need, two letters of recommendation and a copy of the most recent transcript are required.
Target applicant(s): College students. Adult students.
Minimum GPA: 2.5
Amount: $3,500.
Number of awards: 5.
Deadline: April 15.
How to apply: Applications are available online.
Exclusive: Visit www.UltimateScholarshipBook.com and enter code NA66926 for updates on this award.

[670] • Nell Bryant Robinson Scholarship

Phi Upsilon Omicron Inc.
National Office, P.O. Box 50970, Bowling Green, KY 42102-4270
Phone: 270-904-1340
Email: national@phiu.org
http://www.phiu.org
Purpose: To aid Phi Upsilon Omicron members who are pursuing bachelor's degrees in family and consumer sciences.
Eligibility: Preference is given to applicants who are majoring in food and nutrition or dietetics. Selection is based on the overall strength of the application.
Target applicant(s): College students. Adult students.
Amount: $500.
Number of awards: Varies.
Deadline: March 1.
How to apply: Applications are available online. An application form, official transcript, personal statement and three recommendation letters are required.
Exclusive: Visit www.UltimateScholarshipBook.com and enter code PH67026 for updates on this award.

[671] • Nettie Dracup Memorial Scholarship
National Society of Professional Surveyors (NSPS/AAGS)
21 Byte Court, Suite H, Frederick, MD 21702
Phone: 240-439-4615
Email: info@nsps.us.com
https://www.nsps.us.com/page/Scholarships
Purpose: To aid geodetic surveying students.
Eligibility: Applicants must be U.S. citizens who are undergraduate students enrolled in an accredited degree program in geodetic surveying. They must be members of the National Society of Professional Surveyors (NSPS). Selection is based on the applicant's academic achievement, personal statement, recommendations and professional activities.
Target applicant(s): High school students. College students. Adult students.
Amount: $2,000.
Number of awards: 3.
Deadline: January 19.
How to apply: Applications are available online. An application form, official transcript, personal statement, three recommendation letters and proof of ACSM membership are required.
Exclusive: Visit www.UltimateScholarshipBook.com and enter code NA67126 for updates on this award.

[672] • New England FEMARA Scholarship
American Radio Relay League Foundation
225 Main Street, Newington, CT 06111-1494
Phone: 860-594-0200
Email: foundation@arrl.org
https://www.arrl.org/scholarship-program
Purpose: To assist ham radio operators in furthering their educations.
Eligibility: Applicants must have at least a technician ham radio license and be residents of the New England States (Connecticut, Maine, Massachusetts, New Hampshire, Rhode Island or Vermont).
Target applicant(s): High school students. College students. Graduate school students. Adult students.
Amount: $2,000.
Number of awards: Varies.
Deadline: January 10.
How to apply: Applications are available online. Completed applications must be mailed in. They cannot be completed electronically.
Exclusive: Visit www.UltimateScholarshipBook.com and enter code AM67226 for updates on this award.

[673] • NextGen Scholarship
Society for Chartered Property and Casualty Underwriters (CPCU)
720 Providence Road, Malvern, PA 19355
Phone: 800-932-2728
Email: membercenter@cpcusociety.org
https://www.cpcusociety.org/Public/Education/College_Students/NextGen_Scholarship/Public/Education/NextGen.aspx
Purpose: To support risk management students.
Eligibility: Applicants must be full-time undergraduate students majoring in risk management, actuarial science, finance, business or information systems. Students must have a cumulative grade point average of 3.0 or higher. Applicants must also strongly desire to join the risk and insurance industry upon graduation.
Target applicant(s): Junior high students or younger.
Amount: $5,000.
Number of awards: 25.
Deadline: November 6.
How to apply: Applications are available online.
Exclusive: Visit www.UltimateScholarshipBook.com and enter code SO67326 for updates on this award.

[674] • NFMC Gretchen E. Van Roy Music Education Scholarship
National Federation of Music Clubs (FL)
National Federation of Music Clubs, 1646 W Smith Valley Road, Greenwood, IN 46142
Phone: 317-882-4003
Email: cschmidt@en-tel.net
http://www.nfmc-music.org/competitions-awards/
Purpose: To support students majoring in music education.
Eligibility: Applicants must be college juniors majoring in music education and must be affiliated with the National Federation of Music Clubs.
Target applicant(s): College students. Adult students.
Amount: $500-$1,500.
Number of awards: Varies.
Deadline: March 1.
How to apply: Applications are available online.
Exclusive: Visit www.UltimateScholarshipBook.com and enter code NA67426 for updates on this award.

[675] • North American Van Lines Logistics Scholarship
North American Van Lines
Phone: 800-369-9115
https://www.northamerican.com/scholarship
Purpose: To support students pursuing a degree in logistics or supply chain management.
Eligibility: Applicants must be U.S. citizens and enrolled full-time as an undergraduate at an eligible educational institution. Funds must be used for qualified educational expenses. Students should be pursuing a degree in logistics or supply chain management. Applicants will need to submit a 400- to 800-word essay on why they selected a career in logistics/supply chain management. The essay should convey a sincere, personalized tone.
Target applicant(s): High school students. College students. Adult students.
Amount: $1,000.
Number of awards: 3.
Deadline: December 15.
How to apply: Applications are available online and must be submitted along with an official transcript, a verification of enrollment and the essay.
Exclusive: Visit www.UltimateScholarshipBook.com and enter code NO67526 for updates on this award.

[676] • NPPF Still and Multimedia Scholarship
National Press Photographers Association
Still Photographer Scholarship, 120 Hooper Street, Athens, GA 30602-3018
Phone: 706-542-2506
Email: tkenniff@nppa.org
http://www.nppa.org
Purpose: To honor the profession of photojournalism.

Eligibility: Applicants must have completed one year in a full-time four-year college or university with courses in photojournalism, provide a portfolio and demonstrate financial need. Applicants can apply to as many NPPA scholarships as desired, but only one award will be granted per winner.
Target applicant(s): College students. Adult students.
Amount: $2,000.
Number of awards: Varies.
Deadline: January 16.
How to apply: Applications are available online.
Exclusive: Visit www.UltimateScholarshipBook.com and enter code NA67626 for updates on this award.

[677] • NPPF Television News Scholarship
National Press Photographers Foundation Television News Scholarship
120 Hooper Street, Athens, GA 30602-3018
Phone: 706-542-2506
Email: jwbrown@nppf.org
http://www.nppa.org
Purpose: To support students with television news photojournalism potential but with little opportunity and great need.
Eligibility: Applicants must be full-time juniors or seniors at a four-year college or university, provide a portfolio and demonstrate financial need. Applicants must also have courses in TV news photojournalism and continue in this program toward a bachelor's degree. Applicants can apply to as many NPPA scholarships as desired, but only one award will be granted per winner.
Target applicant(s): College students. Adult students.
Amount: $2,000.
Number of awards: 1.
Deadline: February 9.
How to apply: Applications are available online.
Exclusive: Visit www.UltimateScholarshipBook.com and enter code NA67726 for updates on this award.

[678] • Optimist International Oratorical Contest
Optimist International
4494 Lindell Boulevard, St. Louis, MO 63108
Phone: 314-371-6000
Email: programs@optimist.org
https://www.optimist.org/member/scholarships1.cfm
Purpose: To reward students based on their oratorical performance.
Eligibility: Applicants must be students in the U.S., Canada or the Caribbean under the age of 16 as of December 31st of the entry year. Selection is based on an oratorical contest.
Target applicant(s): Junior high students or younger. High school students.
Amount: Up to $22,500.
Number of awards: Varies.
Deadline: Contact the sponsoring Optimist Club to confirm the deadline.
How to apply: Contact your local Optimist Club.
Exclusive: Visit www.UltimateScholarshipBook.com and enter code OP67826 for updates on this award.

[679] • Otto M. Stanfield Legal Scholarship
Unitarian Universalist Association
24 Farnsworth Street, Boston, MA 02210
Phone: 617-742-2100
Email: uufp@uua.org
http://www.uua.org/giving/awards
Purpose: To help Unitarian Universalist students entering or attending law school.
Eligibility: Applicants should be planning to attend or currently attending law school at the graduate level. The award is based on activity with Unitarian Universalism and financial need. Applicants should submit transcripts and recommendations.
Target applicant(s): Graduate school students. Adult students.
Amount: Varies.
Number of awards: Varies.
Deadline: July 31.
How to apply: Applications are available online.
Exclusive: Visit www.UltimateScholarshipBook.com and enter code UN67926 for updates on this award.

[680] • Overseas Press Club Foundation Scholarships/Fellowships
Overseas Press Club Foundation
40 West 45 Street, New York, NY 10036
Phone: 201-493-9087
Email: foundation@opcofamerica.org
http://www.overseaspressclubfoundation.org
Purpose: To encourage undergraduate and graduate students attending American colleges and universities to pursue careers as foreign correspondents.
Eligibility: Scholarships are open to undergraduate and graduate students with an interest in a career as a foreign correspondent. Eligible students must be attending American colleges or universities.
Target applicant(s): College students. Graduate school students. Adult students.
Amount: $3,000-$4,000.
Number of awards: 18.
Deadline: December 1.
How to apply: Applications are available online.
Exclusive: Visit www.UltimateScholarshipBook.com and enter code OV68026 for updates on this award.

[681] • Paul and Helen L. Grauer Scholarship
American Radio Relay League Foundation
225 Main Street, Newington, CT 06111-1494
Phone: 860-594-0200
Email: foundation@arrl.org
https://www.arrl.org/scholarship-program
Purpose: To assist ham radio operators in furthering their educations.
Eligibility: Applicants must have at least a novice ham radio license, be residents and attend school in the ARRL Midwest Division (Iowa, Kansas, Missouri or Nebraska) and be undergraduate or graduate students in electronics, communications or another related field.
Target applicant(s): High school students. College students. Graduate school students. Adult students.
Amount: $1,000.
Number of awards: 1.
Deadline: January 10.
How to apply: Applications are available online. Completed applications must be submitted by mail.

The Ultimate Scholarship Book 2026
Scholarship Directory (Social Sciences)

Exclusive: Visit www.UltimateScholarshipBook.com and enter code AM68126 for updates on this award.

[682] • Paul S. Mills Scholarships
Foundation for Financial Service Professionals (FSP)
1000 Wilson Boulevard, Suite 1890, Arlington, VA 22209
Phone: 610-526-2551
https://www.financialprofoundation.org/paul-s-mills-scholarships
Purpose: To help students pursuing higher education in the financial service field.
Eligibility: Applicants must be U.S. citizens or legal residents living in one of the 50 U.S. states, the District of Columbia or U.S. Territories. Students must be enrolled in a college or university program in the U.S. and have completed the equivalent of one year of credits toward an undergraduate degree or be pursuing a master's or Ph.D. level degree. Students must pursue a course of study in a financial service field and have a FAFSA on file.
Target applicant(s): College students. Graduate school students. Adult students.
Amount: $1,000.
Number of awards: 12.
Deadline: March 31.
How to apply: Applications are available online.
Exclusive: Visit www.UltimateScholarshipBook.com and enter code FO68226 for updates on this award.

[683] • PAVE Student Design Competition
Planning and Visual Education Partnership (PAVE)
8570 Stirling Road, Suite 102-227, Hollywood, FL 33024
Phone: 954-551-9144
Email: info@paveglobal.org
http://paveglobal.org
Purpose: To provide undergraduate students with an opportunity to obtain real-life retail design experience.
Eligibility: Applicants must be undergraduate or graduate students studying in the areas of retail design and planning, visual merchandising, interior design or branding. Students will create a design project based on the given information.
Target applicant(s): College students. Graduate school students. Adult students.
Amount: $1,000-$7,500.
Number of awards: 3.
Deadline: October 31.
How to apply: Application and project details are available online.
Exclusive: Visit www.UltimateScholarshipBook.com and enter code PL68326 for updates on this award.

[684] • Peter and Jody Larkin Legacy Scholarship
National Grocers Association
1005 N. Glebe Road, Suite 250, Arlington, VA 22201
Phone: 225-387-6126
https://www.nationalgrocers.org/foundation/nga-foundation-scholarships/
Purpose: To support students pursuing a degree related to the grocery field.
Eligibility: Applicants must be rising sophomores through postgraduate students, have a minimum 2.5 GPA and be enrolled in a two- or four-year degree-granting institution. Students must major in business, food management, IT or another field related to a career in the grocery industry. Experience in the grocery industry is preferred but not required.
Target applicant(s): College students. Graduate school students. Adult students.
Minimum GPA: 2.5
Amount: $2,500.
Number of awards: 1.
Deadline: April 15.
How to apply: Applications are available online.
Exclusive: Visit www.UltimateScholarshipBook.com and enter code NA68426 for updates on this award.

[685] • PHD Scholarship
American Radio Relay League Foundation
225 Main Street, Newington, CT 06111-1494
Phone: 860-594-0200
Email: foundation@arrl.org
https://www.arrl.org/scholarship-program
Purpose: To assist ham radio operators in furthering their educations.
Eligibility: Applicants must have any class of ham radio license, be residents of the ARRL Midwest Division (Iowa, Kansas, Missouri, Nebraska) and be studying journalism, computer science or electronic engineering. Applicants may also be the children of deceased amateur radio operators.
Target applicant(s): High school students. College students. Adult students.
Amount: $1,000.
Number of awards: 1.
Deadline: January 10.
How to apply: Applications are available online but may not be completed electronically. All completed applications must be mailed.
Exclusive: Visit www.UltimateScholarshipBook.com and enter code AM68526 for updates on this award.

[686] • Pi Lambda Theta Student Support Scholarships
Pi Lambda Theta Scholarships
P.O. Box 7888, Bloomington, IN 47407-7888
Phone: 812-339-1156
Email: scholarships@pdkintl.org
https://pilambda.org/#scholarships
Purpose: To recognize education majors with leadership potential and a dedication to education.
Eligibility: Applicants must be members of Educators Rising, PDK International or Pi Lambda Theta and must be current undergraduate students.
Target applicant(s): College students. Adult students.
Minimum GPA: 3.5
Amount: Up to $2,000.
Number of awards: Varies.
Deadline: April 2.
How to apply: Applications are available online. Transcripts, letters of recommendation and essays are required.
Exclusive: Visit www.UltimateScholarshipBook.com and enter code PI68626 for updates on this award.

[687] • Presidential Scholarships
National Asian Pacific American Bar Association Law Foundation
P.O. Box 65081, Washington, DC 20035
https://www.napabalawfoundation.org/scholarships
Purpose: To support students who demonstrate a commitment to contribute to the Asian Pacific American community.
Eligibility: Applicants must be U.S. citizens or permanent residents and enrolled in an accredited U.S. law school. Students must demonstrate

academic achievement, leadership potential and commitment to serving the Asian Pacific American community. Applicants must provide letters of recommendation along with an essay as part of their application.
Target applicant(s): Graduate school students. Adult students.
Amount: $7,500.
Number of awards: 2.
Deadline: September 4.
How to apply: Applications are available online.
Exclusive: Visit www.UltimateScholarshipBook.com and enter code NA68726 for updates on this award.

[688] • Prize in International Insolvency Studies
International Insolvency Institute
10332 Main Street, PMB 112, Fairfax, VA 22030
Phone: 416-595-2965
Email: ftibando@millerthomson.com
http://www.iiiglobal.org
Purpose: To recognize outstanding international insolvency researchers, commentators and analysts.
Eligibility: Applicants must be undergraduate students, graduate students or practitioners of international insolvency studies who have less than nine years of experience. They must submit original analysis, commentary or legal research on the subject of international insolvency. Selection is based on the overall strength of the submission.
Target applicant(s): College students. Graduate school students. Adult students.
Amount: $1,000-$3,000.
Number of awards: Up to 9.
Deadline: March 31.
How to apply: Application instructions are available online. A scholarly paper is required.
Exclusive: Visit www.UltimateScholarshipBook.com and enter code IN68826 for updates on this award.

[689] • Project Vote Smart National Internship Program
Project Vote Smart
Internship Coordinator, 1153 24th Street, Des Moines, IA 50311
Phone: 515-989-6363
Email: intern@votesmart.org
https://justfacts.votesmart.org/internships/
Purpose: To encourage students and recent college graduates to develop an interest in voter education.
Eligibility: Applicants must be current college students in good standing or recent college graduates. They must be able to approach voter education work with a non-partisan attitude and be willing to commit to a ten-week internship. Selection is based on the overall strength of the application.
Target applicant(s): College students. Adult students.
Amount: Full Tuition.
Number of awards: Varies.
Deadline: Contact the sponsor to confirm the deadline.
How to apply: Applications are available online. An application form, resume, cover letter and three references are required.
Exclusive: Visit www.UltimateScholarshipBook.com and enter code PR68926 for updates on this award.

[690] • Prospanica Foundation Scholarships
Prospanica
11700 Preston Road, Suite 660, #354, Dallas, TX 75230
Phone: 866-276-2140
Email: Scholarships@prospanica.org
https://www.prospanica.org/scholarships
Purpose: To support students of Hispanic descent who are entrepreneurial thinkers.
Eligibility: Applicants must be United States citizens, legal permanent residents or DACA recipients and of Hispanic/Latino heritage. Students must have a minimum 3.0 GPA or 2.75 GPA in combination with work experience and be enrolled or planning to enroll in a postgraduate or undergraduate program in an accredited university business school in the United States or Puerto Rico. Undergraduate applicants must currently be sophomores or higher. Applicants must have a Prospanica membership.
Target applicant(s): College students. Graduate school students. Adult students.
Minimum GPA: 2.75
Amount: Up to $5,000.
Number of awards: Varies.
Deadline: April 30 (Preliminary Round); June 30 (Second Round).
How to apply: Applications are available online.
Exclusive: Visit www.UltimateScholarshipBook.com and enter code PR69026 for updates on this award.

[691] • Quill and Scroll Student Scholarships
Quill and Scroll Society
University of Iowa School of Journalism and Mass Communications, 100 Adler Journalism Building, Iowa City, IA 52242
Phone: 319-335-3457
Email: quill-scroll@uiowa.edu
http://www.quillandscroll.org
Purpose: To aid high school journalists seeking to improve their skills and techniques.
Eligibility: Applicants must be Quill and Scroll members or national winners of the Yearbook Excellence Contest or the International Writing, Photography and Multimedia Contest or Blogging Competition.
Target applicant(s): High school students.
Amount: $250-$1,500.
Number of awards: 5.
Deadline: May 10.
How to apply: Applications are available online.
Exclusive: Visit www.UltimateScholarshipBook.com and enter code QU69126 for updates on this award.

[692] • Raftelis Leadership Scholarships
Raftelis
227 W. Trade Street, Suite 1400, Charlotte, NC 28202
Phone: 866-696-1436
Email: info@raftelis.com
https://www.raftelis.com/who-we-are/giving-back/
Purpose: To support students who have an interest in becoming problem solvers for local governments and municipal water utilities.
Eligibility: Applicants must be college juniors, seniors or graduate students. They must complete an application form that includes a personal statement, one letter of recommendation and transcripts. Applicants must plan to enroll at an accredited institution during the upcoming academic year.
Target applicant(s): College students. Graduate school students. Adult students.

Amount: $5,000.
Number of awards: 10000.
Deadline: December 20.
How to apply: Applications are available online.
Exclusive: Visit www.UltimateScholarshipBook.com and enter code RA69226 for updates on this award.

[693] • Ray and Gertrude Marshall Scholarship
American Culinary Federation
6816 Southpoint Parkway Suite 400, Jacksonville, FL 32216
Phone: 904-824-4468
Email: scholarships@acfchefs.net
http://www.acfchefs.org
Purpose: To assist students in culinary programs.
Eligibility: Applicants must be ACF junior members enrolled in a post-secondary culinary arts program or an ACF apprenticeship program and must have completed at least one grading period. Selection is based on financial need, GPA, recommendations and work experience.
Target applicant(s): College students. Adult students.
Amount: Varies.
Number of awards: Varies.
Deadline: April 30 and October 31.
How to apply: Applications are available online or by written request.
Exclusive: Visit www.UltimateScholarshipBook.com and enter code AM69326 for updates on this award.

[694] • Ray, N0RP and Katie, W0KTE Pautz Scholarship
American Radio Relay League Foundation
225 Main Street, Newington, CT 06111-1494
Phone: 860-594-0200
Email: foundation@arrl.org
https://www.arrl.org/scholarship-program
Purpose: To provide financial assistance to amateur radio operators from the ARRL Midwest Division.
Eligibility: Applicants must be ARRL members with a General Class or higher Amateur Radio License. They must be residents of Iowa, Kansas, Missouri or Nebraska and should major in electronics, computer science or a related field at a four-year institution.
Target applicant(s): High school students. College students. Adult students.
Amount: $500-$1,000.
Number of awards: 1.
Deadline: January 10.
How to apply: Applications are available online.
Exclusive: Visit www.UltimateScholarshipBook.com and enter code AM69426 for updates on this award.

[695] • Reid Blackburn Scholarship
National Press Photographers Foundation
Blackburn Scholarship, 120 Hooper Street, Athens, GA 30602-3018
Phone: 360-759-8027
Email: fay.blackburn@columbian.com
http://www.nppa.org
Purpose: To support photojournalism students.
Eligibility: Applicants must have completed one year at a full-time four-year college or university, provide a portfolio, demonstrate financial need and must have courses in photojournalism and have at least half a year of undergraduate study left. Applicants can apply to as many NPPA scholarships as desired, but only one award will be granted per winner.

Target applicant(s): College students. Adult students.
Amount: $2,000.
Number of awards: Varies.
Deadline: February 9.
How to apply: Applications are available online.
Exclusive: Visit www.UltimateScholarshipBook.com and enter code NA69526 for updates on this award.

[696] • Reiff Law Firm Legal Scholarship
Reiff Law Firm
1500 John F. Kennedy Boulevard #501, Philadelphia, PA 19102
Phone: 215-246-9000
Email: scholarships@reifflawfirm.com
https://www.reifflawfirm.com/legal-scholarship/
Purpose: To support students who are pursuing a legal career.
Eligibility: Applicants must be United States citizens. Students must plan to enroll or be currently enrolled full-time at an accredited college or university in pursuit of a J.D. A minimum 3.0 GPA or higher is required. Applicants must submit a 650-word essay on their goals for employment in the legal field.
Target applicant(s): College students. Graduate school students. Adult students.
Minimum GPA: 3.0
Amount: $1,000.
Number of awards: 1.
Deadline: July 1.
How to apply: Applications are available online.
Exclusive: Visit www.UltimateScholarshipBook.com and enter code RE69626 for updates on this award.

[697] • Richard W. Bendicksen, N7ZL, Memorial Scholarship
American Radio Relay League Foundation
225 Main Street, Newington, CT 06111-1494
Phone: 860-594-0200
Email: foundation@arrl.org
https://www.arrl.org/scholarship-program
Purpose: To provide financial assistance to amateur radio operators.
Eligibility: Applicants must hold an active amateur radio license of any class, and they must be attending a four-year institution of higher learning.
Target applicant(s): High school students. College students. Adult students.
Amount: $1,000.
Number of awards: 1.
Deadline: January 10.
How to apply: Applications are available online.
Exclusive: Visit www.UltimateScholarshipBook.com and enter code AM69726 for updates on this award.

[698] • Risk Management Association Foundation Scholarship
Risk Management Association Foundation Scholarship Program
2005 Market Street, One Commerce Square, Suite 3600, Philadelphia, PA 19103
Phone: 800-677-7621
Email: customers@rmahq.org
https://www.rmahq.org/studentresources/scholarships/
Purpose: To support students who have already completed two years of college.

Eligibility: Applicants must be a U.S. or Canadian citizen who is a current undergraduate student interested in pursuing a career in the banking industry and has completed a minimum of two years of college majoring in accounting, business, finance, economics, banking or related fields of study. Students must be attending full-time and have a minimum 3.0 GPA.
Target applicant(s): College students. Adult students.
Minimum GPA: 3.0
Amount: $1,000 to $5,000.
Number of awards: 75.
Scholarship may be renewable.
Deadline: March 31.
How to apply: Application available online.
Exclusive: Visit www.UltimateScholarshipBook.com and enter code RI69826 for updates on this award.

[699] • Ritchie-Jennings Memorial Scholarship
Association of Certified Fraud Examiners
Scholarships Program Coordinator, The Gregor Building, 716 West Avenue, Austin, TX 78701
Phone: 512-478-9000
Email: memberservices@acfe.com
http://www.acfe.com
Purpose: To support the college education of accounting, business, finance and criminal justice students who may become Certified Fraud Examiners in the future.
Eligibility: Applicants must be full-time undergraduate or graduate students with a declared major or minor in criminal justice, accounting, business or finance. Students must submit three letters of recommendation, with at least one from a Certified Fraud Examiner or local CFE Chapter and must write an essay on why they deserve the scholarship and how fraud awareness will help their career.
Target applicant(s): College students. Graduate school students. Adult students.
Amount: $2,000-$10,000.
Number of awards: Varies.
Deadline: February 5.
How to apply: Applications are available online.
Exclusive: Visit www.UltimateScholarshipBook.com and enter code AS69926 for updates on this award.

[700] • Roger Collins Leadership Scholarship
National Grocers Association
1005 N. Glebe Road, Suite 250, Arlington, VA 22201
Phone: 225-387-6126
https://www.nationalgrocers.org/foundation/nga-foundation-scholarships/
Purpose: To support students pursuing degrees related to the grocery field.
Eligibility: Applicants must be rising sophomores through postgraduate students, have a minimum 2.5 GPA and be enrolled in a two- or four-year degree-granting institution. Students must major in business, food management, IT or another field related to a career in the grocery industry. Experience in the grocery industry is preferred but not required.
Target applicant(s): College students. Graduate school students. Adult students.
Minimum GPA: 2.5
Amount: Varies.
Number of awards: 1.
Deadline: April 15.
How to apply: Applications are available online.
Exclusive: Visit www.UltimateScholarshipBook.com and enter code NA70026 for updates on this award.

[701] • Roller Skating Foundation Scholarship, Current College Student Category
Roller Skating Foundation
Attn.: Scholarship, 6905 Corporate Drive, Indianapolis, IN 46278
Phone: 317-347-2626
Email: foundation@rollerskating.com
https://www.rollerskating.com/scholarships.html
Purpose: To aid sports, hotel and food and beverage management students.
Eligibility: Applicants must be rising undergraduate seniors who are majoring in sports, hotel or food and beverage management. They must have a cumulative GPA of 3.4 or higher on a four-point scale and must demonstrate leadership ability. Selection is based on the overall strength of the application.
Target applicant(s): College students. Adult students.
Minimum GPA: 3.4
Amount: $9,000.
Number of awards: 6.
Deadline: March 31.
How to apply: Applications are available online. An application form, transcript, personal essay, three recommendation letters and income tax information are required.
Exclusive: Visit www.UltimateScholarshipBook.com and enter code RO70126 for updates on this award.

[702] • Ron Culp Scholarship for Mentorship
Public Relations Student Society of America
120 Wall Street, 21st Floor, New York, NY 10005-4024
Phone: 212-460-1474
Email: prssa@prsa.org
https://prssa.prsa.org/scholarships-and-awards/
Purpose: To aid public relations and journalism students who have mentored others wishing to pursue careers in public relations.
Eligibility: Applicants must be members of the Public Relations Student Society of America (PRSSA) who are in good standing. Students must be rising undergraduate seniors who are majoring in journalism, public relations or a related subject at an accredited, four-year postsecondary institution. Applicants must be preparing for careers in public relations and must have mentored others who intend to pursue careers in the field of public relations. Selection is based on the overall strength of the application.
Target applicant(s): College students. Adult students.
Amount: $1,000.
Number of awards: 1.
Deadline: April 30.
How to apply: Applications are available online. Nomination from someone who is familiar with the applicant's mentoring activities is required.
Exclusive: Visit www.UltimateScholarshipBook.com and enter code PU70226 for updates on this award.

[703] • RTNDA President's Scholarship
Radio Television Digital News Association
529 14th Street NW, Suite 1240, Washington, DC 20045
Phone: 202-659-6510
Email: karenh@rtdna.org
http://www.rtdna.org
Purpose: To honor students pursuing careers in radio, television or digital journalism.
Eligibility: Applicants must be full-time college sophomores, juniors or seniors with at least one full academic year remaining. Applicants may be

enrolled in any major as long as their career intent is to pursue a career in radio, television or digital journalism. Applicants may only apply for one RTNDA scholarship.
Target applicant(s): College students. Adult students.
Amount: $2,500.
Number of awards: 2.
Deadline: January 11.
How to apply: Applications are available online.
Exclusive: Visit www.UltimateScholarshipBook.com and enter code RA70326 for updates on this award.

[704] • Ruth Segal Scholarship
Foundation for Outdoor Advertising Research and Education (FOARE)
1850 M Street NW, Suite 1040, Washington, DC 20036
Phone: 202-364-7130
Email: tmfsmith@rcn.com
http://oaaa.org/AboutOAAA/FOARE/FOAREScholarshipProgram.aspx
Purpose: To support students who are pursuing a degree in government affairs, urban affairs, public affairs, political science or a related discipline.
Eligibility: Applicants must be graduating seniors, undergraduate students or graduate students. Selection is primarily based on demonstration of financial need, academic achievement, employment history, community service and extracurricular involvement.
Target applicant(s): High school students. College students. Graduate school students. Adult students.
Amount: $5,000.
Number of awards: 1.
Deadline: June 10.
How to apply: Applications are available online.
Exclusive: Visit www.UltimateScholarshipBook.com and enter code FO70426 for updates on this award.

[705] • Schwan's Food Service Scholarship
School Nutrition Association
120 Waterfront Street, Suite 300, National Harbor, MD 20745
Phone: 301-686-3100
Email: servicecenter@schoolnutrition.org
https://schoolnutrition.org/Membership/AwardsScholarships/
Purpose: To support those entering the school foodservice industry.
Eligibility: Applicants must be School Nutrition Association members for at least one year and be pursuing a field of study related to school foodservice. Applicants must also be employed in school foodservice.
Target applicant(s): High school students. College students. Graduate school students. Adult students.
Amount: Up to $2,500.
Number of awards: Varies.
Scholarship may be renewable.
Deadline: March 29.
How to apply: Applications are available online.
Exclusive: Visit www.UltimateScholarshipBook.com and enter code SC70526 for updates on this award.

[706] • Sharon Stephens Brehm Undergraduate Psychology Scholarships
American Psychological Foundation
750 First Street NE, Washington, DC 20002-4242
Phone: 202-336-5843
Email: foundation@apa.org
https://www.apa.org/apf/funding/grants
Purpose: To reward outstanding psychology undergraduate students who demonstrate financial need.
Eligibility: Applicants must be undergraduates majoring in psychology at an accredited college or university. Students must be enrolled as declared psychology majors with a minimum 3.5 GPA.
Target applicant(s): College students. Adult students.
Minimum GPA: 3.5
Amount: $5,000.
Number of awards: 8.
Deadline: July 10.
How to apply: Applications are available online.
Exclusive: Visit www.UltimateScholarshipBook.com and enter code AM70626 for updates on this award.

[707] • Shawn Carter Foundation Scholarship
Shawn Carter Foundation
Email: scsfapplicant@shawncartersf.com
http://www.shawncartersf.com
Purpose: To assist students at vocational or trade schools.
Eligibility: Applicants must be high school seniors or college students and be between the ages of 18 and 25. Applicants must also be U.S. citizens and have a minimum 2.0 GPA.
Target applicant(s): High school students. College students.
Minimum GPA: 2.0
Amount: Varies.
Number of awards: Varies.
Deadline: April 30.
How to apply: Applications are available online.
Exclusive: Visit www.UltimateScholarshipBook.com and enter code SH70726 for updates on this award.

[708] • Shell Associate Scholarship Program
Shell
P.O. Box 162, 2501 AN, The Hague, NE
Phone: 713-718-6379
Email: shellscholarships@hccsfoundation.org
https://www.shell.us/
Purpose: To support students who are seeking a degree in a technology field.
Eligibility: Applicants must be U.S. citizens and be taking at least six credit hours in the fall and spring. A minimum 2.5 GPA or higher is required. Students should be pursuing a degree in process/production technology, petroleum technology, compressor technology, electrical technology, industrial maintenance technology, instrumentation technology or machinist technology.
Target applicant(s): College students. Adult students.
Minimum GPA: 2.5
Amount: $2,200.
Number of awards: Varies.
Deadline: March 17.
How to apply: Applications are available online.

Exclusive: Visit www.UltimateScholarshipBook.com and enter code SH70826 for updates on this award.

[709] • Shields-Gillespie Scholarship
American Orff-Schulwerk Association (AOSA)
P.O. Box 391089, Cleveland, OH 44139-8089
Phone: 440-543-5366
Email: info@aosa.org
https://aosa.org/resources/scholarships-and-grants/
Purpose: To assist pre-K and kindergarten teachers with program funding, including instruments and training.
Eligibility: Applicants must be a member of AOSA. Applicants must be U.S. citizens or have lived in the United States for the past five years. Programs should focus on music/movement learning.
Target applicant(s): High school students. College students. Graduate school students. Adult students.
Amount: Varies.
Number of awards: Varies.
Deadline: January 15.
How to apply: Applications are available online for AOSA members.
Exclusive: Visit www.UltimateScholarshipBook.com and enter code AM70926 for updates on this award.

[710] • Specialty Equipment Market Association (SEMA) Memorial Scholarship
Specialty Equipment Market Association
1575 S. Valley Vista Drive, Diamond Bar, CA 91765
Phone: 909-396-0289
Email: education@sema.org
http://www.sema.org/scholarships
Purpose: To support the education of students pursuing careers in the automotive aftermarket.
Eligibility: Applicants must show financial need, have a minimum 2.5 GPA and pursue a career in the automotive aftermarket or related field.
Target applicant(s): College students. Graduate school students. Adult students.
Minimum GPA: 2.5
Amount: Up to $5,000.
Number of awards: Varies.
Deadline: March 1.
How to apply: Applications are available online.
Exclusive: Visit www.UltimateScholarshipBook.com and enter code SP71026 for updates on this award.

[711] • SPS Future Teacher Scholarship
Society of Physics Students
One Physics Ellipse, College Park, MD 20740
Phone: 301-209-3007
Email: SPS-Programs@aip.org
https://www.spsnational.org/
Purpose: To provide scholarships to physics majors who are participating in a teacher education program and who intend to pursue a career in physics education.
Eligibility: Applicants must be members of SPS and intend to pursue a career in teaching physics. Students must be undergraduate physics majors at least in their junior year of study at the time of application.
Target applicant(s): College students. Adult students.
Amount: $2,500.
Number of awards: 1.
Deadline: March 15.
How to apply: Applications are available online or from chapter advisors.
Exclusive: Visit www.UltimateScholarshipBook.com and enter code SO71126 for updates on this award.

[712] • Stephen D. Pisinski Memorial Scholarship
Public Relations Student Society of America
120 Wall Street, 21st Floor, New York, NY 10005-4024
Phone: 212-460-1474
Email: prssa@prsa.org
https://prssa.prsa.org/scholarships-and-awards/
Purpose: To aid journalism, public relations and communications students.
Eligibility: Applicants must be members of the Public Relations Student Society of America (PRSSA). Students must be undergraduate juniors or seniors who are majoring in journalism, public relations or communications. Applicants must have a cumulative GPA of 3.3 or higher on a four-point scale. Selection is based on the overall strength of the application.
Target applicant(s): College students. Adult students.
Minimum GPA: 3.3
Amount: $2,000.
Number of awards: 1.
Deadline: April 30.
How to apply: Applications are available online. An application form, official transcript, resume, two writing samples, an essay and two recommendation letters are required.
Exclusive: Visit www.UltimateScholarshipBook.com and enter code PU71226 for updates on this award.

[713] • Steven J. Finkel Service Excellence Scholarship
House of Blues Music Forward Foundation
7060 Hollywood Boulevard, 2nd Floor, Hollywood, CA 90028
Phone: 323-769-4645
Email: info@hobmusicforward.org
https://hobmusicforward.org/program/scholarships/
Purpose: To encourage students who are passionate about the live music customer experience for fans, artists and employees.
Eligibility: Applicants must be full-time juniors or seniors enrolled at an accredited college or university pursuing a career in live entertainment such as: music business management, customer service, hospitality or other related fields. A minimum 3.0 GPA or higher is required. Students must submit a 500-word essay explaining their career goals within the entertainment industry.
Target applicant(s): College students. Adult students.
Minimum GPA: 3.0
Amount: $10,000.
Number of awards: 1.
Deadline: March 31.
How to apply: Applications are available online.
Exclusive: Visit www.UltimateScholarshipBook.com and enter code HO71326 for updates on this award.

[714] • Stuart Cameron and Margaret McLeod Memorial Scholarship

Institute of Management Accountants (IMA)
10 Paragon Drive, Montvale, NJ 07645-1760
Phone: 800-638-4427
Email: students@imanet.org
https://www.imanet.org
Purpose: To help management accounting students.
Eligibility: Applicants must be full- and part-time undergraduate and graduate students, be IMA student members and declare which four- or five-year management accounting, financial management or information technology related program they plan to pursue as a career or list a related field. Candidates should submit applications, resumes, transcripts, two recommendations and statements. Advanced degree students must pass one part of the CMA/CFM certification.
Target applicant(s): College students. Graduate school students. Adult students.
Minimum GPA: 3.0
Amount: $5,000.
Number of awards: 1.
Deadline: March 10.
How to apply: Applications are available online.
Exclusive: Visit www.UltimateScholarshipBook.com and enter code IN71426 for updates on this award.

[715] • Student Success Grants

NEA Foundation
1201 16th Street NW, Washington, DC 20036
Phone: 202-822-7840
Email: NEAFoundation@nea.org
https://www.neafoundation.org
Purpose: To promote the academic achievement of students in U.S. public schools and public higher education institutions by providing funds for teachers.
Eligibility: Applicants must be current public school teachers in PreK-12, public school education support professionals or faculty or staff at public higher education institutions. Preference is given to those who work with economically disadvantaged students and NEA members. The grants may be used for materials, supplies, equipment, transportation, software or scholars-in-residence and in some cases professional development. The work should "engage students in critical thinking and problem-solving that deepens their knowledge of standards-based subject matter."
Target applicant(s): Graduate school students. Adult students.
Amount: Up to $5,000.
Number of awards: Varies.
Deadline: February 1, June 1 and October 15.
How to apply: Applications are available online and may be submitted at any time. Applications are reviewed three times each year on February 1, June 1 and October 15.
Exclusive: Visit www.UltimateScholarshipBook.com and enter code NE71526 for updates on this award.

[716] • Student with a Disability Scholarship

American Speech-Language-Hearing Foundation
2200 Research Boulevard, Rockville, MD 20850
Phone: 301-296-8700
Email: foundationprograms@asha.org
https://www.ashfoundation.org/
Purpose: To support a graduate student with a disability studying communication sciences and disorders.
Eligibility: Master's degree candidates must be in programs accredited by the Council on Academic Accreditation for Audiology and Speech Pathology, but doctoral programs do not have to be accredited. The applicants should submit a transcript, essay, reference form and statement of good standing; be recommended by a faculty or workplace committee and have not received scholarships from the ASHA Foundation. Students must attend their programs full-time.
Target applicant(s): College students. Graduate school students. Adult students.
Amount: $5,000.
Number of awards: 1.
Deadline: May 17.
How to apply: Applications are available online.
Exclusive: Visit www.UltimateScholarshipBook.com and enter code AM71626 for updates on this award.

[717] • Study.com Scholarship for Business Students

Study.com
100 View Street, Suite 202, Mountain View, CA 94041
https://study.com/resources/student-scholarships
Purpose: To support students who plan to pursue higher education.
Eligibility: Applicants must be pursuing a degree in business. Students must be enrolled (or accepted) in an accredited college or university within the United States and plan on continuing next year.
Target applicant(s): College students. Graduate school students. Adult students.
Amount: $1,000.
Number of awards: 1.
Deadline: November 1.
How to apply: Applications are available online.
Exclusive: Visit www.UltimateScholarshipBook.com and enter code ST71726 for updates on this award.

[718] • Sutliff and Stout Law School Scholarship

Sutliff & Stout Law School Scholarship
550 Post Oak Boulevard, Suite 530, Houston, TX 77027
Phone: 281-942-8694
Email: community@sutliffstout.com
https://www.sutliffstout.com/about-us/community/law-school-scholarship/
Purpose: To support students pursuing a law degree.
Eligibility: Applicants must be accepted into or currently enrolled in an ABA-accredited law school in the U.S. Students must write an essay explaining why they want to study law.
Target applicant(s): College students. Graduate school students. Adult students.
Amount: $1,500.
Number of awards: 1.
Deadline: July 26.
How to apply: Applications are available online.
Exclusive: Visit www.UltimateScholarshipBook.com and enter code SU71826 for updates on this award.

[719] • TACTYC Accounting Scholarship
Teachers of Accounting at Two-Year Colleges
Lori Hatchell - TACTYC Treasurer, P.O. Box 69, Greeley, CO 80632-0069
Email: scholarship@tactyc.org
http://www.tactyc.org
Purpose: To aid accounting students who either are pursuing a two-year undergraduate degree or who are moving to a four-year institution after having completed a two-year accounting degree.
Eligibility: Applicants must be undergraduate accounting students. They must be pursuing a two-year degree or must be pursuing a bachelor's degree in accounting after having completed a two-year accounting degree program. Selection is based on recommendations, GPA and stated career goals.
Target applicant(s): College students. Adult students.
Amount: $1,000.
Number of awards: Varies.
Deadline: March 1.
How to apply: Applications are available online. An application form and supporting materials are required.
Exclusive: Visit www.UltimateScholarshipBook.com and enter code TE71926 for updates on this award.

[720] • Teacher Education Scholarship Fund
American Montessori Society
211 E 43rd Street, 7th Fl #262, New York, NY 10017
Phone: 212-358-1250
Email: ams@amshq.org
http://www.amshq.org
Purpose: To support future Montessori teachers.
Eligibility: Applicants must be accepted, are in the process of being accepted or are already enrolled in an AMS-affiliated teacher education program. Financial need, the applicant's personal statement and letters of recommendation are considered.
Target applicant(s): College students. Adult students.
Amount: Varies.
Number of awards: Varies.
Scholarship may be renewable.
Deadline: April 19.
How to apply: Applications are available online.
Exclusive: Visit www.UltimateScholarshipBook.com and enter code AM72026 for updates on this award.

[721] • Teacher of the Year Award
Veterans of Foreign Wars Teacher of the Year Award
406 W. 34th Street, Kansas City, MO 64111
Phone: 816-968-1117
Email: tbeauchamp@vfw.org
http://www.vfw.org
Purpose: To salute the nation's top elementary, junior high and high school teachers who educate their students about citizenship and American history and traditions.
Eligibility: Applicants must be current certified/licensed teachers in grades K-12. Previous winners from the state or national levels are not eligible. Fellow teachers, supervisors, family members or other interested individuals may send in nominations; self-nominations will be accepted.
Target applicant(s): Graduate school students. Adult students.
Amount: $3,000.
Number of awards: 1.
Deadline: October 31.
How to apply: Applications are available online but initial nominations must be sent to the local VFW office. Visit the website for more information.
Exclusive: Visit www.UltimateScholarshipBook.com and enter code VE72126 for updates on this award.

[722] • Timothy S.Y. Lam Foundation Education Scholarships
Timothy S.Y. Lam Foundation
P.O. Box 98141, Las Vegas, NV 89193-8141
Phone: 702-900-7584
Email: info@timothysylam.org
https://www.timothysylam.org/education-scholarships
Purpose: To support students pursuing a career in the hospitality industry.
Eligibility: Applicants must be at least 18 years of age and pursuing a degree or certification in the hospitality industry. An essay is required with the application. There are two deadlines each year: May 15 and November 15.
Target applicant(s): College students. Adult students.
Amount: Up to $2,000.
Number of awards: 7.
Deadline: November 15; February 15; May 15; June 15.
How to apply: Applications are available online, and must include a resume, an essay, one letter of reference, a photo and an official transcript.
Exclusive: Visit www.UltimateScholarshipBook.com and enter code TI72226 for updates on this award.

[723] • TLMI Two/Four Year College and Vocational Degree Program Scholarship
Tag and Label Manufacturers Institute Inc.
TLMI Scholarship Committee, 450 10th Circle North, Nashville, TN 37203
Phone: 615-432-5442
Email: office@tlmi.com
https://tlmi.com/awards-scholarships/educational-and-training-benefits/
Purpose: To aid students who are enrolled in a flexographic printing program of study.
Eligibility: Applicants must be enrolled full-time in a flexographic printing program at a two-year or four-year college or degree-granting technical school. They must have a GPA of 3.0 or higher and have a demonstrated interest in pursuing a career in the tag and label industry. Selection is based on the overall strength of the application.
Target applicant(s): College students. Adult students.
Minimum GPA: 3.0.
Amount: $1,000.
Number of awards: Up to 4.
Deadline: May 1.
How to apply: Applications are available online. An application form, official transcript and personal statement are required.
Exclusive: Visit www.UltimateScholarshipBook.com and enter code TA72326 for updates on this award.

[724] • Tom and Judith Comstock Scholarship
American Radio Relay League Foundation
225 Main Street, Newington, CT 06111-1494
Phone: 860-594-0200
Email: foundation@arrl.org

https://www.arrl.org/scholarship-program
Purpose: To assist ham radio operators in furthering their educations.
Eligibility: Applicants must have any class of ham radio license, be residents of Texas or Oklahoma and be high school seniors accepted at a two- or four-year college or university.
Target applicant(s): High school students. College students. Adult students.
Amount: $2,000.
Number of awards: 1.
Deadline: January 10.
How to apply: Applications are available online but may not be completed electronically. All completed applications must be mailed.
Exclusive: Visit www.UltimateScholarshipBook.com and enter code AM72426 for updates on this award.

[725] • TOPSS Competition for High School Psychology Students

American Psychological Association
750 First Street NE, Washington, DC 20002-4242
Phone: 800-374-2721
https://www.apa.org/apf/funding/scholarships
Purpose: To assist students who are studying psychology.
Eligibility: Applicants must be high school students who have been or are presently enrolled in a psychology course and must write an essay answering a question from the APA. A Teachers of Psychology in Secondary Schools (TOPSS) member must sponsor all candidates, and each school may submit no more than five papers.
Target applicant(s): High school students.
Amount: $300.
Number of awards: 3.
Deadline: March 1.
How to apply: Submission information is available online.
Exclusive: Visit www.UltimateScholarshipBook.com and enter code AM72526 for updates on this award.

[726] • United Commercial Travelers of America (UCT) Scholarship Program

Order of United Commercial Travelers of America
1801 Watermark Drive, Suite 100, P.O. Box 159019, Columbus, OH 43215-8619
Phone: 614-487-9680
Email: aneal@uct.org
https://www.uct.org/doing-good/
Purpose: To support students or teachers who work primarily with students who have intellectual disabilities.
Eligibility: Applicants must be current teachers or current undergraduate students who are pursuing course work to enhance their work with individuals who have intellectual and developmental disabilities. Students must work in North America.
Target applicant(s): College students. Adult students.
Amount: Up to $2,500.
Number of awards: 1.
Scholarship may be renewable.
Deadline: November 15.
How to apply: Applications are available online.
Exclusive: Visit www.UltimateScholarshipBook.com and enter code OR72626 for updates on this award.

[727] • United States Senate Youth Program

William Randolph Hearst Foundation
90 New Montgomery Street, Suite 1212, San Francisco, CA 94105
Phone: 800-841-7048 x 4540
Email: ussyp@hearstfdn.org
http://ussenateyouth.org
Purpose: To expose students to their government in action.
Eligibility: Applicants must be high school juniors or seniors in an elected position at school or in civic or educational offices. USSYP brings the highest level officials from each branch of government together with a group of 104 high school student delegates for an intensive week-long educational program held in Washington, DC.
Target applicant(s): High school students.
Amount: $10,000.
Number of awards: 104.
Deadline: September 27.
How to apply: To apply, contact your high school principal, counselor or state selection contact. State selection contact information is located on the home page of the website.
Exclusive: Visit www.UltimateScholarshipBook.com and enter code WI72726 for updates on this award.

[728] • University of California Public Policy and International Affairs Junior Summer Institute

University of California at Berkeley
UCPPIA Summer Institute, Goldman School of Public Policy, 2607 Hearst Avenue, Berkeley, CA 94720-7320
Phone: 510-642-4670
Email: noah.romero@berkeley.edu
https://gspp.berkeley.edu/programs/undergraduate-programs/ppia-junior-summer-institute
Purpose: To aid students who are interested in pursuing graduate studies in public policy.
Eligibility: Applicants must be U.S. citizens or legal permanent residents who are rising undergraduate seniors who have at least one more semester (or two more quarters) of coursework remaining before graduation. They must be interested in public service careers and must have a demonstrated interest in policy issues that affect underserved populations. They must have overcome obstacles in their pursuit of higher education. Selection is based on the overall strength of the application.
Target applicant(s): College students. Adult students.
Amount: Varies.
Number of awards: 30.
Deadline: November 15.
How to apply: Applications are available online. An application form and personal statement are required.
Exclusive: Visit www.UltimateScholarshipBook.com and enter code UN72826 for updates on this award.

[729] • University of California Public Policy and International Affairs Law Fellowship

University of California at Berkeley
UCPPIA Summer Institute, Goldman School of Public Policy, 2607 Hearst Avenue, Berkeley, CA 94720-7320
Phone: 510-642-4670
Email: noah.romero@berkeley.edu
https://gspp.berkeley.edu/programs/undergraduate-programs/ppia-junior-summer-institute
Purpose: To encourage prospective graduate students to pursue a joint degree in law and public policy.

Eligibility: Applicants must be U.S. citizens or legal permanent residents. They must be rising undergraduate seniors who have at least one more semester (or two more quarters) of coursework remaining before graduation. They must be interested in law and public service careers and must have a demonstrated interest in policy issues that affect underserved populations. They must have overcome obstacles in their pursuit of higher education. Selection is based on the overall strength of the application.
Target applicant(s): College students. Adult students.
Amount: At least $5,000.
Number of awards: 10.
Deadline: November 15.
How to apply: Applications are available online. An application form and personal statement are required.
Exclusive: Visit www.UltimateScholarshipBook.com and enter code UN72926 for updates on this award.

[730] • University of the Aftermarket Foundation Scholarship
Global Automotive Aftermarket Symposium Inc.
c/o Auto Care Association, 7101 Wisconsin Avenue, Suite 1300, Bethesda, MD 20814
Phone: 312-768-7379
Email: uafscholarships@autocare.org
https://automotivescholarships.com/scholarships
Purpose: To support students who intend to have a career in the automotive industry.
Eligibility: Applicants must have graduated from high school or acquired their GED. Students must be enrolled or planning to enroll as a full-time student in a two- or four-year college or an ASE/NATEF certified post-secondary automotive, collision repair or heavy duty program.
Target applicant(s): High school students. College students. Adult students.
Amount: Varies.
Number of awards: Varies.
Deadline: March 31.
How to apply: Applications are available online.
Exclusive: Visit www.UltimateScholarshipBook.com and enter code GL73026 for updates on this award.

[731] • USGIF Scholarship Program
United States Geospatial Intelligence Foundation (USGIF)
13665 Dulles Technology Drive, Suite 150, Herndon, VA 20171
Phone: 888-698-7443
Email: scholarships@usgif.org
https://usgif.org/
Purpose: To assist those who are studying geospatial sciences.
Eligibility: Applicants must be high school seniors or college or graduate students. Selection is based on academic and professional achievement in a field related to geospatial intelligence tradecraft.
Target applicant(s): High school students. College students. Graduate school students. Adult students.
Minimum GPA: 2.5
Amount: $1,000-$15,000.
Number of awards: 20-25.
Deadline: May 31.
How to apply: Applications are available online.
Exclusive: Visit www.UltimateScholarshipBook.com and enter code UN73126 for updates on this award.

[732] • Vern and Elaine Clark Outdoor Advertising Industry
Foundation for Outdoor Advertising Research and Education (FOARE)
1850 M Street NW, Suite 1040, Washington, DC 20036
Phone: 202-364-7130
Email: tmfsmith@rcn.com
http://oaaa.org/AboutOAAA/FOARE/FOAREScholarshipProgram.aspx
Purpose: To support undergraduate and graduate students who are pursuing a career in the outdoor advertising industry.
Eligibility: Applicants must submit a letter of recommendation from someone in the outdoor advertising industry and a letter of recommendation addressing the applicant's community service. Selection is primarily based on academic achievement, career goals and community involvement.
Target applicant(s): High school students. College students. Graduate school students. Adult students.
Amount: $5,000.
Number of awards: 1.
Deadline: June 10.
How to apply: Applications are available online.
Exclusive: Visit www.UltimateScholarshipBook.com and enter code FO73226 for updates on this award.

[733] • Vincent Chin Scholarship
Asian American Journalists Association
1301 K Street, NW, 300W, 3rd Floor, Washington, DC 20005
Email: support@aaja.org
https://www.aaja.org/news-and-resources/scholarships-internships/
Purpose: To support college students interested in pursuing careers in journalism.
Eligibility: Applicants must be undergraduate students enrolled full-time and must be currently taking or planning to take journalism courses and/or pursuing a career in journalism. Applicants are not required to be Asian Americans but must support the mission of the AAJA and be committed to work within the community. Selection is based on the applicant's promise to support the field of journalism and issues faced by Pacific Islanders and Asian Americans. In addition, selection is based on financial need, academic achievement and demonstrated ability in journalism as well as the applicant's resume, two letters of recommendation, essay and work samples.
Target applicant(s): College students. Adult students.
Amount: $1,500.
Number of awards: 1.
Deadline: January 16.
How to apply: Applications are available online.
Exclusive: Visit www.UltimateScholarshipBook.com and enter code AS73326 for updates on this award.

[734] • Wesley-Logan Prize
American Historical Association
400 A Street SE, Washington, DC 20003
Phone: 202-544-2422
Email: info@historians.org
http://www.historians.org
Purpose: To award a prize to a scholarly/literary book focusing on the history of dispersion, relocation, settlement or adjustment of people from Africa or on their return to that continent.

The Ultimate Scholarship Book 2026
Scholarship Directory (Social Sciences)

Eligibility: Books must have been published between May 1 of the previous year and April 30 of the entry year. Entries are mailed directly to committee members.
Target applicant(s): Junior high students or younger. High school students. College students. Graduate school students. Adult students.
Amount: $1,000.
Number of awards: Varies.
Deadline: May 15.
How to apply: Application information is available on approximately March 30.
Exclusive: Visit www.UltimateScholarshipBook.com and enter code AM73426 for updates on this award.

[735] • WIIT Charitable Trust Scholarship
Women in International Trade Charitable Trust
c/o Affinity Strategies, 100 M Street S.E., Suite 600, Washington, DC 20003
Phone: 202-293-2948
Email: info@wiittrust.org
http://www.wiittrust.org
Purpose: To support female undergraduate and graduate students who are pursuing a degree in international trade.
Eligibility: Applicants must submit an essay on a relevant international trade topic (see suggestions below) and can either be a bespoke essay submission or an appropriately formatted existing academic paper from current class works. Students must show a demonstrated interest in international development, international relations, international trade, international economics or international business. Selection is based on the overall strength of the submission. Students must be enrolled at an accredited U.S. educational institution.
Target applicant(s): College students. Graduate school students. Adult students.
Amount: $3,000.
Number of awards: 2.
Deadline: November 1; April 1.
How to apply: Applications are available online.
Exclusive: Visit www.UltimateScholarshipBook.com and enter code WO73526 for updates on this award.

[736] • William (Bill) Ezzell Scholarship
American Institute of Certified Public Accountants
220 Leigh Farm Road, Durham, NC 27707-8110
Phone: 919-402-4500
Email: scholarships@aicpa.org
https://www.aicpa.org
Purpose: To support accounting Ph.D. candidates who demonstrate significant potential to become mentors for the next generation of CPAs.
Eligibility: Applicants must have a minimum of three years of professional accounting experience and earned an undergraduate or a master's degree in accounting. Students must be CPAs and U.S. citizens or permanent residents. Applicants must have either applied to a full-time accounting Ph.D. program and are awaiting word on acceptance, received acceptance into a full-time accounting Ph.D. program or matriculated into a full-time accounting doctoral program and pursuing appropriate coursework.
Target applicant(s): Graduate school students. Adult students.
Amount: $15,000.
Number of awards: 8.
Deadline: June 15.
How to apply: Applications are available online.
Exclusive: Visit www.UltimateScholarshipBook.com and enter code AM73626 for updates on this award.

[737] • William B. Ruggles Right to Work Scholarship
National Institute for Labor Relations Research (NILRR)
William B. Ruggles Scholarship Selection Committee, 5211 Port Royal Road, Suite 510, Springfield, VA 22151
Phone: 703-321-9606
Email: research@nilrr.org
https://nilrr.org/right-to-work-contest/
Purpose: To support students who are dedicated to high journalistic standards.
Eligibility: Applicants must be undergraduate or graduate students majoring in journalism and demonstrate an understanding of the principles of voluntary unionism and the economic and social problems of compulsory unionism.
Target applicant(s): High school students. College students. Graduate school students. Adult students.
Amount: $2,000.
Number of awards: 1.
Deadline: January 31.
How to apply: Applications are available online.
Exclusive: Visit www.UltimateScholarshipBook.com and enter code NA73726 for updates on this award.

[738] • Women Grocers of America (WGA) Mary Macey Scholarship
National Grocers Association
1005 N. Glebe Road, Suite 250, Arlington, VA 22201
Phone: 225-387-6126
https://www.nationalgrocers.org/foundation/nga-foundation-scholarships/
Purpose: To support students pursuing a degree related to the grocery field.
Eligibility: Applicants must be rising sophomores through postgraduate students, have a minimum 2.5 GPA and be enrolled in a two- or four-year degree-granting institution. Students must major in business, food management, IT or another field related to a career in the grocery industry. Experience in the grocery industry is preferred but not required.
Target applicant(s): College students. Graduate school students. Adult students.
Minimum GPA: 2.5
Amount: Varies.
Number of awards: Varies.
Deadline: April 15.
How to apply: Applications are available online.
Exclusive: Visit www.UltimateScholarshipBook.com and enter code NA73826 for updates on this award.

[739] • YASME Foundation Scholarship
American Radio Relay League Foundation
225 Main Street, Newington, CT 06111-1494
Phone: 860-594-0200
Email: foundation@arrl.org
https://www.arrl.org/scholarship-program
Purpose: To support science and engineering students who are involved in amateur radio.
Eligibility: Applicants must have an active amateur radio license. Students must be enrolled in a four-year college or university. Preference will be given to students in the top 10 percent of their class and those who have participated in community service and local amateur radio clubs.
Target applicant(s): High school students. College students. Adult students.

Amount: $5,000.
Number of awards: Varies.
Scholarship may be renewable.
Deadline: January 10.
How to apply: Applications are available online.
Exclusive: Visit www.UltimateScholarshipBook.com and enter code AM73926 for updates on this award.

[740] • Youth Scholarship
Society of Broadcast Engineers
9102 N. Meridian Street, Suite 150, Indianapolis, IN 46260
Phone: 317-846-9000
Email: mclappe@sbe.org
http://www.sbe.org
Purpose: To help students who plan to pursue a career in the technical aspects of broadcasting.
Eligibility: Applicants must be graduating high school seniors who plan to enroll in a technical school, college or university and should pursue studies leading to a career in broadcasting engineering or a related field. Preference is given to members of SBE, but any student may apply. Applicants should submit applications, transcripts, biographies and statements. Recipients must write a paper about broadcast engineering.
Target applicant(s): High school students.
Amount: $2,500.
Number of awards: Varies.
Deadline: July 1.
How to apply: Applications are available online.
Exclusive: Visit www.UltimateScholarshipBook.com and enter code SO74026 for updates on this award.

SCIENCES

[741] • A.O. Putnam Memorial Scholarship
Institute of Industrial and Systems Engineers
3577 Parkway Lane, Suite 200, Norcross, GA 30092
Phone: 800-494-0460
Email: egrimes@iise.org
https://www.iise.org
Purpose: To help undergraduate Institute members who plan to pursue careers in management consulting.
Eligibility: Applicants must be undergraduate students enrolled in a college in the United States, Canada or Mexico with an accredited industrial engineering program, major in industrial engineering and be active members. Preference is given to students who plan to work in management consulting. Students may not apply directly for this scholarship and must be nominated. The award is based on academic ability, character, leadership, potential service to the industrial engineering profession and financial need. Minimum 3.4 GPA required.
Target applicant(s): College students. Adult students.
Minimum GPA: 3.4
Amount: $2,500.
Number of awards: Varies.
Deadline: February 1.
How to apply: Nomination forms are available online.
Exclusive: Visit www.UltimateScholarshipBook.com and enter code IN74126 for updates on this award.

[742] • AAAE Foundation Scholarship
American Association of Airport Executives
The Barclay Building, 601 Madison Street, Alexandria, VA 22314
Phone: 703.824.0504
Email: member.services@aaae.org
https://www.aaae.org
Purpose: To support students of aviation.
Eligibility: Applicants must be enrolled in an aviation program with at least junior standing and at least a 3.0 GPA. Eligibility is unrelated to membership in AAAE. Winners are selected based on academic records, financial need, participation in school and community activities, work experience and a personal statement. Applicants must be recommended by their school.
Target applicant(s): College students. Graduate school students. Adult students.
Minimum GPA: 3.0
Amount: $1,500.
Number of awards: 10.
Deadline: March 15.
How to apply: To obtain an application, contact the scholarship or financial aid office at the college you attend. Scholarship information is usually mailed to universities and colleges in early January.
Exclusive: Visit www.UltimateScholarshipBook.com and enter code AM74226 for updates on this award.

[743] • AACT National Candy Technologists John Kitt Memorial Scholarship Program
Warrell Corp
711 W Water Street, P.O. Box 266, Princeton, WI 54968
Phone: 920-295-6959
Email: aactinfo@gomc.com
https://www.aactcandy.org/awards-scholarships/

Purpose: To aid students with a demonstrated interested in confectionery technology.
Eligibility: Applicants must be rising college sophomores, juniors or seniors at an accredited four-year college or university in North America. They must major in food science, chemical science, biological science or a related area. A GPA of 3.0 or higher is required.
Target applicant(s): College students. Adult students.
Minimum GPA: 3.0
Amount: $2,500.
Number of awards: 1.
Deadline: May 15.
How to apply: Applications are available online. An application form, list of academic, work and other activities, list of honors and awards, statement of goals and transcript are required.
Exclusive: Visit www.UltimateScholarshipBook.com and enter code WA74326 for updates on this award.

[744] • AAGS – NSPS Scholarships
National Society of Professional Surveyors (NSPS/AAGS)
21 Byte Court, Suite H, Frederick, MD 21702
Phone: 240-439-4615
Email: info@nsps.us.com
https://www.nsps.us.com/page/Scholarships
Purpose: To reward excellent surveying and mapping students.
Eligibility: There are several different types of awards. The first is for students enrolled in two-year degree programs in surveying technology. The second is for students enrolled in or accepted to a graduate program in geodetic surveying or geodesy. The third is for students enrolled in four-year degree programs in surveying (or in related areas such as geomatics or surveying engineering). The last type is for students enrolled in a two-year or four-year surveying (or closely related) degree program, either full or part-time. All awards are based on academic record, statement, recommendation letters and professional activities.
Target applicant(s): High school students. College students. Graduate school students. Adult students.
Amount: $2,000-$5,000.
Number of awards: Varies.
Deadline: January 19.
How to apply: Applications are available online.
Exclusive: Visit www.UltimateScholarshipBook.com and enter code NA74426 for updates on this award.

[745] • AAGS Joseph F. Dracup Scholarship Award
National Society of Professional Surveyors (NSPS/AAGS)
21 Byte Court, Suite H, Frederick, MD 21702
Phone: 240-439-4615
Email: info@nsps.us.com
https://www.nsps.us.com/page/Scholarships
Purpose: To aid ACSM members who are enrolled in a four-year degree program in surveying or a closely related subject.
Eligibility: Applicants must be members of AAGS (American Association for Geodetic Surveying). Preference will be given to students whose coursework is significantly focused on geodetic surveying. Students who will be graduating before December of the award disbursement year are ineligible. Selection is based on academic merit, personal statement, recommendations, professional involvement and financial need.
Target applicant(s): High school students. College students. Adult students.
Amount: $2,000.
Number of awards: 1.
Scholarship may be renewable.
Deadline: January 19.
How to apply: Applications are available online. An application form, personal statement, official transcript, three recommendation letters and proof of ACSM membership are required.
Exclusive: Visit www.UltimateScholarshipBook.com and enter code NA74526 for updates on this award.

[746] • AAMA Student Essay Competition
American Association of Medical Assistants
20 North Wacker Drive, Suite 1575, Chicago, IL 60606
Phone: 800-228-2262
Email: info@aama-ntl.org
http://www.aama-ntl.org
Purpose: To reward aspiring medical assistants through an essay competition.
Eligibility: Applicants must be enrolled in and have completed at least one quarter or semester at a college-level medical assisting program accredited by the Commission on Accreditation of Allied Health Education Programs (CAAHEP). Completed entry form and essay (between 400 and 500 words) based on the year s prompt must be submitted by the deadline.
Target applicant(s): College students. Graduate school students. Adult students.
Amount: $1,000.
Number of awards: 1.
Deadline: July 15.
How to apply: Applications are available online.
Exclusive: Visit www.UltimateScholarshipBook.com and enter code AM74626 for updates on this award.

[747] • Abel Wolman Fellowship
American Water Works Association
6666 W. Quincy Avenue, Denver, CO 80235
Phone: 800-926-7337
Email: scholarships@awwa.org
https://www.awwa.org
Purpose: To support doctoral students pursuing advanced training and research in the field of water supply and treatment.
Eligibility: Applicants must obtain a Ph.D. within two years of the award, must be citizens of the U.S., Canada or Mexico and should submit applications, transcripts, GRE scores, three recommendation letters, course of study and description of the dissertation research study and how it pertains to water supply and treatment. The award is based on academics, the connection between the research and water supply and treatment and the applicant's research skills.
Target applicant(s): Graduate school students. Adult students.
Amount: Varies.
Number of awards: Varies.
Scholarship may be renewable.
Deadline: December 20.
How to apply: Applications are available online.
Exclusive: Visit www.UltimateScholarshipBook.com and enter code AM74726 for updates on this award.

[748] • ACAA Educational Foundation Scholarship Program
American Coal Ash Association (ACAA)
9980 S. 300 W., Suite 200, Sandy, UT 84070
Phone: 720-870-7897
Email: info@acaa-usa.org
https://acaa-usa.org/about-acaa/acaa-educational-foundation/

Purpose: To support students interested in coal combustion products research and sustainable use.
Eligibility: Applicants must be graduate and undergraduate students with a demonstrated interest in the management and beneficial use of coal combustion products (CCP). Students must attend a university or college in the U.S. at the time of application. Applicants must have demonstrated excellence in their coursework, grade point average and personal recommendations, and they must write and submit an essay describing their interest in CCP-related issues.
Target applicant(s): College students. Graduate school students. Adult students.
Amount: $1,000 to $5,000.
Number of awards: Varies.
Deadline: June 7.
How to apply: Applications are available online.
Exclusive: Visit www.UltimateScholarshipBook.com and enter code AM74826 for updates on this award.

[749] • Academic Achievement Award
American Water Works Association
6666 W. Quincy Avenue, Denver, CO 80235
Phone: 800-926-7337
Email: scholarships@awwa.org
https://www.awwa.org
Purpose: To recognize contributions to the field of public water supply.
Eligibility: Master's theses and doctoral dissertations that are relevant to the water supply industry are eligible. Unbound manuscripts must be the work of a single author and be submitted during the competition year in which they were submitted for the degree. Students may major in any area as long as the research is directly related to the drinking water supply industry. In addition to the application, students must submit a one-page abstract of the manuscript and a letter of endorsement from the major professor or department chair. The doctoral dissertation awards are $3,000 and $1,500. The master's thesis awards are $3,000 and $1,500.
Target applicant(s): Graduate school students. Adult students.
Amount: $1,500-$3,000.
Number of awards: 4.
Deadline: November 1.
How to apply: Applications are available online.
Exclusive: Visit www.UltimateScholarshipBook.com and enter code AM74926 for updates on this award.

[750] • Academic Education Award
American Association of Occupational Health Nurses (AAOHN) Foundation
330 N. Wabash Avenue, Suite 2000, Chicago, IL 60611
Phone: 312-321-5173
Email: info@aaohn.org
https://www.aaohn.org/AAOHN-Foundation/Grants-Scholarship
Purpose: To provide further education for occupational and environmental health professionals.
Eligibility: Applicants must be registered nurses enrolled full- or part-time in a nationally accredited school of nursing baccalaureate program with an interest in occupational and environmental health or be registered nurses enrolled full- or part-time in a graduate program that has application to occupational and environmental health. Applicants should submit a narrative and letters of recommendation.
Target applicant(s): College students. Graduate school students. Adult students.
Amount: $2,500.
Number of awards: 4.

Scholarship may be renewable.
Deadline: February 28.
How to apply: Applications are available online.
Exclusive: Visit www.UltimateScholarshipBook.com and enter code AM75026 for updates on this award.

[751] • Academy of Nutrition and Dietetics Foundation Student Scholarship
Academy of Nutrition and Dietetics
120 South Riverside Plaza, Suite 2000, Chicago, IL 60606-6995
Phone: 800-877-1600
Email: scholarship@eatright.org
https://eatrightfoundation.org/
Purpose: To encourage students in a dietetic program.
Eligibility: Applicants should be American Dietetic Association members and enrolled in their junior or senior year of a baccalaureate or coordinated program in dietetics or the second year of study in a dietetic technician program, a dietetic internship program or a graduate program. One application form is used for all ADAF scholarships.
Target applicant(s): College students. Graduate school students. Adult students.
Amount: $500-$25,000.
Number of awards: Varies.
Deadline: April 23.
How to apply: Applications are available online.
Exclusive: Visit www.UltimateScholarshipBook.com and enter code AC75126 for updates on this award.

[752] • ACEC New York Scholarship Program
American Council of Engineering Companies of New York
6 Airline Drive, Albany, NY 12205
Phone: 518-452-8611
Email: amanda@acecny.org
https://acecny.org
Purpose: To support students who plan to become consulting engineers.
Eligibility: Applicants must be in their third year of study in a four-year program or their fourth year of study in a five-year program at an engineering school in New York State. They must major in mechanical engineering, electrical engineering, structural engineering, civil engineering, environmental engineering, chemical engineering, engineering technology or surveying. They must plan to make New York State their home and/or career area. Selection is based on work experience (25 percent), college activities and recommendations (15 percent), essay (30 percent) and GPA (30 percent).
Target applicant(s): College students. Adult students.
Amount: $1,000-$10,000.
Number of awards: Varies.
Deadline: January 10.
How to apply: Applications are available online. An application form, essay, transcript and two recommendations are required.
Exclusive: Visit www.UltimateScholarshipBook.com and enter code AM75226 for updates on this award.

[753] • ACI Scholarship
American Concrete Institute
Attn.: ACI Foundation, Scholarship Coordinator, 38800 Country Club Drive, Farmington Hills, MI 48331
Phone: 248-848-3700
Email: scholarships@concrete.org
https://www.acifoundation.org/scholarships.aspx

The Ultimate Scholarship Book 2026
Scholarship Directory (Sciences)

Purpose: To support students who are interested in studying concrete.
Eligibility: Applicants must be nominated by a faculty member who is also a member of ACI in order to receive an application. Students must be full-time undergraduate or graduate students during the award year who plan to study in the U.S. or Canada. Applicants must be proficient in the English language. Students should submit applications via email.
Target applicant(s): College students. Graduate school students. Adult students.
Amount: $3,000-$5,000.
Number of awards: Varies.
Deadline: November 1.
How to apply: Applications are available online.
Exclusive: Visit www.UltimateScholarshipBook.com and enter code AM75326 for updates on this award.

[754] • ACI Student Fellowship Program
American Concrete Institute
Attn.: ACI Foundation, Scholarship Coordinator, 38800 Country Club Drive, Farmington Hills, MI 48331
Phone: 248-848-3700
Email: scholarships@concrete.org
https://www.acifoundation.org/scholarships.aspx
Purpose: To encourage careers in the concrete field.
Eligibility: Applicants must be full-time undergraduate or graduate students nominated by a faculty member who is also a member of the ACI. Students must be studying engineering, construction management or another relevant field. Applicants may live anywhere in the world, but actual study must take place in the U.S. or Canada. Finalists for a fellowship must attend an ACI convention for an interview. In addition to the monetary award, the scholarship also includes conference fees, mentoring and a potential internship.
Target applicant(s): College students. Graduate school students. Adult students.
Amount: Up to $15,000.
Number of awards: Varies.
Scholarship may be renewable.
Deadline: November 1.
How to apply: Applicants must be nominated by an ACI faculty member in order to receive an application.
Exclusive: Visit www.UltimateScholarshipBook.com and enter code AM75426 for updates on this award.

[755] • ADEA/Crest Oral-B Scholarships for Dental Hygiene Students Pursuing Academic Careers
American Dental Education Association
655 K Street NW, Suite 800, Washington, DC 20001
Phone: 202-289-7201
Email: lunde@adea.org
https://www.adea.org/studentawards/
Purpose: To encourage dental hygiene students who are pursuing education beyond an associate degree and who have an interest in academic careers.
Eligibility: Applicants must be enrolled in a baccalaureate degree program or graduate degree program in dental hygiene at an ADEA member institution. Students must show a commitment to pursuing an academic career in dental hygiene and be an ADEA individual member.
Target applicant(s): College students. Graduate school students. Adult students.
Amount: $3,000.
Number of awards: 2.
Deadline: November 1.
How to apply: Applications are available online.
Exclusive: Visit www.UltimateScholarshipBook.com and enter code AM75526 for updates on this award.

[756] • ADEA/Haleon Preventive Dentistry Scholarships
American Dental Education Association
655 K Street NW, Suite 800, Washington, DC 20001
Phone: 202-289-7201
Email: lunde@adea.org
https://www.adea.org/studentawards/
Purpose: To support dental students.
Eligibility: Applicants must be students enrolled at a U.S. or Canadian dental school as full-time students at the time of submission. Students must demonstrate through personal activities and achievements, a strong interest in preventive dentistry and possess a superior academic record. Selections will be limited to students nominated by the dean of his or her dental school or the dean's designate (no more than three nominations are accepted from each school) and are ADEA individual members.
Target applicant(s): High school students. College students. Adult students.
Amount: $2,500.
Number of awards: 12.
Deadline: November 1.
How to apply: Applications are available online.
Exclusive: Visit www.UltimateScholarshipBook.com and enter code AM75626 for updates on this award.

[757] • ADEA/MouthWatch Patti DiGangi Scholarship for Dental Hygiene Innovation
American Dental Education Association
655 K Street NW, Suite 800, Washington, DC 20001
Phone: 202-289-7201
Email: lunde@adea.org
https://www.adea.org/studentawards/
Purpose: To encourage dental hygiene students who are pursuing education beyond an associate degree and who have an interest in academic careers.
Eligibility: Applicants must be enrolled as full-time students in an accredited program in dental hygiene or public health in the U.S. or Canada having completed at least one year of the program. Students must maintain good academic standing and demonstrate achievements in research, community service, leadership, personal growth, etc. that relate to career goals. Selections are limited to an ADEA Individual Member.
Target applicant(s): High school students. College students. Graduate school students. Adult students.
Amount: $1,000.
Number of awards: 1.
Deadline: November 1.
How to apply: Applications are available online.
Exclusive: Visit www.UltimateScholarshipBook.com and enter code AM75726 for updates on this award.

[758] • ADEA/MouthWatch Predoctoral Dental Student Scholarship for Innovation
American Dental Education Association
655 K Street NW, Suite 800, Washington, DC 20001
Phone: 202-289-7201
Email: lunde@adea.org
https://www.adea.org/studentawards/

Purpose: To support dental students.
Eligibility: Applicants must be enrolled as full-time students in an accredited program in dentistry or public health in the U.S. or Canada having completed at least one year of the program. Students must maintain good academic standing and demonstrate achievements in research, community service, leadership, personal growth, etc. that relate to career goals. Selections are limited to an ADEA Individual Member.
Target applicant(s): High school students. College students. Adult students.
Amount: $1,000.
Number of awards: 1.
Deadline: November 1.
How to apply: Applications are available online.
Exclusive: Visit www.UltimateScholarshipBook.com and enter code AM75826 for updates on this award.

[759] • ADEA/Sigma Phi Alpha Linda Devore Scholarship

American Dental Education Association
655 K Street NW, Suite 800, Washington, DC 20001
Phone: 202-289-7201
Email: lunde@adea.org
https://www.adea.org/studentawards/
Purpose: To aid allied dental education students.
Eligibility: Applicants must be members of the American Dental Education Association (ADEA) and be enrolled in a dental hygiene, dental education or public health degree program. They must be in good academic standing and demonstrate leadership in dental education or health care. Selection is based on the overall strength of the application.
Target applicant(s): College students. Graduate school students. Adult students.
Amount: $1,500.
Number of awards: 1.
Deadline: November 1.
How to apply: Applications are available online. An application form, an official transcript, a personal statement and two reference letters are required.
Exclusive: Visit www.UltimateScholarshipBook.com and enter code AM75926 for updates on this award.

[760] • ADHA Institute Scholarship Program

American Dental Hygienists' Association (ADHA) Institute for Oral Health
444 North Michigan Avenue, Suite 400, Chicago, IL 60611
Phone: 312-440-8900
Email: institute@adha.net
https://www.adha.org/ioh/scholarships/
Purpose: To assist students pursuing a career in dental hygiene.
Eligibility: Applicants should be enrolled full-time (unless applying for a part-time scholarship) in an accredited dental hygiene program in the U.S., be finishing their first year and have a minimum 3.0 GPA. Undergraduate students should be active members of the Student American Dental Hygienists' Association or the American Dental Hygienists Association. Graduate students should be active members of the Student American Dental Hygienists' Association or the American Dental Hygienists Association, have a valid dental hygiene license and a bachelor's degree. There should be financial need of at least $1,500, with the exception of the merit-based scholarships.
Target applicant(s): College students. Graduate school students. Adult students.
Minimum GPA: 3.0

Amount: Varies.
Number of awards: Varies.
Deadline: February 2.
How to apply: Applications are available online.
Exclusive: Visit www.UltimateScholarshipBook.com and enter code AM76026 for updates on this award.

[761] • AFCEA Ralph W. Shrader Diversity Scholarships

Armed Forces Communications and Electronics Association (AFCEA)
4114 Legato Road, Suite 1000, Fairfax, VA 22033
Phone: 703-631-6149
http://www.afcea.org
Purpose: Monetary assistance is awarded to graduate students studying electrical, computer, chemical or aerospace engineering, mathematics, physics, computer science, computer technology, electronics, communications technology or engineering or information management systems.
Eligibility: Applicants must be U.S. citizens, full-time postgraduate students working toward a master's degree in electrical, computer, chemical or aerospace engineering, mathematics, physics, computer science, computer technology, electronics, communications technology, communications engineering or information management at an accredited U.S. university. Distance learning or online programs will not qualify. Primary consideration will be given for demonstrated excellence. Applicants do not need to be affiliated with the U.S. military.
Target applicant(s): Graduate school students. Adult students.
Amount: Varies.
Number of awards: Varies.
Deadline: January 1.
How to apply: Applications are available online.
Exclusive: Visit www.UltimateScholarshipBook.com and enter code AR76126 for updates on this award.

[762] • AGC Education and Research Foundation Undergraduate Scholarship

Associated General Contractors (AGC) Education and Research Foundation
2300 Wilson Boulevard, Suite 400, Arlington, VA 22201
Phone: 703-837-5342
Email: info@agc.org
http://www.agcfoundation.org
Purpose: To support rising undergraduate construction and construction-related engineering students pursue their ABET and ACCE-accredited construction and construction-related engineering degrees.
Eligibility: Applicants must be second-year students at a two-year college planning to transfer to a four-year program for the fall, rising college sophomores or juniors in a four-year program or seniors in a five-year program. Juniors and seniors must have one full academic year of study remaining at the time of application submission and be pursuing a B.S. degree in construction or construction-related engineering program.
Target applicant(s): College students. Adult students.
Minimum GPA: 2.0
Amount: $2,500.
Number of awards: 100.
Scholarship may be renewable.
Deadline: November 1.
How to apply: Applications are available online.
Exclusive: Visit www.UltimateScholarshipBook.com and enter code AS76226 for updates on this award.

[763] • AGC Graduate Scholarships
Associated General Contractors of America
2300 Wilson Boulevard, Suite 300, Arlington, VA 22201
Phone: 703-837-5342
Email: patricianm@agc.org
http://www.agc.org
Purpose: Monetary assistance is awarded to college seniors pursuing graduate degrees that will lead to careers in construction or civil engineering.
Eligibility: Applicants must be college seniors enrolled in an undergraduate construction or civil engineering degree program or college graduates with a degree in construction or civil engineering. Applicants must also be enrolled or planning to enroll full-time in a graduate level construction or civil engineering degree program.
Target applicant(s): College students. Graduate school students. Adult students.
Amount: $7,500.
Number of awards: Varies.
Deadline: November 1.
How to apply: Applications are available online.
Exclusive: Visit www.UltimateScholarshipBook.com and enter code AS76326 for updates on this award.

[764] • AGC Undergraduate Scholarships
Associated General Contractors of America
2300 Wilson Boulevard, Suite 300, Arlington, VA 22201
Phone: 703-837-5342
Email: patricianm@agc.org
http://www.agc.org
Purpose: To assist students pursuing studies that lead to a career in construction or civil engineering.
Eligibility: Applicants must be a second-year student at a two-year school planning to transfer to a four-year program, or a rising college sophomore or junior in a four-year program or rising senior in a five-year program enrolled in or planning to enroll in ABET- or ACCE-accredited construction or civil engineering programs pursuing a B.S. degree in construction or construction-related engineering.
Target applicant(s): College students. Adult students.
Amount: $2,500.
Number of awards: Varies.
Scholarship may be renewable.
Deadline: November 1.
How to apply: Applications are available online.
Exclusive: Visit www.UltimateScholarshipBook.com and enter code AS76426 for updates on this award.

[765] • AHIMA Foundation Merit Scholarships
American Health Information Management Association (AHIMA) Foundation
233 N. Michigan Avenue, 21st Floor, Chicago, IL 60601-5809
Phone: 312-233-1131
Email: info@ahimafoundation.org
http://www.ahimafoundation.org
Purpose: To provide merit scholarships to those enrolled in degree programs pursuing health information technology or health information administration.
Eligibility: Applicants must be members of AHIMA, have a minimum 3.0 GPA on a 4.0 scale, have completed 24 credit hours in health information management (HIM) or health information technology (HIT), have at least six credit hours remaining in their course of study and be taking at least six hours per semester in pursuit of the degree. The degrees eligible are AA degrees, BA/BS degrees and those who are credentialed and pursing a master's degree. Scholarships are also available for HIM professionals pursuing graduate degrees in the health information field.
Target applicant(s): College students. Graduate school students. Adult students.
Minimum GPA: 3.0
Amount: $1,000-$2,500.
Number of awards: Varies.
Deadline: May 31.
How to apply: Applications are available online.
Exclusive: Visit www.UltimateScholarshipBook.com and enter code AM76526 for updates on this award.

[766] • AIA/Architects Foundation Diversity Advancement Scholarship
Sir John Soane's Museum Foundation
120 Broadway, 20th Floor, New York, NY 10271
Phone: 212-655-7626
Email: info@soanefoundation.org
https://soanefoundation.org
Purpose: To provide scholarships for students who intend to study architecture and who could not otherwise afford to enter a degree-seeking program.
Eligibility: Applicants must be students from a minority race or ethnicity who intend to study architecture in an NAAB-accredited program. Students who are U.S. residents entering, attending or transferring to an NAAB-accredited program are also eligible.
Target applicant(s): High school students. College students. Adult students.
Amount: $4,000.
Number of awards: Varies.
Scholarship may be renewable.
Deadline: January 19.
How to apply: Applications are available by email. An application form and a recommendation letter are required.
Exclusive: Visit www.UltimateScholarshipBook.com and enter code SI76626 for updates on this award.

[767] • AIAA Foundation Undergraduate Scholarship Program
American Institute of Aeronautics and Astronautics
12700 Sunrise Valley Drive, Suite 200, Reston, VA 20191-5807
Phone: 800-639-AIAA
Email: stephenb@aiaa.org
http://www.aiaa.org
Purpose: AIAA advances the arts, sciences and technology of aeronautics and astronautics.
Eligibility: Applicants must be enrolled in an accredited college or university and have completed at least one semester or quarter of college work with a minimum 3.3 GPA. Applicants must plan to enter a career in science or engineering related to the technical activities of the AIAA. Applicants must be AIAA student members in good standing to apply. Selection is based on scholarship, career goals, recommendations and extracurricular activities.
Target applicant(s): College students. Adult students.
Minimum GPA: 3.3
Amount: Up to $10,000.
Number of awards: Varies.
Scholarship may be renewable.

Deadline: January 31.
How to apply: Applications are available online.
Exclusive: Visit www.UltimateScholarshipBook.com and enter code AM76726 for updates on this award.

[768] • AISI/AIST Foundation Premier Scholarship
Association for Iron and Steel Technology (AIST)
186 Thorn Hill Road, Warrendale, PA 15086-7528
Phone: 724-814-3000
Email: lwharrey@aist.org
https://www.aist.org/students-faculty/scholarships
Purpose: To encourage engineering students to pursue careers in the iron and steel industry.
Eligibility: Applicants must be undergraduate sophomores who are enrolled full-time at an accredited college or university and be majoring in engineering. They must have a GPA of 3.0 or higher on a four-point scale and must have a demonstrated career interest in the iron and steel industry. Selection is based on the overall strength of the application.
Target applicant(s): College students. Adult students.
Minimum GPA: 3.0
Amount: $12,000.
Number of awards: 1.
Scholarship may be renewable.
Deadline: October 14.
How to apply: Applications are available online. An application form, transcript, personal essay and two letters of recommendation are required.
Exclusive: Visit www.UltimateScholarshipBook.com and enter code AS76826 for updates on this award.

[769] • AIST Benjamin F. Fairless Scholarship (AIME)
Association for Iron and Steel Technology (AIST)
186 Thorn Hill Road, Warrendale, PA 15086-7528
Phone: 724-814-3000
Email: lwharrey@aist.org
https://www.aist.org/students-faculty/scholarships
Purpose: To honor the memory of Benjamin F. Fairless, former Chairman of the Board of U.S. Steel Corporation.
Eligibility: Applicants must be enrolled full-time in an accredited university in North America and majoring in engineering, metallurgy or materials science. Applicants must also have a GPA of 2.5 or higher and plan to pursue a career in the iron and steel industry.
Target applicant(s): College students. Adult students.
Minimum GPA: 2.5
Amount: $3,000.
Number of awards: 2.
Deadline: October 14.
How to apply: Applications are available online.
Exclusive: Visit www.UltimateScholarshipBook.com and enter code AS76926 for updates on this award.

[770] • AIST Ronald E. Lincoln Memorial Scholarship
Association for Iron and Steel Technology (AIST)
186 Thorn Hill Road, Warrendale, PA 15086-7528
Phone: 724-814-3000
Email: lwharrey@aist.org
https://www.aist.org/students-faculty/scholarships
Purpose: To honor the memory of Ronald Lincoln and to reward students who demonstrate leadership and innovation.
Eligibility: Applicants must be enrolled full-time in an accredited university in North America and majoring in engineering, metallurgy or materials science. Applicants must also have a GPA of 2.5 or higher and plan to pursue a career in the iron and steel industry.
Target applicant(s): College students. Adult students.
Minimum GPA: 2.5
Amount: $3,000.
Number of awards: 3.
Deadline: October 14.
How to apply: Applications are available online.
Exclusive: Visit www.UltimateScholarshipBook.com and enter code AS77026 for updates on this award.

[771] • AIST Smith Graduate Scholarship
Association for Iron and Steel Technology (AIST)
186 Thorn Hill Road, Warrendale, PA 15086-7528
Phone: 724-814-3000
Email: lwharrey@aist.org
https://www.aist.org/students-faculty/scholarships
Purpose: To aid graduate engineering students who are interested in careers in metallurgy.
Eligibility: Applicants must be full-time graduate students who are enrolled in an engineering degree program at an accredited college or university in the U.S. or Canada. They must have a demonstrated interest in pursuing a career in metallurgy within the iron and steel industry. Selection is based on the overall strength of the application.
Target applicant(s): Graduate school students. Adult students.
Amount: Up to $6,000.
Number of awards: Varies.
Deadline: October 14.
How to apply: Applications are available online. An application form and supporting materials are required.
Exclusive: Visit www.UltimateScholarshipBook.com and enter code AS77126 for updates on this award.

[772] • AIST William E. Schwabe Memorial Scholarship
Association for Iron and Steel Technology (AIST)
186 Thorn Hill Road, Warrendale, PA 15086-7528
Phone: 724-814-3000
Email: lwharrey@aist.org
https://www.aist.org/students-faculty/scholarships
Purpose: To honor the memory of William E. Schwabe, steelmaking pioneer.
Eligibility: Applicants must be enrolled full-time in an accredited university in North America and majoring in engineering, metallurgy or materials science. Applicants must also have a GPA of 2.5 or higher and plan to pursue a career in the iron and steel industry.
Target applicant(s): College students. Adult students.
Minimum GPA: 2.5
Amount: $3,000.
Number of awards: 1.
Deadline: October 14.
How to apply: Applications are available online.
Exclusive: Visit www.UltimateScholarshipBook.com and enter code AS77226 for updates on this award.

[773] • AIST Willy Korf Memorial Fund
Association for Iron and Steel Technology (AIST)
186 Thorn Hill Road, Warrendale, PA 15086-7528
Phone: 724-814-3000
Email: lwharrey@aist.org
https://www.aist.org/students-faculty/scholarships
Purpose: To honor the memory of the late Willy Korf, the founder of the Korf Group, and to assist students who plan to enter the fields of engineering, metallurgy or materials science in the iron and steel industry.
Eligibility: Applicants must be enrolled full-time in an accredited university in North America, and majoring in engineering, metallurgy or materials science. Applicants must also have a GPA of 3.0 or higher and plan to pursue a career in the iron and steel industry.
Target applicant(s): High school students. College students. Adult students.
Minimum GPA: 3.0
Amount: $7,500.
Number of awards: Varies.
Deadline: October 14.
How to apply: Applications are available online.
Exclusive: Visit www.UltimateScholarshipBook.com and enter code AS77326 for updates on this award.

[774] • Alice T. Schafer Mathematics Prize
Association for Women in Mathematics
P.O. Box 40876, Providence, RI 02940
Phone: 401-455-4042
Email: awm@awm-math.org
http://www.awm-math.org
Purpose: To support female students who are studying mathematics.
Eligibility: Nominees must be female college undergraduates and either be U.S. citizens or have a school address in the U.S. Selection is based on performance in advanced mathematics courses and special programs, interest in mathematics, ability to conduct independent work and performance in mathematical competitions at the local or national level.
Target applicant(s): College students. Adult students.
Amount: Up to $1,000.
Number of awards: 5.
Deadline: September 15.
How to apply: Applicants must be nominated.
Exclusive: Visit www.UltimateScholarshipBook.com and enter code AS77426 for updates on this award.

[775] • Alice W. Rooke Scholarship
National Society Daughters of the American Revolution
Committee Services Office, Attn.: Scholarships, 1776 D Street NW, Washington, DC 20006-5303
Phone: 202-628-1776
Email: scholarships@dar.org
https://www.dar.org/national-society/scholarships
Purpose: To assist students in becoming medical doctors.
Eligibility: Applicants must be accepted into or enrolled in a graduate course of study to become a medical doctor. All applicants must obtain a letter of sponsorship from their local DAR chapter. However, affiliation with DAR is not required.
Target applicant(s): Graduate school students. Adult students.
Amount: Up to $5,000.
Number of awards: 1.
Scholarship may be renewable.
Deadline: January 31.
How to apply: Applications are available by written request with a self-addressed, stamped envelope.
Exclusive: Visit www.UltimateScholarshipBook.com and enter code NA77526 for updates on this award.

[776] • Alpha Mu Tau Fraternity Undergraduate Scholarships
American Society for Clinical Laboratory Science
11107 Sunset Hills Road, Suite 100, Reston, VA 20190-5376
Phone: 571-748-3770
Email: awards@ascls.org
http://www.ascls.org
Purpose: To support new professionals in the clinical laboratory sciences.
Eligibility: Applicants must be undergraduate students entering or in their last year of study in an NAACLS-accredited program in Clinical Laboratory Science/Medical Technology or Clinical Laboratory Technician/Medical Laboratory Technician. Applicants must be U.S. citizens or permanent residents of the U.S. Students must be ASCLS members.
Target applicant(s): College students. Adult students.
Amount: $1,000-$4,000.
Number of awards: Varies.
Deadline: April 1.
How to apply: Applications are available online.
Exclusive: Visit www.UltimateScholarshipBook.com and enter code AM77626 for updates on this award.

[777] • Amazon Future Engineer Scholarship
Amazon Future Engineer Scholarship
Scholarship America, One Scholarship Way, Saint Peter, MN 56082
Phone: 800-537-4180
Email: amazonfutureengineer@scholarshipamerica.org
https://scholarshipamerica.org/amazonfutureengineer/
Purpose: To support students interested in careers in computer science or engineering.
Eligibility: Applicants must be U.S. citizens or permanent residents who are high school seniors. Students must plan to pursue a bachelor's degree in computer science, software engineering, computer engineering, mechanical engineering, electrical engineering, robotics or other computer science related field of study at an accredited four-year college or university or an accredited two-year college with the intent to transfer to a four-year institution. Applicants must have a minimum 2.3 GPA and have completed, or be currently enrolled in, a high school or college dual degree course where computer science, engineering or robotics is the subject.
Target applicant(s): High school students.
Minimum GPA: 2.3
Amount: Up to $40,000.
Number of awards: 400.
Scholarship may be renewable.
Deadline: December 19.
How to apply: Applications are available online.
Exclusive: Visit www.UltimateScholarshipBook.com and enter code AM77726 for updates on this award.

[778] • AMBUCS Scholars
AMBUCS
P.O. Box 5127, High Point, NC 27262
Phone: 800-838-1845
Email: ambucs@ambucs.org
http://www.ambucs.org
Purpose: To provide more opportunities for the disabled by encouraging students to become therapists.
Eligibility: Students must be US citizens accepted in a graduate-level program that is accredited by the appropriate therapy profession authority in physical therapy, occupational therapy, speech language pathology or hearing audiology. Assistant or undergraduate programs are not eligible. Awards are based on financial need, commitment to local community, character for compassion and integrity and career objectives.
Target applicant(s): College students. Graduate school students. Adult students.
Amount: $500-$6,000.
Number of awards: Varies.
Deadline: May 1.
How to apply: Applications are available online.
Exclusive: Visit www.UltimateScholarshipBook.com and enter code AM77826 for updates on this award.

[779] • Amelia Earhart Fellowships
Zonta International
1211 West 22nd Street, Suite 900, Oak Brook, IL 60523
Phone: 630-928-1400
Email: zontaintl@zonta.org
https://www.zonta.org
Purpose: To support women in science and engineering.
Eligibility: Applicants must be pursuing graduate PhD/doctoral degrees in aerospace-related sciences and aerospace-related engineering.
Target applicant(s): Graduate school students. Adult students.
Amount: $10,000.
Number of awards: 30.
Deadline: November 15.
How to apply: Applications are available online.
Exclusive: Visit www.UltimateScholarshipBook.com and enter code ZO77926 for updates on this award.

[780] • American Innovations Corrosion Scholarship
National Association of Corrosion Engineers (NACE) International Foundation
15835 Park Ten Place, Houston, TX 77084-5145
Phone: 281-228-6205
Email: nace.foundation@nace.org
https://www.ampp.org/about/emerg-student-outreach/academic-scholarships-program
Purpose: To assist students of the National Association of Corrosion Engineers.
Eligibility: Applicants must be enrolled full-time in an undergraduate program at an accredited, two-year degree-granting college or university located in the U.S. Students must be pursuing a career as a technician or engineer related to corrosion or corrosion control.
Target applicant(s): High school students. College students. Adult students.
Amount: $1,000.
Number of awards: 1.
Deadline: January 4.
How to apply: Applications are available online.
Exclusive: Visit www.UltimateScholarshipBook.com and enter code NA78026 for updates on this award.

[781] • American Water Scholarship
American Water Works Association
6666 W. Quincy Avenue, Denver, CO 80235
Phone: 800-926-7337
Email: scholarships@awwa.org
https://www.awwa.org
Purpose: To support graduate-level students interested in giving service to the water industry.
Eligibility: Applicants must be graduate students working towards a master's or doctoral degree. Students must be planning a career related to the service of the water industry. Selection is based on the overall strength of the application.
Target applicant(s): College students. Graduate school students. Adult students.
Amount: $5,000.
Number of awards: Varies.
Deadline: December 20.
How to apply: Applications are available online.
Exclusive: Visit www.UltimateScholarshipBook.com and enter code AM78126 for updates on this award.

[782] • AMPP Academic Scholarship
National Association of Corrosion Engineers (NACE) International Foundation
15835 Park Ten Place, Houston, TX 77084-5145
Phone: 281-228-6205
Email: nace.foundation@nace.org
https://www.ampp.org/about/emerg-student-outreach/academic-scholarships-program
Purpose: To aid students in the study of corrosion or corrosion control.
Eligibility: Applicants must be enrolled full-time as an undergraduate student at a two- or four-year accredited college or university. Applicants must be pursuing a science or engineering degree. Selection is based on the overall strength of the application.
Target applicant(s): College students. Adult students.
Amount: $5,000.
Number of awards: Up to 3.
Deadline: January 2.
How to apply: Applications are available online. An application form, two recommendation forms, an academic transcript and essay scholarship questions are required.
Exclusive: Visit www.UltimateScholarshipBook.com and enter code NA78226 for updates on this award.

[783] • AMS Graduate Fellowship in the History of Science
American Meteorological Society
Fellowship and Scholarship Department, 45 Beacon Street, Boston, MA 02108-3693
Phone: 617-227-2425
Email: amsinfo@ametsoc.org
https://www.ametsoc.org/ams/index.cfm/information-for/students/ams-scholarships-and-fellowships/
Purpose: To support students writing dissertations on the history of atmospheric or related oceanic or hydrologic sciences.

Eligibility: Applicants must be graduate students who plan to write dissertations on the history of atmospheric or related oceanic or hydrologic sciences. Students must submit a cover letter with vitae, official transcripts, a typed description of the dissertation topic and three letters of recommendation.
Target applicant(s): Graduate school students. Adult students.
Amount: $20,000.
Number of awards: Varies.
Deadline: May 24.
How to apply: Submit materials to address listed.
Exclusive: Visit www.UltimateScholarshipBook.com and enter code AM78326 for updates on this award.

[784] • AMS Graduate Fellowships
American Meteorological Society
Fellowship and Scholarship Department, 45 Beacon Street, Boston, MA 02108-3693
Phone: 617-227-2425
Email: amsinfo@ametsoc.org
https://www.ametsoc.org/ams/index.cfm/information-for/students/ams-scholarships-and-fellowships/
Purpose: To attract students to prepare for careers in the meteorological, oceanic and hydrologic fields.
Eligibility: Applicants must be entering their first year of graduate study the following year and plan to pursue advanced degrees in the atmospheric and related oceanic and hydrologic sciences and have a minimum 3.25 GPA. Awards are based on undergraduate performance. References, transcripts and GRE scores may be sent under separate cover. References can be sent to dfernand@ametsoc.org.
Target applicant(s): College students. Adult students.
Minimum GPA: 3.25
Amount: $25,000.
Number of awards: Varies.
Deadline: January 26.
How to apply: Applications are available online.
Exclusive: Visit www.UltimateScholarshipBook.com and enter code AM78426 for updates on this award.

[785] • AMS Minority Scholarship
American Meteorological Society
Fellowship and Scholarship Department, 45 Beacon Street, Boston, MA 02108-3693
Phone: 617-227-2425
Email: amsinfo@ametsoc.org
https://www.ametsoc.org/ams/index.cfm/information-for/students/ams-scholarships-and-fellowships/
Purpose: To support minority students who have been traditionally underrepresented in the sciences, especially Hispanic, Native American and African American students.
Eligibility: Applicants must be minority students who will be entering their freshman year of college in the following fall and must plan to pursue degrees in the atmospheric or related oceanic and hydrologic sciences. Applicants must submit applications, transcripts, recommendation letters and SAT or equivalent scores. Original materials should be mailed to the closest AMS Local Chapter listed at the bottom of the application, and copies should be mailed to headquarters.
Target applicant(s): High school students.

Amount: $6,000.
Number of awards: Varies.
Scholarship may be renewable.
Deadline: February 23.
How to apply: Applications are available online.
Exclusive: Visit www.UltimateScholarshipBook.com and enter code AM78526 for updates on this award.

[786] • AMS Senior Named Scholarships
American Meteorological Society
Fellowship and Scholarship Department, 45 Beacon Street, Boston, MA 02108-3693
Phone: 617-227-2425
Email: amsinfo@ametsoc.org
https://www.ametsoc.org/ams/index.cfm/information-for/students/ams-scholarships-and-fellowships/
Purpose: To encourage undergraduate students to pursue careers in the atmospheric and related oceanic and hydrologic sciences.
Eligibility: Applicants must be full-time students majoring in the atmospheric or related oceanic or hydrologic science and entering their final undergraduate year, show intent to make the atmospheric or related sciences their career and have a minimum 3.25 GPA. For the Schroeder scholarship, applicants must demonstrate financial need. For the Murphy scholarship, applicants must demonstrate interest in weather forecasting through curricular or extracurricular activities and for the Crow scholarship, applicants must demonstrate interest in applied meteorology. The Glahn scholarship will be awarded to a student with a strong interest in statistical meteorology.
Target applicant(s): College students. Adult students.
Minimum GPA: 3.25
Amount: Up to $10,000.
Number of awards: Varies.
Deadline: March 8.
How to apply: Applications are available online.
Exclusive: Visit www.UltimateScholarshipBook.com and enter code AM78626 for updates on this award.

[787] • AMT Student Scholarship
American Medical Technologists
10700 W. Higgins Road, Suite 150, Rosemont, IL 60018
Phone: 847-823-5169
Email: mail@americanmedtech.org
https://americanmedtech.org/Blog/Blog-Post/apply-for-an-amt-scholarship
Purpose: To provide financial assistance to students interested in medical technology careers.
Eligibility: Applicants must be high school graduates or current seniors planning to attend an accredited institution to pursue an American Medical Technologists-certified career, which includes medical laboratory technology, medical assisting, dental assisting, phlebotomy and office laboratory technician. Applicants must provide evidence of financial need.
Target applicant(s): High school students.
Amount: $500.
Number of awards: 5.
Deadline: April 1.
How to apply: Applications are available online.
Exclusive: Visit www.UltimateScholarshipBook.com and enter code AM78726 for updates on this award.

[788] • Angus Foundation Scholarships
Angus Foundation
3201 Frederick Avenue, St. Joseph, MO 64506
Phone: 816-383-5100
Email: angus@angus.org
https://www.angus.org/foundation
Purpose: To provide scholarships to youth active with the Angus breed.
Eligibility: Applicants must have been members of the National Junior Angus Association and must be junior, regular or life members of the American Angus Association at the time of application. Applicants must be high school seniors or enrolled in a junior college, four-year college or other accredited institution of post-secondary education in an undergraduate program and have a minimum 2.0 GPA. Students may not have reached their 25th birthday by January 1 of the year of application.
Target applicant(s): High school students. College students.
Minimum GPA: 2.0
Amount: $1,000-$5,000.
Number of awards: Varies.
Deadline: May 1.
How to apply: Applications are available online or by written request.
Exclusive: Visit www.UltimateScholarshipBook.com and enter code AN78826 for updates on this award.

[789] • Annual NBNA Scholarships
National Black Nurses Association
8630 Fenton Street, Suite 910, Silver Spring, MD 20910
Phone: 301-589-3200
Email: Info@nbna.org
http://www.nbna.org
Purpose: To promote excellence in education and in continuing education programs for African American nurses and allied health professionals.
Eligibility: Applicants must be African Americans currently enrolled in a nursing program and be in good academic standing, be members of the NBNA, be members of a local chapter and have at least a full year of school remaining. Applicants must submit with their application an essay, references, an official transcript and evidence of participation in student nurse activities and involvement in the African American community.
Target applicant(s): College students. Adult students.
Amount: $1,000-$15,000.
Number of awards: Varies.
Deadline: March 15.
How to apply: Applications are available online.
Exclusive: Visit www.UltimateScholarshipBook.com and enter code NA78926 for updates on this award.

[790] • Annual University Scholarship
Antibodies-online Inc.
321 Jones Boulevard, Limerick, PA 19464
Phone: 877-302-8632
Email: scholarship@antibodies-online.com
https://www.antibodies-online.com/scholarship/
Purpose: To support students who are pursuing degrees in the life sciences.
Eligibility: Applicants must be high school seniors, undergraduates or graduate students enrolled in an accredited college or university for the upcoming fall or spring semester. Students must be majoring in life sciences or related fields. Applicants must submit a 250-word essay on why they decided to pursue a degree in life science and how they plan to further advance this field, as well as a 150-word essay on what their favorite scientific discovery is and why.
Target applicant(s): High school students. College students. Graduate school students. Adult students.
Amount: $1,000.
Number of awards: 2.
Deadline: July 20 and January 20.
How to apply: Applications are available online.
Exclusive: Visit www.UltimateScholarshipBook.com and enter code AN79026 for updates on this award.

[791] • ANS Graduate Scholarship
American Nuclear Society
555 North Kensington Avenue, La Grange Park, IL 60526
Phone: 800-323-3044
Email: hr@ans.org
http://www.ans.org
Purpose: To assist full-time graduate students who are pursuing advanced degrees in a nuclear-related field.
Eligibility: Applicants must be full-time students at an accredited graduate school in a program leading to an advanced degree in nuclear science, nuclear engineering or a nuclear-related field. There are also individual graduate scholarships. Applicants should submit applications, transcripts, recommendation letter and three reference forms.
Target applicant(s): Graduate school students. Adult students.
Amount: $3,000-$5,000.
Number of awards: Varies.
Deadline: February 1.
How to apply: Applications are available online.
Exclusive: Visit www.UltimateScholarshipBook.com and enter code AM79126 for updates on this award.

[792] • ANS Incoming Freshman Scholarships
American Nuclear Society
555 North Kensington Avenue, La Grange Park, IL 60526
Phone: 800-323-3044
Email: hr@ans.org
http://www.ans.org
Purpose: To aid high school seniors who are planning to major in nuclear engineering at the undergraduate level.
Eligibility: Applicants must be graduating high school seniors who have been accepted at an accredited postsecondary institution. They must have plans to major in nuclear engineering. Selection is based on academic merit, personal essay and recommendations.
Target applicant(s): High school students.
Amount: $1,000.
Number of awards: Varies.
Deadline: April 1.
How to apply: Applications are available online. An application form, personal essay, two letters of recommendation and an official transcript are required.
Exclusive: Visit www.UltimateScholarshipBook.com and enter code AM79226 for updates on this award.

[793] • ANS Undergraduate Scholarship
American Nuclear Society
555 North Kensington Avenue, La Grange Park, IL 60526
Phone: 800-323-3044
Email: hr@ans.org
http://www.ans.org

Purpose: To assist undergraduate students who are pursuing careers in the field of nuclear science.
Eligibility: Applicants must be at least sophomores or students who have completed two or more years and will be entering as juniors or seniors in an accredited university and must be enrolled in a program leading to a degree in nuclear science, nuclear engineering or a nuclear-related field. Applicants should submit applications, transcripts, recommendation letter and three reference forms. There are individual undergraduate scholarships for students who have completed two or more years in a course of study leading to a degree in nuclear science, nuclear engineering or a nuclear-related field.
Target applicant(s): College students. Adult students.
Amount: Up to $2,500.
Number of awards: Varies.
Deadline: February 1.
How to apply: Applications are available online.
Exclusive: Visit www.UltimateScholarshipBook.com and enter code AM79326 for updates on this award.

[794] • AOC Scholarships
Association of Old Crows
1000 N. Payne Street, Suite 200, Alexandria, VA 22314-1652
Phone: 703-549-1600
Email: stourangeau@warriorss.com
https://www.crows.org
Purpose: To encourage students interested in strong defense capability emphasizing electronic warfare and information operations.
Eligibility: Applicants must be U.S. citizens enrolled full-time at an accredited college or university in an undergraduate degree program as a junior or senior. Students should be studying engineering or technology with a minimum cumulative GPA of 3.0. Selection is based on interest and potential future contribution to national defense and academic excellence in the STEM area of study.
Target applicant(s): College students. Adult students.
Minimum GPA: 3.0
Amount: $12,500.
Number of awards: 2.
Deadline: April 30.
How to apply: Applications are available online.
Exclusive: Visit www.UltimateScholarshipBook.com and enter code AS79426 for updates on this award.

[795] • AORN Foundation Scholarship Program
Association of Perioperative Registered Nurses
2170 S. Parker Road, Suite 400, Denver, CO 80231
Phone: 800-755-2676
Email: sstokes@aorn.org
https://www.aorn.org/foundation/scholarships-grants
Purpose: To encourage the education of nurses and future nurses.
Eligibility: Applicants must be current nursing students or AORN members accepted to an accredited program and have a minimum 3.0 GPA. Applicants must also demonstrate financial need.
Target applicant(s): College students. Graduate school students. Adult students.
Minimum GPA: 3.0
Amount: Varies.
Number of awards: Varies.
Deadline: June 15.
How to apply: Applications are available online.
Exclusive: Visit www.UltimateScholarshipBook.com and enter code AS79526 for updates on this award.

[796] • AOS Student and Postdoctoral Research Awards
American Ornithologists' Union
Avian Ecology Lab, Archbold Biological Station, 123 Main Drive, Venus, FL 33960
Phone: 863-465-2571
Email: rbowman@archbold-station.org
https://americanornithology.org/awards-grants/
Purpose: To provide research funding for members of the American Ornithologists Union.
Eligibility: Applicants must be members of the AOU and must submit proposals for research projects on avian biology, avian systematics, paleo-ornithology, biogeography, neotropical biology or ornithology.
Target applicant(s): College students. Graduate school students. Adult students.
Amount: Up to $2,500.
Number of awards: Varies.
Deadline: February 2.
How to apply: The submission procedure and tips for writing a proposal are described on the website.
Exclusive: Visit www.UltimateScholarshipBook.com and enter code AM79626 for updates on this award.

[797] • Appaloosa Youth Association Art Contest
Appaloosa Horse Club
Appaloosa Youth Association, 2720 West Pullman Road, Moscow, ID 83843
Phone: 208-882-5578
Email: youth@appaloosa.com
https://www.appaloosa.com/appaloosa-youth-association
Purpose: To allow students to showcase their artistic talents with Appaloosa-themed projects.
Eligibility: Applicants age 18 and under should submit drawings, paintings and hand-built ceramics or sculptures with the Appaloosa theme. There are three age divisions: 10 and under, 11 to 13 and 14 to 18. Awards are based on originality, creativity and the theme.
Target applicant(s): Junior high students or younger. High school students.
Amount: $50-$250.
Number of awards: 9.
Deadline: August 31.
How to apply: Applications are available online.
Exclusive: Visit www.UltimateScholarshipBook.com and enter code AP79726 for updates on this award.

[798] • Apprentice Ecologist Initiative Youth Scholarship Program
Nicodemus Wilderness Project
P.O. Box 40712, Albuquerque, NM 87196-0712
Email: mail@wildernessproject.org
http://www.wildernessproject.org/volunteer_apprentice_ecologist.php
Purpose: To aid ecologically-minded youth.
Eligibility: Applicants must be students who are between the ages of 13 and 21. They must devise and complete an environmental conservation project then write an essay describing the experience. Selection is based on the quality of the project and essay.

Target applicant(s): Junior high students or younger. High school students. College students.
Amount: $1,750.
Number of awards: 3.
Deadline: August 31.
How to apply: Application instructions are available online. An essay and a project photo are required.
Exclusive: Visit www.UltimateScholarshipBook.com and enter code NI79826 for updates on this award.

[799] • ASABE Foundation Engineering Scholarship
American Society of Agricultural and Biological Engineers Foundation
Administrator, Scholarship Fund, 2950 Niles Road, St. Joseph, MI 49085
Phone: 269-429-0300
Email: awards@asabe.org
http://www.asabe.org
Purpose: To assist student members of ASABE.
Eligibility: Applicants must have completed at least one year of undergraduate study and have at least one year of undergraduate study remaining, major in agricultural or biological engineering at an eligible accredited degree program in the U.S. or Canada, have a minimum 2.5 GPA and demonstrate financial need. Students must also be members of ASABE.
Target applicant(s): College students. Adult students.
Minimum GPA: 2.5
Amount: $1,000.
Number of awards: 1.
Deadline: March 15.
How to apply: Application is available online.
Exclusive: Visit www.UltimateScholarshipBook.com and enter code AM79926 for updates on this award.

[800] • ASCA/AISC Student Design Competition
Association of Collegiate Schools of Architecture
1735 New York Avenue NW, Washington, DC 20006
Phone: 202-785-2324
Email: eellis@acsa-arch.org
http://www.acsa-arch.org
Purpose: To encourage innovation in architecture.
Eligibility: Applicants must be architecture students at ACSA member schools in the United States, Canada or Mexico and be college juniors, seniors or graduate students. Students must submit a design project on one of the association's featured themes, and they must work under the direction of a faculty sponsor.
Target applicant(s): College students. Graduate school students. Adult students.
Amount: $1,000-$4,000.
Number of awards: 6.
Deadline: April 10.
How to apply: Applications are available online.
Exclusive: Visit www.UltimateScholarshipBook.com and enter code AS80026 for updates on this award.

[801] • ASDSO Senior Undergraduate Scholarship
Association of State Dam Safety Officials
239 South Limestone Street, Lexington, KY 40508
Phone: 859-550-2788 x 6
Email: info@damsafety.org
https://damsafety.org/apply-scholarship
Purpose: To increase awareness of careers in dam safety.
Eligibility: Applicants must be U.S. citizens who will be full-time seniors in the following school year in an accredited civil engineering program or a related field and show an interest in a career related to dam design, construction or operation. Students must have a minimum 2.5 GPA for the first three years of college, be recommended by their academic advisor and write an essay on what ASDSO is and why dam safety is important. Selection is based on academic achievement, financial need, work experience and activities and essay.
Target applicant(s): College students. Adult students.
Minimum GPA: 2.5
Amount: Up to $20,000.
Number of awards: Varies.
Deadline: March 25.
How to apply: Applications are available online.
Exclusive: Visit www.UltimateScholarshipBook.com and enter code AS80126 for updates on this award.

[802] • ASEV Scholarships
American Society for Enology and Viticulture
P.O. Box 1855, Davis, CA 95617-1855
Phone: 530-753-3142
Email: society@asev.org
http://www.asev.org
Purpose: To support those seeking a degree in enology, viticulture or in a curriculum focusing on a science basic to the wine and grape industry.
Eligibility: Applicants must be undergraduate or graduate students enrolled in or accepted into a full-time accredited four-year university program and must reside in North America (Canada, Mexico or the U.S.). Undergraduate students must be at least juniors for the upcoming academic year and have a minimum 3.0 GPA. Graduate students must have a minimum 3.2 GPA. Applicants must be enrolled in a major or in a graduate group concentrating on enology or viticulture or in a curriculum with a focus on a science basic to the wine and grape industry. The application, transcripts and two letters of recommendation are required.
Target applicant(s): College students. Graduate school students. Adult students.
Minimum GPA: 3.0 for undergraduate students; 3.2 for graduate students
Amount: Varies.
Number of awards: Varies.
Deadline: March 1.
How to apply: Applications are available online, by phone or by email.
Exclusive: Visit www.UltimateScholarshipBook.com and enter code AM80226 for updates on this award.

[803] • ASF Olin Fellowships
Atlantic Salmon Federation
P.O. Box 807, Calais, ME 04619-0807
Phone: 506-529-1033
Email: asfweb@nbnet.nb.ca
http://www.asf.ca
Purpose: To help fund projects that focus on solving problems in Atlantic salmon biology, management and conservation.
Eligibility: Applicants must be studying or actively engaged in salmon management or research. The award is open to U.S. and Canadian applicants.
Target applicant(s): College students. Graduate school students. Adult students.
Amount: $1,000-$3,000.
Number of awards: Varies.
Deadline: March 15.

How to apply: Applications are available by mail.
Exclusive: Visit www.UltimateScholarshipBook.com and enter code AT80326 for updates on this award.

[804] • ASHA Youth Scholarships
American Saddlebred Horse Association Foundation
4083 Iron Works Parkway, Lexington, KY 40511
Phone: 859-259-2742
Email: s.geller@asha.net
https://www.saddlebred.com/about-ashba-giving/grants-scholarships/youth-scholarships
Purpose: To help youths involved with Saddlebreds.
Eligibility: This award is based on academic excellence, financial need, extracurricular activities, community service, involvement with American Saddlebred horses and personal references. An interview may be part of the selection process. Applicants should write an essay about school experiences, special interests, hobbies and American Saddlebred Horse Association activities. Scholarships are given only to high school seniors or recent graduates.
Target applicant(s): High school students.
Amount: Varies.
Number of awards: Varies.
Deadline: June 1.
How to apply: Applications are available online.
Exclusive: Visit www.UltimateScholarshipBook.com and enter code AM80426 for updates on this award.

[805] • ASHRAE Engineering Technology Scholarships
American Society of Heating, Refrigerating and Air-Conditioning Engineers (ASHRAE)
Scholarship Administrator, ASHRAE Inc., 180 Technology Parkway, Peachtree Corners, GA 30092
Phone: 404-636-8400
Email: lbenedict@ashrae.org
https://www.ashrae.org/communities/student-zone/scholarships-and-grants
Purpose: To support students who are interested in pursuing a career in engineering or technology.
Eligibility: Applicants must be full-time undergraduate students pursuing a bachelor's or associate's degree in an engineering or engineering technology program, have a cumulative GPA of 3.0 and be a student member of ASHRAE. Selection is based on the overall strength of the application.
Target applicant(s): College students. Adult students.
Minimum GPA: 3.0
Amount: $5,000-$10,000.
Number of awards: 5.
Scholarship may be renewable.
Deadline: December 1.
How to apply: Applications are available online.
Exclusive: Visit www.UltimateScholarshipBook.com and enter code AM80526 for updates on this award.

[806] • ASHRAE Society Scholarship Program
American Society of Heating, Refrigerating and Air-Conditioning Engineers (ASHRAE)
Scholarship Administrator, ASHRAE Inc., 180 Technology Parkway, Peachtree Corners, GA 30092
Phone: 404-636-8400
Email: lbenedict@ashrae.org
https://www.ashrae.org/communities/student-zone/scholarships-and-grants
Purpose: To support undergraduate students enrolled in an engineering or engineering technology program recognized by ASHRAE.
Eligibility: Applicants must be enrolled full-time in an accredited undergraduate engineering or engineering technology program recognized by ASHRAE. Students must maintain a GPA of no less than 3.0, demonstrate financial need and show a potential service to the HVAC&R profession. Applicants must also meet at least one of three criteria: undergraduate institution hosts a recognized ASHRAE student branch, program of study is accredited by the Accreditation Board for Engineering and Technology (ABET), program of study is accredited by an agency outside the USA that is a signatory of the Washington Accord or has a signed Memorandum of Understanding with ABET.
Target applicant(s): High school students. College students. Adult students.
Minimum GPA: 3.0
Amount: $3,000-$10,000.
Number of awards: 1.
Scholarship may be renewable.
Deadline: December 1.
How to apply: Applications are available online.
Exclusive: Visit www.UltimateScholarshipBook.com and enter code AM80626 for updates on this award.

[807] • ASLA Council of Fellows Scholarships
Landscape Architecture Foundation
1200 17th Street NW, Suite 210, Washington, DC 20036
Phone: 202-331-7070
Email: scholarships@lafoundation.org
https://www.lafoundation.org/what-we-do/scholarships
Purpose: To encourage students who are financially needy or who are from underrepresented groups to pursue careers in landscape architecture.
Eligibility: Applicants must be U.S. citizens or permanent residents. They must be in the third, fourth or fifth year of a Landscape Architecture Accreditation Board (LAAB)-accredited undergraduate degree program in landscape architecture. Selection is based on the overall strength of the application.
Target applicant(s): College students. Adult students.
Amount: $5,000-$10,000.
Number of awards: Up to 4.
Deadline: February 1.
How to apply: Applications are available online. An application form, personal essay, two recommendation letters, financial aid information and an applicant photo are required.
Exclusive: Visit www.UltimateScholarshipBook.com and enter code LA80726 for updates on this award.

[808] • ASME Auxiliary Lucy and Charles W. E. Clarke Scholarship
American Society of Mechanical Engineers (ASME)
Two Park Avenue, New York, NY 10016-5990
Phone: 800-843-2763
Email: lefeverb@asme.org
https://www.asme.org/asme-programs/students-and-faculty/scholarships/scholarships
Purpose: To help FIRST Robotics team members who are interested in pursuing a career in mechanical engineering or mechanical engineering technology.

Eligibility: Applicants must be high school seniors who are FIRST Robotics team members. They must be nominated for the award by an ASME member, an ASME Auxiliary member or a student ASME member who is also involved with FIRST. Students must plan to enroll in an ABET-accredited or similarly accredited mechanical engineering or mechanical engineering technology degree program. They must be able to begin undergraduate studies no later than the fall following graduation from high school. Selection is based on the overall strength of the application.
Target applicant(s): High school students.
Amount: $7,000.
Number of awards: 10.
Deadline: March 15.
How to apply: Applications are available online. An application form, nomination letter, resume or transcript and financial data worksheet are required.
Exclusive: Visit www.UltimateScholarshipBook.com and enter code AM80826 for updates on this award.

[809] • ASME Foundation Scholarships
American Society of Mechanical Engineers (ASME)
Two Park Avenue, New York, NY 10016-5990
Phone: 800-843-2763
Email: lefeverb@asme.org
https://www.asme.org/asme-programs/students-and-faculty/scholarships/scholarships
Purpose: To aid ASME student members who are enrolled in an undergraduate mechanical engineering, mechanical engineering technology or related degree program.
Eligibility: Applicants must be current ASME student members who are currently enrolled in (or have been accepted into) an ABET-accredited (or similarly accredited) undergraduate degree program in mechanical engineering, mechanical engineering technology or a subject related to one of these. They must be rising or current sophomores, juniors or seniors with a minimum 3.5 GPA. Selection is based on academic achievement and professional potential in engineering.
Target applicant(s): College students. Adult students.
Minimum GPA: 3.5
Amount: $11,000.
Number of awards: 1.
Deadline: March 1.
How to apply: Applications are available online through an electronic application system. Current ASME membership, submittal of application through the online system, a transcript and recommendation letters are required.
Exclusive: Visit www.UltimateScholarshipBook.com and enter code AM80926 for updates on this award.

[810] • ASNE Scholarship Program
American Society of Naval Engineers
1423 Powhatan Street, Suite 1, Alexandria, VA 22314
Phone: 703-836-6727
Email: Scholarships@navalengineers.org
http://www.navalengineers.org/Education
Purpose: To encourage college students to enter the field of naval engineering and to provide support to naval engineers pursuing advanced education.
Eligibility: Applications must be for the last year of a full-time or co-op undergraduate program or for one year of full-time graduate study for a designated engineering or physical science degree at an accredited school. Applicants must be U.S. citizens pursuing careers in naval engineering. Graduate student applicants must be members of ASNE. An applicant's academic record, work history, professional promise and interest, extracurricular activities and recommendations are considered. Financial need may be considered.
Target applicant(s): College students. Graduate school students. Adult students.
Amount: Up to $4,000.
Number of awards: Varies.
Deadline: February 12.
How to apply: Applications are available online or by written request.
Exclusive: Visit www.UltimateScholarshipBook.com and enter code AM81026 for updates on this award.

[811] • ASNT Fellowship
American Society for Nondestructive Testing
Awards and Honors Program, 1201 Dublin Road, Suite #G04, Columbus, OH 43215
Phone: 614-274-6003 x 233
Email: awards@asnt.org
http://www.asnt.org
Purpose: To fund research in nondestructive testing.
Eligibility: The award is given to an educational institution to fund research in nondestructive testing (NDT) at the postgraduate level. One proposal per faculty member will be considered annually. Applicants should submit a research proposal, a program of study, description of facilities, budget, background on faculty advisor, and background on a graduate student.
Target applicant(s): Graduate school students. Adult students.
Amount: $20,000.
Number of awards: Up to 5.
Deadline: January 31.
How to apply: Applications are available online.
Exclusive: Visit www.UltimateScholarshipBook.com and enter code AM81126 for updates on this award.

[812] • Association of Federal Communications Consulting Engineers Scholarships
Association of Federal Communications Consulting Engineers
P.O. Box 19333, Washington, DC 20036-0333
Phone: 703-780-4824
Email: scholarships@afcce.org
https://afcce.org/scholarships/
Purpose: To aid full-time undergraduate students attending an accredited college or university in pursuit of a degree in a telecommunications-related subject.
Eligibility: Applicants must be full-time (12+ units per semester) undergraduate or graduate students at an accredited postsecondary institution. They must be rising juniors or above and must be enrolled in a subject that is related to the radio communications consulting engineering field. They are encouraged to acquire an AFCCE member who will act as a sponsor. Selection is based on the overall strength of the application.
Target applicant(s): College students. Graduate school students. Adult students.
Amount: Up to $2,500.
Number of awards: Varies.
Deadline: May 31 (Fall); October 31 (Spring).
How to apply: Applications are available online. An application form, transcript, personal statement and sponsorship by an AFCCE member are required.
Exclusive: Visit www.UltimateScholarshipBook.com and enter code AS81226 for updates on this award.

[813] • Association of Food and Drug Officials Scholarship Award

Association of Food and Drug Officials
155 West Market Street, 3rd Floor, York, PA 17401
Phone: 717-757-2888
Email: afdo@afdo.org
http://www.afdo.org
Purpose: To support college students who are studying food, drug or consumer product safety.
Eligibility: Applicants must be in their third or fourth year of college at an accredited institution and demonstrate a desire to work in a career of research, regulatory work, quality control or teaching in an area related to food, drug or consumer product safety. Applicants must also have demonstrated leadership capabilities, a minimum 3.0 GPA and submit two letters of recommendation from faculty.
Target applicant(s): College students. Adult students.
Minimum GPA: 3.0
Amount: $2,500.
Number of awards: 3.
Deadline: March 31.
How to apply: Applications are available online.
Exclusive: Visit www.UltimateScholarshipBook.com and enter code AS81326 for updates on this award.

[814] • Association of Information Technology Professionals (AITP) Scholarships

Association of Information Technology Professionals (AITP) Scholarships
P.O. Box 583, Omaha, NE 68101
Email: omahaAITP@gmail.com
http://www.aitpomaha.com/scholarship-information.html
Purpose: To support students pursuing information systems and technology education.
Eligibility: Applicants must be enrolling in or currently enrolled in an accredited two- or four-year program in Nebraska, Iowa, Missouri, Kansas, North Dakota or South Dakota with the intent of earning a degree in information systems, computer science or related field.
Target applicant(s): High school students. College students. Adult students.
Amount: $1,000.
Number of awards: Varies.
Deadline: June 1.
How to apply: Applications are available online.
Exclusive: Visit www.UltimateScholarshipBook.com and enter code AS81426 for updates on this award.

[815] • ASTM International Katherine and Bryant Mather Scholarship

ASTM International
100 Barr Harbor Drive, P.O. Box C700, West Conshohocken, PA 19428-2959
Phone: 610-832-9585
Email: awards@astm.org
https://www.astm.org/member-student.html
Purpose: To aid students who are enrolled in degree programs that are related to the cement and concrete technology industry.
Eligibility: Applicants must be full-time undergraduate sophomores, undergraduate juniors, undergraduate seniors or graduate students. They must be enrolled in a degree program that is related to cement construction or concrete materials technology at an accredited institution of higher learning. Selection is based on the overall strength of the application.
Target applicant(s): College students. Graduate school students. Adult students.
Amount: Up to $7,500.
Number of awards: Varies.
Scholarship may be renewable.
Deadline: April 30.
How to apply: Applications are available online. An application form, one reference letter, an official transcript and a personal statement are required.
Exclusive: Visit www.UltimateScholarshipBook.com and enter code AS81526 for updates on this award.

[816] • Astronaut Scholarship

Astronaut Scholarship Foundation
Kennedy Space Center, SR 405, Titusville, FL 32899
Phone: 321-449-4876
Email: info@astronautscholarship.org
http://www.astronautscholarship.org
Purpose: To ensure the United States' continued leadership in science by assisting promising physical science and engineering students.
Eligibility: Applicants must be sophomore, junior or senior undergraduate or graduate students in natural or applied science, engineering or mathematics at Brown University, Colorado School of Mines, Clemson University, Florida Institute of Technology, Georgia Institute of Technology, Harvey Mudd College, Johns Hopkins University, Louisiana State University, Massachusetts Institute of Technology, Miami University, North Carolina State University, North Dakota State University, Ohio State, Pennsylvania State University, Purdue University, Syracuse University, Texas A&M University, Tufts University, University of Arizona, University of Central Florida, University of Chicago, University of Colorado, University of Kansas, University of Kentucky, University of Minnesota, University of Michigan, University of Oklahoma, University of Rochester, University of Southern California, University of Texas at Austin, University of Virginia, University of Washington, University of Wisconsin or Washington University and must be nominated by faculty or staff. Applicants may not directly apply for the scholarship. Students must have excellent grades and performed research or lab work in their field.
Target applicant(s): College students. Graduate school students. Adult students.
Amount: $15,000.
Number of awards: More than 60.
Deadline: March 29.
How to apply: Applicants must be nominated.
Exclusive: Visit www.UltimateScholarshipBook.com and enter code AS81626 for updates on this award.

[817] • AUA Foundation Research Scholars Program

American Foundation for Urologic Disease Inc.
1000 Corporate Boulevard, Linthicum, MD 21090
Phone: 410-689-3750
Email: grants@auafoundation.org
https://www.urologyhealth.org/research/for-researchers
Purpose: To help young men and women who intend to pursue careers in urologic research.
Eligibility: Applicants must be researchers who conduct their research in the U.S. or Canada. Funding is provided for post-doctoral research only.
Target applicant(s): Graduate school students. Adult students.
Amount: $40,000.
Number of awards: Varies.

Deadline: December 13.
How to apply: Applications are available online.
Exclusive: Visit www.UltimateScholarshipBook.com and enter code AM81726 for updates on this award.

[818] • Automotive Hall of Fame Scholarships

Automotive Hall of Fame
Award and Scholarship Programs, 21400 Oakwood Boulevard, Dearborn, MI 48124
Phone: 313-240-4000
http://www.automotivehalloffame.org/scholarships/
Purpose: To assist students interested in automotive careers.
Eligibility: Applicants must be interested in automotive careers. Other requirements vary depending on the specific scholarship. Minimum GPA of 3.0 required.
Target applicant(s): High school students. College students. Adult students.
Minimum GPA: 3.0
Amount: Varies.
Number of awards: Varies.
Deadline: June 30.
How to apply: Applications are available online or by sending a self-addressed, stamped envelope.
Exclusive: Visit www.UltimateScholarshipBook.com and enter code AU81826 for updates on this award.

[819] • Auxiliary Legacy Scholarship

National Society of Professional Engineers
1420 King Street, Alexandria, VA 22314-2794
Phone: 888-285-6773
Email: students@nspe.org
https://www.nspe.org/resources/students/scholarships
Purpose: To aid female students who want to major in engineering.
Eligibility: Applicants must be female college sophomores majoring in engineering. Applicants must be U.S. citizens. Selection is based only on achievement.
Target applicant(s): College students. Adult students.
Amount: $5,000.
Number of awards: 1.
Scholarship may be renewable.
Deadline: April 1.
How to apply: Applications are available online.
Exclusive: Visit www.UltimateScholarshipBook.com and enter code NA81926 for updates on this award.

[820] • Avacare Medical Scholarship

Avacare Medical
1665 Corporate Road West, Lakewood, NJ 08701
Phone: 877-813-7799
Email: scholarships@avacaremedical.com
https://avacaremedical.com/scholarship
Purpose: To reward students who participate in inspiring acts of kindness.
Eligibility: Applicants must be at least 13 years of age, have a minimum 3.0 GPA and be U.S. citizens. Students must be studying or planning on studying a medicine-related field. Students must be at least high school seniors. Selection is based on judges' scores as well as public votes. Submissions may be a blog post, an image or a short video clip and should describe an inspiring act of kindness. Finalists are selected based on content, creativity and quality of work.
Target applicant(s): High school students. College students. Graduate school students. Adult students.
Minimum GPA: 3.0
Amount: $1,000.
Number of awards: 1.
Deadline: December 15.
How to apply: A completed project must be mailed or emailed along with a transcript, full name, email address, phone number and which medical field pursuing.
Exclusive: Visit www.UltimateScholarshipBook.com and enter code AV82026 for updates on this award.

[821] • Aviation Distributors and Manufacturers Association Scholarship Program

Aviation Distributors and Manufacturers Association
100 North 20th Street, Suite 400, Philadelphia, PA 19103-1462
Phone: 215-320-3872
Email: adma@fernley.com
https://www.adma.org/
Purpose: To help students who are planning to pursue careers in aviation.
Eligibility: Applicants must be third- or fourth-year students enrolled at an accredited four-year institution of higher learning and working towards the Bachelor of Science (BS) in aviation management or professional piloting, or must be second-year A&P mechanic students enrolled in an accredited two-year program. They must have a minimum GPA of 3.0. Selection is based on academic achievement, recommendation letters, extracurricular activities, leadership skills and financial need.
Target applicant(s): College students. Adult students.
Minimum GPA: 3.0
Amount: Varies.
Number of awards: Varies.
Deadline: April 22.
How to apply: Applications are available online. An application form, two recommendation letters, a transcript and a personal statement are required.
Exclusive: Visit www.UltimateScholarshipBook.com and enter code AV82126 for updates on this award.

[822] • Aviation Insurance Association Education Foundation Scholarship

Aviation Insurance Association
7200 W. 75th Street, Overland Park, KS 66204
Phone: 913-627-9632
Email: mandie@aiaweb.org
https://aiaweb.org/page/EducationFoundation
Purpose: To help upper division undergraduate aviation students and graduate aviation students.
Eligibility: Applicants must be enrolled in an undergraduate or graduate program in aviation at a school that is a member of the University Aviation Association (UAA). They must have completed at least 45 units of coursework in their degree program, 15 or more of which must be for aviation courses. They must have a GPA of 2.5 or higher. Students must also currently be an intern or recently have completed an internship program within the aviation insurance industry in one of the following areas: agent/broker, underwriter, claims professional or attorney. Awards are given in the spring and fall.
Target applicant(s): College students. Graduate school students. Adult students.
Minimum GPA: 2.5
Amount: $2,500.
Number of awards: 4.

Deadline: Contact the sponsor to confirm the deadline.
How to apply: Applications are available online. Five sets of the following items are required: application form, personal statement, transcript, one letter of recommendation and any FAA certificates (if applicable).
Exclusive: Visit www.UltimateScholarshipBook.com and enter code AV82226 for updates on this award.

[823] • Baroid Scholarship
American Ground Water Trust
50 Pleasant Street, Suite 2, Concord, NH 03301
Phone: 603-228-5444
Email: trustinfo@agwt.org
https://agwt.org/scholarships/
Purpose: To support high school seniors intending to pursue a career in a groundwater-related field.
Eligibility: Applicants must be high school seniors entering an accredited four-year college or university and intending to pursue a career in a ground water-related field.
Target applicant(s): High school students.
Minimum GPA: 3.0
Amount: $2,000.
Number of awards: Varies.
Deadline: June 30.
How to apply: Applications are available online.
Exclusive: Visit www.UltimateScholarshipBook.com and enter code AM82326 for updates on this award.

[824] • Barry M. Goldwater Scholarship and Excellence in Education Program
Barry M. Goldwater Scholarship and Excellence in Education Foundation
6225 Brandon Avenue, Suite 315, Springfield, VA 22150
Phone: 703-756-6012
Email: goldwater@act.org
http://goldwater.scholarsapply.org
Purpose: To assist college students who pursue studies that lead to careers as scientists, mathematicians and engineers.
Eligibility: Applicants must be full-time college sophomores or juniors, U.S. citizens or resident aliens, have a minimum "B" GPA and be in the upper fourth of their class. Award must be used during the junior or senior year of college. Selection is based on potential and intent to pursue careers in mathematics, the natural sciences or engineering.
Target applicant(s): College students. Adult students.
Minimum GPA: 3.0
Amount: Up to $7,500.
Number of awards: Up to 300.
Deadline: January (last Friday).
How to apply: Institutions nominate college sophomores or juniors. Applicants may not apply directly to the foundation.
Exclusive: Visit www.UltimateScholarshipBook.com and enter code BA82426 for updates on this award.

[825] • Battery Division Student Research Award
Electrochemical Society
65 South Main Street, Building D, Pennington, NJ 08534-2839
Phone: 609-737-1902
Email: ecs@electrochem.org
https://www.electrochem.org/student-awards
Purpose: To recognize young engineers and scientists in the field of electrochemical power sources.
Eligibility: Applicants must be accepted or enrolled in a college or university and must submit transcripts, an outline of the proposed research project, a description of how the project is related to the field of electrochemical power sources, a record of achievements in industrial work and a letter of recommendation from the research supervisor. Awards are based on academic performance, past research, proposed research and the recommendation.
Target applicant(s): High school students. College students. Graduate school students. Adult students.
Amount: $1,000.
Number of awards: Varies.
Deadline: January 15.
How to apply: Application materials are described online.
Exclusive: Visit www.UltimateScholarshipBook.com and enter code EL82526 for updates on this award.

[826] • Beef Industry Scholarship
National Cattlemen's Foundation
9110 East Nichols Avenue, Suite 300, Centennial, CO 80112
Phone: 303-694-0305
Email: ncf@beef.org
https://www.nationalcattlemensfoundation.org/scholarships
Purpose: To aid students who are preparing for careers in the beef industry.
Eligibility: Applicants must be graduating high school seniors or college undergraduates, and they must have plans to be enrolled full-time in a two-year or four-year undergraduate program during the upcoming academic year. They must be enrolled in a beef industry-related program of study and have a demonstrated interest in pursuing a career in the beef industry through previous coursework taken, internships completed or other life experiences. They or their families must be members of the National Cattlemen's Beef Association. Selection is based on the strength of the essay, letter of intent and reference letters.
Target applicant(s): High school students. College students. Adult students.
Amount: $1,500.
Number of awards: 10.
Scholarship may be renewable.
Deadline: November 8.
How to apply: Applications are available online. An application form, letter of intent, personal essay and two reference letters are required.
Exclusive: Visit www.UltimateScholarshipBook.com and enter code NA82626 for updates on this award.

[827] • Bill Kane Scholarship, Undergraduate
Shape America
225, Annapolis Junction, , MD 20701
Phone: 800-213-7193
https://www.shapeamerica.org
Purpose: To support health education students.
Eligibility: Applicants must be full-time undergraduate health majors in their sophomore, junior or senior years. They must have a GPA of at least 3.25 and write an essay about what they hope to accomplish as a health educator.
Target applicant(s): College students. Adult students.
Minimum GPA: 3.25
Amount: $1,000.
Number of awards: 1.
Deadline: October 15.
How to apply: Applications are available online.

Exclusive: Visit www.UltimateScholarshipBook.com and enter code SH82726 for updates on this award.

[828] • Biographies of Contemporary Women in Mathematics Essay Contest
Association for Women in Mathematics
P.O. Box 40876, Providence, RI 02940
Phone: 401-455-4042
Email: awm@awm-math.org
http://www.awm-math.org
Purpose: To increase awareness of women's contributions to the mathematical sciences.
Eligibility: Applicants must interview a woman working in a mathematical career and write an essay based on the interview. Applicants may be from the sixth grade to graduate school students.
Target applicant(s): Junior high students or younger. High school students. College students. Adult students.
Amount: Varies.
Number of awards: At least 3.
Deadline: February 1.
How to apply: Applications are available online and must be submitted online.
Exclusive: Visit www.UltimateScholarshipBook.com and enter code AS82826 for updates on this award.

[829] • BMW/SAE Engineering Scholarship
Society of Automotive Engineers International
Scholarships Program, 400 Commonwealth Drive, Warrendale, PA 15096
Phone: 724-776-4841
Email: scholarships@sae.org
https://www.sae.org/participate/scholarships
Purpose: To support engineering students with high potential.
Eligibility: Applicants must be U.S. citizens with a GPA of 3.75 or higher. They must rank in the 90th percentile in math and critical reading on the SAT or ACT and must pursue an engineering or related degree through an ABET-accredited program.
Target applicant(s): High school students.
Minimum GPA: 3.75
Amount: $1,500.
Number of awards: 1.
Scholarship may be renewable.
Deadline: February 28.
How to apply: Applications are available online. An application form, transcript and SAT/ACT scores are required.
Exclusive: Visit www.UltimateScholarshipBook.com and enter code SO82926 for updates on this award.

[830] • Brill Family Scholarship
Society of Women Engineers
130 East Randolph Street, Suite 3500, Chicago, IL 60601
Phone: 877-793-4636
Email: scholarships@swe.org
https://swe.org/scholarships/
Purpose: To encourage women advancing in the field of engineering through a college education.
Eligibility: Applicants must have a minimum 3.0 GPA and be full-time students. Students must be U.S. citizens and plan to study at an ABET-accredited aeronautical/aerospace engineering or biomedical engineering program.
Target applicant(s): College students. Adult students.
Minimum GPA: 3.0
Amount: $3,000.
Number of awards: 1.
Deadline: January 31.
How to apply: Applications are available online.
Exclusive: Visit www.UltimateScholarshipBook.com and enter code SO83026 for updates on this award.

[831] • Bryant L. Bench Carollo Engineers Inc. Scholarship
American Water Works Association
6666 W. Quincy Avenue, Denver, CO 80235
Phone: 800-926-7337
Email: scholarships@awwa.org
https://www.awwa.org
Purpose: To support masters-level students interested in water-energy nexus within the water industry.
Eligibility: Applicants must be pursuing a master's degree. They must also have an interest in water-energy nexus issues in relation to water, water reuse or wastewater. This is a one-time award. Selection is based on the overall strength of the application.
Target applicant(s): College students. Graduate school students. Adult students.
Amount: $10,000.
Number of awards: 1.
Deadline: December 20.
How to apply: Applications are available online.
Exclusive: Visit www.UltimateScholarshipBook.com and enter code AM83126 for updates on this award.

[832] • BSN Scholarship
Association of Rehabilitation Nurses
8735 W. Higgins Road, Suite 300, Chicago, IL 60631-2738
Phone: 800-229-7530
Email: info@rehabnurse.org
https://rehabnurse.org/membership/recognition/scholarship-opportunities
Purpose: To help nurses pursuing a bachelor's of science in nursing.
Eligibility: Applicants must be members of and involved in ARN, enrolled in a bachelor's of science in nursing (BSN) program, have completed at least one course, be currently practicing rehabilitation nursing and have a minimum of two years experience in rehabilitation nursing. Applications, transcripts, a summary of professional and educational goals and achievements and two recommendation letters are required. Applications should be submitted by fax or email.
Target applicant(s): College students. Adult students.
Amount: $1,500.
Number of awards: Varies.
Deadline: June 1.
How to apply: Applications are available online.
Exclusive: Visit www.UltimateScholarshipBook.com and enter code AS83226 for updates on this award.

The Ultimate Scholarship Book 2026
Scholarship Directory (Sciences)

[833] • C.B. Gambrell Undergraduate Scholarship
Institute of Industrial and Systems Engineers
3577 Parkway Lane, Suite 200, Norcross, GA 30092
Phone: 800-494-0460
Email: egrimes@iise.org
https://www.iise.org
Purpose: To help undergraduate industrial engineering students from the U.S.
Eligibility: Applicants must be full-time undergraduate students who have completed their freshman year in an accredited industrial engineering program, have a minimum 3.4 GPA, major in industrial engineering and be active members. Students may not apply directly for this scholarship and must be nominated. The award is based on academic ability, character, leadership, potential service to the industrial engineering profession and financial need.
Target applicant(s): College students. Adult students.
Minimum GPA: 3.4
Amount: $1,000.
Number of awards: 2.
Deadline: February 1.
How to apply: Nomination forms are available online.
Exclusive: Visit www.UltimateScholarshipBook.com and enter code IN83326 for updates on this award.

[834] • Campus Safety Health and Environmental Management Association Scholarship
Campus Safety Health, and Environmental Management Association (CSHEMA)
Scholarship Committee, 7044 South 13th Street, Oak Creek, WI 53154
Phone: 703-234-4141
Email: info@cshema.org
https://www.cshema.org
Purpose: To encourage the study of safety.
Eligibility: Applicants must be full-time undergraduate or graduate students with at least one year left in their degree program. Applicants must also write an essay about health, safety or environmental issues relevant to the university or college campus.
Target applicant(s): High school students. College students. Adult students.
Amount: $3,000.
Number of awards: 1.
Deadline: March 1.
How to apply: Applications are available online.
Exclusive: Visit www.UltimateScholarshipBook.com and enter code CA83426 for updates on this award.

[835] • Careers in Agriculture Scholarship Program
Winfield Solutions LLC
Careers in Agriculture - MS 5735, P.O. Box 64281, St. Paul, MN 55164-0281
Phone: 855-494-6343
Email: info@winfieldsolutionsllc.com
https://learnmore.scholarsapply.org/winfield/
Purpose: To aid high school seniors and college freshmen and sophomores who are interested in pursuing a career in agriculture.
Eligibility: Applicants must be high school seniors who plan to enroll in a two-year or four-year degree program related to agriculture in the fall following graduation or first- or second-year college students pursuing degrees in agronomy, crop production or related fields. Dependents of employees of Winfield Solutions LLC or Land O' Lakes Inc. are ineligible. Selection is based on academic achievement, proven leadership in agriculture and professional interest in the field of agriculture.
Target applicant(s): High school students. College students. Adult students.
Amount: $5,000.
Number of awards: 4.
Deadline: April 17.
How to apply: Applications are available online. An application form, two character evaluations, a transcript and a personal essay are required.
Exclusive: Visit www.UltimateScholarshipBook.com and enter code WI83526 for updates on this award.

[836] • Carville M. Akehurst Memorial Scholarship
Horticultural Research Institute
80 M Street SE, Washington, DC 20003
Phone: 202-789-2900
https://www.hriresearch.org/scholarships
Purpose: To provide scholarships for undergraduate and graduate students who plan to pursue careers in horticulture.
Eligibility: Applicants must be enrolled full-time in a landscaping or horticultural program at a two- or four-year accredited institution and be residents of Maryland, Virginia or West Virginia.
Target applicant(s): College students. Graduate school students. Adult students.
Minimum GPA: 2.7
Amount: Up to $3,500.
Number of awards: 1.
Scholarship may be renewable.
Deadline: May 31.
How to apply: Applications are available online.
Exclusive: Visit www.UltimateScholarshipBook.com and enter code HO83626 for updates on this award.

[837] • Cedarcrest Farms Scholarship
American Jersey Cattle Association
6486 East Main Street, Reynoldsburg, OH 43068-2362
Phone: 614-861-3636
Email: info@usjersey.com
http://www.usjersey.com
Purpose: To aid American Jersey Cattle Association members studying dairy product marketing, large animal veterinary practice, dairy manufacturing or dairy production.
Eligibility: Applicants must be AJCA members studying dairy manufacturing, dairy product marketing, dairy production or large animal veterinary practice at the undergraduate or graduate level. They must have a GPA of 2.5 or above and must plan to pursue a career in agriculture. Selection is based on the overall strength of the application.
Target applicant(s): College students. Graduate school students. Adult students.
Minimum GPA: 2.5
Amount: $1,250.
Number of awards: Varies.
Deadline: July 3.
How to apply: Applications are available online. An application form, transcript and up to two letters of recommendation are required.
Exclusive: Visit www.UltimateScholarshipBook.com and enter code AM83726 for updates on this award.

[838] • Charles H. Bussmann Undergraduate Scholarship

Marine Technology Society
One Thomas Circle, Suite 700, Washington, DC 20005
Phone: 202-717-8705
Email: scholarships@mtsociety.org
https://www.mtsociety.org/scholarships
Purpose: To support Marine Technology Society members who are pursuing an undergraduate degree in a marine-related field.
Eligibility: Applicants must be MTS student members who are accepted for enrollment or enrolled full-time at an educational institution. Selection is based on the overall strength of the application.
Target applicant(s): High school students. College students. Adult students.
Amount: $2,500.
Number of awards: 1.
Deadline: April 15.
How to apply: Applications are available online.
Exclusive: Visit www.UltimateScholarshipBook.com and enter code MA83826 for updates on this award.

[839] • Charlotte McGuire Scholarship

American Holistic Nurses Association
AHNA Office Manager, 2900 SW Plass Court, Topeka, KS 66611-1980
Phone: 800-278-2462 x10
Email: info@ahna.org
http://www.ahna.org
Purpose: To provide scholarships to nurses in undergraduate or graduate nursing programs or other graduate programs related to holistic nursing.
Eligibility: Applicants must be pursuing an education in holistic nursing and be members of the AHNA. Applicants must have a minimum 3.0 GPA.
Target applicant(s): College students. Graduate school students. Adult students.
Minimum GPA: 3.0
Amount: $1,250.
Number of awards: 2.
Deadline: April 15.
How to apply: Applications are available online or from AHNA Headquarters.
Exclusive: Visit www.UltimateScholarshipBook.com and enter code AM83926 for updates on this award.

[840] • ChiroHealthUSA Foxworth Family Scholarship

ChiroHealthUSA
120 Stone Creek Boulevard, Suite 100, Flowood, MS 39232
https://www.chirohealthusa.com/students/foxworth-family-scholarship/
Purpose: To support students studying chiropractic health.
Eligibility: Applicants must be full-time students enrolled in a doctorate of chiropractic program at an accredited U.S. institution and hold a minimum 2.7 GPA. Students must provide two recommendations along with their application.
Target applicant(s): Graduate school students. Adult students.
Minimum GPA: 2.7
Amount: $15,000.
Number of awards: 1.
Deadline: March 30.
How to apply: Applications are available online.
Exclusive: Visit www.UltimateScholarshipBook.com and enter code CH84026 for updates on this award.

[841] • Colgate Bright Smiles, Bright Futures Minority Scholarships

American Dental Hygienists' Association (ADHA) Institute for Oral Health
444 North Michigan Avenue, Suite 400, Chicago, IL 60611
Phone: 312-440-8900
Email: institute@adha.net
https://www.adha.org/ioh/scholarships/
Purpose: To support members of groups underrepresented in dental hygiene programs.
Eligibility: Applicants must have completed one year of an accredited dental hygiene curriculum and be a member of a group that is underrepresented in the field of dental hygiene. Examples of eligible groups include African American, Hispanic, Asian, Native American and male students. Applicants must also demonstrate financial need of at least $1,500, be active members of SADHA or ADHA and submit a goals statement.
Target applicant(s): College students. Adult students.
Amount: $1,250.
Number of awards: Varies.
Deadline: February 2.
How to apply: Applications are available online.
Exclusive: Visit www.UltimateScholarshipBook.com and enter code AM84126 for updates on this award.

[842] • Collegiate Inventors Competition

National Inventors Hall of Fame
3701 Highland Park NW, North Canton, OH 44720
Phone: 330-849-6887
Email: collegiate@invent.org
http://www.invent.org
Purpose: To encourage college students in science, engineering, mathematics, technology and creative invention and to stimulate interest in technology and economic leadership.
Eligibility: Applicants must have been full-time college or university students during part of the 12-month period prior to the entry date. Up to four students may work as a team, and at least one student must meet the full-time criteria. Judging is based on originality and inventiveness, as well as the invention's potential value to society.
Target applicant(s): College students. Graduate school students. Adult students.
Amount: Varies.
Number of awards: Varies.
Deadline: June 1.
How to apply: Applications are available online.
Exclusive: Visit www.UltimateScholarshipBook.com and enter code NA84226 for updates on this award.

The Ultimate Scholarship Book 2026
Scholarship Directory (Sciences)

[843] • Complete Water Solutions Scholarship
Complete Water Solutions
851 West Main Street, Twin Lakes, WI 53181
Phone: 855-787-4200
Email: scholarships@complete-water.com
https://complete-water.com/resources/complete-water-solutions-scholarship
Purpose: To support students who are interested in trades (plumbing, HVAC, boiler operators, electrical), reverse osmosis or water quality.
Eligibility: Applicants must be current or prospective students enrolled in a trade school, water treatment certified training course or an accredited institution in the United States. Students must submit a two- to three-minute video or an essay on a specific subject matter.
Target applicant(s): High school students. College students. Adult students.
Amount: $2,500.
Number of awards: 1.
Deadline: March 1.
How to apply: Applications are available online.
Exclusive: Visit www.UltimateScholarshipBook.com and enter code CO84326 for updates on this award.

[844] • Composites Division/Harold Giles Scholarship
Society of Plastics Engineers
83 Wooster Heights Road Suite 125, Suite 306, Danbury, CT 06810
Phone: 810-986-6131
Email: thomas.miller@ravago.com
https://plasticspioneers.org/scholarships/
Purpose: To aid undergraduate and graduate students who have an interest in the plastics industry.
Eligibility: Applicants must have an interest in the plastics industry, major in or take courses leading to a career in the plastics industry and be in good academic standing. Financial need is considered.
Target applicant(s): College students. Graduate school students. Adult students.
Amount: Varies.
Number of awards: 2.
Deadline: April 30.
How to apply: Applications are available online.
Exclusive: Visit www.UltimateScholarshipBook.com and enter code SO84426 for updates on this award.

[845] • Computational Science Graduate Fellowship
Department of Energy
Krell Institute, 1609 Golden Aspen Drive, Suite 101, Ames, IA 50010
Phone: 515-956-3696
https://www.krellinst.org/csgf/
Purpose: To support students pursuing a Ph.D. in engineering and the physical, computer, mathematical or life sciences.
Eligibility: Applicants must be enrolled at an accredited U.S. college or university during the fellowship period.
Target applicant(s): College students. Graduate school students. Adult students.
Amount: Varies.
Number of awards: Varies.
Scholarship may be renewable.
Deadline: January 16.
How to apply: Applications are available online.
Exclusive: Visit www.UltimateScholarshipBook.com and enter code DE84526 for updates on this award.

[846] • Corrosion Division Morris Cohen Graduate Student Award
Electrochemical Society
65 South Main Street, Building D, Pennington, NJ 08534-2839
Phone: 609-737-1902
Email: ecs@electrochem.org
https://www.electrochem.org/student-awards
Purpose: To recognize graduate research in corrosion science and/or engineering.
Eligibility: Applicants must be graduate students who have completed all the requirements for their degrees within two years prior to the nomination deadline. Nomination may be made by the applicant's research supervisor or someone familiar with the applicant's research work. A summary of the applicant's master's or Ph.D. research work, reports, memberships and involvement with scientific societies, awards, an academic record and reprints of publications are required.
Target applicant(s): Graduate school students. Adult students.
Amount: $2,000.
Number of awards: 1.
Deadline: January 15.
How to apply: Application materials are listed online.
Exclusive: Visit www.UltimateScholarshipBook.com and enter code EL84626 for updates on this award.

[847] • Creative Biolabs Scholarship
Creative Biolabs
45 Ramsey Road, Shirley, NY 11967
Phone: 631-871-5806
Email: marketing@creative-biolabs.com
https://www.creative-biolabs.com/scholarship-program.html
Purpose: To support students pursuing medical and science-related education.
Eligibility: Applicants must be enrolled as a freshman, undergraduate, graduate or doctoral student at an accredited college or university. Students must be pursuing a major in a science-related field. Applicants must have a cumulative grade point average of 3.0 or higher. Students must submit an application, a transcript and an essay. Selection criteria include GPA, learning plan, leadership ability and social concerns.
Target applicant(s): College students. Graduate school students. Adult students.
Minimum GPA: 3.0
Amount: $1,000.
Number of awards: 1.
Deadline: September 30.
How to apply: Applications are available online.
Exclusive: Visit www.UltimateScholarshipBook.com and enter code CR84726 for updates on this award.

[848] • Crest Oral-B Laboratories Dental Hygiene Scholarships
American Dental Hygienists' Association (ADHA) Institute for Oral Health
444 North Michigan Avenue, Suite 400, Chicago, IL 60611
Phone: 312-440-8900
Email: institute@adha.net
https://www.adha.org/ioh/scholarships/

Purpose: To support students pursuing a baccalaureate degree with an interest in research in dental hygiene as well as private and public dental hygiene education.
Eligibility: Applicants must be full-time students at an accredited college or university in the United States pursuing a baccalaureate degree in dental hygiene or a related field and must have completed at least one year of a dental hygiene curriculum. Applicants must also have a strong interest in pursuing research in dental hygiene and promoting private and public dental hygiene education, be active members of the ADHA, have a minimum dental hygiene GPA of 3.5 and have a minimum demonstrated financial need of $1,500. Selection is based on professional and academic excellence and the overall strength of the application.
Target applicant(s): College students. Adult students.
Amount: $1,000.
Number of awards: Varies.
Deadline: January 31.
How to apply: Applications are available online after October 1.
Exclusive: Visit www.UltimateScholarshipBook.com and enter code AM84826 for updates on this award.

[849] • Cummins Scholarship
Society of Women Engineers
130 East Randolph Street, Suite 3500, Chicago, IL 60601
Phone: 877-793-4636
Email: scholarships@swe.org
https://swe.org/scholarships/
Purpose: To support African-American female college engineering students.
Eligibility: Applicants must be U.S. citizens with a 3.0 GPA, be from an under-represented group and be willing to intern. Students must major in automotive engineering, chemical engineering, computer engineering, computer science, electrical engineering, industrial engineering, mechanical engineering, manufacturing engineering, materials science and engineering, industrial systems, metrology or metallurgy.
Target applicant(s): College students. Adult students.
Minimum GPA: 3.0
Amount: $2,500.
Number of awards: 2.
Deadline: January 23.
How to apply: Applications are available online.
Exclusive: Visit www.UltimateScholarshipBook.com and enter code SO84926 for updates on this award.

[850] • Dairy Student Recognition Program
National Dairy Shrine
P.O. Box 68, Fort Atkinson, WI 53538
Phone: 920-863-6333
Email: info@dairyshrine.org
http://www.dairyshrine.org
Purpose: To recognize graduating college seniors planning careers related to dairy.
Eligibility: Applicants must be U.S. citizens planning to enter the fields such as dairy production agriculture, marketing, agricultural law, business, veterinary medicine or environmental science. Selection is based on leadership skills, academic achievement and interest in dairy cattle.
Target applicant(s): College students. Adult students.
Amount: Up to $2,000.
Number of awards: Varies.
Deadline: April 15.
How to apply: Applications are available online, and two applicants per college or university are accepted each year.
Exclusive: Visit www.UltimateScholarshipBook.com and enter code NA85026 for updates on this award.

[851] • Dan L. Meisinger Sr. Memorial Learn to Fly Scholarship
National Air Transportation Foundation Meisinger Scholarship
818 Connecticut Avenue NW, Suite 900, Washington, DC 20006
Phone: 202-774-1535
Email: safety1st@nata.aero
http://www.nata.aero
Purpose: To provide an annual flight training scholarship.
Eligibility: Applicants must be college students enrolled in an aviation program with a B or better GPA and residents of Kansas, Missouri or Illinois will be given preference. Students should be recommended by an aviation professional; independent applications are also considered.
Target applicant(s): College students. Graduate school students. Adult students.
Minimum GPA: 3.0
Amount: $2,500.
Number of awards: Varies.
Deadline: Last Friday in November.
How to apply: Applications are available online.
Exclusive: Visit www.UltimateScholarshipBook.com and enter code NA85126 for updates on this award.

[852] • David A. O Neil Scholarship
Society of Naval Architects and Marine Engineers (SNAME)
99 Canal Center Plaza, Suite 500, Alexandria, VA 22314
Phone: 703-997-6701
Email: scholarships@sname.org
https://www.sname.org/scholarships
Purpose: To aid students who are pursuing a master's degree in a subject that is related to the marine industry.
Eligibility: Applicants must be members of the Society of Naval Architects and Marine Engineers (SNAME). They must be working towards a master's degree in ocean engineering, marine engineering, naval architecture or another marine-related subject. Students who will be receiving their degree before October 1 of the application year are ineligible. Selection is based on the overall strength of the application.
Target applicant(s): College students. Graduate school students. Adult students.
Amount: Up to $20,000.
Number of awards: Varies.
Deadline: February 1.
How to apply: Applications are available online. An application form, transcript, standardized test scores and three recommendation letters are required.
Exclusive: Visit www.UltimateScholarshipBook.com and enter code SO85226 for updates on this award.

The Ultimate Scholarship Book 2026
Scholarship Directory (Sciences)

[853] • David Alan Quick Scholarship
EAA Aviation Center
3000 Poberezny Road, Oshkosh, WI 54902
Phone: 920-426-4800
Email: scholarships@eaa.org
https://www.eaa.org/eaa/learn-to-fly/scholarships
Purpose: To support students in aerospace or aeronautical engineering.
Eligibility: Applicants must be in their junior or senior year at an accredited college or university pursuing a degree in aerospace or aeronautical engineering. Applicants must be involved in school and community activities as well as aviation and be EAA members or be recommended by an EAA member.
Target applicant(s): College students. Adult students.
Amount: $5,000.
Number of awards: 1.
Scholarship may be renewable.
Deadline: March 1.
How to apply: Applications are available online.
Exclusive: Visit www.UltimateScholarshipBook.com and enter code EA85326 for updates on this award.

[854] • David Arver Memorial Scholarship
Aircraft Electronics Association
3570 NE Ralph Powell Road, Lee's Summit, MO 64064
Phone: 816-347-8400
Email: info@aea.net
https://aea.net/educationalfoundation/scholarships.asp
Purpose: To support students who wish to pursue a career in avionics or aircraft repair.
Eligibility: Applicants must be high school seniors or college students who plan to or are attending an accredited school in an avionics or aircraft repair program.
Target applicant(s): High school students. College students. Adult students.
Amount: $1,000.
Number of awards: 1.
Deadline: April 1.
How to apply: Applications are available by contacting the organization for more information.
Exclusive: Visit www.UltimateScholarshipBook.com and enter code AI85426 for updates on this award.

[855] • DEED Funding Opportunities
Demonstration of Energy and Efficiency Developments (DEED)
1875 Connecticut Avenue, NW, Suite 1200, Washington, DC 20009
Phone: 202-467-2960
Email: DEED@publicpower.org
https://www.publicpower.org
Purpose: To support engineering students interested in technical careers.
Eligibility: Applicants must be U.S. citizens attending an accredited college, university or vocational institution full-time and must not be graduating within a year of the application deadline. Selection is based on the overall strength of the application.
Target applicant(s): College students. Graduate school students. Adult students.
Amount: $5,000.
Number of awards: Varies.
Deadline: February 15; October 15.
How to apply: Applications are available online.
Exclusive: Visit www.UltimateScholarshipBook.com and enter code DE85526 for updates on this award.

[856] • Dellums SMART Scholarship
Department of Defense Scholarship-for-Service Program
Phone: 571-633-7940
Email: smart@smartscholarship.org
https://www.smartscholarship.org
Purpose: To support students in STEM fields.
Eligibility: Applicants must be students with no previous college credit who intend to pursue a bachelor's degree. Students must be high school seniors or rising freshmen pursuing a bachelor's degree by the program start date. Applicants must not have any previous college experience.
Target applicant(s): High school students. College students. Adult students.
Minimum GPA: 3.0
Amount: Varies.
Number of awards: Varies.
Deadline: December 5.
How to apply: Applications are available online.
Exclusive: Visit www.UltimateScholarshipBook.com and enter code DE85626 for updates on this award.

[857] • Delta Faucet Company Scholarships
PHCC Educational Foundation
180 South Washington Street, Suite 100, Falls Church, VA 22046
Phone: 800-533-7694
Email: scholarships@naphcc.org
http://www.phccweb.org
Purpose: To elevate the technical and business competence of the plumbing-heating-cooling (p-h-c) industry by awarding scholarships to students who are enrolled in a p-h-c-related major.
Eligibility: Applicants must be students who are currently enrolled or plan to be enrolled in a PHCC-approved plumbing or HVACR apprentice program at an accredited four-year college or university or two-year technical college, community college or trade school. Apprentice program students must also be working full-time for a licensed plumbing or HVAC contractor who is a member of the who is a member of the Plumbing-Heating-Cooling Contractors-National Association. Students must be enrolled in a full-time certificate or degree program at an accredited two-year community college, technical college, or trade school, with a major directly related to the plumbing-heating-cooling (p-h-c) profession such as the following: business management; mechanical CAD design; construction management with a specialty in mechanical construction and plumbing or HVACR installation, service and repair. Applicants can also be enrolled in a full-time undergraduate degree program at an accredited four-year college or university in the following majors: business management; construction management with a specialization in mechanical construction and mechanical engineering.
Target applicant(s): High school students. College students. Adult students.
Amount: $2,500.
Number of awards: Varies.
Deadline: May 1.
How to apply: Applications are available online, by email or by phone.
Exclusive: Visit www.UltimateScholarshipBook.com and enter code PH85726 for updates on this award.

[858] • Desk and Derrick Educational Trust
Desk and Derrick Educational Trust
c/o Natalie Bright, 1415 23rd Street, Canyon, TX 79015
Phone: 281-392-7181
Email: info@theeducationaltrust.org
http://theeducationaltrust.org/
Purpose: To promote studies in the energy industry.
Eligibility: Applicants must be U.S. or Canadian citizens, have completed two years of undergraduate study, have a minimum 3.2 GPA and demonstrate financial need. Students must be pursuing a degree in a field related to the petroleum, energy or allied industries and plan to work full-time in the petroleum, energy or allied industry or research alternative fuels such as coal, electric, solar, wind hydroelectric, nuclear or ethanol.
Target applicant(s): College students. Adult students.
Minimum GPA: 3.2
Amount: Varies.
Number of awards: Varies.
Deadline: April 1.
How to apply: Applications are available online.
Exclusive: Visit www.UltimateScholarshipBook.com and enter code DE85826 for updates on this award.

[859] • DMI Milk Marketing Scholarship
National Dairy Shrine
P.O. Box 68, Fort Atkinson, WI 53538
Phone: 920-863-6333
Email: info@dairyshrine.org
http://www.dairyshrine.org
Purpose: To encourage students to pursue careers in the marketing of dairy foods.
Eligibility: Applicants must be juniors at two- or four-year universities, have a minimum 2.5 GPA and major in dairy science, animal science, agricultural communications, agricultural education, general agriculture or food and nutrition.
Target applicant(s): College students. Adult students.
Minimum GPA: 2.5
Amount: $1,000-$1,500.
Number of awards: Varies.
Deadline: April 15.
How to apply: Applications are available online.
Exclusive: Visit www.UltimateScholarshipBook.com and enter code NA85926 for updates on this award.

[860] • DNA Day Essay Contest
American Society of Human Genetics
6120 Executive Boulevard, Suite 500, Rockville, MD 20852
Phone: 301-634-7300
http://www.ashg.org
Purpose: To support high school students who are interested in genetics.
Eligibility: Applicants must be in grades 9-12 and submit an essay in which they discuss the application of gene therapy in curing or repairing a particular disease or condition. Selection favors presentations that offer well-reasoned arguments, thus exemplifying a student's deep understanding of all concepts related to the essay question.
Target applicant(s): High school students.
Amount: Up to $1,000.
Number of awards: 13.
Deadline: Early March.
How to apply: Applications are available online.
Exclusive: Visit www.UltimateScholarshipBook.com and enter code AM86026 for updates on this award.

[861] • Donald F. and Mildred Topp Othmer Scholarships
American Institute of Chemical Engineers - (AIChE)
120 Wall Street, Floor 23, New York, NY 10005-4020
Phone: 800-242-4363
Email: awards@aiche.org
https://www.aiche.org/community/awards
Purpose: To support AIChE student members.
Eligibility: Applicants must be members of an AIChE Student Chapter or Chemical Engineering Club. Applicants must be nominated by their student chapter advisors. Awards are presented on the basis of academic achievement and involvement in student chapter activities.
Target applicant(s): College students. Graduate school students. Adult students.
Amount: $1,000.
Number of awards: 15.
Deadline: June 15.
How to apply: Applications are available online.
Exclusive: Visit www.UltimateScholarshipBook.com and enter code AM86126 for updates on this award.

[862] • Dorothy Budnek Memorial Scholarship
Association for Radiologic and Imaging Nursing
411 Richmond Street East, Suite 200, Toronto, ON M5A 3S5
Phone: 866-486-2762
Email: info@arinursing.org
https://www.arinursing.org/about/awards-scholarships/
Purpose: To help ARNA members continue their nursing education.
Eligibility: Applicants must be active members of the American Radiological Nurses Association for three years, have a current nursing license and be enrolled in an approved academic program. Students should submit the application, a statement of purpose, two recommendation letters, a transcript which shows a minimum 2.5 GPA, a statement of financial support and a copy of the nursing license.
Target applicant(s): Graduate school students. Adult students.
Minimum GPA: 2.5
Amount: $600.
Number of awards: 1.
Deadline: August 31.
How to apply: Applications are available online.
Exclusive: Visit www.UltimateScholarshipBook.com and enter code AS86226 for updates on this award.

[863] • Dorothy M. and Earl S. Hoffman Award
American Vacuum Society
125 Maiden Lane, 15th Floor, New York, NY 10038
Phone: 212-248-0200
Email: angela@avs.org
http://www.avs.org
Purpose: To recognize excellence in continuing graduate studies in the sciences and technologies related to AVS.
Eligibility: Applicants must be registered graduate students in an accredited academic institution at the time when the applications are due. An application must be submitted online which includes summary of research and an uploaded letter of recommendation. Criteria for selection of the awardee are excellence in research and academic record. The top eight student nominees are invited to present talks on their research to

the Awards Committee in a virtual interview in late summer. After the interview, one of the top three students of the eight finalists will receive the Dorothy M. and Earl S. Hoffman Award. The award consists of reimbursed travel expenses to the international symposium.
Target applicant(s): Graduate school students. Adult students.
Amount: Varies.
Number of awards: 2.
Deadline: March 31.
How to apply: Applications are available online.
Exclusive: Visit www.UltimateScholarshipBook.com and enter code AM86326 for updates on this award.

[864] • Douglas Dockery Thomas Fellowship in Garden History and Design
Landscape Architecture Foundation
1200 17th Street NW, Suite 210, Washington, DC 20036
Phone: 202-331-7070
Email: scholarships@lafoundation.org
https://www.lafoundation.org/what-we-do/scholarships
Purpose: To aid graduate students who are working on research projects related to garden design.
Eligibility: Applicants must be graduate students who are enrolled at a U.S. college or university. They must be researching some aspect of garden design. Selection is based on academic merit and applicability of proposed research to the aims of the Garden Club of America.
Target applicant(s): Graduate school students. Adult students.
Amount: $4,000.
Number of awards: 1.
Deadline: February 1.
How to apply: Application instructions are available online. A cover letter, research proposal, budget proposal, resume and three recommendation letters are required.
Exclusive: Visit www.UltimateScholarshipBook.com and enter code LA86426 for updates on this award.

[865] • Dr. Bart Kamen Memorial FIRST Scholarship
For Inspiration and Recognition of Science and Technology (FIRST)
200 Bedford Street, Manchester, NH 03101
Phone: 603-666-3906
Email: scholarships@firstinspires.org
https://www.firstinspires.org/bart-kamen-scholarship
Purpose: To support undergraduate students pursuing medical education.
Eligibility: Applicants must be high school seniors who have applied or been accepted to a program in biomedical engineering or pre-med studies. Applicants must have participated for a minimum of one year as a team member on a FIRST LEGO league, FIRST Tech Challenge or FIRST Robotics competition team.
Target applicant(s): High school students.
Amount: $10,000.
Number of awards: 4.
Scholarship may be renewable.
Deadline: February 1.
How to apply: Applications are available online.
Exclusive: Visit www.UltimateScholarshipBook.com and enter code FO86526 for updates on this award.

[866] • Dr. Esther Wilkins Scholarship
American Dental Hygienists' Association (ADHA) Institute for Oral Health
444 North Michigan Avenue, Suite 400, Chicago, IL 60611
Phone: 312-440-8900
Email: institute@adha.net
https://www.adha.org/ioh/scholarships/
Purpose: To support students who have completed an entry-level program in dental hygiene and are pursuing additional degrees in order to obtain a career in dental hygiene education.
Eligibility: Applicants must be full-time students at an accredited college or university in the United States pursuing a degree in dental hygiene education or a related field and must have completed at least one year of a dental hygiene curriculum. Applicants must also have completed an entry-level program in dental hygiene and be active members of the ADHA. They must have a minimum 3.0 GPA and have a minimum demonstrated financial need of $1,500. Selection is based on the overall strength of the application.
Target applicant(s): College students. Adult students.
Amount: $1,000.
Number of awards: Varies.
Deadline: January 31.
How to apply: Applications are available online after October 1. An application form and essay are required.
Exclusive: Visit www.UltimateScholarshipBook.com and enter code AM86626 for updates on this award.

[867] • Duane M. Hanson Scholarship
American Society of Heating, Refrigerating and Air-Conditioning Engineers (ASHRAE)
Scholarship Administrator, ASHRAE Inc., 180 Technology Parkway, Peachtree Corners, GA 30092
Phone: 404-636-8400
Email: lbenedict@ashrae.org
https://www.ashrae.org/communities/student-zone/scholarships-and-grants
Purpose: To support engineering students pursuing a degree that will prepare them for an HVAC&R profession.
Eligibility: Applicants must be enrolled in a full-time undergraduate engineering program of study traditionally designed to prepare students for a career in HVAC&R professions. Students must have a GPA of at least 3.0. Applicants must also meet at least one of three criteria: undergraduate institution hosts a recognized ASHRAE student branch, program of study is accredited by the Accreditation Board for Engineering and Technology (ABET), program of study is accredited by an agency outside the U.S. that is a signatory of the Washington Accord or has a signed Memorandum of Understanding with ABET.
Target applicant(s): High school students. College students. Adult students.
Minimum GPA: 3.0
Amount: $5,000.
Number of awards: 1.
Deadline: December 1.
How to apply: Applications are available online.
Exclusive: Visit www.UltimateScholarshipBook.com and enter code AM86726 for updates on this award.

[868] • Dutch and Ginger Arver Scholarship

Aircraft Electronics Association
3570 NE Ralph Powell Road, Lee's Summit, MO 64064
Phone: 816-347-8400
Email: info@aea.net
https://aea.net/educationalfoundation/scholarships.asp
Purpose: To support students who wish to pursue a career in avionics or aircraft repair.
Eligibility: Applicants must be high school seniors or college students who plan to or are attending an accredited school in avionics or aircraft repair.
Target applicant(s): High school students. College students. Adult students.
Amount: $1,000.
Number of awards: 1.
Deadline: April 1.
How to apply: Applications are available by contacting the organization for more information.
Exclusive: Visit www.UltimateScholarshipBook.com and enter code AI86826 for updates on this award.

[869] • Dwight D. Gardner Scholarship

Institute of Industrial and Systems Engineers
3577 Parkway Lane, Suite 200, Norcross, GA 30092
Phone: 800-494-0460
Email: egrimes@iise.org
https://www.iise.org
Purpose: To reward undergraduate members.
Eligibility: Applicants must be undergraduate students enrolled in a college in the United States, Canada or Mexico with an accredited industrial engineering program, major in industrial engineering and be active members. Students may not apply directly for this scholarship and must be nominated. The award is based on academic ability, character, leadership, potential service to the industrial engineering profession and financial need. Applicants must have a minimum 3.4 GPA.
Target applicant(s): College students. Adult students.
Minimum GPA: 3.4
Amount: $2,100.
Number of awards: 13.
Deadline: February 1.
How to apply: Nomination forms are available online.
Exclusive: Visit www.UltimateScholarshipBook.com and enter code IN86926 for updates on this award.

[870] • E. Noel Luddy Scholarship

Association of Federal Communications Consulting Engineers
P.O. Box 19333, Washington, DC 20036-0333
Phone: 703-780-4824
Email: scholarships@afcce.org
https://afcce.org/scholarships/
Purpose: To support students majoring in engineering, broadcasting, telecommunications or related fields.
Eligibility: Applicants must be full-time students working towards an undergraduate degree at an accredited four-year educational institution or a graduate degree through an accredited program in engineering or a field related to broadcasting or telecommunications. Selection is based on the overall strength of the application.
Target applicant(s): College students. Graduate school students. Adult students.
Amount: Up to $2,500.
Number of awards: Varies.
Deadline: October 31 (Spring); June 1 (Fall).
How to apply: Applications are available online. An application form, AFCCE sponsor, personal statement and transcript are required.
Exclusive: Visit www.UltimateScholarshipBook.com and enter code AS87026 for updates on this award.

[871] • E.J. Sierleja Memorial Fellowship

Institute of Industrial and Systems Engineers
3577 Parkway Lane, Suite 200, Norcross, GA 30092
Phone: 800-494-0460
Email: egrimes@iise.org
https://www.iise.org
Purpose: To reward graduate students pursuing advanced studies in the area of transportation.
Eligibility: Applicants must be full-time graduate students, majoring in transportation with a minimum 3.4 GPA, who are IISE active members. Students may not apply directly for this scholarship and must be nominated. The award is based on academic ability, character, leadership, potential service to the industrial engineering profession and financial need. Preference is given to students focusing on rail transportation.
Target applicant(s): Graduate school students. Adult students.
Minimum GPA: 3.4
Amount: $1,300.
Number of awards: 1.
Deadline: February 1.
How to apply: Nomination forms are available online.
Exclusive: Visit www.UltimateScholarshipBook.com and enter code IN87126 for updates on this award.

[872] • Edward D. Hendrickson/SAE Engineering Scholarship

Society of Automotive Engineers International
Scholarships Program, 400 Commonwealth Drive, Warrendale, PA 15096
Phone: 724-776-4841
Email: scholarships@sae.org
https://www.sae.org/participate/scholarships
Purpose: To reward students pursuing an engineering or related science degree.
Eligibility: Students must maintain a 3.75 GPA. Applicants must rank in the 90th percentile in both math and critical reading on either the SAT or the ACT. Scholarship may be renewed for an additional three years. Students must be pursuing their degree through an ABET accredited program.
Target applicant(s): High school students. College students. Adult students.
Minimum GPA: 3.75
Amount: $5,000.
Number of awards: 1.
Scholarship may be renewable.
Deadline: February 28.
How to apply: Applications are available online.
Exclusive: Visit www.UltimateScholarshipBook.com and enter code SO87226 for updates on this award.

[873] • Eight and Forty Lung and Respiratory Nursing Scholarship Fund

American Legion
Attn.: Americanism and Children and Youth Division, P.O. Box 1055, Indianapolis, IN 46206
Phone: 317-630-1249
Email: acy@legion.org
http://www.legion.org
Purpose: To assist registered nurses.
Eligibility: Applicants must plan to be employed full-time in hospitals, clinics or health departments in a position related to lung and respiratory control.
Target applicant(s): College students. Graduate school students. Adult students.
Minimum GPA: 3.0
Amount: $3,000.
Number of awards: Varies.
Deadline: May 15.
How to apply: Applications are available by written request.
Exclusive: Visit www.UltimateScholarshipBook.com and enter code AM87326 for updates on this award.

[874] • Elekta Radiation Therapy Scholarship

American Society of Radiologic Technologists Foundation (ASRT)
ASRT Foundation, 15000 Central Avenue South East, Albuquerque, NM 87123
Phone: 800-444-2778
Email: foundation@asrt.org
https://foundation.asrt.org/what-we-do/scholarships
Purpose: To encourage the best radiation therapy students to pursue a higher education.
Eligibility: Applicants must be members of the American Society of Radiologic Technologists (ASRT) and must be U.S. citizens, national or permanent residents. Students must finish their certificate or program degree by September 1 of the year in which scholarship applications are due. Applicants must be enrolled in an accredited radiologic science program with at least one semester of radiologic studies completed with a 3.0 GPA and be in good standing with ASRT.
Target applicant(s): College students. Adult students.
Minimum GPA: 3.0
Amount: $5,000.
Number of awards: 6.
Scholarship may be renewable.
Deadline: Contact the sponsor to confirm the deadline.
How to apply: Applications are available online.
Exclusive: Visit www.UltimateScholarshipBook.com and enter code AM87426 for updates on this award.

[875] • Elizabeth McLean Memorial Scholarship

Society of Women Engineers
130 East Randolph Street, Suite 3500, Chicago, IL 60601
Phone: 877-793-4636
Email: scholarships@swe.org
https://swe.org/scholarships/
Purpose: To support female students working towards a career in civil engineering.
Eligibility: Applicants must be women majoring in civil engineering with a 3.0 GPA. Students must be in school full-time.
Target applicant(s): College students. Adult students.
Minimum GPA: 3.0
Amount: $1,500.
Number of awards: 1.
Deadline: March 31.
How to apply: Applications are available online.
Exclusive: Visit www.UltimateScholarshipBook.com and enter code SO87526 for updates on this award.

[876] • Elmer J. and Hester Jane Johnson Memorial FFA Scholarship

National FFA Organization
P.O. Box 68960, 6060 FFA Drive, Indianapolis, IN 46268-0960
Phone: 888-332-2668
Email: scholarships@ffa.org
https://www.ffa.org/participate/grants-and-scholarships/
Purpose: To support FFA members working toward a four-year degree in agricultural education.
Eligibility: Applicants must complete the financial portion of the application and be pursuing a four-year degree in agricultural education. Selection is based on financial need, leadership ability and academic ability.
Target applicant(s): High school students. College students.
Amount: $1,000.
Number of awards: 1.
Deadline: January 11.
How to apply: Applications are available online.
Exclusive: Visit www.UltimateScholarshipBook.com and enter code NA87626 for updates on this award.

[877] • Elson T. Killam Memorial Scholarship

New England Water Works Association
125 Hopping Brook Road, Holliston, MA 01746
Phone: 508-893-7979
Email: tmacelhaney@preloadinc.com
http://www.newwa.org
Purpose: To support civil and environmental engineering students who are members of the New England Water Works Association.
Eligibility: Applicants must be enrolled in a civil or environmental engineering degree program and must be members of NEWWA. Students must reside in New England or attend a college/university in New England. Selection is based on the overall strength of the application.
Target applicant(s): High school students. College students. Adult students.
Amount: $1,500.
Number of awards: 1.
Deadline: April 1.
How to apply: Applications are available online. An application form, an official transcript and one recommendation letter are required.
Exclusive: Visit www.UltimateScholarshipBook.com and enter code NE87726 for updates on this award.

[878] • EmPOWERED Scholars Program

American Heart Association
7272 Greenville Avenue, Dallas, TX 75231
Phone: 800-242-8721
Email: inquiries@heart.org
https://www.empoweredtoserve.org/en/capital-access-grant-funding/empowered-scholar
Purpose: To reward students who volunteer in their communities.
Eligibility: Applicants must be currently enrolled college freshmen, sophomores and juniors working to improve community health and wellness. Students must have demonstrated efforts to improve health

equity, including advocating for access to healthy food, volunteering at a health clinic, working in a student health program and fundraising for a cause that promotes health equity. Applicants must have a minimum GPA of 2.0.
Target applicant(s): College students. Adult students.
Amount: $5,000.
Number of awards: Varies.
Deadline: Varies.
How to apply: Applications are available online.
Exclusive: Visit www.UltimateScholarshipBook.com and enter code AM87826 for updates on this award.

[879] • ENA Foundation Undergraduate Scholarship
Emergency Nurses Association
930 E. Woodfield Road, Schaumburg, IL 60173
Phone: 847-460-4100
Email: ena.foundation@ena.org
http://www.ena.org
Purpose: To promote research and education in emergency care.
Eligibility: Applicants must be nurses pursuing baccalaureate degrees in nursing and must have been ENA members for at least 12 months before applying. Selection is based on the application, statement of goals, references and transcript.
Target applicant(s): College students. Adult students.
Minimum GPA: 3.0
Amount: $2,500.
Number of awards: 1.
Deadline: April 26.
How to apply: Applications are available online.
Exclusive: Visit www.UltimateScholarshipBook.com and enter code EM87926 for updates on this award.

[880] • EngineerGirl Essay Contest
National Academy of Engineering
500 Fifth Street NW, Room 1047, Washington, DC 20001
http://www.engineergirl.org
Purpose: To support engineering-minded elementary, middle and high school students.
Eligibility: Applicants must be a student in the third through twelfth grades who submit an essay positing how engineering might positively impact a vulnerable species' life. One submission only; also, employees or those related to or living with employees of the National Academies of Sciences, Engineering and Medicine are prohibited from applying, as are prior winners who wish to reapply within the same category.
Target applicant(s): Junior high students or younger. High school students.
Amount: Up to $1,000.
Number of awards: 3.
Deadline: February 1.
How to apply: Applications are available online.
Exclusive: Visit www.UltimateScholarshipBook.com and enter code NA88026 for updates on this award.

[881] • Engineering Undergraduate Scholarship
American Society for Nondestructive Testing
Awards and Honors Program, 1201 Dublin Road, Suite #G04, Columbus, OH 43215
Phone: 614-274-6003 x 233
Email: awards@asnt.org
http://www.asnt.org
Purpose: To support students studying nondestructive testing.
Eligibility: Applicants must be undergraduate students enrolled in an engineering program and specialize in nondestructive testing (NDT). A nominating letter, transcript, three letters of recommendation and an essay describing the role of NDT/NDE in their career are required.
Target applicant(s): College students. Adult students.
Amount: $3,000.
Number of awards: Varies.
Deadline: January 31.
How to apply: Applications are available online.
Exclusive: Visit www.UltimateScholarshipBook.com and enter code AM88126 for updates on this award.

[882] • Equity in Pharmacy Scholarship
GoodRx
Scholarship America, One Scholarship Way, Saint Peter, MN 56082
Phone: 800-537-4180
Email: goodrx@scholarshipamerica.org
https://www.goodrx.com/scholarship
Purpose: To support students interested in becoming pharmacists and pharmacy technicians.
Eligibility: Applicants must either currently be undergraduates or graduate-level students pursuing pharmacy or pharmacy technician studies at an accredited two- or four-year college, university or vocational-technical school or currently studying towards or have recently received a pharmacy technician certification. Students must have a minimum 3.0 GPA and be from an underrepresented population in the healthcare field.
Target applicant(s): College students. Graduate school students. Adult students.
Minimum GPA: 3.0
Amount: $5,000.
Number of awards: 10.
Deadline: July 7.
How to apply: Applications are available online.
Exclusive: Visit www.UltimateScholarshipBook.com and enter code GO88226 for updates on this award.

[883] • Eugene S. Kropf Scholarship
University Aviation Association - Eugene S. Kropf Scholarship
Kevin R. Kuhlmann, Professor of Aviation and Aerospace Science, Metropolitan State College of Denver, Campus Box 30, P.O. Box 173362, Denver, CO 80217-3362
Phone: 334-844-2434
Email: uaamail@uaa.aero
http://www.uaa.aero/
Purpose: To support students studying an aviation-related curriculum.
Eligibility: Applicants must be U.S. citizens enrolled in an aviation-related curriculum of a two-year or a four-year degree at a UAA member college or university. Students must have a 3.0 GPA and write a 250-word paper on how they can improve aviation education.
Target applicant(s): College students. Adult students.
Minimum GPA: 3.0

Amount: $500.
Number of awards: 1.
Deadline: June 30.
How to apply: Applications are available online.
Exclusive: Visit www.UltimateScholarshipBook.com and enter code UN88326 for updates on this award.

[884] • ExploraVision National Science Competition

ExploraVision
Toshiba/NSTA ExploraVision Awards, 1840 Wilson Boulevard, Arlington, VA 22201
Phone: 800-397-5679
http://www.exploravision.org
Purpose: To encourage students to contemplate the technology of the future through working together and researching the technology and science of today.
Eligibility: Applicants must be citizens or legal residents of the United States or Canada who are no older than 21. Students must enter in teams of two to four. Teams must submit an entry form, an abstract, a description of their project, a bibliography and five sample web pages. Twenty-four teams will be selected as winners based on scientific accuracy, communication, feasibility of vision and creativity of their projects.
Target applicant(s): Junior high students or younger. High school students.
Amount: $10,000.
Number of awards: 48-96.
Deadline: January 31.
How to apply: Applications are available online.
Exclusive: Visit www.UltimateScholarshipBook.com and enter code EX88426 for updates on this award.

[885] • F.W. Beich Beichley Scholarship

American Society of Mechanical Engineers (ASME)
Two Park Avenue, New York, NY 10016-5990
Phone: 800-843-2763
Email: lefeverb@asme.org
https://www.asme.org/asme-programs/students-and-faculty/scholarships/scholarships
Purpose: To support mechanical engineering students.
Eligibility: Applicants must be ASME student members enrolled in an eligible accredited mechanical engineering baccalaureate program. Selection is based on leadership, scholastic ability, potential contribution to the mechanical engineering profession and financial need. The scholarship is only applicable for study in the junior or senior year.
Target applicant(s): College students. Adult students.
Amount: $3,000.
Number of awards: 1.
Deadline: February 15.
How to apply: Applications are available online.
Exclusive: Visit www.UltimateScholarshipBook.com and enter code AM88526 for updates on this award.

[886] • FarmAid FFA Scholarship

National FFA Organization
P.O. Box 68960, 6060 FFA Drive, Indianapolis, IN 46268-0960
Phone: 888-332-2668
Email: scholarships@ffa.org
https://www.ffa.org/participate/grants-and-scholarships/
Purpose: To support students who are FFA members, come from family farms and are pursuing four-year degrees in agriculture.
Eligibility: Applicants must complete the financial analysis part of the application. A minimum GPA of 2.0 is required. Selection is based on the overall strength of the application.
Target applicant(s): High school students. College students.
Minimum GPA: 2.0
Amount: $3,000 over three years.
Number of awards: 6.
Deadline: January 11.
How to apply: A complete application form is required.
Exclusive: Visit www.UltimateScholarshipBook.com and enter code NA88626 for updates on this award.

[887] • Father James B. Macelwane Annual Award in Meteorology

American Meteorological Society
Fellowship and Scholarship Department, 45 Beacon Street, Boston, MA 02108-3693
Phone: 617-227-2425
Email: amsinfo@ametsoc.org
https://www.ametsoc.org/ams/index.cfm/information-for/students/ams-scholarships-and-fellowships/
Purpose: To encourage interest in meteorology among college students.
Eligibility: Applicants must be enrolled as undergraduates and submit an original student paper on an aspect of atmospheric science. No more than two students from any one institution may enter papers in any one contest, and there is no application form needed.
Target applicant(s): College students. Adult students.
Amount: $1,000.
Number of awards: 1.
Deadline: June 14.
How to apply: Submit materials to the address listed.
Exclusive: Visit www.UltimateScholarshipBook.com and enter code AM88726 for updates on this award.

[888] • Feeding Tomorrow General Education Scholarships/Freshman Scholarships

Institute of Food Technologists (IFT)
525 W. Van Buren, Suite 1000, Chicago, IL 60607
Phone: 312-782-8424
Email: ContactUs@applyISTS.com
https://www.ift.org/community/students
Purpose: To help young food scientists who plan to work in industry, government and academia.
Eligibility: Applicants for the freshman scholarships must be academically outstanding high school graduates or seniors who will enter college for the first time in an approved program in food science/technology and must have a minimum 3.0 GPA. All candidates must submit applications, transcripts and a recommendation.
Target applicant(s): High school students.
Minimum GPA: 3.0
Amount: Varies.
Number of awards: Varies.
Deadline: February 26.
How to apply: Applications are available online.
Exclusive: Visit www.UltimateScholarshipBook.com and enter code IN88826 for updates on this award.

[889] • Fellowship Award

Damon Runyon Cancer Research Foundation
One Exchange Plaza, 55 Broadway, Suite 302, New York, NY 10006
Phone: 212-455-0520
Email: awards@damonrunyon.org
http://www.damonrunyon.org
Purpose: To support the training of postdoctoral scientists as they start their research careers.
Eligibility: Applicants must have completed one or more of the following degrees or its equivalent: M.D., Ph.D., M.D./Ph.D., D.D.S. or D.V.M. Applicants should submit an application cover sheet, sponsor's biographical sketch, CV, degree certificate, letter, research proposal, summary of research form, up to three reprints of work and four letters of reference. This is a three-year award with various deadlines and funding. The research must be conducted at a university, hospital or research institution. International candidates may apply to do their research only in the United States.
Target applicant(s): Graduate school students. Adult students.
Amount: $70,000-$76,000 plus expenses.
Number of awards: Varies.
Deadline: December 2.
How to apply: Applications are available online.
Exclusive: Visit www.UltimateScholarshipBook.com and enter code DA88926 for updates on this award.

[890] • Fellowship in Aerospace History

American Historical Association
400 A Street SE, Washington, DC 20003
Phone: 202-544-2422
Email: info@historians.org
http://www.historians.org
Purpose: To provide funding for an academic research project related to aerospace history.
Eligibility: Applicants must possess a doctorate degree in history or a related field or be enrolled in a doctorate program (all coursework completed). One fellow will be appointed for one academic year. The fellow will be expected to write a report and present a paper or lecture on the research at the end of the term.
Target applicant(s): Graduate school students. Adult students.
Amount: $22,550.
Number of awards: At least 1.
Deadline: April 1.
How to apply: Applications are available online.
Exclusive: Visit www.UltimateScholarshipBook.com and enter code AM89026 for updates on this award.

[891] • Foundation for Surgical Technology Medical Mission Scholarship

Association of Surgical Technologists
6 W. Dry Creek Circle, Ste 200, Littleton, CO 80120
Phone: 800-637-7433
Email: scholarships@ast.org
http://ffst.org/
Purpose: To help practitioners with continuing education or medical missionary work.
Eligibility: Applicants must be active AST members, document the educational program or mission program and provide two recommendation letters.
Target applicant(s): Adult students.
Amount: Varies.
Number of awards: Varies.
Deadline: December 31.
How to apply: Applications are available online.
Exclusive: Visit www.UltimateScholarshipBook.com and enter code AS89126 for updates on this award.

[892] • Foundation for Surgical Technology Scholarships

Association of Surgical Technologists
6 W. Dry Creek Circle, Ste 200, Littleton, CO 80120
Phone: 800-637-7433
Email: scholarships@ast.org
http://ffst.org/
Purpose: To support the continuing education of surgical technology students.
Eligibility: Applicants should be enrolled in accredited surgical technology programs and be eligible to sit for the Certified Surgical Technologist examination sponsored by the National Board of Surgical Technology and Surgical Assisting. Applications, transcripts, a minimum 3.0 GPA, essays and recommendation letters are required.
Target applicant(s): College students. Adult students.
Minimum GPA: 3.0
Amount: Varies.
Number of awards: Varies.
Deadline: March 1.
How to apply: Applications are available online.
Exclusive: Visit www.UltimateScholarshipBook.com and enter code AS89226 for updates on this award.

[893] • Frank and Brennie Morgan Prize for Outstanding Research in Mathematics by an Undergraduate Student

American Mathematical Society and Mathematical Association of America
201 Charles Street, Providence, RI 02904
Phone: 401-445-4000
http://www.ams.org/prizes-awards/palist.cgi
Purpose: Awarded to an undergraduate student (or students who have collaborated) for research in the field of mathematics.
Eligibility: Applicants must be undergraduate students at colleges or universities in the United States or its possessions, Canada and Mexico. Students must be nominated.
Target applicant(s): High school students. College students. Adult students.
Amount: $1,200.
Number of awards: 1.
Deadline: May 31.
How to apply: Nomination information is available by email. Questions should be directed to Dr. Martha J. Siegel at the address above. Nominations and submissions should be sent to: Morgan Prize Committee, c/o Robert J. Daverman, American Mathematical Society, 312D Ayres Hall, University of Tennessee, Knoxville, TN 37996.
Exclusive: Visit www.UltimateScholarshipBook.com and enter code AM89326 for updates on this award.

[894] • Frank and Dorothy Miller ASME Auxiliary Scholarships

American Society of Mechanical Engineers (ASME)
Two Park Avenue, New York, NY 10016-5990
Phone: 800-843-2763
Email: lefeverb@asme.org
https://www.asme.org/asme-programs/students-and-faculty/scholarships/scholarships

Purpose: To support U.S. mechanical engineering and mechanical engineering technology undergraduates.
Eligibility: Applicants must be U.S. citizens and residents of North America. They must be juniors or seniors who are enrolled in an ABET-accredited (or equivalent) mechanical engineering, mechanical engineering technology or related program at a U.S. postsecondary institution. They must be ASME student members who are in good standing. Selection is based on leadership, integrity and potential contribution to the field of mechanical engineering.
Target applicant(s): College students. Adult students.
Amount: $2,000.
Number of awards: 2.
Deadline: February 15.
How to apply: The application form is available through ASME's online scholarship application system. This form, an official transcript, a personal statement and up to two recommendation letters are required.
Exclusive: Visit www.UltimateScholarshipBook.com and enter code AM89426 for updates on this award.

[895] • Fred M. Young, Sr./SAE Engineering Scholarship

Society of Automotive Engineers International
Scholarships Program, 400 Commonwealth Drive, Warrendale, PA 15096
Phone: 724-776-4841
Email: scholarships@sae.org
https://www.sae.org/participate/scholarships

Purpose: To support high school seniors who are planning to study engineering at the undergraduate level.
Eligibility: Applicants must be U.S. citizens and must be high school seniors. They must have SAT or ACT scores that rank in the 90th percentile and must have a GPA of 3.75 or higher on a four-point scale. They must plan to enroll in an ABET-accredited undergraduate engineering program. Selection is based on the overall strength of the application.
Target applicant(s): High school students.
Minimum GPA: 3.75
Amount: $1,000.
Number of awards: 1.
Scholarship may be renewable.
Deadline: February 28.
How to apply: Applications are available online. An application form, official transcript and standardized test scores are required.
Exclusive: Visit www.UltimateScholarshipBook.com and enter code SO89526 for updates on this award.

[896] • Freshman Undergraduate Scholarship

American Meteorological Society
Fellowship and Scholarship Department, 45 Beacon Street, Boston, MA 02108-3693
Phone: 617-227-2425
Email: amsinfo@ametsoc.org
https://www.ametsoc.org/ams/index.cfm/information-for/students/ams-scholarships-and-fellowships/

Purpose: To encourage high school students to pursue careers in the atmospheric and related oceanic and hydrologic sciences.
Eligibility: Applicants must enter as full-time freshmen the following fall and major in the atmospheric or related oceanic and hydrologic sciences. Applicants should submit applications, transcripts, recommendation letter and SAT or equivalent scores.
Target applicant(s): High school students.
Amount: $5,000.
Number of awards: Varies.
Scholarship may be renewable.
Deadline: February 3.
How to apply: Applications are available online.
Exclusive: Visit www.UltimateScholarshipBook.com and enter code AM89626 for updates on this award.

[897] • Full-Time Employee Student Scholarship

Air Traffic Control Association
225 Reinekers Lane, Suite 400, Alexandria, VA 22314
Phone: 703-299-2430
Email: info@atca.org
http://www.atca.org

Purpose: To help students in advanced study programs in air traffic control and other aviation disciplines.
Eligibility: Applicants must be full-time employees enrolled in advanced study programs to improve their skills in air traffic control or an aviation discipline.
Target applicant(s): College students. Graduate school students. Adult students.
Amount: $5,000 - $15,000.
Number of awards: Varies.
Deadline: May 1.
How to apply: Applications are available online. An application form, two letters of reference, academic transcripts, an essay and answers to career and leadership questions are required.
Exclusive: Visit www.UltimateScholarshipBook.com and enter code AI89726 for updates on this award.

[898] • Future Leader Scholarship

Association of State Floodplain Managers Foundation (ASFPM)
8301 Excelsior Drive, Madison, WI 53717
Phone: 608-828-3000
Email: asfpmfoundation@floods.org
https://www.asfpmfoundation.org/scholarships/future-leaders-scholarship

Purpose: To support students who will grow to advance the vision of the ASFPM Foundation.
Eligibility: Applicants must be undergraduate students pursuing a course of study related to the vision of the ASFPM Foundation, which includes engineering, planning and biological, earth, and social sciences. Students must be U.S. citizens or have U.S. permanent resident alien status. Applicants must have a cumulative minimum GPA of 2.5 (or equivalent).
Target applicant(s): College students. Adult students.
Minimum GPA: 2.5
Amount: up to $20,000.
Number of awards: Varies.
Deadline: February 1.
How to apply: Applications are available online.
Exclusive: Visit www.UltimateScholarshipBook.com and enter code AS89826 for updates on this award.

[899] • Gabriel A. Hartl Scholarship
Air Traffic Control Association
225 Reinekers Lane, Suite 400, Alexandria, VA 22314
Phone: 703-299-2430
Email: info@atca.org
http://www.atca.org
Purpose: To support air traffic control students.
Eligibility: Applicants must be enrolled half- to full-time in a two- to four-year air traffic control program at an institution approved and/or licensed by the Federal Aviation Administration as directly supporting the FAA's college and training initiative.
Target applicant(s): High school students. College students. Adult students.
Amount: $5,000 - $15,000.
Number of awards: Varies.
Deadline: May 1.
How to apply: Applications are available online.
Exclusive: Visit www.UltimateScholarshipBook.com and enter code AI89926 for updates on this award.

[900] • Gaige Fund Award
American Society of Ichthyologists and Herpetologists
P.O. Box 1897, 810 E 10th St, Lawrence, KS 66044
Phone: 785-865-9405
Email: asih@allenpress.com
https://asih.org/student-awards
Purpose: To support young herpetologists.
Eligibility: Applicants must be members of ASIH and studying for an advanced degree. The award may be used for museum or laboratory study, travel, fieldwork or other activities that will enhance their careers and their contributions to the science of herpetology. Both merit and need will be considered.
Target applicant(s): College students. Graduate school students. Adult students.
Amount: $400-$1,000.
Number of awards: Varies.
Deadline: March 8.
How to apply: Applications are available by email or written request.
Exclusive: Visit www.UltimateScholarshipBook.com and enter code AM90026 for updates on this award.

[901] • Garland Duncan Scholarships
American Society of Mechanical Engineers (ASME)
Two Park Avenue, New York, NY 10016-5990
Phone: 800-843-2763
Email: lefeverb@asme.org
https://www.asme.org/asme-programs/students-and-faculty/scholarships/scholarships
Purpose: To support mechanical engineering students.
Eligibility: Applicants must be ASME student members, be enrolled in an eligible accredited mechanical engineering baccalaureate program, have strong academic performance and be college sophomores, juniors or seniors. Selection is based on character, integrity, leadership, scholastic ability, potential contribution to the mechanical engineering profession and financial need.
Target applicant(s): College students. Adult students.
Amount: $5,000.
Number of awards: 2.
Deadline: February 15.
How to apply: Applications are available online.
Exclusive: Visit www.UltimateScholarshipBook.com and enter code AM90126 for updates on this award.

[902] • Garmin Scholarship
Aircraft Electronics Association
3570 NE Ralph Powell Road, Lee's Summit, MO 64064
Phone: 816-347-8400
Email: info@aea.net
https://aea.net/educationalfoundation/scholarships.asp
Purpose: To support students who wish to pursue a career in avionics and aircraft repair.
Eligibility: Applicants must be high school seniors or college students who plan to or are attending an accredited school in an avionics or aircraft repair program.
Target applicant(s): High school students. College students. Adult students.
Amount: $2,000.
Number of awards: Varies.
Deadline: April 1.
How to apply: Applications are available online.
Exclusive: Visit www.UltimateScholarshipBook.com and enter code AI90226 for updates on this award.

[903] • Gary Wagner, K3OMI, Scholarship
American Radio Relay League Foundation
225 Main Street, Newington, CT 06111-1494
Phone: 860-594-0200
Email: foundation@arrl.org
https://www.arrl.org/scholarship-program
Purpose: To support engineering students who are involved in amateur radio.
Eligibility: Applicants must have an amateur radio license of Novice Class or higher. Students may be pursuing a bachelor's degree in any field of engineering. They must be residents of one of the following states: North Carolina, Virginia, West Virginia, Maryland or Tennessee. Preference will be given to students with financial need.
Target applicant(s): High school students. College students. Adult students.
Amount: $1,000.
Number of awards: 1.
Deadline: January 10.
How to apply: Applications are available online.
Exclusive: Visit www.UltimateScholarshipBook.com and enter code AM90326 for updates on this award.

[904] • GBT Student Observing Support (SOS) Program
National Radio Astronomy Observatory (NRAO)
NRAO Headquarters, 520 Edgemont Road, Charlottesville, VA 22903
Phone: 434-296-0211
Email: info@nrao.edu
https://science.nrao.edu/opportunities/student-programs
Purpose: To support student research at the Robert C. Byrd Green Bank Telescope (GBT).
Eligibility: GBT is the largest fully steerable single aperture antenna. Students begin the application process by completing a preliminary funding proposal form. If the proposal is accepted, they will be informed of further requirements.
Target applicant(s): College students. Graduate school students. Adult students.

The Ultimate Scholarship Book 2026
Scholarship Directory (Sciences)

Amount: Up to $35,000.
Number of awards: Varies.
Deadline: June 5.
How to apply: Applications are available online.
Exclusive: Visit www.UltimateScholarshipBook.com and enter code NA90426 for updates on this award.

[905] • GCSAA Scholars Competition
Golf Course Superintendents Association of America
1421 Research Park Drive, Lawrence, KS 66049
Phone: 800-472-7878
Email: mwright@gcsaa.org
https://www.gcsaa.org/education/scholarships
Purpose: To support students preparing for careers in golf course management.
Eligibility: Applicants must be GCSAA members who are undergraduate students enrolled in an accredited degree program in turf management or a closely related subject. They must have completed at least 24 semester credits or one year of full-time study in their degree program. Selection is based on academic excellence, career potential, recommendations, work history and extracurricular activities.
Target applicant(s): College students. Adult students.
Amount: $500-$6,000.
Number of awards: Varies.
Deadline: June 1.
How to apply: Applications are available online. An application form, personal essay, transcripts and reports from the applicant's academic advisor and golf course superintendent are required.
Exclusive: Visit www.UltimateScholarshipBook.com and enter code GO90526 for updates on this award.

[906] • General James H. Doolittle Scholarship
Communities Foundation of Texas
5500 Caruth Haven Lane, Dallas, TX 75225
Phone: 214-750-4222
Email: info@cftexas.org
https://cftexas.org/scholarships/
Purpose: To support aeronautical engineering and aerospace science students.
Eligibility: Applicants must be undergraduate juniors, undergraduate seniors or graduate students enrolled in a degree program in aerospace science or aeronautical engineering. Students do not need to be Texas residents. Selection is based on the overall strength of the application.
Target applicant(s): College students. Graduate school students. Adult students.
Minimum GPA: 2.75
Amount: Up to $5,000.
Number of awards: Varies.
Deadline: April 1.
How to apply: Applications are available online. An application form and supporting documents are required.
Exclusive: Visit www.UltimateScholarshipBook.com and enter code CO90626 for updates on this award.

[907] • GeneTex Scholarship Program
GeneTex Inc.
2456 Alton Parkway, Irvine, CA 92606
Phone: 949-553-1900
Email: scholarship@genetex.com
http://www.genetex.com/scholarship
Purpose: To support students pursuing STEM degrees.
Eligibility: Applicants must be enrolled at an accredited college or university and be in good standing. Students must be majoring in a STEM (science, technology, engineering or math) area.
Target applicant(s): High school students. College students. Graduate school students. Adult students.
Amount: $2,000.
Number of awards: 1.
Deadline: July 12 (fall); December 1 (spring).
How to apply: Applications are available online.
Exclusive: Visit www.UltimateScholarshipBook.com and enter code GE90726 for updates on this award.

[908] • Geneva Rock Scholarship
Geneva Rock
302 West 5400 South, Suite 200, Murray, UT 84107
https://genevarock.com/scholarship/
Purpose: To support students dedicated to building the future.
Eligibility: Applicants must be currently enrolled or enrolling in an accredited university, college, trade or vocational school pursuing a career in a construction-related field. Students must include a written essay along with their application.
Target applicant(s): College students. Adult students.
Amount: $2,000.
Number of awards: 2.
Deadline: July 1 (Fall); November 15 (Spring).
How to apply: Applications are available online.
Exclusive: Visit www.UltimateScholarshipBook.com and enter code GE90826 for updates on this award.

[909] • George A. Hall / Harold F. Mayfield Grant
Wilson Ornithological Society
Department of Biology and Biomedical Science, Dr. James Chace, Associate Professor, 100 Ochre Point Avenue, Newport, RI 02840-4192
Email: rbpayne@umich.edu
http://www.wilsonsociety.org
Purpose: To assist those who are conducting avian research.
Eligibility: Applicants must be independent researchers without access to funds available at colleges, universities or government agencies and must be non-professionals currently conducting avian research. Applicants must also be willing to present their research results at an annual meeting of the Wilson Ornithological Society.
Target applicant(s): College students. Graduate school students. Adult students.
Amount: $2,000.
Number of awards: 1.
Deadline: February 1.
How to apply: Applications are available online.
Exclusive: Visit www.UltimateScholarshipBook.com and enter code WI90926 for updates on this award.

[910] • Gertrude Cox Scholarship For Women In Statistics

American Statistical Association
Attn: Awards Nominations, 732 North Washington Street, Alexandria, VA 22314-1943
Phone: 703-684-1221
Email: awards@amstat.org
http://www.amstat.org
Purpose: To encourage women to pursue education for careers in statistics.
Eligibility: Applicants must be women who are full-time students in a graduate-level statistics programs.
Target applicant(s): Graduate school students. Adult students.
Amount: $1,000.
Number of awards: 2.
Deadline: February 23.
How to apply: Applications are available online.
Exclusive: Visit www.UltimateScholarshipBook.com and enter code AM91026 for updates on this award.

[911] • Gilbreth Memorial Fellowship

Institute of Industrial and Systems Engineers
3577 Parkway Lane, Suite 200, Norcross, GA 30092
Phone: 800-494-0460
Email: egrimes@iise.org
https://www.iise.org
Purpose: To support graduate student Institute members.
Eligibility: Applicants must be graduate students at an institution in the United States, Canada or Mexico, majoring in industrial engineering or its equivalent and active members. Students may not apply directly for this scholarship and must be nominated. The award is based on academic ability, character, leadership, potential service to the industrial engineering profession and financial need.
Target applicant(s): Graduate school students. Adult students.
Minimum GPA: 3.4
Amount: $3,500.
Number of awards: 4.
Deadline: February 1.
How to apply: Nomination forms are available online.
Exclusive: Visit www.UltimateScholarshipBook.com and enter code IN91126 for updates on this award.

[912] • Giuliano Mazzetti Scholarship

Society of Manufacturing Engineers Education Foundation
One SME Drive, P.O. Box 930, Dearborn, MI 48121
Phone: 313-425-3300
Email: foundation@sme.org
https://www.smeef.org/scholarships
Purpose: To support undergraduate students of manufacturing engineering and technology.
Eligibility: Applicants must be full-time undergraduate students who have completed 30 or more credit hours at a postsecondary institution located in the United States or Canada. They must be studying manufacturing engineering, technology or a related subject and must have plans to pursue a career in one of these same fields. Students must have a GPA of 3.0 or more on a four-point scale. Selection is based on the overall strength of the application.
Target applicant(s): College students. Adult students.
Minimum GPA: 3.0
Amount: Varies.
Number of awards: Varies.
Deadline: February 1.
How to apply: Applications are available online. An application form, personal statement, resume, transcript and two recommendation letters are required.
Exclusive: Visit www.UltimateScholarshipBook.com and enter code SO91226 for updates on this award.

[913] • Gladys Anderson Emerson Scholarship

Iota Sigma Pi (ISP) ND
Professor Kathryn A. Thomasson, Iota Sigma Pi Director for Student Awards, University of North Dakota, Department of Chemistry, P.O. Box 9024, Grand Forks, ND 58202-9024
Phone: 701-777-3199
Email: kthomasson@chem.und.edu
https://www.iotasigmapi.org/
Purpose: To reward achievement in the fields of chemistry and biochemistry by women.
Eligibility: Applicants must have attained junior status at an accredited college or university, be female and be nominated by a member of Iota Sigma Pi.
Target applicant(s): College students. Adult students.
Amount: $2,000.
Number of awards: Up to 2.
Deadline: February 15.
How to apply: Applications are available online.
Exclusive: Visit www.UltimateScholarshipBook.com and enter code IO91326 for updates on this award.

[914] • Gloria Barron Wilderness Society Scholarship

Wilderness Society
1615 M Street NW, Washington, DC 20036
Phone: 800-843-9453
Email: https://wilderness.org
https://wilderness.org
Purpose: To support graduate students pursuing a career in long-term protection of wilderness in the U.S.
Eligibility: Applicants must provide a cover letter, proposal, current resume and letters of recommendation along with the application.
Target applicant(s): Graduate school students. Adult students.
Amount: $25,000.
Number of awards: 2.
Deadline: April 15.
How to apply: Applications are available online.
Exclusive: Visit www.UltimateScholarshipBook.com and enter code WI91426 for updates on this award.

[915] • Gordon Rankin Corrosion Engineering Scholarship

National Association of Corrosion Engineers (NACE) International Foundation
15835 Park Ten Place, Houston, TX 77084-5145
Phone: 281-228-6205
Email: nace.foundation@nace.org
https://www.ampp.org/about/emerg-student-outreach/academic-scholarships-program
Purpose: To aid students in their continued studies in corrosion.

The Ultimate Scholarship Book 2026
Scholarship Directory (Sciences)

Eligibility: Applicants must be U.S. citizens enrolled full-time as an undergraduate at an accredited two or four-year U.S. college or university. Applicants must be enrolled in the study of corrosion or corrosion control and must have a GPA of 3.0 or higher.
Target applicant(s): College students. Adult students.
Minimum GPA: 3.0
Amount: $1,000.
Number of awards: Up to 3.
Deadline: January 2.
How to apply: Applications are available online. An application form, two recommendation forms, an academic transcript and scholarship essay questions are required.
Exclusive: Visit www.UltimateScholarshipBook.com and enter code NA91526 for updates on this award.

[916] • Graduate Research Award (GRA)
American Vacuum Society
125 Maiden Lane, 15th Floor, New York, NY 10038
Phone: 212-248-0200
Email: angela@avs.org
http://www.avs.org
Purpose: To support graduate studies in the sciences and technologies related to the AVS.
Eligibility: The nominee must be a registered graduate student in an accredited academic institution at the time in which the applications are due. Applicants are normally expected not to graduate before the award selection. The top eight student nominees are notified and invited to present talks on their research to the Awards Committee in a virtual interview in late summer. After the interview, the remaining three students of the eight finalists will receive a Graduate Research Award. Criteria for selection of the awardees are excellence in research and academic record. An application must be submitted online, which includes a summary of research and an uploaded letter of recommendation.
Target applicant(s): Graduate school students. Adult students.
Amount: Varies.
Number of awards: 10.
Deadline: March 31.
How to apply: Applications are available online.
Exclusive: Visit www.UltimateScholarshipBook.com and enter code AM91626 for updates on this award.

[917] • Graduate Research Fellowship Program
National Science Foundation
GRF Operations Center, 1818 N Street NW, Suite 600, Washington, DC 20036
Phone: 866-NSF-GRFP
Email: info@nsfgrfp.org
https://www.fastlane.nsf.gov/
Purpose: To assist science and engineering graduate students.
Eligibility: Applicants must be full-time students who have completed no more than 12 months of graduate study and be U.S. citizens, U.S. nationals or permanent residents. The fields of study are interdisciplinary, computer and information science and engineering, mathematical sciences, geosciences, psychology, social sciences, life sciences, chemistry, physics and astronomy and engineering.
Target applicant(s): Graduate school students. Adult students.
Amount: Up to $53,000.
Number of awards: 2,700.
Deadline: October 16; 17; 19 and 20.
How to apply: Applications are available online. An online application form, official transcript and three letters of reference submitted electronically are required.
Exclusive: Visit www.UltimateScholarshipBook.com and enter code NA91726 for updates on this award.

[918] • Graduate Scholarships
Institute of Food Technologists (IFT)
525 W. Van Buren, Suite 1000, Chicago, IL 60607
Phone: 312-782-8424
Email: ContactUs@applyISTS.com
https://www.ift.org/community/students
Purpose: To reward graduate students researching food science or technology.
Eligibility: Applicants should be graduate students pursuing an M.S. and/or Ph.D. at the time the fellowship becomes effective and should research an area of food science or technology. Applications, transcripts and three recommendation letters are required.
Target applicant(s): Graduate school students. Adult students.
Amount: $2,000-$5,000.
Number of awards: Varies.
Deadline: February 26.
How to apply: Applications are available online.
Exclusive: Visit www.UltimateScholarshipBook.com and enter code IN91826 for updates on this award.

[919] • Graduate Student Research Grants
Geological Society of America Graduate Student Research Grants
Matt Dawson, P.O. Box 9140, Boulder, CO 80301-9140
Phone: 303-357-1018
Email: mdawson@geosociety.org
https://www.geosociety.org
Purpose: To support thesis and dissertation research for graduate students in geological science.
Eligibility: Applicants must currently be enrolled in a geological science graduate program at an institution in the United States, Canada, Mexico or Central America. Applicants must also be members of the Geological Society of America (GSA).
Target applicant(s): Graduate school students. Adult students.
Amount: $2,500.
Number of awards: Varies.
Deadline: February 1.
How to apply: Applications are available online.
Exclusive: Visit www.UltimateScholarshipBook.com and enter code GE91926 for updates on this award.

[920] • Graduate Student Scholarship
American Speech-Language-Hearing Foundation
2200 Research Boulevard, Rockville, MD 20850
Phone: 301-296-8700
Email: foundationprograms@asha.org
https://www.ashfoundation.org/
Purpose: To support graduate students in communication sciences and disorders.
Eligibility: Applicants must be full-time graduate students in U.S. communication sciences and disorders programs. Master's degree candidates must be in programs accredited by the Council on Academic Accreditation for Audiology and Speech Pathology, but doctoral programs

do not have to be accredited. Transcripts, an essay, a reference form and a statement of good standing are required.
Target applicant(s): College students. Graduate school students. Adult students.
Amount: $5,000.
Number of awards: Up to 15.
Deadline: May 17.
How to apply: Applications are available online.
Exclusive: Visit www.UltimateScholarshipBook.com and enter code AM92026 for updates on this award.

[921] • Graduate Summer Student Research Assistantship
National Radio Astronomy Observatory (NRAO)
NRAO Headquarters, 520 Edgemont Road, Charlottesville, VA 22903
Phone: 434-296-0211
Email: info@nrao.edu
https://science.nrao.edu/opportunities/student-programs
Purpose: To allow graduate students to perform astronomical research at National Radio Astronomy Observatory (NRAO) sites.
Eligibility: Applicants must be first- or second-year graduate students interested in astronomical research. Recipients work on-site for 10 to 12 weeks, beginning in late May or early June.
Target applicant(s): Graduate school students. Adult students.
Amount: Varies.
Number of awards: Varies.
Deadline: February 1.
How to apply: Applications are available online.
Exclusive: Visit www.UltimateScholarshipBook.com and enter code NA92126 for updates on this award.

[922] • Green Voice Design Competition
Network of the Hospitality Industry
P.O. Box 322, Shawano, WI 54166
Phone: 800-593-6394
https://newh.org/available-scholarships/
Purpose: To support students who create a green design.
Eligibility: Applicants must be interior design or architecture undergraduates in a four-year program or graduate students attending an accredited college. Students must execute a dynamic, creative and cutting-edge design utilizing the best products and technologies, encompassing sustainable topics such as site selection, water efficiency, energy conservation, products/materials and indoor environmental quality. Once selected as winners, applicants must be available to attend the awards event at BDNY.
Target applicant(s): College students. Graduate school students. Adult students.
Amount: $7,500.
Number of awards: Varies.
Deadline: January 8.
How to apply: Applications are available online.
Exclusive: Visit www.UltimateScholarshipBook.com and enter code NE92226 for updates on this award.

[923] • Grow Ag Leaders Scholarship
National FFA Organization
P.O. Box 68960, 6060 FFA Drive, Indianapolis, IN 46268-0960
Phone: 888-332-2668
Email: scholarships@ffa.org
https://www.ffa.org/participate/grants-and-scholarships/
Purpose: To assist students who are FFA members.
Eligibility: Applicants must be high school seniors or students enrolled in college full-time who are planning to attend a vocational, two-year or four-year qualifying agriculture related study program after high school. Students must have a minimum 2.5 GPA and be members of FFA. Applicants must obtain no less than two electronic endorsements from qualifying farmers who live or farm in an eligible county. Selection is based on the overall strength of the application.
Target applicant(s): High school students. College students. Adult students.
Minimum GPA: 2.5
Amount: $1,500.
Number of awards: 352.
Deadline: January 11.
How to apply: Applications are available online.
Exclusive: Visit www.UltimateScholarshipBook.com and enter code NA92326 for updates on this award.

[924] • H.P. Bud Milligan Aviation Scholarship
EAA Aviation Center
3000 Poberezny Road, Oshkosh, WI 54902
Phone: 920-426-4800
Email: scholarships@eaa.org
https://www.eaa.org/eaa/learn-to-fly/scholarships
Purpose: To support excellence among individuals studying aviation.
Eligibility: Applicants must be enrolled in an accredited college, aviation academy or technical school pursuing a course of study focusing on aviation. Applicants must also be involved in school and community activities as well as aviation and be an EAA member or be recommended by an EAA member.
Target applicant(s): High school students. College students. Adult students.
Amount: $5,000.
Number of awards: 1.
Scholarship may be renewable.
Deadline: March 1.
How to apply: Applications are available online.
Exclusive: Visit www.UltimateScholarshipBook.com and enter code EA92426 for updates on this award.

[925] • Harold and Inge Marcus Scholarship
Institute of Industrial and Systems Engineers
3577 Parkway Lane, Suite 200, Norcross, GA 30092
Phone: 800-494-0460
Email: egrimes@iise.org
https://www.iise.org
Purpose: To aid industrial engineering students who are members of the Institute of Industrial Engineers (IIE).
Eligibility: Applicants must be undergraduate industrial engineering students who have been formally nominated for the award by their industrial engineering department heads. They must be full-time students who are active IIE members in good standing and must have an undergraduate GPA of 3.4 or higher on a four-point scale. Selection is

based on academic achievement, integrity, financial need and potential contribution to the industrial engineering field.
Target applicant(s): College students. Adult students.
Minimum GPA: 3.4
Amount: $1,000.
Number of awards: 10.
Deadline: February 1.
How to apply: Applications will be mailed to those who have been formally nominated by their department heads. A formal nomination, an application packet and supporting documents are required.
Exclusive: Visit www.UltimateScholarshipBook.com and enter code IN92526 for updates on this award.

[926] • Harold Bettinger Scholarship
American Floral Endowment
1001 North Fairfax Street, Suite 201, Alexandria, VA 22314
Phone: 703-838-5211
Email: afe@endowment.org
http://endowment.org/scholarships/
Purpose: To aid current horticulture students who are planning to pursue careers in a horticulture-related business.
Eligibility: Applicants must be U.S. or Canadian citizens or residents. They must be graduate students or rising undergraduate sophomores, juniors or seniors. They must have a GPA of 2.0 or higher. They must be horticulture students who are pursuing a major or minor in business or marketing and must have plans to pursue a career in the horticulture business field. Selection is based on the overall strength of the application.
Target applicant(s): College students. Graduate school students. Adult students.
Minimum GPA: 2.0
Amount: Varies.
Number of awards: Varies.
Deadline: May 1.
How to apply: Applications are available online. An application form, two letters of recommendation, a personal statement and a transcript are required.
Exclusive: Visit www.UltimateScholarshipBook.com and enter code AM92626 for updates on this award.

[927] • Harry J. Harwick Scholarship
Medical Group Management Association
104 Inverness Terrace East, Englewood, CO 80112-5306
Phone: 877-275-6462
Email: scholarship@mgma.com
https://www.mgma.com/scholarships
Purpose: To aid undergraduate and graduate students of public health, health care management, health care administration and related areas of medical practice management.
Eligibility: Applicants must be enrolled in an undergraduate or graduate degree program in public health, health care management, health care administration or a related medical practice management subject. Undergraduates must be enrolled in a program that is a member of the Association of University Programs in Health Administration (AUPHA), and graduate students must be enrolled in a program that has been accredited by the Commission on Accreditation of Healthcare Management Education (CAHME). Selection is based on the overall strength of the application.
Target applicant(s): High school students. College students. Graduate school students. Adult students.
Amount: $3,000.
Number of awards: Varies.
Deadline: April 29.
How to apply: Applications are available online. An application form and supporting documents are required.
Exclusive: Visit www.UltimateScholarshipBook.com and enter code ME92726 for updates on this award.

[928] • Health Careers Scholarship
International Order of the King's Daughters and Sons
P.O. Box 1040, 34 Vincent Avenue, Chautauqua, NY 14722
Phone: 716-357-4951
Email: Native-American-director@iokds.org
https://iokds.org/
Purpose: To assist students interested in pursuing health careers.
Eligibility: Applicants must be full-time students pursuing a career in medicine, dentistry, nursing, pharmacy, physical or occupational therapy or medical technologies. R.N. students and those pursuing an M.D. or D.D.S must have completed at least one year of schooling at an accredited institution. All others must be entering at least their third year of school. Pre-med students are not eligible. Applicants must be U.S. or Canadian citizens.
Target applicant(s): College students. Graduate school students. Adult students.
Amount: Varies.
Number of awards: Varies.
Deadline: April 1.
How to apply: Applications are available by sending a self-addressed, stamped legal size envelope.
Exclusive: Visit www.UltimateScholarshipBook.com and enter code IN92826 for updates on this award.

[929] • Helen C. Evans Scholarship
Armenian General Benevolent Union (AGBU)
55 East 59th Street, 7th Floor, New York, NY 10022-1112
Phone: 212-319-6383
Email: scholarship@agbu.org
http://www.agbu.org
Purpose: To support graduate students pursuing studies in the areas of Armenian art, art history, architecture or early Christianity.
Eligibility: Applicants must be enrolled in full-time graduate degree programs pursuing studies in the areas of Armenian art, art history, architecture or early Christianity. Students must demonstrate a strong interest in pursuing world-leading research, teaching and dissemination of future work that will help develop the areas of Armenian art, art history, architecture or early Christianity and related fields. This scholarship is open to students of both Armenian and non-Armenian descent. Applicants must complete and submit a pre-screening form before being invited to apply.
Target applicant(s): Graduate school students. Adult students.
Amount: Up to $5,000.
Number of awards: Varies.
Deadline: May 1.
How to apply: Applications are available online.
Exclusive: Visit www.UltimateScholarshipBook.com and enter code AR92926 for updates on this award.

[930] • Henry Adams Scholarship

American Society of Heating, Refrigerating and Air-Conditioning Engineers (ASHRAE)
Scholarship Administrator, ASHRAE Inc., 180 Technology Parkway, Peachtree Corners, GA 30092
Phone: 404-636-8400
Email: lbenedict@ashrae.org
https://www.ashrae.org/communities/student-zone/scholarships-and-grants
Purpose: To aid undergraduate engineering students who are preparing for careers in the heating, ventilation, air-conditioning and refrigeration (HVACR) industry.
Eligibility: Applicants must be undergraduate engineering or pre-engineering students. They must be enrolled in or accepted into an ABET-accredited school, a school that is accredited by a non-U.S. agency that has entered into a Memorandum of Understanding agreement with ABET or a school that hosts a recognized student branch of the American Society of Heating, Refrigerating and Air-Conditioning Engineers (ASHRAE). The applicant's program of study must offer adequate preparation for a career in the HVACR industry. Applicants must have a GPA of 3.0 or higher and must be ranked in the top 30 percent of their class. Selection is based on the overall strength of the application.
Target applicant(s): High school students. College students. Adult students.
Minimum GPA: 3.0
Amount: $3,000.
Number of awards: 1.
Scholarship may be renewable.
Deadline: December 1.
How to apply: Applications are available online. An application form, official transcript and one recommendation letter are required.
Exclusive: Visit www.UltimateScholarshipBook.com and enter code AM93026 for updates on this award.

[931] • Herbert Levy Memorial Scholarship

Society of Physics Students
One Physics Ellipse, College Park, MD 20740
Phone: 301-209-3007
Email: SPS-Programs@aip.org
https://www.spsnational.org/
Purpose: To provide financial assistance for physics students in any year of undergraduate study.
Eligibility: Applicants must be physics majors, be members of SPS and demonstrate scholarly achievement and financial need.
Target applicant(s): College students. Adult students.
Amount: $2,500.
Number of awards: 1.
Deadline: March 15.
How to apply: Applications are available online or from SPS Chapter Advisors.
Exclusive: Visit www.UltimateScholarshipBook.com and enter code SO93126 for updates on this award.

[932] • Hertz Foundation's Graduate Fellowship Award

Fannie and John Hertz Foundation
Attn: Applications, 2300 First Street, Suite 250, Livermore, CA 94550
Phone: 925-373-1642
Email: askhertz@hertzfoundation.org
http://www.hertzfoundation.org
Purpose: To help graduate students in the applied physical and engineering sciences.
Eligibility: Applicants must be college seniors planning to pursue or graduate students currently pursuing a Ph.D. in the applied physical and engineering sciences or modern biology which applies the physical sciences. Successful applicants must attend one of the foundation's approved schools. The award is based on merit, creativity and potential for research.
Target applicant(s): College students. Graduate school students. Adult students.
Amount: Up to full tuition plus stipend.
Number of awards: Varies.
Scholarship may be renewable.
Deadline: October 27.
How to apply: Applications are available online, by phone or by email.
Exclusive: Visit www.UltimateScholarshipBook.com and enter code FA93226 for updates on this award.

[933] • HIMSS Foundation Scholarship

Healthcare Information and Management Systems Society
230 E. Ohio Street, Suite 500, Chicago, IL 60611-3269
Phone: 312-664-4467
Email: scholarships@himss.org
http://www.himss.org
Purpose: To provide scholarships based on academic achievement and leadership in the field of healthcare information and management systems.
Eligibility: Applicants must be members of HIMSS and study healthcare information and management systems. Scholarships are also available from individual chapters listed on the HIMSS website.
Target applicant(s): College students. Graduate school students. Adult students.
Amount: $5,000.
Number of awards: 2.
Deadline: October 24.
How to apply: Application details are available online.
Exclusive: Visit www.UltimateScholarshipBook.com and enter code HE93326 for updates on this award.

[934] • Holly A. Cornell Scholarship

American Water Works Association
6666 W. Quincy Avenue, Denver, CO 80235
Phone: 800-926-7337
Email: scholarships@awwa.org
https://www.awwa.org
Purpose: To support female and/or minority master's students pursuing advanced training in the field of water supply and treatment.
Eligibility: Applicants must be females and/or minorities who have been accepted to or are current master's degree students in engineering. Applications, transcripts, GRE scores, three recommendation letters, statements and course of study are required. The award is based on academics and leadership.
Target applicant(s): Graduate school students. Adult students.
Amount: $10,000.
Number of awards: 1.
Deadline: December 20.
How to apply: Applications are available online.
Exclusive: Visit www.UltimateScholarshipBook.com and enter code AM93426 for updates on this award.

The Ultimate Scholarship Book 2026
Scholarship Directory (Sciences)

[935] • Houzz Women in Architecture
Houzz Inc.
285 Hamilton Avenue, Palo Alto, CA 94301
Email: scholarships@houzz.com
http://houzz.com/scholarships
Purpose: To support women architecture students.
Eligibility: Applicants must be female students enrolled at a U.S. university as an undergraduate or graduate student. Students must be majoring in architecture.
Target applicant(s): College students. Graduate school students. Adult students.
Amount: $2,500.
Number of awards: 1.
Deadline: March 31.
How to apply: Applications are available online.
Exclusive: Visit www.UltimateScholarshipBook.com and enter code HO93526 for updates on this award.

[936] • Hutton Junior Fisheries Biology Program
American Fisheries Society (AFS)
425 Barlow Place, Suite 110, Bethesda, MD 20814
Phone: 301-897-8616
Email: Hutton@fisheries.org
https://hutton.fisheries.org/
Purpose: To stimulate interest in pursuing fisheries science and aquatic resources among high school students.
Eligibility: Applicants must be a junior or senior in high school. Students must provide official copies of student transcripts. Preference will be given to qualified women and minority applicants.
Target applicant(s): High school students.
Amount: $3,000.
Number of awards: Varies.
Deadline: January 26.
How to apply: Applications are available online.
Exclusive: Visit www.UltimateScholarshipBook.com and enter code AM93626 for updates on this award.

[937] • IBTTA Foundation Scholarship Program
International Bridge, Tunnel and Turnpike Association Foundation
IBTTA Foundation Scholarship Program, Scholarship America, One Scholarship Way, Saint Peter, MN 56082
Phone: 507-931-1682
Email: ibtta@scholarshipamerica.org
https://learnmore.scholarsapply.org/ibtta/
Purpose: To support students who are working towards a transportation-related degree.
Eligibility: Applicants must be current undergraduate college students who have completed at least two full semesters of undergraduate coursework or graduate students. Students must be planning to enroll full-time and have a minimum 2.5 GPA. Applicants must be pursuing a degree in one of the following fields: civil engineering, city and regional planning, construction management, public policy or public administration, structural engineering, finance, accounting, information technology, business management, marketing, communications, operations management or other transportation-related degrees.
Target applicant(s): College students. Graduate school students. Adult students.
Minimum GPA: 2.5
Amount: $5,000.
Number of awards: 6.
Deadline: April 19.
How to apply: Applications are available online.
Exclusive: Visit www.UltimateScholarshipBook.com and enter code IN93726 for updates on this award.

[938] • IISE Council of Fellows Undergraduate Scholarship
Institute of Industrial and Systems Engineers
3577 Parkway Lane, Suite 200, Norcross, GA 30092
Phone: 800-494-0460
Email: egrimes@iise.org
https://www.iise.org
Purpose: To support undergraduate student members.
Eligibility: Applicants must be full-time undergraduate students enrolled in a college in the United States, Canada or Mexico with an accredited industrial engineering program, major in industrial engineering and be active members. Students may not apply directly for this scholarship and must be nominated. The award is based on academic ability, character, leadership, potential service to the industrial engineering profession and financial need. Applicants must have a minimum 3.4 GPA.
Target applicant(s): College students. Adult students.
Minimum GPA: 3.4
Amount: $2,600.
Number of awards: 4.
Deadline: February 1.
How to apply: Nomination forms are available online.
Exclusive: Visit www.UltimateScholarshipBook.com and enter code IN93826 for updates on this award.

[939] • Industrial Electrochemistry and Electrochemical Engineering Student Achievement Award
Electrochemical Society
65 South Main Street, Building D, Pennington, NJ 08534-2839
Phone: 609-737-1902
Email: ecs@electrochem.org
https://www.electrochem.org/student-awards
Purpose: To recognize young engineers and scientists in electrochemical engineering and to encourage the recipients to enter careers in the field.
Eligibility: Applicants must be accepted by or enrolled in a college or university and propose a research project. The application must include transcripts, research outline, statement describing how the project relates to electrochemical engineering, record of industrial work and letter of recommendation from the research supervisor. The award is based on academic performance, research and the recommendation.
Target applicant(s): High school students. College students. Graduate school students. Adult students.
Amount: $1,000.
Number of awards: 1.
Deadline: September 1.
How to apply: Application materials are described online.
Exclusive: Visit www.UltimateScholarshipBook.com and enter code EL93926 for updates on this award.

[940] • Injection Molding Division Scholarship
Society of Plastics Engineers
83 Wooster Heights Road Suite 125, Suite 306, Danbury, CT 06810
Phone: 810-986-6131
Email: thomas.miller@ravago.com
https://plasticspioneers.org/scholarships/
Purpose: To aid students who have employment or academic experience in injection molding.
Eligibility: Applicants must be full-time undergraduate or graduate students who are in good academic standing. They must have experience in injection molding through courses taken, research conducted or formal employment. They must have an interest in the plastics/polymer industry and must have taken courses that would prepare them for a career in this field. Selection is based on academic merit and financial need.
Target applicant(s): High school students. College students. Graduate school students. Adult students.
Amount: $3,000.
Number of awards: 1.
Deadline: April 30.
How to apply: Applications are available online. An application form, three recommendation letters, transcripts, a personal statement, a list of extracurricular activities and honors and employment history are required.
Exclusive: Visit www.UltimateScholarshipBook.com and enter code SO94026 for updates on this award.

[941] • Institute of Electrical and Electronics Engineers Life Members' Fellowship in Electrical History
Institute of Electrical and Electronics Engineers (IEEE)
445 Hoes Lane, Piscataway, NJ 08854
Phone: 732-562-3860
Email: supportieee@ieee.org
http://www.ieee.org/scholarships
Purpose: To support students in engineering and technology-related fields.
Eligibility: Applicants must be studying engineering, computer science and information technology, physical sciences, biological and medical sciences, mathematics, technical communications, education, management or law and policy. The award may be used during one year of full-time graduate work or one year of post-doctoral research. Students must provide a detailed 15-page description of the proposed research, along with three letters of recommendation.
Target applicant(s): College students. Graduate school students. Adult students.
Amount: $25,000.
Number of awards: 1.
Deadline: February 1.
How to apply: Applications are available online.
Exclusive: Visit www.UltimateScholarshipBook.com and enter code IN94126 for updates on this award.

[942] • International Gas Turbine Institute Scholarship
American Society of Mechanical Engineers (ASME)
Two Park Avenue, New York, NY 10016-5990
Phone: 800-843-2763
Email: lefeverb@asme.org
https://www.asme.org/asme-programs/students-and-faculty/scholarships/scholarships
Purpose: To aid American Society of Mechanical Engineers (ASME) student members who are interested in the gas turbine industry.
Eligibility: Applicants must be student members of ASME who are in good standing. They must be enrolled in an accredited undergraduate or graduate degree program in mechanical engineering or aerospace engineering. They must be interested in the turbomachinery, gas turbine or propulsion industry. Preference will be given to those who have employment or research experience in one of the industries. Selection is based on academic achievement and demonstrated interest in the gas turbine industry.
Target applicant(s): High school students. College students. Graduate school students. Adult students.
Amount: $2,000.
Number of awards: 20.
Deadline: February 29.
How to apply: Applications may be completed online. An electronic application form, official transcript, personal statement and one to two recommendation letters are required.
Exclusive: Visit www.UltimateScholarshipBook.com and enter code AM94226 for updates on this award.

[943] • International Student Scholarship
American Speech-Language-Hearing Foundation
2200 Research Boulevard, Rockville, MD 20850
Phone: 301-296-8700
Email: foundationprograms@asha.org
https://www.ashfoundation.org/
Purpose: To support an international graduate student in communication sciences and disorders.
Eligibility: Applicants must be full-time students in the U.S. Master's degree candidates must be in programs accredited by the Council on Academic Accreditation for Audiology and Speech Pathology, but doctoral programs do not have to be accredited. The applicants should submit transcripts, an essay and a reference form.
Target applicant(s): College students. Graduate school students. Adult students.
Amount: $5,000.
Number of awards: Up to 2.
Deadline: May 17.
How to apply: Applications are available online.
Exclusive: Visit www.UltimateScholarshipBook.com and enter code AM94326 for updates on this award.

[944] • International Women's Fishing Association Scholarship
International Women's Fishing Association
P.O. Box 530816, Miami Shores, FL 33153
Email: kelleykeys@aol.com
https://iwfa.memberclicks.net/criteria
Purpose: To help students in graduate programs in the marine sciences.
Eligibility: Applicants must have graduated or have been approved for graduation from an accredited college or university and plan on pursuing a graduate degree in the marine sciences. Selection is based on academic success, personal character, aptitude in the student's area of study and financial need.
Target applicant(s): Graduate school students. Adult students.
Amount: $1,000-$3,000.
Number of awards: Varies.
Deadline: March 1.
How to apply: Applications are available online. Students must include an official transcript, a photo, a letter describing career goals and a list of three people who will be sending letters of recommendation.

The Ultimate Scholarship Book 2026
Scholarship Directory (Sciences)

Exclusive: Visit www.UltimateScholarshipBook.com and enter code IN94426 for updates on this award.

[945] • Intertech Foundation STEM Scholarship
Intertech Foundation
1575 Thomas Center Drive, Eagan, MN 55122
Phone: 651-288-7000
Email: info@intertech.com
https://www.intertech.com/stem-scholarships/
Purpose: To assist college-bound students who have excelled at math and science.
Eligibility: Applicants must be college-bound high school seniors or current college students who are U.S. citizens and have at least a 3.3 GPA. Students must plan to major in computer science in college.
Target applicant(s): High school students. College students. Adult students.
Minimum GPA: 3.3
Amount: $2,500.
Number of awards: 1.
Deadline: April 15.
How to apply: There is no application form. A high school transcript, a resume, two letters of recommendation, a copy of a college acceptance letter and a one-page essay about how the student plans to participate in the professional software development industry are required.
Exclusive: Visit www.UltimateScholarshipBook.com and enter code IN94526 for updates on this award.

[946] • Irene and Daisy MacGregor Memorial Scholarship
National Society Daughters of the American Revolution
Committee Services Office, Attn.: Scholarships, 1776 D Street NW, Washington, DC 20006-5303
Phone: 202-628-1776
Email: scholarships@dar.org
https://www.dar.org/national-society/scholarships
Purpose: To assist students in becoming medical doctors.
Eligibility: Applicants must be accepted into or enrolled in a graduate course of study to become a medical doctor. Those pursuing study in psychiatric nursing at the graduate level at a medical school may also apply, and preference is given to females. All applicants must obtain a letter of sponsorship from their local DAR chapter. However, affiliation with DAR is not required.
Target applicant(s): Graduate school students. Adult students.
Amount: Varies.
Number of awards: 2.
Scholarship may be renewable.
Deadline: January 31.
How to apply: Applications are available by written request with a self-addressed, stamped envelope.
Exclusive: Visit www.UltimateScholarshipBook.com and enter code NA94626 for updates on this award.

[947] • Irene Woodall Graduate Scholarship
American Dental Hygienists' Association (ADHA) Institute for Oral Health
444 North Michigan Avenue, Suite 400, Chicago, IL 60611
Phone: 312-440-8900
Email: institute@adha.net
https://www.adha.org/ioh/scholarships/
Purpose: To support students pursuing a master's degree in dental hygiene.
Eligibility: Applicants must be full-time students at an accredited college or university in the United States pursuing a master's degree in dental hygiene or a related field and must have completed at least one year of a dental hygiene curriculum. Applicants must also be active members of the ADHA, have a minimum 3.5 GPA and have a minimum demonstrated financial need of $1,500. Selection is based on the overall strength of the application.
Target applicant(s): College students. Graduate school students. Adult students.
Amount: $1,000.
Number of awards: 1.
Deadline: February 2.
How to apply: Applications are available online after October 1.
Exclusive: Visit www.UltimateScholarshipBook.com and enter code AM94726 for updates on this award.

[948] • IWSH Essay Scholarship
International Water, Sanitation and Hygiene Foundation
4755 East Philadelphia Street, Ontario, CA 91761
Phone: 909-472-4100
Email: essay@iwsh.org
https://iwsh.org/iwsh-world-plumbing-day-essay-contest
Purpose: To encourage students who have an awareness of the importance of the plumbing industry.
Eligibility: Applicants must be a high school senior or enrolled in an accredited technical school, community college, trade school or four-year accredited college/university. Students must submit an essay between 800 and 1,600 words on the topic listed on the website.
Target applicant(s): High school students. College students. Adult students.
Amount: $1,000-$2,000.
Number of awards: 4.
Deadline: April 30.
How to apply: Applications are available online.
Exclusive: Visit www.UltimateScholarshipBook.com and enter code IN94826 for updates on this award.

[949] • Jackson Laboratory Scholarship
Jackson Laboratory
Training and Education Office, 600 Main Street, Bar Harbor, ME 04609
Phone: 207-288-6250
Email: scholarship@jax.org
https://www.jax.org/scholarship
Purpose: To reward students pursuing a college education in research or medical fields.
Eligibility: Applicants must reside in Connecticut, Maine or in Sacramento County, California and must be pursuing a degree in biomedicine. Students must receive a nomination from a teacher and have financial need or be first-generation college students. Students must also have a 3.5 GPA and be graduating high school seniors.
Target applicant(s): High school students.
Minimum GPA: 3.5
Amount: $10,000.
Number of awards: 3.
Deadline: February 15.
How to apply: Applications are available online.
Exclusive: Visit www.UltimateScholarshipBook.com and enter code JA94926 for updates on this award.

[950] • Jean Theodore Lacordaire Prize

Coleopterists Society
Dr. Darren A. Pollock, Chair, Department of Biology, Eastern New Mexico University, Portales, NM 88130
Phone: 575-562-2862
Email: Darren.Pollock@enmu.edu
http://www.coleopsoc.org/
Purpose: To recognize the work of coleopterists.
Eligibility: Applicants must be graduate students whose papers are nominated for the competition. The papers must be based on the applicant's dissertation research about coleoptera (beetle) systematics or biology published in the preceding calendar year. Self-nominations are not accepted.
Target applicant(s): Graduate school students. Adult students.
Amount: $1,000.
Number of awards: 1.
Deadline: March 1.
How to apply: Application materials are described online.
Exclusive: Visit www.UltimateScholarshipBook.com and enter code CO95026 for updates on this award.

[951] • Jill S. Tietjen P.E. Scholarship

Society of Women Engineers
130 East Randolph Street, Suite 3500, Chicago, IL 60601
Phone: 877-793-4636
Email: scholarships@swe.org
https://swe.org/scholarships/
Purpose: To support female engineering students pursuing a higher education.
Eligibility: Applicants must be currently enrolled in an accredited engineering or engineering technology program with a minimum of a 3.0 GPA. The award is to be used during the sophomore, junior or senior year of college.
Target applicant(s): College students. Adult students.
Minimum GPA: 3.0
Amount: $2,500.
Number of awards: 1.
Deadline: January 31.
How to apply: Applications are available online.
Exclusive: Visit www.UltimateScholarshipBook.com and enter code SO95126 for updates on this award.

[952] • Jimmy A. Young Memorial Education Recognition Award

American Association for Respiratory Care
9425 North MacArthur Boulevard, Suite 100, Irving, TX 75063-4706
Phone: 972-243-2272
Email: info@aarc.org
https://www.aarc.org/your-rt-career/scholarship-loans/
Purpose: To recognize outstanding minority students in respiratory care education programs.
Eligibility: Applicants must be enrolled in an accredited respiratory care education program and have a minimum 3.0 GPA. Students must submit an original paper on respiratory care. Preference is given to minority students.
Target applicant(s): College students. Graduate school students. Adult students.
Minimum GPA: 3.0
Amount: Up to $1,000.
Number of awards: 1.
Deadline: June 1.
How to apply: Applications are available online.
Exclusive: Visit www.UltimateScholarshipBook.com and enter code AM95226 for updates on this award.

[953] • John and Elsa Gracik Scholarships

American Society of Mechanical Engineers (ASME)
Two Park Avenue, New York, NY 10016-5990
Phone: 800-843-2763
Email: lefeverb@asme.org
https://www.asme.org/asme-programs/students-and-faculty/scholarships/scholarships
Purpose: To support mechanical engineering students.
Eligibility: Applicants must be ASME student members, enrolled in an eligible accredited mechanical engineering baccalaureate program and be U.S. citizens. Selection is based on scholastic ability, financial need, character, leadership and potential contribution to the mechanical engineering profession.
Target applicant(s): College students. Adult students.
Amount: $5,000.
Number of awards: 5.
Deadline: February 15.
How to apply: Applications are available online.
Exclusive: Visit www.UltimateScholarshipBook.com and enter code AM95326 for updates on this award.

[954] • John and Muriel Landis Scholarship

American Nuclear Society
555 North Kensington Avenue, La Grange Park, IL 60526
Phone: 800-323-3044
Email: hr@ans.org
http://www.ans.org
Purpose: To assist disadvantaged students in seeking careers in a nuclear-related field.
Eligibility: Applicants must be undergraduate or graduate students enrolled or planning to enroll in a U.S. college or university who are also planning a career in nuclear science, nuclear engineering or another nuclear-related field. High school seniors may apply. Students must have greater than average financial need. Applicants must submit applications, transcripts, sponsor forms and three reference forms.
Target applicant(s): High school students. College students. Graduate school students. Adult students.
Amount: $5,000.
Number of awards: Up to 9.
Deadline: February 1.
How to apply: Applications are available online.
Exclusive: Visit www.UltimateScholarshipBook.com and enter code AM95426 for updates on this award.

[955] • John C. Bajus Scholarship

Marine Technology Society
One Thomas Circle, Suite 700, Washington, DC 20005
Phone: 202-717-8705
Email: scholarships@mtsociety.org
https://www.mtsociety.org/scholarships

Purpose: To support Marine Technology Society members who are pursuing a degree in a marine-related field.
Eligibility: Applicants must be MTS student members who are accepted for enrollment or enrolled full-time in an undergraduate or graduate program. Selection is primarily based on demonstration of commitment to community service and volunteer work.
Target applicant(s): College students. Graduate school students. Adult students.
Amount: $1,000.
Number of awards: 1.
Deadline: April 15.
How to apply: Applications are available online.
Exclusive: Visit www.UltimateScholarshipBook.com and enter code MA95526 for updates on this award.

[956] • John J. McKetta Scholarship
American Institute of Chemical Engineers - (AIChE)
120 Wall Street, Floor 23, New York, NY 10005-4020
Phone: 800-242-4363
Email: awards@aiche.org
https://www.aiche.org/community/awards
Purpose: To support chemical engineering students.
Eligibility: Applicants must be chemical engineering incoming undergraduate juniors or seniors and be planning a career in the chemical engineering process industries. Applicants must also have a minimum 3.0 GPA and be attending an ABET accredited school in the U.S., Canada or Mexico. Selection is based on an essay outlining career goals, leadership in an AIChE student chapter or other university sponsored activity and letters of recommendation. Preference is given to members of AIChE.
Target applicant(s): College students. Adult students.
Minimum GPA: 3.0
Amount: $5,000.
Number of awards: 1.
Deadline: June 15.
How to apply: Applications are available online.
Exclusive: Visit www.UltimateScholarshipBook.com and enter code AM95626 for updates on this award.

[957] • John L. Imhoff Scholarship
Institute of Industrial and Systems Engineers
3577 Parkway Lane, Suite 200, Norcross, GA 30092
Phone: 800-494-0460
Email: egrimes@iise.org
https://www.iise.org
Purpose: To reward a student who has contributed to the development of the industrial engineering profession through international understanding.
Eligibility: Applicants must be pursuing a B.S., master's or doctorate degree in an accredited IE program, and have a minimum 3.4 GPA. Students may not apply directly for this scholarship and must be nominated. An essay describing the candidate's international contributions to industrial engineering and three references are required. IIE membership is not required.
Target applicant(s): College students. Graduate school students. Adult students.
Minimum GPA: 3.4
Amount: $1,500.
Number of awards: 3.
Deadline: February 1.
How to apply: More information is available online.
Exclusive: Visit www.UltimateScholarshipBook.com and enter code IN95726 for updates on this award.

[958] • John Mabry Forestry Scholarship and Paul Webster Forestry Scholarship
Railway Tie Association
110 River Birch Trace, Fayetteville, GA 30215
Phone: 770-460-5553
Email: ties@rta.org
http://www.rta.org
Purpose: To aid forestry school students.
Eligibility: Applicants must be enrolled in an accredited forestry program at a postsecondary institution. They must be in the second year of a two-year technical school program or in the third or fourth year of a four-year college or university program. Students who are in the final year of their program must remain enrolled for the entirety of the academic year. Selection is based on academic merit, leadership ability, stated career goals and financial need.
Target applicant(s): College students. Adult students.
Amount: $5,000.
Number of awards: 2.
Deadline: February 28.
How to apply: Applications are available online. An application form and supporting documents are required.
Exclusive: Visit www.UltimateScholarshipBook.com and enter code RA95826 for updates on this award.

[959] • John S. Marshall Memorial Scholarship
American Institute of Mining, Metallurgical and Petroleum Engineers (AIME)
12999 East Adam Aircraft Circle, Englewood, CO 80112
Phone: 303-325-5185
Email: aime@aimehq.org
http://www.aimehq.org/programs/scholarships
Purpose: To aid mining engineering students.
Eligibility: Applicants must be rising undergraduate juniors or seniors who are enrolled in an ABET-accredited mining engineering degree program on a full-time basis. They must be student members of the Society for Mining, Metallurgy and Exploration (SME). They must have plans to pursue a career in the mining industry and must demonstrate financial need. Selection is based on the overall strength of the application.
Target applicant(s): College students. Adult students.
Amount: Varies.
Number of awards: Varies.
Deadline: October 15.
How to apply: Applications are available online. An application form and two letters of recommendation are required.
Exclusive: Visit www.UltimateScholarshipBook.com and enter code AM95926 for updates on this award.

[960] • John S.W. Fargher, Jr. Scholarship
Institute of Industrial and Systems Engineers
3577 Parkway Lane, Suite 200, Norcross, GA 30092
Phone: 800-494-0460
Email: egrimes@iise.org
https://www.iise.org
Purpose: To reward graduate students in industrial engineering who have demonstrated leadership.
Eligibility: Applicants must be full-time graduate students with at least one full year left who are enrolled in a college in the United States with an accredited industrial engineering program. Candidates must also major in industrial engineering or engineering management and be active members who have demonstrated leadership in industrial engineering-related

activities. Students may not apply directly for this scholarship and must be nominated.
Target applicant(s): Graduate school students. Adult students.
Minimum GPA: 3.0
Amount: $1,000.
Number of awards: 2.
Deadline: February 1.
How to apply: More information is available online.
Exclusive: Visit www.UltimateScholarshipBook.com and enter code IN96026 for updates on this award.

[961] • John V. Wehausen Graduate Scholarship
Society of Naval Architects and Marine Engineers (SNAME)
99 Canal Center Plaza, Suite 500, Alexandria, VA 22314
Phone: 703-997-6701
Email: scholarships@sname.org
https://www.sname.org/scholarships
Purpose: To aid students who are seeking a master's degree in a marine-related subject.
Eligibility: Applicants must be members of the Society of Naval Architects and Marine Engineers (SNAME) or another respected marine society. They must be pursuing a master's degree in naval architecture, ocean engineering, marine engineering or another marine-related subject. Students who will be completing their degree before April 15 of the award disbursement year are ineligible. Selection is based on the overall strength of the application.
Target applicant(s): College students. Graduate school students. Adult students.
Amount: Up to $21,000.
Number of awards: 1.
Deadline: February 1.
How to apply: Applications are available online. An application form, transcript and three reference letters are required.
Exclusive: Visit www.UltimateScholarshipBook.com and enter code SO96126 for updates on this award.

[962] • John Wright Memorial Scholarship
Tree Research and Education Endowment Fund
1755 Park Street, Suite 200, Naperville, IL 60563
Phone: 630-369-8300
Email: treefund@treefund.org
http://www.treefund.org
Purpose: To help undergraduate and technical college students pursuing careers in commercial arboriculture.
Eligibility: Applicants must be high school seniors entering college or community college or returning college students seeking a first bachelor's degree or associate's degree while attending an accredited U.S. college or university. All applicants must plan to enter the arboriculture industry and have a minimum 3.0 GPA. Consideration will be given for honorably discharged veterans and present members of the U.S. Armed Forces, Reserves and National Guard.
Target applicant(s): High school students. College students. Adult students.
Minimum GPA: 3.0
Amount: $5,000.
Number of awards: 1.
Deadline: March 15.
How to apply: Applications are available online.
Exclusive: Visit www.UltimateScholarshipBook.com and enter code TR96226 for updates on this award.

[963] • Johnny Davis Memorial Scholarship
Aircraft Electronics Association
3570 NE Ralph Powell Road, Lee's Summit, MO 64064
Phone: 816-347-8400
Email: info@aea.net
https://aea.net/educationalfoundation/scholarships.asp
Purpose: To support students of avionics and aircraft repair.
Eligibility: Applicants must be high school seniors or college students who plan to or are attending an accredited school in an avionics or aircraft repair program.
Target applicant(s): High school students. College students. Adult students.
Amount: $1,000.
Number of awards: 1.
Deadline: April 1.
How to apply: Applications are available by contacting the organization for more information.
Exclusive: Visit www.UltimateScholarshipBook.com and enter code AI96326 for updates on this award.

[964] • Joseph Frasca Excellence in Aviation Scholarship
University Aviation Association (UAA)
8092 Memphis Avenue, Suite 132, Millington, TN 38053
Phone: 901-563-0505
Email: hello@uaa.aero
https://www.uaa.aero/uaa_scholarships.php
Purpose: To encourage students to reach the highest level of achievement in their aviation studies.
Eligibility: Applicants must be juniors or seniors enrolled at a UAA member college or university with at least a 3.0 GPA. Students must demonstrate excellence in all areas related to aviation and have FAA certification in either aviation maintenance or flight. Applicants must be a member of at least one aviation organization and be involved in aviation activities that demonstrate interest in and enthusiasm for aviation.
Target applicant(s): College students. Adult students.
Minimum GPA: 3.0
Amount: $2,000.
Number of awards: 2.
Deadline: June 30.
How to apply: Applications are available online.
Exclusive: Visit www.UltimateScholarshipBook.com and enter code UN96426 for updates on this award.

[965] • Junior Showmanship Scholarship Program
American Kennel Club
260 Madison Avenue, New York, NY 10016
Phone: 212-696-8200
http://www.akc.org
Purpose: To assist students who are involved with AKC purebred dogs.
Eligibility: Applicants must be under age 18 with an AKC registered purebred dog. Selection is based on involvement with AKC registered dogs, academic achievement and financial need. The scholarship program awards a total of $150,000 annually.
Target applicant(s): Junior high students or younger. High school students.
Amount: Varies.
Number of awards: Varies.
Deadline: March 1.
How to apply: Applications are available online.

Exclusive: Visit www.UltimateScholarshipBook.com and enter code AM96526 for updates on this award.

[966] • Kappa Delta Phi
American Occupational Therapy Foundation
Attn: Jeanne Cooper, 4720 Montgomery Lane, Suite 202, Bethesda, MD 20814
Phone: 240-292-1034
Email: jcooper@aotf.org
https://www.tota.org/scholarships
Purpose: To encourage students who are pursuing post-baccalaureate degrees in occupational therapy.
Eligibility: Applicants must be currently enrolled full-time in an AOTF-accredited occupational therapy program. Students must have completed at least one year of occupational therapy specific course work. Priority is given to students of Arizona, California, Florida, Iowa, Indiana, Kentucky, Missouri and Ohio.
Target applicant(s): College students. Graduate school students. Adult students.
Amount: $2,000.
Number of awards: Varies.
Deadline: October 2.
How to apply: Applications are available online.
Exclusive: Visit www.UltimateScholarshipBook.com and enter code AM96626 for updates on this award.

[967] • Karen O'Neil Memorial Scholarship
Emergency Nurses Association
930 E. Woodfield Road, Schaumburg, IL 60173
Phone: 847-460-4100
Email: ena.foundation@ena.org
http://www.ena.org
Purpose: To promote advanced degrees in emergency nursing.
Eligibility: Applicants must be nurses pursuing an advanced degree and must have been ENA members for at least 12 months before applying.
Target applicant(s): Graduate school students. Adult students.
Amount: $3,000.
Number of awards: 1.
Deadline: April 26.
How to apply: Applications are available online.
Exclusive: Visit www.UltimateScholarshipBook.com and enter code EM96726 for updates on this award.

[968] • Karla Girts Memorial Community Outreach Scholarship
American Dental Hygienists' Association (ADHA) Institute for Oral Health
444 North Michigan Avenue, Suite 400, Chicago, IL 60611
Phone: 312-440-8900
Email: institute@adha.net
https://www.adha.org/ioh/scholarships/
Purpose: To support undergraduate students and those working towards degree completion within the dental hygiene arena who are also committed to work within the geriatric population in an effort to improve the oral health of this population.
Eligibility: Applicants must be full-time students at an accredited college or university in the United States pursuing an associate, baccalaureate or degree completion program in dental hygiene or a related field and must commit to working towards improvement of oral health within the geriatric population. Applicants must have completed at least one year of a dental hygiene curriculum, be active members of the ADHA, have a minimum 3.0 GPA and have a minimum demonstrated financial need of $1,500. Selection is based on the overall strength of the application.
Target applicant(s): College students. Adult students.
Minimum GPA: 3.0
Amount: $2,000.
Number of awards: Varies.
Deadline: January 31.
How to apply: Applications are available online after October 1. An application form and essay are required.
Exclusive: Visit www.UltimateScholarshipBook.com and enter code AM96826 for updates on this award.

[969] • Kenneth Andrew Roe Scholarship
American Society of Mechanical Engineers (ASME)
Two Park Avenue, New York, NY 10016-5990
Phone: 800-843-2763
Email: lefeverb@asme.org
https://www.asme.org/asme-programs/students-and-faculty/scholarships/scholarships
Purpose: To support students who are studying mechanical engineering.
Eligibility: Applicants must be ASME student members, be enrolled in an ABET accredited mechanical engineering baccalaureate program, be North American residents and be U.S. citizens. Applicants must also have strong academic performance, character and integrity. The award is to be used during the junior or senior undergraduate years.
Target applicant(s): College students. Adult students.
Amount: $13,000.
Number of awards: 1.
Deadline: March 22.
How to apply: Applications are available online.
Exclusive: Visit www.UltimateScholarshipBook.com and enter code AM96926 for updates on this award.

[970] • LabRoots Scholarship
LabRoots
18340 Yorba Linda Boulevard, Suite 107 PMB 427, Yorba Linda, CA 92886
https://www.labroots.com/scholarships
Purpose: To support students in STEM studies.
Eligibility: Applicants must be enrolled in or accepted for an undergraduate or graduate degree at a recognized university. Students must be seeking a degree in a STEM field.
Target applicant(s): High school students. College students. Graduate school students. Adult students.
Amount: Varies.
Number of awards: Varies.
Deadline: May 31; July 31.
How to apply: Applications are available online.
Exclusive: Visit www.UltimateScholarshipBook.com and enter code LA97026 for updates on this award.

[971] • Landscape Forms Scholarship in Memory of Peter Lindsay Schaudt, FASLA
Landscape Architecture Foundation
1200 17th Street NW, Suite 210, Washington, DC 20036
Phone: 202-331-7070
Email: scholarships@lafoundation.org
https://www.lafoundation.org/what-we-do/scholarships

Purpose: To aid landscape architecture students.
Eligibility: Applicants must be full-time undergraduate students who are enrolled in a landscape architecture degree program at a school that has been accredited by the Landscape Architectural Accreditation Board (LAAB). They must be in the final year of their degree program. Selection is based on academic merit and creativity.
Target applicant(s): College students. Adult students.
Amount: $5,000.
Number of awards: 1.
Deadline: February 1.
How to apply: Applications are available online. An application form, essay, work samples and two recommendation letters are required.
Exclusive: Visit www.UltimateScholarshipBook.com and enter code LA97126 for updates on this award.

[972] • Larry Williams Photography and AYA Photo Contest
Appaloosa Horse Club
Appaloosa Youth Association, 2720 West Pullman Road, Moscow, ID 83843
Phone: 208-882-5578
Email: youth@appaloosa.com
https://www.appaloosa.com/appaloosa-youth-association
Purpose: To support students who express their love of the Appaloosa through photography.
Eligibility: Applicants must submit multiple photographs in two divisions: 13 and under and 14 to 18.
Target applicant(s): Junior high students or younger. High school students.
Amount: Up to $250.
Number of awards: 6.
Deadline: August 31.
How to apply: Applications are available online.
Exclusive: Visit www.UltimateScholarshipBook.com and enter code AP97226 for updates on this award.

[973] • Larson Aquatic Research Support (LARS)
American Water Works Association
6666 W. Quincy Avenue, Denver, CO 80235
Phone: 800-926-7337
Email: scholarships@awwa.org
https://www.awwa.org
Purpose: To support doctoral and master's students interested in careers in the fields of corrosion control, treatment and distribution of domestic and industrial water supplies, aquatic chemistry and/or environmental chemistry.
Eligibility: Applicants must pursue an advanced (master's or doctoral) degree at an institution of higher education located in Canada, Guam, Puerto Rico, Mexico or the U.S. Applications, resumes, transcripts, GRE scores, three recommendation letters and a course of study are required. Master's students also must submit a statement of educational plans and career objectives or a research plan. Ph.D. students must submit research plans. The master's grant is $5,000, and the doctoral grant is $7,000. The award is based on academics and leadership.
Target applicant(s): Graduate school students. Adult students.
Amount: $5,000-$7,000.
Number of awards: 2.
Deadline: December 20.
How to apply: Applications are available online.
Exclusive: Visit www.UltimateScholarshipBook.com and enter code AM97326 for updates on this award.

[974] • Lawrence C. Fortier Memorial Scholarship
Air Traffic Control Association
225 Reinekers Lane, Suite 400, Alexandria, VA 22314
Phone: 703-299-2430
Email: info@atca.org
http://www.atca.org
Purpose: To help students seeking higher education in air traffic control and other aviation disciplines.
Eligibility: Applicants must be enrolled half- to full-time in a program leading to a bachelor's degree or higher in an aviation-related course of study.
Target applicant(s): High school students. College students. Graduate school students. Adult students.
Amount: $5,000 - $15,000.
Number of awards: Varies.
Deadline: May 1.
How to apply: Applications are available online. An application form, two letters of reference, academic transcripts, an essay and answers to leadership and career questions are required.
Exclusive: Visit www.UltimateScholarshipBook.com and enter code AI97426 for updates on this award.

[975] • Leaders Scholarship
Medical Group Management Association
104 Inverness Terrace East, Englewood, CO 80112-5306
Phone: 877-275-6462
Email: scholarship@mgma.com
https://www.mgma.com/scholarships
Purpose: To support students pursuing advanced degrees in the medical field.
Eligibility: Applicants must be enrolled in a graduate degree program pertaining to medical practice management at a university located in the U.S. Students must include transcripts, two letters of reference, curriculum and resume along with the application.
Target applicant(s): Graduate school students. Adult students.
Amount: $5,000.
Number of awards: 1.
Deadline: May 1.
How to apply: Applications are available online.
Exclusive: Visit www.UltimateScholarshipBook.com and enter code ME97526 for updates on this award.

[976] • Learner Education Women in Mathematics Scholarship
Learner
204 Sandy Bank Road, Media, PA 19063
Phone: 800-654-7390
Email: chris@learnerscholarship.com
https://www.learner.com/scholarship
Purpose: To support female students interested in careers in math-related fields.

The Ultimate Scholarship Book 2026
Scholarship Directory (Sciences)

Eligibility: Applicants must be females who are current high school seniors planning to study or current undergraduate students studying mathematics. An essay on a provided prompt is required to be submitted.
Target applicant(s): High school students. College students. Adult students.
Amount: $1,000.
Number of awards: 1.
Deadline: August 1.
How to apply: Applications are available online.
Exclusive: Visit www.UltimateScholarshipBook.com and enter code LE97626 for updates on this award.

[977] • Lee Tarbox Memorial Scholarship
Aircraft Electronics Association
3570 NE Ralph Powell Road, Lee's Summit, MO 64064
Phone: 816-347-8400
Email: info@aea.net
https://aea.net/educationalfoundation/scholarships.asp
Purpose: To support students of avionics and aircraft repair.
Eligibility: Applicants must be high school seniors or college students who plan to or are attending an accredited school in an avionics or aircraft repair program.
Target applicant(s): High school students. College students. Adult students.
Amount: $2,500.
Number of awards: 1.
Deadline: April 1.
How to apply: Applications are available by contacting the organization for more information.
Exclusive: Visit www.UltimateScholarshipBook.com and enter code AI97726 for updates on this award.

[978] • Lewis C. Hoffman Scholarship
American Ceramic Society
600 North Cleveland Avenue, Suite 210, Westerville, OH 43082
Phone: 866-721-3322
Email: mstout@ceramics.org
http://www.ceramics.org
Purpose: To support undergraduate ceramics and materials science and engineering students.
Eligibility: Applicants must be full-time undergraduates who will have completed 70 or more semester credits (or quarter credit equivalent) at the time of award disbursement. Selection is based on essay response, GPA, recommendation letter, extracurricular involvement and standardized test scores (if available).
Target applicant(s): College students. Adult students.
Amount: $2,000.
Number of awards: 1.
Deadline: May 30.
How to apply: This scholarship does not require an application form. The applicant's essay response, a recommendation letter and a list of extracurricular activities is required.
Exclusive: Visit www.UltimateScholarshipBook.com and enter code AM97826 for updates on this award.

[979] • Libbie H. Hyman Memorial Scholarship
Society for Integrative and Comparative Biology
950 Herndon Parkway, Suite 450, Herndon, VA 20170
Phone: 703-790-1745
https://sicb.org/libbie-h-hyman-memorial-scholarship/
Purpose: To support students seeking field station experience to study invertebrates.
Eligibility: Applicants must be first- or second-year graduate students or advanced undergraduates seeking to carry on invertebrate research at a marine, freshwater or terrestrial field station. Students must complete the application including a proposal, two letters of reference and transcripts.
Target applicant(s): College students. Graduate school students. Adult students.
Amount: Varies.
Number of awards: Varies.
Deadline: February 12.
How to apply: Applications are available online.
Exclusive: Visit www.UltimateScholarshipBook.com and enter code SO97926 for updates on this award.

[980] • Light Metals Division Scholarship
Minerals, Metals and Materials Society
5700 Corporate Drive, Suite 750, Pittsburgh, PA 15237
Phone: 1-724-776-9000
Email: students@tms.org
https://www.tms.org/
Purpose: To aid undergraduate students who are majoring in metallurgical engineering or materials science and engineering.
Eligibility: Applicants must be full-time undergraduate sophomores or juniors who are enrolled in a degree program in metallurgical engineering or materials science and engineering. They must be student members of TMS, The Minerals, Metals and Materials Society. Selection is based on academic merit, extracurricular activities, recommendations and personal statement.
Target applicant(s): College students. Adult students.
Amount: $2,500.
Number of awards: 3.
Deadline: March 15.
How to apply: Applications are available online. An application form, transcript, personal statement and three recommendation letters are required.
Exclusive: Visit www.UltimateScholarshipBook.com and enter code MI98026 for updates on this award.

[981] • Lisa Zaken Award For Excellence
Institute of Industrial and Systems Engineers
3577 Parkway Lane, Suite 200, Norcross, GA 30092
Phone: 800-494-0460
Email: egrimes@iise.org
https://www.iise.org
Purpose: To reward excellence in scholarly activities and leadership related to the industrial engineering profession on campus.
Eligibility: Applicants must be undergraduate or graduate students, have a 3.0 or higher GPA, major in industrial engineering and be active members who have been leaders in IIE. Students may not apply directly for this scholarship and must be nominated. The award is based on academic ability and leadership related to industrial engineering.
Target applicant(s): College students. Graduate school students. Adult students.
Minimum GPA: 3.0

Amount: $1,000.
Number of awards: 1.
Deadline: February 1.
How to apply: Nomination forms are available online.
Exclusive: Visit www.UltimateScholarshipBook.com and enter code IN98126 for updates on this award.

[982] • Lockheed Martin STEM Scholarship Program
Lockheed Martin STEM Scholarship Program
Scholarship America, One Scholarship Way, Saint Peter, MN 56082
Phone: 800-537-4180
Email: lockheedmartin@scholarshipamerica.org
https://lockheedmartin.com/en-us/who-we-are/communities/stem-education/lm-scholarship-program.html
Purpose: To encourage the study of STEM fields.
Eligibility: Applicants must be U.S. citizens who are high school seniors with a GPA of 2.5 or better or current college freshmen or sophomores with a minimum 2.5 GPA. Students must be enrolling full-time at an accredited four-year institution majoring in an engineering field, math, physics, information systems or information assurance.
Target applicant(s): High school students. College students. Adult students.
Minimum GPA: 2.5
Amount: $10,000.
Number of awards: Up to 100.
Deadline: April 1.
How to apply: Applications are available online.
Exclusive: Visit www.UltimateScholarshipBook.com and enter code LO98226 for updates on this award.

[983] • Lois Britt Pork Industry Memorial Scholarship Program
National Pork Producers Council
ATTN: Lois Britt Memorial Pork Industry Scholarship, P.O. Box 10383, Des Moines, IA 50306-9960
Phone: 202-347-3600
Email: invest@nppc.org
https://nppc.org/britt-scholarship/
Purpose: To support students who are preparing for careers in the pork industry.
Eligibility: Applicants must be undergraduates enrolled in either a two-year swine program or a four-year college of agriculture. They must be interested in pursuing a career in the pork industry. Selection is based on the strength of the personal essay.
Target applicant(s): College students. Adult students.
Amount: $2,500.
Number of awards: 10.
Deadline: January 2.
How to apply: Applications are available online. An information sheet, cover letter, personal essay and two reference letters are required.
Exclusive: Visit www.UltimateScholarshipBook.com and enter code NA98326 for updates on this award.

[984] • Long-Term Member Sponsored Scholarship
Society of Automotive Engineers International
Scholarships Program, 400 Commonwealth Drive, Warrendale, PA 15096
Phone: 724-776-4841
Email: scholarships@sae.org
https://www.sae.org/participate/scholarships
Purpose: This scholarship recognizes outstanding SAE student members who actively support SAE and its activities.
Eligibility: Applicants must be college juniors and student members of SAE, major in engineering and actively support SAE and its programs. The scholarship will be awarded purely on the basis of the student's support for SAE and its programs.
Target applicant(s): College students. Adult students.
Amount: $1,000.
Number of awards: Varies.
Deadline: February 28.
How to apply: Applications are available online.
Exclusive: Visit www.UltimateScholarshipBook.com and enter code SO98426 for updates on this award.

[985] • Louis Agassiz Fuertes Award
Wilson Ornithological Society
Department of Biology and Biomedical Science, Dr. James Chace, Associate Professor, 100 Ochre Point Avenue, Newport, RI 02840-4192
Email: rbpayne@umich.edu
http://www.wilsonsociety.org
Purpose: To support ornithologists' research.
Eligibility: Applicants must be students or young professionals doing avian research. Applicants must be willing to report their research results at an annual meeting of the Wilson Ornithological Society.
Target applicant(s): High school students. College students. Graduate school students. Adult students.
Amount: $5,000.
Number of awards: Up to 2.
Deadline: February 1.
How to apply: Applications are available online.
Exclusive: Visit www.UltimateScholarshipBook.com and enter code WI98526 for updates on this award.

[986] • Lowell Loving Undergraduate Scholarship
National Society of Professional Surveyors (NSPS/AAGS)
21 Byte Court, Suite H, Frederick, MD 21702
Phone: 240-439-4615
Email: info@nsps.us.com
https://www.nsps.us.com/page/Scholarships
Purpose: To aid undergraduate surveying and mapping students.
Eligibility: Applicants must be members of the National Society of Professional Surveyors (NSPS). They must be undergraduate juniors or seniors who are enrolled in a surveying and mapping degree program at a four-year institution located in the U.S. They must have a plan of study that includes coursework in two or more of the following areas: spatial measurement system analysis and design, land surveying, photogrammetry and remote sensing or geometric geodesy. Selection is based on academic merit, personal statement, recommendation letters, professional involvement and financial need.
Target applicant(s): College students. Adult students.
Amount: $2,000.
Number of awards: 1.

Scholarship may be renewable.
Deadline: January 19.
How to apply: Applications are available online. An application form, personal statement, proof of ACSM membership, three letters of recommendation and an official transcript are required.
Exclusive: Visit www.UltimateScholarshipBook.com and enter code NA98626 for updates on this award.

[987] • Loy McCandless Marks Scholarship in Tropical Horticulture
Garden Club of America
14 East 60th Street, New York, NY 10022
Phone: 212-753-8287
Email: scholarshipapplications@gcamerica.org
https://www.gcamerica.org/scholarships
Purpose: To promote the study of tropical plants in horticulture and landscape architecture.
Eligibility: Applicants must be U.S. citizens or permanent residents enrolled in a U.S. institution as a graduate or advanced undergraduate. Students must use the award to study abroad within one year.
Target applicant(s): College students. Graduate school students. Adult students.
Amount: $5,000.
Number of awards: 1.
Deadline: January 15.
How to apply: Applications are available online.
Exclusive: Visit www.UltimateScholarshipBook.com and enter code GA98726 for updates on this award.

[988] • Ludo Frevel Crystallography Scholarships
International Centre for Diffraction Data
12 Campus Boulevard, Newtown Square, PA 19073
https://www.icdd.com
Purpose: To support graduate students in crystallography-related fields.
Eligibility: Applicants must be graduate students enrolled in a degree program relating to crystallography. Students must submit a proposed research project along with their application.
Target applicant(s): Graduate school students. Adult students.
Amount: $2,500.
Number of awards: Varies.
Deadline: October 10.
How to apply: Applications are available online.
Exclusive: Visit www.UltimateScholarshipBook.com and enter code IN98826 for updates on this award.

[989] • Mandell and Lester Rosenblatt Undergraduate Scholarship
Society of Naval Architects and Marine Engineers (SNAME)
99 Canal Center Plaza, Suite 500, Alexandria, VA 22314
Phone: 703-997-6701
Email: scholarships@sname.org
https://www.sname.org/scholarships
Purpose: To assist college undergraduates who are studying marine industry fields.
Eligibility: Applicants must be U.S., Canadian or international college students who are members of the SNAME and are working towards degrees in naval architecture, marine engineering, ocean engineering or marine industry related areas fields. An application form, three recommendation letters and an essay are required.

Target applicant(s): College students. Adult students.
Amount: Up to $6,000.
Number of awards: 1.
Scholarship may be renewable.
Deadline: June 1.
How to apply: Applications are available online.
Exclusive: Visit www.UltimateScholarshipBook.com and enter code SO98926 for updates on this award.

[990] • Marliave Fund
Association of Engineering Geologists Foundation Marliave Fund
1954 Mountain Boulevard #13036, Oakland, CA 94611
Phone: 510-990-0059
Email: staff@aegfoundation.org
https://aegfoundation.org/grant-scholarships/
Purpose: To reward outstanding students in engineering geology and geological engineering.
Eligibility: Applicants must be seniors or graduate students in a college or university program directly applicable to geological engineering and be members of the Association of Engineering Geologists.
Target applicant(s): College students. Graduate school students. Adult students.
Amount: Varies.
Number of awards: 1.
Deadline: January 15.
How to apply: Applications are available online or by written request.
Exclusive: Visit www.UltimateScholarshipBook.com and enter code AS99026 for updates on this award.

[991] • Marshall E. McCullough Scholarship
National Dairy Shrine
P.O. Box 68, Fort Atkinson, WI 53538
Phone: 920-863-6333
Email: info@dairyshrine.org
http://www.dairyshrine.org
Purpose: To support students who plan careers in agricultural-related communications.
Eligibility: Applicants must be high school seniors planning to enter a four-year university with intent to major in the dairy or animal sciences with a communications emphasis or agricultural journalism with a dairy or animal science emphasis, and they must intend to work in the dairy industry following graduation.
Target applicant(s): High school students.
Amount: $1,000.
Number of awards: Up to 2.
Deadline: April 15.
How to apply: Applications are available online.
Exclusive: Visit www.UltimateScholarshipBook.com and enter code NA99126 for updates on this award.

[992] • Marvin Mundel Memorial Scholarship
Institute of Industrial and Systems Engineers
3577 Parkway Lane, Suite 200, Norcross, GA 30092
Phone: 800-494-0460
Email: egrimes@iise.org
https://www.iise.org
Purpose: To assist undergraduate engineering students with an interest in work measurement and methods engineering.
Eligibility: Applicants must be full-time undergraduate students enrolled in a college in the United States, Canada or Mexico with an accredited

industrial engineering program, major in industrial engineering and be active members. Students may not apply directly for this scholarship and must be nominated. The award is based on academic ability, character, leadership, potential service to the industrial engineering profession and financial need. Preference is given to students with a demonstrated interest in work measurement and methods engineering.
Target applicant(s): College students. Adult students.
Minimum GPA: 3.4
Amount: $1,000.
Number of awards: 2.
Deadline: February 1.
How to apply: Nomination forms are available online.
Exclusive: Visit www.UltimateScholarshipBook.com and enter code IN99226 for updates on this award.

[993] • Mary Rhein Memorial Scholarship
Mu Alpha Theta Scholarship Committee
c/o University of Oklahoma, 3200 Marshall Avenue, Suite 150, Norman, OK 73019
Phone: 405-325-4489
Email: matheta@ou.edu
https://mualphatheta.org/scholarships
Purpose: To aid graduating high school seniors who are active Mu Alpha Theta members.
Eligibility: Applicants must be graduating high school seniors who are outstanding mathematics students. They must be active Mu Alpha Theta members who have been of service in mathematics and who have participated in local, regional or national mathematics competitions. Applicants must have plans to pursue a mathematics-related career. Selection is based on the overall strength of the application.
Target applicant(s): High school students. College students. Adult students.
Amount: $5,000.
Number of awards: 1.
Deadline: February 1.
How to apply: Applications are available online. An application form, student essay, official transcript and three recommendation letters are required.
Exclusive: Visit www.UltimateScholarshipBook.com and enter code MU99326 for updates on this award.

[994] • Mary V. Munger Scholarship
Society of Women Engineers
130 East Randolph Street, Suite 3500, Chicago, IL 60601
Phone: 877-793-4636
Email: scholarships@swe.org
https://swe.org/scholarships/
Purpose: To support female students working towards a major in engineering.
Eligibility: Applicants must be planning to study at an ABET-accredited program in engineering, technology or computing and have a minimum 3.0 GPA. The award may be used during the junior or senior year of college and is open to re-entry and adult students.
Target applicant(s): College students. Adult students.
Minimum GPA: 3.0
Amount: $6,750.
Number of awards: 1.
Deadline: January 31.
How to apply: Applications are available online.
Exclusive: Visit www.UltimateScholarshipBook.com and enter code SO99426 for updates on this award.

[995] • Materials Processing and Manufacturing Division Scholarship
Minerals, Metals and Materials Society
5700 Corporate Drive, Suite 750, Pittsburgh, PA 15237
Phone: 1-724-776-9000
Email: students@tms.org
https://www.tms.org/
Purpose: To aid undergraduate student members of TMS who are majoring in metallurgical engineering or materials science and engineering.
Eligibility: Applicants must be full-time undergraduate sophomores or juniors whose studies must be focused on the integration of process control technology into manufacturing, materials technology research or the manufacturing process. Selection is based on academic merit, personal statement, recommendations, leadership skills, extracurricular activities and coursework relevance.
Target applicant(s): College students. Adult students.
Amount: $2,500.
Number of awards: 2.
Deadline: March 15.
How to apply: Applications are available online. An application form, personal statement, three recommendation letters and a transcript are required.
Exclusive: Visit www.UltimateScholarshipBook.com and enter code MI99526 for updates on this award.

[996] • Medical Student Research Scholarship
American Academy of Neurology
25 Massachusetts Ave NW, Suite 500J, Washington, DC 20001
Phone: 800-879-1960
Email: ggates@aan.com
https://www.aan.com
Purpose: To support medical students with limited research experience.
Eligibility: Applicants must be medical students with limited research experience relevant to clinical or neuroscience fields who have a supporting preceptor and a project with clearly defined goals. Students must conduct their project through a U.S. or Canadian institution of the student's choice and jointly designed by the student and sponsoring institution.
Target applicant(s): Graduate school students. Adult students.
Amount: Varies.
Number of awards: Varies.
Deadline: July 2.
How to apply: Applications are available online.
Exclusive: Visit www.UltimateScholarshipBook.com and enter code AM99626 for updates on this award.

[997] • Medical Student Training in Aging Research (MSTAR) Program
American Federation for Aging Research (AFAR)
55 West 39th Street, 16th Floor, New York, NY 10018
Phone: 212-703-9977
Email: grants@afar.org

The Ultimate Scholarship Book 2026
Scholarship Directory (Sciences)

http://www.afar.org
Purpose: To support early medical students who demonstrate an interest in geriatric medicine or age-related research with an opportunity to serve under top experts in the field.
Eligibility: Applicants must be osteopathic or allopathic students who have completed at least one year of medical school at a U.S. institution. Students must complete the program at one of 8 National Training Centers and must have a faculty sponsor from their home institution. Check the website for a list of training centers and participating schools. The program lasts 8 to 12 weeks, and monthly stipends are provided.
Target applicant(s): Graduate school students. Adult students.
Amount: $1,980 per month.
Number of awards: Up to 100.
Deadline: Contact the sponsor to confirm the deadline.
How to apply: Applications are available online.
Exclusive: Visit www.UltimateScholarshipBook.com and enter code AM99726 for updates on this award.

[998] • Melvin J. Schiff Fellowship Fund
National Association of Corrosion Engineers (NACE) International Foundation
15835 Park Ten Place, Houston, TX 77084-5145
Phone: 281-228-6205
Email: nace.foundation@nace.org
https://www.ampp.org/about/emerg-student-outreach/academic-scholarships-program
Purpose: To help an outstanding student, professional or technician interested in furthering their knowledge of corrosion and corrosion control.
Eligibility: Applicants must be a permanent resident of the U.S. and be professionals, technicians or full- or part-time students enrolled in an accredited U.S. college or university. Selection is based on the overall strength of the application.
Target applicant(s): College students. Graduate school students. Adult students.
Amount: $1,000.
Number of awards: 1.
Deadline: January 2.
How to apply: Applications are available online. An application form, two recommendation forms, an academic transcript and essay scholarship questions are required.
Exclusive: Visit www.UltimateScholarshipBook.com and enter code NA99826 for updates on this award.

[999] • Melvin R. Green Scholarships
American Society of Mechanical Engineers (ASME)
Two Park Avenue, New York, NY 10016-5990
Phone: 800-843-2763
Email: lefeverb@asme.org
https://www.asme.org/asme-programs/students-and-faculty/scholarships/scholarships
Purpose: To support mechanical engineering students.
Eligibility: Applicants must have outstanding character and integrity, be ASME student members, be enrolled in an eligible accredited mechanical engineering baccalaureate program, be college juniors or seniors, and have strong academic performance. Selection is based on scholastic ability, leadership, financial need and potential contribution to the mechanical engineering profession.
Target applicant(s): College students. Adult students.
Amount: $8,000.
Number of awards: 1.
Deadline: February 15.
How to apply: Applications are available online.
Exclusive: Visit www.UltimateScholarshipBook.com and enter code AM99926 for updates on this award.

[1000] • Mental Health Importance Scholarship
Pettable
P.O. Box 2130, Sparks, NV 89432
Phone: 800-851-7202
Email: elizabeth@pettable.net
https://pettable.com/scholarship
Purpose: To support students who plan to work in the mental health field.
Eligibility: Applicants must be high school, undergraduate and graduate students who believe in the importance of mental health. Students must have a goal of working in the field of mental health or have had their education impacted by adverse effects of mental health. Applicants must write and submit an essay.
Target applicant(s): High school students. College students. Graduate school students. Adult students.
Amount: $1,000.
Number of awards: Varies.
Deadline: December 1.
How to apply: Applications are available online.
Exclusive: Visit www.UltimateScholarshipBook.com and enter code PE100026 for updates on this award.

[1001] • Meredith Thoms Memorial Scholarship
Society of Women Engineers
130 East Randolph Street, Suite 3500, Chicago, IL 60601
Phone: 877-793-4636
Email: scholarships@swe.org
https://swe.org/scholarships/
Purpose: To support female students pursuing a college degree in engineering.
Eligibility: Applicants must be enrolled in an accredited engineering or engineering technology program with a 3.0 GPA. The award may be used during the sophomore, junior or senior year of college.
Target applicant(s): College students. Adult students.
Minimum GPA: 3.0
Amount: $4,500.
Number of awards: 4.
Deadline: January 31.
How to apply: Applications are available online.
Exclusive: Visit www.UltimateScholarshipBook.com and enter code SO100126 for updates on this award.

[1002] • MGMA Midwest Section Scholarship
Medical Group Management Association
104 Inverness Terrace East, Englewood, CO 80112-5306
Phone: 877-275-6462
Email: scholarship@mgma.com
https://www.mgma.com/scholarships
Purpose: To aid MGMA Midwest Section members who are pursuing higher education in a subject that is related to medical practice management.
Eligibility: Applicants must be members of the Medical Group Management Association (MGMA). They must be residents of one of the MGMA Midwest Section states, namely Illinois, Indiana, Iowa, Michigan, Minnesota, Nebraska, North Dakota, Ohio, South Dakota or Wisconsin. They must be undergraduate or graduate students who are enrolled in a

degree program that is related to medical practice management (such as public health, business administration or health care administration). Selection is based on the overall strength of the application.
Target applicant(s): High school students. College students. Graduate school students. Adult students.
Amount: Varies.
Number of awards: Varies.
Deadline: April 29.
How to apply: Applications are available online. An application form and supporting materials are required.
Exclusive: Visit www.UltimateScholarshipBook.com and enter code ME100226 for updates on this award.

[1003] • MGMA Western Section Scholarship
Medical Group Management Association
104 Inverness Terrace East, Englewood, CO 80112-5306
Phone: 877-275-6462
Email: scholarship@mgma.com
https://www.mgma.com/scholarships
Purpose: To aid MGMA Western Section members who are pursuing higher education in subjects that are related to medical practice management.
Eligibility: Applicants must be residents of one of the MGMA Western Section states, namely Alaska, Arizona, California, Colorado, Hawaii, Idaho, Montana, Nevada, New Mexico, Oregon, Utah, Washington or Wyoming. They must be undergraduate or graduate students who are enrolled in a degree program relating to medical practice management (such as public health, business administration or health care administration). Selection is based on the overall strength of the application.
Target applicant(s): High school students. College students. Graduate school students. Adult students.
Amount: Varies.
Number of awards: Varies.
Deadline: April 29.
How to apply: Applications are available online. An application form and supporting materials are required.
Exclusive: Visit www.UltimateScholarshipBook.com and enter code ME100326 for updates on this award.

[1004] • Michael Kidger Memorial Scholarship
Kidger Optics Associates
https://www.kidger.com
Purpose: To support students in the optical design field.
Eligibility: Applicants must be in the optical design field and must have one year remaining of their studies. Students must submit a summary of their academic background and interest in optical design and two letters of recommendation.
Target applicant(s): Graduate school students. Adult students.
Amount: $7,500.
Number of awards: 1.
Deadline: February 28.
How to apply: Applications are available online.
Exclusive: Visit www.UltimateScholarshipBook.com and enter code KI100426 for updates on this award.

[1005] • Michael Moody Fitness Scholarship
Michael Moody Fitness
38 E 5th Avenue, Denver, CO 80203
Phone: 773-484-8094
Email: michael@michaelmoodyfitness.com
http://www.michaelmoodyfitness.com/student-scholarship-chicago/
Purpose: To support students seeking a career in health and fitness related fields.
Eligibility: Applicants must be U.S. citizens or legal residents and be a current high school senior, undergraduate or graduate level student planning on enrolling in an accredited college or university full-time in the upcoming school year. Students should be able to demonstrate that they have outstanding achievement in school, as well as participation and leadership in school activities and work experience. Applicants should be pursuing a degree in one of the following: athletic training, personal training, physical education teaching and coaching, health and physical fitness, exercise science, sports and recreation management, health sciences or another related field.
Target applicant(s): High school students. College students. Graduate school students. Adult students.
Amount: $1,500.
Number of awards: 1.
Deadline: August 1.
How to apply: Applications are available online.
Exclusive: Visit www.UltimateScholarshipBook.com and enter code MI100526 for updates on this award.

[1006] • Mid-Continent Instruments and Avionics Scholarship
Aircraft Electronics Association
3570 NE Ralph Powell Road, Lee's Summit, MO 64064
Phone: 816-347-8400
Email: info@aea.net
https://aea.net/educationalfoundation/scholarships.asp
Purpose: To support students who wish to pursue a career in avionics or aircraft repair.
Eligibility: Applicants must be high school seniors or college students who plan to or are attending an accredited school in an avionics or aircraft repair program.
Target applicant(s): High school students. College students. Adult students.
Amount: $1,000.
Number of awards: 1.
Deadline: April 1.
How to apply: Applications are available by contacting the organization for more information.
Exclusive: Visit www.UltimateScholarshipBook.com and enter code AI100626 for updates on this award.

[1007] • Migrant Health Scholarships
National Center for Farmworker Health Inc.
Migrant Health Scholarship, 1770 FM 967, Buda, TX 78610
Phone: 512-312-2700
Email: favre@ncfh.org
http://www.ncfh.org/scholarships.html
Purpose: To aid migrant health center staff who wish to pursue higher education in health care.
Eligibility: Applicants must be employees at a migrant/community health center. They must be interested in seeking further training in health care. Special consideration will be given to applicants who have a

family background in farm working. Selection is based on demonstrated professional commitment to migrant health, stated career goals and personal experiences.
Target applicant(s): High school students. College students. Graduate school students. Adult students.
Amount: Varies.
Number of awards: Varies.
Deadline: March 29.
How to apply: Applications are available online. An application form and supporting materials are required.
Exclusive: Visit www.UltimateScholarshipBook.com and enter code NA100726 for updates on this award.

[1008] • Minority Fellowship Program
American Nurses Association (ANA)
8515 Georgia Avenue, Suite 400, Silver Spring, MD 20910-3492
Phone: 301-628-5247
Email: mfp@ana.org
http://www.nursingworld.org
Purpose: To provide stipends and tuition assistance to nurses studying minority psychiatric-mental health and substance abuse.
Eligibility: Applicants must be members of the ANA, have their master's degree and plan to pursue doctoral degrees. Eligible applicants must be registered nurses and members of an ethnic/racial minority group.
Target applicant(s): Graduate school students. Adult students.
Amount: Varies.
Number of awards: Varies.
Deadline: April 30.
How to apply: Applications are available online.
Exclusive: Visit www.UltimateScholarshipBook.com and enter code AM100826 for updates on this award.

[1009] • Minority Student Scholarship
American Speech-Language-Hearing Foundation
2200 Research Boulevard, Rockville, MD 20850
Phone: 301-296-8700
Email: foundationprograms@asha.org
https://www.ashfoundation.org/
Purpose: To support a minority graduate student in communication sciences and disorders.
Eligibility: Applicants should be full-time minority graduate students. Master's degree candidates must be in programs accredited by the Council on Academic Accreditation for Audiology and Speech Pathology, but doctoral programs do not have to be accredited. Transcripts, an essay and a reference form are required.
Target applicant(s): College students. Graduate school students. Adult students.
Amount: $5,000.
Number of awards: Up to 2.
Deadline: May 17.
How to apply: Applications are available online.
Exclusive: Visit www.UltimateScholarshipBook.com and enter code AM100926 for updates on this award.

[1010] • MIT THINK Scholarship Program
MIT Tech Fair
Email: think@mit.edu
https://think.mit.edu/#guidelines
Purpose: To support high school students interested in science, technology, engineering and math.
Eligibility: Applicants must be full-time high school students and must be U.S. residents during the academic year. U.S. citizenship is not required and U.S. citizens living outside the country are not eligible. Students must submit a proposal following the provided guidelines and instructions.
Target applicant(s): High school students.
Amount: $1,000.
Number of awards: Varies.
Deadline: January 1.
How to apply: Applications are available online.
Exclusive: Visit www.UltimateScholarshipBook.com and enter code MI101026 for updates on this award.

[1011] • Modeling the Future Challenge
Actuarial Foundation
475 North Martingale Road, Suite 600, Schaumburg, IL 60173
Phone: 847-706-3535
Email: info@actfnd.org
https://actuarialfoundation.org/scholarships/
Purpose: To support students who plan to pursue higher education.
Eligibility: Applicants must be high school students in the U.S. Students who are taking junior or senior-level mathematics classes such as statistics, probability, pre-calc, calculus or other similar high-level math classes are eligible.
Target applicant(s): Junior high students or younger. High school students.
Amount: Up to $60,000.
Number of awards: Varies.
Deadline: November 10.
How to apply: Applications are available online.
Exclusive: Visit www.UltimateScholarshipBook.com and enter code AC101126 for updates on this award.

[1012] • Mollie Butler Memorial Scholarship
Welsh Pony and Cob Society
720 Green Street, Stephens City, VA 22655
Phone: 540-868-7669
Email: info@welshpony.org
https://wpcsa.org/youth/scholarship-application/
Purpose: To support students pursuing education and research in equine-related fields.
Eligibility: Applicants must be graduating high school or attending college, graduate school or professional training in equine fields of study.
Target applicant(s): High school students. College students. Graduate school students. Adult students.
Amount: $500.
Number of awards: Up to 2.
Deadline: July 15.
How to apply: Applications are available online.
Exclusive: Visit www.UltimateScholarshipBook.com and enter code WE101226 for updates on this award.

[1013] • Moody's Mega Math Challenge
Society for Industrial and Applied Mathematics/SIAM
3600 Market Street, 6th Floor, Philadelphia, PA 19104
Phone: 215-382-9800
https://m3challenge.siam.org
Purpose: To support students who complete a math challenge.
Eligibility: Applicants must be from high schools in the United States. Students on the team must be juniors and seniors from the same high school.

Target applicant(s): High school students.
Amount: $5,000-$20,000.
Number of awards: Varies.
Deadline: February 23.
How to apply: Applications are available online.
Exclusive: Visit www.UltimateScholarshipBook.com and enter code SO101326 for updates on this award.

[1014] • MTI Bert Krisher Memorial Scholarship

National Association of Corrosion Engineers (NACE) International Foundation
15835 Park Ten Place, Houston, TX 77084-5145
Phone: 281-228-6205
Email: nace.foundation@nace.org
https://www.ampp.org/about/emerg-student-outreach/academic-scholarships-program
Purpose: To help students pursue careers in materials engineering in the process industries.
Eligibility: Applicants must be enrolled full-time as an undergraduate at an accredited college or university in North America, Europe or Asia. Selection is based on experience, academic achievement, personal and professional activities and overall strength of the application.
Target applicant(s): College students. Adult students.
Amount: $5,000.
Number of awards: Up to 2.
Deadline: January 2.
How to apply: Applications are available online. An application form, three recommendation forms, an academic transcript, a work experience form and essay scholarship questions are required.
Exclusive: Visit www.UltimateScholarshipBook.com and enter code NA101426 for updates on this award.

[1015] • MTS Student Scholarship for Two-Year, Technical, Engineering and Community College Students

Marine Technology Society
One Thomas Circle, Suite 700, Washington, DC 20005
Phone: 202-717-8705
Email: scholarships@mtsociety.org
https://www.mtsociety.org/scholarships
Purpose: To support students who are enrolled at a two-year, technical, engineering or community college in a marine-related field
Eligibility: Applicants must be MTS student members who are accepted for enrollment or enrolled full-time at an educational institution.
Target applicant(s): High school students. College students. Adult students.
Amount: $3,000.
Number of awards: 1.
Deadline: April 15.
How to apply: Applications are available online.
Exclusive: Visit www.UltimateScholarshipBook.com and enter code MA101526 for updates on this award.

[1016] • MTS Student Scholarship for Undergraduate Students

Marine Technology Society
One Thomas Circle, Suite 700, Washington, DC 20005
Phone: 202-717-8705
Email: scholarships@mtsociety.org
https://www.mtsociety.org/scholarships
Purpose: To support Marine Technology Society members who are pursuing an undergraduate degree in a marine-related field.
Eligibility: Applicants must be MTS student members who are accepted for enrollment or enrolled full-time at an educational institution.
Target applicant(s): College students. Adult students.
Amount: $3,000.
Number of awards: 1.
Deadline: April 15.
How to apply: Applications are available online.
Exclusive: Visit www.UltimateScholarshipBook.com and enter code MA101626 for updates on this award.

[1017] • Myrtle and Earl Walker Scholarship

Society of Manufacturing Engineers Education Foundation
One SME Drive, P.O. Box 930, Dearborn, MI 48121
Phone: 313-425-3300
Email: foundation@sme.org
https://www.smeef.org/scholarships
Purpose: To help manufacturing engineering and technology undergraduates.
Eligibility: Applicants must be full-time undergraduate students who are studying manufacturing engineering or technology at an accredited postsecondary institution located in the U.S. or Canada. They must have a GPA of 3.0 or higher on a four-point scale and must have completed 15 or more credit hours. They must have plans to pursue a career in manufacturing engineering or technology. Selection is based on the overall strength of the application.
Target applicant(s): College students. Adult students.
Minimum GPA: 3.0
Amount: Varies.
Number of awards: Varies.
Deadline: February 1.
How to apply: Applications are available online. An application form, personal statement, resume, transcript and two recommendation letters are required.
Exclusive: Visit www.UltimateScholarshipBook.com and enter code SO101726 for updates on this award.

[1018] • N.G. Kaul Memorial Scholarship

New York Water Environment Association Inc.
525 Plum Street, Suite 102, Syracuse, NY 13204
Phone: 877-556-9932
Email: theresa@nywea.org
https://www.nywea.org
Purpose: To support students pursuing advanced degrees in environmental engineering and science.
Eligibility: Applicants must be graduate students pursuing degrees in environmental or civil engineering or environmental science with a concentration on water quality. Students must provide two letters of recommendations, a transcript, a resume and two essays along with their application.
Target applicant(s): Graduate school students. Adult students.
Amount: Up to $5,000.
Number of awards: Varies.
Deadline: February 28.
How to apply: Applications are available online.
Exclusive: Visit www.UltimateScholarshipBook.com and enter code NE101826 for updates on this award.

[1019] • Naomi Brack Student Scholarship

Organization for Associate Degree Nursing National Office
7794 Grow Drive, Pensacola, FL 32514-7072
Phone: 877-966-6236
Email: harriet.mcclung@oadn.org
http://www.oadn.org
Purpose: To aid associate's degree nursing (ADN) students.
Eligibility: Applicants must be currently enrolled in an associate's degree program in nursing at a state-approved institution that is a member of the Organization for Associate Degree Nursing. They must have a GPA of 3.25 or more on a four-point scale and must be active in their school's student nursing association. Selection is based on the overall strength of the application.
Target applicant(s): College students. Adult students.
Minimum GPA: 3.0
Amount: $1,000.
Number of awards: Varies.
Deadline: June 1.
How to apply: Applications are available online. An application form, personal statement, transcript, nomination form and two letters of recommendation are required.
Exclusive: Visit www.UltimateScholarshipBook.com and enter code OR101926 for updates on this award.

[1020] • NAPA Research and Education Foundation Scholarship

National Asphalt Pavement Association
5100 Forbes Boulevard, Lanham, MD 20706-4407
Phone: 888-468-6499
http://www.asphaltpavement.org/
Purpose: To aid engineering and construction students who are interested in hot mix asphalt technology.
Eligibility: Applicants must be U.S. citizens who are enrolled full-time at an accredited postsecondary institution. They must be majoring in construction management, civil engineering or construction engineering. The applicant's school must offer at least one course on hot mix asphalt (HMA) technology. Selection is based on academic achievement, leadership potential, extracurricular involvement and stated career goals.
Target applicant(s): College students. Graduate school students. Adult students.
Amount: Varies.
Number of awards: Varies.
Scholarship may be renewable.
Deadline: November 30.
How to apply: Applications may be requested from the student's state National Asphalt Pavement Association representative. An application form and supporting materials are required.
Exclusive: Visit www.UltimateScholarshipBook.com and enter code NA102026 for updates on this award.

[1021] • National Association for Surface Finishing Scholarships

National Association for Surface Finishing
1155 Fifteenth Street NW, Washington, DC 20005
Phone: 202-457-8401
http://www.nasf.org
Purpose: To support students pursuing the study of surface science.
Eligibility: Applicants must be undergraduate juniors or seniors or graduate students studying chemical engineering, material science, mechanical, metallurgical or environmental engineering or chemistry. Students must have a minimum 3.0 GPA if an undergraduate or 3.3 if a graduate-level student.
Target applicant(s): College students. Graduate school students. Adult students.
Minimum GPA: 3.0 for undergraduate students; 3.3 for graduate students
Amount: $1,500.
Number of awards: 2.
Deadline: March 1.
How to apply: Applications are available online.
Exclusive: Visit www.UltimateScholarshipBook.com and enter code NA102126 for updates on this award.

[1022] • National Aviation Explorer Scholarships

Explorers Learning for Life
1325 West Walnut Hill Lane, P.O. Box 152225, Irving, TX 75015-2225
Phone: 972-580-2433
Email: exploring@lflmail.org
http://www.exploring.org/scholarships/
Purpose: To support students who are pursuing careers in the aviation industry.
Eligibility: Students must be active members of an Aviation Explorer post. Applicants must submit an essay and three letters of recommendation.
Target applicant(s): Junior high students or younger. High school students. College students. Adult students.
Amount: $5,000-$10,000.
Number of awards: Varies.
Deadline: April 30.
How to apply: Applications are available online.
Exclusive: Visit www.UltimateScholarshipBook.com and enter code EX102226 for updates on this award.

[1023] • National Dairy Shrine/Iager Dairy Scholarship

National Dairy Shrine
P.O. Box 68, Fort Atkinson, WI 53538
Phone: 920-863-6333
Email: info@dairyshrine.org
http://www.dairyshrine.org
Purpose: To aid dairy and animal science students who are planning for careers in the dairy industry.
Eligibility: Applicants must be entering the second year of a two-year agricultural college program in dairy or animal science. They must have a GPA of 2.5 or higher on a four-point scale. Selection is based on academic merit, leadership skills and professional commitment to the dairy industry.
Target applicant(s): College students. Adult students.
Minimum GPA: 2.5
Amount: $1,000.
Number of awards: Up to 2.
Deadline: April 15.
How to apply: Applications are available online. An application form, official transcript, personal essay and two recommendation letters are required.
Exclusive: Visit www.UltimateScholarshipBook.com and enter code NA102326 for updates on this award.

[1024] • National Environmental Health Association Graduate Scholarship

National Environmental Health Association and the American Academy of Sanitarians
NEHA/AAS Scholarship, 720 South Colorado Boulevard, Suite 105A, Denver, CO 80246-1910
Phone: 303-802-2200
Email: support@neha.org
http://www.neha.org
Purpose: To encourage commitment to environmental health studies.
Eligibility: Applicants must be enrolled in a graduate program at an accredited institution with a declared curriculum in environmental health sciences and have at least one semester of coursework remaining.
Target applicant(s): Graduate school students. Adult students.
Amount: $3,750.
Number of awards: 1.
Deadline: February 15.
How to apply: Applications are available online.
Exclusive: Visit www.UltimateScholarshipBook.com and enter code NA102426 for updates on this award.

[1025] • National FFA Alumni and Supporters Agricultural Education Scholarship

National FFA Organization
P.O. Box 68960, 6060 FFA Drive, Indianapolis, IN 46268-0960
Phone: 888-332-2668
Email: scholarships@ffa.org
https://www.ffa.org/participate/grants-and-scholarships/
Purpose: To assist students who are FFA members.
Eligibility: Applicants must be members of FFA and FFA alumni. One application is required for all FFA scholarships. Selection is based on the overall strength of the application.
Target applicant(s): High school students. College students. Adult students.
Amount: $1,000.
Number of awards: 1.
Deadline: January 11.
How to apply: Applications are available online.
Exclusive: Visit www.UltimateScholarshipBook.com and enter code NA102526 for updates on this award.

[1026] • National Garden Clubs Scholarship

National Garden Clubs Inc.
4401 Magnolia Avenue, St. Louis, MO 63110
Phone: 314-776-7574
Email: headquarters@gardenclub.org
http://www.gardenclub.org
Purpose: To promote the study of horticulture and related fields.
Eligibility: Applicants must be full-time juniors, seniors, graduate students or sophomores applying for their junior year and major in one of the following fields: agriculture education, horticulture, floriculture, landscape design, botany, biology, plant pathology/science, forestry, agronomy, environmental concerns, economics, environmental conservation, city planning, wildlife science, habitat or forest/systems ecology, land management or related areas. Students must have a minimum 3.25 cumulative GPA and be a U.S. citizen.
Target applicant(s): College students. Graduate school students. Adult students.
Minimum GPA: 3.25
Amount: $4,500.
Number of awards: Up to 45.
Deadline: February 1.
How to apply: Applications are available online and must be mailed to the applicants' state Garden Club scholarship chairman.
Exclusive: Visit www.UltimateScholarshipBook.com and enter code NA102626 for updates on this award.

[1027] • National Horticulture Foundation General Scholarships

National Foliage Foundation
1533 Park Center Drive, Orlando, FL 32835
Phone: 800-375-3642
Email: info@nationalfoliagefoundation.org
https://www.nationalhorticulturefoundation.org/
Purpose: To aid horticulture students who are interested in pursuing careers in foliage growing and marketing.
Eligibility: Applicants must be graduating high school seniors or full-time undergraduate or graduate students. They must be enrolled in or planning to enroll in a horticulture or related degree program and must have a GPA of 2.5 or higher. They must be interested in pursuing a career in foliage marketing or growing. Selection is based on the overall strength of the application.
Target applicant(s): High school students. College students. Graduate school students. Adult students.
Minimum GPA: 2.5
Amount: Varies.
Number of awards: Varies.
Scholarship may be renewable.
Deadline: January 15.
How to apply: Applications are available online. An application form, transcript, two recommendation letters and a personal essay are required.
Exclusive: Visit www.UltimateScholarshipBook.com and enter code NA102726 for updates on this award.

[1028] • National Potato Council Scholarship

National Potato Council
50 F Street NW, Suite 900, Washington, DC 20001
Phone: 202-682-9456
Email: info@nationalpotatocouncil.org
http://www.nationalpotatocouncil.org
Purpose: To aid students pursuing studies that support the potato industry.
Eligibility: Applicants must be graduate agribusiness students. Selection is based on academic achievement, leadership abilities and potato-related areas of graduate study (such as agricultural engineering, agronomy, crop and soil sciences, entomology, food sciences, horticulture and plant pathology).
Target applicant(s): Graduate school students. Adult students.
Amount: $10,000.
Number of awards: 1.
Deadline: June 18.
How to apply: Applications are available online. An application form, essay, transcripts, list of activities and two references are required.
Exclusive: Visit www.UltimateScholarshipBook.com and enter code NA102826 for updates on this award.

[1029] • National Space Club Keynote Scholar
National Space Club
204 E Street NE, Washington, DC 20002
Phone: 202-547-0060
Email: info@spaceclub.org
http://www.spaceclub.org/youth-education.html
Purpose: To aid STEM students.
Eligibility: Applicants must be U.S. citizens and must be high school seniors, undergraduates or graduate students planning to attend or attending an accredited college or university with the intention to follow a course of study related to a career in a science, technology, engineering or math field with a preference for space-related interests. Selection is based on the overall strength of the application.
Target applicant(s): High school students. College students. Graduate school students. Adult students.
Amount: $15,000.
Number of awards: 1.
Deadline: November 1.
How to apply: Applications are available online. An application form, transcripts, two letters of recommendation, statement of intent and video audition are required.
Exclusive: Visit www.UltimateScholarshipBook.com and enter code NA102926 for updates on this award.

[1030] • National Student Nurses' Association Scholarship
National Student Nurses' Association
45 Main Street, Suite 606, Brooklyn, NY 11201
Phone: 718-210-0705
Email: nsna@nsna.org
http://www.nsna.org
Purpose: To promote interest in the nursing field.
Eligibility: Applicants must be currently enrolled in a state-approved school of nursing or pre-nursing in associate degree, baccalaureate, diploma, doctorate or master's programs.
Target applicant(s): College students. Graduate school students. Adult students.
Amount: Up to $10,000.
Number of awards: Varies.
Deadline: January 26.
How to apply: Applications are available online.
Exclusive: Visit www.UltimateScholarshipBook.com and enter code NA103026 for updates on this award.

[1031] • National Young Astronomer Award
Astronomical League
9201 Ward Parkway, Suite 100, Kansas City, MO 64114
Phone: 816-333-7759
Email: horkheimerservice@astroleague.org
https://www.astroleague.org/al/awards/awards.html
Purpose: To support young astronomers.
Eligibility: Applicants must be 14 to 19 years old, not yet enrolled in college at the award deadline and do not have to be members of an astronomy club or of the Astronomical League. International students of the same age are eligible if they are enrolled in a U.S. secondary school on the application deadline. The application consists of the application form, summary of astronomy-related activities and optional exhibits.
Target applicant(s): Junior high students or younger. High school students.
Amount: Varies.
Number of awards: Up to 3.
Deadline: March 31.
How to apply: Applications are available online.
Exclusive: Visit www.UltimateScholarshipBook.com and enter code AS103126 for updates on this award.

[1032] • NAWIC Founders' Undergraduate Scholarship
National Association of Women in Construction
327 South Adams Street, Fort Worth, TX 76104
Phone: 800-552-3506
Email: nawic@nawic.org
http://www.nawic.org
Purpose: To aid undergraduates who are preparing for careers in construction.
Eligibility: Applicants must be full-time, degree-seeking undergraduates who are studying a construction-related subject at a postsecondary institution located in the U.S. or Canada. Students do not need to be female. They must have a cumulative GPA of 3.0 or higher and have plans to pursue a career in a construction-related field. Selection is based on stated career goals, extracurricular activities, work experience, academic achievement and financial need.
Target applicant(s): College students. Adult students.
Minimum GPA: 3.0
Amount: $500 to $2,500.
Number of awards: Varies.
Scholarship may be renewable.
Deadline: February 28.
How to apply: Applications are available online. An application form, transcript, employment history, extracurricular activities list and personal statement are required.
Exclusive: Visit www.UltimateScholarshipBook.com and enter code NA103226 for updates on this award.

[1033] • NBRC/AMP Gareth B. Gish, MS, RRT Memorial and William F. Miller, MD Postgraduate Education Recognition Awards
American Association for Respiratory Care
9425 North MacArthur Boulevard, Suite 100, Irving, TX 75063-4706
Phone: 972-243-2272
Email: info@aarc.org
https://www.aarc.org/your-rt-career/scholarship-loans/
Purpose: To aid qualified respiratory therapists in pursuing advanced degrees.
Eligibility: Applicants must be respiratory therapists who have been accepted into an advanced degree program of a fully accredited school. The application must be accompanied by an original essay describing how the award will aid in achieving an advanced degree and future goals in health care. A minimum 3.0 GPA is required.
Target applicant(s): College students. Graduate school students. Adult students.
Minimum GPA: 3.0
Amount: Up to $5,000.
Number of awards: 1.
Deadline: June 1.
How to apply: Applications are available online.
Exclusive: Visit www.UltimateScholarshipBook.com and enter code AM103326 for updates on this award.

[1034] • NBRC/AMP William W. Burgin, Jr. MD and Robert M. Lawrence, MD Education Recognition Award

American Association for Respiratory Care
9425 North MacArthur Boulevard, Suite 100, Irving, TX 75063-4706
Phone: 972-243-2272
Email: info@aarc.org
https://www.aarc.org/your-rt-career/scholarship-loans/
Purpose: To recognize outstanding students in respiratory care education programs.
Eligibility: Applicants must be third or fourth-year students enrolled in an accredited respiratory therapy program leading to a bachelor's degree and must have a minimum 3.0 GPA. In addition to an original paper dealing with respiratory care, applicants must submit an original essay describing how this award will help them reach their degrees and their future goals in the field of health care.
Target applicant(s): College students. Adult students.
Minimum GPA: 3.0
Amount: Up to $7,500.
Number of awards: 1.
Deadline: June 1.
How to apply: Applications are available online.
Exclusive: Visit www.UltimateScholarshipBook.com and enter code AM103426 for updates on this award.

[1035] • NCAPA Endowment Annual Student Grants

North Carolina Academy of Physician Assistants
Attn.: Kat Nicholas, 1121 Slater Road, Durham, NC 27703
Phone: 800-352-2271
Email: ncapa@ncapa.org
https://ncapa.org/nc-pa-student-scholarships/
Purpose: To aid physician assistant school students.
Eligibility: Applicants must be current student members of the North Carolina Academy of Physician Assistants (NCAPA). They must be rising second- or third-year students in an accredited physician assistant degree program. Selection is based on the overall strength of the application.
Target applicant(s): College students. Adult students.
Amount: Varies.
Number of awards: Varies.
Deadline: July 1.
How to apply: Applications are available online. An application form, financial aid statement, personal essay and official transcript are required.
Exclusive: Visit www.UltimateScholarshipBook.com and enter code NO103526 for updates on this award.

[1036] • NCPA Foundation Presidential Scholarship

National Community Pharmacists Association
NCPA Foundation, 100 Daingerfield Road, Alexandria, VA 22314
Phone: 703-683-8200
Email: info@ncpanet.org
http://www.ncpanet.org
Purpose: To support students who plan to enter the pharmaceutical field.
Eligibility: Applicants must be student members of NCPA and enrolled in a U.S. school or college of pharmacy full-time. Selection is based on academic achievement and leadership.
Target applicant(s): College students. Graduate school students. Adult students.
Amount: $5,000.
Number of awards: Varies.
Deadline: March 15.
How to apply: Applications are available online.
Exclusive: Visit www.UltimateScholarshipBook.com and enter code NA103626 for updates on this award.

[1037] • NDPRB Undergraduate Scholarship Program

National Dairy Promotion and Research Board
c/o Nate Janssen, Dairy Management Inc., 10255 West Higgins Road, Suite 900, Rosemont, IL 60018-5615
Phone: 847-627-3335
Email: nate.janssen@rosedmi.com
http://www.dairy.org
Purpose: To aid undergraduates who are studying a dairy-related subject.
Eligibility: Applicants must be rising undergraduate sophomores, juniors or seniors. They must be majoring in a subject that emphasizes dairy (such as agriculture education, business, communications, economics, food science, journalism, marketing or public relations). Applicants must plan to pursue a career in the dairy industry. Selection is based on stated career goals, academic excellence, dairy-related coursework completed, leadership and integrity.
Target applicant(s): College students. Adult students.
Amount: Up to $3,500.
Number of awards: Up to 11.
Scholarship may be renewable.
Deadline: May 12.
How to apply: Applications are available online. An application form, personal statement, one recommendation letter and an official transcript are required.
Exclusive: Visit www.UltimateScholarshipBook.com and enter code NA103726 for updates on this award.

[1038] • NDS / Klussendorf / McKown Scholarships

National Dairy Shrine
P.O. Box 68, Fort Atkinson, WI 53538
Phone: 920-863-6333
Email: info@dairyshrine.org
http://www.dairyshrine.org
Purpose: To honor students in dairy husbandry fields.
Eligibility: Applicants must be first, second or third year college students at two- or four-year universities, must major in a dairy husbandry field and plan to enter the dairy field.
Target applicant(s): College students. Adult students.
Amount: $1,500.
Number of awards: 7.
Deadline: April 15.
How to apply: Applications are available online.
Exclusive: Visit www.UltimateScholarshipBook.com and enter code NA103826 for updates on this award.

[1039] • NDSEG Fellowship Program

Department of Defense, American Society for Engineering Education
1818 N Street NW, Suite 600, Washington, DC 20036
Phone: 202-331-3546
Email: ndseg@asee.org
https://ndseg.sysplus.com/
Purpose: To award fellowships to those in science and engineering.
Eligibility: Applicants must pursue a doctoral degree in an area of Department of Defense interest: aeronautical and astronautical

engineering, biosciences, chemical engineering, chemistry, civil engineering, cognitive, neural and behavioral sciences, computer and computational sciences, electrical engineering, geosciences, materials science and engineering, mathematics, mechanical engineering, naval architecture and ocean engineering, oceanography and physics. Applicants must have completed no more than one academic year of graduate study as a part-time or full-time student or be in their final year of undergraduate studies. The award is based on academic achievement, personal statements, recommendations and Graduate Record Examination scores. Fellowships may be used only at U.S. institutions of higher education offering doctoral degrees.
Target applicant(s): College students. Graduate school students. Adult students.
Amount: Full tuition plus fees, stipend and medical insurance.
Number of awards: Varies.
Scholarship may be renewable.
Deadline: November 1.
How to apply: Applications are available online.
Exclusive: Visit www.UltimateScholarshipBook.com and enter code DE103926 for updates on this award.

[1040] • NEHA/AAS/APU Scholarship Awards
National Environmental Health Association and the American Academy of Sanitarians
NEHA/AAS Scholarship, 720 South Colorado Boulevard, Suite 105A, Denver, CO 80246-1910
Phone: 303-802-2200
Email: support@neha.org
http://www.neha.org
Purpose: To support students planning careers in environmental health.
Eligibility: Applicants must be either undergraduate or graduate students. The undergraduate scholarships are to be used during the junior or senior year at an Environmental Health Accreditation Council (EHAC) or NEHA member school. The graduate scholarship is available to applicants who are enrolled in a graduate program of study in environmental health sciences and/or public health and have at least one semester of coursework remaining.
Target applicant(s): College students. Graduate school students. Adult students.
Amount: $2,650-$3,750.
Number of awards: 3.
Scholarship may be renewable.
Deadline: February 15.
How to apply: Applications are available online.
Exclusive: Visit www.UltimateScholarshipBook.com and enter code NA104026 for updates on this award.

[1041] • Nellie Yeoh Whetten Award
American Vacuum Society
125 Maiden Lane, 15th Floor, New York, NY 10038
Phone: 212-248-0200
Email: angela@avs.org
http://www.avs.org
Purpose: To recognize and encourage excellence by women in graduate studies in the sciences and technologies of interest to AVS.
Eligibility: The nominee must be a registered female graduate student in an accredited academic institution at the time when the applications are due. The top eight student nominees are notified and invited to present talks on their research to the Awards Committee in a virtual interview in late summer. After the interview, one of the top three students of the eight finalists will receive the Whetten Award. Criteria for selection of the awardee are excellence in research and academic record. An application must be submitted online, which includes a summary of the research and an uploaded letter of recommendation.
Target applicant(s): Graduate school students. Adult students.
Amount: Varies.
Number of awards: 1.
Deadline: May 13.
How to apply: Applications are available online.
Exclusive: Visit www.UltimateScholarshipBook.com and enter code AM104126 for updates on this award.

[1042] • New Century Scholars Doctoral Scholarship
American Speech-Language-Hearing Foundation
2200 Research Boulevard, Rockville, MD 20850
Phone: 301-296-8700
Email: foundationprograms@asha.org
https://www.ashfoundation.org/
Purpose: To support graduate students and researchers who are studying communication sciences and disorders.
Eligibility: Students applying for the scholarship must be enrolled in a research or teaching doctoral program to obtain a Ph.D. or its equivalent. Researchers applying for the grant must have teacher-investigator careers, either in an academic environment or in external research institutions.
Target applicant(s): Graduate school students. Adult students.
Amount: $10,000.
Number of awards: Up to 15.
Deadline: May 15.
How to apply: Applications are available online.
Exclusive: Visit www.UltimateScholarshipBook.com and enter code AM104226 for updates on this award.

[1043] • New Face of Tech Scholarship Program
1,000 Dreams Fund
1875 K Street NW, 4th Floor, Washington, DC 20006
Email: programs@1000dreamsfund.org
https://1000dreamsfund.org
Purpose: To support women students studying science, technology, engineering, arts or math (STEAM).
Eligibility: Applicants must be women students studying science, technology, engineering, arts or math (STEAM). The scholarship award can be used at any accredited college or university.
Target applicant(s): High school students. College students. Adult students.
Amount: $1,500.
Number of awards: Varies.
Deadline: November 22.
How to apply: Applications are available online.
Exclusive: Visit www.UltimateScholarshipBook.com and enter code 1,104326 for updates on this award.

[1044] • Next Swell Scholarship
Next Swell
1177 Queen Street, #2807, Honolulu, HI 96814
Email: Info@thenextswell.org
https://www.thenextswell.org/scholarship
Purpose: To provide academic scholarships to exceptional students pursuing research.

Eligibility: Applicants must be citizens of the U.S. or permanent residents pursuing a graduate degree (master's or Ph.D.). Students must be able to provide proof of attendance (i.e., an academic transcript) or proof of acceptance and have a minimum GPA of 3.5 on a 4.0 scale.
Target applicant(s): College students. Graduate school students. Adult students.
Minimum GPA: 3.5
Amount: $5,000.
Number of awards: Varies.
Deadline: March 15.
How to apply: Applications are available online.
Exclusive: Visit www.UltimateScholarshipBook.com and enter code NE104426 for updates on this award.

[1045] • NFMC Dorothy Dann Bullock Music Therapy Award and the NFMC Ruth B. Robertson Music Therapy Award

National Federation of Music Clubs Bullock and Robertson Awards
Margaret Smith, 2501 Maple Ridge Drive, Tuscaloosa, AL 35406
Phone: 317-882-4003
Email: Margbill1956@att.net
http://www.nfmc-music.org/competitions-awards/
Purpose: To assist students who plan to enter careers in music therapy.
Eligibility: Applicants must be college students majoring in music therapy in schools approved by the National Association of Music Therapists and AMTA. Selection is based on musical talent, skills and training with an emphasis on piano ability in accompanying and sight reading. Other selection criteria are self-reliance, leadership, ability to work with groups and dedication to music therapy as a career. Applicants must be members of the National Federation of Music Clubs.
Target applicant(s): College students. Adult students.
Amount: $650-$1,500.
Number of awards: Varies.
Deadline: March 1.
How to apply: Applications are available online.
Exclusive: Visit www.UltimateScholarshipBook.com and enter code NA104526 for updates on this award.

[1046] • NHSC Scholarship

U.S. Department of Health and Human Services
Health Resources and Services Administration, Bureau of Health Workforce, 5600 Fishers Lane, Rockville, MD 20857
Phone: 800-221-9393
Email: callcenter@hrsa.gov
http://nhsc.hrsa.gov/scholarships
Purpose: To aid students committed to providing health care in communities of great need.
Eligibility: Applicants must be enrolled or accepted into allopathic or osteopathic medical schools, family nurse practitioner programs, nurse-midwifery programs, physician assistant programs or dental school. Upon completion of training, scholars must choose practice sites in federally designated health professional shortage areas for one year for each year of support received.
Target applicant(s): College students. Graduate school students. Adult students.
Amount: Full tuition and fees plus stipend.
Number of awards: Varies.
Scholarship may be renewable.
Deadline: April 25.
How to apply: Applications are available by telephone request.
Exclusive: Visit www.UltimateScholarshipBook.com and enter code U.104626 for updates on this award.

[1047] • NIH Undergraduate Scholarship Program

Office of Intramural Training and Education
National Institute of Health - DHHS, 2 Center Drive, Building 2, Room 2E24, Bethesda, MD 20892-0230
Phone: 800-528-7689
Email: ugsp@nih.gov
http://www.training.nih.gov/programs/ugsp
Purpose: To offer competitive scholarships to students who are committed to careers in biomedical, behavioral and social science health-related research.
Eligibility: Applicants must be enrolled or accepted for enrollment as full-time students at an accredited undergraduate institution, have an underprivileged background and have a minimum 3.3 GPA or be within the top 5 percent of their class. Applicants must also show a commitment to pursuing careers in biomedical, behavioral and social science research at the NIH.
Target applicant(s): College students. Adult students.
Minimum GPA: 3.3
Amount: Up to $20,000.
Number of awards: Varies.
Scholarship may be renewable.
Deadline: March 29.
How to apply: Applications are available online.
Exclusive: Visit www.UltimateScholarshipBook.com and enter code OF104726 for updates on this award.

[1048] • Novus Biologicals Scholarship Program

Novus Biologicals LLC
10771 East Easter Avenue, Centennial, CO 80112
Phone: 303-730-1950
Email: scholarship@novusbio.com
http://www.novusbio.com/scholarship-program.html
Purpose: To reward students who plan to pursue a career in science.
Eligibility: Students must provide a personal statement and a character statement. Applicants must be accepted to or enrolled in a science-related program. Scholarship awarded twice each year.
Target applicant(s): High school students. College students. Graduate school students. Adult students.
Amount: $1,500.
Number of awards: 2.
Deadline: July 19.
How to apply: Applications are available online.
Exclusive: Visit www.UltimateScholarshipBook.com and enter code NO104826 for updates on this award.

[1049] • NPCA Educational Foundation Scholarships

National Precast Concrete Association (NPCA)
1320 City Center Drive, Suite 200, Carmel, IN 46032
Phone: 800-366-7731
Email: mharrell@precast.org
http://precast.org/foundation/scholarships/
Purpose: To aid students who are preparing for careers in the precast concrete industry.
Eligibility: Applicants must be high school seniors or undergraduate students who are enrolled in or planning to enroll in a program of study

that is related to the building, construction or precast concrete industries. Selection is based on the overall strength of the application.
Target applicant(s): High school students. College students. Adult students.
Amount: Up to $20,000.
Number of awards: Varies.
Scholarship may be renewable.
Deadline: March 15.
How to apply: Applications are available online. An application form, transcript and two letters of recommendation are required.
Exclusive: Visit www.UltimateScholarshipBook.com and enter code NA104926 for updates on this award.

[1050] • NPFDA Scholarships
National Poultry and Food Distributors Association
2014 Osborne Road, St. Marys, GA 31558
Phone: 912-439-3603
Email: alina@npfda.org
http://www.npfda.org/npfda-scholarships
Purpose: To aid NPFDA member children and/or employees with their college tuition.
Eligibility: Applicants must be an employee or child of an employee of an NPFDA Member Company and be a rising undergraduate junior or senior who is a full-time student at a U.S. post-secondary institution. Applicants should be pursuing a poultry- or agriculture-related program of study. Selection is based on the overall strength of the application.
Target applicant(s): College students. Adult students.
Amount: $5,000.
Number of awards: 8.
Deadline: April 26.
How to apply: Applications are available online. An application form, official transcript, personal statement and one letter of recommendation are required.
Exclusive: Visit www.UltimateScholarshipBook.com and enter code NA105026 for updates on this award.

[1051] • Nurse Candidate Program
Navy Medicine Professional Development Center
8955 Wood Road, Bethesda, MD 20889-5611
Phone: 301-295-2333
Email: usn.ohstudent@mail.mil
https://www.navy.com/what-to-expect/education-opportunities/undergraduate-degree-opportunities
Purpose: To aid students who are pursuing the bachelor of science in nursing (BSN).
Eligibility: Applicants must be U.S. citizens and be full-time students who have completed two or more years of a four-year bachelor of science in nursing (BSN) degree program at an accredited college or university. They must meet the Navy's physical fitness requirements. Recipients of this award will be required to fulfill an active duty service obligation of up to five years as an officer in the Navy Nurse Corps. Selection is based on the overall strength of the application.
Target applicant(s): College students. Adult students.
Amount: Up to $34,000.
Number of awards: Varies.
Scholarship may be renewable.
Deadline: Contact the sponsor to confirm the deadline.
How to apply: Applications may be obtained by contacting a Navy recruiting officer. An application form and supporting materials are required.
Exclusive: Visit www.UltimateScholarshipBook.com and enter code NA105126 for updates on this award.

[1052] • Nurse Corps Scholarship Program
Health Resources and Services Administration (HRSA)
5600 Fishers Lane, Rockville, MD 20857
Phone: 800-221-9393
Email: gethelp@hrsa.org
http://www.hrsa.gov
Purpose: To aid needy students in obtaining nursing training and education in order to specifically decrease the major shortage of nurses in given health care facilities.
Eligibility: Applicants must be U.S. citizens accepted by or enrolled in a nursing program at an accredited nursing school within the U.S. leading to an associate, baccalaureate or graduate nursing degree or diploma. Applicants must have no federal judgment liens and not be delinquent on a federal debt or have current service commitments. They must begin their nursing program no later than September 30. Selection is based on financial need, academic success, essay answers, resume and letters of recommendation. Preference is given to applicants enrolled full-time in undergraduate or master's nurse practitioner programs. Financial support is provided in exchange for a commitment to serve at least 2 years in a qualifying Nurse Corps site.
Target applicant(s): High school students. College students. Graduate school students. Adult students.
Amount: Full tuition, fees and monthly stipend.
Number of awards: Varies.
Deadline: May 2.
How to apply: Applications are available online. An application form, proof of U.S. citizenship, verification of acceptance report, student aid report, essay answers, resume/curriculum vitae, transcripts and two letters of recommendation are required.
Exclusive: Visit www.UltimateScholarshipBook.com and enter code HE105226 for updates on this award.

[1053] • Nurseries Foundation Award
Oregon Association of Nurseries
29751 SW Town Center Loop West, Wilsonville, OR 97070
Phone: 503-682-5089
Email: onf@oan.org
https://www.oan.org
Purpose: To aid horticulture students.
Eligibility: Applicants must be majoring in horticulture. Selection is based on the overall strength of the application.
Target applicant(s): College students. Adult students.
Amount: $3,000.
Number of awards: 1.
Deadline: April 15.
How to apply: Applications are available online. An application form, an official transcript and three recommendation letters are required.
Exclusive: Visit www.UltimateScholarshipBook.com and enter code OR105326 for updates on this award.

[1054] • Old Guard Oral Presentation Competition
American Society of Mechanical Engineers (ASME)
Two Park Avenue, New York, NY 10016-5990
Phone: 800-843-2763
Email: lefeverb@asme.org
https://www.asme.org/asme-programs/students-and-faculty/scholarships/scholarships

Purpose: To support the professional development of student members of the American Society of Mechanical Engineers (ASME).
Eligibility: Applicants must be certified as ASME student members in good standing. They must be undergraduate engineering students who have been chosen by their student section or academic department head to participate. Applicants must do a 20-minute oral presentation on a relevant engineering topic. Selection is based on presentation content, organization, delivery, effectiveness and discussion.
Target applicant(s): College students. Adult students.
Amount: Varies.
Number of awards: Varies.
Deadline: Contact the sponsor to confirm the deadline.
How to apply: Entry forms are available online. An entry form and oral presentation are required.
Exclusive: Visit www.UltimateScholarshipBook.com and enter code AM105426 for updates on this award.

[1055] • Oliver Moghissi Memorial Scholarship
National Association of Corrosion Engineers (NACE) International Foundation
15835 Park Ten Place, Houston, TX 77084-5145
Phone: 281-228-6205
Email: nace.foundation@nace.org
https://www.ampp.org/about/emerg-student-outreach/academic-scholarships-program
Purpose: To assist students in the National Association of Corrosion Engineers.
Eligibility: Applicants must be enrolled full-time in an undergraduate program focused on the study of chemical engineering at an accredited college or university.
Target applicant(s): High school students. College students. Adult students.
Amount: $2,500.
Number of awards: 2.
Deadline: January 4.
How to apply: Applications are available online.
Exclusive: Visit www.UltimateScholarshipBook.com and enter code NA105526 for updates on this award.

[1056] • Operations and Power Division Scholarship
American Nuclear Society
555 North Kensington Avenue, La Grange Park, IL 60526
Phone: 800-323-3044
Email: hr@ans.org
http://www.ans.org
Purpose: To aid nuclear science and nuclear engineering students.
Eligibility: Applicants must be U.S. citizens or permanent residents and be student members of the American Nuclear Society (ANS). They must be undergraduate or graduate students who have completed two or more years of study toward a four-year degree in nuclear science or nuclear engineering. Students must be enrolled at an accredited U.S. postsecondary institution. Selection is based on academic merit.
Target applicant(s): College students. Adult students.
Amount: $2,500.
Number of awards: 2.
Deadline: February 1.
How to apply: Applications are available online. An application form, transcript and three references are required.
Exclusive: Visit www.UltimateScholarshipBook.com and enter code AM105626 for updates on this award.

[1057] • Outstanding Undergraduate Researchers Award Program
Computing Research Association
1828 L Street NW, Suite 800, Washington, DC 20036-4632
Phone: 202-234-2111
Email: undergradawards@cra.org
https://cra.org/about/awards/
Purpose: To support undergraduates who have completed outstanding research in the field of computing.
Eligibility: Applicants must be undergraduates at a North American college or university and must have conducted some type of computing research. Nominations from two faculty members and a recommendation from the chair of the applicant's home department are also required. Preference is given to undergraduate seniors. Selection is based on the quality of computing research, academic achievement and community involvement.
Target applicant(s): College students. Adult students.
Amount: Up to $1,500.
Number of awards: 4.
Deadline: October 13.
How to apply: The nomination form is available online. A recommendation from the chair of the applicant's home department and nominations from two faculty members are required.
Exclusive: Visit www.UltimateScholarshipBook.com and enter code CO105726 for updates on this award.

[1058] • Paradigm Challenge
Project Paradigm
P.O. Box 27729, Los Angeles, CA 90027
https://www.projectparadigm.org/challenge
Purpose: To encourage youth to use STEM plus kindness, creativity and collaboration to make a difference in the world.
Eligibility: Applicants must be 18 years of age or younger. Students will need to submit a description of 140 characters or less of their idea to reduce waste in their homes, schools, community or around the world.
Target applicant(s): Junior high students or younger. High school students.
Amount: up to $100,000.
Number of awards: 100.
Deadline: May 1.
How to apply: Applications are available online.
Exclusive: Visit www.UltimateScholarshipBook.com and enter code PR105826 for updates on this award.

[1059] • Paros-Digiquartz Scholarship
Marine Technology Society
One Thomas Circle, Suite 700, Washington, DC 20005
Phone: 202-717-8705
Email: scholarships@mtsociety.org
https://www.mtsociety.org/scholarships
Purpose: To support Marine Technology Society members with an interest in marine instrumentation in pursuing post-secondary education.
Eligibility: Applicants must be MTS student members who are accepted for enrollment or enrolled full-time in an undergraduate or graduate program.

Target applicant(s): College students. Graduate school students. Adult students.
Amount: $2,000.
Number of awards: 1.
Deadline: April 15.
How to apply: Applications are available online.
Exclusive: Visit www.UltimateScholarshipBook.com and enter code MA105926 for updates on this award.

[1060] • Path to Pro Scholarship
Home Depot Foundation
https://www.myscholarship.app/home-depot-foundation
Purpose: To support students focused on carpentry, electrical, HVAC, plumbing or construction management studies.
Eligibility: Applicants must be high school seniors, high school graduates or have a GED equivalent. Students must plan to enroll, or be enrolled, in an approved trade-related program at an accredited two-year school in the United States focused on carpentry, electrical, HVAC, plumbing or construction management programs.
Target applicant(s): High school students. College students. Adult students.
Amount: $2,000.
Number of awards: Up to 15.
Deadline: March 31; June 30; September 30; December 31.
How to apply: Applications are available online.
Exclusive: Visit www.UltimateScholarshipBook.com and enter code HO106026 for updates on this award.

[1061] • Paul A. Stewart Grants
Wilson Ornithological Society
Department of Biology and Biomedical Science, Dr. James Chace, Associate Professor, 100 Ochre Point Avenue, Newport, RI 02840-4192
Email: rbpayne@umich.edu
http://www.wilsonsociety.org
Purpose: To promote bird research.
Eligibility: Applicants' proposals should, but are not required to, cover the area of the study of bird movements based on banding, using the analysis and recovery of banded birds, with an emphasis on economic ornithology. Applicants must be willing to present their research results at an annual meeting of the Wilson Ornithological Society.
Target applicant(s): Junior high students or younger. High school students. College students. Graduate school students. Adult students.
Amount: $2,000.
Number of awards: Up to 4.
Deadline: February 1.
How to apply: Applications are available online.
Exclusive: Visit www.UltimateScholarshipBook.com and enter code WI106126 for updates on this award.

[1062] • Payette Sho-Ping Chin Memorial Academic Scholarship
American Institute of Architects
740 15th Street NW, Washington, DC 20005
Phone: 202-787-1001
Email: scholarships@architectsfoundation.org
https://architectsfoundation.org
Purpose: To support women seeking an architectural degree.
Eligibility: Applicants must be female students in their third year of undergraduate or any level of graduate study in an accredited architecture program. Students must have a grade point average of 3.0 or better and be a U.S. citizen.
Target applicant(s): College students. Graduate school students. Adult students.
Minimum GPA: 3.0
Amount: $10,000.
Number of awards: 1.
Deadline: January 19.
How to apply: Applications are available online
Exclusive: Visit www.UltimateScholarshipBook.com and enter code AM106226 for updates on this award.

[1063] • Payzer Scholarship
EAA Aviation Center
3000 Poberezny Road, Oshkosh, WI 54902
Phone: 920-426-4800
Email: scholarships@eaa.org
https://www.eaa.org/eaa/learn-to-fly/scholarships
Purpose: To support students interested in technical careers.
Eligibility: Applicants must be accepted or enrolled in an accredited college or university with an emphasis on technical information and must intend to pursue a career in engineering, mathematics or the physical or biological sciences. Applicants must also be involved in school and community activities as well as aviation and be members of EAA.
Target applicant(s): High school students. College students. Graduate school students. Adult students.
Amount: $5,000.
Number of awards: 1.
Deadline: March 1.
How to apply: Applications are available online.
Exclusive: Visit www.UltimateScholarshipBook.com and enter code EA106326 for updates on this award.

[1064] • Peggy Dixon Two-Year Scholarship
Society of Physics Students
One Physics Ellipse, College Park, MD 20740
Phone: 301-209-3007
Email: SPS-Programs@aip.org
https://www.spsnational.org/
Purpose: To help students seeking a bachelor's degree in physics to transition from a two-year to a four-year program.
Eligibility: Applicants must be members of SPS. Students must have finished at least one semester or quarter of the introductory physics sequence and must be registered in the appropriate subsequent physics classes.
Target applicant(s): College students. Adult students.
Amount: $2,500.
Number of awards: 1.
Deadline: March 15.
How to apply: Applications are available online or from chapter advisors.
Exclusive: Visit www.UltimateScholarshipBook.com and enter code SO106426 for updates on this award.

[1065] • Perennial Plant Association Scholarship
Perennial Plant Association
P.O. Box 6652, Raleigh, NC 27628
Phone: 888-440-3122
Email: perennialplantfoundation@gmail.com
https://perennialplant.org/page/Awards

Purpose: To aid undergraduates who are studying horticulture or a related subject.
Eligibility: Applicants must be enrolled in a two- or four-year degree program while majoring or minoring in horticulture or a related subject. They must have a GPA of 3.0 or higher on a four-point scale. Previous recipients of this scholarship are not eligible. Preference will be given to applicants who are planning to pursue careers in perennials. Selection is based on the overall strength of the application.
Target applicant(s): College students. Adult students.
Minimum GPA: 3.0
Amount: $1,000.
Number of awards: Varies.
Deadline: March 31.
How to apply: Applications are available online. An application form, official transcript, personal statement and three recommendation letters are required.
Exclusive: Visit www.UltimateScholarshipBook.com and enter code PE106526 for updates on this award.

[1066] • Perfect Plants Nursery Scholarship
Perfect Plants
P.O. Box 442, Lloyd, FL 32337
Phone: 850-997-3008
Email: Scholars@myperfectplants.com
https://myperfectplants.com/scholarship-application/
Purpose: To support students pursuing horticultural education.
Eligibility: Applicants must be current or enrolling undergraduate students with a minimum GPA of 3.0 who are pursuing a course of study leading to a career in the horticultural industry. Students must submit an essay and letters of recommendation along with their application and transcripts.
Target applicant(s): High school students. College students. Adult students.
Minimum GPA: 3.0
Amount: $1,000.
Number of awards: 1.
Deadline: August 20.
How to apply: Applications are available online.
Exclusive: Visit www.UltimateScholarshipBook.com and enter code PE106626 for updates on this award.

[1067] • Petroleum Division College Scholarships
ASME International Petroleum Technology Institute
Two Park Avenue, New York, NY 10016-5990
Phone: 800-843-2763
Email: CustomerCare@asme.org
https://www.asme.org/asme-programs/students-and-faculty/scholarships/scholarships
Purpose: To aid undergraduate engineering students who are members of the American Society of Mechanical Engineers (ASME).
Eligibility: Applicants must be ASME student members who are enrolled in an ABET-accredited undergraduate degree program in engineering. They must have an overall GPA of 2.5 or higher on a four-point scale. Selection is based on the overall strength of the application.
Target applicant(s): College students. Adult students.
Minimum GPA: 2.5
Amount: $10,000.
Number of awards: 1.
Deadline: February 15.
How to apply: Applications are available online. An application form, official transcript, personal statement and one recommendation letter are required.
Exclusive: Visit www.UltimateScholarshipBook.com and enter code AS106726 for updates on this award.

[1068] • PHCC Educational Foundation Scholarship
PHCC Educational Foundation
180 South Washington Street, Suite 100, Falls Church, VA 22046
Phone: 800-533-7694
Email: scholarships@naphcc.org
http://www.phccweb.org
Purpose: To elevate the technical and business competence of the plumbing-heating-cooling (p-h-c) industry by awarding scholarships to students who are enrolled in a p-h-c-related major.
Eligibility: Applicants must be currently enrolled or plan to enroll in a p-h-c-related major at an accredited four-year college or university or two-year technical college, community college or trade school. Students enrolled in an approved apprentice program must also be working full-time for a licensed plumbing or HVACR contractor who is a member of the PHCC. Two scholarships will be awarded to students who are enrolled in either a PHCC-approved apprentice program or a full-time certificate or degree program at an accredited two-year community college, technical college or trade school. Three scholarships are awarded to students who are enrolled in an undergraduate degree program at an accredited four-year college or university.
Target applicant(s): High school students. College students. Adult students.
Amount: $1,000-$5,000.
Number of awards: Up to 57.
Deadline: May 1.
How to apply: Applications are available online or by email.
Exclusive: Visit www.UltimateScholarshipBook.com and enter code PH106826 for updates on this award.

[1069] • Phoebe Pember Memorial Scholarship
United Daughters of the Confederacy
328 North Boulevard, Richmond, VA 23220
Phone: 804-355-1636
Email: hqudc@rcn.com
http://www.hqudc.org
Purpose: To aid Confederate descendants who are undergraduate nursing students.
Eligibility: Applicants must be the direct descendant of an eligible Confederate. They must be enrolled in an undergraduate degree program in nursing at an accredited U.S. college or university and have a GPA of 3.0 or higher on a four-point scale. Selection is based on the overall strength of the application.
Target applicant(s): College students. Adult students.
Minimum GPA: 3.0
Amount: Varies.
Number of awards: Varies.
Scholarship may be renewable.
Deadline: Contact the sponsor to confirm the deadline.
How to apply: Applications are available online. An application form, personal statement, official transcript, one letter of recommendation, endorsement from sponsoring UDC Chapter, applicant photo and proof of Confederate ancestry are required.

The Ultimate Scholarship Book 2026
Scholarship Directory (Sciences)

Exclusive: Visit www.UltimateScholarshipBook.com and enter code UN106926 for updates on this award.

[1070] • Physician Assistant Foundation Scholarship

Physician Assistant Foundation
PA Foundation Scholarship Committee, 950 North Washington Street, Alexandria, VA 22314-1552
Phone: 703-519-5686
Email: cshedlock@aapa.org
http://www.aapa.org
Purpose: To support physician assistants.
Eligibility: Applicants must be American Academy of Physician Assistants (AAPA) members and currently enrolled in the professional phase of a PA training program at an ARC-PA-accredited physician assistant program. Students are judged on the basis of financial need, community and professional involvement, goals and academic performance.
Target applicant(s): College students. Adult students.
Amount: $1,000.
Number of awards: 26.
Deadline: March 18.
How to apply: Applications are available online.
Exclusive: Visit www.UltimateScholarshipBook.com and enter code PH107026 for updates on this award.

[1071] • Pioneers of Flight

National Air Transportation Foundation
Pioneers of Flight Scholarship Program, Attn.: Professor Gregory Schwab, Chair, Department of Aerospace Technology, TC 216, Indiana State University, Terre Haute, IN 47809
Email: aeschwab@isugw.indstate.edu
https://www.nata.aero/scholarships/pioneers-of-flight-scholarship
Purpose: To assist students pursuing general aviation as a career.
Eligibility: Applicants must be full-time students at an accredited four-year institution, be sophomores or juniors at the time of application and plan to pursue a career in aviation. Students must have a minimum 3.0 GPA.
Target applicant(s): College students. Adult students.
Minimum GPA: 3.0
Amount: $1,000.
Number of awards: 2.
Deadline: Last Friday in December.
How to apply: Applications are available online.
Exclusive: Visit www.UltimateScholarshipBook.com and enter code NA107126 for updates on this award.

[1072] • PixelPlex Bi-Annual STEM Scholarship

PixelPlex
520 West 28th Street, Suite 31, New York, NY 10001
Phone: 646-490-0772
Email: scholarship@pixelplex.io
https://pixelplex.io/scholarship/
Purpose: To encourage students pursuing education in STEM fields as well as economics and business.
Eligibility: Applicants must be U.S. citizens or permanent residents. Students must be enrolled or accepted into a college or university in the United States. The applicants' field of study must be related to STEM fields, economics or business. An essay is required on a provided prompt.
Target applicant(s): High school students. College students. Graduate school students. Adult students.
Amount: $2,000.
Number of awards: 1.
Deadline: June 5.
How to apply: Applications are available online.
Exclusive: Visit www.UltimateScholarshipBook.com and enter code PI107226 for updates on this award.

[1073] • Plastics Pioneers Association Scholarships

Society of Plastics Engineers
83 Wooster Heights Road Suite 125, Suite 306, Danbury, CT 06810
Phone: 810-986-6131
Email: thomas.miller@ravago.com
https://plasticspioneers.org/scholarships/
Purpose: To aid students who are planning for careers in plastics technology and engineering.
Eligibility: Applicants must be full-time undergraduate students who intend to pursue careers as plastics technicians or engineers. Selection is based on the overall strength of the application.
Target applicant(s): High school students. College students. Adult students.
Amount: $3,000.
Number of awards: Varies.
Deadline: April 30.
How to apply: Applications are available online. An application form, three recommendation letters, a transcript and personal statement are required.
Exclusive: Visit www.UltimateScholarshipBook.com and enter code SO107326 for updates on this award.

[1074] • Polymer Modifiers and Additives Division Scholarships

Society of Plastics Engineers
83 Wooster Heights Road Suite 125, Suite 306, Danbury, CT 06810
Phone: 810-986-6131
Email: thomas.miller@ravago.com
https://plasticspioneers.org/scholarships/
Purpose: To aid students who have an interest in the plastics industry.
Eligibility: Applicants must have an interest in the plastics industry, major in or take courses leading to a career in the plastics industry and be in good academic standing. Financial need is considered.
Target applicant(s): High school students. College students. Adult students.
Amount: Varies.
Number of awards: Varies.
Deadline: April 30.
How to apply: Applications are available online.
Exclusive: Visit www.UltimateScholarshipBook.com and enter code SO107426 for updates on this award.

[1075] • PPG Protective and Marine Coatings Academic Scholarship

National Association of Corrosion Engineers (NACE) International Foundation
15835 Park Ten Place, Houston, TX 77084-5145
Phone: 281-228-6205
Email: nace.foundation@nace.org
https://www.ampp.org/about/emerg-student-outreach/academic-scholarships-program

Purpose: To help students interested in pursuing science and/or engineering degrees.
Eligibility: Applicants must be an undergraduate enrolled full-time at an accredited two- or four-year college or university and must be pursuing a degree with an emphasis on corrosion or coatings. Applicants must have a GPA of 3.0 or higher in their chosen field of study.
Target applicant(s): College students. Adult students.
Minimum GPA: 3.0
Amount: $5,000.
Number of awards: Up to 5.
Deadline: January 2.
How to apply: Applications are available online. An application form, three recommendation forms, an academic transcript and essay scholarship questions are required.
Exclusive: Visit www.UltimateScholarshipBook.com and enter code NA107526 for updates on this award.

[1076] • Predoctoral Fellowship Program

National Gallery of Art
2000B South Club Drive, Landover, MD 20785
Phone: 202-842-6482
Email: thecenter@nga.gov
https://www.nga.gov/research/casva/fellowships.html
Purpose: To support advanced graduate research in the history, theory and criticism of art, architecture and urbanism.
Eligibility: Applicants for predoctoral fellowships must be nominated by the chair of the graduate department of art history or other appropriate departments. Applicants must have completed all departmental requirements, including course work, residency and general and preliminary examinations. Certification in two languages other than English is required. Applicants should submit nomination forms, supporting letters from two individuals and writing samples. There are various fellowships. The David E. Finley Fellowship requires applicants have a significant interest in curatorial work. The Paul Mellon Fellowship is for the completion of a doctoral dissertation in Western art. The Samuel H. Kress Fellowship is for the completion of a doctoral dissertation in European art on a topic before the early nineteenth century. The Wyeth Fellowship is for the completion of a doctoral dissertation that concerns aspects of art of the United States, including native and pre-Revolutionary America. The Ittleson Fellowship is for the completion of a doctoral dissertation in the visual arts in a field other than Western art. The Andrew W. Mellon Fellowship is for the completion of a doctoral dissertation in cross-cultural studies or in a field other than Western art through the twentieth century. The Robert H. and Clarice Smith Fellowship is for research on Northern European art between 1400 and 1700, intended for the advancement or completion of either a doctoral dissertation or a resulting publication. The Chester Dale Fellowships are for the advancement or completion of a doctoral dissertation in any area of Western art, with a preference for modern and contemporary topics. The Center offers a Paul Mellon Postdoctoral Fellowship for recipients of the David E. Finley, Paul Mellon, Samuel H. Kress, Wyeth, Ittleson, Andrew W. Mellon and two-year Chester Dale fellowships if the dissertation has been accepted by June 1 of the residence year. Several candidates for each fellowship will be invited to Washington for interviews.
Target applicant(s): Graduate school students. Adult students.
Amount: $30,000 plus allowances.
Number of awards: 9.
Deadline: November 15.
How to apply: Application materials are described online. Contact your dissertation advisor and departmental chair to obtain nomination forms.
Exclusive: Visit www.UltimateScholarshipBook.com and enter code NA107626 for updates on this award.

[1077] • Predoctoral Research Fellowships

American Epilepsy Society
135 South LaSalle Street, Suite 2850, Chicago, IL 60603
Email: info@aesnet.org
https://www.aesnet.org/research-funding/funding/early-career/predoctoral-research-fellowships
Purpose: To support pre-doctoral students with dissertation research relating to epilepsy.
Eligibility: Applicants must be full-time graduate students pursuing a Ph.D. degree in neuroscience, physiology, pharmacology, psychology, biochemistry, genetics, nursing, pharmacy or other related areas; have a dissertation research project; have a qualified mentor who can supervise the project and have access to resources to conduct the project. The project must be in the U.S. and its territories. The award is based on the quality of the dissertation project, relevance to epilepsy, the applicant's qualifications, the mentor's qualifications and the quality of the proposed environment.
Target applicant(s): Graduate school students. Adult students.
Amount: Up to $30,000.
Number of awards: Varies.
Deadline: January 18.
How to apply: Applicants must submit three recommendation letters including one from the mentor, a statement of intent, a biographical sketch, a cover sheet form, a lay summary, transcripts and a research plan.
Exclusive: Visit www.UltimateScholarshipBook.com and enter code AM107726 for updates on this award.

[1078] • Presidents Scholarship of the Institute of Industrial Engineers

Institute of Industrial and Systems Engineers
3577 Parkway Lane, Suite 200, Norcross, GA 30092
Phone: 800-494-0460
Email: egrimes@iise.org
https://www.iise.org
Purpose: To support undergraduate industrial engineering students.
Eligibility: Applicants must be active student members of the Institute of Industrial Engineers (IIE). They must be full-time undergraduates enrolled in an industrial engineering degree program and have a GPA of 3.4 or higher on a four-point scale. They must have demonstrated leadership skills. Applicants must be nominated by their academic department heads. Selection is based on professional leadership potential, character, financial need and academic merit.
Target applicant(s): College students. Adult students.
Minimum GPA: 3.4
Amount: $1,000.
Number of awards: 1.
Deadline: February 1.
How to apply: Nomination forms are available online. A nomination form completed by the applicant's academic department head is required.
Exclusive: Visit www.UltimateScholarshipBook.com and enter code IN107826 for updates on this award.

[1079] • Pretty Photoshop Actions Bi-annual Scholarship

Pretty Photoshop Actions
Email: scholarship@photoshopactions.com
https://www.photoshopactions.com/pages/pretty-photoshop-actions-scholarship-program
Purpose: To help offset the cost of higher education.

Eligibility: Applicants must be graduating high school seniors or enrolled at a college or university in the U.S. or Canada. Students must create an Adobe Photoshop tutorial essay.
Target applicant(s): High school students. College students. Adult students.
Amount: $500.
Number of awards: 1.
Deadline: October 15.
How to apply: Applications are available online.
Exclusive: Visit www.UltimateScholarshipBook.com and enter code PR107926 for updates on this award.

[1080] • Pulte Group Build Your Future Scholarship Program
National Housing Endowment
1201 15th Street NW, Washington, DC 20005
Phone: 202-266-8069
Email: Scholarships@nahb.org
https://apply.nationalhousingendowment.org
Purpose: To aid U.S. students who plan to pursue careers in the building industry.
Eligibility: Applicants must be U.S. undergraduate freshmen, sophomores or juniors who are enrolled full-time in a housing-related degree program (construction, civil engineering, architecture, building trades or management, etc.). They must have at least one full academic year remaining in their course of study and maintain an overall GPA of at least 2.5 and major GPA of at least 3.0. Preference will be given to applicants who demonstrate financial need or who are members of a building industry-related service or professional organization, especially the National Association of Home Builders. Selection is based on financial need, academic achievement, GPA, work experience, extracurricular activities and professional goals.
Target applicant(s): College students. Adult students.
Minimum GPA: 2.5
Amount: Varies.
Number of awards: Varies.
Scholarship may be renewable.
Deadline: March 31.
How to apply: Applications are available online. An application form, a transcript, two recommendation letters, a list of degree requirements, a personal essay and a statement of financial status are required.
Exclusive: Visit www.UltimateScholarshipBook.com and enter code NA108026 for updates on this award.

[1081] • R&D Systems Scholarship Program
R&D Systems Inc.
614 McKinley Place NE, Minneapolis, MN 55413
Phone: 800-343-7475
Email: scholarship@novusbio.com
https://www.rndsystems.com/grants-scholarships/scholarship-application
Purpose: To support students who are pursuing a degree in a science-related field.
Eligibility: Applicants must be enrolled, or plan to be enrolled, in an undergraduate or graduate level science program.
Target applicant(s): High school students. College students. Graduate school students. Adult students.
Amount: $1,500.
Number of awards: 2.
Deadline: June 16 and December 8.
How to apply: Applications are available online.
Exclusive: Visit www.UltimateScholarshipBook.com and enter code R&108126 for updates on this award.

[1082] • Rain Bird Intelligent Use of Water Scholarship
Landscape Architecture Foundation
1200 17th Street NW, Suite 210, Washington, DC 20036
Phone: 202-331-7070
Email: scholarships@lafoundation.org
https://www.lafoundation.org/what-we-do/scholarships
Purpose: To recognize outstanding landscape architecture students.
Eligibility: Applicants must be college juniors or fourth- or fifth-year seniors who are landscape architecture, horticulture or irrigation science students who have a demonstrated commitment to the landscape architecture profession and exhibit financial need. Applications can only be sent by email.
Target applicant(s): College students. Adult students.
Amount: $5,000.
Number of awards: 1.
Deadline: February 1.
How to apply: Applicants should follow the guidelines.
Exclusive: Visit www.UltimateScholarshipBook.com and enter code LA108226 for updates on this award.

[1083] • Ralph K. Hillquist Honorary SAE Scholarship
Society of Automotive Engineers International
Scholarships Program, 400 Commonwealth Drive, Warrendale, PA 15096
Phone: 724-776-4841
Email: scholarships@sae.org
https://www.sae.org/participate/scholarships
Purpose: To aid mechanical and automotive engineering students.
Eligibility: Applicants must be U.S. citizens and full-time undergraduate juniors who are enrolled in an ABET-accredited mechanical or automotive engineering degree program at a U.S. college or university. They must have a GPA of 3.0 or higher. Preference will be given to applicants who have completed coursework in noise and vibration (e.g., physics, statics, vibration or dynamics). Selection is based on academic merit, leadership and special studies in noise and vibration.
Target applicant(s): College students. Adult students.
Minimum GPA: 3.0
Amount: $1,000.
Number of awards: 1.
Deadline: February 28.
How to apply: Applications are available online. An application form, official transcript and standardized test scores are required.
Exclusive: Visit www.UltimateScholarshipBook.com and enter code SO108326 for updates on this award.

[1084] • Raney Fund Award
American Society of Ichthyologists and Herpetologists
P.O. Box 1897, 810 E 10th St, Lawrence, KS 66044
Phone: 785-865-9405
Email: asih@allenpress.com
https://asih.org/student-awards
Purpose: To support young ichthyologists.
Eligibility: Applicants should be members of ASIH and should be enrolled for an advanced degree, although those with developing careers may receive the award under exceptional circumstances. Awards may be used for museums or laboratory study, travel, fieldwork or other activities that will enhance their professional careers and their contributions to the science of ichthyology. Scholarships are awarded on the basis of merit and need.
Target applicant(s): Graduate school students. Adult students.
Amount: $400-$1,000.
Number of awards: Varies.
Deadline: April 30.
How to apply: Applications are available by email or written request.
Exclusive: Visit www.UltimateScholarshipBook.com and enter code AM108426 for updates on this award.

[1085] • Raymond Davis Scholarship
Society for Imaging Science and Technology
7003 Kilworth Lane, Springfield, VA 22151
Phone: 703-642-9090
Email: info@imaging.org
https://www.imaging.org
Purpose: To support students who are studying imaging science and technology.
Eligibility: Applicants must be full-time graduate or undergraduate students studying photographic or imaging engineering or science who have completed or will complete two academic years of college before the term of the scholarship.
Target applicant(s): College students. Graduate school students. Adult students.
Amount: At least $1,000.
Number of awards: Varies.
Deadline: October 1.
How to apply: Applications are available online.
Exclusive: Visit www.UltimateScholarshipBook.com and enter code SO108526 for updates on this award.

[1086] • Regeneron Science Talent Search
Regeneron Science Talent Search
Society for Science and the Public, 1719 N Street NW, Washington, DC 20036
Phone: 202-785-2255
Email: sts@societyforscience.org
https://student.societyforscience.org/regeneron-sts
Purpose: To recognize excellence in science among the nation's youth and encourage the exploration of science.
Eligibility: Applicants must be high school seniors in the U.S., Puerto Rico, Guam, Virgin Islands, American Samoa, Wake or Midway Islands or the Marianas. U.S. citizens attending foreign schools are also eligible. Applicants must complete college entrance exams and complete individual research projects and provide a report on the research.
Target applicant(s): High school students.
Amount: Up to $250,000.
Number of awards: 40.
Deadline: November 7.
How to apply: Applications are available by request.
Exclusive: Visit www.UltimateScholarshipBook.com and enter code RE108626 for updates on this award.

[1087] • Resident Research Scholarship
American Academy of Neurology
25 Massachusetts Ave NW, Suite 500J, Washington, DC 20001
Phone: 800-879-1960
Email: ggates@aan.com
https://www.aan.com
Purpose: To support neurology residents who are interested in a career in research in neuroscience.
Eligibility: Applicants must be neurology residents who are interested in a career in research in neuroscience. The award is intended to be a springboard into the AAN's Research Program or other programs focused on early-career investigators.
Target applicant(s): Graduate school students. Adult students.
Amount: $3,000.
Number of awards: 3.
Deadline: September 14.
How to apply: Applications are available online.
Exclusive: Visit www.UltimateScholarshipBook.com and enter code AM108726 for updates on this award.

[1088] • Reuben Trane Scholarship
American Society of Heating, Refrigerating and Air-Conditioning Engineers (ASHRAE)
Scholarship Administrator, ASHRAE Inc., 180 Technology Parkway, Peachtree Corners, GA 30092
Phone: 404-636-8400
Email: lbenedict@ashrae.org
https://www.ashrae.org/communities/student-zone/scholarships-and-grants
Purpose: To support engineering undergraduates who are preparing for careers in the heating, ventilation, air-conditioning and refrigeration (HVACR) industry.
Eligibility: Applicants must be attending a school that houses a student branch of the American Society of Heating, Refrigerating and Air-Conditioning Engineers (ASHRAE), is ABET-accredited (U.S. institutions) or is ABET-affiliated (international institutions). Applicants must be undergraduate students who are enrolled in an engineering or pre-engineering curriculum that provides adequate preparation for a career in the HVACR industry. They must have a GPA of 3.0 or higher on a four-point scale or must be in the top 30 percent of their class. Selection is based on the overall strength of the application.
Target applicant(s): High school students. College students. Adult students.
Minimum GPA: 3.0
Amount: $10,000.
Number of awards: 3.
Scholarship may be renewable.
Deadline: December 1.
How to apply: Applications are available online. The application form, official transcript, one letter of recommendation and the evaluation form from an ASHRAE student branch interview (if applicable) are required.
Exclusive: Visit www.UltimateScholarshipBook.com and enter code AM108826 for updates on this award.

[1089] • RevPart STEM Scholarship

RevPart
129 Bethea Road, Suite 402, Fayetteville, GA 30214
Phone: 844-738-7278
Email: info@revpart.com
https://revpart.com/scholarship/
Purpose: To encourage students pursuing a higher education in their chosen study of area of study in a STEM-related field.
Eligibility: Applicants must be current undergraduate or graduate students majoring in a STEM-related field at an accredited college or institution.
Target applicant(s): High school students. College students. Graduate school students. Adult students.
Amount: $500-$2,000.
Number of awards: 3.
Deadline: December 31.
How to apply: Applications are available online.
Exclusive: Visit www.UltimateScholarshipBook.com and enter code RE108926 for updates on this award.

[1090] • Richard J. Stull Student Essay Competition in Healthcare Management

American College of Healthcare Executives
One North Franklin Street, Suite 1700, Chicago, IL 60606
Phone: 312-424-9316
Email: sbrown@ache.org
https://www.ache.org/membership/student-resources
Purpose: To support future healthcare executives.
Eligibility: Applicants must be undergraduate or graduate students enrolled in a healthcare administration degree program at a U.S. or Canadian postsecondary institution that is an American College of Healthcare Executives (ACHE) Higher Education network participant. They must be ACHE student associates or active affiliates. Submitted essays cannot have been published before and must be the sole creation of the applicant. Residents and other postgraduate students are ineligible. Selection is based on relevance of subject matter, creativity, practical applicability of subject matter and clarity.
Target applicant(s): College students. Graduate school students. Adult students.
Amount: Up to $3,000.
Number of awards: 6.
Deadline: December 2.
How to apply: Essay submission guidelines are available online. An essay is required.
Exclusive: Visit www.UltimateScholarshipBook.com and enter code AM109026 for updates on this award.

[1091] • Richard Jensen Scholarship

National Alliance of Independent Crop Consultants
700 Wood Duck Drive, Vonore, TN 37885
Phone: 901-861-0511
Email: AllisonJones@NAICC.org; sjwmackie@gmail.com
https://thefeae.org/scholarships/
Purpose: To aid undergraduate students of crop production.
Eligibility: Applicants must be undergraduate students who are majoring in an agricultural subject that is related to crop production (such as agronomy, horticulture, weed science, soil sciences, entomology or plant pathology). Selection is based on the overall strength of the application.
Target applicant(s): College students. Adult students.
Amount: $3,000.
Number of awards: 1.
Deadline: December 1.
How to apply: Applications are available online. An application form, transcript, proof of enrollment and two reference letters are required.
Exclusive: Visit www.UltimateScholarshipBook.com and enter code NA109126 for updates on this award.

[1092] • Richard L. Davis, FACMPE - Managers Scholarship

Medical Group Management Association
104 Inverness Terrace East, Englewood, CO 80112-5306
Phone: 877-275-6462
Email: scholarship@mgma.com
https://www.mgma.com/scholarships
Purpose: To aid medical practice management professionals who are college students.
Eligibility: Applicants must be current medical practice management professionals who are enrolled in an undergraduate or graduate degree program that is related to medical practice management. Selection is based on the overall strength of the application.
Target applicant(s): College students. Graduate school students. Adult students.
Amount: $2,500.
Number of awards: Varies.
Deadline: April 29.
How to apply: Applications are available online. An application form and supporting materials are required.
Exclusive: Visit www.UltimateScholarshipBook.com and enter code ME109226 for updates on this award.

[1093] • Richard L. Davis, FACMPE/Barbara B. Watson, FACMPE - National Scholarship

Medical Group Management Association
104 Inverness Terrace East, Englewood, CO 80112-5306
Phone: 877-275-6462
Email: scholarship@mgma.com
https://www.mgma.com/scholarships
Purpose: To aid medical practice management students.
Eligibility: Applicants must be undergraduate or graduate students who are enrolled in a degree program that is related to medical practice management (such as healthcare administration, public health or business administration). Selection is based on the overall strength of the application.
Target applicant(s): High school students. College students. Graduate school students. Adult students.
Amount: $2,500.
Number of awards: Varies.
Deadline: May 1.
How to apply: Applications are available online. An application form and supporting materials are required.
Exclusive: Visit www.UltimateScholarshipBook.com and enter code ME109326 for updates on this award.

[1094] • Ridgeline International Community Scholarship

Ridgeline International
8255 Greensboro Drive, Suite 500, McLean, VA 22102
Phone: 703-544-2424
Email: atavares@ridgelineintl.com
https://www.ridgelineintl.com/about#scholarship
Purpose: To reward students who show grit, resilience and agility and take an active role in their community.
Eligibility: Applicants must be graduating high school seniors and current undergraduate students. Students must be pursuing higher education in the science, technology, engineering and math fields. Applicants who are awarded a scholarship may also be considered for future internship and full-time opportunities.
Target applicant(s): High school students. College students. Adult students.
Amount: $5,000.
Number of awards: 3.
Deadline: May 31.
How to apply: Applications are available online.
Exclusive: Visit www.UltimateScholarshipBook.com and enter code RI109426 for updates on this award.

[1095] • RMEL Foundation Scholarships

Rocky Mountain Electrical League
6855 South Havana Street, Suite 430, Centennial, CO 80112
Phone: 303-865-5544
Email: jamessakamoto@rmel.org
https://www.rmel.org
Purpose: To support students pursuing certificate or degree-seeking programs related to the electric energy industry.
Eligibility: Applicants must be U.S. citizens and full-time students pursuing either a certificate, associate or baccalaureate degree in the electric energy arena including: power plant technology, electric line working, power line technology, electrical power technology, electrical line worker technology, electrical distribution systems, utility line technician and traditional or alternative power generation technology. Selection is based on future goals in the electric energy arena, motivation, service and academic performance.
Target applicant(s): High school students. College students. Adult students.
Amount: Up to $3,000.
Number of awards: Varies.
Deadline: February 9.
How to apply: Applications are available online. An application form and transcripts are required.
Exclusive: Visit www.UltimateScholarshipBook.com and enter code RO109526 for updates on this award.

[1096] • Robert B. Oliver ASNT Scholarship

American Society for Nondestructive Testing
Awards and Honors Program, 1201 Dublin Road, Suite #G04, Columbus, OH 43215
Phone: 614-274-6003 x 233
Email: awards@asnt.org
http://www.asnt.org
Purpose: To support students in nondestructive testing.
Eligibility: Applicants must be undergraduate students enrolled in an engineering program and specialize in nondestructive testing (NDT). A nominating letter, transcript and an essay describing the role of NDT/NDE in their career are required. The award is based on creativity, content, format and readability and the student's involvement in a research project.
Target applicant(s): College students. Adult students.
Amount: $2,500.
Number of awards: Up to 3.
Deadline: January 31.
How to apply: Applications are available online.
Exclusive: Visit www.UltimateScholarshipBook.com and enter code AM109626 for updates on this award.

[1097] • Robert E. Thunen Memorial Scholarships

Thunen Scholarship Committee
IES San Francisco Section, Mary-Jane Lawless, 1201 Park Avenue, Suite 100, Emeryville, CA 94608
Phone: 510-655-1200
Email: mlaw@silvermanlight.com
https://www.ies.org/membership/society-awards/
Purpose: To help students who plan to pursue illumination as a career.
Eligibility: Applicants must be full-time junior, senior or graduate students in an accredited four-year college in Northern California, Nevada, Oregon or Washington who plan to pursue illumination as a career. The application, statement of purpose and at least three letters of recommendation are required. Students should review the IES Lighting Handbook to see the available fields of study.
Target applicant(s): College students. Graduate school students. Adult students.
Amount: $2,500.
Number of awards: At least 2.
Deadline: April 1.
How to apply: Applications are available by mail and email.
Exclusive: Visit www.UltimateScholarshipBook.com and enter code TH109726 for updates on this award.

[1098] • Robert N. and Helen H. Herbert Undergraduate Scholarship

Society of Naval Architects and Marine Engineers (SNAME)
99 Canal Center Plaza, Suite 500, Alexandria, VA 22314
Phone: 703-997-6701
Email: scholarships@sname.org
https://www.sname.org/scholarships
Purpose: To assist college undergraduates who are studying marine industry fields.
Eligibility: Applicants must be U.S., Canadian or international college students who are members of the SNAME and are working towards degrees in naval architecture, marine engineering, ocean engineering or marine industry related areas fields. An application form, three recommendation letters and an essay are required.
Target applicant(s): College students. Adult students.
Amount: Up to $6,000.
Number of awards: 1.
Deadline: June 1.
How to apply: Applications are available online.
Exclusive: Visit www.UltimateScholarshipBook.com and enter code SO109826 for updates on this award.

[1099] • Roofing Industry Scholarship - Melvin Kruger Endowed Scholarship

National Roofing Foundation (NRF)
10255 West Higgins Road, Suite 600, Rosemont, IL 60018-5607
Phone: 847-299-9070
http://www.nrca.net
Purpose: To support members of the National Roofing Contractors Association (NRCA).
Eligibility: Applicants must be full-time employees of NRCA member companies or their immediate family members. Students must be high school seniors or graduates or full-time undergraduate students at an accredited two- or four-year post-secondary institution. Applicants must major in a roofing or building construction course of study for a full academic year.
Target applicant(s): High school students. College students. Adult students.
Amount: $5,000.
Number of awards: Up to 12.
Scholarship may be renewable.
Deadline: January 31.
How to apply: Applications are available online.
Exclusive: Visit www.UltimateScholarshipBook.com and enter code NA109926 for updates on this award.

[1100] • Roy J. Shlemon Awards

Geological Society of America Foundation (GSAF)
P.O. Box 9140, Boulder, CO 80301
Phone: 800-472-1988 x1054
Email: info@gsafweb.org
https://www.geosociety.org/gsa
Purpose: To assist graduate students in conducting research in environmental and engineering geology.
Eligibility: Applicants must be members of the Geological Society of America's Engineering Geology Division, and they must be conducting research at the master's or doctoral level.
Target applicant(s): Graduate school students. Adult students.
Amount: Up to $3,000.
Number of awards: At least 2.
Deadline: March 31.
How to apply: Applications are available online.
Exclusive: Visit www.UltimateScholarshipBook.com and enter code GE110026 for updates on this award.

[1101] • Rubber Division Undergraduate Scholarship

American Chemical Society
ACS Scholars Program, 1155 16th Street NW, Washington, DC 20036
Phone: 800-227-5558
Email: scholars@acs.org
http://www.acs.org
Purpose: To aid undergraduate students who are majoring in subjects related to the rubber industry.
Eligibility: Applicants must be rising undergraduate juniors or seniors. They must be majoring in chemistry, chemical engineering, polymer science, mechanical engineering, physics or any other subject that is related to the rubber industry. Selection is based on the overall strength of the application.
Target applicant(s): College students. Adult students.
Amount: $5,000.
Number of awards: 2.
Deadline: March 1.
How to apply: Applications are available online. An application form and supporting materials are required.
Exclusive: Visit www.UltimateScholarshipBook.com and enter code AM110126 for updates on this award.

[1102] • Russell and Sigurd Varian Award

American Vacuum Society
125 Maiden Lane, 15th Floor, New York, NY 10038
Phone: 212-248-0200
Email: angela@avs.org
http://www.avs.org
Purpose: To recognize and encourage excellence in continuing graduate studies in the sciences and technologies of interest to AVS.
Eligibility: The nominee must be a registered graduate student in an accredited academic institution when the applications are due. Applicants are normally expected not to graduate before the award selection. The top eight student nominees are notified and invited to present talks on their research to the Awards Committee in a virtual interview in late summer. After the interview, one of the top three students of the eight finalists will receive the Varian Award. Criteria for selection of the awardee are excellence in research and academic record. An application must be submitted online which includes a summary of research and an uploaded letter of recommendation.
Target applicant(s): Graduate school students. Adult students.
Amount: Varies.
Number of awards: 1.
Deadline: May 13.
How to apply: Applications are available online.
Exclusive: Visit www.UltimateScholarshipBook.com and enter code AM110226 for updates on this award.

[1103] • Ruth Abernathy Presidential Scholarship

Shape America
P.O. Box 225, Annapolis Junction, MD 20701
Phone: 800-213-7193
https://www.shapeamerica.org
Purpose: To honor deserving students in health, physical education, recreation and dance.
Eligibility: Applicants must be members of the American Alliance for Health, Physical Education, Recreation and Dance (AAHPERD), but they may join when applying and must major in health, physical education, recreation or dance. Undergraduate applicants must have a minimum 3.5 GPA and have junior or senior status when applying. Graduate applicants must have a minimum 3.5 GPA and have completed one semester of full-time study. Selection is based on scholastic achievement, leadership, community service and character.
Target applicant(s): College students. Graduate school students. Adult students.
Minimum GPA: 3.5
Amount: $1,250-$1,750.
Number of awards: 5.
Deadline: October 15.
How to apply: Applications are available online.
Exclusive: Visit www.UltimateScholarshipBook.com and enter code SH110326 for updates on this award.

[1104] • RV Learning Center Scholarship Program

Mike Molino RV Learning Center
3930 University Dr., Fairfax, VA 22030
Phone: 703-591-7130
Email: info@rvda.org
https://www.rvda.org/RVLearning/Education/College_Scholarship.aspx
Purpose: To help students who plan to pursue work in the RV industry.
Eligibility: Applicants must be accepted into a four-year college or university as rising sophomores, juniors or senior undergraduates. Students must have a minimum GPA of 2.8, a 1040 SAT or 22 ACT score and a FAFSA on file. Applicants must have a background in the RV industry or a desire to work in the RV business after completing college.
Target applicant(s): College students. Adult students.
Minimum GPA: 2.8
Amount: $2,500.
Number of awards: Varies.
Deadline: July 11.
How to apply: Applications are available online.
Exclusive: Visit www.UltimateScholarshipBook.com and enter code MI110426 for updates on this award.

[1105] • Salvatore J. Monte Thermoplastic Materials and Foams Division Scholarship

Society of Plastics Engineers
83 Wooster Heights Road Suite 125, Suite 306, Danbury, CT 06810
Phone: 810-986-6131
Email: thomas.miller@ravago.com
https://plasticspioneers.org/scholarships/
Purpose: To aid undergraduate students who have a demonstrated interest in thermoplastic materials and foams.
Eligibility: Applicants must be full-time undergraduate and graduate students who are interested in thermoplastic materials and foams. This interest must be shown by relevant internship experiences, jobs held, coursework completed or research undertaken. Selection is based on the overall strength of the application.
Target applicant(s): High school students. College students. Graduate school students. Adult students.
Amount: $2,500.
Number of awards: 1.
Deadline: April 30.
How to apply: Applications are available online. An application form, three references, transcript and personal statement are required.
Exclusive: Visit www.UltimateScholarshipBook.com and enter code SO110526 for updates on this award.

[1106] • Samuel Fletcher Tapman ASCE Student Chapter/Club Scholarship

American Society of Civil Engineers (ASCE)
Attn.: Honors and Awards Program, 1801 Alexander Bell Drive, Reston, VA 20191-4400
Phone: 800-548-2723
Email: awards@asce.org
http://www.asce.org
Purpose: To support worthy civil engineering undergraduate students further their education.
Eligibility: Applicants must be enrolled in an ABET-accredited civil engineering program or related field. Students must be members in good standing of their local ASCE Student Chapters at the time of application submission and award acceptance. Scholarships must be used by sophomore, junior or senior engineering students.
Target applicant(s): College students. Adult students.
Amount: $3,000.
Number of awards: 12.
Scholarship may be renewable.
Deadline: February 10.
How to apply: Applications are available online.
Exclusive: Visit www.UltimateScholarshipBook.com and enter code AM110626 for updates on this award.

[1107] • Schonstedt Scholarship in Surveying

National Society of Professional Surveyors (NSPS/AAGS)
21 Byte Court, Suite H, Frederick, MD 21702
Phone: 240-439-4615
Email: info@nsps.us.com
https://www.nsps.us.com/page/Scholarships
Purpose: To aid surveying students.
Eligibility: Applicants must be members of the American Congress on Surveying and Mapping (ACSM). They must be enrolled in a four-year surveying degree program. Preference will be given to applicants with junior or senior standing. Selection is based on academic merit, personal statement, references and extracurricular activities.
Target applicant(s): College students. Adult students.
Amount: $2,000.
Number of awards: 1.
Scholarship may be renewable.
Deadline: January 19.
How to apply: Applications are available online. An application form, proof of ASCM membership, official transcript, personal statement and three reference letters are required.
Exclusive: Visit www.UltimateScholarshipBook.com and enter code NA110726 for updates on this award.

[1108] • Science Ambassador Scholarship

Cards Against Humanity
1917 North Elston Avenue, Chicago, IL 60642-1219
Phone: 224-623-9009
Email: saraheckhaus@cardsagainsthumanity.com
https://www.scienceambassadorscholarship.org
Purpose: To support women pursuing STEM education.
Eligibility: Applicants must self-identify as female and be graduating high school seniors or currently enrolled full-time undergraduate students. Students must be majoring in a STEM-related field. Applicants must create a video for their application submission.
Target applicant(s): High school students. College students. Adult students.
Amount: Full Tuition.
Number of awards: 1.
Deadline: December 16.
How to apply: Applications are available online.
Exclusive: Visit www.UltimateScholarshipBook.com and enter code CA110826 for updates on this award.

The Ultimate Scholarship Book 2026
Scholarship Directory (Sciences)

[1109] • ScienceSaves Video Scholarship Contest
ScienceSaves
P.O. Box 741, Amherst, NY 14226
Phone: 716-636-4869
https://sciencesaves.org/scholarship/
Purpose: To support students who create a science-related video.
Eligibility: Applicants must create a 20- to 30-second video answering a given question. Students must highlight how science saves in a succinct, creative way with original photos, video clips and text. Applicants must be sure to add #ScienceSaves to their video.
Target applicant(s): High school students.
Amount: $250-$10,000.
Number of awards: 9.
Deadline: May 5.
How to apply: Applications are available online.
Exclusive: Visit www.UltimateScholarshipBook.com and enter code SC110926 for updates on this award.

[1110] • SEE Education Foundation Scholarships
International Society of Explosives Engineers
30325 Bainbridge Road, Cleveland, OH 44139
Phone: 440-349-4400
Email: isee@isee.org
https://isee.org/resources/students/scholarships
Purpose: To aid students who are preparing for careers in the commercial explosives industry.
Eligibility: Applicants must be pursuing a degree from a technical, undergraduate, graduate or doctoral program in fields of education related to the commercial explosives industry. Students should demonstrate financial need. Selection is based on the overall strength of the application.
Target applicant(s): College students. Graduate school students. Adult students.
Amount: Up to $5,000.
Number of awards: Varies.
Deadline: May 15.
How to apply: Applications are available online. An application form, goal statement, income information, two letters of reference and an official transcript are required.
Exclusive: Visit www.UltimateScholarshipBook.com and enter code IN111026 for updates on this award.

[1111] • Sertoma Communicative Disorders Scholarship
Sertoma Inc.
1912 E. Meyer Boulevard, Kansas City, MO 64132
Phone: 816-333-8300
Email: infosertoma@sertomahq.org
http://www.sertoma.org
Purpose: To fund graduate students of audiology and speech-language pathology.
Eligibility: Applicants must be citizens of the U.S. Applicants must also be accepted into a graduate level program in speech language pathology and/or audiology at a college in the U.S. recognized by ASHA's Council and have a minimum 3.5 overall GPA in all undergraduate and graduate-level courses.
Target applicant(s): College students. Graduate school students. Adult students.
Minimum GPA: 3.5
Amount: $1,000.
Number of awards: Varies.
Deadline: March 31.
How to apply: Applications are available online.
Exclusive: Visit www.UltimateScholarshipBook.com and enter code SE111126 for updates on this award.

[1112] • Sigma Phi Alpha Undergraduate Scholarship
American Dental Hygienists' Association (ADHA) Institute for Oral Health
444 North Michigan Avenue, Suite 400, Chicago, IL 60611
Phone: 312-440-8900
Email: institute@adha.net
https://www.adha.org/ioh/scholarships/
Purpose: To aid outstanding Sigma Phi Alpha Dental Hygiene Honor Society students.
Eligibility: Applicants must be members of the Sigma Phi Alpha Dental Hygiene Honor Society who are enrolled in a certificate, associate's degree or bachelor's degree program in dental hygiene at a school that has an active chapter of Sigma Phi Alpha. They must have a major GPA of 3.5 or higher. Selection is based on the overall strength of the application.
Target applicant(s): High school students. College students. Adult students.
Minimum GPA: 3.5
Amount: $1,000.
Number of awards: Varies.
Deadline: February 2.
How to apply: Applications are available online. An application form and supporting materials are required.
Exclusive: Visit www.UltimateScholarshipBook.com and enter code AM111226 for updates on this award.

[1113] • Sir John Soane's Museum Foundation Traveling Grant
Sir John Soane's Museum Foundation
120 Broadway, 20th Floor, New York, NY 10271
Phone: 212-655-7626
Email: info@soanefoundation.org
https://soanefoundation.org
Purpose: To provide scholarships enabling undergraduate students to travel abroad for a focused study of a historic place, period or architecture.
Eligibility: Applicants must be enrolled in undergraduate programs focusing on the history of art, architecture, decorative arts or interior design.
Target applicant(s): High school students. College students. Adult students.
Amount: $10,000.
Number of awards: 2.
Deadline: March 1.
How to apply: Applications are available online.
Exclusive: Visit www.UltimateScholarshipBook.com and enter code SI111326 for updates on this award.

[1114] • SMART Scholarship
American Society for Engineering Education
1818 N. Street, NW, Suite 600, Washington, DC 20036-2479
Phone: 202-331-3500
Email: smart@asee.org
https://www.smartscholarship.org/smart

Purpose: To support undergraduate and graduate students pursuing degrees in Science, Technology, Engineering and Mathematics (STEM) fields.
Eligibility: Applicants must be a U.S. citizen, 18 or older, have a minimum GPA of 3.0, be able to participate in summer internships at the Department of Defense (DoD) and be willing to accept post-graduate work at the DoD. The award includes payment of full tuition, a stipend, a book allowance and room and board.
Target applicant(s): College students. Graduate school students. Adult students.
Minimum GPA: 3.0
Amount: Varies.
Number of awards: Varies.
Scholarship may be renewable.
Deadline: December 1.
How to apply: Applications are available online.
Exclusive: Visit www.UltimateScholarshipBook.com and enter code AM111426 for updates on this award.

[1115] • SMART Scholarship

Department of Defense Scholarship-for-Service Program
Phone: 571-633-7940
Email: smart@smartscholarship.org
https://www.smartscholarship.org
Purpose: To support students in STEM fields.
Eligibility: Applicants must be enrolled at a college or university or have previous college credit and intend to pursue another degree. Students must have a college transcript from a regionally accredited U.S. college or university, have a college transcript by the end of the fall term or intend to pursue a graduate degree in the fall.
Target applicant(s): College students. Graduate school students. Adult students.
Minimum GPA: 3.0
Amount: Varies.
Number of awards: Varies.
Deadline: December 5.
How to apply: Applications are available online.
Exclusive: Visit www.UltimateScholarshipBook.com and enter code DE111526 for updates on this award.

[1116] • SmithGroup J.E.D.I. Scholarship

SmithGroup
Suite 1700, 500 Griswold Street, Detroit, Mi 48226
Phone: 313-983-3600
https://www.smithgroup.com/jedi-scholarship
Purpose: To support students who plan to pursue higher education.
Eligibility: Applicants must be current undergraduate (at least a junior level standing) or graduate students in an accredited architecture, interior design, urban planning, landscape architecture or engineering program (civil/structural, mechanical, electrical and fire protection) in the U.S. and have a minimum GPA of 3.0. Students must be enrolled during the fall semester as scholarships are paid directly to the academic institution. Applicants must be available for a paid summer internship and be legally authorized to work in the U.S.
Target applicant(s): College students. Graduate school students. Adult students.
Minimum GPA: 3.0
Amount: $6,000.
Number of awards: Varies.
Deadline: December 1.
How to apply: Applications are available online.
Exclusive: Visit www.UltimateScholarshipBook.com and enter code SM111626 for updates on this award.

[1117] • SNMTS Paul Cole Scholarship

Society of Nuclear Medicine and Molecular Imaging
Development Office, 1850 Samuel Morse Drive, Reston, VA 20190
Phone: 703-708-9000
Email: tellmer@snmmi.org
http://www.snmmi.org/
Purpose: To promote excellence in healthcare through the support of education and research in nuclear medicine technology.
Eligibility: Applicants must have a minimum 2.5 GPA and be high school seniors or college undergraduates enrolled in or accepted by accredited institutions and be in the nuclear medicine technology field. Applicant must prove financial need.
Target applicant(s): High school students. College students. Graduate school students. Adult students.
Minimum GPA: 2.5
Amount: $1,000.
Number of awards: Varies.
Deadline: February 17.
How to apply: Applications are available online.
Exclusive: Visit www.UltimateScholarshipBook.com and enter code SO111726 for updates on this award.

[1118] • Society of Exploration Geophysicists (SEG) Scholarship

Society of Exploration Geophysicists
Scholarship Committee, SEG Foundation, P.O. Box 702740, Tulsa, OK 74170-2740
Phone: 918-497-5500
Email: scholarships@seg.org
https://seg.org/programs/student-programs/scholarships/
Purpose: To fund individuals who are involved or interested in the field of geophysics.
Eligibility: Applicants must intend to pursue a career in exploration geophysics. Applicants must also be one of the following: A high school student with above average grades planning to enter college the next fall term, an undergraduate whose grades are above average or a graduate student pursuing a career in exploration geophysics in operations, teaching or research.
Target applicant(s): High school students. College students. Graduate school students. Adult students.
Amount: $500-$10,000.
Number of awards: Varies.
Scholarship may be renewable.
Deadline: March 1.
How to apply: Applications are available online or by written request.
Exclusive: Visit www.UltimateScholarshipBook.com and enter code SO111826 for updates on this award.

[1119] • Society of Manufacturing Engineers Directors Scholarship

Society of Manufacturing Engineers Education Foundation
One SME Drive, P.O. Box 930, Dearborn, MI 48121
Phone: 313-425-3300
Email: foundation@sme.org

https://www.smeef.org/scholarships
Purpose: To aid undergraduate manufacturing engineering students.
Eligibility: Applicants must be full-time undergraduates who are enrolled at an accredited U.S. or Canadian postsecondary institution. They must be majoring in manufacturing engineering or a related subject and have completed at least 30 college credit hours. They must have a GPA of 3.5 or higher on a four-point scale and must have plans to pursue a career in manufacturing. Preference will be given to those with proven leadership skills. Selection is based on the overall strength of the application.
Target applicant(s): College students. Adult students.
Minimum GPA: 3.5
Amount: Varies.
Number of awards: Varies.
Deadline: February 1.
How to apply: Applications are available online. An application form and supporting materials are required.
Exclusive: Visit www.UltimateScholarshipBook.com and enter code SO111926 for updates on this award.

[1120] • Society of Plastics Engineers (SPE) Foundation Scholarships

Society of Plastics Engineers
83 Wooster Heights Road Suite 125, Suite 306, Danbury, CT 06810
Phone: 810-986-6131
Email: thomas.miller@ravago.com
https://plasticspioneers.org/scholarships/
Purpose: To aid students who have demonstrated or expressed an interest in the plastics industry.
Eligibility: Applicants must have a demonstrated or expressed interest in the plastics industry and be majoring in or taking courses that would lead to a career in the plastics industry. Applicants must be in good academic standing. Financial need is considered for most scholarships.
Target applicant(s): College students. Graduate school students. Adult students.
Amount: Varies.
Number of awards: Varies.
Scholarship may be renewable.
Deadline: April 30.
How to apply: Applications are available online.
Exclusive: Visit www.UltimateScholarshipBook.com and enter code SO112026 for updates on this award.

[1121] • Society of Vacuum Coaters Foundation Scholarship

Society of Vacuum Coaters Foundation
P.O. Box 10202, Albuquerque, NM 87184-0202
Email: svcfoundation@svc.org
http://www.svcfoundation.org
Purpose: To promote the study of vacuum coating technology.
Eligibility: Applicants must be entering or currently enrolled in studies related to vacuum coating technology at an accredited technical, vocational, two-year, undergraduate or graduate program. Preference is given to those majoring in engineering, physics, materials science or other fields related to vacuum coating. Selection is based on the applicant's field of study, academic achievement, personal qualities and financial need.
Target applicant(s): High school students. College students. Graduate school students. Adult students.
Amount: Up to $5,000.
Number of awards: Varies.
Deadline: October 15.
How to apply: Applications are available online. Two copies of scholarship materials must be submitted including the application form, transcript and two recommendation forms.
Exclusive: Visit www.UltimateScholarshipBook.com and enter code SO112126 for updates on this award.

[1122] • SPIE Optics and Photonics Education Scholarship

SPIE, The International Society for Optical Engineering
P.O. Box 10, Bellingham, WA 98227-0010
Phone: 360-676-3290
Email: scholarships@spie.org
https://www.spie.org/membership/student-services/scholarships
Purpose: To promote students who have the potential to contribute to the field of optics.
Eligibility: Applicants must be high school, undergraduate or graduate students enrolled full-time in programs in the field of optics, photonics or related discipline (e.g., physics or electrical engineering). Students must be members of SPIE, although they may submit a membership application along with the scholarship application, and high school applicants receive a one-year complimentary membership.
Target applicant(s): High school students. College students. Graduate school students. Adult students.
Amount: Up to $11,000.
Number of awards: Varies.
Deadline: February 15.
How to apply: Applications are available online.
Exclusive: Visit www.UltimateScholarshipBook.com and enter code SP112226 for updates on this award.

[1123] • Spring Meadow Proven Winners Scholarship

Horticultural Research Institute
80 M Street SE, Washington, DC 20003
Phone: 202-789-2900
https://www.hriresearch.org/scholarships
Purpose: To help students obtain a degree in horticulture.
Eligibility: Applicants must be enrolled full-time in an undergraduate or graduate landscape horticultural or related program at a two- or four-year accredited institution. Preference is given to those who plan to pursue a career in horticulture. Students must have a 2.25 overall GPA and a 2.7 GPA in their major.
Target applicant(s): College students. Graduate school students. Adult students.
Minimum GPA: 2.25
Amount: Up to $4,000.
Number of awards: 3.
Scholarship may be renewable.
Deadline: May 31.
How to apply: Applications are available online.
Exclusive: Visit www.UltimateScholarshipBook.com and enter code HO112326 for updates on this award.

[1124] • SPS Leadership Scholarships

Society of Physics Students
One Physics Ellipse, College Park, MD 20740
Phone: 301-209-3007
Email: SPS-Programs@aip.org
https://www.spsnational.org/

Purpose: To further the study of physics.
Eligibility: Applicants must be undergraduates at least in their junior year, physics majors and active members of SPS.
Target applicant(s): College students. Adult students.
Amount: $2,500-$6,000.
Number of awards: Varies.
Deadline: March 15.
How to apply: Applications are available online and from SPS Chapter Advisors.
Exclusive: Visit www.UltimateScholarshipBook.com and enter code SO112426 for updates on this award.

[1125] • Steel Intern Scholarships

Association for Iron and Steel Technology (AIST)
186 Thorn Hill Road, Warrendale, PA 15086-7528
Phone: 724-814-3000
Email: lwharrey@aist.org
https://www.aist.org/students-faculty/scholarships
Purpose: To reward students who commit to a paid summer internship at a North American or steel-related company.
Eligibility: Applicants must be citizens of a NAFTA country (USA, Canada, Mexico) and express a strong interest in the iron and steel industry. Students in the following engineering/engineering technology majors may apply: metallurgy, materials science, electrical, mechanical, chemical, industrial, environmental, computer science, data science and safety. Applicants must be freshmen, sophomores, juniors or seniors planning to attend graduate school. Students must be enrolled full-time in a four-year undergraduate or graduate program at an accredited North American university with a minimum 2.5 GPA.
Target applicant(s): College students. Adult students.
Minimum GPA: 2.5
Amount: $7,500.
Number of awards: Up to 50.
Deadline: October 14.
How to apply: Applications are available online.
Exclusive: Visit www.UltimateScholarshipBook.com and enter code AS112526 for updates on this award.

[1126] • Steinman Scholarship

National Society of Professional Engineers
1420 King Street, Alexandria, VA 22314-2794
Phone: 888-285-6773
Email: students@nspe.org
https://www.nspe.org/resources/students/scholarships
Purpose: To aid talented students studying engineering.
Eligibility: Applicants must be undergraduate engineering majors who will enter the junior year and be U.S. citizens. Selection is based on GPA, internship experience, recommendations and ethics essay.
Target applicant(s): College students. Adult students.
Amount: $5,000.
Number of awards: 1.
Deadline: April 1.
How to apply: Applications are available online.
Exclusive: Visit www.UltimateScholarshipBook.com and enter code NA112626 for updates on this award.

[1127] • STEM Scholarship Program

IMEG
623 26th Avenue, Rock Island, IL 61201
Email: scholarship@imegcorp.com
https://imegcorp.com
Purpose: To encourage students who are pursuing a degree which is STEM-related with an engineering focus.
Eligibility: Applicants must be U.S. citizens with demonstrated financial need. Students must be enrolled full-time in their sophomore through senior years at an accredited college or university. Applicants must be pursuing a degree in a STEM related field.
Target applicant(s): College students. Adult students.
Amount: Up to $10,000.
Number of awards: Varies.
Deadline: May 15.
How to apply: Applications are available online.
Exclusive: Visit www.UltimateScholarshipBook.com and enter code IM112726 for updates on this award.

[1128] • Stephanie Carroll Memorial Scholarship

NADONA/LTC
1329 E. Kemper Road, Suite 4100A, Springdale, OH 45246
Phone: 800-222-0539
http://www.nadona.org
Purpose: To support students who are interested in pursuing studies in long-term care or geriatrics.
Eligibility: Applicants must be undergraduate or graduate students enrolled in an accredited nursing program who will make a commitment to practice in long-term care or geriatrics for two years following graduation. Students may submit applications electronically at info@nadona.org. Selection is based on the overall strength of the application.
Target applicant(s): College students. Graduate school students. Adult students.
Amount: Varies.
Number of awards: 1.
Deadline: April 15.
How to apply: Applications are available online.
Exclusive: Visit www.UltimateScholarshipBook.com and enter code NA112826 for updates on this award.

[1129] • Steven G. King Play Environments Scholarship

Landscape Architecture Foundation
1200 17th Street NW, Suite 210, Washington, DC 20036
Phone: 202-331-7070
Email: scholarships@lafoundation.org
https://www.lafoundation.org/what-we-do/scholarships
Purpose: To aid landscape architecture students who are interested in designing play environments.
Eligibility: Applicants must be landscape architecture graduate students or upperclass undergraduate students. They must be enrolled at a college or university that has been accredited by the Landscape Architectural Accreditation Board (LAAB). They must have a demonstrated interest in designing play environments. Selection is based on the overall strength of the application.
Target applicant(s): College students. Graduate school students. Adult students.
Amount: $5,000.
Number of awards: 1.
Deadline: February 1.

How to apply: Applications are available online. An application form, essay, play environment plan and two recommendation letters are required.
Exclusive: Visit www.UltimateScholarshipBook.com and enter code LA112926 for updates on this award.

[1130] • Structural Materials Division Scholarship
Minerals, Metals and Materials Society
5700 Corporate Drive, Suite 750, Pittsburgh, PA 15237
Phone: 1-724-776-9000
Email: students@tms.org
https://www.tms.org/
Purpose: To aid metallurgical and materials science engineering students.
Eligibility: Applicants must be student members of The Minerals, Metals and Materials Society (TMS), be full-time undergraduate sophomores or juniors and be majoring in metallurgical or materials science engineering. Their studies must concentrate on the science and engineering of load-bearing materials. Selection is based on the overall strength of the application.
Target applicant(s): College students. Adult students.
Amount: $2,500.
Number of awards: 1.
Deadline: March 15.
How to apply: Applications are available online. An application form, personal statement, transcript and three recommendation letters are required.
Exclusive: Visit www.UltimateScholarshipBook.com and enter code MI113026 for updates on this award.

[1131] • Student Cash Grant Program
American Society of Certified Engineering Technicians (ASCET)
15621 West 87th Street Parkway, Suite 205, Lenexa, KS 66219
Phone: 773-242-7238
Email: office@ascet.org
https://ascet.org/page/FinancialAid
Purpose: To help engineering technology students.
Eligibility: Applicants must be a student, certified, regular, registered or associate member of the American Society of Certified Engineering Technicians (ASCET) or be high school seniors in the last five months of the academic year who will be enrolled in an engineering technology curriculum no later than six months following the selection for the award. Students must have passing grades in their present curriculum and submit transcripts and a recommendation letter.
Target applicant(s): High school students. College students. Adult students.
Amount: $1,200.
Number of awards: 2.
Deadline: January 30.
How to apply: Applications are available online.
Exclusive: Visit www.UltimateScholarshipBook.com and enter code AM113126 for updates on this award.

[1132] • Student Poster Session Awards
Electrochemical Society
65 South Main Street, Building D, Pennington, NJ 08534-2839
Phone: 609-737-1902
Email: ecs@electrochem.org
https://www.electrochem.org/student-awards
Purpose: To reward students for work related to fields of interest to ECS.
Eligibility: Applicants must be pursuing degrees at any college or university and prepare an abstract on work performed. The applicants must also prepare a poster to present at the society meeting where they will be judged. Two awards are in the categories of electrochemical science and technology and solid-state science and technology.
Target applicant(s): College students. Graduate school students. Adult students.
Amount: Varies.
Number of awards: Varies.
Deadline: Contact the sponsor to confirm the deadline.
How to apply: Application materials are described online.
Exclusive: Visit www.UltimateScholarshipBook.com and enter code EL113226 for updates on this award.

[1133] • Student Research Fellowship Awards
Crohn's and Colitis Foundation of America Inc.
733 Third Avenue, Suite 510, New York, NY 10017
Phone: 800-932-2423
Email: info@ccfa.org
https://www.crohnscolitisfoundation.org/research/grants-fellowships/student-research-awards
Purpose: To stimulate interest in research careers in inflammatory bowel disease by providing salary support for research projects.
Eligibility: Applicants must be undergraduate, graduate or medical students not yet engaged in thesis research. Students must attend an accredited North American school and conduct their research with a mentor. The planned research project must last at least 10 weeks and must be relevant to IBD.
Target applicant(s): College students. Graduate school students. Adult students.
Amount: Up to $2,500.
Number of awards: Up to 16.
Deadline: April 1; November 1.
How to apply: Applications are available online.
Exclusive: Visit www.UltimateScholarshipBook.com and enter code CR113326 for updates on this award.

[1134] • Student Research Scholarships
Bat Conservation International
Phone: 512-327-9721
Email: scholarships@batcon.org
http://www.batcon.org
Purpose: To support students who will contribute to our knowledge about bats.
Eligibility: Applicants must be graduate students and submit a research proposal that addresses a specific area of bat conservation. The application form provides several potential research topics.
Target applicant(s): Graduate school students. Adult students.
Amount: $5,000.
Number of awards: 5.
Deadline: October 31.
How to apply: Applications are available online.
Exclusive: Visit www.UltimateScholarshipBook.com and enter code BA113426 for updates on this award.

[1135] • Summer Undergraduate Research Fellowships
American Physiological Society
Education Office, 9650 Rockville Pike, Bethesda, MD 20814-3991
Phone: 301-634-7787
Email: education@the-aps.org

https://www.physiology.org/?SSO=Y
Purpose: To support full-time summer study for undergraduate students in the laboratory of an established researcher.
Eligibility: Applicants must be enrolled in an undergraduate program, and faculty sponsor must be an active member of APS. Students must have a minimum 3.0 GPA. Fellowships are awarded to students pursuing a career as a basic research scientist.
Target applicant(s): High school students. College students. Adult students.
Minimum GPA: 3.0
Amount: $4,000 stipend plus up to $1,300 travel expenses.
Number of awards: Varies.
Deadline: February 1.
How to apply: Applications are available online.
Exclusive: Visit www.UltimateScholarshipBook.com and enter code AM113526 for updates on this award.

[1136] • Susan Miszkowicz Memorial Scholarship
Society of Women Engineers
130 East Randolph Street, Suite 3500, Chicago, IL 60601
Phone: 877-793-4636
Email: scholarships@swe.org
https://swe.org/scholarships/
Purpose: To support female students working towards a college degree in engineering.
Eligibility: Applicants must be currently enrolled in an accredited engineering, technology or computing program with a minimum of a 3.0 GPA. The award is to be used during the sophomore, junior or senior year of college.
Target applicant(s): College students. Adult students.
Minimum GPA: 3.0
Amount: $1,750.
Number of awards: 1.
Deadline: January 31.
How to apply: Applications are available online.
Exclusive: Visit www.UltimateScholarshipBook.com and enter code SO113626 for updates on this award.

[1137] • Tau Beta Pi/Society of Automotive Engineers Engineering Scholarship
Society of Automotive Engineers International
Scholarships Program, 400 Commonwealth Drive, Warrendale, PA 15096
Phone: 724-776-4841
Email: scholarships@sae.org
https://www.sae.org/participate/scholarships
Purpose: To aid future college students who are planning to major in engineering.
Eligibility: Applicants must be U.S. citizens, be graduating high school seniors and have plans to major in engineering at an ABET-accredited institution. They must have a GPA of 3.75 or higher and must have SAT or ACT scores that rank in the 90th percentile. Selection is based on the overall strength of the application.
Target applicant(s): High school students.
Minimum GPA: 3.75
Amount: $1,500.
Number of awards: 6.
Deadline: February 29.
How to apply: Applications are available online. An application form, official transcript and standardized test scores are required.
Exclusive: Visit www.UltimateScholarshipBook.com and enter code SO113726 for updates on this award.

[1138] • Ted and Holly Rollins Scholarship
Ted Rollins
1001 Morehead Square Drive, Suite 320, Charlotte, NC 28203
Email: caroline@tedrollinsecoscholars.com
https://www.rollinsscholarship.org/
Purpose: To support students pursuing a major related to sustainability.
Eligibility: Applicants must be high school seniors. Students must write and submit an essay about their life story, intended field of study, career and how they will make an impact on the world.
Target applicant(s): High school students.
Amount: $5,000.
Number of awards: 1.
Deadline: December 1.
How to apply: Applications are available online.
Exclusive: Visit www.UltimateScholarshipBook.com and enter code TE113826 for updates on this award.

[1139] • Ted and Ruth Neward Scholarship
Society of Plastics Engineers
83 Wooster Heights Road Suite 125, Suite 306, Danbury, CT 06810
Phone: 810-986-6131
Email: thomas.miller@ravago.com
https://plasticspioneers.org/scholarships/
Purpose: To aid students who have an interest in the plastics industry.
Eligibility: Applicants must be U.S. citizens, have an interest in the plastics industry, major in or take courses leading to a career in the plastics industry and be in good academic standing. Financial need is considered.
Target applicant(s): College students. Graduate school students. Adult students.
Amount: Varies.
Number of awards: Varies.
Deadline: April 30.
How to apply: Applications are available online.
Exclusive: Visit www.UltimateScholarshipBook.com and enter code SO113926 for updates on this award.

[1140] • The Industrial Electrochemistry and Electrochemical Engineering Division H. H. Dow Memorial Student Achievement Award
Electrochemical Society
65 South Main Street, Building D, Pennington, NJ 08534-2839
Phone: 609-737-1902
Email: ecs@electrochem.org
https://www.electrochem.org/student-awards
Purpose: To recognize young engineers and scientists in the fields of electrochemical engineering and applied electrochemistry.
Eligibility: Applicants must be accepted to or enrolled in a graduate program. The application requires transcripts, a description of the research project, a description of how the project relates to electrochemical engineering or applied electrochemistry, a biography, a resume or curriculum vitae and a letter of recommendation from the research supervisor. The award is based on academic performance, research and the recommendation.
Target applicant(s): College students. Graduate school students. Adult students.
Amount: $1,000.

Number of awards: 1.
Deadline: September 1.
How to apply: Application materials are described online.
Exclusive: Visit www.UltimateScholarshipBook.com and enter code EL114026 for updates on this award.

[1141] • Thermo Fisher Scientific Antibody Scholarship

Thermo Fisher Scientific
3747 North Meridian Road, Rockford, IL 61105
Phone: 815-968-0747
Email: antibodyscholarship@thermofisher.com
https://corporate.thermofisher.com/content/tfcorpsite/us/en/index/corporate-social-responsibility/communities/our-giving.html
Purpose: To help students with the expenses related to their pursuit of higher education.
Eligibility: Applicants must be enrolled or accepted for enrollment as an undergraduate or graduate student at an accredited college or university. Students must have a cumulative grade point average of 3.0 and declared a major of one of the following: chemistry, biology, biochemistry or a related life science field. Applicants must be United States citizens or students possessing the appropriate visa status to study in the U.S. Selection is based on the overall strength of the application and any submitted materials.
Target applicant(s): High school students. College students. Graduate school students. Adult students.
Minimum GPA: 3.0
Amount: $5,000-$10,000.
Number of awards: 6.
Deadline: May 3.
How to apply: Applications are available online.
Exclusive: Visit www.UltimateScholarshipBook.com and enter code TH114126 for updates on this award.

[1142] • Thermoplastic Elastomers Special Interest Group Scholarship

Society of Plastics Engineers
83 Wooster Heights Road Suite 125, Suite 306, Danbury, CT 06810
Phone: 810-986-6131
Email: thomas.miller@ravago.com
https://plasticspioneers.org/scholarships/
Purpose: To aid students who have a demonstrated interest in thermoplastic elastomers.
Eligibility: Applicants must be full-time undergraduate or graduate students with a proven interest in thermoplastic elastomers. This interest must be shown by relevant jobs held, internships completed, coursework completed or research undertaken. Selection is based on the overall strength of the application.
Target applicant(s): College students. Graduate school students. Adult students.
Amount: $2,500.
Number of awards: 1.
Deadline: April 30.
How to apply: Applications are available online. An application form, an official transcript, three references and a personal statement are required.
Exclusive: Visit www.UltimateScholarshipBook.com and enter code SO114226 for updates on this award.

[1143] • Thomas E. Powers/Detroit Section Scholarship

Society of Plastics Engineers
83 Wooster Heights Road Suite 125, Suite 306, Danbury, CT 06810
Phone: 810-986-6131
Email: thomas.miller@ravago.com
https://plasticspioneers.org/scholarships/
Purpose: To aid undergraduate students who are interested in the plastics industry.
Eligibility: Applicants must be full-time undergraduate students in good academic standing who have completed coursework in or are majoring in a subject that relates to the plastics industry (such as engineering, polymer science, physics or chemistry). Selection is based on the overall strength of the application.
Target applicant(s): College students. Adult students.
Amount: $500-$5,000.
Number of awards: 1.
Deadline: August 11.
How to apply: Applications are available online. An application form, personal statement, transcript and three recommendation letters are required.
Exclusive: Visit www.UltimateScholarshipBook.com and enter code SO114326 for updates on this award.

[1144] • Thomas M. Stetson Scholarship

American Ground Water Trust
50 Pleasant Street, Suite 2, Concord, NH 03301
Phone: 603-228-5444
Email: trustinfo@agwt.org
https://agwt.org/scholarships/
Purpose: To provide scholarships for high school seniors pursuing careers in a ground water-related field.
Eligibility: Applicants must be high school seniors with intentions to pursue a career in ground water-related field. Applicants must attend a college or university located west of the Mississippi River. A minimum GPA of 3.0 is required.
Target applicant(s): High school students.
Minimum GPA: 3.0
Amount: $2,000.
Number of awards: 1.
Deadline: June 30.
How to apply: Applications are available online.
Exclusive: Visit www.UltimateScholarshipBook.com and enter code AM114426 for updates on this award.

[1145] • Thomas R. Camp Scholarship

American Water Works Association
6666 W. Quincy Avenue, Denver, CO 80235
Phone: 800-926-7337
Email: scholarships@awwa.org
https://www.awwa.org
Purpose: To support students conducting applied research in the drinking water field.
Eligibility: Applicants must pursue graduate degrees at an institution of higher education in Canada, Guam, Puerto Rico, Mexico or the U.S. This is awarded to doctoral students in even years and master's students in odd years. Applicants must submit applications, resumes, transcripts, GRE scores, three recommendation letters, statements and research plans. The award is based on academics and leadership.
Target applicant(s): Graduate school students. Adult students.

Amount: $10,000.
Number of awards: 1.
Deadline: December 20.
How to apply: Applications are available online.
Exclusive: Visit www.UltimateScholarshipBook.com and enter code AM114526 for updates on this award.

[1146] • Tilford Field Studies Scholarship

Association of Engineering Geologists Foundation
Tilford Fund, 4123 Broadway, Suite 817, Oakland, CA 94611
Phone: 510-990-0059
Email: staff@aegfoundation.org
https://www.aegfoundation.org
Purpose: To provide financial assistance for field studies in engineering geology.
Eligibility: Applicants must be members of the Association of Engineering Geologists who are college or graduate students. Applicants are chosen on the basis of scholarship, ability, participation and potential for contributions to the profession.
Target applicant(s): College students. Graduate school students. Adult students.
Amount: Up to $1,500.
Number of awards: 3.
Deadline: January 15.
How to apply: Applications are available online.
Exclusive: Visit www.UltimateScholarshipBook.com and enter code AS114626 for updates on this award.

[1147] • Timothy S. and Palmer W. Bigelow, Jr. Scholarship

Horticultural Research Institute
80 M Street SE, Washington, DC 20003
Phone: 202-789-2900
https://www.hriresearch.org/scholarships
Purpose: To help students from New England who want to pursue a career in horticulture.
Eligibility: Applicants must be seniors in a two-year course and have finished the first year, juniors in a four-year course and have finished the first two years or be graduate students. Undergraduates must have a minimum 2.25 GPA and graduate students a minimum 3.0 GPA. Students must be from Connecticut, Maine, Massachusetts, New Hampshire, Rhode Island or Vermont. Preference will be given to applicants who have financial need and who plan to work in the nursery industry after graduation, including starting a business.
Target applicant(s): College students. Graduate school students. Adult students.
Minimum GPA: 2.25 for undergraduate students; 3.0 for graduate students
Amount: $2,000.
Number of awards: 1.
Deadline: June 1.
How to apply: Applications are available online or by mail.
Exclusive: Visit www.UltimateScholarshipBook.com and enter code HO114726 for updates on this award.

[1148] • TMC/SAE Donald D. Dawson Technical Scholarship

Society of Automotive Engineers International
Scholarships Program, 400 Commonwealth Drive, Warrendale, PA 15096
Phone: 724-776-4841
Email: scholarships@sae.org
https://www.sae.org/participate/scholarships
Purpose: To aid current and future engineering students.
Eligibility: Applicants must be U.S. citizens, be high school seniors or current undergraduate students and be enrolled in or planning to enroll in an ABET-accredited engineering degree program. They must have a GPA of 3.25 or higher and an SAT math score of 600 or higher and a critical reading score of 550 or higher or must have an ACT composite score of 27 or higher. Selection is based on the overall strength of the application.
Target applicant(s): High school students. College students. Adult students.
Minimum GPA: 3.25
Amount: Varies.
Number of awards: 1.
Scholarship may be renewable.
Deadline: February 28.
How to apply: Applications are available online. An application form, personal essay, official transcript and standardized test scores are required.
Exclusive: Visit www.UltimateScholarshipBook.com and enter code SO114826 for updates on this award.

[1149] • TMS Best Paper Contest

Minerals, Metals and Materials Society
5700 Corporate Drive, Suite 750, Pittsburgh, PA 15237
Phone: 1-724-776-9000
Email: students@tms.org
https://www.tms.org/
Purpose: To support the professional development of metallurgy and materials science students.
Eligibility: Applicants must be student members of The Minerals, Metals and Materials Society (TMS). They must prepare and submit a technical essay on a topic that is related to metallurgy or materials science. Selection is based on originality and the quality of research.
Target applicant(s): High school students. College students. Graduate school students. Adult students.
Amount: $250.
Number of awards: 4.
Deadline: March 15.
How to apply: Submission guidelines are available online. A technical essay, cover sheet and faculty endorsement are required.
Exclusive: Visit www.UltimateScholarshipBook.com and enter code MI114926 for updates on this award.

[1150] • TMS Technical Division Student Poster Contest

Minerals, Metals and Materials Society
5700 Corporate Drive, Suite 750, Pittsburgh, PA 15237
Phone: 1-724-776-9000
Email: students@tms.org
https://www.tms.org/
Purpose: To aid student members of the Minerals, Metals and Materials Society.
Eligibility: Applicants must be student members of the Minerals, Metals and Materials Society (TMS), be full-time undergraduate or graduate

The Ultimate Scholarship Book 2026
Scholarship Directory (Sciences)

students and create a poster that addresses a topic that would be of interest for one of the five technical divisions of TMS. Selection is based on the overall strength of the poster.
Target applicant(s): College students. Graduate school students. Adult students.
Amount: Up to $1,000.
Number of awards: 10.
Deadline: December 10.
How to apply: Applications are available online. An application form and poster are required.
Exclusive: Visit www.UltimateScholarshipBook.com and enter code MI115026 for updates on this award.

[1151] • TMS/International Symposium On Superalloys Scholarships
Minerals, Metals and Materials Society
5700 Corporate Drive, Suite 750, Pittsburgh, PA 15237
Phone: 1-724-776-9000
Email: students@tms.org
https://www.tms.org/
Purpose: To aid metallurgical engineering and materials science and engineering students.
Eligibility: Applicants must be student members of the Minerals, Metals and Materials Society (TMS) and be full-time undergraduate or graduate students majoring in metallurgical engineering or materials science and engineering. They must have a demonstrated interest in the high-temperature, high-performance materials used in the gas turbine industry. Selection is based on academic merit, extracurricular activities, relevant coursework completed and recommendation letters.
Target applicant(s): College students. Graduate school students. Adult students.
Amount: $2,000.
Number of awards: 2.
Deadline: March 15.
How to apply: Applications are available online. An application form, transcript, personal essay and three recommendation letters are required.
Exclusive: Visit www.UltimateScholarshipBook.com and enter code MI115126 for updates on this award.

[1152] • Tocris Scholarship
Tocris Bioscience
16144 Westwoods Business Park, Ellisville, MO 63021
Phone: 303-730-1950
Email: scholarship@biotechne.com
https://www.tocris.com/scholarship
Purpose: To support students who plan to pursue a science-related degree in life science, medical science or health science.
Eligibility: Applicants must be residents of the United States, United Kingdom or Canada who are accepted or enrolled in a college or university and plan to pursue a science-related degree in life science, medical science or health science. Students may apply at any level of education including diploma, associate degree, baccalaureate, graduate or PhD.
Target applicant(s): High school students. College students. Graduate school students. Adult students.
Amount: $1,500.
Number of awards: 1.
Deadline: July 19.
How to apply: Applications are available online and must include a transcript and two short answer essays.
Exclusive: Visit www.UltimateScholarshipBook.com and enter code TO115226 for updates on this award.

[1153] • Trent R. Dames and William W. Moore Fellowship
American Society of Civil Engineers (ASCE)
Attn.: Honors and Awards Program, 1801 Alexander Bell Drive, Reston, VA 20191-4400
Phone: 800-548-2723
Email: awards@asce.org
http://www.asce.org
Purpose: To support engineers, earth scientists, professors and graduate students pursuing graduate studies researching new applications and advancements in geotechnical engineering or earth sciences in relation to social, economic, environmental and political issues.
Eligibility: Applicants must be members of ASCE at the time of application submission. Prior fellowship recipients can apply for any additional fellowships provided they meet the current fellowship's eligibility requirements. Completed applications and all supporting material as outlined in the application process must be submitted.
Target applicant(s): Graduate school students. Adult students.
Amount: $6,000.
Number of awards: 2.
Deadline: February 10.
How to apply: Applications are available online.
Exclusive: Visit www.UltimateScholarshipBook.com and enter code AM115326 for updates on this award.

[1154] • Tuskegee Airmen Scholarship Foundation Scholarships
Tuskegee Airmen Scholarship Foundation
1816 S. Figueroa Street, Suite #L5, Los Angeles, CA 90015
Phone: 323-318-0635
Email: info@taisf.org
https://www.taisf.org/scholarship-information.html
Purpose: To aid students who intend to pursue careers in aviation, aerospace engineering, aerospace research or engineering technology.
Eligibility: Applicants must be high school seniors who have a GPA of 3.0 or higher on a four-point scale. They must have a demonstrated interest in pursuing a career in aerospace research, aerospace engineering, aviation or engineering technology. Selection is based on academic merit, extracurricular activities, character and financial need.
Target applicant(s): High school students.
Minimum GPA: 3.0
Amount: $1,500.
Number of awards: 40.
Scholarship may be renewable.
Deadline: January 27.
How to apply: Applications are available by request from the student's local Tuskegee Airmen chapter. An application form, two essays and family income verification are required.
Exclusive: Visit www.UltimateScholarshipBook.com and enter code TU115426 for updates on this award.

[1155] • UAA Janice K. Barden Aviation Scholarship
National Business Aviation Association
1200 G Street NW, Suite 1100, Washington, DC 20005
Phone: 202-783-9250
Email: scholarships@nbaa.org.
https://nbaa.org/professional-development/scholarships/
Purpose: To aid aviation students attending a University Aviation Association (UAA) or National Business Aviation Association (NBAA) member school.

Eligibility: Applicants must be U.S. citizens who are studying a subject that is related to aviation. Selection is based on the overall strength of the application. Applicants must have a minimum 3.0 GPA.
Target applicant(s): College students. Adult students.
Minimum GPA: 3.0
Amount: $1,000.
Number of awards: 5.
Deadline: August 12.
How to apply: Applications are available online. An application form, personal essay, transcript, resume and one recommendation letter are required.
Exclusive: Visit www.UltimateScholarshipBook.com and enter code NA115526 for updates on this award.

[1156] • Undergraduate Award for Excellence in Chemistry
Iota Sigma Pi (ISP) ND
Professor Kathryn A. Thomasson, Iota Sigma Pi Director for Student Awards, University of North Dakota, Department of Chemistry, P.O. Box 9024, Grand Forks, ND 58202-9024
Phone: 701-777-3199
Email: kthomasson@chem.und.edu
https://www.iotasigmapi.org/
Purpose: To reward female undergraduate students for excellence in the field of chemistry study.
Eligibility: Applicants must be female senior chemistry students at an accredited four-year college or university and be nominated by a member of the faculty.
Target applicant(s): College students. Adult students.
Amount: $1,000.
Number of awards: 1.
Deadline: February 15.
How to apply: Applications are available online.
Exclusive: Visit www.UltimateScholarshipBook.com and enter code IO115626 for updates on this award.

[1157] • Undergraduate Engineering Scholarships
American Society of Heating, Refrigerating and Air-Conditioning Engineers (ASHRAE)
Scholarship Administrator, ASHRAE Inc., 180 Technology Parkway, Peachtree Corners, GA 30092
Phone: 404-636-8400
Email: lbenedict@ashrae.org
https://www.ashrae.org/communities/student-zone/scholarships-and-grants
Purpose: To encourage heating, ventilating, air conditioning and refrigeration education.
Eligibility: Applicants must be full-time undergraduates majoring in engineering or pre-engineering in a related course of study approved by the Accreditation Board for Engineering and Technology (ABET) or another accrediting agency recognized by ASHRAE with a minimum 3.0 GPA. Selection is based on leadership, character and potential contribution to the heating, ventilating, air conditioning or refrigeration profession. Applicants must also submit three recommendations from instructors and an official transcript.
Target applicant(s): High school students. College students. Adult students.
Minimum GPA: 3.0
Amount: $3,000-$10,000.
Number of awards: Varies.
Deadline: December 1.
How to apply: Applications are available online.
Exclusive: Visit www.UltimateScholarshipBook.com and enter code AM115726 for updates on this award.

[1158] • Undergraduate Scholarship and Construction Trades Scholarship
National Association of Women in Construction
327 South Adams Street, Fort Worth, TX 76104
Phone: 800-552-3506
Email: nawic@nawic.org
http://www.nawic.org
Purpose: To offer financial aid to students pursuing construction-related degrees.
Eligibility: Applicants must be currently enrolled in a construction-related degree program as full-time students, have at least one term of study remaining in a course of study leading to a degree or an associate degree in a construction-related field, desire a career in a construction-related field and have a minimum 3.0 GPA. Awards are given to male and female students.
Target applicant(s): College students. Adult students.
Minimum GPA: 3.0
Amount: $500-$2,500.
Number of awards: Varies.
Deadline: February 28.
How to apply: Applications are available online.
Exclusive: Visit www.UltimateScholarshipBook.com and enter code NA115826 for updates on this award.

[1159] • Undergraduate Scholarships
Institute of Food Technologists (IFT)
525 W. Van Buren, Suite 1000, Chicago, IL 60607
Phone: 312-782-8424
Email: ContactUs@applyISTS.com
https://www.ift.org/community/students
Purpose: To encourage undergraduate students in food science or technology.
Eligibility: Applicants must be college sophomores, juniors or seniors pursuing an approved program in food science or food technology. An application, a transcript and a recommendation letter are required.
Target applicant(s): College students. Adult students.
Amount: $1,000-$5,000.
Number of awards: 9.
Deadline: February 26.
How to apply: Applications are available online.
Exclusive: Visit www.UltimateScholarshipBook.com and enter code IN115926 for updates on this award.

[1160] • Undergraduate Student Research Grants: South-Central Section
Geological Society of America South-Central Section
P.O. Box 9140, 2801 S. University, Boulder, CO 80301-9140
Phone: 303-357-1000
Email: gsaservice@geosociety.org
https://www.geosociety.org/GSA/Education_Careers/Grants_Scholarships/Undergrad_Grants/GSA/grants/sectionResearch.aspx
Purpose: To provide research grants to undergraduate geology students who are members of GSA.
Eligibility: Applicants must be members of GSA, attend school in the South-Central section and present research at a section meeting or the GSA annual meeting.

The Ultimate Scholarship Book 2026
Scholarship Directory (Sciences)

Target applicant(s): High school students. College students. Adult students.
Amount: Up to $200.
Number of awards: Varies.
Deadline: April 1.
How to apply: Applications are available online.
Exclusive: Visit www.UltimateScholarshipBook.com and enter code GE116026 for updates on this award.

[1161] • Undergraduate Summer Student Research Assistantship

National Radio Astronomy Observatory (NRAO)
NRAO Headquarters, 520 Edgemont Road, Charlottesville, VA 22903
Phone: 434-296-0211
Email: info@nrao.edu
https://science.nrao.edu/opportunities/student-programs
Purpose: To allow students to perform astronomical research at National Radio Astronomy Observatory (NRAO) sites.
Eligibility: Depending on the specific program, applicants must be either undergraduates or graduating college seniors. Recipients work on-site for 10 to 12 weeks, beginning in late May or early June.
Target applicant(s): College students. Adult students.
Amount: Varies.
Number of awards: Varies.
Deadline: February 1.
How to apply: Applications are available online.
Exclusive: Visit www.UltimateScholarshipBook.com and enter code NA116126 for updates on this award.

[1162] • United Parcel Service Scholarship for Female Students

Institute of Industrial and Systems Engineers
3577 Parkway Lane, Suite 200, Norcross, GA 30092
Phone: 800-494-0460
Email: egrimes@iise.org
https://www.iise.org
Purpose: To help female undergraduate engineering students.
Eligibility: Applicants must be full-time female students at an institution in the United States, Canada or Mexico with an accredited industrial engineering program, majoring in industrial engineering or its equivalent and active members. Students may not apply directly for this scholarship and must be nominated. The award is based on academic ability, character, leadership, potential service to the industrial engineering profession and financial need. Applicants must have a minimum 3.4 GPA.
Target applicant(s): College students. Adult students.
Minimum GPA: 3.4
Amount: $4,000.
Number of awards: 2.
Deadline: February 1.
How to apply: Nomination forms are available online.
Exclusive: Visit www.UltimateScholarshipBook.com and enter code IN116226 for updates on this award.

[1163] • USDA/1890 National Scholars Program

U.S. Department of Agriculture
Office of Partnerships and Public Engagement, 1400 Independence Avenue SW, Stop 0601, Washington, DC 20250
Phone: 202-720-6350
Email: 1890init@usda.gov
https://www.usda.gov/youth/career
Purpose: To aid students who are planning to study agriculture or a related subject in college.
Eligibility: Applicants must be U.S. citizens and be rising undergraduate freshmen, sophomores or juniors who have a high school diploma or a GED. They must have a GPA of 3.0 or higher. They must plan to enroll or be enrolled at an 1890 Land Grant institution and have plans to major in agriculture; agriculture business/management; agriculture economics; agricultural engineering/mechanics; agricultural productions and technology; agronomy or crop science; animal science; botany; farm and range management; fish, game or wildlife management; food services/technology; forestry and related services; home economics/nutrition/human development; horticulture; natural resources management; soil conservation/soil science or other related disciplines (e.g., biological sciences, pre-veterinary medicine or computer science). They must also have proven leadership skills and must have experience with community service. Selection is based on the overall strength of the application.
Target applicant(s): High school students. College students. Adult students.
Minimum GPA: 3.0
Amount: Varies.
Number of awards: Varies.
Deadline: March 1.
How to apply: Applications are available by request from the Civil Rights Enforcement and Compliance section of the Animal and Plant Health Inspection Service branch of the USDA. An application form and supporting materials are required.
Exclusive: Visit www.UltimateScholarshipBook.com and enter code U.116326 for updates on this award.

[1164] • Usrey Family Scholarship

Horticultural Research Institute
80 M Street SE, Washington, DC 20003
Phone: 202-789-2900
https://www.hriresearch.org/scholarships
Purpose: To help students who are seeking careers in horticulture.
Eligibility: Applicants must be in an undergraduate or graduate landscape horticulture program or related field at a two or four-year California state university or college. Applicants must also be current, full-time students, academically competitive and have a minimum 2.25 GPA and a minimum 2.7 GPA in the major. Preference is given to applicants who plan to work in the nursery industry after graduation. Applicants must submit applications, cover letters, resumes, transcripts and two recommendation letters.
Target applicant(s): College students. Graduate school students. Adult students.
Minimum GPA: 2.25
Amount: $1,000.
Number of awards: 1.
Deadline: May 31.
How to apply: Applications are available online.
Exclusive: Visit www.UltimateScholarshipBook.com and enter code HO116426 for updates on this award.

[1165] • Vertical Flight Foundation Technical Scholarships

Vertical Flight Foundation
217 N. Washington Street, Alexandria, VA 22314
Phone: 703-684-6777
Email: staff@vtol.org
http://www.vtol.org

Purpose: The Vertical Flight Foundation was founded to support the education in rotorcraft and vertical-takeoff-and-landing aircraft engineering.
Eligibility: Applicants must be full-time students at accredited schools of engineering and submit a transcript with an academic endorsement from a professor or dean. Applicants need not be members of AHS.
Target applicant(s): High school students. College students. Graduate school students. Adult students.
Amount: Up to $6,000.
Number of awards: Varies.
Deadline: February 1.
How to apply: Applications are available online.
Exclusive: Visit www.UltimateScholarshipBook.com and enter code VE116526 for updates on this award.

[1166] • VIP Women in Technology Scholarship
Visionary Integration Professionals
80 Iron Point Circle, Suite 100, Folsom, CA 95630
Phone: 916-985-9625
Email: wits@trustvip.com
https://trustvip.com/company/vip-cares/
Purpose: To aid female students who are preparing for careers in information technology or a related subject.
Eligibility: Applicants must be attending or accepted at a two- or four-year postsecondary institution located in the U.S. They must be planning to pursue a career in information technology or a related field. Selection is based on academic merit, a personal essay and extracurricular activities.
Target applicant(s): High school students. College students. Adult students.
Minimum GPA: 3.0
Amount: Up to $2,500.
Number of awards: Varies.
Deadline: March 31.
How to apply: Applications are available online. An application form, official transcript, personal essay and list of extracurricular activities are required.
Exclusive: Visit www.UltimateScholarshipBook.com and enter code VI116626 for updates on this award.

[1167] • Visiting Medical Student Scholar
American Academy of Neurology
25 Massachusetts Ave NW, Suite 500J, Washington, DC 20001
Phone: 800-879-1960
Email: ggates@aan.com
https://www.aan.com
Purpose: To support U.S. medical students who plan to pursue a neurology visiting student rotation.
Eligibility: Applicants must be third or fourth-year AAN member U.S. medical students who plan to pursue a neurology visiting student rotation. Students must plan on completing their rotation at an LCME/AOA approved U.S. medical school.
Target applicant(s): Graduate school students. Adult students.
Amount: $2,000.
Number of awards: 20.
Deadline: June 4.
How to apply: Applications are available online.
Exclusive: Visit www.UltimateScholarshipBook.com and enter code AM116726 for updates on this award.

[1168] • Walter B. Sinnott Scholarship
American Water Works Association - New York Section
Submit To: Jenny Ingrao, Executive Director, New York Section American Water Works Association, 614 Seventh North Street, Liverpool, NY 13088
Phone: 315-455-2614
Email: jenny@nysawwa.org
https://nysawwa.org/
Purpose: To reward students who are enrolled in a program to study in the water supply field.
Eligibility: Students must be at least a freshman enrolled full-time at an accredited college or university in the United States.
Target applicant(s): College students. Adult students.
Amount: $2,500.
Number of awards: 1.
Deadline: April 7.
How to apply: Applications are available online.
Exclusive: Visit www.UltimateScholarshipBook.com and enter code AM116826 for updates on this award.

[1169] • Welch Scholars Grant
American Osteopathic Foundation (AOF)
142 East Ontario Street, Suite 1450, Chicago, IL 60611
Phone: 312-202-8234
Email: info@aof.org
https://aof.org/grants-awards
Purpose: To support osteopathic medical students.
Eligibility: Applicants must be osteopathic medical students who have successfully completed their first year of studies. Students must be in good academic standing at an accredited College of Osteopathic Medicine. Applicants are chosen based on academic achievement, participation in extracurricular activities and financial need.
Target applicant(s): Graduate school students. Adult students.
Amount: $2,000.
Number of awards: Varies.
Deadline: October 31.
How to apply: Applications are available online.
Exclusive: Visit www.UltimateScholarshipBook.com and enter code AM116926 for updates on this award.

[1170] • William J. Adams, Jr. and Marijane E. Adams Scholarship
American Society of Agricultural and Biological Engineers Foundation
Administrator, Scholarship Fund, 2950 Niles Road, St. Joseph, MI 49085
Phone: 269-429-0300
Email: awards@asabe.org
http://www.asabe.org
Purpose: To aid undergraduate students with an interest in agricultural machinery product design and development.
Eligibility: Applicants must be biological or agricultural engineering majors in eligible accredited programs in the U.S. or Canada. Applicants must also have completed at least one year of undergraduate study and have at least one year of undergraduate study remaining, have a minimum 2.5 GPA, have an interest in agricultural machinery product design and development and demonstrate financial need.
Target applicant(s): College students. Adult students.
Minimum GPA: 2.5
Amount: $2,000.
Number of awards: 1.

Deadline: March 15.
How to apply: Application is by formal letter.
Exclusive: Visit www.UltimateScholarshipBook.com and enter code AM117026 for updates on this award.

[1171] • Williams Companies Academic Scholarship

National Association of Corrosion Engineers (NACE) International Foundation
15835 Park Ten Place, Houston, TX 77084-5145
Phone: 281-228-6205
Email: nace.foundation@nace.org
https://www.ampp.org/about/emerg-student-outreach/academic-scholarships-program
Purpose: To assist students in the National Association of Corrosion Engineers.
Eligibility: Applicants must be enrolled full-time in an undergraduate program engaged in science and/or engineering related to the study of corrosion or corrosion control at an accredited college or university.
Target applicant(s): High school students. College students. Adult students.
Amount: $5,000.
Number of awards: 1.
Deadline: January 4.
How to apply: Applications are available online.
Exclusive: Visit www.UltimateScholarshipBook.com and enter code NA117126 for updates on this award.

[1172] • Women in STEM Scholarship/BHW Scholarship

BHW Group
6011 W. Courtyard Drive, Suite 410, Austin, TX 78730
Phone: 512-220-0035
https://thebhwgroup.com/scholarship
Purpose: To support female students pursuing a degree in a science or mathematics field.
Eligibility: Applicants must be incoming freshmen or currently enrolled female students pursuing an undergraduate or master's degree. Students must be majoring in science, technology, engineering or mathematics. Applicants must be enrolled in a U.S. school and submit an essay and their completed application.
Target applicant(s): High school students. College students. Graduate school students. Adult students.
Amount: $3,000.
Number of awards: 1.
Deadline: April 15.
How to apply: Applications are available online.
Exclusive: Visit www.UltimateScholarshipBook.com and enter code BH117226 for updates on this award.

[1173] • Women's Scholarship

National Strength and Conditioning Association (NSCA) Foundation
1885 Bob Johnson Drive, Colorado Springs, CO 80906
Phone: 800-815-6826
Email: Foundation@nsca.com
http://www.nsca.com/foundation/
Purpose: To encourage women to enter the field of strength and conditioning.
Eligibility: Applicants should be women age 17 and older who have been accepted by an accredited institution for and undergraduate or a graduate degree in strength and conditioning. Applicants must be NSCA members and plan to pursue careers in strength and conditioning. A cover letter of application, application form, resume, transcript, three letters of recommendation and essay are required. The award is based on grades, strength and conditioning experience, NSCA involvement, awards, community involvement, essay and recommendations.
Target applicant(s): High school students. College students. Graduate school students. Adult students.
Amount: $2,000.
Number of awards: Varies.
Deadline: October 15.
How to apply: Application materials are described online.
Exclusive: Visit www.UltimateScholarshipBook.com and enter code NA117326 for updates on this award.

[1174] • Women's Wildlife Management/Conservation Scholarship

National Rifle Association
11250 Waples Mill Road, Fairfax, VA 22030
Phone: 800-672-3888
Email: grantprogram@nrahq.org
https://awards.nra.org/scholarships/
Purpose: To support women who are seeking a career in the wildlife management and conservation field.
Eligibility: Applicants must be full-time female college sophomores, juniors or seniors, have a 3.0 or higher GPA and be majoring in a conservation- or environmental-related degree program. Selection is based on extracurricular activities, community service, work experience, a required essay and the letter of reference.
Target applicant(s): College students. Adult students.
Minimum GPA: 3.0
Amount: $5,000.
Number of awards: Varies.
Scholarship may be renewable.
Deadline: December 15.
How to apply: Applications are submitted online and include a 200- to 300-word essay and at least one letter of recommendation.
Exclusive: Visit www.UltimateScholarshipBook.com and enter code NA117426 for updates on this award.

[1175] • Yanmar/SAE Scholarship

Society of Automotive Engineers International
Scholarships Program, 400 Commonwealth Drive, Warrendale, PA 15096
Phone: 724-776-4841
Email: scholarships@sae.org
https://www.sae.org/participate/scholarships
Purpose: This scholarship is sponsored by the SAE Foundation and the Yanmar Diesel America Corporation.
Eligibility: Applicants must be full-time college juniors pursuing an engineering or related science degree or enrolled in a postgraduate engineering or related science program. Applicants must also pursue a course of study or research related to the conservation of energy in transportation, agriculture and construction and power generation.
Target applicant(s): College students. Graduate school students. Adult students.
Amount: Up to $2,000.
Number of awards: 1.
Scholarship may be renewable.

Deadline: February 28.
How to apply: Applications are available online.
Exclusive: Visit www.UltimateScholarshipBook.com and enter code SO117526 for updates on this award.

[1176] • Youth Incentive Award
Coleopterists Society
Dr. David G. Furth, Entomology, NHB, MRC 165, P.O. Box 37012, Smithsonian Institution, Washington, DC 20013-7012
Phone: 202-633-0990
Email: furthd@si.edu
https://www.coleopsoc.org/society-info/prizes-and-awards/
Purpose: To recognize young people studying beetles.
Eligibility: Applicants should be coleopterists in grades 7-12 and submit individual proposals such as field collecting trips to conduct beetle species inventories or diversity studies, attending workshops or visiting entomology or natural history museums for training and projects on beetles, studying beetle biology, etc. Students are strongly encouraged to find an adult advisor (i.e., teacher, youth group leader, parent) to provide guidance in the proposal development, but the proposal must be written by the applicant. The Coleopterists Society can help establish contacts between applicants and professional coleopterists. The award is based on creativity, educational benefit to the applicant, scientific merit, feasibility and budget. There are two winners: one for grades 7-9 and one for grades 10-12.
Target applicant(s): Junior high students or younger. High school students.
Amount: $400-$800.
Number of awards: 2.
Deadline: November 1.
How to apply: Applications are available online.
Exclusive: Visit www.UltimateScholarshipBook.com and enter code CO117626 for updates on this award.

[1177] • Youth Program
Appaloosa Horse Club
Appaloosa Youth Association, 2720 West Pullman Road, Moscow, ID 83843
Phone: 208-882-5578
Email: youth@appaloosa.com
https://www.appaloosa.com/appaloosa-youth-association
Purpose: To reward student members of the Appaloosa Youth Association or the Appaloosa Horse Club who are pursuing higher education.
Eligibility: Applicants must be members of the Appaloosa Youth Association or the Appaloosa Horse Club and must attend or plan to attend an institute of higher learning. Students may also be the son or daughter of Appaloosa Horse Club members.
Target applicant(s): High school students. College students. Graduate school students. Adult students.
Minimum GPA: 2.5
Amount: $1,000-$2,000.
Number of awards: Varies.
Scholarship may be renewable.
Deadline: April 15.
How to apply: Applications are available online.
Exclusive: Visit www.UltimateScholarshipBook.com and enter code AP117726 for updates on this award.

STATE OF RESIDENCE

[1178] • A.D. Osherman Scholarship Fund
Greater Houston Community Foundation
515 Post Oak Boulevard, Suite 1000, Houston, TX 77027
Phone: 713-333-2200
Email: scholarships@ghcf.org
https://ghcf.org/
Purpose: To support students of Texas in pursuing post-secondary education.
Eligibility: Applicants must demonstrate financial need. A minimum GPA of 2.75 is required. Students must take a minimum of 12 credits in both the fall and spring semesters. Preference is given to minority students, veterans and/or first-generation college students.
Target applicant(s): High school students. College students. Adult students.
Minimum GPA: 2.75
Amount: Up to $3,000.
Number of awards: 4.
Deadline: April 2.
How to apply: Applications are available online.
Exclusive: Visit www.UltimateScholarshipBook.com and enter code GR117826 for updates on this award.

[1179] • Academic Challenge Scholarship
Arkansas Department of Higher Education
423 Main Street, Suite 400, Little Rock, AR 72201
Phone: 501-371-2050
Email: finaid@adhe.arknet.edu
https://sams.adhe.edu/Scholarship
Purpose: To encourage Arkansas high school graduates to enroll in Arkansas colleges and universities.
Eligibility: Applicants must be graduating Arkansas high school seniors who meet academic minimum standards and income requirements. Must submit FAFSA.
Target applicant(s): High school students.
Minimum GPA: 2.25
Amount: $1,000-$5,000.
Number of awards: Varies.
Scholarship may be renewable.
Deadline: July 1.
How to apply: Applications are available through your high school counselor. FAFSA required.
Exclusive: Visit www.UltimateScholarshipBook.com and enter code AR117926 for updates on this award.

[1180] • Academic Excellence Scholarship
State of Wisconsin Higher Educational Aids Board
P.O. Box 7885, Madison, WI 53707
Phone: 608-267-2206
Email: heabmail@wisconsin.gov
https://heab.state.wi.us
Purpose: To assist outstanding Wisconsin students who are planning to attend college in Wisconsin.
Eligibility: Applicants must be high school seniors who plan to enroll full-time at an eligible Wisconsin college or university. The award is given to the student with the highest GPA in each public and private Wisconsin high school.
Target applicant(s): High school students.

Amount: Up to $2,250.
Number of awards: Varies.
Deadline: Contact the sponsor to confirm the deadline.
How to apply: No application is required. Each high school designates the student who has the highest GPA of the graduating high school class.
Exclusive: Visit www.UltimateScholarshipBook.com and enter code ST118026 for updates on this award.

[1181] • Academic Scholars Program

Oklahoma State Regents for Higher Education/Academic Scholars Program
655 Research Parkway, Suite 200, Oklahoma City, OK 73104
Phone: 800-858-1840
Email: studentinfo@osrhe.edu
https://secure.okcollegestart.org/Financial_Aid_Planning/Scholarships/Academic_Scholarships/Academic_Scholars_Program.aspx
Purpose: To assist students in attending Oklahoma colleges and universities.
Eligibility: Applicants can qualify for the program by being Oklahoma or out-of-state students who are named National Merit Scholars, National Merit Finalists or U.S. Presidential Scholars; by being Oklahoma residents who score above the 99.5 percentile on the SAT or ACT or by being nominated by an Oklahoma public college or institution. Applicants must attend an Oklahoma college or university. Selection is based on academic merit.
Target applicant(s): High school students.
Amount: Up to $6,000.
Number of awards: Varies.
Scholarship may be renewable.
Deadline: September 1.
How to apply: Applications are available from the applicant's high school guidance counselor, by telephone request and online. An application form and supporting documents are required.
Exclusive: Visit www.UltimateScholarshipBook.com and enter code OK118126 for updates on this award.

[1182] • Access College Early Scholarship

Nebraska Coordinating Commission for Postsecondary Education
P.O. Box 95005, Lincoln, NE 68509-5005
Phone: 402-471-2847
Email: ritchie.morrow@nebraska.gov
https://ccpe.nebraska.gov/
Purpose: To support Nebraska high school students who are enrolled in early college courses.
Eligibility: Applicants must demonstrate financial need through proof of participation in government aid programs or documentation of recent family hardships. They may be in any year of high school.
Target applicant(s): High school students.
Amount: Full tuition and fees.
Number of awards: Varies.
Scholarship may be renewable.
Deadline: February 15 (Winter); May 15 (Spring); July 15 (Summer); December 15 (Fall).
How to apply: Applications are available online.
Exclusive: Visit www.UltimateScholarshipBook.com and enter code NE118226 for updates on this award.

[1183] • Access to Better Learning and Education Grant Program

Florida Department of Education
Office of Student Financial Assistance, State Scholarship and Grant Programs, 325 West Gaines Street, Suite 1314, Tallahassee, FL 32399-0400
Phone: 888-827-2004
Email: osfa@fldoe.org
https://origin.fldoe.org/finance/financial-aid-scholarships/
Purpose: To help undergraduate students from Florida who want to attend Florida private colleges or universities.
Eligibility: Applicants must be Florida residents for at least a year and first-time undergraduate students enrolled in degree programs (except theology or divinity degrees). Applicants must meet Florida's general state aid eligibility requirements and enroll in at least 12 credit hours per semester. Award renewable for up to nine semesters. Participating institutions determine application procedures, deadlines and student eligibility. The award amount is determined by the Legislature in the General Appropriation Act each year.
Target applicant(s): High school students. College students. Adult students.
Amount: Varies.
Number of awards: Varies.
Scholarship may be renewable.
Deadline: Contact the sponsor to confirm the deadline.
How to apply: Contact the financial aid office at eligible Florida colleges and universities.
Exclusive: Visit www.UltimateScholarshipBook.com and enter code FL118326 for updates on this award.

[1184] • ACEC Colorado Scholarship Program

American Council of Engineering Companies of Colorado
800 Grant Street, Suite 100, Denver, CO 80203
Phone: 303-832-2200
Email: acec@acec-co.org
http://www.acec-co.org
Purpose: To support engineering students.
Eligibility: Applicants must be full-time students pursuing a bachelor's degree in engineering or surveying at an accredited college or university in Colorado. They must be entering their junior, senior or fifth year. Selection is based on GPA (24 points), essay (25 points), work experience (24 points), recommendation (17 points) and extracurricular activities (10 points).
Target applicant(s): College students. Adult students.
Amount: Varies.
Number of awards: Varies.
Deadline: January 12.
How to apply: Applications are available online. An application form, transcript, essay and recommendation are required.
Exclusive: Visit www.UltimateScholarshipBook.com and enter code AM118426 for updates on this award.

[1185] • ACEC Scholarship

American Council of Engineering Companies California (ACEC)
1303 J Street, Suite 450, Sacramento, CA 95814
Phone: 916-441-7991
Email: staff@acec-ca.org
https://www.acec-ca.org/page/ScholarshipApp
Purpose: To support students interested in pursuing a degree in engineering or land surveying.

Eligibility: Applicants must be U.S. citizens, undergraduate students enrolled full-time in an engineering or land surveying program or graduate students enrolled at least half-time. Students must have a minimum GPA of 3.5 in completed engineering/land surveying courses and a minimum overall GPA of 3.2. Selection is made based on the overall strength of the application.
Target applicant(s): College students. Graduate school students. Adult students.
Minimum GPA: 3.2
Amount: Up to $10,000.
Number of awards: Varies.
Deadline: February 2.
How to apply: Applications are available online.
Exclusive: Visit www.UltimateScholarshipBook.com and enter code AM118526 for updates on this award.

[1186] • Advanced Practice Healthcare Scholarship Program
Department of Health Care Access and Information (HCAI)
2020 West El Camino Avenue, Suite 800, Sacramento, CA 95833
Phone: 916-326-3640
Email: hpef-email@oshpd.ca.gov
https://hcai.ca.gov/loans-scholarships-grants/
Purpose: To increase medical care to underserved areas of California by assisting residents who are studying to become dentists, dental hygienists, nurse practitioners, certified midwives and physician assistants.
Eligibility: Applicants must be California residents who have been accepted by or are enrolled in an accredited California program. Financial need, work experience and career goals are considered, and preference is given to applicants who plan to remain in a medically underserved area past the service time. Those selected must sign a two-year service agreement to work in a medically underserved area of California.
Target applicant(s): College students. Graduate school students. Adult students.
Amount: $25,000.
Number of awards: Varies.
Scholarship may be renewable.
Deadline: December 13.
How to apply: Applications are available online.
Exclusive: Visit www.UltimateScholarshipBook.com and enter code DE118626 for updates on this award.

[1187] • AFS Twin City Memorial Scholarship
Foundry Educational Foundation
1695 North Penny Lane, Schaumburg, IL 60173
Phone: 847-490-9200
Email: info@fefinc.org
http://www.fefinc.org/scholarships.html
Purpose: To aid students from Minnesota, western Wisconsin and northern Iowa who are attending a Foundry Education Foundation (FEF) member school.
Eligibility: Applicants must be residents of Minnesota, western Wisconsin or northern Iowa. Preference will be given to students who are completing coursework in a foundry-related subject. Selection is based on the overall strength of the application.
Target applicant(s): College students. Adult students.
Amount: Varies.
Number of awards: Varies.
Deadline: October 3.
How to apply: Applications are available online. An application form and supporting materials are required.
Exclusive: Visit www.UltimateScholarshipBook.com and enter code FO118726 for updates on this award.

[1188] • AFS Wisconsin Past President Scholarship
Foundry Educational Foundation
1695 North Penny Lane, Schaumburg, IL 60173
Phone: 847-490-9200
Email: info@fefinc.org
http://www.fefinc.org/scholarships.html
Purpose: To aid Wisconsin-area students pursuing careers in the cast metal industry.
Eligibility: Students must be enrolled at a Foundry Educational Foundation (FEF) member school, a school located in Wisconsin or a school located in a state adjacent to Wisconsin. They also must have previous work experience, preferably in the cast metal industry. Selection is based on the student's academic record, residential proximity to the AFS Wisconsin Chapter area, the proximity of the student's school to the AFS Wisconsin Chapter area, relevance of the student's degree program to the cast metal industry and relevant work experience.
Target applicant(s): High school students. College students. Adult students.
Amount: Varies.
Number of awards: Varies.
Deadline: December 15.
How to apply: Applications are available online. A completed FEF profile and supporting documents are required.
Exclusive: Visit www.UltimateScholarshipBook.com and enter code FO118826 for updates on this award.

[1189] • AGC of Massachusetts Scholarships
Associated General Contractors of Massachusetts
888 Worcester Street, Suite 40, Wellesley, MA 02482
Phone: 781-786-8917
Email: canoni@agcmass.org
http://www.agcmass.org/scholarships
Purpose: To aid Massachusetts residents who are college sophomores, juniors or seniors and who are enrolled in degree programs related to construction or civil engineering.
Eligibility: Applicants must be undergraduate students at an accredited college or university. They must be legal residents of Massachusetts (though they may attend school outside of the state) and must be enrolled in a degree program related to construction or civil engineering. Selection is based on financial need and the overall strength of the application.
Target applicant(s): College students. Adult students.
Amount: Varies.
Number of awards: Varies.
Scholarship may be renewable.
Deadline: November 1.
How to apply: Applications are available online. An application form and an official transcript are required.
Exclusive: Visit www.UltimateScholarshipBook.com and enter code AS118926 for updates on this award.

[1190] • AGC of Ohio Scholarships
Associated General Contractors of Ohio
1755 Northwest Boulevard, Columbus, OH 43212
Phone: 614-486-6446
Email: parker@agcohio.com
https://agcohio.com/workforce-development/agc-scholarships/

The Ultimate Scholarship Book 2026
Scholarship Directory (State of Residence)

Purpose: To support undergraduate students who are residents of Ohio and interested in pursuing careers in construction-related fields.
Eligibility: Applicants must be U.S. citizens and undergraduate students in at least the second year of a two-year, four-year or five-year degree-seeking program. The minimum GPA requirement is 2.5. Selection is based on the overall strength of the application.
Target applicant(s): College students. Adult students.
Minimum GPA: 2.5
Amount: $1,000.
Number of awards: 7.
Deadline: February 9.
How to apply: Applications are available online. An application form, official college transcripts and essay are required and must be mailed.
Exclusive: Visit www.UltimateScholarshipBook.com and enter code AS119026 for updates on this award.

[1191] • Agnes M. Lindsay Scholarship
Massachusetts Department of Higher Education
Office of Student Financial Assistance, 454 Broadway, Suite 200,
Revere, MA 02151
Phone: 617-727-9420
Email: osfa@osfa.mass.edu
https://www.mass.gov/handbook/massachusetts-financial-aid-programs
Purpose: To provide assistance to Massachusetts students who are from rural parts of the state, demonstrate financial need and attend a Massachusetts public institution of higher education.
Eligibility: Applicants must be permanent Massachusetts residents for at least one year before the beginning of the academic year. Applicants must also be enrolled full-time in an undergraduate program and maintain satisfactory academic progress.
Target applicant(s): High school students. College students. Adult students.
Amount: Varies.
Number of awards: Varies.
Deadline: Contact the sponsor to confirm the deadline.
How to apply: Applications are available by phone.
Exclusive: Visit www.UltimateScholarshipBook.com and enter code MA119126 for updates on this award.

[1192] • Aid for Part-Time Study
New York State Higher Education Services Corporation (HESC)
99 Washington Avenue, Albany, NY 12255
Phone: 888-697-4372
Email: scholarships@hesc.ny.gov
http://www.hesc.ny.gov
Purpose: To assist part-time undergraduate students at New York State institutions.
Eligibility: Applicants must meet income eligibility requirements, be enrolled for at least 3 but less than 12 semester hours per semester or at least 4 but less than 8 semester hours per quarter in an eligible undergraduate program, be New York State residents and be U.S. citizens or eligible noncitizens. Tuition charges must exceed $100 per year, and once payments begin, students must maintain a C average.
Target applicant(s): High school students. College students. Adult students.
Amount: Up to $2,000.
Number of awards: Varies.
Scholarship may be renewable.
Deadline: Contact the college's financial aid office to confirm the deadline.

How to apply: Contact the financial aid office to receive an APTS application.
Exclusive: Visit www.UltimateScholarshipBook.com and enter code NE119226 for updates on this award.

[1193] • Alabama Student Assistance Program
State of Alabama Commission on Higher Education
100 N. Union Street, P.O. Box 302000, Montgomery, AL 36130-2000
Phone: 334-242-1998
https://www.ache.edu
Purpose: To encourage Alabama students to continue their education.
Eligibility: Applicants must be undergraduates who are Alabama residents attending one of the 80 eligible Alabama institutions. The Free Application for Federal Student Aid (FAFSA) is required to be submitted.
Target applicant(s): College students. Adult students.
Amount: $300-$5,000.
Number of awards: Varies.
Deadline: October 1.
How to apply: Applications are available online.
Exclusive: Visit www.UltimateScholarshipBook.com and enter code ST119326 for updates on this award.

[1194] • Alaska Education Grant
Alaska Commission on Postsecondary Education
3030 Vintage Boulevard, Juneau, AK 99801
Phone: 800-441-2962
Email: customer_service@acpe.state.ak.us
http://alaskadvantage.state.ak.us
Purpose: To support Alaska students attending qualifying postsecondary educational institutions in Alaska.
Eligibility: Applicants must be Alaska residents for at least 365 days prior to filing the FAFSA and U.S. citizens or permanent residents. Students must be admitted into an undergraduate degree or vocational certificate program at a qualifying Alaska institution, be enrolled at a minimum half-time status and not have earned a prior baccalaureate degree. Applicants must have a high school diploma or GED.
Target applicant(s): College students. Adult students.
Amount: $500-$4,000.
Number of awards: Varies.
Deadline: As soon as possible after October 1.
How to apply: Applications are available online.
Exclusive: Visit www.UltimateScholarshipBook.com and enter code AL119426 for updates on this award.

[1195] • Alaska Performance Scholarship
Alaska Commission on Postsecondary Education
3030 Vintage Boulevard, Juneau, AK 99801
Phone: 800-441-2962
Email: customer_service@acpe.state.ak.us
http://alaskadvantage.state.ak.us
Purpose: To support Alaska high school students with the cost of postsecondary education expenses.
Eligibility: Applicants must be Alaska residents who graduated from an Alaska high school. Students must file the Free Application for Federal Student Aid (FAFSA).
Target applicant(s): Junior high students or younger.
Amount: Up to $4,755.
Number of awards: 3.
Deadline: July 15.
How to apply: Applications are available online.

Exclusive: Visit www.UltimateScholarshipBook.com and enter code AL119526 for updates on this award.

[1196] • Albert E. and Florence W. Newton Nursing Scholarship

Rhode Island Foundation
One Union Station, Providence, RI 02903
Phone: 401-274-4564
Email: rbogert@rifoundation.org
https://rifoundation.org/grants-scholarships
Purpose: To aid undergraduate nursing students.
Eligibility: Applicants must be undergraduate students seeking a diploma or degree in nursing. They must demonstrate financial need. Preference will be given to Rhode Island residents. Selection is based on academic merit and financial need.
Target applicant(s): High school students. College students. Adult students.
Amount: $500-$5,000.
Number of awards: Varies.
Scholarship may be renewable.
Deadline: May 6.
How to apply: Applications are available online. An application form and supporting materials are required.
Exclusive: Visit www.UltimateScholarshipBook.com and enter code RH119626 for updates on this award.

[1197] • Albert M. Lappin Scholarship

American Legion, Department of Kansas
1314 SW Topeka Boulevard, Topeka, KS 66612
Phone: 785-232-9315
https://kansaslegion.org/
Purpose: To assist the education of needy and worthy children of American Legion and American Legion Auxiliary members.
Eligibility: Applicants must be high school seniors or college freshmen or sophomores who are average or better students. They must be the son or daughter of a veteran and enrolling or enrolled in a post-secondary school in Kansas. A parent must have been a member of the Kansas American Legion or American Legion Auxiliary for the previous three years. In addition, the children of deceased parents are eligible if the parent was a paid member at the time of death. Applicants must submit a 1040 income statement, documentation of parent's veteran status, three letters of recommendation with only one from a teacher, an essay on the topic of "Why I Want to Go to College" and a high school transcript. Applicants must maintain a C average in college and verify enrollment at the start of each semester.
Target applicant(s): High school students. College students. Adult students.
Amount: $1,000.
Number of awards: 1.
Scholarship may be renewable.
Deadline: February 15.
How to apply: Applications are available online.
Exclusive: Visit www.UltimateScholarshipBook.com and enter code AM119726 for updates on this award.

[1198] • Alisa's Angels Scholarship

Alisa's Angels Foundation
5049 E Broadway #308, Tucson, AZ 85711
Phone: 602-381-1400
Email: scholarship@azfoundation.org
http://alisasangels.org
Purpose: To support graduating seniors of Arizona in pursuing post-secondary education.
Eligibility: A minimum GPA of 2.75 is required. Selection is primarily based on demonstration of service to others. Students must submit high school transcripts, an essay describing their service work and a letter of recommendation from a teacher, counselor or faith leader.
Target applicant(s): High school students.
Minimum GPA: 2.75
Amount: $5,000.
Number of awards: Up to 8.
Scholarship may be renewable.
Deadline: March 1.
How to apply: Applications are available online.
Exclusive: Visit www.UltimateScholarshipBook.com and enter code AL119826 for updates on this award.

[1199] • All Iowa Opportunity Scholarship

Iowa College Student Aid Commission
475 SW Fifth Street, Suite D, Des Moines, IA 50309
Phone: 515-725-3400
Email: info@iowacollegeaid.gov
https://www.iowacollegeaid.gov/ScholarshipsAndGrants
Purpose: To recognize Iowa's top students.
Eligibility: Applicants must be Iowa residents who graduated high school in the last two years. Students must demonstrate financial need. Awards may only be used at eligible Iowa institutions. Submit both a FAFSA and an Iowa Financial Aid Application by the deadline to be considered.
Target applicant(s): High school students.
Amount: Up to $5,198.
Number of awards: Varies.
Scholarship may be renewable.
Deadline: March 1.
How to apply: Applications are available online.
Exclusive: Visit www.UltimateScholarshipBook.com and enter code IO119926 for updates on this award.

[1200] • Allan Eldin and Agnes Sutorik Geiger Scholarship Fund

Hawaii Community Foundation - Scholarships
827 Fort Street Mall, Honolulu, HI 96813
Phone: 888-731-3863
Email: scholarships@hcf-hawaii.org
https://www.hawaiicommunityfoundation.org/
Purpose: To support Hawaii students who are pursuing degrees in veterinary science.
Eligibility: Students must have at least a 3.0 GPA, be full-time students and demonstrate financial need.
Target applicant(s): College students. Graduate school students. Adult students.
Minimum GPA: 3.0
Amount: Varies.
Number of awards: Varies.
Deadline: February 28.
How to apply: To apply, register online, complete the online application and select the scholarships to which you wish to apply. In addition, mail the supporting materials: printed confirmation page from the online application, personal statement, copy of Student Aid Report (SAR) available at www.fafsa.ed.gov and official transcript.

The Ultimate Scholarship Book 2026
Scholarship Directory (State of Residence)

Exclusive: Visit www.UltimateScholarshipBook.com and enter code HA120026 for updates on this award.

[1201] • Allan Johnston Memorial Scholarship
Los Alamos National Laboratory Foundation
1112 Plaza del Norte, Espanola, NM 87532
Phone: 505-753-8890
Email: tony@lanlfoundation.org
http://www.lanlfoundation.org
Purpose: To support undergraduate students from northern New Mexico.
Eligibility: Students must have at least a 3.25 cumulative unweighted GPA, and they must have either an SAT score (combined Math plus Critical Reading only) of at least 930 or an ACT score of at least 19. Applicants must submit an essay and two letters of recommendation.
Target applicant(s): High school students. College students. Adult students.
Minimum GPA: 3.25
Amount: $1,000 - $20,000.
Number of awards: Varies.
Deadline: January 16.
How to apply: Applications are available online.
Exclusive: Visit www.UltimateScholarshipBook.com and enter code LO120126 for updates on this award.

[1202] • Allied Healthcare Scholarship Program
Department of Health Care Access and Information (HCAI)
2020 West El Camino Avenue, Suite 800, Sacramento, CA 95833
Phone: 916-326-3640
Email: hpef-email@oshpd.ca.gov
https://hcai.ca.gov/loans-scholarships-grants/
Purpose: To increase the number of allied healthcare professionals working in medically underserved areas of California.
Eligibility: Applicants must be enrolled in a California community college or university and be studying one of the following programs: medical imaging, occupational therapy, physical therapy, respiratory care, social work, pharmacy and diagnostic medical sonography, pharmacy technician, medical laboratory technologist, surgical technician or ultrasound technician. Those selected will complete a one-year service contract or work volunteer hours in a medically underserved area of California. Financial need, work experience, academic achievement and community involvement are considered. Preference is given to those who expect to graduate within two years of application.
Target applicant(s): High school students. College students. Graduate school students. Adult students.
Minimum GPA: 2.0
Amount: Up to $8,000.
Number of awards: Varies.
Scholarship may be renewable.
Deadline: December 13.
How to apply: Applications are available online.
Exclusive: Visit www.UltimateScholarshipBook.com and enter code DE120226 for updates on this award.

[1203] • Alliss Opportunity Grant Program for Adults Returning to College
Minnesota Office of Higher Education Services
1450 Energy Park Drive, Suite 350, Saint Paul, MN 55108-5227
Phone: 651-642-0567
Email: misp.lara@hotmail.com
http://www.ohe.state.mn.us/
Purpose: To support students attending Minnesota state colleges or universities.
Eligibility: Applicants must have financial need and be attending Minnesota State Colleges or Minnesota State Universities. Undergraduate students attending Minnesota State Universities must be enrolled full-time. Applicants should contact the financial aid office at the university they are attending or planning to attend for more information.
Target applicant(s): Adult students.
Amount: Up to $1,100.
Number of awards: Varies.
Deadline: Contact the sponsor to confirm the deadline.
How to apply: Applications are available online.
Exclusive: Visit www.UltimateScholarshipBook.com and enter code MI120326 for updates on this award.

[1204] • Alma White - Delta Kappa Gamma Scholarship
Hawaii Community Foundation - Scholarships
827 Fort Street Mall, Honolulu, HI 96813
Phone: 888-731-3863
Email: scholarships@hcf-hawaii.org
https://www.hawaiicommunityfoundation.org/
Purpose: To support students in Hawaii who are planning careers in teaching.
Eligibility: Applicants must be majoring in education. Students must be a college junior, college senior or graduate student. Minimum 2.7 GPA required.
Target applicant(s): College students. Graduate school students. Adult students.
Minimum GPA: 2.7
Amount: Varies.
Number of awards: Varies.
Deadline: January 31.
How to apply: To apply, register online, complete the online application and select the scholarships to which you wish to apply. In addition, mail the supporting materials: printed confirmation page from the online application, personal statement, copy of Student Aid Report (SAR) available at www.fafsa.ed.gov and official transcript.
Exclusive: Visit www.UltimateScholarshipBook.com and enter code HA120426 for updates on this award.

[1205] • Alyssa McCroskey Memorial Scholarship
California Association on Postsecondary Education and Disability (CAPED)
10073 Valley View Street, #242, Cypress, CA 90630
Phone: 562-397-2810
Email: caped.scholarship.committee@gmail.com
http://www.caped.co/scholarships/
Purpose: To support students with a learning disability who are pursuing higher education.
Eligibility: Applicants must have a verifiable learning disability and be making a positive difference in the lives of other students who are struggling to maintain or regain their mental health. Students must be currently enrolled as a student at a four-year California college or university with a GPA of 2.5 for undergraduates or 3.0 for graduate students. Applicants must have completed at least six semester or eight quarter units as an undergraduate student or three semester or four quarter units as a graduate student.
Target applicant(s): College students. Graduate school students. Adult students.
Minimum GPA: 2.5 for undergraduate students; 3.0 for graduate students

Amount: $1,000.
Number of awards: 1.
Deadline: August 31.
How to apply: Applications are available online.
Exclusive: Visit www.UltimateScholarshipBook.com and enter code CA120526 for updates on this award.

[1206] • Ambassador Minerva Jean Falcon Hawaii Scholarship

Hawaii Community Foundation - Scholarships
827 Fort Street Mall, Honolulu, HI 96813
Phone: 888-731-3863
Email: scholarships@hcf-hawaii.org
https://www.hawaiicommunityfoundation.org/
Purpose: To support students of Filipino ancestry.
Eligibility: Students must be starting their freshman year of college, must attend school in Hawaii and must have a minimum 2.7 GPA.
Target applicant(s): High school students. College students. Adult students.
Minimum GPA: 2.7
Amount: Varies.
Number of awards: Varies.
Deadline: February 28.
How to apply: To apply, register online, complete the online application and select the scholarships to which you wish to apply. In addition, mail the supporting materials: printed confirmation page from the online application, personal statement, copy of Student Aid Report (SAR) available at www.fafsa.ed.gov and official transcript.
Exclusive: Visit www.UltimateScholarshipBook.com and enter code HA120626 for updates on this award.

[1207] • American Council of Engineering Companies of New Jersey Member Organization Scholarship

American Council of Engineering Companies of New Jersey
310 West State Street, Trenton, NJ 08618
Phone: 609-571-9958
Email: info@acecnj.org
https://acecnj.org/awards/scholarship_awards/
Purpose: To help students who are enrolled in engineering or accredited land surveying degree programs.
Eligibility: Applicants must be rising undergraduate juniors or above enrolled in an ABET-accredited bachelor's degree program in engineering, a master's degree program in engineering, a doctoral degree program in engineering or an accredited land surveying program. Master's students must either be enrolled in an ABET-accredited program or must hold a bachelor's degree in engineering from an ABET-accredited school. Doctoral students must hold either an ABET-accredited bachelor's degree or an ABET-accredited master's degree in engineering. They must be U.S. citizens. Selection is based on GPA, personal essay, recommendation letter, work experience and extracurricular involvement.
Target applicant(s): College students. Graduate school students. Adult students.
Amount: Up to $5,000.
Number of awards: Up to 6.
Deadline: February 5.
How to apply: Applications are available online. An application form, a personal essay, an official transcript and one recommendation form are required.
Exclusive: Visit www.UltimateScholarshipBook.com and enter code AM120726 for updates on this award.

[1208] • American Indian Endowed Scholarship

Washington Student Achievement Council
P. O. Box 43430, Olympia, WA 98504-3430
Phone: 360-753-7850
Email: aies@wsac.wa.gov
https://wsac.wa.gov/
Purpose: To help students who have ties to the Native American community and have financial need pay for higher education.
Eligibility: Applicants must have financial need according to a completed Free Application for Federal Student Aid (FAFSA), be residents of Washington state and enroll full-time as an undergraduate or graduate student at an eligible in-state institution.
Target applicant(s): High school students. College students. Graduate school students. Adult students.
Amount: $500-$2,000.
Number of awards: Up to 15.
Scholarship may be renewable.
Deadline: March 1.
How to apply: Applications are available online.
Exclusive: Visit www.UltimateScholarshipBook.com and enter code WA120826 for updates on this award.

[1209] • American Institute of Graphic Arts (AIGA) Honolulu Chapter Scholarship Fund

Hawaii Community Foundation - Scholarships
827 Fort Street Mall, Honolulu, HI 96813
Phone: 888-731-3863
Email: scholarships@hcf-hawaii.org
https://www.hawaiicommunityfoundation.org/
Purpose: To support students majoring in graphic design, visual communication or commercial arts.
Eligibility: Students must be residents of Hawaii.
Target applicant(s): High school students. College students. Adult students.
Minimum GPA: 2.7
Amount: Varies.
Number of awards: Varies.
Deadline: February 28.
How to apply: To apply, register online, complete the online application and select the scholarships to which you wish to apply. In addition, mail the supporting materials: printed confirmation page from the online application, personal statement, copy of Student Aid Report (SAR) available at www.fafsa.ed.gov and official transcript.
Exclusive: Visit www.UltimateScholarshipBook.com and enter code HA120926 for updates on this award.

[1210] • American Legion - Connecticut Oratorical Contest

American Legion, Department of Connecticut
287 West Street, Rocky Hill, CT 06067
Phone: 860-436-9986
Email: deptadj@ctlegion
https://ctlegion.org
Purpose: Scholarship awards are given to high school students who win an oratorical contest on the understanding of the U.S. Constitution.

The Ultimate Scholarship Book 2026
Scholarship Directory (State of Residence)

Eligibility: Applicants must prepare an oration on an assigned topic with specific time constraints. Students will explore the substance and meaning of the Constitution.
Target applicant(s): High school students.
Amount: Varies.
Number of awards: Varies.
Deadline: November 1.
How to apply: Applications are available online.
Exclusive: Visit www.UltimateScholarshipBook.com and enter code AM121026 for updates on this award.

[1211] • American Legion Auxiliary, Department of California Educational Assistance General $1,000 Scholarships
American Legion Auxiliary, Department of California
San Francisco War Memorial Building, 401 Van Ness Avenue, Suite 319, San Francisco, CA 94102-4570
Phone: 415-861-5092
Email: headquarters@calegionaux.org
https://calegionaux.org/scholarships/education-scholarships/
Purpose: To provide support to the children of U.S. Armed Forces members.
Eligibility: One of the applicant's parents must have served in the U.S. Armed Forces during an eligible period. Applicants must be California resident high school seniors or graduates who have had to postpone school due to health or financial reasons and plan to attend a California college or university. Applicants must also demonstrate financial need.
Target applicant(s): High school students.
Amount: $1,000.
Number of awards: 4.
Deadline: March 16.
How to apply: Applications are available online.
Exclusive: Visit www.UltimateScholarshipBook.com and enter code AM121126 for updates on this award.

[1212] • American Legion Auxiliary, Department of California Educational Assistance General $2,000 Scholarships
American Legion Auxiliary, Department of California
San Francisco War Memorial Building, 401 Van Ness Avenue, Suite 319, San Francisco, CA 94102-4570
Phone: 415-861-5092
Email: headquarters@calegionaux.org
https://calegionaux.org/scholarships/education-scholarships/
Purpose: To provide support to children of U.S. Armed Forces members.
Eligibility: One of the applicant's parents must have served in the U.S. Armed Forces during an eligible period. Applicants must attend a California college or university, be California resident high school seniors or graduates who have not begun college because of illness or need and demonstrate need.
Target applicant(s): High school students.
Amount: $2,000.
Number of awards: 1.
Deadline: March 16.
How to apply: Applications are available online.
Exclusive: Visit www.UltimateScholarshipBook.com and enter code AM121226 for updates on this award.

[1213] • American Legion Auxiliary, Department of California Educational Assistance General $500 Scholarships
American Legion Auxiliary, Department of California
San Francisco War Memorial Building, 401 Van Ness Avenue, Suite 319, San Francisco, CA 94102-4570
Phone: 415-861-5092
Email: headquarters@calegionaux.org
https://calegionaux.org/scholarships/education-scholarships/
Purpose: To provide support to the children of U.S. Armed Forces members.
Eligibility: One of applicant's parents must have served in the U.S. Armed Forces during an eligible period. Applicants must be California resident high school seniors or graduates who have had to postpone school due to health or financial reasons and plan to attend a California college or university. Applicants must also demonstrate financial need.
Target applicant(s): High school students. College students. Adult students.
Amount: $500.
Number of awards: 3.
Deadline: March 16.
How to apply: Applications are available online.
Exclusive: Visit www.UltimateScholarshipBook.com and enter code AM121326 for updates on this award.

[1214] • American Legion Department of Arkansas High School Oratorical Scholarship Program
American Legion, Department of Arkansas
Department Oratorical Chairman, Roger Lacy, P.O. Box 3280, Little Rock, AR 72203
Phone: 501-375-1104
Email: alegion@swbell.net
http://www.arlegion.org
Purpose: To enhance high school students' experience with and understanding of the U.S. Constitution. The contest will help develop students' leadership skills and civic appreciation, as well as the ability to deliver thoughtful, insightful orations regarding U.S. citizenship and its inherent responsibilities.
Eligibility: Applicants must be high school students under the age of 20 who are U.S. citizens or legal residents and residents of the state. Students first give an oration within their state and winners compete at the national level. The oration must be related to the Constitution of the United States focusing on the duties and obligations citizens have to the government. It must be in English and be between eight and ten minutes. There is also an assigned topic which is posted on the website, and it should be between three and five minutes.
Target applicant(s): High school students.
Amount: Varies.
Number of awards: Varies.
Deadline: January 5.
How to apply: Applications are available online.
Exclusive: Visit www.UltimateScholarshipBook.com and enter code AM121426 for updates on this award.

[1215] • American Legion Department of Florida General Scholarship
American Legion, Department of Florida
Elizabeth Douglas, Programs Director, 1912A Lee Road, Orlando, FL 32810

Phone: 800-393-3378
Email: mail@floridalegion.org
https://www.floridalegion.org/programs-services/scholarships/
Purpose: To support descendants of American Legion members and deceased veterans.
Eligibility: Applicants must be direct descendants of American Legion members in good standing or deceased U.S. veterans who would have been eligible for membership. They must be seniors at accredited Florida high schools who plan to pursue undergraduate study upon graduation. Funds must be used within four years of graduation, excluding active military service.
Target applicant(s): High school students.
Amount: $500-$2,500.
Number of awards: 7.
Deadline: March 1.
How to apply: Applications are available online. An application form and copy of documentation of the veteran's service are required.
Exclusive: Visit www.UltimateScholarshipBook.com and enter code AM121526 for updates on this award.

[1216] • American Legion Department of Illinois Scholarship

American Legion, Department of Illinois
2720 East Lincoln Street, Bloomington, IL 61704
Phone: 309-663-0361
Email: hdqs@illegion.org
http://www.illegion.org/scholarships/
Purpose: To award scholarships to graduating students enrolled in Illinois high schools.
Eligibility: Applicants must be children or grandchildren of American Legion Illinois members and must be in their senior year of high school. Awards may be used to further education at an accredited college, university or technical school.
Target applicant(s): High school students.
Amount: Varies.
Number of awards: Varies.
Deadline: March 15.
How to apply: Application information is available by contacting the American Legion, Department of Illinois.
Exclusive: Visit www.UltimateScholarshipBook.com and enter code AM121626 for updates on this award.

[1217] • Americanism and Government Scholarship Program

American Legion, Department of Wisconsin
2930 American Legion Drive, P.O. Box 388, Portage, WI 53901
Phone: 608-745-1090
Email: info@wilegion.org
https://wilegion.org/scholarships
Purpose: To reward outstanding performance on the Americanism and Government Test, a 50-question examination based on state and federal government and history.
Eligibility: Participants must be enrolled in a Wisconsin high school and in their sophomore, junior or senior year.
Target applicant(s): High school students.
Amount: $250-$750.
Number of awards: 45.
Deadline: March 15.
How to apply: Application information is available by contacting your local principal, teacher or guidance counselor.
Exclusive: Visit www.UltimateScholarshipBook.com and enter code AM121726 for updates on this award.

[1218] • Ann Griffel Scholarship

Iowa Golf Association
Attn: Ann Griffel Scholarship Committee, 1605 North Ankeny Boulevard, Suite 210, Ankeny, IA 50023
Phone: 888-388-4442
Email: info@iowagolf.org
https://iowagolf.org/scholarships/
Purpose: To support girls who have played golf in Iowa.
Eligibility: Applicants must plan to attend an Iowa college, university or trade school. Selection is based on academic performance, extracurricular activities and leadership qualities.
Target applicant(s): High school students.
Amount: $2,000.
Number of awards: Varies.
Deadline: March 31.
How to apply: Applications are sent to all high school girls' golf coaches in Iowa at the beginning of the year. The application should be mailed with two letters of recommendation, a high school transcript, a photo and a personal essay.
Exclusive: Visit www.UltimateScholarshipBook.com and enter code IO121826 for updates on this award.

[1219] • Anthony Muñoz Scholarship Fund

Anthony Muñoz Foundation
8919 Rossash Road, Cincinnati, OH 45236
Phone: 513-772-4900
Email: Impact@munozfoundation.org
https://www.munozfoundation.org/scholarship-fund/
Purpose: To assist Kentucky, Indiana and Ohio students.
Eligibility: Applicants must be high school seniors who reside in the counties specified by the foundation and plan to attend college in Kentucky, Indiana or Ohio. Students must have a minimum ACT composite score of 18 or at least a 2.5 GPA and must demonstrate academic achievement, leadership and financial need.
Target applicant(s): High school students.
Minimum GPA: 2.5
Amount: $20,000.
Number of awards: Up to 7.
Deadline: April 26.
How to apply: Applications are available online and must be mailed or faxed.
Exclusive: Visit www.UltimateScholarshipBook.com and enter code AN121926 for updates on this award.

[1220] • Antonio Cirino Memorial Scholarship

Rhode Island Foundation
One Union Station, Providence, RI 02903
Phone: 401-274-4564
Email: rbogert@rifoundation.org
https://rifoundation.org/grants-scholarships
Purpose: To support Rhode Island students who are pursuing careers in art education.
Eligibility: Applicants must demonstrate an interest in learning about and practicing art. Preference will be given to visual artists. Students must be enrolled or planning to enroll in a master's or doctoral program that will lead to a career in art education.

The Ultimate Scholarship Book 2026
Scholarship Directory (State of Residence)

Target applicant(s): College students. Graduate school students. Adult students.
Amount: $2,000-$12,000.
Number of awards: Varies.
Scholarship may be renewable.
Deadline: April 15.
How to apply: Applications are available online.
Exclusive: Visit www.UltimateScholarshipBook.com and enter code RH122026 for updates on this award.

[1221] • Arc of Washington State Trust Fund Stipend Award
Arc of Washington State
Attn: Diana Stadden, 2638 State Avenue NE, Olympia, WA 98506
Phone: 360-357-5596
Email: info@arctrustfund.org
http://www.arcwa.org
Purpose: To help students attending school in Alaska, Idaho, Oregon and Washington state who wish to pursue careers working with the developmentally disabled.
Eligibility: Applicants must be undergraduate juniors or above (including graduate-level students) and must be enrolled in a college or university located in Idaho, Washington state, Alaska or Oregon. They must be interested in working with the developmentally disabled. Selection is based on the overall strength of the application.
Target applicant(s): College students. Graduate school students. Adult students.
Amount: Up to $5,000.
Number of awards: Varies.
Deadline: March 15.
How to apply: Applications are available online. An application form, official transcripts, personal statement and two letters of recommendation are required.
Exclusive: Visit www.UltimateScholarshipBook.com and enter code AR122126 for updates on this award.

[1222] • Archibald Rutledge Scholarship Program
South Carolina State Department of Education
1429 Senate Street, Columbia, SC 29201
Phone: 803-734-0323
Email: cpower@ed.sc.gov
http://ed.sc.gov
Purpose: To support students who exhibit academic and artistic excellence.
Eligibility: Applicants must be high school seniors in South Carolina public schools, have attended South Carolina public schools for the past two consecutive years and be U.S. citizens. There are five categories: creative writing, dance, music, theater and visual arts. For the creative writing category, a sonnet, lyric or narrative poem no longer than one page must be submitted. For the dance category, an original, short dance composition of three to ten minutes. For the music category, an original composition of three to ten minutes must be submitted. For the theater category, an original one-act play with a performing time of eight to fifteen minutes. For the visual arts category, an original visual composition must be submitted. Compositions are judged on creativity, originality and quality of expression and content.
Target applicant(s): High school students.
Amount: $2,000.
Number of awards: 5.

Deadline: February 19.
How to apply: Applications are available online. An application form, composition and process folio are required.
Exclusive: Visit www.UltimateScholarshipBook.com and enter code SO122226 for updates on this award.

[1223] • Arizona BPW Foundation Annual Scholarships
Arizona Business and Professional Women's Foundation
P.O. Box 32596, Phoenix, AZ 85064
Email: azbpwfoundation@gmail.com
https://arizonabpwfoundation.org
Purpose: To provide education assistance to women.
Eligibility: Applicants must be women who are returning to school to broaden their job prospects at a community college or trade school in Arizona. They must provide a career goal statement, financial need statement, most recent transcript, most recent income tax return and two letters of recommendation. Students must be at least 19 years old.
Target applicant(s): High school students. College students. Adult students.
Amount: Varies.
Number of awards: Varies.
Deadline: November 24.
How to apply: Applications are available online.
Exclusive: Visit www.UltimateScholarshipBook.com and enter code AR122326 for updates on this award.

[1224] • Arizona National Livestock Show Scholarship
Arizona National Livestock Show
1826 W. McDowell Road, Phoenix, AZ 85007
Phone: 602-258-8568
Email: information@anls.org
https://anls.org/
Purpose: To assist students who participate in the Arizona National Livestock Show.
Eligibility: Applicants must be currently taking at least 12 hours and have completed at least 12 semester hours at a college or university and have a minimum 2.5 GPA.
Target applicant(s): College students. Adult students.
Minimum GPA: 2.5
Amount: $40,000 total for all awards.
Number of awards: Up to 20.
Deadline: March 15.
How to apply: Applications are available online.
Exclusive: Visit www.UltimateScholarshipBook.com and enter code AR122426 for updates on this award.

[1225] • Arkansas Game and Fish Commission Conservation Scholarship
Arkansas Game and Fish Commission
2 Natural Resources Drive, Little Rock, AR 72205
Phone: 800-364-4263
Email: Shawna.Hitchcock@agfc.ar.gov
http://www.agfc.com
Purpose: To aid Arkansas students preparing for careers in natural resources conservation.
Eligibility: Applicants must be Arkansas residents who are high school seniors or undergraduate or graduate-level college students. They must have

a GPA of 2.5 or above and must be planning to pursue a career in natural resources conservation. They cannot have received full scholarship or grant funding from another source. Selection is based on the standardized scoring of each application as a whole.
Target applicant(s): High school students. College students. Graduate school students. Adult students.
Minimum GPA: 2.5
Amount: Up to $2,000 per semester.
Number of awards: Varies.
Scholarship may be renewable.
Deadline: June 15.
How to apply: Applications are available online. An application form, personal statement, essay, official transcript, three personal references, one recommendation letter, photograph and statement of intent to pursue a four-year degree (for those currently attending a two-year institution) are required.
Exclusive: Visit www.UltimateScholarshipBook.com and enter code AR122526 for updates on this award.

[1226] • Arkansas Service Memorial Scholarship Endowment
Arkansas Community Foundation
1400 W. Markham, Suite 206, Little Rock, AR 72201
Phone: 888-220-2723
Email: arcf@arcf.org
http://www.arcf.org
Purpose: To provide financial assistance for students with a parent who died in service to his or her community, state or nation.
Eligibility: Applicants must be Arkansas residents who plan to attend an institution of higher learning in the state. Scholarships are awarded by local Arkansas Community Foundation chapters.
Target applicant(s): High school students. College students. Graduate school students. Adult students.
Amount: $2,500.
Number of awards: Varies.
Scholarship may be renewable.
Deadline: April 1.
How to apply: Applications are available online.
Exclusive: Visit www.UltimateScholarshipBook.com and enter code AR122626 for updates on this award.

[1227] • Aspire Award
Tennessee Student Assistance Corporation
312 Rosa L. Parks Avenue, 9th Floor, Nashville, TN 37243
Phone: 800-342-1663
Email: tsac.aidinfo@tn.gov
https://www.collegefortn.org/about-financial-aid/
Purpose: To provide supplemental support to recipients of the Tennessee HOPE Scholarship.
Eligibility: Applicants must be entering freshmen with a minimum ACT score of 21, minimum SAT score of 980 or minimum 3.0 GPA. Home-schooled applicants must have a minimum ACT score of 21 or SAT score of 980. GED applicants must have a minimum GED score of 525 and minimum ACT score of 21 or SAT score of 980. Independent students or the parents of dependent students must have an adjusted gross income under $36,000.
Target applicant(s): High school students.
Minimum GPA: 3.0
Amount: Up to $750 per semester.
Number of awards: Varies.
Deadline: September 1; February 1.
How to apply: Applications are available through completion of the FAFSA.
Exclusive: Visit www.UltimateScholarshipBook.com and enter code TE122726 for updates on this award.

[1228] • Associate Degree Nursing Scholarship Program
Department of Health Care Access and Information (HCAI)
2020 West El Camino Avenue, Suite 800, Sacramento, CA 95833
Phone: 916-326-3640
Email: hpef-email@oshpd.ca.gov
https://hcai.ca.gov/loans-scholarships-grants/
Purpose: To increase the number of registered nurses working in medically underserved areas of California.
Eligibility: Applicants must be California residents enrolled in an associate degree nursing program at a California school, have a minimum 2.0 GPA and be fluent in a language other than English. Financial need, work experience, community involvement and academic achievement are considered. Preference is given to those who will graduate within two years and to those who plan to remain in a medically underserved area past the service time required. Recipients must sign a two-year service contract to work in a medically underserved area as an RN.
Target applicant(s): High school students. College students. Adult students.
Minimum GPA: 2.0
Amount: Up to $10,000.
Number of awards: Varies.
Scholarship may be renewable.
Deadline: December 13.
How to apply: Applications are available online.
Exclusive: Visit www.UltimateScholarshipBook.com and enter code DE122826 for updates on this award.

[1229] • Associated General Contractors of Connecticut Scholarships
Connecticut Construction Industries Association
912 Silas Deane Highway, Suite 112, Wethersfield, CT 06109
Phone: 860-529-6855
Email: ccia-info@ctconstruction.org
https://www.ctconstruction.org/i4a/pages/index.cfm?pageid=3559
Purpose: To aid students planning to pursue careers in civil engineering or building and construction technology.
Eligibility: Applicants must be high school seniors who intend to enroll in a four-year civil engineering or construction technology program or who plan to complete a construction program at a two-year institution before entering a four-year institution. They must be U.S. citizens or legal residents and must be interested in a career in construction. Selection is based on academic achievement, level of interest in a construction career, work experience, evaluation forms, extracurricular activities and financial need. The award is for two years.
Target applicant(s): High school students. College students. Adult students.
Amount: $2,500.
Number of awards: Varies.
Deadline: February 29.
How to apply: Applications are available online. An application form, two personal evaluation forms, one faculty evaluation form and an official transcript are required.
Exclusive: Visit www.UltimateScholarshipBook.com and enter code CO122926 for updates on this award.

[1230] • Associated General Contractors of Minnesota Scholarships
Associated General Contractors of Minnesota
Capitol Office Building, 525 Park Street, Suite 110, St. Paul, MN 55103-2186
Phone: 651-632-8929
Email: mbeckmann@agcmn.org
http://www.agcmn.org
Purpose: To support outstanding students in Minnesota.
Eligibility: Applicants must attend a Minnesota institution of higher learning with a concentration in construction or construction-related courses. Applications are judged equally on academic performance, career objectives, financial need, personal information and application clarity.
Target applicant(s): College students. Adult students.
Amount: $500-$2,500.
Number of awards: Varies.
Deadline: May 17.
How to apply: Applications are available online. An application form, personal statement, academic core plan, career objectives and recent color photo are required.
Exclusive: Visit www.UltimateScholarshipBook.com and enter code AS123026 for updates on this award.

[1231] • ASWA Seattle Chapter Scholarship
American Society of Women Accountants - Seattle Chapter
800 Fifth Avenue, Suite 101, PMB 237, Seattle, WA 98104-3191
Phone: 206-467-8645
Email: scholarship@aswaseattle.org
http://seattleafwa.org/scholarships/
Purpose: To aid accounting students in Washington state.
Eligibility: Applicants must be part-time or full-time accounting students at an accredited postsecondary institution located in Washington state. Students must have finished at least 30 semester hours (or 45 quarter hours) within four weeks of the application deadline. They must have an overall GPA of 2.0 or higher. The scholarship is open to both male and female students. Selection is based on GPA, stated career goals and financial need.
Target applicant(s): College students. Graduate school students. Adult students.
Minimum GPA: 2.0
Amount: Varies.
Number of awards: Varies.
Deadline: April 30.
How to apply: Applications are available online. An application form, an official transcript, two recommendation letters and financial aid transcripts are required.
Exclusive: Visit www.UltimateScholarshipBook.com and enter code AM123126 for updates on this award.

[1232] • Atsuhiko Tateuchi Memorial Scholarship
Seattle Foundation
1200 Fifth Avenue, Suite 1300, Seattle, WA 98101-3151
Phone: 206-515-2119
Email: scholarships@seattlefoundation.org
http://www.seattlefoundation.org
Purpose: To provide financial assistance for hard-working students from the Pacific Rim states.
Eligibility: Applicants must be high school seniors or undergraduate students from Washington, Oregon, California, Hawaii or Alaska with demonstrated financial need. They must have a GPA of 3.0 or higher. Preference is given to students with Japanese or other Asian ancestry.
Target applicant(s): High school students. College students. Graduate school students. Adult students.
Minimum GPA: 3.0
Amount: $5,000-$15,000.
Number of awards: Varies.
Scholarship may be renewable.
Deadline: March 1.
How to apply: Applications are available online.
Exclusive: Visit www.UltimateScholarshipBook.com and enter code SE123226 for updates on this award.

[1233] • AWAF Scholarships
Association for Women in Architecture Foundation
1315 Storm Parkway, Torrance, CA 90501
Phone: 310-534-8466
Email: awards@awa-foundation.org
https://www.awaplusd.org/awaf-scholarships
Purpose: To support women studying architecture.
Eligibility: Applicants must be female residents of California or attend a California school and must be enrolled in one of the following majors: architecture, landscape architecture, urban and/or land planning, interior design or environmental design. Applicants must also have completed a minimum of 18 units in their major by the application due date. The award is based on grades, personal statement, financial need, recommendations and submitted materials.
Target applicant(s): College students. Graduate school students. Adult students.
Amount: $3,000 to $7,500.
Number of awards: 6.
Deadline: April 19.
How to apply: Applications are available online.
Exclusive: Visit www.UltimateScholarshipBook.com and enter code AS123326 for updates on this award.

[1234] • Bachelor of Science Nursing Scholarship Program
Department of Health Care Access and Information (HCAI)
2020 West El Camino Avenue, Suite 800, Sacramento, CA 95833
Phone: 916-326-3640
Email: hpef-email@oshpd.ca.gov
https://hcai.ca.gov/loans-scholarships-grants/
Purpose: To increase the number of professional nurses practicing in medically underserved areas of California by assisting nursing students attending California schools.
Eligibility: Applicants must be attending a California undergraduate nursing program and be fluent in a language other than English. Financial need, work experience, academic achievement and community involvement are considered. A two-year service agreement to work in a medically underserved area of California is required. Preference is given to those who expect to graduate within two years and to those who plan to remain in a medically underserved area after the service agreement has expired. Applicants must have a minimum 2.0 GPA.
Target applicant(s): College students. Adult students.
Minimum GPA: 2.0
Amount: $10,000.
Number of awards: Varies.
Scholarship may be renewable.
Deadline: December 13.
How to apply: Applications are available online.

Exclusive: Visit www.UltimateScholarshipBook.com and enter code DE123426 for updates on this award.

[1235] • BAFTX Undergraduate Award
British American Foundation of Texas
Email: info@baftx.org
http://www.baftx.org
Purpose: To help offset the cost of higher education for Texas or United Kingdom residents.
Eligibility: Applicants must be residents of Texas or the United Kingdom enrolled as full-time students within Texas or the U.K. and demonstrate financial need. Students must be pursuing a major in science, technology, engineering, math or business and have a minimum GPA of 3.25. Applicants must be able to interview and attend an awards dinner.
Target applicant(s): High school students. College students. Adult students.
Minimum GPA: 3.25
Amount: Varies.
Number of awards: 1.
Deadline: March 31.
How to apply: Applications are available online.
Exclusive: Visit www.UltimateScholarshipBook.com and enter code BR123526 for updates on this award.

[1236] • Ben and Vicky Cayetano Scholarship Fund
Hawaii Community Foundation - Scholarships
827 Fort Street Mall, Honolulu, HI 96813
Phone: 888-731-3863
Email: scholarships@hcf-hawaii.org
https://www.hawaiicommunityfoundation.org/
Purpose: To support exceptional Hawaii students.
Eligibility: Applicants must be upcoming high school graduates in Hawaii. They must have a GPA of 3.5 or higher. Preference is given to students who have overcome financial and social obstacles and to the students with the greatest financial need.
Target applicant(s): High school students.
Minimum GPA: 3.5
Amount: Varies.
Number of awards: Varies.
Deadline: February 28.
How to apply: Applications are available online. An application form, personal statement, copy of FAFSA Student Aid Report, transcript, two letters of recommendation and an essay are required.
Exclusive: Visit www.UltimateScholarshipBook.com and enter code HA123626 for updates on this award.

[1237] • Ben W. Fortson, Jr., Scholarship
Surveying and Mapping Society of Georgia
P.O. Box 113, LaGrange, GA 30241
Phone: 770-947-1767
Email: ginger_samsog@att.net
https://www.samsog.org/mpage/foundation-scholarships
Purpose: To help Georgia undergraduate land surveying students.
Eligibility: Applicants must be Georgia residents enrolled in an undergraduate land surveying program of study at an accredited institution of higher learning. They must have completed at least 20 percent of their program requirements before receiving any scholarship monies awarded. Students must also maintain a 2.4 overall GPA and 2.7 GPA in surveying courses. Preference is given to full-time students seeking a bachelor's degree. Selection is based on the overall strength of the application.
Target applicant(s): College students. Adult students.
Minimum GPA: 2.4
Amount: $3,000.
Number of awards: 1.
Deadline: June 30.
How to apply: Applications are available online. An application form and transcript are required.
Exclusive: Visit www.UltimateScholarshipBook.com and enter code SU123726 for updates on this award.

[1238] • Better Business Bureau of Delaware Foundation Student Ethics Scholarship
Better Business Bureau (BBB) of Delaware Education Foundation
Attn.: Scholarship Committee, 60 Reads Way, New Castle, DE 19720
Phone: 302-221-5259
Email: csauers@delaware.bbb.org
https://www.bbb.org/local/0251/delawarestudentethicsscholarship
Purpose: To assist Delaware high school seniors who exemplify high ethics.
Eligibility: Applicants must demonstrate leadership, community service, personal integrity and academic strength and must plan to attend an accredited college or university. A minimum GPA of 3.0 is required of applicants.
Target applicant(s): High school students.
Minimum GPA: 3.0
Amount: $2,500.
Number of awards: 2.
Deadline: Contact the sponsor to confirm the deadline.
How to apply: Applicants must be nominated by an employee or owner of a company that is accredited by the BBB. An application form, two letters of recommendation, an essay, supporting documentation, a copy of the transcript and certification by sponsor to the BBB are required.
Exclusive: Visit www.UltimateScholarshipBook.com and enter code BE123826 for updates on this award.

[1239] • Betty Bacon Memorial Scholarship
California Association on Postsecondary Education and Disability (CAPED)
10073 Valley View Street, #242, Cypress, CA 90630
Phone: 562-397-2810
Email: caped.scholarship.committee@gmail.com
http://www.caped.co/scholarships/
Purpose: To support students with a learning disability who are pursuing higher education.
Eligibility: Applicants must have a verifiable learning disability and be currently enrolled at a four-year California college or university with a GPA of 2.5 for undergraduates or 3.0 for graduate students. Students must have completed at least six semester or eight quarter units as an undergraduate student or three semester or four quarter units as a graduate student.
Target applicant(s): College students. Graduate school students. Adult students.
Minimum GPA: 2.5 for undergraduate students; 3.0 for graduate students
Amount: $1,000.
Number of awards: 1.
Deadline: August 31.
How to apply: Applications are available online.
Exclusive: Visit www.UltimateScholarshipBook.com and enter code CA123926 for updates on this award.

[1240] • Bick Bickson Scholarship Fund
Hawaii Community Foundation - Scholarships
827 Fort Street Mall, Honolulu, HI 96813
Phone: 888-731-3863
Email: scholarships@hcf-hawaii.org
https://www.hawaiicommunityfoundation.org/
Purpose: To support students pursuing studies in marketing, law or travel.
Eligibility: Applicants must be residents of Hawaii who have need of financial assistance and plan to attend an accredited college or university full-time within the United States as an undergraduate or graduate student. Students must have a 3.0 GPA and plan to major in one of the following areas: marketing, law or travel industry management.
Target applicant(s): High school students. College students. Graduate school students. Adult students.
Minimum GPA: 3.0
Amount: Varies.
Number of awards: Varies.
Deadline: February 28.
How to apply: Applications are available online.
Exclusive: Visit www.UltimateScholarshipBook.com and enter code HA124026 for updates on this award.

[1241] • Big Y Scholarship Programs
Big Y
Scholarship Committee, P.O. Box 7840, Springfield, MA 01102-7840
Phone: 413-504-4047
Email: scholarship@bigy.com
http://www.bigy.com
Purpose: To reward students in the Big Y market area and those affiliated with Big Y.
Eligibility: Applicants must either be Big Y employees or their dependents or must reside or attend school in western or central Massachusetts, Norfolk County, Massachusetts or Connecticut. The scholarships are available to high school seniors, undergraduates, graduates, community college students and adult students. Applicants should submit transcripts, college entrance exam scores and two recommendation letters. Big Y employees must submit one recommendation from their supervisor. Selection is based on achievements, awards, community involvement, leadership positions and class rank. Eight scholarships are available specifically for dependents of law enforcement officers and firefighters.
Target applicant(s): High school students. College students. Graduate school students. Adult students.
Amount: Varies.
Number of awards: 300.
Deadline: February 1.
How to apply: Applications are available at any Big Y location from October through January each year. Applications are also available at guidance offices of schools within Big Y's market area.
Exclusive: Visit www.UltimateScholarshipBook.com and enter code BI124126 for updates on this award.

[1242] • Blossom Kalama Evans Memorial Scholarship Fund
Hawaii Community Foundation - Scholarships
827 Fort Street Mall, Honolulu, HI 96813
Phone: 888-731-3863
Email: scholarships@hcf-hawaii.org
https://www.hawaiicommunityfoundation.org/
Purpose: To support students who are dedicated to serving the native Hawaiian community.
Eligibility: Applicants must be of Hawaiian ancestry, have at least a 2.7 GPA and must be a college junior, college senior or graduate student.
Target applicant(s): College students. Graduate school students. Adult students.
Minimum GPA: 2.7
Amount: Varies.
Number of awards: Varies.
Deadline: February 28.
How to apply: To apply, register online, complete the online application and select the scholarships to which you wish to apply. In addition, mail the supporting materials: printed confirmation page from the online application, personal statement, copy of Student Aid Report (SAR) available at www.fafsa.ed.gov and official transcript.
Exclusive: Visit www.UltimateScholarshipBook.com and enter code HA124226 for updates on this award.

[1243] • Bob C. Powers Scholarship
North Texas Fair and Rodeo
2217 N. Carroll Boulevard, Denton, TX 76201
Phone: 940-387-2632
Email: nkimmey@ntfair.com
https://ntfair.com/get-involved/
Purpose: To support graduating high school seniors by investing in their future.
Eligibility: Applicants must be a high school senior and involved in school, their community and FFA, FHA or 4-H activities. Selection is based on academic achievement, extracurricular activities and financial need.
Target applicant(s): High school students.
Amount: $2,000.
Number of awards: 1.
Deadline: June 1.
How to apply: Applications are available online and must include two letters of recommendation and two photos.
Exclusive: Visit www.UltimateScholarshipBook.com and enter code NO124326 for updates on this award.

[1244] • Bob Eddy Scholarship Program
Connecticut Society of Professional Journalists
Attn.: Paul Singley, P.O. Box 5071, Woodbridge, CT 06525
Phone: 212-683-5700 x364
Email: psingley@ctspj.org
http://connecticutspj.org/
Purpose: To support students interested in journalism careers.
Eligibility: Applicants must be rising college juniors or seniors at a four-year college and Connecticut residents or students at Connecticut schools. They should be able to submit samples of work that shows interest and competency in journalism.
Target applicant(s): College students. Adult students.
Amount: $1,000-$2,500.
Number of awards: 4.
Deadline: April 28.
How to apply: Applications are available online. An application form, transcript, essay and writing samples, tapes or related work in any media are required.
Exclusive: Visit www.UltimateScholarshipBook.com and enter code CO124426 for updates on this award.

[1245] • Bob Stevens Memorial Scholarship
Garden State Scholastic Press Foundation
New Jersey Press Foundation, 840 Bear Tavern Road, Suite 305, West Trenton, NJ 08628-1019
Email: scholarship@gsspa.org
http://www.gsspa.org
Purpose: To support high school journalism students.
Eligibility: Applicants must be graduating New Jersey high school seniors who are nominated by a GSSPA member, have a GPA of 3.0 or higher and have participated in high school journalism for at least two years.
Target applicant(s): High school students.
Minimum GPA: 3.0
Amount: $2,000.
Number of awards: 1.
Deadline: February 7.
How to apply: Applications are available online. An application form, transcript, three or four letters of recommendation and portfolio with work samples are required.
Exclusive: Visit www.UltimateScholarshipBook.com and enter code GA124526 for updates on this award.

[1246] • Boeing Company STEM Scholarship
Independent Colleges of Washington
600 Stewart Street, Suite 600, Seattle, WA 98101
Phone: 206-623-4494
Email: scholarships@icwashington.org
https://icwashington.org/page/scholarships
Purpose: To assist students attending independent Washington colleges.
Eligibility: Applicants must be a junior or senior enrolled at an ICW member institution at the time of the award and be involved with community service. A GPA of 3.25 is required and applicants must be majoring in science, technology, engineering, mathematics, a health care field or be preparing to teach in a STEM field.
Target applicant(s): College students. Adult students.
Minimum GPA: 3.25
Amount: $2,000.
Number of awards: 2.
Deadline: April 12.
How to apply: Applications are available online. An application form, resume, essay, letter of recommendation and transcript are required.
Exclusive: Visit www.UltimateScholarshipBook.com and enter code IN124626 for updates on this award.

[1247] • Boettcher Foundation Scholarship
Boettcher Foundation
600 Seventeenth Street, Suite 2210 South, Denver, CO 80202-5422
Phone: 800-323-9640
Email: scholarships@boettcherfoundation.org
http://boettcherfoundation.org/
Purpose: To recognize dynamic thinkers, doers, and difference makers and encourage them to stay in Colorado for their education so they can positively impact their communities across our state.
Eligibility: Applicants must be graduating Colorado high school seniors who have lived in Colorado for their full junior and senior years of high school, graduates from a Colorado high school and be citizens, legal permanent residents or lawfully present in the United States or meet the requirements and have applied or started the process of applying for citizenship, legal status or lawful presence. They should submit applications, essays, transcripts and standardized test scores. Selection is based on academic merit, intellectual curiosity, demonstration of leadership skills, community service and character.
Target applicant(s): High school students.
Amount: Full tuition.
Number of awards: 50.
Scholarship may be renewable.
Deadline: November 1.
How to apply: Contact high school counselors for more information.
Exclusive: Visit www.UltimateScholarshipBook.com and enter code BO124726 for updates on this award.

[1248] • Bohdan Kolinsky Memorial Sports Journalism Scholarship
Connecticut Sports Writers Alliance
P.O. Box 70, Unionville, CT 06085-0070
Phone: 860-677-0087
Email: rbrtbarton@aol.com
http://www.ctsportswriters.com/
Purpose: To aid aspiring sports journalists.
Eligibility: Applicants must be Connecticut high school seniors, be admitted to an accredited four-year college and plan to pursue studies leading to a career in sports journalism. Students who meet academic standards can receive additional aid.
Target applicant(s): High school students.
Amount: $3,000.
Number of awards: 1.
Scholarship may be renewable.
Deadline: March 22.
How to apply: Applications are available online. An application form, essay, summary of academic and employment history, evidence of good academic standing, letter of recommendation and three samples of published work are required.
Exclusive: Visit www.UltimateScholarshipBook.com and enter code CO124826 for updates on this award.

[1249] • Booz Allen Hawaii Scholarship Fund
Hawaii Community Foundation - Scholarships
827 Fort Street Mall, Honolulu, HI 96813
Phone: 888-731-3863
Email: scholarships@hcf-hawaii.org
https://www.hawaiicommunityfoundation.org/
Purpose: To support undergraduate students in Hawaii.
Eligibility: Students must be residents of Hawaii or dependents of military members stationed there. Applicants must be attending or planning to attend a four-year college or university. Students must have at least a 3.0 GPA.
Target applicant(s): High school students. College students. Adult students.
Minimum GPA: 3.0
Amount: Varies.
Number of awards: Varies.
Deadline: February 28.
How to apply: To apply, register online, complete the online application and select the scholarships to which you wish to apply. In addition, mail the supporting materials: printed confirmation page from the online application, personal statement, copy of Student Aid Report (SAR) available at www.fafsa.ed.gov and official transcript.
Exclusive: Visit www.UltimateScholarshipBook.com and enter code HA124926 for updates on this award.

[1250] • Eagle Scout Scholarship
American Legion, Department of Illinois
P.O. Box 2910, Bloomington, IL 61702-2910
Phone: 309-663-0361
Email: hdqs@illegion.org
http://www.illegion.org/scholarships/
Purpose: To reward a member of the Scouts with a one-year scholarship.
Eligibility: Applicants must be graduating seniors in high school, Senior Scouts or Explorers and residents of Illinois. Students must write an essay on Americanism and/or Scout programs.
Target applicant(s): High school students.
Amount: Up to $1,000.
Number of awards: 3.
Deadline: April 15.
How to apply: Application information is available by contacting your local Scout office or American Legion Scout Chairman.
Exclusive: Visit www.UltimateScholarshipBook.com and enter code AM125026 for updates on this award.

[1251] • Builders Exchange of Billings Scholarship
Montana Community Foundation
P.O. Box 1145, Helena, MT 59624
Phone: 406-443-8313
Email: info@mtcf.org
https://mtcf.org/scholarships/about-scholarships
Purpose: To help students and support philanthropy throughout Montana by helping communities flourish and grow through supporting innovative solutions and creating powerful partnerships.
Eligibility: Applicants must be members of the Builders Exchange of Billings employed by a member or an immediate relation of a member or dependents. Students must be attending an accredited post-secondary educational institution public or private college, university, or college of technology. Applicant must submit essays each limited to 100 words.
Target applicant(s): College students. Adult students.
Minimum GPA: 2.0
Amount: $3,000.
Number of awards: 5.
Deadline: March.
How to apply: Applications are available online.
Exclusive: Visit www.UltimateScholarshipBook.com and enter code MO125126 for updates on this award.

[1252] • Business and Professional Women of Kentucky Foundation Grant
Kentucky Federation of Business and Professional Women
c/o Joanne Story, BPW/KY Foundation Scholarship Chair, 380 Beauchamp Boulevard, Somerset, KY 42503
Phone: 606-875-3200
Email: joanne.story@kctcs.edu
http://bpw-ky.org/
Purpose: To promote economic self-sufficiency for Kentucky women.
Eligibility: Applicants must be Kentucky residents who are at least 18 years of age. They must be employed or planning a career in the Kentucky workforce and attending an institution of higher learning. Individuals may receive a grant no more than once every 24 months.
Target applicant(s): High school students. College students. Adult students.
Amount: Varies.
Number of awards: Varies.
Deadline: April 30 and October 15.
How to apply: Applications are available online.
Exclusive: Visit www.UltimateScholarshipBook.com and enter code KE125226 for updates on this award.

[1253] • Business and Professional Women/Maine Continuing Education Scholarship
Futurama Foundation
c/o Marilyn Ladd, Office Manager, 103 County Road, Oakland, ME 04963
Email: mvladd@colby.edu
http://bpwmefoundation.org/scholarship-program/
Purpose: To provide financial assistance to female students.
Eligibility: Applicants must be Maine residents who have completed at least one year of college or will have done so by the end of the spring semester following application. They must be in good standing or on an approved leave of absence of one year or less at their educational institution. Financial need is required, and the student must have a definite plan to complete the program in which she is enrolled.
Target applicant(s): College students. Adult students.
Amount: $1,500.
Number of awards: Varies.
Deadline: April 13.
How to apply: Applications are available online.
Exclusive: Visit www.UltimateScholarshipBook.com and enter code FU125326 for updates on this award.

[1254] • Byers Scholarship
Keep Iowa Beautiful
300 E. Locust Street, Suite 100, Des Moines, IA 50309
Phone: 515-323-6507
https://keepiowabeautiful.org/grants-scholarships/
Purpose: To support Iowa high school seniors.
Eligibility: Applicants must be graduating high school seniors in Iowa who plan to enroll in an Iowa college or university to study environmental science, community development, landscape architecture, architecture, community planning or marketing and communications.
Target applicant(s): High school students.
Amount: $1,000.
Number of awards: 5.
Deadline: January 31.
How to apply: Applications are available online.
Exclusive: Visit www.UltimateScholarshipBook.com and enter code KE125426 for updates on this award.

[1255] • C. Bertrand and Marian Othmer Schultz Collegiate Scholarship
Nebraska Academy of Sciences Inc.
P.O. Box 22988, Lincoln, NE 68542-2988
Phone: 402-472-2644
Email: nebacad@unl.edu
https://nebraskaacademyofsciences.wildapricot.org/High-School-Scholarships
Purpose: To assist Nebraska college students who are majoring in a natural science.
Eligibility: Applicants must be sophomores or juniors who attend a four-year, accredited college or university in Nebraska and major in a natural

science including chemistry, physics, biology or geology. Students must plan to enter a career in a science-related industry, science teaching or scientific research.
Target applicant(s): College students. Adult students.
Amount: $1,500.
Number of awards: Varies.
Deadline: March 1.
How to apply: Applications are available online. A letter of nomination, transcript and letter describing the applicant's career plans are available.
Exclusive: Visit www.UltimateScholarshipBook.com and enter code NE125526 for updates on this award.

[1256] • Cal Grant A
California Student Aid Commission
Specialized Programs Operations Branch - Chafee, P.O. Box 419027, Rancho Cordova, CA 95741-9027
Phone: 888-224-7268
Email: studentsupport@csac.ca.gov
http://www.csac.ca.gov/
Purpose: To assist California students in obtaining higher education.
Eligibility: Applicants must be California residents who are attending or plan to attend an eligible California college or university pursuing at least two years of coursework. They must enroll for no less than half time and meet program income requirements. They may not have already earned a bachelor's degree or higher, and they must not be in default on a student loan or owe a grant repayment without having made satisfactory arrangements for repayment. Students with a GPA of 3.0 or higher who meet all requirements will receive an entitlement award, and students with a GPA of at least 2.4 may apply for a competitive award.
Target applicant(s): High school students. College students. Adult students.
Minimum GPA: 2.4
Amount: Up to $12,570.
Number of awards: Varies.
Scholarship may be renewable.
Deadline: March 2; September 2.
How to apply: Application materials are available online. A FAFSA and a GPA verification form are required.
Exclusive: Visit www.UltimateScholarshipBook.com and enter code CA125626 for updates on this award.

[1257] • Cal Grant B
California Student Aid Commission
Specialized Programs Operations Branch - Chafee, P.O. Box 419027, Rancho Cordova, CA 95741-9027
Phone: 888-224-7268
Email: studentsupport@csac.ca.gov
http://www.csac.ca.gov/
Purpose: To provide living expenses, tuition and fee assistance for low-income students.
Eligibility: Applicants must be California residents with financial need for attendance at an eligible California college or university. They must enroll for at least half time. A minimum GPA of 2.0 is required. Students who meet financial and eligibility requirements will receive a Cal Grant B entitlement award. Other eligible students can apply for a Cal Grant B competitive award. Competitive award selection is based on family income, education level of parents, GPA, time out of high school and special considerations.
Target applicant(s): High school students. College students. Adult students.
Minimum GPA: 2.0

Amount: Up to $10,868.
Number of awards: Varies.
Scholarship may be renewable.
Deadline: March 2; September 2.
How to apply: Application materials are available online. A FAFSA and a GPA verification form are required.
Exclusive: Visit www.UltimateScholarshipBook.com and enter code CA125726 for updates on this award.

[1258] • Cal Grant C
California Student Aid Commission
Specialized Programs Operations Branch - Chafee, P.O. Box 419027, Rancho Cordova, CA 95741-9027
Phone: 888-224-7268
Email: studentsupport@csac.ca.gov
http://www.csac.ca.gov/
Purpose: To aid students participating in occupational and vocational programs.
Eligibility: Applicants must be California residents. They must enroll in a vocational program at a California community college, independent college or vocational school that is at least four months long. Funds may be received for up to two years. Eligible students will receive an application by mail from the California Student Aid Commission.
Target applicant(s): High school students. College students. Adult students.
Amount: Up to $14,218.
Number of awards: Varies.
Scholarship may be renewable.
Deadline: March 2; September 2.
How to apply: Applications are available by mail. A FAFSA and an application form are required.
Exclusive: Visit www.UltimateScholarshipBook.com and enter code CA125826 for updates on this award.

[1259] • Cal Grant Entitlement Award
California Student Aid Commission
Specialized Programs Operations Branch - Chafee, P.O. Box 419027, Rancho Cordova, CA 95741-9027
Phone: 888-224-7268
Email: studentsupport@csac.ca.gov
http://www.csac.ca.gov/
Purpose: To support California resident students.
Eligibility: Applicants must complete the Free Application for Federal Student Aid (FAFSA) and file a verified grade point average with the California Student Aid Commission. Students must be California residents, be U.S. citizens or eligible noncitizens, meet U.S. Selective Service requirements, attend an eligible California postsecondary institution, be enrolled at least half-time, maintain satisfactory academic progress and not be in default on any student loan. Cal Grant A Entitlement Awards are for undergraduate institutions of not less than two academic years. Cal Grant B Entitlement Awards are for low-income students for living and transportation expenses, supplies and books at institutions of not less than one year. Cal Grant C Awards are for occupational or vocational programs. Cal Grant T Awards are for teacher credential candidates.
Target applicant(s): High school students. College students. Adult students.
Amount: Varies.
Number of awards: Varies.
Deadline: March 2.
How to apply: Applications are available by request.

Exclusive: Visit www.UltimateScholarshipBook.com and enter code CA125926 for updates on this award.

[1260] • California - Hawaii Elks Major Project Undergraduate Scholarship Program for Students with Disabilities

California-Hawaii Elks Association
5450 E. Lamona Avenue, Fresno, CA 93727-2224
Phone: 559-255-4531
Email: chea@chea-elks.org
https://chea-elks.org/youth-activities/scholarships
Purpose: To provide education assistance for students with disabilities.
Eligibility: Applicants must be U.S. citizens and California or Hawaii residents who have a physical, neurological, visual or hearing impairment or a speech/language disorder. They must be high school seniors or graduates or have passed the GED or California High School Proficiency Examination.
Target applicant(s): High school students.
Amount: $1,000-$2,000.
Number of awards: 20-30.
Scholarship may be renewable.
Deadline: March 15.
How to apply: Applications are available online.
Exclusive: Visit www.UltimateScholarshipBook.com and enter code CA126026 for updates on this award.

[1261] • California Fee Waiver Program for Children of Veterans

California Department of Veterans Affairs
1227 O Street, Sacramento, CA 95814
Phone: 800-952-5626
https://www.calvet.ca.gov
Purpose: To provide educational assistance for dependents of veterans.
Eligibility: Applicants must be the children, spouses, unmarried surviving spouses or registered domestic partners of veterans who are deceased or totally disabled due to service-related causes. The veteran must have served during a qualifying war period, and the child must be under 27 years of age (30 if the child is a veteran). There is no age limit for spouses or domestic partners. Children of veterans who have a service-connected disability, had one at the time of death or died of service-related causes may qualify if their income is at or below the national poverty level. In this case, there is no age limit.
Target applicant(s): High school students. College students. Adult students.
Amount: Full tuition.
Number of awards: Varies.
Scholarship may be renewable.
Deadline: Contact the sponsor to confirm the deadline.
How to apply: Applications are available online.
Exclusive: Visit www.UltimateScholarshipBook.com and enter code CA126126 for updates on this award.

[1262] • California Fee Waiver Program for Dependents of Deceased or Disabled National Guard Members

California Department of Veterans Affairs
1227 O Street, Sacramento, CA 95814
Phone: 800-952-5626
https://www.calvet.ca.gov
Purpose: To provide education assistance to dependents of deceased or disabled National Guard members.
Eligibility: Applicants must be dependents or surviving spouses or domestic partners of California National Guard members who were killed or permanently disabled during active duty in service to the state. Spouses or domestic partners must not have remarried or terminated the relationship.
Target applicant(s): High school students. College students. Adult students.
Amount: Full tuition.
Number of awards: Varies.
Scholarship may be renewable.
Deadline: Contact the sponsor to confirm the deadline.
How to apply: Applications are available online.
Exclusive: Visit www.UltimateScholarshipBook.com and enter code CA126226 for updates on this award.

[1263] • California Fee Waiver Program for Recipients of the Medal of Honor and Their Children

California Department of Veterans Affairs
1227 O Street, Sacramento, CA 95814
Phone: 800-952-5626
https://www.calvet.ca.gov
Purpose: To provide financial assistance for Medal of Honor recipients and their families.
Eligibility: Applicants must be Medal of Honor recipients, their children or dependents of a Registered Domestic Partner. Children must meet age, income and residency requirements. This award is only applicable toward undergraduate studies.
Target applicant(s): High school students. College students. Adult students.
Amount: Full tuition.
Number of awards: Varies.
Scholarship may be renewable.
Deadline: Contact the sponsor to confirm the deadline.
How to apply: Applications are available online.
Exclusive: Visit www.UltimateScholarshipBook.com and enter code CA126326 for updates on this award.

[1264] • California Freethought Day High School Essay Scholarship

California Freethought Day
P.O. Box 15464, Sacramento, CA 95851
Phone: 209-610-0651
Email: scholarships@FreethoughtDay.org
https://freethoughtday.org/programs/scholarships/
Purpose: To encourage California students to pursue reason.
Eligibility: Applicants must be California high school students in grades 9-12 who plan to pursue post-secondary education. Students must demonstrate involvement in community organizations and school clubs and have an interest in free speech, science and the separation of church and state. Applicants must write an essay pertaining to fake news.
Target applicant(s): High school students.
Amount: $1,000.
Number of awards: 1.
Deadline: September 16.
How to apply: Applications are available online.
Exclusive: Visit www.UltimateScholarshipBook.com and enter code CA126426 for updates on this award.

[1265] • California Health Sciences Scholarships
Great Minds in STEM (HENAAC)
5211 East Washington Boulevard, Suite 2-320, Los Angeles, CA 90040
Email: info@greatmindsinstem.org
http://www.greatmindsinstem.org
Purpose: To support underrepresented students in California pursuing undergraduate degrees in health-related fields.
Eligibility: Applicants must be U.S. citizens, permanent residents or have Deferred Action for Childhood Arrival (DACA) status. Students must be pursuing a health-related undergraduate degree from an accredited institution in the United States or Puerto Rico with a minimum 3.0 GPA. Applicants must be members of a traditionally underrepresented group in the health sciences. Preference will be given to students pursuing careers in the areas of mental health, rehabilitative, geriatric medical specialties or individuals with disabilities.
Target applicant(s): High school students. College students. Adult students.
Minimum GPA: 3.0
Amount: $1,000.
Number of awards: 1.
Deadline: April 30.
How to apply: Applications are available online.
Exclusive: Visit www.UltimateScholarshipBook.com and enter code GR126526 for updates on this award.

[1266] • California Law Enforcement Personnel Dependents Grant Program
California Student Aid Commission
Specialized Programs Operations Branch - Chafee, P.O. Box 419027, Rancho Cordova, CA 95741-9027
Phone: 888-224-7268
Email: studentsupport@csac.ca.gov
http://www.csac.ca.gov/
Purpose: To provide assistance for the families of deceased or disabled law enforcement personnel.
Eligibility: Applicants must be spouses or children of California peace officers, Department of Corrections or Youth Authority employees or full-time firefighters who were killed or totally disabled due to accident or injury in the line of duty. They must enroll at an accredited California community college, college or university for a minimum of six units. Financial need is required. Awards match the amount of a Cal Grant award.
Target applicant(s): High school students. College students. Adult students.
Amount: $100-$12,192.
Number of awards: Varies.
Scholarship may be renewable.
Deadline: June 30.
How to apply: Applications are available by mail or phone. An application form, copy of FAFSA Student Aid Report and documentation of the law enforcement personnel's death or injury are required.
Exclusive: Visit www.UltimateScholarshipBook.com and enter code CA126626 for updates on this award.

[1267] • California Masonic Foundation Scholarship
California Masonic Foundation
1111 California Street, San Francisco, CA 94108-2284
Phone: 415-776-7000
Email: foundation@californiamasons.org
https://freemason.org/masonic-charities/scholarships/
Purpose: To aid students in pursuit of a higher education.
Eligibility: Applicants must be U.S. citizens, be California residents for at least one year, be current high school seniors with a minimum 3.0 GPA, plan to attend an accredited two- or four-year college or university full-time and demonstrate financial need. There are a number of awards based on residence, career goals and general selection criteria.
Target applicant(s): High school students.
Minimum GPA: 3.0
Amount: Varies.
Number of awards: Varies.
Scholarship may be renewable.
Deadline: January 15.
How to apply: Applications are available online.
Exclusive: Visit www.UltimateScholarshipBook.com and enter code CA126726 for updates on this award.

[1268] • California Oratorical Contest
American Legion, Department of California
1601 7th Street, Sanger, CA 93657
Phone: 415-431-2400
Email: calegion@pacific.net
http://www.calegion.org
Purpose: To enhance high school students' experience with and understanding of the U.S. Constitution. The contest will help develop students' leadership skills and civic appreciation, as well as the ability to deliver thoughtful, insightful orations regarding U.S. citizenship and its inherent responsibilities.
Eligibility: Applicants must be high school students under the age of 20 who are U.S. citizens or legal residents and residents of the state. Students first give an oration within their state and winners compete at the national level. The oration must be related to the Constitution of the United States focusing on the duties and obligations citizens have to the government. It must be in English and be between eight and ten minutes. There is also an assigned topic which is posted on the website, and it should be between three and five minutes.
Target applicant(s): Junior high students or younger. High school students.
Amount: $1,500-$18,000.
Number of awards: Varies.
Deadline: February 25.
How to apply: Applications are available by email.
Exclusive: Visit www.UltimateScholarshipBook.com and enter code AM126826 for updates on this award.

[1269] • California Restaurant Association Educational Foundation General Scholarship
California Restaurant Association
621 Capitol Mall, Suite 2000, Sacramento, CA 95814
Phone: 800-765-4842
Email: craef@calrest.org
https://calrestfoundation.org/scholarships/
Purpose: To aid students with restaurant work experience.
Eligibility: Applicants must be high school seniors or college undergraduates who are California residents and U.S. citizens or permanent residents and be enrolled in at least nine credit hours at an accredited institution of higher learning and have a GPA of 2.5 or higher. Students must plan to enroll in two consecutive semesters and have at least 250 hours of work experience in the restaurant industry.
Target applicant(s): High school students. College students. Adult students.
Minimum GPA: 2.5

The Ultimate Scholarship Book 2026
Scholarship Directory (State of Residence)

Amount: Up to $4,000.
Number of awards: Varies.
Deadline: May 1.
How to apply: Applications are available online. An application form, essay, copy of curriculum, transcript, proof of work experience and one to three letters of recommendation are required.
Exclusive: Visit www.UltimateScholarshipBook.com and enter code CA126926 for updates on this award.

[1270] • California State PTA Volunteer Service Scholarship

California State PTA
2327 L Street, Sacramento, CA 95816-5014
Phone: 916-440-1985
Email: grants@capta.org
http://capta.org/programs-events/scholarships/
Purpose: To support high school seniors who have contributed to the community.
Eligibility: Applicants must attend a public California high school, be high school seniors who have served their school and community and be members of the PTA.
Target applicant(s): High school students.
Amount: $500.
Number of awards: 60.
Deadline: June 1.
How to apply: Applications are available online.
Exclusive: Visit www.UltimateScholarshipBook.com and enter code CA127026 for updates on this award.

[1271] • Candon, Todd and Seabolt Scholarship Fund

Hawaii Community Foundation - Scholarships
827 Fort Street Mall, Honolulu, HI 96813
Phone: 888-731-3863
Email: scholarships@hcf-hawaii.org
https://www.hawaiicommunityfoundation.org/
Purpose: To support Hawaii students who are majoring in accounting or finance.
Eligibility: Students must be in their junior or senior year of college with at least a 3.2 GPA.
Target applicant(s): College students. Adult students.
Minimum GPA: 3.2
Amount: Varies.
Number of awards: Varies.
Deadline: January 31.
How to apply: To apply, register online, complete the online application and select the scholarships to which you wish to apply. In addition, mail the supporting materials: printed confirmation page from the online application, personal statement, copy of Student Aid Report (SAR) available at www.fafsa.ed.gov and official transcript.
Exclusive: Visit www.UltimateScholarshipBook.com and enter code HA127126 for updates on this award.

[1272] • CAPED Excellence Scholarship

California Association for Postsecondary Education and Disability
19197 Golden Valley Road #521, Santa Clarita, CA 91387
Phone: 909-384-8663
Email: caped.scholarship.committee@gmail.com
http://www.caped.co/scholarships/
Purpose: To provide financial assistance to high achievers in academics, community and campus life.
Eligibility: Applicants must have a verifiable disability and demonstrate financial need. A minimum GPA of 2.5 is required for undergraduates and a minimum GPA of 3.0 for graduate students. Applicants must be taking at least six semester units or four quarter units at a public or private California institution of higher learning.
Target applicant(s): High school students. College students. Graduate school students. Adult students.
Minimum GPA: 2.5 for undergraduate students; 3.0 for graduate students
Amount: $1,500.
Number of awards: 1.
Deadline: August 31.
How to apply: Applications are available online.
Exclusive: Visit www.UltimateScholarshipBook.com and enter code CA127226 for updates on this award.

[1273] • CAPPS Memorial Scholarship Program

California Association of Private Postsecondary Schools
2121 Natomas Crossing Drive, Suite 200-442, Sacramento, CA 95834
Phone: 916-447-5500
Email: info@cappsonline.org
https://cappsonline.org/memorial-scholarships/
Purpose: To allow private postsecondary schools to offer tuition scholarships to students.
Eligibility: Applicants must be legal California residents who have fulfilled the admission requirements for the school that is pledging their CAPPS scholarship. Application is restricted to high school and adult students only. Recipients are chosen on the basis of application date and each individual school's judging standards.
Target applicant(s): High school students. College students. Adult students.
Amount: Varies.
Number of awards: 5.
Deadline: July 15.
How to apply: Applications are available online.
Exclusive: Visit www.UltimateScholarshipBook.com and enter code CA127326 for updates on this award.

[1274] • Career Advancement Scholarship

Futurama Foundation
c/o Marilyn Ladd, Office Manager, 103 County Road, Oakland, ME 04963
Email: mvladd@colby.edu
http://bpwmefoundation.org/scholarship-program/
Purpose: To provide financial assistance for women who want to advance their careers.
Eligibility: Applicants must be female Maine residents who are age 30 or older. They must need financial assistance to improve their skills or complete education for career advancement. They must have a definite plan to use their training to improve their chances of advancement, train for a new career or to enter or reenter the job market. Applicants must be officially accepted into their course of study or program.
Target applicant(s): College students. Adult students.
Amount: $2,500.
Number of awards: 1.
Deadline: April 13.
How to apply: Applications are available from your local BPW chapter or your financial aid office.
Exclusive: Visit www.UltimateScholarshipBook.com and enter code FU127426 for updates on this award.

[1275] • Career Based Scholarship
Delaware Department of Education - School Supports
The Townsend Building, 401 Federal Street, Suite 2, Dover, DE 19901-3639
Phone: 800-292-7935
Email: dhec@doe.k12.de.us
https://scholarships.delawarestudentsuccess.org/
Purpose: To support academically-talented Delaware student residents.
Eligibility: Applicants must be full-time undergraduate students enrolled in a bachelor's degree program in a Delaware public or private college in a major leading to a career in a high-need field in Delaware. Students must be residents of Delaware, U.S. citizens or eligible non-citizens enrolled on a full-time basis and who meet their institution's satisfactory academic policy.
Target applicant(s): High school students. College students. Adult students.
Amount: $5,000.
Number of awards: 1.
Deadline: May 15.
How to apply: Applications are available online.
Exclusive: Visit www.UltimateScholarshipBook.com and enter code DE127526 for updates on this award.

[1276] • Career Colleges and Schools of Texas Scholarship Program
Career Colleges and Schools of Texas
Lisa Tomsio, 823 Congress Avenue, Suite 230, Austin, TX 78701
Phone: 512-402-7797
Email: scholars@careerscholarships.org
http://ccst.org/
Purpose: To help Texas high school seniors who want to attend trade or technical schools in the state.
Eligibility: Participating institutions, which are listed on the website, provide scholarships to students who choose to enroll at their schools. Since each school has its own guidelines, applicants should contact a particular school for more information.
Target applicant(s): High school students.
Amount: $1,000.
Number of awards: Varies.
Deadline: Contact the sponsor to confirm the deadline.
How to apply: Applicants should contact their high school counselors or participating schools.
Exclusive: Visit www.UltimateScholarshipBook.com and enter code CA127626 for updates on this award.

[1277] • Cash Grant Program
Massachusetts Department of Higher Education
Office of Student Financial Assistance, 454 Broadway, Suite 200, Revere, MA 02151
Phone: 617-727-9420
Email: osfa@osfa.mass.edu
https://www.mass.gov/handbook/massachusetts-financial-aid-programs
Purpose: To help needy students pay college or university fees and non-state-supported tuition.
Eligibility: Students must be permanent residents of Massachusetts for at least one year before the academic year for which the grant is awarded. Students must also demonstrate financial need, be enrolled in at least three credits per semester in an eligible undergraduate program and not have previously earned a bachelor's degree or higher.
Target applicant(s): High school students. College students. Adult students.
Amount: Up to full tuition.
Number of awards: Varies.
Scholarship may be renewable.
Deadline: Contact the sponsor to confirm the deadline.
How to apply: Applications are available from your financial aid office.
Exclusive: Visit www.UltimateScholarshipBook.com and enter code MA127726 for updates on this award.

[1278] • Categorical Tuition Waiver
Massachusetts Department of Higher Education
Office of Student Financial Assistance, 454 Broadway, Suite 200, Revere, MA 02151
Phone: 617-727-9420
Email: osfa@osfa.mass.edu
https://www.mass.gov/handbook/massachusetts-financial-aid-programs
Purpose: To provide financial support to Massachusetts students who would otherwise not be able to afford higher education.
Eligibility: Applicants must be residents of the state of Massachusetts for at least one year prior to the beginning of the academic year in which the scholarship is used. They also must be members of one of the following groups of people: veterans or active members of the armed forces, Native Americans, senior citizens or clients of either the Massachusetts Rehabilitation Commission or Commission for the Blind. Students must be enrolled in at least three credits per semester in a state undergraduate or certificate program, and they must remain in satisfactory academic standing.
Target applicant(s): High school students. College students. Adult students.
Amount: Up to full tuition.
Number of awards: Varies.
Deadline: Contact the sponsor to confirm the deadline.
How to apply: Applications are available at college financial aid offices.
Exclusive: Visit www.UltimateScholarshipBook.com and enter code MA127826 for updates on this award.

[1279] • Cathay Bank Foundation Scholarship
Asian Pacific Community Fund
1145 Wilshire Boulevard, Suite 105, Los Angeles, CA 90017
Phone: 213-624-6400
Email: scholarships@apcf.org
https://www.apcf.org/scholarships
Purpose: To assist low-income students to pursue higher education.
Eligibility: Applicants must be high school seniors residing in California, Illinois, Maryland, Massachusetts, Nevada, New Jersey, New York, Texas or Washington who are enrolling as first-year students in an accredited four-year college in one of the listed states of residency. Students must have a minimum GPA of 3.0 and have a household income that falls at or below the low-income level. There is no ethnicity requirement.
Target applicant(s): High school students.
Minimum GPA: 3.0
Amount: $2,500.
Number of awards: Up to 20.
Deadline: April 15.
How to apply: Applications are available online.
Exclusive: Visit www.UltimateScholarshipBook.com and enter code AS127926 for updates on this award.

[1280] • CCCAM Scholarships
Competitive Cheer Coaches Association of Michigan
5675 N. Division, Comstock Park, MI 49321
Email: scholarship@cccam.org
https://www.cccam.org/awards/scholarship/
Purpose: To support the pursuit of higher education by competitive cheer athletes.
Eligibility: Applicants must be graduating seniors, be current members of Michigan High School Athletic Association (MHSAA) competitive cheer teams and have a minimum GPA of 3.5 through their junior year. The applicant's cheer team must compete in the annual Scholarship Invitational and the team coach must be a current CCCAM member.
Target applicant(s): High school students.
Minimum GPA: 3.5
Amount: Varies.
Number of awards: Varies.
Deadline: February 11.
How to apply: Applications are available online and must be completed and mailed in with the applicant's short essay, a sealed copy of the high school transcript and two letters of recommendation.
Exclusive: Visit www.UltimateScholarshipBook.com and enter code CO128026 for updates on this award.

[1281] • CDM Constructors Inc. Workforce Development Scholarship
CDM Constructors Inc. Workforce Development Scholarship
Scholarship America, One Scholarship Way, Saint Peter, MN 56082
Phone: 800-537-4180
Email: cdmconstructors@scholarshipamerica.org
https://learnmore.scholarsapply.org/cdmconstructors/
Purpose: To encourage students who plan to continue their education in college or vocational school programs.
Eligibility: Applicants must be high school seniors, high school graduates or current postsecondary undergraduates who plan to enroll full-time in an eligible undergraduate program at an accredited two-year college or vocational technical school. Students must reside or attend school in one of the following states: Texas, California or Florida. Applicants must have a minimum 2.5 GPA. Students must enroll in one of the following eligible majors: electrical, automation, instrumentation and controls, cybersecurity or related discipline.
Target applicant(s): High school students. College students. Adult students.
Minimum GPA: 2.5
Amount: $5,000.
Number of awards: 2.
Deadline: March 7.
How to apply: Applications are available online.
Exclusive: Visit www.UltimateScholarshipBook.com and enter code CD128126 for updates on this award.

[1282] • Central Arizona DX Association Scholarship
American Radio Relay League Foundation
225 Main Street, Newington, CT 06111-1494
Phone: 860-594-0200
Email: foundation@arrl.org
https://www.arrl.org/scholarship-program
Purpose: To provide scholarship assistance to amateur radio operators from Arizona.
Eligibility: Applicants must be Arizona residents with a Technician Class or higher Amateur Radio License. They must have a GPA of 3.2 or higher. Graduating high school seniors receive preference over current college students.
Target applicant(s): High school students. College students. Adult students.
Minimum GPA: 3.2
Amount: $1,000.
Number of awards: 1.
Deadline: January 10.
How to apply: Applications are available online.
Exclusive: Visit www.UltimateScholarshipBook.com and enter code AM128226 for updates on this award.

[1283] • Certificate, License or Other Industry-Recognized Credential
New Hampshire Charitable Foundation
37 Pleasant Street, Concord, NH 03301-4005
Phone: 603-225-6641
Email: jessica.kierstead@nhcf.org
https://www.nhcf.org/how-can-we-help-you/
Purpose: To support students who are pursuing short-term vocational or technical studies.
Eligibility: Applicants must be residents of New Hampshire and be pursuing a certificate, license or other credential in vocational or technical fields such as: automotive technology, plumbing, construction, heating, advanced manufacturing, computer repair, licensed nursing, etc. Preference is given to students whose fields are in the traditional manufacturing trade sector, who have a clear vision of how their education will improve their career goals and who have had little or no other educational training opportunities.
Target applicant(s): College students. Adult students.
Amount: Varies.
Number of awards: Varies.
Deadline: December 13.
How to apply: Applications are available online.
Exclusive: Visit www.UltimateScholarshipBook.com and enter code NE128326 for updates on this award.

[1284] • CESDA Diversity Scholarship
Colorado Educational Services and Development Association
P.O. Box 40214, Denver, CO 80204
Phone: 303-352-3231
Email: questions@cesda.org
https://www.cesda.org/scholarships
Purpose: To provide financial assistance for disadvantaged students.
Eligibility: Applicants must be either first generation college students, members of underrepresented ethnic or racial minorities or show financial need. They must be Colorado residents who are high school seniors at the time of application. Students must have a GPA of 2.8 or higher and enroll in a two- or four-year Colorado college or university in the fall following graduation. They must take at least six credit hours to qualify.
Target applicant(s): High school students.
Minimum GPA: 2.8
Amount: $1,000.
Number of awards: 7.
Deadline: February 15.
How to apply: Applications are available online.
Exclusive: Visit www.UltimateScholarshipBook.com and enter code CO128426 for updates on this award.

[1285] • CEW+ Scholarships
Center for the Education of Women+
330 East Liberty Street, Ann Arbor, MI 48104
Phone: 734-998-7080
Email: contactcew@umich.edu
http://www.cew.umich.edu/
Purpose: To support women who are returning to college after an interruption.
Eligibility: Applicants must be women who are returning to school. For undergraduates one of the following must be met: a minimum 2 year (24 month) consecutive interruption in education anytime since high school, primary caregiver for a minor, older adult or disabled adult or actively engaged in F.E.M.M.E.S., GEECS, SWE, WISE or WISE-RP and working towards a STEM degree. For graduate students one of the following must be met: a minimum 5 year (60 month) consecutive interruption in education anytime since high school, primary caregiver for a minor, older adult or disabled adult or actively engaged in F.E.M.M.E.S., GEECS, SWE, WISE or WISE-RP and working towards a STEM degree. Candidates must be working toward a clear educational goal at any University of Michigan campus. Preference is given to women wishing to study in non-traditional fields such as mathematics, physical sciences and engineering.
Target applicant(s): Graduate school students. Adult students.
Amount: $1,000-$11,000.
Number of awards: Over 70.
Deadline: May 7.
How to apply: Applications are available online.
Exclusive: Visit www.UltimateScholarshipBook.com and enter code CE128526 for updates on this award.

[1286] • Charles Dubose Scholarship
Connecticut Architecture Foundation
370 James Street, Suite 402, New Haven, CT 06513
Phone: 203-865-2195
Email: ctarchfoundation@gmail.com
https://cafct.org/
Purpose: To assist architecture students.
Eligibility: Applicants must have completed two years of an NAAB accredited architecture program leading to a bachelor's degree as of June 30 of the year of application. Students enrolled in non-accredited programs who have been accepted to an NAAB accredited master's degree program, as well as those currently enrolled in such a program, are also eligible. Applicants must be full-time students. Preference is given to students at the University of Pennsylvania, Georgia Institute of Technology and Fontainebleau summer program and to Connecticut residents.
Target applicant(s): College students. Graduate school students. Adult students.
Amount: $1,200-$5,000.
Number of awards: Varies.
Deadline: April 22.
How to apply: Applications are available online. An application form, statement of goals, resume, financial aid information sheet, two letters of reference and submission of a favorite project are required.
Exclusive: Visit www.UltimateScholarshipBook.com and enter code CO128626 for updates on this award.

[1287] • Charles L. Hebner Memorial Scholarship
Delaware Department of Education - School Supports
The Townsend Building, 401 Federal Street, Suite 2, Dover, DE 19901-3639
Phone: 800-292-7935
Email: dhec@doe.k12.de.us
https://scholarships.delawarestudentsuccess.org/
Purpose: To support academically-talented Delaware student residents.
Eligibility: Applicants must be residents of Delaware, U.S. citizens or eligible non-citizens, high school seniors who rank in the upper quarter of their class and score a minimum of 1290 on the SAT and enroll as full-time students in a degree program at a regionally accredited college.
Target applicant(s): High school students.
Amount: $1,250.
Number of awards: 30.
Scholarship may be renewable.
Deadline: February 23.
How to apply: Applications are available online.
Exclusive: Visit www.UltimateScholarshipBook.com and enter code DE128726 for updates on this award.

[1288] • Charles W. and Annette Hill Scholarship
American Legion, Department of Kansas
1314 SW Topeka Boulevard, Topeka, KS 66612
Phone: 785-232-9315
https://kansaslegion.org/
Purpose: To provide financial assistance to needy and worthy children of members of the American Legion.
Eligibility: Applicants must be descendants of an American Legion member with a GPA of at least 3.0. Special consideration will be given to students studying science, engineering or business administration. Applicants must submit three letters of recommendation with only one from a teacher, an essay on "Why I Want to Go to College," a high school transcript, documentation of parent's veteran status and a 1040 income statement. Applicants must maintain a 3.0 GPA in college and verify enrollment at the start of each semester.
Target applicant(s): High school students. College students. Adult students.
Minimum GPA: 3.0
Amount: $1,000.
Number of awards: 1.
Scholarship may be renewable.
Deadline: February 15.
How to apply: Applications are available online.
Exclusive: Visit www.UltimateScholarshipBook.com and enter code AM128826 for updates on this award.

[1289] • Charles W. Riley Fire and Emergency Medical Services Scholarship Program
Maryland Higher Education Commission
Office of Student Financial Assistance, 6 North Liberty Street, Baltimore, MD 21201
Phone: 800-974-1024
Email: osfamail@mhec.state.md.us
https://mhec.maryland.gov
Purpose: To support Maryland students who are majoring and working in firefighting or emergency medical services fields.
Eligibility: Applicants must be active firefighters, ambulance or rescue squad members living and serving in the state of Maryland. Students must attend a Maryland college majoring in fire service technology or emergency medical technology. They must continue to serve throughout college and for one year after graduating.
Target applicant(s): College students. Adult students.
Minimum GPA: 2.5
Amount: At least 1/2 tuition and fees.

The Ultimate Scholarship Book 2026
Scholarship Directory (State of Residence)

Number of awards: Varies.
Scholarship may be renewable.
Deadline: May 1.
How to apply: Applications are available online.
Exclusive: Visit www.UltimateScholarshipBook.com and enter code MA128926 for updates on this award.

[1290] • Chick and Sophie Major Memorial Duck Calling Contest
Stuttgart Arkansas Chamber of Commerce
P.O. Box 1500, 507 S. Main, Stuttgart, AR 72160
Phone: 870-673-1602
Email: stuttgartchamber@centurytel.net
https://stuttgartchamber.com/
Purpose: To assist students who win the duck calling contest.
Eligibility: Applicants must be graduating high school seniors and participate in the annual competition that occurs in Stuttgart, Arkansas.
Target applicant(s): High school students.
Amount: $750-$5,000.
Number of awards: 4.
Deadline: November 24.
How to apply: Details on the competition are available online.
Exclusive: Visit www.UltimateScholarshipBook.com and enter code ST129026 for updates on this award.

[1291] • Children and Youth Scholarships
American Legion, Department of Maine
5 Verti Drive, Winslow, ME 04901-0727
Phone: 207-873-3229
Email: legionme@mainelegion.org
http://www.mainelegion.org/pages/programs/scholarships.php
Purpose: To provide financial support to Maine students.
Eligibility: Applicants must be high school seniors or college students attending or planning to attend an accredited college or vocational school. Applicants must also demonstrate financial need and include two letters of recommendation and a personal statement.
Target applicant(s): High school students. College students. Adult students.
Amount: $500.
Number of awards: 7.
Deadline: May 1.
How to apply: Applications are available online.
Exclusive: Visit www.UltimateScholarshipBook.com and enter code AM129126 for updates on this award.

[1292] • Chiropractic Education Assistance Scholarship
Oklahoma State Regents for Higher Education/Chiropractic Education Assistance Scholarship
655 Research Parkway, Suite 200, Oklahoma City, OK 73104
Phone: 800-858-1840
Email: studentinfo@osrhe.edu
https://secure.okcollegestart.org/Financial_Aid_Planning/Scholarships/Career_Scholarships/Chiropractic_Education_Assistance_Scholarship.aspx
Purpose: To support Oklahoma state residents pursuing chiropractic studies at accredited out-of-state schools.
Eligibility: Applicants must be residents of the state of Oklahoma who have lived in Oklahoma for at least the past five years who are either enrolled or accepted at an accredited school for chiropractic study. Students must have a 3.0 GPA.
Target applicant(s): High school students. College students. Adult students.
Minimum GPA: 3.0
Amount: Up to $6,000.
Number of awards: Varies.
Scholarship may be renewable.
Deadline: May 31.
How to apply: Applications are available online.
Exclusive: Visit www.UltimateScholarshipBook.com and enter code OK129226 for updates on this award.

[1293] • Choose Ohio First Scholarship
Ohio Department of Higher Education
25 South Front Street, Columbus, OH 43215
Phone: 888-833-1133
Email: lreed@highered.ohio.gov
https://highered.ohio.gov/
Purpose: To support Ohio students interested in STEM disciplines and education.
Eligibility: Applicants must be Ohio residents enrolled in full-time or part-time studies seeking undergraduate or graduate degrees or certificates in an eligible STEM field. Students must major in one of the eligible COF programs of study at a participating school.
Target applicant(s): High school students. College students. Graduate school students. Adult students.
Amount: Up to $8,000.
Number of awards: 4,000.
Deadline: Contact the sponsor to confirm the deadline.
How to apply: Applications are available online.
Exclusive: Visit www.UltimateScholarshipBook.com and enter code OH129326 for updates on this award.

[1294] • Christian A. Herter Memorial Scholarship Program
Massachusetts Department of Higher Education
Office of Student Financial Assistance, 454 Broadway, Suite 200, Revere, MA 02151
Phone: 617-727-9420
Email: osfa@osfa.mass.edu
https://www.mass.gov/handbook/massachusetts-financial-aid-programs
Purpose: To provide educational opportunities to Massachusetts students who demonstrate academic promise and a desire to attend post-secondary institutions.
Eligibility: Applicants must be enrolled in a public or private secondary school in the Commonwealth of Massachusetts and be legal residents of the state. Applicants must have a cumulative grade point average of 2.5 and exhibit difficult personal circumstances, high financial need and strong academic promise to continue education beyond the secondary level.
Target applicant(s): High school students.
Minimum GPA: 2.5
Amount: Varies.
Number of awards: Varies.
Scholarship may be renewable.
Deadline: April 12.
How to apply: Applications are available online.
Exclusive: Visit www.UltimateScholarshipBook.com and enter code MA129426 for updates on this award.

[1295] • CIF Scholar-Athlete of the Year
California Interscholastic Federation (CIF)
CIF State Office, Attn.: CIF Scholar-Athlete of the Year, 4658 Duckhorn Drive, Sacramento, CA 95834
Phone: 916-239-4477
Email: info@cifstate.org
http://www.cifstate.org/parents-students/awards_and_scholarships/index
Purpose: To recognize high school student-athletes with exemplary academic and athletic careers and personal standards.
Eligibility: Applicants must be high school seniors with a minimum 3.5 GPA, demonstrate outstanding athletic performance in a minimum of two years of varsity play in California and exhibit character, trustworthiness, respect, responsibility, fairness, caring and citizenship.
Target applicant(s): High school students.
Minimum GPA: 3.5
Amount: $10,000.
Number of awards: 2.
Deadline: March 4.
How to apply: Applications are available by request.
Exclusive: Visit www.UltimateScholarshipBook.com and enter code CA129526 for updates on this award.

[1296] • Clair A. Hill Scholarship
Association of California Water Agencies
980 9th Street, Suite 1000, Sacramento, CA 95814
Phone: 916-441-4545
Email: awards@acwa.com
http://www.acwa.com
Purpose: To support California undergraduates pursuing degrees in a water resources-related subject.
Eligibility: Applicants must be California residents who are rising juniors or seniors at a participating postsecondary institution located in California. They must be pursuing an undergraduate degree in a water resources-related subject and be full-time students enrolled for the entirety of the upcoming school year. Selection is based on professional commitment to the water resources field, academic achievement and financial need.
Target applicant(s): College students. Adult students.
Amount: $5,000.
Number of awards: 1.
Deadline: March 1.
How to apply: Applications are available online. An application form, personal essay, transcript and two to three letters of recommendation are required.
Exclusive: Visit www.UltimateScholarshipBook.com and enter code AS129626 for updates on this award.

[1297] • Clanseer and Anna Johnson Scholarships
Community Foundation of New Jersey
P.O. Box 338, Morristown, NJ 07963-0338
Phone: 973-267-5533
Email: info@cfnj.org
https://cfnj.org/current-funds/student-scholarships/
Purpose: To provide education assistance for disadvantaged African American students.
Eligibility: Applicants must have been born in the United States and be New Jersey residents. They must have an A or B average in science and math-related subjects and maintain above average grades overall. Financial need and merit are considered. Scholarship winners are asked to perform at least ten hours of community service each week for a year following graduation.
Target applicant(s): High school students.
Amount: $6,000.
Number of awards: 4.
Deadline: March 31.
How to apply: Applications are available online.
Exclusive: Visit www.UltimateScholarshipBook.com and enter code CO129726 for updates on this award.

[1298] • Clem Judd, Jr., Memorial Scholarship
Hawaii Lodging and Tourism Association
2270 Kalakaua Avenue, Suite 1702, Honolulu, HI 96815
Phone: 808-923-0407
Email: info@hawaiilodging.org
http://www.hawaiilodging.org/scholarships.html
Purpose: To help Hawaiian residents majoring in hotel management.
Eligibility: Applicants must have a minimum 3.0 GPA, be a resident of Hawaii, be able to prove Hawaiian ancestry and be a junior or senior enrolled full-time at a U.S. university or college.
Target applicant(s): College students. Adult students.
Minimum GPA: 3.0
Amount: $2,000.
Number of awards: Up to 2.
Deadline: April 29.
How to apply: Applications are available by written request beginning February 1.
Exclusive: Visit www.UltimateScholarshipBook.com and enter code HA129826 for updates on this award.

[1299] • Collaborative Teachers Tuition Waiver
Massachusetts Department of Higher Education
Office of Student Financial Assistance, 454 Broadway, Suite 200, Revere, MA 02151
Phone: 617-727-9420
Email: osfa@osfa.mass.edu
https://www.mass.gov/handbook/massachusetts-financial-aid-programs
Purpose: To provide graduate school tuition waivers for Massachusetts teachers who become student teacher mentors.
Eligibility: Applicants must be public school teachers living and working in the state of Massachusetts. They must also agree to mentor a student teacher from a state college or university in their own classroom, and they must be planning to attend graduate school at one of the nine campuses of Massachusetts State College or the University of Massachusetts.
Target applicant(s): Graduate school students. Adult students.
Amount: Varies.
Number of awards: Varies.
Scholarship may be renewable.
Deadline: Contact the sponsor to confirm the deadline.
How to apply: Applications are available at college financial aid offices.
Exclusive: Visit www.UltimateScholarshipBook.com and enter code MA129926 for updates on this award.

[1300] • College Access Program
Kentucky Higher Education Assistance Authority (KHEAA)
P.O. Box 798, Frankfort, KY 40602
Phone: 800-928-8926
Email: blane@kheaa.com
http://www.kheaa.com

Purpose: To aid Kentucky students with financial need.
Eligibility: Applicants must be Kentucky residents, be enrolled at least half-time in undergraduate academic programs and have an Expected Family Contribution (EFC) based on the FAFSA of lower than approximately $3,850.
Target applicant(s): High school students. College students. Adult students.
Amount: Up to $5,300.
Number of awards: Varies.
Deadline: As soon as possible after October 1.
How to apply: Complete the Free Application for Federal Student Aid (FAFSA).
Exclusive: Visit www.UltimateScholarshipBook.com and enter code KE130026 for updates on this award.

[1301] • CollegeInvest 529 Scholarship Program

Colorado Department of Higher Education
1560 Broadway, Suite 1600, Denver, CO 80202
Phone: 303-862-3001
http://highered.colorado.gov/
Purpose: To support Colorado residents who have planned for higher education by saving over the years with a CollegeInvest 529 College Savings Plan.
Eligibility: Applicants must be Colorado residents and the owner of a CollegeInvest 529 College Savings account. Students must have an Expected Family Contribution (EFC) up to $45,000 and complete the FAFSA.
Target applicant(s): College students. Graduate school students. Adult students.
Amount: $2,000.
Number of awards: Varies.
Deadline: September 30.
How to apply: Applications are available online.
Exclusive: Visit www.UltimateScholarshipBook.com and enter code CO130126 for updates on this award.

[1302] • Collegiate Scholarship

Texas 4-H Youth Development Foundation
4180 Highway 6, College Station, TX 77845
Phone: 979-845-1211
Email: texas4h@ag.tamu.edu
https://texas4-h.tamu.edu/
Purpose: To support undergraduate students in Texas.
Eligibility: Applicants must have actively participated in a 4-H program during their high school years. They must be currently enrolled full-time with at least a 2.7 GPA. Recipients must have completed at least 30 credit hours by the time scholarship payments begin. Awards are based on financial need, academic achievement and 4-H experience.
Target applicant(s): College students. Adult students.
Minimum GPA: 2.7
Amount: Varies.
Number of awards: Varies.
Deadline: February 15.
How to apply: Applications are available online.
Exclusive: Visit www.UltimateScholarshipBook.com and enter code TE130226 for updates on this award.

[1303] • Colorado Council Volunteerism and Community Service Scholarship

Colorado Council Volunteerism and Community Service
P.O. Box 3383, Pagosa Springs, CO 81147
Phone: 970-264-2231
Email: mthompson@pagosa.k12.co.us
http://www.coloradocouncil.org/scholarship
Purpose: To support Colorado students interested in community service who are pursuing higher education.
Eligibility: Applicants must be graduating high school seniors who have been residents of Colorado for their final two years of high school. Students must be accepted at a Colorado Council Member Institution and be enrolled as a full-time student within six months after graduation from high school.
Target applicant(s): High school students.
Minimum GPA: 2.5
Amount: $1,500.
Number of awards: 16.
Deadline: March 15.
How to apply: Applications are available online.
Exclusive: Visit www.UltimateScholarshipBook.com and enter code CO130326 for updates on this award.

[1304] • Colorado Masons Benevolent Fund Scholarships

Colorado Masons Benevolent Fund Association
P.O. Box 703, Westminster, CO 80036-0703
Phone: 719-623-5349
Email: education@cmbfa.org
https://grandlodgeofcolorado.org/philanthropy/scholarships
Purpose: To help Colorado students.
Eligibility: Applicants must be graduating seniors from a Colorado public high school planning to attend a Colorado postsecondary institution. Selection is based on leadership, maturity, need and scholastic ability without reference to race, creed, color, sex or Masonic relationship.
Target applicant(s): High school students.
Amount: Up to $7,000.
Number of awards: Varies.
Scholarship may be renewable.
Deadline: April 15.
How to apply: Applications are available online.
Exclusive: Visit www.UltimateScholarshipBook.com and enter code CO130426 for updates on this award.

[1305] • Colorado Oratorical Contest

American Legion, Department of Colorado
7465 E. 1st Avenue, Suite D, Denver, CO 80230
Phone: 303-366-5201
Email: drivercoach69@yahoo.com
http://www.coloradolegion.org
Purpose: To enhance high school students' experience with and understanding of the U.S. Constitution. The contest will help develop students' leadership skills and civic appreciation, as well as the ability to deliver thoughtful, insightful orations regarding U.S. citizenship and its inherent responsibilities.
Eligibility: Applicants must be high school students under the age of 20 who are U.S. citizens or legal residents and residents of the state. Students first give an oration within their state and winners compete at the national

level. The oration must be related to the Constitution of the United States focusing on the duties and obligations citizens have to the government. It must be in English and be between eight and ten minutes. There is also an assigned topic which is posted on the website, and it should be between three and five minutes.
Target applicant(s): Junior high students or younger. High school students.
Amount: Varies.
Number of awards: Varies.
Deadline: November 22.
How to apply: Applications are available online.
Exclusive: Visit www.UltimateScholarshipBook.com and enter code AM130526 for updates on this award.

[1306] • Colorado Student Grant
Colorado Department of Higher Education
1560 Broadway, Suite 1600, Denver, CO 80202
Phone: 303-862-3001
http://highered.colorado.gov/
Purpose: To assist Colorado student residents.
Eligibility: Applicants must be Colorado residents who plan to enroll or are enrolled in eligible programs at eligible Colorado postsecondary institutions. Applicants must make satisfactory academic progress and have not defaulted in educational loans or grants. Awards are need-based and merit-based and are made by institutions to students.
Target applicant(s): High school students. College students. Adult students.
Amount: Varies.
Number of awards: Varies.
Deadline: As soon as possible after October 1.
How to apply: Contact your financial aid office.
Exclusive: Visit www.UltimateScholarshipBook.com and enter code CO130626 for updates on this award.

[1307] • Colorado Women's Education Foundation
Colorado Women's Education Foundation
P.O. Box 1189, Boulder, CO 80306-1189
Phone: 303-443-2573
Email: office@cwef.org
https://www.cwef.org
Purpose: To provide education assistance for adult women.
Eligibility: Applicants must be women who are 25 years of age or older, United States citizens and Colorado residents for at least 12 months prior to the application deadline. They must be enrolled in or attending an accredited college, university or vocational training institution and reside in Colorado while completing their program.
Target applicant(s): College students. Adult students.
Amount: At least $1,000.
Number of awards: At least 20.
Scholarship may be renewable.
Deadline: April 30.
How to apply: Applications are available online.
Exclusive: Visit www.UltimateScholarshipBook.com and enter code CO130726 for updates on this award.

[1308] • Communities Foundation of Oklahoma Scholarships
Communities Foundation of Oklahoma
P.O. Box 21210, Oklahoma City, OK 73156
Phone: 405-488-1450
Email: aklososky@cfok.org
https://cfok.org/students/
Purpose: To support Oklahoma students.
Eligibility: Applicants must be high school seniors, college students, graduate students or adult students who live in or attend school in Oklahoma. Students must complete the universal scholarship application to be eligible for one of the 700 scholarships awarded annually.
Target applicant(s): High school students. College students. Graduate school students. Adult students.
Amount: Up to full tuition.
Number of awards: 700.
Deadline: March 15.
How to apply: Applications are available online.
Exclusive: Visit www.UltimateScholarshipBook.com and enter code CO130826 for updates on this award.

[1309] • Community Banker Association of Illinois Annual Essay Scholarship Program
Community Banker Association of Illinois
901 Community Drive, Springfield, IL 62703-5184
Phone: 800-736-2224
Email: bobbiw@cbai.com
https://www.cbai.com
Purpose: To assist Illinois high school seniors.
Eligibility: Applicants must write essays and be sponsored by a participating CBAI member bank. There is an essay topic related to community banking, and the short essays are judged on understanding of community banking philosophy, accurate information, clear and concise sentences, logical organization, proper grammar, correct punctuation and spelling and conclusion/summary.
Target applicant(s): High school students.
Amount: Up to $4,000.
Number of awards: 24.
Deadline: March 1.
How to apply: A list of participating banks and more information is available by email.
Exclusive: Visit www.UltimateScholarshipBook.com and enter code CO130926 for updates on this award.

[1310] • Community Scholarship Fund
Hawaii Community Foundation - Scholarships
827 Fort Street Mall, Honolulu, HI 96813
Phone: 888-731-3863
Email: scholarships@hcf-hawaii.org
https://www.hawaiicommunityfoundation.org/
Purpose: To assist college and graduate students majoring in arts, education, humanities or social science.
Eligibility: Applicants must demonstrate accomplishment, motivation, initiative, vision and intention to work in Hawaii and major in the arts, architecture, education, humanities or social science.
Target applicant(s): High school students. College students. Graduate school students. Adult students.
Minimum GPA: 3.3
Amount: Varies.
Number of awards: Varies.

The Ultimate Scholarship Book 2026
Scholarship Directory (State of Residence)

Deadline: February 28.
How to apply: To apply, register online, complete the online application and select the scholarships to which you wish to apply. In addition, mail the supporting materials: printed confirmation page from the online application, personal statement, copy of Student Aid Report (SAR) available at www.fafsa.ed.gov and official transcript.
Exclusive: Visit www.UltimateScholarshipBook.com and enter code HA131026 for updates on this award.

[1311] • Competitive Scholarships
New Mexico Higher Education Department
2044 Galisteo Street, Suite 4, Santa Fe, NM 87505-2100
Phone: 505-476-8400
Email: cesaria.tapia1@state.nm.us
https://hed.state.nm.us/financial-aid
Purpose: To provide a financial incentive for exceptional out-of-state students to attend college in New Mexico.
Eligibility: Applicants must be non-residents of the state of New Mexico, and they must be willing to enroll full-time in a public four-year university in New Mexico. Students applying to Eastern New Mexico University, New Mexico Highlands University, New Mexico Institute of Mining and Technology or Western New Mexico University must have one of the following combinations: a GPA of at least 3.0 and an ACT score of at least 23, or a GPA of at least 3.5 and an ACT of at least 20. Students applying to the University of New Mexico or New Mexico State University must have either an ACT score of 26 and a GPA of 3.0 or an ACT score of 23 and a GPA of 3.5.
Target applicant(s): High school students. College students. Adult students.
Minimum GPA: 3.0
Amount: $100 per semester.
Number of awards: Varies.
Scholarship may be renewable.
Deadline: Contact the sponsor to confirm the deadline.
How to apply: Applications are available at college financial aid offices.
Exclusive: Visit www.UltimateScholarshipBook.com and enter code NE131126 for updates on this award.

[1312] • Confederation of Oregon School Administrators Scholarships
Coalition of Oregon School Administrators
707 13th Street SE, Suite 100, Salem, OR 97301
Phone: 503-581-3141
Email: sara@oasc.org
https://www.cosa.k12.or.us/
Purpose: To provide financial assistance to Oregon students who plan to attend Oregon colleges or universities.
Eligibility: Applicants must be graduating seniors at an Oregon public high school who plan to attend a public or private institution of higher learning in the state. They must have a minimum 3.5 GPA, be active in school and community activities and be endorsed by a COSA member.
Target applicant(s): High school students.
Minimum GPA: 3.5
Amount: $1,000.
Number of awards: 2.
Deadline: March 1.
How to apply: Applications are available online.
Exclusive: Visit www.UltimateScholarshipBook.com and enter code CO131226 for updates on this award.

[1313] • Connecticut Building Congress Scholarships
Connecticut Building Congress Scholarship Fund Inc.
c/o DiBlasi Associates P.C., 500 Purdy Hill Road, Monroe, CT 06468
Phone: 203-452-1331
Email: tomd@diblasi-engrs.com
https://cbc-ct.org/cbc_scholarship/
Purpose: To aid students pursuing degrees in construction fields.
Eligibility: Applicants must be graduating seniors at Connecticut high schools and Connecticut residents. Students must be entering associate, bachelor's or master's degree programs in architecture, engineering, construction management, surveying, planning or another construction-related course of study.
Target applicant(s): High school students.
Amount: $2,500 to $4,000.
Number of awards: Varies.
Scholarship may be renewable.
Deadline: March 1.
How to apply: Applications are available online. An application form, essay, transcript and FAFSA Student Aid Report are required.
Exclusive: Visit www.UltimateScholarshipBook.com and enter code CO131326 for updates on this award.

[1314] • Cora Aguda Manayan Fund
Hawaii Community Foundation - Scholarships
827 Fort Street Mall, Honolulu, HI 96813
Phone: 888-731-3863
Email: scholarships@hcf-hawaii.org
https://www.hawaiicommunityfoundation.org/
Purpose: To support Hawaii students of Filipino ancestry who are dedicated to helping others.
Eligibility: Students must be majoring in a health-related field. Preference may be given to students who are attending school in Hawaii. Applicants must have a minimum 3.0 GPA and have financial need.
Target applicant(s): High school students. College students. Adult students.
Minimum GPA: 3.0
Amount: Varies.
Number of awards: Varies.
Deadline: February 28.
How to apply: To apply, register online, complete the online application and select the scholarships to which you wish to apply. In addition, mail the supporting materials: printed confirmation page from the online application, personal statement, copy of Student Aid Report (SAR) available at www.fafsa.ed.gov and official transcript.
Exclusive: Visit www.UltimateScholarshipBook.com and enter code HA131426 for updates on this award.

[1315] • COSA Youth Development Program Scholarships
Coalition of Oregon School Administrators
707 13th Street SE, Suite 100, Salem, OR 97301
Phone: 503-581-3141
Email: sara@oasc.org
https://www.cosa.k12.or.us/
Purpose: To provide financial assistance for Oregon students.
Eligibility: Applicants must be students at an Oregon public high school who are active in their communities and schools. They must have a minimum 3.5 GPA and plan to attend an Oregon college or university. A field of study must be chosen. An endorsement from a COSA member

is required, and the student must enroll in college the fall after high school graduation.
Target applicant(s): High school students.
Minimum GPA: 3.5
Amount: $1,000.
Number of awards: 6.
Deadline: March 1.
How to apply: Applications are available online, from your high school guidance counselor and the COSA office. An application form, one-page autobiography, letter of recommendation from a COSA member and transcript are required.
Exclusive: Visit www.UltimateScholarshipBook.com and enter code CO131526 for updates on this award.

[1316] • Courageous Heart Scholarship
Texas 4-H Youth Development Foundation
4180 Highway 6, College Station, TX 77845
Phone: 979-845-1211
Email: texas4h@ag.tamu.edu
https://texas4-h.tamu.edu/
Purpose: To support Texas high school students who have overcome serious obstacles related to health, family or education.
Eligibility: Applicants must be current active members and have actively participated in a 4-H program for two of the past three years. They must have formally applied to a Texas college or university, and they must meet all requirements for admission. Students must provide documentation of the obstacles they have faced.
Target applicant(s): High school students.
Amount: $5,000.
Number of awards: Varies.
Deadline: February 15.
How to apply: Applications are available online.
Exclusive: Visit www.UltimateScholarshipBook.com and enter code TE131626 for updates on this award.

[1317] • Crumley Roberts Next Step Scholarship
Crumley Roberts, Attorneys at Law
2400 Freeman Mill Road, Greensboro, NC 27406
Phone: 336-728-6219
https://www.crlegalteam.com/the-roberts-center/leadership-advancement-and-scholarships/
Purpose: To support North Carolina, South Carolina and Alabama community college students who plan to transfer to accredited four-year institutions of higher learning.
Eligibility: Applicants must be community college students in North Carolina, South Carolina, Georgia and Alabama who will be transferring to an accredited four-year college or university in the coming fall.
Target applicant(s): College students. Adult students.
Minimum GPA: 3.2
Amount: $2,500.
Number of awards: 1.
Deadline: January 31.
How to apply: Applications are available to be printed online but must then be mailed. An application form, two letters of recommendation, a transcript and an essay are required.
Exclusive: Visit www.UltimateScholarshipBook.com and enter code CR131726 for updates on this award.

[1318] • CTA Cesar E. Chavez and Dolores Huerta Education Award Program
California Teachers Association (CTA)
CTA Human Rights Department, P.O. Box 921, Burlingame, CA 94011-0921
Phone: 650-697-1400
Email: scholarships@cta.org
https://www.cta.org/for-educators/scholarships-awards
Purpose: To honor Cesar Chavez by rewarding students and teachers who follow his vision and guiding principles.
Eligibility: A student or group of up to five students must submit an essay or visual piece under the supervision of a teacher or professor who is a member of the CTA. Students may be in kindergarten through high school or in community college. All works must focus on topics such as non-violence and their relationship to Chavez's legacy. Visit the website for a complete list of topics and specific essay and visual arts submission requirements.
Target applicant(s): Junior high students or younger. High school students. College students. Adult students.
Amount: Up to $550.
Number of awards: Varies.
Deadline: March 1.
How to apply: Applications are available online.
Exclusive: Visit www.UltimateScholarshipBook.com and enter code CA131826 for updates on this award.

[1319] • CTAHPERD Gibson-Laemel Scholarship
Connecticut Association of Health, Physical Education, Recreation and Dance
c/o Janice Skene, CTAHPERD Scholarship Chair, Buttonball Lane School, 376 Buttonball Lane, Glastonbury, CT 06033
Phone: 860-652-7276
Email: skenej@glastonburyus.org
http://www.ctahperd.org
Purpose: To support students majoring in areas related to physical education.
Eligibility: Applicants must be Connecticut students who have declared a major in health, physical education, recreation or dance. Students must be college juniors or seniors, maintain a GPA of 2.7 or higher and be CTAHPERD members.
Target applicant(s): College students. Adult students.
Minimum GPA: 2.7
Amount: $1,000.
Number of awards: Varies.
Deadline: June 15.
How to apply: Applications are available online. An application form, personal statement, transcript and two letters of recommendation are required.
Exclusive: Visit www.UltimateScholarshipBook.com and enter code CO131926 for updates on this award.

[1320] • Cynthia and Alan Baran Fine Arts and Music Scholarship Fund
Community Foundation of Middle Tennessee
3833 Cleghorn Avenue, Suite 400, Nashville, TN 37215-2519
Phone: 888-540-5200
Email: pcole@cfmt.org
https://www.cfmt.org
Purpose: To aid students in pursuing careers in visual arts and music.

Eligibility: Applicants must be current students at an accredited college or university, take at least six credit hours and be enrolled in a bachelor's of fine art, bachelor's of studio art, master's of fine art or bachelor's or master's in music program. Art students must major in painting, drawing, sculpture, ceramics, photography or printmaking. Preference for music scholarships is given to those studying acoustic mandolin or acoustic guitar. A minimum GPA of 3.0 is required.
Target applicant(s): College students. Graduate school students. Adult students.
Minimum GPA: 3.0
Amount: Varies.
Number of awards: Varies.
Deadline: February 1.
How to apply: Applications are available online. An application form, transcript, essay, Student Aid Report and two appraisal forms are required.
Exclusive: Visit www.UltimateScholarshipBook.com and enter code CO132026 for updates on this award.

[1321] • Daniel E. Lambert Memorial Scholarship
American Legion, Department of Maine
5 Verti Drive, Winslow, ME 04901-0727
Phone: 207-873-3229
Email: legionme@mainelegion.org
http://www.mainelegion.org/pages/programs/scholarships.php
Purpose: To support the descendants of veterans who demonstrate financial need and who are residents of Maine.
Eligibility: Applicants must be enrolled in an accredited college or vocational technical school and be U.S. citizens. A parent or grandparent must be a veteran, verified by a copy of military discharge papers with the application. Applicants must have good character and believe in the American way of life.
Target applicant(s): College students. Adult students.
Amount: $1,000.
Number of awards: 2.
Deadline: May 1.
How to apply: Applications are available online.
Exclusive: Visit www.UltimateScholarshipBook.com and enter code AM132126 for updates on this award.

[1322] • Daniels Scholarship Program
Daniels Fund
101 Monroe Street, Denver, CO 80206
Phone: 303-393-7220
http://www.danielsfund.org
Purpose: To support students who have a proven record of character strength, leadership and a commitment to their communities in accomplishing their goal of obtaining a post-secondary education.
Eligibility: Applicants must be graduating high school seniors enrolling in any nonprofit accredited college or university and be a resident of Colorado, New Mexico, Utah or Wyoming. Students must submit a FAFSA to demonstrate financial need, have a minimum 2.0 GPA and earn an ACT score of 17 and minimum SAT Math score of 470 along with a minimum SAT Critical Reading score of 450.
Target applicant(s): High school students.
Minimum GPA: 2.0
Amount: Varies.
Number of awards: Varies.
Scholarship may be renewable.
Deadline: October 15.
How to apply: Applications are available online.

Exclusive: Visit www.UltimateScholarshipBook.com and enter code DA132226 for updates on this award.

[1323] • David E. Simon Scholarship
Indiana Golf Association
P.O. Box 26159, Indianapolis, IN 46226
Phone: 317-738-9696
Email: astrong@indianagolf.org
https://www.indianagolf.org/scholarships/
Purpose: To aid those students who have worked at an Indiana golf facility in their pursuit of a college education.
Eligibility: Applicants must be seniors in high school, have worked in an Indiana golf facility in the previous 12 months, have a 3.0 GPA, display strong character and prove financial need. Selection is based on financial need, personal essay and academic achievement.
Target applicant(s): High school students.
Minimum GPA: 3.0
Amount: $5,000.
Number of awards: Varies.
Deadline: March 30.
How to apply: Applications are available online and must include an IRS 1040 form, high school transcript, personal essay and at least one letter of reference. In addition to the main application form, students should submit the academic evaluation form and employment evaluation form.
Exclusive: Visit www.UltimateScholarshipBook.com and enter code IN132326 for updates on this award.

[1324] • DC Tuition Assistance Grant Program
Government of the District of Columbia
DC Tuition Assistance Grant Program, 1050 First Street NE, Fifth Floor, Washington, DC 20002
Phone: 877-485-6751
Email: osse@dc.gov
http://osse.dc.gov
Purpose: To provide financial assistance to students in the District of Columbia who wish to attend either a public university in a different state or a historically black college or university.
Eligibility: Applicants must be residents who have lived in the District of Columbia for at least 12 months prior to the beginning of their freshman year of college. Applicants must also either plan to or be currently enrolled at least half-time in an undergraduate or certificate program.
Target applicant(s): High school students. College students.
Amount: Up to $10,000.
Number of awards: Varies.
Scholarship may be renewable.
Deadline: August 18.
How to apply: Applications are available online.
Exclusive: Visit www.UltimateScholarshipBook.com and enter code GO132426 for updates on this award.

[1325] • Delaware Educational Benefits for Children of Deceased Veterans and Others
Delaware Department of Education - School Supports
The Townsend Building, 401 Federal Street, Suite 2, Dover, DE 19901-3639
Phone: 800-292-7935
Email: dhec@doe.k12.de.us
https://scholarships.delawarestudentsuccess.org/
Purpose: To assist children of deceased veterans.

Eligibility: Applicants must be U.S. citizens or eligible non-citizens who have been Delaware residents for at least three years prior to application. They must be the child of an armed forces member who died from a service-related cause, is/was a prisoner of war or has been declared missing in action; a state police officer whose death was service-related or a Department of Transportation employee who worked on the state highway system whose death was job-related. Applicants must be 16 to 24 years of age. Priority is given to students attending a Delaware public college, followed by students attending Delaware private colleges and those attending out-of-state institutions. Those attending private or out-of-state colleges must pursue majors that are not offered by Delaware public colleges.
Target applicant(s): High school students. College students.
Amount: Full tuition.
Number of awards: Varies.
Scholarship may be renewable.
Deadline: May 15.
How to apply: Applications are available online. An application form is required.
Exclusive: Visit www.UltimateScholarshipBook.com and enter code DE132526 for updates on this award.

[1326] • Delaware Scholarship Incentive Program
Delaware Department of Education - School Supports
The Townsend Building, 401 Federal Street, Suite 2, Dover, DE 19901-3639
Phone: 800-292-7935
Email: dhec@doe.k12.de.us
https://scholarships.delawarestudentsuccess.org/
Purpose: To assist Delaware student residents.
Eligibility: Applicants must be legal residents of Delaware and U.S. citizens or eligible non-citizens who are enrolled full-time at a regionally-accredited undergraduate institution in Delaware or Pennsylvania. Other undergraduate and graduate students will be considered if their major is not available at a public college in Delaware. Students must demonstrate substantial financial need and have a minimum 2.5 GPA. Applicants must also submit the Free Application for Federal Student Aid (FAFSA).
Target applicant(s): High school students. College students. Graduate school students. Adult students.
Minimum GPA: 2.5
Amount: $1,000.
Number of awards: Varies.
Scholarship may be renewable.
Deadline: May 15.
How to apply: Delaware residents are automatically considered for the scholarship when their FAFSA form is received.
Exclusive: Visit www.UltimateScholarshipBook.com and enter code DE132626 for updates on this award.

[1327] • Delaware Solid Waste Authority John P. Pat Healy Scholarship
Delaware Solid Waste Authority
1128 South Bradford Street, Dover, DE 19904
Phone: 302-739-5361
Email: info@dswa.com
https://dswa.com/scholarship/
Purpose: To aid Delaware students who are preparing for careers in environmental engineering or environmental science.
Eligibility: Applicants must be Delaware residents, U.S. citizens or eligible non-citizens and full-time students. They must be high school seniors or undergraduate students majoring in or planning to major in environmental sciences or environmental engineering at a Delaware college or university. They also must complete a Free Application for Federal Student Aid (FAFSA) form for the upcoming school year. Selection is based on academic achievement, leadership skills, extracurricular involvement and financial need.
Target applicant(s): High school students. College students. Adult students.
Amount: $2,500.
Number of awards: Varies.
Scholarship may be renewable.
Deadline: April 30.
How to apply: Applications are available online. An application form, personal essay, transcript and FAFSA are required.
Exclusive: Visit www.UltimateScholarshipBook.com and enter code DE132726 for updates on this award.

[1328] • Delegate Scholarship
Maryland Higher Education Commission
Office of Student Financial Assistance, 6 North Liberty Street, Baltimore, MD 21201
Phone: 800-974-1024
Email: osfamail@mhec.state.md.us
https://mhec.maryland.gov
Purpose: To assist Maryland undergraduate and graduate students who can demonstrate financial need.
Eligibility: Applicants must be legal residents of the state of Maryland and complete the Free Application for Federal Student Aid (FAFSA). They must show financial need if the Office of Student Financial Assistance (OFSA) makes the award for the applicant's delegate. Applicants must be or must plan to be degree-seeking students at a Maryland institution. Selection is based on the overall strength of the application.
Target applicant(s): High school students. College students. Graduate school students. Adult students.
Amount: Up to $29,600.
Number of awards: Varies.
Scholarship may be renewable.
Deadline: March 1.
How to apply: Complete and file the Free Application for Federal Student Aid (FAFSA). Contact delegate's office for specific application forms. The Office of Student Financial Assistance (OSFA) can provide a list of all state legislators. An application form and supporting documents are required.
Exclusive: Visit www.UltimateScholarshipBook.com and enter code MA132826 for updates on this award.

[1329] • Dennis Schoepp Memorial Scholarship
Funeral Service Foundation
13625 Bishop's Drive, Brookfield, WI 53005-6607
Phone: 877-402-5900
Email: info@funeralservicefoundation.org
https://www.funeralservicefoundation.org/academicscholarships/
Purpose: To aid students with tuition costs associated with mortuary science education.
Eligibility: Applicants must be a student of funeral service from Montana and be enrolled full- or part-time in an American Board of Funeral Service Education accredited program. Selection is based on the overall strength of the application.
Target applicant(s): College students. Graduate school students. Adult students.
Minimum GPA: 2.0
Amount: $2,500-$5,000.
Number of awards: Varies.

Deadline: April 1; November 1.
How to apply: Applications are available online. An application form, essay, academic transcript and video submissions are required.
Exclusive: Visit www.UltimateScholarshipBook.com and enter code FU132926 for updates on this award.

[1330] • Department of Children and Families (DCF) Foster Child Tuition Waiver and Fee Assistance Program

Massachusetts Department of Higher Education
Office of Student Financial Assistance, 454 Broadway, Suite 200, Revere, MA 02151
Phone: 617-727-9420
Email: osfa@osfa.mass.edu
https://www.mass.gov/handbook/massachusetts-financial-aid-programs
Purpose: To provide financial support to Massachusetts foster children who are pursuing higher education.
Eligibility: Applicants must be current or former foster children who were placed in Massachusetts state custody for at least 12 months due to a Care and Protection Petition. They must not have been adopted or returned home, and they must be 24 years old or younger. Students must be enrolled as full-time undergraduates at a state-supported school.
Target applicant(s): High school students. College students. Adult students.
Amount: Full tuition.
Number of awards: Varies.
Deadline: Contact the sponsor to confirm the deadline.
How to apply: Applications are available at college financial aid offices.
Exclusive: Visit www.UltimateScholarshipBook.com and enter code MA133026 for updates on this award.

[1331] • Dianne E. H. Wilcox Scholarship Fund

Community Foundation Serving Western Virginia
P.O. Box 1159, Roanoke, VA 24006
Phone: 540-985-0204
https://www.cfwesternva.org/for-students/scholarship-listings/
Purpose: To assist students in the Western Virginia area.
Eligibility: Applicants must be Virginia residents. Students must enroll full-time in an accredited two- or four-year college or university.
Target applicant(s): High school students. College students. Graduate school students. Adult students.
Amount: $1,000.
Number of awards: 1.
Deadline: January 12.
How to apply: Applications are available online.
Exclusive: Visit www.UltimateScholarshipBook.com and enter code CO133126 for updates on this award.

[1332] • Dick Griffiths Memorial Scholarship

California Association on Postsecondary Education and Disability (CAPED)
10073 Valley View Street, #242, Cypress, CA 90630
Phone: 562-397-2810
Email: caped.scholarship.committee@gmail.com
http://www.caped.co/scholarships/
Purpose: To support students with a learning disability in math who are pursuing higher education.
Eligibility: Applicants must have a verifiable learning disability in math and be currently enrolled as a student at a California college or university with a GPA of 2.5 for undergraduates or 3.0 for graduate students. Students must have completed at least six semester or eight quarter units as an undergraduate student or three semester or four quarter units as a graduate student.
Target applicant(s): College students. Graduate school students. Adult students.
Minimum GPA: 2.5 for undergraduate students; 3.0 for graduate students
Amount: $1,000.
Number of awards: 1.
Deadline: August 31.
How to apply: Applications are available online.
Exclusive: Visit www.UltimateScholarshipBook.com and enter code CA133226 for updates on this award.

[1333] • District of Columbia Tuition Assistance Grant

DC Tuition Assistance Grant Office
1050 1st Street NE, Fifth Floor, Washington, DC 20002
Phone: 202-727-2824
Email: osse@dc.gov
https://osse.dc.gov/
Purpose: To make attending out-of-state, private and Historically Black schools more affordable for DC residents.
Eligibility: Applicants must be residents of Washington, DC for at least 12 months before the start of their freshman year of college, high school graduates or GED recipients, enrolled at least half-time at an eligible institution and be 24 years of age or younger. Applicants must maintain satisfactory academic progress, not have defaulted on student loans, have registered with the Selective Service, be U.S. citizens or permanent residents, have not already received a B.A. or B.S. and have not been incarcerated. The award provides up to $10,000 a year for the difference between in-state and out-of-state tuition at public four year institutions in the U.S. and up to $2,500 per year for private colleges in DC, private Historically Black Colleges and Universities or two-year colleges nationwide.
Target applicant(s): High school students. College students.
Amount: $2,500-$10,000.
Number of awards: Varies.
Scholarship may be renewable.
Deadline: August 18.
How to apply: Applications are available online.
Exclusive: Visit www.UltimateScholarshipBook.com and enter code DC133326 for updates on this award.

[1334] • Don't Mess with Texas Scholarship

Don't Mess with Texas
Sherry Matthews Advocacy, 200 South Congress Avenue, Austin, TX 78704
Phone: 512-476-4368
Email: scholarship@dontmesswithtexas.org
https://www.dontmesswithtexas.org/education-overview/scholarships/
Purpose: To support students concerned about litter.
Eligibility: Students must be a Texas high school senior who wants to attend a two- or four-year college or university in Texas. To apply for the scholarship, students must complete the application and one or two essays and submit two letters of recommendation (one from a school-related source and the other from a non-school related source).
Target applicant(s): High school students.
Amount: $5,000.

Number of awards: Varies.
Deadline: April 2.
How to apply: Applications are available online.
Exclusive: Visit www.UltimateScholarshipBook.com and enter code DO133426 for updates on this award.

[1335] • Dorian De Long Arts and Music Scholarship

Jefferson County Education Association
12650 W. 64th Avenue, Unit E195, Arvada, CO 80004
Email: educate@ddamscholarship.com
https://www.ddamscholarship.com
Purpose: To support students who are pursuing a degree in the arts.
Eligibility: Applicants must be graduating Colorado high school seniors who are pursuing the study of arts.
Target applicant(s): High school students.
Amount: $1,500-$2,500.
Number of awards: 1.
Scholarship may be renewable.
Deadline: March 1.
How to apply: Applications are available online.
Exclusive: Visit www.UltimateScholarshipBook.com and enter code JE133526 for updates on this award.

[1336] • Doris and Clarence Glick Classical Music Scholarship

Hawaii Community Foundation - Scholarships
827 Fort Street Mall, Honolulu, HI 96813
Phone: 888-731-3863
Email: scholarships@hcf-hawaii.org
https://www.hawaiicommunityfoundation.org/
Purpose: To provide financial assistance for Hawaii students of classical music.
Eligibility: Applicants must be majoring in music with an emphasis on classical music. They must have a GPA of 2.7 or higher, and they must describe their program of study as it relates to classical music in their personal statement.
Target applicant(s): High school students. College students. Graduate school students. Adult students.
Minimum GPA: 2.7
Amount: Varies.
Number of awards: Varies.
Deadline: February 28.
How to apply: To apply, register online, complete the online application and select the scholarships to which you wish to apply. In addition, mail the supporting materials: printed confirmation page from the online application, personal statement, copy of Student Aid Report (SAR) available at www.fafsa.ed.gov and official transcript.
Exclusive: Visit www.UltimateScholarshipBook.com and enter code HA133626 for updates on this award.

[1337] • Dorothy D. Greer Journalist of the Year Scholarship Competition

Colorado Student Media Association
Jack Kennedy, CSMA Executive Director, 9253 Sori Lane, Highlands Ranch, CO 80126
Phone: 303-550-4755
Email: jpkjournalism@gmail.com
http://colostudentmedia.com/
Purpose: To support outstanding young journalists.
Eligibility: Applicants must be Colorado high school seniors whose schools are members of the Colorado Student Media Association. Students must have worked on their yearbook or newspaper for at least two years. A GPA of 3.0 or higher is required. Selection criteria include neatness (10 percent), quality of work (40 percent), personal statement (20 percent), letters of recommendation (20 percent) and grades (10 percent).
Target applicant(s): High school students.
Minimum GPA: 3.0
Amount: Up to $3,000.
Number of awards: 1.
Deadline: February 15.
How to apply: Applications are available online. An application form, personal statement, transcript, three to four letters of recommendation, samples of published work and action photo are required.
Exclusive: Visit www.UltimateScholarshipBook.com and enter code CO133726 for updates on this award.

[1338] • Douvas Memorial Scholarship

Wyoming Department of Education
2300 Capitol Avenue, Hathaway Building, 2nd Floor, Cheyenne, WY 82002-0050
Phone: 307-777-3469
Email: laurie.hernandez@wyo.gov
http://edu.wyoming.gov
Purpose: To assist first generation Americans in obtaining higher education.
Eligibility: Applicants must have been born in the United States but have parents who were born outside the country. They must be high school seniors or between the ages of 18 and 22, and they must be Wyoming residents. They must attend a Wyoming community college or the University of Wyoming.
Target applicant(s): High school students. College students.
Amount: $500.
Number of awards: 1.
Deadline: May 3.
How to apply: Applications are available online.
Exclusive: Visit www.UltimateScholarshipBook.com and enter code WY133826 for updates on this award.

[1339] • Dr. and Mrs. Arthur F. Sullivan Fund

Connecticut Community Foundation Center for Philanthropy
43 Field Street, Waterbury, CT 06702
Phone: 203-753-1315
Email: scholarships@conncf.org
http://www.conncf.org
Purpose: To provide financial assistance to students who are entering or enrolled in medical school.
Eligibility: Applicants must be accepted to or enrolled in medical school. They must reside in the Connecticut Community Foundation's service area and demonstrate exemplary academic achievement. Scholarship awarded in even years.
Target applicant(s): College students. Graduate school students. Adult students.
Amount: Varies.
Number of awards: Varies.
Deadline: March 15.
How to apply: Applications are available online.
Exclusive: Visit www.UltimateScholarshipBook.com and enter code CO133926 for updates on this award.

[1340] • Dr. Edison and Sallie Miyawaki Scholarship Fund

Hawaii Community Foundation - Scholarships
827 Fort Street Mall, Honolulu, HI 96813
Phone: 888-731-3863
Email: scholarships@hcf-hawaii.org
https://www.hawaiicommunityfoundation.org/
Purpose: To reward students with outstanding achievement in extracurricular activities.
Eligibility: Applicants must be Hawaii residents who plan to attend an accredited institution of higher learning. They must have a GPA between 2.5 and 3.0, demonstrate financial need and participate in an extracurricular sports program.
Target applicant(s): High school students. College students. Graduate school students. Adult students.
Minimum GPA: 2.5
Amount: Varies.
Number of awards: Varies.
Deadline: January 31.
How to apply: To apply, register online, complete the online application and select the scholarships to which you wish to apply. In addition, mail the supporting materials: printed confirmation page from the online application, personal statement, copy of Student Aid Report (SAR) available at www.fafsa.ed.gov and official transcript.
Exclusive: Visit www.UltimateScholarshipBook.com and enter code HA134026 for updates on this award.

[1341] • Dr. Hans and Clara Zimmerman Foundation Education Scholarship

Hawaii Community Foundation - Scholarships
827 Fort Street Mall, Honolulu, HI 96813
Phone: 888-731-3863
Email: scholarships@hcf-hawaii.org
https://www.hawaiicommunityfoundation.org/
Purpose: To provide financial assistance to Hawaii students who want to study education.
Eligibility: Applicants major in education with an emphasis in teaching. They must have a GPA of 2.8 or higher, demonstrate good character and be full-time students. Preference is given to students of Hawaiian ethnicity and to students with at least two years of teaching experience. Applicants must discuss their teaching philosophies in their personal statement.
Target applicant(s): High school students. College students. Graduate school students. Adult students.
Minimum GPA: 2.8
Amount: Varies.
Number of awards: Varies.
Deadline: February 28.
How to apply: To apply, register online, complete the online application and select the scholarships to which you wish to apply. In addition, mail the supporting materials: printed confirmation page from the online application, personal statement, copy of Student Aid Report (SAR) available at www.fafsa.ed.gov and official transcript.
Exclusive: Visit www.UltimateScholarshipBook.com and enter code HA134126 for updates on this award.

[1342] • Dr. Hans and Clara Zimmerman Foundation Health Scholarships

Hawaii Community Foundation - Scholarships
827 Fort Street Mall, Honolulu, HI 96813
Phone: 888-731-3863
Email: scholarships@hcf-hawaii.org
https://www.hawaiicommunityfoundation.org/
Purpose: To provide financial assistance to Hawaii students who want to study in health fields.
Eligibility: Applicants must plan to major in a health-related field other than sports medicine, non-clinical psychology or social work at a U.S. college or university. They must be full-time college juniors, college seniors or graduate students, and they must have a GPA of 3.0 or higher.
Target applicant(s): College students. Graduate school students. Adult students.
Minimum GPA: 3.0
Amount: Varies.
Number of awards: Varies.
Deadline: February 28.
How to apply: To apply, register online, complete the online application and select the scholarships to which you wish to apply. In addition, mail the supporting materials: printed confirmation page from the online application, personal statement, copy of Student Aid Report (SAR) available at www.fafsa.ed.gov and official transcript.
Exclusive: Visit www.UltimateScholarshipBook.com and enter code HA134226 for updates on this award.

[1343] • Dr. Ralph E. White Graduating Senior Scholarship

California State PTA
2327 L Street, Sacramento, CA 95816-5014
Phone: 916-440-1985
Email: grants@capta.org
http://capta.org/programs-events/scholarships/
Purpose: To support students who intend to pursue a career in a medical field.
Eligibility: Applicants must be California residents and high school seniors graduating from a California high school. Students must be a member of their school PTA/PTSA in good standing and a council, district or state PTA board member. An essay is required to be submitted on a provided prompt.
Target applicant(s): High school students.
Amount: $500.
Number of awards: 2.
Deadline: February 1.
How to apply: Applications are available online.
Exclusive: Visit www.UltimateScholarshipBook.com and enter code CA134326 for updates on this award.

[1344] • Dr. William S. Boyd Scholarship

Chiropractic Association of Louisiana
10636 Timberlake Drive, Baton Rouge, LA 70810
Phone: 225-769-5560
Email: Melissa-chiroassoclaoffice@gmail.com
https://www.cal-online.org/scholarship-info
Purpose: To aid Louisiana chiropractic students.
Eligibility: Applicants must be Louisiana residents who are juniors or seniors at a CCE-accredited chiropractic college located in Louisiana. They must have a GPA of 2.75 or higher and must intend to work in

Louisiana after graduation. Selection is based on the overall strength of the application.
Target applicant(s): College students. Adult students.
Minimum GPA: 2.75
Amount: Varies.
Number of awards: At least 1.
Deadline: June 30.
How to apply: Applications are available by request from the CAL. An application form, three letters of recommendation and an endorsement from a current member of the CAL are required.
Exclusive: Visit www.UltimateScholarshipBook.com and enter code CH134426 for updates on this award.

[1345] • Duke Award Scholarship
Outrigger Duke Kahanamoku Foundation
P.O. Box 160924, 4354 Pahoa Avenue, Honolulu, HI 96816
Phone: 808-545-4880
Email: info@dukefoundation.org
https://www.dukefoundation.org/
Purpose: To support Hawaii students who are involved in water sports.
Eligibility: Applicants must be nominated by a school or athletic official. Each school may nominate up to 3 candidates to be considered for the Duke Award. While financial need is not a requirement of the Duke Award, it may be weighed as a determining factor.
Target applicant(s): High school students. College students. Adult students.
Minimum GPA: 3.0
Amount: Up to $15,000.
Number of awards: 1.
Deadline: February 1.
How to apply: Applications are available online.
Exclusive: Visit www.UltimateScholarshipBook.com and enter code OU134526 for updates on this award.

[1346] • E.H. Marth Food Protection and Food Science Scholarship
WAFP Scholarship Committee
c/o Tera Montgomery, 1 University Plaza, Platteville, WI 53818
Phone: 608-342-6027
Email: montgomeryt@uwplatt.edu
http://www.wifoodprotection.org/scholarships.php
Purpose: To support students who are preparing for careers that are related to food or environmental sanitation.
Eligibility: Applicants must be Wisconsin residents who are enrolled at or have been accepted into a postsecondary institution that is either located in the state of Wisconsin or that has a reciprocal enrollment agreement with Wisconsin. They must be or plan to be enrolled full-time in an undergraduate academic program that is related to food science, environmental sanitation or dairy science. Selection is based on the overall strength of the application.
Target applicant(s): College students. Adult students.
Amount: $3,000.
Number of awards: 1.
Scholarship may be renewable.
Deadline: June 30.
How to apply: Applications are available online. An application form, official transcript and letter of recommendation are required.
Exclusive: Visit www.UltimateScholarshipBook.com and enter code WA134626 for updates on this award.

[1347] • Eagle Scout of the Year
American Legion, Department of Wisconsin
2930 American Legion Drive, P.O. Box 388, Portage, WI 53901
Phone: 608-745-1090
Email: info@wilegion.org
https://wilegion.org/scholarships
Purpose: To reward outstanding service as an Eagle Scout at the state level.
Eligibility: Applicants must demonstrate outstanding service in community, church and school and must be at least 15 years of age, in high school and either members of a troop chartered by the American Legion/Auxiliary or sons or grandsons of members of the American Legion/Auxiliary. Students must have received the Eagle Scout Award as well as the Scout religious emblem. Scholarships may be used to attend a state-accredited college, university or other school above the high school level.
Target applicant(s): High school students.
Amount: $2,500-$10,000.
Number of awards: Varies.
Deadline: March 1.
How to apply: Applications are available from the local Legion Post or from the Wisconsin American Legion Headquarters.
Exclusive: Visit www.UltimateScholarshipBook.com and enter code AM134726 for updates on this award.

[1348] • Early Childhood Educators Scholarship
Massachusetts Department of Higher Education
Office of Student Financial Assistance, 454 Broadway, Suite 200, Revere, MA 02151
Phone: 617-727-9420
Email: osfa@osfa.mass.edu
https://www.mass.gov/handbook/massachusetts-financial-aid-programs
Purpose: To support the education of Massachusetts teachers employed in early childhood settings.
Eligibility: Applicants must be legal residents of Massachusetts who have worked as early childhood educators in the state for at least one year prior to receiving the scholarship. They must continue working in the profession while enrolled in school and upon completion of the degree. Students must be enrolled in Early Childhood Education or a related undergraduate program, and they cannot have any previously earned bachelor's degrees.
Target applicant(s): College students. Graduate school students. Adult students.
Amount: Varies.
Number of awards: Varies.
Scholarship may be renewable.
Deadline: October 1.
How to apply: Applications are available online.
Exclusive: Visit www.UltimateScholarshipBook.com and enter code MA134826 for updates on this award.

[1349] • Early College for ME
Early College for ME
Maine Community College System, 323 State Street, Augusta, ME 04330-7131
Phone: 207-629-4000
Email: mpour@mccs.me.edu
https://www.mccs.me.edu/
Purpose: To help high school students who are undecided about college.
Eligibility: Applicants must be in their junior year at one of the 74 Maine high schools participating in the program. The list of schools is online at http://www.earlycollege.me.edu/participating.html. Students must

be Maine residents for at least one year prior to entering the first year of college and must have not yet made plans for college and yet be capable of succeeding at a community college. High schools may also take financial need into consideration when selecting students for the program as well as whether or not the student is the first one to attend college in their family. The program provides community college courses in the senior year of high school, as available, as well as financial aid for a one-year or two-year degree program at a Maine community college.
Target applicant(s): High school students.
Amount: Up to $2,000.
Number of awards: Varies.
Deadline: Contact the sponsor to confirm the deadline.
How to apply: Speak with your guidance counselor at your high school about entering the program.
Exclusive: Visit www.UltimateScholarshipBook.com and enter code EA134926 for updates on this award.

[1350] • Ed and Charlotte Rodgers Scholarships
Alabama Road Builders Association Inc.
630 Adams Avenue, Montgomery, AL 36104
Phone: 334-832-4331
Email: lexie@alarba.org
https://www.alrba.org/Scholarship
Purpose: To support financially needy civil engineering students.
Eligibility: Applicants must be full-time civil engineering students who have completed their sophomore year of college. They must be in good standing academically, have a good GPA and demonstrate financial need. Selection is based on leadership skills, awards received and extracurricular involvements.
Target applicant(s): College students. Adult students.
Amount: $2,000.
Number of awards: Up to 6.
Deadline: September 15.
How to apply: Applications are available online. An application form, a recent photo and a personal essay are required.
Exclusive: Visit www.UltimateScholarshipBook.com and enter code AL135026 for updates on this award.

[1351] • Edmund F. Maxwell Foundation Scholarship
Edmund F. Maxwell Foundation
P.O. Box 55548, Seattle, WA 98155
Email: support@maxwell.org
http://www.maxwell.org
Purpose: To assist high-achieving students who follow the ideals of Edmund F. Maxwell: ability, aptitude and citizenship.
Eligibility: Applicants must be from western Washington, plan to attend an accredited independent school that is primarily not tax-funded and have a minimum SAT score of 1200. Students must submit a FAFSA form and demonstrate financial need.
Target applicant(s): High school students.
Amount: Up to $5,000.
Number of awards: Varies.
Scholarship may be renewable.
Deadline: May 10.
How to apply: Applications are available online.
Exclusive: Visit www.UltimateScholarshipBook.com and enter code ED135126 for updates on this award.

[1352] • Educational Award/Graduating High School Female
New York State Women's 600 Club
Connie Canfield, Chairman, 1288 Scribner Hollow Road, East Jewett, NY 12424-5538
Phone: 518-589-5319
Email: cmc600ed@gmail.com
http://www.bowlny.com/
Purpose: To support New York graduating high school senior female bowlers as they embark on their college careers.
Eligibility: Applicant must be a member of a league or high school bowling team certified by USBC. Applicants must also have bowled at least 39 games in the current season or 18 games during the current high school season. Each applicant must also be sponsored by a current member of the New York State Women's 600 Bowling Club.
Target applicant(s): High school students.
Amount: Varies.
Number of awards: Varies.
Deadline: March 1.
How to apply: Applications are available online and consist of forms to be completed by the applicant, a league official, a school official and the NYSW 600 member sponsor.
Exclusive: Visit www.UltimateScholarshipBook.com and enter code NE135226 for updates on this award.

[1353] • Educational Excellence Scholarship
Kentucky Higher Education Assistance Authority (KHEAA)
P.O. Box 798, Frankfort, KY 40602
Phone: 800-928-8926
Email: blane@kheaa.com
http://www.kheaa.com
Purpose: To reward outstanding Kentucky high school students.
Eligibility: Applicants must have a minimum 2.5 GPA, be graduating from eligible Kentucky high schools and meet high school graduation requirements. The scholarship amount is based on high school GPA and ACT composite score.
Target applicant(s): High school students.
Minimum GPA: 2.5
Amount: Up to $500.
Number of awards: Varies.
Scholarship may be renewable.
Deadline: As soon as possible after October 1.
How to apply: High schools send eligible students' GPAs to the Kentucky Department of Education. There is no application for this award.
Exclusive: Visit www.UltimateScholarshipBook.com and enter code KE135326 for updates on this award.

[1354] • Educational Opportunity Fund (EOF) Grant
New Jersey Commission on Higher Education
P.O. Box 542, Trenton, NJ 08625
Phone: 609-292-4310
Email: meverett@che.state.nj.us
http://www.state.nj.us/highereducation
Purpose: To support underprivileged students in New Jersey.
Eligibility: Applicants must be able to show financial need and a background of family poverty, and they cannot exceed the established maximum income. They must be enrolled full-time in one of the participating public or private colleges in New Jersey, and they must have been residents of the state for at least 12 months prior to enrollment. Students pursuing a bachelor's degree cannot have any prior baccalaureate

degrees, and students pursuing a two-year degree cannot have any previous associate's degrees. Applicants must not major in theology or divinity.
Target applicant(s): High school students. College students. Graduate school students. Adult students.
Amount: $200-$2,500.
Number of awards: Varies.
Scholarship may be renewable.
Deadline: Contact the sponsor to confirm the deadline.
How to apply: Applications are available from campus EOF directors.
Exclusive: Visit www.UltimateScholarshipBook.com and enter code NE135426 for updates on this award.

[1355] • Educational Training Voucher Programs for Foster Youth

Foster Care to Success
23811 Chagrin Boulevard, Suite 210, Cleveland, OH 44122
Phone: 800-585-6188
Email: support@statevoucher.org
http://www.fc2success.org/programs/scholarships-and-grants/
Purpose: To support foster care students pursuing a higher education.
Eligibility: Applicants must have been in foster care for their 18th birthday and have aged out at that time, been adopted from foster care with the adoption finalized after their 16th birthday, or have their foster care case closed between the ages of 18 and 21. Students must be residents of Alabama, Arizona, Colorado, Maryland, Missouri, New York, North Carolina, Ohio or the District of Columbia. Students must be a U.S. citizen with assets worth less than $10,000. Applicants must be at least 17 but younger than 21 to apply for the first time. Students must have been accepted into a degree, certificate or other accredited program at a college, university, technical or vocational school.
Target applicant(s): High school students. College students. Adult students.
Amount: $2,500-$5,000.
Number of awards: Varies.
Scholarship may be renewable.
Deadline: March 31.
How to apply: Applications are available online.
Exclusive: Visit www.UltimateScholarshipBook.com and enter code FO135526 for updates on this award.

[1356] • Educator Support Scholarship

Delaware Department of Education - School Supports
The Townsend Building, 401 Federal Street, Suite 2, Dover, DE 19901-3639
Phone: 800-292-7935
Email: dhec@doe.k12.de.us
https://scholarships.delawarestudentsuccess.org/
Purpose: To support academically-talented Delaware student residents.
Eligibility: Applicants must be full-time graduate or undergraduate students attending a Delaware public or private college who intend to pursue a career in education (in a classroom or as a specialist) in specific certifications identified as areas of need in Delaware schools. Students must be residents of Delaware, U.S. citizens or eligible non-citizens enrolled on a full-time basis and who meet their institution's satisfactory academic policy.
Target applicant(s): High school students. College students. Graduate school students. Adult students.
Amount: $5,000.
Number of awards: 1.
Deadline: May 15.
How to apply: Applications are available online.
Exclusive: Visit www.UltimateScholarshipBook.com and enter code DE135626 for updates on this award.

[1357] • Educators for Maine Program

Finance Authority of Maine
5 Community Drive, Augusta, ME 04330
Phone: 207-623-3263
Email: Education@FAMEmaine.com
https://www.famemaine.com/
Purpose: To support Maine students pursuing careers in education or child care and planning to work in Maine after graduation.
Eligibility: Applicants must be Maine residents and graduating high school seniors or undergraduate and graduate students accepted into post-secondary degree programs. Students must be enrolled full-time as undergraduates or as graduate students enrolled at least half-time in an accredited U.S. college or university. Applicants must have a minimum 3.0 GPA and be pursuing initial certification as a teacher, including speech pathology or child-care-provider qualifications.
Target applicant(s): High school students. College students. Graduate school students. Adult students.
Minimum GPA: 3.0
Amount: Up to $4,000.
Number of awards: Varies.
Scholarship may be renewable.
Deadline: May 1.
How to apply: Applications are available online.
Exclusive: Visit www.UltimateScholarshipBook.com and enter code FI135726 for updates on this award.

[1358] • Edward L. Simeth Scholarships

Tool, Die and Machining Association of Wisconsin
W175 N11117 Stonewood Drive, Suite 280, Germantown, WI 53022
Phone: 262-532-2440
Email: toolmaker@TDMAW.org
https://tdmaw.org/Scholarships-Available!
Purpose: To support Wisconsin students who are enrolled in a machine tool operations or tool and die training program at an accredited technical school.
Eligibility: Applicants must be Wisconsin residents, and they must have a high school diploma or GED. They must have completed at least one semester at an accredited technical school located in Wisconsin or pursuing a state apprenticeship and be enrolled in a machine tool operations or tool and die program. Selection is based on the overall strength of the application.
Target applicant(s): College students. Adult students.
Minimum GPA: 3.0
Amount: Up to $500 per semester.
Number of awards: Varies.
Scholarship may be renewable.
Deadline: July 15 (Fall); December 1 (Spring).
How to apply: Applications are available online. An application form, an official transcript and two references are required.
Exclusive: Visit www.UltimateScholarshipBook.com and enter code TO135826 for updates on this award.

[1359] • Edward Payson and Bernice Piilani Irwin Scholarship

Hawaii Community Foundation - Scholarships
827 Fort Street Mall, Honolulu, HI 96813
Phone: 888-731-3863
Email: scholarships@hcf-hawaii.org
https://www.hawaiicommunityfoundation.org/
Purpose: To provide financial assistance to Hawaii students who are pursuing careers in journalism.
Eligibility: Applicants must be college juniors, college seniors or graduate students majoring in journalism or communications. They must have a GPA of 2.75 or higher.
Target applicant(s): College students. Graduate school students. Adult students.
Minimum GPA: 2.75
Amount: Varies.
Number of awards: Varies.
Deadline: February 28.
How to apply: To apply, register online, complete the online application and select the scholarships to which you wish to apply. In addition, mail the supporting materials: printed confirmation page from the online application, personal statement, copy of Student Aid Report (SAR) available at www.fafsa.ed.gov and official transcript.
Exclusive: Visit www.UltimateScholarshipBook.com and enter code HA135926 for updates on this award.

[1360] • Eizo and Toyo Sakumoto Trust Scholarship

Hawaii Community Foundation - Scholarships
827 Fort Street Mall, Honolulu, HI 96813
Phone: 888-731-3863
Email: scholarships@hcf-hawaii.org
https://www.hawaiicommunityfoundation.org/
Purpose: To assist Hawaiian students of Japanese ancestry.
Eligibility: Applicants must be Hawaii residents of primarily Japanese ancestry who were born in the state and who are a graduate level student at a college or university in Hawaii. They must have a GPA of 3.5 or higher and prove financial need.
Target applicant(s): Graduate school students. Adult students.
Minimum GPA: 3.5
Amount: Varies.
Number of awards: Varies.
Deadline: February 28.
How to apply: To apply, register online, complete the online application and select the scholarships to which you wish to apply. In addition, mail the supporting materials: printed confirmation page from the online application, personal statement, copy of Student Aid Report (SAR) available at www.fafsa.ed.gov and official transcript.
Exclusive: Visit www.UltimateScholarshipBook.com and enter code HA136026 for updates on this award.

[1361] • Ellison Onizuka Memorial Scholarship Fund

Hawaii Community Foundation - Scholarships
827 Fort Street Mall, Honolulu, HI 96813
Phone: 888-731-3863
Email: scholarships@hcf-hawaii.org
https://www.hawaiicommunityfoundation.org/
Purpose: To provide financial assistance to Hawaii students who plan to major in aerospace engineering.
Eligibility: Applicants must be graduating high school in the year of application and plan to pursue a degree in aerospace engineering or a related field. Students must have a GPA of 3.0, and their transcripts must list their SAT scores.
Target applicant(s): High school students.
Minimum GPA: 3.0
Amount: Varies.
Number of awards: Varies.
Deadline: February 28.
How to apply: To apply, register online, complete the online application and select the scholarships to which you wish to apply. In addition, mail the supporting materials: printed confirmation page from the online application, two letters of recommendation, personal statement, copy of Student Aid Report (SAR) available at www.fafsa.ed.gov and official transcript. The personal statement must describe participation in extracurricular activities, clubs and community service.
Exclusive: Visit www.UltimateScholarshipBook.com and enter code HA136126 for updates on this award.

[1362] • Emily M. Hewitt and Stephen K. Stocking Memorial Scholarship

Calaveras Big Trees Association
P.O. Box 1196, Arnold, CA 95223
Phone: 209-795-3840
Email: info@bigtrees.org
http://www.bigtrees.org
Purpose: To support students who are committed to communicating a love of nature and an understanding of the need to practice conservation.
Eligibility: Applicants must be enrolled full-time in an accredited California post-secondary educational institution and must have career goals that are related to communicating and interpreting nature's wonder. Students pursuing degrees in environmental protection, forestry, wildlife and fisheries biology, parks and recreation, park management, environmental law and public policy, environmental art and California history are encouraged to apply. Selection is based on dedication to the ideals of the scholarship and financial need.
Target applicant(s): High school students. College students. Graduate school students. Adult students.
Amount: $3,000.
Number of awards: 2.
Deadline: April 15.
How to apply: Students must submit a statement of personal and career goals, a resume (and portfolio if applicable) and transcripts of all college work completed to date. On the cover page, include your name, address, phone number and college major.
Exclusive: Visit www.UltimateScholarshipBook.com and enter code CA136226 for updates on this award.

[1363] • Engineering Foundation of Wisconsin Scholarship

Wisconsin Society of Professional Engineers
7044 South 13th Street, Oak Creek, WI 53154
Phone: 414-908-4950
Email: customercare@wspe.org
http://www.wspe.org
Purpose: To aid Wisconsin high school seniors who are planning to pursue education and careers in engineering.
Eligibility: Applicants must be current high school seniors who are U.S. citizens and Wisconsin residents. They must plan to enroll in an

undergraduate engineering program at an ABET-accredited school and must intend to pursue careers in engineering after graduating. They must have a GPA of 3.0 or more and an ACT composite score of at least 24. Selection is based on GPA, ACT score, class rank, extracurricular involvement, honors, personal essay and any AP or college-level courses taken.
Target applicant(s): High school students.
Minimum GPA: 3.0
Amount: $2,500.
Number of awards: 4.
Deadline: December 16.
How to apply: Applications are available online. An application form, transcript and personal essay are required.
Exclusive: Visit www.UltimateScholarshipBook.com and enter code WI136326 for updates on this award.

[1364] • Engineers Foundation of Ohio General Fund Scholarship

Engineers Foundation of Ohio
400 South Fifth Street, Suite 300, Columbus, OH 43215-5430
Phone: 614-223-1177
Email: efo@ohioengineer.com
http://www.ohioengineer.com
Purpose: To aid Ohio engineering students.
Eligibility: Applicants must be U.S. citizens and residents of Ohio. They must be rising juniors or seniors enrolled full-time in an ABET-accredited engineering program that leads to the bachelor of science or its equivalent. They must have a GPA of 3.0 or higher on a 4-point scale. Selection is based on academic achievement, extracurricular involvements and financial need.
Target applicant(s): College students. Adult students.
Minimum GPA: 3.0
Amount: $1,000.
Number of awards: 1.
Deadline: February 15.
How to apply: Applications are available online. An application form, personal essay, faculty evaluation and transcript are required.
Exclusive: Visit www.UltimateScholarshipBook.com and enter code EN136426 for updates on this award.

[1365] • Epsilon Sigma Alpha

College Foundation of North Carolina
2917 Highwoods Boulevard, Raleigh, NC 27604
Phone: 866-866-2362
https://www.cfnc.org/pay-for-college/apply-for-financial-aid/
Purpose: To provide financial assistance to students who want to work with exceptional children.
Eligibility: Applicants must be enrolled in an accredited college or university, either at the undergraduate level or as a North Carolina teacher seeking training, and must be training to work with special needs children up to the age of 21 in an educational setting. They must agree to teach at a North Carolina public school for at least one year after graduation.
Target applicant(s): College students. Graduate school students. Adult students.
Amount: $500-$2,500.
Number of awards: Varies.
Deadline: February 1.
How to apply: Applications are available online.
Exclusive: Visit www.UltimateScholarshipBook.com and enter code CO136526 for updates on this award.

[1366] • ERC Eco Scholarship Fund

Environmental Research Center
3111 Camino Del Rio North, Suite 400, San Diego, CA 92108
Phone: 619-500-3090
Email: ERCprograms@gmail.com
http://www.erc501c3.org
Purpose: To support graduating high school seniors residing in California who intend to major in an environmental studies program.
Eligibility: Applicants must be U.S. citizens and residents of California who are graduating high school seniors. Students must be accepted to a California college or university and intend to pursue a degree in environmental studies. A minimum high school GPA of 3.25 is required and applicants must have completed at least one high school science class in addition to the minimum amount required for graduation.
Target applicant(s): High school students.
Minimum GPA: 3.25
Amount: $1,000.
Number of awards: Varies.
Deadline: There is no deadline for submission, as scholarships are distributed on an ongoing basis.
How to apply: Applications are available online.
Exclusive: Visit www.UltimateScholarshipBook.com and enter code EN136626 for updates on this award.

[1367] • Esther Kanagawa Memorial Art Scholarship

Hawaii Community Foundation - Scholarships
827 Fort Street Mall, Honolulu, HI 96813
Phone: 888-731-3863
Email: scholarships@hcf-hawaii.org
https://www.hawaiicommunityfoundation.org/
Purpose: To provide financial assistance to Hawaii students who are majoring in fine arts.
Eligibility: Applicants must be current high school seniors who plan to major in fine arts at an accredited college or university. They must have a GPA of 2.7 or higher and demonstrate financial need and good character.
Target applicant(s): High school students.
Minimum GPA: 2.7
Amount: Varies.
Number of awards: Varies.
Deadline: February 28.
How to apply: To apply, register online, complete the online application and select the scholarships to which you wish to apply. In addition, mail the supporting materials: printed confirmation page from the online application, personal statement, copy of Student Aid Report (SAR) available at www.fafsa.ed.gov and official transcript.
Exclusive: Visit www.UltimateScholarshipBook.com and enter code HA136726 for updates on this award.

[1368] • Exemption for Highest Ranking High School Graduate

Texas Higher Education Coordinating Board
1200 East Anderson Lane, Austin, TX 78752
Phone: 888-311-8881.
Email: pamela.harris@thecb.state.tx.us
http://www.collegeforalltexans.com
Purpose: To support students who are the top graduate of their high school class.
Eligibility: Applicant must be a resident, nonresident or foreign student of Texas and intending on attending a Texas public college or university.

The Ultimate Scholarship Book 2026
Scholarship Directory (State of Residence)

Students must provide documentation of their high school ranking. Applicants will receive full tuition for their first year of college.
Target applicant(s): High school students.
Amount: Full Tuition.
Number of awards: Varies.
Deadline: Contact the sponsor to confirm the deadline.
How to apply: Applications are available online.
Exclusive: Visit www.UltimateScholarshipBook.com and enter code TE136826 for updates on this award.

[1369] • Exemption for Texas Veterans (Hazelwood Exemption)
Texas Higher Education Coordinating Board
1200 East Anderson Lane, Austin, TX 78752
Phone: 888-311-8881.
Email: pamela.harris@thecb.state.tx.us
http://www.collegeforalltexans.com
Purpose: To support qualified veterans with educational benefits at public institutions of higher education in Texas.
Eligibility: Applicants must be a qualified veteran, spouse or dependent child to qualify for this exemption. Students must have been accepted to a Texas public college or university. Applicants must provide proof of GI Bill benefits. Students must enroll in the Hazlewood On-Line database as part of the exemption process.
Target applicant(s): College students. Adult students.
Amount: Up to 150 semester hours.
Number of awards: 1.
Scholarship may be renewable.
Deadline: Check with your school on application deadline policies.
How to apply: Applications are available online.
Exclusive: Visit www.UltimateScholarshipBook.com and enter code TE136926 for updates on this award.

[1370] • Exemption from Tuition Fees for Dependents of Kentucky Veterans
Kentucky Department of Veterans Affairs
Attn.: Tuition Waiver Coordinator, 321 West Main Street, Suite 390, Louisville, KY 40202
Phone: 502-595-4447
Email: barbaraa.hale@ky.gov
https://veterans.ky.gov
Purpose: To support the families of Kentucky veterans.
Eligibility: Applicants must be children, stepchildren, adopted children, spouses or unremarried widows or widowers of qualifying Kentucky veterans. The veteran must have died on active duty or as a result of a service-connected disability, be 100 percent disabled from service, be totally disabled with wartime service or be deceased and have served during wartime. Children of veterans must be 26 years of age or younger.
Target applicant(s): High school students. College students. Adult students.
Amount: Full tuition.
Number of awards: Varies.
Deadline: Contact the sponsor to confirm the deadline.
How to apply: Applications are available online. An application form, birth or marriage certificate, veteran's discharge certificate, death certificate or disability award letter and evidence of Kentucky residency are required.
Exclusive: Visit www.UltimateScholarshipBook.com and enter code KE137026 for updates on this award.

[1371] • F. Koehnen Ltd. Scholarship Fund
Hawaii Community Foundation - Scholarships
827 Fort Street Mall, Honolulu, HI 96813
Phone: 888-731-3863
Email: scholarships@hcf-hawaii.org
https://www.hawaiicommunityfoundation.org/
Purpose: To provide financial assistance to students whose parents or grandparents are employed in Hawaiian retail establishments.
Eligibility: Applicants must be Hawaii high school graduates with a GPA of 2.0 or higher. They must be children or grandchildren of retail employees on the island of Hawaii.
Target applicant(s): High school students. College students. Graduate school students. Adult students.
Minimum GPA: 2.0
Amount: Varies.
Number of awards: Varies.
Deadline: February 28.
How to apply: To apply, register online, complete the online application and select the scholarships to which you wish to apply. In addition, mail the supporting materials: printed confirmation page from the online application, personal statement, copy of Student Aid Report (SAR) available at www.fafsa.ed.gov and official transcript.
Exclusive: Visit www.UltimateScholarshipBook.com and enter code HA137126 for updates on this award.

[1372] • Family District 1 Scholarships
American Hellenic Education Progressive Association
1909 Q Street NW, Suite 500, Washington, DC 20009
Phone: 202-232-6300
Email: admin@ahepa.org
https://ahepa.org/education/
Purpose: To provide financial assistance for those pursuing higher education.
Eligibility: Applicants must be graduating seniors, high school graduates or current undergraduate or graduate students who plan to attend a college or university full-time during the calendar year of application. They must be residents of Alabama, Georgia, Mississippi, South Carolina, Tennessee or Florida.
Target applicant(s): High school students. College students. Graduate school students. Adult students.
Amount: Varies.
Number of awards: Varies.
Deadline: March 31.
How to apply: Applications are available online. The current application must be used and must be sent by certified mail and return receipt requested.
Exclusive: Visit www.UltimateScholarshipBook.com and enter code AM137226 for updates on this award.

[1373] • Fellowship on Women and Public Policy
Center for Women in Government and Civil Society
University at Albany, SUNY, 135 Western Avenue, Draper Hall 302, Albany, NY 12222
Phone: 518-442-3900
http://www.cwig.albany.edu
Purpose: To encourage New York state graduate students to pursue jobs in public policy.
Eligibility: Students must be enrolled in a graduate program at an accredited college or university in New York and have completed at least 12 credits before applying but not be scheduled to graduate before the

internship, and must have minimum 3-5 years work/internship experience and minimum 3.0 GPA. Applicants must demonstrate an interest in improving the status of women and underrepresented populations.
Target applicant(s): Graduate school students. Adult students.
Minimum GPA: 3.0
Amount: $12,000 stipend and tuition assistance.
Number of awards: Varies.
Deadline: September 1.
How to apply: Applications are available online.
Exclusive: Visit www.UltimateScholarshipBook.com and enter code CE137326 for updates on this award.

[1374] • Fields of Learning Scholarship
Fields of Learning
9357 Sperry Road, Kirtland Hills, OH 44060
Phone: 440-256-3757
http://www.fieldsoflearning.org
Purpose: To encourage students who wish to pursue education following high school and have an interest in high school football.
Eligibility: Applicants must write an essay of 700 to 1,500 words based on a true story about what the student has learned related to high school football. Students must intend to use the funds for post high school education within one year of graduating high school. Applicants can be in grades nine through twelve. Students do not have to be on the football team to apply.
Target applicant(s): High school students.
Amount: $1,000.
Number of awards: 5.
Deadline: March 31.
How to apply: Applications are available online.
Exclusive: Visit www.UltimateScholarshipBook.com and enter code FI137426 for updates on this award.

[1375] • First Generation Matching Grant Program
Florida Department of Education
Office of Student Financial Assistance, State Scholarship and Grant Programs, 325 West Gaines Street, Suite 1314, Tallahassee, FL 32399-0400
Phone: 888-827-2004
Email: osfa@fldoe.org
https://origin.fldoe.org/finance/financial-aid-scholarships/
Purpose: To help Florida undergraduate students with financial need who are enrolled in state universities and whose parents have not earned bachelor's degrees.
Eligibility: Applicants must submit applications and the Free Application for Federal Student Aid (FAFSA). Each university determines its own deadline.
Target applicant(s): High school students. College students. Adult students.
Amount: Varies.
Number of awards: Varies.
Deadline: Contact the sponsor to confirm the deadline.
How to apply: Applications are at the financial aid offices of state universities.
Exclusive: Visit www.UltimateScholarshipBook.com and enter code FL137526 for updates on this award.

[1376] • First-Year Teacher Scholarships
Texas Retired Teachers Foundation
Attn.: Scholarship Committee, 313 E. 12th Street, Suite 220, Austin, TX 78701
Phone: 512-476-1622
Email: info@trtf.org
https://trtf.org/
Purpose: To assist new Texas teachers.
Eligibility: Applicants must be employed in a Texas public-school district and be teaching in the classroom.
Target applicant(s): High school students. College students. Graduate school students. Adult students.
Amount: $1,000.
Number of awards: 35.
Deadline: January 26.
How to apply: Applications are available online.
Exclusive: Visit www.UltimateScholarshipBook.com and enter code TE137626 for updates on this award.

[1377] • Florida Bright Futures Scholarship Program
Florida Department of Education
Office of Student Financial Assistance, State Scholarship and Grant Programs, 325 West Gaines Street, Suite 1314, Tallahassee, FL 32399-0400
Phone: 888-827-2004
Email: osfa@fldoe.org
https://origin.fldoe.org/finance/financial-aid-scholarships/
Purpose: Lottery-funded scholarships are awarded to Florida high school seniors as reward for academic achievements and to assist with postsecondary education.
Eligibility: Applicants must earn a Florida high school diploma or equivalent, have not been found guilty or plead no contest to a felony charge and meet the award's academic requirements. Applicants must also be Florida residents, U.S. citizens or eligible noncitizens and be accepted by and enrolled in an eligible Florida public or private college or vocational school at least quarter time. Application must be completed during the senior year of high school.
Target applicant(s): High school students.
Amount: Varies.
Number of awards: Varies.
Deadline: August 31.
How to apply: Apply by completing the Florida Financial Aid Application. The application is available online at www.floridastudentfinancialaid.org or from your high school guidance counselor.
Exclusive: Visit www.UltimateScholarshipBook.com and enter code FL137726 for updates on this award.

[1378] • Florida Engineers in Construction Scholarship
Florida Engineering Society
125 South Gadsden Street, Tallahassee, FL 32302-0750
Phone: 850-224-7121
Email: allen@fleng.org
https://www.fleng.org
Purpose: To aid Florida engineering majors who are interested in careers in construction.
Eligibility: Applicants must be undergraduate juniors or seniors enrolled or accepted in an accredited degree program in engineering at a Florida university. They must have a GPA of at least 3.0 on a 4.0 scale and must have

The Ultimate Scholarship Book 2026
Scholarship Directory (State of Residence)

plans to pursue a career in construction. Please include a recommendation by an engineering faculty member. Selection is based on the overall strength of the application.
Target applicant(s): College students. Adult students.
Minimum GPA: 3.0
Amount: $1,000.
Number of awards: 1.
Deadline: April 19.
How to apply: Applications are available online. An application form, a transcript and one letter of recommendation are required.
Exclusive: Visit www.UltimateScholarshipBook.com and enter code FL137826 for updates on this award.

[1379] • Florida Governor's Black History Month Essay Contest
Volunteer Florida
Black History Month Committee, 1545 Raymond Diehl Road, Suite 250, Tallahassee, FL 32308
Phone: 850-414-7400
Email: info@volunteerflorida.org
http://www.floridablackhistory.com
Purpose: To promote Black History Month.
Eligibility: Applicants must be Florida students in grades 4-12 and compose an essay on the given topic. Winners receive a four-year full scholarship to a Florida state college or university and a trip to the Governor's Black History Month celebration.
Target applicant(s): Junior high students or younger. High school students.
Amount: Full tuition.
Number of awards: 3.
Scholarship may be renewable.
Deadline: February 7.
How to apply: Applications are available online. A parental waiver, essay and student's contact information are required.
Exclusive: Visit www.UltimateScholarshipBook.com and enter code VO137926 for updates on this award.

[1380] • Florida Oratorical Contest
American Legion, Department of Florida
Elizabeth Douglas, Programs Director, 1912A Lee Road, Orlando, FL 32810
Phone: 800-393-3378
Email: mail@floridalegion.org
https://www.floridalegion.org/programs-services/scholarships/
Purpose: To enhance high school students' experience with and understanding of the U.S. Constitution. The contest will help develop students' leadership skills and civic appreciation, as well as the ability to deliver thoughtful, insightful orations regarding U.S. citizenship and its inherent responsibilities.
Eligibility: Applicants must be high school students under the age of 20 who are U.S. citizens or legal residents and residents of the state. Students first give an oration within their state and winners compete at the national level. The oration must be related to the Constitution of the United States focusing on the duties and obligations citizens have to the government. It must be in English and be between eight and ten minutes. There is also an assigned topic which is posted on the website, and it should be between three and five minutes.
Target applicant(s): Junior high students or younger. High school students.
Amount: $500-$18,000.
Number of awards: Varies.
Deadline: March 30.
How to apply: Applications are available by contacting the local American Legion Post.
Exclusive: Visit www.UltimateScholarshipBook.com and enter code AM138026 for updates on this award.

[1381] • Florida Student Assistance Grant Program
Florida Department of Education
Office of Student Financial Assistance, State Scholarship and Grant Programs, 325 West Gaines Street, Suite 1314, Tallahassee, FL 32399-0400
Phone: 888-827-2004
Email: osfa@fldoe.org
https://origin.fldoe.org/finance/financial-aid-scholarships/
Purpose: To help degree-seeking, Florida resident, undergraduate students who have financial need and who are enrolled in participating postsecondary institutions.
Eligibility: There are three student financial aid programs: The Florida Public Student Assistance Grant is for students who attend state universities and public community colleges. The Florida Private Student Assistance Grant is for students who attend eligible private, non-profit, four-year colleges and universities. The Florida Postsecondary Student Assistance Grant is for students who attend eligible degree-granting private colleges and universities that are ineligible under the Florida Private Student Assistance Grant. High school students in the top 20 percent of their classes receive priority funding.
Target applicant(s): High school students. College students. Adult students.
Amount: At least $200.
Number of awards: Varies.
Scholarship may be renewable.
Deadline: Contact the sponsor to confirm the deadline.
How to apply: Applicants must submit the Free Application for Federal Student Aid (FAFSA).
Exclusive: Visit www.UltimateScholarshipBook.com and enter code FL138126 for updates on this award.

[1382] • Ford Opportunity Program
Ford Family Foundation Scholarship Office
44 Club Road, Suite 100, Eugene, OR 97401
Phone: 541-485-6211
Email: fordscholarships@tfff.org
https://www.tfff.org/
Purpose: To assist single parents pursuing higher education.
Eligibility: Applicants must be residents of Oregon or Siskiyou County, California and parents or adult learners 25 years of age or older. Students must be seeking an associate or bachelor's degree at an eligible public or private college and have not previously earned a bachelor's degree. Applicants must have at least one year remaining in their degree program and plan to enroll full-time in their state of residence.
Target applicant(s): Adult students.
Amount: Varies.
Number of awards: Varies.
Scholarship may be renewable.
Deadline: March 1.
How to apply: Applications are available online.
Exclusive: Visit www.UltimateScholarshipBook.com and enter code FO138226 for updates on this award.

[1383] • Foster Child Grant Program
Massachusetts Department of Higher Education
Office of Student Financial Assistance, 454 Broadway, Suite 200, Revere, MA 02151
Phone: 617-727-9420
Email: osfa@osfa.mass.edu
https://www.mass.gov/handbook/massachusetts-financial-aid-programs
Purpose: To assist children who have lived in foster homes in obtaining higher education.
Eligibility: Applicants must be placed in the custody of the Department of Social Services and be permanent residents of the state of Massachusetts. Students must be younger than 25 years of age at the start of the academic year and apply for financial aid.
Target applicant(s): High school students. College students. Graduate school students.
Amount: Up to $6,000.
Number of awards: Varies.
Scholarship may be renewable.
Deadline: Contact the sponsor to confirm the deadline.
How to apply: Applications are available by phone from the Massachusetts Office of Student Financial Assistance or from your social worker.
Exclusive: Visit www.UltimateScholarshipBook.com and enter code MA138326 for updates on this award.

[1384] • Four-year or Bachelor's Degree Program
New Hampshire Charitable Foundation
37 Pleasant Street, Concord, NH 03301-4005
Phone: 603-225-6641
Email: jessica.kierstead@nhcf.org
https://www.nhcf.org/how-can-we-help-you/
Purpose: To support New Hampshire students who are seeking a four-year degree program.
Eligibility: Applicants must be New Hampshire residents who are enrolling in a four-year degree program. Students must prove financial need. Selection is based on need, academic merit, community service, extracurricular activities and work experience.
Target applicant(s): High school students. College students. Adult students.
Amount: $250-$7,500.
Number of awards: Varies.
Deadline: April 12 (under 24); For those over 24: December 13.
How to apply: Applications are available online.
Exclusive: Visit www.UltimateScholarshipBook.com and enter code NE138426 for updates on this award.

[1385] • Four-Year Undergraduate Scholarships
Los Alamos National Laboratory Foundation
1112 Plaza del Norte, Espanola, NM 87532
Phone: 505-753-8890
Email: tony@lanlfoundation.org
http://www.lanlfoundation.org
Purpose: To support students from northern New Mexico who have demonstrated leadership skills in their homes, schools and communities.
Eligibility: Students must have at least a 3.25 cumulative unweighted GPA, and be residents of Northern New Mexico in Los Alamos, Mora, Rio Arriba, San Miguel, Sandoval, Santa Fe, or Taos Counties. Applicants must submit an essay and two letters of recommendation.
Target applicant(s): High school students. College students. Adult students.
Minimum GPA: 3.25
Amount: Varies.
Number of awards: 4.
Scholarship may be renewable.
Deadline: January 16.
How to apply: Applications are available online.
Exclusive: Visit www.UltimateScholarshipBook.com and enter code LO138526 for updates on this award.

[1386] • Frances Koop Parsons/AT&T Pioneers Memorial Scholarship
Oklahoma State Regents for Higher Education
655 Research Parkway, Suite 200, Oklahoma City, OK 73104
Phone: 405-225-9100
Email: studentinfo@osrhe.edu
http://www.okhighered.org
Purpose: To assist Oklahoma students in obtaining their education goals.
Eligibility: Applicants must be Oklahoma residents and first-time freshmen with a minimum 3.0 high school GPA. Students must enroll full-time at an eligible Oklahoma post-secondary institution and have a family income not exceeding $75,000. Preference will be given to students with a strong volunteer and leadership background.
Target applicant(s): High school students.
Minimum GPA: 3.0
Amount: $1,000.
Number of awards: 1.
Deadline: March 25.
How to apply: Applications are available online.
Exclusive: Visit www.UltimateScholarshipBook.com and enter code OK138626 for updates on this award.

[1387] • Frances L. Macartney Porter Fund
Rhode Island Foundation
One Union Station, Providence, RI 02903
Phone: 401-274-4564
Email: rbogert@rifoundation.org
https://rifoundation.org/grants-scholarships
Purpose: To encourage single parents from Rhode Island to pursue higher education.
Eligibility: Applicants must be single parents who are residents of Rhode Island or are attending a Rhode Island institution of higher learning. Students can be enrolled in certificate programs or degree granting programs. Preference will be given to applicants enrolled in trade schools.
Target applicant(s): College students. Adult students.
Amount: $1,000-$4,000.
Number of awards: Varies.
Scholarship may be renewable.
Deadline: April 15.
How to apply: Applications are available online.
Exclusive: Visit www.UltimateScholarshipBook.com and enter code RH138726 for updates on this award.

[1388] • Friends of the California State Fair Scholarship Program
California State Fair
1600 Exposition Boulevard, Sacramento, CA 95815
Phone: 916-263-3247
Email: scholarship@calexpo.com

The Ultimate Scholarship Book 2026
Scholarship Directory (State of Residence)

https://calexpostatefair.com/participate/friends-of-the-ca-state-fair/scholarship/
Purpose: To reward and motivate well-rounded, high-achieving California students.
Eligibility: Applicants must be enrolled or plan to enroll in a four-year accredited California institution of higher learning. They must have a GPA of 3.0 or higher and have a valid California ID.
Target applicant(s): High school students. College students. Adult students.
Minimum GPA: 3.0
Amount: Up to $2,500.
Number of awards: Varies.
Deadline: March 1.
How to apply: Applications are available online.
Exclusive: Visit www.UltimateScholarshipBook.com and enter code CA138826 for updates on this award.

[1389] • Future Ready Iowa Grant
Future Ready Iowa
Email: frigrants@iwd.iowa.gov
https://www.futurereadyiowa.gov
Purpose: To support Iowa students who have previously earned at least half the credits necessary for an eligible bachelor's degree that leads to a high-demand job.
Eligibility: Applicants must have applied for all other available financial aid and have not been enrolled in post-secondary education for two or more years. Eligible institutions are accredited Iowa colleges or universities that offer bachelor's degree programs aligned with high-demand jobs.
Target applicant(s): College students. Adult students.
Amount: Varies.
Number of awards: Varies.
Deadline: As soon as possible after October 1.
How to apply: Applications are available online.
Exclusive: Visit www.UltimateScholarshipBook.com and enter code FU138926 for updates on this award.

[1390] • Future Ready Iowa Last-Dollar Scholarship
Future Ready Iowa
Email: frigrants@iwd.iowa.gov
https://www.futurereadyiowa.gov
Purpose: To support Iowa students with higher education expenses.
Eligibility: Applicants must be recent high school graduates enrolling in an eligible program full-time, recent high school graduates who are enrolling in an eligible program part-time and are employed in an approved work-based learning program or adult learners 20 years of age or older starting an eligible program at least part-time. Students must have applied for all other available financial aid and plan to earn a credential for a high-demand job. Eligible institutions are Iowa community colleges or accredited private colleges in Iowa that offer qualified programs of study.
Target applicant(s): High school students. College students. Adult students.
Amount: Varies.
Number of awards: Varies.
Deadline: December 31.
How to apply: Applications are available online.
Exclusive: Visit www.UltimateScholarshipBook.com and enter code FU139026 for updates on this award.

[1391] • GEAR UP Idaho Scholarship 3
Idaho State Board of Education
650 West State Street, 3rd Floor, Boise, ID 83702
Phone: 208-334-2270
Email: Joy.Miller@osbe.idaho.gov
https://boardofed.idaho.gov/scholarships/
Purpose: Monetary assistance is provided to Idaho resident high school students for freshman expenses at Idaho colleges or universities.
Eligibility: Applicants must have graduated from an Idaho high school, be entering freshmen at an eligible Idaho college or university, be residents of Idaho and have a minimum 3.0 GPA or minimum ACT score of 20. Applicants must also be younger than 22 years old and complete at least 12 credits per semester with a minimum 2.5 GPA to remain eligible for renewal.
Target applicant(s): High school students.
Minimum GPA: 3.0
Amount: Varies.
Number of awards: Varies.
Scholarship may be renewable.
Deadline: March 1.
How to apply: Contact eligible college or university financial aid office.
Exclusive: Visit www.UltimateScholarshipBook.com and enter code ID139126 for updates on this award.

[1392] • General Assembly Merit Scholarship
Tennessee Student Assistance Corporation
312 Rosa L. Parks Avenue, 9th Floor, Nashville, TN 37243
Phone: 800-342-1663
Email: tsac.aidinfo@tn.gov
https://www.collegefortn.org/about-financial-aid/
Purpose: To provide supplemental support to recipients of the Tennessee HOPE Scholarship.
Eligibility: Students graduating from public schools or category 1, 2 and 3 private schools must have at least a 3.75 GPA and either a 29 on the ACT or a 1280 on the SAT. Home-schooled or non-category 1, 2 or 3 private school students must complete at least 12 college credit hours while in high school, and they must have at least a 3.0 GPA in those courses. Recipients of the Aspire Award are not eligible.
Target applicant(s): High school students.
Minimum GPA: 3.75
Amount: Up to $1,500.
Number of awards: Varies.
Deadline: September 1; February 1.
How to apply: Applications are available through completion of the FAFSA.
Exclusive: Visit www.UltimateScholarshipBook.com and enter code TE139226 for updates on this award.

[1393] • George and Donna Nigh Public Service Scholarship
Oklahoma State Regents for Higher Education/George and Donna Nigh Public Service Scholarship
University of Central Oklahoma, ADM 104C, Box 109, 100 N. University Drive, Edmond, OK 73034
Phone: 405-974-2626
Email: cpainter1@uco.edu
https://secure.okcollegestart.org/Financial_Aid_Planning/Scholarships
Purpose: To support Oklahoma students who are pursuing a career in public service.

Eligibility: Applicants must be residents of the state of Oklahoma who are enrolled full-time in an undergraduate program at an Oklahoma college or university. Students must be enrolled in a program leading to a career in public service and must demonstrate exceptional academic achievement.
Target applicant(s): College students. Adult students.
Amount: $1,000.
Number of awards: Varies.
Deadline: January 12.
How to apply: Applications are available online.
Exclusive: Visit www.UltimateScholarshipBook.com and enter code OK139326 for updates on this award.

[1394] • George Mason Business Scholarship Fund
Hawaii Community Foundation - Scholarships
827 Fort Street Mall, Honolulu, HI 96813
Phone: 888-731-3863
Email: scholarships@hcf-hawaii.org
https://www.hawaiicommunityfoundation.org/
Purpose: To assist Hawaii students who are majoring in business administration.
Eligibility: Applicants must be seniors at a Hawaiian college or university and have a GPA of 3.0 or higher. They must discuss why they have chosen to pursue a business career and how they expect to make a difference in the business world in their personal statement.
Target applicant(s): College students. Adult students.
Minimum GPA: 3.0
Amount: Varies.
Number of awards: Varies.
Deadline: January 31.
How to apply: To apply, register online, complete the online application and select the scholarships to which you wish to apply. In addition, mail the supporting materials: printed confirmation page from the online application, personal statement, copy of Student Aid Report (SAR) available at www.fafsa.ed.gov and official transcript.
Exclusive: Visit www.UltimateScholarshipBook.com and enter code HA139426 for updates on this award.

[1395] • Georgia HOPE GED Grant
Georgia Student Finance Commission
2082 East Exchange Place, Tucker, GA 30084
Phone: 800-505-4732
Email: gsfcinfo@gsfc.org
https://www.gafutures.org
Purpose: To support students who earned a GED diploma awarded by the Technical College System of Georgia (TCSG).
Eligibility: Applicants must have a GED diploma from the Technical College System of Georgia, be U.S. citizens or eligible non-citizens, be a Georgia resident and enroll at an eligible postsecondary institution in Georgia.
Target applicant(s): Adult students.
Amount: $500.
Number of awards: Varies.
Deadline: The last day of the school term or a student's withdrawal date; whichever occurs first.
How to apply: Applications are available online.
Exclusive: Visit www.UltimateScholarshipBook.com and enter code GE139526 for updates on this award.

[1396] • Georgia HOPE Grant
Georgia Student Finance Commission
2082 East Exchange Place, Tucker, GA 30084
Phone: 800-505-4732
Email: gsfcinfo@gsfc.org
https://www.gafutures.org
Purpose: To support Georgia residents who are working towards a certificate or diploma at an eligible college or university in Georgia.
Eligibility: Applicants must be U.S. citizens or eligible non-citizens, be a legal resident of Georgia and working towards a certificate or diploma at an eligible college or university in Georgia.
Target applicant(s): High school students. College students. Adult students.
Amount: Varies.
Number of awards: Varies.
Scholarship may be renewable.
Deadline: The last day of the school term or a student's withdrawal date; whichever occurs first.
How to apply: Applications are available online.
Exclusive: Visit www.UltimateScholarshipBook.com and enter code GE139626 for updates on this award.

[1397] • Georgia Oratorical Contest
American Legion, Department of Georgia
3035 Mt. Zion Road, Stockbridge, GA 30281
Phone: 678-289-8883
Email: amerlegga@bellsouth.net
http://departmentofgeorgiaoratorical.weebly.com/
Purpose: To enhance high school students' experience with and understanding of the U.S. Constitution. The contest will help develop students' leadership skills and civic appreciation, as well as the ability to deliver thoughtful, insightful orations regarding U.S. citizenship and its inherent responsibilities.
Eligibility: Applicants must be high school students under the age of 20 who are U.S. citizens or legal residents and residents of the state. Students first give an oration within their state and winners compete at the national level. The oration must be related to the Constitution of the United States focusing on the duties and obligations citizens have to the government. It must be in English and be between eight and ten minutes. There is also an assigned topic which is posted on the website, and it should be between three and five minutes.
Target applicant(s): Junior high students or younger. High school students.
Amount: Up to $1,300.
Number of awards: Varies.
Deadline: March 3.
How to apply: Applications are available by contacting the local American Legion Post.
Exclusive: Visit www.UltimateScholarshipBook.com and enter code AM139726 for updates on this award.

[1398] • Georgia Press Educational Foundation Scholarships
Georgia Press Educational Foundation Inc.
Georgia Press Building, 3066 Mercer University Drive, Suite 200, Atlanta, GA 30343-4137
Phone: 770-454-6776
Email: sireland@gapress.org
https://gapress.org/scholarships-internships/
Purpose: To aid students interested in newspaper journalism.

The Ultimate Scholarship Book 2026
Scholarship Directory (State of Residence)

Eligibility: Applicants must be high school seniors or undergraduate students who have been Georgia residents for three years, or their parents must have been Georgia residents for two years. Students must attend a Georgia college or university, demonstrate financial need and be recommended by a counselor, principal, professor or Georgia Press Association member.
Target applicant(s): High school students. College students. Adult students.
Amount: $1,500-$2,000.
Number of awards: Varies.
Deadline: March 1.
How to apply: Applications are available online. An application form, transcript, copy of SAT scores, copy of tax return, anticipated budget, school photograph and letter of recommendation are required.
Exclusive: Visit www.UltimateScholarshipBook.com and enter code GE139826 for updates on this award.

[1399] • Georgia Thespians Achievement Scholarships
Georgia Thespians
2897 North Druid Hills Road, Box 225, Atlanta, GA 30329
Phone: 678-910-4487
Email: scholarships@gathespians.org
https://www.gathespians.org/scholarships
Purpose: To support outstanding thespians.
Eligibility: Applicants must be Georgia high school juniors or seniors and perform an audition in one of the following categories: acting, technical theatre, singing or theatre education.
Target applicant(s): High school students.
Amount: $2,000.
Number of awards: 5.
Deadline: December 4.
How to apply: Applications are available online. An application form and resume of thespian troupe experience are required.
Exclusive: Visit www.UltimateScholarshipBook.com and enter code GE139926 for updates on this award.

[1400] • Georgia Tuition Equalization Grant
Georgia Student Finance Commission
2082 East Exchange Place, Tucker, GA 30084
Phone: 800-505-4732
Email: gsfcinfo@gsfc.org
https://www.gafutures.org
Purpose: To support Georgia resident students.
Eligibility: Applicants must be full-time students at eligible private colleges or universities in Georgia and be U.S. citizens and legal residents of the state of Georgia.
Target applicant(s): College students. Adult students.
Amount: $283 per quarter or $425 per semester.
Number of awards: Varies.
Scholarship may be renewable.
Deadline: July 1.
How to apply: Applications are available online.
Exclusive: Visit www.UltimateScholarshipBook.com and enter code GE140026 for updates on this award.

[1401] • Gilbert Matching Student Grant
Massachusetts Department of Higher Education
Office of Student Financial Assistance, 454 Broadway, Suite 200, Revere, MA 02151
Phone: 617-727-9420
Email: osfa@osfa.mass.edu
https://www.mass.gov/handbook/massachusetts-financial-aid-programs
Purpose: To assist needy students in attending private institutions of higher education or nursing schools.
Eligibility: Students must be permanent residents of Massachusetts, demonstrate financial need, maintain satisfactory academic progress and attend an eligible Massachusetts institution. Applicants must not have earned a bachelor's or professional degree, nor a first diploma from a hospital or professional nursing program.
Target applicant(s): High school students. College students. Adult students.
Amount: $200-$2,500.
Number of awards: Varies.
Scholarship may be renewable.
Deadline: Contact the sponsor to confirm the deadline.
How to apply: Applications are available from your school's financial aid office.
Exclusive: Visit www.UltimateScholarshipBook.com and enter code MA140126 for updates on this award.

[1402] • Golden Apple Scholars of Illinois (Illinois Scholars Program)
Golden Apple Foundation
8 South Michigan Avenue, Chicago, IL 60603
Phone: 312-407-0006
http://www.goldenapple.org
Purpose: To offer scholarships to promising students pursuing teaching degrees.
Eligibility: Applicants must be Illinois high school seniors or college sophomores at one of the 53 partner universities in Illinois who are interested in teaching. There are a limited number of spots for college sophomores, and all college students must be nominated by a university liaison. A minimum GPA of 2.5 is required. Students must commit to teaching in an Illinois school of need for five years after graduation.
Target applicant(s): High school students. College students. Adult students.
Minimum GPA: 2.5
Amount: Up to $23,000.
Number of awards: Varies.
Scholarship may be renewable.
Deadline: April 1.
How to apply: Applications are available by calling 312-407-0433, extension 105.
Exclusive: Visit www.UltimateScholarshipBook.com and enter code GO140226 for updates on this award.

[1403] • Golden LEAF Scholars Program – Two-Year Colleges
College Foundation of North Carolina
2917 Highwoods Boulevard, Raleigh, NC 27604
Phone: 866-866-2362
https://www.cfnc.org/pay-for-college/apply-for-financial-aid/
Purpose: To provide need-based financial assistance to North Carolina community college students.

Eligibility: Applicants must be residents of one of the 73 eligible counties and meet specific income requirements as evidenced by FAFSA information (for curriculum students) or the federal TRIO formula (for occupational education students). Degree-seeking students must be enrolled at least half-time.
Target applicant(s): High school students. College students. Adult students.
Amount: Up to $2,250 per year.
Number of awards: Varies.
Scholarship may be renewable.
Deadline: Contact the financial aid office of the community college.
How to apply: Applications are available online.
Exclusive: Visit www.UltimateScholarshipBook.com and enter code CO140326 for updates on this award.

[1404] • Good Eats Scholarship Fund
Hawaii Community Foundation - Scholarships
827 Fort Street Mall, Honolulu, HI 96813
Phone: 888-731-3863
Email: scholarships@hcf-hawaii.org
https://www.hawaiicommunityfoundation.org/
Purpose: To provide financial assistance to Hawaii students pursuing degrees in agriculture and culinary arts, and to encourage them to return to Hawaii upon graduation.
Eligibility: Applicants must be Hawaii residents who plan to study culinary arts or agriculture at a college or university in the continental United States. They must have a GPA of 2.7 or higher and demonstrate interest in food production and preparation through their school or community activities.
Target applicant(s): High school students. College students. Adult students.
Minimum GPA: 2.7
Amount: Varies.
Number of awards: Varies.
Deadline: February 28.
How to apply: To apply, register online, complete the online application and select the scholarships to which you wish to apply. In addition, mail the supporting materials: printed confirmation page from the online application, personal statement, copy of Student Aid Report (SAR) available at www.fafsa.ed.gov and official transcript.
Exclusive: Visit www.UltimateScholarshipBook.com and enter code HA140426 for updates on this award.

[1405] • Gorgas Scholarship Competition
Alabama Junior Academy of Science
c/o Dr. Ellen Buckner, CHS 1506, Samford University, 800 Lakeshore Drive, Birmingham, AL 35229
Phone: 205-910-9877
Email: ebbuckner@gmail.com
http://alabamajunioracademyofscience.org/
Purpose: To aid Alabama residents who are planning to pursue higher education in science.
Eligibility: Applicants must be Alabama residents who are high school seniors and have completed a scientific research project and an accompanying report of no more than 20 pages. They must have completed all college entrance requirements by October 1 of the year of application submission. Selection is based on the quality of the scientific research paper that is submitted as part of the application.
Target applicant(s): High school students.
Amount: Up to $10,000.
Number of awards: Varies.
Deadline: December 19.
How to apply: Applications are available online. An entry form, research paper, official transcript, one letter of recommendation and additional research-related documentation are required.
Exclusive: Visit www.UltimateScholarshipBook.com and enter code AL140526 for updates on this award.

[1406] • Governor Guinn Millennium Scholarship Program
Nevada Office of the State Treasurer
101 N. Carson Street, Suite 4, Carson City, NV 89701
Phone: 702-486-3383
Email: MillenniumScholars@nevadatreasurer.gov
http://www.nevadatreasurer.gov/Programs/Programs/
Purpose: To assist students who have attained high academic achievement in a Nevada high school.
Eligibility: Applicants must graduate from a Nevada public or private high school with a GPA of 3.25 or higher, pass all areas of the Nevada High School Proficiency Exam and have been a resident of Nevada for at least two years in high school.
Target applicant(s): College students. Adult students.
Minimum GPA: 3.25
Amount: $10,000.
Number of awards: 2.
Scholarship may be renewable.
Deadline: The date of high school graduation.
How to apply: Applications are not required. Your school district will submit your name to the State Treasurer's office if you are eligible.
Exclusive: Visit www.UltimateScholarshipBook.com and enter code NE140626 for updates on this award.

[1407] • Governor's Cup Scholarship
Idaho State Board of Education
650 West State Street, 3rd Floor, Boise, ID 83702
Phone: 208-334-2270
Email: Joy.Miller@osbe.idaho.gov
https://boardofed.idaho.gov/scholarships/
Purpose: Monetary assistance is provided to Idaho resident high school seniors planning to attend state colleges.
Eligibility: Applicants must be Idaho high school seniors planning to attend Idaho colleges or universities full-time and have a minimum 2.8 GPA. Public service is a significant factor.
Target applicant(s): High school students.
Minimum GPA: 2.8
Amount: Up to $5,000.
Number of awards: 25.
Scholarship may be renewable.
Deadline: March 1.
How to apply: Applications are available online.
Exclusive: Visit www.UltimateScholarshipBook.com and enter code ID140726 for updates on this award.

[1408] • Governor's Distinguished Scholarship
Arkansas Department of Higher Education
423 Main Street, Suite 400, Little Rock, AR 72201
Phone: 501-371-2050
Email: finaid@adhe.arknet.edu
https://sams.adhe.edu/Scholarship

The Ultimate Scholarship Book 2026
Scholarship Directory (State of Residence)

Purpose: To assist outstanding Arkansas high school graduates to encourage them to attend postsecondary schools in Arkansas.
Eligibility: Applicants must be Arkansas graduating high school seniors who will attend an Arkansas college or university. Selection is based on academic achievement, test scores and leadership. A minimum ACT score of 32, SAT score of 1410 or 3.5 GPA in academic courses is required.
Target applicant(s): High school students.
Minimum GPA: 3.5
Amount: Up to $10,000.
Number of awards: Varies.
Scholarship may be renewable.
Deadline: March 1.
How to apply: Applications are available through your high school counselor and online.
Exclusive: Visit www.UltimateScholarshipBook.com and enter code AR140826 for updates on this award.

[1409] • GPB Art Harris Scholarship
Great Plains Bank
5909 NW Expressway, Suite 400, Oklahoma City, OK 73132
Phone: 405-720-4813
Email: lhopkins@gpbankok.net
https://www.gpbankok.com
Purpose: To support students pursuing a higher education who live in the Great Plains Bank service area.
Eligibility: Applicants must be graduating high school seniors within the Great Plains Bank service area who have at least a 2.0 GPA. Students must have need of financial assistance and be residents of Oklahoma state and citizens of the United States. An essay is required as part of the application process.
Target applicant(s): High school students.
Minimum GPA: 2.0
Amount: $5,000.
Number of awards: 1.
Deadline: April 1.
How to apply: Applications are available online.
Exclusive: Visit www.UltimateScholarshipBook.com and enter code GR140926 for updates on this award.

[1410] • Graduate Tuition Waiver
Massachusetts Department of Higher Education
Office of Student Financial Assistance, 454 Broadway, Suite 200, Revere, MA 02151
Phone: 617-727-9420
Email: osfa@osfa.mass.edu
https://www.mass.gov/handbook/massachusetts-financial-aid-programs
Purpose: To provide financial support to Massachusetts graduate students.
Eligibility: Students must be enrolled in graduate level courses at a Massachusetts public school that is not a community college. Applicants must not owe any refunds on previously received financial aid, and they must not have defaulted on any government loans.
Target applicant(s): Graduate school students. Adult students.
Amount: Varies.
Number of awards: Varies.

Deadline: Contact the sponsor to confirm the deadline.
How to apply: Applications are available at college financial aid offices.
Exclusive: Visit www.UltimateScholarshipBook.com and enter code MA141026 for updates on this award.

[1411] • Granville P. Meade Scholarship
Virginia Department of Education
P.O. Box 2120, Richmond, VA 23218
Phone: 804-225-3349
Email: joseph.wharff@doe.virginia.gov
http://www.doe.virginia.gov/
Purpose: To support graduating high school seniors in Virginia.
Eligibility: Students must have been born in Virginia, and they must plan to attend a public or private Virginia school. They must demonstrate financial need, academic achievement, extracurricular activities and good character. Recipients must maintain a 2.5 GPA.
Target applicant(s): High school students.
Minimum GPA: 2.5
Amount: $2,000.
Number of awards: Varies.
Scholarship may be renewable.
Deadline: March 3.
How to apply: Applications are available online.
Exclusive: Visit www.UltimateScholarshipBook.com and enter code VI141126 for updates on this award.

[1412] • Greater Kanawha Valley Foundation Scholarship Program
Greater Kanawha Valley Foundation
1600 Huntington Square, 900 Lee Street, East, Charleston, WV 25301
Phone: 304-346-3620
Email: shoover@tgkvf.org
https://tgkvf.org/scholarship-information/
Purpose: To provide financial assistance to prospective college students from the state of West Virginia.
Eligibility: Applicants must be residents of West Virginia, be full-time students (12 hours) and demonstrate good moral character. Many awards are available, and each individual award may have additional eligibility requirements. Applicants must have a minimum 2.5 GPA and an ACT score of at least 20.
Target applicant(s): High school students. College students. Adult students.
Minimum GPA: 2.5
Amount: Varies.
Number of awards: Varies.
Scholarship may be renewable.
Deadline: February 1.
How to apply: Applications are available online.
Exclusive: Visit www.UltimateScholarshipBook.com and enter code GR141226 for updates on this award.

[1413] • Greenhouse Scholars Scholarship
Greenhouse Scholars
1820 Folsom Street, Boulder, CO 80302
Phone: 303-459-5482
Email: scholars@greenhousescholars.org
http://www.greenhousescholars.org
Purpose: To provide personal, professional and financial support to high-performing, under-resourced students who are leaders and contributors to their communities.

Eligibility: Applicants must be high school seniors who plan to attend a four-year college or university. They must be U.S. citizens or permanent residents who reside and attend school in Colorado, Georgia, Illinois, New York or North Carolina. They must have an unweighted GPA of 3.5 or higher, and they must demonstrate leadership, perseverance and financial need. Their household income must be $70,000 a year or less. Winners participate in the Whole Person Program which includes Summer Symposium, Mentorship, Professional Networking, Impact and Internship programming and more!
Target applicant(s): High school students.
Minimum GPA: 3.5
Amount: Up to $5,000.
Number of awards: Varies.
Scholarship may be renewable.
Deadline: November 21.
How to apply: Applications are available online.
Exclusive: Visit www.UltimateScholarshipBook.com and enter code GR141326 for updates on this award.

[1414] • Grossman Scholarship
Volunteers for Outdoor Colorado
600 South Marion Parkway, Denver, CO 80209
Phone: 303-715-1010
Email: scholarships@voc.org
https://www.voc.org/grossman-scholarship
Purpose: To support students committed to caring for our environment's natural resources.
Eligibility: Applicants must be Colorado residents and graduating high school seniors, graduate students or non-traditional students. Students must be pursuing a degree program with an environmental, natural resource, climate or outdoor industry emphasis at an accredited four-year college or university, two-year community college or a certificate program offered by an accredited college or university within the state of Colorado. Applicants must demonstrate a commitment to caring for our environment's natural resources within their personal, educational and/or professional time.
Target applicant(s): High school students. College students. Graduate school students. Adult students.
Amount: $5,000-$10,000.
Number of awards: 6.
Deadline: February 26.
How to apply: Applications are available online.
Exclusive: Visit www.UltimateScholarshipBook.com and enter code VO141426 for updates on this award.

[1415] • Gump and Ayers Scholarship
Utah State Chapter P.E.O.
Email: peoutah.gumpayers@gmail.com
https://www.peoutah.org/
Purpose: To support Utah single mothers pursuing higher education.
Eligibility: Applicants must be Utah residents who are single mothers. Students must be high school graduates and provide proof of enrollment in an accredited Utah university or college. Applicants must have realistic future goals and demonstrate financial need. Students must be recommended by a Utah P.E.O. chapter.
Target applicant(s): College students. Adult students.
Amount: Varies.
Number of awards: Varies.
Deadline: March 5.
How to apply: Applications are available online.
Exclusive: Visit www.UltimateScholarshipBook.com and enter code UT141526 for updates on this award.

[1416] • Guy M. Wilson Scholarship
American Legion, Department of Michigan
212 N. Verlinden Avenue, Suite A, Lansing, MI 48915
Phone: 517-371-4720 x11
Email: programs@michiganlegion.org
http://www.michiganlegion.org
Purpose: To aid students who are the sons or daughters or grandchildren of veterans who plan to attend a Michigan college.
Eligibility: Applicants must be residents of Michigan who are planning to attend a Michigan college or university and who are the sons or daughters or grandchildren of veterans. Students must have a minimum GPA of 2.5 and must have demonstrated financial need. Applicants must provide proof of a parent's military service record and an indication of their abilities to fulfill their goals and intentions. They should send scholarship information to their county district committee person.
Target applicant(s): High school students.
Minimum GPA: 2.5
Amount: $500.
Number of awards: Varies.
Deadline: January 22.
How to apply: Applications are available online.
Exclusive: Visit www.UltimateScholarshipBook.com and enter code AM141626 for updates on this award.

[1417] • H-E-B Scholarships for UIL Participants
Sports in Action
405 State Highway 121, Suite A-200, Lewisville, TX 75067
Phone: 972-898-8585
Email: uil@registermyathlete.com
http://www.sportsinaction.com/scholarship/
Purpose: To reward students for their community service and involvement.
Eligibility: Applicants must be current Texas high school seniors with a minimum 3.3 GPA. Students must have participated in a UIL competition as high school students and have been active in community service programs. Awards are distributed as follows: five students who competed in athletics, five students who competed in music and five students who competed in academic events.
Target applicant(s): High school students.
Minimum GPA: 3.3
Amount: $2,000.
Number of awards: 15.
Deadline: February 2.
How to apply: Applications are available online.
Exclusive: Visit www.UltimateScholarshipBook.com and enter code SP141726 for updates on this award.

[1418] • H. W. Almen/West OKC Rotary Scholarship
Oklahoma City Community Foundation
1000 North Broadway, Oklahoma City, OK 73102
Phone: 405-235-5603
Email: scholarships@occf.org
https://occf.org/scholarships/
Purpose: To support students from the state of Oklahoma with furthering their education.
Eligibility: Applicants must be a graduating senior from an Oklahoma high school. Students must have a 2.75 GPA or higher to be considered for this award. Financial need is considered and applicant's family income

cannot exceed $100,000. Students must provide a written statement that focuses on how their local Rotary Club supports their local community.
Target applicant(s): High school students.
Minimum GPA: 2.75
Amount: $5,000.
Number of awards: 1.
Deadline: March 1.
How to apply: Applications are available online.
Exclusive: Visit www.UltimateScholarshipBook.com and enter code OK141826 for updates on this award.

[1419] • H.L. Taylor Scholarship Program
Iowa PTA
P.O. Box 10634, Cedar Rapids, IA 52410
Phone: 319-573-0049
Email: execdir@iowapta.org
https://iowapta.org/programs-events/
Purpose: To support Iowa students pursuing post-secondary education.
Eligibility: Applicants must be graduating high school seniors in Iowa whose school district has an active PTA at any level of education. Students must be residents of Iowa and plan to enroll at an accredited Iowa post-secondary institution.
Target applicant(s): High school students.
Amount: $500.
Number of awards: Varies.
Deadline: February 1.
How to apply: Applications are available online.
Exclusive: Visit www.UltimateScholarshipBook.com and enter code IO141926 for updates on this award.

[1420] • H.M. Muffly Memorial Scholarship
Colorado Nurses Foundation
2851 S. Parker Road, Suite 1210, Aurora, CO 80014
Phone: 720-457-1191
Email: sonja.hix-cortina@civicamanagement.com
https://www.coloradonursesfoundation.com/
Purpose: To aid nursing students working towards bachelor's, master's or doctoral degrees.
Eligibility: Applicants must be Colorado residents who are planning to practice nursing in Colorado. They must be juniors or seniors working towards the Bachelor of Science in Nursing (BSN); Registered Nurses (RNs) pursuing the bachelor's degree or higher in a school of nursing; practicing RNs pursuing a doctoral degree in nursing or second- or third-year Doctor of Nursing Practice (DNP) students. Undergraduates must have a GPA of 3.25 or higher, and graduate students must have a GPA of 3.5 or higher. Selection is based on GPA, financial need, recommendations, community involvement and commitment to professional practice in Colorado.
Target applicant(s): College students. Graduate school students. Adult students.
Minimum GPA: 3.25 for undergraduate students; 3.5 for graduate students
Amount: $2,000.
Number of awards: 1.
Deadline: October 14.
How to apply: Applications are available online. An application form, schedule of classes, two recommendation letters, financial need statement, transcript and personal essay are required.
Exclusive: Visit www.UltimateScholarshipBook.com and enter code CO142026 for updates on this award.

[1421] • Harriet Hayes Austin Memorial Scholarship for Nursing
Topeka Community Foundation
5431 SW 29th Street, Suite 300, Topeka, KS 66614
Phone: 785-272-4804
Email: info@topekacommunityfoundation.org
https://topekacommunityfoundation.org/college-students-apply-here
Purpose: To aid students who are pursuing the Bachelor of Science in Nursing (BSN) degree at an accredited postsecondary institution located in Kansas.
Eligibility: Applicants must be U.S. citizens who are enrolled in or who plan to enroll in a BSN program at an accredited school located in Kansas. They must demonstrate financial need. Preference is given to Kansas residents. Selection is based on the overall strength of the application.
Target applicant(s): High school students. College students. Adult students.
Amount: $1,000.
Number of awards: 5.
Deadline: February 5.
How to apply: Applications are available online. An application form, official transcript, one letter of recommendation, personal statements, financial analysis form and proof of U.S. citizenship are required.
Exclusive: Visit www.UltimateScholarshipBook.com and enter code TO142126 for updates on this award.

[1422] • Harry Alan Gregg Foundation Grants
Harry Alan Gregg Foundation Grants
1 Verney Drive, Greenfield, NH 03047
Phone: 603-547-3311
Email: hgf@crotchedmountain.org
https://harrygreggfoundation.org/grantinfo/
Purpose: To provide financial assistance for the disabled.
Eligibility: Applicants must be New Hampshire residents with physical, intellectual or emotional disabilities or their families. Funds may be used for a variety of purposes but must benefit the person with a disability. Selection is based on need. Applications are reviewed multiple times a year.
Target applicant(s): High school students. College students. Graduate school students. Adult students.
Amount: Up to $1,200.
Number of awards: Varies.
Deadline: March 24; July 28; November 24.
How to apply: Applications are available online. Documentation of the expense must be provided before payment will be made.
Exclusive: Visit www.UltimateScholarshipBook.com and enter code HA142226 for updates on this award.

[1423] • Harry Barfield KBA Scholarship Program
Kentucky Broadcasters Association
101 Enterprise Drive, Frankfort, KY 40601
Phone: 888-843-5221
Email: kba@kba.org
http://www.kba.org
Purpose: To aid aspiring young broadcasters.
Eligibility: Applicants must be attending a college or university in Kentucky and major or plan to major in broadcasting or telecommunications. Preference is given to second semester sophomores, and funds are awarded in the junior year and renewable for the senior year. Applicants should have a minimum 3.0 GPA, although some consideration will be given to those with lower GPAs who have exceptional credentials otherwise.
Target applicant(s): College students. Adult students.

Minimum GPA: 3.0
Amount: $3,500.
Number of awards: 4.
Scholarship may be renewable.
Deadline: April 1.
How to apply: Applications are available online. An application form, transcript, essay, list of extracurricular activities and letter of recommendation are required.
Exclusive: Visit www.UltimateScholarshipBook.com and enter code KE142326 for updates on this award.

[1424] • Hattie Tedrow Memorial Fund Scholarship
American Legion, Department of North Dakota
405 W. Maine Avenue, Suite 4A, P.O. Box 5057, West Fargo, ND 58078
Phone: 701-293-3120
Email: Americanism@legion.org
https://www.ndlegion.org/scholarships/
Purpose: To support descendants of veterans.
Eligibility: Applicants must be high school seniors, North Dakota residents and U.S. citizens. They must be direct descendants of veterans with honorable service in the U.S. military.
Target applicant(s): High school students.
Amount: Up to $2,000.
Number of awards: Varies.
Deadline: April 1.
How to apply: Applications are available by mail. An application form, essay and proof of veteran's military service are required.
Exclusive: Visit www.UltimateScholarshipBook.com and enter code AM142426 for updates on this award.

[1425] • Hawaii Community Foundation Scholarships
Hawaii Community Foundation - Scholarships
827 Fort Street Mall, Honolulu, HI 96813
Phone: 888-731-3863
Email: scholarships@hcf-hawaii.org
https://www.hawaiicommunityfoundation.org/
Purpose: To help Hawaii residents who show financial need.
Eligibility: The Hawaii Community Foundation Scholarship Program has over 200 different scholarship funds covering areas such as vocational education, those in foster care, ethnicity, religion and major. Applicants must be Hawaii residents who plan to attend nonprofit two- or four-year colleges as either full-time undergraduate or graduate students. Applicants must also have academic achievement and good moral character. A personal statement, Student Aid Report, transcript, recommendation letter and essay may be required depending on the specific scholarship.
Target applicant(s): High school students. College students. Graduate school students. Adult students.
Amount: Varies.
Number of awards: Varies.
Deadline: February 28.
How to apply: Applications are available online.
Exclusive: Visit www.UltimateScholarshipBook.com and enter code HA142526 for updates on this award.

[1426] • Hawaii High School Athletic Association Hall of Honor
Hawaii High School Athletic Association
P.O. Box 62029, Honolulu, HI 96839
Phone: 808-800-4092
Email: info@hhsaa.org
http://www.sportshigh.com
Purpose: To support Hawaii high school seniors who are athletes.
Eligibility: Applicants must be graduating high school seniors and athletes in any organized sport in Hawaii. Selection is based primarily on sports achievements. Factors considered include contributions to the team, sportsmanship, character, participation in school activities and community involvement.
Target applicant(s): High school students.
Amount: $2,000.
Number of awards: 12.
Deadline: May 13.
How to apply: Applications are available by written request.
Exclusive: Visit www.UltimateScholarshipBook.com and enter code HA142626 for updates on this award.

[1427] • Hawaii Pizza Hut Scholarship Fund
Hawaii Community Foundation - Scholarships
827 Fort Street Mall, Honolulu, HI 96813
Phone: 888-731-3863
Email: scholarships@hcf-hawaii.org
https://www.hawaiicommunityfoundation.org/
Purpose: To support students in Hawaii with financial need.
Eligibility: Applicants must be Hawaii residents, attend a two- or four-year college or university and have a GPA between 3.0 and 3.5.
Target applicant(s): High school students. College students. Adult students.
Minimum GPA: 3.0
Amount: Varies.
Number of awards: Varies.
Deadline: January 31.
How to apply: To apply, register online, complete the online application and select the scholarships to which you wish to apply. In addition, mail the supporting materials: printed confirmation page from the online application, personal statement, copy of Student Aid Report (SAR) available at www.fafsa.ed.gov and official transcript.
Exclusive: Visit www.UltimateScholarshipBook.com and enter code HA142726 for updates on this award.

[1428] • Hawaii Rotary Youth Foundation Scholarship
Hawaii Rotary Youth Foundation
3536 Harding Avenue, Honolulu, HI 96816
Phone: 808-735-1073
Email: office@hawaiirotaryyouthfoundation.org
https://www.hawaiirotaryyouthfoundation.org
Purpose: To encourage graduating high school seniors from Hawaii to pursue a higher education.
Eligibility: Applicants must be graduating high school seniors sponsored by a District 5000 Rotary Club in the state of Hawaii. Students must plan to enroll full-time at a four-year college or university in the United States. Applicants must be U.S. citizens and residents of Hawaii.
Target applicant(s): High school students.
Amount: $5,000.
Number of awards: Varies.

Deadline: February 1.
How to apply: Applications are available online.
Exclusive: Visit www.UltimateScholarshipBook.com and enter code HA142826 for updates on this award.

[1429] • Hawaii Society of Certified Public Accountants Scholarship Fund

Hawaii Community Foundation - Scholarships
827 Fort Street Mall, Honolulu, HI 96813
Phone: 888-731-3863
Email: scholarships@hcf-hawaii.org
https://www.hawaiicommunityfoundation.org/
Purpose: To provide financial assistance for those pursuing degrees in accounting.
Eligibility: Applicants must be college juniors, college seniors or graduate students attending an accredited four-year Hawaii institution of higher learning with a major or concentration in accounting. They must have a minimum GPA of 3.0.
Target applicant(s): College students. Graduate school students. Adult students.
Minimum GPA: 3.0
Amount: Varies.
Number of awards: Varies.
Deadline: January 31.
How to apply: To apply, register online, complete the online application and select the scholarships to which you wish to apply. In addition, mail the supporting materials: printed confirmation page from the online application, personal statement, copy of Student Aid Report (SAR) available at www.fafsa.ed.gov and official transcript.
Exclusive: Visit www.UltimateScholarshipBook.com and enter code HA142926 for updates on this award.

[1430] • Helping Heroes Grant

Tennessee Student Assistance Corporation
312 Rosa L. Parks Avenue, 9th Floor, Nashville, TN 37243
Phone: 800-342-1663
Email: tsac.aidinfo@tn.gov
https://www.collegefortn.org/about-financial-aid/
Purpose: To support students who are U.S. veterans who were honorably discharged or who are a former or current member of a reserve or Tennessee National Guard unit.
Eligibility: Applicants must be honorably discharged veterans who have formally served the armed forces of the United States or a former or current member of a reserve or Tennessee National Guard unit who was called into active military service of the United States. Students must be residents of Tennessee and enroll at an eligible two-year or four-year post-secondary institution.
Target applicant(s): College students. Graduate school students. Adult students.
Amount: $1,000.
Number of awards: Varies.
Deadline: February 1 (Spring); May 1 (Summer); September 2 (Fall).
How to apply: Applications are available online.
Exclusive: Visit www.UltimateScholarshipBook.com and enter code TE143026 for updates on this award.

[1431] • Henry A. Zuberano Scholarship

Hawaii Community Foundation - Scholarships
827 Fort Street Mall, Honolulu, HI 96813
Phone: 888-731-3863
Email: scholarships@hcf-hawaii.org
https://www.hawaiicommunityfoundation.org/
Purpose: To assist Hawaii students who are majoring in political science, international relations, international business or public administration.
Eligibility: Applicants must have a GPA of 2.7 or higher.
Target applicant(s): High school students. College students. Adult students.
Minimum GPA: 2.7
Amount: Varies.
Number of awards: Varies.
Deadline: February 28.
How to apply: To apply, register online, complete the online application and select the scholarships to which you wish to apply. In addition, mail the supporting materials: printed confirmation page from the online application, personal statement, copy of Student Aid Report (SAR) available at www.fafsa.ed.gov and official transcript.
Exclusive: Visit www.UltimateScholarshipBook.com and enter code HA143126 for updates on this award.

[1432] • Henry Sachs Foundation Scholarship

Henry Sachs Foundation
90 S. Cascade Avenue, Suite 1410, Colorado Springs, CO 80903
Phone: 719-633-2353
Email: info@sachsfoundation.org
https://www.sachsfoundation.org
Purpose: To aid African-American high school students in Colorado to obtain a college education.
Eligibility: Applicants must be African-American residents of Colorado for at least five years. Applicants must be either seniors in high school or have graduated in the last three years but are not currently attending college. Awards are based on high school grade point average and financial need. If selected, applicants must attend a personal interview in order to receive the grant money.
Target applicant(s): High school students. College students. Adult students.
Minimum GPA: 3.0
Amount: $10,000.
Number of awards: Varies.
Scholarship may be renewable.
Deadline: March 15.
How to apply: Applications are available online.
Exclusive: Visit www.UltimateScholarshipBook.com and enter code HE143226 for updates on this award.

[1433] • Herb It Forward Scholarship

Herb It Forward Foundation
1149 W Lancaster Avenue, Suite U3, Bryn Mawr, PA 19010
Phone: 855-766-1446
Email: Info@Herbie.com
https://www.herbie.com
Purpose: To encourage students who grew up in challenging environments, yet have an optimistic outlook, a desire to help others, and a passion for community service.
Eligibility: Applicants must be residents of the United States between the ages of 17 and 25, and also residents of Philadelphia or the Philadelphia area counties. Students must be residents of the counties of Philadelphia, Bucks, Montgomery, Chester and Delaware in Pennsylvania and Camden, Gloucester and Burlington counties in New Jersey. Applicants must be graduating or have already graduated from high school and attending or planning on attending an accredited program at a college, vocational or technical school. Financial need is strongly considered. Students must

explain on the application how they have helped their community in the past and how their future career path will help their community.
Target applicant(s): High school students. College students.
Amount: $1,000-$5,000.
Number of awards: 30.
Scholarship may be renewable.
Deadline: February 5.
How to apply: Applications are available online.
Exclusive: Visit www.UltimateScholarshipBook.com and enter code HE143326 for updates on this award.

[1434] • Herbert Hoover Uncommon Student Award
Hoover Presidential Foundation
P.O. Box 696, West Branch, IA 52358
Phone: 800-828-0475
Email: info@hooverpf.org
http://www.hooverpresidentialfoundation.org
Purpose: To honor Herbert Hoover by rewarding students who live up to his ideal of the "uncommon man."
Eligibility: Applicants must be juniors in an Iowa high school or be homeschooled. Students must submit a project proposal and two letters of recommendation. Recipients must attend a weekend program during the summer and are expected to complete the proposed project. Grades, essays and test scores are not considered.
Target applicant(s): High school students.
Amount: Up to $11,500.
Number of awards: Up to 15.
Deadline: April 1.
How to apply: Applications are available online.
Exclusive: Visit www.UltimateScholarshipBook.com and enter code HO143426 for updates on this award.

[1435] • Herman J. Smith Scholarship
National Housing Endowment
1201 15th Street NW, Washington, DC 20005
Phone: 202-266-8069
Email: Scholarships@nahb.org
https://apply.nationalhousingendowment.org
Purpose: To aid students who are planning for careers in mortgage finance or the construction industry.
Eligibility: Applicants must be full-time undergraduate or graduate students attending an accredited four-year institution. They must have at least one more year of study to complete after the date of award disbursement; fifth-year seniors are ineligible for this award. They must be majoring in and planning to pursue a career in mortgage finance, construction management or another construction-related subject. Preference is given to Texas residents, students who attend school in Texas and current members of their school's National Association of Home Builders student chapter. Selection is based on academic merit, recommendations, work experience, extracurricular activities, career goals and financial need.
Target applicant(s): College students. Graduate school students. Adult students.
Amount: Varies.
Number of awards: Varies.

Scholarship may be renewable.
Deadline: March 31.
How to apply: Applications are available online. An application form, course schedule, official transcripts and three recommendation letters are required.
Exclusive: Visit www.UltimateScholarshipBook.com and enter code NA143526 for updates on this award.

[1436] • Herman Sani Scholarship
Iowa Golf Association
Attn: Ann Griffel Scholarship Committee, 1605 North Ankeny Boulevard, Suite 210, Ankeny, IA 50023
Phone: 888-388-4442
Email: info@iowagolf.org
https://iowagolf.org/scholarships/
Purpose: To assist Iowa college-bound students as they further their education.
Eligibility: Applicant must be a high school senior with a background in golf. Selection is based on academic achievement, extracurricular activities and leadership qualities. Selection is not based on golf accomplishments or abilities.
Target applicant(s): High school students.
Amount: $2,000.
Number of awards: Varies.
Scholarship may be renewable.
Deadline: March 31.
How to apply: Applications are available online and include a personal essay, two letters of recommendation and an official transcript.
Exclusive: Visit www.UltimateScholarshipBook.com and enter code IO143626 for updates on this award.

[1437] • Hermine Solt Student Scholarship
Pennsylvania Association of Educational Office Professionals (PAEOP)
Lenore Filipovic, Phoenixville Area School District, 386 City Line Avenue, Phoenixville, PA 19460
Email: herminsoltstudentscholarship@gmail.com
https://www.paeop.com/page/68
Purpose: To support students in Pennsylvania who are pursuing a higher education in a business-related field.
Eligibility: Applicants must be graduating high school seniors from either a Pennsylvania high school or Pennsylvania cyber charter school with a 3.0 GPA. Students must attend an approved post-secondary institution, college or university majoring in the business field.
Target applicant(s): High school students.
Minimum GPA: 3.0
Amount: $500.
Number of awards: Varies.
Deadline: March 20.
How to apply: Applications are available online.
Exclusive: Visit www.UltimateScholarshipBook.com and enter code PE143726 for updates on this award.

[1438] • Hideko and Zenzo Matsuyama Scholarship Fund
Hawaii Community Foundation - Scholarships
827 Fort Street Mall, Honolulu, HI 96813
Phone: 888-731-3863
Email: scholarships@hcf-hawaii.org
https://www.hawaiicommunityfoundation.org/

The Ultimate Scholarship Book 2026
Scholarship Directory (State of Residence)

Purpose: To provide financial assistance for high school graduates who are seeking higher education.
Eligibility: Applicants must be graduates of Hawaiian high schools or GED recipients who plan to attend a college or university in Hawaii or the continental U.S. full-time. They must have a GPA of 3.0 or higher. Applicants must be of Japanese ancestry.
Target applicant(s): High school students. College students. Adult students.
Minimum GPA: 3.0
Amount: Varies.
Number of awards: Varies.
Deadline: January 31.
How to apply: To apply, register online, complete the online application and select the scholarships to which you wish to apply. In addition, mail the supporting materials: printed confirmation page from the online application, personal statement, copy of Student Aid Report (SAR) available at www.fafsa.ed.gov and official transcript.
Exclusive: Visit www.UltimateScholarshipBook.com and enter code HA143826 for updates on this award.

[1439] • High School Senior Essay Contest
Masonic Charity Foundation of Oklahoma
P.O. Box 2406, Edmond, OK 73083
Phone: 405-348-7500
Email: information@mcfok.org
https://www.mcfok.org/programs/
Purpose: To support high school seniors attending Oklahoma public schools.
Eligibility: Applicants must be high school seniors attending an Oklahoma public school. An original essay submission of 1,000-1,250 words is required on a provided topic. Selection is based on adherence to the prescribed topic, organization of material, interest, originality, spelling, grammar, punctuation and neatness.
Target applicant(s): High school students.
Amount: Up to $2,000.
Number of awards: 10.
Deadline: October 31.
How to apply: Applications are available online.
Exclusive: Visit www.UltimateScholarshipBook.com and enter code MA143926 for updates on this award.

[1440] • High Technology Scholar/Intern Tuition Waiver
Massachusetts Department of Higher Education
Office of Student Financial Assistance, 454 Broadway, Suite 200, Revere, MA 02151
Phone: 617-727-9420
Email: osfa@osfa.mass.edu
https://www.mass.gov/handbook/massachusetts-financial-aid-programs
Purpose: To provide financial aid and internship connections to computer technology and engineering students in Massachusetts.
Eligibility: Students must be enrolled in an undergraduate program at a Massachusetts public college and must not have previously earned a bachelor's degree. Applicants must have approval from the company or organization that is funding the scholarship. Students must not owe refunds on any previous financial aid or have any defaulted government loans.
Target applicant(s): High school students. College students. Adult students.
Amount: Up to full tuition.
Number of awards: Varies.
Deadline: Contact the sponsor to confirm the deadline.
How to apply: Applications are available at college financial aid offices.
Exclusive: Visit www.UltimateScholarshipBook.com and enter code MA144026 for updates on this award.

[1441] • Higher Education Academic Scholarship Program (Bright Flight)
Missouri Student Assistance Resource Services (MOSTARS)
Missouri Department of Higher Education, Attn: Bright Flight, P.O. Box 1469, Jefferson City, MO 65102
Phone: 800-473-6757
Email: info@dhe.mo.gov
http://dhe.mo.gov/ppc/grants/
Purpose: This merit-based program encourages top-ranked high school seniors to attend approved Missouri postsecondary schools.
Eligibility: Applicants must be U.S. citizens or eligible noncitizens, Missouri residents and have an ACT or SAT score within the top 3 percent of all Missouri students taking those tests. Applicants must be high school seniors who enroll as first-time, full-time students at an approved Missouri postsecondary school.
Target applicant(s): High school students.
Amount: Up to $3,000.
Number of awards: Varies.
Scholarship may be renewable.
Deadline: Contact the sponsor to confirm the deadline.
How to apply: For an application contact your high school counselor or MOSTARS.
Exclusive: Visit www.UltimateScholarshipBook.com and enter code MI144126 for updates on this award.

[1442] • Higher Education Adult Part-Time Student (HEAPS) Grant Program
West Virginia Higher Education Policy Commission
1018 Kanawha Boulevard, East, Suite 700, Charleston, WV 25301
Phone: 304-558-2101
Email: jacob.abrams@wvhepc.edu
http://www.wvhepc.edu/
Purpose: To assist adult West Virginia students.
Eligibility: Applicants must be West Virginia residents, be U.S. citizens or permanent residents, be enrolled or accepted for enrollment in an undergraduate institution on a part-time basis and demonstrate financial need.
Target applicant(s): High school students. College students. Adult students.
Amount: $2,000.
Number of awards: Varies.
Scholarship may be renewable.
Deadline: As soon as possible after October 1.
How to apply: Complete the Free Application for Federal Student Aid (FAFSA).
Exclusive: Visit www.UltimateScholarshipBook.com and enter code WE144226 for updates on this award.

[1443] • Higher Education Legislative Plan (HELP)
Mississippi Office of Student Financial Aid
3825 Ridgewood Road, Jackson, MS 39211-6453
Phone: 800-327-2980
Email: sfa@ihl.state.ms.us

https://www.msfinancialaid.org/
Purpose: To assist financially needy Mississippi students to afford tuition.
Eligibility: Applicants must be U.S. citizens or eligible noncitizens, Mississippi residents and have a minimum college GPA of 2.5 and have graduated from high school within the past two years. Applicants must be attending an eligible Mississippi institution, must have a minimum ACT score of 20 and must document an average gross income of $39,500 or less over the prior two years, and must have the results of a processed Student Aid Report (SAR). Students who file the Free Application for Federal Student Aid (FAFSA) will receive a SAR report.
Target applicant(s): High school students. College students. Adult students.
Minimum GPA: 2.5
Amount: Full tuition.
Number of awards: Varies.
Scholarship may be renewable.
Deadline: March 31.
How to apply: Contact the Mississippi Office of Student Financial Aid for an application.
Exclusive: Visit www.UltimateScholarshipBook.com and enter code MI144326 for updates on this award.

[1444] • Ho'omaka Hou – A New Beginning Fund
Hawaii Community Foundation - Scholarships
827 Fort Street Mall, Honolulu, HI 96813
Phone: 888-731-3863
Email: scholarships@hcf-hawaii.org
https://www.hawaiicommunityfoundation.org/
Purpose: To support students who have overcome substance abuse or other difficulties in their lives.
Eligibility: Applicants must show financial need. Students must attend college or technical school in Hawaii. Minimum 2.7 GPA required.
Target applicant(s): High school students. College students. Adult students.
Minimum GPA: 2.7
Amount: Varies.
Number of awards: Varies.
Deadline: February 28.
How to apply: Applications are available online. In addition, mail the supporting materials: personal statement, one letter of recommendation, copy of Student Aid Report (SAR) available at www.fafsa.ed.gov and official transcript.
Exclusive: Visit www.UltimateScholarshipBook.com and enter code HA144426 for updates on this award.

[1445] • Homeschoolers' Support Association Scholarship
Washington Homeschool Organization
P.O. Box 66960, Seattle, WA 98166-0960
https://washhomeschool.org/
Purpose: To support Washington homeschooled students with their pursuits of higher education.
Eligibility: Applicants must be homeschooled and members of the Washington Homeschool Organization. Students must be graduating and continuing their post-secondary education in Washington. An essay on a provided prompt is required.
Target applicant(s): High school students.
Amount: $1,000.
Number of awards: 1.
Deadline: March 31.
How to apply: Applications are available online.
Exclusive: Visit www.UltimateScholarshipBook.com and enter code WA144526 for updates on this award.

[1446] • Honors Award
Louisiana Office of Student Financial Assistance
605 N. Fifth Street, Baton Rouge, LA 70802
Phone: 800-259-5626 x1012
Email: custserv@la.gov
https://mylosfa.la.gov/students-parents/scholarships-grants/tops/
Purpose: To aid Louisiana student residents.
Eligibility: Applicants must be Louisiana residents and U.S. citizens, apply during their senior year in high school, use the award at a Louisiana college or university, have a minimum 3.0 GPA and have a minimum ACT score of 27 or equivalent SAT score.
Target applicant(s): High school students.
Minimum GPA: 3.0
Amount: Full tuition plus $800 stipend.
Number of awards: Varies.
Scholarship may be renewable.
Deadline: July 1.
How to apply: The application is the Free Application for Federal Student Aid (FAFSA). ACT or SAT scores must also be reported.
Exclusive: Visit www.UltimateScholarshipBook.com and enter code LO144626 for updates on this award.

[1447] • HOPE Scholarship Program
Georgia Student Finance Commission
2082 East Exchange Place, Tucker, GA 30084
Phone: 800-505-4732
Email: gsfcinfo@gsfc.org
https://www.gafutures.org
Purpose: To support students attending Georgia institutions.
Eligibility: Applicants must have graduated from high school and be attending or planning to attend college in Georgia. Students must be U.S. citizens or eligible non-citizens, be a legal resident of the state of Georgia and have a minimum 3.0 GPA. Students should submit applications as early as possible.
Target applicant(s): High school students. College students. Adult students.
Minimum GPA: 3.0
Amount: Varies.
Number of awards: Varies.
Scholarship may be renewable.
Deadline: Last day of classes.
How to apply: Applications are available online.
Exclusive: Visit www.UltimateScholarshipBook.com and enter code GE144726 for updates on this award.

[1448] • HospitalityMaine Scholarship
HospitalityMaine
45 Melville Street, Augusta, ME 04330
Phone: 207-623-2178
Email: cassidy@hospitalitymaine.com
https://www.hospitalitymaine.com/scholarship
Purpose: To support students enrolled in hospitality-related programs.
Eligibility: Applicants must be Maine residents and accepted to an accredited institution of higher learning with specialties in hotel administration or culinary sciences. Students must plan to begin a career in hospitality upon completion of their degrees.

The Ultimate Scholarship Book 2026
Scholarship Directory (State of Residence)

Target applicant(s): High school students. College students. Adult students.
Amount: Varies.
Number of awards: Varies.
Deadline: April 12.
How to apply: Applications are available from the Maine Innkeepers Association.
Exclusive: Visit www.UltimateScholarshipBook.com and enter code HO144826 for updates on this award.

[1449] • Houston Livestock Show and Rodeo Scholarships

Houston Livestock Show and Rodeo
Educational Programs Department, P.O. Box 20070, Houston, TX 77225-0070
Phone: 832-667-1285
Email: scholarship@rodeohouston.com
https://www.rodeohouston.com/Educational-Support/Scholarships
Purpose: To support graduating high school students who are Texas residents.
Eligibility: Applicants must be U.S. citizens and be graduating high school seniors from public schools who have completed a current FAFSA. Applicants must also plan to attend and have applied to an accredited, not-for-profit university in Texas after graduation. SAT or ACT scores are required. Selection is based on financial need, academic performance and demonstrated leadership. Multiple types of scholarships are available. Specific eligibility criteria and deadlines differ for each scholarship.
Target applicant(s): High school students.
Amount: Varies.
Number of awards: Varies.
Deadline: January 31.
How to apply: Applications are available online. A copy of the application and other required documentation (varies for each scholarship) must be mailed to the Office of Educational Programs.
Exclusive: Visit www.UltimateScholarshipBook.com and enter code HO144926 for updates on this award.

[1450] • Howard P. Rawlings Educational Assistance (EA) Grant

Maryland Higher Education Commission
Office of Student Financial Assistance, 6 North Liberty Street, Baltimore, MD 21201
Phone: 800-974-1024
Email: osfamail@mhec.state.md.us
https://mhec.maryland.gov
Purpose: To help Maryland students who demonstrate financial need.
Eligibility: Applicants (and their parents, if applicants are dependents) must be residents of the state of Maryland. They must be high school seniors or undergraduate students and must be or plan to become full-time, degree-seeking students. They must complete the Free Application for Federal Student Aid (FAFSA) and must demonstrate financial need. Selection is based on financial need.
Target applicant(s): High school students. College students. Adult students.
Amount: Up to $3,000.
Number of awards: Varies.
Scholarship may be renewable.
Deadline: March 1.
How to apply: To apply, applicants must fill out and submit the FAFSA.
Exclusive: Visit www.UltimateScholarshipBook.com and enter code MA145026 for updates on this award.

[1451] • Howard P. Rawlings Guaranteed Access (GA) Grant

Maryland Higher Education Commission
Office of Student Financial Assistance, 6 North Liberty Street, Baltimore, MD 21201
Phone: 800-974-1024
Email: osfamail@mhec.state.md.us
https://mhec.maryland.gov
Purpose: To help Maryland students with financial need afford college.
Eligibility: Applicants and their parents must both be legal residents of the state of Maryland. Applicants must be U.S. citizens or eligible noncitizens, complete the Free Application for Federal Student Aid (FAFSA) and the Guaranteed Access (GA) Grant application. Applicants and families must also meet the established income limits to qualify.
Target applicant(s): High school students.
Amount: Up to $20,000.
Number of awards: Varies.
Scholarship may be renewable.
Deadline: March 1.
How to apply: Complete the FAFSA.
Exclusive: Visit www.UltimateScholarshipBook.com and enter code MA145126 for updates on this award.

[1452] • Hugh A. Smith Scholarship Fund

American Legion, Department of Kansas
1314 SW Topeka Boulevard, Topeka, KS 66612
Phone: 785-232-9315
https://kansaslegion.org/
Purpose: To provide assistance to needy and worthy children of American Legion and American Legion Auxiliary members.
Eligibility: Applicants must be average or better students who are high school seniors or college freshmen or sophomores enrolling or enrolled in a post-secondary school in Kansas. They must be the son or daughter of a veteran, and a parent must have been a member of the Kansas American Legion or American Legion Auxiliary for the past three years. The children of deceased parents are also eligible if the parent was a paid member at the time of death. Applicants must submit three letters of recommendation, including one from a teacher, an essay on "Why I Want to Go to College," high school transcript, a 1040 income statement and documentation of parent's veteran status.
Target applicant(s): High school students. College students. Adult students.
Amount: $500.
Number of awards: Varies.
Deadline: February 15.
How to apply: Applications are available online.
Exclusive: Visit www.UltimateScholarshipBook.com and enter code AM145226 for updates on this award.

[1453] • IAD Foundation Scholarships

Iowa Automobile Dealers Foundation for Education
1111 Office Park Road, West Des Moines, IA 50265
Phone: 515-440-7625
Email: mcason@iada.com
https://iada.com/about/iad-foundation-for-education/
Purpose: To support Iowa students pursuing automotive-related studies.

Eligibility: Applicants must be Iowa high school graduates enrolling in a two- or four-year post-secondary institution to pursue automotive-related studies.
Target applicant(s): High school students.
Amount: Varies.
Number of awards: 9.
Deadline: March 1.
How to apply: Applications are available online.
Exclusive: Visit www.UltimateScholarshipBook.com and enter code IO145326 for updates on this award.

[1454] • ICCA Scholarships

Iowa Cheerleading Coaches' Association
Attn.: JoEllen Wesselmann, P.O. Box 207, Huxley, IA 50124
Phone: 515-494-3541
Email: iccajo@hotmail.com
http://iowacheercoaches.org/
Purpose: To aid graduating Iowa cheerleaders who display outstanding scholastic achievement in their pursuit of higher education.
Eligibility: Applicants must be a high school senior and have a coach who is a current member of the Iowa Cheerleading Coaches' Association. Students must also have a 3.5 GPA or higher. Selection is based on academic achievement, leadership and community involvement.
Target applicant(s): High school students.
Minimum GPA: 3.5
Amount: $500.
Number of awards: Varies.
Deadline: February 15.
How to apply: Applications are available online and include the basic application, the one page essay, activity listing, cheerleading coach letter of recommendation, additional letter of recommendation and letter from high school counselor verifying grade point average.
Exclusive: Visit www.UltimateScholarshipBook.com and enter code IO145426 for updates on this award.

[1455] • Idaho State Broadcasters Association Scholarships

Idaho State Broadcasters Association
1674 Hill Road, Suite 3, Boise, ID 83702
Phone: 208-345-3072
Email: isba@qwestoffice.net
http://www.idahobroadcasters.org
Purpose: To aid students planning careers in broadcasting.
Eligibility: Applicants must be enrolled full-time in an Idaho college or university, have exhibited superior potential in activities or courses related to broadcasting and be respected among their peer groups. Students must have a GPA of 2.0 or higher in the first two years of college and a GPA of 2.5 in the last two years.
Target applicant(s): College students. Adult students.
Minimum GPA: 2.0 for first two years of college; 2.5 for last two years of college
Amount: $1,000.
Number of awards: 3.
Deadline: March 15.
How to apply: Applications are available online. An application form, letter of recommendation, transcript and essay are required.
Exclusive: Visit www.UltimateScholarshipBook.com and enter code ID145526 for updates on this award.

[1456] • Illinois AMVETS Ladies Auxiliary Memorial Scholarship

Illinois AMVETS Service Foundation
AMVETS Department of Illinois, 2200 South Sixth Street, Springfield, IL 62703
Phone: 217-528-4713
Email: crystal@ilamvets.org
http://www.ilamvets.org
Purpose: To provide financial assistance to children and grandchildren of U.S. veterans and members of the military.
Eligibility: Applicants must be Illinois high school seniors who have taken the SAT or ACT, and they must be the children or grandchildren of veterans who were honorably discharged after September 15, 1940 or who are currently serving in the military.
Target applicant(s): High school students.
Amount: Varies.
Number of awards: Varies.
Deadline: March 1.
How to apply: Applications are available online.
Exclusive: Visit www.UltimateScholarshipBook.com and enter code IL145626 for updates on this award.

[1457] • Illinois AMVETS Ladies Auxiliary Worchid Scholarship

Illinois AMVETS Service Foundation
AMVETS Department of Illinois, 2200 South Sixth Street, Springfield, IL 62703
Phone: 217-528-4713
Email: crystal@ilamvets.org
http://www.ilamvets.org
Purpose: To provide financial assistance for students whose parents are U.S. veterans.
Eligibility: Applicants must be Illinois high school seniors whose mother or father is now deceased but had served after September 15, 1940, and was Honorably Discharged. Death of the parent does not have to be from military action or as a result of a service-related disability. Applicants must also have taken the SAT or ACT.
Target applicant(s): High school students.
Amount: Varies.
Number of awards: Varies.
Deadline: March 1.
How to apply: Applications are available online.
Exclusive: Visit www.UltimateScholarshipBook.com and enter code IL145726 for updates on this award.

[1458] • Illinois AMVETS Sad Sacks Nursing Scholarship

Illinois AMVETS Service Foundation
AMVETS Department of Illinois, 2200 South Sixth Street, Springfield, IL 62703
Phone: 217-528-4713
Email: crystal@ilamvets.org
http://www.ilamvets.org
Purpose: To assist Illinois students who are pursuing a career in nursing.
Eligibility: Applicants must be Illinois high school seniors who have been accepted into a nursing program or students who are already attending nursing school in Illinois. They must have financial need and a satisfactory academic record, character and activity record. Dependents of deceased or disabled veterans receive priority.

Target applicant(s): High school students. College students. Adult students.
Amount: Varies.
Number of awards: Varies.
Deadline: March 1.
How to apply: Applications are available online.
Exclusive: Visit www.UltimateScholarshipBook.com and enter code IL145826 for updates on this award.

[1459] • Illinois AMVETS Service Foundation Scholarship

Illinois AMVETS Service Foundation
AMVETS Department of Illinois, 2200 South Sixth Street, Springfield, IL 62703
Phone: 217-528-4713
Email: crystal@ilamvets.org
http://www.ilamvets.org
Purpose: To help Illinois students pay for college.
Eligibility: Applicants must be Illinois high school seniors who have taken the SAT or ACT. Preference is given to students who are the children or grandchildren of Illinois veterans.
Target applicant(s): High school students.
Amount: $2,000.
Number of awards: Varies.
Deadline: March 1.
How to apply: Applications are available online.
Exclusive: Visit www.UltimateScholarshipBook.com and enter code IL145926 for updates on this award.

[1460] • Illinois Association for Health, Physical Education, Recreation and Dance Scholarships

Illinois Association for Health, Physical Education, Recreation and Dance
P.O. Box 865, Alton, IL 62002
Phone: 217-245-6413
Email: iahperd@gmail.com
https://www.iahperd.org/grants/student-scholarships
Purpose: To support physical education students.
Eligibility: Applicants must be full-time junior or senior level undergraduate students at colleges or universities in Illinois and must major in health, physical education, recreation or dance. Students must have been members of IAHPERD since December 1 of the previous year and may receive this award no more than twice.
Target applicant(s): College students. Adult students.
Amount: $1,500-$2,000.
Number of awards: 6.
Scholarship may be renewable.
Deadline: June 1.
How to apply: Applications are available online. An application form, cover letter, resume, essay, transcript and two letters of recommendation are required.
Exclusive: Visit www.UltimateScholarshipBook.com and enter code IL146026 for updates on this award.

[1461] • Illinois Department of Children and Family Services Scholarship Program

Illinois Department of Children and Family Services
406 E. Monroe Street, Springfield, IL 62701
Phone: 217-557-5805
https://www2.illinois.gov/dcfs/
Purpose: To support students who have been under the guardianship of the Department of Children and Family Services.
Eligibility: Applicants must be between 16 and 21 years of age as of the application deadline and have a diploma from an accredited high school or a GED by the end of the current school year. Students must be in the Subsidized Guardianship Program, or the department must have court-ordered legal guardianship or have had legal guardianship for the applicant before adoption was finalized. Recipients must attend an Illinois state community college or university.
Target applicant(s): High school students. College students.
Amount: Varies.
Number of awards: 53.
Scholarship may be renewable.
Deadline: March 31.
How to apply: Applications are available online. An application form, transcript or copy of GED, SAT or ACT scores, three letters of recommendation and a college transcript (if applicable) are required.
Exclusive: Visit www.UltimateScholarshipBook.com and enter code IL146126 for updates on this award.

[1462] • Illinois Veteran Grant Program

Illinois Student Assistance Commission
1755 Lake Cook Road, Deerfield, IL 60015-5209
Phone: 800-899-4722
https://www.isac.org
Purpose: To support Illinois veterans with their higher education expenses.
Eligibility: Applicants must be Illinois residents and have served at least one year of federal active duty service in the Armed Forces of the United States, which may include the Illinois National Guard and the Reserve component of the Armed Forces, or have served in a foreign country in a time of hostilities in that country or have been medically discharged for service related reasons.
Target applicant(s): College students. Adult students.
Amount: Varies.
Number of awards: Varies.
Deadline: Contact the sponsor to confirm the deadline.
How to apply: Applications are available online.
Exclusive: Visit www.UltimateScholarshipBook.com and enter code IL146226 for updates on this award.

[1463] • Incentive Program for Aspiring Teachers

Massachusetts Department of Higher Education
Office of Student Financial Assistance, 454 Broadway, Suite 200, Revere, MA 02151
Phone: 617-727-9420
Email: osfa@osfa.mass.edu
https://www.mass.gov/handbook/massachusetts-financial-aid-programs
Purpose: To provide financial support for Massachusetts college students who are studying to become teachers.
Eligibility: Applicants must be in their third or fourth year at a public college in the state of Massachusetts, and they must be enrolled in a field with teacher shortages. They must have a 3.0 GPA in general education courses, and they must remain in satisfactory academic standing while receiving the scholarship. Students must agree to work in a public school in Massachusetts for two years after earning a bachelor's degree.
Target applicant(s): College students. Adult students.
Minimum GPA: 3.0
Amount: Full tuition.
Number of awards: Varies.

Scholarship may be renewable.
Deadline: Contact the sponsor to confirm the deadline.
How to apply: Applications are available at college financial aid offices.
Exclusive: Visit www.UltimateScholarshipBook.com and enter code MA146326 for updates on this award.

[1464] • Independence Excavating, A DiGeronimo Company Scholarship

Associated General Contractors of Ohio
1755 Northwest Boulevard, Columbus, OH 43212
Phone: 614-486-6446
Email: parker@agcohio.com
https://agcohio.com/workforce-development/agc-scholarships/
Purpose: To aid students who are preparing for construction-related careers at postsecondary institutions located in Ohio, Pennsylvania and West Virginia.
Eligibility: Applicants must be U.S. citizens. They must be in at least the second year of study in a two-year, four-year or five-year undergraduate degree program that is related to construction. They must be enrolled at a postsecondary institution located in West Virginia, Pennsylvania or Ohio and have a GPA of 2.5 or higher. Applicants must have plans to work in the construction industry. Selection is based on the overall strength of the application.
Target applicant(s): College students. Adult students.
Minimum GPA: 2.5
Amount: Varies.
Number of awards: Varies.
Deadline: February 9.
How to apply: Applications are available online. An application form, transcript and personal essay are required.
Exclusive: Visit www.UltimateScholarshipBook.com and enter code AS146426 for updates on this award.

[1465] • Indiana Broadcasters Association College Scholarships

Indiana Broadcasters Association
P.O. Box 902, Carmel, IN 46082
Phone: 317-770-0970
Email: sam@indianabroadcasters.org
https://www.indianabroadcasters.org/scholarships/
Purpose: To support student broadcasters.
Eligibility: Applicants must be Indiana residents and current college students with a 3.0 or higher GPA. Students must be actively participating in a college broadcast facility or working for a commercial broadcast facility and be attending an IBA member institution that has a radio/TV facility on campus and/or offers majors in telecommunications or broadcast journalism.
Target applicant(s): College students. Adult students.
Minimum GPA: 3.0
Amount: $5,000.
Number of awards: 10.
Deadline: February 15.
How to apply: Applications are available online. An application form, essay and transcript request form are required.
Exclusive: Visit www.UltimateScholarshipBook.com and enter code IN146526 for updates on this award.

[1466] • Indiana Golf Foundation Scholarship

Indiana Golf Association
P.O. Box 26159, Indianapolis, IN 46226
Phone: 317-738-9696
Email: astrong@indianagolf.org
https://www.indianagolf.org/scholarships/
Purpose: To support youth who have participated in the Indiana Junior Golf Program.
Eligibility: Applicants must be high school seniors who have participated in the Indiana Junior Golf Program for at least two years, have a 3.0 GPA or higher, display strong character and have financial need. Selection is based on these criteria as well as a personal essay.
Target applicant(s): High school students.
Minimum GPA: 3.0
Amount: $2,500.
Number of awards: Varies.
Deadline: March 24.
How to apply: Applications are available online and must also include the personal essay, high school transcript, IRS Form 1040 and at least one letter of recommendation.
Exclusive: Visit www.UltimateScholarshipBook.com and enter code IN146626 for updates on this award.

[1467] • Indiana Oratorical Contest

American Legion, Department of Indiana
5440 Herbert Lord Road, Indianapolis, IN 46216
Phone: 317-630-1300
Email: programs@indlegion.org
http://www.indianalegion.org
Purpose: To enhance high school students' experience with and understanding of the U.S. Constitution. The contest will help develop students' leadership skills and civic appreciation, as well as the ability to deliver thoughtful, insightful orations regarding U.S. citizenship and its inherent responsibilities.
Eligibility: Applicants must be high school students under the age of 20 who are U.S. citizens or legal residents and residents of the state. Students first give an oration within their state and winners compete at the national level. The oration must be related to the Constitution of the United States focusing on the duties and obligations citizens have to the government. It must be in English and be between eight and ten minutes. There is also an assigned topic which is posted on the website, and it should be between three and five minutes.
Target applicant(s): High school students.
Amount: $200-$3,400.
Number of awards: Varies.
Deadline: February 21.
How to apply: Application information is available from the local American Legion Post and online.
Exclusive: Visit www.UltimateScholarshipBook.com and enter code AM146726 for updates on this award.

[1468] • Inspired to Teach

Oklahoma State Regents for Higher Education/Inspired to Teach
655 Research Parkway, Suite 200, Oklahoma City, OK 73104
Phone: 800-858-1840
Email: studentinfo@osrhe.edu
https://www.okcollegestart.org/Financial_Aid_Planning/Scholarships/Career_Scholarships/Inspired_to_Teach.aspx
Purpose: To encourage students to become comprehensively trained teachers in Oklahoma public schools.

Eligibility: Applicants must graduate from a high school, homeschool or earn a GED; meet higher education admission standards at a public or private Oklahoma university with an accredited Oklahoma teacher education program, or a community college with an approved articulation agreement with an accredited Oklahoma university teacher education program; declare a major in an accredited Oklahoma university teacher education program with a degree leading to a standard teaching certificate, or declare a major at an Oklahoma community college with an approved Inspired to Teach articulation agreement leading to a standard teaching certificate. Applicants must maintain Satisfactory Academic Progress (SAP) and a minimum 2.5 GPA throughout matriculation and agree to teach in an Oklahoma public school district (PK-12) upon graduation.
Target applicant(s): High school students. College students. Adult students.
Minimum GPA: 2.5
Amount: Up to $25,500.
Number of awards: Varies.
Deadline: Contact the sponsor to confirm the deadline.
How to apply: Applications are submitted by the nominating institution.
Exclusive: Visit www.UltimateScholarshipBook.com and enter code OK146826 for updates on this award.

[1469] • Iowa 4-H College Scholarships
Iowa 4-H Foundation
Extension 4-H Youth Building, 1259 Stange Road, Ames, IA 50011-1002
Phone: 515-294-4443
https://www.iowa4hfoundation.org
Purpose: To assist Iowa 4-H participants to pursue higher education.
Eligibility: Applicants must be Iowa residents and 4-H members who are enrolling in or currently enrolled in an Iowa post-secondary institution. Students must submit two letters of recommendation along with their materials.
Target applicant(s): High school students. College students. Adult students.
Amount: Varies.
Number of awards: Varies.
Deadline: March 1.
How to apply: Applications are available online.
Exclusive: Visit www.UltimateScholarshipBook.com and enter code IO146926 for updates on this award.

[1470] • Iowa Newspaper Association Scholarships
Iowa Newspaper Association
319 E 5th Street, Des Moines, IA 50309
Phone: 515-244-2145
Email: ina@inanews.com
http://www.inanews.com
Purpose: To support students preparing for careers in the newspaper industry.
Eligibility: Applicants must be Iowa residents who are high school seniors or current college students and must attend an in-state college or university. Students must plan to work in the newspaper industry in Iowa upon completion of their degrees.
Target applicant(s): High school students. College students. Adult students.
Amount: $500-$1,000.
Number of awards: Varies.
Deadline: February 16.
How to apply: Applications are available online. An application form, two letters of reference, personal statement and two writing samples are required.
Exclusive: Visit www.UltimateScholarshipBook.com and enter code IO147026 for updates on this award.

[1471] • Iowa Oratorical Contest
American Legion, Department of Iowa
720 Lyon Street, Des Moines, IA 50309
Phone: 800-365-8387
Email: programs@ialegion.org
https://www.ialegion.org/oratorical/
Purpose: To enhance high school students' experience with and understanding of the U.S. Constitution. The contest will help develop students' leadership skills and civic appreciation, as well as the ability to deliver thoughtful, insightful orations regarding U.S. citizenship and its inherent responsibilities.
Eligibility: Applicants must be high school students under the age of 20 who are U.S. citizens or legal residents and residents of the state. Students first give an oration within their state and winners compete at the national level. The oration must be related to the Constitution of the United States focusing on the duties and obligations citizens have to the government. It must be in English and be between eight and ten minutes. There is also an assigned topic which is posted on the website, and it should be between three and five minutes.
Target applicant(s): High school students.
Amount: Up to $18,000.
Number of awards: Varies.
Deadline: Contact the sponsor to confirm the deadline.
How to apply: Applications are available online.
Exclusive: Visit www.UltimateScholarshipBook.com and enter code AM147126 for updates on this award.

[1472] • Iowa PGA Foundation Charlie Burkart Scholarship
Iowa PGA Foundation
3184 HWY 22 Riverside, Riverside, IA 52327
https://www.iowapgajuniorgolf.com/charlie-burkart/
Purpose: To assist Iowa student golf athletes to pursue post-secondary education.
Eligibility: Applicants must reside within the boundaries of the Iowa PGA section, including the cities of Monmouth, Macomb, Galesburg, Moline, Rock Island, Kewanee and Galena. Students must demonstrate an interest in golf, community involvement and financial need.
Target applicant(s): High school students. College students. Adult students.
Amount: $1,500.
Number of awards: 1.
Scholarship may be renewable.
Deadline: June 18.
How to apply: Applications are available online.
Exclusive: Visit www.UltimateScholarshipBook.com and enter code IO147226 for updates on this award.

[1473] • Iowa Physician Assistant Society Scholarship
Iowa Physician Assistant Society
6919 Vista Drive, West Des Moines, IA 50266
Phone: 515-282-8192
Email: info@iapasociety.org

https://www.iapasociety.org/index.php/students/scholarship-information
Purpose: To aid Iowa students who are enrolled in a physician assistant degree program.
Eligibility: Applicants must be enrolled in an approved Physician Assistant (PA) degree program at a postsecondary institution located in Iowa. They must have had an outstanding undergraduate academic record, strong leadership skills and a well-developed knowledge of the role of the professional physician assistant. Selection is based on academic merit, demonstrated leadership ability, commitment to the field of physician assisting, extracurricular activities and professional awareness.
Target applicant(s): College students. Adult students.
Amount: $1,000.
Number of awards: 5.
Deadline: September 5.
How to apply: Applications are available online. An application form, transcript and personal statement are required.
Exclusive: Visit www.UltimateScholarshipBook.com and enter code IO147326 for updates on this award.

[1474] • Iowa Pork Foundation Scholarship
Iowa Pork Producers Association
1636 NW 114th Street, P.O. Box 71009, Clive, IA 50325
Phone: 800-372-7675
Email: info@iowapork.org
http://www.iowapork.org
Purpose: To aid Iowa agriculture students who are interested in the pork industry.
Eligibility: Applicants must be Iowa residents who are enrolled at or who plan to enroll at a two-year or four-year postsecondary institution located in Iowa. They must be majoring in or have plans to major in an agriculture-related undergraduate program that focuses on swine production. They must maintain a GPA of 2.5 or higher. Selection is based on the overall strength of the application.
Target applicant(s): High school students. College students. Adult students.
Minimum GPA: 2.5
Amount: $1,000.
Number of awards: Varies.
Scholarship may be renewable.
Deadline: April 1.
How to apply: Applications are available online. An application form, two recommendation letters and a transcript are required.
Exclusive: Visit www.UltimateScholarshipBook.com and enter code IO147426 for updates on this award.

[1475] • Iowa Scholarship for the Arts
Iowa Arts Council
600 E. Locust, Des Moines, IA 50319-0290
Phone: 515-281-6412
https://iowaculture.gov/arts/grants
Purpose: To aid outstanding young artists.
Eligibility: Applicants must be Iowa residents and graduating high school seniors and show proven artistic ability in dance, literature, music, theatre, traditional arts or visual arts. Students must be accepted full-time to an accredited Iowa college or university and must major in one of the aforementioned areas.
Target applicant(s): High school students.
Amount: $3,000.
Number of awards: Varies.
Deadline: April 1.
How to apply: Applications are available online. An application form, two letters of recommendation and an essay are required.
Exclusive: Visit www.UltimateScholarshipBook.com and enter code IO147526 for updates on this award.

[1476] • Iowa Thespian Chapter Board Senior Scholarships
Iowa Thespian Chapter
Leslie LaCorte, Iowa Thespian Treasurer, Davenport North High School, 626 West 53rd Street, Davenport, IA 52806
Phone: 563-332-5151
Email: myattw@pleasval.k12.ia.us
http://www.iowathespians.org
Purpose: To aid promising young thespians.
Eligibility: Applicants must be Iowa high school seniors and have an overall GPA of 2.0 or higher with a GPA of 3.0 or higher in arts-related classes. Students must be members of the International Thespian Society in good standing. Applicants must plan to major or minor in theatre, film, radio and television, broadcasting, music or dance. Applicants must also perform an audition at the Iowa Thespian Festival in the performance, technical or theatre educator category.
Target applicant(s): High school students.
Minimum GPA: 2.0
Amount: $1,000.
Number of awards: Varies.
Deadline: October 19.
How to apply: Applications are available from the Iowa Thespian Society. An application form and resume are required.
Exclusive: Visit www.UltimateScholarshipBook.com and enter code IO147626 for updates on this award.

[1477] • Iowa Tuition Grants
Iowa College Student Aid Commission
475 SW Fifth Street, Suite D, Des Moines, IA 50309
Phone: 515-725-3400
Email: info@iowacollegeaid.gov
https://www.iowacollegeaid.gov/ScholarshipsAndGrants
Purpose: To help students attend Iowa's independent colleges and universities.
Eligibility: Applicants must be enrolled in or planning to enroll at least part-time in an eligible Iowa college or university and demonstrate financial need. Priority is given to the neediest applicants.
Target applicant(s): High school students. College students. Adult students.
Amount: Up to $6,800.
Number of awards: Varies.
Scholarship may be renewable.
Deadline: July 1.
How to apply: Complete the Free Application for Federal Student Aid (FAFSA).
Exclusive: Visit www.UltimateScholarshipBook.com and enter code IO147726 for updates on this award.

[1478] • Iowa Vocational-Technical Tuition Grants
Iowa College Student Aid Commission
475 SW Fifth Street, Suite D, Des Moines, IA 50309
Phone: 515-725-3400
Email: info@iowacollegeaid.gov
https://www.iowacollegeaid.gov/ScholarshipsAndGrants

The Ultimate Scholarship Book 2026
Scholarship Directory (State of Residence)

Purpose: To aid those Iowa residents enrolled in vocational-technical programs at community colleges.
Eligibility: Applicants must be enrolled in or planning to enroll in a career education or option course for 3 credit hours consisting of at least 15 weeks duration at an Iowa area community college and be U.S. citizens or permanent residents. Applicants must prove financial need.
Target applicant(s): High school students. College students. Adult students.
Amount: Up to $1,000.
Number of awards: Varies.
Scholarship may be renewable.
Deadline: July 1.
How to apply: Complete the Free Application for Federal Student Aid (FAFSA).
Exclusive: Visit www.UltimateScholarshipBook.com and enter code IO147826 for updates on this award.

[1479] • Irving W. Cook, WA0CGS, Scholarship
American Radio Relay League Foundation
225 Main Street, Newington, CT 06111-1494
Phone: 860-594-0200
Email: foundation@arrl.org
https://www.arrl.org/scholarship-program
Purpose: To provide scholarship assistance to Kansas residents who are amateur radio operators.
Eligibility: Applicants must be residents of Kansas and holders of an active amateur radio license of any class. Preference is given to students who are studying electronics, communications or a related subject at the baccalaureate level or higher.
Target applicant(s): College students. Graduate school students. Adult students.
Amount: $1,000.
Number of awards: 1.
Deadline: January 10.
How to apply: Applications are available online.
Exclusive: Visit www.UltimateScholarshipBook.com and enter code AM147926 for updates on this award.

[1480] • ISAA Scholarship Program
Iowa State Archery Association
ISAA Scholarship Program, Jan Kostka, Chair, 1425 Plymouth Road, Mason City, IA 50401
Email: jankostka@mac.com
http://www.isaaproam.com
Purpose: To aid students who have participated in the Iowa State Archery Association as they continue their education beyond high school.
Eligibility: Applicants must be a high school senior, have obtained a GED or be a full-time college student. The student must have been an active member of ISAA for at least two years. Selection is based on participation in ISAA activities, academic achievement, financial need, community involvement and the reference letters.
Target applicant(s): High school students. College students. Graduate school students. Adult students.
Amount: Up to $1,000.
Number of awards: Varies.
Deadline: February 8.
How to apply: Applications are available online.
Exclusive: Visit www.UltimateScholarshipBook.com and enter code IO148026 for updates on this award.

[1481] • Ivomec Generations of Excellence Internship and Scholarship Program
Texas CattleWomen
Erin Worrell, 657 Blue Oak Trail, Harper, TX 78631
Phone: 512-413-1616
Email: worrellerin@gmail.com
https://txcattlewomen.org/programs
Purpose: To aid Texas students who are preparing for careers in the beef industry.
Eligibility: Applicants must be permanent residents of Texas and be graduate students or rising undergraduate juniors or seniors who are enrolled at a Texas college or university. They must be majoring in agriculture or a related subject, must have a background in beef cattle and have a GPA of 2.5 or higher. Selection is based on the overall strength of the application.
Target applicant(s): College students. Graduate school students. Adult students.
Minimum GPA: 2.5
Amount: $1,000.
Number of awards: 1.
Deadline: June 1.
How to apply: Applications are available online. An application form and supporting materials are required.
Exclusive: Visit www.UltimateScholarshipBook.com and enter code TE148126 for updates on this award.

[1482] • J.R. Popalisky Scholarship
American Water Works Association - Missouri Section
https://awwa-mo.org
Purpose: To aid Missouri students whose coursework is related to the water supply industry.
Eligibility: Applicants must be U.S. citizens who are enrolled at an accredited college or university located in Missouri. They must have completed coursework in subjects relating to the water supply industry (such as environmental engineering, civil engineering or environmental science). Students who are receiving funding from an employer are ineligible. Selection is based on coursework relevance, GPA, financial need, recommendations, personal essay and extracurricular activities.
Target applicant(s): College students. Adult students.
Amount: $1,000.
Number of awards: At least 1.
Deadline: February 28.
How to apply: Applications are available online. An application form, personal essay and a financial analysis form are required.
Exclusive: Visit www.UltimateScholarshipBook.com and enter code AM148226 for updates on this award.

[1483] • Jack E. Barger, Sr. Memorial Nursing Scholarship
Nursing Foundation of Pennsylvania
3605 Vartan Way, Suite 204, Harrisburg, PA 17110
Phone: 717-827-4369
Email: info@thenfp.org
http://www.thenfp.org/scholarships/
Purpose: To aid Pennsylvania nursing undergraduates who are serving in the military, are veterans, are military spouses, are veterans' spouses or who are the children of active duty military or veterans.

Eligibility: Candidates must be residents of Pennsylvania and must be enrolled in an undergraduate nursing program at an institution located in Pennsylvania. They must be active duty military, veterans, military spouses, veterans' spouses or the children of active duty military or veterans. Candidates are nominated for this award by the deans and department heads in the school of nursing at their institutions. Selection of award recipients will be determined by lottery.
Target applicant(s): High school students. College students. Adult students.
Amount: $1,000.
Number of awards: 6.
Deadline: March 31.
How to apply: Candidates are not required to submit an application for this award. Instead, the dean or department head of the candidate's school must submit a formal nomination to the scholarship committee.
Exclusive: Visit www.UltimateScholarshipBook.com and enter code NU148326 for updates on this award.

[1484] • Jack F. Tolbert Memorial Student Grant Program

Maryland Higher Education Commission
Office of Student Financial Assistance, 6 North Liberty Street,
Baltimore, MD 21201
Phone: 800-974-1024
Email: osfamail@mhec.state.md.us
https://mhec.maryland.gov
Purpose: To assist students who are attending or planning to attend a private career school.
Eligibility: Students and their parents if they are dependents must be residents of Maryland. Applicants must also enroll at an approved private career school in the state for at least 18 hours per week.
Target applicant(s): High school students. College students. Adult students.
Amount: Up to $500.
Number of awards: Varies.
Scholarship may be renewable.
Deadline: Varies.
How to apply: Students apply by completing the Free Application for Federal Student Aid (FAFSA) and turning it in to the financial aid office of the career school they will attend.
Exclusive: Visit www.UltimateScholarshipBook.com and enter code MA148426 for updates on this award.

[1485] • Jack Hughes Education Scholarship

California Nevada Racquetball Association
Terry Rogers, CNRA Scholarship Chairperson, 8317 Divernon Avenue, Las Vegas, NV 89149
Email: info@californianevadaracquetball.org
http://www.californiaracquetball.org
Purpose: To help graduating seniors and college undergraduates who are USA Racquetball (USAR) members expand racquetball.
Eligibility: Applicants must be high school seniors who will be graduating or college undergraduates. Students must reside in California or Nevada and demonstrate a desire to expand racquetball. Applicants must also be current USAR members.
Target applicant(s): High school students. College students. Adult students.
Amount: Varies.
Number of awards: Varies.
Deadline: August 15.
How to apply: Applications are available online.
Exclusive: Visit www.UltimateScholarshipBook.com and enter code CA148526 for updates on this award.

[1486] • James Anderson Logan Jr. and Betty Ann McFarland Logan Scholarship Fund

Oklahoma City Community Foundation
1000 North Broadway, Oklahoma City, OK 73102
Phone: 405-235-5603
Email: scholarships@occf.org
https://occf.org/scholarships/
Purpose: To support Oklahoma students who are single parents.
Eligibility: Applicants must be single parents who have legal custody and have sole responsibility for the care of at least one child age 26 or younger, as long as the child is still on the parent's insurance. Students must be from the state of Oklahoma attending college at a four-year, two-year or vocational technical school. Preference is given to students with financial need.
Target applicant(s): College students. Adult students.
Amount: $2,000.
Number of awards: 1.
Deadline: March 1.
How to apply: Applications are available online.
Exclusive: Visit www.UltimateScholarshipBook.com and enter code OK148626 for updates on this award.

[1487] • James B. Morris Scholarship

James B. Morris Scholarship Fund
P.O. Box 12145, Des Moines, IA 50312
http://www.morrisscholarship.org
Purpose: To support Iowa minority students pursuing post-secondary education.
Eligibility: Applicants must be U.S. citizens of a minority ethnic status who are either Iowa high school graduates attending any U.S. college or university or non-Iowa residents who are attending an Iowa college or university. Students must have a minimum GPA of 2.5.
Target applicant(s): High school students. College students. Graduate school students. Adult students.
Minimum GPA: 2.5
Amount: Varies.
Number of awards: Varies.
Deadline: February 29.
How to apply: Applications are available online.
Exclusive: Visit www.UltimateScholarshipBook.com and enter code JA148726 for updates on this award.

[1488] • James H. Dunn, Jr. Memorial Fellowship

Governor's Office of the State of Illinois Dunn Fellowship
Dunn Fellowship Program, 207 State House, Springfield, IL 62706
Phone: 217-782-0244
Email: GOV.DunnFellowshipApp@illinois.gov
https://gov.illinois.gov/about/opportunities.html
Purpose: To provide college graduates with an opportunity to experience daily operations in state government for one year.
Eligibility: Fellows must possess a bachelor's degree. Fellows will be assigned to various posts in the Governor's office or in an office under the governor's jurisdiction.
Target applicant(s): College students. Adult students.
Amount: Up to $41,588.
Number of awards: Varies.
Deadline: February 14.

How to apply: Applications are available online or by mail.
Exclusive: Visit www.UltimateScholarshipBook.com and enter code GO148826 for updates on this award.

[1489] • James J. Burns and C.A. Haynes Textile Scholarship

Rhode Island Foundation
One Union Station, Providence, RI 02903
Phone: 401-274-4564
Email: rbogert@rifoundation.org
https://rifoundation.org/grants-scholarships
Purpose: To support students who are planning to work in the textile industry.
Eligibility: Students must be currently enrolled in a textile program. They must demonstrate financial need or academic excellence. Preference will be given to students whose parents are members of the National Association of Textile Supervisors.
Target applicant(s): High school students. College students. Graduate school students. Adult students.
Amount: $1,000.
Number of awards: Varies.
Deadline: April 15.
How to apply: Applications are available online.
Exclusive: Visit www.UltimateScholarshipBook.com and enter code RH148926 for updates on this award.

[1490] • James S. Davis Memorial Scholarship

National Foliage Foundation
1533 Park Center Drive, Orlando, FL 32835
Phone: 800-375-3642
Email: info@nationalfoliagefoundation.org
https://www.nationalhorticulturefoundation.org/
Purpose: To aid students pursuing higher education in horticulture or a related discipline in Florida.
Eligibility: Applicants must be rising freshmen or undergraduates at an accredited postsecondary institution located in Florida. They must be full-time students who are enrolled in or who are planning to enroll in a degree program in horticulture or a related subject. They must have a GPA of 2.0 or higher. Selection is based on the overall strength of the application.
Target applicant(s): High school students. College students. Adult students.
Minimum GPA: 2.0
Amount: Varies.
Number of awards: Varies.
Scholarship may be renewable.
Deadline: January 15.
How to apply: Applications are available online. An application form, transcript, personal essay and two letters of recommendation are required.
Exclusive: Visit www.UltimateScholarshipBook.com and enter code NA149026 for updates on this award.

[1491] • James V. Day Scholarship

American Legion, Department of Maine
5 Verti Drive, Winslow, ME 04901-0727
Phone: 207-873-3229
Email: legionme@mainelegion.org
http://www.mainelegion.org/pages/programs/scholarships.php
Purpose: To provide financial assistance to the children or grandchildren of American Legion, Department of Maine members.
Eligibility: Applicants must be U.S. citizens, residents of Maine and graduating high school seniors. They must be enrolled in an accredited college or vocational technical school and provide evidence of financial need. Applicants must demonstrate good character and a belief in the American way of life.
Target applicant(s): High school students.
Amount: $500.
Number of awards: 2.
Deadline: May 1.
How to apply: Applications are available online.
Exclusive: Visit www.UltimateScholarshipBook.com and enter code AM149126 for updates on this award.

[1492] • Jean Lee/Jeff Marvin Collegiate Scholarships

Indiana Association for Health, Physical Education, Recreation and Dance
2007 Wilno Drive, Marion, IN 46952
Phone: 765-664-8319
Email: hatch@cometck.com
https://indianashape.org/scholarships/
Purpose: To aid students pursuing degrees in physical education-related fields.
Eligibility: Applicants must be attending an Indiana college or university and be upcoming juniors or seniors who are majoring in health education, physical education, recreation, dance education or allied areas.
Target applicant(s): College students. Adult students.
Amount: $1,000.
Number of awards: 6.
Deadline: February 1.
How to apply: Applications are available online. An application form, goals statement, statement of need, list of activities during college attendance, philosophy statement and two letters of recommendation are required.
Exclusive: Visit www.UltimateScholarshipBook.com and enter code IN149226 for updates on this award.

[1493] • Jimmie L. Dean Scholarship

Jimmie L. Dean Scholarship Foundation Inc.
20 East 5th Street, Suite 1200G, Tulsa, OK 74103
Email: info@jimmiedeanfoundation.org
https://jimmiedeanfoundation.org
Purpose: To encourage Oklahoma students to pursue education.
Eligibility: Applicants must be legal residents and have lived in Oklahoma for the past six years. Students must be graduating from an Oklahoma high school or have completed graduation requirements through homeschooling. Applicants must be attending an Oklahoma college, university or technical school as a full-time, first-time student.
Target applicant(s): High school students.
Amount: Up to $10,000.
Number of awards: Varies.
Scholarship may be renewable.
Deadline: April 30.
How to apply: Applications are available online.
Exclusive: Visit www.UltimateScholarshipBook.com and enter code JI149326 for updates on this award.

[1494] • Jimmy Rane Foundation Scholarships
Jimmy Rane Foundation
P.O. Box 40, Abbeville, AL 36310
Phone: 800-310-4053
Email: contactus@applyists.com
http://www.jimmyranefoundation.org
Purpose: To support students who are planning to pursue undergraduate degrees.
Eligibility: Applicants must be high school seniors or college freshmen or sophomores who are residents of Alabama, Arkansas, Delaware, Florida, Georgia, Iowa, Kansas, Kentucky, Louisiana, Maryland, Mississippi, Missouri, Nebraska, New Jersey, New York, North Carolina, Ohio, Oklahoma, Pennsylvania, South Carolina, Tennessee, Texas, Virginia, West Virginia or the District of Columbia. Students must have a minimum GPA of 3.0 for high school seniors or 2.75 for college students. Selection is based on academic excellence, community involvement, leadership skills, awards and honors and financial need.
Target applicant(s): High school students. College students.
Minimum GPA: 3.0 for high school seniors; 2.75 for college students
Amount: $500-$5,000.
Number of awards: Varies.
Deadline: February 7.
How to apply: Applications are available online.
Exclusive: Visit www.UltimateScholarshipBook.com and enter code JI149426 for updates on this award.

[1495] • JJ Klein Scholarship Fund
Alaska Community Foundation
3201 C Street, Suite 110, Anchorage, AK 99503
Phone: 907-334-6700
Email: scholarships@alaskacf.org
https://alaskacf.org/scholarships/
Purpose: To assist Alaskan students.
Eligibility: Applicants must be Alaskan high school graduates pursuing post-secondary education with a minimum 2.0 GPA who are enrolled full-time in an accredited institute of higher education or vocational school for the upcoming academic year. Students must demonstrate financial need and motivation to succeed.
Target applicant(s): High school students. College students. Adult students.
Minimum GPA: 2.0
Amount: Up to $10,000.
Number of awards: 2.
Deadline: March 15.
How to apply: Applications are available online.
Exclusive: Visit www.UltimateScholarshipBook.com and enter code AL149526 for updates on this award.

[1496] • Joe Foss, An American Hero Scholarship
Sioux Falls Area Community Foundation
The Depot at Cherapa Place, 200 N. Cherapa Place, Sioux Falls, SD 57103-2205
Phone: 605-336-7055
Email: tlatza@sfacf.org
https://www.sfacf.org/grants-scholarships/scholarships
Purpose: To support high school seniors who have strong values, courage and patriotism.
Eligibility: Applicants must have at least a 3.5 GPA and an ACT score of 21 or above. Students must reside in South Dakota.
Target applicant(s): High school students.
Minimum GPA: 3.5
Amount: $1,000.
Number of awards: 6.
Deadline: March 15.
How to apply: Applications are available online.
Exclusive: Visit www.UltimateScholarshipBook.com and enter code SI149626 for updates on this award.

[1497] • Johanna Drew Cluney Fund
Hawaii Community Foundation - Scholarships
827 Fort Street Mall, Honolulu, HI 96813
Phone: 888-731-3863
Email: scholarships@hcf-hawaii.org
https://www.hawaiicommunityfoundation.org/
Purpose: To aid students pursuing vocational education.
Eligibility: Applicants must be Hawaii residents who are enrolled full-time in vocational degree programs at a University of Hawaii school and who have a minimum 2.0 GPA. They must be first-time degree seekers who plan to enter the workforce upon graduation.
Target applicant(s): College students. Adult students.
Minimum GPA: 2.0
Amount: Varies.
Number of awards: Varies.
Deadline: January 31.
How to apply: Applications are available online. An application form, personal statement and letter of recommendation are required.
Exclusive: Visit www.UltimateScholarshipBook.com and enter code HA149726 for updates on this award.

[1498] • John and Abigail Adams Scholarship
Massachusetts Department of Higher Education
Office of Student Financial Assistance, 454 Broadway, Suite 200, Revere, MA 02151
Phone: 617-727-9420
Email: osfa@osfa.mass.edu
https://www.mass.gov/handbook/massachusetts-financial-aid-programs
Purpose: To attract high-performing high school seniors to Massachusetts public institutions of higher education and to reward previous achievements.
Eligibility: Applicants must be permanent residents of Massachusetts, score in the Advanced category in one category of the 10th grade MCAS test and in the Proficient or Advanced category in the other and have a combined MCAS score in the top 25 percent of their school district. Scholarship winners must maintain a 3.0 or higher GPA for continued eligibility.
Target applicant(s): High school students.
Minimum GPA: 3.0
Amount: Up to full tuition.
Number of awards: Varies.
Scholarship may be renewable.
Deadline: As soon as possible after October 1.
How to apply: No application is necessary, but students must complete the Free Application for Federal Student Aid.

The Ultimate Scholarship Book 2026
Scholarship Directory (State of Residence)

Exclusive: Visit www.UltimateScholarshipBook.com and enter code MA149826 for updates on this award.

[1499] • John and Anne Clifton Scholarship
Hawaii Community Foundation - Scholarships
827 Fort Street Mall, Honolulu, HI 96813
Phone: 888-731-3863
Email: scholarships@hcf-hawaii.org
https://www.hawaiicommunityfoundation.org/
Purpose: To assist students pursuing vocational degrees.
Eligibility: Applicants must be enrolled in a vocational program at a University of Hawaii school and have at least a 2.0 GPA.
Target applicant(s): High school students. College students. Adult students.
Minimum GPA: 2.0
Amount: Varies.
Number of awards: Varies.
Deadline: February 28.
How to apply: Applications are available online.
Exclusive: Visit www.UltimateScholarshipBook.com and enter code HA149926 for updates on this award.

[1500] • John D. and Virginia Riesch Scholarship
Wisconsin Medical Society Foundation
P.O. Box 1109, Madison, WI 53701
Phone: 608-442-3800
Email: foundation@wismed.org
https://foundation.wismed.org/wisconsin/
Purpose: To aid students who are training to become physicians or nurses.
Eligibility: Applicants must be U.S. citizens. They must be full-time students enrolled in a medical school or nursing degree program at an accredited Wisconsin college or university. Rising undergraduate freshmen, undergraduate medical students and nursing students enrolled in a less than two-year program are ineligible. Preference will be given to Wisconsin residents and to applicants who are planning to practice in Wisconsin. Selection is based on academic merit, personal qualities, recommendations and financial need.
Target applicant(s): College students. Graduate school students. Adult students.
Amount: Varies.
Number of awards: 2.
Deadline: February 1.
How to apply: Applications are available online. An application form, personal statement, transcript and two recommendation letters are required.
Exclusive: Visit www.UltimateScholarshipBook.com and enter code WI150026 for updates on this award.

[1501] • John Dawe Dental Education Fund
Hawaii Community Foundation - Scholarships
827 Fort Street Mall, Honolulu, HI 96813
Phone: 888-731-3863
Email: scholarships@hcf-hawaii.org
https://www.hawaiicommunityfoundation.org/
Purpose: To provide financial assistance to Hawaii students pursuing careers in dental professions.
Eligibility: Applicants must be enrolled full-time in a school of dentistry, dental hygiene or dental assisting. They must have a GPA of 2.7 or higher. Two letters of recommendation and a letter from the applicant's school confirming enrollment in the dentistry or dental hygiene program are required.
Target applicant(s): High school students. College students. Adult students.
Minimum GPA: 2.7
Amount: Varies.
Number of awards: Varies.
Deadline: February 28.
How to apply: To apply, register online, complete the online application and select the scholarships to which you wish to apply. In addition, mail the supporting materials: printed confirmation page from the online application, personal statement, copy of Student Aid Report (SAR) available at www.fafsa.ed.gov and official transcript.
Exclusive: Visit www.UltimateScholarshipBook.com and enter code HA150126 for updates on this award.

[1502] • John R. Lillard VAOC Scholarship
Virginia Department of Aviation
VAOC Scholarship, Attn: Betty Wilson, 5702 Gulfstream Road, Richmond, VA 23250-2422
Phone: 804-236-3624
Email: director@doav.virginia.gov
https://doav.virginia.gov/
Purpose: To aid Virginia high school seniors who are planning for careers in aviation.
Eligibility: Applicants must be Virginia high school seniors who have an unweighted GPA of 3.5 or higher. They must be accepted into or enrolled in an aviation-related program at an accredited postsecondary institution and must have plans to pursue a career in aviation. Selection is based on academic merit, personal essay, leadership skills and financial need.
Target applicant(s): High school students.
Minimum GPA: 3.5
Amount: $3,000.
Number of awards: Varies.
Deadline: March 1.
How to apply: Applications are available online. An application form, personal essay, official transcript, verification of college acceptance or enrollment, list of extracurricular activities and up to three recommendation letters are required.
Exclusive: Visit www.UltimateScholarshipBook.com and enter code VI150226 for updates on this award.

[1503] • John Schwartz Scholarship
American Institute of Wine and Food - Pacific Northwest Chapter
213-37 39th Avenue, Box 216, Bayside, NY 11361
Phone: 800-274-2493
Email: bsteinmetz100@hotmail.com
http://www.aiwf.org
Purpose: To aid students pursuing culinary degrees.
Eligibility: Applicants must have been Washington State residents for at least two years, be enrolled in a Washington State accredited culinary or winemaking arts program and have a GPA of 3.0 or higher.
Target applicant(s): College students. Adult students.
Minimum GPA: 3.0
Amount: $1,000.
Number of awards: 1.
Deadline: Contact the sponsor to confirm the deadline.
How to apply: Applications are available from your school's culinary or winemaking arts department. An application form, resume and references are required.

Exclusive: Visit www.UltimateScholarshipBook.com and enter code AM150326 for updates on this award.

[1504] • John W. Rogers Memorial Scholarship
Missouri Bankers Foundation
P.O. Box 57, 207 East Capitol Avenue, Jefferson City, MO 65101
Phone: 573-636-8151
Email: rpreston@mobankers.com
https://www.mobankers.com
Purpose: To aid high school seniors who are planning to pursue higher education in agriculture or a banking-related subject.
Eligibility: Applicants must be graduating high school seniors who have plans to major in agriculture or a banking-related subject at the postsecondary level. Preference will be given to applicants who are planning to attend the University of Missouri-Columbia. Selection is based on the overall strength of the application.
Target applicant(s): High school students.
Amount: $1,000.
Number of awards: 7.
Deadline: March 1.
How to apply: Applications are available online. An application form, official transcript, ACT scores, a list of extracurricular activities and two recommendation letters are required.
Exclusive: Visit www.UltimateScholarshipBook.com and enter code MI150426 for updates on this award.

[1505] • Jose Marti Scholarship Challenge Grant
Florida Department of Education
Office of Student Financial Assistance, State Scholarship and Grant Programs, 325 West Gaines Street, Suite 1314, Tallahassee, FL 32399-0400
Phone: 888-827-2004
Email: osfa@fldoe.org
https://origin.fldoe.org/finance/financial-aid-scholarships/
Purpose: To help Florida students in need who are of Hispanic origin.
Eligibility: Applicants must have been born in or have a natural parent who was born in either Mexico or Spain, or a Hispanic country of the Caribbean, Central or South America, regardless of race. Students must plan to attend Florida public or eligible private institutions as undergraduate or graduate students, but graduating high school seniors get preference.
Target applicant(s): High school students. College students. Graduate school students. Adult students.
Minimum GPA: 3.0
Amount: $2,000.
Number of awards: Varies.
Scholarship may be renewable.
Deadline: April 1.
How to apply: Applicants must submit the initial student Florida Financial Aid Application by April 1 and the Free Application for Federal Student Aid (FAFSA) by May 15.
Exclusive: Visit www.UltimateScholarshipBook.com and enter code FL150526 for updates on this award.

[1506] • Judge William F. Cooper Scholarship
Center for Scholarship Administration
4320 Wade Hampton Boulevard, Suite G, Taylors, SC 29687-0031
Phone: 864-268-3363
Email: allisonleewagoner@bellsouth.net
https://www.csascholars.org/index.php
Purpose: To provide financial assistance to female students from Georgia who plan to attend college.
Eligibility: Applicants must be high school seniors who have financial need. Students must have an acceptable GPA and plan to study in any field except law, theology or medicine. Nursing is acceptable.
Target applicant(s): High school students.
Amount: Varies.
Number of awards: Varies.
Scholarship may be renewable.
Deadline: February 26.
How to apply: Applications are available online.
Exclusive: Visit www.UltimateScholarshipBook.com and enter code CE150626 for updates on this award.

[1507] • KAB Broadcast Scholarship Program
Kansas Association of Broadcasters
Scholarship Committee, 534 S Kansas Avenue, Suite 1105, Topeka, KS 66603
Phone: 785-235-1307
Email: kent@kab.net
https://kab.net/kab-foundation/
Purpose: To support future broadcasters.
Eligibility: Applicants must be Kansas residents and be attending a Kansas college or university the fall semester after application. Those attending four-year institutions must be entering the junior or senior year, and those attending two-year institutions must be entering their sophomore year. Students must enroll in a broadcast or related curriculum for at least 12 hours. A GPA of 2.5 or greater is required.
Target applicant(s): College students. Adult students.
Minimum GPA: 2.5
Amount: Up to $20,000.
Number of awards: Varies.
Deadline: May 1.
How to apply: Applications are available online. An application form, essay and up to three letters of recommendation are required.
Exclusive: Visit www.UltimateScholarshipBook.com and enter code KA150726 for updates on this award.

[1508] • Kansas Agricultural Aviation Association Scholarship
Kansas Agricultural Aviation Association
P.O. Box 585, Colwich, KS 67030
Phone: 316-796-1180
Email: grossflying@hotmail.com
http://www.ksagaviation.org
Purpose: To aid Kansas students who are pursuing higher education in Kansas.
Eligibility: Applicants must be Kansas residents and high school graduates who are planning to enroll at a Kansas postsecondary institution. They must be recommended for the award by a member of the Kansas Agricultural Aviation Association (KAAA) and must demonstrate financial need. Preference will be given to students who are majoring in or planning to major in agriculture, agricultural business, aviation or engineering. Selection is based on academic merit and financial need.
Target applicant(s): High school students.
Amount: $2,500.
Number of awards: 1.
Deadline: January 31.

The Ultimate Scholarship Book 2026
Scholarship Directory (State of Residence)

How to apply: Applications are available online. An application form, transcript, financial need statement and two recommendation letters are required.
Exclusive: Visit www.UltimateScholarshipBook.com and enter code KA150826 for updates on this award.

[1509] • Kansas Career Technical Workforce Grant
Kansas Board of Regents
Curtis State Office Building, Suite 520, 1000 SW Jackson Street,
Topeka, KS 66612
Phone: 785-430-4255
Email: dlindeman@ksbor.org
http://www.kansasregents.org/students/student_financial_aid
Purpose: To assist Kansas students attending vocational colleges.
Eligibility: Applicants must be enrolled in approved vocational programs and take the vocational exam. Selection is based on exam scores. Students must register for the vocational exam by the scholarship deadline.
Target applicant(s): High school students. College students. Adult students.
Amount: Up to $1,000.
Number of awards: Varies.
Scholarship may be renewable.
Deadline: May 1.
How to apply: Applications are available online.
Exclusive: Visit www.UltimateScholarshipBook.com and enter code KA150926 for updates on this award.

[1510] • Kansas Comprehensive Grants
Kansas Board of Regents
Curtis State Office Building, Suite 520, 1000 SW Jackson Street,
Topeka, KS 66612
Phone: 785-430-4255
Email: dlindeman@ksbor.org
http://www.kansasregents.org/students/student_financial_aid
Purpose: To help needy Kansas students attend Kansas colleges and universities.
Eligibility: Applicants must be enrolled full-time at an eligible Kansas institution. Selection is based on financial need.
Target applicant(s): College students. Adult students.
Amount: Up to $10,000.
Number of awards: Varies.
Deadline: April 1.
How to apply: Complete the Free Application for Federal Student Aid (FAFSA).
Exclusive: Visit www.UltimateScholarshipBook.com and enter code KA151026 for updates on this award.

[1511] • Kansas Ethnic Minority Scholarship
Kansas Board of Regents
Curtis State Office Building, Suite 520, 1000 SW Jackson Street,
Topeka, KS 66612
Phone: 785-430-4255
Email: dlindeman@ksbor.org
http://www.kansasregents.org/students/student_financial_aid
Purpose: To aid outstanding Kansas minority students with financial need.
Eligibility: Applicants must be African American, Native Indian or Alaskan Native, Asian or Pacific Islander or Hispanic. Priority is given to graduating high school seniors. Applicants must have one of the following: a minimum ACT score of 21 or SAT score of 990, a minimum 3.0 GPA, a top 33 percent ranking in their high school class, completion of Kansas Scholars Curriculum, selection by National Merit Corporation or selection by College Board as a Hispanic Scholar.
Target applicant(s): High school students.
Minimum GPA: 3.0
Amount: Up to $1,850.
Number of awards: Varies.
Scholarship may be renewable.
Deadline: May 1.
How to apply: Applications are available online.
Exclusive: Visit www.UltimateScholarshipBook.com and enter code KA151126 for updates on this award.

[1512] • Kansas Nursing Service Scholarship
Kansas Board of Regents
Curtis State Office Building, Suite 520, 1000 SW Jackson Street,
Topeka, KS 66612
Phone: 785-430-4255
Email: dlindeman@ksbor.org
http://www.kansasregents.org/students/student_financial_aid
Purpose: To encourage Kansas students to enroll in LPN or RN nursing programs.
Eligibility: Applicants must be accepted to a Kansas nursing program and enrolled in a LPN or RN program. Students must sign an agreement with the State of Kansas to practice nursing at a specific facility one year for each year of scholarship support. Applicants must complete and submit the FAFSA.
Target applicant(s): College students. Adult students.
Amount: Up to $4,500.
Number of awards: Varies.
Deadline: May 1.
How to apply: Applications are available online.
Exclusive: Visit www.UltimateScholarshipBook.com and enter code KA151226 for updates on this award.

[1513] • Kansas Oratorical Contest
American Legion, Department of Kansas
1314 SW Topeka Boulevard, Topeka, KS 66612
Phone: 785-232-9315
https://kansaslegion.org/
Purpose: To enhance high school students' experience with and understanding of the U.S. Constitution. The contest will help develop students' leadership skills and civic appreciation, as well as the ability to deliver thoughtful, insightful orations regarding U.S. citizenship and its inherent responsibilities.
Eligibility: Applicants must be high school students under the age of 20 who are U.S. citizens or legal residents and residents of the state. Students first give an oration within their state and winners compete at the national level. The oration must be related to the Constitution of the United States focusing on the duties and obligations citizens have to the government. It must be in English and be between eight and ten minutes. There is also an assigned topic which is posted on the website, and it should be between three and five minutes.
Target applicant(s): High school students.
Amount: $150-$1,000.
Number of awards: Varies.
Deadline: March 16.
How to apply: Applications are available from schools and local American Legion Posts.
Exclusive: Visit www.UltimateScholarshipBook.com and enter code AM151326 for updates on this award.

[1514] • Kansas Osteopathic Medical Service Scholarship

Kansas Board of Regents
Curtis State Office Building, Suite 520, 1000 SW Jackson Street,
Topeka, KS 66612
Phone: 785-430-4255
Email: dlindeman@ksbor.org
http://www.kansasregents.org/students/student_financial_aid
Purpose: To encourage students to establish osteopathic practices in rural Kansas.
Eligibility: Applicants must be Kansas residents and enrolled at nationally accredited osteopathic schools. Students must establish practices in rural areas of Kansas. Preference goes to first-year students. Applicants must complete a program application and the designated financial aid application.
Target applicant(s): Graduate school students. Adult students.
Amount: $15,000.
Number of awards: Varies.
Deadline: May 15.
How to apply: Applications are available online.
Exclusive: Visit www.UltimateScholarshipBook.com and enter code KA151426 for updates on this award.

[1515] • Kansas State Scholarship

Kansas Board of Regents
Curtis State Office Building, Suite 520, 1000 SW Jackson Street,
Topeka, KS 66612
Phone: 785-430-4255
Email: dlindeman@ksbor.org
http://www.kansasregents.org/students/student_financial_aid
Purpose: To aid needy Kansas students designated as state scholars.
Eligibility: Applicants must have taken the ACT, completed the Regents Scholars Curriculum and be graduating seniors. Applicants are ranked by an index combining ACT score and GPA. The top students are chosen.
Target applicant(s): High school students. College students. Adult students.
Amount: $1,000.
Number of awards: 2,500.
Scholarship may be renewable.
Deadline: August 1.
How to apply: Complete the Free Application for Federal Student Aid (FAFSA).
Exclusive: Visit www.UltimateScholarshipBook.com and enter code KA151526 for updates on this award.

[1516] • Kansas Teacher Service Scholarship

Kansas Board of Regents
Curtis State Office Building, Suite 520, 1000 SW Jackson Street,
Topeka, KS 66612
Phone: 785-430-4255
Email: dlindeman@ksbor.org
http://www.kansasregents.org/students/student_financial_aid
Purpose: To support students pursuing bachelor's or master's degree programs who are planning to teach (K-12) in an underserved geographic area in Kansas.
Eligibility: Applicants must be residents of Kansas and be attending a Kansas higher education institution. Students must be enrolled in a program leading to licensure as a teacher in an identified hard-to-fill discipline or underserved geographic area in Kansas. Applicants may also be currently licensed teachers enrolled in a program leading to a new endorsement or enrolled in a program leading to a master's degree in an identified hard-to-fill discipline or underserved geographic area. The FAFSA and the State of Kansas Student Aid application must be completed.
Target applicant(s): College students. Graduate school students. Adult students.
Amount: Up to $5,830.
Number of awards: Varies.
Deadline: June 1.
How to apply: Applications are available online.
Exclusive: Visit www.UltimateScholarshipBook.com and enter code KA151626 for updates on this award.

[1517] • Karen Ann Shopis-Fox Memorial Scholarship

American Society of Landscape Architects
CTASLA Scholarship Committee, P.O. Box 209197, New Haven, CT 06520
Phone: 800-878-1474
Email: scholarships@ctasla.org
http://www.ctasla.org
Purpose: To support students who are studying landscape architecture or environmental education.
Eligibility: Applicants must be Connecticut residents and be enrolled in an accredited post-secondary landscape architecture or environmental education program. Both undergraduate and graduate students may apply.
Target applicant(s): College students. Graduate school students. Adult students.
Amount: $2,500.
Number of awards: Varies.
Deadline: April 26.
How to apply: Applications are available online. An application form, transcript, personal statement and letter of recommendation are required.
Exclusive: Visit www.UltimateScholarshipBook.com and enter code AM151726 for updates on this award.

[1518] • Kathryn D. Sullivan Earth and Marine Science Fellowship

South Carolina Space Grant Consortium
Department of Geology and Environmental Sciences, College of Charleston, 66 George Street, Charleston, SC 29424
Phone: 843-953-5463
Email: scozzarot@cofc.edu
https://scspacegrant.cofc.edu/scholarshipsandfellowships
Purpose: To aid graduate students who are studying the natural sciences, technology or engineering.
Eligibility: Applicants must be U.S. citizens and be either full-time graduate students enrolled in an accredited consortium member institution or successful applicants for full-time admission to a Master's or Doctorate program in an accredited consortium member institution. Selection is based on recommendation letters, academic merit, faculty sponsorship and stated academic goals and interests in science, technology and engineering.
Target applicant(s): Graduate school students. Adult students.
Amount: $16,000.
Number of awards: 1.
Deadline: January 29.
How to apply: Applications are available online. An application form, personal essay, two recommendation letters, a transcript and a resume are required.

The Ultimate Scholarship Book 2026
Scholarship Directory (State of Residence)

Exclusive: Visit www.UltimateScholarshipBook.com and enter code SO151826 for updates on this award.

[1519] • KEM Electric Cooperative Scholarships for Students Attending High School Outside the Service Area
KEM Electric
107 S. Broadway, P.O. Box 790, Linton, ND 58552
Email: info@kemelectric.com
https://www.kemelectric.com/scholarships
Purpose: To assist students in the North Dakota area.
Eligibility: Applicants must be graduating seniors from a homeschool setting, GED setting, or a school outside of the Kem Electric service area.
Target applicant(s): High school students. College students. Adult students.
Amount: $500.
Number of awards: 1.
Deadline: February 9.
How to apply: Applications are available online.
Exclusive: Visit www.UltimateScholarshipBook.com and enter code KE151926 for updates on this award.

[1520] • Kentucky Tuition Grant
Kentucky Higher Education Assistance Authority (KHEAA)
P.O. Box 798, Frankfort, KY 40602
Phone: 800-928-8926
Email: blane@kheaa.com
http://www.kheaa.com
Purpose: To provide grants to Kentucky residents to attend the Commonwealth's independent colleges.
Eligibility: Applicants must be full-time students enrolled at eligible private institutions. Students must not be enrolled in divinity, theology or religious education degree programs. This is a need-based program.
Target applicant(s): High school students. College students. Adult students.
Amount: Up to $3,200.
Number of awards: Varies.
Deadline: As soon as possible after October 1.
How to apply: Complete the Free Application for Federal Student Aid (FAFSA).
Exclusive: Visit www.UltimateScholarshipBook.com and enter code KE152026 for updates on this award.

[1521] • Kentucky Veterans Tuition Waiver Program
Kentucky Department of Veterans Affairs
Attn.: Tuition Waiver Coordinator, 321 West Main Street, Suite 390, Louisville, KY 40202
Phone: 502-595-4447
Email: barbaraa.hale@ky.gov
https://veterans.ky.gov
Purpose: To assist the families of Kentucky veterans in obtaining higher education.
Eligibility: Applicants must be Kentucky residents and be children, stepchildren, adopted children, spouses or unremarried widows/widowers of Kentucky veterans and must be age 26 or younger. The veteran must have died in active duty or as a result of a service-connected disability, have a service-connected 100 percent disability, have served during wartime and be totally disabled or have died for any reason.

Target applicant(s): High school students. College students. Adult students.
Amount: Full tuition waiver.
Number of awards: Varies.
Scholarship may be renewable.
Deadline: Contact the sponsor to confirm the deadline.
How to apply: Applications are available online.
Exclusive: Visit www.UltimateScholarshipBook.com and enter code KE152126 for updates on this award.

[1522] • Kibbie Grant (Iowa Skilled Workforce Shortage Tuition Grant)
Iowa College Student Aid Commission
475 SW Fifth Street, Suite D, Des Moines, IA 50309
Phone: 515-725-3400
Email: info@iowacollegeaid.gov
https://www.iowacollegeaid.gov/ScholarshipsAndGrants
Purpose: To support Iowa students enrolled in community college.
Eligibility: Applicants must be Iowa residents enrolled in an Iowa community college. Students must be enrolled in at least three credit hours in a qualified program of study and demonstrate financial need.
Target applicant(s): High school students. College students. Adult students.
Amount: Up to $3,000.
Number of awards: Varies.
Deadline: July 1.
How to apply: Applications are available online.
Exclusive: Visit www.UltimateScholarshipBook.com and enter code IO152226 for updates on this award.

[1523] • Kittie M. Fairey Educational Fund Scholarships
Center for Scholarship Administration Inc.
Kittie M. Fairey Educational Fund Scholarship Program, 4320 Wade Hampton Boulevard, Suite G, Taylors, SC 29687-0031
Phone: 864-268-3363
Email: allison@csascholars.org
https://www.csascholars.org/index.php
Purpose: To help South Carolina high school seniors who want to attend colleges or universities in the state.
Eligibility: Applicants must be South Carolina high school seniors with a combined SAT score of 1800 or composite ACT score of 26 who plan to be full-time students at an accredited college or university in South Carolina. Selection is based on academic merit and financial need, and the applicant's parents' adjusted gross income must not exceed $40,000. A transcript, recommendation letter, essay and parents' tax documents are required.
Target applicant(s): High school students.
Minimum GPA: 3.0
Amount: Varies.
Number of awards: Varies.
Scholarship may be renewable.
Deadline: February 7.
How to apply: Applications are available online.
Exclusive: Visit www.UltimateScholarshipBook.com and enter code CE152326 for updates on this award.

[1524] • Kokosing Construction Co. Scholarship
Associated General Contractors of Ohio
1755 Northwest Boulevard, Columbus, OH 43212
Phone: 614-486-6446
Email: parker@agcohio.com
https://agcohio.com/workforce-development/agc-scholarships/
Purpose: To support undergraduate students who are residents of Ohio and interested in pursuing careers in construction-related fields.
Eligibility: Applicants must be U.S. citizens and undergraduate students in at least the second year of a two-year, four-year or five-year degree seeking program. The minimum GPA requirement is 2.5. Selection is based on the overall strength of the application.
Target applicant(s): College students. Adult students.
Minimum GPA: 2.5
Amount: $1,000.
Number of awards: 1.
Deadline: February 9.
How to apply: Applications are available online. An application form, official college transcripts and essay are required and must be mailed.
Exclusive: Visit www.UltimateScholarshipBook.com and enter code AS152426 for updates on this award.

[1525] • Lambeth Family Scholarship
Seattle Foundation
1200 Fifth Avenue, Suite 1300, Seattle, WA 98101-3151
Phone: 206-515-2119
Email: scholarships@seattlefoundation.org
http://www.seattlefoundation.org
Purpose: To aid students who are pursuing higher education in computer science, the natural sciences, business, mathematics or engineering.
Eligibility: Applicants must be enrolled in a degree-granting program in business, computer science, engineering, mathematics or the natural sciences. Selection is based on the overall strength of the application.
Target applicant(s): High school students. College students. Adult students.
Amount: $3,000.
Number of awards: 8.
Deadline: January 16.
How to apply: Applications are available online. An application form and supporting documents are required.
Exclusive: Visit www.UltimateScholarshipBook.com and enter code SE152526 for updates on this award.

[1526] • Laura N. Dowsett Fund
Hawaii Community Foundation - Scholarships
827 Fort Street Mall, Honolulu, HI 96813
Phone: 888-731-3863
Email: scholarships@hcf-hawaii.org
https://www.hawaiicommunityfoundation.org/
Purpose: To support Hawaii students who are majoring in occupational therapy.
Eligibility: Applicants must be college juniors, college seniors or graduate students. Minimum 2.7 GPA required.
Target applicant(s): College students. Graduate school students. Adult students.
Minimum GPA: 2.7
Amount: Varies.
Number of awards: Varies.
Deadline: February 28.
How to apply: To apply, register online, complete the online application and select the scholarships to which you wish to apply. In addition, mail the supporting materials: printed confirmation page from the online application, personal statement, copy of Student Aid Report (SAR) available at www.fafsa.ed.gov and official transcript.
Exclusive: Visit www.UltimateScholarshipBook.com and enter code HA152626 for updates on this award.

[1527] • Laurene Ann Opdyke Nursing Scholarship
Oklahoma City Community Foundation
1000 North Broadway, Oklahoma City, OK 73102
Phone: 405-235-5603
Email: scholarships@occf.org
https://occf.org/scholarships/
Purpose: To support students pursuing bachelor of nursing programs.
Eligibility: Applicants must be admitted into a bachelor of nursing program and apply during their sophomore or junior year of school. Students may also be pursuing a diploma nursing program leading toward licensure as a professional registered nurse. Applicants must have a minimum 3.0 GPA. Preference will be given to applicants with financial need.
Target applicant(s): College students. Adult students.
Minimum GPA: 3.0
Amount: $2,500.
Number of awards: 1.
Scholarship may be renewable.
Deadline: February 15.
How to apply: Applications are available online.
Exclusive: Visit www.UltimateScholarshipBook.com and enter code OK152726 for updates on this award.

[1528] • Lawrence C. Yeardley Scholarship
Greater Kanawha Valley Foundation
1600 Huntington Square, 900 Lee Street, East, Charleston, WV 25301
Phone: 304-346-3620
Email: shoover@tgkvf.org
https://tgkvf.org/scholarship-information/
Purpose: To provide financial assistance to West Virginia residents who are interested in pursuing a college education.
Eligibility: Applicants must be residents of West Virginia, be full-time students (12 credit hours) and possess good moral character and proven academic achievement.
Target applicant(s): High school students. College students. Adult students.
Amount: $2,500.
Number of awards: Varies.
Scholarship may be renewable.
Deadline: February 1.
How to apply: Applications are available online.
Exclusive: Visit www.UltimateScholarshipBook.com and enter code GR152826 for updates on this award.

[1529] • Leaders Advancing and Helping Communities Scholarship
Leaders Advancing and Helping Communities
5275 Kenilworth Street, Dearborn, MI 48126-3197
Phone: 888-315-5242
Email: assistant@lahc.org
https://lahc.org/scholarship-program/

The Ultimate Scholarship Book 2026
Scholarship Directory (State of Residence)

Purpose: To encourage all high school seniors to get a higher education.
Eligibility: Applicants must be U.S. citizens, Michigan residents, be high school seniors and have a GPA of 3.5 or higher. Students do not need to be Lebanese Americans to apply. Applicants must demonstrate financial need.
Target applicant(s): High school students.
Minimum GPA: 3.5
Amount: Varies.
Number of awards: Varies.
Deadline: March 31.
How to apply: Applications are available online.
Exclusive: Visit www.UltimateScholarshipBook.com and enter code LE152926 for updates on this award.

[1530] • Leadership for Diversity Scholarship
California School Library Association
6444 E. Spring Street #247, Long Beach, CA 90815-1553
Phone: 888-655-8480
Email: info@csla.net
http://csla.net/awards/
Purpose: To encourage diversity in the library media teacher profession.
Eligibility: Applicants must be members of a traditionally underrepresented group attending or planning to attend an accredited library media teacher credential program and plan to work in California for three years after completing the program. Applicants must provide a 250-word statement about their qualifications, career goals, financial situation and commitment to supporting multicultural students and two letters of reference.
Target applicant(s): High school students. College students. Graduate school students. Adult students.
Amount: $1,500.
Number of awards: 1.
Deadline: November 7.
How to apply: Applications are available online.
Exclusive: Visit www.UltimateScholarshipBook.com and enter code CA153026 for updates on this award.

[1531] • LEAF Scholarships
California Landscape Contractors Association
1491 River Park Drive, Suite 100, Sacramento, CA 95815
Phone: 916-830-2780
Email: leaf@clca.org
https://www.clca.org
Purpose: To support ornamental horticulture students.
Eligibility: Applicants must attend an accredited California community college or state university and take a minimum of six credits.
Target applicant(s): College students. Adult students.
Amount: Varies.
Number of awards: Varies.
Deadline: April 15.
How to apply: Applications are available online. An application form, transcript and three letters of reference are required.
Exclusive: Visit www.UltimateScholarshipBook.com and enter code CA153126 for updates on this award.

[1532] • Legislative for Future Excellence (LIFE) Scholarship Program
South Carolina Commission on Higher Education
1122 Lady Street, Suite 400, Columbia, SC 29201
Phone: 803-737-2260
https://www.che.sc.gov
Purpose: Monetary assistance is provided to South Carolina resident students pursuing higher education.
Eligibility: Applicants must graduate from a high school in South Carolina or outside of South Carolina if a parent is a legal resident of South Carolina, attend an eligible South Carolina public or private college full-time and be a resident of South Carolina. Entering freshmen must meet two of the following: have a minimum 3.0 GPA, a minimum SAT score of 1100 or ACT score of 24 or graduate in the top 30 percent of their class.
Target applicant(s): High school students. College students. Adult students.
Minimum GPA: 3.0
Amount: Up to full tuition.
Number of awards: Varies.
Scholarship may be renewable.
Deadline: As soon as possible after October 1.
How to apply: Your college will determine your eligibility based on your high school transcript. There is no application form.
Exclusive: Visit www.UltimateScholarshipBook.com and enter code SO153226 for updates on this award.

[1533] • Legislative Lottery Scholarships
New Mexico Higher Education Department
2044 Galisteo Street, Suite 4, Santa Fe, NM 87505-2100
Phone: 505-476-8400
Email: cesaria.tapia1@state.nm.us
https://hed.state.nm.us/financial-aid
Purpose: To support graduating New Mexico high school seniors with financial need.
Eligibility: Applicants must be graduating high school seniors in New Mexico, enroll full-time at an eligible New Mexico public college or university and maintain a minimum 2.5 GPA during the first college semester.
Target applicant(s): High school students.
Amount: Partial Tuition.
Number of awards: Varies.
Scholarship may be renewable.
Deadline: Contact the college's financial aid office to confirm the deadline.
How to apply: Contact your financial aid office.
Exclusive: Visit www.UltimateScholarshipBook.com and enter code NE153326 for updates on this award.

[1534] • Lemieux-Lovejoy Youth Scholarship
Futurama Foundation
c/o Marilyn Ladd, Office Manager, 103 County Road, Oakland, ME 04963
Email: mvladd@colby.edu
http://bpwmefoundation.org/scholarship-program/
Purpose: To honor the memory of Rachel E. Lemieux and to provide financial assistance to Maine high school seniors and recent graduates.
Eligibility: Applicants must be female Maine residents who are high school seniors or who have recently graduated from high school.
Target applicant(s): High school students.
Amount: $2,500.
Number of awards: 1.
Deadline: April 13.
How to apply: Applications are available from your local BPW chapter.
Exclusive: Visit www.UltimateScholarshipBook.com and enter code FU153426 for updates on this award.

[1535] • Leo Bourassa Scholarship

Virginia Lakes and Watersheds Association
VLWA Scholarship Committee, CH2M HILL, 5701 Cleveland Street, Suite 200, Virginia Beach, VA 23462
Phone: 757-671-6222
Email: scholarship@vlwa.org
http://www.vlwa.org
Purpose: To acknowledge students for their accomplishments in the field of water resources.
Eligibility: Applicants must be Virginia residents and students in good standing at an accredited college or university in the state. They must complete at least two semesters of undergraduate study by the award date. They must also be full-time undergraduate or full- or part-time graduate students enrolled in curriculum related to water resources.
Target applicant(s): College students. Graduate school students. Adult students.
Amount: $500-$3,000.
Number of awards: Varies.
Deadline: April 1.
How to apply: Applications are available online.
Exclusive: Visit www.UltimateScholarshipBook.com and enter code VI153526 for updates on this award.

[1536] • Leo H. Grether Memorial Scholarship

Iowa High School Music Association
P.O. Box 10, Boone, IA 50036
http://www.ihsma.org
Purpose: To support Iowa students pursuing vocal music education.
Eligibility: Applicants must be Iowa residents and graduating high school seniors enrolling in college to pursue a vocal music education major. Students must submit a recording of two selections and essay along with their application materials.
Target applicant(s): High school students.
Amount: $2,500.
Number of awards: 1.
Deadline: April 15.
How to apply: Applications are available online.
Exclusive: Visit www.UltimateScholarshipBook.com and enter code IO153626 for updates on this award.

[1537] • Liam Hood Scholarship Fund

Alaska Community Foundation
3201 C Street, Suite 110, Anchorage, AK 99503
Phone: 907-334-6700
Email: scholarships@alaskacf.org
https://alaskacf.org/scholarships/
Purpose: To assist Alaskan students.
Eligibility: Applicants must be Alaska residents who are graduating high school seniors and have a minimum GPA of 3.0.
Target applicant(s): High school students. College students. Adult students.
Minimum GPA: 3.0
Amount: $5,000.
Number of awards: 1.
Deadline: March 15.
How to apply: Applications are available online.
Exclusive: Visit www.UltimateScholarshipBook.com and enter code AL153726 for updates on this award.

[1538] • Licensed Vocational Nurse to Associate Degree Nursing Scholarship

Health Professions Education Foundation
400 R Street, Suite 460, Sacramento, CA 95811
Phone: 916-326-3640
Email: stran@oshpd.ca.gov
https://hcai.ca.gov/loans-scholarships-grants/
Purpose: To aid licensed vocational nurses in California who are pursuing an associate's degree in nursing.
Eligibility: Applicants must be licensed vocational nurses (LVNs) who are enrolled in or have been accepted into an accredited associate's degree in nursing (ADN) program in the state of California. They must be attending or planning to attend school at least part-time (six or more credits per semester) and must commit to two years of nursing practice in an underserved area of California after graduation. Selection is based on the overall strength of the application.
Target applicant(s): College students. Adult students.
Amount: Up to $8,000.
Number of awards: Varies.
Deadline: October 31.
How to apply: Applications are available online. An application form, official transcript, personal statement, financial information, two recommendation letters and proof of vocational nurse licensure are required.
Exclusive: Visit www.UltimateScholarshipBook.com and enter code HE153826 for updates on this award.

[1539] • Lila M. Van Sweringen Student Scholarship

Educational Office Professionals of Ohio
Mrs. Carla Huntsinger, Scholarship Chairperson, 100 Scarlet Oaks Drive, Cincinnati, OH 45241
https://eopo-oh.org/scholarships/
Purpose: To support high school seniors and college students from Ohio who are pursuing a higher education in an office-related career.
Eligibility: Applicants must be residents of Ohio who are either current college students or high school seniors who will be attending a post-secondary institution in the fall of the next school year. Students must be pursuing an office-related career.
Target applicant(s): High school students. College students. Adult students.
Amount: $1,000.
Number of awards: Varies.
Deadline: January 10.
How to apply: Applications are available online.
Exclusive: Visit www.UltimateScholarshipBook.com and enter code ED153926 for updates on this award.

[1540] • Lilly Endowment Community Scholarship Program

Independent Colleges of Indiana
30 South Meridian Street, Suite 800, Indianapolis, IN 46204
Phone: 317-236-6090
Email: smartchoice@icindiana.org
http://www.icindiana.org
Purpose: To raise the level of education in Indiana.
Eligibility: Applicants must be Indiana high school seniors who have been accepted into a full-time bachelor's degree program at an accredited public or private institution of higher learning in Indiana.
Target applicant(s): High school students.
Amount: Full tuition plus fees and $900 book stipend.

The Ultimate Scholarship Book 2026
Scholarship Directory (State of Residence)

Number of awards: 142.
Scholarship may be renewable.
Deadline: Contact the sponsor to confirm the deadline.
How to apply: Applications are available online and from local Indiana Community Foundations.
Exclusive: Visit www.UltimateScholarshipBook.com and enter code IN154026 for updates on this award.

[1541] • Lily and Catello Sorrentino Memorial Scholarship

Rhode Island Foundation
One Union Station, Providence, RI 02903
Phone: 401-274-4564
Email: rbogert@rifoundation.org
https://rifoundation.org/grants-scholarships
Purpose: To assist adult students who are continuing their undergraduate studies at colleges or universities in Rhode Island.
Eligibility: Applicants must be residents of Rhode Island, be over 25 years of age and attend a non-parochial college or university in the state.
Target applicant(s): College students. Adult students.
Amount: $1,000-$1,500.
Number of awards: 1.
Scholarship may be renewable.
Deadline: April 15.
How to apply: Applications are available online.
Exclusive: Visit www.UltimateScholarshipBook.com and enter code RH154126 for updates on this award.

[1542] • Linda Craig Memorial Scholarship Presented by St. Vincent Sports Performance

Pacers Foundation
Linda Craig Memorial Scholarship Committee, 125 S. Pennsylvania Street, Indianapolis, IN 46204
Phone: 317-917-2500
Email: bill.benner@pacers.com
http://www.pacersfoundation.org/
Purpose: To support Indiana students interested in sports medicine, physical therapy and related fields.
Eligibility: Applicants must be U.S. citizens who have completed at least one full year of an undergraduate program majoring in medicine, sports medicine, physical therapy or a related area. They must have a GPA of at least 3.0 and demonstrate outstanding character, integrity and leadership. Applicants may not have received a full scholarship from any other organization.
Target applicant(s): College students. Adult students.
Minimum GPA: 3.0
Amount: $2,500.
Number of awards: 3.
Deadline: April 26.
How to apply: Applications are available online.
Exclusive: Visit www.UltimateScholarshipBook.com and enter code PA154226 for updates on this award.

[1543] • Linly Heflin Scholarship

Linly Heflin Unit
13 Office Park Circle, Suite 8, Mountain Brook, AL 35223
Phone: 205-871-8171
Email: linlyheflinscholarship@gmail.com
https://www.linlyheflin.org/
Purpose: To support Alabama female students with their pursuits of undergraduate studies.
Eligibility: Applicants must be female Alabama residents and U.S. citizens who have significant economic need and sound academic records. Students must attend or plan to attend a four-year Alabama college or university for undergraduate studies that is accredited by the Southern Association of Colleges and Schools.
Target applicant(s): High school students. College students. Adult students.
Amount: $10,000.
Number of awards: Varies.
Deadline: January 10.
How to apply: Applications are available online.
Exclusive: Visit www.UltimateScholarshipBook.com and enter code LI154326 for updates on this award.

[1544] • Lloyd F. Hutt Scholarship

Lake Michigan Credit Union
Phone: 616-242-9790
https://www.lmcu.org/about/community-relations/hutt-scholarship/
Purpose: To support Michigan or Florida students or members or children of members of the credit union.
Eligibility: Applicants must be residents of Michigan or Florida or members of Lake Michigan Credit Union or the children of members. Students must be high school seniors who plan to enter a trade school, college or university.
Target applicant(s): High school students.
Amount: $2,000.
Number of awards: 20.
Deadline: January 5.
How to apply: Applications are available online.
Exclusive: Visit www.UltimateScholarshipBook.com and enter code LA154426 for updates on this award.

[1545] • Loan Assistance Repayment Program Primary Care Services

Maryland Higher Education Commission
Office of Student Financial Assistance, 6 North Liberty Street, Baltimore, MD 21201
Phone: 800-974-1024
Email: osfamail@mhec.state.md.us
https://mhec.maryland.gov
Purpose: To support primary care physicians and medical residents.
Eligibility: Medical resident applicants must be graduates of a Maryland college, and they must have at least one year remaining in a primary care residency program. Physician applicants must have a valid primary care license and currently work in an underserved area of Maryland. All applicants must have outstanding loans on which they have not defaulted. Specialization in one of the following fields is required: general internal medicine, family practice medicine, general pediatrics, obstetrics/gynecology or gynecology. Applicants must agree to work in an underserved area of Maryland for two to four years after winning the scholarship and completing their residency.
Target applicant(s): Graduate school students. Adult students.
Amount: Up to $50,000.
Number of awards: Varies.
Scholarship may be renewable.
Deadline: April 15.
How to apply: Applications are available from the Department of Health and Mental Hygiene.

[1546] • Lois Livingston McMillen Memorial Fund
Connecticut Community Foundation Center for Philanthropy
43 Field Street, Waterbury, CT 06702
Phone: 203-753-1315
Email: scholarships@conncf.org
http://www.conncf.org
Purpose: To provide financial assistance to women who are studying or plan to study art, especially painting or design.
Eligibility: Applicants must be women who plan to study art at an accredited college or university, or in an artist-in-residence program. They must also live in the Connecticut Community Foundation's service area.
Target applicant(s): High school students. College students. Adult students.
Amount: Varies.
Number of awards: Varies.
Scholarship may be renewable.
Deadline: March 15.
How to apply: Applications are available online.
Exclusive: Visit www.UltimateScholarshipBook.com and enter code CO154626 for updates on this award.

[1547] • Lori Rhett Memorial Scholarship
National Association for Campus Activities
13 Harbison Way, Columbia, SC 29212
Phone: 803-732-6222
Email: info@naca.org
https://www.naca.org/resources/scholarships-grants/scholarships.html
Purpose: The scholarship recognizes the achievements of student leaders who are undergraduate or graduate students.
Eligibility: Applicants must be U.S. citizens and have a minimum GPA of 2.5. Students must hold a significant campus leadership position and demonstrate significant leadership skills and abilities. Applicants must also be making significant contributions through on- or off-campus volunteering and must attend school in Alaska, Idaho, Montana, Oregon or Washington.
Target applicant(s): College students. Graduate school students. Adult students.
Minimum GPA: 2.5
Amount: $500.
Number of awards: 1.
Deadline: November 30.
How to apply: Applications are available online.
Exclusive: Visit www.UltimateScholarshipBook.com and enter code NA154726 for updates on this award.

[1548] • Los Alamos Employees' Scholarship
Los Alamos National Laboratory Foundation
1112 Plaza del Norte, Espanola, NM 87532
Phone: 505-753-8890
Email: tony@lanlfoundation.org
http://www.lanlfoundation.org
Purpose: To provide financial assistance for students in northern New Mexico who plan to pursue undergraduate degrees in fields of study that will benefit the community.
Eligibility: Selection is based on academic performance, including the pursuit in high school of a rigorous course of study, GPA and standardized test scores, varied extracurricular and community service activities, strong critical thinking skills and career goals that are relevant to the needs of the northern New Mexico community. Some consideration is also given to financial need, ethnic diversity and equally representing all the regions of northern New Mexico. Applicants must have a minimum 3.25 GPA and either minimum score of 19 on the ACT or 930 on the SAT (Math and Critical Reading).
Target applicant(s): College students. Adult students.
Minimum GPA: 3.25
Amount: Varies.
Number of awards: Varies.
Scholarship may be renewable.
Deadline: January 16.
How to apply: Applications are available online.
Exclusive: Visit www.UltimateScholarshipBook.com and enter code LO154826 for updates on this award.

[1549] • Lottery Tuition Assistance Program
South Carolina Commission on Higher Education
1122 Lady Street, Suite 400, Columbia, SC 29201
Phone: 803-737-2260
https://ed.sc.gov/newsroom/scholarships/
Purpose: To assist South Carolina residents attending a two-year public or independent institution of higher learning.
Eligibility: Applicants must complete the Free Application for Federal Student Aid (FAFSA), be residents of South Carolina and be enrolled as a degree-seeking student in a minimum of six credit hours at an eligible two-year technical institution, a USC two-year regional campus or Spartanburg Methodist College.
Target applicant(s): High school students. College students. Adult students.
Amount: Up to $1,200 per term.
Number of awards: Varies.
Deadline: As soon as possible after October 1.
How to apply: Applications are available by telephone request.
Exclusive: Visit www.UltimateScholarshipBook.com and enter code SO154926 for updates on this award.

[1550] • Louis B. Russell Scholarship
Indiana State Teachers Association
150 W. Market Street, Suite 900, Indianapolis, IN 46204
Phone: 844-275-4782
Email: ccherry@ista-in.org
https://www.ista-in.org/our-profession/scholarships-awards
Purpose: To provide financial assistance to ethnic minorities who are seeking vocational or technical education.
Eligibility: Applicants must be ethnic minority high school seniors who plan to pursue education in the area of industrial arts, vocational education or technical education at an accredited college or university.
Target applicant(s): High school students.
Amount: $1,000.
Number of awards: 1.
Scholarship may be renewable.
Deadline: March 1.
How to apply: Applications are available online.
Exclusive: Visit www.UltimateScholarshipBook.com and enter code IN155026 for updates on this award.

[1551] • Louisiana Go Grant

Louisiana Office of Student Financial Assistance
605 N. Fifth Street, Baton Rouge, LA 70802
Phone: 800-259-5626 x1012
Email: custserv@la.gov
https://mylosfa.la.gov/students-parents/scholarships-grants/tops/
Purpose: To help students from moderate and low income families afford a college education.
Eligibility: Applicants must be Louisiana residents who have been admitted and enrolled in an undergraduate program at a Louisiana public or private college or university. They must be first-time freshmen or adult students who have not been enrolled in credit-bearing courses for at least one academic year. Financial need is required.
Target applicant(s): High school students. College students. Adult students.
Amount: Up to $3,000.
Number of awards: Varies.
Deadline: As soon as possible after October 1.
How to apply: All eligible students who have filed a Free Application for Federal Student Aid are considered for this grant.
Exclusive: Visit www.UltimateScholarshipBook.com and enter code LO155126 for updates on this award.

[1552] • Louisiana Memorial Scholarship

American Radio Relay League Foundation
225 Main Street, Newington, CT 06111-1494
Phone: 860-594-0200
Email: foundation@arrl.org
https://www.arrl.org/scholarship-program
Purpose: To provide financial assistance to Louisiana students who are amateur radio operators.
Eligibility: Applicants must hold a Technician Class or higher Amateur Radio License and either be Louisiana residents or attend school in Louisiana. They must have a GPA of 3.0 or higher. Only students who are accepted to or enrolled in a four-year college or university are eligible.
Target applicant(s): High school students. College students. Adult students.
Minimum GPA: 3.0
Amount: $750.
Number of awards: 1.
Deadline: January 10.
How to apply: Applications are available online.
Exclusive: Visit www.UltimateScholarshipBook.com and enter code AM155226 for updates on this award.

[1553] • Luso-American Education Foundation General Youth Scholarship

Luso-American Education Foundation
P.O. Box 2967, Dublin, CA 94568
Phone: 925-828-3883
Email: odom@luso-american.org
https://luso-american.org/education/
Purpose: To provide educational opportunities for Portuguese students.
Eligibility: Applicants must be residents of California and high school students who are of Portuguese descent with a GPA of 3.5 or higher, or who are taking classes in the Portuguese language with a GPA of 3.0 or higher. They must be enrolled in a college, university, trade or business school and have taken the SAT or ACT. Two letters of recommendation are required.
Target applicant(s): High school students.
Minimum GPA: 3.0
Amount: $1,000-$4,000.
Number of awards: Varies.
Deadline: March 1.
How to apply: Applications are available by phone, fax, mail or email.
Exclusive: Visit www.UltimateScholarshipBook.com and enter code LU155326 for updates on this award.

[1554] • Mabel Mayforth Scholarship

Federated Garden Clubs of Vermont Inc.
c/o Marybeth Tevis, Scholarship Chair, 973 Stock Farm Road, Randolph, VT 05060
Phone: 802-728-6083
Email: marybeth@eravt.com
http://www.vermontfgcv.com
Purpose: To support students who are studying in fields related to plants.
Eligibility: Applicants must be Vermont residents who are college juniors, seniors or graduate students and must major horticulture, landscape, design, conservation, forestry, agronomy, plant pathology or biology with a special interest in plants, ecology and allied subjects. They must be full-time students at an accredited institution with a GPA of 3.0 or higher. Previous winners may reapply.
Target applicant(s): College students. Graduate school students. Adult students.
Minimum GPA: 3.0
Amount: $1,000.
Number of awards: Varies.
Deadline: February 1.
How to apply: Applications are available online. An application form, list of extracurricular activities, letter of application, transcript and three letters of recommendation are required.
Exclusive: Visit www.UltimateScholarshipBook.com and enter code FE155426 for updates on this award.

[1555] • Mackinac Scholarship

American Society of Civil Engineers-Michigan Section
ASCE Michigan Section Scholarships, 215 N. Walnut Street, Lansing, MI 48933
Phone: 517-332-2066
Email: cschmitz@acecmi.org
https://branches.asce.org/michigan-se/other-asce-scholarships
Purpose: To aid Michigan civil engineering students.
Eligibility: Applicants must be U.S. citizens and Michigan residents. They must be rising undergraduate juniors or seniors who are enrolled full-time in an ABET-accredited civil engineering degree program. They must have a GPA of 2.5 or higher on a four-point scale. Selection is based on academic achievement, personal qualities and financial need.
Target applicant(s): College students. Adult students.
Minimum GPA: 2.5
Amount: $10,000.
Number of awards: 1.
Deadline: May (Memorial Day).
How to apply: Applications are available online. An application form and an official transcript are required.
Exclusive: Visit www.UltimateScholarshipBook.com and enter code AM155526 for updates on this award.

[1556] • Maine Community Foundation Scholarship Program
Maine Community Foundation
245 Main Street, Ellsworth, ME 04605
Phone: 207-667-9735
Email: jwarren@mainecf.org
https://www.mainecf.org
Purpose: To provide financial assistance to Maine students.
Eligibility: There are a number of scholarships in this program for Maine traditional and adult students to attend private high schools, undergraduate colleges or graduate schools. Many are limited to residents of a specific county or graduates of a certain high school.
Target applicant(s): High school students. College students. Graduate school students. Adult students.
Amount: Varies.
Number of awards: Varies.
Deadline: Contact the sponsor to confirm the deadline.
How to apply: Applications are available online.
Exclusive: Visit www.UltimateScholarshipBook.com and enter code MA155626 for updates on this award.

[1557] • Maine Demolay and Pine Tree Youth Foundation Scholarships
Maine Demolay and Pine Tree Youth Foundation
Benjamin Weisner, 83 High Street Apartment 4, Auburn, ME 04210
Phone: 207-773-5184
Email: grandlodge@mainemason.org
https://pinetreeyouth.org/scholarships/
Purpose: To support Maine high school seniors.
Eligibility: Applicants must be graduating high school seniors and undergraduate students from Maine. Students must submit a short essay and demonstrate educational and civic achievement.
Target applicant(s): High school students. College students. Adult students.
Amount: Varies.
Number of awards: Varies.
Deadline: March 30.
How to apply: Applications are available online.
Exclusive: Visit www.UltimateScholarshipBook.com and enter code MA155726 for updates on this award.

[1558] • Maine Health Professionals Loan Program
Finance Authority of Maine
5 Community Drive, Augusta, ME 04330
Phone: 207-623-3263
Email: Education@FAMEmaine.com
https://www.famemaine.com/
Purpose: To support Maine students pursuing postgraduate medical, dental, and veterinary education.
Eligibility: Applicants must be Maine residents (for purposes other than education) for one year prior to matriculation into medical school. Students must be admitted to a program of allopathic, osteopathic, veterinary medicine or dentistry at an accredited institution of medical education.
Target applicant(s): Graduate school students. Adult students.
Amount: Up to $25,000.
Number of awards: Varies.
Scholarship may be renewable.
Deadline: May 31.
How to apply: Applications are available online.
Exclusive: Visit www.UltimateScholarshipBook.com and enter code FI155826 for updates on this award.

[1559] • Maine State Society Foundation Scholarship
Maine State Society Foundation of Washington, DC
6508 Bowie Drive, Springfield, VA 22150
Email: mssfscholarship@gmail.com
https://mainestatesociety.org/foundation/
Purpose: To provide financial assistance to Maine students.
Eligibility: Applicants or their parents must have been born in or have been a legal resident of Maine for at least four years. Applicants must be full-time students who are at least sophomores and must attend an accredited, non-profit college or university in Maine.
Target applicant(s): College students.
Minimum GPA: 3.0
Amount: At least $1,000.
Number of awards: Varies.
Deadline: March 15.
How to apply: Applications are available by mail and online.
Exclusive: Visit www.UltimateScholarshipBook.com and enter code MA155926 for updates on this award.

[1560] • Maine Veterans Dependents Educational Benefits
Bureau of Veterans' Services
117 State House Station, Augusta, ME 04333-0117
Phone: 207-430-6035
Email: mainebvs@maine.gov
http://www.maine.gov/veterans/
Purpose: To provide the opportunity for dependents of veterans to obtain higher education.
Eligibility: Applicants must be spouses or children of a veteran in the state of Maine. They must be at least 16 years old, be high school graduates and be residents of the state of Maine for the last 5 years. They must be pursuing a college degree. Benefits must be awarded prior to the dependent's 22nd birthday, unless he is serving in the U.S. Armed Forces, in which case they may be awarded until his 26th birthday.
Target applicant(s): High school students. College students. Adult students.
Amount: Full Tuition.
Number of awards: Varies.
Scholarship may be renewable.
Deadline: Contact the sponsor to confirm the deadline.
How to apply: Applications are available online.
Exclusive: Visit www.UltimateScholarshipBook.com and enter code BU156026 for updates on this award.

[1561] • Maison Law California Scholarship
Maison Law Personal Injury Lawyer
525 West Main Street, Suite B-1033, Visalia, CA 93291
Phone: 559-396-3889
Email: maisonlawscholarshipprogram@gmail.com
https://maisonlaw.com/community/scholarship/
Purpose: To support students who have suffered a serious injury.
Eligibility: Applicants must be graduating, college-bound high school seniors or be currently enrolled in an accredited college or university

The Ultimate Scholarship Book 2026
Scholarship Directory (State of Residence)

with a minimum 3.0 GPA. Students are required to submit an essay on a provided prompt.
Target applicant(s): High school students. College students. Graduate school students. Adult students.
Minimum GPA: 3.0
Amount: $2,000.
Number of awards: 1.
Deadline: May 1.
How to apply: Applications are available online.
Exclusive: Visit www.UltimateScholarshipBook.com and enter code MA156126 for updates on this award.

[1562] • Mamoru and Aiko Takitani Foundation Scholarship
Mamoru and Aiko Takitani Foundation
P.O. Box 10687, Honolulu, HI 96816-0687
Phone: 808-228-0209
Email: info@takitanifoundation.org
http://www.takitani.org
Purpose: To provide financial assistance to graduating seniors for their undergraduate education.
Eligibility: Applicants must be graduating high school seniors and Hawaii residents. Applicants must also demonstrate scholastic achievement, participation in activities and have been accepted into an accredited institution. Community service and financial need are also considered.
Target applicant(s): High school students.
Amount: $2,000-$10,000.
Number of awards: Varies.
Scholarship may be renewable.
Deadline: February 1.
How to apply: Contact your high school guidance counselor.
Exclusive: Visit www.UltimateScholarshipBook.com and enter code MA156226 for updates on this award.

[1563] • Margaret A. Pemberton Scholarship
Black Nurses Association of Greater Washington, DC Area Inc.
P.O. Box 55285, Washington, DC 20040
Phone: 202-291-8866
Email: contactus@bnaofgwdca.org
https://www.bnaofgwdca.org
Purpose: To aid Washington, DC students who are planning to pursue higher education in nursing.
Eligibility: Applicants must be U.S. citizens, be graduating seniors who are students at a Washington, DC high school and be accepted into a National League for Nursing bachelor's degree program at a U.S. postsecondary institution. They must have a GPA of 2.8 or higher and must demonstrate financial need. Selection is based on the overall strength of the application.
Target applicant(s): High school students.
Minimum GPA: 2.8
Amount: Varies.
Number of awards: 1.
Deadline: April 15.
How to apply: Applications are available online. An application form, personal statement, official transcript, copy of college acceptance letter and two recommendation letters are required.
Exclusive: Visit www.UltimateScholarshipBook.com and enter code BL156326 for updates on this award.

[1564] • Margaret A. Stafford Nursing Scholarship
Delaware Community Foundation
P.O. Box 1636, Wilmington, DE 19899
Phone: 302-571-8004
Email: rgentsch@delcf.org
http://www.delcf.org
Purpose: To aid Delaware students who are pursuing higher education in nursing.
Eligibility: Applicants must be Delaware residents who are enrolled in or who have been accepted into a nursing degree program at an accredited college or university. Selection is based on the overall strength of the application.
Target applicant(s): High school students. College students. Adult students.
Amount: Varies.
Number of awards: Varies.
Deadline: March 15.
How to apply: Applications are available online. An application form, transcript, personal statement and two recommendation letters are required.
Exclusive: Visit www.UltimateScholarshipBook.com and enter code DE156426 for updates on this award.

[1565] • MARILN Professional Scholarship Award
Massachusetts/Rhode Island League for Nursing
Award Committee, P.O. Box 407, Westwood, MA 02090
Phone: 781-366-0722
Email: nursing.mariln@gmail.com
https://mariln.nursingnetwork.com/
Purpose: To aid Massachusetts and Rhode Island practical nursing students.
Eligibility: Applicants must be Massachusetts or Rhode Island residents and have lived in Massachusetts or Rhode Island for at least four years before having entered that practical nursing program. They must be full-time students who have completed two consecutive semesters of their program of study. Selection is based on stated career goals and professional potential.
Target applicant(s): College students. Adult students.
Amount: Varies.
Number of awards: Varies.
Deadline: September 15.
How to apply: Applications are available online. An application form, official transcript, personal essay and two recommendation letters are required.
Exclusive: Visit www.UltimateScholarshipBook.com and enter code MA156526 for updates on this award.

[1566] • Marion Maccarrell Scott Scholarship
Hawaii Community Foundation - Scholarships
827 Fort Street Mall, Honolulu, HI 96813
Phone: 888-731-3863
Email: scholarships@hcf-hawaii.org
https://www.hawaiicommunityfoundation.org/
Purpose: To support graduating high school students in Hawaii who are committed to world peace.
Eligibility: Applicants must have attended a public high school in Hawaii, and they must plan to attend college on the U.S. mainland. Students must have at least a 2.8 GPA.
Target applicant(s): High school students.
Minimum GPA: 2.8

Amount: Varies.
Number of awards: Varies.
Deadline: February 28.
How to apply: To apply, register online, complete the online application and select the scholarships to which you wish to apply. In addition, mail the supporting materials: printed confirmation page from the online application, personal statement, essay, copy of Student Aid Report (SAR) available at www.fafsa.ed.gov and official transcript.
Exclusive: Visit www.UltimateScholarshipBook.com and enter code HA156626 for updates on this award.

[1567] • Marlin R. Scarborough Memorial Scholarship
South Dakota Board of Regents
306 East Capitol Ave, Suite 200, Pierre, SD 57501-2545
Phone: 605-773-3455
Email: info@sdbor.edu
http://www.sdbor.edu
Purpose: To support undergraduate students in South Dakota.
Eligibility: Applicants must submit an essay detailing their leadership qualities, academic achievements and community service. Students must attend a public South Dakota university with at least a 3.5 GPA, and they must be in their junior year at the time they receive the scholarship funding.
Target applicant(s): College students. Adult students.
Minimum GPA: 3.5
Amount: $1,500.
Number of awards: 1.
Deadline: Contact the sponsor to confirm the deadline.
How to apply: Applications are available online.
Exclusive: Visit www.UltimateScholarshipBook.com and enter code SO156726 for updates on this award.

[1568] • Marvin L. Zuidema Scholarship Award
American Society of Civil Engineers-Michigan Section
ASCE Michigan Section Scholarships, 215 N. Walnut Street, Lansing, MI 48933
Phone: 517-332-2066
Email: cschmitz@acecmi.org
https://branches.asce.org/michigan-se/other-asce-scholarships
Purpose: To aid American Society of Civil Engineers (ASCE) student members in Michigan who have contributed meaningfully to student civil engineering activities.
Eligibility: Applicants must be U.S. citizens, Michigan residents and rising juniors or seniors who are enrolled full-time in an ABET-accredited civil engineering degree program. They must have a GPA of 2.5 or higher on a four-point scale and have made a notable contribution to civil engineering student activities. Selection is based on academic merit.
Target applicant(s): College students. Adult students.
Minimum GPA: 2.5
Amount: $1,500.
Number of awards: 1.
Deadline: May 27.
How to apply: Applications are available online. An application form and an official transcript are required.
Exclusive: Visit www.UltimateScholarshipBook.com and enter code AM156826 for updates on this award.

[1569] • Mary Ann K. Murtha Memorial Scholarship
American Legion Auxiliary, Department of New York
112 State Street, Suite 1310, Albany, NY 12207
Phone: 518-463-1162
Email: nyalaeducation@gmail.com
http://www.deptny.org/?page_id=2128
Purpose: To provide financial assistance to students whose parents, grandparents or great-grandparents served in the Armed Forces during wartime.
Eligibility: Applicants must be children, grandchildren or great-grandchildren of Armed Forces veterans who served during World War I, World War II, the Korean Conflict, the Vietnam War, Grenada/Lebanon, Panama, the Persian Gulf and War on Terrorism. Students must be high school seniors, U.S. citizens and New York State residents.
Target applicant(s): High school students.
Amount: $1,000.
Number of awards: 1.
Deadline: March 1.
How to apply: Applications are available online.
Exclusive: Visit www.UltimateScholarshipBook.com and enter code AM156926 for updates on this award.

[1570] • Mary Benevento/CTAHPERD Scholarship
Connecticut Association of Health, Physical Education, Recreation and Dance
c/o Janice Skene, CTAHPERD Scholarship Chair, Buttonball Lane School, 376 Buttonball Lane, Glastonbury, CT 06033
Phone: 860-652-7276
Email: skenej@glastonburyus.org
http://www.ctahperd.org
Purpose: To aid Connecticut students who are planning to pursue higher education in school health teaching, physical education, recreation or dance.
Eligibility: Applicants must be U.S. citizens and Connecticut residents. They must be high school seniors who are planning to pursue a bachelor's degree in school health teaching, physical education, recreation or dance at an accredited Connecticut postsecondary institution. Selection is based on academic merit, professional potential and character.
Target applicant(s): High school students.
Amount: $1,000.
Number of awards: Varies.
Deadline: June 15.
How to apply: Applications are available online. An application form, transcript, personal statement and one letter of recommendation are required.
Exclusive: Visit www.UltimateScholarshipBook.com and enter code CO157026 for updates on this award.

[1571] • Mary Eileen Dixey Scholarship
American Occupational Therapy Foundation
Attn: Jeanne Cooper, 4720 Montgomery Lane, Suite 202, Bethesda, MD 20814
Phone: 240-292-1034
Email: jcooper@aotf.org
https://www.tota.org/scholarships
Purpose: To aid New Hampshire occupational therapy students.
Eligibility: Applicants must be New Hampshire residents who are members of the American Occupational Therapy Association (AOTA). They must be enrolled full-time in an accredited occupational therapy program at the associate's or master's degree level in the state of New

The Ultimate Scholarship Book 2026
Scholarship Directory (State of Residence)

Hampshire. Master's level students must be enrolled in a first professional degree program and must have completed at least one year of study to be eligible. Selection is based on the overall strength of the application.
Target applicant(s): College students. Graduate school students. Adult students.
Amount: Varies.
Number of awards: Varies.
Deadline: October 2.
How to apply: Applications are available online. An application form, two personal references and a program director statement are required.
Exclusive: Visit www.UltimateScholarshipBook.com and enter code AM157126 for updates on this award.

[1572] • Mary Keith Duff Memorial Scholarship
Travis Credit Union
P.O. Box 2069, Vacaville, CA 95696
Phone: 707-449-4000
https://www.traviscu.org/community/events-seminars-community-education/scholarships/
Purpose: To assist members of the Travis Credit Union.
Eligibility: Applicants must be graduating high school seniors and have a minimum 3.0 GPA. Selection is based on GPA, honors and awards, employment and community service, leadership and extracurricular activities, essay and financial need. Students must plan to enroll in a two-year or four-year college or university full-time or with 12 or more credits or units.
Target applicant(s): High school students.
Minimum GPA: 3.0
Amount: $2,000.
Number of awards: 22.
Deadline: February 28.
How to apply: Applications are available online between January 1 and March 5 of each year.
Exclusive: Visit www.UltimateScholarshipBook.com and enter code TR157226 for updates on this award.

[1573] • Mary Macon McGuire Scholarship
General Federation of Women's Clubs of Virginia
P.O. Box 8750, Richmond, VA 23226
Phone: 804-288-3724
Email: scholarships@gfwcvirginia.org
https://gfwcvirginia.org/
Purpose: To support Virginia women who are returning to school in order to better support their families.
Eligibility: Applicants must be a female head of household and a resident of Virginia. Students must be currently enrolled in a course of study at an accredited Virginia school. Students must submit an essay and three letters of recommendation. Applicants must show financial need.
Target applicant(s): College students. Adult students.
Amount: $2,500.
Number of awards: 2.
Deadline: March 15.
How to apply: Applications are available online.
Exclusive: Visit www.UltimateScholarshipBook.com and enter code GE157326 for updates on this award.

[1574] • Masonic Scholarship Program
Grand Lodge of Iowa, A.F. and A.M.
Iowa Masonic Library and Museum, 813 First Avenue SE, P.O. Box 279, Cedar Rapids, IA 52406-0279
Phone: 319-365-1438
Email: scholarships@gl-iowa.org
https://grandlodgeofiowa.org/
Purpose: To reward high school seniors from Iowa public high schools for academics and leadership skills.
Eligibility: Applicants must be pursuing a post-secondary education in any state at an institution which provides a two-year or four-year college program or vocational training. They do not need to have a Masonic connection. Selection is based on academic record, communication skills and financial need, but the most important is service to school and community with an emphasis on leadership roles. Finalists will be asked to appear before the committee for personal interviews.
Target applicant(s): High school students.
Amount: Varies.
Number of awards: 60.
Deadline: February 1.
How to apply: Applications are available online or from guidance departments at Iowa public high schools.
Exclusive: Visit www.UltimateScholarshipBook.com and enter code GR157426 for updates on this award.

[1575] • Masonry Institute of Iowa Foundation Scholarship Program
Masonry Institute of Iowa
6919 Vista Drive, West Des Moines, IA 50266
Email: admin@masonryinstituteofiowa.org
https://masonryinstituteofiowa.wildapricot.org/Scholarships
Purpose: To support students pursuing construction, architecture and engineering.
Eligibility: Applicants must be current Iowa high school or college students attending an Iowa institution and pursuing a program related to construction, engineering, masonry or architecture.
Target applicant(s): High school students. College students. Adult students.
Amount: $500 up to $1,000.
Number of awards: Varies.
Deadline: February 1.
How to apply: Applications are available online.
Exclusive: Visit www.UltimateScholarshipBook.com and enter code MA157526 for updates on this award.

[1576] • Massachusetts Community Colleges Access Grant
Massachusetts Community Colleges
85 Devonshire Street, 7th Floor, Boston, MA 02109
Phone: 617-542-2911
Email: info@masscc.org
http://www.masscc.org/student-resources/financial-aid-resources
Purpose: To make a Massachusetts community college education accessible for all.
Eligibility: Applicants must be pursuing an associate degree at a Massachusetts community college. Students whose household income is $36,000 per year or less are eligible to receive funds to cover full tuition and fees.
Target applicant(s): High school students. College students. Adult students.
Amount: Up to full tuition.
Number of awards: Varies.
Deadline: Contact the sponsor to confirm the deadline.

How to apply: Applications are available from Massachusetts community college financial aid offices.
Exclusive: Visit www.UltimateScholarshipBook.com and enter code MA157626 for updates on this award.

[1577] • Massachusetts Part-Time Grant
Massachusetts Department of Higher Education
Office of Student Financial Assistance, 454 Broadway, Suite 200, Revere, MA 02151
Phone: 617-727-9420
Email: osfa@osfa.mass.edu
https://www.mass.gov/handbook/massachusetts-financial-aid-programs
Purpose: To aid Massachusetts part-time undergraduate students.
Eligibility: Applicants must U.S. citizens or eligible non-citizens who have been Massachusetts residents for at least one year. They must be enrolled in an undergraduate degree or certificate program on a part-time basis (6 to 11 credits per semester) at a Massachusetts postsecondary institution. They must not owe refund money on an educational grant or have any defaulted student loans. Applicants who have earned a bachelor's or professional degree previously are ineligible.
Target applicant(s): High school students. College students. Adult students.
Amount: At least $200.
Number of awards: Varies.
Scholarship may be renewable.
Deadline: As soon as possible after October 1.
How to apply: Application is made by completing the FAFSA and then contacting your financial aid office.
Exclusive: Visit www.UltimateScholarshipBook.com and enter code MA157726 for updates on this award.

[1578] • Massachusetts Student Broadcaster Scholarship
Massachusetts Broadcasters Association
43 Riverside Avenue, PMB 401, Medford, MA 02155
Phone: 800-471-1875
Email: jordan@massbroadcasters.org
http://www.massbroadcasters.org
Purpose: To support student broadcasters.
Eligibility: Applicants must be Massachusetts residents who are enrolled or plan to enroll in an accredited institution of higher learning that offers degrees in television and radio broadcasting. Students must meet their school's definition of a full-time student. Selection is based on financial need, academic merit, community service, extracurricular activities and work experience.
Target applicant(s): High school students. College students. Adult students.
Amount: $2,500-$5,000.
Number of awards: Varies.
Deadline: April 12.
How to apply: Applications are available online. An application form, transcript and financial statement are required.
Exclusive: Visit www.UltimateScholarshipBook.com and enter code MA157826 for updates on this award.

[1579] • MASSGrant
Massachusetts Department of Higher Education
Office of Student Financial Assistance, 454 Broadway, Suite 200, Revere, MA 02151
Phone: 617-727-9420
Email: osfa@osfa.mass.edu
https://www.mass.gov/handbook/massachusetts-financial-aid-programs
Purpose: To provide need-based financial assistance to undergraduate students who reside in Massachusetts and who are enrolled in and pursuing a program of higher education.
Eligibility: Applicants must be permanent legal residents of Massachusetts and have an Expected Family Contribution (EFC) between $0 and $5,198. Applicants must be enrolled as full-time students in a certificate, associate or bachelor's degree program and not have received a prior bachelor's degree or its equivalent.
Target applicant(s): High school students. College students. Adult students.
Amount: Varies.
Number of awards: Varies.
Scholarship may be renewable.
Deadline: May 1.
How to apply: Complete and submit the Free Application for Federal Student Aid (FAFSA).
Exclusive: Visit www.UltimateScholarshipBook.com and enter code MA157926 for updates on this award.

[1580] • Master's, Ph.D. or Other Advanced Degree Program
New Hampshire Charitable Foundation
37 Pleasant Street, Concord, NH 03301-4005
Phone: 603-225-6641
Email: jessica.kierstead@nhcf.org
https://www.nhcf.org/how-can-we-help-you/
Purpose: To support New Hampshire students who are seeking graduate level studies.
Eligibility: Applicants must be New Hampshire residents who are enrolling in graduate level studies, including master's, Ph.D. or another advanced degree program. Selection is based on financial need, academic merit, community service, school activities and work experience. Students must file a FAFSA and submit a copy of the SAR with the application.
Target applicant(s): Graduate school students. Adult students.
Amount: Varies.
Number of awards: Varies.
Deadline: April 12.
How to apply: Applications are available online.
Exclusive: Visit www.UltimateScholarshipBook.com and enter code NE158026 for updates on this award.

[1581] • Math and Science Teaching Incentive Scholarships
New York State Higher Education Services Corporation (HESC)
99 Washington Avenue, Albany, NY 12255
Phone: 888-697-4372
Email: scholarships@hesc.ny.gov
http://www.hesc.ny.gov

Purpose: To support students in New York who are planning careers in math or science secondary education.
Eligibility: Applicants must have at least a 2.5 GPA. Recipients must agree to work for at least five years after graduation as a secondary school science or math teacher in New York.
Target applicant(s): College students. Graduate school students. Adult students.
Minimum GPA: 2.5
Amount: Up to full tuition.
Number of awards: Varies.
Scholarship may be renewable.
Deadline: As soon as possible after October 1.
How to apply: Applications are available online.
Exclusive: Visit www.UltimateScholarshipBook.com and enter code NE158126 for updates on this award.

[1582] • May T. Henry Scholarship Fund
Stride Bank
Wealth Management Division, P.O. Box 3448, Enid, OK 73702-3448
Phone: 580-233-3535
Email: customerservice@stridebank.com
https://stridebank.com/scholarships.html
Purpose: To support students who plan to attend post-secondary education institutions in Oklahoma.
Eligibility: Applicants must be high school seniors who plan to attend a college, university or technical school supported by the state of Oklahoma. Students must have graduated from an accredited high school or equivalent institution and not be related to any member of the selection committee.
Target applicant(s): High school students.
Amount: $1,000.
Number of awards: Varies.
Deadline: April 1.
How to apply: Applications are available online.
Exclusive: Visit www.UltimateScholarshipBook.com and enter code ST158226 for updates on this award.

[1583] • MCEC Technical Scholarship
Grand Lodge of Iowa, A.F. and A.M.
Iowa Masonic Library and Museum, 813 First Avenue SE, P.O. Box 279, Cedar Rapids, IA 52406-0279
Phone: 319-365-1438
Email: scholarships@gl-iowa.org
https://grandlodgeofiowa.org/
Purpose: To support Iowa students pursuing trade education.
Eligibility: Applicants must be graduating high school seniors in Iowa who plan to enroll in a mechanical or trade course of study at an accredited Iowa community college.
Target applicant(s): High school students.
Amount: Varies.
Number of awards: Varies.
Deadline: February 1.
How to apply: Applications are available online.
Exclusive: Visit www.UltimateScholarshipBook.com and enter code GR158326 for updates on this award.

[1584] • McLean Scholarship for Nursing and Physician Assistant Majors
Association of Independent Colleges and Universities of Pennsylvania
101 North Front Street, Harrisburg, PA 17101-1404
Phone: 717-232-8649
Email: klinger@aicup.org
https://www.aicup.org/philanthropy/aicup-scholarships/
Purpose: To aid undergraduates who are studying to become nurses and physician assistants.
Eligibility: Applicants must be full-time undergraduates who are majoring in nursing or physician assisting at an Association of Independent Colleges and Universities of Pennsylvania (AICUP) member school. They must have a GPA of 3.0 or higher and must have proven leadership skills. Selection is based on the overall strength of the application.
Target applicant(s): College students. Adult students.
Minimum GPA: 3.0
Amount: $4,500.
Number of awards: 7.
Deadline: June 1.
How to apply: Applications are available online. An application form and personal essay are required.
Exclusive: Visit www.UltimateScholarshipBook.com and enter code AS158426 for updates on this award.

[1585] • Medallion Fund
New Hampshire Charitable Foundation
37 Pleasant Street, Concord, NH 03301-4005
Phone: 603-225-6641
Email: jessica.kierstead@nhcf.org
https://www.nhcf.org/how-can-we-help-you/
Purpose: To improve the skilled workforce in areas of need in New Hampshire.
Eligibility: Applicants must be enrolling in an accredited vocational or technical program that does not lead to a bachelor's or advanced degree. They must be legal residents of New Hampshire and intend to work in a vocational or technical career when their schooling is complete. Preference is given to those who plan to go into the manufacturing trade sector or have little or no other opportunities for training or education.
Target applicant(s): High school students. College students. Adult students.
Amount: Varies.
Number of awards: Varies.
Deadline: December 13.
How to apply: Applications are available online.
Exclusive: Visit www.UltimateScholarshipBook.com and enter code NE158526 for updates on this award.

[1586] • Medical Loan-For-Service Program
New Mexico Higher Education Department
2044 Galisteo Street, Suite 4, Santa Fe, NM 87505-2100
Phone: 505-476-8400
Email: cesaria.tapia1@state.nm.us
https://hed.state.nm.us/financial-aid
Purpose: To encourage New Mexico students interested in becoming doctors.

Eligibility: Applicants must be New Mexico residents and accepted into a medical school within New Mexico. Students must demonstrate financial need and be enrolled at least half-time. Applicants must declare their intent to practice as a health professional in a designated shortage area within the state of New Mexico. For every year of service provided in a designated shortage area within New Mexico, a portion of the loan will be forgiven.
Target applicant(s): Graduate school students. Adult students.
Amount: Up to $25,000.
Number of awards: Varies.
Scholarship may be renewable.
Deadline: July 1.
How to apply: Applications are available online.
Exclusive: Visit www.UltimateScholarshipBook.com and enter code NE158626 for updates on this award.

[1587] • MEFA UPlan Prepaid Tuition Waiver Program

Massachusetts Educational Financing Authority
160 Federal Street, 4th Floor, Boston, MA 02110
Phone: 800-449-6332
Email: info@mefa.org
https://www.mefa.org
Purpose: To provide financial aid in the form of tuition waivers to Massachusetts students who prepay their tuition at lower rates.
Eligibility: Applicants must be planning to attend a school in the state of Massachusetts which participates in the UPlan program.
Target applicant(s): Junior high students or younger. High school students. College students. Adult students.
Amount: Varies.
Number of awards: Varies.
Scholarship may be renewable.
Deadline: Contact the sponsor to confirm the deadline.
How to apply: Applications are available online.
Exclusive: Visit www.UltimateScholarshipBook.com and enter code MA158726 for updates on this award.

[1588] • Mellinger Scholarships

Edward Arthur Mellinger Educational Foundation Inc.
1025 E. Broadway, P.O. Box 770, Monmouth, IL 61462
Phone: 309-734-2419
Email: info@mellinger.org
http://www.mellinger.org
Purpose: The E. A. Mellinger Foundation supports education as a memorial to its namesake.
Eligibility: Applicants must live in western Illinois or eastern Iowa, submit the FAFSA form and demonstrate financial need and attend an accredited university. Awards are based on academic achievement. Part-time students are also eligible for scholarships, and loans are also available to graduate students.
Target applicant(s): High school students. College students. Adult students.
Amount: Varies.
Number of awards: Varies.
Scholarship may be renewable.
Deadline: May 1.
How to apply: Applications are available by mail or online. Application forms are only available from February 1 to May 1 each year.
Exclusive: Visit www.UltimateScholarshipBook.com and enter code ED158826 for updates on this award.

[1589] • Mexican Scholarship Fund

Central Indiana Community Foundation
615 North Alabama Street, Suite 119, Indianapolis, IN 46204-1498
Phone: 317-634-2423
Email: scholarships@cicf.org
http://www.cicf.org
Purpose: To provide financial assistance to Indiana residents of Mexican descent.
Eligibility: Applicants must have a minimum GPA of 3.0, demonstrate academic promise and demonstrate financial need. Preference is given to students of Mexican descent. Awards may be used for tuition, required fees or room and board.
Target applicant(s): High school students.
Minimum GPA: 3.0
Amount: Varies.
Number of awards: Varies.
Deadline: February 1.
How to apply: Applications are available online.
Exclusive: Visit www.UltimateScholarshipBook.com and enter code CE158926 for updates on this award.

[1590] • MFA Foundation Scholarships

MFA Incorporated
201 Ray Young Drive, Columbia, MO 65201
Phone: 573-874-5111
https://www.mfafoundation.com/
Purpose: To aid Midwest college-bound high school seniors.
Eligibility: Applicants must be high school seniors who live in an area where a sponsoring MFA agency is located. They must have plans to enroll full-time at an accredited college or university no later than September 1 of the application year. Selection is based on character, extracurricular activities and financial need.
Target applicant(s): High school students.
Amount: $2,000.
Number of awards: Varies.
Deadline: February 15.
How to apply: Applications are available by request from the applicant's high school counselor. An application form and supporting materials are required.
Exclusive: Visit www.UltimateScholarshipBook.com and enter code MF159026 for updates on this award.

[1591] • Michael Curry Summer Internship Program

Governor's Office of the State of Illinois Michael Curry Summer Internship Program
207 State House, Springfield, IL 62706
https://gov.illinois.gov/about/opportunities.html
Purpose: To provide internships for college juniors, seniors or graduate students.
Eligibility: Applicants must be Illinois residents. Recipients work full-time in an agency under the jurisdiction of the Governor for 10 weeks during the summer.
Target applicant(s): College students. Graduate school students. Adult students.
Amount: $2,600 stipend.
Number of awards: Varies.
Deadline: April 7.
How to apply: Applications are available online or by mail.

The Ultimate Scholarship Book 2026
Scholarship Directory (State of Residence)

Exclusive: Visit www.UltimateScholarshipBook.com and enter code GO159126 for updates on this award.

[1592] • Michigan Competitive Scholarship
Michigan Student Aid
Student Scholarships and Grants, P.O. Box 30462, Lansing, MI 48909-7962
Phone: 888-447-2687
Email: ssg@michigan.gov
http://www.michigan.gov/mistudentaid/
Purpose: To assist students who plan to attend a Michigan public or private college.
Eligibility: Applicants must be Michigan residents since July 1 of the previous calendar year and have received a qualifying score on the ACT and a minimum 2.0 GPA. Applicants must also demonstrate financial need and be enrolled in an approved Michigan college or university. Applicants cannot be pursuing a degree in theology, divinity or religious education. This award is based on both financial need and academic merit.
Target applicant(s): High school students. College students. Adult students.
Minimum GPA: 2.0
Amount: Varies.
Number of awards: Varies.
Scholarship may be renewable.
Deadline: May 1.
How to apply: File a Free Application for Federal Student Aid (FAFSA).
Exclusive: Visit www.UltimateScholarshipBook.com and enter code MI159226 for updates on this award.

[1593] • Michigan Council of Women in Technology University Scholarship
Michigan Council of Women in Technology Foundation
Attn.: Scholarship Committee, One Towne Square, Suite 690, Southfield, MI 48076
Phone: 248-218-2578
Email: scholarships@mcwt.org
https://mcwt.org/programs/list/University-Initiatives/Scholarship-Program
Purpose: To support female information technology students.
Eligibility: Applicants must be high school seniors or undergraduate or graduate students who are Michigan residents and U.S. citizens with a GPA of 3.0 or higher. Students must be enrolled in a full-time undergraduate or graduate degree program in a major such as information systems, computer science, computer engineering, software engineering, computer information systems, digital forensics or software engineering. (Note: This is not a complete list.) Applicants must maintain program requirements and will be subject to verification.
Target applicant(s): High school students. College students. Graduate school students. Adult students.
Minimum GPA: 3.0
Amount: Varies.
Number of awards: Varies.
Scholarship may be renewable.
Deadline: January 31.
How to apply: Applications are available online. An application form, transcript, two letters of recommendation and research project description (for research grant applicants only) are required.
Exclusive: Visit www.UltimateScholarshipBook.com and enter code MI159326 for updates on this award.

[1594] • Michigan Engineering Scholarships
Michigan Society of Professional Engineers
PO Box 160, Parma, MI 49269
Phone: 517-487-9388
Email: dfnedervelt@outlook.com
https://www.michiganspe.org/scholarships/
Purpose: To aid Michigan students who are planning to pursue an undergraduate degree in engineering.
Eligibility: Applicants must be U.S. citizens, residents of Michigan and high school seniors. They must be accepted at an ABET-accredited college or university in Michigan and must have plans to pursue a degree in engineering. Students must have a GPA of 3.0 or higher for both the 10th and 11th grade years and a minimum composite ACT score of 26 or higher. Selection is based on GPA, ACT score, personal essay, extracurricular activities, any college-level coursework completed and honors received.
Target applicant(s): High school students.
Minimum GPA: 3.0
Amount: Varies.
Number of awards: Varies.
Deadline: February 17.
How to apply: Applications are available online. An application form, personal essay and official transcript are required.
Exclusive: Visit www.UltimateScholarshipBook.com and enter code MI159426 for updates on this award.

[1595] • Michigan Oratorical Contest
American Legion, Department of Michigan
212 N. Verlinden Avenue, Suite A, Lansing, MI 48915
Phone: 517-371-4720 x11
Email: programs@michiganlegion.org
http://www.michiganlegion.org
Purpose: To enhance high school students' experience with and understanding of the U.S. Constitution. The contest will help develop students' leadership skills and civic appreciation, as well as the ability to deliver thoughtful, insightful orations regarding U.S. citizenship and its inherent responsibilities.
Eligibility: Applicants must be high school students under the age of 20 who are U.S. citizens or legal residents and residents of the state. Students first give an oration within their state and winners compete at the national level. The oration must be related to the Constitution of the United States focusing on the duties and obligations citizens have to the government. It must be in English and be between eight and ten minutes. There is also an assigned topic which is posted on the website, and it should be between three and five minutes.
Target applicant(s): High school students.
Amount: Up to $2,000.
Number of awards: Varies.
Deadline: December 9.
How to apply: Application information is available online under the link "Forms and Applications."
Exclusive: Visit www.UltimateScholarshipBook.com and enter code AM159526 for updates on this award.

[1596] • Michigan Tuition Grant
Michigan Student Aid
Student Scholarships and Grants, P.O. Box 30462, Lansing, MI 48909-7962
Phone: 888-447-2687
Email: ssg@michigan.gov
http://www.michigan.gov/mistudentaid/

Purpose: To assist Michigan students who are pursuing higher education in Michigan.
Eligibility: Applicants must be U.S. citizens, permanent residents or approved refugees. They must be Michigan residents who have lived there since at least July 1 of the previous calendar year and must be undergraduate students who are attending an approved Michigan college or university at least part-time. They must demonstrate financial need and not be in default on a federal student loan. Applicants who are pursuing degrees in divinity, theology or religious education are ineligible. Selection is based on financial need.
Target applicant(s): College students. Adult students.
Amount: Up to full tuition.
Number of awards: Varies.
Scholarship may be renewable.
Deadline: May 1.
How to apply: Application is made by filing the FAFSA.
Exclusive: Visit www.UltimateScholarshipBook.com and enter code MI159626 for updates on this award.

[1597] • Michigan Tuition Incentive Program
Michigan Department of Treasury
P.O. Box 30462, Lansing, MI 48909-7962
Phone: 888-447-2687
Email: mistudentaid@michigan.gov
http://www.michigan.gov/
Purpose: To encourage Michigan students to complete high school and seek higher education.
Eligibility: Applicants must be upcoming high school graduates or GED recipients under the age of 20 and also must have received Medicaid for 24 months in a 36 month period after their 12th birthday. Qualifying students will receive an acceptance form, which must be returned to the Office of Scholarships and Grants to become eligible. The program covers tuition and mandatory fees for students pursuing an associate degree and up to $2,000 for studies in pursuit of a four-year degree.
Target applicant(s): High school students.
Amount: Up to full tuition.
Number of awards: Varies.
Scholarship may be renewable.
Deadline: August 31.
How to apply: Applications are available from the Michigan Department of Human Services.
Exclusive: Visit www.UltimateScholarshipBook.com and enter code MI159726 for updates on this award.

[1598] • Middle School Essay Contest
American Legion, Department of Virginia
1708 Commonwealth Avenue, Richmond, VA 23230
Phone: 804-353-6606
http://www.valegion.org
Purpose: To promote citizenship in young Virginia students.
Eligibility: Applicants must be middle school students and write an essay on an assigned topic. The essay should be written at the student's desk during school time and will be evaluated based on originality, sincerity and the student's ability to communicate meaning.
Target applicant(s): Junior high students or younger.
Amount: $50-$250.
Number of awards: 2.
Deadline: December 21.
How to apply: Applications are available online and from sponsoring Posts.
Exclusive: Visit www.UltimateScholarshipBook.com and enter code AM159826 for updates on this award.

[1599] • Midwest Student Exchange Program
Midwestern Higher Education Compact
105 Fifth Avenue South, Suite 450, Minneapolis, MN 55401
Phone: 612-677-2777
Email: msep@mhec.org
http://msep.mhec.org
Purpose: The program aims to increase higher education options for Midwestern students and families within the region.
Eligibility: Applicants must currently live in Illinois, Indiana, Kansas, Minnesota, Missouri, Nebraska, North Dakota, Ohio or Wisconsin and wish to attend a participating school in one of these states outside their own. Other eligibility requirements vary depending on the state and school. Awards are tuition reduction for out-of-state schools in the participating region.
Target applicant(s): High school students. College students. Graduate school students. Adult students.
Amount: Varies.
Number of awards: Varies.
Scholarship may be renewable.
Deadline: Contact the sponsor to confirm the deadline.
How to apply: Students must clearly mark that they are an MSEP student when applying to the school of their choice.
Exclusive: Visit www.UltimateScholarshipBook.com and enter code MI159926 for updates on this award.

[1600] • Mikkelson Foundation Scholarship
Mikkelson Foundation
P.O. Box 768, Monument, CO 80132
http://mikkelsonfoundation.org
Purpose: To support graduating seniors of Colorado in pursuing a degree in engineering, physical or biological sciences or mathematics.
Eligibility: Applicants must have a minimum GPA of 3.7 and a minimum SAT score of 1200 or a minimum ACT score of 28. Students must submit three letters of recommendation, official transcripts and a personal essay.
Target applicant(s): High school students.
Minimum GPA: 3.7
Amount: $3,000.
Number of awards: 3.
Deadline: April 14.
How to apply: Applications are available online.
Exclusive: Visit www.UltimateScholarshipBook.com and enter code MI160026 for updates on this award.

[1601] • Mildred Towle Scholarship - Study Abroad
Hawaii Community Foundation - Scholarships
827 Fort Street Mall, Honolulu, HI 96813
Phone: 888-731-3863
Email: scholarships@hcf-hawaii.org
https://www.hawaiicommunityfoundation.org/
Purpose: To support Hawaii students who plan to study abroad.
Eligibility: Applicants must study abroad as a junior, senior or graduate student. Students must have at least a 3.0 GPA. Preference will be given to applicants pursuing studies in the social sciences regarding international understanding and interracial fellowship. Applicants must prove financial need.
Target applicant(s): College students. Graduate school students. Adult students.

The Ultimate Scholarship Book 2026
Scholarship Directory (State of Residence)

Minimum GPA: 3.0
Amount: Varies.
Number of awards: Varies.
Deadline: February 28.
How to apply: To apply, register online, complete the online application and select the scholarships to which you wish to apply. In addition, mail the supporting materials: printed confirmation page from the online application, personal statement, copy of Student Aid Report (SAR) available at www.fafsa.ed.gov and official transcript.
Exclusive: Visit www.UltimateScholarshipBook.com and enter code HA160126 for updates on this award.

[1602] • Mildred Towle Scholarship for African-Americans

Hawaii Community Foundation - Scholarships
827 Fort Street Mall, Honolulu, HI 96813
Phone: 888-731-3863
Email: scholarships@hcf-hawaii.org
https://www.hawaiicommunityfoundation.org/
Purpose: To support African American students who are attending colleges in Hawaii.
Eligibility: Students must have at least a 3.0 GPA.
Target applicant(s): High school students. College students. Adult students.
Minimum GPA: 3.0
Amount: Varies.
Number of awards: Varies.
Deadline: February 28.
How to apply: To apply, register online, complete the online application and select the scholarships to which you wish to apply. In addition, mail the supporting materials: printed confirmation page from the online application, personal statement, copy of Student Aid Report (SAR) available at www.fafsa.ed.gov and official transcript.
Exclusive: Visit www.UltimateScholarshipBook.com and enter code HA160226 for updates on this award.

[1603] • Milton Fisher Scholarship for Innovation and Creativity

Milton Fisher Scholarship for Innovation and Creativity
Renee B. Fisher Foundation, c/o Community Foundation for Greater New Haven, 70 Audubon Street, 5th Floor, New Haven, CT 06510
Phone: 203-777-2386
Email: info@mfscholarship.org
http://mfscholarship.org/
Purpose: To reward and encourage innovative problem solving.
Eligibility: Applicants must be high school juniors or seniors or must be entering or in the first year of an undergraduate degree program. Students must be Connecticut or New York City residents who attend or plan to attend an institution in the U.S. or students who attend or plan to attend a Connecticut or New York City institution of higher learning. Students must have come up with a solution to a problem faced by their school, community or family; solve an artistic, scientific or technical problem or develop a new group that serves an important need.
Target applicant(s): High school students. College students. Adult students.
Amount: $1,000 to $5,000.
Number of awards: 8-10.
Scholarship may be renewable.
Deadline: May 15.
How to apply: Applications are available online.

Exclusive: Visit www.UltimateScholarshipBook.com and enter code MI160326 for updates on this award.

[1604] • Minnesota Academic Excellence Scholarship

Minnesota Office of Higher Education Services
1450 Energy Park Drive, Suite 350, Saint Paul, MN 55108-5227
Phone: 651-642-0567
Email: misp.lara@hotmail.com
http://www.ohe.state.mn.us/
Purpose: To help students who have demonstrated outstanding ability, achievement and potential in selected areas of study.
Eligibility: Applicants must be Minnesota residents who have been admitted to a full-time program in an approved Minnesota college or university. Applicants must have demonstrated achievement in one of the following subjects: English or creative writing, fine arts, foreign language, math, science or social science.
Target applicant(s): High school students. College students. Adult students.
Amount: Up to full tuition.
Number of awards: Varies.
Scholarship may be renewable.
Deadline: Contact the sponsor to confirm the deadline.
How to apply: For information about the status of this program, applicants should contact the schools they wish to attend.
Exclusive: Visit www.UltimateScholarshipBook.com and enter code MI160426 for updates on this award.

[1605] • Minnesota Division Izaak Walton League Scholarship

Izaak Walton League of America-Minnesota Division
6601 Auto Club Road, Bloomington, MN 55438
Phone: 651-221-0215
Email: ikes@minnesotaikes.org
http://www.minnesotaikes.org
Purpose: To aid Minnesota residents who are studying environmental or conservation subjects in college.
Eligibility: Applicants must be U.S. citizens and Minnesota residents. They must be in the second year or higher of a college degree program in environmental science, environmental education, conservation, environmental law, wildlife management or a related subject. Selection is based on academic merit and financial need.
Target applicant(s): College students. Adult students.
Amount: Up to $1,000.
Number of awards: Varies.
Deadline: May 1.
How to apply: Applications are available online. An application form, transcript, personal essay, resume and two letters of recommendation are required.
Exclusive: Visit www.UltimateScholarshipBook.com and enter code IZ160526 for updates on this award.

[1606] • Minnesota Hockey Scholarship

Minnesota Hockey
Executive Director, Minnesota Hockey Scholarship Committee, 317 Washington Street, St. Paul, MN 55102
Phone: 651-602-5727
Email: info@minnesotahockey.org
http://www.minnesotahockey.org

Purpose: To support hockey students who wish to further their education beyond high school.
Eligibility: Applicants must be residents of Minnesota, high school seniors, participate on a youth Junior Gold team or a girls' 19 and under team of an affiliate association of Minnesota Hockey and have a minimum GPA of 2.0. Selection is based on academic achievement, a personal essay and the letters of recommendation.
Target applicant(s): High school students.
Minimum GPA: 2.0
Amount: $1,500.
Number of awards: Varies.
Deadline: March 6.
How to apply: Applications are available online.
Exclusive: Visit www.UltimateScholarshipBook.com and enter code MI160626 for updates on this award.

[1607] • Minnesota Indian Scholarship Program

Minnesota Office of Higher Education Services
1450 Energy Park Drive, Suite 350, Saint Paul, MN 55108-5227
Phone: 651-642-0567
Email: misp.lara@hotmail.com
http://www.ohe.state.mn.us/
Purpose: To provide money to help Native American students pay for higher education.
Eligibility: Applicants must be at least one-fourth Native American, Minnesota residents and members of a federally recognized Indian tribe. Applicants must be a high school graduate or possess a GED and have been accepted by an approved college, university or vocational school in Minnesota.
Target applicant(s): High school students. College students. Graduate school students. Adult students.
Amount: Up to $6,000.
Number of awards: Varies.
Scholarship may be renewable.
Deadline: July 1.
How to apply: This award is administered by the Minnesota Department of Children, Families, and Learning (CFL), and must be approved by the Minnesota Indian Scholarship Committee. To receive an application, contact your local tribal education office.
Exclusive: Visit www.UltimateScholarshipBook.com and enter code MI160726 for updates on this award.

[1608] • Minnesota Masonic Charities Vocational Scholarship

Minnesota Masonic Charities
11501 Masonic Home Drive, Bloomington, MN 55437-3699
Phone: 952-948-6200
Email: scholarships@mnmasonic.org
https://mnmasoniccharities.org/
Purpose: To support Minnesota students pursuing vocational or technical education.
Eligibility: Applicants must be Minnesota residents and have graduated from a Minnesota high school. Students must be enrolled in or planning to enroll in an accredited vocational, technical or trade school program or a two-year community college seeking an associate degree.
Target applicant(s): High school students. College students. Adult students.
Amount: Up to $2,500.
Number of awards: 40.
Scholarship may be renewable.
Deadline: February 15.
How to apply: Applications are available online.
Exclusive: Visit www.UltimateScholarshipBook.com and enter code MI160826 for updates on this award.

[1609] • Minnesota Oratorical Contest

American Legion, Department of Minnesota
Department of Minnesota, 20 West 12th Street, Room 300-A, St. Paul, MN 55155
Phone: 651-291-1800
Email: department@mnlegion.org
https://mnlegion.org/programs/
Purpose: To enhance high school students' experience with and understanding of the U.S. Constitution. The contest will help develop students' leadership skills and civic appreciation, as well as the ability to deliver thoughtful, insightful orations regarding U.S. citizenship and its inherent responsibilities.
Eligibility: Applicants must be high school students under the age of 20 who are U.S. citizens or legal residents and residents of the state. Students first give an oration within their state and winners compete at the national level. The oration must be related to the Constitution of the United States focusing on the duties and obligations citizens have to the government. It must be in English and be between eight and ten minutes. There is also an assigned topic which is posted on the website, and it should be between three and five minutes.
Target applicant(s): High school students.
Amount: Up to $25,000.
Number of awards: 4.
Deadline: February 24.
How to apply: Application information is available by email.
Exclusive: Visit www.UltimateScholarshipBook.com and enter code AM160926 for updates on this award.

[1610] • Minnesota State Grant

Minnesota Office of Higher Education Services
1450 Energy Park Drive, Suite 350, Saint Paul, MN 55108-5227
Phone: 651-642-0567
Email: misp.lara@hotmail.com
http://www.ohe.state.mn.us/
Purpose: To aid Minnesota students who are pursuing higher education in Minnesota.
Eligibility: Applicants must be U.S. citizens or permanent residents who are Minnesota residents. They must be high school graduates, GED recipients or at least 17 years old by the end of the academic year. They must be enrolled in a diploma, certificate or degree program for at least three credits at an eligible Minnesota school. Applicants who are in default of a federal or state SELF student loan are ineligible, as are those who owe the Office of Higher Education for the overpayment of a state grant. They cannot have earned a baccalaureate degree previously or be more than 30 days past due on child support payments. Selection is based on financial need.
Target applicant(s): High school students. College students. Adult students.
Amount: Up to $12,345.
Number of awards: Varies.
Scholarship may be renewable.
Deadline: June 30.
How to apply: Application is made by filing the FAFSA.
Exclusive: Visit www.UltimateScholarshipBook.com and enter code MI161026 for updates on this award.

[1611] • Minority Scholarship
Ohio News Media Foundation
1335 Dublin Road, Suite 216-B, Columbus, OH 43215
Phone: 614-486-6677
Email: ariggs@ohionews.org
https://ohionews.org/aws/ONA/pt/sp/scholarships
Purpose: To support minority graduating high school seniors from Ohio who are pursuing a degree in a journalism-related field at an Ohio college or university.
Eligibility: Applicants must be African American, Hispanic, Asian American or American Indian high school students graduating from an Ohio high school and must be enrolled at an Ohio college or university for the upcoming fall. Students must have at least a 2.5 GPA and be majoring in a journalism-related field such as journalism, advertising or marketing. Applicants must write an autobiography as part of their essay, must get recommendations and may submit work samples.
Target applicant(s): High school students.
Minimum GPA: 2.5
Amount: $1,000.
Number of awards: 1.
Deadline: May 20.
How to apply: Applications are available online.
Exclusive: Visit www.UltimateScholarshipBook.com and enter code OH161126 for updates on this award.

[1612] • Minority Teaching Fellows Program
Tennessee Student Assistance Corporation
312 Rosa L. Parks Avenue, 9th Floor, Nashville, TN 37243
Phone: 800-342-1663
Email: tsac.aidinfo@tn.gov
https://www.collegefortn.org/about-financial-aid/
Purpose: To support minority Tennessee students pursuing degrees in education.
Eligibility: Applicants must be minority Tennessee residents and U.S. citizens and classified as college juniors, seniors or graduate students. Students must be full-time undergraduate students or at least half-time graduate students enrolled in courses creditable to teacher certification. Applicants must not be a licensed teacher and have a minimum 2.5 GPA.
Target applicant(s): College students. Graduate school students. Adult students.
Minimum GPA: 2.5
Amount: $5,000.
Number of awards: Varies.
Deadline: April 15.
How to apply: Applications are available online.
Exclusive: Visit www.UltimateScholarshipBook.com and enter code TE161226 for updates on this award.

[1613] • Minority Undergraduate Retention Grant
State of Wisconsin Higher Educational Aids Board
P.O. Box 7885, Madison, WI 53707
Phone: 608-267-2206
Email: heabmail@wisconsin.gov
https://heab.state.wi.us
Purpose: To support minority Wisconsin students with their higher education expenses.
Eligibility: Applicants must be minority Wisconsin residents who are undergraduate students. Students must be enrolled at least half-time in independent, tribal or Wisconsin Technical College institutions. Applicants can not be first year undergraduate students.
Target applicant(s): College students. Adult students.
Amount: $250-$2,500.
Number of awards: Varies.
Deadline: As soon as possible after October 1.
How to apply: Applications are available online.
Exclusive: Visit www.UltimateScholarshipBook.com and enter code ST161326 for updates on this award.

[1614] • Mississippi Association of Broadcasters Scholarship Program
Mississippi Association of Broadcasters
Scholarship Committee, 855 South Pear Orchard Road, Suite 403, Ridgeland, MS 39157
Phone: 601-957-9121
Email: info@msbroadcasters.org
https://www.msbroadcasters.org/
Purpose: To support students involved in broadcasting.
Eligibility: Applicants must be Mississippi residents and be enrolled in an accredited broadcast curriculum at a Mississippi two- or four-year college.
Target applicant(s): College students. Adult students.
Amount: $1,500.
Number of awards: Varies.
Deadline: October 30.
How to apply: Applications are available online. An application form, essay and up to three letters of recommendation are required.
Exclusive: Visit www.UltimateScholarshipBook.com and enter code MI161426 for updates on this award.

[1615] • Mississippi Eminent Scholars Grant (MESG)
Mississippi Office of Student Financial Aid
3825 Ridgewood Road, Jackson, MS 39211-6453
Phone: 800-327-2980
Email: sfa@ihl.state.ms.us
https://www.msfinancialaid.org/
Purpose: To recognize academically high performing Mississippi students.
Eligibility: Applicants must be U.S. citizens or eligible noncitizens and current legal residents of Mississippi who are enrolled as full-time, first-time-in-college undergraduates. Applicants must have a high school GPA of 3.5 and a minimum ACT of 29. National Merit/National Achievement semifinalists with a 3.5 grade point average qualify without the test score.
Target applicant(s): High school students. College students. Adult students.
Minimum GPA: 3.5
Amount: $2,500.
Number of awards: Varies.
Scholarship may be renewable.
Deadline: September 15.
How to apply: Applicants must complete an MTAG/MESG application and either a FAFSA or a Statement of Certification (a waiver for completing the FAFSA).
Exclusive: Visit www.UltimateScholarshipBook.com and enter code MI161526 for updates on this award.

[1616] • Mississippi Scholarship
American Radio Relay League Foundation
225 Main Street, Newington, CT 06111-1494
Phone: 860-594-0200
Email: foundation@arrl.org

https://www.arrl.org/scholarship-program
Purpose: To provide financial assistance to Mississippi students who are amateur radio operators and are studying electronics or communications.
Eligibility: Applicants must be licensed amateur radio operators and residents of Mississippi who attend an institution of higher learning in Mississippi. They must be seeking a bachelor's degree or higher in electronics, communication or a related field, and they must be under 30 years old.
Target applicant(s): High school students. College students. Graduate school students. Adult students.
Amount: $500.
Number of awards: 1.
Deadline: January 10.
How to apply: Applications are available online.
Exclusive: Visit www.UltimateScholarshipBook.com and enter code AM161626 for updates on this award.

[1617] • Mississippi Tuition Assistance Grant (MTAG)
Mississippi Office of Student Financial Aid
3825 Ridgewood Road, Jackson, MS 39211-6453
Phone: 800-327-2980
Email: sfa@ihl.state.ms.us
https://www.msfinancialaid.org/
Purpose: To assist financially needy Mississippi students to afford tuition.
Eligibility: Applicants must be current legal residents of Mississippi who are enrolled as full-time undergraduates. Applicants must have a high school grade-point average of 2.5 and a minimum ACT of 15.
Target applicant(s): High school students. College students. Adult students.
Minimum GPA: 2.5
Amount: $500-$1,000.
Number of awards: Varies.
Scholarship may be renewable.
Deadline: September 15.
How to apply: Applicants must complete an MTAG/MESG application and either a FAFSA or a Statement of Certification (a waiver for completing the FAFSA).
Exclusive: Visit www.UltimateScholarshipBook.com and enter code MI161726 for updates on this award.

[1618] • Missouri 4-H Foundation Scholarships
Missouri 4-H Foundation
109 Whitten Hall, Columbia, MO 65211
Phone: 573-882-2680
Email: 4hfoundation@missouri.edu
https://extension.missouri.edu/programs/missouri-4-h-foundation/scholarships
Purpose: To aid present and former Missouri 4-H members who are preparing for careers in veterinary medicine and animal science.
Eligibility: Applicants must be Missouri residents who are present or former members of 4-H and who are rising undergraduate freshmen. They must have a GPA of 2.5 or higher on a four-point scale. Selection is based on 4-H achievements, stated career goals and financial need.
Target applicant(s): High school students.
Minimum GPA: 2.5

Amount: $500-$2,500.
Number of awards: 60.
Deadline: March 1.
How to apply: Applications are available online. An application form, transcript, financial information and essay are required.
Exclusive: Visit www.UltimateScholarshipBook.com and enter code MI161826 for updates on this award.

[1619] • Missouri Oratorical Contest
American Legion, Department of Missouri
P.O. Box 179, Jefferson City, MO 65102
Phone: 800-846-9023
Email: bmayberry@missourilegion.org
http://www.missourilegion.org/
Purpose: To enhance high school students' experience with and understanding of the U.S. Constitution. The contest will help develop students' leadership skills and civic appreciation, as well as the ability to deliver thoughtful, insightful orations regarding U.S. citizenship and its inherent responsibilities.
Eligibility: Applicants must be high school students under the age of 20 who are U.S. citizens or legal residents and residents of the state. Students first give an oration within their state and winners compete at the national level. The oration must be related to the Constitution of the United States focusing on the duties and obligations citizens have to the government. It must be in English and be between eight and ten minutes. There is also an assigned topic which is posted on the website, and it should be between three and five minutes.
Target applicant(s): High school students.
Amount: $2,000-$20,000.
Number of awards: Varies.
Deadline: November 30.
How to apply: Application information is available by email.
Exclusive: Visit www.UltimateScholarshipBook.com and enter code AM161926 for updates on this award.

[1620] • Missouri State Thespian Scholarships
Missouri State Thespians
Attn.: Jennifer Forrest-James, 419 Sorrento Drive, Ballwin, MO 63021
Email: mstscholarships@gmail.com
https://missourithespians.org
Purpose: To support young Missouri thespians.
Eligibility: Applicants must be high school seniors, International Thespians members and delegates to the conference. Students must have a GPA of 2.5 or higher and audition in the category of performance, technical or theatre education.
Target applicant(s): High school students.
Minimum GPA: 2.5
Amount: $1,000.
Number of awards: Up to 11.
Deadline: November 1.
How to apply: Applications are available online. An application form is required.
Exclusive: Visit www.UltimateScholarshipBook.com and enter code MI162026 for updates on this award.

[1621] • Mitch Daniels Early Graduation Scholarship

Indiana Commission for Higher Education
101 West Ohio Street, Suite 300, Indianapolis, IN 46204-4206
Phone: 888-528-4719
Email: awards@che.in.gov
https://www.in.gov/che/
Purpose: To support Indiana students who graduate from a publicly supported high school at least one year early.
Eligibility: Applicants must be Indiana residents and U.S. citizens or eligible non-citizens. Students must have attended a publicly supported high school on a full-time equivalency basis for at least the last two semesters before the student graduated and been awarded a minimum of a Core 40 high school diploma by the end of grade 11. Applicants must enroll as full-time, degree-seeking students at an eligible institution.
Target applicant(s): High school students.
Amount: $4,000.
Number of awards: Varies.
Deadline: August 31.
How to apply: Applications are available online.
Exclusive: Visit www.UltimateScholarshipBook.com and enter code IN162126 for updates on this award.

[1622] • Mitchell Scholarship

Mitchell Institute
75 Washington Avenue, Suite 2E, Portland, ME 04101
Phone: 207-773-7700
Email: info@mitchellinstitute.org
http://mitchellinstitute.org/scholarship/
Purpose: To provide educational opportunities to students in Maine.
Eligibility: Applicants must be legal residents of Maine graduating from a public high school in Maine and attending a two- or four-year program at an accredited college. Scholarships are based on academic performance, community service and financial need. One scholarship is given out at every Maine public high school, with one extra scholarship per county intended for first-generation college students. While the deadline for the application is April 1, supporting materials have a deadline of May 1.
Target applicant(s): High school students.
Amount: $2,500-$10,000.
Number of awards: Varies.
Scholarship may be renewable.
Deadline: April 1.
How to apply: Applications are available online.
Exclusive: Visit www.UltimateScholarshipBook.com and enter code MI162226 for updates on this award.

[1623] • Monetary Award Program (MAP)

Illinois Department of Public Health
Center for Rural Health, 525-535 West Jefferson Street, Springfield, IL 62761
Phone: 217-782-4977
Email: dph.nesp@illinois.gov
http://www.dph.illinois.gov
Purpose: To provide grants to eligible Illinois undergraduate students.
Eligibility: Applicants must be residents of Illinois, enrolled at a MAP-approved Illinois institution and carry a minimum of three hours per term. Applicants must also demonstrate financial need and maintain satisfactory academic progress.
Target applicant(s): High school students. College students. Adult students.
Amount: Varies.
Number of awards: Varies.
Scholarship may be renewable.
Deadline: April 1.
How to apply: Complete the Free Application for Federal Student Aid (FAFSA).
Exclusive: Visit www.UltimateScholarshipBook.com and enter code IL162326 for updates on this award.

[1624] • Montana CattleWomen Scholarship

Montana CattleWomen Inc.
Attn.: Marilyn Roen, Scholarship Committee Chair, 2606 North 17th Road, Worden, MT 59088
Phone: 406-442-3420
Email: lorrie@mtbeef.org
https://montanacattlewomen.org/resources
Purpose: To support a Montana university or college student whose major field of study benefits the livestock industry.
Eligibility: Applicants must be from Montana and currently enrolled as a sophomore or higher in an accredited university or college in Montana. Students must have a cumulative grade point average of 2.7 or more and demonstrate a need for financial assistance. Selection is based on demonstrated need and the student's potential to benefit the livestock industry. Preference is given to students from an agricultural background and/or members or children of members of Montana CattleWomen.
Target applicant(s): College students. Adult students.
Minimum GPA: 2.7
Amount: $1,000.
Number of awards: 1.
Deadline: May 1.
How to apply: Application instructions are available online. A personal resume, academic resume, high school and college transcripts, essay, applicant photo, photo of family living situation and three recommendation letters are required.
Exclusive: Visit www.UltimateScholarshipBook.com and enter code MO162426 for updates on this award.

[1625] • Montana University System Honor Scholarship

Montana University System
Student Financial Services (SFS), Scholarship Department, P.O. Box 203101, Helena, MT 59620-3201
Phone: 800-537-7508
https://mus.edu/Prepare/Pay/Scholarships/
Purpose: To reward Montana high school seniors with outstanding academic achievement.
Eligibility: Applicants must have a 3.4 or higher GPA, meet specific college preparatory requirements and have been enrolled in an accredited Montana high school for at least three years prior to graduation, including their senior year. Applicants must also be accepted to and attend a Montana public university or community college.
Target applicant(s): High school students.
Minimum GPA: 3.4
Amount: Up to $20,000.
Number of awards: Up to 200.
Scholarship may be renewable.
Deadline: March 15.
How to apply: Applications are available from your high school guidance counselor.

Exclusive: Visit www.UltimateScholarshipBook.com and enter code MO162526 for updates on this award.

[1626] • Moody Scholar Program
Moody Foundation
2302 Post Office, St # 704, Galveston, TX 77550
https://moodyf.org/moody-scholars/
Purpose: To support students enrolled in a Texas college.
Eligibility: Applicants must be ranked in the top 25 percent of their graduating class. Award is renewable for up to four years of undergraduate work. Evidence of financial need is required.
Target applicant(s): High school students.
Minimum GPA: 3.0
Amount: $4,000.
Number of awards: 80.
Scholarship may be renewable.
Deadline: November 30.
How to apply: Applications are available online.
Exclusive: Visit www.UltimateScholarshipBook.com and enter code MO162626 for updates on this award.

[1627] • MSAA Scholarship Program
Minnesota State Archery Association
c/o Cheri Irlbeck, MSAA Secretary, 33266 County Hwy 4, Sanborn, MN 56083
Phone: 507-640-1683
Email: secretary.msaa@mnarchery.org
http://www.mnarchery.org
Purpose: To promote the sport of archery and encourage outstanding students to attend the college of their choice.
Eligibility: Students must apply as a senior in high school or within the first three years of college. The applicant must be a Minnesota State Archery Association member in good standing.
Target applicant(s): High school students. College students. Adult students.
Amount: $500.
Number of awards: 2.
Deadline: June 15.
How to apply: Applications are available online.
Exclusive: Visit www.UltimateScholarshipBook.com and enter code MI162726 for updates on this award.

[1628] • MSPE Kenneth B. Fishbeck, P.E., Memorial Grant
Michigan Society of Professional Engineers
P.O. Box 160, Parma, MI 49269
Phone: 517-487-9388
Email: dfnedervelt@outlook.com
https://www.michiganspe.org/scholarships/
Purpose: To aid Michigan students planning to pursue higher education in engineering.
Eligibility: Applicants must be high school seniors who are Michigan residents and U.S. citizens. They must have a GPA of 3.0 or higher for the sophomore and junior years of high school and a composite ACT score of 26 or higher. Students must be accepted into a Michigan institution of higher learning that has an ABET-accredited engineering degree program. Selection is based on personal essay, awards and recognitions, GPA, ACT scores and any college-level coursework completed.
Target applicant(s): High school students.
Minimum GPA: 3.0

Amount: Varies.
Number of awards: Varies.
Deadline: February 17.
How to apply: Applications are available online. An application form, transcript, personal essay and ACT score report are required.
Exclusive: Visit www.UltimateScholarshipBook.com and enter code MI162826 for updates on this award.

[1629] • Murray Watson Jr. Scholarship
Brazos Education Lending
5609 Crosslake Parkway, Waco, TX 76712
Email: info@brazos.us.com
https://studentloans.com/scholarship/
Purpose: To recognize and reward academically talented and highly motivated Texas students.
Eligibility: Applicants must be graduating high school seniors, current college students or graduate students at least 17 years of age and residents of Texas. Applicants must have a minimum 3.3 GPA or equivalent and be accepted to or currently enrolled in an accredited college or university in the U.S. Applicants must submit a personal letter that describes their career and educational goals. A list of activities or a current resume and a copy of an academic transcript are also required.
Target applicant(s): High school students. College students. Graduate school students. Adult students.
Minimum GPA: 3.3
Amount: $5,000.
Number of awards: 12.
Deadline: May only apply once in an academic year (defined as August - July).
How to apply: Applications are available online.
Exclusive: Visit www.UltimateScholarshipBook.com and enter code BR162926 for updates on this award.

[1630] • Music Committee Scholarship
American Legion, Department of Kansas
1314 SW Topeka Boulevard, Topeka, KS 66612
Phone: 785-232-9315
https://kansaslegion.org/
Purpose: To support Kansas students who have distinguished themselves in the field of music.
Eligibility: Applicants must be Kansas residents who are currently high school seniors. They must have a proven talent and background in music and be planning to major or minor in music at an approved Kansas post-secondary institution. Applicants must also be average or better students. Three letters of recommendation with only one from a music teacher, a 1040 income statement, a high school transcript and a statement describing why they are applying for the scholarship are required. The scholarship will be awarded in two installments; recipients must maintain a C average to receive the second installment.
Target applicant(s): High school students.
Amount: $1,000.
Number of awards: 1.
Deadline: February 15.
How to apply: Applications are available online.
Exclusive: Visit www.UltimateScholarshipBook.com and enter code AM163026 for updates on this award.

Scholarship Directory (State of Residence)

[1631] • My Action Plan for College Young Scholars Initiative
My Action Plan for College
P.O. Box 121, Hull, MA 02045
Phone: 508-631-0936
Email: ernest@mapforcollege.com
https://mapforcollege.com/scholarships/
Purpose: To support 8th graders who plan to attend college.
Eligibility: Students must be current eighth graders with a goal to attend college one day. Applicants must submit a 250-300 word hand-written essay including the topics of academic and extra-curricular plans for college. Selection is based on the overall strength of the application.
Target applicant(s): Junior high students or younger.
Amount: $125-$750.
Number of awards: 6.
Deadline: September 5.
How to apply: Essays should be submitted by mail.
Exclusive: Visit www.UltimateScholarshipBook.com and enter code MY163126 for updates on this award.

[1632] • NACA Northern Plains Regional Student Leadership Scholarship
National Association for Campus Activities
13 Harbison Way, Columbia, SC 29212
Phone: 803-732-6222
Email: info@naca.org
https://www.naca.org/resources/scholarships-grants/scholarships.html
Purpose: To help students who are working toward undergraduate or graduate degrees that lead to careers in student activities or services.
Eligibility: Applicants must be undergraduate students taking at least six credits per semester and be enrolled in or have previously earned a degree from a college or university in Wisconsin or the Upper Peninsula of Michigan. Applicants must also have demonstrated leadership and service to their campus community.
Target applicant(s): College students. Adult students.
Amount: $500.
Number of awards: Varies.
Deadline: November 30.
How to apply: Applications are available online.
Exclusive: Visit www.UltimateScholarshipBook.com and enter code NA163226 for updates on this award.

[1633] • NACA South Student Leadership Scholarships
National Association for Campus Activities
13 Harbison Way, Columbia, SC 29212
Phone: 803-732-6222
Email: info@naca.org
https://www.naca.org/resources/scholarships-grants/scholarships.html
Purpose: To provide financial assistance to Southeast student leaders.
Eligibility: Students must hold a significant campus leadership position, demonstrate significant leadership skills and abilities and make significant contributions through on- or off-campus volunteering. Students must attend school in Alabama, Florida, Georgia, Mississippi, North Carolina, South Carolina, Tennessee, Virginia or Puerto Rico.
Target applicant(s): College students. Adult students.
Amount: Varies.
Number of awards: Up to 4.
Deadline: November 30.
How to apply: Applications are available online.
Exclusive: Visit www.UltimateScholarshipBook.com and enter code NA163326 for updates on this award.

[1634] • NADCA Indiana Chapter 25 Scholarship
Foundry Educational Foundation
1695 North Penny Lane, Schaumburg, IL 60173
Phone: 847-490-9200
Email: info@fefinc.org
http://www.fefinc.org/scholarships.html
Purpose: To aid Indiana region students who have a demonstrated interest in the die cast and cast metal industries.
Eligibility: Applicants must be residents of Indiana or of a state that is adjacent to Indiana. They must be enrolled at an Indiana school or at a Foundry Educational Foundation (FEF) member school located in a state adjacent to Indiana. They must have prior work experience in manufacturing, the die casting industry or the cast metal industry. Preference will be given to applicants who are studying a subject related to the die casting industry. Selection is based on the overall strength of the application.
Target applicant(s): High school students. College students. Adult students.
Amount: Varies.
Number of awards: Varies.
Deadline: October 7.
How to apply: Applications are available online. An application form and supporting documents are required.
Exclusive: Visit www.UltimateScholarshipBook.com and enter code FO163426 for updates on this award.

[1635] • Nancy Penn Lyons Scholarship Fund
Community Foundation for Greater Atlanta Inc.
50 Hurt Plaza, Suite 449, Atlanta, GA 30303
Phone: 404-688-5525
Email: info@cfgreateratlanta.org
https://cfgreateratlanta.org/scholarships/
Purpose: To provide assistance to needy students who have been accepted to prestigious or out-of-state universities.
Eligibility: Applicants must be graduating high school seniors who have been Georgia residents for at least one year. They must have an ACT score of 22 or higher or an SAT composite score of 1000 or higher and a GPA of 3.0 or greater. They must have participated in community service and have financial need, and they must not be attending a public institution in the state of Georgia.
Target applicant(s): High school students.
Minimum GPA: 3.0
Amount: $6,000.
Number of awards: 5.
Scholarship may be renewable.
Deadline: March 1.
How to apply: Applications are available online.
Exclusive: Visit www.UltimateScholarshipBook.com and enter code CO163526 for updates on this award.

[1636] • Nathaniel Alston Student Achievement Award
Pennsylvania Society of Physician Assistants
P.O. Box 128, Greensburg, PA 15601
Phone: 724-836-6411
Email: hohpac@windstream.net

https://pspa.net/
Purpose: To aid outstanding physician assistant students attending school in Pennsylvania.
Eligibility: Applicants must be current students in good standing who are enrolled in an accredited physician assistant program in the state of Pennsylvania. They must be current Pennsylvania Society of Physician Assistants (PSPA) members who demonstrate outstanding leadership and participation in their schools and communities. Selection is based on the overall strength of the application.
Target applicant(s): Graduate school students. Adult students.
Amount: $2,000.
Number of awards: Varies.
Deadline: June 30.
How to apply: Applications are available online. An application form and personal essay are required.
Exclusive: Visit www.UltimateScholarshipBook.com and enter code PE163626 for updates on this award.

[1637] • NCRA Scholarship
North Carolina Racquetball Association (NCRA)
195 Hill Lane, Sneads Ferry, NC 28460
Phone: 910-327-4441
Email: ncra@ncracquetball.com
http://www.ncracquetball.com
Purpose: To support those NCRA junior racquetball participants who wish to pursue higher education after high school.
Eligibility: Applicants must be NCRA members in good standing, be a senior in high school or a college undergraduate and have a "B" overall grade point average.
Target applicant(s): High school students. College students. Adult students.
Minimum GPA: 3.0
Amount: $500.
Number of awards: 4.
Deadline: June 15.
How to apply: Applications are available online or by calling the NCRA office. The application includes a release form, at least one letter of reference, the teacher report form, a personal essay, an official transcript and a photo.
Exclusive: Visit www.UltimateScholarshipBook.com and enter code NO163726 for updates on this award.

[1638] • NDVA Waiver of Tuition
Nebraska Department of Veterans' Affairs
State Service Office, 3800 Village Drive, P.O. Box 85816, Lincoln, NE 68501-5816
Phone: 402-420-4021
Email: ndva@nebraska.gov
https://veterans.nebraska.gov/
Purpose: To provide assistance to children and spouses of Nebraska veterans.
Eligibility: Applicants must be the children, stepchildren, spouses or widows of veterans who died of a service-connected injury or illness, became totally and permanently disabled as a result of military service or was classified as MIA or POW during armed conflict after August 4th, 1964. They must be Nebraska residents and attend a state college, university or community college.
Target applicant(s): High school students. College students. Adult students.
Amount: Full tuition.
Number of awards: Varies.
Scholarship may be renewable.
Deadline: Prior to the start of any term.
How to apply: Applications are available from your County Veterans Service Officer.
Exclusive: Visit www.UltimateScholarshipBook.com and enter code NE163826 for updates on this award.

[1639] • Nebraska Academy of Sciences High School Scholarships
Nebraska Academy of Sciences Inc.
P.O. Box 22988, Lincoln, NE 68542-2988
Phone: 402-472-2644
Email: nebacad@unl.edu
https://nebraskaacademyofsciences.wildapricot.org/High-School-Scholarships
Purpose: To assist Nebraska high school students.
Eligibility: There are six scholarships given to Nebraska high school seniors including those who plan to study geology, earth sciences, prairie and soil conservation, climate and environmental change and business and the environment.
Target applicant(s): High school students.
Amount: $300-$750.
Number of awards: Varies.
Deadline: March 1.
How to apply: Applications are available online. Requirements vary by the individual award.
Exclusive: Visit www.UltimateScholarshipBook.com and enter code NE163926 for updates on this award.

[1640] • Nebraska Actuaries Club Scholarship
Nebraska Actuaries Club
Ben Bosco, 7505 N. 117th Cir, Omaha, NE 68142
Email: bennyb_07@yahoo.com
https://www.nebraskaactuariesclub.org/scholarships.html
Purpose: To aid Nebraska students who plan to major in actuarial science or a related subject.
Eligibility: Applicants must be U.S. high school seniors who are planning to attend an accredited college or university located in the state of Nebraska. They must be planning to major in actuarial science, economics, mathematics or statistics and must intend to pursue an actuarial career. Applicants must have demonstrated mathematical ability. Selection is based on the overall strength of the application.
Target applicant(s): High school students.
Amount: $2,000-$4,000.
Number of awards: 4.
Deadline: March 31.
How to apply: Applications are available online. An application form, recommendation letter and standardized test scores are required.
Exclusive: Visit www.UltimateScholarshipBook.com and enter code NE164026 for updates on this award.

[1641] • Nebraska Elks Association Vocational Scholarship
Nebraska State Elks Association
Dr. Candace Walton, Attn: Vocational Scholarship, 4019 Cannon Road, Grand Island, NE 68803
https://www.nebraskaelks.org/
Purpose: To support Nebraska students pursuing vocational studies.

Eligibility: Applicants must be graduating high school seniors from a Nebraska high school. Students must intend to study a vocational program at a community college or other two-year programs. Applicants must be U.S. citizens.
Target applicant(s): High school students.
Amount: Varies.
Number of awards: Varies.
Deadline: February 15.
How to apply: Applications are available online.
Exclusive: Visit www.UltimateScholarshipBook.com and enter code NE164126 for updates on this award.

[1642] • Ned McWherter Scholars Program
Tennessee Student Assistance Corporation
312 Rosa L. Parks Avenue, 9th Floor, Nashville, TN 37243
Phone: 800-342-1663
Email: tsac.aidinfo@tn.gov
https://www.collegefortn.org/about-financial-aid/
Purpose: To assist outstanding Tennessee students who are planning to attend a Tennessee college or university.
Eligibility: Applicants must be U.S. citizens or legal residents and Tennessee residents who are graduating high school seniors. They must have plans to attend an eligible Tennessee undergraduate institution full-time and have a GPA of 3.5 or higher. Applicants must have a combined math and reading SAT score of at least 1280 or an ACT composite score of 29 or higher. Selection is based on the overall strength of the application.
Target applicant(s): High school students.
Minimum GPA: 3.5
Amount: $6,000.
Number of awards: Varies.
Scholarship may be renewable.
Deadline: February 15.
How to apply: Applications are available online. An application form, official transcripts and standardized test scores are required.
Exclusive: Visit www.UltimateScholarshipBook.com and enter code TE164226 for updates on this award.

[1643] • Need Based Tuition Waiver Program
Massachusetts Department of Higher Education
Office of Student Financial Assistance, 454 Broadway, Suite 200, Revere, MA 02151
Phone: 617-727-9420
Email: osfa@osfa.mass.edu
https://www.mass.gov/handbook/massachusetts-financial-aid-programs
Purpose: To support Massachusetts students who are in need of supplemental financial aid.
Eligibility: Applicants must live in the state of Massachusetts for at least one year prior to the beginning of the school year, and they must be enrolled in a state-funded college. They must be in an undergraduate program with at least three credits per semester. Students must not owe any refunds on prior scholarships and cannot have any defaulted government loans. They must also be able to show proof of financial need.
Target applicant(s): High school students. College students. Adult students.
Amount: Up to full tuition.
Number of awards: Varies.
Deadline: Contact the financial aid office at the institution applicant is attending or plans to attend.
How to apply: Applications are available at college financial aid offices.
Exclusive: Visit www.UltimateScholarshipBook.com and enter code MA164326 for updates on this award.

[1644] • Nevada Women's Fund Scholarships
Nevada Women's Fund
770 Smithridge Drive, Suite 300, Reno, NV 89502
Phone: 775-786-2335
Email: info@nevadawomensfund.org
http://www.nevadawomensfund.org
Purpose: To improve the lives of women and children in northern Nevada.
Eligibility: Northern Nevada residents and those attending northern Nevada schools receive preference. Applicants must be enrolled in an accredited two or four year degree or certifying program, will take a minimum of 6 to 8 credits per semester and have a cumulative GPA of 3.0.
Target applicant(s): High school students. College students. Graduate school students. Adult students.
Minimum GPA: 3.0
Amount: $500-$5,000.
Number of awards: Varies.
Deadline: January 6.
How to apply: Applications are available online or from several offices listed on the website.
Exclusive: Visit www.UltimateScholarshipBook.com and enter code NE164426 for updates on this award.

[1645] • New England Regional Student Program
New England Board of Higher Education
45 Temple Place, Boston, MA 02111
Phone: 617-357-9620
Email: rsp@nebhe.org
http://www.nebhe.org
Purpose: The program lowers tuition rates for New England students who must travel out of state for their desired major.
Eligibility: Students must be residents of Connecticut, Maine, Massachusetts, New Hampshire, Rhode Island or Vermont and attend a school in another of those states that offers an RSP program in their major. The major must not be available at an in-school state.
Target applicant(s): High school students. College students. Graduate school students. Adult students.
Amount: Varies.
Number of awards: Varies.
Scholarship may be renewable.
Deadline: Contact the sponsor to confirm the deadline.
How to apply: Students should note that they are interested in the RSP program on their regular college application.
Exclusive: Visit www.UltimateScholarshipBook.com and enter code NE164526 for updates on this award.

[1646] • New Hampshire Charitable Foundation Statewide Student Aid Program
New Hampshire Charitable Foundation
37 Pleasant Street, Concord, NH 03301-4005
Phone: 603-225-6641
Email: jessica.kierstead@nhcf.org
https://www.nhcf.org/how-can-we-help-you/
Purpose: To allow New Hampshire students to access over 50 scholarship and loan opportunities through a single application.
Eligibility: Applicants must be New Hampshire residents who plan to pursue a bachelor's degree or graduate students of any age. They must enroll at least half-time to qualify.

Target applicant(s): High school students. College students. Graduate school students. Adult students.
Amount: $100-$7,500.
Number of awards: Varies.
Deadline: April 12 (under 24); For those over 24: December 15.
How to apply: Applications are available online.
Exclusive: Visit www.UltimateScholarshipBook.com and enter code NE164626 for updates on this award.

[1647] • New Jersey Oratorical Contest

American Legion, Department of New Jersey
171 Jersey Street, Build #5, 2nd Floor, Trenton, NJ 08611
Phone: 609-695-5418
Email: adjutant@njamericanlegion.org
https://www.njamericanlegion.org/family-and-youth
Purpose: To enhance high school students' experience with and understanding of the U.S. Constitution. The contest will help develop students' leadership skills and civic appreciation, as well as the ability to deliver thoughtful, insightful orations regarding U.S. citizenship and its inherent responsibilities.
Eligibility: Applicants must be high school students under the age of 20 who are U.S. citizens or legal residents and residents of the state. Students first give an oration within their state and winners compete at the national level. The oration must be related to the Constitution of the United States focusing on the duties and obligations citizens have to the government. It must be in English and be between eight and ten minutes. There is also an assigned topic which is posted on the website, and it should be between three and five minutes.
Target applicant(s): High school students.
Amount: Up to $25,000.
Number of awards: Varies.
Deadline: February 3.
How to apply: Application information is available by email: ray@njamericanlegion.org.
Exclusive: Visit www.UltimateScholarshipBook.com and enter code AM164726 for updates on this award.

[1648] • New Jersey State Elks Special Children's Committee Scholarship

New Jersey State Elks
665 Rahway Avenue, P.O. Box 1596, Woodbridge, NJ 07095
Phone: 732-326-1300
Email: ndame788@aol.com
http://www.njelks.org/index.php/our-programs/scholarship-information
Purpose: To assist students with physical handicaps in obtaining higher education.
Eligibility: Applicants must be New Jersey residents and high school seniors with physical handicaps. They must demonstrate financial need and excellent academic standing.
Target applicant(s): High school students.
Amount: $4,000-$10,000.
Number of awards: 4.
Scholarship may be renewable.
Deadline: April 25.
How to apply: Applications are available online or by phone.
Exclusive: Visit www.UltimateScholarshipBook.com and enter code NE164826 for updates on this award.

[1649] • New Jersey World Trade Center Scholarship

New Jersey Higher Education Student Assistance Authority
P.O. Box 540, Trenton, NJ 08625
Phone: 800-792-8670
Email: clientservices@hesaa.org
http://www.hesaa.org
Purpose: To support the children and spouses of those who died as a result of the World Trade Center attack.
Eligibility: Applicants must be a dependent child or spouse of a New Jersey resident who was killed in the September 11, 2001 attack, died from resulting injuries or exposure to the attack site or are missing and presumed dead as a result of the attack. Students must be full-time undergraduates, and they may attend any eligible school in the U.S.
Target applicant(s): High school students. College students. Adult students.
Amount: Full tuition.
Number of awards: Varies.
Scholarship may be renewable.
Deadline: March 1.
How to apply: Applications are available online.
Exclusive: Visit www.UltimateScholarshipBook.com and enter code NE164926 for updates on this award.

[1650] • New Mexico Scholars

New Mexico Higher Education Department
2044 Galisteo Street, Suite 4, Santa Fe, NM 87505-2100
Phone: 505-476-8400
Email: cesaria.tapia1@state.nm.us
https://hed.state.nm.us/financial-aid
Purpose: To support New Mexico undergraduate students with financial need attend postsecondary institutions in New Mexico.
Eligibility: Applicants must be undergraduate students attending selected New Mexico public institutions or designated private non-profit colleges, meet family income requirements, be under the age of 22 and have graduated in the top 5 percent of their high school class, have a minimum ACT score of 25 or a minimum 1140 SAT score. Students must be enrolled full time.
Target applicant(s): College students.
Amount: Up to full tuition.
Number of awards: Varies.
Scholarship may be renewable.
Deadline: Contact the college's financial aid office to confirm the deadline.
How to apply: Contact your financial aid office. Must complete a FAFSA.
Exclusive: Visit www.UltimateScholarshipBook.com and enter code NE165026 for updates on this award.

[1651] • New York Legion Auxiliary Department Scholarship

American Legion Auxiliary, Department of New York
112 State Street, Suite 1310, Albany, NY 12207
Phone: 518-463-1162
Email: nyalaeducation@gmail.com
http://www.deptny.org/?page_id=2128
Purpose: To assist students whose parents, grandparents or great-grandparents served in the Armed Forces during wartime.
Eligibility: Applicants must be children, grandchildren or great-grandchildren of veterans who served in the Armed Forces during World War I, World War II, the Korean Conflict, the Vietnam War, Grenada/Lebanon, Panama, the Persian Gulf or War on Terrorism. Students must

be high school seniors or graduates and be New York State residents and U.S. citizens.
Target applicant(s): High school students.
Amount: $1,000.
Number of awards: 1.
Deadline: March 1.
How to apply: Applications are available online.
Exclusive: Visit www.UltimateScholarshipBook.com and enter code AM165126 for updates on this award.

[1652] • New York Legion Auxiliary District Scholarships

American Legion Auxiliary, Department of New York
112 State Street, Suite 1310, Albany, NY 12207
Phone: 518-463-1162
Email: nyalaeducation@gmail.com
http://www.deptny.org/?page_id=2128
Purpose: To provide financial assistance to children, grandchildren and great-grandchildren of war veterans.
Eligibility: Applicants must be children, grandchildren or great-grandchildren of Armed Forces veterans of World War I, World War II, the Korean Conflict, the Vietnam War, Grenada/Lebanon, Panama, the Persian Gulf or War on Terrorism. Students must be high school seniors and must be U.S. citizens and New York State residents.
Target applicant(s): High school students.
Amount: $1,000.
Number of awards: 1.
Deadline: March 1.
How to apply: Applications are available online.
Exclusive: Visit www.UltimateScholarshipBook.com and enter code AM165226 for updates on this award.

[1653] • New York Oratorical Contest

American Legion, Department of New York
1304 Park Boulevard, Troy, NY 12180
Phone: 518-463-2215
Email: info@nylegion.org
https://nylegion.net/programs-services/
Purpose: To enhance high school students' experience with and understanding of the U.S. Constitution. The contest will help develop students' leadership skills and civic appreciation, as well as the ability to deliver thoughtful, insightful orations regarding U.S. citizenship and its inherent responsibilities.
Eligibility: Applicants must be high school students under the age of 20 who are U.S. citizens or legal residents and residents of the state. Students first give an oration within their state and winners compete at the national level. The oration must be related to the Constitution of the United States focusing on the duties and obligations citizens have to the government. It must be in English and be between eight and ten minutes. There is also an assigned topic which is posted on the website, and it should be between three and five minutes.
Target applicant(s): High school students.
Amount: $2,000-$6,000.
Number of awards: 4.
Deadline: March 8.
How to apply: Application information is available by contacting the local American Legion Post.
Exclusive: Visit www.UltimateScholarshipBook.com and enter code AM165326 for updates on this award.

[1654] • New York State Association of Agricultural Fairs/New York State Showpeople's Association Scholarships

New York State Association of Agricultural Fairs
Norma W. Hamilton, Executive Secretary, 67 Verbeck Avenue, Schaghticoke, NY 12154
Phone: 518-753-4956
Email: carousels4@aol.com
http://nyfairs.org/scholarships.htm
Purpose: To aid New York students who are preparing for careers in agriculture, fair management or the outdoor amusement business.
Eligibility: Applicants must be New York state residents or must attend school in the state of New York and must be high school seniors or current undergraduate students. They can be enrolled in or planning to enroll in any degree program but additional consideration may be given to those pursuing degrees in agriculture, fair management or the outdoor amusement business. They must be attending or planning to attend an accredited postsecondary institution and must be active in local fairs. Selection is based on fair participation, leadership, citizenship and essay.
Target applicant(s): High school students. College students. Adult students.
Amount: $1,500.
Number of awards: Up to 10.
Deadline: Second Friday in April.
How to apply: Applications are available online. An application form, personal essay, two recommendation letters and a transcript are required.
Exclusive: Visit www.UltimateScholarshipBook.com and enter code NE165426 for updates on this award.

[1655] • New York State Society of Physician Assistants Scholarship

New York State Society of Physician Assistants
N83 W13410 Leon Road, Menomonee Falls, WI 53051
Email: info@nysspa.org
http://www.nysspa.org
Purpose: To aid New York State Society of Physician Assistants (NYSSPA) student members.
Eligibility: Applicants must be NYSSPA members who are currently enrolled in an ARC-PA accredited physician assistant degree program in the state of New York. They must be in the professional phase of their degree program. Previous NYSSPA Scholarship winners, NYSSPA board members and NYSSPA committee chairs are ineligible. Selection is based on academic achievement, financial need and professional activities.
Target applicant(s): College students. Graduate school students. Adult students.
Amount: $1,500.
Number of awards: Varies.
Deadline: August 31.
How to apply: Applications are available online. An application form, one reference letter, a personal essay and a financial aid award letter are required.
Exclusive: Visit www.UltimateScholarshipBook.com and enter code NE165526 for updates on this award.

[1656] • New York State USBC Scholarships

New York State USBC
55 Edgewood Drive, Batavia, NY 14020
Phone: 585-343-3736
Email: bowlny300@yahoo.com
https://www.bowlny.com/youth_scholarships.php
Purpose: To assist bowlers in New York.

Eligibility: Applicants must be members of a New York State USBC Youth certified league and be high school seniors. Selection includes academic and extracurricular achievement.
Target applicant(s): High school students.
Amount: Up to $4,000.
Number of awards: Varies.
Scholarship may be renewable.
Deadline: April 1.
How to apply: Applications are available online.
Exclusive: Visit www.UltimateScholarshipBook.com and enter code NE165626 for updates on this award.

[1657] • New York State USBC Spirit Awards
New York State USBC
55 Edgewood Drive, Batavia, NY 14020
Phone: 585-343-3736
Email: bowlny300@yahoo.com
https://www.bowlny.com/youth_scholarships.php
Purpose: To assist bowlers in grades 8-11 in New York.
Eligibility: Applicants must demonstrate sportsmanship, commitment and leadership.
Target applicant(s): Junior high students or younger. High school students.
Amount: $250-$750.
Number of awards: 3.
Deadline: April 1.
How to apply: Bowlers are nominated by their bowling coach.
Exclusive: Visit www.UltimateScholarshipBook.com and enter code NE165726 for updates on this award.

[1658] • New York Women in Communications Foundation Scholarships
New York Women in Communications Foundation
660 International Drive, Suite 600, McLean, VA 22102
Phone: 212-251-7255
Email: info@nywici.org
http://www.nywici.org/students/scholarships
Purpose: To support high school, college and graduate students currently residing in New York, New Jersey, Connecticut or Pennsylvania with the pursuit of a degree in a communications-related field.
Eligibility: Applicants are required to have a minimum GPA of 3.2 and must be majoring, declaring a major or pursuing an advanced degree in a communications-related field at an accredited college or university in the United States. Graduate students must already be members of New York Women in Communications.
Target applicant(s): High school students. College students. Graduate school students. Adult students.
Minimum GPA: 3.2
Amount: $10,000.
Number of awards: 18-20.
Deadline: January 19.
How to apply: Applications are available online.
Exclusive: Visit www.UltimateScholarshipBook.com and enter code NE165826 for updates on this award.

[1659] • Nightingale Awards of Pennsylvania Scholarship
Nightingale Awards of Pennsylvania
2400 Ardmore Boulevard, Suite 302, Pittsburgh, PA 15221
Phone: 412-871-3353
Email: info@nightingaleawards.org
http://www.nightingaleawards.org/scholarships/
Purpose: To support Pennsylvania nursing students.
Eligibility: Applicants must be Pennsylvania residents who are enrolled in or have been accepted into a Pennsylvania nursing program in licensed practical nursing, registered nursing or graduate-level nursing practice. They must have completed at least one course in nursing and must have a B average or better. Previous recipients of this scholarship are ineligible. Selection is based on academic achievement, leadership ability, extracurricular activities and professional dedication to nursing.
Target applicant(s): College students. Graduate school students. Adult students.
Minimum GPA: 3.0
Amount: Varies.
Number of awards: Varies.
Deadline: April 15.
How to apply: Applications are available online. An application form, official transcript, two recommendation letters, a copy of the applicant's nursing program acceptance letter, a personal statement and a research proposal abstract (Ph.D. applicants only) are required.
Exclusive: Visit www.UltimateScholarshipBook.com and enter code NI165926 for updates on this award.

[1660] • Nissan Scholarship
Nissan North America
P.O. Box 685003, Franklin, TN 37068
Phone: 800-647-7261
Email: webmaster@nissanusa.com
https://www.nissanusa.com
Purpose: To assist Mississippi high school seniors in attending public two-year or four-year colleges.
Eligibility: Applicants must have a minimum GPA of 2.5 and a minimum ACT score of 20 or SAT score of 820, have demonstrated financial need and be accepted as a full-time student at a Mississippi public college or university.
Target applicant(s): High school students.
Minimum GPA: 2.5
Amount: Full tuition.
Number of awards: Varies.
Deadline: March 1.
How to apply: No application is necessary. However, students must mail an essay, resume, high school transcript with ACT or SAT score and FAFSA results to Mississippi Office of Student Financial Aid, 3825 Ridgewood Road, Jackson, MS 39211-6453.
Exclusive: Visit www.UltimateScholarshipBook.com and enter code NI166026 for updates on this award.

[1661] • NJ Student Tuition Assistance Reward Scholarship (STARS)
New Jersey Higher Education Student Assistance Authority
P.O. Box 540, Trenton, NJ 08625
Phone: 800-792-8670
Email: clientservices@hesaa.org
http://www.hesaa.org

The Ultimate Scholarship Book 2026
Scholarship Directory (State of Residence)

Purpose: To support community college students in New Jersey who graduated from high school with excellent academic standing.
Eligibility: Applicants must have graduated from a New Jersey high school in the top 20 percent of their class, and they must have been state residents for at least 12 months prior to graduation. Students must enroll full-time in their home county college by the fifth semester after graduating from high school.
Target applicant(s): High school students.
Minimum GPA: 3.0
Amount: Up to full tuition.
Number of awards: Varies.
Scholarship may be renewable.
Deadline: September 15.
How to apply: Applications are available at college financial aid offices.
Exclusive: Visit www.UltimateScholarshipBook.com and enter code NE166126 for updates on this award.

[1662] • NJ Student Tuition Assistance Reward Scholarship II
New Jersey Higher Education Student Assistance Authority
P.O. Box 540, Trenton, NJ 08625
Phone: 800-792-8670
Email: clientservices@hesaa.org
http://www.hesaa.org
Purpose: To support NJ STARS students who are transferring to four-year colleges.
Eligibility: Applicants must be county college graduates with an associate's degree, and they must have a GPA of at least 3.0. They must either be NJ STARS recipients or have other full state or federal aid during the semester in which they graduate. Students must be enrolled full-time at a New Jersey four-year college within two semesters of graduation.
Target applicant(s): College students. Adult students.
Minimum GPA: 3.0
Amount: Up to $2,500 a year.
Number of awards: Varies.
Scholarship may be renewable.
Deadline: September 15.
How to apply: Applications are available at college financial aid offices.
Exclusive: Visit www.UltimateScholarshipBook.com and enter code NE166226 for updates on this award.

[1663] • NJCDCA Scholarship
New Jersey Cheerleading and Dance Coaches Association
Doug Linden, 276 Stamets Road, Milford, NJ 08848
Phone: 908-797-6262
Email: doug.linden@njcdca.com
https://www.njcheerleading.com
Purpose: To recognize New Jersey senior cheerleaders and dancers for their academic achievements and athletic excellence.
Eligibility: Applicants must be a high school senior and member of a cheer or dance team that is a New Jersey Cheerleading and Dance Coaches Association member. Selection is based on academic and athletic achievement, community involvement, personal essay and coach recommendation.
Target applicant(s): High school students.
Amount: Varies.
Number of awards: Varies.
Deadline: December 15.
How to apply: Applications are available online and include the application form, a personal essay, an official high school transcript and a coach recommendation form.
Exclusive: Visit www.UltimateScholarshipBook.com and enter code NE166326 for updates on this award.

[1664] • NJSCA High School Scholarship
New Jersey School Counselor Association Inc.
Sheila Brewer, NJSCA High School Awards Chair, 5 Split Rock Place, Moorestown, NJ 08057
Phone: 609-893-8141
Email: sbrewer@pemb.org
http://www.njsca.org
Purpose: To spread awareness of the importance of the role of school counselors.
Eligibility: Applicants must be New Jersey residents who will be graduating in the year of application. They must have been accepted to and plan to enroll in an institution of higher learning. A 300-500 word essay is required.
Target applicant(s): High school students.
Amount: Varies.
Number of awards: Varies.
Deadline: April 3.
How to apply: Applications are available online.
Exclusive: Visit www.UltimateScholarshipBook.com and enter code NE166426 for updates on this award.

[1665] • NMASBO High School Scholarships
New Mexico Association of School Business Officials
P.O. Box 7535, Albuquerque, NM 87194-7535
Phone: 505-923-3283
Email: info@nmasbo.org
https://nmasbo.org
Purpose: To support graduating high school seniors in New Mexico.
Eligibility: Students must have at least a 3.0 GPA. Applicants must submit an essay and two letters of recommendation. Students must plan to attend a New Mexico college or university on a full-time basis.
Target applicant(s): High school students.
Minimum GPA: 3.0
Amount: $1,500.
Number of awards: 6.
Deadline: March 1.
How to apply: Applications are available online.
Exclusive: Visit www.UltimateScholarshipBook.com and enter code NE166526 for updates on this award.

[1666] • NNM American Society of Mechanical Engineers Scholarship
Los Alamos National Laboratory Foundation
1112 Plaza del Norte, Espanola, NM 87532
Phone: 505-753-8890
Email: tony@lanlfoundation.org
http://www.lanlfoundation.org
Purpose: To support undergraduate students from northern New Mexico who are majoring in mechanical engineering.
Eligibility: Students must have at least a 3.25 GPA, and they must have either an SAT score (combined Math plus Critical Reading only) of at least 930 or an ACT score of at least 19. Applicants must submit an essay and two letters of recommendation.

Target applicant(s): High school students. College students. Adult students.
Minimum GPA: 3.25
Amount: $1,000-$20,000.
Number of awards: Varies.
Deadline: January 16.
How to apply: Applications are available online.
Exclusive: Visit www.UltimateScholarshipBook.com and enter code LO166626 for updates on this award.

[1667] • Norman and Ruth Good Educational Endowment

Lincoln Community Foundation
215 Centennial Mall South, Suite 100, Lincoln, NE 68508
Phone: 402-474-2345
Email: robertm@lcf.org
http://www.lcf.org/scholarships
Purpose: To assist Nebraska students.
Eligibility: Applicants must be attending a private college in Nebraska and must be in their junior or senior year. Applicants may not apply if the scholarship money is to be used for summer programs or schools that are not valid degree-granting institutions.
Target applicant(s): College students. Adult students.
Minimum GPA: 2.5
Amount: $2,000.
Number of awards: Varies.
Scholarship may be renewable.
Deadline: March 15.
How to apply: Applications are available online.
Exclusive: Visit www.UltimateScholarshipBook.com and enter code LI166726 for updates on this award.

[1668] • Norman S. and Betty M. Fitzhugh Fund

Greater Kanawha Valley Foundation
1600 Huntington Square, 900 Lee Street, East, Charleston, WV 25301
Phone: 304-346-3620
Email: shoover@tgkvf.org
https://tgkvf.org/scholarship-information/
Purpose: To provide financial assistance to West Virginia residents wishing to earn a college degree.
Eligibility: Applicants must be full-time students (12 hours) and demonstrate good moral character and academic excellence. Students must have a minimum 2.5 GPA and minimum ACT score of 20.
Target applicant(s): High school students. College students. Adult students.
Minimum GPA: 2.5
Amount: $1,000.
Number of awards: 1.
Scholarship may be renewable.
Deadline: February 1.
How to apply: Applications are available online or by email.
Exclusive: Visit www.UltimateScholarshipBook.com and enter code GR166826 for updates on this award.

[1669] • North Carolina 4-H Development Fund Scholarships

North Carolina 4-H Youth Development
Shannon McCollum, Extension 4-H Associate, NCCES 4-H/FCS Team, NCSU Campus Box 7655, Raleigh, NC 27695
Phone: 919-515-8486
Email: shannon_mccollum@ncsu.edu
https://nc4h.ces.ncsu.edu/
Purpose: To help North Carolina students who have been involved with the 4-H Club who want to go to college in the state.
Eligibility: Applicants must be enrolling as undergraduates at a four-year North Carolina college or university or a junior or community college in the state, provided the program of study is transferable to a four-year college. Students must also have a strong record of 4-H Club participation, have an excellent high school academic record and show an aptitude for college work through SAT scores. An application form, transcript, photo page and two recommendation letters are required. For some of the awards, financial need is necessary. Some awards have geographic restrictions to regions of the state while others are for a degree program or a specific college or university. Some scholarships are renewable.
Target applicant(s): High school students.
Amount: Varies.
Number of awards: Varies.
Scholarship may be renewable.
Deadline: February 1.
How to apply: Applications are available through each county cooperative extension office in North Carolina by phone or online.
Exclusive: Visit www.UltimateScholarshipBook.com and enter code NO166926 for updates on this award.

[1670] • North Carolina Community College Grant

College Foundation of North Carolina
2917 Highwoods Boulevard, Raleigh, NC 27604
Phone: 866-866-2362
https://www.cfnc.org/pay-for-college/apply-for-financial-aid/
Purpose: To assist North Carolina community college students.
Eligibility: Applicants must be North Carolina residents, demonstrate financial need and attend a North Carolina community college for at least six credit hours per semester. Selection is based on financial need.
Target applicant(s): College students. Adult students.
Amount: Up to $2,200.
Number of awards: Varies.
Deadline: As soon as possible after October 1.
How to apply: Application is made by completing the FAFSA.
Exclusive: Visit www.UltimateScholarshipBook.com and enter code CO167026 for updates on this award.

[1671] • North Carolina Education Lottery Scholarship

College Foundation of North Carolina
2917 Highwoods Boulevard, Raleigh, NC 27604
Phone: 866-866-2362
https://www.cfnc.org/pay-for-college/apply-for-financial-aid/
Purpose: To provide financial assistance to North Carolina residents with financial need who are attending North Carolina colleges and universities.
Eligibility: Applicants must be enrolled for at least six credit hours per semester in an undergraduate degree-seeking program at an eligible North Carolina institution and meet satisfactory academic progress requirements. Students who meet the same criteria as the Federal Pell Grant are eligible for the scholarship. Awards are given on a rolling basis, and students should

apply as soon as possible after October 1 when the FAFSA is available. The deadline is the priority deadline of the college.
Target applicant(s): College students. Adult students.
Amount: Up to $3,768.
Number of awards: Varies.
Deadline: December 1.
How to apply: Qualified students who submit the Free Application for Federal Student Aid (FAFSA) will be considered.
Exclusive: Visit www.UltimateScholarshipBook.com and enter code CO167126 for updates on this award.

[1672] • North Carolina Oratorical Contest
American Legion, Department of North Carolina
4 N. Blount Street, P.O. Box 26657, Raleigh, NC 27611-6657
Phone: 919-832-7506
Email: nclegion@nc.rr.com
https://nclegion.org
Purpose: To enhance high school students' experience with and understanding of the U.S. Constitution. The contest will help develop students' leadership skills and civic appreciation, as well as the ability to deliver thoughtful, insightful orations regarding U.S. citizenship and its inherent responsibilities.
Eligibility: Applicants must be high school students under the age of 20 who are U.S. citizens or legal residents and residents of the state. Students first give an oration within their state and winners compete at the national level. The oration must be related to the Constitution of the United States focusing on the duties and obligations citizens have to the government. It must be in English and be between eight and ten minutes. There is also an assigned topic which is posted on the website, and it should be between three and five minutes.
Target applicant(s): High school students.
Amount: $20,00-$25,000.
Number of awards: Varies.
Deadline: April 21-23.
How to apply: Application information is available by contacting the local post by email.
Exclusive: Visit www.UltimateScholarshipBook.com and enter code AM167226 for updates on this award.

[1673] • North Dakota Career Builders Scholarship
North Dakota University System Career Builders Scholarship
North Dakota University System, 10th Floor, State Capitol, 600 East Boulevard Avenue, Dept. 215, Bismarck, ND 58505-0230
Phone: 701-328-2960
Email: ndfinaid@ndus.edu
https://ndus.edu/paying-for-college/
Purpose: To support students interested in high-need and emerging occupations in North Dakota.
Eligibility: Applicants must be enrolled in programs at the associate's level and below or other programs, up to and including bachelor programs, that are four semesters or six quarters in length. Students must be enrolled in a qualifying certificate or degree program at a North Dakota institution that directly relates to high-need occupations. Applicants must live in North Dakota and work within North Dakota for three years following program completion to retain the scholarship.
Target applicant(s): College students. Adult students.
Minimum GPA: 2.5
Amount: Varies.
Number of awards: Varies.
Deadline: Contact the sponsor to confirm the deadline.
How to apply: Applications are available online.
Exclusive: Visit www.UltimateScholarshipBook.com and enter code NO167326 for updates on this award.

[1674] • North Dakota Dollars for Scholars
North Dakota Dollars for Scholars
P.O. Box 5509, Bismarck, ND 58506-5509
Phone: 701-328-5702
Email: statedirector@nddfs.org
https://northdakota.dollarsforscholars.org/index.php
Purpose: To support North Dakota students with their post-secondary education expenses.
Eligibility: Applicants must have graduated from a North Dakota high school or were home educated in North Dakota.
Target applicant(s): High school students. College students. Graduate school students. Adult students.
Amount: Up to $2,500.
Number of awards: Varies.
Deadline: April 1.
How to apply: Applications are available online.
Exclusive: Visit www.UltimateScholarshipBook.com and enter code NO167426 for updates on this award.

[1675] • North Dakota Jaycee JCI Senate Scholarship
North Dakota Jaycee JCI Senate
1372 32nd Street South #7, Fargo, ND 58103
Email: angiejelinek@hotmail.com
https://usjcisenate.org/index.php/scholarship-program
Purpose: To assist North Dakota students.
Eligibility: Applicants must be high school seniors who are planning to attend a two- or four-year college or a trade/technical college.
Target applicant(s): High school students.
Amount: $300.
Number of awards: 4.
Deadline: January 17.
How to apply: Applications are available online.
Exclusive: Visit www.UltimateScholarshipBook.com and enter code NO167526 for updates on this award.

[1676] • North Dakota Scholars Program
North Dakota University System
10th Floor, State Capitol, 600 East Boulevard Avenue, Dept. 215, Bismarck, ND 58505-0230
Phone: 701-328-2960
Email: ndus.inquiry@ndus.edu
https://ndus.edu/paying-for-college/
Purpose: To assist outstanding North Dakota high school students.
Eligibility: Applicants must be North Dakota high school seniors who have scored in the top 5 percent of all students in North Dakota who have taken the ACT by July 1 in the calendar year preceding college enrollment. They must have plans to attend a North Dakota postsecondary institution. Selection is based on academic merit.
Target applicant(s): High school students.
Amount: Full tuition.
Number of awards: Varies.
Scholarship may be renewable.
Deadline: July 1.
How to apply: Applications are available by written request. An application form and supporting documents are required.

Exclusive: Visit www.UltimateScholarshipBook.com and enter code NO167626 for updates on this award.

[1677] • North Dakota Scholarship

North Dakota Department of Public Instruction
600 E. Boulevard Avenue, Bismarck, ND 58505
Phone: 701-328-2244
Email: dpischoolapproval@nd.gov
https://www.nd.gov/dpi/north-dakota-scholarship-requirements-and-information
Purpose: To assist North Dakota high school seniors pursuing post-secondary education at a North Dakota college or university.
Eligibility: Applicants must plan to enroll full-time at an accredited North Dakota postsecondary institution and maintain a minimum 2.75 college GPA. The scholarship may not exceed $6,000 nor extend beyond six years. For additional scholarship criteria, see the information at the website listed below.
Target applicant(s): High school students.
Minimum GPA: 2.75
Amount: Up to $6,000.
Number of awards: Varies.
Scholarship may be renewable.
Deadline: June 7.
How to apply: Application instructions are available from your counselor.
Exclusive: Visit www.UltimateScholarshipBook.com and enter code NO167726 for updates on this award.

[1678] • North Dakota School Counseling Association

North Dakota School Counselor Association
1601 College Drive, Devils Lake, ND 58301
Email: shaina.hess@k12.nd.us
http://www.ndsca.us/awards.html
Purpose: To support North Dakota students pursuing post-secondary education.
Eligibility: Applicants must be graduating seniors from a North Dakota high school. Students must submit an application signed by their school counselor, write an essay and provide a letter of recommendation.
Target applicant(s): High school students.
Amount: $1,000.
Number of awards: Varies.
Deadline: December 1.
How to apply: Applications are available online.
Exclusive: Visit www.UltimateScholarshipBook.com and enter code NO167826 for updates on this award.

[1679] • North Dakota State Student Incentive Grant

North Dakota University System
10th Floor, State Capitol, 600 East Boulevard Avenue, Dept. 215, Bismarck, ND 58505-0230
Phone: 701-328-2960
Email: ndus.inquiry@ndus.edu
https://ndus.edu/paying-for-college/
Purpose: To assist North Dakota students who have financial need.
Eligibility: Applicants must be U.S. citizens or permanent residents. They must be North Dakota residents who are high school graduates or GED recipients and enrolled as full-time students in a North Dakota undergraduate program that lasts for at least one academic year. They must be first-time undergraduate students who have no defaulted student loans and who owe no Title IV grant or loan refunds. Selection is based on financial need.
Target applicant(s): High school students. College students. Adult students.
Amount: Varies.
Number of awards: Varies.
Scholarship may be renewable.
Deadline: As soon as possible after October 1.
How to apply: Application is made by completing the Free Application for Federal Student Aid (FAFSA).
Exclusive: Visit www.UltimateScholarshipBook.com and enter code NO167926 for updates on this award.

[1680] • North Texas State Fair Association Scholarship

North Texas Fair and Rodeo
2217 N. Carroll Boulevard, Denton, TX 76201
Phone: 940-387-2632
Email: nkimmey@ntfair.com
https://ntfair.com/get-involved/
Purpose: To support high school senior students by investing in their future.
Eligibility: Applicants must be high school seniors who have actively participated in school, community, FFA, FHA or 4-H activities. Selection is based on academic success, extracurricular involvement and financial need.
Target applicant(s): High school students.
Amount: $2,000.
Number of awards: Varies.
Deadline: June 1.
How to apply: Applications are available online and should include two letters of recommendation and two photos.
Exclusive: Visit www.UltimateScholarshipBook.com and enter code NO168026 for updates on this award.

[1681] • Northrop Grumman Scholarship

Society of Women Engineers
130 East Randolph Street, Suite 3500, Chicago, IL 60601
Phone: 877-793-4636
Email: scholarships@swe.org
https://swe.org/scholarships/
Purpose: To support high school seniors who reside in a community where Northrop Grumman has a major presence and who intend to pursue a career in engineering, computer science, mathematics or physics.
Eligibility: Scholarships are available for students living in each of Maryland's 23 counties, one scholarship for a student living in the city of Baltimore and two scholarships for applicants living in specific counties/communities from the following states: Alabama, California, Colorado, Florida, Illinois, New York, Ohio, Utah or Virginia. Applicants must have a minimum composite SAT score of 1150 or ACT score of 27 and a minimum GPA of 3.5.
Target applicant(s): College students. Adult students.
Minimum GPA: 3.5
Amount: $4,500.
Number of awards: 5.
Scholarship may be renewable.
Deadline: January 31.
How to apply: Applications are available online.

The Ultimate Scholarship Book 2026
Scholarship Directory (State of Residence)

Exclusive: Visit www.UltimateScholarshipBook.com and enter code SO168126 for updates on this award.

[1682] • Nursing Education Scholarship Program
Illinois Student Assistance Commission
1755 Lake Cook Road, Deerfield, IL 60015
Phone: 800-899-4722
Email: collegezone@isac.org
https://www.isac.org
Purpose: To increase the number of nurses in Illinois.
Eligibility: Applicants must be Illinois residents, having lived in the state for one year prior to applying and be U.S. citizens or permanent residents. Applicants must be accepted to or enrolled in an approved nursing program and demonstrate financial need. Scholarship recipients must agree to work as a nurse in Illinois after graduation.
Target applicant(s): High school students. College students. Graduate school students. Adult students.
Amount: Up to full tuition.
Number of awards: Varies.
Scholarship may be renewable.
Deadline: April 30.
How to apply: Applications are available online.
Exclusive: Visit www.UltimateScholarshipBook.com and enter code IL168226 for updates on this award.

[1683] • Nursing Incentive Scholarship Fund
Kentucky Board of Nursing
312 Whittington Parkway, Suite 300, Louisville, KY 40222-5172
Phone: 800-305-2042
https://kbn.ky.gov
Purpose: To support Kentucky students pursuing nursing education.
Eligibility: Applicants must be Kentucky residents accepted to a nursing program who are completing core nursing courses. Students in prelicensure and BSN completion programs must complete a minimum of 15 credit hours and nine credit hours if in a graduate nursing program. Applicants must maintain a high enough GPA to allow continuation in the program. Recipients must work as a full-time nurse in Kentucky for one year for each academic year funded.
Target applicant(s): College students. Graduate school students. Adult students.
Amount: $1,500-$3,000.
Number of awards: Varies.
Deadline: June 8.
How to apply: Applications are available online.
Exclusive: Visit www.UltimateScholarshipBook.com and enter code KE168326 for updates on this award.

[1684] • Nursing Loan-For-Service Program
New Mexico Higher Education Department
2044 Galisteo Street, Suite 4, Santa Fe, NM 87505-2100
Phone: 505-476-8400
Email: cesaria.tapia1@state.nm.us
https://hed.state.nm.us/financial-aid
Purpose: To support New Mexico students interested in nursing.
Eligibility: Applicants must be New Mexico residents and accepted into a nursing program at a New Mexico public college or university. Students must demonstrate financial need and be enrolled at least half-time. Applicants must declare their intent to practice as a health professional in a designated shortage area within the state of New Mexico. For every year of service provided in a designated shortage area within New Mexico, a portion of the loan will be forgiven.
Target applicant(s): College students. Graduate school students. Adult students.
Amount: Up to $16,000.
Number of awards: Varies.
Scholarship may be renewable.
Deadline: July 1.
How to apply: Applications are available online.
Exclusive: Visit www.UltimateScholarshipBook.com and enter code NE168426 for updates on this award.

[1685] • Nursing Student Loan
State of Wisconsin Higher Educational Aids Board
P.O. Box 7885, Madison, WI 53707
Phone: 608-267-2206
Email: heabmail@wisconsin.gov
https://heab.state.wi.us
Purpose: To encourage Wisconsin students to become licensed nurses.
Eligibility: Applicants must be Wisconsin residents who are undergraduate or graduate students enrolled at least half-time at an eligible in-state institution that prepares them to be licensed as nurses either RN or LPN. Students must agree to be employed as licensed nurses in the state of Wisconsin. For each of the first two years the applicants work as nurses or nurse educators and meet the eligibility criteria, 25 percent of the loan is forgiven.
Target applicant(s): College students. Graduate school students. Adult students.
Amount: Up to $3,000.
Number of awards: Varies.
Deadline: As soon as possible after October 1.
How to apply: Applications are available online.
Exclusive: Visit www.UltimateScholarshipBook.com and enter code ST168526 for updates on this award.

[1686] • NYWEA Major Environmental Career Scholarship
New York Water Environment Association Inc.
525 Plum Street, Suite 102, Syracuse, NY 13204
Phone: 877-556-9932
Email: theresa@nywea.org
https://www.nywea.org
Purpose: To support New York students who are planning to pursue a bachelor's degree in an environment-related subject.
Eligibility: Applicants must be residents of the state of New York and must be high school seniors who plan to enroll full-time in an environment-related bachelor's degree program no later than the fall following graduation. The programs could include but are not limited to environmental engineering, civil engineering with an environmental minor, chemical engineering with an environmental minor, hydrogeology with an environmental emphasis or biology or microbiology with an environmental emphasis. Selection is based on the overall strength of the application.
Target applicant(s): High school students.
Amount: $12,000.
Number of awards: 1.
Deadline: February 28.
How to apply: Applications are available online. An application form, official transcript, two recommendation letters and two personal essays are required.
Exclusive: Visit www.UltimateScholarshipBook.com and enter code NE168626 for updates on this award.

[1687] • Ohio Classical Conference Scholarship for Prospective Latin Teachers

Ohio Classical Conference
c/o Kelly Kusch, Covington Latin School, 21 East Eleventh Street, Covington, KY 41011
https://ohioclassicalconference.org/occ-scholarships-4/
Purpose: To aid Ohio students who are planning for careers as Latin teachers.
Eligibility: Applicants must be undergraduate students who are residents of Ohio or who are enrolled at an accredited Ohio postsecondary institution, or can be graduates of Ohio high schools pursuing study at accredited colleges or universities elsewhere in the U.S. They must have sophomore standing or above and be taking courses that provide preparation for a career as a K-12 Latin teacher. Selection is based on the overall strength of the application.
Target applicant(s): College students. Adult students.
Amount: $1,500.
Number of awards: 1.
Deadline: April 1.
How to apply: Applications are available online. An application form, official transcript, two recommendation letters, course schedule and personal statement are required.
Exclusive: Visit www.UltimateScholarshipBook.com and enter code OH168726 for updates on this award.

[1688] • Ohio Section Scholarships

Institute of Transportation Engineers - Ohio Section
1391 West 5th Avenue, PMB 157, Columbus, OH 43212
Phone: 614-898-7100
Email: gburch@hntb.com
http://ohioite.org/Scholarship
Purpose: To aid students who are enrolled in a degree program that is related to transportation engineering.
Eligibility: Applicants must be full-time students who are attending an ABET-accredited college or university located in the state of Ohio. They must be enrolled in a civil engineering or other transportation-related degree program and have a GPA of 2.5 or higher. Selection is based on academic achievement, stated career goals and extracurricular activities.
Target applicant(s): College students. Graduate school students. Adult students.
Minimum GPA: 2.5
Amount: $1,000.
Number of awards: 1.
Deadline: October 18.
How to apply: Applications are available online. An application form, personal statement, official transcript and one recommendation letter are required.
Exclusive: Visit www.UltimateScholarshipBook.com and enter code IN168826 for updates on this award.

[1689] • Ohio State Association/AOTF Scholarships

American Occupational Therapy Foundation
Attn: Jeanne Cooper, 4720 Montgomery Lane, Suite 202, Bethesda, MD 20814
Phone: 240-292-1034
Email: jcooper@aotf.org
https://www.tota.org/scholarships
Purpose: To aid Ohio occupational therapy students who are members of the American Occupational Therapy Foundation.
Eligibility: Applicants must be Ohio residents who are enrolled in an accredited occupational therapy associate's or first professional degree program at a school located in Ohio. Selection is based on the overall strength of the application.
Target applicant(s): College students. Graduate school students. Adult students.
Amount: Varies.
Number of awards: 3.
Deadline: October 2.
How to apply: Applications are available online. An application form, two personal references and a letter from the student's academic program director are required.
Exclusive: Visit www.UltimateScholarshipBook.com and enter code AM168926 for updates on this award.

[1690] • Ohio Turfgrass Foundation Scholarships

Ohio Turfgrass Foundation
Scholarships Committee, 2710 North Star Road, Columbus, OH 43221
Phone: 614-285-4683
Email: info@ohioturfgrass.org
https://ohioturfgrass.org
Purpose: To aid Ohio students who are pursuing higher education in subjects related to the turfgrass industry.
Eligibility: Applicants must be Ohio undergraduate or graduate students who are enrolled in a degree program that is related to turfgrass science. They must have a cumulative GPA of 2.5 or higher and a major GPA of 2.75 or higher. Selection is based on academic merit, professional commitment to the turfgrass industry and financial need.
Target applicant(s): College students. Graduate school students. Adult students.
Minimum GPA: 2.5
Amount: Varies.
Number of awards: Varies.
Deadline: November 1.
How to apply: Applications are available online. An application form, transcript and two recommendation letters are required.
Exclusive: Visit www.UltimateScholarshipBook.com and enter code OH169026 for updates on this award.

[1691] • Oklahoma Association of Broadcasters Scholarship

Oklahoma Association of Broadcasters
6520 North Western, Suite 104, Oklahoma City, OK 73116
Phone: 405-848-0771
Email: struby@oabok.org
https://oabok.org/careerseducation/scholarships/
Purpose: To support students attending an Oklahoma college or university majoring in broadcasting.
Eligibility: Applicants must be juniors or seniors at an Oklahoma college or university majoring in broadcasting. Students must be enrolled in at least 12 credit hours and maintain a B average in all courses. Applicants must be planning to enter the broadcast industry upon graduation.
Target applicant(s): College students. Adult students.
Minimum GPA: 3.0
Amount: $2,000.
Number of awards: Varies.
Deadline: February 9.
How to apply: Applications are available online.

Scholarship Directory (State of Residence)

Exclusive: Visit www.UltimateScholarshipBook.com and enter code OK169126 for updates on this award.

[1692] • Oklahoma Foundation for Excellence Academic All-State Scholarships

Oklahoma Foundation for Excellence
101 Park Avenue, Suite 420, Oklahoma City, OK 73102-7201
Phone: 405-236-0006
Email: info@ofe.org
http://www.ofe.org
Purpose: To reward Oklahoma students who have high academic achievement.
Eligibility: Applicants must be high school seniors who are nominated by their school principals or superintendents. They must have an ACT score of 30 or higher or an SAT score of 1370 or higher or be a semi-finalist for a National Merit, National Achievement or National Hispanic Scholarship. An essay is required.
Target applicant(s): High school students.
Amount: $1,500.
Number of awards: 100.
Deadline: December 3.
How to apply: Applications are available from your school.
Exclusive: Visit www.UltimateScholarshipBook.com and enter code OK169226 for updates on this award.

[1693] • Oklahoma Hall of Fame Scholarship

Oklahoma Hall of Fame
1400 Classen Drive, Oklahoma City, OK 73106
Phone: 405-235-4458
Email: gmc@oklahomahof.com
https://oklahomahof.com/scholarships
Purpose: To support Oklahoma high school seniors committed to attending an Oklahoma college or university.
Eligibility: Applicants must be Oklahoma high school seniors committed to attending an Oklahoma college or university. Students must be nominated for this scholarship by teachers, administrators or any adult not related to the student. Selection is based on the student's leadership roles, civic or community involvement, academic achievement and knowledge of and pride for Oklahoma.
Target applicant(s): High school students.
Amount: $6,000.
Number of awards: 1.
Deadline: September 22.
How to apply: Applications are available online.
Exclusive: Visit www.UltimateScholarshipBook.com and enter code OK169326 for updates on this award.

[1694] • Oklahoma Rural Rehabilitation Corporation Scholarships

Oklahoma Rural Rehabilitation Corporation
401 South Lewis Street, Stillwater, OK 74074-3518
Phone: 405-377-2010
Email: orrcjudy@att.net
http://www.orrcinc.com/scholarships.html
Purpose: To support rural high school graduates entering any private or public college or technical school in Oklahoma.
Eligibility: Applicants must be a rural Oklahoma resident and meet the state of Oklahoma requirements to graduate high school. Students must be entering any private or public college or technical school in Oklahoma during the following term.
Target applicant(s): High school students.
Amount: $200 up to $500.
Number of awards: Varies.
Deadline: April 15.
How to apply: Applications are available online.
Exclusive: Visit www.UltimateScholarshipBook.com and enter code OK169426 for updates on this award.

[1695] • Oklahoma Schools Insurance Group (OSIG) Scholarship

Oklahoma Schools Insurance Group (OSIG)
OSIG Scholarship Committee, P.O. Box 3068, Tulsa, OK 74101-3068
Phone: 866-444-0061
Email: OSIGdirector@gmail.com
https://osig.org/scholarships
Purpose: To support graduating high school seniors from each quadrant in the state of Oklahoma
Eligibility: Applicants must be graduating high school seniors enrolled in an OSIG member school in good standing. An essay submission on a provided topic, transcripts, letters of recommendation and ACT/SAT scores are required.
Target applicant(s): High school students.
Amount: $1,000-$2,000.
Number of awards: 12.
Deadline: March 4.
How to apply: Applications are available online.
Exclusive: Visit www.UltimateScholarshipBook.com and enter code OK169526 for updates on this award.

[1696] • Oklahoma Society of Land Surveyors Scholarships

Oklahoma Society of Land Surveyors
13905 Twin Ridge Road, Edmond, OK 73034
Phone: 405-202-5792
Email: osls@osls.org
https://www.osls.org
Purpose: To aid those who are preparing for careers in land surveying.
Eligibility: Applicants must be high school seniors who are planning to study land surveying in college, or they must be working toward licensure under the direct supervision of a professional land surveyor. High school seniors must be Oklahoma residents who have a GPA of 2.5 or higher. Applicants who are already working in the field must be associate members of the Oklahoma Society of Land Surveyors (OSLS) and must be recommended by a registered professional land surveyor. Selection is based on citizenship, leadership and commitment to professional land surveying.
Target applicant(s): High school students. College students. Adult students.
Minimum GPA: 2.5
Amount: Varies.
Number of awards: Varies.
Deadline: May 15.
How to apply: Applications are available online. An application form, official transcript, ACT scores and one recommendation letter are required.
Exclusive: Visit www.UltimateScholarshipBook.com and enter code OK169626 for updates on this award.

[1697] • Oklahoma State Fair Inc. Scholarship Program

Oklahoma State Fair
3001 General Pershing Boulevard, Oklahoma City, OK 73107
Phone: 405-948-6829
Email: Hkinyon@okstatefair.com
http://www.okstatefair.com
Purpose: To encourage Oklahoma students to continue their education.
Eligibility: Applicants must be graduating seniors from an accredited high school or homeschool in Oklahoma. Students must attend a college, university, vocation or technical school in Oklahoma. Applicants must be U.S. citizens and legal residents of Oklahoma. Students must have verifiable Oklahoma State Fair involvement beyond regular attendance in the areas of livestock, equine, creative arts competitions or other related forms of involvement.
Target applicant(s): High school students.
Amount: $2,500.
Number of awards: 10.
Deadline: March 8.
How to apply: Applications are available online.
Exclusive: Visit www.UltimateScholarshipBook.com and enter code OK169726 for updates on this award.

[1698] • Oklahoma Tuition Aid Grant Program (OTAG)

Oklahoma State Regents for Higher Education/Oklahoma Tuition Aid Grant Program (OTAG)
655 Research Parkway, Suite 200, Oklahoma City, OK 73104
Phone: 800-858-1840
Email: studentinfo@osrhe.edu
https://secure.okcollegestart.org/Financial_Aid_Planning/Oklahoma_Grants/Oklahoma_Tuition_Aid_Grant.aspx
Purpose: To assist Oklahoma undergraduates who are pursuing higher education in Oklahoma.
Eligibility: Applicants must be Oklahoma residents who are attending eligible undergraduate institutions in Oklahoma. They must demonstrate financial need. Qualified undocumented immigrants may be considered for this award.
Target applicant(s): High school students. College students. Adult students.
Amount: Up to $3,000.
Number of awards: Varies.
Deadline: May be school determined.
How to apply: Application is made by completing the FAFSA.
Exclusive: Visit www.UltimateScholarshipBook.com and enter code OK169826 for updates on this award.

[1699] • Oklahoma Tuition Equalization Grant Program (OTEG)

Oklahoma State Regents for Higher Education (OTEG)
655 Research Parkway, Suite 200, Oklahoma City, OK 73104
Phone: 800-858-1840
Email: studentinfo@osrhe.edu
https://secure.okcollegestart.org/Financial_Aid_Planning/Oklahoma_Grants/Oklahoma_Tuition_Equalization_Grant.aspx
Purpose: To provide financial assistance for Oklahoma residents who are attending eligible private institutions in the state.
Eligibility: Applicants must be enrolled in an undergraduate program at a private institution of higher learning full-time. They must have a family income of no more than $50,000, make satisfactory academic progress and not have already earned a bachelor's degree.
Target applicant(s): High school students. College students. Adult students.
Amount: $2,000.
Number of awards: Varies.
Deadline: As soon as possible after October 1, 2025.
How to apply: Eligible students who file a Free Application for Federal Student Aid (FAFSA) will be considered.
Exclusive: Visit www.UltimateScholarshipBook.com and enter code OK169926 for updates on this award.

[1700] • Oklahoma Youth with Promise Scholarship Fund

Oklahoma City Community Foundation
1000 North Broadway, Oklahoma City, OK 73102
Phone: 405-235-5603
Email: scholarships@occf.org
https://occf.org/scholarships/
Purpose: To provide educational assistance to students who graduated while in foster care.
Eligibility: Applicants must be graduates of Oklahoma high schools who were in the custody of the Oklahoma Department of Human Services at the time of graduation. They must have a minimum GPA of 2.0. Financial need is considered.
Target applicant(s): High school students. College students. Adult students.
Minimum GPA: 2.0
Amount: $3,000.
Number of awards: Varies.
Deadline: June 1.
How to apply: Applications are available online.
Exclusive: Visit www.UltimateScholarshipBook.com and enter code OK170026 for updates on this award.

[1701] • Oklahoma's Promise

Oklahoma State Regents for Higher Education/Oklahoma's Promise
655 Research Parkway, Suite 200, Oklahoma City, OK 73104
Phone: 800-858-1840
Email: studentinfo@osrhe.edu
https://www.okhighered.org/okpromise
Purpose: To assist qualified Oklahoma students in paying for college.
Eligibility: Applicants must be Oklahoma residents who are enrolled in the eighth, ninth, tenth or eleventh grade at an Oklahoma high school (homeschool students must be age 13, 14, 15 or 16). Applicants must be students whose parents' federal adjusted gross income does not exceed $60,000 with one or two dependent children; or $70,000 with three or four dependent children; or $80,000 with five or more dependent children.
Target applicant(s): Junior high students or younger. High school students.
Minimum GPA: 2.5
Amount: Full Tuition.
Number of awards: Varies.
Scholarship may be renewable.
Deadline: July 1.
How to apply: Applications are available online.
Exclusive: Visit www.UltimateScholarshipBook.com and enter code OK170126 for updates on this award.

[1702] • Oliver Joel and Ellen Pell Denny Healthcare Scholarship Fund

Winston-Salem Foundation
751 West Fourth Street, Suite 200, Winston-Salem, NC 27101
Phone: 336-725-2382
Email: StudentAid@wsfoundation.org
http://www.wsfoundation.org
Purpose: To aid North Carolina allied health students.
Eligibility: Applicants must be residents of North Carolina. They must be studying a subject in the field of allied health at an accredited postsecondary institution and have a GPA of 2.5 or higher. They must be seeking a first-time certificate, diploma, associate's degree or bachelor's degree. Master's degree holders are ineligible. Applicants must demonstrate financial need. Preference will be given to residents of Davidson, Davie, Forsyth, Stokes, Surry, Wilkes and Yadkin counties. Selection is based on the overall strength of the application.
Target applicant(s): High school students. College students. Adult students.
Minimum GPA: 2.5
Amount: Varies.
Number of awards: Varies.
Deadline: April 1.
How to apply: Applications are available online. An application form, official transcript, tax forms and financial aid award letter are required.
Exclusive: Visit www.UltimateScholarshipBook.com and enter code WI170226 for updates on this award.

[1703] • One Family Scholars Program

One Family Inc.
423 West Broadway, Suite 402, Boston, MA 02127
Phone: 617-423-0504
Email: scholars@onefamilyinc.org
http://www.onefamilyinc.org
Purpose: To provide financial support, mentoring, leadership development and other resources for Massachusetts low income single parents who are returning to school.
Eligibility: Applicants must be a single parent with a child under the age of 18 and have family earnings which fall 200 percent or more below the poverty level. They should have clear and obtainable career goals as well as the proven desire and ability to complete the chosen academic program. Students must continue to remain residents of the state of Massachusetts throughout the program, and they must remain active in attendance at required meetings, workshops and retreats. Applicants must be referred by two organizations that they are currently involved with or be endorsed by a partnering organization from One Family's network.
Target applicant(s): College students. Adult students.
Amount: Varies.
Number of awards: Varies.
Scholarship may be renewable.
Deadline: July 16.
How to apply: Applications are available by phone.
Exclusive: Visit www.UltimateScholarshipBook.com and enter code ON170326 for updates on this award.

[1704] • Opportunity Award

Louisiana Office of Student Financial Assistance
605 N. Fifth Street, Baton Rouge, LA 70802
Phone: 800-259-5626 x1012
Email: custserv@la.gov
https://mylosfa.la.gov/students-parents/scholarships-grants/tops/
Purpose: To aid Louisiana student residents.
Eligibility: Applicants must be Louisiana residents, U.S. citizens, have a minimum 2.5 GPA, have a minimum ACT score of 20 or equivalent SAT score and apply during their senior year in high school. Applicants must use the award at a Louisiana college or university.
Target applicant(s): High school students.
Minimum GPA: 2.5
Amount: Up to full tuition.
Number of awards: Varies.
Scholarship may be renewable.
Deadline: July 1.
How to apply: The application is the Free Application for Federal Student Aid (FAFSA). ACT or SAT scores must also be reported.
Exclusive: Visit www.UltimateScholarshipBook.com and enter code LO170426 for updates on this award.

[1705] • Opportunity Grant

Washington State Board for Community and Technical Colleges
P.O. Box 42495, 1300 Quince Street SE, Olympia, WA 98504-2495
Phone: 360-704-4400
Email: kwheeler@sbctc.edu
http://www.sbctc.edu/
Purpose: To assist Washington adult students.
Eligibility: Applicants must be adult students with financial need who are attending a community or technical college and who have a minimum 2.0 GPA. The grant provides funding for up to 45 credits over a maximum of three years and up to $1,000 for books and supplies per year. In addition, there are support services such as tutoring, career advising, emergency transportation and emergency child care.
Target applicant(s): High school students. College students. Adult students.
Minimum GPA: 2.0
Amount: Full tuition.
Number of awards: Varies.
Scholarship may be renewable.
Deadline: Contact the Opportunity Grant Coordinator at your community or technical college.
How to apply: Applicants must complete the Free Application for Federal Student Aid (FAFSA). Contact your college for more information.
Exclusive: Visit www.UltimateScholarshipBook.com and enter code WA170526 for updates on this award.

[1706] • Oratorical Contest Scholarship

American Legion, Department of Nebraska
Department Headquarters, P.O. Box 5205, Lincoln, NE 68505
Phone: 402-464-6338
Email: actsecylegion@windstream.net
http://www.nebraskalegion.net
Purpose: To encourage students to work hard to gain a comprehensive understanding of the Constitution of the United States of America. This contest also seeks to encourage high school students to become leaders, build effective communication skills and learn of and accept any and all responsibilities associated with being an American citizen.
Eligibility: Students, current and under age twenty, must be current attendees or residents of the state where they are to participate in the contest. Students must compete at the local American Legion Post level. The winner will then move on to the district contest, with the winners advancing to the area competition. Four winners will move forward to the state finals each January. Winners will be awarded for each of these competitions, however the national scholarship awards will be awarded to the top three students in the final round of the national contest.

Target applicant(s): Junior high students or younger. High school students.
Amount: $2,00-$20,000.
Number of awards: Varies.
Deadline: April 1.
How to apply: There is no application for this program.
Exclusive: Visit www.UltimateScholarshipBook.com and enter code AM170626 for updates on this award.

[1707] • Oregon Army National Guard
Oregon Army National Guard
Oregon Military Department, 1776 Militia Way SE, Salem, OR 97301
Phone: 800-452-7500
http://www.oregonarmyguard.com
Purpose: To support students from Oregon who are in the National Guard.
Eligibility: Students must serve in the Oregon Army National Guard. The educational program provides tuition and expenses for vocational school, distance learning, alternative credit programs or college. The Student Loan Repayment Program helps students in repaying up to $50,000. Students must take the Armed Services Vocational Aptitude Battery (ASVAB).
Target applicant(s): High school students. College students. Graduate school students. Adult students.
Amount: Varies.
Number of awards: Varies.
Scholarship may be renewable.
Deadline: Contact the sponsor to confirm the deadline.
How to apply: Applications are available online.
Exclusive: Visit www.UltimateScholarshipBook.com and enter code OR170726 for updates on this award.

[1708] • Oregon Farm Bureau Memorial Scholarships
Oregon Farm Bureau
1320 Capitol Street NE, Suite 200, Salem, OR 97301
Phone: 503-399-1701
Email: scholarship@oregonfb.org.
http://www.oregonfb.org
Purpose: To aid Oregon high school graduates who are preparing for careers in agriculture or forestry.
Eligibility: Applicants must be Oregon high school or home school graduates with a full year of completed college coursework. Students must be enrolled in a degree program that is related to agriculture or forestry. Selection is based on the overall strength of the application.
Target applicant(s): College students. Adult students.
Minimum GPA: 3.0
Amount: Varies.
Number of awards: 10-16.
Deadline: March 1.
How to apply: Applications are available online. An application form, transcript and three letters of recommendation are required.
Exclusive: Visit www.UltimateScholarshipBook.com and enter code OR170826 for updates on this award.

[1709] • OROS Scholarship
Organization of Rural Oklahoma Schools
P.O. Box 199, Dewar, OK 74431
Phone: 918-694-1572
https://www.orosok.org
Purpose: To support students in rural Oklahoma schools.
Eligibility: Applicants must be graduating high school seniors whose school is a registered member of Organization of Rural Oklahoma Schools. Scholarship will be awarded to one student from each quadrant of the state of Oklahoma.
Target applicant(s): High school students.
Amount: $2,500.
Number of awards: Varies.
Deadline: March 1.
How to apply: Applications are available online and must be submitted through the high school.
Exclusive: Visit www.UltimateScholarshipBook.com and enter code OR170926 for updates on this award.

[1710] • Our First Amendment Freedoms Art and Essay Contest
Anti-Defamation League Midwest
120 South LaSalle, Suite 1150, Chicago, IL 60603
Phone: 312-533-3939
Email: midwest@adl.org
https://chicago.adl.org/fivefreedoms/
Purpose: To support students interested in the First Amendment.
Eligibility: Applicants must be 6th to 12th grade students in Illinois, Wisconsin, Indiana, Minnesota, North Dakota or South Dakota. Students must submit an essay or artwork related to the First Amendment. Selection is based on the overall strength of the submission.
Target applicant(s): Junior high students or younger. High school students.
Amount: Up to $5,000.
Number of awards: Up to 14.
Deadline: December 31.
How to apply: Applications are available online.
Exclusive: Visit www.UltimateScholarshipBook.com and enter code AN171026 for updates on this award.

[1711] • Page Education Foundation Grants
Page Education Foundation
901 North 3rd Street, Suite 355, Minneapolis, MN 55458
Phone: 612-332-0406
https://www.page-ed.org/what-we-do/page-grant/
Purpose: To support students of color in Minnesota.
Eligibility: Applicants must be students of color who graduated from a Minnesota high school. Students must be enrolling full-time at an accredited Minnesota post-secondary institution and be willing to complete a minimum of 50 hours of volunteer tutoring for children.
Target applicant(s): High school students. College students. Graduate school students. Adult students.
Amount: Up to $2,500.
Number of awards: Varies.
Deadline: April 1.
How to apply: Applications are available online.
Exclusive: Visit www.UltimateScholarshipBook.com and enter code PA171126 for updates on this award.

[1712] • Palmetto Fellows Scholarship Program
South Carolina Commission on Higher Education
1122 Lady Street, Suite 400, Columbia, SC 29201
Phone: 803-737-2260
https://www.che.sc.gov

The Ultimate Scholarship Book 2026
Scholarship Directory (State of Residence)

Purpose: Monetary assistance is awarded to academically talented South Carolina high school seniors in an effort to encourage them to go to South Carolina colleges.
Eligibility: Applicants must have a minimum SAT score of 1200 or ACT score of 27, have a minimum 3.5 GPA, rank in the top 6 percent of their class, be residents of South Carolina, be enrolled in a public or private high school, be U.S. citizens or permanent residents and plan to attend a college in South Carolina.
Target applicant(s): High school students.
Minimum GPA: 3.5
Amount: Up to $7,500.
Number of awards: Varies.
Scholarship may be renewable.
Deadline: As soon as possible after October 1.
How to apply: Applications are available through your high school guidance office.
Exclusive: Visit www.UltimateScholarshipBook.com and enter code SO171226 for updates on this award.

[1713] • Paraprofessional Teacher Preparation Grant
Massachusetts Department of Higher Education
Office of Student Financial Assistance, 454 Broadway, Suite 200,
Revere, MA 02151
Phone: 617-727-9420
Email: osfa@osfa.mass.edu
https://www.mass.gov/handbook/massachusetts-financial-aid-programs
Purpose: To assist Massachusetts public school paraprofessionals who wish to become certified as full-time teachers.
Eligibility: Applicants must be employed for at least two years as a paraprofessional in a Massachusetts public school and enroll in an undergraduate program leading to teacher certification, or be employed as a paraprofessional for less than two years and enroll in an undergraduate course of study leading to teacher certification in a high need discipline. Applicants must not have previously earned a bachelor's degree.
Target applicant(s): High school students. College students. Adult students.
Amount: Up to $7,500.
Number of awards: Varies.
Scholarship may be renewable.
Deadline: September 1.
How to apply: Applications are available online.
Exclusive: Visit www.UltimateScholarshipBook.com and enter code MA171326 for updates on this award.

[1714] • Part-Time Grant
Maryland Higher Education Commission
Office of Student Financial Assistance, 6 North Liberty Street,
Baltimore, MD 21201
Phone: 800-974-1024
Email: osfamail@mhec.state.md.us
https://mhec.maryland.gov
Purpose: To assist part-time, degree-seeking undergraduates.
Eligibility: All applicants and their parents (if applicants are dependents of their parents) must be Maryland residents. Part-time applicants must complete the Free Application for Federal Student Aid (FAFSA) and contact the financial aid office of the college attending and request to be considered for the Part-Time Grant. Selection is based on financial need. Recommended to apply as soon after January 1 as possible.

Target applicant(s): High school students. College students. Adult students.
Amount: $200-$2,000.
Number of awards: Varies.
Scholarship may be renewable.
Deadline: March 1.
How to apply: Applications are available by request from the applicant's financial aid office. An application form and a completed FAFSA are required.
Exclusive: Visit www.UltimateScholarshipBook.com and enter code MA171426 for updates on this award.

[1715] • Part-Time Grants
Vermont Student Assistance Corporation
Scholarships, P.O. Box 2000, Winooski, VT 05404
Phone: 800-642-3177
Email: info@vsac.org
https://www.vsac.org/pay/student-aid-options/scholarships
Purpose: To assist Vermont part-time undergraduate students.
Eligibility: Applicants must be Vermont residents enrolled in or planning to enroll in an undergraduate degree or certificate program part-time (for less than 12 credits per semester). Those who have earned a bachelor's degree previously are ineligible. Selection is based on financial need.
Target applicant(s): High school students. College students. Adult students.
Amount: Varies.
Number of awards: Varies.
Deadline: February 15.
How to apply: Applications are available online. An application form, a completed FAFSA and supporting documents are required.
Exclusive: Visit www.UltimateScholarshipBook.com and enter code VE171526 for updates on this award.

[1716] • Part-Time TAP Program
New York State Higher Education Services Corporation (HESC)
99 Washington Avenue, Albany, NY 12255
Phone: 888-697-4372
Email: scholarships@hesc.ny.gov
http://www.hesc.ny.gov
Purpose: To support undergraduate students in the state of New York.
Eligibility: Applicants may attend the State University of New York, the City University of New York or any other public New York school. Students must be enrolled in 6-12 credits per semester, and they must have at least a 2.0 GPA. Applicants must have earned 12 credits per semester in at least two consecutive prior semesters. Students must demonstrate financial need through the FAFSA.
Target applicant(s): College students. Adult students.
Minimum GPA: 2.0
Amount: Varies.
Number of awards: Varies.
Scholarship may be renewable.
Deadline: June 30.
How to apply: Applications are available online.
Exclusive: Visit www.UltimateScholarshipBook.com and enter code NE171626 for updates on this award.

[1717] • Part-Time Tuition Aid Grant
New Jersey Higher Education Student Assistance Authority
P.O. Box 540, Trenton, NJ 08625
Phone: 800-792-8670

Email: clientservices@hesaa.org
http://www.hesaa.org
Purpose: To support part-time students who are attending county colleges in New Jersey.
Eligibility: Applicants must be residents of New Jersey for at least 12 months prior to college enrollment. They cannot have any previous degrees or defaulted student loans. Students must be enrolled in 6-11 credits per semester at an approved New Jersey county college, and they cannot be majoring in theology or divinity.
Target applicant(s): High school students. College students. Adult students.
Amount: Up to full tuition.
Number of awards: Varies.
Scholarship may be renewable.
Deadline: September 15 (Fall and Full-year) and February 15 (Spring).
How to apply: Applications are available through completion of the FAFSA.
Exclusive: Visit www.UltimateScholarshipBook.com and enter code NE171726 for updates on this award.

[1718] • Past Department Presidents' Junior Scholarship Award

American Legion Auxiliary, Department of California
San Francisco War Memorial Building, 401 Van Ness Avenue, Suite 319, San Francisco, CA 94102-4570
Phone: 415-861-5092
Email: headquarters@calegionaux.org
https://calegionaux.org/scholarships/education-scholarships/
Purpose: To reward American Legion Auxiliary Juniors.
Eligibility: Applicants must be California resident high school students planning to attend a California college or university, be American Legion Auxiliary members with three years as a Junior and be the children, grandchildren or great grandchildren of a veteran.
Target applicant(s): High school students.
Amount: Varies.
Number of awards: 1.
Deadline: Contact the sponsor to confirm the deadline.
How to apply: Applications are available online.
Exclusive: Visit www.UltimateScholarshipBook.com and enter code AM171826 for updates on this award.

[1719] • Patty and Melvin Alperin First Generation Scholarship

Rhode Island Foundation
One Union Station, Providence, RI 02903
Phone: 401-274-4564
Email: rbogert@rifoundation.org
https://rifoundation.org/grants-scholarships
Purpose: To provide opportunities for students whose parents did not graduate from college.
Eligibility: Applicants must be Rhode Island high school seniors and first-generation college students. They must be enrolled in an accredited institution of higher learning that offers either two-year or four-year degrees.
Target applicant(s): High school students.
Amount: $1,000-$1,500.
Number of awards: Varies.
Scholarship may be renewable.
Deadline: April 15.
How to apply: Applications are available online.
Exclusive: Visit www.UltimateScholarshipBook.com and enter code RH171926 for updates on this award.

[1720] • Pauahi Foundation Public Scholarships

Ke Ali'i Pauahi Foundation
567 South King Street, Suite 160, Honolulu, HI 96813
Phone: 808-534-3966
Email: scholarships@pauahi.org
http://www.pauahi.org
Purpose: To support students pursuing higher education.
Eligibility: Applicants must be attending a two- or four-year accredited institution in the state of Hawaii or the mainland United States enrolled in a classified, degree seeking program. Students must be enrolled full-time as undergraduates or graduates.
Target applicant(s): High school students. College students. Graduate school students. Adult students.
Amount: Varies.
Number of awards: Varies.
Deadline: January 31.
How to apply: Applications are available online.
Exclusive: Visit www.UltimateScholarshipBook.com and enter code KE172026 for updates on this award.

[1721] • Paul Flaherty Athletic Scholarship

American Legion, Department of Kansas
1314 SW Topeka Boulevard, Topeka, KS 66612
Phone: 785-232-9315
https://kansaslegion.org/
Purpose: To support student athletes.
Eligibility: Applicants must be high school seniors who have participated in high school athletics. Students must be average or better students and submit three letters of recommendation, one of which must be from a coach, a high school transcript, a 1040 income statement and an essay on the topic, "Why I Want to Go to College."
Target applicant(s): High school students.
Amount: $250.
Number of awards: 1.
Deadline: July 15.
How to apply: Applications are available online.
Exclusive: Visit www.UltimateScholarshipBook.com and enter code AM172126 for updates on this award.

[1722] • Paulina L. Sorg Scholarship

Hawaii Community Foundation - Scholarships
827 Fort Street Mall, Honolulu, HI 96813
Phone: 888-731-3863
Email: scholarships@hcf-hawaii.org
https://www.hawaiicommunityfoundation.org/
Purpose: To support nursing or physical therapy students in Hawaii.
Eligibility: Applicants must be college juniors, college seniors or graduate students attending full-time in a physical therapy degree program with a minimum 2.7 GPA.
Target applicant(s): College students. Graduate school students. Adult students.
Minimum GPA: 2.7
Amount: Varies.
Number of awards: Varies.
Deadline: February 28.
How to apply: To apply, register online, complete the online application and select the scholarships to which you wish to apply. In addition, mail

The Ultimate Scholarship Book 2026
Scholarship Directory (State of Residence)

the supporting materials: printed confirmation page from the online application, personal statement, copy of Student Aid Report (SAR) available at www.fafsa.ed.gov and official transcript.
Exclusive: Visit www.UltimateScholarshipBook.com and enter code HA172226 for updates on this award.

[1723] • Pennsylvania American Legion Essay Contest

American Legion, Department of Pennsylvania
P.O. Box 2324, Harrisburg, PA 17105-2324
Phone: 717-730-9100
Email: hq@pa-legion.com
http://www.pa-legion.com
Purpose: To encourage Pennsylvania high school students to develop research and writing skills.
Eligibility: Applicants must be Pennsylvania students who are in grades 9 through 12. They must submit an essay of 500 to 1,000 words on a topic that is determined by the scholarship committee. Selection is based on essay grammar, spelling, originality and factual accuracy.
Target applicant(s): High school students.
Amount: $2,500-$3,500.
Number of awards: Varies.
Deadline: January 9.
How to apply: Entry instructions are available online. An essay and cover page are required.
Exclusive: Visit www.UltimateScholarshipBook.com and enter code AM172326 for updates on this award.

[1724] • Pennsylvania Business Education Association Scholarship

Pennsylvania Business Education Association
c/o Renee Hughes, PBEA Scholarship Chair, 506 Pine Hill Drive, Pine Grove, PA 17963
Email: rhughes@pgasd.com
http://www.pbea.info
Purpose: To aid Pennsylvania business teacher education students.
Eligibility: Applicants must be enrolled in a business teacher education program at a postsecondary institution located in Pennsylvania. They must be pursuing an undergraduate degree, master's degree or teaching certificate in the subject. They must have a GPA of 3.0 or higher. Selection is based on the overall strength of the application.
Target applicant(s): College students. Graduate school students. Adult students.
Minimum GPA: 3.0
Amount: Up to $1,000.
Number of awards: 1.
Deadline: October 15.
How to apply: Applications are available online. An application form, official transcript, personal statement and three recommendation letters are required.
Exclusive: Visit www.UltimateScholarshipBook.com and enter code PE172426 for updates on this award.

[1725] • Pennsylvania Educational Gratuity Program

Pennsylvania Department of Military and Veterans Affairs
Building P-0-47, Fort Indiantown Gap, Annville, PA 17003-5002
Phone: 717-861-8910
Email: Ra-eg@pa.gov
http://www.dmva.pa.gov
Purpose: To provide financial assistance to children of veterans.
Eligibility: Applicants must be dependents of honorably discharged veterans who served during wartime or armed conflict and have service-connected disabilities or who died in service during war or armed conflict. They must be 16 to 23 years of age and have lived in and attended school in Pennsylvania for five years prior to application, and they must demonstrate financial need.
Target applicant(s): High school students. College students.
Amount: Up to $500.
Number of awards: Varies.
Scholarship may be renewable.
Deadline: Contact the sponsor to confirm the deadline.
How to apply: Applications are available from your local Department of Military and Veterans Affairs.
Exclusive: Visit www.UltimateScholarshipBook.com and enter code PE172526 for updates on this award.

[1726] • Pennsylvania Land Surveyors' Foundation Scholarship

Pennsylvania Society of Land Surveyors
10340 Democracy Lane, Fairfax, VA 22030
Phone: 717-412-1946
Email: psls@psls.org
http://www.psls.org/scholarship
Purpose: To aid Pennsylvania students who are planning for careers as land surveyors.
Eligibility: Applicants must be U.S. citizens and residents of Pennsylvania. They must be accepted into or enrolled in a two- or four-year degree program in land surveying. Selection is based on academic merit, statement of purpose, extracurricular activities and recommendations.
Target applicant(s): High school students. College students. Adult students.
Amount: Varies.
Number of awards: Varies.
Deadline: April 30.
How to apply: Applications are available online. An application form, transcript, standardized test scores (high school applicants only) and a guidance counselor evaluation form are required.
Exclusive: Visit www.UltimateScholarshipBook.com and enter code PE172626 for updates on this award.

[1727] • Pennsylvania Masonic Youth Foundation Scholarships

Pennsylvania Masonic Youth Foundation
Masonic Conference Center, Patton Hall, 1244 Bainbridge Road, Elizabethtown, PA 17022-9423
Phone: 800-266-8424
Email: pmyf@pagrandlodge.com
https://pmyf.org/
Purpose: To assist students in pursuing higher education.
Eligibility: Applicants must be working toward a two- or four-year college degree, graduate degree or trade school education. This award is open to students regardless of Masonic ties, age, race or religion.
Target applicant(s): High school students. College students. Adult students.
Amount: Varies.
Number of awards: Varies.
Deadline: March 15.
How to apply: Applications are available by mail.

Exclusive: Visit www.UltimateScholarshipBook.com and enter code PE172726 for updates on this award.

[1728] • Pennsylvania Oratorical Contest
American Legion, Department of Pennsylvania
P.O. Box 2324, Harrisburg, PA 17105-2324
Phone: 717-730-9100
Email: hq@pa-legion.com
http://www.pa-legion.com
Purpose: To enhance high school students' experience with and understanding of the U.S. Constitution. The contest will help develop students' leadership skills and civic appreciation, as well as the ability to deliver thoughtful, insightful orations regarding U.S. citizenship and its inherent responsibilities.
Eligibility: Applicants must be high school students under the age of 20 who are U.S. citizens or legal residents and residents of the state. Students first give an oration within their state and winners compete at the national level. The oration must be related to the Constitution of the United States focusing on the duties and obligations citizens have to the government. It must be in English and be between eight and ten minutes. There is also an assigned topic which is posted on the website, and it should be between three and five minutes.
Target applicant(s): High school students.
Amount: $4,000-$7,500.
Number of awards: 3.
Deadline: December 3.
How to apply: Applications are available from school coordinators and online.
Exclusive: Visit www.UltimateScholarshipBook.com and enter code AM172826 for updates on this award.

[1729] • Pennsylvania Society of Tax and Accounting Professionals Scholarships
Pennsylvania Society of Tax and Accounting Professionals
20 Erford Road, Suite 200A, Lemoyne, PA 17043
Phone: 800-270-3352
Email: info@pstap.org
http://www.pstap.org/
Purpose: To aid Pennsylvania accounting students.
Eligibility: Applicants must be full-time undergraduate students who are enrolled at a college or university located in Pennsylvania. They must be majoring in accounting, must have completed 60 credits or more of their degree program and must have a GPA of 3.0. Selection is based on academic achievement, leadership, extracurricular activities and financial need.
Target applicant(s): College students. Adult students.
Minimum GPA: 3.0
Amount: $2,000-$3,000.
Number of awards: 3.
Deadline: October 31.
How to apply: Applications are available online. An application form and an official transcript are required.
Exclusive: Visit www.UltimateScholarshipBook.com and enter code PE172926 for updates on this award.

[1730] • Pennsylvania State Bowling Association Scholarship Program
Pennsylvania State Bowling Association
100 Dutch Hill Road, Bloomsburg, PA 17815
Phone: 570-784-9142
Email: psbasect@ptd.net
https://bowlpa.com
Purpose: To support those students who have participated in the USBC Youth or USBC league in Pennsylvania as they pursue a college education.
Eligibility: Students must be a graduating senior or have recently graduated with the intent to begin collegiate studies. Applicants must have a minimum GPA of 2.0. Selection is based on academic achievements, involvement in bowling and non-bowling activities and financial need.
Target applicant(s): High school students.
Minimum GPA: 2.0
Amount: $1,500.
Number of awards: 4.
Scholarship may be renewable.
Deadline: February 28.
How to apply: Applications are available online. In addition to the form, applicants must submit an official high school transcript and a brief autobiography detailing academic as well as extracurricular achievements.
Exclusive: Visit www.UltimateScholarshipBook.com and enter code PE173026 for updates on this award.

[1731] • Pennsylvania State Grant Program
Pennsylvania Higher Education Assistance Agency (PHEAA)
Pennsylvania State Grant Program, P.O. Box 8157, Harrisburg, PA 17105-8157
Phone: 800-692-7392
Email: granthelp@pheaa.org
https://www.pheaa.org/grants/state-grant-program/index.shtml
Purpose: To assist Pennsylvania undergraduates who demonstrate financial need.
Eligibility: Applicants must be current Pennsylvania residents who have lived in the state for at least 12 consecutive months. They must be graduates of an approved high school or GED recipients and be enrolled in or plan to enroll in a two-year or longer degree program at an approved college or university. They must be enrolled for at least six credit hours per academic term and must meet financial need criteria. Applicants who have earned a bachelor's degree previously or who have a defaulted student loan are ineligible. Selection is based on financial need.
Target applicant(s): High school students. College students. Adult students.
Amount: Varies.
Number of awards: Varies.
Deadline: May 1; August 1; August 15.
How to apply: Applications are available online. An application form, a completed FAFSA and supporting documents are required.
Exclusive: Visit www.UltimateScholarshipBook.com and enter code PE173126 for updates on this award.

[1732] • Pennsylvania Targeted Industry Program
Pennsylvania Higher Education Assistance Agency (PHEAA)
Pennsylvania State Grant Program, P.O. Box 8157, Harrisburg, PA 17105-8157
Phone: 800-692-7392
Email: granthelp@pheaa.org
https://www.pheaa.org/grants/state-grant-program/index.shtml
Purpose: To support Pennsylvania students interested in energy, health, advanced materials and diversified manufacturing or agriculture and food production careers.
Eligibility: Applicants must be U.S. citizens or eligible non-citizens and residents of Pennsylvania. Students must have received a high school diploma, GED or recognized homeschool certificate and filed the FAFSA. Applicants must be enrolled at least half-time and demonstrate financial need.

The Ultimate Scholarship Book 2026
Scholarship Directory (State of Residence)

Target applicant(s): College students. Graduate school students. Adult students.
Amount: Up to $5,000.
Number of awards: Varies.
Deadline: May 1.
How to apply: Applications are available online.
Exclusive: Visit www.UltimateScholarshipBook.com and enter code PE173226 for updates on this award.

[1733] • PenSPRA Scholarship
Pennsylvania School Public Relations Association
Shelly Belcher, Communications Coordinator, Peters Township School District, 631 East McMurray Road, McMurray, PA 15317
Phone: 724-941-6251 x7205
Email: belchers@pt-sd.org
https://penspra.com/
Purpose: To support Pennsylvania students pursuing a career in the communications field.
Eligibility: Applicants must be Pennsylvania public high school students with a 3.0 GPA who are pursuing a degree in communications or a related field such as public relations, journalism, English, advertising or graphic arts. Students must have been accepted to or applied to a college, university, technical school or other institution of higher learning. Applicants must live within one of PenSPRA's three regions (Eastern, Central and Western).
Target applicant(s): High school students.
Minimum GPA: 3.0
Amount: $1,000.
Number of awards: 2.
Deadline: March 31.
How to apply: Applications are available online.
Exclusive: Visit www.UltimateScholarshipBook.com and enter code PE173326 for updates on this award.

[1734] • PG&E Better Together STEM Scholarship Program
PG&E Better Together STEM Scholarship Program, Scholarship America
One Scholarship Way, Saint Peter, MN 56082
Phone: 800-537-4180
Email: pge@scholarshipamerica.org
https://pge.com/scholarships
Purpose: To encourage students from California to further their studies in STEM-related fields.
Eligibility: Applicants must be PG&E customers who are either high school seniors, current college students, veterans or adults returning to school studying one of the following STEM related careers: Engineering (electrical, mechanical, computer, industrial or environmental), computer science/information systems, cyber security or environmental sciences. Students must intend to be full-time undergraduate students for the entire upcoming school year working toward their first degree at a PG&E Partner School in California.
Target applicant(s): High school students. College students. Adult students.
Amount: Up to $10,000.
Number of awards: 40.
Scholarship may be renewable.
Deadline: March 15.
How to apply: Applications are available online.
Exclusive: Visit www.UltimateScholarshipBook.com and enter code PG173426 for updates on this award.

[1735] • Phyllis V. Roberts Scholarship
General Federation of Women's Clubs of Virginia
P.O. Box 8750, Richmond, VA 23226
Phone: 804-288-3724
Email: scholarships@gfwcvirginia.org
https://gfwcvirginia.org/
Purpose: To support undergraduate and graduate students in the field of food and nutritional sciences.
Eligibility: Applicants must be Virginia residents and have a minimum 3.0 GPA. Students will need to submit a short essay explaining why they have chosen an undergraduate or graduate degree in the field of agricultural sciences, animal and poultry sciences, wildlife conservation or forestry. Applicants should have a goal of helping to address food insecurity in our communities.
Target applicant(s): College students. Graduate school students. Adult students.
Minimum GPA: 3.0
Amount: $1,000.
Number of awards: Varies.
Deadline: March 15.
How to apply: The application is available online and must include three letters of reference, a college verification of GPA, a resume and the short essay.
Exclusive: Visit www.UltimateScholarshipBook.com and enter code GE173526 for updates on this award.

[1736] • Pinnacol Foundation Scholarship Program
Pinnacol Foundation
7501 E. Lowry Boulevard, Denver, CO 80230
Phone: 303-361-4775
Email: pinnacolfoundation@pinnacol.com
https://www.pinnacolfoundation.org/apply-for-a-scholarship
Purpose: To provide assistance for students whose parent was killed or injured in a work-related accident.
Eligibility: Applicants must be dependents of workers killed or permanently injured in compensable work-related accidents during employment with Colorado-based employers. They must be between the ages of 16 and 25 and have a diploma or GED or be high school seniors in good standing with a minimum GPA of 2.0. Letter of recommendation, essay, transcripts and documentation of the parent's injury or death are required.
Target applicant(s): High school students. College students.
Minimum GPA: 2.0
Amount: $4,700.
Number of awards: Varies.
Scholarship may be renewable.
Deadline: February 15.
How to apply: Applications are available online.
Exclusive: Visit www.UltimateScholarshipBook.com and enter code PI173626 for updates on this award.

[1737] • Plan NH Scholarship and Fellowship Program
Plan New Hampshire
273 Corporate Drive, Suite 100, Portsmouth, NH 03801
Phone: 603-452-7526
Email: info@plannh.org
https://plannh.org/programs/scholarship-and-fellowship
Purpose: To support students who foster excellence in the planning and design of New Hampshire's development.

Eligibility: Applicants must be residents of New Hampshire and be pursuing a degree in or related to: architecture, landscape architecture, studio art, engineering, interior design, construction-related field or trade, environmental science, land or community planning or historic preservation. Students must be current college undergraduate or graduate level students with a superior grade point average. Applicants must also prove leadership experience, work excellence and dedication to life's work in their field with a focus on the New England area.
Target applicant(s): College students. Graduate school students. Adult students.
Amount: $2,500-$5,000.
Number of awards: Varies.
Deadline: April 12.
How to apply: Applications are available online.
Exclusive: Visit www.UltimateScholarshipBook.com and enter code PL173726 for updates on this award.

[1738] • PRSA-Hawai'i/Roy Leffingwell Public Relations Scholarship

Hawaii Community Foundation - Scholarships
827 Fort Street Mall, Honolulu, HI 96813
Phone: 888-731-3863
Email: scholarships@hcf-hawaii.org
https://www.hawaiicommunityfoundation.org/
Purpose: To support Hawaii students who are pursuing careers in public relations.
Eligibility: Applicants must be college juniors, college seniors or graduate students. They must be majoring in public relations, journalism or communications. A minimum GPA of 2.7 is required.
Target applicant(s): College students. Graduate school students. Adult students.
Minimum GPA: 2.7
Amount: Varies.
Number of awards: Varies.
Deadline: February 28.
How to apply: To apply, register online, complete the online application and select the scholarships to which you wish to apply. In addition, mail the supporting materials: printed confirmation page from the online application, personal statement, copy of Student Aid Report (SAR) available at www.fafsa.ed.gov and official transcript.
Exclusive: Visit www.UltimateScholarshipBook.com and enter code HA173826 for updates on this award.

[1739] • R. Flake Shaw Scholarship

North Carolina Farm Bureau
Attn: R. Flake Shaw Scholarship, P.O. Box 27766, Raleigh, NC 27611
Phone: 919-782-1705
Email: ncfbscholarship@ncfb.org
http://www.ncfb.org
Purpose: To aid North Carolina students who are preparing for careers in agriculture.
Eligibility: Applicants must be North Carolina students who are pursuing an associate's or bachelor's degree in an agriculture-related subject. They must be planning to pursue a career in agriculture and demonstrate leadership ability and financial need. Preference will be given to applicants who are the family members of Farm Bureau members. Selection is based on academic merit, character, stated career goals and financial need.
Target applicant(s): High school students. College students. Adult students.
Amount: $1,000-$5,000.
Number of awards: 12.
Scholarship may be renewable.
Deadline: March 4.
How to apply: Applications are available online. An application form, transcript, personal statement and financial information are required.
Exclusive: Visit www.UltimateScholarshipBook.com and enter code NO173926 for updates on this award.

[1740] • R. Preston Woodruff, Jr. Scholarships

Arkansas Student Loan Authority
3801 Woodland Heights, Suite 200, Little Rock, AR 72212
Phone: 800-443-6030
Email: info@asla.info
https://www.asla.info/scholarships
Purpose: To support students who live in Arkansas or are planning to attend school there.
Eligibility: Students must be a resident of Arkansas and be enrolled or planning to enroll in an undergraduate program at a postsecondary education institution in Arkansas with at least a half-time schedule. Applicants must be a high school senior or current college student.
Target applicant(s): High school students. College students. Adult students.
Amount: $1,000.
Number of awards: Varies.
Scholarship may be renewable.
Deadline: April 1.
How to apply: Applications are available online.
Exclusive: Visit www.UltimateScholarshipBook.com and enter code AR174026 for updates on this award.

[1741] • R.W. Bob Holden Scholarship

Hawaii Hotel Industry Foundation
Attn.: Scholarship Committee, 2270 Kalakaua Avenue, Suite 1506, Honolulu, HI 96815
Phone: 808-923-0407
http://www.hawaiilodging.org/scholarships.html
Purpose: To reward students enrolled in a college or university majoring in hotel or lodging management program.
Eligibility: Applicants must be Hawaii residents. Students must be enrolled as full-time juniors or seniors attending an accredited university or college in the United States.
Target applicant(s): College students. Adult students.
Minimum GPA: 3.0
Amount: $2,000.
Number of awards: 1.
Deadline: April 29.
How to apply: Applications are available online.
Exclusive: Visit www.UltimateScholarshipBook.com and enter code HA174126 for updates on this award.

[1742] • Rae Lee Siporin Award

Los Alamos National Laboratory Foundation
1112 Plaza del Norte, Espanola, NM 87532
Phone: 505-753-8890
Email: tony@lanlfoundation.org
http://www.lanlfoundation.org
Purpose: To support undergraduate students from northern New Mexico.
Eligibility: Students must have at least a 3.25 GPA, and they must have either an SAT score (combined Math plus Critical Reading only) of at least 930 or an ACT score of at least 19. Applicants must submit an essay and two letters of recommendation.

Target applicant(s): High school students. College students. Adult students.
Minimum GPA: 3.25
Amount: $1,000 - $20,000.
Number of awards: Varies.
Deadline: January 16.
How to apply: Applications are available online.
Exclusive: Visit www.UltimateScholarshipBook.com and enter code LO174226 for updates on this award.

[1743] • Ranelius Scholarship Program
Minnesota Turkey Growers Association
Scholarship Selection Committee, 108 Marty Drive, Suite 1, Buffalo, MN 55313-5546
Phone: 763-682-2171
Email: bseverns@minnesotaturkey.com
https://minnesotaturkey.com/
Purpose: To aid Minnesota students who are preparing for careers in the poultry industry.
Eligibility: Applicants must be Minnesota residents. They must be enrolled in or planning to enroll in a postsecondary educational program that provides adequate preparation for a career in the turkey or poultry industry. Preference will be given to applicants who have not won the award previously, members of the Minnesota Turkey Growers Association (MTGA), family members of MTGA members and employees of MTGA members. Selection is based on academic merit, extracurricular activities and demonstrated interest in the poultry industry.
Target applicant(s): High school students. College students. Adult students.
Amount: $3,000.
Number of awards: Varies.
Scholarship may be renewable.
Deadline: March 1.
How to apply: Applications are available online. An application form, personal essay and one recommendation letter are required.
Exclusive: Visit www.UltimateScholarshipBook.com and enter code MI174326 for updates on this award.

[1744] • Ray Anthony Peacock Scholarship
Ray A. Peacock Foundation
P.O. Box 8153, Houston, TX 77288-8153
Phone: 281-793-7358
Email: rapscholarship@comcast.net
http://www.rapscholarship.com
Purpose: To support graduating seniors of Texas in pursuing post-secondary education.
Eligibility: Applicants must demonstrate excellent writing skills, a history of community or public service and have unmet financial need. A minimum GPA of 3.0 is required. Students must submit an essay about their goals and accomplishments, transcripts and two letters of recommendation.
Target applicant(s): High school students.
Minimum GPA: 3.0
Amount: Varies.
Number of awards: Varies.
Deadline: March 1.
How to apply: Applications are available online.
Exclusive: Visit www.UltimateScholarshipBook.com and enter code RA174426 for updates on this award.

[1745] • Raymond F. Cain Scholarship Fund
Hawaii Community Foundation - Scholarships
827 Fort Street Mall, Honolulu, HI 96813
Phone: 888-731-3863
Email: scholarships@hcf-hawaii.org
https://www.hawaiicommunityfoundation.org/
Purpose: To support students in Hawaii who are majoring in fields related to landscape architecture.
Eligibility: Applicants must have at least a 2.7 GPA, and they must have financial need.
Target applicant(s): High school students. College students. Graduate school students. Adult students.
Minimum GPA: 2.7
Amount: Varies.
Number of awards: Varies.
Deadline: February 28.
How to apply: To apply, register online, complete the online application and select the scholarships to which you wish to apply. In addition, mail the supporting materials: printed confirmation page from the online application, personal statement, copy of Student Aid Report (SAR) available at www.fafsa.ed.gov and official transcript.
Exclusive: Visit www.UltimateScholarshipBook.com and enter code HA174526 for updates on this award.

[1746] • Raymond J. Faust Scholarship
American Water Works Association - Michigan Section
Attn.: Faust Scholarship Committee, P.O. Box 150469, Grand Rapids, MI 49515
Phone: 517-292-2912
Email: feedback@mi-water.org
http://www.mi-water.org/?page=Scholarships
Purpose: To aid Michigan Section American Water Works Association members who are preparing for careers in the water utility industry.
Eligibility: Applicants must be members of the Michigan Section of the American Water Works Association (AWWA). They must be current water utility employees, the dependents of current water utility employees or prospective water utility professionals. They must be pursuing or planning to pursue a college degree in a subject that relates to the drinking water field. Selection is based on commitment to the water supply industry.
Target applicant(s): High school students. College students. Adult students.
Amount: Varies.
Number of awards: Varies.
Deadline: July 1.
How to apply: Applications are available online. An application form is required.
Exclusive: Visit www.UltimateScholarshipBook.com and enter code AM174626 for updates on this award.

[1747] • Raymond T. Wellington, Jr. Memorial Scholarship
American Legion Auxiliary, Department of New York
112 State Street, Suite 1310, Albany, NY 12207
Phone: 518-463-1162
Email: nyalaeducation@gmail.com
http://www.deptny.org/?page_id=2128
Purpose: To provide financial assistance to students who are children, grandchildren and great-grandchildren of war veterans.
Eligibility: Applicants must be children, grandchildren or great grand-children of Armed Forces veterans who served in World War II, the Korean

Conflict, the Vietnam War, Grenada/Lebanon, Panama, the Persian Gulf or War on Terrorism. Students must be high school seniors or high school graduates and must be U.S. citizens and New York State residents.
Target applicant(s): High school students.
Amount: $1,000.
Number of awards: 1.
Deadline: March 1.
How to apply: Applications are available online.
Exclusive: Visit www.UltimateScholarshipBook.com and enter code AM174726 for updates on this award.

[1748] • RBC Wealth Management Colorado Scholarship
Denver Foundation
1009 Grant Street, Denver, CO 80203
Phone: 303-300-1790
Email: information@denverfoundation.org
https://denverfoundation.org/scholarships/scholarship-opportunities/
Purpose: To provide assistance to outstanding Colorado high school seniors who plan to pursue degrees in science, engineering or math.
Eligibility: Applicants must be graduating seniors at a Colorado high school who have a 3.75 minimum GPA and have completed college preparatory coursework.
Target applicant(s): High school students.
Minimum GPA: 3.75
Amount: $5,000.
Number of awards: 5.
Deadline: March 1.
How to apply: Applications are available online.
Exclusive: Visit www.UltimateScholarshipBook.com and enter code DE174826 for updates on this award.

[1749] • Reach Higher Finish Line Scholarship
Oklahoma State Regents for Higher Education Reach Higher Finish Line Scholarship
655 Research Parkway, Suite 200, Oklahoma City, OK 73104
Phone: 800-858-1840
Email: reachhigher@osrhe.edu
https://reachhigherok.org/finishlineok/
Purpose: To support adult students who want to return to college or university to complete their degrees, college certificates or micro-credentials in several ways.
Eligibility: Applicants are strongly encouraged but not required to complete the FAFSA. Award recipients must enroll in a minimum of three credit hours per semester with priority given to those enrolled in six credit hours. Reach Higher students must maintain a minimum of a 2.0 retention/graduation GPA or the minimum GPA required for the specific program by the institution. Applicants must be within 45 credits or fewer of completion of an approved degree at a Reach Higher institution and must be an Oklahoma resident.
Target applicant(s): Adult students.
Amount: Varies.
Number of awards: Varies.
Scholarship may be renewable.
Deadline: Varies.
How to apply: Applications are available online. The Reach Higher institutional representatives will review applications and select scholarship recipients. The institution will notify scholarship award recipients.
Exclusive: Visit www.UltimateScholarshipBook.com and enter code OK174926 for updates on this award.

[1750] • Reach Higher Montana Scholarships
Reach Higher Montana
40 West 6th Avenue, Helena, MT 59601
Phone: 406-422-1275
https://reachhighermontana.org/pay-for-school/scholarships
Purpose: To support students from Montana who are pursuing a higher education.
Eligibility: Applicants must be graduating high school seniors from Montana or residents of Montana who graduated from a Montana high school and are currently attending a college or university in Montana. Students must be attending at least half-time with a 2.5 GPA.
Target applicant(s): High school students. College students. Adult students.
Minimum GPA: 2.5
Amount: $2,000.
Number of awards: 50.
Deadline: March 1.
How to apply: Applications are available online.
Exclusive: Visit www.UltimateScholarshipBook.com and enter code RE175026 for updates on this award.

[1751] • Red Boucher Scholarship
Alaska Community Foundation
3201 C Street, Suite 110, Anchorage, AK 99503
Phone: 907-334-6700
Email: scholarships@alaskacf.org
https://alaskacf.org/scholarships/
Purpose: To support graduating seniors and graduates of Alaskan high schools in pursuing a degree in technology education and/or training.
Eligibility: Applicants must be enrolled full-time in a technology related program by the beginning of the semester in which the award is granted. A minimum GPA of 3.0 is required. Preference is given to students with demonstrated financial need.
Target applicant(s): High school students. College students. Adult students.
Minimum GPA: 3.0
Amount: $500.
Number of awards: Varies.
Deadline: January 20.
How to apply: Applications are available online.
Exclusive: Visit www.UltimateScholarshipBook.com and enter code AL175126 for updates on this award.

[1752] • Regional University Baccalaureate Scholarship
Oklahoma State Regents for Higher Education/Regional University Baccalaureate Scholarship
655 Research Parkway, Suite 200, Oklahoma City, OK 73104
Phone: 800-858-1840
Email: studentinfo@osrhe.edu
https://secure.okcollegestart.org/Financial_Aid_Planning/Scholarships/Academic_Scholarships/Regional_University_Baccalaureate_Scholarship.aspx
Purpose: To provide financial assistance to students of regional universities.
Eligibility: Applicants must be Oklahoma residents who are enrolled in a bachelor's degree program at one of the following schools: Cameron University, East Central University, Langston University, Northeastern State University, Northwestern Oklahoma State University, Oklahoma Panhandle State University, Rogers State University, Southeastern

Oklahoma State University, Southwestern Oklahoma State University, University of Central Oklahoma or the University of Science and Arts of Oklahoma. They must also either have an ACT score of 30 or higher or be a National Merit Semifinalist or Commended Student.
Target applicant(s): High school students.
Amount: $3,500.
Number of awards: Varies.
Scholarship may be renewable.
Deadline: May 17.
How to apply: Applications are available from your university.
Exclusive: Visit www.UltimateScholarshipBook.com and enter code OK175226 for updates on this award.

[1753] • Retail Chapter Award II and III
Oregon Association of Nurseries
29751 SW Town Center Loop West, Wilsonville, OR 97070
Phone: 503-682-5089
Email: onf@oan.org
https://www.oan.org
Purpose: To aid students who are majoring in ornamental horticulture or a related subject.
Eligibility: Applicants must be majoring in ornamental horticulture or a related subject. Selection is based on the overall strength of the application.
Target applicant(s): College students. Adult students.
Amount: $2,000.
Number of awards: 1.
Deadline: April 15.
How to apply: Applications are available online. An application form, official transcript and three references letters are required.
Exclusive: Visit www.UltimateScholarshipBook.com and enter code OR175326 for updates on this award.

[1754] • Rhode Island Foundation Association of Former Legislators Scholarship
Rhode Island Foundation
One Union Station, Providence, RI 02903
Phone: 401-274-4564
Email: rbogert@rifoundation.org
https://rifoundation.org/grants-scholarships
Purpose: To assist Rhode Island high school seniors with an excellent track record of community service.
Eligibility: Applicants must be Rhode Island high school seniors who have been accepted into college, have demonstrated need and have a substantial amount of community service.
Target applicant(s): High school students.
Amount: $1,000-$1,500.
Number of awards: 1.
Scholarship may be renewable.
Deadline: April 15.
How to apply: Applications are available online.
Exclusive: Visit www.UltimateScholarshipBook.com and enter code RH175426 for updates on this award.

[1755] • Rhode Island Promise Scholarship
Rhode Island Office of the Postsecondary Commissioner
560 Jefferson Boulevard, Suite 100, Warwick, RI 02886
Phone: 401-736-1100
https://www.riopc.edu
Purpose: To assist outstanding Rhode Island high school students.
Eligibility: Applicants must be graduating Rhode Island high school seniors who plan to attend a postsecondary institution full-time and demonstrate academic achievement and financial need.
Target applicant(s): High school students.
Minimum GPA: 2.5
Amount: Varies.
Number of awards: Varies.
Scholarship may be renewable.
Deadline: May 1.
How to apply: Complete the Free Application for Federal Student Aid (FAFSA).
Exclusive: Visit www.UltimateScholarshipBook.com and enter code RH175526 for updates on this award.

[1756] • Richard D. Johnson Memorial Post-Secondary Scholarship
American Legion, Department of Alaska
1550 Charter Circle, Anchorage, AK 99508
Phone: 907-278-8598
Email: office@alaskalegion.org
http://www.alaskalegion.org
Purpose: To support graduating high school seniors with their post-secondary education to prepare for the future.
Eligibility: Applicants must be average students involved in school, church and community activities with strong beliefs in the importance of patriotic organizations such as the American Legion. They must have a GPA between 2.0 and 3.0 with an improving outlook on life. Students must show need and have set goals upon graduating from high school. A minimum 500-word essay is required.
Target applicant(s): High school students. College students. Adult students.
Minimum GPA: 2.0
Amount: $1,000.
Number of awards: 1.
Deadline: March 30.
How to apply: Applications are available online.
Exclusive: Visit www.UltimateScholarshipBook.com and enter code AM175626 for updates on this award.

[1757] • Richard D. Wiegers Scholarship
Illinois Real Estate Educational Foundation
P.O. Box 2607, Springfield, IL 62708
Phone: 866-854-7333
Email: lclayton@ilreef.org
https://www.ilreef.org/scholarships/
Purpose: To aid Illinois students who are preparing for careers in business, law and finance.
Eligibility: Applicants must be Illinois residents who are attending an Illinois college or university. They must be graduate students who are majoring in business or undergraduate students who are majoring in business, finance or pre-law studies. Selection is based on academic merit, stated career goals, references and financial need.
Target applicant(s): College students. Graduate school students. Adult students.
Amount: Up to $1,000.
Number of awards: Varies.
Deadline: April 1.
How to apply: Applications are available online. An application form, official transcript, two reference letters, a personal statement and course of study outline are required.

Exclusive: Visit www.UltimateScholarshipBook.com and enter code IL175726 for updates on this award.

[1758] • Richard E. Bangert Business Award
Independent Colleges of Washington
600 Stewart Street, Suite 600, Seattle, WA 98101
Phone: 206-623-4494
Email: scholarships@icwashington.org
https://icwashington.org/page/scholarships
Purpose: To aid business students who are attending one of the Independent Colleges of Washington (ICW) member institutions.
Eligibility: Applicants must be attending an Independent Colleges of Washington (ICW) member institution, namely Whitworth University, St. Martin's University, Gonzaga University, Pacific Lutheran University, Whitman College, University of Puget Sound, Walla Walla University, Heritage University, Seattle University or Seattle Pacific University. They must be rising undergraduate juniors or seniors who are majoring in business or a related subject and must demonstrate financial need. Selection is based on the overall strength of the application.
Target applicant(s): College students. Adult students.
Amount: $2,875.
Number of awards: 4.
Deadline: April 12.
How to apply: Applications are available online. An application form, resume, one recommendation letter, transcript and personal essay are required.
Exclusive: Visit www.UltimateScholarshipBook.com and enter code IN175826 for updates on this award.

[1759] • Richard Goolsby Scholarship Fund
Foundation for the Carolinas
220 North Tryon Street, Charlotte, NC 28202
Phone: 704-973-4500
Email: mmccrorey@fftc.org
https://www.fftc.org/scholarships
Purpose: To support students who are interested in the plastics industry.
Eligibility: Applicants must be full-time graduate students or rising undergraduate sophomores, juniors or seniors. They must have completed science, business or engineering coursework related to plastics and must be interested in the plastics industry. Selection is based on the overall strength of the application.
Target applicant(s): College students. Graduate school students. Adult students.
Amount: Varies.
Number of awards: Varies.
Deadline: March 1.
How to apply: Applications are available online. An application form and supporting materials are required.
Exclusive: Visit www.UltimateScholarshipBook.com and enter code FO175926 for updates on this award.

[1760] • Ritchie M. Gregory Fund
Hawaii Community Foundation - Scholarships
827 Fort Street Mall, Honolulu, HI 96813
Phone: 888-731-3863
Email: scholarships@hcf-hawaii.org
https://www.hawaiicommunityfoundation.org/
Purpose: To support students who are majoring in art.
Eligibility: Applicants must be residents of Hawaii, demonstrate financial need and have a minimum 2.7 GPA. Students must also plan to attend an accredited two- or four-year college or university full-time as an undergraduate or graduate student.
Target applicant(s): High school students. College students. Graduate school students. Adult students.
Minimum GPA: 2.7
Amount: Varies.
Number of awards: Varies.
Deadline: February 28.
How to apply: To apply, register online, complete the online application and select the scholarships to which you wish to apply. In addition, mail the supporting materials: printed confirmation page from the online application, personal statement, copy of Student Aid Report (SAR) available at www.fafsa.ed.gov and official transcript.
Exclusive: Visit www.UltimateScholarshipBook.com and enter code HA176026 for updates on this award.

[1761] • Road to Safety Scholarship Contest
Metzger Wickersham Injury Lawyers
Attn: Road to Safety Scholarship Contest, 2321 Paxton Church Road, Harrisburg, PA 17110
Phone: 717-268-4288
Email: road2safety@mwke.com
https://www.mwke.com
Purpose: To encourage students to take a stand against dangerous driving.
Eligibility: Applicants must be graduating, college-bound high school seniors in Pennsylvania. Students must submit a project sending a message about the dangers of drunk driving and/or distracted driving.
Target applicant(s): High school students.
Amount: $500-$1,000.
Number of awards: 3.
Deadline: April 15.
How to apply: Applications are available online.
Exclusive: Visit www.UltimateScholarshipBook.com and enter code ME176126 for updates on this award.

[1762] • Robanna Fund
Hawaii Community Foundation - Scholarships
827 Fort Street Mall, Honolulu, HI 96813
Phone: 888-731-3863
Email: scholarships@hcf-hawaii.org
https://www.hawaiicommunityfoundation.org/
Purpose: To support Hawaii students who plan to work in health care.
Eligibility: Applicants must be in an undergraduate health-related program and have a minimum GPA of 2.7. Students must also demonstrate financial need and plan to attend an accredited two- or four-year college full-time.
Target applicant(s): High school students. College students. Graduate school students. Adult students.
Minimum GPA: 2.7
Amount: Varies.
Number of awards: Varies.
Deadline: February 28.
How to apply: To apply, register online, complete the online application and select the scholarships to which you wish to apply. In addition, mail the supporting materials: printed confirmation page from the online application, personal statement, copy of Student Aid Report (SAR) available at www.fafsa.ed.gov and official transcript.
Exclusive: Visit www.UltimateScholarshipBook.com and enter code HA176226 for updates on this award.

The Ultimate Scholarship Book 2026
Scholarship Directory (State of Residence)

[1763] • Robert D. Blue Scholarship
Robert D. Blue Scholarship
Michael L. Fitzgerald, Treasurer of State, State Capitol Building, Des Moines, IA 50319
Phone: 515-281-7003
Email: rdbluescholarship@iowa.gov
http://www.rdblue.org/scholarship/
Purpose: To provide financial assistance to deserving Iowa students.
Eligibility: Applicants must be Iowa residents who plan to attend an Iowa institution of higher learning the following school year. They may be high school seniors or current college students. An essay and two references are required.
Target applicant(s): High school students. College students. Adult students.
Amount: $500-$1,000.
Number of awards: Varies.
Deadline: May 10.
How to apply: Applications are available online.
Exclusive: Visit www.UltimateScholarshipBook.com and enter code RO176326 for updates on this award.

[1764] • Robert R. Robinson Memorial Scholarship
Michigan Townships Association
512 Westshire Drive, Lansing, MI 48917
Phone: 517-321-6467
http://www.michigantownships.org
Purpose: To aid Michigan students who are planning for careers in public administration.
Eligibility: Applicants must be undergraduate juniors, undergraduate seniors or graduate students who are attending a Michigan college or university. They must be majoring in public administration and must have plans to pursue a career in that field. Selection is based on academic merit, extracurricular activities and stated career goals.
Target applicant(s): College students. Graduate school students. Adult students.
Amount: Up to $1,000.
Number of awards: Varies.
Deadline: May 31.
How to apply: Applications are available online. An application form, one letter of recommendation, a personal essay and a resolution of support from a Michigan township board are required.
Exclusive: Visit www.UltimateScholarshipBook.com and enter code MI176426 for updates on this award.

[1765] • Roberta B. Willis Scholarship - Need and Merit-Based Award
Connecticut Office of Higher Education
450 Columbus Boulevard, Hartford, CT 06103
Phone: 860-947-1800
http://www.ctohe.org
Purpose: To aid Connecticut residents with higher education expenses.
Eligibility: Applicants must be a high school senior or high school graduate with a high school junior year class rank of 20 percent or better. Students must have a minimum SAT score of 1800 or ACT score of 27 and plan to attend a Connecticut public or non-profit private college. Selection is based on financial need and academic merit.
Target applicant(s): High school students.
Amount: Up to $4,500.
Number of awards: Varies.
Deadline: Contact college financial aid office to confirm the deadline.
How to apply: Applications are available through high school guidance offices. An application form and Free Application for Federal Student Aid are required.
Exclusive: Visit www.UltimateScholarshipBook.com and enter code CO176526 for updates on this award.

[1766] • Roberta B. Willis Scholarship - Need-Based Award
Connecticut Office of Higher Education
450 Columbus Boulevard, Hartford, CT 06103
Phone: 860-947-1800
http://www.ctohe.org
Purpose: To aid Connecticut residents with higher education expenses.
Eligibility: Applicants must be attending a public or non-profit private Connecticut college or university and be enrolled in full-time study in a two- or four-year program. Students must have a federal Expected Family Contribution within the allowable range. Selection is based on need.
Target applicant(s): College students. Adult students.
Amount: $4,650-$5,250.
Number of awards: Varies.
Deadline: February 15.
How to apply: A Free Application for Federal Student Aid is required.
Exclusive: Visit www.UltimateScholarshipBook.com and enter code CO176626 for updates on this award.

[1767] • Rockefeller State Wildlife Scholarship
Louisiana Office of Student Financial Assistance
605 N. Fifth Street, Baton Rouge, LA 70802
Phone: 800-259-5626 x1012
Email: custserv@la.gov
https://mylosfa.la.gov/students-parents/scholarships-grants/tops/
Purpose: To assist Louisiana students in wildlife, forestry or marine science.
Eligibility: Applicants must be Louisiana residents for at least one year, be enrolled as full-time undergraduate or graduate students in a Louisiana public college or university, earn a degree in wildlife, forestry or marine science and have a minimum 2.5 GPA (3.0 if a graduate level student). Applicants must also submit the Free Application for Federal Student Aid (FAFSA) and be U.S. citizens.
Target applicant(s): College students. Graduate school students. Adult students.
Minimum GPA: 2.5 for undergraduate students; 3.0 for graduate students
Amount: Up to $12,000.
Number of awards: Varies.
Scholarship may be renewable.
Deadline: July 1.
How to apply: Applications are available online or by written request.
Exclusive: Visit www.UltimateScholarshipBook.com and enter code LO176726 for updates on this award.

[1768] • Rosa L. Parks Scholarships
Rosa L. Parks Scholarship Foundation
160 W. Fort Street, Detroit, MI 48226
Phone: 313-222-2538
Email: info@rosaparksscholarship.org
https://www.rosaparksscholarship.org/
Purpose: To provide education funds for students who hold ideals close to those of Rosa Parks.

Eligibility: Applicants must be Michigan high school seniors who will graduate by August of the application year. They must have a GPA of 2.5 or higher and have taken the SAT or ACT. An essay is required.
Target applicant(s): High school students.
Minimum GPA: 2.5
Amount: $2,000.
Number of awards: 40.
Deadline: March 1.
How to apply: Applications are available online.
Exclusive: Visit www.UltimateScholarshipBook.com and enter code RO176826 for updates on this award.

[1769] • Rosedale Post 346 Scholarship
American Legion, Department of Kansas
1314 SW Topeka Boulevard, Topeka, KS 66612
Phone: 785-232-9315
https://kansaslegion.org/
Purpose: To assist the children of members of the Kansas American Legion or American Legion Auxiliary.
Eligibility: Applicants must be high school seniors or college freshmen or sophomores who are enrolling or enrolled in an approved post-secondary school. They also must be average or better students who are the children of veterans. The children of deceased parents are also eligible if the parent was a paid member at the time of death. Applicants must submit three letters of recommendation with at least one from a teacher, an essay on "Why I Want to Go to College," a 1040 income statement, documentation of parent's veteran status and a certified high school transcript.
Target applicant(s): High school students. College students. Adult students.
Amount: $750-$1,500.
Number of awards: 2.
Deadline: February 15.
How to apply: Applications are available online.
Exclusive: Visit www.UltimateScholarshipBook.com and enter code AM176926 for updates on this award.

[1770] • Rosemary and Nellie Ebrie Fund
Hawaii Community Foundation - Scholarships
827 Fort Street Mall, Honolulu, HI 96813
Phone: 888-731-3863
Email: scholarships@hcf-hawaii.org
https://www.hawaiicommunityfoundation.org/
Purpose: To assist college and graduate students who have Hawaiian ancestry or were born or have been a long-time residents of the Island.
Eligibility: Applicants must be residents of the Island of Hawaii and be of Hawaiian or part-Hawaiian ancestry. Applicants must also submit a four-sheet application and financial form, personal statement, recommendations and transcript.
Target applicant(s): High school students. College students. Graduate school students. Adult students.
Minimum GPA: 2.7
Amount: Varies.
Number of awards: Varies.
Deadline: February 28.
How to apply: Applications are available by written request.
Exclusive: Visit www.UltimateScholarshipBook.com and enter code HA177026 for updates on this award.

[1771] • Rosewood Family Scholarship Program
Florida Department of Education
Office of Student Financial Assistance, State Scholarship and Grant Programs, 325 West Gaines Street, Suite 1314, Tallahassee, FL 32399-0400
Phone: 888-827-2004
Email: osfa@fldoe.org
https://origin.fldoe.org/finance/financial-aid-scholarships/
Purpose: To help Florida minority students especially direct descendants of Rosewood families.
Eligibility: Applicants must be full-time, undergraduate students who attend state universities, public community colleges or public postsecondary vocational-technical schools. Direct descendants of Rosewood families affected by the incidents of January 1923 receive preference. The descendants must provide family information on the Florida Financial Aid Application.
Target applicant(s): High school students. College students. Adult students.
Amount: Up to $6,100.
Number of awards: 50.
Scholarship may be renewable.
Deadline: April 1.
How to apply: Applicants must submit the Initial Student Florida Financial Aid Applications online by April 1. Florida residents must submit the Free Application for Federal Student Aid (FAFSA) online by May 15. Non-residents must submit the FAFSA in time to receive the Student Aid Report (SAR) from the processor and send a copy of the SAR to the Office of Student Financial Assistance by May 15.
Exclusive: Visit www.UltimateScholarshipBook.com and enter code FL177126 for updates on this award.

[1772] • Roshan Rahbari Scholarship Fund
Silicon Valley Community Foundation
2440 W. El Camino Real, Suite 300, Mountain View, CA 94040
Phone: 650-450-5400
Email: scholarships@siliconvalleycf.org
https://www.siliconvalleycf.org
Purpose: To support students from the Silicon Valley area.
Eligibility: Applicants must be current residents of California. Students must be current community college students transferring to a four-year college or university on a part-time or full-time basis with a minimum 3.0 GPA. Applicants must demonstrate service to community or school and financial need. Students must display character qualities such as integrity, compassion and generosity.
Target applicant(s): College students. Adult students.
Minimum GPA: 3.0
Amount: Up to $5,000.
Number of awards: Up to 4.
Scholarship may be renewable.
Deadline: June 2.
How to apply: Applications are available online.
Exclusive: Visit www.UltimateScholarshipBook.com and enter code SI177226 for updates on this award.

[1773] • Roy W. Likins Scholarship
American Water Works Association - Florida Section
1300 Ninth Street, Suite B-124, St. Cloud, FL 34769
Phone: 407-957-8448
Email: marjoriecraig@polk-county.net
https://www.fsawwa.org

The Ultimate Scholarship Book 2026
Scholarship Directory (State of Residence)

Purpose: To aid Florida students who are preparing for careers in the drinking water industry.
Eligibility: Applicants must be undergraduate upperclassmen or graduate students who are enrolled at an accredited postsecondary institution located in Florida. They must be majoring in a subject that is related to the drinking water industry and have a GPA of 3.0 or higher on a four-point scale. Previous recipients of this award are ineligible. Selection is based on academic achievement, extracurricular activities, character and stated career goals.
Target applicant(s): College students. Graduate school students. Adult students.
Minimum GPA: 3.0
Amount: $5,000.
Number of awards: 10.
Scholarship may be renewable.
Deadline: June 30.
How to apply: Applications are available online. An application form, personal statement, official transcript and two recommendation letters are required.
Exclusive: Visit www.UltimateScholarshipBook.com and enter code AM177326 for updates on this award.

[1774] • Russ Brannen/KENT FEEDS Memorial Beef Scholarship

Iowa Foundation for Agricultural Advancement
Winner's Circle Scholarships, c/o SGI, 30805 595th Avenue,
Cambridge, IA 50046
Phone: 515-291-3941
Email: linda@slweldon.net
https://ifaa.org/scholarships.php
Purpose: To aid incoming freshmen at Iowa four-year colleges and universities.
Eligibility: Applicants must be incoming freshmen at an Iowa four-year college or university. They must have been actively involved in FFA beef cattle projects. Preference will be given to applicants who have experience in cattle showmanship contests and expositions. Selection is based on livestock project participation, academic merit and leadership.
Target applicant(s): High school students.
Amount: $1,500.
Number of awards: 1.
Deadline: April 1.
How to apply: Applications are available online. An application form, extracurricular activities list and personal essay are required.
Exclusive: Visit www.UltimateScholarshipBook.com and enter code IO177426 for updates on this award.

[1775] • Ruth Lutes Bachmann Scholarship

Grand Lodge of Missouri: Ancient, Free and Accepted Masons
6033 Masonic Drive, Suite B, Columbia, MO 65202-6568
Phone: 573-474-8561
Email: grlodge@momason.org
http://momason.org/scholarships/
Purpose: To aid Missouri high school seniors who are planning to become nurses or school teachers.
Eligibility: Applicants must have plans to pursue higher education in nursing or school teaching. Selection is based on academic merit and promise.
Target applicant(s): High school students.
Minimum GPA: 3.0
Amount: $1,000.
Number of awards: 1.
Scholarship may be renewable.
Deadline: March 1.
How to apply: Applications are available online. An application form, personal statement, transcript and standardized test scores are required.
Exclusive: Visit www.UltimateScholarshipBook.com and enter code GR177526 for updates on this award.

[1776] • Safety Essay Contest

American Legion, Department of New Jersey
171 Jersey Street, Build #5, 2nd Floor, Trenton, NJ 08611
Phone: 609-695-5418
Email: adjutant@njamericanlegion.org
https://www.njamericanlegion.org/family-and-youth
Purpose: To reward students for exceptional essays regarding safety.
Eligibility: Applicants must be in the 6th, 7th or 8th grade and enrolled in a New Jersey school.
Target applicant(s): Junior high students or younger.
Amount: Up to $250.
Number of awards: 4.
Deadline: January 19.
How to apply: Application information is available from the local Department.
Exclusive: Visit www.UltimateScholarshipBook.com and enter code AM177626 for updates on this award.

[1777] • Samsung@First Scholars

Silicon Valley Community Foundation
2440 W. El Camino Real, Suite 300, Mountain View, CA 94040
Phone: 650-450-5400
Email: scholarships@siliconvalleycf.org
https://www.siliconvalleycf.org
Purpose: To support students from the Silicon Valley area.
Eligibility: Applicants must be current undergraduate students entering their sophomore, junior or senior year, undergraduate seniors accepted into a master's program or current master's students. Students must be planning to enroll on a full-time basis in a California, public four-year college or university and declare a major in science, technology, engineering or math (STEM) with preference given to computer science and engineering (CISE) and engineering majors. Applicants must have a minimum 3.0 GPA. Preference will be given to students enrolling in a school in the greater Bay Area which includes the following counties: Santa Clara, San Mateo, San Francisco, Marin, Alameda, Contra Costa, Napa, Solano or Sonoma.
Target applicant(s): College students. Graduate school students. Adult students.
Minimum GPA: 3.0
Amount: Up to $15,000.
Number of awards: Up to 3.
Deadline: February 29.
How to apply: Applications are available online.
Exclusive: Visit www.UltimateScholarshipBook.com and enter code SI177726 for updates on this award.

[1778] • Schlutz Family Beef Breeding Scholarship
Iowa Foundation for Agricultural Advancement
Winner's Circle Scholarships, c/o SGI, 30805 595th Avenue,
Cambridge, IA 50046
Phone: 515-291-3941
Email: linda@slweldon.net
https://ifaa.org/scholarships.php
Purpose: To aid Iowa entering undergraduate freshmen who have experience in beef projects.
Eligibility: Applicants must be rising undergraduate freshmen at an Iowa postsecondary institution. They must have experience in beef projects and activities. Preference will be given to applicants who demonstrate an interest in continuing an involvement in the beef cattle industry after graduation from college. Selection is based on the overall strength of the application.
Target applicant(s): College students. Adult students.
Amount: $2,000.
Number of awards: 1.
Deadline: April 1.
How to apply: Applications are available online. An application form and supporting materials are required.
Exclusive: Visit www.UltimateScholarshipBook.com and enter code IO177826 for updates on this award.

[1779] • Schneider-Emanuel American Legion Scholarship
American Legion, Department of Wisconsin
2930 American Legion Drive, P.O. Box 388, Portage, WI 53901
Phone: 608-745-1090
Email: info@wilegion.org
https://wilegion.org/scholarships
Purpose: To award scholarships to American Legion members and their children or grandchildren and members of the Sons of the American Legion or Auxiliary.
Eligibility: Applicants must have graduated from an accredited Wisconsin high school and plan to earn an undergraduate degree at a U.S. college or university. Applicants must also have participated in one or more American Legion-sponsored activities listed in the eligibility requirements.
Target applicant(s): High school students. College students. Adult students.
Minimum GPA: 3.0
Amount: $1,000.
Number of awards: 3.
Deadline: March 1.
How to apply: Applications are available online.
Exclusive: Visit www.UltimateScholarshipBook.com and enter code AM177926 for updates on this award.

[1780] • Scholars for Excellence in Child Care
Oklahoma State Regents for Higher Education/Scholars for Excellence in Child Care
655 Research Parkway, Suite 200, Oklahoma City, OK 73104
Phone: 866-343-3881
Email: gmcpherson@osrhe.edu
https://www.okhighered.org/scholars/
Purpose: To aid child care professionals in Oklahoma who wish to pursue credentials in child development and early childhood education.
Eligibility: Applicants must be child care professionals in Oklahoma. They must be pursuing or planning to pursue additional education or credentials in early childhood education or child development. Selection is based on the overall strength of the application.
Target applicant(s): College students. Adult students.
Amount: Varies.
Number of awards: Varies.
Deadline: Contact the sponsor to confirm the deadline.
How to apply: Applications are available online. An application form and supporting materials are required.
Exclusive: Visit www.UltimateScholarshipBook.com and enter code OK178026 for updates on this award.

[1781] • Scholarships for Academic Excellence
New York State Higher Education Services Corporation (HESC)
99 Washington Avenue, Albany, NY 12255
Phone: 888-697-4372
Email: scholarships@hesc.ny.gov
http://www.hesc.ny.gov
Purpose: To assist outstanding New York State high school graduates.
Eligibility: Applicants must be New York residents who are high school graduates, enrolled full-time in an eligible undergraduate program in New York State and are U.S. citizens or eligible noncitizens. Selection is based on grades in Regents exams.
Target applicant(s): College students. Adult students.
Amount: $500-$1,500.
Number of awards: 8,000.
Scholarship may be renewable.
Deadline: As soon as possible after October 1.
How to apply: Students are nominated by their high schools.
Exclusive: Visit www.UltimateScholarshipBook.com and enter code NE178126 for updates on this award.

[1782] • Scholarships in Mathematics Education
Illinois Council of Teachers of Mathematics
ICTM Scholarship, c/o Sue and Randy Pippen, 24807 Winterberry Lane, Plainfield, IL 60585
Email: scholarships@ictm.org
https://www.ictm.org/ictm-scholarships
Purpose: To aid Illinois mathematics education students.
Eligibility: Applicants must be enrolled at an accredited Illinois postsecondary institution in an undergraduate mathematics education curriculum that provides preparation for becoming a teacher. They must be rising juniors or seniors who have a GPA of 3.0 or higher on a four-point scale. Applicants must be pursuing a first bachelor's degree. Selection is based on the overall strength of the application.
Target applicant(s): College students. Adult students.
Minimum GPA: 3.0
Amount: $1,500.
Number of awards: 3.
Deadline: May 9.
How to apply: Applications are available online. An application form, lesson planning form, personal essay, two recommendation letters and a transcript are required.
Exclusive: Visit www.UltimateScholarshipBook.com and enter code IL178226 for updates on this award.

The Ultimate Scholarship Book 2026
Scholarship Directory (State of Residence)

[1783] • Senator Patricia K. McGee Nursing Faculty Scholarship
New York State Higher Education Services Corporation (HESC)
99 Washington Avenue, Albany, NY 12255
Phone: 888-697-4372
Email: scholarships@hesc.ny.gov
http://www.hesc.ny.gov
Purpose: To increase the number of nursing educators and clinical faculty members in the State of New York.
Eligibility: Applicants must be U.S. citizens or eligible non-citizens and residents of New York for one year or more. They must be registered nurses who are licensed in New York, and they must be accepted into a graduate nursing program at an approved college or university in New York. Students must also agree to four years of service as nursing faculty in the state.
Target applicant(s): Graduate school students. Adult students.
Amount: Up to $20,000.
Number of awards: Varies.
Scholarship may be renewable.
Deadline: February 1.
How to apply: Applications are available online after June of each year.
Exclusive: Visit www.UltimateScholarshipBook.com and enter code NE178326 for updates on this award.

[1784] • Senatorial Scholarship
Maryland Higher Education Commission
Office of Student Financial Assistance, 6 North Liberty Street, Baltimore, MD 21201
Phone: 800-974-1024
Email: osfamail@mhec.state.md.us
https://mhec.maryland.gov
Purpose: To assist Maryland undergraduate and graduate students who can demonstrate financial need.
Eligibility: Applicants must be U.S. citizens or eligible noncitizens, legal residents of the state of Maryland and complete the Free Application for Federal Student Aid (FAFSA). Some senators have supplementary forms. Contact your area's senator's office for complete details. All applicants must enroll at a two- or four-year Maryland college or university as degree-seeking undergraduate or graduate student, or attend certain private career schools. Applicants must show financial need. High school applicants must also take the SAT or the ACT.
Target applicant(s): High school students. College students. Graduate school students. Adult students.
Amount: $400-$12,617.
Number of awards: Varies.
Scholarship may be renewable.
Deadline: March 1.
How to apply: Complete and file the Free Application for Federal Student Aid (FAFSA). Contact senator for specific application forms. The Office of Student Financial Assistance (OSFA) can provide a list of all State legislators.
Exclusive: Visit www.UltimateScholarshipBook.com and enter code MA178426 for updates on this award.

[1785] • SGT Felix M. Del Greco, Jr. Memorial Scholarship
Connecticut National Guard Foundation Inc.
State Armory, 360 Broad Street, Hartford, CT 06105-3795
Phone: 860-241-1550
Email: scholarship.committee@ctngfoundation.org
https://ctngfi.org/
Purpose: To provide financial assistance to children of Connecticut National Guard members.
Eligibility: Applicants must be sons or daughters of a member of the Connecticut Army National Guard. They must be enrolled in or plan to attend an accredited degree or technical program.
Target applicant(s): High school students. College students. Adult students.
Amount: $4,000.
Number of awards: 3.
Deadline: March 15.
How to apply: Applications are available online.
Exclusive: Visit www.UltimateScholarshipBook.com and enter code CO178526 for updates on this award.

[1786] • Shipley Rose Buckner Memorial Scholarship
Funeral Service Foundation
13625 Bishop's Drive, Brookfield, WI 53005-6607
Phone: 877-402-5900
Email: info@funeralservicefoundation.org
https://www.funeralservicefoundation.org/academicscholarships/
Purpose: To aid female Tennessee students with tuition costs of mortuary science education programs.
Eligibility: Applicants must be enrolled as a funeral service student full- or part-time in an American Board of Funeral Service Education accredited program. Selection is based on the overall strength of the application.
Target applicant(s): College students. Graduate school students. Adult students.
Minimum GPA: 2.0
Amount: $2,500-$5,000.
Number of awards: Varies.
Deadline: April 1; November 1.
How to apply: Applications are available online. An application form, essay, academic transcript and video submissions are required.
Exclusive: Visit www.UltimateScholarshipBook.com and enter code FU178626 for updates on this award.

[1787] • Shirley McKown Scholarship Fund
Hawaii Community Foundation - Scholarships
827 Fort Street Mall, Honolulu, HI 96813
Phone: 888-731-3863
Email: scholarships@hcf-hawaii.org
https://www.hawaiicommunityfoundation.org/
Purpose: To support Hawaii students who are majoring in journalism, advertising or public relations.
Eligibility: Applicants must be attending a four-year college or university with at least a 3.0 GPA. They must be college juniors, college seniors or graduate students.
Target applicant(s): College students. Graduate school students. Adult students.
Minimum GPA: 3.0
Amount: Varies.
Number of awards: Varies.
Deadline: February 28.
How to apply: To apply, register online, complete the online application and select the scholarships to which you wish to apply. In addition, mail the supporting materials: printed confirmation page from the online application, personal statement, copy of Student Aid Report (SAR) available at www.fafsa.ed.gov and official transcript.

Exclusive: Visit www.UltimateScholarshipBook.com and enter code HA178726 for updates on this award.

[1788] • Shook Construction Harry F. Gaeke Memorial Scholarship

Associated General Contractors of Ohio
1755 Northwest Boulevard, Columbus, OH 43212
Phone: 614-486-6446
Email: parker@agcohio.com
https://agcohio.com/workforce-development/agc-scholarships/
Purpose: To aid students preparing for careers in the construction industry.
Eligibility: Applicants must be U.S. citizens either living in or attending school in Ohio, Kentucky or Indiana. They must be in at least the second year of an undergraduate degree program that is related to construction and have a GPA of 2.5 or higher. Selection is based on the overall strength of the application.
Target applicant(s): College students. Adult students.
Minimum GPA: 2.5
Amount: $1,000.
Number of awards: 1.
Deadline: February 9.
How to apply: Applications are available online. An application form, transcript and personal essay are required.
Exclusive: Visit www.UltimateScholarshipBook.com and enter code AS178826 for updates on this award.

[1789] • Shuichi, Katsu and Itsuyo Suga Scholarship

Hawaii Community Foundation - Scholarships
827 Fort Street Mall, Honolulu, HI 96813
Phone: 888-731-3863
Email: scholarships@hcf-hawaii.org
https://www.hawaiicommunityfoundation.org/
Purpose: To support Hawaii students who are majoring in math, physics or science and technology.
Eligibility: Applicants must have at least a 3.0 GPA.
Target applicant(s): High school students. College students. Graduate school students. Adult students.
Minimum GPA: 3.0
Amount: Varies.
Number of awards: Varies.
Deadline: January 31.
How to apply: To apply, register online, complete the online application and select the scholarships to which you wish to apply. In addition, mail the supporting materials: printed confirmation page from the online application, personal statement, copy of Student Aid Report (SAR) available at www.fafsa.ed.gov and official transcript.
Exclusive: Visit www.UltimateScholarshipBook.com and enter code HA178926 for updates on this award.

[1790] • Sioux Falls Area Retired Teachers Scholarship

Sioux Falls Area Community Foundation
The Depot at Cherapa Place, 200 N. Cherapa Place, Sioux Falls, SD 57103-2205
Phone: 605-336-7055
Email: tlatza@sfacf.org
https://www.sfacf.org/grants-scholarships/scholarships
Purpose: To aid South Dakota students who are majoring in education.
Eligibility: Applicants must be rising undergraduate juniors or seniors who are majoring in education at an accredited South Dakota college or university. They must have a GPA of 2.5 or better, demonstrate financial need, participate in extracurricular activities and display a commitment to the teaching profession. Selection is based on the overall strength of the application.
Target applicant(s): College students. Adult students.
Minimum GPA: 2.5
Amount: $1,500.
Number of awards: 1.
Deadline: December 15.
How to apply: Applications are available from the applicant's financial aid office or guidance counselor. An application form and supporting materials are required.
Exclusive: Visit www.UltimateScholarshipBook.com and enter code SI179026 for updates on this award.

[1791] • Sister Helen Marie Pellicer Scholarship

Florida Academy of Nutrition and Dietetics Foundation
Scholarship Chair, P.O. Box 12608, Tallahassee, FL 32317-2608
Phone: 850-386-8850
Email: cstapell@eatrightflorida.org
http://www.eatrightflorida.org
Purpose: To aid Florida dietetics students.
Eligibility: Applicants must be U.S. citizens or permanent residents, Florida residents and undergraduate upperclassmen who are majoring in dietetics. They must have a GPA of 2.5 or higher on a four-point scale. Selection is based on the overall strength of the application.
Target applicant(s): College students. Adult students.
Minimum GPA: 2.5
Amount: $1,000.
Number of awards: 1.
Deadline: October 12.
How to apply: Applications are available online. An application form, official transcript and two recommendation letters are required.
Exclusive: Visit www.UltimateScholarshipBook.com and enter code FL179126 for updates on this award.

[1792] • Sister Mary Petronia Van Straten Scholarship for Pre-Service Teachers

Wisconsin Mathematics Council Inc.
W175 N11117 Stonewood Drive, Suite 204, Germantown, WI 53022
Phone: 262-437-0174
Email: wismath@teamwi.com
http://www.wismath.org
Purpose: To aid Wisconsin teacher education students.
Eligibility: Applicants must be Wisconsin legal residents, be enrolled in a teacher education program and have completed or be in the process of completing a course in mathematics teaching methods. They must have a GPA of 3.0 or higher. Selection is based on the overall strength of the application.
Target applicant(s): College students. Adult students.
Minimum GPA: 3.0
Amount: $2,000.
Number of awards: 1.
Deadline: March 1.
How to apply: Applications are available online. An application form, official transcript, two letters of recommendation, a plan of study and a personal essay are required.

The Ultimate Scholarship Book 2026
Scholarship Directory (State of Residence)

Exclusive: Visit www.UltimateScholarshipBook.com and enter code WI179226 for updates on this award.

[1793] • Six Meter Club of Chicago Scholarship
American Radio Relay League Foundation
225 Main Street, Newington, CT 06111-1494
Phone: 860-594-0200
Email: foundation@arrl.org
https://www.arrl.org/scholarship-program
Purpose: To support Illinois residents who are involved in amateur radio.
Eligibility: Applicants must have an active amateur radio license in any class. Students must be enrolled in an Illinois university or technical school for undergraduate study. A minimum GPA of 2.5 is preferred.
Target applicant(s): High school students. College students. Adult students.
Minimum GPA: 2.5
Amount: $500.
Number of awards: 1.
Deadline: January 10.
How to apply: Applications are available online.
Exclusive: Visit www.UltimateScholarshipBook.com and enter code AM179326 for updates on this award.

[1794] • Smart Choices Scholarship Program
Washington Interscholastic Activities Association (WIAA)
435 Main Avenue South, Renton, WA 98057
Phone: 425-687-8585
Email: smartchoices@wiaa.com
http://www.wiaa.com/
Purpose: To support graduating seniors who have proven excellence in activities, academics, leadership and community service.
Eligibility: Applicants must be high school seniors, have a minimum GPA of 3.2 and participate in a WIAA high school sport or activity during the current school year. Applicants must also be dairy consumers. Selection will be based on academic achievement, leadership and community service.
Target applicant(s): High school students.
Minimum GPA: 3.2
Amount: $1,000-$5,000.
Number of awards: 15.
Deadline: March 15.
How to apply: Applications are available online.
Exclusive: Visit www.UltimateScholarshipBook.com and enter code WA179426 for updates on this award.

[1795] • Smith Diversity Scholarship
Lutheran Family Services of Nebraska
124 South 24th Street, Omaha, NE 56102
Phone: 402-681-7024
Email: mmcdowell@lfs.neb.org
https://www.onelfs.org/sds/
Purpose: To support graduating high school seniors from low-income, minority families who are residents of Nebraska.
Eligibility: Applicants must be a resident of Nebraska at time of graduation. Students must show financial need. Preference will be given to applicants from disadvantaged ethnic backgrounds that do not identify as Caucasian.
Target applicant(s): High school students.
Amount: Up to $25,000.
Number of awards: Varies.
Scholarship may be renewable.
Deadline: January 28.
How to apply: Applications are available online.
Exclusive: Visit www.UltimateScholarshipBook.com and enter code LU179526 for updates on this award.

[1796] • Smith Scholarship Program
Smith Scholarship Foundation
400 Caldwell Trace, Birmingham, AL 35242
Phone: 205-202-4076
Email: appsupport@smithscholarships.com
http://www.smithscholarships.com
Purpose: To provide assistance for students who face financial, physical or emotional challenges and who have participated in volunteer work or assisted their families.
Eligibility: Applicants must be seniors at an Alabama high school and plan to attend an Alabama four-year college the following fall. Students must also write two essays about their future plans and their community service or family assistance endeavors and provide three letters of recommendation. A minimum C+ GPA is required.
Target applicant(s): High school students.
Minimum GPA: 2.33
Amount: Up to $20,000.
Number of awards: Varies.
Deadline: January 13.
How to apply: Applications are available online or by mail.
Exclusive: Visit www.UltimateScholarshipBook.com and enter code SM179626 for updates on this award.

[1797] • Society of American Military Engineers, Albuquerque Post Scholarship
New Mexico Engineering Foundation
P.O. Box 3828, Albuquerque, NM 87190-3828
Email: scholarship@nmef.net
http://www.nmef.net
Purpose: To support New Mexico students who plan to pursue college degrees in science, engineering or mathematics.
Eligibility: Applicants must be high school seniors and residents of New Mexico. They must plan to enroll in a math, science or engineering undergraduate degree program. Selection is based on academic achievement, leadership experiences at school, involvement in the community and financial need.
Target applicant(s): High school students.
Amount: $2,000.
Number of awards: 2.
Deadline: June 1.
How to apply: Applications are available online. An application form, a transcript and one letter of recommendation are required.
Exclusive: Visit www.UltimateScholarshipBook.com and enter code NE179726 for updates on this award.

[1798] • Sons of Italy Grand Lodge of California Italian Language Study Grant
Order Sons of Italy in America, Grand Lodge of California
Attention: Scholarship Commission, 5051 Mission Street, San Francisco, CA 94112-3473
Phone: 626-222-7768
Email: rgeorev@aol.com
http://www.osiaca.org/Scholarships/How-To-Apply

Purpose: To support students of Italian ancestry graduating from public or private high schools in California, Nevada and Klamath Falls, Oregon with a 30-day summer study abroad program in Italy.
Eligibility: Applicants must be of at least partial Italian ancestry and be enrolled at a college or trade school for the upcoming fall semester. Applicants must also have finished a foreign language course in high school. Selection is based on academic performance, leadership activities, financial need, essay detailing Italian ancestry, a personal statement and letters of recommendation.
Target applicant(s): High school students.
Amount: Up to $5,000.
Number of awards: Varies.
Deadline: March 1.
How to apply: Applications are available online. An application, personal statement, SAT/PSAT/ACT scores, GPA, record of activities, transcript and two letters of recommendation are required.
Exclusive: Visit www.UltimateScholarshipBook.com and enter code OR179826 for updates on this award.

[1799] • Sons of Italy Grand Lodge of College Scholarship
Order Sons of Italy in America, Grand Lodge of California
Attention: Scholarship Commission, 5051 Mission Street, San Francisco, CA 94112-3473
Phone: 626-222-7768
Email: rgeorev@aol.com
http://www.osiaca.org/Scholarships/How-To-Apply
Purpose: To support students of Italian ancestry graduating from public or private high schools in California, Nevada and Klamath Falls, Oregon.
Eligibility: Applicants must be of at least partial Italian ancestry and be enrolled at a college or trade school for the upcoming fall semester. Selection is based on academic performance, leadership activities, financial need, essay detailing Italian ancestry, a personal statement and letters of recommendation.
Target applicant(s): High school students.
Amount: $500-$5,000.
Number of awards: Varies.
Deadline: March 1.
How to apply: Applications are available online. An application, personal statement, SAT/PSAT/ACT scores, GPA, record of activities, transcript and two letters of recommendation are required.
Exclusive: Visit www.UltimateScholarshipBook.com and enter code OR179926 for updates on this award.

[1800] • South Carolina Farm Bureau Foundation Scholarships
South Carolina Farm Bureau Foundation
P.O. Box 754, Columbia, SC 29202-0754
Email: sanderson@scfb.org
http://www.scfb.org
Purpose: To aid agriculture students from South Carolina Farm Bureau member families.
Eligibility: Applicants must be from a South Carolina Farm Bureau member family. They must be rising undergraduate sophomores, juniors or seniors. They must be majoring in agriculture or a related subject. Selection is based on commitment to the field of agriculture, character and demonstrated leadership ability.
Target applicant(s): College students. Adult students.
Amount: $3,000.
Number of awards: 6.
Deadline: April 30.
How to apply: Applications are available by request from the South Carolina Farm Bureau. An application form and supporting materials are required.
Exclusive: Visit www.UltimateScholarshipBook.com and enter code SO180026 for updates on this award.

[1801] • South Carolina Hope Scholarship
South Carolina Commission on Higher Education
1122 Lady Street, Suite 400, Columbia, SC 29201
Phone: 803-737-2260
https://www.che.sc.gov
Purpose: Monetary assistance is provided to those freshmen who do not qualify for LIFE or Palmetto Fellows Scholarships.
Eligibility: Applicants must attend an eligible South Carolina public or private college full-time, be South Carolina residents and have a minimum 3.0 GPA. The award is only applicable to the first year of college.
Target applicant(s): High school students.
Minimum GPA: 3.0
Amount: Up to $2,800.
Number of awards: Varies.
Deadline: As soon as possible after October 1.
How to apply: Your college will determine your eligibility based on your high school transcript. There is no application form.
Exclusive: Visit www.UltimateScholarshipBook.com and enter code SO180126 for updates on this award.

[1802] • South Carolina Nurses Foundation Nurses Care Scholarship
South Carolina Nurses Foundation Inc.
Chairperson, SCNF Awards Committee, 1821 Gadsden Street, Columbia, SC 29201
Email: scnursesfoundation@gmail.com
http://www.scnursesfoundation.org
Purpose: To aid South Carolina nursing students.
Eligibility: Applicants must be South Carolina residents and be enrolled in an undergraduate registered nurse (RN) degree program or a graduate degree program in nursing. They must be in good academic standing, have plans to practice nursing in South Carolina after graduation and must demonstrate financial need. Selection is based on the overall strength of the application.
Target applicant(s): College students. Graduate school students. Adult students.
Amount: Varies.
Number of awards: 2.
Deadline: June 15.
How to apply: Applications are available online. An application form, personal statement, transcript and two recommendation letters are required.
Exclusive: Visit www.UltimateScholarshipBook.com and enter code SO180226 for updates on this award.

[1803] • South Carolina Tuition Grants Program
South Carolina Tuition Grants Commission
111 Executive Center Drive, Suite 242, Columbia, SC 29210
Phone: 803-896-1120
Email: info@sctuitiongrants.org
https://sctuitiongrants.org/
Purpose: To assist students who wish to attend independent South Carolina colleges.

The Ultimate Scholarship Book 2026
Scholarship Directory (State of Residence)

Eligibility: Students must be legal residents of South Carolina with financial need. High school seniors must graduate in the top 75 percent of their class or score a minimum of 900 on the SAT or 19 on the ACT. College applicants must complete and pass a minimum of 24 semester hours each year.
Target applicant(s): High school students. College students. Adult students.
Minimum GPA: 2.7
Amount: Up to $3,200.
Number of awards: Varies.
Scholarship may be renewable.
Deadline: June 30.
How to apply: Fill out the FAFSA, which is available online.
Exclusive: Visit www.UltimateScholarshipBook.com and enter code SO180326 for updates on this award.

[1804] • South Dakota Free Tuition for Veterans and Others Who Performed War Service
South Dakota Board of Regents
306 East Capitol Ave, Suite 200, Pierre, SD 57501-2545
Phone: 605-773-3455
Email: info@sdbor.edu
http://www.sdbor.edu
Purpose: To allow veterans and others who served in war the opportunity to receive higher education.
Eligibility: Applicants must be veterans or others who performed active war service. They must South Dakota residents who qualify for resident tuition and not be entitled to have their tuition or expenses paid by the United States.
Target applicant(s): College students. Adult students.
Amount: Full tuition.
Number of awards: Varies.
Scholarship may be renewable.
Deadline: Contact the sponsor to confirm the deadline.
How to apply: Applications are available from your financial aid office.
Exclusive: Visit www.UltimateScholarshipBook.com and enter code SO180426 for updates on this award.

[1805] • Southern Scholarship Foundation Scholarship
Southern Scholarship Foundation
322 Stadium Drive, Tallahassee, FL 32304
Phone: 850-222-3833
Email: Admissions@SouthernScholarship.org
http://www.southernscholarship.org
Purpose: To provide rent-free housing scholarships to students attending specific Florida institutions.
Eligibility: Applicants must have financial need, have a minimum 3.0 GPA, demonstrate high character and attend or plan to attend Florida A&M University, Florida Gulf Coast University, Florida State University, the University of Florida, Tallahassee Community College or Santa Fe Community College.
Target applicant(s): High school students. College students.
Minimum GPA: 3.0
Amount: Room and board.
Number of awards: Varies.
Scholarship may be renewable.
Deadline: April 1 (Fall); November 1 (Spring).
How to apply: Applications are available online.

Exclusive: Visit www.UltimateScholarshipBook.com and enter code SO180526 for updates on this award.

[1806] • Spillman-Bischoff Scholarship
Georgia Association for Nursing Education Inc.
P.O. Box 3844, LaGrange, GA 30241
Email: ganegeneral@gmail.com
http://gane.nursingnetwork.com
Purpose: To support Georgia students pursuing nursing education.
Eligibility: Applicants must be currently enrolled in an accredited program in nursing and a resident of Georgia. Students must demonstrate financial need, have a minimum 2.5 GPA, and provide two letters of reference. All non-RN applicants must have completed one year of study.
Target applicant(s): College students. Adult students.
Minimum GPA: 2.5
Amount: Varies.
Number of awards: Varies.
Deadline: December 17.
How to apply: Applications are available online.
Exclusive: Visit www.UltimateScholarshipBook.com and enter code GE180626 for updates on this award.

[1807] • Stanley O. McNaughton Community Service Award
Independent Colleges of Washington
600 Stewart Street, Suite 600, Seattle, WA 98101
Phone: 206-623-4494
Email: scholarships@icwashington.org
https://icwashington.org/page/scholarships
Purpose: To reward students who are committed to community service and who attend an independent college of Washington.
Eligibility: Applicants must be juniors or seniors who have participated in community service in high school and college. Students attending Gonzaga University, Heritage University, Pacific Lutheran University, Saint Martin's University, Seattle Pacific University, Seattle University, University of Puget Sound, Walla Walla University, Whitman College or Whitworth University are eligible.
Target applicant(s): College students. Adult students.
Amount: $2,400.
Number of awards: 5.
Deadline: April 12.
How to apply: Applications are available online or from your school's financial aid office.
Exclusive: Visit www.UltimateScholarshipBook.com and enter code IN180726 for updates on this award.

[1808] • Stanley Z. Koplik Certificate of Mastery Tuition Waiver Program
Massachusetts Department of Higher Education
Office of Student Financial Assistance, 454 Broadway, Suite 200, Revere, MA 02151
Phone: 617-727-9420
Email: osfa@osfa.mass.edu
https://www.mass.gov/handbook/massachusetts-financial-aid-programs

Purpose: To support Massachusetts students who have demonstrated academic merit.
Eligibility: Applicants must be currently enrolled in a public high school in Massachusetts. Students must receive an "Advanced" score on at least one part of the 10th grade MCAS test, and they must score "Proficient" on all of the other sections. They must also have good scores on at least two AP exams, two SAT II exams or combinations of one of those tests and other achievements determined by the Koplik program. Students must maintain a 3.3 GPA while participating in the scholarship.
Target applicant(s): High school students.
Minimum GPA: 3.3
Amount: Up to full tuition.
Number of awards: Varies.
Scholarship may be renewable.
Deadline: Contact the Koplik coordinator at your high school.
How to apply: Applications are available from high schools.
Exclusive: Visit www.UltimateScholarshipBook.com and enter code MA180826 for updates on this award.

[1809] • State Employees Association of North Carolina (SEANC) Scholarships

SEANC Scholarship Foundation
1621 Midtown Place, Raleigh, NC 27609
Phone: 919-833-6436
Email: cwilson@seanc.org
https://www.seanc.org/scholarship
Purpose: To provide financial assistance to SEANC members, their spouses and their children who plan to attend college.
Eligibility: Applicants must be the spouses or children of members and demonstrate either financial need or merit, or applicants must be members working full-time and enrolled in six or more semester hours of undergraduate work or three or more hours of graduate work. Students who are spouses or children must be enrolled full-time.
Target applicant(s): High school students. College students. Graduate school students. Adult students.
Amount: Varies.
Number of awards: Varies.
Deadline: April 15.
How to apply: Applications are available online or from your guidance counselor or financial aid office.
Exclusive: Visit www.UltimateScholarshipBook.com and enter code SE180926 for updates on this award.

[1810] • State Need-based Grants

South Carolina Commission on Higher Education
1122 Lady Street, Suite 400, Columbia, SC 29201
Phone: 803-737-2260
https://www.che.sc.gov
Purpose: Monetary assistance for higher education is provided to South Carolina resident students.
Eligibility: Applicants must be obtaining their first baccalaureate or professional degree, complete the Free Application for Federal Student Aid (FAFSA) and be residents of South Carolina. Students must have a minimum 2.0 GPA and be enrolled in their first one-year program, first associate's degree, first program leading to a baccalaureate degree, first baccalaureate degree or first professional degree to be eligible.
Target applicant(s): High school students. College students. Adult students.
Minimum GPA: 2.0
Amount: Up to $3,500.
Number of awards: Varies.
Scholarship may be renewable.
Deadline: As soon as possible after October 1.
How to apply: Complete the FAFSA and contact your college's financial aid office if you plan to attend a public college or the South Carolina Commission on Higher Education if you plan to attend a private college.
Exclusive: Visit www.UltimateScholarshipBook.com and enter code SO181026 for updates on this award.

[1811] • State of Hawai`i B Plus Scholarship

University of Hawaii - Office of Student Affairs
Attn: UH System Scholarship Office, 2444 Dole Street, Bachman Annex 9, Room 5, Honolulu, HI 96822
Phone: 808-956-4642
Email: scholars@hawaii.edu
https://westoahu.hawaii.edu/financial-aid/
Purpose: To support Hawaii residents with higher education expenses.
Eligibility: Applicants must be Hawaii residents who graduated from high school after 2005. Students must have a minimum 3.0 GPA, have completed a rigorous high school curriculum and demonstrate financial need.
Target applicant(s): College students. Adult students.
Minimum GPA: 3.0
Amount: Varies.
Number of awards: Varies.
Deadline: March 1.
How to apply: Applications are available online.
Exclusive: Visit www.UltimateScholarshipBook.com and enter code UN181126 for updates on this award.

[1812] • State of Maine Grant Program

Maine Education Assistance Division
Finance Authority of Maine (FAME), 5 Community Drive, P.O. Box 949, Augusta, ME 04332
Phone: 800-228-3734
Email: education@famemaine.com
http://www.famemaine.com
Purpose: To support Maine undergraduate students who have financial need.
Eligibility: Applicants must be U.S. citizens or eligible non-citizens, be Maine residents and submit the Free Application for Federal Student Aid (FAFSA) by May 1. They must have an Expected Family Contribution (EFC) of $5,000 or less. Selection is based on financial need.
Target applicant(s): High school students. College students. Adult students.
Amount: $2,500.
Number of awards: Varies.
Scholarship may be renewable.
Deadline: May 1.
How to apply: Application is made by completing the FAFSA.
Exclusive: Visit www.UltimateScholarshipBook.com and enter code MA181226 for updates on this award.

[1813] • State Work Study

Washington Student Achievement Council
P. O. Box 43430, Olympia, WA 98504-3430
Phone: 360-753-7850
Email: aies@wsac.wa.gov
https://wsac.wa.gov/
Purpose: To help low and middle income students earn money for college while gaining work experience.

The Ultimate Scholarship Book 2026
Scholarship Directory (State of Residence)

Eligibility: Applicants must have demonstrated financial need according to the FAFSA or WASFA, enroll at least half-time in an eligible undergraduate or graduate program, be authorized to work in the United States and not be seeking a degree in theology.
Target applicant(s): High school students. College students. Graduate school students. Adult students.
Amount: $2,000-$5,000 per year.
Number of awards: Varies.
Scholarship may be renewable.
Deadline: June 30.
How to apply: Eligible students who have filed a Free Application for Federal Student Aid (FAFSA) will be considered.
Exclusive: Visit www.UltimateScholarshipBook.com and enter code WA181326 for updates on this award.

[1814] • Stephen Phillips Memorial Scholarship Fund
Stephen Phillips Memorial Scholarship Fund
P.O. Box 870, Salem, MA 01970
Phone: 978-744-2111
Email: staff@spscholars.org
http://phillips-scholarship.org/
Purpose: To aid New England residents pursuing higher education.
Eligibility: Applicants must be U.S. residents or resident aliens who are permanent residents of Connecticut, Massachusetts, Maine, New Hampshire, Rhode Island or Vermont. They must be enrolled in a demanding undergraduate course of study pursuing their first degrees. A GPA of 3.0 or higher is required. Applicants must demonstrate citizenship, character, serious-mindedness and financial need.
Target applicant(s): High school students. College students. Adult students.
Minimum GPA: 3.0
Amount: $3,000-$17,000.
Number of awards: Varies.
Deadline: May 1.
How to apply: Applications are available online. An application form, essay, transcript, counselor or professor recommendation, additional letter of recommendation, FAFSA Student Aid Report, financial aid award letter, documentation of college costs and student's and parents' tax forms are required.
Exclusive: Visit www.UltimateScholarshipBook.com and enter code ST181426 for updates on this award.

[1815] • Sterling Scholar Awards of Utah
Deseret News-KSL Broadcast Group Sterling Scholar
55 North 300 West, Suite 800, Salt Lake City, UT 84145
Phone: 801-323-4223
Email: michaelsonj@deseretmgt.com
http://www.sterlingscholar.org
Purpose: To aid outstanding Utah students.
Eligibility: Applicants must be Utah public high school seniors. They must be nominated by their schools in one of 14 categories. Selection is based on scholarship (50 percent), leadership (25 percent) and community service/citizenship (25 percent).
Target applicant(s): High school students.
Amount: Varies.
Number of awards: Varies.
Deadline: March 30.
How to apply: Applications are available from your school's Sterling Awards organizer. An ID page, application form, transcript, proof of ACT scores, principal's report, standardized test data sheet and letter of recommendation are required.
Exclusive: Visit www.UltimateScholarshipBook.com and enter code DE181526 for updates on this award.

[1816] • Steve Fasteau Past Presidents' Scholarship
California Association for Postsecondary Education and Disability
19197 Golden Valley Road #521, Santa Clarita, CA 91387
Phone: 909-384-8663
Email: caped.scholarship.committee@gmail.com
http://www.caped.co/scholarships/
Purpose: To support disabled students.
Eligibility: Applicants must be college students with high academic achievement. They must demonstrate leadership and dedication to the advancement of students with disabilities in higher education. Undergraduate students must have a minimum GPA of 2.5 and at least six semester units, and graduate students must have a minimum GPA of 3.0 and at least three semester units from a public or private California college or university.
Target applicant(s): College students. Graduate school students. Adult students.
Minimum GPA: 2.5 for undergraduate students; 3.0 for graduate students
Amount: $1,500.
Number of awards: 1.
Deadline: August 31.
How to apply: Applications are available online. An application form, letter of application, letter of recommendation, verification of disability, transcript and proof of enrollment are required.
Exclusive: Visit www.UltimateScholarshipBook.com and enter code CA181626 for updates on this award.

[1817] • Student Incentive Grants
New Mexico Higher Education Department
2044 Galisteo Street, Suite 4, Santa Fe, NM 87505-2100
Phone: 505-476-8400
Email: cesaria.tapia1@state.nm.us
https://hed.state.nm.us/financial-aid
Purpose: To support New Mexico undergraduate students with financial need to attend postsecondary institutions in New Mexico.
Eligibility: Applicants must be New Mexico resident undergraduate students and attend public and selected private nonprofit postsecondary institutions in New Mexico at least half-time. Students must also be U.S. citizens.
Target applicant(s): College students. Adult students.
Amount: $200-$2,500.
Number of awards: Varies.
Deadline: Contact the college's financial aid office to confirm the deadline.
How to apply: Submit the FAFSA and contact your financial aid office. Deadlines are set by individual institutions.
Exclusive: Visit www.UltimateScholarshipBook.com and enter code NE181726 for updates on this award.

[1818] • Susan Bunch Memorial Scholarship
California Association on Postsecondary Education and Disability (CAPED)
10073 Valley View Street, #242, Cypress, CA 90630
Phone: 562-397-2810
Email: caped.scholarship.committee@gmail.com
http://www.caped.co/scholarships/

Purpose: To support students with a learning disability who are pursuing a higher education.
Eligibility: Applicants must have a verifiable learning disability and be currently enrolled as a student at a California college or university with a GPA of 2.5 for undergraduates or 3.0 for graduate students. Students must have completed at least six semester or eight quarter units as an undergraduate student or three semester or four quarter units as a graduate student.
Target applicant(s): College students. Graduate school students. Adult students.
Minimum GPA: 2.5 for undergraduate students; 3.0 for graduate students
Amount: $1,000.
Number of awards: 1.
Deadline: August 31.
How to apply: Applications are available online.
Exclusive: Visit www.UltimateScholarshipBook.com and enter code CA181826 for updates on this award.

[1819] • Susan Howard Community Service Award

British American Foundation of Texas
Email: info@baftx.org
http://www.baftx.org
Purpose: To support Texas students with a passion for community service.
Eligibility: Applicants must be residents of Texas or the U.K. enrolled as full-time students within the Texas or U.K. education systems. Students must demonstrate financial need, be 11 to 21 years old and be currently working on an inspiring community service project.
Target applicant(s): Junior high students or younger. High school students. College students.
Amount: $5,000.
Number of awards: 1.
Deadline: March 31.
How to apply: Applications are available online.
Exclusive: Visit www.UltimateScholarshipBook.com and enter code BR181926 for updates on this award.

[1820] • Susan Thompson Buffett Foundation Scholarship Program

Susan Thompson Buffett Foundation
808 Conagra Drive, Omaha, NE 68102
Phone: 402-943-1383
Email: scholarships@stbfoundation.org
https://buffettscholarships.org/eligibility-selection
Purpose: To support Nebraska students with financial need attend college.
Eligibility: Applicants must live in Nebraska, meet in-state residency requirements and be Nebraska high school or GED graduates. Students must have a minimum 2.0 GPA in high school, be in need of financial assistance and be a first-time freshman planning to attend a Nebraska public college.
Target applicant(s): High school students. College students. Adult students.
Minimum GPA: 2.0
Amount: Varies.
Number of awards: Varies.
Scholarship may be renewable.
Deadline: February 1.
How to apply: Applications are available online.
Exclusive: Visit www.UltimateScholarshipBook.com and enter code SU182026 for updates on this award.

[1821] • Sussman-Miller Educational Assistance Award

Albuquerque Community Foundation (ACF)
P.O. Box 25266, Albuquerque, NM 87125-0266
Phone: 505-883-6240
Email: dominic@abqcf.org
https://abqcf.org/scholarships/
Purpose: To assist New Mexico high school graduates and college undergraduates.
Eligibility: Students must be New Mexico residents for a minimum of one year, have been awarded a financial package that does not satisfy demonstrated need and be accepted by and have chosen to attend a U.S. post-secondary, accredited, nonprofit educational institution full-time. High school applicants need to graduate from an accredited public or private high school and have a 3.0 minimum GPA. Undergraduate applicants must have completed a minimum of one semester of undergraduate study with a 2.5 minimum GPA and cannot be applying for residency in another state.
Target applicant(s): High school students. College students. Adult students.
Minimum GPA: 3.0 for high school students; 2.5 for undergraduate students
Amount: Up to $8,000.
Number of awards: Varies.
Deadline: April 4 (Spring); June 6 (Summer).
How to apply: Applications are available online.
Exclusive: Visit www.UltimateScholarshipBook.com and enter code AL182126 for updates on this award.

[1822] • T. Eugene Young Montana's Promise Scholarship

Montana Community Foundation
P.O. Box 1145, Helena, MT 59624
Phone: 406-443-8313
Email: info@mtcf.org
https://mtcf.org/scholarships/about-scholarships
Purpose: To help students and support philanthropy throughout Montana by helping communities flourish and grow through supporting innovative solutions and creating powerful partnerships.
Eligibility: Applicants must be high school seniors graduating from a Montana high school with a minimum 3.0 or higher GPA and be willing to go to college to study (STEM) science, technology, engineering, mathematics or healthcare. Students must be attending an accredited post-secondary educational institution, (university, college, community college, college of technology or technical school) and preference will be given to those applicants who plan to attend a university or college in Montana.
Target applicant(s): High school students. College students. Adult students.
Minimum GPA: 3.0
Amount: $1,000.
Number of awards: 25.
Deadline: March 31.
How to apply: Applications are available online.
Exclusive: Visit www.UltimateScholarshipBook.com and enter code MO182226 for updates on this award.

The Ultimate Scholarship Book 2026
Scholarship Directory (State of Residence)

[1823] • Talent Incentive Program Grant
State of Wisconsin Higher Educational Aids Board
P.O. Box 7885, Madison, WI 53707
Phone: 608-267-2206
Email: heabmail@wisconsin.gov
https://heab.state.wi.us
Purpose: To assist Wisconsin students who have financial need.
Eligibility: Applicants must be Wisconsin residents who are first-time college freshmen at a Wisconsin postsecondary institution. They must be enrolled at least part-time and must demonstrate financial need. Selection is based on financial need.
Target applicant(s): High school students. College students. Adult students.
Amount: $600-$1,800.
Number of awards: Varies.
Scholarship may be renewable.
Deadline: As soon as possible after October 1.
How to apply: Applicants must complete the FAFSA and must be nominated for this award by their financial aid office or by a Wisconsin Educational Opportunities Program (WEOP) counselor.
Exclusive: Visit www.UltimateScholarshipBook.com and enter code ST182326 for updates on this award.

[1824] • Teacher Loan Program
State of Wisconsin Higher Educational Aids Board
P.O. Box 7885, Madison, WI 53707
Phone: 608-267-2206
Email: heabmail@wisconsin.gov
https://heab.state.wi.us
Purpose: To encourage Wisconsin students to become teachers in identified shortage areas.
Eligibility: Applicants must be Wisconsin residents who are undergraduate sophomores, juniors or seniors. Students must be enrolled at least half-time at a University of Wisconsin System institution or a non-profit, independent college or university in the state of Wisconsin and have a minimum 3.0 GPA. Applicants must be pursuing programs leading to teacher licensure in a discipline identified as a teacher shortage area for the state of Wisconsin. Students who participate in this program must agree to teach full-time in an elementary or secondary school in the city of Milwaukee or in a county defined as "rural". For each year the applicants meet all forgiveness criteria requirements, 25 percent of the loan is forgiven.
Target applicant(s): College students. Adult students.
Minimum GPA: 3.0
Amount: Up to $10,000.
Number of awards: Varies.
Deadline: Contact the sponsor to confirm the deadline.
How to apply: Applications are available online.
Exclusive: Visit www.UltimateScholarshipBook.com and enter code ST182426 for updates on this award.

[1825] • Teacher Loan-For-Service Program
New Mexico Higher Education Department
2044 Galisteo Street, Suite 4, Santa Fe, NM 87505-2100
Phone: 505-476-8400
Email: cesaria.tapia1@state.nm.us
https://hed.state.nm.us/financial-aid
Purpose: To encourage New Mexico students interested in becoming teachers.
Eligibility: Applicants must be New Mexico residents and accepted into a teaching or an alternative licensure teacher preparation program at a New Mexico public college or university. Students must be enrolled as undergraduates or graduates at least half-time and demonstrate financial need. Applicants must declare their intent to practice as a teacher in a designated shortage area within the state of New Mexico.
Target applicant(s): College students. Graduate school students. Adult students.
Amount: Up to $4,000.
Number of awards: Varies.
Scholarship may be renewable.
Deadline: July 1.
How to apply: Applications are available online.
Exclusive: Visit www.UltimateScholarshipBook.com and enter code NE182526 for updates on this award.

[1826] • Teacher Scholarship Program
Kentucky Higher Education Assistance Authority (KHEAA)
P.O. Box 798, Frankfort, KY 40602
Phone: 800-928-8926
Email: blane@kheaa.com
http://www.kheaa.com
Purpose: To support Kentucky students pursuing teacher certification at participating Kentucky colleges.
Eligibility: Applicants must be U.S. citizens and Kentucky residents. Students must be admitted to a teacher education program pursuing initial teacher certification at a participating Kentucky college or a certified teacher (primary through grade 12) pursuing additional certification for classroom teaching. Applicants must demonstrate financial need and meet satisfactory academic progress. Students must teach one semester at a Kentucky public or certified non-public school for each semester the scholarship is received. The FAFSA must be filed.
Target applicant(s): College students. Graduate school students. Adult students.
Amount: Up to $3,000.
Number of awards: Varies.
Deadline: May 1.
How to apply: Applications are available online.
Exclusive: Visit www.UltimateScholarshipBook.com and enter code KE182626 for updates on this award.

[1827] • Teacher Shortage Employment Incentive Program
Oklahoma State Regents for Higher Education
655 Research Parkway, Suite 200, Oklahoma City, OK 73104
Phone: 405-225-9100
Email: studentinfo@osrhe.edu
http://www.okhighered.org
Purpose: To encourage students who major in mathematics or science to serve as teachers of mathematics and science in Oklahoma public secondary schools.
Eligibility: Applicants must be willing to teach mathematics or science at an Oklahoma public secondary school for at least five years. Students must complete an approved professional teacher education program from an Oklahoma accredited teacher education unit which must include a student teaching requirement. Applicants must also hold a valid certificate to teach mathematics or science at the secondary level.
Target applicant(s): College students. Adult students.
Amount: Varies.
Number of awards: Varies.
Deadline: No later than the date of their graduation.
How to apply: Applications are available online.

Exclusive: Visit www.UltimateScholarshipBook.com and enter code OK182726 for updates on this award.

[1828] • Tech High School Alumni Association/ W.O. Cheney Merit Scholarship
Community Foundation for Greater Atlanta Inc.
50 Hurt Plaza, Suite 449, Atlanta, GA 30303
Phone: 404-688-5525
Email: info@cfgreateratlanta.org
https://cfgreateratlanta.org/scholarships/
Purpose: To aid future college students who are planning to major in engineering, mathematics or one of the physical sciences.
Eligibility: Applicants must be U.S. citizens, Georgia residents and high school seniors who have been accepted at an accredited four-year postsecondary institution. They must be planning to major in mathematics, one of the physical sciences or engineering and must be full-time students who have a proven interest in community service. They must have an SAT composite (math and critical reading) score of 1300 or higher and must either be in the top 10 percent of their class or have a GPA of 3.0 or higher. Selection is based on the overall strength of the application.
Target applicant(s): High school students.
Minimum GPA: 3.0
Amount: $5,000 a year.
Number of awards: Up to 4.
Scholarship may be renewable.
Deadline: February 15.
How to apply: Applications are available online. An application form and supporting materials are required.
Exclusive: Visit www.UltimateScholarshipBook.com and enter code CO182826 for updates on this award.

[1829] • Technical Certification Scholarship
Texas 4-H Youth Development Foundation
4180 Highway 6, College Station, TX 77845
Phone: 979-845-1211
Email: texas4h@ag.tamu.edu
https://texas4-h.tamu.edu/
Purpose: To support Texas high school seniors who plan to pursue a technical program.
Eligibility: Applicants must be current active members and have actively participated in a 4-H program for at least two of the past three years. They must have formally applied to a Texas college or university, and they must meet all requirements for admission. Students must not have any plans to continue their college education after completion of a technical program.
Target applicant(s): High school students.
Amount: Varies.
Number of awards: Varies.
Deadline: February 15.
How to apply: Applications are available online.
Exclusive: Visit www.UltimateScholarshipBook.com and enter code TE182926 for updates on this award.

[1830] • Ted and Nora Anderson Scholarships
American Legion, Department of Kansas
1314 SW Topeka Boulevard, Topeka, KS 66612
Phone: 785-232-9315
https://kansaslegion.org/
Purpose: To support worthy and needy children of American Legion and American Legion Auxiliary members as they pursue their educations.
Eligibility: Applicants must be high school seniors or college freshmen or sophomores who are average or better students. They must be enrolling or enrolled in a post-secondary school in Kansas and the son or daughter of a veteran. At least one parent must have been a member of the Kansas American Legion or American Legion Auxiliary for the past three years. The children of deceased parents are also eligible as long as the parent was a paid member at the time of death. Applicants must submit three letters of recommendation with only one from a teacher, a 1040 income statement, documentation of parent's veteran status, an essay on "Why I Want to Go to College" and a high school transcript.
Target applicant(s): High school students. College students. Adult students.
Amount: $500.
Number of awards: 4.
Deadline: February 15.
How to apply: Applications are available online.
Exclusive: Visit www.UltimateScholarshipBook.com and enter code AM183026 for updates on this award.

[1831] • Ted Brickley/Bernice Shickora Scholarship
New Jersey Chapter of the American Society of Safety Engineers
Liberty Mutual Insurance Company, Attn.: Frank Gesualdo, 7 Becker Farm Road, 2nd Floor, Roseland, NJ 07068
Email: scholarship@njasse.org
http://nj.asse.org/scholarship/
Purpose: To aid New Jersey students who are majoring in industrial hygiene, occupational safety, environmental science or a related subject.
Eligibility: Applicants must be New Jersey residents who are enrolled at an accredited New Jersey college or university and must be graduate students or rising undergraduate juniors or seniors. They must be majoring in industrial hygiene, occupational safety, environmental science or a related subject and must be involved in extracurricular activities pertaining to occupational safety. They must have a major GPA of 2.5 or higher on a four-point scale. Selection is based on the overall strength of the application.
Target applicant(s): College students. Graduate school students. Adult students.
Minimum GPA: 2.5
Amount: $1,000.
Number of awards: 2.
Deadline: April 15; November 15.
How to apply: Applications are available online. An application form, transcript and one reference letter are required.
Exclusive: Visit www.UltimateScholarshipBook.com and enter code NE183126 for updates on this award.

[1832] • Tennessee Funeral Directors Association Memorial Scholarship
Tennessee Funeral Directors Association
Scholarship Committee, 1616 Church Street, Suite A, Nashville, TN 37203
Phone: 615-321-8792
Email: office@tnfda.org
http://www.tnfda.org
Purpose: To aid funeral service and mortuary science students who are residents of Tennessee.
Eligibility: Applicants must be U.S. citizens and legal residents of Tennessee. They must be enrolled full time in a funeral service or mortuary science program at a school that has been accredited by the American Board of Funeral Service Education (ABFSE). They must have completed one term of their program and must have at least one term remaining in their

program. They must have plans to practice in Tennessee after graduating. Selection is based on the overall strength of the application.
Target applicant(s): College students. Adult students.
Amount: Varies.
Number of awards: Varies.
Deadline: Contact the sponsor to confirm the deadline.
How to apply: Applications are available online. An application form, transcript, copies of federal income tax forms, one recommendation letter and a personal essay are required.
Exclusive: Visit www.UltimateScholarshipBook.com and enter code TE183226 for updates on this award.

[1833] • Tennessee HOPE Lottery Scholarship
Tennessee Student Assistance Corporation
312 Rosa L. Parks Avenue, 9th Floor, Nashville, TN 37243
Phone: 800-342-1663
Email: tsac.aidinfo@tn.gov
https://www.collegefortn.org/about-financial-aid/
Purpose: To support undergraduate students in Tennessee.
Eligibility: Applicants must be entering freshmen and either have at least a 3.0 GPA, a score of 21 on the ACT or a score of 980 on the SAT. GED students must also score at least a 525 on the GED test. Home-schooled students and some private school students must meet additional requirements. Applicants must be Tennessee residents as classified pursuant to TCA 49-8-104.
Target applicant(s): High school students.
Minimum GPA: 3.0
Amount: Up to $6,000.
Number of awards: Varies.
Scholarship may be renewable.
Deadline: February 1 (Spring and Summer); September 1 (Fall).
How to apply: Applications are available through completion of the FAFSA.
Exclusive: Visit www.UltimateScholarshipBook.com and enter code TE183326 for updates on this award.

[1834] • Tennessee Student Assistance Awards
Tennessee Student Assistance Corporation
312 Rosa L. Parks Avenue, 9th Floor, Nashville, TN 37243
Phone: 800-342-1663
Email: tsac.aidinfo@tn.gov
https://www.collegefortn.org/about-financial-aid/
Purpose: To aid Tennessee students.
Eligibility: Applicants must be Tennessee residents who have applied for federal aid and have an Expected Family Contribution of $5,846 or less. They must be enrolled at least half time at an eligible Tennessee institution of higher learning and maintain satisfactory academic progress. They may not be in default on a loan or owe a refund on any grant previously received for education.
Target applicant(s): High school students. College students. Adult students.
Amount: Up to $4,000.
Number of awards: Varies.
Scholarship may be renewable.
Deadline: As soon as possible after October 1.
How to apply: Applications are available online. A Free Application for Federal Student Aid (FAFSA) is required.
Exclusive: Visit www.UltimateScholarshipBook.com and enter code TE183426 for updates on this award.

[1835] • Terrel H. Bell Education Scholarship
Utah System of Higher Education
New Century Scholarship, P.O. Box 145116, Salt Lake City, UT 84114-5116
Phone: 801-321-7221
Email: newcentury@ushe.edu
https://ushe.edu/
Purpose: To support students planning to pursue a degree in education.
Eligibility: Applicants must be undergraduate and graduate students who meet required academic standards and are enrolled in at least six credits. Students must plan to pursue a degree in education and intend to work in a Utah public school. Applicants must study in an approved teacher preparation program or in an approved program that prepares them to become a speech-language pathologist or another licensed professional providing services in a public school to students with disabilities.
Target applicant(s): College students. Graduate school students. Adult students.
Amount: Varies.
Number of awards: Varies.
Deadline: Contact the sponsor to confirm the deadline.
How to apply: Applications are available online.
Exclusive: Visit www.UltimateScholarshipBook.com and enter code UT183526 for updates on this award.

[1836] • Texas 4-H Opportunity Scholarship Program – Baccalaureate Scholarships
Texas 4-H Youth Development Foundation
4180 Highway 6, College Station, TX 77845
Phone: 979-845-1211
Email: texas4h@ag.tamu.edu
https://texas4-h.tamu.edu/
Purpose: To support Texas 4-H members who are planning to pursue a bachelor's degree.
Eligibility: Students must be high school seniors who have actively participated in a Texas 4-H program during the current year and at least two of the three previous years. They must have formally applied to a Texas college or university, and they must meet the school's admission requirements. Applicants must have a score of at least 1350 on the SAT or 19 on the ACT. Students must provide information about their 4-H achievements, financial need, community service participation and leadership skills.
Target applicant(s): High school students.
Amount: $3,000-$20,000.
Number of awards: Varies.
Deadline: February 15.
How to apply: Applications are available online.
Exclusive: Visit www.UltimateScholarshipBook.com and enter code TE183626 for updates on this award.

[1837] • Texas Association FCCLA Regional Scholarship
Family, Career and Community Leaders of America - Texas Association
1107 West 45th Street, Austin, TX 78756
Phone: 512-306-0099
Email: fccla@texasfccla.org
https://www.texasfccla.org/scholarships-1
Purpose: To aid Texas students who are planning to major in family and consumer sciences.
Eligibility: Applicants must be members of Texas Association, Family, Career and Community Leaders of America (FCCLA). They must be

planning to major in family and consumer sciences in college. Selection is based on the overall strength of the application.
Target applicant(s): High school students.
Amount: $1,000.
Number of awards: 5.
Deadline: February 1.
How to apply: Applications are available online. An application form, transcript, personal essay and standardized test scores are required.
Exclusive: Visit www.UltimateScholarshipBook.com and enter code FA183726 for updates on this award.

[1838] • Texas Broadcast Education Foundation Scholarships
Texas Association of Broadcasters
502 E. 11th Street, Suite 200, Austin, TX 78701
Phone: 512-322-9944
Email: craig@tab.org
https://www.tab.org/scholarships
Purpose: To support promising Texas students.
Eligibility: Applicants must be TAB student members or attend a TAB member college or university. All eligible applicants must have a GPA of 3.0 or higher and enroll full-time in a program that emphasizes radio or television broadcasting or communications at a college or university in Texas.
Target applicant(s): High school students. College students. Graduate school students. Adult students.
Minimum GPA: 3.0
Amount: $3,000-$5,000.
Number of awards: 9.
Deadline: Contact the sponsor to confirm the deadline.
How to apply: Applications are available online. An application form is required.
Exclusive: Visit www.UltimateScholarshipBook.com and enter code TE183826 for updates on this award.

[1839] • Texas Elks State Association Four-Year Scholarship Program
Texas Elks State Association (TESA)
Pollard RV Park, 1961 FM 1586, Gonzales, TX 78629
Phone: 830-263-461
Email: tecsi@gvec.net
https://texaselks.org/tesa-scholarships
Purpose: To support Texas students.
Eligibility: Applicants must be seniors in Texas high schools who are not in the top 5 percent of their class. They must be U.S. citizens and Texas residents.
Target applicant(s): High school students.
Amount: $1,250.
Number of awards: 6.
Scholarship may be renewable.
Deadline: March 8.
How to apply: Applications are available online. An application form, transcript, SAT or ACT scores, applicant statement and parent statement are required.
Exclusive: Visit www.UltimateScholarshipBook.com and enter code TE183926 for updates on this award.

[1840] • Texas Elks State Association Teenager of the Year Scholarship
Texas Elks State Association (TESA)
Pollard RV Park, 1961 FM 1586, Gonzales, TX 78629
Phone: 830-263-461
Email: tecsi@gvec.net
https://texaselks.org/tesa-scholarships
Purpose: To support outstanding high school students.
Eligibility: Applicants must be graduating high school seniors from Texas. Selection criteria include SAT/ACT scores, honors and awards, participation and leadership in extracurricular activities and neatness and organization of application.
Target applicant(s): High school students.
Amount: $1,000-$2,500.
Number of awards: 6.
Deadline: March 8.
How to apply: Applications are available online. An application form and documentation of awards and activities are required.
Exclusive: Visit www.UltimateScholarshipBook.com and enter code TE184026 for updates on this award.

[1841] • Texas Elks State Association Vocational Grant Program
Texas Elks State Association (TESA)
Pollard RV Park, 1961 FM 1586, Gonzales, TX 78629
Phone: 830-263-461
Email: tecsi@gvec.net
https://texaselks.org/tesa-scholarships
Purpose: To support students pursuing vocational education.
Eligibility: Applicants must be U.S. citizens and Texas residents 18 years of age or older. They must plan to enroll full-time in a two-year or less vocational or technical program that results in a certificate, diploma or associate's degree.
Target applicant(s): High school students. College students. Adult students.
Amount: Varies.
Number of awards: Varies.
Deadline: March 8.
How to apply: Applications are available online. An application form, personal statement, letter from parent or other person with knowledge of family background, letter of recommendation and grade or work records for previous two years are required.
Exclusive: Visit www.UltimateScholarshipBook.com and enter code TE184126 for updates on this award.

[1842] • Texas Fifth-Year Accounting Student Scholarship Program
Texas Higher Education Coordinating Board
1200 East Anderson Lane, Austin, TX 78752
Phone: 888-311-8881.
Email: pamela.harris@thecb.state.tx.us
http://www.collegeforalltexans.com
Purpose: To aid Texas students who are preparing for careers as certified public accountants (CPAs).
Eligibility: Applicants must be Texas residents who are enrolled at an accredited, non-profit postsecondary institution located in Texas. By the time of award disbursement, they must have completed at least 120 credit hours of college coursework with at least 15 of those being from accounting courses. They must plan to take the exam to become a certified public

accountant (CPA), and they must demonstrate financial need. Selection is based on the overall strength of the application.
Target applicant(s): College students. Adult students.
Amount: Up to $5,000.
Number of awards: Varies.
Deadline: Contact the sponsor to confirm the deadline.
How to apply: Applications are available from the applicant's college financial aid office or department of accounting. An application form and supporting materials are required.
Exclusive: Visit www.UltimateScholarshipBook.com and enter code TE184226 for updates on this award.

[1843] • Texas History Essay Scholarship

Sons of the Republic of Texas
1717 8th Street, Bay City, TX 77414
Phone: 979-245-6644
http://www.srttexas.org/community.html
Purpose: To aid high school students and promote awareness of Texas history.
Eligibility: Applicants must be graduating seniors. They must submit an essay exploring the relevance of Texas history in the building of the state. Selection is based on research, originality and organization.
Target applicant(s): High school students.
Amount: $2,000-$4,000.
Number of awards: 3.
Deadline: January 31.
How to apply: Applications are available online. An application form and essay are required.
Exclusive: Visit www.UltimateScholarshipBook.com and enter code SO184326 for updates on this award.

[1844] • Texas International Fishing Tournament Inc. Scholarship

Texas International Fishing Tournament
P.O. Box 2715, South Padre Island, TX 78597
Phone: 956-943-8438
Email: info@tift.org
https://www.tift.org/content.php?id=7759
Purpose: To support college level anglers in their pursuit of completing undergraduate studies.
Eligibility: Applicants must be a college undergraduate (freshman through senior), have at least a 2.25 GPA and have been involved with the Texas International Fishing Tournament. Selection is based on past involvement with T.I.F.T., academic achievement and an essay.
Target applicant(s): College students. Adult students.
Minimum GPA: 2.25
Amount: $2,000.
Number of awards: Varies.
Scholarship may be renewable.
Deadline: March 1.
How to apply: Applications are available online.
Exclusive: Visit www.UltimateScholarshipBook.com and enter code TE184426 for updates on this award.

[1845] • Texas Occupational Therapy Association Scholarships

American Occupational Therapy Foundation
Attn: Jeanne Cooper, 4720 Montgomery Lane, Suite 202, Bethesda, MD 20814
Phone: 240-292-1034
Email: jcooper@aotf.org
https://www.tota.org/scholarships
Purpose: To aid Texas occupational therapy students.
Eligibility: Applicants must be members of the Texas Occupational Therapy Association (TOTA). They must be Texas residents who are enrolled in an occupational therapy certificate, associate's or professional degree program at an accredited Texas school. Selection is based on the overall strength of the application.
Target applicant(s): College students. Adult students.
Amount: Varies.
Number of awards: 2.
Deadline: October 2.
How to apply: Applications are available by request from Jeanne Cooper, who is the scholarship coordinator at the American Occupational Therapy Association. An application form and supporting materials are required.
Exclusive: Visit www.UltimateScholarshipBook.com and enter code AM184526 for updates on this award.

[1846] • Texas Oratorical Contest

American Legion, Department of Texas
P.O. Box 140527, Austin, TX 78714
Phone: 512-472-4138
Email: programs@txlegion.org
https://txlegion.org/programs/oratorical/
Purpose: To enhance high school students' experience with and understanding of the U.S. Constitution. The contest will help develop students' leadership skills and civic appreciation, as well as the ability to deliver thoughtful, insightful orations regarding U.S. citizenship and its inherent responsibilities.
Eligibility: Applicants must be high school students under the age of 20 who are U.S. citizens or legal residents and residents of the state. Students first give an oration within their state and winners compete at the national level. The oration must be related to the Constitution of the United States focusing on the duties and obligations citizens have to the government. It must be in English and be between three and five minutes. There is also an assigned topic which is posted on the website, and it should be between three and five minutes.
Target applicant(s): High school students.
Amount: $500-$20,000.
Number of awards: Varies.
Deadline: February 19.
How to apply: Application information is available online or by contacting the local post.
Exclusive: Visit www.UltimateScholarshipBook.com and enter code AM184626 for updates on this award.

[1847] • Texas Public Educational Grant

Texas Higher Education Coordinating Board
1200 East Anderson Lane, Austin, TX 78752
Phone: 888-311-8881.
Email: pamela.harris@thecb.state.tx.us
http://www.collegeforalltexans.com
Purpose: To assist Texas students who have financial need.
Eligibility: Applicants must attend a public college or university in Texas and demonstrate financial need. Individual institutions determine additional eligibility criteria. Selection is based on financial need.

Target applicant(s): High school students. College students. Graduate school students. Adult students.
Amount: Varies.
Number of awards: Varies.
Deadline: As soon as possible after October 1.
How to apply: Application is made by completing the FAFSA and contacting your school's financial aid office.
Exclusive: Visit www.UltimateScholarshipBook.com and enter code TE184726 for updates on this award.

[1848] • Thaddeus Colson and Isabelle Saalwaechter Fitzpatrick Memorial Scholarship

Community Foundation of Louisville
Waterfront Plaza, West Tower, 325 West Main Street, Suite 1110, Louisville, KY 40202
Phone: 502-585-4649
Email: ebonyo@cflouisville.org
https://www.cflouisville.org/scholarships/
Purpose: To aid female undergraduates in Kentucky who are majoring in environment-related subjects.
Eligibility: Applicants must be female Kentucky residents who are attending a public college or university in Kentucky. They must be full-time undergraduate students who are rising sophomores, juniors or seniors and be majoring in a subject that is related to the environment (such as agriculture, horticulture, environmental engineering, biology or environmental studies). They must have a GPA of 3.0 or higher. Selection is based on the overall strength of the application.
Target applicant(s): College students. Adult students.
Minimum GPA: 3.0
Amount: Varies.
Number of awards: Varies.
Deadline: February 29.
How to apply: Applications are available online. An application form and supporting materials are required.
Exclusive: Visit www.UltimateScholarshipBook.com and enter code CO184826 for updates on this award.

[1849] • Tongan Cultural Society Scholarship

Hawaii Community Foundation - Scholarships
827 Fort Street Mall, Honolulu, HI 96813
Phone: 888-731-3863
Email: scholarships@hcf-hawaii.org
https://www.hawaiicommunityfoundation.org/
Purpose: To support students of Tongan ancestry.
Eligibility: Applicants must attend school in Hawaii and must maintain a minimum 2.7 GPA.
Target applicant(s): High school students. College students. Graduate school students. Adult students.
Minimum GPA: 2.7
Amount: Varies.
Number of awards: Varies.
Deadline: February 28.
How to apply: To apply, register online, complete the online application and select the scholarships to which you wish to apply. In addition, mail the supporting materials: printed confirmation page from the online application, personal statement, copy of Student Aid Report (SAR) available at www.fafsa.ed.gov and official transcript.
Exclusive: Visit www.UltimateScholarshipBook.com and enter code HA184926 for updates on this award.

[1850] • TOPS Performance Award

Louisiana Office of Student Financial Assistance
605 N. Fifth Street, Baton Rouge, LA 70802
Phone: 800-259-5626 x1012
Email: custserv@la.gov
https://mylosfa.la.gov/students-parents/scholarships-grants/tops/
Purpose: To aid Louisiana student residents.
Eligibility: Applicants must be Louisiana residents, U.S. citizens, apply during their senior year in high school, use the award at a Louisiana college or university, have a minimum 3.0 GPA and have a minimum ACT score of 23 or an equivalent SAT score.
Target applicant(s): High school students.
Minimum GPA: 3.0
Amount: Tuition plus a $400 stipend.
Number of awards: Varies.
Scholarship may be renewable.
Deadline: July 1.
How to apply: The application is the Free Application for Federal Student Aid (FAFSA). ACT or SAT scores must also be reported.
Exclusive: Visit www.UltimateScholarshipBook.com and enter code LO185026 for updates on this award.

[1851] • TOPS Tech Award

Louisiana Office of Student Financial Assistance
605 N. Fifth Street, Baton Rouge, LA 70802
Phone: 800-259-5626 x1012
Email: custserv@la.gov
https://mylosfa.la.gov/students-parents/scholarships-grants/tops/
Purpose: To assist Louisiana resident students.
Eligibility: Applicants must be Louisiana residents, apply during their senior year in a public high school and pursue an industry-based occupational or vocational credential in a public college or university that meets certain standards. They must also have a minimum 2.5 GPA, score at least 15 on the English and Mathematics subsections of the ACT PLAN Assessment, have at least minimum passing scores in English and Mathematics on the GEE and have prepared a five-year education and career plan.
Target applicant(s): High school students.
Minimum GPA: 2.5
Amount: Up to full tuition.
Number of awards: Varies.
Scholarship may be renewable.
Deadline: July 1.
How to apply: Applications are available online or from guidance counselors.
Exclusive: Visit www.UltimateScholarshipBook.com and enter code LO185126 for updates on this award.

[1852] • Towards EXcellence, Access and Success (TEXAS) Grant Program

Texas Higher Education Coordinating Board
1200 East Anderson Lane, Austin, TX 78752
Phone: 888-311-8881.
Email: pamela.harris@thecb.state.tx.us
http://www.collegeforalltexans.com
Purpose: To assist Texas students who have financial need.
Eligibility: Applicants must be Texas residents and high school graduates. They must demonstrate financial need by having an Expected Family Contribution (EFC) of $4,000 or less. They must be enrolled at a public, non-profit Texas college or university and cannot have earned more than

30 semester credits at the time of application submission. Those who have earned an associate's degree at a Texas two-year institution and who intend to enroll in a Texas bachelor's degree program within 12 months of graduation are also eligible. Selection is based on financial need.
Target applicant(s): High school students. College students. Adult students.
Amount: Varies.
Number of awards: Varies.
Scholarship may be renewable.
Deadline: January 15.
How to apply: Application is made by completing the FAFSA.
Exclusive: Visit www.UltimateScholarshipBook.com and enter code TE185226 for updates on this award.

[1853] • Township Officials of Illinois Scholarship-Undergraduate Scholarship

Township Officials of Illinois
3217 Northfield Drive, Springfield, IL 62702
Phone: 217-744-2212
Email: bryantoi@toi.org
http://www.toi.org
Purpose: To promote the ideas of quality local government and civic duty and to recruit young people into the TOI.
Eligibility: Applicants must be high school seniors attending an Illinois college or university in the fall and must have a minimum 3.0 GPA.
Target applicant(s): High school students. College students. Graduate school students. Adult students.
Minimum GPA: 3.0
Amount: $500.
Number of awards: 1.
Deadline: May 17.
How to apply: Applications are available online in January.
Exclusive: Visit www.UltimateScholarshipBook.com and enter code TO185326 for updates on this award.

[1854] • Treacy Foundation Scholarship

Treacy Foundation
P.O. Box 1479, Helena, MT 59624
Email: director@treacyfoundation.org
https://treacyfoundation.org/scholarships/
Purpose: To reward starting freshmen and sophomore students from the state of Montana.
Eligibility: Applicants must be either a starting freshman or sophomore. Students must be residents of Montana.
Target applicant(s): High school students. College students. Adult students.
Amount: $3,000.
Number of awards: Varies.
Scholarship may be renewable.
Deadline: April 29.
How to apply: Applications are available online.
Exclusive: Visit www.UltimateScholarshipBook.com and enter code TR185426 for updates on this award.

[1855] • Tuition Aid Grant

New Jersey Higher Education Student Assistance Authority
P.O. Box 540, Trenton, NJ 08625
Phone: 800-792-8670
Email: clientservices@hesaa.org
http://www.hesaa.org
Purpose: To support New Jersey students who are unable to pay the full cost of tuition.
Eligibility: Students must be residents of New Jersey for at least 12 months prior to college enrollment, enroll in an approved New Jersey school and remain in school full-time in an undergraduate program. Applicants cannot have any previous degrees, and they cannot be enrolled in theology or divinity programs.
Target applicant(s): High school students. College students. Adult students.
Amount: Up to full tuition.
Number of awards: Varies.
Scholarship may be renewable.
Deadline: September 15.
How to apply: Applications are available through completion of the FAFSA.
Exclusive: Visit www.UltimateScholarshipBook.com and enter code NE185526 for updates on this award.

[1856] • Tuition Assistance Program (TAP)

New York State Higher Education Services Corporation (HESC)
99 Washington Avenue, Albany, NY 12255
Phone: 888-697-4372
Email: scholarships@hesc.ny.gov
http://www.hesc.ny.gov
Purpose: To assist New York resident students in attending in-state postsecondary institutions.
Eligibility: Applicants must be U.S. citizens or eligible noncitizens, be legal residents of New York State, study full-time at an eligible New York State postsecondary institution as undergraduate or graduate students, meet income eligibility requirements and maintain a "C" average in college.
Target applicant(s): High school students. College students. Graduate school students. Adult students.
Minimum GPA: 2.0
Amount: Up to $5,665.
Number of awards: Varies.
Scholarship may be renewable.
Deadline: February 15.
How to apply: Complete the Free Application for Federal Student Aid (FAFSA), include a New York school on the application and then complete the Express TAP Application.
Exclusive: Visit www.UltimateScholarshipBook.com and enter code NE185626 for updates on this award.

[1857] • Tuition Equalization Grant Program

Texas Higher Education Coordinating Board
1200 East Anderson Lane, Austin, TX 78752
Phone: 888-311-8881.
Email: pamela.harris@thecb.state.tx.us
http://www.collegeforalltexans.com
Purpose: To assist students with financial need who are attending private, non-profit colleges or universities in Texas.
Eligibility: Applicants must be Texas residents or nonresident National Merit Finalists. They must be enrolled at a private, non-profit Texas institution in a first associate's, bachelor's, master's or doctoral degree program. Applicants cannot be athletic scholarship recipients and must demonstrate financial need. Applicants must maintain at least a 2.5 GPA and must complete 24 credit hours per year. Selection is based on financial need.
Target applicant(s): High school students. College students. Graduate school students. Adult students.

Minimum GPA: 2.5
Amount: Up to $3,873.
Number of awards: Varies.
Deadline: January 15.
How to apply: Application is made by completing the FAFSA.
Exclusive: Visit www.UltimateScholarshipBook.com and enter code TE185726 for updates on this award.

[1858] • Tuition Reduction for Non-Resident Nursing Students

Maryland Higher Education Commission
Office of Student Financial Assistance, 6 North Liberty Street,
Baltimore, MD 21201
Phone: 800-974-1024
Email: osfamail@mhec.state.md.us
https://mhec.maryland.gov
Purpose: To support non-resident nursing students who are attending college in Maryland.
Eligibility: Applicants cannot be residents of the state of Maryland, but they must be enrolled in a two-year or four-year undergraduate nursing program in Maryland. Students must agree to work full-time at a Maryland hospital after graduation, for a period of four years for full-time students and two years for part-time students.
Target applicant(s): High school students. College students. Adult students.
Amount: Varies.
Number of awards: Varies.
Scholarship may be renewable.
Deadline: Contact the sponsor to confirm the deadline.
How to apply: Applications are available online.
Exclusive: Visit www.UltimateScholarshipBook.com and enter code MA185826 for updates on this award.

[1859] • Tuition Waiver for Foster Care Recipients

Maryland Higher Education Commission
Office of Student Financial Assistance, 6 North Liberty Street,
Baltimore, MD 21201
Phone: 800-974-1024
Email: osfamail@mhec.state.md.us
https://mhec.maryland.gov
Purpose: To assist students who have resided in foster care in attending a public college.
Eligibility: Applicants must be under age 25 and have been in an out-of-home placement when they graduated from high school or have lived in foster care on their 14th birthday and subsequently been adopted.
Target applicant(s): High school students. College students.
Amount: Up to full tuition.
Number of awards: Varies.
Scholarship may be renewable.
Deadline: March 1.
How to apply: Students may apply by filing the FAFSA and contacting the financial aid office at the institution they plan to attend.
Exclusive: Visit www.UltimateScholarshipBook.com and enter code MA185926 for updates on this award.

[1860] • Tuttle Construction Inc. Tiny Rauch Scholarship

Associated General Contractors of Ohio
1755 Northwest Boulevard, Columbus, OH 43212
Phone: 614-486-6446
Email: parker@agcohio.com
https://agcohio.com/workforce-development/agc-scholarships/
Purpose: To support students who are residents of Ohio pursuing degrees in construction-related fields or employees of Tuttle Services Inc. or immediate family.
Eligibility: Applicants must be U.S. citizens and undergraduate students in at least the second year of a two-year, four-year or five-year degree seeking program. The minimum GPA requirement is 2.5. Selection is based on the overall strength of the application.
Target applicant(s): College students. Adult students.
Minimum GPA: 2.5
Amount: $1,000.
Number of awards: 1.
Deadline: February 9.
How to apply: Applications are available online. An application form, official college transcripts and essay are required and must be mailed.
Exclusive: Visit www.UltimateScholarshipBook.com and enter code AS186026 for updates on this award.

[1861] • Tweet Coleman Aviation Scholarship

American Association of University Women - Honolulu Branch
P.O. Box 22331, Honolulu, HI 96823-2331
Phone: 808-537-4702
Email: aviation@aauwhonolulu.org
https://www.aauwhonolulu.org/scholarship-and-grants
Purpose: To aid females in the state of Hawaii in earning a Federal Aviation Administration (FAA) Pilot Certificate.
Eligibility: Applicants must be a female living in Hawaii (only residence is Hawaii) or stationed in Hawaii with the military. Applicants must also be a college graduate (associate degree or higher) or currently enrolled in a college or university in Hawaii. Students must be working on an FAA Pilot Certificate and possess an FAA "Solo Flight" endorsement.
Target applicant(s): College students. Adult students.
Amount: Varies.
Number of awards: Varies.
Deadline: April 30.
How to apply: Applications are available by online request. An application form and supporting materials are required.
Exclusive: Visit www.UltimateScholarshipBook.com and enter code AM186126 for updates on this award.

[1862] • Twenty-first Century Scholars Program

Indiana Commission for Higher Education
101 West Ohio Street, Suite 300, Indianapolis, IN 46204-4206
Phone: 888-528-4719
Email: awards@che.in.gov
https://www.in.gov/che/
Purpose: To support Indiana middle school students from families with low to moderate incomes.
Eligibility: Applicants must be in 7th or 8th grade at a school recognized by the Indiana Department of Education. Students must be below the maximum income requirements, be wards of the state or county or be in

foster care. Scholarship funds may only be used at eligible Indiana colleges or technical schools.
Target applicant(s): Junior high students or younger.
Minimum GPA: 2.5
Amount: Up to full tuition.
Number of awards: Varies.
Scholarship may be renewable.
Deadline: June 30.
How to apply: Applications are available at Indiana middle schools.
Exclusive: Visit www.UltimateScholarshipBook.com and enter code IN186226 for updates on this award.

[1863] • Two-year or Associate Degree Program
New Hampshire Charitable Foundation
37 Pleasant Street, Concord, NH 03301-4005
Phone: 603-225-6641
Email: jessica.kierstead@nhcf.org
https://www.nhcf.org/how-can-we-help-you/
Purpose: To support New Hampshire students who are attending a two-year or short-term training program.
Eligibility: Applicants must have completed high school or earned a GED and plan to attend a short-term training program. Students will need to submit a copy of the Student Aid Report received from submitting the FAFSA. Preference is given to those who have successfully completed prior educational work or who are entering professions in the STEM fields such as: computer science, advanced manufacturing, clinical health care, engineering, engineering technology, graphic design (CAD), etc.
Target applicant(s): College students. Adult students.
Amount: $100-$3,500.
Number of awards: Varies.
Deadline: December 13.
How to apply: Applications are available online.
Exclusive: Visit www.UltimateScholarshipBook.com and enter code NE186326 for updates on this award.

[1864] • UMSA Foundation Scholarship Program
Upper Midwest Security Alliance (UMSA)
P.O. Box 130935, Roseville, MN 55113
https://umsafoundation.org/foundation/umsa-scholarship-program/
Purpose: To provide financial assistance in security and risk-related industries.
Eligibility: Applicants must be residents of or attend schools in the upper Midwest states. Students must be high school seniors or enrolled in a college or university for undergraduate or graduate study. Applicants must be in any of the following fields: business continuity and disaster recovery, cybersecurity, governance, risk and compliance or physical security.
Target applicant(s): Junior high students or younger.
Amount: $1,000 - $3,000.
Number of awards: 12.
Deadline: February 28.
How to apply: Applications are available online.
Exclusive: Visit www.UltimateScholarshipBook.com and enter code UP186426 for updates on this award.

[1865] • Unitil Scholarship Fund
Unitil
Attn.: Kristen Anderson/Scholarship Committee, 6 Liberty Lane West, Hampton, NH 03842
Phone: 603-772-0775
http://unitil.com/our-community/unitil-scholarship-fund
Purpose: To support students who live in Maine, New Hampshire or Massachusetts.
Eligibility: Applicants must attend school and reside in one of the cities or towns in Unitil service territories and must have a declared major or concentration in science, technology, math or engineering.
Target applicant(s): College students. Adult students.
Amount: $5,000.
Number of awards: 6.
Deadline: March 31.
How to apply: Applications are available online.
Exclusive: Visit www.UltimateScholarshipBook.com and enter code UN186526 for updates on this award.

[1866] • University Journalism Scholarships
Ohio News Media Foundation
1335 Dublin Road, Suite 216-B, Columbus, OH 43215
Phone: 614-486-6677
Email: ariggs@ohionews.org
https://ohionews.org/aws/ONA/pt/sp/scholarships
Purpose: To support students pursuing a journalism-related major at an Ohio college or university.
Eligibility: Applicants must be enrolled in an Ohio college or university and be majoring in a journalism-related field such as journalism, advertising or marketing. Students must have at least a 2.5 GPA and write an essay as part of their application showcasing their writing skill along with including work samples related to degree.
Target applicant(s): College students. Adult students.
Minimum GPA: 2.5
Amount: $1,000.
Number of awards: Varies.
Deadline: May 20.
How to apply: Applications are available online.
Exclusive: Visit www.UltimateScholarshipBook.com and enter code OH186626 for updates on this award.

[1867] • Upper Midwest Chapter Scholarships
National Academy of Television Arts and Sciences-Upper Midwest Foundation
7319 Hunters Run, Eden Prairie, MN 55346
Phone: 952-474-7126
Email: info@midwestemmys.org
https://midwestemmys.org/student-awards/scholarships/
Purpose: To aid students interested in television, broadcasting and electronic media careers.
Eligibility: Applicants must be high school seniors who live in Minnesota, North Dakota, South Dakota, Iowa or Wisconsin. They must have applied or been accepted to a college or university that offers a broadcasting, television or other electronic media curriculum and intend to pursue one of these fields. A GPA of 3.0 or higher is preferred, but not required.
Target applicant(s): High school students.
Amount: $1,500.
Number of awards: Varies.
Deadline: February 2.
How to apply: Applications are available online. An application form is required.
Exclusive: Visit www.UltimateScholarshipBook.com and enter code NA186726 for updates on this award.

[1868] • Urban Scholars Award
New Jersey Higher Education Student Assistance Authority
P.O. Box 540, Trenton, NJ 08625
Phone: 800-792-8670
Email: clientservices@hesaa.org
http://www.hesaa.org
Purpose: To support New Jersey high school seniors from urban or economically depressed areas.
Eligibility: Applicants must be New Jersey residents for at least 12 months prior to college enrollment, and they must enroll full-time in an approved state college. Students must show outstanding academic achievement in high school through SAT scores and transcripts. Applicants must have a minimum 3.0 GPA and be in the top five percent of their class.
Target applicant(s): High school students.
Minimum GPA: 3.0
Amount: Varies.
Number of awards: Varies.
Scholarship may be renewable.
Deadline: Contact the sponsor to confirm the deadline.
How to apply: Applications are available from high school guidance counselors.
Exclusive: Visit www.UltimateScholarshipBook.com and enter code NE186826 for updates on this award.

[1869] • Utah Association of Independent Insurance Agents Scholarship
Utah Association of Independent Insurance Agents
4885 South 900 East, Suite 302, Salt Lake City, UT 84117
Phone: 801-269-1200
Email: info@uaiia.org
https://www.utahia.org/Education/Pages/Scholarships/
Purpose: To aid college-bound Utah high school seniors.
Eligibility: Applicants must be Utah high school seniors. They must have a GPA of 3.0 or higher and must be active in extracurricular activities. Selection is based on the overall strength of the application.
Target applicant(s): High school students.
Minimum GPA: 3.0
Amount: $500-$3,000.
Number of awards: At least 3.
Deadline: April 1.
How to apply: Applications are available online. An application form, transcript and applicant photo are required.
Exclusive: Visit www.UltimateScholarshipBook.com and enter code UT186926 for updates on this award.

[1870] • Utah Young Humanitarian Award
Youthlinc
1166 East Brickyard Road, Salt Lake City, UT 84106
Phone: 801-467-4417
https://www.youthlinc.org/yha
Purpose: To reward outstanding humanitarian service.
Eligibility: Applicants must be U.S. citizens, legal residents or have DACA status and be either Utah high school juniors or seniors or be enrolled as a full-time undergraduate student at an accredited college or university in Utah.
Target applicant(s): High school students. College students. Adult students.
Amount: $1,500 up to $7,500.
Number of awards: 10.
Deadline: March 1.
How to apply: Applications are available online.
Exclusive: Visit www.UltimateScholarshipBook.com and enter code YO187026 for updates on this award.

[1871] • Valedictorian Program Tuition Waiver
Massachusetts Department of Higher Education
Office of Student Financial Assistance, 454 Broadway, Suite 200, Revere, MA 02151
Phone: 617-727-9420
Email: osfa@osfa.mass.edu
https://www.mass.gov/handbook/massachusetts-financial-aid-programs
Purpose: To provide comprehensive financial aid to Massachusetts valedictorians.
Eligibility: Applicants must be designated as a valedictorian by a public or private high school in the state of Massachusetts, and they must be residents of the state for at least one year prior to the beginning of the school year. Students must enroll in a Massachusetts public college and meet individual requirements for the program imposed by the school. They cannot owe refunds on previous financial aid or have any defaulted government loans.
Target applicant(s): High school students.
Amount: Full tuition.
Number of awards: Varies.
Scholarship may be renewable.
Deadline: Contact the financial aid office at the institution applicant is attending or plans to attend.
How to apply: Applications are available at college financial aid offices.
Exclusive: Visit www.UltimateScholarshipBook.com and enter code MA187126 for updates on this award.

[1872] • Vermont Incentive Grants
Vermont Student Assistance Corporation
Scholarships, P.O. Box 2000, Winooski, VT 05404
Phone: 800-642-3177
Email: info@vsac.org
https://www.vsac.org/pay/student-aid-options/scholarships
Purpose: To assist Vermont students who are attending college full-time.
Eligibility: Applicants must be Vermont residents who are accepted into or enrolled in an undergraduate degree program, a certificate program, a Doctor of Veterinary Medicine degree program or a University of Vermont College of Medicine degree program. They must attend or plan to attend school full-time. Applicants who have earned a bachelor's degree previously are ineligible. Selection is based on financial need.
Target applicant(s): High school students. College students. Adult students.
Amount: Varies.
Number of awards: Varies.
Deadline: March 1.
How to apply: Applications are available online. An application form and a completed FAFSA are required.
Exclusive: Visit www.UltimateScholarshipBook.com and enter code VE187226 for updates on this award.

[1873] • Vermont Oratorical Contest
American Legion, Department of Vermont
P.O. Box 396, 126 State Street, Montpelier, VT 05601-0396
Phone: 802-223-7131
Email: alvthq@myfairpoint.net
http://www.vtlegion.org

Purpose: To enhance high school students' experience with and understanding of the U.S. Constitution. The contest will help develop students' leadership skills and civic appreciation, as well as the ability to deliver thoughtful, insightful orations regarding U.S. citizenship and its inherent responsibilities.
Eligibility: Applicants must be high school students under the age of 20 who are U.S. citizens or legal residents and residents of the state. Students must first give an oration within their state and winners compete at the national level. The oration must be related to the Constitution of the United States focusing on the duties and obligations citizens have to the government. It must be in English and be between eight and ten minutes. There is also an assigned topic which is posted on the website, and it should be between three and five minutes.
Target applicant(s): High school students.
Amount: Varies.
Number of awards: Varies.
Deadline: October 14.
How to apply: Applications are available from district representatives.
Exclusive: Visit www.UltimateScholarshipBook.com and enter code AM187326 for updates on this award.

[1874] • Vermont Sheriffs' Association Scholarship

Vermont Student Assistance Corporation
Scholarships, P.O. Box 2000, Winooski, VT 05404
Phone: 800-642-3177
Email: info@vsac.org
https://www.vsac.org/pay/student-aid-options/scholarships
Purpose: To aid Vermont residents who are studying to become police officers.
Eligibility: Applicants must be Vermont residents. They must be enrolled in a law enforcement degree program at an accredited school that has been approved for federal Title IV funding. They must have plans to become police officers. Selection is based on academic merit, essay and financial need.
Target applicant(s): High school students. College students. Graduate school students. Adult students.
Amount: $1,000.
Number of awards: 1.
Deadline: February 14.
How to apply: Applications are available online. An application form, official transcript, personal essay and financial aid information are required.
Exclusive: Visit www.UltimateScholarshipBook.com and enter code VE187426 for updates on this award.

[1875] • Vernon T. Swain, P.E./Robert E. Chute, P.E. Scholarship

Maine Society of Professional Engineers
Colin C. Hewett, P.E., Chairman, Scholarship Committee, P.O. Box 318, Winthrop, ME 04364
Email: chewett@ahgeng.com
http://www.mespe.org
Purpose: To aid Maine students who are preparing for careers in engineering.
Eligibility: Applicants must be Maine residents who are graduating high school seniors. They must have plans to enroll in an ABETEAC-accredited degree program in engineering and to pursue a career in engineering. Applicants must have applied to at least one school that offers engineering degrees. These are the minimum acceptable standardized test scores: SAT Math 600, SAT Writing 500, SAT Critical Reading 500, ACT Math 29, ACT English 25, PAA Quantitative 750 and PAA Verbal 640. Selection is based on standardized test scores, GPA, personal essay, recommendations, extracurricular activities and work experience.
Target applicant(s): High school students.
Amount: At least $2,500.
Number of awards: 2.
Deadline: March 22.
How to apply: Applications are available online. An application form, official transcript, personal statement, two recommendation letters and official SAT or ACT scores are required.
Exclusive: Visit www.UltimateScholarshipBook.com and enter code MA187526 for updates on this award.

[1876] • Veterans Tuition Awards

New York State Higher Education Services Corporation (HESC)
99 Washington Avenue, Albany, NY 12255
Phone: 888-697-4372
Email: scholarships@hesc.ny.gov
http://www.hesc.ny.gov
Purpose: To assist veterans in obtaining higher education.
Eligibility: Applicants must be veterans from New York State who have been honorably discharged and served in Indochina between December 22, 1961 and May 7, 1975, the Persian Gulf on or after August 2, 1990 or Afghanistan on or after September 11, 2001. Applicants must also have applied for the Tuition Assistant Program if studying full-time and the Federal Pell Grant whether studying full-time or part-time, unless enrolled in a vocational training program.
Target applicant(s): College students. Graduate school students. Adult students.
Amount: Up to full tuition.
Number of awards: Varies.
Scholarship may be renewable.
Deadline: June 30.
How to apply: Applications are available from your institution's financial aid office or by phone from HESC.
Exclusive: Visit www.UltimateScholarshipBook.com and enter code NE187626 for updates on this award.

[1877] • VHSL Achievement Award

Virginia High School League
1642 State Farm Boulevard, Charlottesville, VA 22911
https://www.vhsl.org/scholarships/
Purpose: To support students who have made outstanding achievements in sports, academics or courageousness.
Eligibility: Students must be from a Virginia high school in Group 1A through 6A. Applicants must show participation in VHSL activities and other school or community activities. They must have at least a 3.0 GPA.
Target applicant(s): High school students.
Minimum GPA: 3.0
Amount: $1,500.
Number of awards: 19.
Deadline: March 15.
How to apply: Applications are available online.
Exclusive: Visit www.UltimateScholarshipBook.com and enter code VI187726 for updates on this award.

[1878] • Victoria S. and Bradley L. Geist Foundation

Hawaii Community Foundation - Scholarships
827 Fort Street Mall, Honolulu, HI 96813
Phone: 888-731-3863
Email: scholarships@hcf-hawaii.org
https://www.hawaiicommunityfoundation.org/
Purpose: To support students who have been in the Hawaii foster care system.
Eligibility: Applicants must be residents of Hawaii. Students must not have been legally adopted before the age of 18.
Target applicant(s): High school students. College students. Adult students.
Amount: Varies.
Number of awards: Varies.
Scholarship may be renewable.
Deadline: February 28.
How to apply: Applications are available online. In addition, mail the supporting materials: confirmation letter from a case worker, personal statement and official transcript.
Exclusive: Visit www.UltimateScholarshipBook.com and enter code HA187826 for updates on this award.

[1879] • Vietnam Veterans' Scholarship

New Mexico Higher Education Department
2044 Galisteo Street, Suite 4, Santa Fe, NM 87505-2100
Phone: 505-476-8400
Email: cesaria.tapia1@state.nm.us
https://hed.state.nm.us/financial-aid
Purpose: To support Vietnam veterans who are attending college in New Mexico.
Eligibility: Applicants must have been honorably discharged from the armed forces, and they must have received a Vietnam campaign medal for serving in Vietnam anytime between August 5, 1964 and the official end of the war. Students must be attending either a public school or one of the following private schools in New Mexico: the College of Santa Fe, St. John's College or the College of the Southwest. They must have been New Mexico residents when entering the armed forces or have lived in the state for at least 10 years.
Target applicant(s): College students. Graduate school students. Adult students.
Amount: Full tuition.
Number of awards: Varies.
Scholarship may be renewable.
Deadline: Contact the sponsor to confirm the deadline.
How to apply: Applications are available at college financial aid offices.
Exclusive: Visit www.UltimateScholarshipBook.com and enter code NE187926 for updates on this award.

[1880] • Virginia Commonwealth Award

State Council of Higher Education for Virginia
101 N. 14th Street, 10th Floor, James Monroe Building, Richmond, VA 23219
Phone: 804-225-2600
Email: communications@schev.edu
https://www.schev.edu/financial-aid/financial-aid
Purpose: To assist Virginia students.
Eligibility: Undergraduate applicants must be admitted to a Virginia public two- or four-year college or university, be enrolled at least half-time, be residents of Virginia, be U.S. citizens or eligible noncitizens and demonstrate financial need. Graduate applicants must be enrolled full-time in an eligible Virginia graduate degree program. The selection process varies by school.
Target applicant(s): High school students. College students. Graduate school students. Adult students.
Amount: Up to full tuition.
Number of awards: Varies.
Scholarship may be renewable.
Deadline: March 1.
How to apply: Application instructions are available by request from the student's financial aid office.
Exclusive: Visit www.UltimateScholarshipBook.com and enter code ST188026 for updates on this award.

[1881] • Virginia Daughters of the American Revolution Scholarships

Virginia Daughters of the American Revolution
DAR Scholarship Committee, Anne E. Starling, State Chairman, 2308 Krossridge Court, North Chesterfield, VA 23236
Phone: 757-479-4167
Email: gandbatkinson@cox.net
https://www.virginiadar.org/about/#scholarships
Purpose: To support Virginia high school students in pursuing higher education.
Eligibility: Applicants must be high school seniors and U.S. citizens who are sponsored by a Virginia DAR chapter. They may pursue an undergraduate degree in any field except nursing at any Virginia college or university.
Target applicant(s): High school students.
Amount: $2,500.
Number of awards: 4.
Deadline: January 12.
How to apply: Applications are available online. An application form, letter of sponsorship, written statement, transcript, financial need form and letter of recommendation are required.
Exclusive: Visit www.UltimateScholarshipBook.com and enter code VI188126 for updates on this award.

[1882] • Virginia Guaranteed Assistance Program

State Council of Higher Education for Virginia
101 N. 14th Street, 10th Floor, James Monroe Building, Richmond, VA 23219
Phone: 804-225-2600
Email: communications@schev.edu
https://www.schev.edu/financial-aid/financial-aid
Purpose: To provide a financial incentive for economically disadvantaged students to consider attending college.
Eligibility: Applicants must have graduated from a Virginia high school with at least a 2.5 GPA, and they must be enrolled full-time in a two-year or four-year college in the state. Students must be classified as dependents. Preference will be given to students with the greatest financial need.
Target applicant(s): High school students. College students. Adult students.
Minimum GPA: 2.5
Amount: Up to full tuition.
Number of awards: Varies.
Scholarship may be renewable.
Deadline: As soon as possible after October 1.

The Ultimate Scholarship Book 2026
Scholarship Directory (State of Residence)

How to apply: Applications are available at college financial aid offices.
Exclusive: Visit www.UltimateScholarshipBook.com and enter code ST188226 for updates on this award.

[1883] • Virginia High School League Charles E. Savedge Journalism Scholarship
Virginia High School League
1642 State Farm Boulevard, Charlottesville, VA 22911
https://www.vhsl.org/scholarships/
Purpose: To support student journalists in Virginia.
Eligibility: Applicants must be active members of a high school newspaper, yearbook or other publication. Students must be in their senior year and have plans to study journalism in college.
Target applicant(s): High school students.
Amount: $500.
Number of awards: Varies.
Deadline: March 1.
How to apply: Applications are available online.
Exclusive: Visit www.UltimateScholarshipBook.com and enter code VI188326 for updates on this award.

[1884] • Virginia Part-Time Assistance Program
State Council of Higher Education for Virginia
101 N. 14th Street, 10th Floor, James Monroe Building, Richmond, VA 23219
Phone: 804-225-2600
Email: communications@schev.edu
https://www.schev.edu/financial-aid/financial-aid
Purpose: To assist part-time Virginia students who have financial need.
Eligibility: Applicants must be Virginia residents. They must attend a school in Virginia's community college system part-time (one to eight credit hours per term) and must demonstrate financial need. Selection is based on financial need.
Target applicant(s): High school students. College students. Adult students.
Amount: Up to full tuition.
Number of awards: Varies.
Deadline: June 30.
How to apply: Applications are available from the student's financial aid office. An application form and supporting materials are required.
Exclusive: Visit www.UltimateScholarshipBook.com and enter code ST188426 for updates on this award.

[1885] • Virginia Sheriffs' Institute Scholarship
Virginia Sheriffs' Institute
951 East Byrd Street, Suite 905, Richmond, VA 23219
Phone: 804-225-7152
Email: vsavsi@virginiasherrifs.org
http://vasheriffsinstitute.org
Purpose: To aid Virginia criminal justice students.
Eligibility: Applicants must be residents of an eligible Virginia locality. They must be accepted or enrolled at a Virginia college or university and must be majoring in or planning to major in criminal justice. Selection is based on the overall strength of the application.
Target applicant(s): High school students. College students. Adult students.
Amount: Varies.
Number of awards: Varies.
Deadline: May 1.
How to apply: Applications are available online. An application form, transcript, letter of recommendation from applicant's local sheriff, personal essay, proof of college acceptance (incoming freshmen only) and standardized test scores (incoming freshmen only) are required.
Exclusive: Visit www.UltimateScholarshipBook.com and enter code VI188526 for updates on this award.

[1886] • Virginia Tuition Assistance Grant Program
State Council of Higher Education for Virginia
101 N. 14th Street, 10th Floor, James Monroe Building, Richmond, VA 23219
Phone: 804-225-2600
Email: communications@schev.edu
https://www.schev.edu/financial-aid/financial-aid
Purpose: To assist Virginia students who are attending eligible private postsecondary institutions in Virginia.
Eligibility: Applicants must be Virginia residents and enrolled full-time as undergraduate, graduate or professional school students at an eligible private, non-profit Virginia postsecondary institution. Applicants who are enrolled in a religious or theological degree program are ineligible as are graduate students who are enrolled in a degree program that is not related to health care. Selection is based on the overall strength of the application.
Target applicant(s): High school students. College students. Graduate school students. Adult students.
Amount: Up to $12,500 per year.
Number of awards: Varies.
Scholarship may be renewable.
Deadline: July 31.
How to apply: Applications are available by request from the student's college financial aid office. An application form and supporting materials are required.
Exclusive: Visit www.UltimateScholarshipBook.com and enter code ST188626 for updates on this award.

[1887] • Vocational Nurse Scholarship
Health Professions Education Foundation
400 R Street, Suite 460, Sacramento, CA 95811
Phone: 916-326-3640
Email: stran@oshpd.ca.gov
https://hcai.ca.gov/loans-scholarships-grants/
Purpose: To aid California vocational nursing students.
Eligibility: Applicants must be accepted or enrolled in an accredited California vocational nurse (VN) degree program and must be enrolled full-time. They must maintain a GPA of 2.0 or higher while enrolled in the degree program and must commit to two years of practice in an underserved area of California after graduation. Selection is based on academic merit, stated career goals, community involvement, work experience and financial need.
Target applicant(s): College students. Adult students.
Minimum GPA: 2.0
Amount: Up to $4,000.
Number of awards: Varies.
Deadline: December 13.
How to apply: Applications are available online. An application form, personal statement, official transcript, two recommendation letters and financial information are required.
Exclusive: Visit www.UltimateScholarshipBook.com and enter code HE188726 for updates on this award.

[1888] • W.P. Black Scholarship Fund
Greater Kanawha Valley Foundation
1600 Huntington Square, 900 Lee Street, East, Charleston, WV 25301
Phone: 304-346-3620
Email: shoover@tgkvf.org
https://tgkvf.org/scholarship-information/
Purpose: To aid West Virginia students.
Eligibility: Applicants must be residents of West Virginia who are full-time students, have a minimum 2.5 GPA, have a minimum ACT score of 20, be of good moral character and demonstrate significant financial need.
Target applicant(s): High school students. College students. Adult students.
Minimum GPA: 2.5
Amount: $2,000.
Number of awards: 62.
Scholarship may be renewable.
Deadline: February 1.
How to apply: Applications are available online.
Exclusive: Visit www.UltimateScholarshipBook.com and enter code GR188826 for updates on this award.

[1889] • Wallace S. and Wilma K. Laughlin Foundation Trust Scholarships
Nebraska Funeral Directors Association
Wallace S. and Wilma K. Laughlin Foundation Trust, 521 First Street, P.O. Box 10, Milford, NE 68405
Phone: 402-761-2217
Email: staff@nefda.org
https://www.nefda.org/scholarship-information
Purpose: To aid Nebraska students of mortuary science.
Eligibility: Applicants must be residents of Nebraska and must be graduating seniors at a Nebraska high school or they must be graduates of a Nebraska high school. They must be entering or current students of mortuary science, reside in Nebraska for at least three years after completing their mortuary science degree programs and intend to practice mortuary science. Selection is based on applicant interview.
Target applicant(s): High school students. College students. Adult students.
Amount: At least $1,000.
Number of awards: Varies.
Deadline: June 15.
How to apply: Applications are available online. An application form, transcript, recommendation letter and proof that all pre-mortuary science state requirements have been met are required.
Exclusive: Visit www.UltimateScholarshipBook.com and enter code NE188926 for updates on this award.

[1890] • Washington BPW Foundation Mature Woman Educational Scholarship
Washington Business and Professional Women's Foundation
Attn: Scholarship Committee Chairman, S. Tellock, 1914 NW 87th Circle, Vancouver, WA 98665
Phone: 360-714-8901
Email: WSBPW_Foundation@bpwwa.org
https://wsbpwfoundation.org/
Purpose: To assist non-traditional female students.
Eligibility: Applicants must be female students age 30 or older who are pursuing retraining or continuing education. Students must be U.S. citizens and Washington state residents for at least two years and must be accepted into a program at an accredited Washington state institution of higher learning or enrolled in an accredited online program from a Washington state school. They must demonstrate scholastic ability and financial need.
Target applicant(s): College students. Adult students.
Amount: $1,500.
Number of awards: Varies.
Deadline: March 15.
How to apply: Applications are available online. An application form, essay, proof of income, financial aid and expense estimates, three letters of recommendation, transcript and proof of acceptance or enrollment are required.
Exclusive: Visit www.UltimateScholarshipBook.com and enter code WA189026 for updates on this award.

[1891] • Washington College Grant
Washington Student Achievement Council
P. O. Box 43430, Olympia, WA 98504-3430
Phone: 360-753-7850
Email: aies@wsac.wa.gov
https://wsac.wa.gov/
Purpose: To assist low-income students to pursue undergraduate degrees or train for new careers.
Eligibility: Applicants must be Washington residents who have a family income of 100 percent or less of the state median and be pursuing a certificate, associate's degree or bachelor's degree. Students can use the financial aid at Washington's eligible institutions, including public two- and four-year colleges and universities and many accredited private/independent colleges, universities and career schools in the state, as well as for approved apprenticeship programs.
Target applicant(s): High school students. College students. Adult students.
Amount: Varies.
Number of awards: Varies.
Deadline: June 30.
How to apply: Eligible students who have filed a Free Application for Federal Student Aid (FAFSA) are considered.
Exclusive: Visit www.UltimateScholarshipBook.com and enter code WA189126 for updates on this award.

[1892] • Washington Health Corps
Washington Student Achievement Council
P. O. Box 43430, Olympia, WA 98504-3430
Phone: 360-753-7850
Email: aies@wsac.wa.gov
https://wsac.wa.gov/
Purpose: To attract health professionals to work in rural and under served communities in Washington state.
Eligibility: Applicants must be employed, or be under contract to be employed, at an eligible site, provide proof of eligible student debt and sign a contract to serve a minimum of two or three years. A full list of eligible professions can be found on the Washington Health Corps website.
Target applicant(s): College students. Adult students.
Amount: Up to $75,000.
Number of awards: Varies.
Scholarship may be renewable.
Deadline: March 8.
How to apply: Applications are available online.
Exclusive: Visit www.UltimateScholarshipBook.com and enter code WA189226 for updates on this award.

[1893] • Washington Oratorical Contest
American Legion, Department of Washington
P.O. Box 3917, Lacey, WA 98509
Phone: 360-491-4373
Email: americanismchairman@americanism-alwa.org
http://www.walegion.org/index.php?id=8
Purpose: To enhance high school students' experience with and understanding of the U.S. Constitution. The contest will help develop students' leadership skills and civic appreciation, as well as the ability to deliver thoughtful, insightful orations regarding U.S. citizenship and its inherent responsibilities.
Eligibility: Applicants must be high school students under the age of 20 who are U.S. citizens or legal residents and residents of the state. Students first give an oration within their state and winners compete at the national level. The oration must be related to the Constitution of the United States focusing on the duties and obligations citizens have to the government. It must be in English and be between eight and ten minutes. There is also an assigned topic which is posted on the website, and it should be between three and five minutes.
Target applicant(s): High school students.
Amount: Up to $2,000.
Number of awards: 4.
Deadline: March 28-29.
How to apply: Application information is available online.
Exclusive: Visit www.UltimateScholarshipBook.com and enter code AM189326 for updates on this award.

[1894] • Washington State Auto Dealers Association Bright Future Scholarship
Washington State Auto Dealers Association (WSADA) Scholarship Program
621 SW Grady Way, Renton, WA 98057
Phone: 206-433-6300
Email: info@wsada.org
http://www.wsada.org/community/scholarships
Purpose: To provide financial assistance for business majors.
Eligibility: Applicants must be high school seniors enrolled in a Washington State public or private high school or be home-schooled and reside in Washington State. Students must plan to use their scholarship within the 12 months following the award by enrolling in any public or private school, vocational institution, community college or four-year college or university.
Target applicant(s): High school students.
Amount: $3,000.
Number of awards: 6.
Deadline: April 26.
How to apply: Applications are available online and must also include two letters of reference, a resume and an essay.
Exclusive: Visit www.UltimateScholarshipBook.com and enter code WA189426 for updates on this award.

[1895] • Washington State College Bound Scholarship
Washington Student Achievement Council
P. O. Box 43430, Olympia, WA 98504-3430
Phone: 360-753-7850
Email: aies@wsac.wa.gov
https://wsac.wa.gov/
Purpose: To provide an incentive for students and their families who might not consider college due to financial concerns.
Eligibility: Applicants must be Washington students in the seventh or eighth grades who are eligible for free or reduced-price lunch, and they must sign a pledge to participate in the program. The student's family income must be 65 percent or less of the state's median income when he or she graduates high school, and his or her GPA must be 2.0 or higher in order to receive the scholarship.
Target applicant(s): Junior high students or younger.
Minimum GPA: 2.0
Amount: Full tuition at public rates, some fees and $500 for books.
Number of awards: Varies.
Scholarship may be renewable.
Deadline: Contact the sponsor to confirm the deadline.
How to apply: Applications are available online.
Exclusive: Visit www.UltimateScholarshipBook.com and enter code WA189526 for updates on this award.

[1896] • Washington State Governors' Scholarship for Foster Youth
College Success Foundation
1605 NW Sammamish Road, Suite 100, Issaquah, WA 98027
Phone: 425-416-2000
Email: info@collegesuccessfoundation.org
http://www.collegesuccessfoundation.org
Purpose: To assist Washington state youth in an open dependency court order.
Eligibility: Applicants must be high school seniors, have a minimum 2.0 GPA, have resided in Washington for at least three years prior to graduation and plan to enroll full-time in an eligible Washington public or private college or university.
Target applicant(s): High school students.
Minimum GPA: 2.0
Amount: $2,000-$4,000.
Number of awards: 40-50.
Deadline: May 15.
How to apply: Applications are available online.
Exclusive: Visit www.UltimateScholarshipBook.com and enter code CO189626 for updates on this award.

[1897] • Washington State PTA Scholarship
Washington State PTA
2003 65th Avenue West, Tacoma, WA 98466-6215
Phone: 253-565-2153
Email: wapta@wastatepta.org
http://www.wastatepta.org
Purpose: To provide financial assistance to graduates of Washington public high schools.
Eligibility: Applicants must meet maximum household income requirements and be entering their freshman year of college. Academic performance and community service are also considered.
Target applicant(s): High school students.
Minimum GPA: 3.2
Amount: $2,500.
Number of awards: Varies.
Deadline: February 15.
How to apply: Applications are available online.
Exclusive: Visit www.UltimateScholarshipBook.com and enter code WA189726 for updates on this award.

[1898] • Washington Women In Need
Washington Women In Need
232 5th Avenue South, Kirkland, WA 98033
Email: programs@wwin.org
https://www.wwin.org
Purpose: To empower women in Washington State to achieve economic stability through higher education and living wage careers.
Eligibility: Applicants must be female or identify as female Washington residents and U.S. citizens or permanent residents admitted to an approved and accredited Washington state college or university. Students must demonstrate financial need and exhibit qualities reflective of the WWIN program. Applicants must be 18 years of age or older and pursuing an undergraduate degree.
Target applicant(s): College students. Adult students.
Amount: Up to $20,000.
Number of awards: Varies.
Scholarship may be renewable.
Deadline: April 18.
How to apply: Applications are available online.
Exclusive: Visit www.UltimateScholarshipBook.com and enter code WA189826 for updates on this award.

[1899] • Werks Mobile Scholarship
Werks Mobile
2511 N. Hiatus Road, Suite 157, Hollywood, FL 33026-1301
Phone: 954-233-1630
Email: scholarship@werksmobile.com
https://werksmobile.com/scholarship/
Purpose: To support students who reside in the mobile company's service area.
Eligibility: Applicants must have received a Pell Grant during the current year. Students must have demonstrated financial need. Applicants must reside in any of the following states: California, Florida, Texas, New York, Illinois or Virginia.
Target applicant(s): High school students. College students. Graduate school students. Adult students.
Amount: $5,000.
Number of awards: 200.
Deadline: Last day of each month.
How to apply: Applications are available online.
Exclusive: Visit www.UltimateScholarshipBook.com and enter code WE189926 for updates on this award.

[1900] • West Virginia Engineering, Science and Technology Scholarship
West Virginia Higher Education Policy Commission PROMISE Scholarship
1018 Kanawha Boulevard, East, Suite 700, Charleston, WV 25301
Phone: 304-558-2101
Email: canderson@hepc.wvnet.edu
https://secure.cfwv.com
Purpose: To assist West Virginia students interested in obtaining a degree in engineering, science or technology and committed to the pursuit of a career in West Virginia.
Eligibility: Applicants must be enrolled or accepted for enrollment at time of application. Students must agree to work full-time in an engineering, science or technology field in West Virginia for one year for each year the scholarship was received or begin an approved program of community service related to specific fields. Applicants must demonstrate financial need.
Target applicant(s): High school students. College students. Adult students.
Minimum GPA: 3.0
Amount: $3,000.
Number of awards: Varies.
Scholarship may be renewable.
Deadline: March 1.
How to apply: Applications are available online.
Exclusive: Visit www.UltimateScholarshipBook.com and enter code WE190026 for updates on this award.

[1901] • West Virginia Higher Education Grant
West Virginia Higher Education Policy Commission
1018 Kanawha Boulevard, East, Suite 700, Charleston, WV 25301
Phone: 304-558-2101
Email: jacob.abrams@wvhepc.edu
http://www.wvhepc.edu/
Purpose: To assist West Virginia students who have financial need.
Eligibility: Applicants must be U.S. citizens or permanent residents and West Virginia residents who have lived in the state for at least 12 months before the application submission date. They must be high school graduates or GED recipients who are enrolled full-time in an undergraduate degree program at a participating postsecondary institution located in West Virginia or Pennsylvania. They must demonstrate financial need. Applicants who have earned a bachelor's degree previously are ineligible. Selection is based on financial need.
Target applicant(s): College students. Adult students.
Amount: Up to $2,700.
Number of awards: Varies.
Scholarship may be renewable.
Deadline: April 15.
How to apply: Application is made by completing the FAFSA.
Exclusive: Visit www.UltimateScholarshipBook.com and enter code WE190126 for updates on this award.

[1902] • West Virginia PROMISE Scholarship
West Virginia Higher Education Policy Commission PROMISE Scholarship
1018 Kanawha Boulevard, East, Suite 700, Charleston, WV 25301
Phone: 304-558-2101
Email: canderson@hepc.wvnet.edu
https://secure.cfwv.com
Purpose: To assist outstanding West Virginia high school students who are planning to attend college in the state.
Eligibility: Applicants must be West Virginia residents and high school seniors or GED recipients who are planning to attend a West Virginia postsecondary institution. They must have a GPA of 3.0 or higher or a GED score of 2500 or higher. Applicants must also have a combined reading and math SAT score of 1020 or higher or a composite ACT score of 22 or higher. Selection is based on academic merit and financial need.
Target applicant(s): High school students.
Minimum GPA: 3.0
Amount: Up to $5,200.
Number of awards: Varies.
Scholarship may be renewable.
Deadline: March 1.
How to apply: Applications are available online. An application form, supporting materials and a completed FAFSA are required.
Exclusive: Visit www.UltimateScholarshipBook.com and enter code WE190226 for updates on this award.

[1903] • West Virginia PTA Scholarship

West Virginia PTA
P.O. Box 3557, Parkersburg, WV 26103-3557
Phone: 304-420-9576
http://www.westvirginiapta.org/scholarship
Purpose: To support graduating seniors of West Virginia in pursuing post-secondary education.
Eligibility: A minimum GPA of 2.0 is required. Applicants must submit official transcripts, letters of recommendation and an essay describing their educational goals. Selection is primarily based on academic achievement, extracurricular involvement and community service.
Target applicant(s): High school students.
Minimum GPA: 2.0
Amount: $500.
Number of awards: Varies.
Deadline: February 1.
How to apply: Applications are available online.
Exclusive: Visit www.UltimateScholarshipBook.com and enter code WE190326 for updates on this award.

[1904] • Willa S. Bellamy Scholarship

Government Finance Officers Association of South Carolina
Attn.: Scholarship Committee, P.O. Box 80549, Charleston, SC 29416
Phone: 803-881-8600
Email: scholarship@gfoasc.org
https://gfoasc.org
Purpose: To aid South Carolina students who are interested in government finance careers.
Eligibility: Applicants must be South Carolina residents who are rising undergraduate sophomores, juniors or seniors at an accredited public college or university located in South Carolina. They must be majoring in accounting, finance or business administration with a concentration in accounting or finance. They must have a GPA of 3.0 or higher and must be full-time students. Selection is based on the overall strength of the application.
Target applicant(s): College students. Adult students.
Minimum GPA: 3.0
Amount: $2,000.
Number of awards: 1.
Deadline: April 7.
How to apply: Applications are available online. An application form, transcript and one recommendation letter are required.
Exclusive: Visit www.UltimateScholarshipBook.com and enter code GO190426 for updates on this award.

[1905] • Willard H. Erwin, Jr. Scholarship

Greater Kanawha Valley Foundation
1600 Huntington Square, 900 Lee Street, East, Charleston, WV 25301
Phone: 304-346-3620
Email: shoover@tgkvf.org
https://tgkvf.org/scholarship-information/
Purpose: To aid West Virginia state college and university students.
Eligibility: Applicants must be undergraduate students who are enrolled at a state-run college or university located in West Virginia. They must demonstrate financial need. Preference will be given to sophomores, juniors, seniors, part-time students, full-time students and health care finance students. Selection is based on the overall strength of the application.
Target applicant(s): College students. Adult students.
Amount: Up to $1,000.
Number of awards: 1.
Scholarship may be renewable.
Deadline: February 1.
How to apply: Applications are available online. An application form, transcript, one recommendation letter and income tax information are required.
Exclusive: Visit www.UltimateScholarshipBook.com and enter code GR190526 for updates on this award.

[1906] • William A. Crawford Minority Teacher Scholarship

Indiana Commission for Higher Education
101 West Ohio Street, Suite 300, Indianapolis, IN 46204-4206
Phone: 888-528-4719
Email: awards@che.in.gov
https://www.in.gov/che/
Purpose: To support students in Indiana who are pursuing degrees in teaching, special education, physical therapy or occupational therapy.
Eligibility: Applicants must be enrolled or planning to enroll in college full-time. Students must have at least a 2.0 GPA, and financial need may be considered. Preference will be given to black and Hispanic students. Students must agree to work in the state of Indiana for a period of time after graduation.
Target applicant(s): High school students. College students. Adult students.
Minimum GPA: 2.0
Amount: Varies.
Number of awards: Varies.
Scholarship may be renewable.
Deadline: August 31.
How to apply: Applications are available at the financial aid office of the institution.
Exclusive: Visit www.UltimateScholarshipBook.com and enter code IN190626 for updates on this award.

[1907] • William and Gertrude Fradkin Memorial Scholarship

Los Alamos National Laboratory Foundation
1112 Plaza del Norte, Espanola, NM 87532
Phone: 505-753-8890
Email: tony@lanlfoundation.org
http://www.lanlfoundation.org
Purpose: To support students of northern New Mexico enrolled in or attending a post-secondary institution of higher learning.
Eligibility: Applicants must be permanent residents of northern New Mexico with a minimum GPA of 3.25 and a minimum ACT score of 19 or minimum combined math and critical reading SAT score of 930. Applicants must be enrolled in or currently attending a post-secondary institution of higher learning. Selection is based on academic success, ability to utilize critical thinking skills and leadership skills. Financial need is also considered but not a requirement for eligibility.
Target applicant(s): High school students. College students. Adult students.
Minimum GPA: 3.25
Amount: $1,000-$20,000.
Number of awards: Varies.
Deadline: January 16.
How to apply: Applications are available online. An application form, transcripts, SAT and ACT scores, two letter of recommendation, a 250-word essay and wallet-size photograph are required.

Exclusive: Visit www.UltimateScholarshipBook.com and enter code LO190726 for updates on this award.

[1908] • William and Sara Jenne' Scholarship
Montana State Elks Association
Robert J. Byers, Attn: Scholarship, P.O. Box 1274, Polson, MT 59860
http://www.mtelks.org
Purpose: To support undergraduate students in Montana.
Eligibility: Students must have completed one year of college or technical school with at least 30 semester hours, and they must have at least a 2.0 GPA. Applicants must show financial need and good character.
Target applicant(s): College students. Adult students.
Minimum GPA: 2.0
Amount: Varies.
Number of awards: Varies.
Deadline: June 1.
How to apply: Applications are available online.
Exclusive: Visit www.UltimateScholarshipBook.com and enter code MO190826 for updates on this award.

[1909] • William D. and Jewell Brewer Scholarship
American Legion, Department of Michigan
212 N. Verlinden Avenue, Suite A, Lansing, MI 48915
Phone: 517-371-4720 x11
Email: programs@michiganlegion.org
http://www.michiganlegion.org
Purpose: To support Michigan students who are the sons, daughters or grandchildren of veterans.
Eligibility: Applicants must be sons, daughters or grandchildren of wartime veterans, residents of Michigan, have a minimum 2.5 GPA and plan to attend a college or university. Scholarships are based on financial need, academic standing and applicants' goals. Applicants must also provide proof of a parent's military service record. They should send scholarship information to the county district committee person.
Target applicant(s): High school students. College students. Adult students.
Minimum GPA: 2.5
Amount: $500.
Number of awards: Varies.
Deadline: January 22.
How to apply: Applications are available online.
Exclusive: Visit www.UltimateScholarshipBook.com and enter code AM190926 for updates on this award.

[1910] • William G. Saletic Scholarship
Independent Colleges of Washington
600 Stewart Street, Suite 600, Seattle, WA 98101
Phone: 206-623-4494
Email: scholarships@icwashington.org
https://icwashington.org/page/scholarships
Purpose: To provide financial assistance to students who are studying politics or history at an independent college of Washington.
Eligibility: Applicants must be juniors or seniors who are studying or majoring in politics or history. Students attending Gonzaga University, Heritage University, Pacific Lutheran University, Saint Martin's University, Seattle Pacific University, Seattle University, University of Puget Sound, Walla Walla University, Whitman College or Whitworth University are eligible.
Target applicant(s): College students. Adult students.
Amount: $1,700.
Number of awards: 1.
Deadline: April 12.
How to apply: Applications are available online or from your school's financial aid office.
Exclusive: Visit www.UltimateScholarshipBook.com and enter code IN191026 for updates on this award.

[1911] • William James and Dorothy Bading Lanquist Fund
Hawaii Community Foundation - Scholarships
827 Fort Street Mall, Honolulu, HI 96813
Phone: 888-731-3863
Email: scholarships@hcf-hawaii.org
https://www.hawaiicommunityfoundation.org/
Purpose: To support students who are majoring in physical sciences and related fields.
Eligibility: Applicants must be residents of Hawaii and be able to demonstrate financial need. Applicants must attend full-time an accredited, two or four year, not-for-profit institution in the U.S. (including U.S. territories) in an undergraduate or graduate level program in Physical Sciences (excluding Biological and Social Sciences). Applicants must have a minimum 3.0 GPA.
Target applicant(s): High school students. College students. Graduate school students. Adult students.
Minimum GPA: 3.0
Amount: Varies.
Number of awards: Varies.
Deadline: January 31.
How to apply: To apply, register online, complete the online application and select the scholarships to which you wish to apply. In addition, mail the supporting materials: printed confirmation page from the online application, personal statement, copy of Student Aid Report (SAR) available at www.fafsa.ed.gov and official transcript.
Exclusive: Visit www.UltimateScholarshipBook.com and enter code HA191126 for updates on this award.

[1912] • William L. Boyd, IV, Effective Access to Student Education Program
Florida Department of Education
Office of Student Financial Assistance, State Scholarship and Grant Programs, 325 West Gaines Street, Suite 1314, Tallahassee, FL 32399-0400
Phone: 888-827-2004
Email: osfa@fldoe.org
https://origin.fldoe.org/finance/financial-aid-scholarships/
Purpose: Provides monetary assistance to Florida undergraduate college students enrolled at eligible, private, non-profit Florida schools.
Eligibility: Applicants must attend an eligible private, nonprofit Florida college or university, be Florida residents and not be in default on any state or federal grant, loan or scholarship. Requirements vary by institution.
Target applicant(s): High school students. College students. Adult students.
Amount: $3,000.
Number of awards: Varies.
Scholarship may be renewable.
Deadline: As soon as possible after October 1.
How to apply: Contact your financial aid office.
Exclusive: Visit www.UltimateScholarshipBook.com and enter code FL191226 for updates on this award.

The Ultimate Scholarship Book 2026
Scholarship Directory (State of Residence)

[1913] • Winifred R. Reynolds Educational Scholarship
Denver Foundation
1009 Grant Street, Denver, CO 80203
Phone: 303-300-1790
Email: information@denverfoundation.org
https://denverfoundation.org/scholarships/scholarship-opportunities/
Purpose: To support graduate students pursuing a degree related to early childhood education.
Eligibility: Applicants must have financial need, be residents of Colorado and have a minimum 3.5 GPA for the graduate work they have completed. Students must be pursuing a graduate degree in early childhood education, child development or an equivalent field.
Target applicant(s): College students. Graduate school students. Adult students.
Minimum GPA: 3.5
Amount: $1,000.
Number of awards: Varies.
Scholarship may be renewable.
Deadline: March 1.
How to apply: Applications are available online.
Exclusive: Visit www.UltimateScholarshipBook.com and enter code DE191326 for updates on this award.

[1914] • Winner's Circle Scholarships
Iowa Foundation for Agricultural Advancement
Winner's Circle Scholarships, c/o SGI, 30805 595th Avenue, Cambridge, IA 50046
Phone: 515-291-3941
Email: linda@slweldon.net
https://ifaa.org/scholarships.php
Purpose: To aid Iowa students who have been active in 4-H or FFA.
Eligibility: Applicants must be Iowa residents, be incoming freshmen at an Iowa college or university and have experience in 4-H and/or FFA livestock projects. They must have plans to major in animal science, agriculture or a related subject. Preference will be given to applicants from Polk County. Selection is based on the overall strength of the application.
Target applicant(s): High school students.
Amount: Up to $5,000.
Number of awards: Varies.
Deadline: April 1.
How to apply: Applications are available online. An application form and supporting materials are required.
Exclusive: Visit www.UltimateScholarshipBook.com and enter code IO191426 for updates on this award.

[1915] • Wisconsin Amusement and Music Operators Scholarships
Wisconsin Amusement and Music Operators
P.O. Box 259506, Madison, WI 53725
Phone: 800-827-8011
Email: info@wamo.net
http://wamo.net/
Purpose: To assist students of Wisconsin technical schools.
Eligibility: Applicants must be enrolled in or accepted for a minimum of six credits or plan to attend one of the 16 Wisconsin Technical College campuses. They must be family members, employees or players of a WAMO member business. They must have a recommendation from a WAMO member.
Target applicant(s): High school students. College students. Adult students.
Amount: Varies.
Number of awards: Varies.
Deadline: Contact the sponsor to confirm the deadline.
How to apply: Applications are available online. Two copies of application form, a transcript and two letters of recommendation are required.
Exclusive: Visit www.UltimateScholarshipBook.com and enter code WI191526 for updates on this award.

[1916] • Wisconsin Broadcasters Association Foundation Student Scholarship Program
Wisconsin Broadcasters Association
Linda Baun, WBA Foundation, 44 E. Mifflin Street, Suite 900, Madison, WI 53703
Phone: 608-255-2600
Email: contact@wi-broadcasters.org
https://www.wbafoundation.org/
Purpose: To assist broadcasting students.
Eligibility: Applicants must attend a public or private college or university, a broadcast or media school or Wisconsin technical college. They must major in broadcasting, communications or a related field and have completed 60 credits by the application deadline. Students must have graduated from a Wisconsin high school or be attending a Wisconsin institution of higher learning. They must plan a career in radio or television broadcasting and must not have previously won a WBA scholarship.
Target applicant(s): College students. Adult students.
Amount: $1,500-$2,500.
Number of awards: 4.
Deadline: November 1.
How to apply: Applications are available online. An application form, transcript, essay and two letters of recommendation are required.
Exclusive: Visit www.UltimateScholarshipBook.com and enter code WI191626 for updates on this award.

[1917] • Wisconsin Higher Education Grant
State of Wisconsin Higher Educational Aids Board
P.O. Box 7885, Madison, WI 53707
Phone: 608-267-2206
Email: heabmail@wisconsin.gov
https://heab.state.wi.us
Purpose: To assist Wisconsin students who have financial need.
Eligibility: Applicants must be Wisconsin residents and certificate- or degree-seeking undergraduate students with financial need who are enrolled at least part-time. They must be attending a Wisconsin technical college, tribal college or University of Wisconsin system institution. Selection is based on financial need.
Target applicant(s): High school students. College students. Adult students.
Amount: $250-$3,000.
Number of awards: Varies.
Scholarship may be renewable.
Deadline: As soon as possible after October 1.
How to apply: Application is made by completing the FAFSA.
Exclusive: Visit www.UltimateScholarshipBook.com and enter code ST191726 for updates on this award.

The Ultimate Scholarship Book 2026
Scholarship Directory (State of Residence)

[1918] • Wisconsin National Guard Tuition Grant
Wisconsin Department of Military Affairs
WIAR-G1-ED, P.O. Box 8111, Madison, WI 53708-8111
Phone: 608-242-3159
Email: karen.behling@wisconsin.gov
http://dma.wi.gov
Purpose: To help Wisconsin National Guard members with their education.
Eligibility: Applicants must be Wisconsin National Guard enlisted members and warrant officers in good standing who do not have a bachelor's degree. Recipients may use the grant at any campus of the University of Wisconsin System, a public institution of higher education under the Minnesota-Wisconsin student reciprocity agreement or an accredited institution of higher education in Wisconsin.
Target applicant(s): High school students. College students. Adult students.
Minimum GPA: 2.0
Amount: Full tuition.
Number of awards: Varies.
Scholarship may be renewable.
Deadline: Contact the sponsor to confirm the deadline.
How to apply: Applications are available online and are due no later than 90 days after the end of each course or term.
Exclusive: Visit www.UltimateScholarshipBook.com and enter code WI191826 for updates on this award.

[1919] • Wisconsin Oratorical Scholarship Program
American Legion, Department of Wisconsin
2930 American Legion Drive, P.O. Box 388, Portage, WI 53901
Phone: 608-745-1090
Email: info@wilegion.org
https://wilegion.org/scholarships
Purpose: To enhance high school students' experience with and understanding of the U.S. Constitution. The contest will help develop students' leadership skills and civic appreciation, as well as the ability to deliver thoughtful, insightful orations regarding U.S. citizenship and its inherent responsibilities.
Eligibility: Applicants must be high school students under the age of 20 who are U.S. citizens or legal residents and residents of the state. Students first give an oration within their state and winners compete at the national level. The oration must be related to the Constitution of the United States focusing on the duties and obligations citizens have to the government. It must be in English and be between eight and ten minutes. There is also an assigned topic which is posted on the website, and it should be between three and five minutes.
Target applicant(s): High school students.
Amount: Up to $5,000.
Number of awards: Varies.
Deadline: Contact the sponsor to confirm the deadline.
How to apply: Application information is available by contacting the local American Legion Post.
Exclusive: Visit www.UltimateScholarshipBook.com and enter code AM191926 for updates on this award.

[1920] • Wisconsin Veterans Education Reimbursement Grants
Wisconsin Department of Veterans Affairs
201 West Washington Avenue, P.O. Box 7843, Madison, WI 53707-7843
Phone: 800-947-8387
Email: WDVAWeb@dva.wisconsin.gov
http://www.dva.state.wi.us
Purpose: To support Wisconsin veterans.
Eligibility: Applicants must be Wisconsin residents and must have served in the U.S. armed forces in active duty for two consecutive years, completed their initial active service obligations, accumulated at least 90 days of active duty during wartime or have received or become qualified to receive an expeditionary or service medal. Students must have received an honorable discharge and be working toward a degree or certificate. A minimum 2.0 GPA is required. Funds are awarded upon course completion.
Target applicant(s): College students. Adult students.
Minimum GPA: 2.0
Amount: Up to full tuition.
Number of awards: Varies.
Deadline: No later than 60 days after the start of classes.
How to apply: Applications are available online. An application form is required.
Exclusive: Visit www.UltimateScholarshipBook.com and enter code WI192026 for updates on this award.

[1921] • Wisconsin Women in Government Undergraduate Scholarship
Wisconsin Women in Government Inc.
P.O. Box 2543, Madison, WI 53701
Phone: 608-848-2321
Email: info@wiscwomeningovernment.org
http://wiscwomeningovernment.org/
Purpose: To aid Wisconsin women who are planning for careers in government and public service.
Eligibility: Applicants must be female Wisconsin residents who are undergraduate students at a participating Wisconsin college or university. They must be interested in government, public service or political careers and demonstrate financial need. Selection is based on academic merit, leadership, initiative, communication skills, extracurricular activities and commitment to public service.
Target applicant(s): College students. Adult students.
Minimum GPA: 2.0
Amount: Up to $3,000.
Number of awards: Varies.
Scholarship may be renewable.
Deadline: June 14.
How to apply: Applications are available online. An application form, transcript, two recommendation letters and financial aid information are required.
Exclusive: Visit www.UltimateScholarshipBook.com and enter code WI192126 for updates on this award.

[1922] • Women in STEM Award
British American Foundation of Texas
Email: info@baftx.org
http://www.baftx.org
Purpose: To support students from Texas pursuing STEM education.
Eligibility: Applicants must be residents of Texas enrolled as full-time undergraduate students within the Texas education system with demonstrated financial need. Students must be majoring in STEM with a GPA of 3.25 or higher.
Target applicant(s): College students. Graduate school students. Adult students.
Minimum GPA: 3.25
Amount: $5,000.

Number of awards: 1.
Deadline: March 31.
How to apply: Applications are available online.
Exclusive: Visit www.UltimateScholarshipBook.com and enter code BR192226 for updates on this award.

[1923] • Workforce Shortage Student Assistance Grant Program
Maryland Higher Education Commission
Office of Student Financial Assistance, 6 North Liberty Street, Baltimore, MD 21201
Phone: 800-974-1024
Email: osfamail@mhec.state.md.us
https://mhec.maryland.gov
Purpose: To support students in Maryland who plan to work in jobs which are needed on a statewide or regional basis.
Eligibility: Applicants must be currently enrolled or planning to enroll in a Maryland postsecondary school. Dependent students must have parents who also live in Maryland. Eligible majors are chosen to address current state or regional needs and usually include the following: child care, human services, teaching, nursing, physical and occupational therapy and public service. Students must agree to begin working within that employment field within one year of graduation at a rate of one year for every year that the scholarship was granted.
Target applicant(s): High school students. College students. Graduate school students. Adult students.
Amount: Up to $4,000.
Number of awards: Varies.
Scholarship may be renewable.
Deadline: July 15.
How to apply: Applications are available online in January.
Exclusive: Visit www.UltimateScholarshipBook.com and enter code MA192326 for updates on this award.

[1924] • World Trade Center Memorial Scholarship
New York State Higher Education Services Corporation (HESC)
99 Washington Avenue, Albany, NY 12255
Phone: 888-697-4372
Email: scholarships@hesc.ny.gov
http://www.hesc.ny.gov
Purpose: To support the families and dependents of those who were injured or died as a result of the attacks on September 11, 2001.
Eligibility: Applicants must be full-time undergraduate students. Students must attend school in the state of New York, but they may be residents of any state or country.
Target applicant(s): College students. Adult students.
Amount: Varies.
Number of awards: Varies.
Scholarship may be renewable.
Deadline: June 30.
How to apply: Applications are available online.
Exclusive: Visit www.UltimateScholarshipBook.com and enter code NE192426 for updates on this award.

[1925] • WTS Minnesota Chapter Scholarships
Women's Transportation Seminar (WTS) - Minnesota Chapter
University of Minnesota, 200 Center for Transportation Studies, 511 Washington Avenue SE, Minneapolis, MN 55455
Email: Lyssa.Leitner@co.washington.mn.us
https://www.wtsinternational.org/chapters/minnesota/scholarships
Purpose: To aid women who are pursuing higher education in a transportation-related subject.
Eligibility: Applicants must be women who are enrolled in an undergraduate or graduate degree program that is related to transportation. They either must be attending a school located in Minnesota, or must be North Dakota, South Dakota or Iowa students who have lived in Minnesota at some point during the past five years. They must have plans to pursue a career in the transportation field, and must have a GPA of 3.0 or higher. Selection is based on academic merit, transportation-related activities and career goals.
Target applicant(s): College students. Graduate school students. Adult students.
Minimum GPA: 3.0
Amount: $2,000.
Number of awards: 3.
Deadline: December 16.
How to apply: Applications are available online. An application form, official transcript, proof of enrollment, one letter of recommendation and a personal essay are required.
Exclusive: Visit www.UltimateScholarshipBook.com and enter code WO192526 for updates on this award.

[1926] • Xello High School Scholarship
Wisconsin School Counselor Association
2820 Walton Commons, Suite 103, Madison, WI 53718
Phone: 608-204-9825
Email: nechodomk@gmail.com
https://www.wscaweb.org/awards-scholarships/scholarships/
Purpose: To support Wisconsin students.
Eligibility: Applicants must be seniors at a public or private Wisconsin high school. They must plan to attend an institution of higher learning in the school year following graduation.
Target applicant(s): High school students.
Amount: $500.
Number of awards: 4.
Deadline: December 11.
How to apply: Applications are available online. An application form and essay are required.
Exclusive: Visit www.UltimateScholarshipBook.com and enter code WI192626 for updates on this award.

[1927] • You've Got a Friend in Pennsylvania Scholarship
American Radio Relay League Foundation
225 Main Street, Newington, CT 06111-1494
Phone: 860-594-0200
Email: foundation@arrl.org
https://www.arrl.org/scholarship-program
Purpose: To support Pennsylvania students who are involved in amateur radio.
Eligibility: Applicants must have an amateur radio license in General Class or higher and an active American Radio Relay League membership. Applicants must have an "A" or equivalent GPA.
Target applicant(s): High school students. College students. Adult students.
Minimum GPA: 3.6
Amount: $1,000.
Number of awards: 1.
Deadline: January 10.
How to apply: Applications are available online.

Exclusive: Visit www.UltimateScholarshipBook.com and enter code AM192726 for updates on this award.

[1928] • Zagunis Student Leader Scholarship
National Association for Campus Activities
13 Harbison Way, Columbia, SC 29212
Phone: 803-732-6222
Email: info@naca.org
https://www.naca.org/resources/scholarships-grants/scholarships.html
Purpose: To provide financial assistance to student leaders.
Eligibility: Applicants must be current undergraduate or graduate students who hold a significant campus leadership position, demonstrate significant leadership skills and abilities and make significant contributions through on- or off-campus volunteering. Students must attend school in Kentucky, Michigan, Ohio, West Virginia or western Pennsylvania.
Target applicant(s): College students. Graduate school students. Adult students.
Minimum GPA: 3.0
Amount: Varies.
Number of awards: Varies.
Deadline: November 30.
How to apply: Applications are available online.
Exclusive: Visit www.UltimateScholarshipBook.com and enter code NA192826 for updates on this award.

[1929] • Zell Miller Scholarship
Georgia Student Finance Commission
2082 East Exchange Place, Tucker, GA 30084
Phone: 800-505-4732
Email: gsfcinfo@gsfc.org
https://www.gafutures.org
Purpose: To support students attending Georgia institutions.
Eligibility: Applicants must have graduated from high school and be attending or planning to attend college in Georgia. Students must be U.S. citizens or eligible non-citizens, be a legal resident of the state of Georgia, have a minimum 3.7 GPA and an ACT composite score of 26 or a SAT total test score of 1200. Students should submit applications as early as possible.
Target applicant(s): High school students.
Minimum GPA: 3.7
Amount: Varies.
Number of awards: Varies.
Scholarship may be renewable.
Deadline: Last day of the school term or a student's withdrawal date; whichever occurs first.
How to apply: Applications are available online.
Exclusive: Visit www.UltimateScholarshipBook.com and enter code GE192926 for updates on this award.

MEMBERSHIP

[1930] • 4-H Youth in Action
National 4-H Council
7100 Connecticut Avenue, Chevy Chase, MD 20815
Phone: 301-961-2800
Email: youthinaction@4-h.org
https://4-h.org/parents/4-h-youth-in-action-awards/
Purpose: To recognize dynamic young leaders among 4-H members.
Eligibility: Applicants must be current or former 4-H members between the ages of 15-19 years old. Students must create a one-minute video relating to their leadership in one of the 4-H pillar areas and provide the following: several short essays, photos supporting their entry and proof of 4-H involvement. One award will be given in each of four pillar areas: agriculture, civic engagement, healthy living and STEM.
Target applicant(s): High school students. College students.
Amount: $5,000.
Number of awards: 4.
Deadline: April 1.
How to apply: Applications are available online.
Exclusive: Visit www.UltimateScholarshipBook.com and enter code NA193026 for updates on this award.

[1931] • Adrianna Andreini Scholarship
American Quarter Horse Foundation
Scholarship Program, 2601 East Interstate 40, Amarillo, TX 79104
Phone: 806-378-5029
Email: foundation@aqha.org
https://www.aqha.com/scholarships1
Purpose: To support AQHA members with their higher education expenses.
Eligibility: Applicants must be current AQHA or AQHYA members with a minimum 2.5 GPA. Members must apply beginning from their sophomore year of college. Current or previous AQHF scholarship students are not eligible to receive this scholarship. Funding for this scholarship may be applied to a four-year undergraduate and or two-year graduate-level degree program of the student's choice.
Target applicant(s): College students. Graduate school students. Adult students.
Minimum GPA: 2.5
Amount: $8,750.
Number of awards: Varies.
Deadline: January 15.
How to apply: Applications are available online.
Exclusive: Visit www.UltimateScholarshipBook.com and enter code AM193126 for updates on this award.

[1932] • AFSA Financial Aid Scholarships
American Foreign Service Association (AFSA)
2101 East Street NW, Washington, DC 20037
Phone: 202-944-5504
Email: dec@afsa.org
http://www.afsa.org/afsa-scholarships
Purpose: To provide financial aid to university students who are the children or dependents of Foreign Service employees.
Eligibility: Applicants must be dependents of U.S. government Foreign Service employees with a minimum 2.0 GPA. Students must attend or plan to attend full-time an undergraduate U.S. college, university, community college, art school, conservatory or other post-secondary institution.

Applicants must submit applications, transcripts and financial need reports. Recipients must complete their undergraduate degree within four years and must demonstrate financial need.
Target applicant(s): High school students. College students. Adult students.
Minimum GPA: 2.0
Amount: $1,500-$6,000.
Number of awards: Varies.
Scholarship may be renewable.
Deadline: March 11.
How to apply: Applications are available after November 1.
Exclusive: Visit www.UltimateScholarshipBook.com and enter code AM193226 for updates on this award.

[1933] • AFSA/AAFSW Merit Awards
American Foreign Service Association (AFSA)
2101 East Street NW, Washington, DC 20037
Phone: 202-944-5504
Email: dec@afsa.org
http://www.afsa.org/afsa-scholarships
Purpose: To recognize the academic and artistic achievements of high school seniors who are the children or dependents of Foreign Service employees.
Eligibility: Applicants must be dependents of U.S. government Foreign Service employees who are members of AFSA or AAFSW. Students must be high school seniors with a minimum 2.0 GPA. Applicants can also submit an art entry under the categories of visual arts, musical arts, drama, dance or creative writing. Awards are based on GPA, SAT scores, a two-page essay, letters of recommendation and extra-curricular activities.
Target applicant(s): High school students.
Minimum GPA: 2.0
Amount: $1,500-$3,500.
Number of awards: Varies.
Deadline: March 11.
How to apply: Applications are available online after November 1.
Exclusive: Visit www.UltimateScholarshipBook.com and enter code AM193326 for updates on this award.

[1934] • AFSCME Family Scholarship
American Federation of State, County and Municipal Employees (AFSCME), AFL-CIO
Attn.: Education Department, 1625 L Street NW, Washington, DC 20036-5687
Phone: 202-429-5080
Email: education@afscme.org
https://www.afscme.org/members/scholarships
Purpose: To offer financial assistance to the dependents of AFSCME members.
Eligibility: Applicants must be graduating high school seniors who are the daughters, sons or financially dependent grandchildren of AFSCME members who intend to enroll in a full-time, four-year degree program in any accredited college or university. Applicants should submit applications, essays, transcripts, test scores and recommendation letters. Selection is based on information provided on the application form, high school transcript, SAT/ACT scores and a required essay.
Target applicant(s): High school students.
Amount: $2,000.
Number of awards: 10.
Scholarship may be renewable.
Deadline: December 31.
How to apply: Applications are available online and by written request.

Exclusive: Visit www.UltimateScholarshipBook.com and enter code AM193426 for updates on this award.

[1935] • Allan Jerome Burry Scholarship
United Methodist Church
P.O. Box 340007, Nashville, TN 37203-0007
Phone: 615-340-7400
Email: umscholar@gbhem.org
https://www.gbhem.org/scholarships/
Purpose: To support students in ministry or chaplaincy programs who are members of the United Methodist Church.
Eligibility: Applicants must be college undergraduates who show evidence of financial need, leadership qualities, academic excellence and church participation. They must have a GPA of 3.0 or higher. Students must have been active members of the United Methodist Church for at least three years and be nominated by the campus chaplain or minister.
Target applicant(s): College students. Adult students.
Minimum GPA: 3.0
Amount: $1,000.
Number of awards: Varies.
Deadline: March 30.
How to apply: Applications are available from campus ministers or chaplains.
Exclusive: Visit www.UltimateScholarshipBook.com and enter code UN193526 for updates on this award.

[1936] • ALPA Scholarship Program
Air Line Pilots Association, International
7950 Jones Branch Drive, Suite 400S, McLean, VA 22102
Phone: 703-689-2270
Email: communications@alpa.org
https://www.alpa.org/resources/alpa-scholarship-programs
Purpose: To support the children of medically retired, long-term disabled or deceased pilot members of the Air Line Pilots Association.
Eligibility: Applicants must be pursuing a baccalaureate degree. Selection is based on academic achievements and financial need. The award is renewable for four years with a minimum 3.0 GPA.
Target applicant(s): High school students. College students. Adult students.
Minimum GPA: 3.0
Amount: $15,000.
Number of awards: 1.
Scholarship may be renewable.
Deadline: April 1.
How to apply: Applications are available by mail.
Exclusive: Visit www.UltimateScholarshipBook.com and enter code AI193626 for updates on this award.

[1937] • American Association of State Troopers (AAST) Scholarship
American Association of State Troopers (AAST) Inc.
1949 Raymond Diehl Road, Tallahassee, FL 32308
Phone: 800-765-5456
http://www.statetroopers.org
Purpose: To support dependents of AAST trooper members.
Eligibility: Applicants must be a dependent (child by natural birth, child legally adopted, stepchild or claimed dependent on income tax) of a trooper member. Student AAST member parent must have been a member in good standing for two consecutive years prior to application deadline.

Target applicant(s): High school students. College students. Adult students.
Minimum GPA: 3.0
Amount: $500.
Number of awards: 1.
Scholarship may be renewable.
Deadline: July 31.
How to apply: Applications are available online.
Exclusive: Visit www.UltimateScholarshipBook.com and enter code AM193726 for updates on this award.

[1938] • American Legion Eagle Scout of the Year
American Legion
Attn.: Americanism and Children and Youth Division, P.O. Box 1055, Indianapolis, IN 46206
Phone: 317-630-1249
Email: acy@legion.org
http://www.legion.org
Purpose: To provide scholarships for Eagle Scouts.
Eligibility: Applicants must have received the Eagle Scout Award, be active members of their religious institutions, have received the appropriate Scouts religious emblem, demonstrate citizenship, be at least 15 years old and be high school students. Nominations are due March 1.
Target applicant(s): High school students.
Amount: $2,500-$10,000.
Number of awards: 4.
Deadline: March 1.
How to apply: Applications are available online.
Exclusive: Visit www.UltimateScholarshipBook.com and enter code AM193826 for updates on this award.

[1939] • AMVETS National Ladies Auxiliary Scholarship
AMVETS National Ladies Auxiliary Headquarters
Attn.: Scholarship Officer, 4647 Forbes Boulevard, Lanham, MD 20706
Phone: 301-459-6255
http://amvetsaux.org/scholarships/
Purpose: To promote educational opportunities for students interested in or involved with a national service organization.
Eligibility: Applicants must be a current member of or the child or grandchild of a current member of the AMVETS Ladies Auxiliary. Students must be at least sophomores at an accredited college or university.
Target applicant(s): College students. Adult students.
Amount: $750-$1,000.
Number of awards: 7.
Deadline: July 1.
How to apply: Applications are available by mail.
Exclusive: Visit www.UltimateScholarshipBook.com and enter code AM193926 for updates on this award.

[1940] • AQHF General Scholarship
American Quarter Horse Foundation
Scholarship Program, 2601 East Interstate 40, Amarillo, TX 79104
Phone: 806-378-5029
Email: foundation@aqha.org
https://www.aqha.com/scholarships1
Purpose: To support AQHA members with their higher education expenses.
Eligibility: Applicants must be current members of AQHA or AQHYA with a minimum 2.5 GPA. Members must apply while enrolled at an accredited college or university. Current or previous AQHF scholarship recipients are not eligible to receive this scholarship. Funding for this scholarship may be applied to either a two- or four-year degree program, including the student's undergraduate or graduate studies.
Target applicant(s): High school students. College students. Graduate school students. Adult students.
Minimum GPA: 2.5
Amount: Up to $9,000.
Number of awards: Varies.
Deadline: January 15.
How to apply: Applications are available online.
Exclusive: Visit www.UltimateScholarshipBook.com and enter code AM194026 for updates on this award.

[1941] • AQHF Youth Scholarship
American Quarter Horse Foundation
Scholarship Program, 2601 East Interstate 40, Amarillo, TX 79104
Phone: 806-378-5029
Email: foundation@aqha.org
https://www.aqha.com/scholarships1
Purpose: To support AQHA members with their higher education expenses.
Eligibility: Applicants must be members of AQHA or AQHYA who have completed a minimum of three years of cumulative membership and ranked within the upper 25 percent of their high school graduating class while exhibiting an affinity for the advancement of the American Quarter Horse and demonstrating leadership potential. Members must be high school or home-schooled seniors when applying. Students currently enrolled as first-year college freshmen are not eligible for consideration. Current or previous AQHF scholarship recipients are not eligible to receive this scholarship. Recipients must maintain a minimum 2.5 GPA, and funds for this scholarship will be applied to a four-year undergraduate degree program of the student's choice.
Target applicant(s): High school students. College students. Adult students.
Minimum GPA: 2.5
Amount: $8,000.
Number of awards: 5.
Deadline: January 15.
How to apply: Applications are available online.
Exclusive: Visit www.UltimateScholarshipBook.com and enter code AM194126 for updates on this award.

[1942] • ARA Scholarship
ARA Scholarship Foundation Inc.
ARA Scholarship Advisor, 9113 Church Street, Manassas, VA 20110
Phone: 571-208-0428
Email: Kelly@a-r-a.org
http://www.a-r-a.org
Purpose: To support the children of Automotive Recyclers Association (ARA) members.
Eligibility: Applicants must be high school seniors and/or planning to attend college full-time and have earned a minimum 3.0 GPA in their last educational program. Applicants must also be the children of employees of a Direct Member of ARA who were hired at least one year prior to March 15 of the application year. Scholarships are based on academic merit, not financial need.
Target applicant(s): High school students. College students. Graduate school students. Adult students.

The Ultimate Scholarship Book 2026
Scholarship Directory (Membership)

Minimum GPA: 3.0
Amount: $1,000-$2,000.
Number of awards: Varies.
Scholarship may be renewable.
Deadline: March 15.
How to apply: Applications are available online and by email request.
Exclusive: Visit www.UltimateScholarshipBook.com and enter code AR194226 for updates on this award.

[1943] • Arthur M. and Berdena King Eagle Scout Contest

National Society, Sons of the American Revolution
809 West Main Street, Louisville, KY 40202
Phone: 502-589-1776
Email: coggins.sar@gmail.com
https://www.sar.org/education/
Purpose: To reward exceptional students who have reached the status of Eagle Scout.
Eligibility: Applicants must have reached Eagle Scout status, must currently be registered in an active unit and can't have reached their 19th birthday during the year of application. Applicants can apply multiple years as long as they are under the age limit, but the maximum award amount is $10,000. Applicants usually apply at the chapter level. Applicants will be required to submit an essay and four-generation ancestor chart with their application.
Target applicant(s): Junior high students or younger. High school students.
Amount: $200-$10,000.
Number of awards: 15.
Deadline: December 31.
How to apply: Applications are available online.
Exclusive: Visit www.UltimateScholarshipBook.com and enter code NA194326 for updates on this award.

[1944] • Association of Flight Attendants Annual Scholarship

Association of Flight Attendants
501 Third Street NW, Washington, DC 20001
Phone: 202-434-1300
Email: info@afacwa.org
http://www.afacwa.org/
Purpose: To provide financial assistance to the children of members of the AFA.
Eligibility: Applicants must be the dependents of AFA members in good standing. Applicants must also be in the top 15 percent of their class, have or expect to have excellent SAT/ACT scores, demonstrate financial need and provide a 300-word essay along with the completed application.
Target applicant(s): High school students.
Amount: Varies.
Number of awards: Varies.
Scholarship may be renewable.
Deadline: April 10.
How to apply: Applications are available online.
Exclusive: Visit www.UltimateScholarshipBook.com and enter code AS194426 for updates on this award.

[1945] • Assured Life Association National Scholarship

Assured Life Association
Scholarship Committee, P.O. Box 3169, Englewood, CO 80155
Phone: 800-777-9777 x 3773
Email: scholarship@assuredlife.org
http://assuredlife.org
Purpose: To support students seeking a college education.
Eligibility: Applicants must be certificate holders or children or grandchildren of certificate holders of Assured Life Association of Greenwood Village, Colorado. Students must be seniors in high school, undergraduates or graduates students taking at least 12 credit hours. Applicants are required to submit a 250- to 500-word essay on the given topic.
Target applicant(s): High school students. College students. Graduate school students. Adult students.
Amount: $500-$2,500.
Number of awards: 60-70.
Deadline: May 15.
How to apply: Applications are available online and must include an official transcript, a current list of extracurricular activities, a recent photo of the applicant and the certificate information of the certificate holder.
Exclusive: Visit www.UltimateScholarshipBook.com and enter code AS194526 for updates on this award.

[1946] • AWSM Internship and Scholarship

Association for Women in Sports Media
7742 Spalding Drive #377, Norcross, GA 30092
Email: awsminternship@gmail.com
http://awsmonline.org/internships-scholarships
Purpose: To encourage females interested in sports media careers.
Eligibility: Applicants must be female students working full-time toward a graduate or undergraduate degree with the goal of becoming a sports writer, editor, broadcaster or public relations representative. Applicants must submit a resume, an essay on a memorable experience in sports or sports media, three references, two letters of recommendation and up to five samples of their work. Application fee is waived for AWSM members.
Target applicant(s): College students. Graduate school students. Adult students.
Amount: $1,000 plus paid internship.
Number of awards: Varies.
Deadline: November 30.
How to apply: Applications are available online.
Exclusive: Visit www.UltimateScholarshipBook.com and enter code AS194626 for updates on this award.

[1947] • Bernard Rotberg Memorial Scholarship Fund

Jewish War Veterans of the USA
1811 R Street NW, Washington, DC 20009
Phone: 202-265-6280
Email: jwv@jwv.org
https://jwvusafoundation.org/
Purpose: To provide scholarships for descendants of members of the Jewish War Veterans of the USA.
Eligibility: Applicants must be a direct descendant of a JWV member in good standing. Candidates must also have been accepted to an accredited college, university or nursing school, be in the upper 25 percent of their class and be active in activities at school and within the Jewish community.
Target applicant(s): High school students.

Amount: $1,000.
Number of awards: 1.
Deadline: May 19.
How to apply: Applications are available online and should be submitted by the applicant's school to the department commander in the local post.
Exclusive: Visit www.UltimateScholarshipBook.com and enter code JE194726 for updates on this award.

[1948] • Boon San Kitty Scholarship

American Quarter Horse Foundation
Scholarship Program, 2601 East Interstate 40, Amarillo, TX 79104
Phone: 806-378-5029
Email: foundation@aqha.org
https://www.aqha.com/scholarships1
Purpose: To support AQHA members with their higher education expenses.
Eligibility: Applicants must be current AQHA or AQHYA members with a minimum 3.0 GPA. Members must apply during their senior year of high school. Current or previous AQHF scholarship recipients are not eligible to receive this scholarship. Funding for this scholarship will be applied to a four-year undergraduate degree program of the student's choice.
Target applicant(s): High school students. College students. Adult students.
Minimum GPA: 3.0
Amount: $7,500.
Number of awards: Varies.
Deadline: January 15.
How to apply: Applications are available online.
Exclusive: Visit www.UltimateScholarshipBook.com and enter code AM194826 for updates on this award.

[1949] • Boys and Girls Clubs of America National Youth of the Year Award

Boys and Girls Clubs of America
1275 Peachtree Street NE, Atlanta, GA 30309
Phone: 404-487-5700
Email: info@bgca.org
https://www.bgca.org/programs/youth-of-the-year
Purpose: To reward club members who demonstrate good academic performance, perform services for both their club and community and who are active in both family and spiritual life.
Eligibility: Applicants must be a member of a BGCA and be selected by their local club to compete for the regional and national scholarships. Regional and national awards are renewable up to four years.
Target applicant(s): High school students.
Amount: $2,500-$50,000.
Number of awards: Varies.
Scholarship may be renewable.
Deadline: Contact the sponsor to confirm the deadline.
How to apply: Contact your local club for more information.
Exclusive: Visit www.UltimateScholarshipBook.com and enter code BO194926 for updates on this award.

[1950] • Carroll C. Hall Memorial Scholarship

Tau Kappa Epsilon Educational Foundation
7439 Woodland Drive, Suite 100, Indianapolis, IN 46278
Phone: 317-872-6533
Email: tkeogc@tke.org
https://www.tke.org/foundation/scholarships
Purpose: To reward a member of Tau Kappa Epsilon for outstanding academic achievement and for leadership within the organization, campus or community.
Eligibility: Applicants must have a minimum 3.0 GPA and be undergraduates seeking a degree in education or science with the intention of pursuing a career in teaching or the sciences.
Target applicant(s): High school students. College students. Adult students.
Minimum GPA: 3.0
Amount: $400.
Number of awards: 1.
Deadline: March 15.
How to apply: Applications are available online.
Exclusive: Visit www.UltimateScholarshipBook.com and enter code TA195026 for updates on this award.

[1951] • Catholic United Financial College Tuition Scholarship

Catholic United Financial
Scholarship Program, 3499 Lexington Avenue North, St. Paul, MN 55126
Phone: 800-568-6670
Email: engage@catholicunited.org
http://www.catholicunitedfinancial.org
Purpose: To reward members of the Catholic United Financial.
Eligibility: Applicants must be members of the Catholic United Financial for at least two years prior to the date of application, have completed high school and be entering their first or second year in any accredited college, university, state college or technical college other than a private, non-Catholic college/university. Those attending a Catholic college are eligible for a $300 award and those attending a non-Catholic college are eligible for a $500 award.
Target applicant(s): High school students. College students. Adult students.
Amount: $300-$500.
Number of awards: Varies.
Deadline: April 30.
How to apply: Applications are available online.
Exclusive: Visit www.UltimateScholarshipBook.com and enter code CA195126 for updates on this award.

[1952] • Chairman's Award

National Association of Blacks in Criminal Justice
1801 Fayetteville Street, 106 Whiting Criminal Justice Building, P.O. Box 20011-C, Durham, NC 27707
Phone: 919-683-1801
Email: Office@NABCJ.org
https://nabcj.org/
Purpose: To support an individual who has shown leadership and dedication and made contributions to NABCJ at the chapter or regional level.
Eligibility: Applicants must be nominated by a member of NABCJ.
Target applicant(s): College students. Adult students.
Amount: Varies.
Number of awards: 1.
Deadline: March 15.
How to apply: Nomination applications are available online.
Exclusive: Visit www.UltimateScholarshipBook.com and enter code NA195226 for updates on this award.

[1953] • Champions for Christ Scholarship

Champions for Christ Foundation
P.O. Box 786, Greenville, SC
Phone: 864-294-0800
http://championsforchrist.us/
Purpose: To support students going into full-time Christian ministry.
Eligibility: Applicants must be enrolled at a U.S. educational institution. Selection is based on the overall strength of the application.
Target applicant(s): College students. Adult students.
Amount: Varies.
Number of awards: Varies.
Deadline: July 1 and November 1.
How to apply: Applications are available online.
Exclusive: Visit www.UltimateScholarshipBook.com and enter code CH195326 for updates on this award.

[1954] • Charles R. Walgreen Jr. Leadership Award

Tau Kappa Epsilon Educational Foundation
7439 Woodland Drive, Suite 100, Indianapolis, IN 46278
Phone: 317-872-6533
Email: tkeogc@tke.org
https://www.tke.org/foundation/scholarships
Purpose: To honor Charles R. Walgreen's support of Tau Kappa Epsilon by recognizing academic achievement in members.
Eligibility: Applicants must be initiated Tau Kappa Epsilon members in good standing and full-time students. They must have a GPA of at least 3.0 and demonstrate leadership in their chapter, campus and community. Applicants must also include a statement describing how they have benefited from TKE membership.
Target applicant(s): High school students. College students. Adult students.
Minimum GPA: 3.0
Amount: $1,400.
Number of awards: 1.
Deadline: March 15.
How to apply: Applications are available online.
Exclusive: Visit www.UltimateScholarshipBook.com and enter code TA195426 for updates on this award.

[1955] • Charlie Logan Scholarship Program for Dependents

Seafarers International Union of North America
Seafarers Health and Benefits Plan, Capital Gateway Drive, Camp Springs, Camp Springs, MD 20746
Phone: 301-899-0675
http://www.seafarers.org
Purpose: To offer scholarships to the dependents of members of the SIU.
Eligibility: Applicants must be the dependent children or spouses of members of the Seafarers International Union. The union member must be eligible for the Seafarer's Plan and must have credit for three years with an employer who is obligated to make a contribution to the Seafarer's Plan on behalf of the employee. Recipients may attend any U.S.-accredited institution. Selection is based on a review of secondary school records, SAT or ACT test scores, college transcripts, if any, character references, extracurricular activities and autobiography.
Target applicant(s): High school students. College students. Adult students.
Amount: $20,000.
Number of awards: 5.
Scholarship may be renewable.
Deadline: April 17.
How to apply: Applications are available by written request.
Exclusive: Visit www.UltimateScholarshipBook.com and enter code SE195526 for updates on this award.

[1956] • CNH Industrial Aftermarket Solutions Scholarship

National FFA Organization
P.O. Box 68960, 6060 FFA Drive, Indianapolis, IN 46268-0960
Phone: 888-332-2668
Email: scholarships@ffa.org
https://www.ffa.org/participate/grants-and-scholarships/
Purpose: To assist students who are FFA members.
Eligibility: Applicants must be members of FFA. One application is required for all FFA scholarships. Selection is based on the overall strength of the application.
Target applicant(s): High school students. College students. Adult students.
Amount: $10,000.
Number of awards: 4.
Deadline: January 11.
How to apply: Applications are available online.
Exclusive: Visit www.UltimateScholarshipBook.com and enter code NA195626 for updates on this award.

[1957] • Community College Transition Award

National Society of Collegiate Scholars (NSCS)
2000 M Street NW, Suite 600, Washington, DC 20036
Phone: 202-265-9000
Email: nscs@nscs.org
https://nscs.org/scholarships/
Purpose: To aid NSCS members in attaining their goals and to recognize their achievements in academics, leadership and service.
Eligibility: Applicants must be outstanding community college students transferring to a four-year college. Selection is based on the overall strength of the application.
Target applicant(s): College students. Adult students.
Amount: $1,000.
Number of awards: 3.
Deadline: May 25.
How to apply: Applications are available online.
Exclusive: Visit www.UltimateScholarshipBook.com and enter code NA195726 for updates on this award.

[1958] • CWA Joe Beirne Foundation Scholarship

Communications Workers of America
501 Third Street NW, Washington, DC 20001
Phone: 202-434-1100
Email: kadams@cwa-union.org
http://www.cwa-union.org
Purpose: To provide scholarships for CWA members and their families.
Eligibility: Applicants may be Communications Workers of America (CWA) members, their spouses, their children or their grandchildren. Applicants must be high school graduates or at least high school students who will graduate during the year in which they apply. Winners are selected by a lottery drawing. This is a two-year scholarship.
Target applicant(s): High school students. College students. Graduate school students. Adult students.
Amount: $4,000.

Number of awards: Varies.
Scholarship may be renewable.
Deadline: April 30.
How to apply: Contact a CWA Local or write (referencing CWA local number, member name and Social Security number) for an application. Applications are available online.
Exclusive: Visit www.UltimateScholarshipBook.com and enter code CO195826 for updates on this award.

[1959] • David B. Durkee Memorial Scholarship Program
Bakery Confectionary Tobacco Workers and Grain Millers (BCTGM) International Union
Scholarship Program, 10401 Connecticut Avenue, Kensington, MD 20895-3961
Phone: 301-933-8600
http://www.bctgm.org
Purpose: To provide scholarships for the members and families of members of BTGCM.
Eligibility: Applicants must be members of the BCTGM in good standing or the children of such members. The scholarships are also open to office employees and children of those employed at the International Union office. Applicants must be high school students who will be attending an accredited college, technical college or vocational school for the first time, high school graduates who have never attended college or BCTGM members who have never applied to the program before who are currently enrolled or planning to begin or resume their studies in the fall. All applicants are required to take the SAT or an equivalent, such as the ACT.
Target applicant(s): High school students. College students. Graduate school students. Adult students.
Amount: $5,000.
Number of awards: 5.
Deadline: January 31.
How to apply: Applications are available through your local BCTGM union office.
Exclusive: Visit www.UltimateScholarshipBook.com and enter code BA195926 for updates on this award.

[1960] • Delta Gamma Foundation Scholarship
Delta Gamma Foundation
3250 Riverside Drive, P.O. Box 21397, Columbus, OH 43221
Phone: 614-481-8169
Email: dgscholarships08@aol.com
http://www.deltagamma.org
Purpose: To support student members.
Eligibility: Applicants must be initiated members of Delta Gamma, have maintained a 3.0 GPA and have completed three semesters or five quarters of college coursework. Applicants should also be active participants in chapter, campus and community leadership activities. Awards are based on academic achievement and participation in activities.
Target applicant(s): College students. Adult students.
Minimum GPA: 3.0
Amount: Varies.
Number of awards: Varies.
Deadline: March 1.
How to apply: Applications are available online.
Exclusive: Visit www.UltimateScholarshipBook.com and enter code DE196026 for updates on this award.

[1961] • Delta Phi Epsilon Educational Foundation Scholarship
Delta Phi Epsilon Educational Foundation
16A Worthington Drive, Maryland Heights, MO 63043
Phone: 314-275-2626
Email: fausbury@dphie.org
https://dphie.org
Purpose: To reward members of Delta Phi Epsilon.
Eligibility: Applicants must be members or the sons or daughters of members of Delta Phi Epsilon who are applying for undergraduate or graduate study. The award is based on service and involvement, academics and financial need. Applicants should submit transcripts, letters of introduction and financial need, autobiographical sketches, two recent photos, at least two letters of recommendation and the contact information of the financial aid director for the school.
Target applicant(s): High school students. College students. Graduate school students. Adult students.
Amount: Varies.
Number of awards: Varies.
Deadline: December 31.
How to apply: Applications are available online.
Exclusive: Visit www.UltimateScholarshipBook.com and enter code DE196126 for updates on this award.

[1962] • Diller Teen Tikkun Olam Awards
Helen Diller Family Foundation
121 Stuart Street, San Francisco, CA 94105
Phone: 415-684-8618
Email: DillerTeenAwards@sfjcf.org
https://www.dillerteenawards.org/
Purpose: To assist Jewish teens who have demonstrated leadership and participation in community service projects that exemplify the value of tikkun olam (repair of the world).
Eligibility: Applicants must be Jewish teens, U.S. residents and between 13 and 19 years old. Two references and an application form are required. Teens' projects can help either the Jewish community or the general community as long as they have not been remunerated for their services. Teens may be nominated by any community member who knows the importance of their project except family members or may also nominate themselves.
Target applicant(s): Junior high students or younger. High school students. College students.
Amount: $36,000.
Number of awards: Up to 15.
Deadline: January 9.
How to apply: Applications are available online.
Exclusive: Visit www.UltimateScholarshipBook.com and enter code HE196226 for updates on this award.

[1963] • Diocese of the Armenian Church of America (Eastern) Scholarships
Diocese of the Armenian Church of America (Eastern)
630 Second Avenue, New York, NY 10016
Phone: 212-686-0710
Email: mariab@armeniandiocese.org
https://armenianchurch.us/scholarships/
Purpose: To support young Armenian Church members who are seeking higher education.
Eligibility: Applicants must be Armenian Americans who are currently attending or plan to attend a four-year college or university. Preference is

given to applicants who are U.S. citizens and are active in the Armenian Church.
Target applicant(s): High school students. College students. Adult students.
Amount: Varies.
Number of awards: Varies.
Deadline: May 19.
How to apply: Applications are available from the Diocese of the Armenian Church of America (Eastern).
Exclusive: Visit www.UltimateScholarshipBook.com and enter code DI196326 for updates on this award.

[1964] • Donald A. and John R. Fisher Memorial Scholarship
Tau Kappa Epsilon Educational Foundation
7439 Woodland Drive, Suite 100, Indianapolis, IN 46278
Phone: 317-872-6533
Email: tkeogc@tke.org
https://www.tke.org/foundation/scholarships
Purpose: To recognize academic achievement and leadership in honor of father and son members Donald A. and John R. Fisher.
Eligibility: Applicants must be initiated Tau Kappa Epsilon members in good standing and full-time students with a GPA of at least 3.0. They must demonstrate outstanding leadership in their chapter, campus and community. Applicants must also include a statement describing how they have benefited from TKE membership.
Target applicant(s): College students. Adult students.
Minimum GPA: 3.0
Amount: $800.
Number of awards: 1.
Deadline: March 15.
How to apply: Applications are available online.
Exclusive: Visit www.UltimateScholarshipBook.com and enter code TA196426 for updates on this award.

[1965] • Emergency Educational Fund Grants
Elks National Foundation Headquarters
2750 North Lakeview Avenue, Chicago, IL 60614
Phone: 773-755-4732
Email: scholarship@elks.org
https://www.elks.org/scholars/
Purpose: To assist children of deceased and incapacitated Elks.
Eligibility: Applicants must be the children of deceased or incapacitated Elks who were/are members in good standing for at least one year, unmarried, under 23 years old and full-time undergraduate students at a U.S. school. Applicants must also demonstrate financial need.
Target applicant(s): High school students. College students.
Amount: Up to $5,000.
Number of awards: Varies.
Scholarship may be renewable.
Deadline: December 31.
How to apply: Applications are available from the local Elks Lodge or by phone or e-mail request.
Exclusive: Visit www.UltimateScholarshipBook.com and enter code EL196526 for updates on this award.

[1966] • Emmett J. Doerr Memorial Scout Scholarship
National Catholic Committee on Scouting
Attn: Elizabeth Olivas/Emmett J. Doerr Memorial Scout Scholarship,
P.O. Box 934, Rociada, NM 87742
Phone: 972-580-2114
Email: nccs@scouting.org
http://www.nccs-bsa.org/index.php/college-scholarship
Purpose: To help scouts in a Scouting America program with their college education.
Eligibility: Applicants must be practicing Catholics and full-time high school seniors who hold a leadership role in their scouting unit and are actively involved with a Scout Troop, Varsity Scout Team, Venturing Crew or Sea Scout Ship. Students must have provided service to their community, school, scouting and home parish and earned the Ad Altare Dei, Pope Pius XII Religious Award or Light is Life (Eastern Rite) Religious Emblem. Applicants must also have earned the Eagle Scout, Summit Award or Quartermaster Award.
Target applicant(s): High school students.
Amount: Up to $5,000.
Number of awards: 7.
Deadline: March 1.
How to apply: Applications are available online. An application form, official high school transcript, four letters of recommendation and a photo are required.
Exclusive: Visit www.UltimateScholarshipBook.com and enter code NA196626 for updates on this award.

[1967] • Eugene C. Beach Memorial Scholarship
Tau Kappa Epsilon Educational Foundation
7439 Woodland Drive, Suite 100, Indianapolis, IN 46278
Phone: 317-872-6533
Email: tkeogc@tke.org
https://www.tke.org/foundation/scholarships
Purpose: To reward a member of Tau Kappa Epsilon for outstanding academic achievement and leadership within the chapter, campus and community.
Eligibility: Applicants must have a minimum GPA of 3.0.
Target applicant(s): College students. Adult students.
Minimum GPA: 3.0
Amount: $300.
Number of awards: 1.
Deadline: March 15.
How to apply: Applications are available online.
Exclusive: Visit www.UltimateScholarshipBook.com and enter code TA196726 for updates on this award.

[1968] • Fadel Educational Foundation Annual Award Program
Fadel Educational Foundation
Phone: 484-694-1783
http://www.fadelfoundation.org
Purpose: To support Muslim U.S. citizens and permanent residents.
Eligibility: Applicants must be non-incarcerated students pursuing higher education. Selection is based on need and merit. Applicants should provide application forms, two teacher recommendation forms, one masjid official recommendation letter and financial need reports.
Target applicant(s): High school students. College students. Graduate school students. Adult students.
Amount: Up to $3,500.

Number of awards: Varies.
Deadline: May 29.
How to apply: Applications are available online.
Exclusive: Visit www.UltimateScholarshipBook.com and enter code FA196826 for updates on this award.

[1969] • Farm Credit Services of America Collegiate Scholarship

National FFA Organization
P.O. Box 68960, 6060 FFA Drive, Indianapolis, IN 46268-0960
Phone: 888-332-2668
Email: scholarships@ffa.org
https://www.ffa.org/participate/grants-and-scholarships/
Purpose: To assist students who are FFA members.
Eligibility: Applicants must be members of FFA. One application is required for all FFA scholarships.
Target applicant(s): High school students. College students. Adult students.
Amount: $2,000.
Number of awards: 32.
Deadline: January 11.
How to apply: Applications are available online.
Exclusive: Visit www.UltimateScholarshipBook.com and enter code NA196926 for updates on this award.

[1970] • FEEA Scholarship Program

Federal Employee Education and Assistance Fund
1641 Prince Street, Alexandria, VA 22314
Phone: 202-554-0007x102
https://feea.org/our-programs/scholarships/
Purpose: The FEEA scholarship program aids current, civilian, federal and postal employees and their dependents and spouses.
Eligibility: Applicants must be current civilian, federal and postal employees and their dependents, including spouses. Applicants must also be enrolled or plan to enroll in an accredited post secondary school, have a minimum 3.0 GPA and may be high school seniors, college students or graduate students.
Target applicant(s): High school students. College students. Graduate school students. Adult students.
Minimum GPA: 3.0
Amount: $1,000-$5,000.
Number of awards: At least 200.
Deadline: March 14.
How to apply: Applications are available online or by sending a self-addressed and stamped envelope.
Exclusive: Visit www.UltimateScholarshipBook.com and enter code FE197026 for updates on this award.

[1971] • First in the Family Scholarship

National Society of Collegiate Scholars (NSCS)
2000 M Street NW, Suite 600, Washington, DC 20036
Phone: 202-265-9000
Email: nscs@nscs.org
https://nscs.org/scholarships/
Purpose: To aid NSCS members with achieving their goals and to recognize their academic, service and leadership achievements.
Eligibility: Applicants must be the first person in their family to attend college. Selection is based on the overall strength of the application.
Target applicant(s): College students. Adult students.
Amount: Varies.
Number of awards: Varies.
Deadline: January 30.
How to apply: Applications are available online.
Exclusive: Visit www.UltimateScholarshipBook.com and enter code NA197126 for updates on this award.

[1972] • Fleet Reserve Association Scholarship

Fleet Reserve Association (FRA)
FRA Scholarship Administrator, 125 N. West Street, Alexandria, VA 22314
Phone: 800-372-1924
Email: fra@fra.org
https://www.fra.org/essay
Purpose: To provide financial support for post-secondary education to FRA members and their dependents and grandchildren.
Eligibility: Applicants must be either FRA members or the dependents or grandchildren of an FRA member who is in good standing or was in good standing at the time of death. Applicants are judged on the basis of leadership skills, financial need, academic record and character.
Target applicant(s): High school students. College students. Graduate school students. Adult students.
Amount: Up to $5,000.
Number of awards: Varies.
Deadline: April 15.
How to apply: Applications are available online.
Exclusive: Visit www.UltimateScholarshipBook.com and enter code FL197226 for updates on this award.

[1973] • Ford Motor Company Fund and Ford Trucks Built Ford Tough - FFA Scholarship Program

National FFA Organization
P.O. Box 68960, 6060 FFA Drive, Indianapolis, IN 46268-0960
Phone: 888-332-2668
Email: scholarships@ffa.org
https://www.ffa.org/participate/grants-and-scholarships/
Purpose: To provide educational assistance to FFA members.
Eligibility: Applicants must be high school seniors who plan to pursue a two- or four-year degree in any major. They must apply online and obtain a signature and dealer code from a local participating Ford Truck dealer. If there is no participating Ford dealer in the applicant's area, he or she may obtain a signature from any local Ford dealer and be eligible for one of five national scholarships.
Target applicant(s): High school students.
Amount: $1,000.
Number of awards: Up to 500.
Deadline: January 11.
How to apply: Applications are available online.
Exclusive: Visit www.UltimateScholarshipBook.com and enter code NA197326 for updates on this award.

[1974] • Fourth Degree Pro Deo and Pro Patria Scholarships

Knights of Columbus
Department of Scholarships, 1 Columbus Plaza, New Haven, CT 06510-3326
Phone: 203-752-4000
Email: info@kofc.org
https://www.kofc.org/en/what-we-do/scholarships
Purpose: To provide aid to members or the children of members of the Knights of Columbus.
Eligibility: Applicants must be members or the children of current or deceased members of the Knights of Columbus or, in some cases, be members of the Columbian Squires. Applicants must be entering their freshmen year at a U.S. Catholic college.
Target applicant(s): High school students.
Amount: $1,500.
Number of awards: Varies.
Scholarship may be renewable.
Deadline: April 1.
How to apply: Applications are available by mail.
Exclusive: Visit www.UltimateScholarshipBook.com and enter code KN197426 for updates on this award.

[1975] • Frank S. Land Scholarships

DeMolay Foundation
10200 NW Ambassador Drive, Kansas City, MO 64153
Phone: 800-336-6529
Email: demolay@demolay.org
https://demolay.org/
Purpose: To reward DeMolay members.
Eligibility: Applicants must be active male members of DeMolay and be under the age of 21. DeMolay is an organization with more than 1,000 chapters in the world that helps prepare young men ages 12 to 21 to "lead successful, happy and productive lives." The group aims to help members develop civic awareness, personal responsibility and leadership skills.
Target applicant(s): Junior high students or younger. High school students. College students.
Amount: Varies.
Number of awards: Varies.
Deadline: April 15.
How to apply: Applications are available online.
Exclusive: Visit www.UltimateScholarshipBook.com and enter code DE197526 for updates on this award.

[1976] • Gaston/Nolle Scholarships

Alpha Chi
8 Shackleford Plaza Suite 200, Little Rock, AR 72211
Phone: 800-477-4225
Email: office@alphachihonor.org
https://alphachihonor.org/scholarships
Purpose: To assist Alpha Chi members who are entering their senior year of undergraduate study.
Eligibility: Applicants must be members of Alpha Chi who are enrolled full-time in a bachelor's degree program.
Target applicant(s): College students. Adult students.
Amount: $2,000-$3,000.
Number of awards: 10.
Deadline: March 5.
How to apply: Application requirements are available online, and applicants must be nominated by the faculty sponsor.
Exclusive: Visit www.UltimateScholarshipBook.com and enter code AL197626 for updates on this award.

[1977] • GCSAA Legacy Awards

Golf Course Superintendents Association of America
1421 Research Park Drive, Lawrence, KS 66049
Phone: 800-472-7878
Email: mwright@gcsaa.org
https://www.gcsaa.org/education/scholarships
Purpose: To support the children and grandchildren of GCSAA members.
Eligibility: The applicant's parents or grandparents must have been GCSAA members for five or more consecutive years. Applicants must also be full-time college students or high school seniors already accepted into a postsecondary school.
Target applicant(s): High school students. College students. Adult students.
Amount: $1,500.
Number of awards: Varies.
Deadline: April 15.
How to apply: Applications are available by contacting Pam Smith at 800-472-7878, x3678.
Exclusive: Visit www.UltimateScholarshipBook.com and enter code GO197726 for updates on this award.

[1978] • George Heller Memorial Scholarship Fund of the SAG-AFTRA Foundation

Screen Actors Guild - American Federation of Television and Radio Artists
5757 Wilshire Boulevard, 7th Floor, Los Angeles, CA 90036
Phone: 855-724-2387
Email: sagaftrainfo@sagaftra.org
https://sagaftra.foundation/scholarships/
Purpose: To support AFTRA members and their children.
Eligibility: Applicants must be AFTRA members in good standing with five years of membership or the children of members. Scholarships are awarded based on academic achievement and financial need and can be used to study any academic field or for professional training in the performing arts at an accredited higher education institution.
Target applicant(s): High school students. College students. Graduate school students. Adult students.
Amount: Up to $2,500.
Number of awards: Up to 15.
Deadline: March 31.
How to apply: Applications are available online.
Exclusive: Visit www.UltimateScholarshipBook.com and enter code SC197826 for updates on this award.

[1979] • Glass, Molders, Pottery, Plastics and Allied Workers Memorial Scholarship Fund

International Scholarship and Tuition Services Inc.
GMP Memorial Scholarship Fund, 1321 Murfreesboro Road, Suite 800, Nashville, TN 37217
Phone: 855-670-4787
Email: contactus@applyists.com
http://www.gmpiu.org
Purpose: To provide financial assistance to the children of members.

Eligibility: Applicants must be children, step-children or legally-adopted children of Glass, Molders, Pottery, Plastics and Allied Workers members.
Target applicant(s): High school students. College students. Adult students.
Amount: $2,000-$4,000.
Number of awards: 10.
Scholarship may be renewable.
Deadline: March 1.
How to apply: Applications are available by written request or by contacting your local union office.
Exclusive: Visit www.UltimateScholarshipBook.com and enter code IN197926 for updates on this award.

[1980] • Golden Key Graduate Scholar Award
Golden Key International Honour Society
Scholarship Program Administrators, 2302 Parklake Drive, Suite 630, Atlanta, GA 30345
Phone: 800-377-2401
Email: support@goldenkey.org
https://scholarships.goldenkey.org/
Purpose: To support Golden Key members' graduate studies at accredited universities in the U.S. or abroad.
Eligibility: Applicant must be a Golden Key member, be enrolled in a graduate program or an undergraduate who will be enrolled in a graduate program in the next academic year. Selection is based on future academic and career goals, as well as how the applicant plans to create change in the future. Applicants must display academic achievement, leadership, service and involvement with the local Golden Key chapter.
Target applicant(s): College students. Graduate school students. Adult students.
Amount: $1,500.
Number of awards: Varies.
Deadline: December 15.
How to apply: Applications are available online.
Exclusive: Visit www.UltimateScholarshipBook.com and enter code GO198026 for updates on this award.

[1981] • Golden Key Outstanding Member Award
Golden Key International Honour Society
Scholarship Program Administrators, 2302 Parklake Drive, Suite 630, Atlanta, GA 30345
Phone: 800-377-2401
Email: support@goldenkey.org
https://scholarships.goldenkey.org/
Purpose: To support Golden Key members with their higher education expenses.
Eligibility: Applicants must be Golden Key members. Emphasis will be placed on how a member has demonstrated exceptional achievement in all three Golden Key pillars.
Target applicant(s): High school students. College students. Graduate school students. Adult students.
Amount: $500.
Number of awards: Varies.
Deadline: June 15.
How to apply: Applications are available online.
Exclusive: Visit www.UltimateScholarshipBook.com and enter code GO198126 for updates on this award.

[1982] • Golden Key Undergraduate Achievement Award
Golden Key International Honour Society
Scholarship Program Administrators, 2302 Parklake Drive, Suite 630, Atlanta, GA 30345
Phone: 800-377-2401
Email: support@goldenkey.org
https://scholarships.goldenkey.org/
Purpose: To support Golden Key members pursuing undergraduate studies.
Eligibility: Applicants must be Golden Key members. Students must be currently enrolled as undergraduates. Applicants must have a minimum 3.5 GPA. Emphasis will be placed upon academic excellence and how they live out the values of Golden Key on a daily basis.
Target applicant(s): High school students. College students. Adult students.
Minimum GPA: 3.5
Amount: $1,000.
Number of awards: Varies.
Deadline: June 15.
How to apply: Applications are available online.
Exclusive: Visit www.UltimateScholarshipBook.com and enter code GO198226 for updates on this award.

[1983] • Golden Key Undergraduate Achievement Scholarship
Golden Key International Honour Society
Scholarship Program Administrators, 2302 Parklake Drive, Suite 630, Atlanta, GA 30345
Phone: 800-377-2401
Email: support@goldenkey.org
https://scholarships.goldenkey.org/
Purpose: To aid degree-seeking Golden Key members.
Eligibility: Applicants must be Golden Key members who are enrolled in an undergraduate degree program with a 3.5 minimum GPA. Selection is based on academic achievement, leadership skills and service to the community.
Target applicant(s): College students. Adult students.
Minimum GPA: 3.5
Amount: $1,000.
Number of awards: Varies.
Deadline: June 15.
How to apply: Applications are available online. An application form, official transcript, resume, personal statement and one recommendation letter are required.
Exclusive: Visit www.UltimateScholarshipBook.com and enter code GO198326 for updates on this award.

[1984] • Guistwhite Scholarships
Phi Theta Kappa Honor Society
1625 Eastover Drive, Jackson, MS 39211
Phone: 601-987-5741
Email: scholarship.programs@ptk.org
http://www.ptk.org
Purpose: To aid Phi Theta Kappa members who plan to pursue bachelor's degrees.
Eligibility: Applicants must be active members of Phi Theta Kappa who will remain enrolled at a community college through December of the application year. They must have completed at least 30 semester credits (or 45 quarter credits) over the past five years and must have maintained a

GPA of 3.5 or higher on a four-point scale over the past five years. Students must have plans to transfer to a four-year postsecondary institution during the calendar year following the submission of the scholarship application and must have junior status at the time of transfer. Applicants must have a community college record that is free of any disciplinary action and must not have a criminal record. Selection is based on academic merit and Phi Theta Kappa participation.
Target applicant(s): College students. Adult students.
Minimum GPA: 3.5
Amount: $5,000.
Number of awards: Up to 15.
Deadline: December 1.
How to apply: Applications are available online. An application form, official transcript, two recommendation letters and personal essay are required.
Exclusive: Visit www.UltimateScholarshipBook.com and enter code PH198426 for updates on this award.

[1985] • Helen B. and Lewis E. Goldstein Scholarship Fund
Jewish Community Federation and Endowment Fund
121 Steuart Street, San Francisco, CA 94105
Phone: 415-777-0411
https://jewishfed.org/how-we-help/scholarships/college-scholarships
Purpose: To support Jewish students who pursue continuing education.
Eligibility: Applicants must be Jewish undergraduate or graduate students currently enrolled at an accredited four-year institution in the U.S. Preference is given to immigrants and students enrolled in a professional school. Applicants must demonstrate academic merit.
Target applicant(s): College students. Graduate school students. Adult students.
Amount: Up to $10,000.
Number of awards: 1.
Deadline: March 31.
How to apply: Applications are available online.
Exclusive: Visit www.UltimateScholarshipBook.com and enter code JE198526 for updates on this award.

[1986] • Hites Transfer Scholarship
Phi Theta Kappa Honor Society
1625 Eastover Drive, Jackson, MS 39211
Phone: 601-987-5741
Email: scholarship.programs@ptk.org
http://www.ptk.org
Purpose: To aid Phi Theta Kappa members who intend to transfer to a four-year postsecondary institution.
Eligibility: Applicants must be Phi Theta Kappa members who are in good standing, have a GPA of 3.5 or higher and have completed 50 or more semester credits over the past five years. Students must be enrolled at an accredited community college through March of the application year, have plans to transfer to a four-year postsecondary institution in the fall and have plans to pursue a bachelor's degree on a full-time basis. Applicants cannot have a criminal record. Selection is based on the overall strength of the application.
Target applicant(s): College students. Adult students.
Minimum GPA: 3.5
Amount: $7,500.
Number of awards: Up to 10.
Deadline: December 1.
How to apply: Applications are available online. An application form and supporting documents are required.
Exclusive: Visit www.UltimateScholarshipBook.com and enter code PH198626 for updates on this award.

[1987] • Hoard's Dairyman FFA Scholarship
National FFA Organization
P.O. Box 68960, 6060 FFA Drive, Indianapolis, IN 46268-0960
Phone: 888-332-2668
Email: scholarships@ffa.org
https://www.ffa.org/participate/grants-and-scholarships/
Purpose: To support FFA members working toward four-year degrees in agricultural journalism or dairy science.
Eligibility: Applicants specializing in agricultural communications are preferred. Selection is based on the overall strength of the application.
Target applicant(s): High school students. College students.
Amount: $1,000.
Number of awards: 1.
Deadline: January 11.
How to apply: Applications are available online.
Exclusive: Visit www.UltimateScholarshipBook.com and enter code NA198726 for updates on this award.

[1988] • Howard Coughlin Memorial Scholarship Fund
Office and Professional Employees International Union
80 Eighth Avenue, Suite 201, New York, NY 10011
Phone: 212-367-0902
Email: stoffice@opeiu.org
http://www.opeiu.org
Purpose: To offer scholarships to OPEIU members and their children.
Eligibility: Applicants must either be members of OPEIU in good standing, or the children, stepchildren or legally adopted children of an OPEIU member in good standing or associate members. Applicants must also be high school seniors, high school graduates entering a college, university or a recognized technical or vocational post-secondary school as full-time students or presently in a college, university or a recognized technical or vocational post-secondary school as a full-time or part-time student. Part-time scholarships are defined as a minimum of three credits and no more than two courses. Selection is based on transcripts, high school class rank and SAT/ACT scores or evidence of an equivalent exam by a recognized technical or vocational post-secondary school.
Target applicant(s): High school students. College students. Adult students.
Amount: $662-$6,500.
Number of awards: 20.
Scholarship may be renewable.
Deadline: March 29.
How to apply: Applications are available at the local union office, at the secretary-treasurer's office of the International Union or online.
Exclusive: Visit www.UltimateScholarshipBook.com and enter code OF198826 for updates on this award.

[1989] • IAM Scholarship
International Association of Machinists and Aerospace Workers Scholarship Program, 9000 Machinists Place, Room 204, Upper Marlboro, MD 20772-2687
Phone: 301-967-4500
Email: scholarship@iamaw.org
https://www.goiam.org/departments/headquarters/scholarships/

Purpose: To offer scholarships to members of the International Association of Machinists and Aerospace Workers (IAM) and their children.
Eligibility: Applicants must be an IAM member who has two years of continuous good standing membership or the child of a member who has two years of continuous good standing membership. Applicants may be entering college or vocational/technical school as a freshman or at a higher level with some college credits already completed. Grades, attitude, references, test scores, activities and participation in local lodge are considered in selecting scholarship recipients.
Target applicant(s): High school students. College students. Adult students.
Amount: $1,000-$2,000.
Number of awards: Varies.
Deadline: February 10.
How to apply: Applications are available by written request.
Exclusive: Visit www.UltimateScholarshipBook.com and enter code IN198926 for updates on this award.

[1990] • IFSA Foundation Scholarship Award
International Flight Services Association (IFSA)
1100 Johnson Ferry Road, Suite 300, Atlanta, GA 30342
Phone: 678-303-3009
Email: kjohnson@ifsa.aero
https://ifsa.apex.aero/foundation/
Purpose: To aid students whose parents are members of the International Flight Services Association.
Eligibility: Applicants must be the children of International Flight Services Association (IFSA) members who are enrolled or planning to enroll at an accredited college or university. They must be attending or planning to attend school on an at least a part-time basis and have a minimum GPA of 3.0. Selection is based on academic achievement and the applicant's interest in pursuing higher education.
Target applicant(s): High school students. College students. Adult students.
Minimum GPA: 3.0
Amount: Varies.
Number of awards: Varies.
Deadline: June 2.
How to apply: Applications are available online. An application form, official transcript, three recommendation letters, a personal essay and proof of college acceptance or enrollment are required.
Exclusive: Visit www.UltimateScholarshipBook.com and enter code IN199026 for updates on this award.

[1991] • Induction Recognition Award
National Society of Collegiate Scholars (NSCS)
2000 M Street NW, Suite 600, Washington, DC 20036
Phone: 202-265-9000
Email: nscs@nscs.org
https://nscs.org/scholarships/
Purpose: To help NSCS members achieve their goals and recognize their academic, service and leadership achievements.
Eligibility: Applicants must be new college undergraduate members who attend their induction ceremony and become actively involved in their chapter. Selection is based on the overall strength of the application.
Target applicant(s): College students. Adult students.
Amount: Varies.
Number of awards: Varies.
Deadline: January 30.
How to apply: Applications are available online.
Exclusive: Visit www.UltimateScholarshipBook.com and enter code NA199126 for updates on this award.

[1992] • ISF Policy Scholarship Program
Islamic Scholarship Fund
1935 Addison Street, Suite A, Berkeley, CA 94704
Phone: 650-995-6782
Email: contact@islamicscholarshipfund.org
https://islamicscholarshipfund.org/policy-scholarship/
Purpose: To aid Muslim students in pursuing degrees in humanities, social sciences, liberal arts and law.
Eligibility: Applicants must be accepted by or attend a top-ranked four-year college or university for undergraduate or graduate studies. They must be practicing Muslims and U.S. citizens or permanent residents. They must have college junior standing or higher and maintain a minimum GPA of 3.0. Applicants should be active members of their communities. Selection is based on academic record, school and extracurricular activities, extenuating circumstances and a personal interview.
Target applicant(s): College students. Graduate school students. Adult students.
Minimum GPA: 3.0
Amount: $3,000-$10,000.
Number of awards: Varies.
Deadline: Late March.
How to apply: Applications are available online.
Exclusive: Visit www.UltimateScholarshipBook.com and enter code IS199226 for updates on this award.

[1993] • Islamic Society of North America Scholarships
Islamic Society of North America
6555 S. County Road 750 E, Plainfield, IN 46168
Phone: 317-839-8157
http://www.isna.net/scholarships/
Purpose: To reward students for their academic performance and community development work.
Eligibility: Applicants must be U.S. citizens or permanent residents attending a U.S. based accredited college or university. Students must be actively engaged in their community.
Target applicant(s): High school students. College students. Graduate school students. Adult students.
Amount: Varies.
Number of awards: Varies.
Deadline: June 30.
How to apply: Applications are available online.
Exclusive: Visit www.UltimateScholarshipBook.com and enter code IS199326 for updates on this award.

[1994] • James B. Carey Scholarship
International Union of Electronic, Electrical, Salaried, Machine and Furniture Workers-Communications Workers of America
2701 Dryden Road, Dayton, OH 45439
Phone: 937-298-9984
https://www.iue-cwa.org/scholarships
Purpose: To support students who are or are related to IUE-CWA members or employees.
Eligibility: Applicants must have IUE-CWA membership either directly or through a parent or grandparent. Students must be at the undergraduate level at an accredited college.

Target applicant(s): High school students. College students. Adult students.
Amount: $4,000.
Number of awards: 5.
Deadline: April 30.
How to apply: Applications are available online.
Exclusive: Visit www.UltimateScholarshipBook.com and enter code IN199426 for updates on this award.

[1995] • James E. Breining Scholarship Award
Explorers Learning for Life
1325 West Walnut Hill Lane, P.O. Box 152225, Irving, TX 75015-2225
Phone: 972-580-2433
Email: exploring@lflmail.org
http://www.exploring.org/scholarships/
Purpose: To encourage Law Enforcement Explorers to attend college.
Eligibility: Applicants must be active Law Enforcement Explorers in good standing who demonstrate a meaningful contribution to society, impeccable character and ethics and leadership abilities in both Law Enforcement Exploring and the community. The award is given in even-numbered years.
Target applicant(s): High school students. College students. Adult students.
Amount: At least $1,500.
Number of awards: Varies.
Deadline: June 15.
How to apply: Applications are available online.
Exclusive: Visit www.UltimateScholarshipBook.com and enter code EX199526 for updates on this award.

[1996] • James Rust Scholarship
Triangle Education Foundation
Chairman, Scholarship and Loan Committee, 120 S. Center Street, Plainfield, IN 46168
Phone: 317-837-9641
Email: TEF@Triangle.org
http://www.triangleef.org/
Purpose: To help deserving active members of Triangle Fraternity in completing their education.
Eligibility: Applicants must be active members of the Triangle Fraternity who have completed at least two full academic years of school and will be undergraduates in the school year following their application. Selection is based on financial need, grades and participation in campus and Triangle activities. Preference is given to applicants in engineering and the hard sciences. Applicants must have at least a 3.0 GPA.
Target applicant(s): College students. Adult students.
Minimum GPA: 3.0
Amount: $6,500.
Number of awards: 1.
Deadline: April 5.
How to apply: Applications are available online.
Exclusive: Visit www.UltimateScholarshipBook.com and enter code TR199626 for updates on this award.

[1997] • John Kelly Labor Studies Scholarship Fund
Office and Professional Employees International Union
80 Eighth Avenue, Suite 201, New York, NY 10011
Phone: 212-367-0902
Email: stoffice@opeiu.org
http://www.opeiu.org
Purpose: To offer scholarships to OPEIU members and associate members.
Eligibility: Applicants must be members of OPEIU in good standing or associate members for at least two years, and applicants must be either undergraduate or graduate students in one of the following areas of study: labor studies, industrial relations, union leadership and administration or non-degree programs sponsored by the National Labor College at the George Meany Center or similar institution. The selections shall be based on the recommendations of an academic scholarship committee.
Target applicant(s): College students. Graduate school students. Adult students.
Amount: $3,250.
Number of awards: 8.
Deadline: March 29.
How to apply: Applications are available by phone or written request from the local union office, at the secretary-treasurer's office of the International Union or online.
Exclusive: Visit www.UltimateScholarshipBook.com and enter code OF199726 for updates on this award.

[1998] • John L. Dales Scholarship Fund
Screen Actors Guild Foundation
5757 Wilshire Boulevard, Suite 124, Los Angeles, CA 90036
Phone: 323-549-6649
Email: dlloyd@sag.org
https://sagaftra.foundation/
Purpose: To award scholarships to the families of the SAG.
Eligibility: Applicants must be a member of the Screen Actors Guild or a child of a member of the Screen Actors Guild. Transitional scholarships are open to members under the age of 26 who have been a member of the Screen Actors Guild for five years and have a lifetime earnings of $30,000. The parent of an applicant must have ten vested years of pension credits or lifetime earnings of $150,000 earned in the Guild's jurisdiction. Children of members are eligible for standard scholarships and must also be under age 26. Applicants must submit an essay of 350 to 750 words on a topic of their choice. The award may be used during college or graduate school.
Target applicant(s): High school students. College students. Graduate school students.
Amount: Varies.
Number of awards: Varies.
Deadline: March 15.
How to apply: Applications are available online.
Exclusive: Visit www.UltimateScholarshipBook.com and enter code SC199826 for updates on this award.

[1999] • John W. McDevitt (Fourth Degree) Scholarship Fund
Knights of Columbus
Department of Scholarships, 1 Columbus Plaza, New Haven, CT 06510-3326
Phone: 203-752-4000
Email: info@kofc.org
https://www.kofc.org/en/what-we-do/scholarships
Purpose: To provide financial assistance to college students who are Knights of Columbus members or family members of a member.
Eligibility: Applicants must be a Knights of Columbus member, or the wife, widow or child of a member in good standing. New applicants must also be entering their freshman year at a Catholic college or university.
Target applicant(s): High school students.
Amount: $1,500.

Number of awards: Varies.
Scholarship may be renewable.
Deadline: April 1.
How to apply: Applications are available by mail.
Exclusive: Visit www.UltimateScholarshipBook.com and enter code KN199926 for updates on this award.

[2000] • Jones-Laurence Award for Scholastic Achievement

Sigma Alpha Epsilon (SAE)
Dave Sandell, Sigma Alpha Epsilon Foundation Scholarships, 1856 Sheridan Road, Evanston, IL 60201-3837
Phone: 847-475-1856
Email: foundation@sae.net.
https://www.sae.net/foundation/scholarship-program/
Purpose: To improve scholarship among active Sigma Alpha Epsilon members.
Eligibility: Applicants must be brothers of Sigma Alpha Epsilon in good standing and must be pursuing full-time undergraduate or graduate study. This award is merit-based, with an emphasis on combining academic excellence, leadership, service and campus involvement. Applicants are nominated by their chapters and have a minimum 3.9 GPA.
Target applicant(s): College students. Graduate school students. Adult students.
Minimum GPA: 3.9
Amount: $1,000-$3,000.
Number of awards: 2.
Deadline: March 1.
How to apply: Applications are available online.
Exclusive: Visit www.UltimateScholarshipBook.com and enter code SI200026 for updates on this award.

[2001] • Junior Member Loyalty Scholarship

American Legion Auxiliary
3450 Founders Road, Indianapolis, IN 46268
Phone: 317-569-4500
Email: alahq@alaforveterans.org
https://www.legion-aux.org/scholarships
Purpose: To reward American Legion Auxiliary Junior members who retain their membership into adulthood.
Eligibility: Applicants must have been Junior members of the American Legion Auxiliary, held membership in the American Legion Auxiliary for the past three consecutive years and be a paid member for the current membership year. Students must be traditional college students with no interruption in education in at least the first semester of college but have not obtained a bachelor's degree. Applicants must have a minimum 3.0 GPA.
Target applicant(s): College students. Adult students.
Minimum GPA: 3.0
Amount: $2,500.
Number of awards: 10.
Deadline: March 1.
How to apply: Applications are available online.
Exclusive: Visit www.UltimateScholarshipBook.com and enter code AM200126 for updates on this award.

[2002] • Kiwanis Children's Fund Scholarship

Circle K International
3636 Woodview Trace, Indianapolis, IN 46268
Email: scholarships@kiwanis.org
https://www.kiwanis.org/who-we-are/kiwanis-childrens-fund/
Purpose: This scholarship is in memory of Harry S. Himmel, deceased President Emeritus of the Kiwanis International Foundation. Recipients should demonstrate dedication and leadership within the organization.
Eligibility: Applicants must be Key Club or Circle K members who appear on the international roster, are currently enrolled in college or are college-bound and have completed 100 service hours with the organization. Key Club members must have also held an elected officer position within the organization.
Target applicant(s): High school students. College students. Adult students.
Minimum GPA: 3.0
Amount: $2,500.
Number of awards: 2.
Deadline: February 1.
How to apply: Applications are available online.
Exclusive: Visit www.UltimateScholarshipBook.com and enter code CI200226 for updates on this award.

[2003] • Kyutaro and Yasuo Abiko Memorial Scholarship

Japanese American Citizens League (JACL)
1765 Sutter Street, San Francisco, CA 94115
Phone: 415-921-5225
Email: jacl@jacl.org
http://www.jacl.org
Purpose: To aid National Japanese American Citizens League (JACL) members who are pursuing higher education.
Eligibility: Applicants must be National JACL members who are enrolled as full-time undergraduates at a U.S. institution of higher learning. Preference will be given to applicants who are studying agriculture or journalism. Selection is based on the overall strength of the application.
Target applicant(s): High school students. College students. Adult students.
Amount: Varies.
Number of awards: Varies.
Deadline: April 1.
How to apply: Applications are available online. An application form, official transcript, personal statement, one recommendation letter and proof of JACL membership are required.
Exclusive: Visit www.UltimateScholarshipBook.com and enter code JA200326 for updates on this award.

[2004] • Legacy Award

Elks National Foundation Headquarters
2750 North Lakeview Avenue, Chicago, IL 60614
Phone: 773-755-4732
Email: scholarship@elks.org
https://www.elks.org/scholars/
Purpose: To assist the descendants of Elk members.
Eligibility: Applicants must be children or grandchildren (including step-children/grandchildren and legal wards) of Elk members in good standing and be high school seniors planning to attend accredited U.S. postsecondary institutions (with the exception of some non-U.S. Elks Lodges). Applicants must also take or have taken the SAT or ACT. The selection committee will evaluate applicants on the core values of

knowledge, charity, community and integrity. Financial need is not a consideration.
Target applicant(s): High school students.
Amount: $4,000.
Number of awards: Varies.
Deadline: February 5.
How to apply: Applications are available from local Elks Lodges, online or by written request.
Exclusive: Visit www.UltimateScholarshipBook.com and enter code EL200426 for updates on this award.

[2005] • Lillian and Arthur Dunn Scholarship
National Society Daughters of the American Revolution
Committee Services Office, Attn.: Scholarships, 1776 D Street NW, Washington, DC 20006-5303
Phone: 202-628-1776
Email: scholarships@dar.org
https://www.dar.org/national-society/scholarships
Purpose: To assist the children of members with their education.
Eligibility: Applicants must be sons or daughters of current women members of NSDAR, must be U.S. citizens and plan to attend an accredited U.S. college or university. All applicants must obtain a letter of sponsorship from their local DAR chapter.
Target applicant(s): High school students. College students. Adult students.
Amount: $2,500.
Number of awards: Varies.
Scholarship may be renewable.
Deadline: January 31.
How to apply: Applications are available by written request with a self-addressed, stamped envelope.
Exclusive: Visit www.UltimateScholarshipBook.com and enter code NA200526 for updates on this award.

[2006] • Literacy Grants
Honor Society of Phi Kappa Phi
7576 Goodwood Boulevard, Baton Rouge, LA 70806
Phone: 800-804-9880
Email: kpartin@phikappaphi.org
http://www.phikappaphi.org
Purpose: To award grants to Phi Kappa Phi members and chapters to offer literacy programs.
Eligibility: The project leader must be a member of Phi Kappa Phi. Previous winners have provided books and book bags to literacy programs, organized literacy fairs and conducted research on literacy.
Target applicant(s): College students. Graduate school students. Adult students.
Amount: Up to $2,500.
Number of awards: Varies.
Deadline: April 1.
How to apply: Applications are available online.
Exclusive: Visit www.UltimateScholarshipBook.com and enter code HO200626 for updates on this award.

[2007] • Maids of Athena Scholarships
Maids of Athena
1909 Q Street NW, Suite 500, Washington, DC 20009
Phone: 202-232-6300
Email: moagrandlodge@gmail.com
https://www.maidsofathena.org/scholarships
Purpose: To support members of the Maids of Athena.
Eligibility: Students must demonstrate financial need and academic achievement. Applicants must be high school seniors, college undergraduates or graduate students. Selection is based on academic achievement, financial need and participation in the organization.
Target applicant(s): High school students. College students. Graduate school students. Adult students.
Amount: Varies.
Number of awards: Varies.
Deadline: May 31.
How to apply: Applications are available online.
Exclusive: Visit www.UltimateScholarshipBook.com and enter code MA200726 for updates on this award.

[2008] • Margaret A. Haines Telephony Scholarship
American Quarter Horse Foundation
Scholarship Program, 2601 East Interstate 40, Amarillo, TX 79104
Phone: 806-378-5029
Email: foundation@aqha.org
https://www.aqha.com/scholarships1
Purpose: To support AQHA members with their higher education expenses.
Eligibility: Applicants must be members of AQHA for at least one year and be attending an AVMA-accredited college of veterinary medicine with studies focused on equine medicine and or surgery and have a minimum 3.0 GPA. Students must pursue an equine-focused veterinary practice. Applicants must be enrolled as third-year veterinary school students when applying. Funding for this scholarship will be applied to the student's last year of the veterinary program.
Target applicant(s): College students. Adult students.
Minimum GPA: 3.0
Amount: Varies.
Number of awards: Varies.
Deadline: January 15.
How to apply: Applications are available online.
Exclusive: Visit www.UltimateScholarshipBook.com and enter code AM200826 for updates on this award.

[2009] • Margaret Jerome Sampson Scholarship
Phi Upsilon Omicron Inc.
National Office, P.O. Box 50970, Bowling Green, KY 42102-4270
Phone: 270-904-1340
Email: national@phiu.org
http://www.phiu.org
Purpose: To aid Phi Upsilon Omicron members who are working toward bachelor's degrees in family and consumer sciences.
Eligibility: Applicants must be Phi Upsilon Omicron (Phi U) members. They must be full-time students who are enrolled in a family and consumer sciences degree program at the baccalaureate level. Preference will be given to applicants who are majoring in food and nutrition or dietetics. Selection is based on academic merit, participation in Phi U and stated career goals.
Target applicant(s): College students. Adult students.
Amount: $5,650.
Number of awards: Up to 8.
Deadline: March 1.
How to apply: Applications are available online. An application form, three recommendation letters, an official transcript and a financial statement are required.

Exclusive: Visit www.UltimateScholarshipBook.com and enter code PH200926 for updates on this award.

[2010] • Martin Luther King, Jr. Memorial Scholarship
California Teachers Association (CTA)
CTA Human Rights Department, P.O. Box 921, Burlingame, CA 94011-0921
Phone: 650-697-1400
Email: scholarships@cta.org
https://www.cta.org/for-educators/scholarships-awards
Purpose: To encourage ethnic minority students to become teachers and support the continuing education of ethnic minority teachers.
Eligibility: Applicants must be African American, American Indian/Alaska Native, Asian/Pacific Islander or Hispanic students pursuing a teaching-related career in public education. Candidates must also be active members of the California Teachers Association or Student California Teachers Association or the dependents of an active, retired-life or deceased California Teachers Association member.
Target applicant(s): High school students. College students. Graduate school students. Adult students.
Amount: Up to $6,000.
Number of awards: Varies.
Deadline: February 23.
How to apply: Applications are available online.
Exclusive: Visit www.UltimateScholarshipBook.com and enter code CA201026 for updates on this award.

[2011] • Mary E. Bivins Religious Scholarship
Mary E. Bivins Foundation
2311 West 16th Avenue, Amarillo, TX 79102
Phone: 806-379-9400
Email: info@bivinsfoundation.org
https://www.bivinsfoundation.org/scholarship/scholarship-program/
Purpose: To assist students pursuing Christian ministry.
Eligibility: Applicants must be graduate students pursuing a master's degree in a field that prepares them to preach the Christian religion.
Target applicant(s): Graduate school students. Adult students.
Amount: $3,500.
Number of awards: 1.
Deadline: February 23.
How to apply: Applications are available online.
Exclusive: Visit www.UltimateScholarshipBook.com and enter code MA201126 for updates on this award.

[2012] • Michael J. Quill Scholarship Fund
Transport Worker Union of America, AFL-CIO
Michael J. Quill Scholarship Fund, 1220 19th Street NW, Suite 600, Washington, DC 20036
Phone: 202-719-3900
http://www.twu.org
Purpose: To provide financial assistance to the dependents of TWU members.
Eligibility: Applicants must be high school seniors and may be the children of present, retired or deceased TWU members in good standing or meet other eligibility requirements. Recipients are selected by a public drawing.
Target applicant(s): High school students.
Amount: $4,800.
Number of awards: 15.

Scholarship may be renewable.
Deadline: May 3.
How to apply: Applications are available from local unions and the union publication. They're also available online.
Exclusive: Visit www.UltimateScholarshipBook.com and enter code TR201226 for updates on this award.

[2013] • Modern Woodmen of America Scholarship
Modern Woodmen of America
1701 1st Avenue, P.O. Box 2005, Rock Island, IL 61204
Phone: 309-786-6481
Email: memberservice@modern-woodmen.org
https://learnmore.scholarsapply.org/impact/
Purpose: To support beneficial members of Modern Woodmen.
Eligibility: Applicants must be high school seniors and be beneficial members of Modern Woodmen for at least two years. Applicants should be in the upper half of their graduating class. There are national, regional and one-time awards.
Target applicant(s): High school students.
Amount: Up to $10,000.
Number of awards: Varies.
Deadline: February 5.
How to apply: Applications are available online.
Exclusive: Visit www.UltimateScholarshipBook.com and enter code MO201326 for updates on this award.

[2014] • Moris J. and Betty Kaplun Essay Contest
Kaplun Foundation
Essay Contest Committee, P.O. Box 234428, Great Neck, NY 11023
Email: info@kaplunfoundation.org
http://www.kaplunfoundation.org
Purpose: To reward essays about Jewish-related topics.
Eligibility: Applicants must be in grades 7 through 12. Grades 7 through 9 are level one, and grades 10 through 12 are level two. Applicants must submit essays on Jewish-related topics listed on the website, and essays must be typed, double-spaced and a minimum of 250 words. Level one essays may not be more than 1,000 words. Level two essays may not be more than 1,500 words. A recent level one topic has been, "What person of importance to the Jewish people, past or present, would you like to meet and why?" A recent level two topic has been, "Antisemitism plagues all Jews regardless of religious adherence. How do you see yourself reacting to it?"
Target applicant(s): Junior high students or younger. High school students.
Amount: $500-$1,800.
Number of awards: 12.
Deadline: March 13.
How to apply: Essays must be submitted by mail.
Exclusive: Visit www.UltimateScholarshipBook.com and enter code KA201426 for updates on this award.

[2015] • Mortar Board National Foundation Fellowship
Mortar Board National Foundation
1200 Chambers Road, #201, Columbus, OH 43212
Phone: 614-488-4094
Email: mortarboard@mortarboard.org
http://www.mortarboard.org
Purpose: To support Mortar Board members pursuing post-graduate degrees who exemplify the tenets of scholarship, leadership and dedication to service at their college Alma Mater.

Eligibility: Applicants must be current or former members of Mortar Board entering a post-graduate degree program who have not previously been awarded a Mortar National Foundation Fellowship. They must complete the online application, submit two letters of recommendation and a current, official transcript. Fellowship recipients must be ready to begin and complete the year of post-graduate study upon acceptance of the fellowship award.
Target applicant(s): College students. Adult students.
Amount: $3,000-$5,000.
Number of awards: 12.
Deadline: March 15.
How to apply: Applications are available online.
Exclusive: Visit www.UltimateScholarshipBook.com and enter code MO201526 for updates on this award.

[2016] • Mortin Scholarship

Triangle Education Foundation
Chairman, Scholarship and Loan Committee, 120 S. Center Street, Plainfield, IN 46168
Phone: 317-837-9641
Email: TEF@Triangle.org
http://www.triangleef.org/
Purpose: To help deserving active members of Triangle Fraternity in completing their education.
Eligibility: Applicants must be active members of the Triangle Fraternity enrolled in a course of study leading to a degree. Applicants must have at least a 3.0 GPA, have completed at least two full academic years of school and be undergraduates in the year following their application. Selection is based on financial need, grades and participation in campus and Triangle activities.
Target applicant(s): College students. Adult students.
Minimum GPA: 3.0
Amount: Varies.
Number of awards: 1.
Deadline: April 5.
How to apply: Applications are available online.
Exclusive: Visit www.UltimateScholarshipBook.com and enter code TR201626 for updates on this award.

[2017] • National Eagle Scout Association Scholarship

National Eagle Scout Association, Scouting America
1325 West Walnut Hill Lane, P.O. Box 152079, Irving, TX 75015
Phone: 972-580-2000
Email: nesa@scouting.org
https://nesa.org/scholarships/
Purpose: To support Eagle Scouts.
Eligibility: Applicants must be Eagle Scouts who have received credentials from the national office. Students must demonstrate active participation in school, Scouting activities and community service.
Target applicant(s): High school students.
Amount: $5,000.
Number of awards: Varies.
Scholarship may be renewable.
Deadline: January 31.
How to apply: Applications are available online. An application form, transcript and letter of recommendation from a scout leader are required.
Exclusive: Visit www.UltimateScholarshipBook.com and enter code NA201726 for updates on this award.

[2018] • National FFA Combined Scholarship

National FFA Organization
P.O. Box 68960, 6060 FFA Drive, Indianapolis, IN 46268-0960
Phone: 888-332-2668
Email: scholarships@ffa.org
https://www.ffa.org/participate/grants-and-scholarships/
Purpose: To provide financial assistance to students who have livestock backgrounds and are seeking degrees in animal science, agricultural education and agribusiness.
Eligibility: Applicants must be current FFA members and high school seniors or college students planning to enroll or currently enrolled full-time. Students only need to complete the online application one time to be considered for all FFA-administered scholarships. The application requires information about the student's activities and a 1,000-word essay. Awards may be used for books, supplies, tuition, fees and room and board.
Target applicant(s): High school students. College students.
Amount: $400.
Number of awards: 1.
Deadline: January 11.
How to apply: Applications are available online.
Exclusive: Visit www.UltimateScholarshipBook.com and enter code NA201826 for updates on this award.

[2019] • National Honor Society Scholarship

National Honor Society
c/o National Association of Secondary School Principals, 1904 Association Drive, Reston, VA 20191
Phone: 703-860-0200
Email: nhs@nhs.us
https://www.nhs.us/students/the-nhs-scholarship
Purpose: To recognize NHS members.
Eligibility: Applicants must be senior National Honor Society members. Applicants must demonstrate character, scholarship, service and leadership.
Target applicant(s): High school students.
Amount: $3,200-$25,000.
Number of awards: 600.
Deadline: November 26.
How to apply: Application forms are available from your local NHS chapter adviser.
Exclusive: Visit www.UltimateScholarshipBook.com and enter code NA201926 for updates on this award.

[2020] • National Presbyterian College Scholarship

Presbyterian Church (USA)
100 Witherspoon Street, Louisville, KY 40202
Phone: 800-728-7228
Email: finaid@pcusa.org
https://www.presbyterianmission.org/grants/
Purpose: To recognize young students preparing to enter as full-time incoming freshmen in one of the participating colleges related to the Presbyterian Church.
Eligibility: Applicants must be members of the Presbyterian Church, U.S. citizens or permanent residents and high school seniors planning to attend a participating college related to PCUSA. Applicants must also demonstrate financial need and take the SAT or ACT exam no later than December 15 of their senior year in high school. Applicants must have recommendations from both their church pastors and high school guidance counselors.
Target applicant(s): High school students.

Minimum GPA: 3.0
Amount: Up to $1,500.
Number of awards: Varies.
Scholarship may be renewable.
Deadline: May 15.
How to apply: Applications are available online.
Exclusive: Visit www.UltimateScholarshipBook.com and enter code PR202026 for updates on this award.

[2021] • National Propane Gas Foundation
National Propane Gas Foundation
1899 L Street, NW, Suite 350, Washington, DC 20036
Phone: 202-355-1328
Email: jcasey@npga.org
https://www.npga.org/organization/scholarship-fund/
Purpose: To support the educational opportunities of dependent children of employees of National Propane Gas Association (NPGA) member companies.
Eligibility: Applicants must be high school seniors or undergraduate students and have a 2.6 or higher GPA. Selection is based on academic achievement, letters of recommendation, extra curricular activity involvement, employment experience and financial need.
Target applicant(s): High school students. College students. Adult students.
Minimum GPA: 2.6
Amount: $1,000-$2,000.
Number of awards: Varies.
Deadline: February 15.
How to apply: Applications are only available online. In addition to the application form, students must submit an official transcript and have two letters of recommendation mailed directly to NPGA.
Exclusive: Visit www.UltimateScholarshipBook.com and enter code NA202126 for updates on this award.

[2022] • NESA Hall/McElwain Merit Scholarships
National Eagle Scout Association, Scouting America
1325 West Walnut Hill Lane, P.O. Box 152079, Irving, TX 75015
Phone: 972-580-2000
Email: nesa@scouting.org
https://nesa.org/scholarships/
Purpose: To assist Eagle Scouts.
Eligibility: Applicants must have received credentials from the national office. They must be graduating high school seniors or college freshmen, sophomores or juniors. A minimum SAT score of 1200 or ACT score of 28 is required. Applicants must have demonstrated leadership ability in scouting and a record of participation in activities outside of scouting.
Target applicant(s): High school students. College students. Adult students.
Amount: Up to $5,000.
Number of awards: Varies.
Deadline: January 31.
How to apply: Applications are available online. An application form, transcript and letter of recommendation from a scout leader are required.
Exclusive: Visit www.UltimateScholarshipBook.com and enter code NA202226 for updates on this award.

[2023] • NESA Lawrence S. and Mabel Cooke Scholarship
National Eagle Scout Association, Scouting America
1325 West Walnut Hill Lane, P.O. Box 152079, Irving, TX 75015
Phone: 972-580-2000
Email: nesa@scouting.org
https://nesa.org/scholarships/
Purpose: To provide scholarship funds for students who have earned the rank of Eagle Scout in Scouting America.
Eligibility: Applicants must be high school seniors who plan to enroll as full-time college students at a four-year, non-military college or university and have achieved the rank of Eagle Scout in the Scouts program. Students must demonstrate academic performance, financial need and active participation in school and Scouting activities.
Target applicant(s): High school students.
Amount: $6,250-$12,000.
Number of awards: 4.
Scholarship may be renewable.
Deadline: January 31.
How to apply: Applications are available online.
Exclusive: Visit www.UltimateScholarshipBook.com and enter code NA202326 for updates on this award.

[2024] • NIADA Scholarship
National Independent Automobile Dealers Association
5215 N. O'Connor Boulevard 11th Floor, Suite 11-104, Irving, TX 75039
Phone: 817-640-3838
Email: rachel@niada.com
https://niada.com/foundation/
Purpose: To support high school seniors with academic achievement and ties to NIADA members.
Eligibility: Applicants must be high school seniors with an outstanding academic record. Students must have a desire to work in the automotive industry.
Target applicant(s): High school students.
Amount: $3,500.
Number of awards: 4.
Deadline: March 26.
How to apply: Applications are available online and should be submitted to the state association.
Exclusive: Visit www.UltimateScholarshipBook.com and enter code NA202426 for updates on this award.

[2025] • Non-Traditional Student Scholarship
American Legion Auxiliary
3450 Founders Road, Indianapolis, IN 46268
Phone: 317-569-4500
Email: alahq@alaforveterans.org
https://www.legion-aux.org/scholarships
Purpose: To support students resuming formal schooling after an interruption.
Eligibility: Applicants must be members of The American Legion, the American Legion Auxiliary or Sons of The American Legion and be undergraduate students who are enrolled in at least six hours per semester or four hours per quarter. Applicants must also be students resuming formal schooling after an interruption or who have had at least one year of college schooling and need financial assistance to continue their degree. Selection is based on financial need, scholastic achievement, character and goals.
Target applicant(s): Adult students.

Amount: $2,000.
Number of awards: 5.
Deadline: March 1.
How to apply: Applications are available online.
Exclusive: Visit www.UltimateScholarshipBook.com and enter code AM202526 for updates on this award.

[2026] • NSCS Grad School Award
National Society of Collegiate Scholars (NSCS)
2000 M Street NW, Suite 600, Washington, DC 20036
Phone: 202-265-9000
Email: nscs@nscs.org
https://nscs.org/scholarships/
Purpose: To aid NSCS members and alumni in attaining their goals and to recognize their achievements in academics, service and leadership.
Eligibility: Applicants must be current or accepted graduate students. Selection is based on the overall strength of the application.
Target applicant(s): Graduate school students. Adult students.
Amount: $2,500.
Number of awards: 5.
Deadline: June 29.
How to apply: Applications are available online.
Exclusive: Visit www.UltimateScholarshipBook.com and enter code NA202626 for updates on this award.

[2027] • Opportunity Scholarships for Lutheran Laywomen
Women of the Evangelical Lutheran Church in America
8765 W. Higgins Road, Chicago, IL 60631
Phone: 800-638-3522 x2730
Email: women.elca@elca.org
http://www.womenoftheelca.org
Purpose: To assist Lutheran women in studying for careers other than ordained ministry.
Eligibility: Applicants must be U.S. citizens, members of the Evangelical Lutheran Church in America (ELCA) and at least 21 years of age. They must also have had an interruption in education of two years or more since graduating from high school. There are four scholarships awarded with individual criteria including for women of color; for women studying for ELCA service abroad; graduate students preparing for careers in Christian service and for undergraduate, graduate, professional or vocational study.
Target applicant(s): College students. Graduate school students. Adult students.
Amount: Varies.
Number of awards: Varies.
Deadline: April 5.
How to apply: Applications are available online.
Exclusive: Visit www.UltimateScholarshipBook.com and enter code WO202726 for updates on this award.

[2028] • Owens-Bell Award
National Association of Blacks in Criminal Justice
1801 Fayetteville Street, 106 Whiting Criminal Justice Building, P.O. Box 20011-C, Durham, NC 27707
Phone: 919-683-1801
Email: Office@NABCJ.org
https://nabcj.org/
Purpose: To reward an individual NABCJ member for outstanding chapter development and leadership.
Eligibility: Applicants must be nominated by a member of NABCJ.
Target applicant(s): High school students. College students. Adult students.
Amount: Varies.
Number of awards: 1.
Deadline: March 15.
How to apply: Nomination applications are available online.
Exclusive: Visit www.UltimateScholarshipBook.com and enter code NA202826 for updates on this award.

[2029] • Phi Delta Kappa (PDK) Educational Foundation Scholarship Program
Phi Delta Kappa International
P.O. Box 7888, Bloomington, IN 47407
Email: scholarships@pdkintl.org
https://pdkintl.org
Purpose: To aid prospective educators who are affiliated with one of PDK's membership associations - Educators Rising High School, Educators Rising Collegiate, Pi Lambda Theta, and the PDK Association.
Eligibility: Applicants must be high school seniors through graduate students and must be a member in good standing of one of the following associations: Educators Rising, Educators Rising Collegiate, Pi Lambda Theta and/or PDK Association; pursuing a career in public education and enrolled in an institution of higher education full- or part-time for the fall semester of the application year.
Target applicant(s): High school students. College students. Graduate school students. Adult students.
Amount: $500-$4,000.
Number of awards: Varies.
Deadline: April 2.
How to apply: Applications are available online. An application form and supporting materials are required.
Exclusive: Visit www.UltimateScholarshipBook.com and enter code PH202926 for updates on this award.

[2030] • Phi Kappa Phi Fellowship
Honor Society of Phi Kappa Phi
7576 Goodwood Boulevard, Baton Rouge, LA 70806
Phone: 800-804-9880
Email: kpartin@phikappaphi.org
http://www.phikappaphi.org
Purpose: To provide fellowships for Phi Kappa Phi members entering their first year of graduate or professional studies.
Eligibility: Applicants may enter any professional or graduate field and must not have completed one full term of graduate study. Selection is based on academic achievement, service, leadership, letters of recommendation, personal statement and career goals.
Target applicant(s): College students. Graduate school students. Adult students.
Amount: $8,500-$35,000.
Number of awards: 62.
Deadline: April 15.
How to apply: Applications are available online.
Exclusive: Visit www.UltimateScholarshipBook.com and enter code HO203026 for updates on this award.

[2031] • Presbyterian Church USA Student Opportunity Scholarships
Presbyterian Church (USA)
100 Witherspoon Street, Louisville, KY 40202

Phone: 800-728-7228
Email: finaid@pcusa.org
https://www.presbyterianmission.org/grants/
Purpose: To aid students pursuing disciplines that further the mission of the Presbyterian Church.
Eligibility: Applicants must be members of the Presbyterian Church (USA) who have completed their first year of college. They must be enrolled full-time and have a GPA of 2.5 or greater. Students must be pursuing a bachelor's degree in education, health service/science, religious studies, sacred music or social service/sciences. Financial need is required. Preference is given to members of racial and ethnic minorities.
Target applicant(s): College students. Adult students.
Minimum GPA: 2.5
Amount: Up to $4,000.
Number of awards: Varies.
Scholarship may be renewable.
Deadline: May 13.
How to apply: Applications are available by mail or email.
Exclusive: Visit www.UltimateScholarshipBook.com and enter code PR203126 for updates on this award.

[2032] • Rebecca Palmer Eagle Scout Scholarship Endowment

National Eagle Scout Association, Scouting America
1325 West Walnut Hill Lane, P.O. Box 152079, Irving, TX 75015
Phone: 972-580-2000
Email: nesa@scouting.org
https://nesa.org/scholarships/
Purpose: To support Scouts who have achieved Eagle Scout rank.
Eligibility: Applicants must be registered Scouts with an Eagle rank and demonstrate active participation in school, Scouting activities and community service.
Target applicant(s): High school students.
Amount: $3,500.
Number of awards: 3.
Scholarship may be renewable.
Deadline: January 31.
How to apply: Applications are available online.
Exclusive: Visit www.UltimateScholarshipBook.com and enter code NA203226 for updates on this award.

[2033] • Religious Liberty Essay Scholarship Contest

Baptist Joint Committee for Religious Liberty (BJC)
Essay Contest, 200 Maryland Avenue, NE, Washington, DC 20002
Phone: 202-544-4226
Email: cwatson@bjconline.org
https://bjconline.org/contest/
Purpose: To reward students who have written outstanding essays on religious liberty.
Eligibility: Applicants must be high school juniors or seniors. Students must submit an essay relating to religious freedom. Selection is based on the overall strength of the essay.
Target applicant(s): High school students.
Amount: $500-$2,000.
Number of awards: 3.
Deadline: March 15.
How to apply: Applications are available online.
Exclusive: Visit www.UltimateScholarshipBook.com and enter code BA203326 for updates on this award.

[2034] • Rev. Dr. Karen Layman Gift of Hope Scholarship

United Methodist Church
P.O. Box 340007, Nashville, TN 37203-0007
Phone: 615-340-7400
Email: umscholar@gbhem.org
https://www.gbhem.org/scholarships/
Purpose: To support United Methodist students who are leaders in the church.
Eligibility: Applicants must have been full, active members and leaders in the United Methodist Church for at least three years. They must be U.S. citizens, permanent residents or members of the Central Conferences. Students must be enrolled in a full-time undergraduate degree program at an accredited U.S. institution with a GPA of 3.0 or higher.
Target applicant(s): High school students. College students. Adult students.
Minimum GPA: 3.0
Amount: $1,000.
Number of awards: Varies.
Deadline: March 30.
How to apply: Applications are available online. An application form, transcript, essay and three letters of recommendation are required.
Exclusive: Visit www.UltimateScholarshipBook.com and enter code UN203426 for updates on this award.

[2035] • Richard F. Walsh, Alfred W. DiTolla, Harold P. Spivak Foundation Award

International Alliance of Theatrical Stage Employees, Artists and Allied Crafts of the U.S.
207 West 25th Street, 4th Floor, New York, NY 10001
http://iatse.net/member-benefits/scholarship-foundation
Purpose: To provide scholarships for the children of IATSE members.
Eligibility: Applicants must be the sons or daughters of IATSE members in good standing, be high school seniors and apply for admission to an accredited college or university full-time leading towards a bachelor's degree.
Target applicant(s): High school students.
Amount: $10,000.
Number of awards: 5.
Scholarship may be renewable.
Deadline: December 31.
How to apply: Applications are available by written request (through an online form).
Exclusive: Visit www.UltimateScholarshipBook.com and enter code IN203526 for updates on this award.

[2036] • Robert G. Porter Post-Secondary Scholarships

American Federation of Teachers
555 New Jersey Avenue NW, Washington, DC 20001
Phone: 202-879-4400
https://www.aft.org/member-benefits/education-learning-opportunities
Purpose: To provide scholarships to AFT members' dependents.
Eligibility: Applicants must be graduating high school seniors. The award is merit-based and will consider academics, community service and performance on the required labor-related essay. Applicants' parents or guardians must be AFT members for at least one year.
Target applicant(s): High school students.

Amount: $1,000-$2,000.
Number of awards: Varies.
Scholarship may be renewable.
Deadline: March 31.
How to apply: Applications are available by written request.
Exclusive: Visit www.UltimateScholarshipBook.com and enter code AM203626 for updates on this award.

[2037] • Robert G. Porter Scholars Program for Members
American Federation of Teachers
555 New Jersey Avenue NW, Washington, DC 20001
Phone: 202-879-4400
https://www.aft.org/member-benefits/education-learning-opportunities
Purpose: To provide grants to AFT members.
Eligibility: Applicants must be AFT members who have been in good standing for at least one year and intend to pursue courses in their field of work. Applicants must submit an essay on a labor-related topic.
Target applicant(s): High school students.
Amount: $8,000.
Number of awards: 4.
Deadline: March 31.
How to apply: Applications are available by written request.
Exclusive: Visit www.UltimateScholarshipBook.com and enter code AM203726 for updates on this award.

[2038] • S. Frank Bud Raftery Scholarship
IUPAT International Office
7234 Parkway Drive, Hanover, MD 21076
Phone: 410-564-5900
Email: mail@iupat.org
https://www.iupat.org/for-members/benefits/scholarships/
Purpose: To provide scholarships for the children of IUPAT members.
Eligibility: Applicants must be the children or legally-adopted dependents of an IUPAT member in good standing. Selection is based on a 1,000- to 2,000-word essay on a subject chosen by the IUPAT.
Target applicant(s): High school students. College students. Adult students.
Amount: $2,000.
Number of awards: 10.
Deadline: May 29.
How to apply: Applications are available by written request.
Exclusive: Visit www.UltimateScholarshipBook.com and enter code IU203826 for updates on this award.

[2039] • Sam Rose Memorial Scholarship
Ladies Auxiliary of the Fleet Reserve Association
LA FRA National Scholarship Chairman, Kelly Pena RPWC, P.O. Box 9572, San Jose, CA 95157
Phone: 408-642-7722
Email: penakelly66@gmail.com
https://la-fra.org
Purpose: To support the descendants of Fleet Reserve Association members.
Eligibility: Applicants must have a deceased father or grandfather who was a member of the Fleet Reserve Association or was eligible for membership at the time of death.

Target applicant(s): High school students. College students. Adult students.
Amount: Varies.
Number of awards: Varies.
Deadline: April 15.
How to apply: Applications are available online.
Exclusive: Visit www.UltimateScholarshipBook.com and enter code LA203926 for updates on this award.

[2040] • Sandra Jo Hornick Scholarship
Kappa Delta Pi Educational Foundation
3707 Woodview Trace, Indianapolis, IN 46268-1158
Phone: 800-284-3167
Email: foundation@kdp.org
http://www.kdp.org
Purpose: To aid Kappa Delta Pi members who are studying education.
Eligibility: Applicants must be active members of Kappa Delta Pi. They must be undergraduate students who are majoring in education. Selection is based on the overall strength of the application.
Target applicant(s): College students. Adult students.
Amount: $1,250.
Number of awards: 1.
Deadline: April 28.
How to apply: Applications are available online. An application form, transcript, one reference letter, a personal essay and the applicant's Kappa Delta Pi membership number are required.
Exclusive: Visit www.UltimateScholarshipBook.com and enter code KA204026 for updates on this award.

[2041] • Service Employees International Union Scholarships
Service Employees International Union
c/o Scholarship Program Administrators Inc., P.O. Box 23737, Nashville, TN 37202-3737
Phone: 800-424-8592
http://www.seiu1.org/scholarships/
Purpose: To give financial assistance to members of the SEIU and their children.
Eligibility: For the $2,000 scholarship, applicants must be members or the children of members of SEIU who have been in good standing for at least three years. Applicants must also be enrolled in an accredited college or university and should not have completed more than one year of college. For the $10,000 scholarship, applicants must be members or the children of members of SEIU returning full time to an accredited college or university as a sophomore, junior or senior or attending an accredited community college, trade or technical school. All applicants must read a report online and answer questions.
Target applicant(s): High school students. College students. Adult students.
Amount: Up to $10,000.
Number of awards: 13.
Deadline: April 5.
How to apply: Applications are available online.
Exclusive: Visit www.UltimateScholarshipBook.com and enter code SE204126 for updates on this award.

[2042] • Shasta Head Start Alumni Scholarship
Shasta Head Start Child Development Inc.
375 Lake Boulevard, Suite 100, Redding, CA 96003
http://www.shastaheadstart.org

Purpose: To support students who were once participants of Head Start and are now pursuing a higher education.
Eligibility: Applicants must have been members of a Head Start program who are now high school seniors enrolling in post-secondary institutions. Students must have a 3.0 GPA and have shown an interest in the welfare of the children and families in their community.
Target applicant(s): High school students.
Minimum GPA: 3.0
Amount: $1,000.
Number of awards: 1.
Deadline: April 12.
How to apply: Applications are available online.
Exclusive: Visit www.UltimateScholarshipBook.com and enter code SH204226 for updates on this award.

[2043] • Shawn Maree Vaillant Memorial Scholarship

American Quarter Horse Foundation
Scholarship Program, 2601 East Interstate 40, Amarillo, TX 79104
Phone: 806-378-5029
Email: foundation@aqha.org
https://www.aqha.com/scholarships
Purpose: To support AQHA members with their higher education expenses.
Eligibility: Applicants must be current members of AQHA or AQHYA who exemplify the qualities gained through horsemanship activities, including outstanding leadership and communication skills, as well as courage, determination and compassion. Members may apply during their senior year of high school or while enrolled at an accredited college or university and must maintain a minimum 3.0 GPA. Students may reside in the U.S. or Canada. Funding for this scholarship may be applied to either a two- or four-year degree program of the student's choice. Past AQHF scholarship recipients are eligible to reapply for this scholarship.
Target applicant(s): High school students. College students. Graduate school students. Adult students.
Minimum GPA: 3.0
Amount: $1,500.
Number of awards: 1.
Scholarship may be renewable.
Deadline: January 15.
How to apply: Applications are available online.
Exclusive: Visit www.UltimateScholarshipBook.com and enter code AM204326 for updates on this award.

[2044] • Sheet Metal Workers' International Scholarship Fund

Sheet Metal Workers' International Association
1750 New York Avenue NW, 6th Floor, Washington, DC 20006-5389
Phone: 202-662-0858
Email: scholarship@smart-union.org
https://smart-union.org/why-join-smart/scholarships/
Purpose: To provide scholarships for members of the SMWIA and their families.
Eligibility: Applicants must be SMWIA members, covered employees, or dependent spouses or children under the age of 25 of SMWIA members or covered employees. Applicants must also be full-time students or accepted to be full-time students at an accredited college or university. Only qualified applicants from local unions that participate in the one-cent check off are eligible for these four-year scholarships. Selection is based on information on SMWIA membership, including information on the local union's jurisdiction and family member's SMWIA membership, high school transcript, SAT/ACT scores or college transcript if already enrolled in college, an essay on the importance of SMWIA to the applicant's family and a letter of recommendation.
Target applicant(s): High school students. College students.
Amount: $6,000.
Number of awards: 34.
Scholarship may be renewable.
Deadline: March 1.
How to apply: Applications are available by email and written request.
Exclusive: Visit www.UltimateScholarshipBook.com and enter code SH204426 for updates on this award.

[2045] • Shropshire Scholarship

Civitan
Civitan International Foundation, P.O. Box 382857, Birmingham, AL 35213-0744
Phone: 205-591-8910
Email: emily@civitan.org
http://www.civitan.org
Purpose: The Shropshire Scholarship assists deserving Civitan members who will pursue careers that further the ideals of Civitan International, such as working toward world peace and unity, fighting for justice and building better citizenship.
Eligibility: Applicants must be a Civitan, Campus Civitan or Junior Civitan and must have been a member for at least two years, be enrolled in a college or university and pursue careers which help further the ideals of Civitan International.
Target applicant(s): High school students. College students. Graduate school students. Adult students.
Amount: $5,000.
Number of awards: Varies.
Deadline: January 31.
How to apply: Applications are available online.
Exclusive: Visit www.UltimateScholarshipBook.com and enter code CI204526 for updates on this award.

[2046] • Sigma Phi Epsilon Balanced Man Scholarship

Sigma Phi Epsilon Fraternity (National)
310 South Boulevard, Richmond, VA 23220
Phone: 804-353-1901
Email: scholarships@sigep.net
http://sigep.org/scholarships
Purpose: To reward students who balance academics with healthy living.
Eligibility: Applicants must be male incoming freshmen or current undergraduates at one of the universities offering the scholarship. Students must exhibit academic excellence, leadership skills and a commitment to health and well-being.
Target applicant(s): High school students. College students. Adult students.
Amount: $500-$1,000.
Number of awards: Varies.
Deadline: June 1.
How to apply: Applications are available online.
Exclusive: Visit www.UltimateScholarshipBook.com and enter code SI204626 for updates on this award.

[2047] • Spirit of Youth Scholarship for Junior Members

American Legion Auxiliary
3450 Founders Road, Indianapolis, IN 46268
Phone: 317-569-4500
Email: alahq@alaforveterans.org
https://www.legion-aux.org/scholarships
Purpose: To assist Junior members of the American Legion Auxiliary.
Eligibility: Applicants must be or have been Junior members of the American Legion Auxiliary for three years, be high school seniors, have a minimum 3.0 GPA and demonstrate character. Selection is based on character/leadership (30 percent), essay/application (30 percent) and scholarship (40 percent).
Target applicant(s): High school students.
Minimum GPA: 3.0
Amount: $5,000.
Number of awards: 5.
Scholarship may be renewable.
Deadline: March 1.
How to apply: Applications are available online.
Exclusive: Visit www.UltimateScholarshipBook.com and enter code AM204726 for updates on this award.

[2048] • Stanfield and D'Orlando Art Scholarship

Unitarian Universalist Association
24 Farnsworth Street, Boston, MA 02210
Phone: 617-742-2100
Email: uufp@uua.org
http://www.uua.org/giving/awards
Purpose: To help graduate and undergraduate Unitarian Universalist artists.
Eligibility: Applicants must be preparing for a career in fine arts which includes painting, drawing, photography and sculpture. Applicants must submit applications, transcripts, recommendations, slide portfolios and a list of works.
Target applicant(s): College students. Graduate school students. Adult students.
Amount: Varies.
Number of awards: Varies.
Deadline: February 15.
How to apply: Applications are available online.
Exclusive: Visit www.UltimateScholarshipBook.com and enter code UN204826 for updates on this award.

[2049] • Stanley A. Doran Memorial Scholarship

Fleet Reserve Association (FRA)
FRA Scholarship Administrator, 125 N. West Street, Alexandria, VA 22314
Phone: 800-372-1924
Email: fra@fra.org
https://www.fra.org/essay
Purpose: To provide financial aid to the dependents of FRA members.
Eligibility: Applicants must be the dependent children of a member in good standing of the FRA or a member who was in good standing at time of death. Recipients are selected on the basis of academic achievement, leadership skills, financial need and character.
Target applicant(s): High school students. College students. Graduate school students. Adult students.
Amount: Up to $5,000.
Number of awards: Varies.
Deadline: April 15.
How to apply: Applications are available online.
Exclusive: Visit www.UltimateScholarshipBook.com and enter code FL204926 for updates on this award.

[2050] • Starfleet Scholarships

STARFLEET Scholarship Program
c/o Tammy Wilcox, Director, 316 Dublin Road, Asheboro, NC 27203
Email: scholarships@sfi.org
http://sfi.org
Purpose: To assist members of the International Star Trek Fan Association.
Eligibility: Applicants must have been members of Starfleet for at least one year prior to applying and must be attending or planning to attend a community college, four-year college, technical school, junior college or graduate school. Awards are given in the categories of medicine, engineering, performing arts, international studies, business, science, education, writing, law enforcement and general studies.
Target applicant(s): High school students. College students. Graduate school students. Adult students.
Amount: $1,000.
Number of awards: Varies.
Deadline: June 15.
How to apply: Applications are available online. An application form, a personal essay, three letters of recommendation and a transcript are required.
Exclusive: Visit www.UltimateScholarshipBook.com and enter code ST205026 for updates on this award.

[2051] • Student CTA (SCTA) Scholarship in Honor of L. Gordon Bittle

California Teachers Association (CTA)
CTA Human Rights Department, P.O. Box 921, Burlingame, CA 94011-0921
Phone: 650-697-1400
Email: scholarships@cta.org
https://www.cta.org/for-educators/scholarships-awards
Purpose: To support members of the Student California Teachers Association.
Eligibility: Applicants must be planning to work in public education and have a minimum 3.5 high school GPA or show high academic achievement in college coursework, explaining any special circumstances affecting their grades. Students must be active members of Student CTA. Scholarships are based on a personal statement, school and community activities and letters of recommendation.
Target applicant(s): High school students. College students. Graduate school students. Adult students.
Minimum GPA: 3.5
Amount: $5,000.
Number of awards: Up to 3.
Deadline: February 9.
How to apply: Applications are available online.
Exclusive: Visit www.UltimateScholarshipBook.com and enter code CA205126 for updates on this award.

[2052] • Tall Club International Scholarship

Tall Clubs International Foundation Inc.
c/o Carolyn Goldstein, 1555 CR 2103, Weimar, TX 78962
Phone: 888-468-2552
Email: tci-scholarships@tall.org
http://www.tall.org

Purpose: To support students of tall stature.
Eligibility: Applicants must be high school seniors under the age of 21 attending or planning to attend a two- or four-year institution of higher learning for their first year of college. Female applicants must meet the height requirement of 5'10" and male applicants must meet the requirement of 6'2". Applicants must live within the geographic area of a participating club. Note: We do not recommend applying to scholarships that charge application fees. However, some scholarships of this type charge fees and are included for completeness.
Target applicant(s): High school students.
Amount: Up to $1,000.
Number of awards: Varies.
Deadline: March 1.
How to apply: Applications are available by emailing the closest TCI club.
Exclusive: Visit www.UltimateScholarshipBook.com and enter code TA205226 for updates on this award.

[2053] • Tau Beta Pi Scholarships
Tau Beta Pi Association
Attn.: D. Stephen Pierre Jr., P.E., P.O. Box 2697, Knoxville, TN 37901-2697
Phone: 865-546-4578
Email: fellowships@tbp.org
http://www.tbp.org
Purpose: To assist members who are studying engineering.
Eligibility: Applicants must be undergraduate members of Tau Beta Pi and be juniors at the time of application who are planning to remain in or return to school for a senior year of full-time study in engineering.
Target applicant(s): College students. Adult students.
Amount: $2,000.
Number of awards: Varies.
Deadline: April 1.
How to apply: Applications are available online.
Exclusive: Visit www.UltimateScholarshipBook.com and enter code TA205326 for updates on this award.

[2054] • Terrill Graduate Fellowship
Phi Sigma Kappa International Headquarters
2925 E. 96th Street, Indianapolis, IN 46240
Phone: 317-573-5420
Email: vershun@phisigmakappa.org
https://phisigmakappa.org/undergrads/programs/scholarships/
Purpose: To award money to graduating seniors and alumni members entering graduate school or members already enrolled in graduate school.
Eligibility: Applicants must graduate from college by August of the year during which they apply, plan to begin graduate or professional study during the next academic year or already be in graduate school and have a minimum B GPA for all undergraduate work. Scholarships are awarded based on scholastic performance.
Target applicant(s): College students. Graduate school students. Adult students.
Minimum GPA: 3.0
Amount: $5,000-$10,000.
Number of awards: 2.
Deadline: January 31.
How to apply: Applications are available online.
Exclusive: Visit www.UltimateScholarshipBook.com and enter code PH205426 for updates on this award.

[2055] • Tractor Supply Company Endowment
National FFA Organization
P.O. Box 68960, 6060 FFA Drive, Indianapolis, IN 46268-0960
Phone: 888-332-2668
Email: scholarships@ffa.org
https://www.ffa.org/participate/grants-and-scholarships/
Purpose: To assist students who are FFA members.
Eligibility: Applicants must be members of FFA. One application is required for all FFA scholarships. Selection is based on the overall strength of the application.
Target applicant(s): High school students. College students. Adult students.
Amount: $4,000.
Number of awards: 1.
Deadline: January 11.
How to apply: Applications are available online.
Exclusive: Visit www.UltimateScholarshipBook.com and enter code NA205526 for updates on this award.

[2056] • Tri Delta Undergraduate Scholarship
Tri Delta
Delta Delta Delta Foundation, 14951 North Dallas Parkway, Suite 500, Dallas, TX 75254
Phone: 817-633-8001
Email: info@trideltaeo.org
http://www.tridelta.org
Purpose: To offer scholarships to undergraduate members.
Eligibility: Applicants must be undergraduates enrolled full-time in good standing with the organization. Selection is based on academic achievement, chapter involvement, campus/community involvement, financial need and future promise.
Target applicant(s): College students. Adult students.
Amount: $1,000 up to $10,000.
Number of awards: 120.
Deadline: March 1.
How to apply: Applications are available online.
Exclusive: Visit www.UltimateScholarshipBook.com and enter code TR205626 for updates on this award.

[2057] • Truckload Carriers Association Scholarship Fund
Truckload Carriers Association
c/o TCA Scholarship Fund, 555 East Braddock Road, Alexandria, VA 22314
Phone: 703-838-1950
Email: TCA@truckload.org
http://www.truckload.org
Purpose: To support college students affiliated with the trucking industry.
Eligibility: Applicants must attend or plan to attend college, be in good standing and be the children, grandchildren or spouses of an employee of a trucking company; applicants may also be the children, grandchildren or spouses of an independent contractor or independent contractors affiliated with a trucking company and attending a four-year college.
Target applicant(s): High school students. College students. Adult students.
Minimum GPA: 3.3
Amount: $2,725-$6,250.
Number of awards: Varies.
Deadline: April 3.
How to apply: Applications are available online.

Exclusive: Visit www.UltimateScholarshipBook.com and enter code TR205726 for updates on this award.

[2058] • Tuition Exchange Scholarships
Tuition Exchange
3 Bethesda Metro Center, Suite 700, Bethesda, MD 20814
Phone: 202-518-0135
Email: info@tuitionexchange.org
http://www.tuitionexchange.org
Purpose: To assist the children or other family members of the faculty and staff at participating colleges and universities to encourage employment of parents and guardians in higher education.
Eligibility: Eligibility varies by institution. Applicants must be family members of the home institution where they are applying. However specific details about employment status, years of service or other requirements are determined solely by the home institution.
Target applicant(s): High school students. College students. Adult students.
Amount: Up to full tuition.
Number of awards: Varies.
Scholarship may be renewable.
Deadline: Contact the sponsor to confirm the deadline.
How to apply: Applications are available from the liaison officer at the home institution.
Exclusive: Visit www.UltimateScholarshipBook.com and enter code TU205826 for updates on this award.

[2059] • UCC Seminarian Scholarship
United Church of Christ
Pat Lyden, Associate Director Grant and Scholarship Administration, 700 Prospect Avenue, Cleveland, OH 44115
Phone: 216-736-2166
Email: scholarships@ucc.org
http://www.ucc.org/scholarships
Purpose: To support members of the United Church of Christ who are preparing for ministry.
Eligibility: Applicants must be members of a United Church of Christ congregation for at least one year prior to receipt of the scholarship. They must be currently enrolled in an ATS accredited seminary in a course of study to become an ordained minister, and they must maintain at least a B average to receive and keep the scholarship. Applicants should be able to show that they have demonstrated leadership abilities in a church or academic environment. Students must also agree to serve the United Church of Christ or one of its partners after the completion of their studies.
Target applicant(s): College students. Graduate school students. Adult students.
Minimum GPA: 3.0
Amount: Varies.
Number of awards: 6.
Scholarship may be renewable.
Deadline: March 1.
How to apply: Applications are available by mail.
Exclusive: Visit www.UltimateScholarshipBook.com and enter code UN205926 for updates on this award.

[2060] • UFCW Scholarship Program
United Food and Commercial Workers Union
Scholarship Program - Education Office, 1775 K Street NW, Washington, DC 20006
Email: cfscholarship@ufcw.org
http://www.ufcw.org
Purpose: To provide financial assistance for members of the UFCW and their children.
Eligibility: Applicants must be members of good standing of the UFCW with a membership of one continuous year or more or the unmarried children of a member. Applicants must also be graduating high school in the year of the competition and be less than 20 years old. Academic achievement, community involvement and essays are part of the selection process.
Target applicant(s): High school students.
Amount: Up to $2,000.
Number of awards: Varies.
Scholarship may be renewable.
Deadline: May 12.
How to apply: Applications are available online.
Exclusive: Visit www.UltimateScholarshipBook.com and enter code UN206026 for updates on this award.

[2061] • UMWA-Lorin E. Kerr Scholarships
United Mine Workers of America/BCOA T.E.F.
18354 Quantico Gateway Drive, Suite 200, Triangle, VA 22172
Phone: 703-291-2400
Email: info@umwa.org
https://umwa.org/
Purpose: To offer scholarships to UMWA members and their families.
Eligibility: Applicants must be UMWA members or dependents who pursue undergraduate degrees. Selection is based on academic potential and financial need.
Target applicant(s): High school students. College students. Adult students.
Amount: $2,500.
Number of awards: 2.
Deadline: February 16.
How to apply: Applications are available online.
Exclusive: Visit www.UltimateScholarshipBook.com and enter code UN206126 for updates on this award.

[2062] • Undergraduate Scholarship
Delta Sigma Pi
330 South Campus Avenue, Oxford, OH 45056-2405
Phone: 513-523-1907
Email: centraloffice@dspnet.org
http://www.deltasigmapi.org
Purpose: To assist student members.
Eligibility: Applicants must be members in good standing of Delta Sigma Pi with at least one semester or quarter of undergraduate studies remaining. Applicants are judged on scholastic achievement, financial need, fraternal service, service activities, letters of recommendation and overall presentation of required materials.
Target applicant(s): College students. Adult students.
Amount: $350-$5,000.
Number of awards: Varies.
Deadline: June 1.
How to apply: Applications are available online.
Exclusive: Visit www.UltimateScholarshipBook.com and enter code DE206226 for updates on this award.

[2063] • Undergraduate Scholarships

American Baptist Churches USA
1075 First Avenue, King of Prussia, PA 19406
Phone: 800-222-3872888.79.A
Email: communications@abhms.org
http://abhms.org/ministries/developing-leaders/education-scholarships/
Purpose: To support American Baptist students pursuing educational opportunities.
Eligibility: Applicants must be members of an American Baptist church for at least one year before applying for aid, be enrolled at an accredited educational institution in the U.S. or Puerto Rico, be U.S. citizens and retain a 2.75 GPA to remain eligible for the scholarships.
Target applicant(s): High school students. College students. Adult students.
Minimum GPA: 2.75
Amount: Varies.
Number of awards: Varies.
Scholarship may be renewable.
Deadline: April 15.
How to apply: Applications are available by request.
Exclusive: Visit www.UltimateScholarshipBook.com and enter code AM206326 for updates on this award.

[2064] • Union Plus Scholarship

Union Plus
1100 1st Street NE, Suite 850, Washington, DC 20002
Email: scholarships@unionplus.org
http://www.unionplus.org
Purpose: To help the families of union members.
Eligibility: Applicants must be members of unions participating in a Union Plus program or the spouses or children of such union members. Applicants must be accepted to or attending an undergraduate course of study at an accredited college or university, community college or recognized technical or trade school. Selection is based on academic ability, social awareness, financial need and appreciation of labor. Minimum 3.0 GPA is required.
Target applicant(s): High school students. College students. Graduate school students. Adult students.
Minimum GPA: 3.0
Amount: $500-$4,000.
Number of awards: Varies.
Deadline: January 31.
How to apply: Applications are available online.
Exclusive: Visit www.UltimateScholarshipBook.com and enter code UN206426 for updates on this award.

[2065] • United Agribusiness League and United Agricultural Benefit Trust Scholarships

United Agribusiness League
54 Corporate Park, Irvine, CA 92606
Phone: 800-223-4590
Email: jlopez@unitedag.org
https://www.unitedag.org
Purpose: To aid undergraduate students who are affiliated with the United Agribusiness League (UAL) or the United Agricultural Benefit Trust (UABT).
Eligibility: Applicants must be current undergraduate students at an accredited college or university and must be affiliated with the United Agribusiness League (UAL) or the United Agricultural Benefit Trust (UABT) through a member or an employee of a member. They must have a minimum 2.5 GPA. Selection is based on the overall strength of the application.
Target applicant(s): College students. Adult students.
Minimum GPA: 2.5
Amount: Varies.
Number of awards: 40.
Deadline: December 31.
How to apply: Applications are available online. An application form, three reference letters, a personal essay and a resume are required.
Exclusive: Visit www.UltimateScholarshipBook.com and enter code UN206526 for updates on this award.

[2066] • United Methodist General Scholarship

United Methodist Church
P.O. Box 340007, Nashville, TN 37203-0007
Phone: 615-340-7400
Email: umscholar@gbhem.org
https://www.gbhem.org/scholarships/
Purpose: To support students who are members of a United Methodist Church.
Eligibility: Applicants must be active, full members of a United Methodist Church for at least one year prior to applying, be admitted to a full-time degree program in an accredited college or university and have a minimum 2.5 GPA. Students must also be U.S. citizens or permanent residents and be undergraduate, graduate or doctoral students. Supporting documents are due by May 1.
Target applicant(s): College students. Graduate school students. Adult students.
Minimum GPA: 2.5
Amount: $500-$2,000.
Number of awards: Varies.
Deadline: March 13.
How to apply: Applications are available online.
Exclusive: Visit www.UltimateScholarshipBook.com and enter code UN206626 for updates on this award.

[2067] • United Transportation Union Scholarships

United Transportation Union Insurance Association
UTUIA Scholarship Program, 24950 Country Club Boulevard, Suite 340, North Olmsted, OH 44070-5333
http://www.utuia.org
Purpose: To provide financial aid to the children and grandchildren of UTU/UTUIA members.
Eligibility: Applicants must be at least high school seniors or the equivalent and be age 25 or less. Applicants must also be UTU or UTUIA-insured members, the children or grandchildren of a UTU or UTUIA-insured member or the children of a deceased UTU or UTUIA-insured member. UTU or UTUIA-insured members must be U.S. residents. Applicants must be accepted for admittance or already enrolled for at least 12 credit hours per quarter or semester at a recognized institution of higher learning (university, college or junior college, nursing or technical school offering college credit). Scholarships are awarded on the basis of chance, not grades. A UTUIA scholar, however, is expected to maintain a satisfactory academic record to keep the scholarship for the full four years.
Target applicant(s): High school students. College students.
Amount: $2,000.
Number of awards: 50.
Scholarship may be renewable.
Deadline: March 31.

[2068] • Utility Workers Union of America Scholarships

Utility Workers Union of America
1300 L Street NW, Suite 1200, Washington, DC 20005
Phone: 202-899-2851
Email: rfarley@aflcio.org
http://uwua.net/
Purpose: To offer scholarships to the children of UWUA members.
Eligibility: Applicants must be the sons or daughters of active Utility Workers Union members. Recipients are selected from those who participate in the National Merit Scholarship Competition by taking the PSAT/NMSQT as high school juniors, completing high school and enrolling in a regionally accredited college in the United States.
Target applicant(s): High school students.
Amount: $2,000-$10,000.
Number of awards: Varies.
Scholarship may be renewable.
Deadline: April 26.
How to apply: Applications are available online.
Exclusive: Visit www.UltimateScholarshipBook.com and enter code UT206826 for updates on this award.

[2069] • VFW Scout of the Year Scholarship

Veterans of Foreign Wars
406 West 34th Street, Kansas City, MO 64111
Phone: 816-968-1117
Email: kharmer@vfw.org
https://www.vfw.org/community/youth-and-education
Purpose: To reward an outstanding Scout, Venture Scout, Sea Scout or Girl Scout.
Eligibility: Applicants must have received the Eagle Scout Award, the Girl Scout Gold Award, the Venture Silver Award or the Sea Scout Quartermaster Award and demonstrated practical citizenship. Applicants must also have reached their 15th birthday and be enrolled in high school.
Target applicant(s): High school students.
Amount: Up to $5,000.
Number of awards: 3.
Deadline: March 1.
How to apply: Applications are available online.
Exclusive: Visit www.UltimateScholarshipBook.com and enter code VE206926 for updates on this award.

[2070] • Walter L. Mitchell Memorial Scholarship Awards

International Chemical Workers Union Council/UFCW
Research and Education Department, Walter L. Mitchell Memorial Scholarship Awards, 1655 West Market Street, Akron, OH 44313
Phone: 330-926-1444
Email: dburdette@icwuc.org
http://www.icwuc.org
Purpose: To offer scholarships to the children or step-children of members of the UFCW.
Eligibility: Applicants must be children or step-children of members of at least a year who intend to enter college the fall following application. Recipients are selected on the basis of biographical information, ACT/SAT scores and high school records.
Target applicant(s): High school students.
Amount: $1,500.
Number of awards: 12.
Deadline: March 8.
How to apply: Applications are available online.
Exclusive: Visit www.UltimateScholarshipBook.com and enter code IN207026 for updates on this award.

[2071] • Warren Poslusny Award for Outstanding Achievement

Sigma Alpha Epsilon (SAE)
Dave Sandell, Sigma Alpha Epsilon Foundation Scholarships, 1856 Sheridan Road, Evanston, IL 60201-3837
Phone: 847-475-1856
Email: foundation@sae.net.
https://www.sae.net/foundation/scholarship-program/
Purpose: To recognize collegians who have demonstrated outstanding leadership and service and have exemplified a dedication to the values established by the founders of Sigma Alpha Epsilon.
Eligibility: Applicants must be brothers of Sigma Alpha Epsilon in good standing, have a minimum 3.0 GPA and be pursuing full-time undergraduate or graduate study. This award is merit-based, with an emphasis on combining academic excellence, leadership, service and campus involvement.
Target applicant(s): College students. Graduate school students. Adult students.
Minimum GPA: 3.0
Amount: $2,000-$4,000.
Number of awards: 9..
Deadline: March 1.
How to apply: Contact the coordinator of educational programs and services.
Exclusive: Visit www.UltimateScholarshipBook.com and enter code SI207126 for updates on this award.

[2072] • Wenderoth Undergraduate Scholarship

Phi Sigma Kappa International Headquarters
2925 E. 96th Street, Indianapolis, IN 46240
Phone: 317-573-5420
Email: vershun@phisigmakappa.org
https://phisigmakappa.org/undergrads/programs/scholarships/
Purpose: To give financial aid to college sophomore and junior members.
Eligibility: Applicants must be sophomores or juniors in college for the year that the scholarship will apply to, have completed two semesters or three quarters of study and have a minimum B GPA. Scholarships are awarded on the basis of academic accomplishments and essays.
Target applicant(s): College students. Adult students.
Minimum GPA: 3.0
Amount: $2,500-$5,000.
Number of awards: 2.
Deadline: January 31.
How to apply: Applications are available online.
Exclusive: Visit www.UltimateScholarshipBook.com and enter code PH207226 for updates on this award.

[2073] • William C. Doherty Scholarship Fund
National Association of Letter Carriers
100 Indiana Avenue NW, Washington, DC 20001-2144
Phone: 202-393-4695
Email: nalcinf@nalc.org
https://www.nalc.org/member-benefits/benefits-for-members/scholarships
Purpose: To offer scholarships to the children of members of the Letter Carriers Union.
Eligibility: Applicants must be the children or legally adopted children of an active, retired or deceased letter carrier and high school seniors. Applicants' parents must be members in good standing at least one year prior to applying. Selection is based on SAT/ACT scores, high school transcript and questionnaire.
Target applicant(s): High school students.
Amount: $4,000.
Number of awards: 5.
Scholarship may be renewable.
Deadline: December 31.
How to apply: Preliminary applications are available online.
Exclusive: Visit www.UltimateScholarshipBook.com and enter code NA207326 for updates on this award.

[2074] • Women in Aviation International Scholarship
Women in Aviation International
1864 Dayton Germantown Pike, Unit 4, Germantown, OH 45327
Phone: 937-839-4647
Email: dwallace@wai.org
http://www.wai.org
Purpose: To assist students pursuing aviation and aerospace education.
Eligibility: Applicants must be members of Women in Aviation International. Students must write a resume and an essay and provide two recommendation letters.
Target applicant(s): High school students. College students. Adult students.
Amount: Varies.
Number of awards: Varies.
Deadline: October 12.
How to apply: Applications are available online.
Exclusive: Visit www.UltimateScholarshipBook.com and enter code WO207426 for updates on this award.

[2075] • Women in United Methodist History Writing Award
General Commission on Archives and History, The United Methodist Church
P.O. Box 127, 36 Madison Avenue, Madison, NJ 07940
Phone: 973-408-3189
Email: research@gcah.org
https://gcah.org/research/grants-awards/
Purpose: To reward research and writing on the history of women in The United Methodist Church.
Eligibility: Applicants must submit completed, original manuscripts no longer than 20 double-spaced, typewritten pages with footnotes and bibliography about the history of women in the United Methodist Church or its antecedents.
Target applicant(s): High school students. College students. Graduate school students. Adult students.
Amount: $200.
Number of awards: 1.
Deadline: March 17.
How to apply: Send the manuscript to the General Secretary at the address listed.
Exclusive: Visit www.UltimateScholarshipBook.com and enter code GE207526 for updates on this award.

[2076] • Young Christian Leaders Scholarship
Young Christian Leaders
144 Woodbury Road, Woodbury, NY 11797
Phone: 516-693-5790
Email: info@yclscholarship.org
http://www.yclscholarship.org
Purpose: To support emerging young Christian students.
Eligibility: Applicants must be a high school senior or full-time current college student who is a permanent resident of New York, New Jersey or Connecticut and is an active member of their local church (college students who attend school away from their home will be evaluated on an individual basis). A minimum 3.0 GPA is required. The scholarship is awarded on a monthly basis with a deadline of the 15th of each month.
Target applicant(s): High school students. College students.
Minimum GPA: 3.0
Amount: $1,000.
Number of awards: 12.
Deadline: 15th of each month.
How to apply: Applications are available online.
Exclusive: Visit www.UltimateScholarshipBook.com and enter code YO207626 for updates on this award.

[2077] • Youth of the Year Award
National Exchange Club
3050 West Central Avenue, Toledo, OH 43606
Phone: 419-535-3232
Email: info@nationalexchangeclub.org
http://www.nationalexchangeclub.org
Purpose: To recognize students who excel in academics, leadership and community service.
Eligibility: Applicants are chosen by their local Exchange Clubs. The process begins with the Youth of the Month Awards. At the end of the year, a Youth of the Year nominee is selected from Youth of the Month winners. Applicants are judged based on participation in activities, community service, special achievements/awards, grades and a required essay. To be eligible to win, applicants must be able to attend the national convention to accept the award.
Target applicant(s): High school students.
Amount: Varies.
Number of awards: Varies.
Deadline: Contact the sponsor to confirm the deadline.
How to apply: Applications are available online.
Exclusive: Visit www.UltimateScholarshipBook.com and enter code NA207726 for updates on this award.

[2078] • Youth Partners Accessing Capital
Alpha Kappa Alpha Educational Advancement Foundation Inc.
5656 S. Stony Island Avenue, Chicago, IL 60637
Phone: 800-653-6528
Email: akaeaf@akaeaf.net
https://akaeaf.org/scholarships
Purpose: To provide financial assistance to Alpha Kappa Alpha members with exceptional academic achievement or extreme financial need.

Eligibility: Applicants must be Alpha Kappa Alpha members who are in their sophomore year of college or higher with a GPA of 3.0 or higher. They must have either high academic achievement or extreme financial need, and they must participate in leadership, volunteer, civic or campus activities.
Target applicant(s): College students. Adult students.
Minimum GPA: 3.0
Amount: Varies.
Number of awards: Varies.
Deadline: April 15.
How to apply: Applications are available online.
Exclusive: Visit www.UltimateScholarshipBook.com and enter code AL207826 for updates on this award.

ETHNICITY/RACE/GENDER/FAMILY STATUS

[2079] • A.T. Anderson Memorial Scholarship
American Indian Science and Engineering Society
4263 Montgomery Boulevard, NE, Suite 200, Albuquerque, NM 87109
Phone: 505-765-1052
http://www.aises.org/scholarships
Purpose: To support students studying any STEM related degree.
Eligibility: Applicants must be: an enrolled citizen or a descendant of an enrolled citizen of a federal or state recognized American Indian Tribe or Alaska Native Village; or Native Hawaiian or descendant from a Native Hawaiian; or Pacific Islander or descendant from Pacific Islander; or Indigenous person of Canada. Students must be full-time undergraduate or graduate students at an accredited two-year or four-year college or university with a minimum 3.0 GPA pursuing any STEM related degree.
Target applicant(s): College students. Graduate school students. Adult students.
Minimum GPA: 3.0
Amount: $1,000-$2,000.
Number of awards: Varies.
Deadline: April 30.
How to apply: Applications are available online.
Exclusive: Visit www.UltimateScholarshipBook.com and enter code AM207926 for updates on this award.

[2080] • AAUW Educational Foundation Career Development Grants
American Association of University Women (AAUW) Educational Foundation
Dept. 60, 301 ACT Drive, Iowa City, IA 52243-4030
Phone: 319-337-1716 x60
Email: aauw@act.org
https://www.aauw.org
Purpose: To support college-educated women who need additional training to advance their careers, re-enter the workforce or change careers.
Eligibility: Applicants must be U.S. citizens, hold a bachelor's degree and enroll in courses at a regionally-accredited program related to their professional development, including two- and four-year colleges, technical schools and distance learning programs and have earned the degree at least five years prior to application. Special preference is given to women of color, AAUW members and women pursuing their first advanced degree or credentials in a nontraditional field.
Target applicant(s): College students. Graduate school students. Adult students.
Amount: $2,000-$20,000.
Number of awards: Varies.
Deadline: November 15.
How to apply: Applications are available online from August 1-November 15.
Exclusive: Visit www.UltimateScholarshipBook.com and enter code AM208026 for updates on this award.

[2081] • Abe and Esther Hagiwara Student Aid Award
Japanese American Citizens League (JACL)
1765 Sutter Street, San Francisco, CA 94115
Phone: 415-921-5225
Email: jacl@jacl.org

http://www.jacl.org
Purpose: To aid students who otherwise would have to delay or terminate their education due to lack of financing.
Eligibility: Applicants must be National JACL members and must be attending a college, university, trade school, business school or any other institution of higher learning. A personal statement, letter of recommendation, academic performance, work experience and community involvement are considered. Applicants should have extreme financial need.
Target applicant(s): High school students. College students. Adult students.
Amount: Varies.
Number of awards: Varies.
Deadline: April 1.
How to apply: Applications are available online.
Exclusive: Visit www.UltimateScholarshipBook.com and enter code JA208126 for updates on this award.

[2082] • Achievers in Technology Program

Sankofatech
3560 Webstar Avenue, Bronx, NY 10467
Email: ait@sankofatech.org
https://sankofatech.org/ait/
Purpose: To support students of African descent who are interested in technology careers.
Eligibility: Applicants must be entering a U.S. college or university as a first-year student and demonstrate an interest in pursuing a tech career. Students must be of African descent and come from a low-income household.
Target applicant(s): High school students.
Amount: $2,000.
Number of awards: 6.
Deadline: April 27.
How to apply: Applications are available online.
Exclusive: Visit www.UltimateScholarshipBook.com and enter code SA208226 for updates on this award.

[2083] • Actuarial Diversity Scholarship

Actuarial Foundation
475 North Martingale Road, Suite 600, Schaumburg, IL 60173
Phone: 847-706-3535
Email: info@actfnd.org
https://actuarialfoundation.org/scholarships/
Purpose: To promote diversity through an annual scholarship program for African American, Hispanic and Native American Indian students and encourage academic achievements by awarding scholarships to full-time undergraduate and graduate students pursuing a degree in the actuarial profession.
Eligibility: Applicants must have at least one birth parent who is a member of one of the minority groups listed and a minimum GPA of 3.0. High school seniors must have a minimum ACT math score of 28 or SAT math score of 620. An award will be provided in the recipient's name to any accredited U.S. educational institution to cover educational expenses. An application, a personal statement, a letter of recommendation and official or unofficial school transcripts are accepted.
Target applicant(s): High school students. College students. Graduate school students. Adult students.
Minimum GPA: 3.0
Amount: Varies.
Number of awards: Varies.
Scholarship may be renewable.
Deadline: June 1.
How to apply: Applications are available online.
Exclusive: Visit www.UltimateScholarshipBook.com and enter code AC208326 for updates on this award.

[2084] • Ada I. Pressman Memorial Scholarship

Society of Women Engineers
130 East Randolph Street, Suite 3500, Chicago, IL 60601
Phone: 877-793-4636
Email: scholarships@swe.org
https://swe.org/scholarships/
Purpose: To support female engineering students.
Eligibility: Applicants may major in any type of engineering. They must be U.S. citizens and must be college sophomores, juniors, seniors or graduate students. A GPA of 3.0 or higher is required.
Target applicant(s): College students. Graduate school students. Adult students.
Minimum GPA: 3.0
Amount: $6,000.
Number of awards: 9.
Deadline: January 31.
How to apply: Applications are available online. An application form is required.
Exclusive: Visit www.UltimateScholarshipBook.com and enter code SO208426 for updates on this award.

[2085] • Admiral Grace Murray Hopper Memorial Scholarships

Society of Women Engineers
130 East Randolph Street, Suite 3500, Chicago, IL 60601
Phone: 877-793-4636
Email: scholarships@swe.org
https://swe.org/scholarships/
Purpose: To support women in engineering.
Eligibility: Applicants must be females who are enrolled in their freshman year at an accredited engineering or computer science program. They must have a GPA of 3.5 or higher.
Target applicant(s): High school students. College students. Adult students.
Minimum GPA: 3.5
Amount: $5,100.
Number of awards: 1.
Deadline: March 31.
How to apply: Applications are available online. An application form is required.
Exclusive: Visit www.UltimateScholarshipBook.com and enter code SO208526 for updates on this award.

[2086] • Adolph Van Pelt Scholarship

Association on American Indian Affairs
Lisa Wyzlic, Director of Scholarship Programs, 966 Hungerford Drive, Suite 12-B, Rockville, MD 20850
Phone: 240-314-7155
Email: lw.aaia@indian-affairs.org
https://www.indian-affairs.org/nativescholarship.html
Purpose: To assist Native American/Alaska Native undergraduate students based on merit and financial need.
Eligibility: Applicants must be full-time students and provide proof of tribal enrollment, a Certificate of Indian Blood (showing 1/4 Indian blood) and an essay on educational goals.

Target applicant(s): High school students. College students. Adult students.
Minimum GPA: 2.5
Amount: Varies.
Number of awards: Varies.
Scholarship may be renewable.
Deadline: May 31.
How to apply: Applications are available online.
Exclusive: Visit www.UltimateScholarshipBook.com and enter code AS208626 for updates on this award.

[2087] • Afro-Academic, Cultural, Technological and Scientific Olympics (ACT-SO)
NAACP ACT-SO Achievement Program
4805 Mt. Hope Drive, Baltimore, MD 21215
Phone: 410-580-5777
https://naacp.org/our-work/youth-programs/act-so-achievement-program
Purpose: To recognize and reward the academic and cultural achievements of African American high school students.
Eligibility: Students must be in grades 9 through 12, 19 years of age or younger and of African-American descent. They must compete in one of 26 categories including business, sciences, humanities and performing and visual arts. Winners receive scholarships, internships and apprenticeships.
Target applicant(s): High school students.
Amount: Varies.
Number of awards: Varies.
Deadline: April 1.
How to apply: Applications are available from the NAACP.
Exclusive: Visit www.UltimateScholarshipBook.com and enter code NA208726 for updates on this award.

[2088] • Against The Grain Artistic Scholarship
Against The Grain
Email: outreach@againstthegrainproductions.com
http://againstthegrainproductions.com/
Purpose: To support Asian American students pursuing degrees in visual or performing arts.
Eligibility: Applicants must be at least 25 percent Asian and/or Pacific Islander ethnicity and citizens or national or legal permanent residents of the U.S. Students must be high school seniors or current college students enrolled full-time at an accredited U.S. vocational, community or four-year college or university. Applicants must be pursuing majors in visual or performing arts and have a minimum 3.0 GPA. Students must demonstrate leadership abilities through community service, extracurricular or other activities.
Target applicant(s): High school students. College students. Graduate school students. Adult students.
Minimum GPA: 3.0
Amount: $1,000.
Number of awards: 1.
Deadline: May 31.
How to apply: Applications are available online.
Exclusive: Visit www.UltimateScholarshipBook.com and enter code AG208826 for updates on this award.

[2089] • AGBU US Graduate Scholarship
Armenian General Benevolent Union (AGBU)
55 East 59th Street, 7th Floor, New York, NY 10022-1112
Phone: 212-319-6383
Email: scholarship@agbu.org
http://www.agbu.org
Purpose: To support graduate students of Armenian heritage.
Eligibility: Applicants must be of Armenian heritage, be a full-time student at a U.S. college/university and have earned a minimum 3.5 GPA in undergraduate study.
Target applicant(s): Graduate school students. Adult students.
Minimum GPA: 3.5
Amount: $5,000.
Number of awards: 3.
Scholarship may be renewable.
Deadline: July 1.
How to apply: Applications are available online.
Exclusive: Visit www.UltimateScholarshipBook.com and enter code AR208926 for updates on this award.

[2090] • Agnes Jones Jackson Scholarship
National Association for the Advancement of Colored People
4805 Mt. Hope Drive, Baltimore, MD 21215
Phone: 410-580-5777
https://naacp.org/find-resources/scholarships-awards-internships/scholarships
Purpose: To reward NAACP members with financial need.
Eligibility: Students must be members of the NAACP, U.S. citizens and attending an accredited U.S. college. Undergraduates must attend college full-time, while graduates may be full- or part-time students. High school seniors and undergraduates must have a minimum 2.5 GPA while graduate students must have a minimum 3.0 GPA. Applicants must demonstrate financial need according to the formula in the application form.
Target applicant(s): High school students. College students. Graduate school students.
Minimum GPA: 2.5 for high school seniors and undergraduate students; 3.0 for graduate students
Amount: $2,000.
Number of awards: Varies.
Scholarship may be renewable.
Deadline: May 21.
How to apply: Applications are available online.
Exclusive: Visit www.UltimateScholarshipBook.com and enter code NA209026 for updates on this award.

[2091] • Agnes Missirian Scholarship
Armenian International Women's Association
65 Main Street, #3A, Watertown, MA 02472
Phone: 617-926-0171
Email: aiwainc@aol.com
http://aiwainternational.org/
Purpose: To honor the memory of Professor Agnes Missirian and assist Armenian women in obtaining higher education.
Eligibility: Applicants must be full-time students at accredited colleges or universities who are females of Armenian descent. They must be juniors, seniors or graduate students. Awards are based on financial need and merit.
Target applicant(s): College students. Graduate school students. Adult students.
Amount: $2,000.
Number of awards: 1.

Deadline: April 22.
How to apply: Applications are available online.
Exclusive: Visit www.UltimateScholarshipBook.com and enter code AR209126 for updates on this award.

[2092] • AHEPA Educational Foundation National Scholarship Program
American Hellenic Education Progressive Association
1909 Q Street NW, Suite 500, Washington, DC 20009
Phone: 202-232-6300
Email: admin@ahepa.org
https://ahepa.org/education/
Purpose: To assist Hellenic students.
Eligibility: Applicants must be members of the AHEPA family or be related to someone who is a member. Students must be of Hellenic descent and/or Phil-Hellene, the son or daughter of a member in good standing of AHEPA, the Maids of Athena, the Daughters of Penelope or the Sons of Pericles.
Target applicant(s): High school students. College students. Graduate school students. Adult students.
Amount: Up to $2,000.
Number of awards: 1.
Deadline: March 31.
How to apply: Applications are available online.
Exclusive: Visit www.UltimateScholarshipBook.com and enter code AM209226 for updates on this award.

[2093] • AICPA Fellowship for Minority Doctoral Students
American Institute of Certified Public Accountants
220 Leigh Farm Road, Durham, NC 27707-8110
Phone: 919-402-4500
Email: scholarships@aicpa.org
https://www.aicpa.org
Purpose: To support minority students who demonstrate significant potential to become accounting educators.
Eligibility: Applicants must be minority full-time students who have applied to a doctoral program or have been accepted to a doctoral program and plan to pursue the CPA exam.
Target applicant(s): Graduate school students. Adult students.
Amount: $15,000.
Number of awards: 23.
Deadline: June 15.
How to apply: Applications are available online.
Exclusive: Visit www.UltimateScholarshipBook.com and enter code AM209326 for updates on this award.

[2094] • AICPA Scholarship for Minority Accounting Students
American Institute of Certified Public Accountants
220 Leigh Farm Road, Durham, NC 27707-8110
Phone: 919-402-4500
Email: scholarships@aicpa.org
https://www.aicpa.org
Purpose: To encourage minority students to become certified public accountants (CPAs).
Eligibility: Applicants must be African-American, Native American, Latino or Asian American students who are majoring in accounting. They must be full-time students who have completed at least 30 credits overall and at least six credits in accounting. They must have a GPA of 3.0 or higher and must have plans to become a certified public accountant (CPA). Selection is based on academic merit, leadership, volunteer experience and commitment to becoming a CPA.
Target applicant(s): College students. Graduate school students. Adult students.
Minimum GPA: 3.0
Amount: Up to $5,000.
Number of awards: Varies.
Scholarship may be renewable.
Deadline: March 15.
How to apply: Applications are available online. An application form and a personal essay are required.
Exclusive: Visit www.UltimateScholarshipBook.com and enter code AM209426 for updates on this award.

[2095] • AISES Intel Scholarship
American Indian Science and Engineering Society
4263 Montgomery Boulevard, NE, Suite 200, Albuquerque, NM 87109
Phone: 505-765-1052
http://www.aises.org/scholarships
Purpose: To support the advancement of AISES (American Indian Science and Engineering Society) members who are American Indian, Alaska Natives or Native Hawaiians working towards degrees in the STEM disciplines (science, technology, engineering and math).
Eligibility: Applicants must be AISES members who are also members of an enrolled citizen or a decedent of an enrolled citizen of a federal or state recognized American Indian Tribe or Alaska Native Village; or Native Hawaiian or decedent from a Native Hawaiian; or Pacific Islander or decedent from Pacific Islander; or Indigenous person of Canada. They must also be enrolled as full-time undergraduate or graduate students at a four-year academic institution or at a two-year institution working towards an academic degree. Students must major in one of the following fields: chemistry, computer science, computer engineering, electrical engineering, electrical and computer engineering, mechanical engineering, neuroscience, physics, chemical engineering or material engineering or science. The minimum GPA requirement is 3.0. Selection is based on the quality of the application.
Target applicant(s): College students. Graduate school students. Adult students.
Minimum GPA: 3.0
Amount: $5,000-$10,000.
Number of awards: Varies.
Deadline: May 31.
How to apply: Applications are available online. An application form, official transcripts, an essay, two letters of recommendation, tribal enrollment documentation and resume are required.
Exclusive: Visit www.UltimateScholarshipBook.com and enter code AM209526 for updates on this award.

[2096] • Allogan Slagle Memorial Scholarship
Association on American Indian Affairs
Lisa Wyzlic, Director of Scholarship Programs, 966 Hungerford Drive, Suite 12-B, Rockville, MD 20850
Phone: 240-314-7155
Email: lw.aaia@indian-affairs.org
https://www.indian-affairs.org/nativescholarship.html
Purpose: To assist Native American/Alaska Native undergraduate and graduate students from tribes that are not recognized by the federal government.

The Ultimate Scholarship Book 2026
Scholarship Directory (Ethnicity / Race / Gender / Family Situation)

Eligibility: Applicants must submit a financial need analysis form, Certificate of Indian Blood or documents proving their lineal descent, proof of tribal enrollment, essay, two letters of recommendation, current financial aid award letter, transcripts and class schedule.
Target applicant(s): High school students. College students. Graduate school students. Adult students.
Minimum GPA: 2.5
Amount: Varies.
Number of awards: Varies.
Deadline: May 31.
How to apply: Applications are available online.
Exclusive: Visit www.UltimateScholarshipBook.com and enter code AS209626 for updates on this award.

[2097] • Ally Financial Law Scholars
Congressional Black Caucus Foundation
1720 Massachusetts Avenue NW, Washington, DC 20036
Phone: 202-263-2800
Email: info@cbcfinc.org
https://www.cbcfinc.org/scholarships/
Purpose: To support students who demonstrate leadership ability through exemplary community service and academic talent.
Eligibility: Applicants must be U.S. residents and incoming full-time students at an accredited law school. Students must demonstrate commitment to the legal profession, exhibit leadership and be active within the community.
Target applicant(s): High school students. College students. Adult students.
Amount: $60,000.
Number of awards: Varies.
Deadline: March 15.
How to apply: Applications are available online.
Exclusive: Visit www.UltimateScholarshipBook.com and enter code CO209726 for updates on this award.

[2098] • American Chemical Society Scholars Program
American Chemical Society
ACS Scholars Program, 1155 16th Street NW, Washington, DC 20036
Phone: 800-227-5558
Email: scholars@acs.org
http://www.acs.org
Purpose: To encourage minority students to pursue careers in the sciences and to help them acquire the skills necessary for success in these fields.
Eligibility: Applicants must be African American, Hispanic/Latino or American Indian and graduating high school seniors or college freshmen, sophomores or juniors enrolled full-time at an accredited institution. Students must major in chemistry, biochemistry, chemical engineering or a chemically-related science and plan to work in a chemistry-related field. Those entering pre-med programs or pursuing pharmacy degrees are not eligible. A minimum GPA of 3.0 or "B" or better with high academic achievement in chemistry or science is required. Students must also demonstrate financial need through the Free Application for Federal Student Aid (FAFSA).
Target applicant(s): High school students. College students. Adult students.
Minimum GPA: 3.0
Amount: Up to $5,000.
Number of awards: Varies.
Scholarship may be renewable.
Deadline: March 1.
How to apply: Applications are available online.
Exclusive: Visit www.UltimateScholarshipBook.com and enter code AM209826 for updates on this award.

[2099] • American Indian Services Scholarship
American Indian Services
3115 East Lion Lane, Suite 320, Salt Lake City, UT 84121
Phone: 801-375-1777
Email: scholarship@americanindianservices.org
https://www.americanindianservices.org/scholarships
Purpose: To support Native American students in pursuing post-secondary education.
Eligibility: Applicant must be an enrolled member of a U.S. Federally Recognized American Indian or Alaska Native Tribe or lineal descendant of a base roll member. A minimum GPA of 2.25 is required. Students must be undergraduate students who have earned fewer than 150 credits.
Target applicant(s): College students. Adult students.
Minimum GPA: 2.25
Amount: Varies.
Number of awards: Varies.
Deadline: February 1; April 1; July 1; November 1.
How to apply: Applications are available online.
Exclusive: Visit www.UltimateScholarshipBook.com and enter code AM209926 for updates on this award.

[2100] • Anne Maureen Whitney Barrow Memorial Scholarship
Society of Women Engineers
130 East Randolph Street, Suite 3500, Chicago, IL 60601
Phone: 877-793-4636
Email: scholarships@swe.org
https://swe.org/scholarships/
Purpose: To support female engineering students.
Eligibility: Applicants must be enrolled in an accredited engineering or computer science program. A minimum GPA of 3.5 is required.
Target applicant(s): High school students. College students. Adult students.
Minimum GPA: 3.5
Amount: $9,000.
Number of awards: 1.
Scholarship may be renewable.
Deadline: March 31.
How to apply: Applications are available online.
Exclusive: Visit www.UltimateScholarshipBook.com and enter code SO210026 for updates on this award.

[2101] • APIA Scholarship Program
APIA Scholars
1850 M Street NW, Suite 245, Washington, DC 20036
Phone: 202-986-6892
Email: applicant@apiasf.org
https://apiascholars.org/scholarship/apia-scholarship/
Purpose: To support students with the expenses related to their undergraduate studies.
Eligibility: Applicants must be able to describe their ethnicity, heritage or ancestry in relation to the countries, territories or lands in Asia or the Pacific Islands. Students must be enrolling or continuing as a degree-seeking undergraduate student in a U.S. accredited college or university and have a minimum 2.7 GPA. Applicants must be citizens, nationals or legal permanent residents of the United States.

Target applicant(s): High school students. College students. Adult students.
Minimum GPA: 2.7
Amount: Up to $20,000.
Number of awards: Varies.
Deadline: January 9.
How to apply: Applications are available online.
Exclusive: Visit www.UltimateScholarshipBook.com and enter code AP210126 for updates on this award.

[2102] • Aritzia Scholarship
Stonewall Community Foundation
1270 Broadway, Suite 501, New York, NY 10001
Phone: 212-457-1341
Email: scholarships@stonewallfoundation.org
https://stonewallfoundation.org
Purpose: To support LGBTQIA people in pursuing post-secondary education.
Eligibility: Applicants must identify as lesbian, gay, bisexual, transgender, queer, intersex, asexual or two-spirit and be currently enrolled in an undergraduate or graduate school in the United States. Students must study, plan to work in, or demonstrate a commitment to the fields of fashion design, retail management, mental health or social justice advocacy.
Target applicant(s): College students. Graduate school students. Adult students.
Amount: $5,000.
Number of awards: 4.
Deadline: May 5.
How to apply: Applications are available online.
Exclusive: Visit www.UltimateScholarshipBook.com and enter code ST210226 for updates on this award.

[2103] • ARS Undergraduate Scholarship
Armenian Relief Society of Eastern USA (ARS)
80 Bigelow Avenue, Suite 200, Watertown, MA 02472
Phone: 617-926-3801
https://arseastusa.org/
Purpose: To support students of Armenian descent who are attending a four-year college.
Eligibility: Applicant must be of Armenian descent. Applicants must be an undergraduate student who has completed at least one college semester at an accredited four-year college or university in the United States or enrolled in a two-year college and transferring to a four-year college or university as a full time student in the fall. A letter from an Armenian community leader or representative that attests to the applicant's activity or contributions to the Armenian Community is required.
Target applicant(s): College students. Adult students.
Amount: $1,000.
Number of awards: 12.
Deadline: April 1.
How to apply: Applications are available online.
Exclusive: Visit www.UltimateScholarshipBook.com and enter code AR210326 for updates on this award.

[2104] • ASA Scholarships
Armenian Students' Association of America
333 Atlantic Avenue, Warwick, RI 02888
Phone: 401-461-6114
Email: headasa@asainc.org
http://www.asainc.org
Purpose: To provide scholarships for students of Armenian descent.
Eligibility: Applicants must be college sophomores or beyond in the year of application and be of Armenian descent. Note: We do not recommend applying to scholarships that charge application fees. However, some scholarships of this type charge fees and are included for completeness.
Target applicant(s): College students. Adult students.
Amount: Varies.
Number of awards: Varies.
Deadline: March 15.
How to apply: Request forms for applications are available online.
Exclusive: Visit www.UltimateScholarshipBook.com and enter code AR210426 for updates on this award.

[2105] • Asian and Pacific Islander American Scholarships
Asian and Pacific Islander American Scholarship Fund
2025 M Street NW, Suite 610, Washington, DC 20036
Phone: 202-986-6892
Email: info@apiasf.org
http://www.apiasf.org
Purpose: To provide financial assistance to Asian and Pacific Island Americans.
Eligibility: Applicants must be of Asian or Pacific Islander ethnicity as defined by the U.S. Census, and they must be legal citizens, nationals or permanent residents of the United States. Citizens of the Marshall Islands, Micronesia and Palau are also eligible. Applicants must be enrolling full-time as a first-year degree-seeking student in an accredited college or university in the U.S. They must have a GPA of 2.7 or higher or have earned a GED, and they must apply for federal financial aid.
Target applicant(s): High school students.
Minimum GPA: 2.7
Amount: $2,500-$20,000.
Number of awards: Varies.
Deadline: January 9.
How to apply: Applications are available online.
Exclusive: Visit www.UltimateScholarshipBook.com and enter code AS210526 for updates on this award.

[2106] • Association of Cuban Engineers Scholarship Foundation Scholarships
Association of Cuban-American Engineers Scholarship Foundation
P.O. Box 941436, Miami, FL 33194-1436
Phone: 305-597-9858
https://www.cubanamericanengineers.com/students/applications-for-scholarships-and-membership/
Purpose: To help undergraduate and graduate students of Hispanic heritage who are pursuing degrees in engineering.
Eligibility: Applicants must be U.S. citizens or legal residents of Hispanic heritage who have completed at least 30 units of coursework towards a bachelor's degree or higher in engineering at an ABET-accredited institution located in the United States or Puerto Rico. They must have a GPA of 3.0 or higher and must be current, full-time students (carrying 12 or more semester hours if an undergraduate and 6 or more semester hours as a graduate student). Selection is based on the overall strength of the application.
Target applicant(s): College students. Graduate school students. Adult students.
Minimum GPA: 3.0
Amount: Varies.
Number of awards: Varies.

The Ultimate Scholarship Book 2026
Scholarship Directory (Ethnicity / Race / Gender / Family Situation)

Deadline: September 15.
How to apply: Applications are available online. An application form, official transcript and financial aid award letter are required.
Exclusive: Visit www.UltimateScholarshipBook.com and enter code AS210626 for updates on this award.

[2107] • B.J. Harrod Scholarships
Society of Women Engineers
130 East Randolph Street, Suite 3500, Chicago, IL 60601
Phone: 877-793-4636
Email: scholarships@swe.org
https://swe.org/scholarships/
Purpose: To aid female engineering students.
Eligibility: Applicants may major in any type of engineering at an accredited institution of higher learning. They must be freshmen and have a GPA of 3.5 or higher.
Target applicant(s): College students. Adult students.
Minimum GPA: 3.5
Amount: $3,000.
Number of awards: 1.
Deadline: March 31.
How to apply: Applications are available online. An application form is required.
Exclusive: Visit www.UltimateScholarshipBook.com and enter code SO210726 for updates on this award.

[2108] • B.K. Krenzer Reentry Scholarship
Society of Women Engineers
130 East Randolph Street, Suite 3500, Chicago, IL 60601
Phone: 877-793-4636
Email: scholarships@swe.org
https://swe.org/scholarships/
Purpose: To support reentering female engineering students.
Eligibility: Applicants must have been out of school and out of the job market for at least two years. They must enroll in an accredited engineering or computer science program. A GPA of 3.0 or higher is required. Preference is given to degreed engineers.
Target applicant(s): College students. Adult students.
Minimum GPA: 3.0
Amount: $3,750.
Number of awards: 1.
Deadline: March 31.
How to apply: Applications are available online. An application form is required.
Exclusive: Visit www.UltimateScholarshipBook.com and enter code SO210826 for updates on this award.

[2109] • BIPOC Scholarship
Point Foundation
P.O. Box 60108, Los Angeles, CA 90060
Phone: 833-887-6462
Email: info@pointfoundation.org
http://www.pointfoundation.org
Purpose: To support students who are members of black, indigenous and people of color (BIPOC) communities who identify as LGBTQ.
Eligibility: Applicants must be members of black, indigenous and people of color (BIPOC) communities who identify as LGBTQ. Students must be enrolled in community college, four-year college or university or graduate program maintaining a full-time or part-time course load. Applicants must demonstrate a proven commitment to furthering their education.
Target applicant(s): High school students. College students. Graduate school students. Adult students.
Amount: $1,500.
Number of awards: 1.
Deadline: March 7.
How to apply: Applications are available online.
Exclusive: Visit www.UltimateScholarshipBook.com and enter code PO210926 for updates on this award.

[2110] • BrandSource Scholarship
Foster Love-Together We Rise
560 West Lambert Road, Brea, CA 92821
Phone: 714-202-7629
Email: ta@togetherwerise.org
https://academics.fosterlove.com/brandsource-scholars/
Purpose: To encourage students in foster care to pursue higher education.
Eligibility: Applicants must be U.S. citizens between the ages of 17 to 25 years and been in public or private foster care for the 12 months leading up to their 18th birthday or have been adopted or placed in legal guardianship after the 13th birthday or been orphaned for at least one year by the age of 18. Students must be graduating high school seniors, have graduated, passed a GED or on track to complete a GED. Applicants must have been accepted into or expect acceptance into an accredited two-year public or nonprofit college or vocational-technical school with the intent to enroll on a full-time basis. Students must be majoring in a two-year trade degree or certification within one of the following fields: appliance repair, carpentry, cabinet making, electrician, plumbing, equipment operator, electronics repair and industrial mechanics service.
Target applicant(s): High school students. College students.
Amount: Up to $5,500.
Number of awards: 10.
Scholarship may be renewable.
Deadline: Contact the sponsor to confirm the deadline.
How to apply: Applications are available online.
Exclusive: Visit www.UltimateScholarshipBook.com and enter code FO211026 for updates on this award.

[2111] • Burlington Northern Santa Fe (BNSF) Foundation Scholarship
American Indian Science and Engineering Society
4263 Montgomery Boulevard, NE, Suite 200, Albuquerque, NM 87109
Phone: 505-765-1052
http://www.aises.org/scholarships
Purpose: To provide a four-year scholarship for an American Indian student attending an accredited four-year college or university in a state where Burlington Northern Santa Fe operates.
Eligibility: Applicants must reside in one of the following states: Arizona, California, Colorado, Kansas, Minnesota, Montana, New Mexico, North Dakota, Oklahoma, Oregon, South Dakota, Texas, Arkansas, Louisiana, Utah, Nevada, Wyoming, Illinois, Missouri, Nebraska, Wisconsin, Iowa or Washington. Students must also major in one of the following areas: business, engineering, math, medicine/health administration, natural/physical sciences, technology or education and belong to AISES. Applicants must be full-time undergraduate or graduate students at an accredited college or university with a 3.0 minimum GPA.
Target applicant(s): High school students. College students. Graduate school students. Adult students.
Minimum GPA: 3.0
Amount: $2,500 for 4 years.
Number of awards: Varies.

Scholarship may be renewable.
Deadline: April 30.
How to apply: Applications are available online.
Exclusive: Visit www.UltimateScholarshipBook.com and enter code AM211126 for updates on this award.

[2112] • Cafe Bustelo El Cafe Del Futuro Scholarship
Hispanic Association of Colleges and Universities (HACU)
8415 Datapoint Drive, Suite 400, San Antonio, TX 78229
Phone: 210-692-3805
Email: scholarship@hacu.net
http://www.hacu.net/hacu/scholarships.asp
Purpose: To support students who are of Latino heritage.
Eligibility: Applicants must be at least 18 years old, a U.S. citizen or permanent legal resident and be of Latino descent. Students must be enrolled full-time in an undergraduate or graduate level program at a four-year HACU-member institution in the United States, Washington, DC, or Puerto Rico. Students will submit a 500-word essay on the topic outlined on the website pertaining to Latino heritage, goals and future community service.
Target applicant(s): College students. Graduate school students. Adult students.
Amount: $5,000.
Number of awards: Varies.
Deadline: July 3.
How to apply: Applications are available online.
Exclusive: Visit www.UltimateScholarshipBook.com and enter code HI211226 for updates on this award.

[2113] • California Chafee Grant for Foster Youth
California Student Aid Commission
Specialized Programs Operations Branch - Chafee, P.O. Box 419027, Rancho Cordova, CA 95741-9027
Phone: 888-224-7268
Email: studentsupport@csac.ca.gov
http://www.csac.ca.gov/
Purpose: To provide educational assistance for students who have been in foster care in California.
Eligibility: Applicants must be current or former foster youth who are under 22 years of age as of July 1 of the award year. Dependency must have been established by the court between the ages of 16 and 18. Financial need is required. Applicants must enroll at least half-time in a program that is at least one academic year long, and they must attend class regularly and maintain good grades.
Target applicant(s): High school students. College students.
Amount: Up to $5,000.
Number of awards: Varies.
Scholarship may be renewable.
Deadline: July 31.
How to apply: Applications are available online and applicants must also complete a FAFSA.
Exclusive: Visit www.UltimateScholarshipBook.com and enter code CA211326 for updates on this award.

[2114] • Casey Family Scholarship
Casey Family
23811 Chagrin Boulevard, Suite 210, Cleveland, OH 44122
Phone: 571-203-0270
Email: info@fc2success.org
http://www.fc2success.org/our-programs/information-for-students/
Purpose: To support foster care students pursuing a higher education.
Eligibility: Applicants must have been in foster care for the year prior to their 18th birthday; or have been adopted or placed into legal guardianship from foster care after their 16th birthday; or they must have been orphaned for at least one year at the time of their 18th birthday. Students must have been accepted into an accredited post-secondary school. Applicants must have been in foster care or orphaned while living in the United States.
Target applicant(s): High school students. College students. Graduate school students. Adult students.
Amount: Up to $10,000.
Number of awards: Varies.
Scholarship may be renewable.
Deadline: Varies.
How to apply: Applications are available online.
Exclusive: Visit www.UltimateScholarshipBook.com and enter code CA211426 for updates on this award.

[2115] • Catching the Dream Native American Scholarship Fund
Catching the Dream
Attn.: Scholarship Affairs Office, 8200 Mountain Road NE, Suite 103, Albuquerque, NM 87110
Phone: 505-262-2351
Email: CTD4deanchavers@aol.com
https://catchingthedream.org
Purpose: To support American Indian students pursuing higher education.
Eligibility: Applicants must be undergraduate or graduate students who are 1/4 or more American Indian, enrolled in a U.S. tribe and attend or plan to attend an accredited institution on a full-time basis. Students must excel academically, have received high ACT or SAT scores and demonstrate a strong commitment to the Indian community. Selection is based on the strength of the overall application.
Target applicant(s): College students. Adult students.
Amount: $5,000.
Number of awards: Varies.
Deadline: March 15 (Summer); April 30 (Fall); September 15 (Spring).
How to apply: Applications are available online.
Exclusive: Visit www.UltimateScholarshipBook.com and enter code CA211526 for updates on this award.

[2116] • CBC Spouses Essay Contest
Congressional Black Caucus Foundation
1720 Massachusetts Avenue NW, Washington, DC 20036
Phone: 202-263-2800
Email: info@cbcfinc.org
https://www.cbcfinc.org/scholarships/
Purpose: To support students who demonstrate leadership ability through exemplary community service and academic talent.
Eligibility: Applicants must be high school juniors and seniors (grades 11 and 12) and reside in a district represented by a Congressional Black Caucus Member. Students must be U.S. citizens or legal permanent residents. Applicants must be Black or African-American.
Target applicant(s): High school students.
Amount: Varies.
Number of awards: Varies.
Deadline: March 29.
How to apply: Applications are available online.
Exclusive: Visit www.UltimateScholarshipBook.com and enter code CO211626 for updates on this award.

[2117] • CBC Spouses Performing Arts Scholarship
Congressional Black Caucus Foundation
1720 Massachusetts Avenue NW, Washington, DC 20036
Phone: 202-263-2800
Email: info@cbcfinc.org
https://www.cbcfinc.org/scholarships/
Purpose: To support students who are pursuing careers in performing arts.
Eligibility: Applicants must be African American students who have at least a 2.5 GPA, and they must be enrolled or accepted into a full-time undergraduate degree program. Applicants must show leadership qualities and community service participation.
Target applicant(s): High school students. College students. Graduate school students. Adult students.
Minimum GPA: 2.5
Amount: $5,000.
Number of awards: Varies.
Deadline: March 31.
How to apply: Applications are available online.
Exclusive: Visit www.UltimateScholarshipBook.com and enter code CO211726 for updates on this award.

[2118] • CBCF Reducing the Financial Barrier Scholarship
Congressional Black Caucus Foundation
1720 Massachusetts Avenue NW, Washington, DC 20036
Phone: 202-263-2800
Email: info@cbcfinc.org
https://www.cbcfinc.org/scholarships/
Purpose: To support students who demonstrate leadership ability through exemplary community service and academic talent.
Eligibility: Applicants must be U.S. citizens or legal permanent residents enrolled full-time at an accredited two- or four-year college or university or a vocational-technical school. Students must have a minimum of 2.5 GPA on a 4.0 scale. Applicants must be Black or African American and must have a FAFSA on file.
Target applicant(s): College students. Adult students.
Minimum GPA: 2.5
Amount: $10,000.
Number of awards: 1.
Deadline: March 15.
How to apply: Applications are available online.
Exclusive: Visit www.UltimateScholarshipBook.com and enter code CO211826 for updates on this award.

[2119] • CHCI United Health Foundation Scholar-Intern Program
Congressional Hispanic Caucus Institute Inc.
300 M Street SE, 5th Floor, Suite 510, Washington, DC 20003
Phone: 202-543-1771
Email: shernandez@chci.org
http://www.chci.org
Purpose: To reward Latino students who are interested in careers in the healthcare industry.
Eligibility: Applicants must be Latinos focused on the healthcare industry who are currently enrolled full-time at an accredited community college, four-year university or graduate or professional program. Students must have at least one more full year of their program remaining when they apply, must have a minimum 3.0 GPA and must demonstrate financial need.
Target applicant(s): College students. Graduate school students. Adult students.
Minimum GPA: 3.0
Amount: $3,125-$3,750.
Number of awards: Varies.
Deadline: March 1.
How to apply: Applications are available online.
Exclusive: Visit www.UltimateScholarshipBook.com and enter code CO211926 for updates on this award.

[2120] • Cherokee Nation/Tribal Council At-Large Scholarship
Cherokee Nation
800 S. Muskogee Avenue, Tahlequah, OK 74464
Phone: 918-207-0950
Email: contact@cherokeenationfoundation.org
https://www.cherokeenationfoundation.org/scholarships
Purpose: To aid undergraduate students who are members of the Cherokee Nation.
Eligibility: Applicants must be citizens of the Cherokee Nation. They must be undergraduate students who are attending a not-for-profit educational institution. Selection is based on the overall strength of the application.
Target applicant(s): College students. Adult students.
Amount: Varies.
Number of awards: Varies.
Deadline: January 31.
How to apply: Applications are available online. An application form and supporting materials are required.
Exclusive: Visit www.UltimateScholarshipBook.com and enter code CH212026 for updates on this award.

[2121] • Chevron Corporate Scholars Program
United Negro College Fund (UNCF)
1805 7th Street NW, Washington, DC 20001
Phone: 800-331-2244
Email: kenya.gray@uncf.org
https://uncf.org/scholarships
Purpose: To support current high school seniors who will be attending a UNCF member institution.
Eligibility: Applicants must be graduating high school seniors enrolled to attend a Historically Black College or University. Students must have a minimum GPA of 2.8 on a 4.0 scale and exhibit interest in enrolling in a STEM field or major.
Target applicant(s): High school students.
Minimum GPA: 2.8
Amount: Up to $15,000.
Number of awards: Varies.
Scholarship may be renewable.
Deadline: September 16.
How to apply: Applications are available online.
Exclusive: Visit www.UltimateScholarshipBook.com and enter code UN212126 for updates on this award.

[2122] • Chief Manuelito Scholarship Program
Office of Navajo Nation Scholarship and Financial Assistance
P.O. Box 1870, Window Rock, Window Rock, AZ 86515
Phone: 928-871-7444
https://onnsfa.org/

Purpose: The scholarship was created to help high-achieving Navajo students.
Eligibility: Applicants must be high school graduates who have completed required courses including Navajo Language and have been admitted to a post-secondary institution. Undergraduate students who have completed 24 credit hours with a minimum 3.0 GPA are also eligible.
Target applicant(s): High school students. College students. Adult students.
Minimum GPA: 3.0
Amount: $7,000.
Number of awards: Varies.
Scholarship may be renewable.
Deadline: Nov 25; June 25.
How to apply: Applications are available online and must be submitted to your agency, which is listed online.
Exclusive: Visit www.UltimateScholarshipBook.com and enter code OF212226 for updates on this award.

[2123] • Citizen Potawatomi Nation Tribal Scholarship

Citizen Potawatomi Nation
1601 S. Gordon Cooper Drive, Shawnee, OK 74801
Phone: 405-275-3121
Email: college@potawatomi.org
https://www.potawatomi.org/services/community/
Purpose: To assist Citizen Potawatomi Nation tribal members who are pursuing higher education.
Eligibility: Applicants must be Citizen Potawatomi Nation tribal members who are enrolled full or part-time in an undergraduate or graduate academic degree program at an accredited, not-for-profit postsecondary institution. Selection is based on the overall strength of the application.
Target applicant(s): High school students. College students. Graduate school students. Adult students.
Amount: $750-$2,000 per semester.
Number of awards: Varies.
Scholarship may be renewable.
Deadline: February 15; June 15; September 15.
How to apply: Applications are available online. An application form, proof of enrollment, federal tax return information and transcript are required.
Exclusive: Visit www.UltimateScholarshipBook.com and enter code CI212326 for updates on this award.

[2124] • Colgate-Palmolive Make the U Educational Grant

Hispanic Heritage Foundation Colgate-Palmolive Haz la U
1001 Pennsylvania Ave NW, Washington, DC 20004
Phone: 202-558-9473
Email: info@hispanicheritage.org
https://www.colgate.com/en-us/mission/make-the-u
Purpose: To support Hispanic students who excel in the classroom and their community by providing them with funds to further their education.
Eligibility: Applicants must have Hispanic heritage, have a minimum 3.0 GPA and be graduating high school seniors. Students must be role models in their communities and must also be permanent residents, DACA, U.S. citizens or eligible non-citizens.
Target applicant(s): High school students.
Minimum GPA: 3.0
Amount: $2,000-$10,000.
Number of awards: 31.
Deadline: November 3.
How to apply: Applications are available online.
Exclusive: Visit www.UltimateScholarshipBook.com and enter code HI212426 for updates on this award.

[2125] • Conference of Minority Transportation Officials (COMTO) National Scholarship

Conference of Minority Transportation Officials
1330 Braddock Place, Suite 203, Alexandria, VA 22314
Phone: 202-506-2917
Email: info@comtonational.org
https://comto.org/programs-events
Purpose: To support graduating high school students whose parents are COMTO members and college or graduate students who are studying fields related to transportation.
Eligibility: Applicants must have at least a 3.0 GPA. High school students must be accepted into a college or technical school, and their parents must have been COMTO members in good standing for at least the past year. College students must have at least 60 credits, and graduate students must have at least 15 credits.
Target applicant(s): High school students. College students. Graduate school students. Adult students.
Amount: $500 - $6,000.
Number of awards: Varies.
Deadline: December 31.
How to apply: Applications are available online.
Exclusive: Visit www.UltimateScholarshipBook.com and enter code CO212526 for updates on this award.

[2126] • Congressional Black Caucus Spouses Education Scholarship

Congressional Black Caucus Foundation
1720 Massachusetts Avenue NW, Washington, DC 20036
Phone: 202-263-2800
Email: info@cbcfinc.org
https://www.cbcfinc.org/scholarships/
Purpose: To support students who are pursuing undergraduate or graduate degrees.
Eligibility: Applicants must be African American students attending or planning to attend school on a full-time basis. Students must have at least a 2.5 GPA, and they must demonstrate leadership and community service participation.
Target applicant(s): High school students. College students. Graduate school students. Adult students.
Minimum GPA: 2.5
Amount: Varies.
Number of awards: Varies.
Deadline: March 31.
How to apply: Applications are available online.
Exclusive: Visit www.UltimateScholarshipBook.com and enter code CO212626 for updates on this award.

[2127] • Congressional Black Caucus Spouses Visual Arts Scholarship

Congressional Black Caucus Foundation
1720 Massachusetts Avenue NW, Washington, DC 20036
Phone: 202-263-2800
Email: info@cbcfinc.org
https://www.cbcfinc.org/scholarships/

The Ultimate Scholarship Book 2026
Scholarship Directory (Ethnicity / Race / Gender / Family Situation)

Purpose: To support students who are pursuing careers in visual arts.
Eligibility: Applicants must be African American students, have at least a 2.5 GPA and be enrolled at or accepted into a full-time undergraduate degree program. Applicants must show leadership qualities and community service participation.
Target applicant(s): High school students. College students. Graduate school students. Adult students.
Minimum GPA: 2.5
Amount: $5,000.
Number of awards: Varies.
Deadline: March 31.
How to apply: Applications are available online.
Exclusive: Visit www.UltimateScholarshipBook.com and enter code CO212726 for updates on this award.

[2128] • CRA All-Access Scholarship
Charles River Associates
40 Burton Hills Boulevard, Suite 170, Nashville, TN 37215
https://www.crai.com/about-us/community-advancement/all-access-initiative/cra-all-access-scholarship/
Purpose: To support female students and students from underrepresented communities or socioeconomically challenging backgrounds.
Eligibility: Applicants must be attending an accredited university on a full-time basis and currently enrolled as a sophomore. Students must be majoring in economics, business or STEM and have a minimum overall 3.5 GPA or a minimum 3.2 GPA in their declared major. Applicants must demonstrate leadership, community service and a commitment to diversity, inclusion and equity. Students must show financial need.
Target applicant(s): College students. Adult students.
Minimum GPA: 3.5
Amount: $5,000.
Number of awards: 12.
Deadline: April 22.
How to apply: Applications are available online.
Exclusive: Visit www.UltimateScholarshipBook.com and enter code CH212826 for updates on this award.

[2129] • Creative Sole Scholarship
National Association for the Advancement of Colored People
4805 Mt. Hope Drive, Baltimore, MD 21215
Phone: 410-580-5777
https://naacp.org/find-resources/scholarships-awards-internships/scholarships
Purpose: To encourage Black students and students of color pursuing undergraduate degrees.
Eligibility: Applicants must be U.S. citizens or residents, Black or a person of color and members of the NAACP. Students must be currently enrolled full-time or accepted to an accredited college or university in the U.S. or graduating high school seniors with a minimum 3.0 GPA. Applicants must demonstrate an interest in pursuing a career in the creative fields such as one of the following: art, music, journalism, marketing, design, communications, architecture or film.
Target applicant(s): High school students. College students. Adult students.
Minimum GPA: 3.0
Amount: $5,000.
Number of awards: 1.
Scholarship may be renewable.
Deadline: June 2.
How to apply: Applications are available online.
Exclusive: Visit www.UltimateScholarshipBook.com and enter code NA212926 for updates on this award.

[2130] • Development Fund for Black Students in Science and Technology
Development Fund for Black Students in Science and Technology
2705 Bladensburg Road NE, Washington, DC 20018
http://www.dfbsstscholarship.org/dfb_sch.html
Purpose: To support African-American students studying scientific fields.
Eligibility: Applicants must be U.S. citizens or permanent residents and undergraduate African-American students at a Historically Black College majoring in a technical field such as engineering or math. Students must demonstrate financial need and provide an essay along with their application materials.
Target applicant(s): High school students. College students. Adult students.
Amount: Up to $3,000.
Number of awards: 1.
Deadline: June 15.
How to apply: Applications are available online.
Exclusive: Visit www.UltimateScholarshipBook.com and enter code DE213026 for updates on this award.

[2131] • Distinguished Young Women Scholarship Program
Distinguished Young Women
751 Government Street, Mobile, AL 36602
Phone: 251-438-3621
Email: lynne@ajm.org
http://distinguishedyw.org/scholarships/
Purpose: To provide scholarship opportunities and encourage personal development for high school girls through a competitive pageant stressing academics and talent as well as self-expression and fitness.
Eligibility: Teen girls are selected from state competitions to participate in a national pageant. Contestants are judged on a combination of scholastics, personal interview, talent, fitness and self-expression. Applicants should be a high school student at least in their sophomore year. Students must be U.S. citizens, have never been married and have never been pregnant.
Target applicant(s): High school students.
Amount: Varies.
Number of awards: Varies.
Deadline: Contact the sponsor to confirm the deadline.
How to apply: Applications are available online.
Exclusive: Visit www.UltimateScholarshipBook.com and enter code DI213126 for updates on this award.

[2132] • Diversity Advocacy Council Scholarship
American Society for Clinical Laboratory Science
11107 Sunset Hills Road, Suite 100, Reston, VA 20190-5376
Phone: 571-748-3770
Email: awards@ascls.org
http://www.ascls.org
Purpose: To assist minority students in becoming clinical laboratory scientists and clinical laboratory technicians.
Eligibility: Applicants must be minority students accepted to an NAACLS-accredited Clinical Laboratory Science/Medical Technology program or a Clinical Laboratory Technician/Medical Laboratory Technician program. They must also demonstrate financial need.
Target applicant(s): High school students. College students. Adult students.

Amount: Varies.
Number of awards: Varies.
Deadline: April 1.
How to apply: Applications are available online.
Exclusive: Visit www.UltimateScholarshipBook.com and enter code AM213226 for updates on this award.

[2133] • Dr. Ivy M. Parker Memorial Scholarship
Society of Women Engineers
130 East Randolph Street, Suite 3500, Chicago, IL 60601
Phone: 877-793-4636
Email: scholarships@swe.org
https://swe.org/scholarships/
Purpose: To aid female undergraduates who are majoring in engineering.
Eligibility: Applicants must be full-time students who are enrolled in an ABET-accredited engineering program. They must be rising juniors or seniors who have a GPA of 3.0 or higher on a four-point scale. Applicants cannot be currently receiving another scholarship awarded by the Society of Women Engineers (SWE), and they cannot be receiving full funding from another source (such as an employee reimbursement program or the U.S. military). Selection is based on academic merit and financial need.
Target applicant(s): College students. Adult students.
Minimum GPA: 3.0
Amount: $1,500.
Number of awards: 1.
Deadline: January 31.
How to apply: Applications are available online. An application form, official transcript and two letters of recommendation are required.
Exclusive: Visit www.UltimateScholarshipBook.com and enter code SO213326 for updates on this award.

[2134] • Dr. Juan Andrade, Jr. Scholarship
United States Hispanic Leadership Institute
431 S. Dearborn Street, Suite 1203, Chicago, IL 60605
Phone: 312-427-8683
https://www.ushli.org
Purpose: To support Hispanic students in pursuing post-secondary education.
Eligibility: Applicants must be enrolled or accepted for enrollment as a full-time student at an accredited educational institution in the U.S. Students must have demonstrated financial need and at least one parent of Hispanic ancestry. Applicants must submit letters of recommendation, grade transcripts, a resume and several essays.
Target applicant(s): High school students. College students. Adult students.
Amount: $500-$1,000.
Number of awards: Varies.
Deadline: November 30.
How to apply: Applications are available online.
Exclusive: Visit www.UltimateScholarshipBook.com and enter code UN213426 for updates on this award.

[2135] • Drs. James and Wanda Trefil Science Scholarship
Kosciuszko Foundation
15 East 65th Street, New York, NY 10021-6595
Phone: 212-734-2130
http://www.thekf.org
Purpose: To support American students of Polish descent.
Eligibility: Applicants must be U.S. citizens or legal permanent residents of Polish descent who are full-time undergraduate freshmen, sophomores or juniors at the time of application. Students must have a minimum GPA of 3.5 and be pursuing a major in physics, chemistry, biology, astronomy, earth science or another similar area.
Target applicant(s): College students. Adult students.
Minimum GPA: 3.5
Amount: $5,000.
Number of awards: 1.
Deadline: March 4.
How to apply: Applications are available online.
Exclusive: Visit www.UltimateScholarshipBook.com and enter code KO213526 for updates on this award.

[2136] • Edie Windsor Coding Scholarship
Lesbians Who Tech
Email: edie@lesbianswhotech.org
https://lesbianswhotech.org/codingscholarship/
Purpose: To inspire future generations of LGBTQ, technical women and non-binary individuals.
Eligibility: Applicants must identify as part of the LGBTQ, non-binary or transgender communities. Students must be interested in coding as a future career.
Target applicant(s): High school students. College students. Adult students.
Amount: Varies.
Number of awards: Varies.
Deadline: Contact the sponsor to confirm the deadline.
How to apply: Applications are available online.
Exclusive: Visit www.UltimateScholarshipBook.com and enter code LE213626 for updates on this award.

[2137] • EDSA Diversity Scholarships
Landscape Architecture Foundation
1200 17th Street NW, Suite 210, Washington, DC 20036
Phone: 202-331-7070
Email: scholarships@lafoundation.org
https://www.lafoundation.org/what-we-do/scholarships
Purpose: To aid minority students of landscape architecture.
Eligibility: Applicants must be members of an ethnic, cultural or racial minority. They must be landscape architecture students who are in the final two years of their undergraduate degree program or who are graduate students of landscape architecture. Selection is based on the overall strength of the application.
Target applicant(s): College students. Graduate school students. Adult students.
Amount: $5,000.
Number of awards: 2.
Deadline: February 1.
How to apply: Applications are available online. An application form, personal essay, three work samples, two recommendation letters and an applicant photo are required.
Exclusive: Visit www.UltimateScholarshipBook.com and enter code LA213726 for updates on this award.

[2138] • Education Scholarship
Polish Roman Catholic Union of America
984 North Milwaukee Avenue, Chicago, IL 60642-9981
Phone: 800-772-8632
Email: scholarships@prcua.org
https://www.prcua.org/scholarships/
Purpose: To support students of the Polish American community in their higher education pursuits.
Eligibility: Applicants must have completed their freshman year of undergraduate studies and be sophomores, juniors and seniors enrolled full-time in undergraduate study or those students enrolled in graduate or professional degree programs. Students must be citizens of the United States or permanent residents with a minimum 3.0 GPA on a 4.0 scale or a minimum 4.0 on a 5.0 scale. An essay submission on a provided prompt is required.
Target applicant(s): College students. Graduate school students. Adult students.
Minimum GPA: 3.0
Amount: $500-$25,000.
Number of awards: Varies.
Deadline: June 1.
How to apply: Applications are available online.
Exclusive: Visit www.UltimateScholarshipBook.com and enter code PO213826 for updates on this award.

[2139] • Education Support Award
Patsy Takemoto Mink Education Foundation
P.O. Box 769, Granby, MA 01033
http://patsyminkfoundation.org
Purpose: To support low-income mothers in pursuing post-secondary education.
Eligibility: Applicants must be females who are at least 17 years old. Students must be mothers with minor children pursuing a first degree at a postsecondary level of education and degree program must add to level of education accomplished. Selection is primarily based on demonstration of financial need, personal circumstances, educational and professional goals and community involvement.
Target applicant(s): High school students. College students. Graduate school students. Adult students.
Amount: Up to $5,000.
Number of awards: 5.
Deadline: August 1.
How to apply: Applications are available online.
Exclusive: Visit www.UltimateScholarshipBook.com and enter code PA213926 for updates on this award.

[2140] • Eugene and Elinor Kotur Scholarship Trust Fund
Ukrainian Fraternal Association
371 N. 9th Avenue, Scranton, PA 18504-2005
Phone: 570-342-0937
http://www.members.tripod.com/~ufa_home
Purpose: To support Ukrainian students.
Eligibility: Applicants must be in their sophomore year of college or higher at one of 30 participating schools. They must be of Ukrainian descent and have been members of the Ukrainian Fraternal Association for two years.
Target applicant(s): College students. Graduate school students. Adult students.
Amount: At least $1,000.
Number of awards: Varies.
Deadline: Contact the sponsor to confirm the deadline.
How to apply: Applications are available by mail or phone.
Exclusive: Visit www.UltimateScholarshipBook.com and enter code UK214026 for updates on this award.

[2141] • Florence Young Memorial Scholarship
Association on American Indian Affairs
Lisa Wyzlic, Director of Scholarship Programs, 966 Hungerford Drive, Suite 12-B, Rockville, MD 20850
Phone: 240-314-7155
Email: lw.aaia@indian-affairs.org
https://www.indian-affairs.org/nativescholarship.html
Purpose: To provide financial assistance to Native Americans who are working toward a master's degree in art, public health or law.
Eligibility: Applicants must be full-time students from the continental U.S. or Alaska.
Target applicant(s): Graduate school students. Adult students.
Amount: Varies.
Number of awards: Varies.
Deadline: May 31.
How to apply: Applications are available online.
Exclusive: Visit www.UltimateScholarshipBook.com and enter code AS214126 for updates on this award.

[2142] • Foundation Scholarships
CIRI Foundation
3201 C Street, Suite 506, Anchorage, AK 99503
Phone: 800-764-3382
Email: tcf@thecirifoundation.org
http://www.thecirifoundation.org
Purpose: To provide financial aid for Alaska Natives.
Eligibility: Applicants must be qualified Alaska Native beneficiaries who plan to attend or are currently attending undergraduate or graduate institutions. There are a number of awards based on field of study or career goal. Applicants must submit applications, proof of eligibility, reference letter, transcripts, purpose statements and proof of enrollment.
Target applicant(s): High school students. College students. Graduate school students. Adult students.
Amount: Varies.
Number of awards: Varies.
Scholarship may be renewable.
Deadline: June 30 and December 31.
How to apply: Applications are available online.
Exclusive: Visit www.UltimateScholarshipBook.com and enter code CI214226 for updates on this award.

[2143] • Frontline Families Scholarship
Frontline Families Scholarship Program
Scholarship America, One Scholarship Way, Saint Peter, MN 56082
Phone: 800-537-4180
Email: frontlinefamilies@scholarshipamerica.org
https://learnmore.scholarsapply.org/frontlinefamilies/
Purpose: To support students who are the surviving family members of frontline healthcare workers and volunteers who lost their lives in the fight against COVID-19.
Eligibility: Applicants must be high school seniors, high school graduates or current college undergraduates. Students must be the child of a deceased frontline health care worker who died from Covid-19 while employed at a medical facility. Applicants must be planning to enroll in full-time or

part-time undergraduate study at an accredited two- or four-year college, university or vocational-technical school.
Target applicant(s): High school students. College students. Adult students.
Amount: $1,000-$2,500.
Number of awards: 200.
Deadline: February 15.
How to apply: Applications are available online.
Exclusive: Visit www.UltimateScholarshipBook.com and enter code FR214326 for updates on this award.

[2144] • Full Circle Scholarship
American Indian College Fund
8333 Greenwood Boulevard, Denver, CO 80221
Phone: 303-426-8900
https://collegefund.org/
Purpose: To support American Indian and Alaska Native students seeking undergraduate and graduate degrees.
Eligibility: Applicants must be enrolled full-time in a certificate, associate's, bachelor's or graduate program at an accredited tribal, public or private college or university. Students must be registered as an enrolled member of a federal or state-recognized tribe or a descendant of at least one grandparent or parent who is an enrolled tribal member. Applicants must have a minimum 2.0 GPA.
Target applicant(s): College students. Graduate school students. Adult students.
Minimum GPA: 2.0
Amount: Varies.
Number of awards: Varies.
Deadline: May 31.
How to apply: Applications are available online.
Exclusive: Visit www.UltimateScholarshipBook.com and enter code AM214426 for updates on this award.

[2145] • Gamma Mu Scholarships Program
Gamma Mu Foundation
P.O Box 23520, Fort Lauderdale, FL 33307-3520
Phone: 866-463-6007
Email: scholarships@gammamufoundation.org
https://gammamufoundation.org/
Purpose: To support gay men who want to further their education at a college, university or vocational or professional training program.
Eligibility: Applicants must be male students under 35 years of age who identify themselves as gay and are U.S. citizens. Students must have graduated from high school or received their GED Certificate by June of the application year.
Target applicant(s): High school students. College students. Graduate school students. Adult students.
Amount: $1,000-$2,500.
Number of awards: 2.
Deadline: March 31.
How to apply: Applications are available online.
Exclusive: Visit www.UltimateScholarshipBook.com and enter code GA214526 for updates on this award.

[2146] • Gates Scholarship
Gates Foundation
P.O. Box 10500, Fairfax, VA 22031
Phone: 877-690-4677
https://www.thegatesscholarship.org/scholarship
Purpose: To provide outstanding minority students with opportunities to complete their undergraduate college educations.
Eligibility: Applicants must be U.S. citizens or permanent residents who are high school seniors with a minimum GPA of 3.3. Students must be African-American, American Indian/Alaska Native, Asian and Pacific Islander American and/or Hispanic American, plan to enroll in a four-year degree program and be Pell-eligible.
Target applicant(s): High school students.
Minimum GPA: 3.3
Amount: Varies.
Number of awards: 300.
Deadline: September 15.
How to apply: Applications are available online.
Exclusive: Visit www.UltimateScholarshipBook.com and enter code GA214626 for updates on this award.

[2147] • GEM MS Engineering Fellowship Program
National GEM Consortium
1430 Duke Street, Alexandria, VA 22314
Phone: 703-562-3646
Email: info@gemfellowship.org
http://www.gemfellowship.org
Purpose: To provide fellowships for minority engineering and computer science students pursuing master's degrees.
Eligibility: Applicants must be college seniors or graduate students majoring in engineering or computer science and be members of one of the following minority groups: African American, Native American or Latino or other Hispanic American. Students must also be U.S. citizens or permanent residents, have a minimum 2.8 GPA and agree to intern for two summers with a GEM employer.
Target applicant(s): College students. Graduate school students. Adult students.
Minimum GPA: 2.8
Amount: Up to $16,000.
Number of awards: Varies.
Deadline: November 8.
How to apply: Applications are available online. The deadline for Part I is October 1, and the deadline for part II is November 13.
Exclusive: Visit www.UltimateScholarshipBook.com and enter code NA214726 for updates on this award.

[2148] • General Society of Mayflower Descendants (GSMD) Scholarship
General Society of Mayflower Descendants
P.O. Box 3297, Plymouth, MA 02361
Phone: 508-746-3188
Email: scholarships@themayflowersociety.org
https://themayflowersociety.org/about/about/scholarship-information/
Purpose: To assist high school seniors who are Mayflower descendants.
Eligibility: Applicants must plan to attend a four-year college or university or a two-year community college and must obtain a valid GSMD membership number. Recipients typically are in the top 10 percent of their class and score in the 75th percentile or higher on the SAT or ACT.
Target applicant(s): High school students.
Amount: $2,500-$5,000.
Number of awards: 3.
Deadline: March 1.
How to apply: Applications are available online.
Exclusive: Visit www.UltimateScholarshipBook.com and enter code GE214826 for updates on this award.

The Ultimate Scholarship Book 2026
Scholarship Directory (Ethnicity / Race / Gender / Family Situation)

[2149] • Generation Google Scholarship
Google Inc.
1600 Amphitheatre Parkway, Mountain View, CA 94043
https://buildyourfuture.withgoogle.com/scholarships/
Purpose: To encourage students who are aspiring computer scientists to become leaders in their field.
Eligibility: Applicants must either be a graduating high school senior or be currently enrolled as an undergraduate or graduate student. Students must be enrolled as computer science or computer engineering majors, exhibit strong leadership skills and demonstrate a passion for computer science and technology. Applicants must be from an underrepresented group in computer science such as African American, Hispanic, American Indian or Filipino/Native Hawaiian/Pacific Islander.
Target applicant(s): High school students. College students. Graduate school students. Adult students.
Amount: Up to $10,000.
Number of awards: Varies.
Deadline: May 19.
How to apply: Applications are available online.
Exclusive: Visit www.UltimateScholarshipBook.com and enter code GO214926 for updates on this award.

[2150] • Gentlemen Showcase
Network of Enlightened Women
1360 East Capitol Street NE, Washington, DC 20003
Phone: 517-310-5388
Email: franchetta@enlightenedwomen.org
http://enlightenedwomen.org
Purpose: To recognize and honor young gentlemen across the country.
Eligibility: Individuals nominated must be at least 18 years of age and not more than 40 years of age. Nominees must be enrolled in undergraduate or graduate programs and provide a student email address.
Target applicant(s): High school students. College students. Graduate school students. Adult students.
Amount: $200.
Number of awards: 5.
Deadline: February 5-9.
How to apply: Applications are available online.
Exclusive: Visit www.UltimateScholarshipBook.com and enter code NE215026 for updates on this award.

[2151] • George Choy Memorial/Gay Asian Pacific Alliance (GAPA) Scholarship
Horizons Foundation
550 Montgomery Street, Suite 700, San Francisco, CA 94111
Phone: 415-398-2333
Email: info@horizonsfoundation.org
https://www.horizonsfoundation.org/
Purpose: To assist Bay Area gay, lesbian, bisexual and transgender Asian and Pacific Islander graduating high school students.
Eligibility: Applicants should have at least 25 percent Asian/Pacific Islander ancestry, in the process of applying to or currently attending a college, university or vocational school and reside in one of the nine Bay Area counties (Alameda, Contra Costa, Marin, San Francisco, San Mateo, Santa Clara, Napa, Sonoma or Solano). Preference is given to those who are lesbian, gay, bisexual or transgender or who are involved in the LGBT community.
Target applicant(s): High school students. College students. Adult students.
Minimum GPA: 2.75
Amount: Up to $1,000.
Number of awards: Varies.
Deadline: July 12.
How to apply: Applications are available by phone.
Exclusive: Visit www.UltimateScholarshipBook.com and enter code HO215126 for updates on this award.

[2152] • Goldie Bateson Scholarship
Ladies Professional Golf Association
100 International Golf Drive, Daytona Beach, FL 32124-1092
Phone: 386-274-6200
Email: info@lpgafoundation.org
http://www.lpga.com/lpga-foundation/scholarships
Purpose: To support junior age females who play golf or have an interest in learning the game of golf.
Eligibility: Applicants must be between 7 and 17 years of age and have an interest in playing golf or be currently involved in golf. Students must reside within one of the LPGA T&CP Midwest Section States. Selection is based on the personal essay and letters of recommendation.
Target applicant(s): Junior high students or younger. High school students.
Amount: $250.
Number of awards: 10.
Deadline: October 11.
How to apply: Applications are available online and include a personal essay and two letters of recommendation.
Exclusive: Visit www.UltimateScholarshipBook.com and enter code LA215226 for updates on this award.

[2153] • HBCU NREI Scholarship
Congressional Black Caucus Foundation
1720 Massachusetts Avenue NW, Washington, DC 20036
Phone: 202-263-2800
Email: info@cbcfinc.org
https://www.cbcfinc.org/scholarships/
Purpose: To support students at HBCUs.
Eligibility: Applicants must be Black or African-American and be U.S. citizens or legal permanent residents. Students must attend an accredited HBCU during the academic year of the scholarship award. Applicants must have a minimum GPA of 3.0 on a 4.0 scale, demonstrate a commitment to social justice, exhibit leadership and be active in the community.
Target applicant(s): College students. Adult students.
Minimum GPA: 3.0
Amount: $10,000.
Number of awards: Varies.
Deadline: March 15.
How to apply: Applications are available online.
Exclusive: Visit www.UltimateScholarshipBook.com and enter code CO215326 for updates on this award.

[2154] • Health Professions Pre-Graduate Scholarship Program
Indian Health Service
Scholarship Program Office, 5600 Fishers Lane, Mail Stop: OHR (11E53A), Rockville, MD 20857
Phone: 301-443-2349
Email: michael.bartholomew@ihs.gov
https://www.ihs.gov/scholarship/scholarships/
Purpose: To aid Native Americans and Alaska Natives who are enrolled in selected health-related pre-professional degree programs.

Eligibility: Applicants must be U.S. citizens who are enrolled in or accepted into a pre-medicine, pre-dentistry, pre-optometry, pre-podiatry or other health-related pre-professional degree program. Applicants must have plans to work in the Native American or Alaska Native community as a health care provider in the chosen field of study. Selection is based on academic achievement, recommendation letters and the applicant's stated career goals. Applicant must have a minimum 2.0 GPA.
Target applicant(s): High school students. College students. Adult students.
Minimum GPA: 2.0
Amount: Full tuition and fees.
Number of awards: Varies.
Scholarship may be renewable.
Deadline: Contact the sponsor to confirm the deadline.
How to apply: Applications are available online. An application form, course curriculum outline, two recommendation forms, proof of Native American/Alaska Native status, an official transcript, proof of acceptance into an academic program and other supporting documents are required.
Exclusive: Visit www.UltimateScholarshipBook.com and enter code IN215426 for updates on this award.

[2155] • Health Professions Preparatory Scholarship Program

Indian Health Service
Scholarship Program Office, 5600 Fishers Lane, Mail Stop: OHR (11E53A), Rockville, MD 20857
Phone: 301-443-2349
Email: michael.bartholomew@ihs.gov
https://www.ihs.gov/scholarship/scholarships/
Purpose: To aid Native Americans and Alaska Natives who are preparing for careers in one of the health professions.
Eligibility: Applicants must be U.S. citizens accepted into or enrolled in a compensatory or pre-professional general education course of study at an accredited college or university. The applicant must be studying or have plans to study a subject that has been designated as a priority career category by the Indian Health Service. Applicants must plan to serve Native American or Alaska Native communities as a professional healthcare provider after completing the necessary training. Selection is based on academic achievement, recommendation letters and stated career goals.
Target applicant(s): College students. Adult students.
Minimum GPA: 2.0
Amount: Varies.
Number of awards: Varies.
Scholarship may be renewable.
Deadline: February 28.
How to apply: Applications are available online. An application form, two letters of recommendation, proof of Native American or Alaska Native status, an official transcript, proof of acceptance into a postsecondary educational program and other supporting documents are required.
Exclusive: Visit www.UltimateScholarshipBook.com and enter code IN215526 for updates on this award.

[2156] • Helene M. Overly Memorial Graduate Scholarship

Women's Transportation Seminar (WTS) International
1701 K Street NW, Suite 800, Washington, DC 20006
Phone: 202-955-5085
Email: membership@wtsinternational.org
https://www.wtsinternational.org/mission/wts-foundation/scholarships
Purpose: To support women pursuing careers in the transportation industry with their higher education expenses.
Eligibility: Applicants must be women enrolled in graduate studies in transportation or the related fields of engineering, planning, finance or logistics. Selection is based on the applicant's academic record, transportation-related activities or job skills and specific transportation goals.
Target applicant(s): Graduate school students. Adult students.
Amount: $5,000.
Number of awards: 1.
Deadline: Varies based on local chapter deadline.
How to apply: Applications are available through a local chapter.
Exclusive: Visit www.UltimateScholarshipBook.com and enter code WO215626 for updates on this award.

[2157] • Henry Salvatori Scholarship

Order Sons of Italy in America (OSIA)
219 E Street NE, Washington, DC 20002
Phone: 202-547-2900
Email: scholarships@osia.org
https://osdia.org/
Purpose: To support students who demonstrate exceptional leadership, distinguished scholarship and respect for the principles upon which our nation was founded.
Eligibility: Applicants must be U.S. citizens of Italian descent who are graduating high school seniors who are planning to attend an undergraduate program at a four-year, accredited college or university for the upcoming fall semester. Students must write an essay as part of the application process.
Target applicant(s): High school students.
Amount: Varies.
Number of awards: 1.
Deadline: March 7.
How to apply: Applications are available online.
Exclusive: Visit www.UltimateScholarshipBook.com and enter code OR215726 for updates on this award.

[2158] • Herbert Lehman Education Fund Scholarship

NAACP Legal Defense and Educational Fund Inc.
40 Rector Street, 5th Floor, New York, NY 10006
Phone: 212-965-2200
Email: scholarships@naacpldf.org
https://www.naacpldf.org/about-us/ldf-scholarships/
Purpose: To support African American students who are attending college for the first time.
Eligibility: Applicants must have a strong academic record and clear educational goals, and they must show leadership potential through involvement in school and extracurricular activities. Students must show good character through positive recommendations from teachers, employers or community representatives.
Target applicant(s): High school students. College students. Adult students.
Amount: $3,000.
Number of awards: Varies.
Scholarship may be renewable.
Deadline: April 1.
How to apply: Applications are available by sending a written request.
Exclusive: Visit www.UltimateScholarshipBook.com and enter code NA215826 for updates on this award.

[2159] • Hispanic Heritage Youth Awards
Hispanic Heritage Awards Foundation
1001 Pennsylvania Avenue NW, Washington, DC 20004
Phone: 202-861-9797
Email: contact@hispanicheritageawards.org
http://hispanicheritage.org/
Purpose: To promote Hispanic excellence and recognize the contributions of Hispanic American youth.
Eligibility: Applicants must be high school seniors who are U.S. citizens or permanent residents, reside in Atlanta, Chicago, Dallas, Houston, Los Angeles, Miami, New York City, Philadelphia, Phoenix, San Diego, San Jose and Washington, DC and have Hispanic parentage (Hispanic parentage can be one parent of Mexican, Central American, Cuban, Puerto Rican, South American, Spanish or Caribbean Hispanic descent). Selection criteria include achievement in the applicant's discipline, involvement in community, ability to overcome adversity and character. The disciplines are: Academic Excellence, Sports, the Arts, Literature/Journalism, Mathematics, Leadership/Community Service and Science and Technology.
Target applicant(s): High school students.
Minimum GPA: 3.0
Amount: Varies.
Number of awards: Varies.
Deadline: November 3.
How to apply: Applications are available by request.
Exclusive: Visit www.UltimateScholarshipBook.com and enter code HI215926 for updates on this award.

[2160] • Hispanic Scholarship Fund
Hispanic Scholarship Fund (HSF)
1411 W. 190th Street, Suite 700, Gardena, CA 90248
Phone: 877-473-4636
Email: info@hsf.net
https://www.hsf.net/scholarship
Purpose: To support students of Hispanic heritage.
Eligibility: Applicants must be high school seniors, entering college students or current college undergraduate or graduate students who are of Hispanic heritage and U.S. citizens or permanent residents. Students must have a GPA of 3.0 or higher and plan to enroll full-time in a degree program at a two- or four-year accredited institution in the U.S., Puerto Rico, the Virgin Islands or Guam in the upcoming academic year. Applicants must also apply for federal financial aid and be pursuing their first undergraduate or graduate degree.
Target applicant(s): High school students. College students. Graduate school students. Adult students.
Minimum GPA: 3.0
Amount: $500-$5,000.
Number of awards: Varies.
Deadline: February 15.
How to apply: Applications are available online.
Exclusive: Visit www.UltimateScholarshipBook.com and enter code HI216026 for updates on this award.

[2161] • Hispanic Serving Institutions Scholarship
American Institute for Foreign Study
AIFS Abroad, 1 High Ridge Park, Stamford, CT 06905
Phone: 800-727-2437
Email: AIFSAbroad@aifs.com
https://www.aifsabroad.com/scholarships.asp
Purpose: To support students who plan to pursue higher education.
Eligibility: Applicants must be students at Hispanic Serving Institutions. Students must be AIFS Abroad study abroad and/or intern students. Applicants must have at least a 3.0 minimum cumulative GPA.
Target applicant(s): High school students. College students. Adult students.
Minimum GPA: 3.0
Amount: Up to $2,000.
Number of awards: 3.
Deadline: April 15 for fall; October 1 for spring.
How to apply: Applications are available online.
Exclusive: Visit www.UltimateScholarshipBook.com and enter code AM216126 for updates on this award.

[2162] • Historically Black College and University Scholarship
American Institute for Foreign Study
AIFS Abroad, 1 High Ridge Park, Stamford, CT 06905
Phone: 800-727-2437
Email: AIFSAbroad@aifs.com
https://www.aifsabroad.com/scholarships.asp
Purpose: To support students who plan to study abroad.
Eligibility: Applicants must be AIFS Abroad study abroad and/or intern students. Students must have at least 3.0 minimum cumulative GPA. Applicants must attend an institution designated as a Historically Black College or University.
Target applicant(s): High school students. College students. Adult students.
Minimum GPA: 3.0
Amount: Up to $2,000.
Number of awards: Varies.
Deadline: April 15 for fall; October 1 for spring.
How to apply: Applications are available online.
Exclusive: Visit www.UltimateScholarshipBook.com and enter code AM216226 for updates on this award.

[2163] • Honeywell International Inc. Scholarships
Society of Women Engineers
130 East Randolph Street, Suite 3500, Chicago, IL 60601
Phone: 877-793-4636
Email: scholarships@swe.org
https://swe.org/scholarships/
Purpose: To aid female students planning to pursue undergraduate degrees in computer science and engineering.
Eligibility: Applicants must be female U.S. citizens. They must be rising undergraduate sophomores, juniors or seniors and must plan to major in computer science, computer engineering, electrical engineering, chemical engineering, manufacturing engineering, mechanical engineering, architectural engineering, aerospace engineering, industrial engineering or materials science and engineering. Applicants must demonstrate financial need. Selection is based on the overall strength of the application. A minimum 3.5 GPA is required.
Target applicant(s): College students. Adult students.
Minimum GPA: 3.5
Amount: $5,000.
Number of awards: 3.
Deadline: January 31.
How to apply: Applications are available online. An application form and supporting documents are required.
Exclusive: Visit www.UltimateScholarshipBook.com and enter code SO216326 for updates on this award.

[2164] • Hopi Scholarship Program
Hopi Tribe Grants and Scholarship Program
P.O. Box 123, Kykotsmovi, AZ 86039
Phone: 800-762-9630
Email: heef@hopieducationfund.org
http://www.hopieducationfund.org
Purpose: To help Hopi students with academic achievement.
Eligibility: Applicants must be enrolled members of the Hopi tribe, be high school graduates or have earned a GED, have been accepted to a regionally accredited college and plan to attend full-time and have completed the Free Application for Federal Student Aid. Students must be in the top 10 percent of their high school class or score 930 on the SAT or 21 on the ACT as entering freshmen; have a minimum 3.0 GPA as undergraduates or have a minimum 3.2 GPA as graduate, post graduate or professional degree students. Applications, statements of goals, financial needs analysis, proof of Hopi enrollment and transcripts are required.
Target applicant(s): High school students. College students. Graduate school students. Adult students.
Minimum GPA: 3.0 for undergraduate students; 3.2 for graduate students
Amount: Varies.
Number of awards: Varies.
Deadline: April 15; July 15; October 15; December 15.
How to apply: Applications are available by mail.
Exclusive: Visit www.UltimateScholarshipBook.com and enter code HO216426 for updates on this award.

[2165] • HSC Foundation Scholarship
Hispanic Scholarship Consortium
314 E. Highland Mall Boulevard #103, Austin, TX 78752
Phone: 512-368-2956
https://www.hispanicscholar.org/
Purpose: To support Hispanic graduating seniors who are pursuing a degree in science, technology, engineering or mathematics.
Eligibility: Applicants must be enrolled full-time. A minimum GPA of 2.5 is required. Selection is based on the overall strength of the application.
Target applicant(s): High school students. College students. Adult students.
Minimum GPA: 2.5
Amount: $2,000.
Number of awards: 1.
Scholarship may be renewable.
Deadline: April 30.
How to apply: Applications are available online.
Exclusive: Visit www.UltimateScholarshipBook.com and enter code HI216526 for updates on this award.

[2166] • Hsiao Memorial Social Sciences Scholarship
Asian Pacific Community Fund
1145 Wilshire Boulevard, Suite 105, Los Angeles, CA 90017
Phone: 213-624-6400
Email: scholarships@apcf.org
https://www.apcf.org/scholarships
Purpose: To encourage Asian American and Pacific Islander students.
Eligibility: Applicants must be graduate students attending a U.S.-based college or university in the current academic year. Students must be of Asian heritage and have financial need. Applicants must have a minimum GPA of 3.0.
Target applicant(s): Graduate school students. Adult students.
Amount: $1,000.
Number of awards: 1.
Deadline: April 26.
How to apply: Applications are available online.
Exclusive: Visit www.UltimateScholarshipBook.com and enter code AS216626 for updates on this award.

[2167] • Hubertus W.V. Wellems Scholarship for Male Students
National Association for the Advancement of Colored People
4805 Mt. Hope Drive, Baltimore, MD 21215
Phone: 410-580-5777
https://naacp.org/find-resources/scholarships-awards-internships/scholarships
Purpose: To aid male students who are studying certain math and science subjects at the undergraduate and graduate levels.
Eligibility: Applicants must be U.S. citizens who are high school seniors, undergraduates or graduate students. They must be enrolled in or plan to enroll in a mathematics, chemistry, physics or engineering degree program at an accredited four-year institution of higher learning located in the U.S. Undergraduate applicants must be full-time students. High school seniors and undergraduate students must have a GPA of 2.5 or higher, and graduate students must have a GPA of 3.0 or higher. All applicants must demonstrate financial need. Selection is based on the overall strength of the application.
Target applicant(s): High school students. College students. Graduate school students. Adult students.
Minimum GPA: 2.5 for high school seniors and undergraduate students; 3.0 for graduate students
Amount: $3,000.
Number of awards: 20-40.
Deadline: May 21.
How to apply: Applications are available online. An application form, personal essay, official transcript and two letters of recommendation are required.
Exclusive: Visit www.UltimateScholarshipBook.com and enter code NA216726 for updates on this award.

[2168] • Ida M. Pope Memorial Scholarship
Hawaii Community Foundation - Scholarships
827 Fort Street Mall, Honolulu, HI 96813
Phone: 888-731-3863
Email: scholarships@hcf-hawaii.org
https://www.hawaiicommunityfoundation.org/
Purpose: To assist female students of Hawaiian ancestry in obtaining higher education.
Eligibility: Applicants must attend an accredited college or university and have a GPA of 3.5 or higher. Students must also major in health, science, education, counseling or social work.
Target applicant(s): High school students. College students. Adult students.
Minimum GPA: 3.5
Amount: Varies.
Number of awards: Varies.
Deadline: February 28.
How to apply: To apply, register online, complete the online application and select the scholarships to which you wish to apply. In addition, mail the supporting materials: printed confirmation page from the online application, personal statement, copy of Student Aid Report (SAR) available at www.fafsa.ed.gov and official transcript.
Exclusive: Visit www.UltimateScholarshipBook.com and enter code HA216826 for updates on this award.

[2169] • Intellia Therapeutics - UNCF Scholarship
United Negro College Fund (UNCF)
1805 7th Street NW, Washington, DC 20001
Phone: 800-331-2244
Email: kenya.gray@uncf.org
https://uncf.org/scholarships
Purpose: To support full-time students pursuing higher education.
Eligibility: Applicants must be African American, Hispanic or Native American enrolled full-time at any accredited four-year college or university. Students must be pursuing degrees in life sciences in one of the following: biochemistry, biomedical engineering, biology, chemistry, chemical and physical biology, cellular, molecular and developmental biology, plant biology entomology or microbiology with a minimum 2.75 GPA. Applicants must demonstrate unmet financial need and submit the FAFSA.
Target applicant(s): College students. Graduate school students. Adult students.
Minimum GPA: 2.75.
Amount: $5,000.
Number of awards: 7.
Deadline: June 5.
How to apply: Applications are available online.
Exclusive: Visit www.UltimateScholarshipBook.com and enter code UN216926 for updates on this award.

[2170] • Jackie Robinson Foundation Scholarship Program
Jackie Robinson Foundation
3 W. 35th Street, 11th Floor, New York, NY 10001
Phone: 212-290-8600
Email: general@jackierobinson.org
http://www.jackierobinson.org
Purpose: To help minority students who have shown leadership skills in their communities.
Eligibility: Applicants must be minority high school seniors with demonstrated financial need, leadership potential and academic achievement and who have already been accepted to a four-year college or university. Students must also be U.S. citizens and have a minimum SAT score of 1000 or composite ACT score of 22.
Target applicant(s): High school students.
Amount: Up to $28,000.
Number of awards: Varies.
Deadline: January 10.
How to apply: Applications are available online.
Exclusive: Visit www.UltimateScholarshipBook.com and enter code JA217026 for updates on this award.

[2171] • James M. and Erma T. Freemont Foundation Scholarship Program
James M. and Erma T. Freemont Foundation
P.O. Box 82563, Hapeville, GA 30354
http://www.freemontfoundation.com
Purpose: To support students who demonstrate involvement and leadership.
Eligibility: Applicants must be graduating high school seniors, undergraduate or graduate students who are planning to attend or are attending an HBCU. Students must demonstrate outstanding academic achievement, leadership and volunteerism in their community and participation in extracurricular school activities.
Target applicant(s): High school students. College students. Graduate school students. Adult students.
Amount: Varies.
Number of awards: Varies.
Deadline: February 2.
How to apply: Applications are available online.
Exclusive: Visit www.UltimateScholarshipBook.com and enter code JA217126 for updates on this award.

[2172] • Japanese American Citizens League Entering Freshman Awards
Japanese American Citizens League (JACL)
1765 Sutter Street, San Francisco, CA 94115
Phone: 415-921-5225
Email: jacl@jacl.org
http://www.jacl.org
Purpose: To recognize and encourage education as a key to greater opportunities among JACL members.
Eligibility: Applicants must be National JACL members and must be planning to attend a college, university, trade school, business school or any other institution of higher learning at the undergraduate level. A personal statement, letter of recommendation, academic performance, work experience and community involvement will all be considered.
Target applicant(s): High school students.
Amount: Varies.
Number of awards: Varies.
Deadline: March 1.
How to apply: Applications are available through local JACL chapters, regional offices, National JACL Headquarters and website.
Exclusive: Visit www.UltimateScholarshipBook.com and enter code JA217226 for updates on this award.

[2173] • Japanese American Citizens League Graduate Awards
Japanese American Citizens League (JACL)
1765 Sutter Street, San Francisco, CA 94115
Phone: 415-921-5225
Email: jacl@jacl.org
http://www.jacl.org
Purpose: To provide monetary assistance for graduate studies to JACL members.
Eligibility: Applicants must be National JACL members and must attend a college or university at the graduate level. A personal statement, letter of recommendation, academic performance, work experience and community involvement are considered.
Target applicant(s): Graduate school students. Adult students.
Amount: Varies.
Number of awards: Varies.
Deadline: April 1.
How to apply: Applications are available online and by sending a self-addressed, stamped envelope.
Exclusive: Visit www.UltimateScholarshipBook.com and enter code JA217326 for updates on this award.

[2174] • Japanese American Citizens League Law Scholarships
Japanese American Citizens League (JACL)
1765 Sutter Street, San Francisco, CA 94115
Phone: 415-921-5225
Email: jacl@jacl.org
http://www.jacl.org
Purpose: To help JACL members who are studying law.
Eligibility: Applicants must be National JACL members and must be studying law at a college or university. A personal statement, letter of recommendation, academic performance, work experience and community involvement will all be considered.
Target applicant(s): Graduate school students. Adult students.
Amount: Varies.
Number of awards: Varies.
Deadline: April 1.
How to apply: Applications are available online and by sending a self-addressed, stamped envelope.
Exclusive: Visit www.UltimateScholarshipBook.com and enter code JA217426 for updates on this award.

[2175] • Japanese American Citizens League Undergraduate Awards
Japanese American Citizens League (JACL)
1765 Sutter Street, San Francisco, CA 94115
Phone: 415-921-5225
Email: jacl@jacl.org
http://www.jacl.org
Purpose: To recognize and encourage education as a key to greater opportunities among JACL members.
Eligibility: Applicants must be National JACL members and must be attending a college, university, trade school, business school or any other institution of higher learning at the undergraduate level. A personal statement, letter of recommendation, academic performance, work experience and community involvement will all be considered.
Target applicant(s): College students. Adult students.
Amount: Varies.
Number of awards: Varies.
Deadline: March 1.
How to apply: Applications are available through local JACL chapters, regional offices, National JACL Headquarters and website.
Exclusive: Visit www.UltimateScholarshipBook.com and enter code JA217526 for updates on this award.

[2176] • Jeannette Rankin National Scholar Grant
Jeannette Rankin Foundation
1 Huntington Road, Suite 701, Athens, GA 30606
Phone: 706-208-1211
Email: info@rankinfoundation.org
http://www.rankinfoundation.org
Purpose: To support the education of low-income women 35 years or older.
Eligibility: Applicants must be women 35 years of age or older, plan to obtain an undergraduate or vocational education and meet maximum household income guidelines.
Target applicant(s): College students. Adult students.
Amount: Varies.
Number of awards: Varies.
Scholarship may be renewable.
Deadline: February 16.
How to apply: Applications are available online.
Exclusive: Visit www.UltimateScholarshipBook.com and enter code JE217626 for updates on this award.

[2177] • Judith Resnik Memorial Scholarship
Society of Women Engineers
130 East Randolph Street, Suite 3500, Chicago, IL 60601
Phone: 877-793-4636
Email: scholarships@swe.org
https://swe.org/scholarships/
Purpose: To help female undergraduates who are majoring in astronautical, aeronautical or aerospace engineering.
Eligibility: Applicants must be rising undergraduate sophomores, juniors or seniors and have a GPA of 3.0 or higher on a four-point scale. They must be enrolled in an ABET-accredited degree program in aeronautical engineering, aerospace engineering or astronautical engineering. They cannot be receiving a renewable scholarship from the Society of Women Engineers. Applicants who are receiving full funding from another source (such as the U.S. military or an employee reimbursement plan) are ineligible. Selection is based on the overall strength of the application.
Target applicant(s): College students. Adult students.
Minimum GPA: 3.0
Amount: $4,000.
Number of awards: 1.
Deadline: January 31.
How to apply: Applications are available online. An application form, official transcript and two recommendation letters are required.
Exclusive: Visit www.UltimateScholarshipBook.com and enter code SO217726 for updates on this award.

[2178] • Julianne Malveaux Scholarship
National Association of Negro Business and Professional Women's Clubs Inc.
1806 New Hampshire Avenue NW, Washington, DC 20009
Phone: 202-483-4206
Email: education@nanbpwc.org
http://www.nanbpwc.org
Purpose: To award scholarships to college students majoring in journalism, economics or a related field.
Eligibility: Applicants must be African American females enrolled as sophomores or juniors at an accredited college or university and have a minimum 3.0 GPA. Students may major in related fields such as public policy or creative writing.
Target applicant(s): College students. Adult students.
Minimum GPA: 3.0
Amount: Varies.
Number of awards: Varies.
Deadline: March 29.
How to apply: Applications are available online.
Exclusive: Visit www.UltimateScholarshipBook.com and enter code NA217826 for updates on this award.

[2179] • Kenneth W. Payne Student Prize
Association for Queer Anthropology (AQA)
Email: payne.prize@gmail.com
http://queeranthro.org/awards/the-kenneth-w-payne-student-prize/
Purpose: To encourage LGBT students interested in any of the four fields of anthropology.

The Ultimate Scholarship Book 2026
Scholarship Directory (Ethnicity / Race / Gender / Family Situation)

Eligibility: Applicants must be undergraduates or graduate students who are members of the LGBT community. Students must be studying any of the four fields of anthropology. Research papers as well as visual media are eligible for submission for this competition.
Target applicant(s): College students. Graduate school students. Adult students.
Amount: $500.
Number of awards: 1.
Deadline: June 1.
How to apply: Applications are available online.
Exclusive: Visit www.UltimateScholarshipBook.com and enter code AS217926 for updates on this award.

[2180] • Knights of Lithuania Scholarship Program
Knights of Lithuania Scholarship Program
c/o Mikalina Tambasco, Committee Chair, 14 Pine Avenue, Johnstown, NY 12095
Phone: 518-705-1165
Email: mikalina@hotmail.com
https://www.knightsoflithuania.org/scholarship-fund
Purpose: To assist Lithuanian-Americans in obtaining higher education.
Eligibility: Applicants must be members of the Knights of Lithuania for at least two years. They must receive recommendations from their council president or vice president, a pastor or spiritual adviser and a former teacher in addition to a separate character reference.
Target applicant(s): High school students. College students. Graduate school students. Adult students.
Amount: Varies.
Number of awards: Varies.
Deadline: June 30.
How to apply: Applications are available online.
Exclusive: Visit www.UltimateScholarshipBook.com and enter code KN218026 for updates on this award.

[2181] • Korean Ancestry Grant
William Orr Dingwall Foundation
P.O. Box 57088, Washington, DC 20037
Email: kag@dingwallfoundation.org
http://www.dingwallfoundation.org
Purpose: To aid students of Asian ancestry.
Eligibility: Applicants must be of Asian ancestry and have at least one Asian grandparent. They must be entering or current undergraduate students. Preference will be given to applicants of Korean ancestry. Selection is based on the overall strength of the application.
Target applicant(s): High school students. College students. Adult students.
Amount: Up to $10,000.
Number of awards: 24.
Scholarship may be renewable.
Deadline: April 1.
How to apply: Applications are available online. An application form, official transcript, personal statement and two recommendation letters are required.
Exclusive: Visit www.UltimateScholarshipBook.com and enter code WI218126 for updates on this award.

[2182] • LAGRANT Scholarship Program
LAGRANT Foundation
633 W. 5th Street, 48th Floor, Los Angeles, CA 90071
Phone: 323-469-8680
http://www.lagrantfoundation.org
Purpose: To support minority students who are seeking degrees in advertising, graphic design, marketing or public relations.
Eligibility: Applicants must be African American/Black, Asian American/Pacific Islander, Hispanic/Latino or Native American/Alaskan Native. Students must be U.S. citizens, permanent residents, AB-540 students or DACA recipients. Applicants must be full-time students at an accredited four-year institution in the U.S. A minimum 3.0 GPA or higher is required. Students must submit an essay with their application.
Target applicant(s): College students. Graduate school students. Adult students.
Minimum GPA: 3.0
Amount: $2,500-$3,750.
Number of awards: 50.
Deadline: February 28.
How to apply: Applications are available online.
Exclusive: Visit www.UltimateScholarshipBook.com and enter code LA218226 for updates on this award.

[2183] • Larry Whiteside Scholarship
National Association of Black Journalists
1100 Knight Hall, Suite 3101, College Park, MD 20742
Phone: 301-405-7520
Email: iwashington@nabj.org
https://nabjonline.org/student-services/
Purpose: To assist students who are planning for careers in sports journalism.
Eligibility: Applicants must be student members of the National Association of Black Journalists (NABJ). They must be graduate students or rising undergraduate juniors or seniors at an accredited four-year institution who are planning to pursue careers in sports journalism. They must be majoring in journalism or communications or must have demonstrated an interest in journalism by working for a media outlet. They must have a major GPA of 2.5 or higher. Selection is based on the overall strength of the application.
Target applicant(s): College students. Graduate school students. Adult students.
Minimum GPA: 2.5
Amount: $5,000.
Number of awards: 1.
Deadline: February 28.
How to apply: Applications are available online. An application form, resume, official transcript, personal essay, three writing samples and three references are required.
Exclusive: Visit www.UltimateScholarshipBook.com and enter code NA218326 for updates on this award.

[2184] • Laurel Hester Memorial Scholarship
LEAGUE Foundation
Email: info@leaguefoundation.org
https://www.leaguefoundation.org/
Purpose: To support LGBTQ+ graduating high school seniors who are entering their first year of institutions of higher learning.
Eligibility: Applicants must be self-identified LGBTQ+ graduating high school seniors with a minimum 3.0 GPA who are attending an accredited college, university, or vocational school within the United States or Canada. Students must be citizens of the United States.
Target applicant(s): High school students.
Minimum GPA: 3.0
Amount: Varies.
Number of awards: 1.

Deadline: April 1.
How to apply: Applications are available online.
Exclusive: Visit www.UltimateScholarshipBook.com and enter code LE218426 for updates on this award.

[2185] • LEAGUE Foundation Scholarship
LEAGUE Foundation
Email: info@leaguefoundation.org
https://www.leaguefoundation.org/
Purpose: To support students from the LGBTQ+ community pursuing higher education.
Eligibility: Applicants must be openly self-identified members of the LGBTQ+ community and United States citizens or legal immigrants. Students must be graduating high school seniors planning to enroll in an accredited college, university or vocational school within the United States or Canada with a minimum 3.0 GPA. Applicants must provide a detailed list of community involvement with heavier weight given to those activities and leadership roles relating directly to the LGBTQ+ communities.
Target applicant(s): High school students.
Minimum GPA: 3.0
Amount: Varies.
Number of awards: Up to 9.
Deadline: April 15.
How to apply: Applications are available online.
Exclusive: Visit www.UltimateScholarshipBook.com and enter code LE218526 for updates on this award.

[2186] • LGBTQ+ Student Scholarship from Study.com
Study.com
100 View Street, Suite 202, Mountain View, CA 94041
https://study.com/resources/student-scholarships
Purpose: To support LGBTQ+ students.
Eligibility: Applicants must be LGBTQ+ students enrolled (or accepted) in an accredited college or university within the United States, pursuing an undergraduate or graduate degree in any field of study and planning on continuing the next year. Students must have a minimum of 30 semester or 45 quarter hours to complete.
Target applicant(s): College students. Graduate school students. Adult students.
Amount: $1,000.
Number of awards: Varies.
Deadline: May 31.
How to apply: Applications are available online.
Exclusive: Visit www.UltimateScholarshipBook.com and enter code ST218626 for updates on this award.

[2187] • Lillian Moller Gilbreth Memorial Scholarship
Society of Women Engineers
130 East Randolph Street, Suite 3500, Chicago, IL 60601
Phone: 877-793-4636
Email: scholarships@swe.org
https://swe.org/scholarships/
Purpose: To aid female students who are majoring in engineering.
Eligibility: Applicants must be rising undergraduate juniors or seniors who are enrolled in an ABET-accredited engineering degree program. They must have a GPA of 3.0 or higher on a four-point scale. Applicants cannot be receiving full academic funding from another source, and they cannot be receiving another renewable SWE scholarship at the time of award disbursement. Selection is based on the overall strength of the application.
Target applicant(s): College students. Adult students.
Minimum GPA: 3.0
Amount: $19,000.
Number of awards: 1.
Scholarship may be renewable.
Deadline: January 31.
How to apply: Applications are available online. An application form, official transcript and two letters of recommendation are required.
Exclusive: Visit www.UltimateScholarshipBook.com and enter code SO218726 for updates on this award.

[2188] • Live Your Dream Awards Program
Soroptimist International of the Americas
1709 Spruce Street, Philadelphia, PA 19103
Phone: 215-893-9000
Email: siahq@soroptimist.org
https://www.soroptimist.org/our-work/live-your-dream-awards/
Purpose: To assist women entering or re-entering the workforce with educational and skills training support.
Eligibility: Applicants must be attending or been accepted by a vocational/skills training program or an undergraduate degree program. Applicants must be the women heads of household who provide the primary source of financial support for their families and demonstrate financial need. Applicants must submit their application to the appropriate regional office.
Target applicant(s): High school students. College students. Adult students.
Amount: Up to $16,000.
Number of awards: Varies.
Deadline: November 15.
How to apply: Applications are available online.
Exclusive: Visit www.UltimateScholarshipBook.com and enter code SO218826 for updates on this award.

[2189] • Lucy Kasparian Aharonian Scholarship
Armenian International Women's Association
65 Main Street, #3A, Watertown, MA 02472
Phone: 617-926-0171
Email: aiwainc@aol.com
http://aiwainternational.org/
Purpose: To aid female students of Armenian descent who are studying selected subjects.
Eligibility: Applicants must be full-time undergraduate juniors, undergraduate seniors or graduate students who are enrolled at an accredited postsecondary institution. They must be pursuing a degree in architecture, computer science, engineering, mathematics or technology. Selection is based on academic merit and financial need.
Target applicant(s): College students. Graduate school students. Adult students.
Amount: $2,000.
Number of awards: 3.
Deadline: April 22.
How to apply: Applications are available online. An application form and supporting materials are required.
Exclusive: Visit www.UltimateScholarshipBook.com and enter code AR218926 for updates on this award.

[2190] • LULAC General Awards
League of United Latin American Citizens
1133 19th Street NW, Suite 1000, Washington, DC 20036
Phone: 202-835-9646
Email: scholarships@lnesc.org
https://www.lnesc.org
Purpose: To provide assistance to Latino students who are seeking or plan to seek degrees.
Eligibility: Students must have applied to or be enrolled in a two- or four-year college or graduate school and be U.S. citizens or legal residents. Grades and academic achievement may be considered, but emphasis is placed on motivation, sincerity and integrity as demonstrated by the interview and essay.
Target applicant(s): High school students. College students. Graduate school students. Adult students.
Amount: $250-$1,000.
Number of awards: Varies.
Deadline: March 31.
How to apply: Applications are available online.
Exclusive: Visit www.UltimateScholarshipBook.com and enter code LE219026 for updates on this award.

[2191] • LULAC Honors Awards
League of United Latin American Citizens
1133 19th Street NW, Suite 1000, Washington, DC 20036
Phone: 202-835-9646
Email: scholarships@lnesc.org
https://www.lnesc.org
Purpose: To provide assistance to Latino students of all levels of education.
Eligibility: Applicants must be U.S. citizens or legal residents, have applied to or attend a college or graduate school and have a GPA of 3.0 or better. Applicants who are entering freshmen must also have an ACT score of 23 or higher or an SAT score of 1100 or higher.
Target applicant(s): High school students. College students. Graduate school students. Adult students.
Minimum GPA: 3.0
Amount: $500-$2,000.
Number of awards: Varies.
Deadline: March 31.
How to apply: Applications are available from LULAC.
Exclusive: Visit www.UltimateScholarshipBook.com and enter code LE219126 for updates on this award.

[2192] • MAES Scholarship Program
Society of Mexican American Engineers and Scientists Inc. (MAES)
711 W. Bay Area Boulevard, Suite #206, Webster, TX 77598-4051
Phone: 281-557-3677
Email: execdir@maes-natl.org
http://mymaes.org/programs/
Purpose: To assist Hispanic students in the fields of science and engineering.
Eligibility: Applicants must be current Hispanic MAES student members who are full-time undergraduate and graduate students in an accredited U.S. college or university majoring in science or engineering. Community college applicants must be enrolled in majors that are transferable to a four-year institution offering bachelor's degrees. There are various scholarships in the program. Some sponsors require students to be U.S. citizens or permanent residents. Awards are based on financial need, academic achievement, personal qualities, strengths and leadership abilities. Applicants should submit applications, financial information, recommendations and transcripts.
Target applicant(s): High school students. College students. Graduate school students. Adult students.
Amount: Varies.
Number of awards: Varies.
Deadline: March 15.
How to apply: Applications are available online.
Exclusive: Visit www.UltimateScholarshipBook.com and enter code SO219226 for updates on this award.

[2193] • MALDEF Law School Scholarship
Mexican American Legal Defense and Educational Fund
634 South Spring Street, 11th Floor, Los Angeles, CA 90014
Phone: 213-629-2512
Email: lawscholarships@maldef.org
https://www.maldef.org
Purpose: To support law school students in funding their education.
Eligibility: Applicants must be enrolled full-time at an accredited U.S. law school. Selection is primarily based on demonstration of academic achievement, extracurricular involvement, financial need and commitment to the advancement of Latino civil rights. Students must submit transcripts, letters of recommendation and a personal statement.
Target applicant(s): College students. Graduate school students. Adult students.
Amount: $2,000-$10,000.
Number of awards: 5-15.
Deadline: January 19.
How to apply: Applications are available online.
Exclusive: Visit www.UltimateScholarshipBook.com and enter code ME219326 for updates on this award.

[2194] • Marcus Garvey Scholarship
Malcolm Frierson Foundation
P.O. Box 271221, Flower Mound, TX 75027
Email: mfrierson@gmail.com
https://www.malcolmfrierson.com/
Purpose: To encourage students who identify as being of African descent and who demonstrate leadership and service.
Eligibility: Applicants must identify as being of African descent and plan on enrolling as a first-time student at an accredited U.S. college or university. Students must have a minimum high school GPA of 3.0 and demonstrate leadership and commitment to service.
Target applicant(s): High school students. College students. Adult students.
Minimum GPA: 3.0
Amount: $1,000.
Number of awards: 1.
Deadline: July 1.
How to apply: Applications are available online.
Exclusive: Visit www.UltimateScholarshipBook.com and enter code MA219426 for updates on this award.

[2195] • Margaret McNamara Education Grants
Margaret Mcnamara Memorial Fund
Margaret McNamara Education Grants, 1818 H Street NW, MSN J2-202, Washington, DC 20433
https://www.mmeg.org/

Purpose: To provide financial assistance to women from developing countries who are currently studying to earn an undergraduate or graduate degree in the U.S. or Canada.
Eligibility: Applicants must be citizens of low or middle income country, have a proven track record of professional or volunteer services towards improving well-being of women and children and be U.S. or Canadian residents at the time of application. Students must be at least 25 years of age.
Target applicant(s): College students. Graduate school students. Adult students.
Amount: $5,000-$15,000.
Number of awards: Varies.
Deadline: January 15.
How to apply: Applications are available online.
Exclusive: Visit www.UltimateScholarshipBook.com and enter code MA219526 for updates on this award.

[2196] • Marilynn Smith Scholarship
Ladies Professional Golf Association
100 International Golf Drive, Daytona Beach, FL 32124-1092
Phone: 386-274-6200
Email: info@lpgafoundation.org
http://www.lpga.com/lpga-foundation/scholarships
Purpose: To support female high school senior golf participants who wish to play competitive golf in college.
Eligibility: Applicants must have played at least 50 percent of their high school team's schedule or played competitive junior golf for the past two years. Students must also be U.S. citizens or legal residents, have a minimum 3.2 GPA, be accepted to attend a college or university and plan on playing competitive golf while attending college. Selection is based on the personal essay, letters of reference and financial need.
Target applicant(s): High school students.
Minimum GPA: 3.2
Amount: $5,000.
Number of awards: 1.
Deadline: January 31.
How to apply: Applications are available online and must include the official application form, three letters of reference, official high school transcript and the personal essay.
Exclusive: Visit www.UltimateScholarshipBook.com and enter code LA219626 for updates on this award.

[2197] • Mark Ando and Ito Family Scholarship
Far West Athletic Trainers' Association/District 8
Ned Bergert, Committee Chair
Phone: 714-501-3858
Email: contact@fwatad8.org
http://www.fwatad8.org/
Purpose: To aid students of Asian descent in California, Hawaii and Nevada who are pursuing higher education in athletic training.
Eligibility: Applicants must be District 8 student members of the National Athletic Trainers' Association (NATA) who are of Asian descent. They must be enrolled in an undergraduate- or graduate-level athletic training program. Community college applicants and all other applicants must have a GPA of 3.2 or higher on a four-point scale. Non-community college undergraduates must be sponsored by a certified athletic trainer and must have junior standing. All applicants must have plans to pursue a career in athletic training. Selection is based on academic merit, extracurricular activities, leadership potential and athletic training achievement.
Target applicant(s): College students. Graduate school students. Adult students.
Minimum GPA: 3.2

Amount: Varies.
Number of awards: Varies.
Deadline: March 15.
How to apply: Applications are available online. An application form, an official transcript and a personal essay are required.
Exclusive: Visit www.UltimateScholarshipBook.com and enter code FA219726 for updates on this award.

[2198] • Mary Gunther Memorial Scholarship
Society of Women Engineers
130 East Randolph Street, Suite 3500, Chicago, IL 60601
Phone: 877-793-4636
Email: scholarships@swe.org
https://swe.org/scholarships/
Purpose: To aid students who plan to major in engineering.
Eligibility: Applicants must be female rising undergraduate freshmen, sophomores, juniors or seniors who intend to major in engineering at an ABET-accredited school. They must be full-time students who have a GPA of 3.5 or higher on a four-point scale. Preference will be given to students majoring in architectural engineering or environmental engineering. Selection is based on the overall strength of the application.
Target applicant(s): High school students. College students. Adult students.
Minimum GPA: 3.5
Amount: $7,000.
Number of awards: 2.
Deadline: February 1; March 20 (freshmen).
How to apply: Applications are available online. An application form, transcript, proof of college acceptance and two recommendation letters are required.
Exclusive: Visit www.UltimateScholarshipBook.com and enter code SO219826 for updates on this award.

[2199] • Mary Quan Moy Ing Memorial Scholarship
Asian American Journalists Association
1301 K Street, NW, 300W, 3rd Floor, Washington, DC 20005
Email: support@aaja.org
https://www.aaja.org/news-and-resources/scholarships-internships/
Purpose: Monetary assistance is awarded to a high school senior pursuing college studies that lead to a journalism career.
Eligibility: Applicants must be high school seniors intending to major in journalism. Students must also demonstrate a commitment to the field of journalism, sensitivity to Asian American issues as demonstrated by community involvement, journalistic ability, scholastic ability and financial need.
Target applicant(s): High school students.
Amount: $2,000.
Number of awards: 1.
Deadline: January 16.
How to apply: Applications are available online.
Exclusive: Visit www.UltimateScholarshipBook.com and enter code AS219926 for updates on this award.

[2200] • Mas Family Scholarships
Jorge Mas Canosa Freedom Foundation
Attn: Mas Family Scholarships, P.O. Box 14-1898, Coral Gables, FL 33114-1898
Phone: 305-507-7323
Email: jmcff@jmcff.org
http://jmcff.org/

Purpose: To aid undergraduate and graduate students of Cuban descent who are studying selected subjects.
Eligibility: Applicants must be majoring in or have plans to major in business, communications, economics, engineering, international relations or journalism. They must demonstrate leadership potential and a commitment to success in a democratic, free enterprise society. Selection is based on academic merit, personal essay, leadership ability, professional potential and character.
Target applicant(s): High school students. College students. Graduate school students. Adult students.
Minimum GPA: 3.5
Amount: Varies.
Number of awards: Varies.
Scholarship may be renewable.
Deadline: January 15.
How to apply: Applications are available online. An application form, official transcript, SAT scores, personal essay, three recommendation forms, proof of Cuban descent, proof of college acceptance (for incoming freshmen only), cost of tuition statement and statement of financial need are required.
Exclusive: Visit www.UltimateScholarshipBook.com and enter code JO220026 for updates on this award.

[2201] • Maureen L. and Howard N. Blitman, P.E., Scholarship

National Society of Professional Engineers
1420 King Street, Alexandria, VA 22314-2794
Phone: 888-285-6773
Email: students@nspe.org
https://www.nspe.org/resources/students/scholarships
Purpose: To encourage minority students to pursue careers in engineering.
Eligibility: Applicants must be African-American, Hispanic or Native American high school seniors who have been accepted into an accredited engineering program at a four-year institution. Students are evaluated based on academic achievement, community involvement and recommendations and must have a minimum 3.5 GPA.
Target applicant(s): High school students.
Minimum GPA: 3.5
Amount: $5,000.
Number of awards: 1.
Deadline: April 1.
How to apply: Applications are available online.
Exclusive: Visit www.UltimateScholarshipBook.com and enter code NA220126 for updates on this award.

[2202] • MCCA Lloyd M. Johnson, Jr. Scholarship Program

Minority Corporate Counsel Association (MCCA)
1111 Pennsylvania Avenue, NW, Washington, DC 20004
Phone: 202-739-5901
Email: contactus@applyists.com
https://mcca.com/pipeline/scholarship-program/
Purpose: To support first-year entering law students.
Eligibility: Applicants must be diverse students entering their first year of law school full-time at an accredited institution. They must have a GPA of at least 3.2 and demonstrate financial need.
Target applicant(s): College students. Graduate school students. Adult students.
Minimum GPA: 3.2
Amount: $10,000.
Number of awards: Up to 10.
Scholarship may be renewable.
Deadline: April 10.
How to apply: Applications are available online.
Exclusive: Visit www.UltimateScholarshipBook.com and enter code MI220226 for updates on this award.

[2203] • Medicus Student Exchange

Swiss Benevolent Society of New York
Scholarship Committee, 420 Lexington Ave, Suite 430, New York, NY 10170
Email: scholarship@sbsny.org
https://www.sbsny.org/
Purpose: To provide need and merit-based scholarships for students from Swiss-American backgrounds.
Eligibility: Applicants or one of their parents must be a Swiss national. The Medicus grant for study in Switzerland is only open to U.S. residents and is a need-based award. Applicants must be college juniors or seniors or graduate-level students accepted to a Swiss university or the Federal Institute of Technology. Note: We do not recommend applying to scholarships that charge application fees. However, some scholarships of this type charge fees and are included for completeness.
Target applicant(s): College students. Graduate school students. Adult students.
Amount: Varies.
Number of awards: Varies.
Deadline: March 31.
How to apply: Applications are available online.
Exclusive: Visit www.UltimateScholarshipBook.com and enter code SW220326 for updates on this award.

[2204] • Meritage Homes Scholarship

Society of Women Engineers
130 East Randolph Street, Suite 3500, Chicago, IL 60601
Phone: 877-793-4636
Email: scholarships@swe.org
https://swe.org/scholarships/
Purpose: To support rising college juniors and seniors with their higher education expenses.
Eligibility: Applicants must be African American U.S. citizens or permanent residents. Students must be currently classified as college sophomores or juniors and plan to be enrolled as full-time college juniors or seniors at any UNCF member institution or other accredited HBCU with a minimum 2.5 GPA. Applicants must complete the FAFSA and demonstrate unmet financial need.
Target applicant(s): College students. Adult students.
Minimum GPA: 2.5
Amount: $4,400.
Number of awards: 10.
Deadline: June 11.
How to apply: Applications are available online.
Exclusive: Visit www.UltimateScholarshipBook.com and enter code SO220426 for updates on this award.

[2205] • Minority Scholarship

National Strength and Conditioning Association (NSCA) Foundation
1885 Bob Johnson Drive, Colorado Springs, CO 80906
Phone: 800-815-6826
Email: Foundation@nsca.com
http://www.nsca.com/foundation/

Purpose: To encourage minorities to enter the field of strength and conditioning.
Eligibility: Applicants must be African American, Hispanic, Asian American or Native American students working toward a graduate degree related to strength and conditioning. Students must be NSCA members for one year before applying and be pursuing careers in strength and conditioning. Applications are evaluated based on grades, courses, experience, honors, recommendations and involvement in the community and with NSCA.
Target applicant(s): High school students. College students. Graduate school students. Adult students.
Amount: $2,000.
Number of awards: Varies.
Deadline: October 15.
How to apply: Applications are available with membership.
Exclusive: Visit www.UltimateScholarshipBook.com and enter code NA220526 for updates on this award.

[2206] • Minority Scholarship Award for Physical Therapy Students

American Physical Therapy Association
1111 North Fairfax Street, Alexandria, VA 22314
Phone: 703-684-2782
Email: honorsandawards@apta.org
https://www.apta.org/for-students/scholarships-awards
Purpose: To aid minority physical therapy students.
Eligibility: Applicants must be U.S. citizens or legal permanent residents. They must be African-American, Hispanic, Native American, Pacific Islander, Native Hawaiian or Alaska Native. They must be in the final year of an accredited or developing professional physical therapist program at the time of award disbursement. Students must demonstrate academic excellence, service to minority affairs and career potential. Selection is based on the overall strength of the application.
Target applicant(s): Graduate school students. Adult students.
Amount: $2,500.
Number of awards: Varies.
Deadline: December 1.
How to apply: Applications are available online. An application form, official transcript, personal essay and three letters of reference are required.
Exclusive: Visit www.UltimateScholarshipBook.com and enter code AM220626 for updates on this award.

[2207] • Minority Scholarship Awards for College Students

American Institute of Chemical Engineers - (AIChE)
120 Wall Street, Floor 23, New York, NY 10005-4020
Phone: 800-242-4363
Email: awards@aiche.org
https://www.aiche.org/community/awards
Purpose: To aid minority students who are majoring in chemical engineering.
Eligibility: Applicants must be members of a minority group that is underrepresented in the field of chemical engineering (African-American, Latino, Native American, Alaska Native or Pacific Islander). They must be student members of the American Institute of Chemical Engineers (AIChE) and must be undergraduates who are majoring in chemical engineering. Selection is based on academic merit, stated career goals, AIChE participation and financial need.
Target applicant(s): College students. Adult students.
Amount: $1,000.
Number of awards: Varies.
Deadline: May 15.
How to apply: Applications are available online. An application form and supporting materials are required.
Exclusive: Visit www.UltimateScholarshipBook.com and enter code AM220726 for updates on this award.

[2208] • Minority Scholarship Awards for Incoming College Freshmen

American Institute of Chemical Engineers - (AIChE)
120 Wall Street, Floor 23, New York, NY 10005-4020
Phone: 800-242-4363
Email: awards@aiche.org
https://www.aiche.org/community/awards
Purpose: To offer financial aid to minority students in chemical engineering.
Eligibility: Applicants must be members of a minority group (i.e. African American, Hispanic, Native American or Alaskan Native) that is underrepresented in chemical engineering. Applicants must also be high school graduates during the academic year of application and plan to enroll in a four-year college or university. Applicants are encouraged to major in science or engineering. Selection is also based on academic record, reason for choosing science or engineering, work or activities and financial need.
Target applicant(s): High school students.
Amount: $1,000.
Number of awards: 10.
Deadline: May 15.
How to apply: Applications are available online or by telephone or written request.
Exclusive: Visit www.UltimateScholarshipBook.com and enter code AM220826 for updates on this award.

[2209] • Minority Serving Institution Grants

Council on International Educational Exchange (CIEE)
600 Southborough Drive, Suite 104, South Portland, Portland, ME 04106
Phone: 207-553-4000
Email: contact@ciee.org
http://www.ciee.org
Purpose: To aid underrepresented students who wish to study abroad.
Eligibility: Applicants must be CIEE Study Center participants. They must be students who are self-identified as being from a group that is underrepresented in study abroad programs. Selection is based on the overall strength of the application.
Target applicant(s): College students. Adult students.
Amount: Up to $2,000.
Number of awards: Varies.
Deadline: April 1.
How to apply: Applications are available online. An application form, financial aid information and an essay are required.
Exclusive: Visit www.UltimateScholarshipBook.com and enter code CO220926 for updates on this award.

[2210] • Molitoris Leadership Scholarship for Undergraduates

Women's Transportation Seminar (WTS) International
1701 K Street NW, Suite 800, Washington, DC 20006
Phone: 202-955-5085
Email: membership@wtsinternational.org
https://www.wtsinternational.org/mission/wts-foundation/scholarships

Purpose: To aid female undergraduates who are pursuing transportation-related degrees.
Eligibility: Applicants must be currently enrolled in a transportation-related degree program, have a GPA of 3.0 or higher and have plans to pursue a career in the field of transportation. Selection is based on academic merit, proven leadership in transportation-related activities and stated career goals.
Target applicant(s): College students. Adult students.
Minimum GPA: 3.0
Amount: $5,000.
Number of awards: 1.
Deadline: March 10.
How to apply: Applications are available from local WTS chapters by request. An application form and supporting materials are required.
Exclusive: Visit www.UltimateScholarshipBook.com and enter code WO221026 for updates on this award.

[2211] • Morris K. Udall Scholarship
Morris K. Udall Foundation
434 E. University Boulevard, Suite 300, Tucson, AZ 85705
Phone: 520-901-8500
Email: info@udall.gov
http://www.udall.gov
Purpose: To aid students committed to careers related to the environment, tribal public policy or Native American health care.
Eligibility: Students must be juniors or sophomores studying full-time for an associate's or bachelor's degree at an accredited two- or four-year institution. They must be U.S. citizens, nationals or permanent residents and be committed to a career related to the environment, tribal public policy or Native American health care. Students must be nominated by a college or university faculty representative and must have a grade point average equivalent to a "B" or higher. Selection is based on demonstrated commitment to the environment, tribal public policy or Native American healthcare. Selection is also based on the potential of the applicant to make significant contributions, leadership, character, desire to make a difference and demonstration of diverse interests and activities.
Target applicant(s): College students. Adult students.
Minimum GPA: 3.0
Amount: Up to $7,000.
Number of awards: 55.
Scholarship may be renewable.
Deadline: March 6.
How to apply: Applications are available online. An application form, essay, college transcript(s) and three recommendation letters are required.
Exclusive: Visit www.UltimateScholarshipBook.com and enter code MO221126 for updates on this award.

[2212] • Mutual of Omaha Actuarial Scholarship for Minority Students
Mutual of Omaha
Mutual of Omaha Plaza, Strategic Staffing - Actuarial Recruitment, Omaha, NE 68175
Phone: 402-351-3300
https://www.mutualofomaha.com/careers/
Purpose: To support undergraduate students who are preparing for actuarial careers.
Eligibility: Applicants must be African-American, Native American, Hispanic, Asian American or from another underrepresented minority group. They must be U.S. citizens, permanent residents, temporary residents, asylees or refugees and must be full-time undergraduate students who have completed 24 or more credit hours (including 18 or more graded hours). They must be pursuing a degree in mathematics or an actuarial-related subject and must have a GPA of 3.4 or more. Applicants must have plans to pursue a career in an actuarial field and must have passed at least one actuarial exam. Scholarship recipients must be willing to complete a summer internship at the Mutual of Omaha offices in Omaha. Selection is based on the overall strength of the application.
Target applicant(s): High school students. College students. Adult students.
Minimum GPA: 3.4
Amount: $5,000.
Number of awards: Varies.
Scholarship may be renewable.
Deadline: October 20.
How to apply: Applications are available online. An application form, personal statement, one recommendation letter and a resume are required.
Exclusive: Visit www.UltimateScholarshipBook.com and enter code MU221226 for updates on this award.

[2213] • NAHN Scholarship
National Association of Hispanic Nurses
1500 Sunday Drive, Suite 102, Raleigh, NC 27607
Phone: 919-573-5443
Email: info@thehispanicnurses.org
https://www.nahnnet.org
Purpose: To aid Hispanic nursing students who demonstrate the potential to make contributions to the nursing profession and who will act as positive role models for other nursing students.
Eligibility: Applicants must be members of the NAHN and be enrolled in a diploma, associate, baccalaureate, graduate or practical/vocational nursing program.
Target applicant(s): College students. Graduate school students. Adult students.
Minimum GPA: 3.0
Amount: Varies.
Number of awards: Varies.
Deadline: March 26.
How to apply: Applications are available online or by mail.
Exclusive: Visit www.UltimateScholarshipBook.com and enter code NA221326 for updates on this award.

[2214] • National and Chapter Scholarships
American Hellenic Education Progressive Association
1909 Q Street NW, Suite 500, Washington, DC 20009
Phone: 202-232-6300
Email: admin@ahepa.org
https://ahepa.org/education/
Purpose: To support projects furthering the goals of AHEPA: studies concerning Hellenism, Hellenic culture or Greek-American life.
Eligibility: Applicants must be high school seniors, college students, post-graduate students or adult students of Greek descent.
Target applicant(s): Graduate school students. Adult students.
Amount: Up to $2,000.
Number of awards: Varies.
Scholarship may be renewable.
Deadline: June 16.
How to apply: Applications are available online.
Exclusive: Visit www.UltimateScholarshipBook.com and enter code AM221426 for updates on this award.

[2215] • National Association of Black Accountants National Scholarship Program

National Association of Black Accountants
6406 Ivy Lane, Suite 200B, Greenbelt, MD 20770
Phone: 301-474-NABA
Email: memberservices@nabainc.org
https://www.nabainc.org/scholarship
Purpose: To support African Americans and other minorities in the accounting and finance professions.
Eligibility: Applicants must be ethnic minorities currently enrolled as full-time undergraduates in accounting, finance or business or as graduate students in a Master's of Accountancy program. Applicants must also be NABA members and have a minimum 3.5 major GPA and 3.3 cumulative GPA.
Target applicant(s): College students. Graduate school students. Adult students.
Minimum GPA: 3.3
Amount: $1,000-$10,000.
Number of awards: 150.
Deadline: February 15.
How to apply: Applications are available online.
Exclusive: Visit www.UltimateScholarshipBook.com and enter code NA221526 for updates on this award.

[2216] • National Foster Parent Association (NFPA) Youth Scholarship

National Foster Parent Association (NFPA)
14508 Owen-Tech Boulevard, Suite 129, Austin, TX 78728
Phone: 800-557-5238
Email: scholarships@nfpaonline.org
https://nfpaonline.org
Purpose: To support foster youth.
Eligibility: Applicants must be foster children, adopted children or biological children of currently licensed foster parents who are high school seniors planning to attend a college or university.
Target applicant(s): High school students.
Amount: $500.
Number of awards: Up to 6.
Deadline: April 1.
How to apply: Applications are available online.
Exclusive: Visit www.UltimateScholarshipBook.com and enter code NA221626 for updates on this award.

[2217] • National Gymnastics Foundation Men's Scholarship

USA Gymnastics
Men's Scholarship Program, 132 E. Washington Street, Suite 700, Indianapolis, IN 46204
Phone: 317-237-5050
Email: dmcintyre@usagym.org
https://usagym.org/men/scholarships/
Purpose: To support competitive USA Gymnastics athlete members by helping to fund college or post-secondary education.
Eligibility: Applicants must be USA Gymnastics members and pursuing college or post-secondary education.
Target applicant(s): High school students. College students. Adult students.
Amount: Varies.
Number of awards: Varies.
Deadline: May 15.
How to apply: Applications are available online.
Exclusive: Visit www.UltimateScholarshipBook.com and enter code US221726 for updates on this award.

[2218] • National Hispanic Health Professional Student Scholarship

National Hispanic Health Foundation
The New York Academy of Medicine, 1216 Fifth Avenue, Room 457, New York, NY 10029
Phone: 212-419-3686
Email: nhhf@nhmafoundation.org
http://www.nhmafoundation.org
Purpose: To support Hispanic students who are planning to pursue careers in health care.
Eligibility: Applicants must be students who are fully enrolled in a postsecondary degree program in medical (allopathic or osteopathic), dentistry, pharmacy, PA, public health or health policy or nursing. Undergraduate BSN students are also eligible to apply. Selection is based on academic achievement, leadership skills and commitment to improving health care in the Hispanic community.
Target applicant(s): Graduate school students. Adult students.
Amount: $5,000.
Number of awards: 15-20.
Deadline: September 15.
How to apply: Applications are available online. An application form and supporting materials are required.
Exclusive: Visit www.UltimateScholarshipBook.com and enter code NA221826 for updates on this award.

[2219] • National Italian American Foundation Scholarship

National Italian American Foundation
1860 19th Street NW, Washington, DC 20009
Phone: 202-387-0600
Email: scholarships@niaf.org
https://www.niaf.org/programs/scholarships/
Purpose: To support Italian American students.
Eligibility: Applicants must be Italian American students who demonstrate outstanding academic achievement and must either be a member or child of a member. Applicants must also plan to be or currently be enrolled in an accredited institution of higher education, have a minimum 3.5 GPA and be U.S. citizens or permanent residents.
Target applicant(s): High school students. College students. Adult students.
Minimum GPA: 3.5
Amount: $2,500-$12,000.
Number of awards: Varies.
Deadline: March 1.
How to apply: Applications are available online.
Exclusive: Visit www.UltimateScholarshipBook.com and enter code NA221926 for updates on this award.

[2220] • National Scholarship

National Association of Negro Business and Professional Women's Clubs Inc.
1806 New Hampshire Avenue NW, Washington, DC 20009
Phone: 202-483-4206
Email: education@nanbpwc.org
http://www.nanbpwc.org

Purpose: To award scholarships to aspiring business and professional college or university students.
Eligibility: Applicants must be African American graduating high school seniors and have a minimum 3.0 GPA. Students must submit a transcript, an application form, two letters of recommendation and an essay that is at least 300 words on "Why is education important to me?"
Target applicant(s): High school students.
Minimum GPA: 3.0
Amount: Varies.
Number of awards: Varies.
Deadline: March 29.
How to apply: Applications are available online.
Exclusive: Visit www.UltimateScholarshipBook.com and enter code NA222026 for updates on this award.

[2221] • Native American Education Grant
Presbyterian Church (USA)
100 Witherspoon Street, Louisville, KY 40202
Phone: 800-728-7228
Email: finaid@pcusa.org
https://www.presbyterianmission.org/grants/
Purpose: To aid Alaska Natives and Native Americans pursuing full-time post-secondary education.
Eligibility: Applicants must be U.S. citizens who are high school graduates or G.E.D. recipients and demonstrate financial need and must have a minimum 2.5 GPA. Applicants must present proof of tribal membership, and preference will be given to active members of the Presbyterian Church. Students are selected based on the availability of funds and best match to donor restrictions. The deadline for students applying to renew the grant is May 1. Awards for new students will be offered on a funds available basis after May 1.
Target applicant(s): College students. Adult students.
Minimum GPA: 2.5
Amount: Up to $1,500.
Number of awards: Varies.
Scholarship may be renewable.
Deadline: May 15.
How to apply: Applications are available online.
Exclusive: Visit www.UltimateScholarshipBook.com and enter code PR222126 for updates on this award.

[2222] • Native American Scholarship
International Order of the King's Daughters and Sons
P.O. Box 1040, 34 Vincent Avenue, Chautauqua, NY 14722
Phone: 716-357-4951
Email: Native-American-director@iokds.org
https://iokds.org/
Purpose: To support Native American students with their post-secondary education.
Eligibility: Applicants must be Native Americans enrolled or planning to enroll at a technical school, vocational school, college or university for undergraduate studies. Students must provide a tribal registration number.
Target applicant(s): High school students. College students. Adult students.
Amount: $1,000.
Number of awards: 1.
Deadline: March 1.
How to apply: Applications are available online.
Exclusive: Visit www.UltimateScholarshipBook.com and enter code IN222226 for updates on this award.

[2223] • NativeVision Scholarships
NativeVision
Johns Hopkins Center for American Indian Health, 415 North Washington Street, 4th Floor, Baltimore, MD Baltimore
Phone: 410-955-6931
Email: mhammen@jhu.edu
http://www.nativevision.org/Scholarship_Recipients/Scholarship_Recipients.html
Purpose: To support Native American students with their educational expenses.
Eligibility: Applicants must be Native American students entering their first year of college and have a minimum 3.0 GPA.
Target applicant(s): High school students.
Minimum GPA: 3.0
Amount: $5,000.
Number of awards: 4.
Deadline: May 19.
How to apply: Applications are available online.
Exclusive: Visit www.UltimateScholarshipBook.com and enter code NA222326 for updates on this award.

[2224] • NCTA and AWMF Scholarship
Alliance for Women in Media
2365 Harrodsburg Road, Suite A325, Lexington, KY 40504
Phone: 202-750-3664
Email: info@allwomeninmedia.org
https://allwomeninmedia.org/foundation/scholarships/
Purpose: To support female undergraduate and graduate students studying media, journalism, English, communications and related fields.
Eligibility: Applicants must be attending an accredited college or university in the United States in the fall of application year. Students must submit a 750- to 1,000-word essay on a suggested topic.
Target applicant(s): College students. Graduate school students. Adult students.
Amount: $10,000.
Number of awards: 1.
Deadline: May 1.
How to apply: Applications are available online.
Exclusive: Visit www.UltimateScholarshipBook.com and enter code AL222426 for updates on this award.

[2225] • NCWIT Award for Aspirations in Computing
National Center for Women and Information Technology (NCWIT)
University of Colorado, Campus Box 322 UCB, Boulder, CO 80309
Phone: 303-735-6671
Email: aspirations@ncwit.org
http://www.ncwit.org
Purpose: To recognize young women who are interested in technology-related pursuits.
Eligibility: Applicants must be U.S. residents and be female high school students. They must be interested in technology-related subjects. Selection is based on aptitude for computing and internet technology, leadership skills, academic merit and educational goals.
Target applicant(s): High school students.
Amount: Varies.
Number of awards: Varies.
Deadline: November 8.
How to apply: Applications are available online. An application form and supporting materials are required.

Exclusive: Visit www.UltimateScholarshipBook.com and enter code NA222526 for updates on this award.

[2226] • New York Ramblers Scholarship
New York Ramblers Soccer Club
2 Gold Street, Apartment 21C, New York, NY 10038
Email: committee@nyramblers.com
https://nyramblers.com/scholarship/
Purpose: To support undergraduate student athletes of all sports who are members or allies of the LGBTQIA2S+ community.
Eligibility: Applicants must be open and self-identified lesbian, gay, bisexual, transgender, queer or intersex persons or a demonstrated and committed ally to the community. Students must be between the ages of 15 and 21 years of age and athletes in any sport or athletic activity. Applicants must be graduating high school students who plan to attend a recognized undergraduate college or university in the United States or are already matriculated U.S. undergraduate college students.
Target applicant(s): High school students. College students.
Amount: $2,500.
Number of awards: 2.
Deadline: May 1.
How to apply: Applications are available online.
Exclusive: Visit www.UltimateScholarshipBook.com and enter code NE222626 for updates on this award.

[2227] • NOAA Educational Partnership Program Undergraduate Scholarships
NOAA Educational Partnership Program - Office of Education
Herbert C Hoover Building, 14th Street and Constitution Avenue NW, Room 6863, Washington, DC 20230
Phone: 202-482-3384
Email: epp.usp@noaa.gov
https://www.noaa.gov/office-education
Purpose: To aid undergraduates who are attending a minority-serving institution and are pursuing undergraduate degrees in subjects related to the atmospheric, oceanic or environmental sciences.
Eligibility: Applicants must be U.S. citizens and full-time undergraduates who are in the second year of a four-year degree program or in the third year of a five-year degree program. They must be attending an accredited minority-serving institution (MSI), and they must have a GPA of 3.2 or higher on a four-point scale. Applicants must be majoring in a discipline that is related to environmental, atmospheric or oceanic sciences. Selection is based on relevant coursework completed, stated career goals, recommendations and extracurricular activities.
Target applicant(s): College students. Adult students.
Minimum GPA: 3.2
Amount: Up to $45,000.
Number of awards: Varies.
Scholarship may be renewable.
Deadline: January 31.
How to apply: Applications are available online. An application form, two personal essays, two recommendation letters and an official transcript are required.
Exclusive: Visit www.UltimateScholarshipBook.com and enter code NO222726 for updates on this award.

[2228] • OCA/UPS Gold Mountain Scholarship
OCA (formerly Organization of Chinese Americans)
900 19th Street NW, 6th Floor, Washington, DC 20036
Phone: 202-223-5500
Email: kent.tong@ocanational.org.
https://www.ocanational.org/scholarships
Purpose: To support first generation Asian American students.
Eligibility: Applicants must be Asian Pacific Americans who intend to begin college in the fall of the year of application and must demonstrate significant financial need. Applicants must also be the first in their family to attend college and have a minimum 3.0 GPA.
Target applicant(s): High school students.
Minimum GPA: 3.0
Amount: $2,000.
Number of awards: 15.
Deadline: April 21.
How to apply: Applications are available online or by written request.
Exclusive: Visit www.UltimateScholarshipBook.com and enter code OC222826 for updates on this award.

[2229] • Olay Face the Stem Gap Scholarship
Olay Face the Stem
Phone: 800-285-5170
https://www.olay.com/commitments
Purpose: To support female students interested in STEM related degrees.
Eligibility: Applicants must be female women of color who are U.S. citizens or legal residents. Students must be enrolled as full-time undergraduate sophomores at any U.S. located, accredited, four-year college or university and have a minimum 3.0 GPA. Applicants must be pursuing a degree program related to science, technology, engineering or math.
Target applicant(s): College students. Adult students.
Minimum GPA: 3.0
Amount: $2,500.
Number of awards: Varies.
Scholarship may be renewable.
Deadline: June 29.
How to apply: Applications are available online.
Exclusive: Visit www.UltimateScholarshipBook.com and enter code OL222926 for updates on this award.

[2230] • Olive Lynn Salembier Memorial Reentry Scholarship
Society of Women Engineers
130 East Randolph Street, Suite 3500, Chicago, IL 60601
Phone: 877-793-4636
Email: scholarships@swe.org
https://swe.org/scholarships/
Purpose: To aid female engineering students.
Eligibility: Applicants must be females who have been out of the engineering workforce and out of school for a minimum of two years prior to reentry. Applicants must have a GPA of 3.0 or higher on a four-point scale except for first year reentry. Selection is based on the overall strength of the application.
Target applicant(s): High school students. College students. Graduate school students. Adult students.
Minimum GPA: 3.0
Amount: $2,000.
Number of awards: 1.
Deadline: March 31.

How to apply: Applications are available online. An application form and supporting materials are required.
Exclusive: Visit www.UltimateScholarshipBook.com and enter code SO223026 for updates on this award.

[2231] • P.E.O. International Peace Scholarship
P.E.O. International
3700 Grand Avenue, Des Moines, IA 50312
Phone: 515-255-3153
http://www.peointernational.org
Purpose: To assist women from countries other than the U.S. or Canada in their graduate studies within North America.
Eligibility: Applicants must be female, attend a North American graduate school or Cottey College and be from a country other than the U.S. or Canada. Eligibility must be established by submitting an eligibility form between August 15 and December 15.
Target applicant(s): College students. Graduate school students. Adult students.
Amount: Up to $12,500.
Number of awards: Varies.
Scholarship may be renewable.
Deadline: February 1.
How to apply: Applicants must first submit an eligibility form, available online. If found eligible, students will be mailed application materials.
Exclusive: Visit www.UltimateScholarshipBook.com and enter code P.223126 for updates on this award.

[2232] • P.E.O. Program for Continuing Education
P.E.O. International
3700 Grand Avenue, Des Moines, IA 50312
Phone: 515-255-3153
http://www.peointernational.org
Purpose: To assist women whose education has been interrupted.
Eligibility: Applicants must be women who are resuming studies to improve their marketable skills due to changing demands in their lives. They must have financial need and cannot use the funds to pay living expenses or repay educational loans. They must be sponsored by a P.E.O. chapter and be citizens and students of the United States or Canada. They must have had at least two consecutive years as a non-student in their adult lives and be able to complete their educational goals in two consecutive years or less. Doctoral degree students are not eligible.
Target applicant(s): College students. Graduate school students. Adult students.
Amount: $3,000.
Number of awards: Varies.
Deadline: 8 weeks before the start of classes.
How to apply: Applications are available from your local P.E.O. Chapter. An application form, income and expense statement and chapter recommendation are required. See the website to locate the nearest P.E.O. Chapter.
Exclusive: Visit www.UltimateScholarshipBook.com and enter code P.223226 for updates on this award.

[2233] • P.O. Pistilli Undergraduate Scholarship for Advancement in Computer Science and Electrical Engineering
Design Automation Conference/Association for Computing Machinery
Professor Andrew B. Kahng, P.O. Pistilli Scholarship Director, Department of Computer Science and Engineering, UCSD, 9500 Gilman Drive #0404, La Jolla, CA 92093-0404
Phone: 858-822-4884
Email: abk@cs.ucsd.edu
https://www.dac.com/Attend/Students-Scholarships
Purpose: To promote professions in electrical engineering, computer engineering and computer science among underrepresented groups.
Eligibility: Applicants must be high school seniors who are from an underrepresented group (African American, Hispanic, Native American, women or disabled). Students must have a minimum 3.0 GPA, have demonstrated high achievement in math and science courses and have financial need. Applicants must also intend to pursue a career in electrical engineering, computer engineering or computer science.
Target applicant(s): High school students.
Minimum GPA: 3.0
Amount: $4,000.
Number of awards: Up to 7.
Scholarship may be renewable.
Deadline: May 1.
How to apply: Applications are available online. An application form, three letters of recommendation, an official transcript, a personal letter, a copy of tax returns and a copy of the FAFSA are required.
Exclusive: Visit www.UltimateScholarshipBook.com and enter code DE223326 for updates on this award.

[2234] • Paumanauke Native American Indian Scholarship
Paumanauke Native American Festival Inc.
2005 Merrick Road, Suite 221, Attn.: Tony Moon Hawk Langhorn, Merrick, NY 11566
Email: info@paumanauke.org
http://www.paumanauke.org
Purpose: To encourage Native American Indians to finish their college educations.
Eligibility: Applicants must be members of a Native American Indian tribe who are enrolled full-time at a college, university or other accredited post-secondary institution. Selection is based on the overall strength of the application.
Target applicant(s): College students. Graduate school students. Adult students.
Amount: $500-$750.
Number of awards: 6.
Deadline: June 1.
How to apply: Applications are available online.
Exclusive: Visit www.UltimateScholarshipBook.com and enter code PA223426 for updates on this award.

[2235] • Pega Scholars Program
Pega Scholars Program
Scholarship America, One Scholarship Way, Saint Peter, MN 56082
Phone: 507-931-1682
Email: pegascholars@scholarshipamerica.org
https://learnmore.scholarsapply.org/pegascholars
Purpose: To support future technologists from diverse communities around the globe.
Eligibility: Applicants must be current high school or secondary school graduates or current university students pursuing a degree in computer science, technology or a related field. Students must plan to enroll in part-time or full-time undergraduate study at a two-, three- or four-year accredited institution. Applicants must reside in one of the following countries: USA, Canada, Brazil, United Kingdom, The Netherlands, India or Australia. Students must self-identify with one or more of the

following: women; LGBTQIA+; person with disability; military veteran; Indigenous; Native American or Alaskan Native; Asian American; Black; African American; Hispanic or Latino/Latina; Native Hawaiian or other Pacific Islander.
Target applicant(s): High school students. College students. Adult students.
Amount: $1,500.
Number of awards: 10.
Deadline: June 20.
How to apply: Applications are available online.
Exclusive: Visit www.UltimateScholarshipBook.com and enter code PE223526 for updates on this award.

[2236] • Performing Arts Scholarship

Armenian General Benevolent Union (AGBU)
55 East 59th Street, 7th Floor, New York, NY 10022-1112
Phone: 212-319-6383
Email: scholarship@agbu.org
http://www.agbu.org
Purpose: To support students of Armenian descent who demonstrate exceptional artistic accomplishment.
Eligibility: Applicants must be full-time undergraduate and graduate students of Armenian descent worldwide who are pursuing studies in the field of performing arts and enrolled in highly selective colleges and universities. Students must have a minimum 3.5 GPA and submit examples of their artistic experience in the form of audio/visual recordings.
Target applicant(s): College students. Graduate school students. Adult students.
Minimum GPA: 3.5
Amount: $1,000-$5,000.
Number of awards: Varies.
Deadline: June 1.
How to apply: Applications are available online.
Exclusive: Visit www.UltimateScholarshipBook.com and enter code AR223626 for updates on this award.

[2237] • Phyllis G. Meekins Scholarship

Ladies Professional Golf Association
100 International Golf Drive, Daytona Beach, FL 32124-1092
Phone: 386-274-6200
Email: info@lpgafoundation.org
http://www.lpga.com/lpga-foundation/scholarships
Purpose: To support a female high school senior golf participant of a recognized minority background in pursuit of a college education.
Eligibility: Applicants must have a minimum 3.0 GPA and be U.S. citizens or legal residents. Students must also have been accepted to a college or university and plan to play competitive golf at the collegiate level. Selection is based on financial need.
Target applicant(s): High school students.
Minimum GPA: 3.0
Amount: $5,000.
Number of awards: 2.
Deadline: January 31.
How to apply: Applications are available online.
Exclusive: Visit www.UltimateScholarshipBook.com and enter code LA223726 for updates on this award.

[2238] • Point Community College Scholarship

Point Foundation
P.O. Box 60108, Los Angeles, CA 90060
Phone: 833-887-6462
Email: info@pointfoundation.org
http://www.pointfoundation.org
Purpose: To support LGBTQ students attending a community college.
Eligibility: Applicants must be LGBTQ, be enrolled or intending to enroll in an accredited community college in the U.S. and intend to transfer to a bachelor's degree program. Students are assessed on academic performance, leadership skills, financial need, personal goals and the applicant's involvement in the LGBTQ community. Consideration is also given to students who have lost the social support of their families and/or communities as a result of revealing their sexual orientation, gender identity or gender expression.
Target applicant(s): High school students. College students. Adult students.
Amount: $4,800 per year.
Number of awards: 34.
Deadline: February 22.
How to apply: Applications are available online.
Exclusive: Visit www.UltimateScholarshipBook.com and enter code PO223826 for updates on this award.

[2239] • Point Flagship Scholarship

Point Foundation
P.O. Box 60108, Los Angeles, CA 90060
Phone: 833-887-6462
Email: info@pointfoundation.org
http://www.pointfoundation.org
Purpose: To support LGBTQ students pursuing an undergraduate or graduate degree.
Eligibility: Applicants must be LGBTQ and be at least seniors in high school and enrolled or intending to enroll in an accredited college or university in the U.S. Students are assessed on academic performance, leadership skills, financial need, personal goals and the applicant's involvement in the LGBTQ community. Consideration is also given to students who have lost the social support of their families and/or communities as a result of revealing their sexual orientation, gender identity or gender expression. Point Scholarships are awarded on a last provider basis, meaning that Point fills in the gaps and provides funds not provided by other scholarships, grants, loans, work/study programs, etc. It is the responsibility of those selected as Point Scholars to annually secure as much other funding as possible.
Target applicant(s): High school students. College students. Adult students.
Amount: $3,000.
Number of awards: 1.
Scholarship may be renewable.
Deadline: December 5.
How to apply: Applications are available online.
Exclusive: Visit www.UltimateScholarshipBook.com and enter code PO223926 for updates on this award.

[2240] • Polish National Alliance Scholarship

Polish National Alliance
Educational Department, 6100 Cicero Avenue, Chicago, IL 60646
Phone: 800-621-3723
Email: pna@pna-znp.org
http://www.pna-znp.org

Purpose: To assist members of the Polish National Alliance with their undergraduate studies.
Eligibility: Applicants must be college sophomores, juniors or seniors and have been paying members in good standing with the Polish National Association for at least three years and must have a minimum 3.0 GPA. If the applicant has been in good standing with the PNA for at least two years, his or her parents must have been paying PNA members for at least five years. Applicants must have a minimum $10,000 permanent insurance plan at the PNA.
Target applicant(s): College students. Adult students.
Minimum GPA: 3.0
Amount: Varies.
Number of awards: Varies.
Scholarship may be renewable.
Deadline: April 15.
How to apply: Applications are available by email at mary.srodon@pna-znp.org.
Exclusive: Visit www.UltimateScholarshipBook.com and enter code PO224026 for updates on this award.

[2241] • PRSA Diversity Multicultural Scholarship
Public Relations Student Society of America
120 Wall Street, 21st Floor, New York, NY 10005-4024
Phone: 212-460-1474
Email: prssa@prsa.org
https://prssa.prsa.org/scholarships-and-awards/
Purpose: To aid minority communications students.
Eligibility: Applicants must be of African-American, Latino, Asian, Native American, Alaska Native or Pacific Islander descent. They must be undergraduate students who are majoring or minoring in public relations at an accredited four-year institution. They must be full-time students who have a GPA of 3.0 or higher on a four-point scale. Selection is based on the overall strength of the application.
Target applicant(s): College students. Adult students.
Minimum GPA: 3.0
Amount: $1,500.
Number of awards: 2.
Deadline: April 30.
How to apply: Applications are available online. An application form, official transcript, essay and one recommendation letter are required.
Exclusive: Visit www.UltimateScholarshipBook.com and enter code PU224126 for updates on this award.

[2242] • Religious Studies Scholarship
Armenian General Benevolent Union (AGBU)
55 East 59th Street, 7th Floor, New York, NY 10022-1112
Phone: 212-319-6383
Email: scholarship@agbu.org
http://www.agbu.org
Purpose: To support graduate students of Armenian descent who are pursuing religious studies.
Eligibility: Applicants must be graduate students of Armenian descent worldwide who are pursuing religious studies. Students must be enrolled in full-time degree programs at seminaries or highly selective colleges or universities with a minimum 3.0 GPA.
Target applicant(s): Graduate school students. Adult students.
Minimum GPA: 3.0
Amount: Up to $5,000.
Number of awards: Varies.
Deadline: June 1.
How to apply: Applications are available online.

Exclusive: Visit www.UltimateScholarshipBook.com and enter code AR224226 for updates on this award.

[2243] • Richard R. Tufenkian Memorial Scholarship
Armenian Educational Foundation Inc.
600 W. Broadway, Suite 130, Glendale, CA 91204
Phone: 818-242-4154
Email: aef@aefweb.org
http://www.aefweb.org
Purpose: To support Armenian undergraduate students.
Eligibility: Applicants must be full-time undergraduate students of Armenian descent at U.S. universities, have a minimum 3.0 GPA, demonstrate financial need and be involved in the Armenian community. Tax returns, transcripts, two reference letters, essays and applications are required.
Target applicant(s): High school students. College students. Adult students.
Minimum GPA: 3.0
Amount: $3,000.
Number of awards: 3.
Deadline: April 30.
How to apply: Applications are available online.
Exclusive: Visit www.UltimateScholarshipBook.com and enter code AR224326 for updates on this award.

[2244] • Ron Brown Scholar Program
CAP Charitable Foundation
Ron Brown Scholar Program, 1160 Pepsi Place, Suite 206, Charlottesville, VA 22901
Phone: 434-964-1588
Email: franh@ronbrown.org
http://www.ronbrown.org
Purpose: To award scholarships to academically talented, highly motivated African American high school seniors.
Eligibility: Applicants must be African American collegebound high school seniors. Selection is based on academic promise, leadership, communication skills, school and community involvement and financial need.
Target applicant(s): High school students.
Amount: Up to $40,000.
Number of awards: 20-25.
Scholarship may be renewable.
Deadline: December 1.
How to apply: Applications are available online.
Exclusive: Visit www.UltimateScholarshipBook.com and enter code CA224426 for updates on this award.

[2245] • Ruth D. Peterson Fellowship for Racial and Ethnic Diversity
American Society of Criminology
1314 Kinnear Road, Suite 212, Columbus, OH 43212-1156
Email: ronet@udel.edu
https://www.asc41.com
Purpose: To encourage minorities to study criminology or criminal justice.
Eligibility: Applicants must be African American, Asian American, Latino or Native American. Recipients must have been accepted into a doctoral studies program. Selection is based on curriculum vitae, college transcripts,

financial need, references and letter describing career plans, experiences and interest in criminology.
Target applicant(s): Graduate school students. Adult students.
Amount: $8,000.
Number of awards: Up to 3.
Deadline: Contact the sponsor to confirm the deadline.
How to apply: Applications are available by written request.
Exclusive: Visit www.UltimateScholarshipBook.com and enter code AM224526 for updates on this award.

[2246] • Sahara Hope Scholarship For Women Empowered To Change The World

Cosmoforge
Phone: 916-619-0209
Email: launch@cosmoforge.io
https://cosmoforge.io/sahara-hope-scholarship-for-women-empowered-to-change-the-world/
Purpose: To support female students inspiring to change the world.
Eligibility: Applicants must be female students currently enrolled in an undergraduate or graduate degree program at an accredited university. Students must have a minimum GPA of 3.0 and reside in the United States.
Target applicant(s): College students. Graduate school students. Adult students.
Minimum GPA: 3.0
Amount: $500-$1,000.
Number of awards: 2.
Deadline: November 15.
How to apply: Applications are available online.
Exclusive: Visit www.UltimateScholarshipBook.com and enter code CO224626 for updates on this award.

[2247] • Sharon D. Banks Memorial Undergraduate Scholarship

Women's Transportation Seminar (WTS) International
1701 K Street NW, Suite 800, Washington, DC 20006
Phone: 202-955-5085
Email: membership@wtsinternational.org
https://www.wtsinternational.org/mission/wts-foundation/scholarships
Purpose: To help women pursuing transportation careers with their higher education expenses.
Eligibility: Applicants must be women enrolled in undergraduate programs related to transportation studies. Selection is based on the applicant's academic record, transportation-related activities, job skills and specific transportation goals.
Target applicant(s): College students. Adult students.
Amount: $4,000.
Number of awards: 1.
Deadline: Varies based on local chapter deadlines.
How to apply: Applications are available through a local chapter.
Exclusive: Visit www.UltimateScholarshipBook.com and enter code WO224726 for updates on this award.

[2248] • SHPE Scholarship Program

Society of Hispanic Professional Engineers
13181 Crossroads Parkway North, Suite 220, City of Industry, CA 91746
Phone: 323-725-3970
Email: scholarships@shpe.org
https://shpe.org/engage/programs/scholarshpe/
Purpose: To aid Hispanic students who are majoring in STEM related fields.
Eligibility: Applicants must be members of the Society of Hispanic Professional Engineers (SHPE). They must be graduating high school seniors, current undergraduates or entering graduate students who are pursuing degrees in STEM related fields. They must have a GPA of 2.75 or higher. Selection is based on the overall strength of the application.
Target applicant(s): High school students. College students. Graduate school students. Adult students.
Minimum GPA: 2.75
Amount: Varies.
Number of awards: Varies.
Deadline: April 14.
How to apply: Applications are available online. An application form, official transcript, resume, personal statement and two recommendation letters are required.
Exclusive: Visit www.UltimateScholarshipBook.com and enter code SO224826 for updates on this award.

[2249] • SpeakOUT's LGBTQ+ Scholarship

SpeakOUT
P.O. Box 301223, Boston, MA 02130
Phone: 877-223-9390
Email: info@speakoutboston.org
https://www.speakoutboston.org
Purpose: To support LGBTQ+ students in pursuit of post-secondary education.
Eligibility: Applicants must be undergraduate LGBTQ+ students or high school students entering a college, university, community college or training program by the fall. Students must be residents of New England and have a minimum 3.0 GPA.
Target applicant(s): High school students. College students. Adult students.
Minimum GPA: 3.0
Amount: $500.
Number of awards: 3.
Deadline: March 31.
How to apply: Applications are available online.
Exclusive: Visit www.UltimateScholarshipBook.com and enter code SP224926 for updates on this award.

[2250] • St. Andrew's Society of Washington, DC Scholarship

St. Andrew's Society of Washington, DC
Chairman, Scholarships Committee, P.O. Box 7849, Washington, DC 20044
Email: scholarships@saintandrewsociety.org
http://www.saintandrewsociety.org/scholarships/
Purpose: To assist students of Scottish birth or descent.
Eligibility: Applicants must be of Scottish birth or descent and be able to cite their Scottish descent. U.S. citizens must be permanent residents of the District of Columbia, Delaware, Maryland, New Jersey, North Carolina, West Virginia, Pennsylvania or Virginia. Students must also demonstrate financial need and academic achievement. Attention will be given to work that enhances the "knowledge of Scottish history or culture."
Target applicant(s): College students. Graduate school students. Adult students.
Amount: Varies.
Number of awards: Varies.

Deadline: April 30.
How to apply: Applications are available online.
Exclusive: Visit www.UltimateScholarshipBook.com and enter code ST225026 for updates on this award.

[2251] • Stantec Equity and Diversity Scholarship
Stantec
International Scholarship and Tuition Services Inc. (ISTS), 1321 Murfreesboro Road, Suite 800, Nashville, TN 37217
Email: askstantec@stantec.com
https://www.stantec.com/en/about/community-engagement/scholarships/equity-diversity-scholarship
Purpose: To support the creation of a critical mass of talented students that will fully represent the STEAM fields.
Eligibility: Applicants must be enrolled in a college, university or post-secondary institution in pursuit of a bachelor's degree and pursuing a STEAM (science, technology, engineering, arts and mathematics) major. Students must be a historically underrepresented population/group such as BIPOC (Black, Indigenous, and People of Color), members of the LGBTQ2+ community, people with disabilities, veterans and first-generation college students.
Target applicant(s): High school students. College students. Adult students.
Amount: $1,500-$10,000.
Number of awards: Varies.
Deadline: October 13.
How to apply: Applications are available online.
Exclusive: Visit www.UltimateScholarshipBook.com and enter code ST225126 for updates on this award.

[2252] • STEM Scholarship
Great Minds in STEM (HENAAC)
5211 East Washington Boulevard, Suite 2-320, Los Angeles, CA 90040
Email: info@greatmindsinstem.org
http://www.greatmindsinstem.org
Purpose: To support students pursuing STEM or health related degrees.
Eligibility: Applicants must be enrolled in a STEM- or health-related undergraduate or graduate program at an accredited two- or four-year college or university in the U.S. or its territories. Students must have a minimum 2.5 GPA for non-merit-based scholarship or a minimum 3.0 GPA for merit-based scholarships. Applicants may be enrolled full-time or part-time and be pursuing a science, technology, engineering or math degree. Students must be of Hispanic descent and/or must demonstrate significant leadership or service within the underserved community. Applicants must demonstrate merit through academic achievements, leadership and campus or community activities.
Target applicant(s): High school students. College students. Graduate school students. Adult students.
Minimum GPA: 2.5
Amount: $500 to $5,000.
Number of awards: 1.
Deadline: April 30.
How to apply: Applications are available online.
Exclusive: Visit www.UltimateScholarshipBook.com and enter code GR225226 for updates on this award.

[2253] • Striving Solo Parent Scholarship
Daniel R. Bacalis P.C.
669 Airport Freeway, Suite 307, Hurst, TX 76053
Phone: 817-498-4105
Email: scholarship@dbacalis.com
https://www.dbacalis.com/scholarship
Purpose: To support students who are single parents with their pursuits of higher education.
Eligibility: Applicants must be single parents and U.S. citizens or permanent residents. Students must be enrolled in an accredited university or college within the United States with a minimum 3.0 GPA. An essay on a provided prompt is required.
Target applicant(s): High school students. College students. Graduate school students. Adult students.
Minimum GPA: 3.0
Amount: $1,000.
Number of awards: 1.
Deadline: March 14.
How to apply: Applications are available online.
Exclusive: Visit www.UltimateScholarshipBook.com and enter code DA225326 for updates on this award.

[2254] • Study.com Scholarship for Black Students
Study.com
100 View Street, Suite 202, Mountain View, CA 94041
https://study.com/resources/student-scholarships
Purpose: To support African American students.
Eligibility: Applicants must be of African descent, accepted by or enrolled in a college or university within the United States and plan on continuing the next year. Students must have a minimum of 30 semester or 45 quarter hours to complete.
Target applicant(s): High school students.
Amount: $2,000.
Number of awards: Varies.
Deadline: May 31.
How to apply: Applications are available online.
Exclusive: Visit www.UltimateScholarshipBook.com and enter code ST225426 for updates on this award.

[2255] • Study.com Scholarship for Moms
Study.com
100 View Street, Suite 202, Mountain View, CA 94041
https://study.com/resources/student-scholarships
Purpose: To support students who are mothers.
Eligibility: Applicants must be moms, accepted by or enrolled in a college or university within the United States and planning on continuing the next year. Students must have a minimum of 30 semester or 45 quarter hours to complete.
Target applicant(s): High school students. College students. Graduate school students. Adult students.
Amount: $1,000.
Number of awards: 1.
Deadline: November 1.
How to apply: Applications are available online.
Exclusive: Visit www.UltimateScholarshipBook.com and enter code ST225526 for updates on this award.

[2256] • Study.com Scholarship for Women in STEM

Study.com
100 View Street, Suite 202, Mountain View, CA 94041
https://study.com/resources/student-scholarships
Purpose: To support women in STEM.
Eligibility: Applicants must be women pursuing a degree with STEM (Science, Technology, Engineering, or Mathematics) programs with emphasis, such as biology, computer science, mechanical engineering, math, etc. Students must be enrolled (or accepted) in an accredited college or university within the United States and planning on continuing the next year.
Target applicant(s): High school students.
Amount: $2,000.
Number of awards: Varies.
Deadline: May 31.
How to apply: Applications are available online.
Exclusive: Visit www.UltimateScholarshipBook.com and enter code ST225626 for updates on this award.

[2257] • Study.com Single Parent Scholarship

Study.com
100 View Street, Suite 202, Mountain View, CA 94041
https://study.com/resources/student-scholarships
Purpose: To support single parent students.
Eligibility: Applicants must be single parents, accepted by or enrolled in a college or university within the United States and planning on continuing the next year. Students must have a minimum of 30 semester or 45 quarter hours to complete.
Target applicant(s): High school students. College students. Graduate school students. Adult students.
Amount: $1,000.
Number of awards: 1.
Deadline: November 1.
How to apply: Applications are available online.
Exclusive: Visit www.UltimateScholarshipBook.com and enter code ST225726 for updates on this award.

[2258] • Sunflower Initiative Scholarship

Sunflower Initiative
P.O. Box 378, Bedford, VA 24523
https://www.thesunflowerinitiative.com/scholarship/
Purpose: To support female students seeking post-secondary education.
Eligibility: Applicants must be female and planning to start her undergraduate education at a women's college in the following academic year. Women who have already completed a semester of college or more are not eligible. A minimum 3.7 GPA and either a SAT composite score of 1350 or an ACT composite score of 27 or higher with no single ACT score below 25 are required.
Target applicant(s): High school students.
Minimum GPA: 3.7
Amount: $10,000.
Number of awards: 1.
Deadline: February 1.
How to apply: Applications are available online.
Exclusive: Visit www.UltimateScholarshipBook.com and enter code SU225826 for updates on this award.

[2259] • SWE Past Presidents Scholarship

Society of Women Engineers
130 East Randolph Street, Suite 3500, Chicago, IL 60601
Phone: 877-793-4636
Email: scholarships@swe.org
https://swe.org/scholarships/
Purpose: To aid female engineering students.
Eligibility: Applicants must be U.S. citizens and be graduate students or undergraduate sophomores, juniors or seniors. They must be enrolled in an ABET-accredited engineering degree program and have a GPA of 3.0 or higher on a four-point scale. Selection is based on the overall strength of the application.
Target applicant(s): College students. Graduate school students. Adult students.
Minimum GPA: 3.0
Amount: $6,500.
Number of awards: 1.
Deadline: January 31.
How to apply: Applications are available online. An application form and supporting materials are required.
Exclusive: Visit www.UltimateScholarshipBook.com and enter code SO225926 for updates on this award.

[2260] • Taiwanese American Scholarship Fund

Taiwanese American Scholarship Fund
P.O. Box 60074, Pasadena, CA 91116-6074
Email: kfan@apcf.org
https://tascholarshipfund.org/
Purpose: To assist Taiwanese American students with financial need.
Eligibility: Applicants must be U.S. citizens or permanent residents and direct blood descendants of a Taiwanese citizen. Students must also be high school seniors or first-year college students planning to attend a university or college as full-time 1st or 2nd year students in the United States, have a minimum 3.0 GPA and have a household income level below the federal, state or county low-income level.
Target applicant(s): High school students. College students. Adult students.
Minimum GPA: 3.0
Amount: $7,500.
Number of awards: 10.
Scholarship may be renewable.
Deadline: April 15.
How to apply: Applications are available online.
Exclusive: Visit www.UltimateScholarshipBook.com and enter code TA226026 for updates on this award.

[2261] • Tampax Flow It Forward Scholarship

United Negro College Fund (UNCF)
1805 7th Street NW, Washington, DC 20001
Phone: 800-331-2244
Email: kenya.gray@uncf.org
https://uncf.org/scholarships
Purpose: To support African American college juniors attending an HBCU pursuing careers in healthcare.
Eligibility: Applicants must be African American U.S. citizens, nationals or permanent residents. Students must be enrolled as full-time college juniors at any four-year HBCU with a minimum 3.5 GPA. Applicants must demonstrate a commitment to community service in the health sector and a desire to specialize in any medical field that impacts women's

health, with a focus on the health of the Black community. Students must complete the FAFSA and demonstrate unmet financial need.
Target applicant(s): College students. Adult students.
Minimum GPA: 3.5
Amount: Up to $10,000.
Number of awards: Varies.
Deadline: August 15.
How to apply: Applications are available online.
Exclusive: Visit www.UltimateScholarshipBook.com and enter code UN226126 for updates on this award.

[2262] • TE Connectivity African Heritage Scholarship
TE Connectivity African Heritage Scholarship
Scholarship America, One Scholarship Way, Saint Peter, MN 56082
Phone: 507-931-1682
Email: teconnectivity-african-heritage@scholarshipamerica.org
https://te.com/scholarships
Purpose: To support African American students pursuing degrees in STEM and related fields.
Eligibility: Applicants must be college sophomores who self-identify as black or African American or multiracial. Students must be pursuing a degree in Science, Technology, Engineering, Mathematics (STEM), operations management, supply chain, finance or information technology. Applicants must demonstrate financial need and have a minimum 3.0 GPA.
Target applicant(s): College students. Adult students.
Minimum GPA: 3.0
Amount: Up to $22,500.
Number of awards: 14.
Deadline: November 10.
How to apply: Applications are available online.
Exclusive: Visit www.UltimateScholarshipBook.com and enter code TE226226 for updates on this award.

[2263] • TheDream.US Scholarship
TheDream.US
One Scholarship Way, Saint Peter, MN 56082
Phone: 507-931-1682
Email: TheDream.US@applyISTS.com
http://thedream.us
Purpose: To support immigrant students in pursuing post-secondary education.
Eligibility: Applicants must be graduating seniors who intend to enroll full-time in an associate's or bachelor's degree program at one of TheDream. US Partner Colleges. Students must have come to the U.S. before their 16th birthday and must demonstrate significant unmet financial need.
Target applicant(s): High school students. College students. Adult students.
Minimum GPA: 2.5
Amount: Up to $33,000.
Number of awards: Varies.
Scholarship may be renewable.
Deadline: February 29.
How to apply: Applications are available online.
Exclusive: Visit www.UltimateScholarshipBook.com and enter code TH226326 for updates on this award.

[2264] • Thurgood Marshall College Scholarship Fund
Thurgood Marshall Scholarship Fund
901 F Street NW, Suite 300, Washington, DC 20004
Phone: 202-507-4851
Email: deshuandra.walker@tmcf.org
https://www.tmcf.org/students-alumni/scholarships/
Purpose: To provide support to the nation's 47 historically black public colleges and universities by offering merit-based scholarships.
Eligibility: Applicants must be currently enrolled or planning to enroll as full-time students at one of the 47 TMSF member schools and have a minimum 3.0 high school GPA. Applicants must demonstrate a commitment to academic excellence and community service and show financial need. Winners need to maintain a 3.0 GPA for the duration of the scholarship. Applicants must submit a head shot photograph, letters of recommendation, essay and resume.
Target applicant(s): High school students. College students. Graduate school students. Adult students.
Minimum GPA: 3.0
Amount: $3,100.
Number of awards: Varies.
Scholarship may be renewable.
Deadline: March 27.
How to apply: Applications are available through the member schools.
Exclusive: Visit www.UltimateScholarshipBook.com and enter code TH226426 for updates on this award.

[2265] • Tracking Foundation Multi-Year Scholarship Program
Congressional Black Caucus Foundation
1720 Massachusetts Avenue NW, Washington, DC 20036
Phone: 202-263-2800
Email: info@cbcfinc.org
https://www.cbcfinc.org/scholarships/
Purpose: To support students who demonstrate leadership ability through exemplary community service and academic talent.
Eligibility: Applicants must be U.S. citizens or legal permanent residents. Students must be preparing to pursue or currently pursuing an undergraduate degree full-time at an accredited college or university. Applicants must have a minimum 2.5 GPA on a 4.0 scale, exhibit leadership and be active in the community and be Black or African American.
Target applicant(s): High school students. College students. Adult students.
Minimum GPA: 2.5
Amount: $40,000.
Number of awards: Varies.
Deadline: March 15.
How to apply: Applications are available online.
Exclusive: Visit www.UltimateScholarshipBook.com and enter code CO226526 for updates on this award.

[2266] • Tracking Foundation Scholars Scholarship Program
Congressional Black Caucus Foundation
1720 Massachusetts Avenue NW, Washington, DC 20036
Phone: 202-263-2800
Email: info@cbcfinc.org
https://www.cbcfinc.org/scholarships/

Purpose: To support students who demonstrate leadership ability through exemplary community service and academic talent.
Eligibility: Applicants must be U.S. citizens or legal permanent residents preparing to pursue or currently pursuing a graduate or doctoral degree full-time at an accredited college or university. Students must have a minimum 3.0 GPA on a 4.0 scale, exhibit leadership and be active in the community. Applicants must be Black or African American.
Target applicant(s): Graduate school students. Adult students.
Minimum GPA: 3.0
Amount: $20,000.
Number of awards: Varies.
Deadline: March 15.
How to apply: Applications are available online.
Exclusive: Visit www.UltimateScholarshipBook.com and enter code CO226626 for updates on this award.

[2267] • Traub-Dicker Rainbow Scholarship

Stonewall Community Foundation
1270 Broadway, Suite 501, New York, NY 10001
Phone: 212-457-1341
Email: scholarships@stonewallfoundation.org
https://stonewallfoundation.org
Purpose: To support lesbian women in pursuing post-secondary education.
Eligibility: Applicants must be incoming or current college students in any year of study, including graduate school. Selection is primarily based on demonstration of academic achievement, community service and desire to make a difference.
Target applicant(s): High school students. College students. Graduate school students. Adult students.
Amount: $4,000.
Number of awards: Varies.
Deadline: June 10.
How to apply: Applications are available online.
Exclusive: Visit www.UltimateScholarshipBook.com and enter code ST226726 for updates on this award.

[2268] • Tribal College and University (TCU) Scholarships

American Indian College Fund
8333 Greenwood Boulevard, Denver, CO 80221
Phone: 303-426-8900
https://collegefund.org/
Purpose: To support American Indian and Alaska Native students pursuing undergraduate and graduate degrees at tribal colleges.
Eligibility: Applicants must be American Indian and Alaska Native college students seeking undergraduate and graduate degrees at tribal colleges. Scholarships are awarded by each Tribal College or University. Students should contact their school's financial aid office to learn more.
Target applicant(s): High school students. College students. Graduate school students. Adult students.
Amount: Varies.
Number of awards: Varies.
Deadline: May 31.
How to apply: Applications are available online.
Exclusive: Visit www.UltimateScholarshipBook.com and enter code AM226826 for updates on this award.

[2269] • Truman D. Picard Scholarship

Intertribal Timber Council
Attn.: Education Committee, 1112 NE 21st Avenue, Suite 4, Portland, OR 97232-2114
Phone: 503-282-4296
Email: intertribaltimbercouncil@gmail.com
http://www.itcnet.org/about_us/scholarships.html
Purpose: To promote the field of natural resources.
Eligibility: Applicants must be high school seniors or college students and must pursue the natural resources field. Applicants must submit a resume, letters of reference, validated enrollment in Tribe/Native Alaska Corporation and a letter about their interest in natural resources, educational background, academic achievements and financial need.
Target applicant(s): High school students. College students. Adult students.
Amount: $2,000-$2,500.
Number of awards: Varies.
Deadline: January 26.
How to apply: There is no official application form.
Exclusive: Visit www.UltimateScholarshipBook.com and enter code IN226926 for updates on this award.

[2270] • U.S. Lacrosse Native American Scholarships

Tewaaraton Foundation
128 Birch Lane, Manhasset, NY 11030
Phone: 202-255-1485
Email: Andy@Tewaaraton.com
http://www.tewaaraton.com
Purpose: To acknowledge and reward students' academic and athletic achievement in the sport of lacrosse.
Eligibility: Applicants must be a member of the Iroquois community, enrolled in a secondary school and in good academic standing. Scholarships are awarded based on academic achievement, athletic performance and ambition.
Target applicant(s): High school students.
Amount: $5,000.
Number of awards: 2.
Deadline: April 10.
How to apply: Applications are available online. An application form, an essay, two letters of recommendation, a high school transcript and a photograph of the applicant are required.
Exclusive: Visit www.UltimateScholarshipBook.com and enter code TE227026 for updates on this award.

[2271] • UNCF Healthcare Workforce Diversity Program Certification

United Negro College Fund (UNCF)
1805 7th Street NW, Washington, DC 20001
Phone: 800-331-2244
Email: kenya.gray@uncf.org
https://uncf.org/scholarships
Purpose: To support students interested in healthcare careers.
Eligibility: Applicants must be African American U.S. citizens, nationals or permanent residents. Students must be pursuing a certification or a two-

year associates degree in healthcare-related STEM fields. Applicants must complete the FAFSA and demonstrate unmet financial need.
Target applicant(s): College students. Adult students.
Amount: Up to $5,000.
Number of awards: Varies.
Deadline: March 28.
How to apply: Applications are available online.
Exclusive: Visit www.UltimateScholarshipBook.com and enter code UN227126 for updates on this award.

[2272] • United Parcel Service Scholarship for Minority Students
Institute of Industrial and Systems Engineers
3577 Parkway Lane, Suite 200, Norcross, GA 30092
Phone: 800-494-0460
Email: egrimes@iise.org
https://www.iise.org
Purpose: To help minority undergraduate students in industrial engineering.
Eligibility: Applicants must be full-time undergraduate minority students enrolled in a college in the United States, Canada or Mexico with an accredited industrial engineering program, have at least a 3.4 GPA, major in industrial engineering and be active members. Students may not apply directly for this scholarship and must be nominated. The award is based on academic ability, character, leadership, potential service to the industrial engineering profession and financial need.
Target applicant(s): College students. Adult students.
Minimum GPA: 3.4
Amount: $4,000.
Number of awards: 2.
Deadline: February 1.
How to apply: Nomination forms are available online.
Exclusive: Visit www.UltimateScholarshipBook.com and enter code IN227226 for updates on this award.

[2273] • Upakar Foundation Indian American Community College Scholarship
Upakar Foundation
9710 Traville Gateway Dr, Box 401, Rockville, MD 20850
Email: upakarfoundation@hotmail.com
http://www.upakar.org/scholarships/
Purpose: To support Indian-American graduating seniors in pursuing post-secondary education at a community college.
Eligibility: Applicants must have been born in India or have at least one parent born in India. Students must be U.S. citizens or U.S. Green Card holders. A minimum GPA of 3.6 is required.
Target applicant(s): High school students.
Minimum GPA: 3.6
Amount: Up to $8,000.
Number of awards: Varies.
Scholarship may be renewable.
Deadline: April 30.
How to apply: Applications are available online.
Exclusive: Visit www.UltimateScholarshipBook.com and enter code UP227326 for updates on this award.

[2274] • UPS Hallmark Scholarship
U.S. Pan Asian American Chamber of Commerce
1329 18th Street NW, Washington, DC 20036
Phone: 800-696-7818
Email: celeb@uspaacc.com
https://celebrasianconference.com/scholarships
Purpose: To provide financial assistance to Asian American students.
Eligibility: Applicants must be high school seniors at least 16 years of age who are of Asian or Pacific heritage. They must be U.S. citizens or permanent residents and plan to enroll full-time at an accredited college or university in the United States in the fall following graduation. A minimum GPA of 3.3 is required, and applicants should demonstrate academic excellence, leadership, community service involvement and financial need.
Target applicant(s): High school students.
Minimum GPA: 3.3
Amount: $3,000-$5,000.
Number of awards: Up to 12.
Deadline: March 1.
How to apply: Applications are available online.
Exclusive: Visit www.UltimateScholarshipBook.com and enter code U.227426 for updates on this award.

[2275] • William and Charlotte Cadbury Award
National Medical Fellowships Inc.
347 Fifth Avenue, Suite 510, New York, NY 10016
Phone: 212-483-8880
Email: scholarships@nmfonline.org
https://nmfonline.org/about-our-scholarships-and-awards/programs/
Purpose: To reward minority medical students with outstanding achievement.
Eligibility: Applicants must be senior minority medical students at an accredited U.S. medical school. Students must demonstrate outstanding academic achievement, leadership and community service.
Target applicant(s): Graduate school students. Adult students.
Amount: $5,000.
Number of awards: 1.
Deadline: Contact the sponsor to confirm the deadline.
How to apply: Applications are available online.
Exclusive: Visit www.UltimateScholarshipBook.com and enter code NA227526 for updates on this award.

[2276] • Women In Defense WID Scholar
Women In Defense
HORIZONS Foundation, c/o National Defense Industrial Association, 2111 Wilson Boulevard, Suite 400, Arlington, VA 22201
Phone: 703-247-2552
Email: jcasey@ndia.org
https://www.womenindefense.net
Purpose: To encourage women to pursue careers supporting national security.
Eligibility: Applicants must be women currently enrolled or expected to be enrolled in an accredited university or college by the next academic term. Students must have attained at least junior-level status and demonstrate an interest in pursuing a career related to national security or defense. Applicants must have demonstrated financial need, have a minimum grade point average of 3.25 and be U.S. citizens.
Target applicant(s): College students. Adult students.
Minimum GPA: 3.25
Amount: Varies.
Number of awards: Varies.

Deadline: April 1.
How to apply: Applications are available online.
Exclusive: Visit www.UltimateScholarshipBook.com and enter code WO227626 for updates on this award.

[2277] • WomenIn Scholarship
Academy of Interactive Arts and Sciences (AIAS)
c/o Randy Pausch Scholarship, 9800 S. La Cienega Boulevard, 14th Floor, Inglewood, CA 90301
Phone: 310-484-2560
Email: gabriel@interactive.org
http://www.interactive.org
Purpose: To support female students who plan to pursue careers in the interactive entertainment industry.
Eligibility: Applicants must be pursuing careers in game development or the business of interactive entertainment. Students must be full-time undergraduate or graduate students attending an accredited college or university or working as early professionals (within their first four years in the industry) in the U.S. Applicants must have a minimum GPA of 3.3 on a 4.0 scale and submit pertinent documents.
Target applicant(s): College students. Graduate school students. Adult students.
Amount: Varies.
Number of awards: Varies.
Deadline: May 31.
How to apply: Applications are available online.
Exclusive: Visit www.UltimateScholarshipBook.com and enter code AC227726 for updates on this award.

[2278] • Worthy Women's Professional Studies Scholarship
Worthy
25 West 45th Street, 2nd Floor, New York, NY 10036
Phone: 888-222-0208
Email: scholarships@worthy.com
https://www.worthy.com/about/scholarship/
Purpose: To assist women who have enrolled in continuing education professional studies to pursue their passion.
Eligibility: Applicants must be a permanent resident of the U.S., identify as a female, be over the age of 30 and be enrolled in a continuing education professional studies program. A 300- to 500-word essay is required on one of three provided topics.
Target applicant(s): College students. Adult students.
Amount: $1,000-$2,500.
Number of awards: 3.
Deadline: December 4.
How to apply: Applications are available online. A 300- to 500-word essay on one of three topics provided is required.
Exclusive: Visit www.UltimateScholarshipBook.com and enter code WO227826 for updates on this award.

[2279] • Write Your Future Scholarship
National Association for the Advancement of Colored People
4805 Mt. Hope Drive, Baltimore, MD 21215
Phone: 410-580-5777
https://naacp.org/find-resources/scholarships-awards-internships/scholarships
Purpose: To encourage Black students and students of color, who identify as female and are pursuing an undergraduate degrees.
Eligibility: Applicants must be Black students or students of color and identify as female. Students must be graduating high school seniors enrolling in an accredited four-year, tax-exempt academic institution. Applicants must be NAACP members and current participants in an active ACT-SO program.
Target applicant(s): High school students.
Amount: $10,000.
Number of awards: 1.
Deadline: June 2.
How to apply: Applications are available online.
Exclusive: Visit www.UltimateScholarshipBook.com and enter code NA227926 for updates on this award.

[2280] • X Society Awards Scholarship
National Association for the Advancement of Colored People
4805 Mt. Hope Drive, Baltimore, MD 21215
Phone: 410-580-5777
https://naacp.org/find-resources/scholarships-awards-internships/scholarships
Purpose: To encourage Black students and students of color pursuing undergraduate degrees.
Eligibility: Applicants must be U.S. citizens or residents, Black or a person of color and members of the NAACP. Students must be enrolled full-time or accepted to an accredited college or university in the U.S. or graduating high school seniors with a minimum 3.0 GPA. Applicants must demonstrate an interest in pursuing a career in the visual/performing arts field such as one of the following: film, theatre, fashion, photography, graphic design, dance, music, journalism or mass communications.
Target applicant(s): High school students. College students. Adult students.
Minimum GPA: 3.0
Amount: $8,000.
Number of awards: 1.
Deadline: June 2.
How to apply: Applications are available online.
Exclusive: Visit www.UltimateScholarshipBook.com and enter code NA228026 for updates on this award.

[2281] • Young Women in Public Affairs Award
Zonta International
1211 West 22nd Street, Suite 900, Oak Brook, IL 60523
Phone: 630-928-1400
Email: zontaintl@zonta.org
https://www.zonta.org
Purpose: To encourage young women to participate in politics and public service.
Eligibility: Applicants must be young women between the ages of 16 and 19. District award winners receive at least $1,000, and international award winners receive $4,000. Selection is based on volunteerism, volunteer leadership and dedication to "advancing the status of women worldwide." Club deadlines vary. The April 1 deadline is the date by which applications must be received by the District Governor.
Target applicant(s): High school students.
Amount: $1,000-$5,000.
Number of awards: Varies.
Deadline: Contact the sponsor to confirm the deadline.
How to apply: Applications are available online or from your local Zonta Club.
Exclusive: Visit www.UltimateScholarshipBook.com and enter code ZO228126 for updates on this award.

DISABILITY / ILLNESS

[2282] • AbbVie Immunology Scholarship
AbbVie Immunology Scholarship
Scholarship America, One Scholarship Way, Saint Peter, MN 56082
Phone: 507-931-0651
Email: abbvieimmunology@scholarshipamerica.org
https://abbvieimmunologyscholarship.com/
Purpose: To support students who are living with chronic inflammatory diseases.
Eligibility: Applicants must be U.S. citizens or legal and permanent residents of the U.S. who have been diagnosed with one of the following conditions: ankylosing spondylitis, atopic dermatitis, Crohn's disease, hidradenitis suppurativa, juvenile idiopathic arthritis, plaque psoriasis, psoriatic arthritis, rheumatoid arthritis, ulcerative colitis or uveitis. Students must plan to enroll full-time in an undergraduate or graduate level program at an accredited college, university or technical school in the U.S. for the upcoming school year.
Target applicant(s): High school students. College students. Graduate school students. Adult students.
Amount: Up to $15,000.
Number of awards: Varies.
Deadline: December 1.
How to apply: Applications are available online.
Exclusive: Visit www.UltimateScholarshipBook.com and enter code AB228226 for updates on this award.

[2283] • American Council of the Blind Scholarships
American Council of the Blind
Scholarship Program, 1703 North Beauregard Street, Suite 420, Alexandria, VA 22311
Phone: 202-467-5081
Email: info@acb.org
http://www.acb.org
Purpose: To reward outstanding blind students.
Eligibility: Students must be legally blind in both eyes and admitted full-time to a post-secondary academic or vocational program. A minimum GPA of 3.3 is required, except in extenuating circumstances. Students who work full-time and attend school part-time may apply for the John Hebner Memorial Scholarship. Scholarship recipients are expected to attend a national convention if they are over 18.
Target applicant(s): High school students. College students. Graduate school students. Adult students.
Minimum GPA: 3.3
Amount: $2,000-$7,500.
Number of awards: Up to 20.
Deadline: February 14.
How to apply: Applications are available online and by phone.
Exclusive: Visit www.UltimateScholarshipBook.com and enter code AM228326 for updates on this award.

[2284] • Anne Ford Scholarship Program
National Center for Learning Disabilities
1220 L Street NW, Suite 100, Box #168, Washington, DC 20005
Phone: 301-966-2234
Email: afscholarship@ncld.org
http://www.ncld.org
Purpose: To provide financial assistance to high school seniors with learning disabilities who plan to pursue undergraduate degrees.
Eligibility: Applicants must be U.S. citizens who are academically successful in public or private secondary schools and with an identified learning disability. Students must have a minimum 3.0 GPA. Financial need is considered.
Target applicant(s): High school students.
Minimum GPA: 3.0
Amount: $2,500.
Number of awards: 1.
Deadline: April 13.
How to apply: Applications are available online.
Exclusive: Visit www.UltimateScholarshipBook.com and enter code NA228426 for updates on this award.

[2285] • Baer Reintegration Scholarship
Baer Reintegration Scholarship
P.O. Box 35218, Philadelphia, PA 19128
Phone: 800-809-8202
Email: baerscholarships@reintegration.com
http://www.reintegration.com
Purpose: To provide aid to students with schizophrenia or similar disorders who are seeking to advance themselves academically and vocationally.
Eligibility: Applicants must have been diagnosed with schizophrenia, schizophreniform, schizoaffective disorder or bipolar disorder, be undergoing medical treatment for their disease(s) and be involved in other rehabilitative efforts, such as working part-time or volunteering with a civic organization.
Target applicant(s): High school students. College students. Graduate school students. Adult students.
Amount: Varies.
Number of awards: Varies.
Deadline: January 31.
How to apply: Applications are available online or by phone, mail or email.
Exclusive: Visit www.UltimateScholarshipBook.com and enter code BA228526 for updates on this award.

[2286] • BMO Capital Markets Lime Connect Equity Through Education Scholarship
Lime Connect
590 Madison Avenue, 21st Floor, New York, NY 10022
Phone: 212-521-4469
https://www.limeconnect.com/programs/page/scholarships
Purpose: To support undergraduate and graduate students with disabilities in pursuing a career in financial services.
Eligibility: Applicants must be enrolled full-time in a finance, business, engineering, mathematics, physics, statistics or related program in the U.S. or Canada. Students must submit university transcripts, resume, an essay explaining their career goals and a letter of recommendation. Selection is based on the overall strength of the application.
Target applicant(s): College students. Graduate school students. Adult students.
Amount: $10,000.
Number of awards: 1.
Deadline: February 1.
How to apply: Applications are available online.
Exclusive: Visit www.UltimateScholarshipBook.com and enter code LI228626 for updates on this award.

[2287] • Boomer Esiason Foundation General Academic Scholarship
Boomer Esiason Foundation
c/o Chris McEwan, 483 10th Avenue, Suite 300, New York, NY 10018
Phone: 646-292-7930
Email: jcahillbef@aol.com
http://www.esiason.org/cf-living/scholarships
Purpose: To provide assistance to students with cystic fibrosis.
Eligibility: Applicants may be pursuing undergraduate or graduate degrees. They must demonstrate financial need. Selection is based on scholastic achievement, character, leadership, community service and financial need.
Target applicant(s): High school students. College students. Graduate school students. Adult students.
Amount: $10,000.
Number of awards: 20.
Deadline: April 18.
How to apply: Applications are available online. An application form, recent photo, letter from doctor, essay, transcript, tuition breakdown and W2 from both parents are required.
Exclusive: Visit www.UltimateScholarshipBook.com and enter code BO228726 for updates on this award.

[2288] • Cancer Fighter Scholarship
Student Mover Against Cancer (SMAC)
P.O. Box 676, Scotch Plains, NJ 07076
Email: scholarship@supportsmac.org
https://www.supportsmac.org/cfscholarship
Purpose: To support students who encountered difficulties with cancer.
Eligibility: Applicants must be graduating seniors from a public or private high school planning to attend a post-high school institution (two or four-year college, vocational or technical school) within the U.S. Students must have battled cancer themselves, helped a loved one or friend through their fight or have been leaders in their school and community in the fight against cancer.
Target applicant(s): High school students.
Amount: $1,000.
Number of awards: 10.
Deadline: April 1.
How to apply: Applications are available online.
Exclusive: Visit www.UltimateScholarshipBook.com and enter code ST228826 for updates on this award.

[2289] • Cancer for College Scholarships
Cancer for College
1050 University Avenue, Suite E107 #705, San Diego, CA 92103
Phone: 760-599-5096
Email: applications@cancerforcollege.org
https://www.cancerforcollege.org/
Purpose: To support current and former cancer patients and amputees.
Eligibility: Applicants must have received a cancer diagnosis at some point in their life. Students must be attending an accredited college in the United States and have a family income of less than $150,000 per year.
Target applicant(s): High school students. College students. Adult students.
Amount: $5,000.
Number of awards: Varies.
Scholarship may be renewable.
Deadline: January 31.
How to apply: Applications are available online. An application form, summary of cancer treatment, personal statement, details of college financing and two letters of recommendation are required.
Exclusive: Visit www.UltimateScholarshipBook.com and enter code CA228926 for updates on this award.

[2290] • Challenge Met Scholarship
American Radio Relay League Foundation
225 Main Street, Newington, CT 06111-1494
Phone: 860-594-0200
Email: foundation@arrl.org
https://www.arrl.org/scholarship-program
Purpose: To provide assistance to amateur radio operators with learning disabilities.
Eligibility: Applicants must be licensed amateur radio operators who are accepted to or enrolled in a two- or four-year college, technical school or university. Preference is given to students with documented learning disabilities who are putting forth effort.
Target applicant(s): High school students. College students. Adult students.
Amount: $500.
Number of awards: 1.
Deadline: January 10.
How to apply: Applications are available online.
Exclusive: Visit www.UltimateScholarshipBook.com and enter code AM229026 for updates on this award.

[2291] • Duane Buckley Memorial Scholarship
American Council of the Blind
Scholarship Program, 1703 North Beauregard Street, Suite 420, Alexandria, VA 22311
Phone: 202-467-5081
Email: info@acb.org
http://www.acb.org
Purpose: To assist students who work to overcome challenges.
Eligibility: Applicants must be legally blind college freshmen. A letter of recommendation, autobiographical sketch and copies of transcripts are required.
Target applicant(s): College students. Adult students.
Minimum GPA: 3.0
Amount: $1,000.
Number of awards: 1.
Deadline: February 14.
How to apply: Applications are available online.
Exclusive: Visit www.UltimateScholarshipBook.com and enter code AM229126 for updates on this award.

[2292] • Dyslexia/Auditory Processing Disorder Scholarship
Gemm Learning
877 Post Road E., Suite 2, Westport, CT 06880
Phone: 203-292-5410
https://www.gemmlearning.com/about/scholarship-opportunities
Purpose: To support students with dyslexia in pursuing post-secondary education.
Eligibility: Applicants must be enrolled or planning on enrolling at a U.S. or Canada based educational institution. Students must submit an essay explaining what it's like to live with dyslexia. Selection is based on the overall strength of the submission.

The Ultimate Scholarship Book 2026
Scholarship Directory (Disability / Illness)

Target applicant(s): High school students. College students. Adult students.
Amount: $1,000.
Number of awards: 1.
Deadline: October 31.
How to apply: Applications are available online.
Exclusive: Visit www.UltimateScholarshipBook.com and enter code GE229226 for updates on this award.

[2293] • Elizabeth Nash Foundation Scholarship Program
Elizabeth Nash Foundation
P.O. Box 1260, Los Gatos, CA 95031-1260
Email: info@elizabethnashfoundation.org
http://www.elizabethnashfoundation.org
Purpose: To support students with cystic fibrosis.
Eligibility: Applicants must be current or entering graduate or undergraduate students at an accredited U.S. institution of higher learning. They must be U.S. citizens, and they must be pursuing a bachelor's degree or higher. Selection criteria include scholastic achievement, character, leadership, community service, service to cystic fibrosis-related causes and financial need.
Target applicant(s): High school students. College students. Graduate school students. Adult students.
Amount: $1,000-$2,500.
Number of awards: Varies.
Deadline: April 1.
How to apply: Applications are available online. An application form, essay, letter of recommendation, documentation of cystic fibrosis diagnosis, transcript, copy of FAFSA and details of tuition costs are required.
Exclusive: Visit www.UltimateScholarshipBook.com and enter code EL229326 for updates on this award.

[2294] • Eric Dostie Memorial College Scholarship
NuFACTOR
41093 County Center Drive, Temecula, CA 92591
Phone: 800-323-6832
Email: info@kelleycom.com
https://www.kelleycom.com/scholarships/
Purpose: To assist students who suffer from hemophilia or related bleeding disorders as well as their immediate families.
Eligibility: Applicants must be individuals with hemophilia or related to said individuals, enrolled full-time in an accredited college or university and demonstrate academic achievement, financial need and a history of community service.
Target applicant(s): High school students. College students. Adult students.
Amount: $1,000.
Number of awards: 10.
Deadline: March 1.
How to apply: Applications are available after November 1 by telephone or mail.
Exclusive: Visit www.UltimateScholarshipBook.com and enter code NU229426 for updates on this award.

[2295] • Fred Scheigert Scholarships
Council of Citizens with Low Vision International
1155 15th Street NW, Suite 1004, Washington, DC 20005
Phone: 800-733-2258
Email: ncclv@yahoo.com
http://www.cclvi.org
Purpose: To provide educational assistance for students with low vision.
Eligibility: Applicants must be registered in a full-time undergraduate or graduate course of study at a college, trade or vocational school. They must have a GPA of 3.2 or higher. Those with extenuating circumstances may be exempt from these requirements. Applicants must have 20/70 or worse vision in the better eye with the best possible correction, or a field of vision of 30 degrees or less.
Target applicant(s): High school students. College students. Graduate school students. Adult students.
Minimum GPA: 3.2
Amount: $3,000.
Number of awards: 4.
Deadline: March 15.
How to apply: Applications are available online.
Exclusive: Visit www.UltimateScholarshipBook.com and enter code CO229526 for updates on this award.

[2296] • George H. Nofer Scholarship for Law and Public Policy
Alexander Graham Bell Association for the Deaf and Hard of Hearing
Youth and Family Programs Manager, 3417 Volta Place NW, Washington, DC 20007
Phone: 202-337-5220
Email: scholarships@agbell.org
http://www.agbell.org
Purpose: To assist graduate students with moderate to profound hearing loss.
Eligibility: Applicants must attend or be accepted to attend full-time an accredited law school or a master's or doctoral program in public policy or public administration and must use spoken language as the primary mode of communication. Students must also have a pre-lingual and bilateral hearing loss. Applications are available online.
Target applicant(s): Graduate school students. Adult students.
Amount: $5,000.
Number of awards: Up to 3.
Deadline: March 15.
How to apply: Applications are available online.
Exclusive: Visit www.UltimateScholarshipBook.com and enter code AL229626 for updates on this award.

[2297] • Graeme Clark Scholarship
Cochlear Americas
The Graeme Clark Scholarship, 13059 East Peakview Avenue, Centennial, CO 80111
Phone: 303-790-9010
http://www.cochlearamericas.com
Purpose: To support cochlear implant recipients.
Eligibility: Applicants must have received a Nucleus cochlear implant. They may be high school seniors, current college students, students who have been accepted into an institution of higher learning or graduate students. Students must pursue a minimum of a three-year undergraduate degree at an accredited university. Criteria for selection include academic achievement and commitment to leadership and humanity. A minimum GPA of 2.5 is required for all applicants.
Target applicant(s): High school students. College students. Graduate school students. Adult students.
Minimum GPA: 2.5
Amount: $2,000.
Number of awards: Varies.

Deadline: September 30.
How to apply: Applications are available online. An application form, transcript, proof of university admission, list of activities and awards, personal statement, proof of age and citizenship and three letters of reference are required.
Exclusive: Visit www.UltimateScholarshipBook.com and enter code CO229726 for updates on this award.

[2298] • Guthrie-Koch PKU Scholarship
National PKU News
6869 Woodlawn Avenue NE #116, Seattle, WA 98115
Phone: 206-525-8140
Email: scholarship@pkunews.org
https://pkunews.org/guthrie-koch-scholarship/
Purpose: In honor of the doctor who created the newborn screening test for PKU, the scholarship gives support to bright students living with PKU.
Eligibility: Students must have PKU, follow the diet and attend an accredited school. Financial need is considered along with academic excellence.
Target applicant(s): High school students. College students.
Amount: Varies.
Number of awards: Varies.
Deadline: February 1.
How to apply: Applications are available online after July 1 each year.
Exclusive: Visit www.UltimateScholarshipBook.com and enter code NA229826 for updates on this award.

[2299] • Help America Hear Scholarship
Help America Hear Inc.
P.O. Box 1245, Smithtown, NY 11787
Phone: 888-580-8886
Email: info@helpamericahear.org
https://helpamericahear.org/scholarship/
Purpose: To encourage students with hearing loss to reach their full potential.
Eligibility: Applicants must be high school seniors. Students must have hearing loss which requires the use of hearing aids or cochlear implants in their daily life. An essay on a provided prompt is required.
Target applicant(s): High school students.
Amount: $4,000.
Number of awards: 1.
Deadline: April 7.
How to apply: Applications are available online.
Exclusive: Visit www.UltimateScholarshipBook.com and enter code HE229926 for updates on this award.

[2300] • HIV-Positive Scholarship
STDcheck.com
Phone: 800-456-2323
https://www.stdcheck.com/scholarship-application.php
Purpose: To support students who are HIV-positive.
Eligibility: Applicants must be U.S. citizens who are currently enrolled or will be enrolled the following semester full-time at an accredited college or university in the U.S. Students will need to provide proof that they are HIV-positive. Applicants must also submit an essay on how HIV was contracted, how it has affected their life and what they wish those living without HIV knew about living with the virus. The scholarship is awarded monthly.
Target applicant(s): High school students. College students. Adult students.
Amount: $250-$5,000.
Number of awards: Varies.
Deadline: Monthly.
How to apply: Applications are available online and must include the essay, proof of HIV-positive status and an official transcript.
Exclusive: Visit www.UltimateScholarshipBook.com and enter code ST230026 for updates on this award.

[2301] • Incight Scholarship
Incight Education
P.O. Box 82056, Portland, OR 97282
Phone: 971-244-0305
Email: scholarship@incight.org
https://www.incight.org/scholarship
Purpose: To support students with physical or learning disabilities who are residents of Oregon, Washington or California.
Eligibility: Applicants must have a documented disability that may include physical, learning or cognitive. Students must also attend a trade school, college or university on a full-time basis. Recipients are placed with internships related to their field of study.
Target applicant(s): High school students. College students. Graduate school students. Adult students.
Amount: $500-$2,500.
Number of awards: Varies.
Scholarship may be renewable.
Deadline: April 15.
How to apply: Applications are available online.
Exclusive: Visit www.UltimateScholarshipBook.com and enter code IN230126 for updates on this award.

[2302] • Jaime Guttenberg All Abilities Scholarship
Orange Ribbons for Jaime
5944 Coral Ridge Drive, Suite 301, Coral Springs, FL 33076
Phone: 561-750-1500
Email: info@orangeribbonsforjaime.org
https://orangeribbonsforjaime.org/scholarship/
Purpose: To support students with a diagnosis of a special need or disability.
Eligibility: Applicants must have a diagnosis of a special need or disability such as, but not limited to autism, down's syndrome, cerebral palsy or limb deficiency. Students must have a high school diploma and be applying to any post-high school program such as, but not limited to, university, college, technical school, trade school or vocational training. A writing submission on a provided topic is required.
Target applicant(s): High school students.
Amount: Varies.
Number of awards: Varies.
Deadline: March 31.
How to apply: Applications are available online.
Exclusive: Visit www.UltimateScholarshipBook.com and enter code OR230226 for updates on this award.

[2303] • Kevin Child Scholarship
National Hemophilia Foundation
7 Penn Plaza, Suite 1204, New York, NY 10001
http://www.hemophilia.org
Purpose: To support students who have been diagnosed with hemophilia A or B.
Eligibility: Applicants must be high school seniors or enrolled undergraduate students.

Target applicant(s): High school students. College students. Adult students.
Amount: $1,000.
Number of awards: 1.
Deadline: June 4.
How to apply: Applications are available online.
Exclusive: Visit www.UltimateScholarshipBook.com and enter code NA230326 for updates on this award.

[2304] • Lighthouse Guild Scholarships

Lighthouse Guild
Scholarship Awards, 250 West 64th Street, New York, NY 10023
Phone: 212-769-7833
Email: scholars@lighthouseguild.org
https://www.lighthouseguild.org/
Purpose: To assist blind or partially-sighted collegiate or college-bound students.
Eligibility: Applicants must be legally blind. Visual requirements include a best corrected visual acuity of 20/200 or less in the better eye and/or a visual field of less than 20 degrees in the better eye and be in one of three categories: college-bound high school student, undergraduate college student or graduate student. They must also be U.S. citizens and residents and attend an accredited college or university in the U.S. or its territories. Selection is based on academic and personal achievements.
Target applicant(s): High school students. College students. Graduate school students. Adult students.
Amount: Up to $10,000.
Number of awards: Up to 17.
Deadline: April 15.
How to apply: Applications are available online.
Exclusive: Visit www.UltimateScholarshipBook.com and enter code LI230426 for updates on this award.

[2305] • Lime Connect Pathways Scholarship for High School Seniors with Disabilities

Lime Connect
590 Madison Avenue, 21st Floor, New York, NY 10022
Phone: 212-521-4469
https://www.limeconnect.com/programs/page/scholarships
Purpose: To support high school seniors with disabilities.
Eligibility: Applicants must be current high school seniors in the U.S. or Canada and have or consider themselves to have a visible or invisible disability. Students must be accepted to, or applied and awaiting acceptance to, a four-year university or college in the U.S. or Canada and intend to enroll full-time.
Target applicant(s): High school students.
Amount: $1,000.
Number of awards: Varies.
Deadline: June 1.
How to apply: Applications are available online.
Exclusive: Visit www.UltimateScholarshipBook.com and enter code LI230526 for updates on this award.

[2306] • Little People of America Scholarships

Little People of America
617 Broadway #518, Suite 218, Sonoma, CA 95476
Phone: 888-572-2001
Email: info@lpaonline.org
http://www.lpaonline.org
Purpose: To aid those affected by dwarfism.
Eligibility: Applicants may be junior high, high school or college students who have been involved with Little People of America. Preference is given in the following order: LPA members with medically diagnosed dwarfism, immediate family members of LPA members diagnosed with dwarfism and non-LPA members with dwarfism.
Target applicant(s): Junior high students or younger. High school students. College students. Graduate school students. Adult students.
Amount: $250-$1,000.
Number of awards: 3.
Deadline: April 15.
How to apply: Applications are available online. An application form, personal statement and three letters of recommendation are required.
Exclusive: Visit www.UltimateScholarshipBook.com and enter code LI230626 for updates on this award.

[2307] • Marion Huber Learning Through Listening Awards

Learning Ally
20 Roszel Road, Princeton, NJ 08540
Phone: 800-221-4792
Email: naa@LearningAlly.org
https://www.learningally.org/
Purpose: To assist learning-disabled high school seniors.
Eligibility: Applicants must demonstrate leadership skills, scholarship and a desire to help others and attend a two- or four-year college or vocational school. Students must have a specific learning disability and be registered with RFB&D for at least one year prior to the application deadline.
Target applicant(s): High school students.
Minimum GPA: 3.0
Amount: $2,000-$6,000.
Number of awards: 6.
Deadline: January 31.
How to apply: Applications are available online.
Exclusive: Visit www.UltimateScholarshipBook.com and enter code LE230726 for updates on this award.

[2308] • Mary P. Oenslanger Scholastic Achievement Awards

Learning Ally
20 Roszel Road, Princeton, NJ 08540
Phone: 800-221-4792
Email: naa@LearningAlly.org
https://www.learningally.org/
Purpose: Assistance for graduate study is awarded to blind college senior students or graduate students who have shown leadership skills, scholarship and a desire to help others.
Eligibility: Applicants must be blind or visually impaired, Learning Ally members and college seniors and graduate students.
Target applicant(s): College students. Graduate school students. Adult students.
Minimum GPA: 3.0
Amount: $1,000-$6,000.
Number of awards: 9.
Deadline: January 31.
How to apply: Applications are available online.
Exclusive: Visit www.UltimateScholarshipBook.com and enter code LE230826 for updates on this award.

[2309] • Michael A. Hunter Memorial Scholarship Fund

Orange County Community Foundation
4041 MacArthur Boulevard, Suite 510, Newport Beach, CA 92660
Phone: 949-553-4202
Email: info@oc-cf.org
https://www.oc-cf.org/grants-scholarships-overview/scholarships/
Purpose: To support students from the Orange County area.
Eligibility: Applicants must be high school seniors or current college students who are leukemia/lymphoma patients and/or are the children of non-surviving leukemia/lymphoma patients. Applicants must be full-time students with a GPA of at least 3.0 and demonstrate financial need. They must submit an essay describing how leukemia or lymphoma has impacted their life, a doctor's note verifying the leukemia or lymphoma diagnosis and two letters of recommendation.
Target applicant(s): High school students. College students. Adult students.
Minimum GPA: 3.0
Amount: $2,000-$5,000.
Number of awards: Varies.
Deadline: March 16.
How to apply: Applications are available online.
Exclusive: Visit www.UltimateScholarshipBook.com and enter code OR230926 for updates on this award.

[2310] • Millie Brother Scholarship

Children of Deaf Adults, International
Dr. Jennie E. Pyers, Assistant Professor of Psychology, Wellesley College, 106 Central Street, SCI480, Wellesley, MA 02481
Phone: 781-283-3736
Email: scholarships@coda-international.org
https://www.coda-international.org/scholarships
Purpose: To assist hearing children of deaf parents to pursue post-secondary educational opportunities.
Eligibility: Applicants must be graduating high school seniors and the hearing children of deaf parents. Applicants must submit a transcript, letters of recommendation and essay. Essays should describe applicants' Coda experience and future career goals.
Target applicant(s): High school students. College students. Adult students.
Amount: $3,000.
Number of awards: 2.
Deadline: February 29.
How to apply: Applications are available online.
Exclusive: Visit www.UltimateScholarshipBook.com and enter code CH231026 for updates on this award.

[2311] • National Collegiate Cancer Foundation Scholarship

National Collegiate Cancer Foundation
4858 Battery Lane, #216, Bethesda, MD 20814
Phone: 240-515-6262
Email: info@collegiatecancer.org
http://www.collegiatecancer.org
Purpose: To provide financial assistance to college students who have been diagnosed with cancer.
Eligibility: Applicants must demonstrate financial need. Selection is based on financial need, quality of essay and recommendations, demonstrating a "will win" attitude and overall story of cancer survivorship.
Target applicant(s): High school students. College students. Graduate school students. Adult students.
Amount: $1,000.
Number of awards: Varies.
Deadline: May 19.
How to apply: Applications are available online.
Exclusive: Visit www.UltimateScholarshipBook.com and enter code NA231126 for updates on this award.

[2312] • National Federation of the Blind Scholarship

National Federation of the Blind
200 East Wells Street, Baltimore, MD 21230
Phone: 410-659-9314
Email: scholarships@nfb.org
https://nfb.org
Purpose: The National Federation of the Blind offers thirty scholarships to exceptional blind scholars.
Eligibility: Applicants must be legally blind and pursue a full-time postsecondary study in the following semester in the U.S. One scholarship may be given to a part-time student. There are no additional restrictions for most of the scholarships. However, a few require study in certain fields or other special traits. Awards are based on academic excellence, community service and financial need. Applicants must reside in the United States or Puerto Rico and attend college in the United States or Puerto Rico. Students make one application for any of the 30 awards; the members of the NFB Scholarship Committee choose the 30 winners and decide which person will receive which award. Legally blind means one is blind in both eyes according to the legal definition, which is available on the organization's website.
Target applicant(s): High school students. College students. Graduate school students. Adult students.
Amount: $8,000.
Number of awards: 30.
Deadline: March 31.
How to apply: Applications are available online.
Exclusive: Visit www.UltimateScholarshipBook.com and enter code NA231226 for updates on this award.

[2313] • National Scholarship Competition for Disabled College Students

disABLEDperson Inc.
P.O. Box 230636, Encinitas, CA 92023
Phone: 760-420-1269
Email: info@disabledperson.com
https://www.disabledperson.com/scholarships/info
Purpose: To support disabled students in pursuing their undergraduate studies.
Eligibility: Applicants must be enrolled full-time in a two- or four-year college. Students must provide proof of disability through the Disability Student Services department at their school. Applicants must also include an essay with their application. Selection is based on the overall strength of the application.
Target applicant(s): College students. Adult students.
Amount: $2,000.
Number of awards: 1.
Deadline: March 15.
How to apply: Applications are available online.
Exclusive: Visit www.UltimateScholarshipBook.com and enter code DI231326 for updates on this award.

[2314] • NFMC Hinda Honigman Award for the Blind

National Federation of Music Clubs (NC)
Bobbye Guyton, 2400 Coronado Drive, Hoover, AL 35226
Phone: 205-822-6117
Email: rag2400@aol.com
http://www.nfmc-music.org/competitions-awards/
Purpose: To support blind instrumentalists or vocalists.
Eligibility: Applicants must be between the ages of 16 and 25, be an instrumentalist or vocalist and submit an affidavit from an ophthalmologist stating that they are blind. Applicants must also be affiliated with the National Federation of Music Clubs.
Target applicant(s): High school students. College students. Graduate school students. Adult students.
Amount: $500-$1,500.
Number of awards: 2.
Deadline: February 1.
How to apply: Applications are available online.
Exclusive: Visit www.UltimateScholarshipBook.com and enter code NA231426 for updates on this award.

[2315] • Northwestern Mutual Foundation Childhood Cancer Sibling Scholarship

Northwestern Mutual Foundation Childhood Cancer Sibling Scholarship
Scholarship America, One Scholarship Way, Saint Peter, MN 56082
Phone: 507-931-1682
Email: nmsibling@scholarshipamerica.org
https://learnmore.scholarsapply.org/nmsibling
Purpose: To support students whose siblings have been affected by cancer.
Eligibility: Applicants must be U.S. citizens ages 25 or younger and siblings of individuals who have been affected by pediatric cancer, whether they have survived, passed away or are currently in treatment. Students must have a minimum 2.5 GPA, demonstrate financial need and plan to enroll full-time for undergraduate study.
Target applicant(s): High school students. College students.
Minimum GPA: 2.5
Amount: $5,000.
Number of awards: 25.
Scholarship may be renewable.
Deadline: February 1.
How to apply: Applications are available online.
Exclusive: Visit www.UltimateScholarshipBook.com and enter code NO231526 for updates on this award.

[2316] • Optimist International Communications Contest

Optimist International
4494 Lindell Boulevard, St. Louis, MO 63108
Phone: 314-371-6000
Email: programs@optimist.org
https://www.optimist.org/member/scholarships1.cfm
Purpose: To reward students based on their communications performance.
Eligibility: Applicants must be students up to grade 12 in the U.S. and Canada, to CEGEP in Quebec and to grade 13 in the Caribbean who are recognized by their schools as deaf or hard of hearing.
Target applicant(s): High school students.
Amount: $2,500.
Number of awards: Varies.
Deadline: June 15.
How to apply: Contact your local Optimist Club.
Exclusive: Visit www.UltimateScholarshipBook.com and enter code OP231626 for updates on this award.

[2317] • P. Buckley Moss Endowed Scholarship

P. Buckley Moss Foundation for Children's Education
74 Poplar Grove Lane, Mathews, VA 23109
Phone: 800-430-1320
Email: foundation@mossfoundation.org
http://mossfoundation.org
Purpose: To support students with learning disabilities to pursue visual arts education.
Eligibility: Applicants must be graduating high school seniors with a language-related learning disability who are enrolling in an accredited two- or four-year college or university. Students must be pursuing a career in the visual arts and demonstrate financial need.
Target applicant(s): High school students.
Amount: $1,000.
Number of awards: 1.
Deadline: March 31.
How to apply: Applications are available online.
Exclusive: Visit www.UltimateScholarshipBook.com and enter code P.231726 for updates on this award.

[2318] • Paul and Ellen Ruckes Scholarship

American Foundation for the Blind Scholarship Committee
1000 Fifth Avenue, Suite 350, Huntington, WV 25701
Phone: 800-232-5463
Email: afbinfo@afb.net
http://www.afb.org
Purpose: To support visually impaired engineering, computer science, life sciences or physical sciences students.
Eligibility: Applicants must be U.S. citizens who are blind or visually impaired. They must be undergraduate or graduate students who are majoring in computer science, life sciences, physical sciences or engineering. Selection is based on the overall strength of the application.
Target applicant(s): High school students. College students. Graduate school students. Adult students.
Amount: $2,000.
Number of awards: 2.
Deadline: February 14.
How to apply: Applications are available online. An application form, official transcript, personal statement, two reference letters, proof of college acceptance, proof of U.S. citizenship and proof of legal blindness are required.
Exclusive: Visit www.UltimateScholarshipBook.com and enter code AM231826 for updates on this award.

[2319] • RAREis Scholarship

RAREis Scholarship Fund
Scholarship America, One Scholarship Way, Saint Peter, MN 56082
Phone: 507-931-1682
Email: rareis@scholarshipamerica.org
https://learnmore.scholarsapply.org/rareis/
Purpose: To support students diagnosed with a rare disease.
Eligibility: Applicants must be U.S. residents who have been diagnosed by a physician as having any form of rare disease regardless of treatment status and provide a diagnosis verification form. Students must be at least 17 years of age and plan to enroll full-time or part-time in undergraduate

or graduate study at an accredited two- or four-year college, university or vocational-technical/trade school. An essay submission on a provided prompt is required.
Target applicant(s): High school students. College students. Graduate school students. Adult students.
Amount: $5,000.
Number of awards: 70.
Deadline: April 13.
How to apply: Applications are available online.
Exclusive: Visit www.UltimateScholarshipBook.com and enter code RA231926 for updates on this award.

[2320] • Rudolph Dillman Memorial Scholarship
American Foundation for the Blind Scholarship Committee
1000 Fifth Avenue, Suite 350, Huntington, WV 25701
Phone: 800-232-5463
Email: afbinfo@afb.net
http://www.afb.org
Purpose: To aid blind or visually impaired students who are preparing for careers in the rehabilitation or education of the blind or visually impaired.
Eligibility: Applicants must be U.S. citizens who are blind or visually impaired. They must be undergraduate or graduate students who are preparing for careers in the education or rehabilitation of visually impaired or blind people. Previous recipients of this award are ineligible. Selection is based on the overall strength of the application.
Target applicant(s): College students. Graduate school students. Adult students.
Amount: $2,500.
Number of awards: 4.
Deadline: February 14.
How to apply: Applications are available online. An application form, official transcript, personal essay, two recommendation letters, proof of legal blindness and proof of U.S. citizenship are required.
Exclusive: Visit www.UltimateScholarshipBook.com and enter code AM232026 for updates on this award.

[2321] • Salix Gastrointestinal Health Scholars Award
Salix Pharmaceuticals
400 Somerset Corporate Boulevard, Bridgewater, NJ 08807
Phone: 908-927-1190
Email: salixcommunications@salix.com
https://www.salix.com/scholarship
Purpose: To support students living with gastrointestinal disease.
Eligibility: Applicants must be undergraduates, graduate students, working parents or single parents who have been diagnosed with gastrointestinal disease. Students must have applied to, been accepted to or be currently attending a qualifying institution in pursuit of an undergraduate, vocational/technical or graduate degree. An essay submission on a provided topic is required.
Target applicant(s): High school students. College students. Adult students.
Amount: Up to $10,000.
Number of awards: 10.
Deadline: May 6.
How to apply: Applications are available online.
Exclusive: Visit www.UltimateScholarshipBook.com and enter code SA232126 for updates on this award.

[2322] • Scholarships for Survivors
Patient Advocate Foundation
421 Butler Farm Road, Hampton, VA 23666
Phone: 800-532-5274
Email: scholarship@patientadvocate.org
http://www.patientadvocate.org
Purpose: This group of scholarships seeks to assist students who have been diagnosed with cancer or another life-threatening illness.
Eligibility: Students must be under the age of 25 and have been diagnosed with or be actively treated for their life-threatening illness in the past five years. If awarded a scholarship, the student must maintain a 3.0 GPA, be enrolled full time and perform 20 hours of community service each year.
Target applicant(s): High school students. College students.
Minimum GPA: 3.0
Amount: $3,000.
Number of awards: 12.
Scholarship may be renewable.
Deadline: March 8.
How to apply: Applications are available online.
Exclusive: Visit www.UltimateScholarshipBook.com and enter code PA232226 for updates on this award.

[2323] • Sertoma Scholarship for Students Who Are Hard of Hearing or Deaf
Sertoma Inc.
1912 E. Meyer Boulevard, Kansas City, MO 64132
Phone: 816-333-8300
Email: infosertoma@sertomahq.org
http://www.sertoma.org
Purpose: The organization's focus is to concentrate on communicative disorders.
Eligibility: Applicants must be entering or continuing as full-time undergraduates in the U.S., show proof that they have a clinically significant (40dB) bilateral hearing loss and have a minimum 3.2 GPA for all high school and college courses.
Target applicant(s): High school students. College students. Adult students.
Minimum GPA: 3.2
Amount: $1,000.
Number of awards: Varies.
Deadline: April 01.
How to apply: Applications are available online.
Exclusive: Visit www.UltimateScholarshipBook.com and enter code SE232326 for updates on this award.

[2324] • Soozie Courter Hemophilia Scholarship Program
Pfizer
Hemophilia Scholarship Program, 7 Penn Plaza, Suite 1204, New York, NY 10001
Phone: 212-328-3700
https://www.hemophilia.org/community-resources/financial-assistance/scholarships
Purpose: To provide financial assistance to students with hemophilia.
Eligibility: Applicants must be high school seniors or graduates, GED recipients or college or vocational school students who have been diagnosed with hemophilia A or B.
Target applicant(s): High school students. College students. Graduate school students. Adult students.

Amount: $2,500-$5,000.
Number of awards: 13.
Deadline: May 31.
How to apply: Applications are available online.
Exclusive: Visit www.UltimateScholarshipBook.com and enter code PF232426 for updates on this award.

[2325] • Student Award Program of FSD

Foundation for Science and Disability
503 N.W. 89 Street, Gainesville, FL 32607
http://stemd.org
Purpose: To support students with disabilities in completing a science project or thesis in any field of mathematics, science, medicine, engineering or computer science.
Eligibility: Applicants must be graduate students or senior undergraduates who have been accepted to graduate school. Students must submit two letters of recommendation and an essay outlining their professional goals and aspirations and the purpose for which the grant would be used. Selection is based on the overall strength of the application.
Target applicant(s): College students. Graduate school students. Adult students.
Amount: $1,000.
Number of awards: 1.
Deadline: December 1.
How to apply: Applications are available online.
Exclusive: Visit www.UltimateScholarshipBook.com and enter code FO232526 for updates on this award.

[2326] • Susanna and Lucy DeLaurentis Charitable Foundation Memorial Scholarships

Susanna DeLaurentis Charitable Foundation
SDCF, P.O. Box 11208, Elkins Park, PA 19027
Phone: 215-635-9405
http://thesusannafoundation.org/scholarships/apply.php
Purpose: To support graduating seniors who have faced chronic disease or other serious health issues in pursuing post-secondary education.
Eligibility: Applicants must submit high school transcripts, verification of health condition from a medical professional, a letter of recommendation and a personal statement. Selection is primarily based on academic achievement and extracurricular involvement.
Target applicant(s): High school students.
Amount: $1,000.
Number of awards: 1.
Deadline: Third Friday in April.
How to apply: Applications are available online.
Exclusive: Visit www.UltimateScholarshipBook.com and enter code SU232626 for updates on this award.

[2327] • Tony Coelho Media Scholarship

American Association of People with Disabilities (AAPD)
2013 H Street, NW, 5th Floor, Washington, DC 20006
Phone: 800-840-8844
Email: scholarship@aapd.com
http://www.aapd.com
Purpose: To support students with disabilities pursuing a career in the entertainment industry.
Eligibility: Applicants must be second year associate's degree students, undergraduate students in their sophomore year or higher or graduate students with disabilities who are interested in pursuing a career in the communications, media or entertainment industry.
Target applicant(s): College students. Graduate school students. Adult students.
Amount: $5,625.
Number of awards: 8.
Deadline: May 8.
How to apply: Applications are available online.
Exclusive: Visit www.UltimateScholarshipBook.com and enter code AM232726 for updates on this award.

[2328] • TPA Scholarship Trust for the Hearing Impaired

TPA Scholarship Trust for the Deaf and Near Deaf
2041 Exchange Drive, Saint Charles, MO 63303
Phone: 314-371-0533
Email: support@tpahq.org
http://www.tpahq.org
Purpose: To provide financial aid to children and adults who are deaf or hearing impaired and who need assistance in obtaining mechanical devices, treatment or specialized education.
Eligibility: Applicants must suffer from deafness or hearing impairment. Completed applications must be returned to the Trust by the end of each quarter. Applications are reviewed on the last day of each quarter and recipients will be notified within 30 days of the decision.
Target applicant(s): Junior high students or younger. High school students. College students. Graduate school students. Adult students.
Amount: Varies.
Number of awards: Varies.
Deadline: March 31; June 30; September 30; December 31.
How to apply: Applications are available by written request or online.
Exclusive: Visit www.UltimateScholarshipBook.com and enter code TP232826 for updates on this award.

[2329] • UCB Family Epilepsy Scholarship Program

UCB Family Epilepsy Scholarship Program
1421 East Broad Street, Suite 340, Fuquay-Varina, NC 27526
Phone: 866-825-1920
Email: ucbepilepsyscholarship@summitmedcomm.com
https://ucbepilepsyscholarship.com
Purpose: To provide financial assistance to people with epilepsy who wish to obtain higher education.
Eligibility: Applicants must be U.S. citizens or legal and permanent residents who have epilepsy, or family members or caregivers of persons with epilepsy. They must be graduating high school in the year of application or have already graduated and be enrolled in or awaiting acceptance from a U.S. institution of higher learning. They must have demonstrated academic achievement, participate in extracurricular activities and be positive role models.
Target applicant(s): High school students. College students. Graduate school students. Adult students.
Amount: $5,000-$10,000.
Number of awards: 33.
Deadline: March 15.
How to apply: Applications are available online.
Exclusive: Visit www.UltimateScholarshipBook.com and enter code UC232926 for updates on this award.

[2330] • Vitality Medical's Student Disability Scholarship

Vitality Medical
Attn.: Vitality Medical Scholars, 7910 S. 3500 E., Suite C, Salt Lake City, UT 84121
Phone: 800-397-5899
http://www.vitalitymedical.com/scholarship
Purpose: To encourage outstanding students who make an impact on their school and community.
Eligibility: Applicants must be a high school senior or currently enrolled undergraduate student. Students should be 16 years old or older and have at least a 3.0 GPA. Applicants do not have to have a disability to enter. A poem and personal statement on how using disability aids have added vitality to your life are required.
Target applicant(s): High school students. College students. Adult students.
Minimum GPA: 3.0
Amount: $500.
Number of awards: varies.
Deadline: September 15.
How to apply: Application information available online. Poem, personal statement and transcript must be submitted by mail.
Exclusive: Visit www.UltimateScholarshipBook.com and enter code VI233026 for updates on this award.

[2331] • Wells Fargo Scholarship Program for People with Disabilities

Wells Fargo Scholarship Program for People with Disabilities, Scholarship America
One Scholarship Way, Saint Peter, MN 56082
Phone: 844-402-0357
Email: pwdscholarship@scholarshipamerica.org
https://learnmore.scholarsapply.org/pwdscholarship/
Purpose: To support students with disabilities in the career path of their choice.
Eligibility: Applicants must have an identified disability, a long-term or recurring issue that impacts one or more major life activities. Students must be either high school seniors or current undergraduate students enrolled full- or half-time at an accredited two- or four-year college or university in the U.S. A GPA of 3.0 or higher is required.
Target applicant(s): High school students. College students. Adult students.
Minimum GPA: 3.0
Amount: Up to $2,500.
Number of awards: Up to 35.
Scholarship may be renewable.
Deadline: March 20.
How to apply: Applications are available online.
Exclusive: Visit www.UltimateScholarshipBook.com and enter code WE233126 for updates on this award.

[2332] • William and Dorothy Ferrell Scholarship

Association for Education and Rehabilitation of the Blind and Visually Impaired
AER Scholarship Committee, 1703 N. Beauregard Street, Suite 440, Alexandria, VA 22311
Phone: 703-671-4500
Email: scholarships@aerbvi.org
https://aerbvi.org
Purpose: To assist visually-impaired students who plan to assist others who are visually impaired.
Eligibility: Applicants must be legally blind, with a vision of 20/200 or less in the best eye or 20 degrees or less in the visual field. Applicants must also study in college or a similar institution in the field of services for the blind or visually impaired. Scholarships are only awarded in even-numbered years.
Target applicant(s): College students. Graduate school students. Adult students.
Amount: $1,000.
Number of awards: 2.
Deadline: April 15.
How to apply: Applications are available online or by phone request.
Exclusive: Visit www.UltimateScholarshipBook.com and enter code AS233226 for updates on this award.

Scholarship Indexes

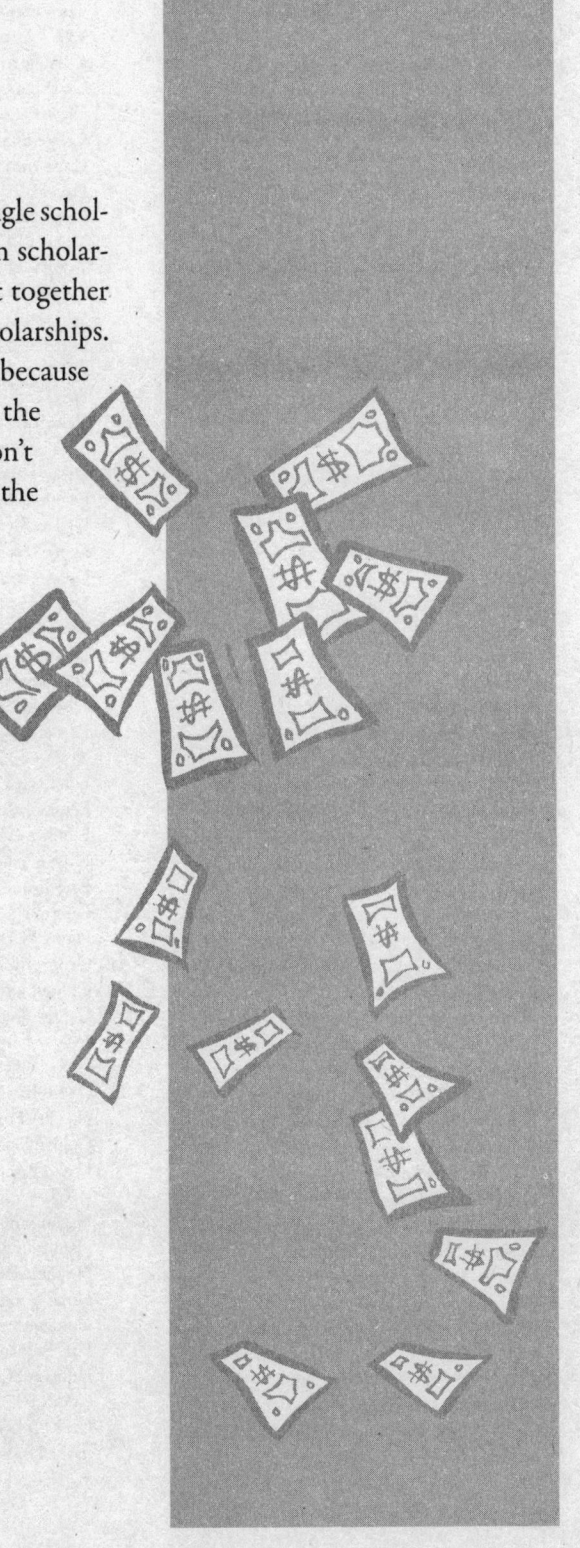

What would you rather do: read the description of every single scholarship in this book or use an index to quickly zero in on scholarships that fit you? That's what we thought, which is why we put together a set of indexes that make it easy for you to find the perfect scholarships. We strongly recommend that you use all of the indexes. This is because every scholarship can be categorized in numerous ways and often the decision is unavoidably subjective. So to make sure that you don't miss out on a great scholarship, spend the time to consult each of the following indexes:

General Category Index..................................552-567
Field of Study Index......................................568-584
Career Index..585-595
Interests / Hobbies Index...............................595-598
Special Circumstances Index..........................598-599
State of Residence Index...............................600-608
Athletics Index...608
Military Related Index..................................609-610
Ethnicity / Race Index..................................610-614
Religion Index..614
Disability Index..615
Membership Index.......................................615-619
Sponsor Index..619-647
Scholarship Name Index...............................647-663

The Ultimate Scholarship Book 2026
General Category Index

GENERAL CATEGORY INDEX

This is one of the most useful indexes since it organizes the scholarships by common fields of study or career areas. It does not list any state specific scholarships since there is another index just for state of residence.

ACADEMICS/GENERAL
Also See Scholarships Listed Under:
Leadership
Public Service/Community Service

$1,000 All Star Verified Scholarship • 1
$1,000 College JumpStart Gratitude Scholarship • 2
$1,000 College JumpStart Love of Learning Scholarship • 3
$1,000 College JumpStart Pay It Forward Scholarship • 4
$1,000 College JumpStart Show Grit Scholarship • 5
$1,000 GK Tanabe Student Scholarship • 6
$1,000 Moolahspot Scholarship • 7
$1,000 Scholarship Detective Launch Scholarship • 8
1 for 2 Education Foundation Scholarship • 9
1Dental Scholarship • 11
A+A Altruism + All Good Deeds Scholarship • 14
Aaliyah Lee Scholarship • 15
Abacus Life Scholarship • 18
Abe and Esther Hagiwara Student Aid Award • 2081
Act of Kindness Scholarship • 20
Adult Learner Scholarship from Study.com • 21
Adult Skills Education Award • 22
AFSA National Essay Contest • 24
Ag Day Essay Contest • 25
Agota M. Bardos Award • 26
AIERF Graduate Scholarship • 522
AIFS Green Ambassador Scholarship • 28
Akash Kuruvilla Memorial Scholarship • 35
Alpha Kappa Alpha Financial Need Scholars • 38
American Bar Association Law Day Art Contest • 40
Americanism Essay Contest • 43
AU Student Contest • 56
Barbizon's College Tuition Scholarship • 59
Be the Boss Scholarship • 60
Beyond the Boroughs Scholarship • 61
BMTX Financial Empowerment Scholarship • 63
Boomer Benefits Scholarship • 66
Bright!Tax Global Scholar Initiative • 67
Building Bridges Scholarship • 69
Burger King Scholars Program • 70
C.I.P. Scholarship • 71
CareerFitter Scholarship • 74
Carson Scholars • 76
Cashtelligent Financial Literacy Scholarship • 77
Chinese American Citizens Alliance Essay Contest • 83
Christophers Video Contest for College Students • 84
CIA Undergraduate Scholarship Program • 85
CJ Pony Parts Scholarship Video Contest • 86
Clubs of America Scholarship Award for Career Success • 87

Coca-Cola Community College Academic Team • 90
Coca-Cola Scholars Program • 91
College Prep Scholarship for High School Juniors • 92
Completing the Dream Scholarship • 94
Congress Bundestag Youth Exchange Program • 95
Coolidge Scholarship • 97
Corporate Culture Scholarship • 98
Corporate Office Interiors Scholarship Contest • 99
Courage to Grow Scholarship • 100
Craig Dickinson Memorial Scholarship • 102
Create Real Impact Contest • 103
Create-a-Greeting-Card Scholarship • 104
Crossword Hobbyist Crossword Scholarship • 105
Davidson Fellows Scholarships • 110
Davis-Putter Scholarship Fund • 111
Delete Cyberbullying Beyond School Walls Scholarship • 112
Delete Cyberbullying Mental Health Awareness Scholarship • 113
Delete Cyberbullying Social Media Scholarship • 114
Dell Scholars Program • 115
Delta Theta Chi Sorority National Memorial Scholarship • 116
Denes I. Bardos Award • 117
Digital Privacy Scholarship • 118
Dollars for Scholars Scholarship • 124
Don't Text and Drive Scholarship • 126
DoSomething Monthly Scholarships • 127
E-waste Scholarship • 131
Eco-Warrior Scholarship • 133
Education Accessibility Scholarship • 135
Educational Advancement Foundation Merit Scholarship • 136
Educational Training Voucher Programs for Foster Youth • 1355
Eon Essay Contest • 138
Equitable Excellence Scholarship • 139
Families of Freedom Scholarship Fund • 142
FMAA Scholarship Program • 144
Foreclosure Scholarship Program • 147
Fulbright Grants • 149
Future Without Speciesism Cash Award • 150
George Montgomery/NRA Youth Wildlife Art Contest • 154
George S. and Stella M. Knight Essay Contest • 155
Global Citizen Scholarship • 157
GMR Transcription Academic Scholarship • 159
Go City Education Scholarship • 161
Golden Door Scholars • 162
H and P Veterans Helping Veterans Scholarship • 165
Hagan Scholarship • 167
Hamilton Award • 168
Hispanic Heritage Youth Awards • 2159
Horatio Alger National Scholarship Program • 174
Humane Studies Fellowship: Flexible Support for PhD Students • 175
Humane Studies Fellowship: Graduate Sabbatical Grants • 176
IAPMO Essay Scholarship Contest • 177
In the Driver's Seat • 181

Industrial Metal Service Scholarship • 183
International College Counselors Scholarship • 184
Iowa Student Loan Midwest Senior Scholarship • 185
Jack Kent Cooke Foundation College Scholarship Program • 187
Jane Austen Society of North America Essay Contest • 189
Japanese American Citizens League Entering Freshman Awards • 2172
Japanese American Citizens League Undergraduate Awards • 2175
John F. Kennedy Profile in Courage Essay Contest • 625
John S. Linakis Scholarship • 192
Kemper Human Rights Education Foundation • 199
LA Tutors Innovation in Education Scholarship • 202
Leadership Essay Contest • 203
Life Lessons Scholarship Program • 204
Live Mas Scholarship • 205
LULAC National Scholastic Achievement Awards • 207
Marshall Memorial Fellowship • 213
Marshall Scholar • 214
Mensa Foundation Scholarship Program • 221
Mometrix College Scholarship • 226
Most Valuable Student Scholarships • 230
National College Match Program • 234
National Honor Society Scholarship • 2019
National Marbles Tournament Scholarship • 236
National Merit Scholarship Program and National Achievement Scholarship Program • 237
National Oratorical Contest • 238
Naval Intelligence Essay Contest • 244
Nicholas Virgilio Haiku and Senryu Contest • 257
Odenza Marketing Group Scholarship • 262
Oleg Fastovsky Outstanding Citizenship Scholarship • 263
Patriot's Pen Youth Essay Contest • 473
Paul and Daisy Soros Fellowships for New Americans • 265
Pilot International Scholarship • 269
Play! Pokemon Scholarship • 271
Project Yellow Light/Hunter Garner Scholarship • 273
Pulse of Perseverance Scholarship • 275
RealtyHop Scholarship • 278
RentHop's College and University Scholarship • 279
Return 2 College Scholarship • 280
Rhodes Scholar • 281
Rover Sitter Scholarship • 285
Rubincam Youth Writing Competition • 286
Russel R. Taylor Foundation Scholarship • 287
Sallie Mae Bridging the Dream Scholarship • 288
Sandra Hancock Scholarship • 290
Sarah Josephine Langstaff Memorial Scholarship • 291
Scholars Helping Collars Scholarship • 293
Scholarship America Dream Award • 294
Shari Simon Greenberg Community Scholarship • 300

Sigma Phi Epsilon Balanced Man Scholarship • 2046
Sir Cyril Taylor Legacy Scholarship • 302
Sloane Stephens Doc and Glo Scholarship • 303
Soliant's Sunrise Scholarship • 305
Spirit of Giving Scholarship • 308
Stamps Scholars • 309
Steps For Change Scholarship • 310
Stokes Educational Scholarship Program • 311
Stossel in the Classroom Essay Contest • 312
Stossel in the Classroom Video Contest • 313
Stuck at Prom Scholarship • 314
Student Video Contest • 317
Student View Scholarship • 318
StudentCam Competition • 319
Study.com College Scholarship for Homeschool Students • 320
Study.com Community College Student Scholarship • 321
Study.com Online Graduate Degree Scholarship • 322
Study.com Online Undergraduate Degree Scholarship • 323
Study.com Scholarship for Nontraditional Students • 327
Study.com Scholarship for Transfer Students • 328
Sunflower Initiative Scholarship • 2258
SuperCollege Scholarship • 330
Tattoo Journal Ink Scholarship • 335
Technology Addiction Awareness Scholarship • 336
Telluride Association Summer Seminars (TASS) • 337
Thiel Fellowship Grant • 338
Think For Yourself College Scholarship Essay Contest • 339
Thurgood Marshall College Scholarship Fund • 2264
Truth Change Maker Awards • 343
U.S. Bank Scholarship Program • 344
U.S. JCI Senate Scholarship Grants • 345
U.S. Western Digital STEM Scholarship • 346
Unboxing Your Life Video Scholarship • 348
Undergraduate Transfer Scholarship • 349
United States Hispanic Leadership Institute Denny's Hungry for Education • 351
USMA Metric Scholarship Award • 360
Voice of Democracy Audio Essay Contests • 363
VRG Scholarship • 365
Waggle Human-Pet Bond Scholarship Opportunity • 368
Watson Travel Fellowship • 370
We The Future Contest • 372
Women in STEM Scholarship • 378
Women on Par Scholarship • 380
Young Scholars Program • 384

ACCOUNTING/FINANCE
Also See Scholarships Listed Under:
Business/Management
Mathematics
Accounting and Financial Women's Alliance Foundation Scholarship • 513
AICPA Foundation Scholarship for Future CPAs • 518
AICPA Foundation Two-year Transfer Scholarship • 519
AICPA John L. Carey Scholarship • 520
AWSCPA Scholarship • 536
Goldberg-Miller Public Finance Scholarship • 594
IMA Memorial Education Fund Scholarship • 610
Laurels Fund Scholarship • 633
National Academic Scholarships • 661
National Association of Black Accountants National Scholarship Program • 2215
Prize in International Insolvency Studies • 688
Ritchie-Jennings Memorial Scholarship • 699
Stuart Cameron and Margaret McLeod Memorial Scholarship • 714
TACTYC Accounting Scholarship • 719
William (Bill) Ezzell Scholarship • 736

AEROSPACE/AVIATION
Also See Scholarships Listed Under:
Engineering
Mathematics
AAAE Foundation Scholarship • 742
AFCEA Ralph W. Shrader Diversity Scholarships • 761
AFCEA ROTC Scholarships • 23
AIAA Foundation Undergraduate Scholarship Program • 767
Astronaut Scholarship • 816
Aviation Distributors and Manufacturers Association Scholarship Program • 821
Aviation Insurance Association Education Foundation Scholarship • 822
Dan L. Meisinger Sr. Memorial Learn to Fly Scholarship • 851
David Alan Quick Scholarship • 853
David Arver Memorial Scholarship • 854
Dutch and Ginger Arver Scholarship • 868
Eugene S. Kropf Scholarship • 883
Fellowship in Aerospace History • 890
Full-Time Employee Student Scholarship • 897
Gabriel A. Hartl Scholarship • 899
Garmin Scholarship • 902
General James H. Doolittle Scholarship • 906
H.P. Bud Milligan Aviation Scholarship • 924
Johnny Davis Memorial Scholarship • 963
Joseph Frasca Excellence in Aviation Scholarship • 964
Judith Resnik Memorial Scholarship • 2177
Kansas Agricultural Aviation Association Scholarship • 1508
Lawrence C. Fortier Memorial Scholarship • 974
Lee Tarbox Memorial Scholarship • 977
Mid-Continent Instruments and Avionics Scholarship • 1006
National Aviation Explorer Scholarships • 1022
Payzer Scholarship • 1063
Pioneers of Flight • 1071
UAA Janice K. Barden Aviation Scholarship • 1155
Vertical Flight Foundation Technical Scholarships • 1165
Women in Aviation International Scholarship • 2074

AGRICULTURE/HORTICULTURE/ANIMALS
Also See Scholarships Listed Under:
Biological Sciences/Life Sciences
Forestry/Wildlife
Angus Foundation Scholarships • 788
Appaloosa Youth Association Art Contest • 797
ASABE Foundation Engineering Scholarship • 799
ASEV Scholarships • 802
ASF Olin Fellowships • 803
ASHA Youth Scholarships • 804
Association of Food and Drug Officials Scholarship Award • 813
Beef Industry Scholarship • 826
Careers in Agriculture Scholarship Program • 835
Carville M. Akehurst Memorial Scholarship • 836
Cedarcrest Farms Scholarship • 837
Dairy Student Recognition Program • 850
DMI Milk Marketing Scholarship • 859
Elmer J. and Hester Jane Johnson Memorial FFA Scholarship • 876
FarmAid FFA Scholarship • 886
Feeding Tomorrow General Education Scholarships/Freshman Scholarships • 888
GCSAA Scholars Competition • 905
Graduate Scholarships • 918
Grow Ag Leaders Scholarship • 923
Harold Bettinger Scholarship • 926
Hoard's Dairyman FFA Scholarship • 1987
Hutton Junior Fisheries Biology Program • 936
Iowa Pork Foundation Scholarship • 1474
James S. Davis Memorial Scholarship • 1490
JFLF Awards Programs • 620
John W. Rogers Memorial Scholarship • 1504
John Wright Memorial Scholarship • 962
Junior Showmanship Scholarship Program • 965
Kansas Agricultural Aviation Association Scholarship • 1508
Larry Williams Photography and AYA Photo Contest • 972
LEAF Scholarships • 1531
Lois Britt Pork Industry Memorial Scholarship Program • 983
Loy McCandless Marks Scholarship in Tropical Horticulture • 987
Mabel Mayforth Scholarship • 1554
Marshall E. McCullough Scholarship • 991
Missouri 4-H Foundation Scholarships • 1618
National Dairy Shrine/Iager Dairy Scholarship • 1023
National FFA Alumni and Supporters Agricultural Education Scholarship • 1025
National Garden Clubs Scholarship • 1026
National Horticulture Foundation General Scholarships • 1027
National Potato Council Scholarship • 1028
NDPRB Undergraduate Scholarship Program • 1037
NDS / Klussendorf / McKown Scholarships • 1038
North Texas State Fair Association Scholarship • 1680
NPFDA Scholarships • 1050
Nurseries Foundation Award • 1053
Perennial Plant Association Scholarship • 1065
Perfect Plants Nursery Scholarship • 1066
Richard Jensen Scholarship • 1091
Spring Meadow Proven Winners Scholarship • 1123
Timothy S. and Palmer W. Bigelow, Jr. Scholarship • 1147
Undergraduate Scholarships • 1159

The Ultimate Scholarship Book 2026
General Category Index

USDA/1890 National Scholars Program • 1163
Usrey Family Scholarship • 1164
William J. Adams, Jr. and Marijane E. Adams Scholarship • 1170
Yanmar/SAE Scholarship • 1175
Youth Program • 1177

Architecture/Landscape
Also See Scholarships Listed Under:
Agriculture/Horticulture/Animals

ACI Student Fellowship Program • 754
AIA/Architects Foundation Diversity Advancement Scholarship • 766
ASCA/AISC Student Design Competition • 800
ASLA Council of Fellows Scholarships • 807
ASTM International Katherine and Bryant Mather Scholarship • 815
AWAF Scholarships • 1233
Charles Dubose Scholarship • 1286
Douglas Dockery Thomas Fellowship in Garden History and Design • 864
EDSA Diversity Scholarships • 2137
Green Voice Design Competition • 922
Helen C. Evans Scholarship • 929
Houzz Women in Architecture • 935
Karen Ann Shopis-Fox Memorial Scholarship • 1517
Landscape Forms Scholarship in Memory of Peter Lindsay Schaudt, FASLA • 971
National Garden Clubs Scholarship • 1026
Payette Sho-Ping Chin Memorial Academic Scholarship • 1062
Predoctoral Fellowship Program • 1076
Rain Bird Intelligent Use of Water Scholarship • 1082
Robert E. Thunen Memorial Scholarships • 1097
Sir John Soane's Museum Foundation Traveling Grant • 1113
SmithGroup J.E.D.I. Scholarship • 1116
Steven G. King Play Environments Scholarship • 1129

Athletics/Outdoors
Also See Scholarships Listed Under:
Leadership

AAU Karate Scholarship • 16
AAUS Student Scholarships • 17
AHHS Foundation Scholarship • 27
All-American Scholars (Cheerleading) • 36
All-American Scholars (Football) • 37
American Legion Baseball Scholarship • 41
Ann Griffel Scholarship • 1218
Babe Ruth League Scholarships • 57
Banana George Blair Ambassador Scholarship • 58
Big Al Wagner Western Region Scholarship • 62
Bob Warnicke Scholarship • 64
Bodie McDowell Scholarship • 545
Carolyn Hines Memorial Scholarship Program • 75
CCA Christian Cheer Nationals • 78
CCCAM Scholarships • 1280
Challenge Scholarship • 79
CIF Scholar-Athlete of the Year • 1295
Collegiate Championship Award Program • 93
CPI Highest Point Hunt Seat Rider • 101
Curt Greene Memorial Scholarship • 106
Curwen-Guidry-Blackburn Scholarship Fund • 107

Dinah Shore Scholarship • 119
Dixie Boys Baseball Scholarship Program • 120
Dixie Softball Scholarships • 121
Dixie Youth Scholarship Program • 122
Dizzy Dean Scholarship • 123
Dr. James Earl Kennamer Scholarship • 128
Dwight F. Davis Memorial Scholarship • 129
Dwight Mosley Scholarship Award • 130
Earl Anthony Memorial Scholarships • 132
Educational Award/Graduating High School Female • 1352
Ethnic Minority and Women's Enhancement Scholarship • 140
Eve Kraft Education and College Scholarship • 141
FMC Skaters Scholarship • 145
Gift for Life Scholarships • 156
GNC Nutritional Research Grant • 160
Goldie Bateson Scholarship • 2152
Graduate Research Grant - Master and Doctoral • 164
H. U. Lee Scholarship • 166
Hawaii High School Athletic Association Hall of Honor • 1426
HD Hogan Rodeo Scholarship • 170
Heisman High School Scholarship • 171
Helen Gee Chin Scholarship Foundation Scholarship • 172
Herman Sani Scholarship • 1436
High School Scholarship • 173
Hispanic Heritage Youth Awards • 2159
ICCA Scholarships • 1454
IEA Founders College Scholarship Awards • 178
IEA Zone Specific Scholarships • 179
Ike Foundation Scholarship • 180
Indiana Golf Foundation Scholarship • 1466
Individual Scholarship Program • 182
ISIA Education Foundation Scholarship • 186
Jack Hughes Education Scholarship • 1485
John J. Smith Graduate School Scholarship • 191
Justin Dignam Memorial Scholarship • 197
Kevin Higgins College Scholarship • 200
Lou Manzione Scholarship • 206
Marian Wood Baird College Scholarship • 208
Marilynn Smith Scholarship • 2196
Marsh Scholarship Fund • 212
Memorial Fund Scholarships • 219
Metro Youth Football Association Scholarship • 222
Minnesota Hockey Scholarship • 1606
Minority Scholarship • 2205
MSAA Scholarship Program • 1627
NABF Scholarship Program • 231
NATA Scholarship • 233
National Gymnastics Foundation Men's Scholarship • 2217
National Intercollegiate Rodeo Foundation Scholarship • 235
National Scholarship Program • 239
National Sportsmanship Award • 240
National Table Tennis Scholarship • 241
NCAA Division II Degree Completion Award Program • 252
NCAA Postgraduate Scholarship • 253
NCRA Scholarship • 1637
New York State USBC Scholarships • 1656
New York State USBC Spirit Awards • 1657

NFAA Scholarship Program • 256
NJCDCA Scholarship • 1663
NSCA Scholarship • 261
Pacific Academy Foundation Scholarship • 264
Pennsylvania State Bowling Association Scholarship Program • 1730
PGA WORKS John and Tamara Lundgren Scholars Program • 268
Phyllis G. Meekins Scholarship • 2237
Pony Alumni Scholarship • 272
Race Entry Student Scholarship • 276
Rawhide Scholarship • 277
Rhodes Scholar • 281
Richard Avila Scholarship • 282
Roller Skating Foundation Scholarship, High School Student Category • 283
Rosalind P. Walter College Scholarship • 284
SASS Scholarship Foundation Scholarships • 292
Scholastic Honors Team • 297
Scott Hamilton Skaters Education Fund • 298
Smart Choices Scholarship Program • 1794
Southern Region/Elmer Stailing Scholarship • 307
Sweet Karen Alumni Scholarship • 332
Tampa Bay Buccaneers Foundation Girls in Football Scholarship • 334
Texas International Fishing Tournament Inc. Scholarship • 1844
Tim Olson Memorial Scholarship • 340
Trapshooting Hall of Fame College Scholarships • 341
USA Roller Sports Scholarship Fund • 353
USA Water Ski and Wake Sports Foundation Scholarships • 354
USAR Scholarship • 355
USBC Alberta E. Crowe Star of Tomorrow • 356
USBC Annual Zeb Scholarship • 357
USBC Chuck Hall Star of Tomorrow • 358
USBC Youth Ambassador of the Year • 359
Wade Trophy • 367
Walter Byers Graduate Scholarship • 369
WBCA Coaches' All-America • 371
William J. Goaziou Scholarship • 375
Women Divers Hall of Fame Scholarships and Grants • 377
Women's Scholarship • 1173
Women's Western Golf Foundation Scholarship • 383
Zale Parry Scholarship • 385

Biological Sciences/Life Sciences
Also See Scholarships Listed Under:
Agriculture/Horticulture/Animals
Chemistry
Forestry/Wildlife
Medicine/Nursing/Health Profession

Angus Foundation Scholarships • 788
Annual University Scholarship • 790
AOS Student and Postdoctoral Research Awards • 796
ASABE Foundation Engineering Scholarship • 799
Astronaut Scholarship • 816
Barry M. Goldwater Scholarship and Excellence in Education Program • 824
C. Bertrand and Marian Othmer Schultz Collegiate Scholarship • 1255

Charles H. Bussmann Undergraduate Scholarship • 838
Davidson Fellows Scholarships • 110
DNA Day Essay Contest • 860
Drs. James and Wanda Trefil Science Scholarship • 2135
Gaige Fund Award • 900
GEM MS Engineering Fellowship Program • 2147
George A. Hall / Harold F. Mayfield Grant • 909
Gorgas Scholarship Competition • 1405
Graduate Research Fellowship Program • 917
Hertz Foundation's Graduate Fellowship Award • 932
International Women's Fishing Association Scholarship • 944
Jean Theodore Lacordaire Prize • 950
John C. Bajus Scholarship • 955
LabRoots Scholarship • 970
Libbie H. Hyman Memorial Scholarship • 979
Louis Agassiz Fuertes Award • 985
Ludo Frevel Crystallography Scholarships • 988
MAES Scholarship Program • 2192
Mollie Butler Memorial Scholarship • 1012
MTS Student Scholarship for Two-Year, Technical, Engineering and Community College Students • 1015
MTS Student Scholarship for Undergraduate Students • 1016
National Garden Clubs Scholarship • 1026
NDSEG Fellowship Program • 1039
Next Swell Scholarship • 1044
NIH Undergraduate Scholarship Program • 1047
Novus Biologicals Scholarship Program • 1048
Paros-Digiquartz Scholarship • 1059
Paul A. Stewart Grants • 1061
Payzer Scholarship • 1063
Raney Fund Award • 1084
Regeneron Science Talent Search • 1086
Science Ambassador Scholarship • 1108
Student Research Scholarships • 1134
William J. Adams, Jr. and Marijane E. Adams Scholarship • 1170
Youth Incentive Award • 1176

BUSINESS/MANAGEMENT
Also See Scholarships Listed Under:
Accounting/Finance
Marketing
Leadership

A.J. Grisanti Memorial Scholarship • 509
Academic Merit Scholarships • 512
Actuarial Diversity Scholarship • 2083
Adult Students in Scholastic Transition (ASIST) • 517
Alice L. Haltom Educational Fund Scholarship • 523
Allied Van Lines Scholarship • 524
Alpha Kappa Psi Scholarships • 526
Betsy Plank/PRSSA Scholarship • 540
CardRates.com Financial Futures Scholarship • 552
Executive Women International Scholarship Program • 578
FOARE Scholarship Program • 580
Francis X. Crowley Scholarship • 581
Fund for American Studies Internships • 586

Gary Yoshimura Scholarship • 590
Harry A. Applegate Scholarship • 599
Henry Belin du Pont Dissertation Fellowship • 601
Hermine Solt Student Scholarship • 1437
Humane Studies Fellowship: Flexible Support for PhD Students • 175
Humane Studies Fellowship: Graduate Sabbatical Grants • 176
IMA Memorial Education Fund Scholarship • 610
James A. Turner, Jr. Memorial Scholarship • 616
Jane M. Klausman Women in Business Scholarship Fund • 618
Joe Perdue Scholarship • 622
John W. Rogers Memorial Scholarship • 1504
Lawrence G. Foster Award for Excellence in Public Relations • 634
Material Handling Education Foundation • 647
MBA Fellowship • 648
Microsoft Office Specialist World Championship • 652
National Academic Scholarships • 661
National Association of Black Accountants National Scholarship Program • 2215
National Scholarship • 2220
National Scholarship Program • 665
North American Van Lines Logistics Scholarship • 675
Office Supply Scholarship • 470
Paul S. Mills Scholarships • 682
Prospanica Foundation Scholarships • 690
Risk Management Association Foundation Scholarship • 698
Ritchie-Jennings Memorial Scholarship • 699
Stuart Cameron and Margaret McLeod Memorial Scholarship • 714
Study.com Scholarship for Business Students • 717
Undergraduate Scholarship • 2062
Vern and Elaine Clark Outdoor Advertising Industry • 732
WIIT Charitable Trust Scholarship • 735

CHEMISTRY
Also See Scholarships Listed Under:
Biological Sciences/Life Sciences
Engineering
Medicine/Nursing/Health Professions
Sciences/Physical Sciences

AACT National Candy Technologists John Kitt Memorial Scholarship Program • 743
American Chemical Society Scholars Program • 2098
AMS Graduate Fellowships • 784
Astronaut Scholarship • 816
Composites Division/Harold Giles Scholarship • 844
Davidson Fellows Scholarships • 110
Donald F. and Mildred Topp Othmer Scholarships • 861
Gladys Anderson Emerson Scholarship • 913
Gorgas Scholarship Competition • 1405
Graduate Research Fellowship Program • 917
Hubertus W.V. Wellems Scholarship for Male Students • 2167
John J. McKetta Scholarship • 956
Larson Aquatic Research Support (LARS) • 973
Minority Scholarship Awards for Incoming College Freshmen • 2208

National Association for Surface Finishing Scholarships • 1021
NDSEG Fellowship Program • 1039
Polymer Modifiers and Additives Division Scholarships • 1074
Regeneron Science Talent Search • 1086
Rubber Division Undergraduate Scholarship • 1101
Society of Plastics Engineers (SPE) Foundation Scholarships • 1120
Student Poster Session Awards • 1132
Ted and Ruth Neward Scholarship • 1139
The Industrial Electrochemistry and Electrochemical Engineering Division H. H. Dow Memorial Student Achievement Award • 1140
Undergraduate Award for Excellence in Chemistry • 1156

COMMUNICATIONS
Also See Scholarships Listed Under:
English/Writing
Journalism/Broadcasting

AFCEA Ralph W. Shrader Diversity Scholarships • 761
ARRL Foundation General Fund Scholarship • 534
Bill Gove Scholarship • 399
Bill, W2ONV and Ann Salerno Memorial Scholarship • 542
Bodie McDowell Scholarship • 545
Carole J. Streeter, KB9JBR, Scholarship • 553
Cavett Robert Scholarship • 405
Charles Clarke Cordle Memorial Scholarship • 555
Charles N. Fisher Memorial Scholarship • 556
Dayton Amateur Radio Association Scholarship • 565
Distinguished Service Award for Students • 567
DMI Milk Marketing Scholarship • 859
Don Riebhoff Memorial Scholarship • 568
Dr. James L. Lawson Memorial Scholarship • 570
Edmond A. Metzger Scholarship • 575
Fred R. McDaniel Memorial Scholarship • 583
Fund for American Studies Internships • 586
Hispanic Heritage Youth Awards • 2159
IFEC Scholarships Award • 608
IRARC Memorial, Joseph P. Rubino, WA4MMD, Scholarship • 615
John Bayliss Radio Scholarship • 623
Julianne Malveaux Scholarship • 2178
K2TEO Martin J. Green, Sr. Memorial Scholarship • 628
L. Phil and Alice J. Wicker Scholarship • 631
L.B. Cebik, W4RNL and Jean Cebik, N4TZP Memorial Scholarship • 632
Mary Lou Brown Scholarship • 646
Massachusetts Student Broadcaster Scholarship • 1578
Media Fellows Program • 649
Mississippi Association of Broadcasters Scholarship Program • 1614
NCTA and AWMF Scholarship • 2224
New England FEMARA Scholarship • 672
Optimist International Communications Contest • 2316
Optimist International Oratorical Contest • 678
Paul and Helen L. Grauer Scholarship • 681

The Ultimate Scholarship Book 2026
General Category Index

PHD Scholarship • 685
Print and Graphics Scholarship • 478
Ray, N0RP and Katie, W0KTE Pautz Scholarship • 694
Richard W. Bendicksen, N7ZL, Memorial Scholarship • 697
Student with a Disability Scholarship • 716
Tom and Judith Comstock Scholarship • 724
YASME Foundation Scholarship • 739
Youth Scholarship • 740

COMPUTER AND INFORMATION SCIENCE
Also See Scholarships Listed Under:
Engineering
Mathematics
Sciences/Physical Sciences

Admiral Grace Murray Hopper Memorial Scholarships • 2085
AFCEA Ralph W. Shrader Diversity Scholarships • 761
AFCEA ROTC Scholarships • 23
Amazon Future Engineer Scholarship • 777
Anne Maureen Whitney Barrow Memorial Scholarship • 2100
AOC Scholarships • 794
Association of Information Technology Professionals (AITP) Scholarships • 814
Astronaut Scholarship • 816
Davidson Fellows Scholarships • 110
Dellums SMART Scholarship • 856
Generation Google Scholarship • 2149
Google SVA Scholarship • 163
Graduate Research Fellowship Program • 917
HIMSS Foundation Scholarship • 933
HSC Foundation Scholarship • 2165
Intertech Foundation STEM Scholarship • 945
Mary V. Munger Scholarship • 994
Michigan Council of Women in Technology University Scholarship • 1593
National Academic Scholarships • 661
National Space Club Keynote Scholar • 1029
NCWIT Award for Aspirations in Computing • 2225
Outstanding Undergraduate Researchers Award Program • 1057
PixelPlex Bi-Annual STEM Scholarship • 1072
Pretty Photoshop Actions Bi-annual Scholarship • 1079
Raymond Davis Scholarship • 1085
Regeneron Science Talent Search • 1086
Science Ambassador Scholarship • 1108
SMART Scholarship • 1114
SMART Scholarship • 1115
Stokes Educational Scholarship Program • 311
Susan Miszkowicz Memorial Scholarship • 1136
VIP Women in Technology Scholarship • 1166

CONSTRUCTION TRADES
Also See Scholarships Listed Under:
Vocational/Technical

AAGS Joseph F. Dracup Scholarship Award • 745
AGC Graduate Scholarships • 763
AGC of Ohio Scholarships • 1190
AGC Undergraduate Scholarships • 764
Associated General Contractors of Minnesota Scholarships • 1230
Complete Water Solutions Scholarship • 843
Connecticut Building Congress Scholarships • 1313
Delta Faucet Company Scholarships • 857
Geneva Rock Scholarship • 908
Herman J. Smith Scholarship • 1435
Independence Excavating, A DiGeronimo Company Scholarship • 1464
IWSH Essay Scholarship • 948
Kokosing Construction Co. Scholarship • 1524
NAWIC Founders' Undergraduate Scholarship • 1032
NPCA Educational Foundation Scholarships • 1049
Path to Pro Scholarship • 1060
PHCC Educational Foundation Scholarship • 1068
Pulte Group Build Your Future Scholarship Program • 1080
Roofing Industry Scholarship - Melvin Kruger Endowed Scholarship • 1099
Shook Construction Harry F. Gaeke Memorial Scholarship • 1788
Tuttle Construction Inc. Tiny Rauch Scholarship • 1860
Undergraduate Scholarship and Construction Trades Scholarship • 1158
Yanmar/SAE Scholarship • 1175

CULINARY ARTS
Also See Scholarships Listed Under:
Food Services
Hospitality/Travel/Tourism

American Culinary Federation Scholarships • 528
IFEC Scholarships Award • 608
IFSEA Worthy Goal Scholarship • 609
John Schwartz Scholarship • 1503
Ray and Gertrude Marshall Scholarship • 693

DENTISTRY
Also See Scholarships Listed Under:
Medicine/Nursing/Health Professions

ADEA/Haleon Preventive Dentistry Scholarships • 756
ADEA/MouthWatch Patti DiGangi Scholarship for Dental Hygiene Innovation • 757
ADEA/MouthWatch Predoctoral Dental Student Scholarship for Innovation • 758
ADHA Institute Scholarship Program • 760
Colgate Bright Smiles, Bright Futures Minority Scholarships • 841
Crest Oral-B Laboratories Dental Hygiene Scholarships • 848
Dr. Esther Wilkins Scholarship • 866
Irene Woodall Graduate Scholarship • 947
Karla Girts Memorial Community Outreach Scholarship • 968
NHSC Scholarship • 1046

DISABILITY
Also See Scholarships Listed Under:
Academics/General

AbbVie Immunology Scholarship • 2282
American Council of the Blind Scholarships • 2283
Anne Ford Scholarship Program • 2284
Baer Reintegration Scholarship • 2285
BMO Capital Markets Lime Connect Equity Through Education Scholarship • 2286
Boomer Esiason Foundation General Academic Scholarship • 2287
Cancer Fighter Scholarship • 2288
Cancer for College Scholarships • 2289
Challenge Met Scholarship • 2290
Duane Buckley Memorial Scholarship • 2291
Dyslexia/Auditory Processing Disorder Scholarship • 2292
Elizabeth Nash Foundation Scholarship Program • 2293
Eric Dostie Memorial College Scholarship • 2294
Fred Scheigert Scholarships • 2295
George H. Nofer Scholarship for Law and Public Policy • 2296
Graeme Clark Scholarship • 2297
Guthrie-Koch PKU Scholarship • 2298
Help America Hear Scholarship • 2299
HIV-Positive Scholarship • 2300
Incight Scholarship • 2301
Jaime Guttenberg All Abilities Scholarship • 2302
Kevin Child Scholarship • 2303
Lighthouse Guild Scholarships • 2304
Lime Connect Pathways Scholarship for High School Seniors with Disabilities • 2305
Little People of America Scholarships • 2306
Marion Huber Learning Through Listening Awards • 2307
Mary P. Oenslanger Scholastic Achievement Awards • 2308
Michael A. Hunter Memorial Scholarship Fund • 2309
Millie Brother Scholarship • 2310
National Collegiate Cancer Foundation Scholarship • 2311
National Federation of the Blind Scholarship • 2312
National Scholarship Competition for Disabled College Students • 2313
NFMC Hinda Honigman Award for the Blind • 2314
Northwestern Mutual Foundation Childhood Cancer Sibling Scholarship • 2315
Optimist International Communications Contest • 2316
P. Buckley Moss Endowed Scholarship • 2317
Paul and Ellen Ruckes Scholarship • 2318
RAREis Scholarship • 2319
Rudolph Dillman Memorial Scholarship • 2320
Salix Gastrointestinal Health Scholars Award • 2321
Scholarships for Survivors • 2322
Sertoma Scholarship for Students Who Are Hard of Hearing or Deaf • 2323
Soozie Courter Hemophilia Scholarship Program • 2324
Steve Fasteau Past Presidents' Scholarship • 1816
Student Award Program of FSD • 2325
Student with a Disability Scholarship • 716
Susanna and Lucy DeLaurentis Charitable Foundation Memorial Scholarships • 2326
Tony Coelho Media Scholarship • 2327
TPA Scholarship Trust for the Hearing Impaired • 2328
UCB Family Epilepsy Scholarship Program • 2329
Vitality Medical's Student Disability Scholarship • 2330

Wells Fargo Scholarship Program for People with Disabilities • 2331
William and Dorothy Ferrell Scholarship • 2332

EDUCATION/TEACHING
Also See Scholarships Listed Under:
Academics/General
English/Writing
Public Administration/Social Work
Public Service/Community Service

ACLS Fellowships • 514
DMI Milk Marketing Scholarship • 859
Dr. Robert Hawkins Memorial Scholarship • 571
FTEE Scholarship: Undergraduate Major in Technology and Engineering Education • 585
Fulbright Grants • 149
Future Journalism Teacher Scholarship • 588
International Technology Engineering Educators Association Scholarship - FTEE/Undergraduate • 614
Learning and Leadership Grants • 635
Litherland/ITEEA Scholarship • 640
Maley/FTEE Teacher Professional Development Scholarship • 644
NACA Mid Atlantic Graduate Student Scholarship • 658
NEA-Retired Jack Kinnaman Memorial Scholarship • 669
NFMC Gretchen E. Van Roy Music Education Scholarship • 674
Pi Lambda Theta Student Support Scholarships • 686
Prize in Ethics Essay Contest • 479
Robert G. Porter Post-Secondary Scholarships • 2036
Shields-Gillespie Scholarship • 709
SPS Future Teacher Scholarship • 711
Student Success Grants • 715
Teacher Education Scholarship Fund • 720
Teacher of the Year Award • 721
Truman Scholar • 342
United Commercial Travelers of America (UCT) Scholarship Program • 726

ENGINEERING
Also See Scholarships Listed Under:
Aerospace/Aviation
Computer and Information Science
Sciences/Physical Sciences

A.O. Putnam Memorial Scholarship • 741
AAGS - NSPS Scholarships • 744
Abel Wolman Fellowship • 747
ACAA Educational Foundation Scholarship Program • 748
Academic Achievement Award • 749
ACEC Colorado Scholarship Program • 1184
ACEC New York Scholarship Program • 752
ACEC Scholarship • 1185
ACI Scholarship • 753
ACI Student Fellowship Program • 754
Ada I. Pressman Memorial Scholarship • 2084
Admiral Grace Murray Hopper Memorial Scholarships • 2085
AFCEA Ralph W. Shrader Diversity Scholarships • 761
AFCEA ROTC Scholarships • 23
AGC Education and Research Foundation Undergraduate Scholarship • 762

AGC Graduate Scholarships • 763
AGC Undergraduate Scholarships • 764
AIAA Foundation Undergraduate Scholarship Program • 767
AISI/AIST Foundation Premier Scholarship • 768
AIST Benjamin F. Fairless Scholarship (AIME) • 769
AIST Ronald E. Lincoln Memorial Scholarship • 770
AIST Smith Graduate Scholarship • 771
AIST William E. Schwabe Memorial Scholarship • 772
AIST Willy Korf Memorial Fund • 773
Amelia Earhart Fellowships • 779
American Council of Engineering Companies of New Jersey Member Organization Scholarship • 1207
American Innovations Corrosion Scholarship • 780
American Water Scholarship • 781
AMPP Academic Scholarship • 782
Anne Maureen Whitney Barrow Memorial Scholarship • 2100
ANS Graduate Scholarship • 791
ANS Incoming Freshman Scholarships • 792
ANS Undergraduate Scholarship • 793
ASABE Foundation Engineering Scholarship • 799
ASDSO Senior Undergraduate Scholarship • 801
ASHRAE Engineering Technology Scholarships • 805
ASHRAE Society Scholarship Program • 806
ASME Auxiliary Lucy and Charles W. E. Clarke Scholarship • 808
ASME Foundation Scholarships • 809
ASNE Scholarship Program • 810
ASNT Fellowship • 811
Associated General Contractors of Connecticut Scholarships • 1229
Association of Cuban Engineers Scholarship Foundation Scholarships • 2106
Association of Federal Communications Consulting Engineers Scholarships • 812
ASTM International Katherine and Bryant Mather Scholarship • 815
Astronaut Scholarship • 816
Automotive Hall of Fame Scholarships • 818
Auxiliary Legacy Scholarship • 819
AWAF Scholarships • 1233
B.J. Harrod Scholarships • 2107
B.K. Krenzer Reentry Scholarship • 2108
Baroid Scholarship • 823
Barry M. Goldwater Scholarship and Excellence in Education Program • 824
Battery Division Student Research Award • 825
BMW/SAE Engineering Scholarship • 829
Brill Family Scholarship • 830
Bryant L. Bench Carollo Engineers Inc. Scholarship • 831
C.B. Gambrell Undergraduate Scholarship • 833
Collegiate Inventors Competition • 842
Composites Division/Harold Giles Scholarship • 844
Computational Science Graduate Fellowship • 845
Corrosion Division Morris Cohen Graduate Student Award • 846

Cummins Scholarship • 849
David A. O Neil Scholarship • 852
David Alan Quick Scholarship • 853
Davidson Fellows Scholarships • 110
DEED Funding Opportunities • 855
Delaware Solid Waste Authority John P. Pat Healy Scholarship • 1327
Desk and Derrick Educational Trust • 858
Donald F. and Mildred Topp Othmer Scholarships • 861
Dorothy M. and Earl S. Hoffman Award • 863
Dr. Ivy M. Parker Memorial Scholarship • 2133
Dr. James L. Lawson Memorial Scholarship • 570
Duane M. Hanson Scholarship • 867
Dwight D. Gardner Scholarship • 869
E. Noel Luddy Scholarship • 870
E.J. Sierleja Memorial Fellowship • 871
Ed and Charlotte Rodgers Scholarships • 1350
Edmond A. Metzger Scholarship • 575
Edward D. Hendrickson/SAE Engineering Scholarship • 872
Elizabeth McLean Memorial Scholarship • 875
Elson T. Killam Memorial Scholarship • 877
EngineerGirl Essay Contest • 880
Engineering Undergraduate Scholarship • 881
Engineers Foundation of Ohio General Fund Scholarship • 1364
F.W. Beich Beichley Scholarship • 885
Francis X. Crowley Scholarship • 581
Frank and Dorothy Miller ASME Auxiliary Scholarships • 894
Fred M. Young, Sr./SAE Engineering Scholarship • 895
Fred R. McDaniel Memorial Scholarship • 583
Future Leader Scholarship • 898
Garland Duncan Scholarships • 901
Gary Wagner, K3OMI, Scholarship • 903
GEM MS Engineering Fellowship Program • 2147
Gilbreth Memorial Fellowship • 911
Giuliano Mazzetti Scholarship • 912
Gordon Rankin Corrosion Engineering Scholarship • 915
Graduate Research Award (GRA) • 916
Graduate Research Fellowship Program • 917
Harold and Inge Marcus Scholarship • 925
Henry Adams Scholarship • 930
Hertz Foundation's Graduate Fellowship Award • 932
Holly A. Cornell Scholarship • 934
Honeywell International Inc. Scholarships • 2163
HSC Foundation Scholarship • 2165
Hubertus W.V. Wellems Scholarship for Male Students • 2167
IBTTA Foundation Scholarship Program • 937
IISE Council of Fellows Undergraduate Scholarship • 938
Industrial Electrochemistry and Electrochemical Engineering Student Achievement Award • 939
Injection Molding Division Scholarship • 940
Institute of Electrical and Electronics Engineers Life Members' Fellowship in Electrical History • 941
International Gas Turbine Institute Scholarship • 942
J.R. Popalisky Scholarship • 1482
James Rust Scholarship • 1996

The Ultimate Scholarship Book 2026
General Category Index

Jill S. Tietjen P.E. Scholarship • 951
John and Elsa Gracik Scholarships • 953
John and Muriel Landis Scholarship • 954
John J. McKetta Scholarship • 956
John L. Imhoff Scholarship • 957
John S. Marshall Memorial Scholarship • 959
John S.W. Fargher, Jr. Scholarship • 960
John V. Wehausen Graduate Scholarship • 961
Kenneth Andrew Roe Scholarship • 969
LabRoots Scholarship • 970
Larson Aquatic Research Support (LARS) • 973
Lewis C. Hoffman Scholarship • 978
Light Metals Division Scholarship • 980
Lillian Moller Gilbreth Memorial Scholarship • 2187
Lisa Zaken Award For Excellence • 981
Lockheed Martin STEM Scholarship Program • 982
Long-Term Member Sponsored Scholarship • 984
Lowell Loving Undergraduate Scholarship • 986
Mackinac Scholarship • 1555
MAES Scholarship Program • 2192
Mandell and Lester Rosenblatt Undergraduate Scholarship • 989
Marliave Fund • 990
Marvin Mundel Memorial Scholarship • 992
Mary Gunther Memorial Scholarship • 2198
Mary V. Munger Scholarship • 994
Materials Processing and Manufacturing Division Scholarship • 995
Maureen L. and Howard N. Blitman, P.E., Scholarship • 2201
Melvin J. Schiff Fellowship Fund • 998
Melvin R. Green Scholarships • 999
Meredith Thoms Memorial Scholarship • 1001
Michael Kidger Memorial Scholarship • 1004
Michigan Engineering Scholarships • 1594
Minority Scholarship Awards for College Students • 2207
Minority Scholarship Awards for Incoming College Freshmen • 2208
Molitoris Leadership Scholarship for Undergraduates • 2210
MTI Bert Krisher Memorial Scholarship • 1014
Myrtle and Earl Walker Scholarship • 1017
N.G. Kaul Memorial Scholarship • 1018
NAPA Research and Education Foundation Scholarship • 1020
National Environmental Health Association Graduate Scholarship • 1024
National Space Club Keynote Scholar • 1029
NDSEG Fellowship Program • 1039
Nellie Yeoh Whetten Award • 1041
Old Guard Oral Presentation Competition • 1054
Olive Lynn Salembier Memorial Reentry Scholarship • 2230
Oliver Moghissi Memorial Scholarship • 1055
Operations and Power Division Scholarship • 1056
P.O. Pistilli Undergraduate Scholarship for Advancement in Computer Science and Electrical Engineering • 2233
Payzer Scholarship • 1063
Petroleum Division College Scholarships • 1067
Plastics Pioneers Association Scholarships • 1073
Polymer Modifiers and Additives Division Scholarships • 1074

PPG Protective and Marine Coatings Academic Scholarship • 1075
Presidents Scholarship of the Institute of Industrial Engineers • 1078
Ralph K. Hillquist Honorary SAE Scholarship • 1083
Raymond Davis Scholarship • 1085
Regeneron Science Talent Search • 1086
Reuben Trane Scholarship • 1088
RMEL Foundation Scholarships • 1095
Robert B. Oliver ASNT Scholarship • 1096
Robert E. Thunen Memorial Scholarships • 1097
Robert N. and Helen H. Herbert Undergraduate Scholarship • 1098
Russell and Sigurd Varian Award • 1102
RV Learning Center Scholarship Program • 1104
Salvatore J. Monte Thermoplastic Materials and Foams Division Scholarship • 1105
Samuel Fletcher Tapman ASCE Student Chapter/Club Scholarship • 1106
Schonstedt Scholarship in Surveying • 1107
Science Ambassador Scholarship • 1108
SEE Education Foundation Scholarships • 1110
SMART Scholarship • 1114
Society of Exploration Geophysicists (SEG) Scholarship • 1118
Society of Manufacturing Engineers Directors Scholarship • 1119
Society of Plastics Engineers (SPE) Foundation Scholarships • 1120
Society of Vacuum Coaters Foundation Scholarship • 1121
SPIE Optics and Photonics Education Scholarship • 1122
Steel Intern Scholarships • 1125
Steinman Scholarship • 1126
Stokes Educational Scholarship Program • 311
Structural Materials Division Scholarship • 1130
Student Cash Grant Program • 1131
Student Poster Session Awards • 1132
Susan Miszkowicz Memorial Scholarship • 1136
SWE Past Presidents Scholarship • 2259
Tau Beta Pi Scholarships • 2053
Tau Beta Pi/Society of Automotive Engineers Engineering Scholarship • 1137
Ted and Ruth Neward Scholarship • 1139
The Industrial Electrochemistry and Electrochemical Engineering Division H. H. Dow Memorial Student Achievement Award • 1140
Thermoplastic Elastomers Special Interest Group Scholarship • 1142
Thomas E. Powers/Detroit Section Scholarship • 1143
Thomas M. Stetson Scholarship • 1144
Thomas R. Camp Scholarship • 1145
Tilford Field Studies Scholarship • 1146
TMC/SAE Donald D. Dawson Technical Scholarship • 1148
TMS Best Paper Contest • 1149
TMS Technical Division Student Poster Contest • 1150
TMS/International Symposium On Superalloys Scholarships • 1151
Trent R. Dames and William W. Moore Fellowship • 1153

Tuskegee Airmen Scholarship Foundation Scholarships • 1154
Undergraduate Engineering Scholarships • 1157
United Parcel Service Scholarship for Female Students • 1162
United Parcel Service Scholarship for Minority Students • 2272
Vernon T. Swain, P.E./Robert E. Chute, P.E. Scholarship • 1875
Vertical Flight Foundation Technical Scholarships • 1165
Walter B. Sinnott Scholarship • 1168
William J. Adams, Jr. and Marijane E. Adams Scholarship • 1170
Williams Companies Academic Scholarship • 1171
Yanmar/SAE Scholarship • 1175
Youth Scholarship • 740

ENGLISH/WRITING

Also See Scholarships Listed Under:
Academics/General
Education/Teaching
Communications
Journalism/Broadcasting
Library Science

ACES Education Fund Scholarship • 386
ACES Scholarships • 387
Amy Lowell Poetry Travelling Scholarship • 395
Anthem Essay Contest • 396
Atlas Shrugged Essay Contest • 398
Bill Gove Scholarship • 399
Cavett Robert Scholarship • 405
Clauder Competition Prize • 408
Crossword Hobbyist Crossword Scholarship • 105
CTA Cesar E. Chavez and Dolores Huerta Education Award Program • 1318
Davidson Fellows Scholarships • 110
Disney Entertainment Writing Program • 413
Global Citizen Scholarship • 157
Heinlein Society Scholarship Program • 433
Henry Salvatori Scholarship • 2157
Hispanic Heritage Youth Awards • 2159
Huntington Fellowships • 606
Huntington-British Academy Fellowships for Study in Great Britain • 607
ILA Jeanne S. Chall Research Fellowship • 441
John F. Kennedy Profile in Courage Essay Contest • 625
Julianne Malveaux Scholarship • 2178
Mensa Foundation Scholarship Program • 221
Minnesota Academic Excellence Scholarship • 1604
Moris J. and Betty Kaplun Essay Contest • 2014
National High School Poetry Contest/Easterday Poetry Award • 462
New York Life Award • 466
Optimist International Essay Contest • 471
Patriot's Pen Youth Essay Contest • 473
Platt Family Scholarship Prize Essay Contest • 474
Prize in Ethics Essay Contest • 479
Ruth Lilly and Dorothy Sargent Rosenberg Poetry Fellowship Program • 481
Scholastic Art and Writing Portfolio Award • 483
SuperCollege Scholarship • 330
Taylor/Blakeslee University Fellowships • 492
The Fountainhead Essay Contest • 493

United States Hispanic Leadership Institute Denny's Hungry for Education • 351
Voice of Democracy Audio Essay Contests • 363

ETHNIC AND AREA STUDIES
Also See Scholarships Listed Under:
Foreign Language
Social Science/History
Bridging Scholarships for Study Abroad in Japan • 400
Carl A. Ross Student Paper Award • 404
Council on International Educational Exchange (CIEE) Scholarships • 411
DAAD/AICGS Research Fellowship Program • 412
Diversity Achievement Scholarship • 414
Dumbarton Oaks Fellowships • 418
Fellowships/Grants to Study in Scandinavia • 424
Finlandia Foundation National Student Scholarships Program • 426
Fulbright Grants • 149
Gilman International Scholarship • 429
IACI/NUIG Visiting Fellowship in Irish Studies • 436
ICWA Fellowship Program • 437
Junior Fellowships • 450
Marshall Memorial Fellowship • 213
Marshall Scholar • 214
National Italian American Foundation Scholarship • 2219
Study Abroad Europe Scholarship • 491

FOOD SERVICES
Also See Scholarships Listed Under:
Culinary Arts
Hospitality/Travel/Tourism
Asparagus Club, Thomas K. Zaucha Scholarship • 535
Bob Richardson Legacy Scholarship • 544
California Restaurant Association Educational Foundation General Scholarship • 1269
Charlie and Becky Bray Legacy Scholarship • 557
FMS Solutions Holdings LLC Legacy Scholarship • 579
IFEC Scholarships Award • 608
IFSEA Worthy Goal Scholarship • 609
James Beard Foundation Scholarship • 617
Kimberly-Clark Corporation Legacy Scholarship • 629
Mondelez International Legacy Scholarship • 656
Nancy Curry Scholarship • 659
NextGen Scholarship • 673
Peter and Jody Larkin Legacy Scholarship • 684
Roger Collins Leadership Scholarship • 700
Schwan's Food Service Scholarship • 705
Women Grocers of America (WGA) Mary Macey Scholarship • 738

FOREIGN LANGUAGE
Also See Scholarships Listed Under:
Ethnic and Area Studies
ACL/NJCL National Greek Examination Scholarship • 388
ACL/NJCL National Latin Examination Scholarships • 389
Bridging Scholarships for Study Abroad in Japan • 400
Council on International Educational Exchange (CIEE) Scholarships • 411

Fellowships for Regular Program in Greece • 423
Language Grants • 451
Nadia Christensen Prize • 461
National Junior Classical League (NJCL) Scholarships • 463
National Latin Exam Scholarship • 464
Stokes Educational Scholarship Program • 311
Student Translation Award • 490
Translation Prize Competition • 495

FORESTRY/WILDLIFE
Also See Scholarships Listed Under:
Agriculture/Horticulture/Animals
Biological Sciences/Life Sciences
AOS Student and Postdoctoral Research Awards • 796
Apprentice Ecologist Initiative Youth Scholarship Program • 798
ASF Olin Fellowships • 803
Campus Safety Health and Environmental Management Association Scholarship • 834
Federal Junior Duck Stamp Program and Scholarship Competition • 422
George A. Hall / Harold F. Mayfield Grant • 909
Gloria Barron Wilderness Society Scholarship • 914
John Mabry Forestry Scholarship and Paul Webster Forestry Scholarship • 958
John Wright Memorial Scholarship • 962
Louis Agassiz Fuertes Award • 985
Minnesota Division Izaak Walton League Scholarship • 1605
National Garden Clubs Scholarship • 1026
Paul A. Stewart Grants • 1061
Rockefeller State Wildlife Scholarship • 1767
Student Research Scholarships • 1134
Truman D. Picard Scholarship • 2269
Women's Wildlife Management/Conservation Scholarship • 1174

GRAPHIC ARTS
Also See Scholarships Listed Under:
Performing Arts/Music/Drama/Visual Arts
CardsDirect Future Designer Scholarship • 401
Dorian De Long Arts and Music Scholarship • 1335
FFTA Scholarship Competition • 425
Lions International Peace Poster Contest • 455
Print and Graphics Scholarship • 478
Student Design Competition • 489

HOSPITALITY/TRAVEL/TOURISM
Also See Scholarships Listed Under:
Business/Management
American Express Scholarship Competition • 529
Ecolab Scholarship Competition • 573
HospitalityMaine Scholarship • 1448
IFEC Scholarships Award • 608
Incoming Freshman Scholarship • 612
Roller Skating Foundation Scholarship, Current College Student Category • 701
Steven J. Finkel Service Excellence Scholarship • 713
Timothy S.Y. Lam Foundation Education Scholarships • 722

JOURNALISM/BROADCASTING
Also See Scholarships Listed Under:
Communications
BEA National Scholarships in Broadcasting • 537
Bob East Scholarship • 543
Bob Eddy Scholarship Program • 1244
Bob Stevens Memorial Scholarship • 1245
Bodie McDowell Scholarship • 545
Bohdan Kolinsky Memorial Sports Journalism Scholarship • 1248
Carole Simpson Scholarship • 554
Chester Burger Scholarship for Excellence in Public Relations • 558
College Photographer of the Year • 561
College Television Awards • 409
Dr. Jack G. Shaheen Media Scholarship • 569
Ed Bradley Scholarship • 574
Fund for American Studies Internships • 586
Harry Barfield KBA Scholarship Program • 1423
Hedy Lamarr Achievement Award for Emerging Leaders in Entertainment Technology • 432
Hispanic Heritage Youth Awards • 2159
Idaho State Broadcasters Association Scholarships • 1455
Iowa Newspaper Association Scholarships • 1470
John D. Graham Scholarship • 624
Julianne Malveaux Scholarship • 2178
KAB Broadcast Scholarship Program • 1507
Kit C. King Graduate Scholarship Fund • 630
Lee Thornton Scholarship • 636
Lou and Carole Prato Sports Reporting Scholarship • 642
Marshall E. McCullough Scholarship • 991
Mary Quan Moy Ing Memorial Scholarship • 2199
Minority Scholarship • 1611
National Press Club Scholarship for Journalism Diversity • 664
NPPF Still and Multimedia Scholarship • 676
NPPF Television News Scholarship • 677
Overseas Press Club Foundation Scholarships/Fellowships • 680
PRSA Diversity Multicultural Scholarship • 2241
Quill and Scroll Student Scholarships • 691
Reid Blackburn Scholarship • 695
Ron Culp Scholarship for Mentorship • 702
RTNDA President's Scholarship • 703
Scholastic Art and Writing Portfolio Award • 483
Stephen D. Pisinski Memorial Scholarship • 712
Texas Broadcast Education Foundation Scholarships • 1838
University Journalism Scholarships • 1866
Upper Midwest Chapter Scholarships • 1867
Vincent Chin Scholarship • 733
William B. Ruggles Right to Work Scholarship • 737

LAW
Also See Scholarships Listed Under:
Leadership
AALL Educational Scholarships • 510
ABF Summer Undergraduate Research Fellowship Program • 511
American Bar Association Law Day Art Contest • 40
American Bar Association Law Student Writing Competition • 527

The Ultimate Scholarship Book 2026
General Category Index

American Legion Auxiliary, Department of California Educational Assistance General $1,000 Scholarships • 1211
American Legion Auxiliary, Department of California Educational Assistance General $2,000 Scholarships • 1212
Earl Warren Scholarship • 572
George A. Strait Minority Scholarship • 591
Giles Sutherland Rich Memorial Scholarship • 592
Honorable William Conner Writing Competition • 603
Humane Studies Fellowship: Flexible Support for PhD Students • 175
Humane Studies Fellowship: Graduate Sabbatical Grants • 176
Japanese American Citizens League Law Scholarships • 2174
Jonathan Jasper Wright Award • 194
Legal Opportunity Scholarship Fund • 637
LexisNexis / John R. Johnson Memorial Scholarship Endowment • 638
LimNexus Scholarship • 639
MALDEF Law School Scholarship • 2193
Mary Church Terrell Award • 215
Medgar Evers Award • 218
NCRA A to Z Scholarship • 667
NCRA CASE Student Scholarship • 668
Otto M. Stanfield Legal Scholarship • 679
Presidential Scholarships • 687
Reiff Law Firm Legal Scholarship • 696
Sutliff and Stout Law School Scholarship • 718
University of California Public Policy and International Affairs Junior Summer Institute • 728
University of California Public Policy and International Affairs Law Fellowship • 729
William L. Hastie Award • 376

LEADERSHIP
Also See Scholarships Listed Under:
Academics/General
Public Service/Community Service
Public Administration/Social Work
Coca-Cola Scholars Program • 91
GE-Reagan Foundation Scholarship Program • 151
Hispanic Heritage Youth Awards • 2159
Lori Rhett Memorial Scholarship • 1547
Markley Scholarship • 211
Marshall Memorial Fellowship • 213
Most Valuable Student Scholarships • 230
National Merit Scholarship Program and National Achievement Scholarship Program • 237
Newman Civic Fellow Awards • 254
Scholarships for Student Leaders • 296
SuperCollege Scholarship • 330

LIBRARY SCIENCE
Also See Scholarships Listed Under:
English/Writing
AALL Educational Scholarships • 510
Begun Scholarship • 539
Beverly Murphy MLA Scholarship for Underrepresented Students • 541
Bound to Stay Bound Books Scholarship • 547
CLA Scholarship For BIPOC Students in Memory of Edna Yelland • 559
Frederic G. Melcher Scholarship • 584
George A. Strait Minority Scholarship • 591
Gwendolyn S. Cruzat MLA Scholarship • 597
LexisNexis / John R. Johnson Memorial Scholarship Endowment • 638

MARKETING
Also See Scholarships Listed Under:
Business/Management
Betsy Plank/PRSSA Scholarship • 540
Caples Student Campaign of the Year Award • 551
DMI Milk Marketing Scholarship • 859
Executive Women International Scholarship Program • 578
Gary Yoshimura Scholarship • 590
Harry A. Applegate Scholarship • 599
IFEC Scholarships Award • 608
LAGRANT Scholarship Program • 2182
Lawrence G. Foster Award for Excellence in Public Relations • 634
National Scholarship • 2220
PAVE Student Design Competition • 683

MATHEMATICS
Also See Scholarships Listed Under:
Accounting/Finance
Computer And Information Science
Aerospace/Aviation
Sciences/Physical Sciences
Actuarial Diversity Scholarship • 2083
AFCEA Ralph W. Shrader Diversity Scholarships • 761
AFCEA ROTC Scholarships • 23
Alice T. Schafer Mathematics Prize • 774
Astronaut Scholarship • 816
Barry M. Goldwater Scholarship and Excellence in Education Program • 824
Biographies of Contemporary Women in Mathematics Essay Contest • 828
Collegiate Inventors Competition • 842
Davidson Fellows Scholarships • 110
Frank and Brennie Morgan Prize for Outstanding Research in Mathematics by an Undergraduate Student • 893
Gertrude Cox Scholarship For Women In Statistics • 910
Graduate Research Fellowship Program • 917
Hispanic Heritage Youth Awards • 2159
HSC Foundation Scholarship • 2165
Hubertus W.V. Wellems Scholarship for Male Students • 2167
LabRoots Scholarship • 970
Learner Education Women in Mathematics Scholarship • 976
Mary Rhein Memorial Scholarship • 993
Minnesota Academic Excellence Scholarship • 1604
Modeling the Future Challenge • 1011
Moody's Mega Math Challenge • 1013
National Space Club Keynote Scholar • 1029
NDSEG Fellowship Program • 1039
Paradigm Challenge • 1058
Payzer Scholarship • 1063
Regeneron Science Talent Search • 1086
Science Ambassador Scholarship • 1108
SMART Scholarship • 1114
Stokes Educational Scholarship Program • 311

MEDICINE/NURSING/HEALTH PROFESSIONS
Also See Scholarships Listed Under:
Biological Sciences/Life Sciences
Chemistry
Dentistry
AAMA Student Essay Competition • 746
Academic Education Award • 750
Academy of Nutrition and Dietetics Foundation Student Scholarship • 751
ADEA/Crest Oral-B Scholarships for Dental Hygiene Students Pursuing Academic Careers • 755
ADEA/Sigma Phi Alpha Linda Devore Scholarship • 759
AHIMA Foundation Merit Scholarships • 765
Alice W. Rooke Scholarship • 775
Alpha Mu Tau Fraternity Undergraduate Scholarships • 776
AMBUCS Scholars • 778
AMT Student Scholarship • 787
Annual NBNA Scholarships • 789
AORN Foundation Scholarship Program • 795
Arc of Washington State Trust Fund Stipend Award • 1221
Association of Food and Drug Officials Scholarship Award • 813
AUA Foundation Research Scholars Program • 817
Avacare Medical Scholarship • 820
Bill Kane Scholarship, Undergraduate • 827
BSN Scholarship • 832
Campus Safety Health and Environmental Management Association Scholarship • 834
Charlotte McGuire Scholarship • 839
ChiroHealthUSA Foxworth Family Scholarship • 840
CTAHPERD Gibson-Laemel Scholarship • 1319
Dorothy Budnek Memorial Scholarship • 862
Dr. Bart Kamen Memorial FIRST Scholarship • 865
Eight and Forty Lung and Respiratory Nursing Scholarship Fund • 873
Elekta Radiation Therapy Scholarship • 874
EmPOWERED Scholars Program • 878
ENA Foundation Undergraduate Scholarship • 879
Equity in Pharmacy Scholarship • 882
Foundation for Surgical Technology Medical Mission Scholarship • 891
Foundation for Surgical Technology Scholarships • 892
Graduate Student Scholarship • 920
Gwendolyn S. Cruzat MLA Scholarship • 597
H.M. Muffly Memorial Scholarship • 1420
Harriet Hayes Austin Memorial Scholarship for Nursing • 1421
Harry J. Harwick Scholarship • 927
Health Careers Scholarship • 928
Health Professions Pre-Graduate Scholarship Program • 2154
Health Professions Preparatory Scholarship Program • 2155
HIMSS Foundation Scholarship • 933
Illinois Association for Health, Physical Education, Recreation and Dance Scholarships • 1460
International Student Scholarship • 943

Iowa Physician Assistant Society Scholarship • 1473
Irene and Daisy MacGregor Memorial Scholarship • 946
Jack E. Barger, Sr. Memorial Nursing Scholarship • 1483
Jackson Laboratory Scholarship • 949
Jean Lee/Jeff Marvin Collegiate Scholarships • 1492
Jimmy A. Young Memorial Education Recognition Award • 952
John D. and Virginia Riesch Scholarship • 1500
Kappa Delta Phi • 966
Karen O'Neil Memorial Scholarship • 967
Leaders Scholarship • 975
Linda Craig Memorial Scholarship Presented by St. Vincent Sports Performance • 1542
Margaret A. Pemberton Scholarship • 1563
Margaret A. Stafford Nursing Scholarship • 1564
MARILN Professional Scholarship Award • 1565
Medical Student Research Scholarship • 996
Medical Student Training in Aging Research (MSTAR) Program • 997
Mental Health Importance Scholarship • 1000
MGMA Midwest Section Scholarship • 1002
MGMA Western Section Scholarship • 1003
Michael Moody Fitness Scholarship • 1005
Migrant Health Scholarships • 1007
Minority Fellowship Program • 1008
Minority Scholarship Award for Physical Therapy Students • 2206
Minority Student Scholarship • 1009
NAHN Scholarship • 2213
Naomi Brack Student Scholarship • 1019
National Hispanic Health Professional Student Scholarship • 2218
National Student Nurses' Association Scholarship • 1030
NBRC/AMP Gareth B. Gish, MS, RRT Memorial and William F. Miller, MD Postgraduate Education Recognition Awards • 1033
NBRC/AMP William W. Burgin, Jr. MD and Robert M. Lawrence, MD Education Recognition Award • 1034
NCAPA Endowment Annual Student Grants • 1035
NCPA Foundation Presidential Scholarship • 1036
NEHA/AAS/APU Scholarship Awards • 1040
New Century Scholars Doctoral Scholarship • 1042
NFMC Dorothy Dann Bullock Music Therapy Award and the NFMC Ruth B. Robertson Music Therapy Award • 1045
NHSC Scholarship • 1046
NIH Undergraduate Scholarship Program • 1047
Nurse Candidate Program • 1051
Nurse Corps Scholarship Program • 1052
Phoebe Pember Memorial Scholarship • 1069
Physician Assistant Foundation Scholarship • 1070
Predoctoral Research Fellowships • 1077
Resident Research Scholarship • 1087
Richard J. Stull Student Essay Competition in Healthcare Management • 1090
Richard L. Davis, FACMPE - Managers Scholarship • 1092
Richard L. Davis, FACMPE/Barbara B. Watson, FACMPE - National Scholarship • 1093
Robert G. Porter Post-Secondary Scholarships • 2036
Ruth Abernathy Presidential Scholarship • 1103
Sertoma Communicative Disorders Scholarship • 1111
Sigma Phi Alpha Undergraduate Scholarship • 1112
SNMTS Paul Cole Scholarship • 1117
Stephanie Carroll Memorial Scholarship • 1128
Student Research Fellowship Awards • 1133
Summer Undergraduate Research Fellowships • 1135
Visiting Medical Student Scholar • 1167
Welch Scholars Grant • 1169
William and Charlotte Cadbury Award • 2275
Women's Scholarship • 1173

MILITARY/POLICE/FIRE
Also See Scholarships Listed Under:
Leadership

100th Infantry Battalion Memorial Scholarship Fund • 10
1st Marine Division Association Scholarship • 12
25th Infantry Division Association Educational Scholarship • 13
ACJA/Lambda Alpha Epsilon Scholarship • 19
AFCEA ROTC Scholarships • 23
Air Force ROTC ASCP • 29
Air Force ROTC High School Scholarship Program • 30
Air Force ROTC In-College Program • 31
Air Force ROTC Professional Officer Course-Early Release Program • 32
Air Force ROTC SOAR Program • 33
Airmen Memorial Foundation Scholarship Program • 34
America's 911 Foundation Scholarship • 39
American Legion Auxiliary, Department of California Educational Assistance General $1,000 Scholarships • 1211
American Legion Auxiliary, Department of California Educational Assistance General $2,000 Scholarships • 1212
American Legion Auxiliary, Department of California Educational Assistance General $500 Scholarships • 1213
American Legion Legacy Scholarships • 42
AMVETS Children/Grandchildren Scholarships • 46
AMVETS National Scholarships for Veterans • 47
Anchor Scholarship Foundation Scholarship • 48
Armed Services YMCA Annual Essay Contest • 49
Army Emergency Relief's MG James Ursano Scholarship Program • 50
Army Engineer Memorial Awards • 51
Army Nurse Corps Association Scholarships • 52
Army ROTC Advanced Course • 53
Army ROTC Four-Year Scholarship Program • 54
Army ROTC Green To Gold Scholarship Program • 55
ASNE Scholarship Program • 810
Brown Hudner Navy Scholarship • 68
Capt. James J. Regan Scholarship • 72
Captain Caliendo College Assistance Fund • 73
Chief Master Sergeants of the Air Force Scholarships • 80
Chief Petty Officer Scholarship Fund • 81
Children of Warriors National Presidents' Scholarship • 82
Coast Guard College Student Pre-Commissioning Initiative • 88
Coast Guard Foundation Scholarship Fund • 89
Congressional Medal of Honor Society Scholarships • 96
Daedalian Foundation Scholarship Program • 108
Daughters of the Cincinnati Scholarship • 109
Dolphin Scholarships • 125
Edith Nourse Rogers STEM Scholarship • 134
EOD Warrior Foundation Scholarship • 137
Exemption from Tuition Fees for Dependents of Kentucky Veterans • 1370
First Cavalry Division Foundation Scholarship • 143
Folds of Honor Higher Education Scholarship • 146
Fraternal Order of Eagles Memorial Foundation • 148
Gene Carte Student Paper Competition • 152
General Henry H. Arnold Education Grant Program • 153
Google SVA Scholarship • 163
Guy M. Wilson Scholarship • 1416
H and P Veterans Helping Veterans Scholarship • 165
Hanscom Air Force Base Spouses' Club Scholarship • 169
Jack E. Barger, Sr. Memorial Nursing Scholarship • 1483
John F. Duffy Scholarship/Grant Program • 190
Jon C. Ladda Memorial Foundation Scholarship • 193
Jonathan Jasper Wright Award • 194
Joseph P. and Helen T. Cribbins Scholarship • 195
Judith Haupt Member's Child Scholarship • 196
Kathern F. Gruber Scholarship Program • 198
La Fra Scholarship • 201
Leadership Essay Contest • 203
Marine Corps League Scholarships • 209
Marine Corps Scholarship Foundation Scholarship • 210
Mary Church Terrell Award • 215
Mary Paolozzi Member's Scholarship • 216
Medgar Evers Award • 218
Memorial Scholarship Fund • 220
Mike and Gail Donley Spouse Scholarship • 223
Military Award Program (MAP) • 224
Military Family Support Trust Scholarships • 225
Montgomery GI Bill - Active Duty • 227
Montgomery GI Bill - Selected Reserve • 228
Montgomery GI Bill Tuition Assistance Top-Up • 229
NACOP Scholarship • 232
Naval Enlisted Reserve Association Scholarships • 242
Naval Helicopter Association Scholarship • 243
Naval Intelligence Essay Contest • 244
Navy College Fund • 246
Navy Supply Corps Foundation Scholarship • 247
Navy-Marine Corps ROTC College Program • 248

The Ultimate Scholarship Book 2026
General Category Index

Navy-Marine Corps ROTC Four-Year Scholarships • 249
Navy-Marine Corps ROTC Two-Year Scholarships • 250
Navy/Marine Corps/Coast Guard (NMCCG) Enlisted Dependent Spouse Scholarship • 251
Next Gen Scholars Award • 255
Non Commissioned Officers Association Scholarships • 258
NROTC Nurse Corps Scholarship • 259
NROTC Scholarship Program • 260
Past Department Presidents' Junior Scholarship Award • 1718
Patriot's Pen Youth Essay Contest • 473
Pauline Langkamp Memorial Scholarship • 266
Pennsylvania Educational Gratuity Program • 1725
Ritchie-Jennings Memorial Scholarship • 699
Ruth D. Peterson Fellowship for Racial and Ethnic Diversity • 2245
Scholarships for Military Children • 295
Seabee Memorial Scholarship • 299
Sheryl A. Horak Memorial Scholarship • 301
Sons of Union Veterans of the Civil War Scholarships • 306
Student Paper Competition • 316
Study.com Scholarship for Children of First Responders • 324
Study.com Scholarship for Military Members and Veterans • 325
Study.com Scholarship for Military Spouses and Children • 326
Subic Bay-Cubi Point Scholarship • 329
Supplemental Education Grant (SEG) • 331
Tailhook Educational Foundation Scholarship • 333
UDT-SEAL Scholarship • 347
United Daughters of the Confederacy Scholarships • 350
VA Essay Scholarship • 361
Veterans Caucus Scholarship • 362
W. H. Howie McClennan Scholarship • 366
Wells Fargo Veterans Scholarship Program • 373
William D. and Jewell Brewer Scholarship • 1909
William L. Hastie Award • 376
Wisconsin Veterans Education Reimbursement Grants • 1920
Women Marines Association Scholarship Program • 379
Women's Army Corps Veterans Association Scholarship • 381
Women's Overseas Service League Scholarships for Women • 382

ORGANIZATIONS/CLUBS/EMPLOYERS
Also See Scholarships Listed Under:
Unions

4-H Youth in Action • 1930
Adrianna Andreini Scholarship • 1931
AFSA Financial Aid Scholarships • 1932
AFSA/AAFSW Merit Awards • 1933
AHIMA Foundation Merit Scholarships • 765
American Association of State Troopers (AAST) Scholarship • 1937
American Legion Eagle Scout of the Year • 1938
AMVETS National Ladies Auxiliary Scholarship • 1939
Angus Foundation Scholarships • 788
Annual NBNA Scholarships • 789
AOS Student and Postdoctoral Research Awards • 796
AQHF General Scholarship • 1940
AQHF Youth Scholarship • 1941
ARA Scholarship • 1942
Arthur M. and Berdena King Eagle Scout Contest • 1943
ASABE Foundation Engineering Scholarship • 799
ASNE Scholarship Program • 810
Assured Life Association National Scholarship • 1945
AWSM Internship and Scholarship • 1946
Bernard Rotberg Memorial Scholarship Fund • 1947
Betsy Plank/PRSSA Scholarship • 540
Bob Warnicke Scholarship • 64
Boon San Kitty Scholarship • 1948
Boys and Girls Clubs of America National Youth of the Year Award • 1949
Carroll C. Hall Memorial Scholarship • 1950
Chairman's Award • 1952
Charles R. Walgreen Jr. Leadership Award • 1954
CNH Industrial Aftermarket Solutions Scholarship • 1956
Community College Transition Award • 1957
Delta Gamma Foundation Scholarship • 1960
Delta Phi Epsilon Educational Foundation Scholarship • 1961
Donald A. and John R. Fisher Memorial Scholarship • 1964
Donald F. and Mildred Topp Othmer Scholarships • 861
Elmer J. and Hester Jane Johnson Memorial FFA Scholarship • 876
Elson T. Killam Memorial Scholarship • 877
Emergency Educational Fund Grants • 1965
Emmett J. Doerr Memorial Scout Scholarship • 1966
ENA Foundation Undergraduate Scholarship • 879
Eugene C. Beach Memorial Scholarship • 1967
F.W. Beich Beichley Scholarship • 885
Farm Credit Services of America Collegiate Scholarship • 1969
FarmAid FFA Scholarship • 886
FEEA Scholarship Program • 1970
First in the Family Scholarship • 1971
Fleet Reserve Association Scholarship • 1972
Ford Motor Company Fund and Ford Trucks Built Ford Tough - FFA Scholarship Program • 1973
Fourth Degree Pro Deo and Pro Patria Scholarships • 1974
Frank S. Land Scholarships • 1975
Gaige Fund Award • 900
Gamma Theta Upsilon-Geographical Honor Society Scholarships • 589
Garland Duncan Scholarships • 901
Gary Yoshimura Scholarship • 590
Gaston/Nolle Scholarships • 1976
GCSAA Legacy Awards • 1977
GCSAA Scholars Competition • 905
Golden Key Graduate Scholar Award • 1980
Golden Key Outstanding Member Award • 1981
Golden Key Undergraduate Achievement Award • 1982
Golden Key Undergraduate Achievement Scholarship • 1983
Guistwhite Scholarships • 1984
Harold and Inge Marcus Scholarship • 925
Hites Transfer Scholarship • 1986
Hoard's Dairyman FFA Scholarship • 1987
IFSA Foundation Scholarship Award • 1990
Induction Recognition Award • 1991
International Gas Turbine Institute Scholarship • 942
James E. Breining Scholarship Award • 1995
James Rust Scholarship • 1996
John and Elsa Gracik Scholarships • 953
John J. McKetta Scholarship • 956
John W. McDevitt (Fourth Degree) Scholarship Fund • 1999
Jones-Laurence Award for Scholastic Achievement • 2000
Junior Member Loyalty Scholarship • 2001
Karen O'Neil Memorial Scholarship • 967
Kenneth Andrew Roe Scholarship • 969
Kiwanis Children's Fund Scholarship • 2002
Kyutaro and Yasuo Abiko Memorial Scholarship • 2003
Lawrence G. Foster Award for Excellence in Public Relations • 634
Legacy Award • 2004
Lillian and Arthur Dunn Scholarship • 2005
Literacy Grants • 2006
Long-Term Member Sponsored Scholarship • 984
Maids of Athena Scholarships • 2007
Margaret A. Haines Telephony Scholarship • 2008
Margaret Jerome Sampson Scholarship • 2009
Marliave Fund • 990
Martin Luther King, Jr. Memorial Scholarship • 2010
Melvin R. Green Scholarships • 999
Modern Woodmen of America Scholarship • 2013
Mortar Board National Foundation Fellowship • 2015
Mortin Scholarship • 2016
Nancy Curry Scholarship • 659
Nancy McManus Washington Internship Scholarships • 660
National Eagle Scout Association Scholarship • 2017
National FFA Combined Scholarship • 2018
National Honor Society Scholarship • 2019
National Propane Gas Foundation • 2021
National Scholarship Program • 239
Navy Supply Corps Foundation Scholarship • 247
NESA Hall/McElwain Merit Scholarships • 2022
NESA Lawrence S. and Mabel Cooke Scholarship • 2023
NFMC Dorothy Dann Bullock Music Therapy Award and the NFMC Ruth B. Robertson Music Therapy Award • 1045
NFMC Lynn Freeman Olson Composition Awards • 467
NFMC Wendell Irish Viola Award • 468
NIADA Scholarship • 2024
Non-Traditional Student Scholarship • 2025
NSCS Grad School Award • 2026
Owens-Bell Award • 2028

Phi Delta Kappa (PDK) Educational Foundation Scholarship Program • 2029
Phi Kappa Phi Fellowship • 2030
Physician Assistant Foundation Scholarship • 1070
Raney Fund Award • 1084
Rebecca Palmer Eagle Scout Scholarship Endowment • 2032
Ruth Abernathy Presidential Scholarship • 1103
Sam Rose Memorial Scholarship • 2039
Sandra Jo Hornick Scholarship • 2040
Schwan's Food Service Scholarship • 705
Shasta Head Start Alumni Scholarship • 2042
Shawn Maree Vaillant Memorial Scholarship • 2043
Shropshire Scholarship • 2045
Sigma Phi Epsilon Balanced Man Scholarship • 2046
Spirit of Youth Scholarship for Junior Members • 2047
Stanley A. Doran Memorial Scholarship • 2049
Starfleet Scholarships • 2050
Stella Blum Research Grant • 486
Stillman Kelley/Thelma Byrum Awards • 487
Student CTA (SCTA) Scholarship in Honor of L. Gordon Bittle • 2051
Student Paper Competition • 316
Tall Club International Scholarship • 2052
Tau Beta Pi Scholarships • 2053
Terrill Graduate Fellowship • 2054
Thelma A. Robinson Award in Ballet • 494
Tilford Field Studies Scholarship • 1146
Tractor Supply Company Endowment • 2055
Tri Delta Undergraduate Scholarship • 2056
Truckload Carriers Association Scholarship Fund • 2057
Tuition Exchange Scholarships • 2058
Undergraduate Scholarship • 2062
Undergraduate Scholarships • 498
United Agribusiness League and United Agricultural Benefit Trust Scholarships • 2065
VFW Scout of the Year Scholarship • 2069
Warren Poslusny Award for Outstanding Achievement • 2071
Wenderoth Undergraduate Scholarship • 2072
Women in Aviation International Scholarship • 2074
Youth of the Year Award • 2077
Youth Partners Accessing Capital • 2078
Youth Program • 1177

Performing Arts/Music/Drama/Visual Arts
Also See Scholarships Listed Under:
English/Writing
Graphic Arts

Adobe Design Circle Scholarships • 390
AFSA/AAFSW Merit Awards • 1933
AGL Over the Rainbow Scholarship • 391
AIGA Worldstudio Scholarships • 392
Alexia Foundation Student Grants • 393
AMCA Music Scholarship • 394
Archibald Rutledge Scholarship Program • 1222
ASCAP Foundation Morton Gould Young Composer Awards • 397
AWAF Scholarships • 1233
Bob East Scholarship • 543
Bodie McDowell Scholarship • 545
Career Center • 402
Career Transition for Dancers Undergraduate Studies Scholarship • 403
Children in Need Scholarship • 406
Christopher L. Hunt Scholarship • 407
College Photographer of the Year • 561
College Television Awards • 409
Congressional Black Caucus Spouses Visual Arts Scholarship • 2127
ConnectHER Film Festival • 410
Cynthia and Alan Baran Fine Arts and Music Scholarship Fund • 1320
Davidson Fellows Scholarships • 110
Dolly Parton Songwriters Award • 415
Doodle for Google • 416
Dr. Kenny D. Hasija Scholarship • 417
Educational Theatre Association Board of Directors Scholarship • 419
Expressions Challenge by Walgreens • 420
Fashion Scholarship Fund Scholarships • 421
Federal Junior Duck Stamp Program and Scholarship Competition • 422
FFTA Scholarship Competition • 425
Frame My Future Scholarship Contest • 427
Future Theatre Educator Scholarship • 428
George Heller Memorial Scholarship Fund of the SAG-AFTRA Foundation • 1978
Georgia Thespians Achievement Scholarships • 1399
Glenn Miller Scholarship Competition • 430
Great Khalid Performing Arts Scholarship • 431
Hedy Lamarr Achievement Award for Emerging Leaders in Entertainment Technology • 432
Herb Alpert Young Jazz Composer Awards • 434
Herblock Award for Editorial Cartoon • 435
Hispanic Heritage Youth Awards • 2159
Huntington Fellowships • 606
Huntington-British Academy Fellowships for Study in Great Britain • 607
IDSA Undergraduate and Graduate Scholarships • 438
IFDA Leaders Commemorative Scholarship • 439
IFDA Student Member Scholarship • 440
IFEC Scholarships Award • 608
Illustrators of the Future • 442
International Trumpet Guild Conference Scholarship • 443
Iowa Scholarship for the Arts • 1475
Iowa Thespian Chapter Board Senior Scholarships • 1476
Jack Kent Cooke Young Artist Award • 444
Jaime Guttenberg Dance Scholarship • 445
JFLF Awards Programs • 620
Joel Polsky Academic Achievement Award • 446
John F. and Anna Lee Stacey Scholarship Fund for Art Education • 447
John L. Dales Scholarship Fund • 1998
John Lennon Scholarship Competition • 448
Julius and Esther Stulberg International String Competition • 449
Kit C. King Graduate Scholarship Fund • 630
Laura Ziegler Scholarship • 452
Legacy Scholarship for Undergraduates • 453
Leiber and Stoller Scholarship for Songwriters • 454
Leo H. Grether Memorial Scholarship • 1536
Lotte Lenya Competition • 456
Luce/ACLS Dissertation Fellowships in American Art • 457
Marian A. Smith Costume Award • 458
Mary Bowman Arts in Activism Award • 459
Michael J. Peitz Leadership Scholarship • 460
Minnesota Academic Excellence Scholarship • 1604
Missouri State Thespian Scholarships • 1620
National Vocal Competition for Young Opera Singers • 465
NFMC Dorothy Dann Bullock Music Therapy Award and the NFMC Ruth B. Robertson Music Therapy Award • 1045
NFMC Gretchen E. Van Roy Music Education Scholarship • 674
NFMC Hinda Honigman Award for the Blind • 2314
NFMC Lynn Freeman Olson Composition Awards • 467
NFMC Wendell Irish Viola Award • 468
NPPF Still and Multimedia Scholarship • 676
NPPF Television News Scholarship • 677
Ocean Awareness Contest • 469
Office Supply Scholarship • 470
Part-Time Student Scholarship • 472
Playwright Discovery Award • 475
Poster Contest for High School Students • 476
Princess Grace Awards • 477
Print and Graphics Scholarship • 478
Reid Blackburn Scholarship • 695
Ruth Abernathy Presidential Scholarship • 1103
Ruth Clark Furniture Design Scholarship • 480
Sara Tucker Study Grant • 482
Scholastic Art and Writing Portfolio Award • 483
Senior Fellowship Program • 484
Sir John Soane's Museum Foundation Traveling Grant • 1113
Stanfield and D'Orlando Art Scholarship • 2048
State of the Arts Scholarship • 485
Stella Blum Research Grant • 486
Stillman Kelley/Thelma Byrum Awards • 487
Stuck at Prom Scholarship • 314
Student Academy Awards Competition • 488
Thelma A. Robinson Award in Ballet • 494
Tricia LeVangie Green/Sustainable Design Scholarship • 496
Ukulele Festival Hawaii's College Scholarship Program • 497
Undergraduate Scholarships • 498
Vectorworks Design Scholarship • 499
Vercille Voss IFDA Graduate Student Scholarship • 500
Visiting Senior Fellowship Program • 501
VMSD Scholarship • 502
Women Band Directors International College Scholarships • 503
Wyland National Art Challenge • 504
You Can t Label People, but You Can Label Products Essay and Label Design Scholarship • 505
Young American Creative Patriotic Art Contest • 506
Young Filmmakers Contest • 507
Zicklin Contracting Restoration Awareness Scholarship • 508

The Ultimate Scholarship Book 2026
General Category Index

PSYCHOLOGY
Also See Scholarships Listed Under:
Social Science/History
  APF Dr. Christine Blasey Ford Grant • 530
  APF/COGDOP Graduate Student Scholarships • 531
  APF/Division 54 Lizette Peterson-Homer Injury Prevention Grant • 532
  David H. and Beverly A. Barlow Grant • 564
  Future Counselors of America Scholarship • 587
  Graduate Research Fellowship Program • 917
  Sharon Stephens Brehm Undergraduate Psychology Scholarships • 706
  TOPSS Competition for High School Psychology Students • 725

PUBLIC ADMINISTRATION/SOCIAL WORK
Also See Scholarships Listed Under:
Leadership
Education/Teaching
Public Service/Community Service
  Boren Scholarships • 546
  Byron Hanke Fellowship • 549
  Fund for American Studies Internships • 586
  Graduate Scholarship Program • 595
  John F. Kennedy Profile in Courage Essay Contest • 625
  Julianne Malveaux Scholarship • 2178
  National Academic Scholarships • 661
  National Foundation Scholarships • 662
  National Washington Crossing Foundation Scholarship • 666
  Project Vote Smart National Internship Program • 689
  Raftelis Leadership Scholarships • 692
  Ruth Segal Scholarship • 704
  Shasta Head Start Alumni Scholarship • 2042
  Truman Scholar • 342
  United States Senate Youth Program • 727

PUBLIC SERVICE/COMMUNITY SERVICE
Also See Scholarships Listed Under:
Academics/General
Leadership
Education/Teaching
  Americorps National Civilian Community Corps • 44
  Americorps Vista • 45
  Arthur M. and Berdena King Eagle Scout Contest • 1943
  Bonner Scholars Program • 65
  Coca-Cola Scholars Program • 91
  Colorado Council Volunteerism and Community Service Scholarship • 1303
  Gloria Barron Prize for Young Heroes • 158
  Hispanic Heritage Youth Awards • 2159
  Horatio Alger National Scholarship Program • 174
  Imagine America High School Scholarship Program • 611
  James M. and Virginia M. Smyth Scholarship • 188
  Japanese American Citizens League Entering Freshman Awards • 2172
  Japanese American Citizens League Undergraduate Awards • 2175
  Markley Scholarship • 211
  Mason Lighthouse Scholarship • 217
  National Honor Society Scholarship • 2019
  Navin Narayan College Scholarship • 245

  Newman Civic Fellow Awards • 254
  Pedro Zamora Young Leaders Scholarship • 267
  Pilot Pen G2 Overachievers Student Grant • 270
  Prudential Emerging Visionaries • 274
  Samuel Huntington Public Service Award • 289
  Sodexo Stephen J. Brady STOP Hunger Scholarship • 304
  Student Activist Awards • 315
  SuperCollege Scholarship • 330
  Thurgood Marshall College Scholarship Fund • 2264
  Truman Scholar • 342
  United States Senate Youth Program • 727
  Urban Fellows Program • 352
  Voyager Scholarship, The Obama-Chesky Scholarship for Public Service • 364
  White House Fellows Program • 374
  Women's Overseas Service League Scholarships for Women • 382

RACE/ETHNICITY/GENDER/FAMILY STATUS
Also See Scholarships Listed Under:
Academics/General
  A.T. Anderson Memorial Scholarship • 2079
  AAUW Educational Foundation Career Development Grants • 2080
  Abe and Esther Hagiwara Student Aid Award • 2081
  Achievers in Technology Program • 2082
  Actuarial Diversity Scholarship • 2083
  Ada I. Pressman Memorial Scholarship • 2084
  Admiral Grace Murray Hopper Memorial Scholarships • 2085
  Adolph Van Pelt Scholarship • 2086
  Adult Students in Scholastic Transition (ASIST) • 517
  Afro-Academic, Cultural, Technological and Scientific Olympics (ACT-SO) • 2087
  Against The Grain Artistic Scholarship • 2088
  AGBU US Graduate Scholarship • 2089
  Agnes Jones Jackson Scholarship • 2090
  Agnes Missirian Scholarship • 2091
  AHEPA Educational Foundation National Scholarship Program • 2092
  AICPA Fellowship for Minority Doctoral Students • 2093
  AICPA Scholarship for Minority Accounting Students • 2094
  AISES Intel Scholarship • 2095
  Alice T. Schafer Mathematics Prize • 774
  Alice W. Rooke Scholarship • 775
  Allogan Slagle Memorial Scholarship • 2096
  Ally Financial Law Scholars • 2097
  American Chemical Society Scholars Program • 2098
  American Indian Services Scholarship • 2099
  AMS Minority Scholarship • 785
  Anne Maureen Whitney Barrow Memorial Scholarship • 2100
  Annual NBNA Scholarships • 789
  APIA Scholarship Program • 2101
  Aritzia Scholarship • 2102
  ARS Undergraduate Scholarship • 2103
  ASA Scholarships • 2104
  Asian and Pacific Islander American Scholarships • 2105

  Association of Cuban Engineers Scholarship Foundation Scholarships • 2106
  Auxiliary Legacy Scholarship • 819
  AWAF Scholarships • 1233
  B.J. Harrod Scholarships • 2107
  B.K. Krenzer Reentry Scholarship • 2108
  Beverly Murphy MLA Scholarship for Underrepresented Students • 541
  Biographies of Contemporary Women in Mathematics Essay Contest • 828
  BIPOC Scholarship • 2109
  BrandSource Scholarship • 2110
  Burlington Northern Santa Fe (BNSF) Foundation Scholarship • 2111
  Cafe Bustelo El Cafe Del Futuro Scholarship • 2112
  California Chafee Grant for Foster Youth • 2113
  Casey Family Scholarship • 2114
  Catching the Dream Native American Scholarship Fund • 2115
  CBC Spouses Essay Contest • 2116
  CBC Spouses Performing Arts Scholarship • 2117
  CBCF Reducing the Financial Barrier Scholarship • 2118
  CHCI United Health Foundation Scholar-Intern Program • 2119
  Cherokee Nation/Tribal Council At-Large Scholarship • 2120
  Chevron Corporate Scholars Program • 2121
  Chief Manuelito Scholarship Program • 2122
  Citizen Potawatomi Nation Tribal Scholarship • 2123
  Colgate-Palmolive Make the U Educational Grant • 2124
  Conference of Minority Transportation Officials (COMTO) National Scholarship • 2125
  Congressional Black Caucus Spouses Education Scholarship • 2126
  Congressional Black Caucus Spouses Visual Arts Scholarship • 2127
  CRA All-Access Scholarship • 2128
  Creative Sole Scholarship • 2129
  Development Fund for Black Students in Science and Technology • 2130
  Distinguished Young Women Scholarship Program • 2131
  Diversity Advocacy Council Scholarship • 2132
  Dr. Ivy M. Parker Memorial Scholarship • 2133
  Dr. Juan Andrade, Jr. Scholarship • 2134
  Drs. James and Wanda Trefil Science Scholarship • 2135
  Edie Windsor Coding Scholarship • 2136
  EDSA Diversity Scholarships • 2137
  Education Scholarship • 2138
  Education Support Award • 2139
  Eugene and Elinor Kotur Scholarship Trust Fund • 2140
  Florence Young Memorial Scholarship • 2141
  Foundation Scholarships • 2142
  Frontline Families Scholarship • 2143
  Full Circle Scholarship • 2144
  Gamma Mu Scholarships Program • 2145
  Gates Scholarship • 2146
  GEM MS Engineering Fellowship Program • 2147
  General Society of Mayflower Descendants (GSMD) Scholarship • 2148

Generation Google Scholarship • 2149
Gentlemen Showcase • 2150
George Choy Memorial/Gay Asian Pacific Alliance (GAPA) Scholarship • 2151
Gladys Anderson Emerson Scholarship • 913
Goldie Bateson Scholarship • 2152
HBCU NREI Scholarship • 2153
Health Professions Pre-Graduate Scholarship Program • 2154
Health Professions Preparatory Scholarship Program • 2155
Helene M. Overly Memorial Graduate Scholarship • 2156
Henry Sachs Foundation Scholarship • 1432
Henry Salvatori Scholarship • 2157
Herbert Lehman Education Fund Scholarship • 2158
Hispanic Heritage Youth Awards • 2159
Hispanic Scholarship Fund • 2160
Hispanic Serving Institutions Scholarship • 2161
Historically Black College and University Scholarship • 2162
Honeywell International Inc. Scholarships • 2163
Hopi Scholarship Program • 2164
HSC Foundation Scholarship • 2165
Hsiao Memorial Social Sciences Scholarship • 2166
Hubertus W.V. Wellems Scholarship for Male Students • 2167
Ida M. Pope Memorial Scholarship • 2168
Intellia Therapeutics - UNCF Scholarship • 2169
Jackie Robinson Foundation Scholarship Program • 2170
James M. and Erma T. Freemont Foundation Scholarship Program • 2171
Japanese American Citizens League Entering Freshman Awards • 2172
Japanese American Citizens League Graduate Awards • 2173
Japanese American Citizens League Law Scholarships • 2174
Japanese American Citizens League Undergraduate Awards • 2175
Jeannette Rankin National Scholar Grant • 2176
Jimmy A. Young Memorial Education Recognition Award • 952
Jonathan Jasper Wright Award • 194
Judith Resnik Memorial Scholarship • 2177
Julianne Malveaux Scholarship • 2178
Kansas Ethnic Minority Scholarship • 1511
Kenneth W. Payne Student Prize • 2179
Knights of Lithuania Scholarship Program • 2180
Korean Ancestry Grant • 2181
LAGRANT Scholarship Program • 2182
Larry Whiteside Scholarship • 2183
Laurel Hester Memorial Scholarship • 2184
Laurels Fund Scholarship • 633
LEAGUE Foundation Scholarship • 2185
Legal Opportunity Scholarship Fund • 637
LGBTQ+ Student Scholarship from Study.com • 2186
Lillian Moller Gilbreth Memorial Scholarship • 2187
Live Your Dream Awards Program • 2188
Lucy Kasparian Aharonian Scholarship • 2189
LULAC General Awards • 2190

LULAC Honors Awards • 2191
MAES Scholarship Program • 2192
MALDEF Law School Scholarship • 2193
Marcus Garvey Scholarship • 2194
Margaret McNamara Education Grants • 2195
Marilynn Smith Scholarship • 2196
Mark Ando and Ito Family Scholarship • 2197
Mary Church Terrell Award • 215
Mary Gunther Memorial Scholarship • 2198
Mary Quan Moy Ing Memorial Scholarship • 2199
Mas Family Scholarships • 2200
Maureen L. and Howard N. Blitman, P.E., Scholarship • 2201
MCCA Lloyd M. Johnson, Jr. Scholarship Program • 2202
Medgar Evers Award • 218
Medicus Student Exchange • 2203
Meritage Homes Scholarship • 2204
Minnesota Indian Scholarship Program • 1607
Minorities and Women Educational Scholarship • 654
Minority Fellowship Program • 655
Minority Scholarship • 2205
Minority Scholarship Award for Physical Therapy Students • 2206
Minority Scholarship Awards for College Students • 2207
Minority Scholarship Awards for Incoming College Freshmen • 2208
Minority Serving Institution Grants • 2209
Minority Student Scholarship • 1009
Molitoris Leadership Scholarship for Undergraduates • 2210
Morris K. Udall Scholarship • 2211
Mutual of Omaha Actuarial Scholarship for Minority Students • 2212
NAHN Scholarship • 2213
National and Chapter Scholarships • 2214
National Association of Black Accountants National Scholarship Program • 2215
National Foster Parent Association (NFPA) Youth Scholarship • 2216
National Gymnastics Foundation Men's Scholarship • 2217
National Hispanic Health Professional Student Scholarship • 2218
National Italian American Foundation Scholarship • 2219
National Scholarship • 2220
Native American Education Grant • 2221
Native American Scholarship • 2222
NativeVision Scholarships • 2223
NCTA and AWMF Scholarship • 2224
NCWIT Award for Aspirations in Computing • 2225
New York Ramblers Scholarship • 2226
NOAA Educational Partnership Program Undergraduate Scholarships • 2227
OCA/UPS Gold Mountain Scholarship • 2228
Olay Face the Stem Gap Scholarship • 2229
Olive Lynn Salembier Memorial Reentry Scholarship • 2230
P.E.O. International Peace Scholarship • 2231
P.E.O. Program for Continuing Education • 2232

P.O. Pistilli Undergraduate Scholarship for Advancement in Computer Science and Electrical Engineering • 2233
Paumanauke Native American Indian Scholarship • 2234
Pega Scholars Program • 2235
Performing Arts Scholarship • 2236
Phyllis G. Meekins Scholarship • 2237
Point Community College Scholarship • 2238
Point Flagship Scholarship • 2239
Polish National Alliance Scholarship • 2240
PRSA Diversity Multicultural Scholarship • 2241
Religious Studies Scholarship • 2242
Richard R. Tufenkian Memorial Scholarship • 2243
Ron Brown Scholar Program • 2244
Ruth D. Peterson Fellowship for Racial and Ethnic Diversity • 2245
Sahara Hope Scholarship For Women Empowered To Change The World • 2246
Sharon D. Banks Memorial Undergraduate Scholarship • 2247
SHPE Scholarship Program • 2248
SpeakOUT's LGBTQ+ Scholarship • 2249
St. Andrew's Society of Washington, DC Scholarship • 2250
Stantec Equity and Diversity Scholarship • 2251
STEM Scholarship • 2252
Striving Solo Parent Scholarship • 2253
Study.com Scholarship for Black Students • 2254
Study.com Scholarship for Moms • 2255
Study.com Scholarship for Women in STEM • 2256
Study.com Single Parent Scholarship • 2257
Sunflower Initiative Scholarship • 2258
SWE Past Presidents Scholarship • 2259
Taiwanese American Scholarship Fund • 2260
Tampax Flow It Forward Scholarship • 2261
TE Connectivity African Heritage Scholarship • 2262
TheDream.US Scholarship • 2263
Thurgood Marshall College Scholarship Fund • 2264
Tracking Foundation Multi-Year Scholarship Program • 2265
Tracking Foundation Scholars Scholarship Program • 2266
Traub-Dicker Rainbow Scholarship • 2267
Tribal College and University (TCU) Scholarships • 2268
Truman D. Picard Scholarship • 2269
U.S. Lacrosse Native American Scholarships • 2270
UNCF Healthcare Workforce Diversity Program Certification • 2271
United Parcel Service Scholarship for Minority Students • 2272
Upakar Foundation Indian American Community College Scholarship • 2273
UPS Hallmark Scholarship • 2274
VIP Women in Technology Scholarship • 1166
William and Charlotte Cadbury Award • 2275
William L. Hastie Award • 376
Women In Defense WID Scholar • 2276
Women's Overseas Service League Scholarships for Women • 382

The Ultimate Scholarship Book 2026
General Category Index

WomenIn Scholarship • 2277
Worthy Women's Professional Studies Scholarship • 2278
Write Your Future Scholarship • 2279
X Society Awards Scholarship • 2280
Young Women in Public Affairs Award • 2281

Real Estate
Also See Scholarships Listed Under:
Business/Management

AIERF College Scholarship • 521
AIERF Graduate Scholarship • 522
CREW Network Foundation Scholarship • 562
International Facility Management Association Foundation Scholarship Program • 613
Mildred C. Hanson SIOR Memorial Scholarship • 653
Minorities and Women Educational Scholarship • 654

Religion and Churches
Also See Scholarships Listed Under:
Academics/General

Allan Jerome Burry Scholarship • 1935
California Masonic Foundation Scholarship • 1267
Catholic United Financial College Tuition Scholarship • 1951
CCA Christian Cheer Nationals • 78
Champions for Christ Scholarship • 1953
Diller Teen Tikkun Olam Awards • 1962
Diocese of the Armenian Church of America (Eastern) Scholarships • 1963
Fadel Educational Foundation Annual Award Program • 1968
Helen B. and Lewis E. Goldstein Scholarship Fund • 1985
ISF Policy Scholarship Program • 1992
Islamic Society of North America Scholarships • 1993
Mary E. Bivins Religious Scholarship • 2011
Moris J. and Betty Kaplun Essay Contest • 2014
National Presbyterian College Scholarship • 2020
Opportunity Scholarships for Lutheran Laywomen • 2027
Otto M. Stanfield Legal Scholarship • 679
Presbyterian Church USA Student Opportunity Scholarships • 2031
Religious Liberty Essay Scholarship Contest • 2033
Rev. Dr. Karen Layman Gift of Hope Scholarship • 2034
Stanfield and D'Orlando Art Scholarship • 2048
UCC Seminarian Scholarship • 2059
Undergraduate Scholarships • 2063
United Methodist General Scholarship • 2066
Women in United Methodist History Writing Award • 2075
Young Christian Leaders Scholarship • 2076

Sciences/Physical Sciences
Also See Scholarships Listed Under:
Engineering
Chemistry
Computer and Information Science
Mathematics

AFCEA Ralph W. Shrader Diversity Scholarships • 761

AFCEA ROTC Scholarships • 23
AIAA Foundation Undergraduate Scholarship Program • 767
American Chemical Society Scholars Program • 2098
AMS Graduate Fellowship in the History of Science • 783
AMS Graduate Fellowships • 784
AMS Minority Scholarship • 785
AMS Senior Named Scholarships • 786
ANS Graduate Scholarship • 791
ANS Undergraduate Scholarship • 793
ASNE Scholarship Program • 810
Astronaut Scholarship • 816
Barry M. Goldwater Scholarship and Excellence in Education Program • 824
Battery Division Student Research Award • 825
Collegiate Inventors Competition • 842
Corrosion Division Morris Cohen Graduate Student Award • 846
Creative Biolabs Scholarship • 847
Davidson Fellows Scholarships • 110
ERC Eco Scholarship Fund • 1366
ExploraVision National Science Competition • 884
Father James B. Macelwane Annual Award in Meteorology • 887
Fellowship Award • 889
Freshman Undergraduate Scholarship • 896
GBT Student Observing Support (SOS) Program • 904
GEM MS Engineering Fellowship Program • 2147
GeneTex Scholarship Program • 907
Gorgas Scholarship Competition • 1405
Graduate Research Fellowship Program • 917
Graduate Student Research Grants • 919
Graduate Summer Student Research Assistantship • 921
Herbert Levy Memorial Scholarship • 931
Hertz Foundation's Graduate Fellowship Award • 932
Hispanic Heritage Youth Awards • 2159
HSC Foundation Scholarship • 2165
Industrial Electrochemistry and Electrochemical Engineering Student Achievement Award • 939
James Rust Scholarship • 1996
John and Muriel Landis Scholarship • 954
MAES Scholarship Program • 2192
Marliave Fund • 990
Michael Kidger Memorial Scholarship • 1004
Minnesota Academic Excellence Scholarship • 1604
MIT THINK Scholarship Program • 1010
National Space Club Keynote Scholar • 1029
National Young Astronomer Award • 1031
NDSEG Fellowship Program • 1039
New Face of Tech Scholarship Program • 1043
Novus Biologicals Scholarship Program • 1048
Payzer Scholarship • 1063
Peggy Dixon Two-Year Scholarship • 1064
R&D Systems Scholarship Program • 1081
Regeneron Science Talent Search • 1086
RevPart STEM Scholarship • 1089
Ridgeline International Community Scholarship • 1094
Robert E. Thunen Memorial Scholarships • 1097

Roy J. Shlemon Awards • 1100
Science Ambassador Scholarship • 1108
ScienceSaves Video Scholarship Contest • 1109
SMART Scholarship • 1114
Society of Exploration Geophysicists (SEG) Scholarship • 1118
SPS Future Teacher Scholarship • 711
SPS Leadership Scholarships • 1124
STEM Scholarship Program • 1127
Student Poster Session Awards • 1132
Summer Undergraduate Research Fellowships • 1135
Ted and Holly Rollins Scholarship • 1138
The Industrial Electrochemistry and Electrochemical Engineering Division H. H. Dow Memorial Student Achievement Award • 1140
Thermo Fisher Scientific Antibody Scholarship • 1141
Tilford Field Studies Scholarship • 1146
Tocris Scholarship • 1152
Undergraduate Student Research Grants: South-Central Section • 1160
Undergraduate Summer Student Research Assistantship • 1161
Women in STEM Scholarship/BHW Scholarship • 1172

Social Science/History
Also See Scholarships Listed Under:
Education/Teaching
English/Writing
Foreign Language
Ethnic and Area Studies
State of Residence

ACOR-CAORC Fellowship • 515
Adelle and Erwin Tomash Fellowship in the History of Information Processing • 516
Ally Financial Public Policy Scholars • 525
ARIT Fellowships for Research in Turkey • 533
BSA Research Fellowship • 548
DAAD/AICGS Research Fellowship Program • 412
Darrel Hess Community College Geography Scholarship • 563
Davidson Fellows Scholarships • 110
Don Riebhoff Memorial Scholarship • 568
Fellowship in Aerospace History • 890
Fellowships for Regular Program in Greece • 423
Fund for American Studies Internships • 586
Gamma Theta Upsilon-Geographical Honor Society Scholarships • 589
Gene Carte Student Paper Competition • 152
Graduate Research Fellowship Program • 917
Harrell Family Fellowship • 598
Harry S. Truman Research Grant • 600
Henry Belin du Pont Dissertation Fellowship • 601
Herbert Hoover Research Travel Grant Award • 602
Humane Studies Fellowship: Flexible Support for PhD Students • 175
Humane Studies Fellowship: Graduate Sabbatical Grants • 176
Humane Studies Fellowship: Publication Accelerator Grants • 605
Huntington Fellowships • 606
Huntington-British Academy Fellowships for Study in Great Britain • 607

Jennifer C. Groot Fellowship • 619
John F. Kennedy Profile in Courage Essay Contest • 625
Joseph S. Rumbaugh Historical Oration Contest • 626
Julianne Malveaux Scholarship • 2178
Junior Fellowships • 627
Lou Hochberg Awards • 643
Memorial Classic Golf Tournament Scholarship • 650
Minnesota Academic Excellence Scholarship • 1604
Minority Fellowship Program • 655
Moody Research Grant • 657
Nancy McManus Washington Internship Scholarships • 660
National Academic Scholarships • 661
National History Day Contest • 663
Nettie Dracup Memorial Scholarship • 671
NIH Undergraduate Scholarship Program • 1047
Robert G. Porter Post-Secondary Scholarships • 2036
Ruth D. Peterson Fellowship for Racial and Ethnic Diversity • 2245
TLMI Two/Four Year College and Vocational Degree Program Scholarship • 723
USGIF Scholarship Program • 731
Wesley-Logan Prize • 734
Women in United Methodist History Writing Award • 2075

UNIONS
Also See Scholarships Listed Under:
Organizations/Clubs/Employers
AFSCME Family Scholarship • 1934
ALPA Scholarship Program • 1936
Association of Flight Attendants Annual Scholarship • 1944
Career Center • 402
Career Transition for Dancers Undergraduate Studies Scholarship • 403
Charlie Logan Scholarship Program for Dependents • 1955
CWA Joe Beirne Foundation Scholarship • 1958
David B. Durkee Memorial Scholarship Program • 1959
George Heller Memorial Scholarship Fund of the SAG-AFTRA Foundation • 1978
Glass, Molders, Pottery, Plastics and Allied Workers Memorial Scholarship Fund • 1979
Howard Coughlin Memorial Scholarship Fund • 1988
IAM Scholarship • 1989
James B. Carey Scholarship • 1994
John Kelly Labor Studies Scholarship Fund • 1997
John L. Dales Scholarship Fund • 1998
Michael J. Quill Scholarship Fund • 2012
Richard F. Walsh, Alfred W. DiTolla, Harold P. Spivak Foundation Award • 2035
Robert G. Porter Post-Secondary Scholarships • 2036
Robert G. Porter Scholars Program for Members • 2037
S. Frank Bud Raftery Scholarship • 2038
Service Employees International Union Scholarships • 2041
Sheet Metal Workers' International Scholarship Fund • 2044
UFCW Scholarship Program • 2060
UMWA-Lorin E. Kerr Scholarships • 2061
Union Plus Scholarship • 2064
United Transportation Union Scholarships • 2067
Utility Workers Union of America Scholarships • 2068
W. H. Howie McClennan Scholarship • 366
Walter L. Mitchell Memorial Scholarship Awards • 2070
William B. Ruggles Right to Work Scholarship • 737
William C. Doherty Scholarship Fund • 2073

VOCATIONAL/TECHNICAL
Also See Scholarships Listed Under:
Construction Trades
Engineering
Computer and Information Science
Abe and Esther Hagiwara Student Aid Award • 2081
AGC Undergraduate Scholarships • 764
Army Emergency Relief's MG James Ursano Scholarship Program • 50
Automotive Hall of Fame Scholarships • 818
Beauty Changes Lives Foundation Scholarships • 538
Cal Grant Entitlement Award • 1259
California - Hawaii Elks Association Vocational Grants • 550
Catholic United Financial College Tuition Scholarship • 1951
Clifford H. Ted Rees Jr. Scholarship • 560
David Arver Memorial Scholarship • 854
Delta Faucet Company Scholarships • 857
DEWALT Trades Scholarship • 566
Dutch and Ginger Arver Scholarship • 868
Educational Foundation Scholarship • 576
Edward L. Simeth Scholarships • 1358
EGIA Foundation Scholarship Program • 577
Frank M. Coda Scholarship • 582
Garmin Scholarship • 902
GoFoodservice Scholarship • 593
Great Scholarship Program • 596
H.P. Bud Milligan Aviation Scholarship • 924
Horatio Alger Career and Technical Scholarship • 604
IAM Scholarship • 1989
Imagine America High School Scholarship Program • 611
Iowa Vocational-Technical Tuition Grants • 1478
James A. Turner, Jr. Memorial Scholarship • 616
Jeannette Rankin National Scholar Grant • 2176
JFLF Awards Programs • 620
Joe Francis Haircare Scholarship Program • 621
Johnny Davis Memorial Scholarship • 963
Kansas Career Technical Workforce Grant • 1509
Lee Tarbox Memorial Scholarship • 977
Live Your Dream Awards Program • 2188
Lockheed Martin Vocational Scholarship Program • 641
Lottery Tuition Assistance Program • 1549
Maple Flooring Manufacturers Association Scholarship • 645
MCEC Technical Scholarship • 1583

Medallion Fund • 1585
Merchants Exchange of Portland Scholarship • 651
Mid-Continent Instruments and Avionics Scholarship • 1006
Montgomery GI Bill - Active Duty • 227
Nell Bryant Robinson Scholarship • 670
PHCC Educational Foundation Scholarship • 1068
Shawn Carter Foundation Scholarship • 707
Shell Associate Scholarship Program • 708
Specialty Equipment Market Association (SEMA) Memorial Scholarship • 710
Undergraduate Scholarship and Construction Trades Scholarship • 1158
United Transportation Union Scholarships • 2067
University of the Aftermarket Foundation Scholarship • 730

The Ultimate Scholarship Book 2026
Field of Study Index

FIELD OF STUDY INDEX

This index organizes the scholarships by fields of study. It lists both general areas of study (in bold) as well as specific areas of study. If you cannot find a specific area of study that matches your major simply look at the scholarships under the closest matching general area.

In addition to this index be sure to use the Career Index since many scholarships are targeted to specific careers but do not have specific field of study requirements.

ACCOUNTING
See: BUSINESS, MANAGEMENT AND MARKETING

ACTING
See: VISUAL AND PERFORMING ARTS

ACTUARIAL SCIENCE
See: BUSINESS, MANAGEMENT AND MARKETING

ADULT DEVELOPMENT AND AGING
See: FAMILY AND CONSUMER SCIENCES / HUMAN SCIENCES

ADVERTISING
See: COMMUNICATION AND JOURNALISM

AEROSPACE, AERONAUTICAL AND ASTRONAUTICAL ENGINEERING
See: ENGINEERING

AFRICAN STUDIES
See: AREA, ETHNIC, CULTURAL AND GENDER STUDIES

AGRICULTURAL / BIOLOGICAL ENGINEERING AND BIOENGINEERING
See: ENGINEERING

AGRICULTURE AND RELATED SCIENCES
ASEV Scholarships • 802
ASF Olin Fellowships • 803
Careers in Agriculture Scholarship Program • 835
Carville M. Akehurst Memorial Scholarship • 836
Chevron Corporate Scholars Program • 2121
Dairy Student Recognition Program • 850
Dellums SMART Scholarship • 856
Edith Nourse Rogers STEM Scholarship • 134
Emily M. Hewitt and Stephen K. Stocking Memorial Scholarship • 1362
FarmAid FFA Scholarship • 886
Feeding Tomorrow General Education Scholarships/Freshman Scholarships • 888
Good Eats Scholarship Fund • 1404
Grow Ag Leaders Scholarship • 923
Hoard's Dairyman FFA Scholarship • 1987
Iowa Pork Foundation Scholarship • 1474
Ivomec Generations of Excellence Internship and Scholarship Program • 1481
Kansas Agricultural Aviation Association Scholarship • 1508
Lois Britt Pork Industry Memorial Scholarship Program • 983
Mabel Mayforth Scholarship • 1554
Mollie Butler Memorial Scholarship • 1012
National Garden Clubs Scholarship • 1026
NDS / Klussendorf / McKown Scholarships • 1038
Novus Biologicals Scholarship Program • 1048
Ohio Turfgrass Foundation Scholarships • 1690
Oregon Farm Bureau Memorial Scholarships • 1708
R. Flake Shaw Scholarship • 1739
SMART Scholarship • 1115
South Carolina Farm Bureau Foundation Scholarships • 1800
Spring Meadow Proven Winners Scholarship • 1123
Study.com Scholarship for Women in STEM • 2256
T. Eugene Young Montana's Promise Scholarship • 1822
Thaddeus Colson and Isabelle Saalwaechter Fitzpatrick Memorial Scholarship • 1848
USDA/1890 National Scholars Program • 1163
Winner's Circle Scholarships • 1914
Yanmar/SAE Scholarship • 1175

AGRICULTURE AND RELATED SCIENCES -- AGRICULTURAL AND FOOD PRODUCTS PROCESSING
E.H. Marth Food Protection and Food Science Scholarship • 1346
Iowa Pork Foundation Scholarship • 1474
Pennsylvania Targeted Industry Program • 1732
Undergraduate Scholarships • 1159

AGRICULTURE AND RELATED SCIENCES -- AGRICULTURAL BUSINESS AND MANAGEMENT
DMI Milk Marketing Scholarship • 859
Iowa Pork Foundation Scholarship • 1474
National Potato Council Scholarship • 1028

AGRICULTURE AND RELATED SCIENCES -- ANIMAL SCIENCES
Iowa Pork Foundation Scholarship • 1474
Louis Agassiz Fuertes Award • 985
National Dairy Shrine/Iager Dairy Scholarship • 1023
National FFA Combined Scholarship • 2018
Phyllis V. Roberts Scholarship • 1735

AGRICULTURE AND RELATED SCIENCES -- APPLIED HORTICULTURE AND HORTICULTURAL BUSINESS SERVICES
Emily M. Hewitt and Stephen K. Stocking Memorial Scholarship • 1362
Harold Bettinger Scholarship • 926
James S. Davis Memorial Scholarship • 1490
LEAF Scholarships • 1531
Loy McCandless Marks Scholarship in Tropical Horticulture • 987
National FFA Combined Scholarship • 2018
National Horticulture Foundation General Scholarships • 1027
Nurseries Foundation Award • 1053
Perennial Plant Association Scholarship • 1065
Perfect Plants Nursery Scholarship • 1066
Rain Bird Intelligent Use of Water Scholarship • 1082
Retail Chapter Award II and III • 1753
Timothy S. and Palmer W. Bigelow, Jr. Scholarship • 1147
Usrey Family Scholarship • 1164

AGRICULTURE AND RELATED SCIENCES -- FOOD SCIENCE AND TECHNOLOGY
AACT National Candy Technologists John Kitt Memorial Scholarship Program • 743
Asparagus Club, Thomas K. Zaucha Scholarship • 535
Association of Food and Drug Officials Scholarship Award • 813
Bob Richardson Legacy Scholarship • 544
Charlie and Becky Bray Legacy Scholarship • 557
E.H. Marth Food Protection and Food Science Scholarship • 1346
FMS Solutions Holdings LLC Legacy Scholarship • 579
Graduate Scholarships • 918
Iowa Pork Foundation Scholarship • 1474
Kimberly-Clark Corporation Legacy Scholarship • 629
Mondelez International Legacy Scholarship • 656
Peter and Jody Larkin Legacy Scholarship • 684
Phyllis V. Roberts Scholarship • 1735
Roger Collins Leadership Scholarship • 700
Undergraduate Scholarships • 1159
Women Grocers of America (WGA) Mary Macey Scholarship • 738

AGRONOMY AND CROP SCIENCE
See: AGRICULTURE AND RELATED SCIENCES

AIRLINE / COMMERCIAL / PROFESSIONAL PILOT AND FLIGHT CREW
See: TRANSPORTATION AND MATERIALS MOVING

AMERICAN HISTORY
See: HISTORY

ANIMAL SCIENCES
See: AGRICULTURE AND RELATED SCIENCES

ANTHROPOLOGY
See: SOCIAL SCIENCES

APPLIED HORTICULTURE AND HORTICULTURAL BUSINESS SERVICES
See: AGRICULTURE AND RELATED SCIENCES

AQUACULTURE
See: AGRICULTURE AND RELATED SCIENCES

ARCHITECTURE
See: ARCHITECTURE AND RELATED SERVICES

ARCHITECTURE AND RELATED SERVICES
A.T. Anderson Memorial Scholarship • 2079
AIA/Architects Foundation Diversity Advancement Scholarship • 766
ASCA/AISC Student Design Competition • 800
Associated General Contractors of Minnesota Scholarships • 1230
AWAF Scholarships • 1233
Byers Scholarship • 1254
Carville M. Akehurst Memorial Scholarship • 836
Connecticut Building Congress Scholarships • 1313
Houzz Women in Architecture • 935
Lucy Kasparian Aharonian Scholarship • 2189

Masonry Institute of Iowa Foundation Scholarship Program • 1575
National Garden Clubs Scholarship • 1026
Payette Sho-Ping Chin Memorial Academic Scholarship • 1062
Plan NH Scholarship and Fellowship Program • 1737
Robert E. Thunen Memorial Scholarships • 1097
SmithGroup J.E.D.I. Scholarship • 1116
Spring Meadow Proven Winners Scholarship • 1123
Vectorworks Design Scholarship • 499
You Can t Label People, but You Can Label Products Essay and Label Design Scholarship • 505

ARCHITECTURE AND RELATED SERVICES -- ARCHITECTURE
Charles Dubose Scholarship • 1286
Green Voice Design Competition • 922
Helen C. Evans Scholarship • 929
Maple Flooring Manufacturers Association Scholarship • 645
Pulte Group Build Your Future Scholarship Program • 1080
VMSD Scholarship • 502

ARCHITECTURE AND RELATED SERVICES -- CITY / URBAN, COMMUNITY AND REGIONAL PLANNING
IBTTA Foundation Scholarship Program • 937

ARCHITECTURE AND RELATED SERVICES -- ENVIRONMENTAL DESIGN / ARCHITECTURE
Karen Ann Shopis-Fox Memorial Scholarship • 1517
National Foundation Scholarships • 662

ARCHITECTURE AND RELATED SERVICES -- INTERIOR ARCHITECTURE
Green Voice Design Competition • 922
Predoctoral Fellowship Program • 1076

ARCHITECTURE AND RELATED SERVICES -- LANDSCAPE ARCHITECTURE
ASLA Council of Fellows Scholarships • 807
EDSA Diversity Scholarships • 2137
John Wright Memorial Scholarship • 962
Karen Ann Shopis-Fox Memorial Scholarship • 1517
Landscape Forms Scholarship in Memory of Peter Lindsay Schaudt, FASLA • 971
Loy McCandless Marks Scholarship in Tropical Horticulture • 987
Mabel Mayforth Scholarship • 1554
Rain Bird Intelligent Use of Water Scholarship • 1082
Raymond F. Cain Scholarship Fund • 1745
Steven G. King Play Environments Scholarship • 1129
Timothy S. and Palmer W. Bigelow, Jr. Scholarship • 1147
Usrey Family Scholarship • 1164

AREA, ETHNIC, CULTURAL AND GENDER STUDIES
ACOR-CAORC Fellowship • 515
AGBU US Graduate Scholarship • 2089
Bridging Scholarships for Study Abroad in Japan • 400
Carl A. Ross Student Paper Award • 404
DAAD/AICGS Research Fellowship Program • 412
Dumbarton Oaks Fellowships • 418
Fellowships for Regular Program in Greece • 423
National and Chapter Scholarships • 2214
Wesley-Logan Prize • 734

ART HISTORY, CRITICISM AND CONSERVATION
See: VISUAL AND PERFORMING ARTS

ASIAN STUDIES / CIVILIZATION
See: AREA, ETHNIC, CULTURAL AND GENDER STUDIES

ATHLETIC TRAINING / TRAINER
See: HEALTH PROFESSIONS AND RELATED CLINICAL SCIENCES

AUTOMOBILE / AUTOMOTIVE MECHANICS TECHNOLOGY / TECHNICIAN
See: MECHANIC AND REPAIR TECHNOLOGIES / TECHNICIANS

AVIATION / AIRWAY MANAGEMENT AND OPERATIONS
See: TRANSPORTATION AND MATERIALS MOVING

AVIONICS MAINTENANCE TECHNOLOGY / TECHNICIAN
See: MECHANIC AND REPAIR TECHNOLOGIES / TECHNICIANS

BIOCHEMISTRY, BIOPHYSICS AND MOLECULAR BIOLOGY
See: BIOLOGICAL AND BIOMEDICAL SCIENCES

BIOLOGICAL AND BIOMEDICAL SCIENCES
A.T. Anderson Memorial Scholarship • 2079
ACOR-CAORC Fellowship • 515
Annual University Scholarship • 790
ASABE Foundation Engineering Scholarship • 799
ASF Olin Fellowships • 803
Astronaut Scholarship • 816
Brown Hudner Navy Scholarship • 68
Chevron Corporate Scholars Program • 2121
Computational Science Graduate Fellowship • 845
CRA All-Access Scholarship • 2128
Davidson Fellows Scholarships • 110
Dellums SMART Scholarship • 856
DNA Day Essay Contest • 860
Drs. James and Wanda Trefil Science Scholarship • 2135
Edith Nourse Rogers STEM Scholarship • 134
Gaige Fund Award • 900
Gladys Anderson Emerson Scholarship • 913
Gorgas Scholarship Competition • 1405
Graduate Research Fellowship Program • 917
Hertz Foundation's Graduate Fellowship Award • 932
HSC Foundation Scholarship • 2165
Ida M. Pope Memorial Scholarship • 2168
Institute of Electrical and Electronics Engineers Life Members' Fellowship in Electrical History • 941
Kathryn D. Sullivan Earth and Marine Science Fellowship • 1518
LabRoots Scholarship • 970
Lambeth Family Scholarship • 1525
Mabel Mayforth Scholarship • 1554
MAES Scholarship Program • 2192
Maple Flooring Manufacturers Association Scholarship • 645
Mikkelson Foundation Scholarship • 1600
Minnesota Academic Excellence Scholarship • 1604
National Garden Clubs Scholarship • 1026
NDSEG Fellowship Program • 1039
New Face of Tech Scholarship Program • 1043
Olay Face the Stem Gap Scholarship • 2229
Paul A. Stewart Grants • 1061
Paul and Ellen Ruckes Scholarship • 2318
Payzer Scholarship • 1063
R&D Systems Scholarship Program • 1081
RBC Wealth Management Colorado Scholarship • 1748
RevPart STEM Scholarship • 1089
Samsung@First Scholars • 1777
Science Ambassador Scholarship • 1108
SHPE Scholarship Program • 2248
SMART Scholarship • 1115
Society of American Military Engineers, Albuquerque Post Scholarship • 1797
STEM Scholarship • 2252
STEM Scholarship Program • 1127
Student Award Program of FSD • 2325
Study.com Scholarship for Women in STEM • 2256
Summer Undergraduate Research Fellowships • 1135
Thaddeus Colson and Isabelle Saalwaechter Fitzpatrick Memorial Scholarship • 1848
West Virginia Engineering, Science and Technology Scholarship • 1900
Women in STEM Scholarship • 378
YASME Foundation Scholarship • 739

BIOLOGICAL AND BIOMEDICAL SCIENCES -- BIOCHEMISTRY, BIOPHYSICS AND MOLECULAR BIOLOGY
American Chemical Society Scholars Program • 2098
Creative Biolabs Scholarship • 847
Intellia Therapeutics - UNCF Scholarship • 2169
Ludo Frevel Crystallography Scholarships • 988
Thermo Fisher Scientific Antibody Scholarship • 1141

BIOLOGICAL AND BIOMEDICAL SCIENCES -- BIOLOGY / BIOLOGICAL SCIENCES, GENERAL
AACT National Candy Technologists John Kitt, Memorial Scholarship Program • 743
Choose Ohio First Scholarship • 1293
Creative Biolabs Scholarship • 847
Intellia Therapeutics - UNCF Scholarship • 2169
NOAA Educational Partnership Program Undergraduate Scholarships • 2227

The Ultimate Scholarship Book 2026
Field of Study Index

NYWEA Major Environmental Career Scholarship • 1686
Thermo Fisher Scientific Antibody Scholarship • 1141
USDA/1890 National Scholars Program • 1163

BIOLOGICAL AND BIOMEDICAL SCIENCES -- BIOTECHNOLOGY
American Chemical Society Scholars Program • 2098
Joseph P. and Helen T. Cribbins Scholarship • 195

BIOLOGICAL AND BIOMEDICAL SCIENCES -- BOTANY / PLANT BIOLOGY
Mabel Mayforth Scholarship • 1554
USDA/1890 National Scholars Program • 1163

BIOLOGICAL AND BIOMEDICAL SCIENCES -- ENTOMOLOGY
Intellia Therapeutics - UNCF Scholarship • 2169
Jean Theodore Lacordaire Prize • 950
Youth Incentive Award • 1176

BIOLOGICAL AND BIOMEDICAL SCIENCES -- MARINE BIOLOGY AND BIOLOGICAL OCEANOGRAPHY
Charles H. Bussmann Undergraduate Scholarship • 838
International Women's Fishing Association Scholarship • 944
John C. Bajus Scholarship • 955
Libbie H. Hyman Memorial Scholarship • 979
Mandell and Lester Rosenblatt Undergraduate Scholarship • 989
MTS Student Scholarship for Two-Year, Technical, Engineering and Community College Students • 1015
MTS Student Scholarship for Undergraduate Students • 1016
Next Swell Scholarship • 1044
NOAA Educational Partnership Program Undergraduate Scholarships • 2227
Paros-Digiquartz Scholarship • 1059
Robert N. and Helen H. Herbert Undergraduate Scholarship • 1098
Rockefeller State Wildlife Scholarship • 1767
Zale Parry Scholarship • 385

BIOLOGICAL AND BIOMEDICAL SCIENCES -- MICROBIOLOGICAL SCIENCES AND IMMUNOLOGY
Creative Biolabs Scholarship • 847
Intellia Therapeutics - UNCF Scholarship • 2169
NYWEA Major Environmental Career Scholarship • 1686

BIOLOGICAL AND BIOMEDICAL SCIENCES -- ZOOLOGY / ANIMAL BIOLOGY
George A. Hall / Harold F. Mayfield Grant • 909
Libbie H. Hyman Memorial Scholarship • 979
Louis Agassiz Fuertes Award • 985

BIOMEDICAL / MEDICAL ENGINEERING
See: ENGINEERING

BIOTECHNOLOGY
See: BIOLOGICAL AND BIOMEDICAL SCIENCES

BOTANY / PLANT BIOLOGY
See: BIOLOGICAL AND BIOMEDICAL SCIENCES

BROADCAST JOURNALISM
See: COMMUNICATION AND JOURNALISM

BUSINESS, MANAGEMENT AND MARKETING
Betsy Plank/PRSSA Scholarship • 540
Burlington Northern Santa Fe (BNSF) Foundation Scholarship • 2111
Christopher L. Hunt Scholarship • 407
CRA All-Access Scholarship • 2128
Hermine Solt Student Scholarship • 1437
IBTTA Foundation Scholarship Program • 937
James A. Turner, Jr. Memorial Scholarship • 616
Jane M. Klausman Women in Business Scholarship Fund • 618
Joe Perdue Scholarship • 622
Lambeth Family Scholarship • 1525
Lawrence G. Foster Award for Excellence in Public Relations • 634
Mas Family Scholarships • 2200
MBA Fellowship • 648
Mildred C. Hanson SIOR Memorial Scholarship • 653
National Academic Scholarships • 661
National Association of Black Accountants National Scholarship Program • 2215
National Scholarship • 2220
Prospanica Foundation Scholarships • 690
Study.com Scholarship for Business Students • 717
UMSA Foundation Scholarship Program • 1864

BUSINESS, MANAGEMENT AND MARKETING -- ACCOUNTING
Accounting and Financial Women's Alliance Foundation Scholarship • 513
AICPA Fellowship for Minority Doctoral Students • 2093
AICPA Foundation Scholarship for Future CPAs • 518
AICPA Foundation Two-year Transfer Scholarship • 519
AICPA John L. Carey Scholarship • 520
AICPA Scholarship for Minority Accounting Students • 2094
ASWA Seattle Chapter Scholarship • 1231
AWSCPA Scholarship • 536
Candon, Todd and Seabolt Scholarship Fund • 1271
CardRates.com Financial Futures Scholarship • 552
CREW Network Foundation Scholarship • 562
Hawaii Society of Certified Public Accountants Scholarship Fund • 1429
IBTTA Foundation Scholarship Program • 937
Laurels Fund Scholarship • 633
PAVE Student Design Competition • 683
Pennsylvania Society of Tax and Accounting Professionals Scholarships • 1729
Risk Management Association Foundation Scholarship • 698
Ritchie-Jennings Memorial Scholarship • 699
TACTYC Accounting Scholarship • 719
TE Connectivity African Heritage Scholarship • 2262
Washington State Auto Dealers Association Bright Future Scholarship • 1894
Willa S. Bellamy Scholarship • 1904
William (Bill) Ezzell Scholarship • 736

BUSINESS, MANAGEMENT AND MARKETING -- ACTUARIAL SCIENCE
Actuarial Diversity Scholarship • 2083
Mutual of Omaha Actuarial Scholarship for Minority Students • 2212
Nebraska Actuaries Club Scholarship • 1640
NextGen Scholarship • 673

BUSINESS, MANAGEMENT AND MARKETING -- BUSINESS ADMINISTRATION AND MANAGEMENT, GENERAL
BMO Capital Markets Lime Connect Equity Through Education Scholarship • 2286
CardRates.com Financial Futures Scholarship • 552
George Mason Business Scholarship Fund • 1394
IBTTA Foundation Scholarship Program • 937
PixelPlex Bi-Annual STEM Scholarship • 1072
Richard D. Wiegers Scholarship • 1757
Richard E. Bangert Business Award • 1758
Risk Management Association Foundation Scholarship • 698
Washington State Auto Dealers Association Bright Future Scholarship • 1894
Willa S. Bellamy Scholarship • 1904

BUSINESS, MANAGEMENT AND MARKETING -- CONSTRUCTION MANAGEMENT
Associated General Contractors of Minnesota Scholarships • 1230
Herman J. Smith Scholarship • 1435
Maple Flooring Manufacturers Association Scholarship • 645
NAPA Research and Education Foundation Scholarship • 1020

BUSINESS, MANAGEMENT AND MARKETING -- FINANCE, GENERAL
Accounting and Financial Women's Alliance Foundation Scholarship • 513
BMO Capital Markets Lime Connect Equity Through Education Scholarship • 2286
Candon, Todd and Seabolt Scholarship Fund • 1271
CardRates.com Financial Futures Scholarship • 552
Hawaii Society of Certified Public Accountants Scholarship Fund • 1429
Herman J. Smith Scholarship • 1435
IBTTA Foundation Scholarship Program • 937
Laurels Fund Scholarship • 633
NextGen Scholarship • 673
Paul S. Mills Scholarships • 682
Prize in International Insolvency Studies • 688
Richard D. Wiegers Scholarship • 1757
Risk Management Association Foundation Scholarship • 698
Ritchie-Jennings Memorial Scholarship • 699
TE Connectivity African Heritage Scholarship • 2262

Washington State Auto Dealers Association Bright Future Scholarship • 1894
Willa S. Bellamy Scholarship • 1904

BUSINESS, MANAGEMENT AND MARKETING -- HOSPITALITY ADMINISTRATION / MANAGEMENT, GENERAL
A.J. Grisanti Memorial Scholarship • 509
Clem Judd, Jr., Memorial Scholarship • 1298
GoFoodservice Scholarship • 593
R.W. Bob Holden Scholarship • 1741
Roller Skating Foundation Scholarship, Current College Student Category • 701
Timothy S.Y. Lam Foundation Education Scholarships • 722

BUSINESS, MANAGEMENT AND MARKETING -- INTERNATIONAL BUSINESS / TRADE / COMMERCE
Don Riebhoff Memorial Scholarship • 568
Henry A. Zuberano Scholarship • 1431
Louisiana Memorial Scholarship • 1552
Merchants Exchange of Portland Scholarship • 651
Washington State Auto Dealers Association Bright Future Scholarship • 1894
WIIT Charitable Trust Scholarship • 735

BUSINESS, MANAGEMENT AND MARKETING -- MANAGEMENT INFORMATION SYSTEMS, GENERAL
Alice L. Haltom Educational Fund Scholarship • 523
NextGen Scholarship • 673

BUSINESS, MANAGEMENT AND MARKETING -- MARKETING / MARKETING MANAGEMENT, GENERAL
Bick Bickson Scholarship Fund • 1240
Byers Scholarship • 1254
Gary Yoshimura Scholarship • 590
IBTTA Foundation Scholarship Program • 937
LAGRANT Scholarship Program • 2182
PAVE Student Design Competition • 683

BUSINESS, MANAGEMENT AND MARKETING -- RESTAURANT / FOOD SERVICES MANAGEMENT
A.J. Grisanti Memorial Scholarship • 509
Asparagus Club, Thomas K. Zaucha Scholarship • 535
Bob Richardson Legacy Scholarship • 544
Charlie and Becky Bray Legacy Scholarship • 557
FMS Solutions Holdings LLC Legacy Scholarship • 579
IFSEA Worthy Goal Scholarship • 609
Kimberly-Clark Corporation Legacy Scholarship • 629
Mondelez International Legacy Scholarship • 656
Peter and Jody Larkin Legacy Scholarship • 684
Roger Collins Leadership Scholarship • 700
Timothy S.Y. Lam Foundation Education Scholarships • 722
Women Grocers of America (WGA) Mary Macey Scholarship • 738

BUSINESS, MANAGEMENT AND MARKETING -- SALES, DISTRIBUTION AND MARKETING OPERATIONS, GENERAL
PAVE Student Design Competition • 683
Washington State Auto Dealers Association Bright Future Scholarship • 1894

BUSINESS, MANAGEMENT AND MARKETING -- TOURISM AND TRAVEL SERVICES MANAGEMENT
Academic Merit Scholarships • 512
Bick Bickson Scholarship Fund • 1240
Timothy S.Y. Lam Foundation Education Scholarships • 722

CENTRAL / MIDDLE AND EASTERN EUROPEAN STUDIES
See: AREA, ETHNIC, CULTURAL AND GENDER STUDIES

CHEMICAL ENGINEERING
See: ENGINEERING

CHEMISTRY
See: PHYSICAL SCIENCES

CHILD DEVELOPMENT
See: FAMILY AND CONSUMER SCIENCES / HUMAN SCIENCES

CHINESE LANGUAGE AND LITERATURE
See: FOREIGN LANGUAGES, LITERATURES AND LINGUISTICS

CHIROPRACTIC
See: HEALTH PROFESSIONS AND RELATED CLINICAL SCIENCES

CHRISTIAN STUDIES
See: PHILOSOPHY AND RELIGIOUS STUDIES

CITY / URBAN, COMMUNITY AND REGIONAL PLANNING
See: ARCHITECTURE AND RELATED SERVICES

CIVIL ENGINEERING
See: ENGINEERING

CLINICAL / MEDICAL LABORATORY SCIENCE AND ALLIED PROFESSIONS
See: HEALTH PROFESSIONS AND RELATED CLINICAL SCIENCES

COMMUNICATION AND JOURNALISM
Bill Gove Scholarship • 399
Bodie McDowell Scholarship • 545
Cavett Robert Scholarship • 405
Charles Clarke Cordle Memorial Scholarship • 555
Charles N. Fisher Memorial Scholarship • 556
Dr. Jack G. Shaheen Media Scholarship • 569
Dr. James L. Lawson Memorial Scholarship • 570
Edward Payson and Bernice Piilani Irwin Scholarship • 1359
Fred R. McDaniel Memorial Scholarship • 583
Irving W. Cook, WA0CGS, Scholarship • 1479
Julianne Malveaux Scholarship • 2178
L. Phil and Alice J. Wicker Scholarship • 631
Lee Thornton Scholarship • 636
Mary Quan Moy Ing Memorial Scholarship • 2199
Mas Family Scholarships • 2200
Minority Scholarship • 1611
Mississippi Association of Broadcasters Scholarship Program • 1614
Mississippi Scholarship • 1616
NCTA and AWMF Scholarship • 2224
New York Women in Communications Foundation Scholarships • 1658
Paul and Helen L. Grauer Scholarship • 681
PenSPRA Scholarship • 1733
University Journalism Scholarships • 1866
William B. Ruggles Right to Work Scholarship • 737

COMMUNICATION AND JOURNALISM -- ADVERTISING
AIGA Worldstudio Scholarships • 392
FOARE Scholarship Program • 580
LAGRANT Scholarship Program • 2182
Shirley McKown Scholarship Fund • 1787
Vern and Elaine Clark Outdoor Advertising Industry • 732

COMMUNICATION AND JOURNALISM -- BROADCAST JOURNALISM
Dr. Jack G. Shaheen Media Scholarship • 569
Harry Barfield KBA Scholarship Program • 1423
KAB Broadcast Scholarship Program • 1507
Oklahoma Association of Broadcasters Scholarship • 1691
Texas Broadcast Education Foundation Scholarships • 1838

COMMUNICATION AND JOURNALISM -- JOURNALISM
AGBU US Graduate Scholarship • 2089
Chester Burger Scholarship for Excellence in Public Relations • 558
Dr. Jack G. Shaheen Media Scholarship • 569
John D. Graham Scholarship • 624
Kit C. King Graduate Scholarship Fund • 630
NPPF Still and Multimedia Scholarship • 676
NPPF Television News Scholarship • 677
PHD Scholarship • 685
Reid Blackburn Scholarship • 695
Ron Culp Scholarship for Mentorship • 702
Shirley McKown Scholarship Fund • 1787
Stephen D. Pisinski Memorial Scholarship • 712
Virginia High School League Charles E. Savedge Journalism Scholarship • 1883

COMMUNICATION AND JOURNALISM -- MASS COMMUNICATION / MEDIA STUDIES
Dr. Jack G. Shaheen Media Scholarship • 569
PRSA Diversity Multicultural Scholarship • 2241
Stephen D. Pisinski Memorial Scholarship • 712

COMMUNICATION AND JOURNALISM -- PUBLIC RELATIONS / IMAGE MANAGEMENT
Chester Burger Scholarship for Excellence in Public Relations • 558
Gary Yoshimura Scholarship • 590
John D. Graham Scholarship • 624
LAGRANT Scholarship Program • 2182
Ron Culp Scholarship for Mentorship • 702
Shirley McKown Scholarship Fund • 1787
Stephen D. Pisinski Memorial Scholarship • 712

COMMUNICATION DISORDERS, GENERAL
See: HEALTH PROFESSIONS AND RELATED CLINICAL SCIENCES

The Ultimate Scholarship Book 2026
Field of Study Index

COMPUTER AND INFORMATION SCIENCES

A.T. Anderson Memorial Scholarship • 2079
Adelle and Erwin Tomash Fellowship in the History of Information Processing • 516
AFCEA Ralph W. Shrader Diversity Scholarships • 761
AFCEA ROTC Scholarships • 23
Association of Information Technology Professionals (AITP) Scholarships • 814
Astronaut Scholarship • 816
BAFTX Undergraduate Award • 1235
Boeing Company STEM Scholarship • 1246
CDM Constructors Inc. Workforce Development Scholarship • 1281
Chevron Corporate Scholars Program • 2121
Computational Science Graduate Fellowship • 845
Cummins Scholarship • 849
Davidson Fellows Scholarships • 110
Dellums SMART Scholarship • 856
Edith Nourse Rogers STEM Scholarship • 134
GEM MS Engineering Fellowship Program • 2147
Generation Google Scholarship • 2149
GeneTex Scholarship Program • 907
Google SVA Scholarship • 163
Graduate Research Fellowship Program • 917
High Technology Scholar/Intern Tuition Waiver • 1440
Institute of Electrical and Electronics Engineers Life Members' Fellowship in Electrical History • 941
Intertech Foundation STEM Scholarship • 945
Kathryn D. Sullivan Earth and Marine Science Fellowship • 1518
Lockheed Martin STEM Scholarship Program • 982
Lockheed Martin Vocational Scholarship Program • 641
Lucy Kasparian Aharonian Scholarship • 2189
MAES Scholarship Program • 2192
Mary V. Munger Scholarship • 994
Michigan Council of Women in Technology University Scholarship • 1593
National Academic Scholarships • 661
NDSEG Fellowship Program • 1039
Northrop Grumman Scholarship • 1681
Olay Face the Stem Gap Scholarship • 2229
Pega Scholars Program • 2235
PHD Scholarship • 685
Ray, N0RP and Katie, W0KTE Pautz Scholarship • 694
RevPart STEM Scholarship • 1089
Science Ambassador Scholarship • 1108
SHPE Scholarship Program • 2248
SMART Scholarship • 1114
SMART Scholarship • 1115
STEM Scholarship • 2252
Stokes Educational Scholarship Program • 311
Study.com Scholarship for Women in STEM • 2256
Susan Miszkowicz Memorial Scholarship • 1136
T. Eugene Young Montana's Promise Scholarship • 1822
UMSA Foundation Scholarship Program • 1864
West Virginia Engineering, Science and Technology Scholarship • 1900
Women in STEM Award • 1922
Women in STEM Scholarship • 378
Women in STEM Scholarship/BHW Scholarship • 1172

COMPUTER AND INFORMATION SCIENCES -- COMPUTER SCIENCE

Admiral Grace Murray Hopper Memorial Scholarships • 2085
AISES Intel Scholarship • 2095
Amazon Future Engineer Scholarship • 777
Anne Maureen Whitney Barrow Memorial Scholarship • 2100
Burlington Northern Santa Fe (BNSF) Foundation Scholarship • 2111
Honeywell International Inc. Scholarships • 2163
Joseph P. and Helen T. Cribbins Scholarship • 195
Lambeth Family Scholarship • 1525
Paul and Ellen Ruckes Scholarship • 2318
PG&E Better Together STEM Scholarship Program • 1734
Steel Intern Scholarships • 1125
Student Award Program of FSD • 2325
Student Poster Session Awards • 1132
Unitil Scholarship Fund • 1865
Women In Defense WID Scholar • 2276

COMPUTER AND INFORMATION SCIENCES -- COMPUTER SYSTEMS NETWORKING AND TELECOMMUNICATIONS

Harry Barfield KBA Scholarship Program • 1423
PG&E Better Together STEM Scholarship Program • 1734

COMPUTER AND INFORMATION SCIENCES -- INFORMATION TECHNOLOGY

Brown Hudner Navy Scholarship • 68
Choose Ohio First Scholarship • 1293
CRA All-Access Scholarship • 2128
IBTTA Foundation Scholarship Program • 937
New Face of Tech Scholarship Program • 1043
PixelPlex Bi-Annual STEM Scholarship • 1072
Ridgeline International Community Scholarship • 1094
Samsung@First Scholars • 1777
STEM Scholarship Program • 1127
TE Connectivity African Heritage Scholarship • 2262

COMPUTER ENGINEERING, GENERAL
See: ENGINEERING

COMPUTER INSTALLATION AND REPAIR TECHNOLOGY / TECHNICIAN
See: MECHANIC AND REPAIR TECHNOLOGIES / TECHNICIANS

CONSTRUCTION / HEAVY EQUIPMENT / EARTHMOVING EQUIPMENT OPERATION
See: TRANSPORTATION AND MATERIALS MOVING

CONSTRUCTION MANAGEMENT
See: BUSINESS, MANAGEMENT AND MARKETING

CONSTRUCTION TRADES

ACI Student Fellowship Program • 754
AGC Education and Research Foundation Undergraduate Scholarship • 762
AGC of Massachusetts Scholarships • 1189
AGC of Ohio Scholarships • 1190
Associated General Contractors of Connecticut Scholarships • 1229
Associated General Contractors of Minnesota Scholarships • 1230
Connecticut Building Congress Scholarships • 1313
Delta Faucet Company Scholarships • 857
Johanna Drew Cluney Fund • 1497
Kokosing Construction Co. Scholarship • 1524
Masonry Institute of Iowa Foundation Scholarship Program • 1575
MCEC Technical Scholarship • 1583
Path to Pro Scholarship • 1060
PHCC Educational Foundation Scholarship • 1068
Plan NH Scholarship and Fellowship Program • 1737
Pulte Group Build Your Future Scholarship Program • 1080
Roofing Industry Scholarship - Melvin Kruger Endowed Scholarship • 1099
Texas Elks State Association Vocational Grant Program • 1841
Tuttle Construction Inc. Tiny Rauch Scholarship • 1860
Undergraduate Scholarship and Construction Trades Scholarship • 1158

COOKING AND RELATED CULINARY ARTS, GENERAL
See: PERSONAL AND CULINARY SERVICES

CRIMINAL JUSTICE / POLICE SCIENCE
See: SECURITY AND PROTECTIVE SERVICES

CRIMINOLOGY
See: SOCIAL SCIENCES

DANCE, GENERAL
See: VISUAL AND PERFORMING ARTS

DENTAL SUPPORT SERVICES AND ALLIED PROFESSIONS
See: HEALTH PROFESSIONS AND RELATED CLINICAL SCIENCES

DENTISTRY
See: HEALTH PROFESSIONS AND RELATED CLINICAL SCIENCES

DESIGN AND VISUAL COMMUNICATIONS, GENERAL
See: VISUAL AND PERFORMING ARTS

DIETETICS / DIETITIAN
See: HEALTH PROFESSIONS AND RELATED CLINICAL SCIENCES

DIVINITY / MINISTRY
See: THEOLOGY AND RELIGIOUS VOCATIONS

DRAMA AND DRAMATICS / THEATRE ARTS, GENERAL
See: VISUAL AND PERFORMING ARTS

ECOLOGY
See: BIOLOGICAL AND BIOMEDICAL SCIENCES

ECONOMICS, GENERAL
See: SOCIAL SCIENCES

EDUCATION
Alma White - Delta Kappa Gamma Scholarship • 1204
Bill Kane Scholarship, Undergraduate • 827
Burlington Northern Santa Fe (BNSF) Foundation Scholarship • 2111
Community Scholarship Fund • 1310
Dr. Hans and Clara Zimmerman Foundation Education Scholarship • 1341
Educators for Maine Program • 1357
Epsilon Sigma Alpha • 1365
Future Journalism Teacher Scholarship • 588
Ida M. Pope Memorial Scholarship • 2168
Kansas Teacher Service Scholarship • 1516
Minority Teaching Fellows Program • 1612
NEA-Retired Jack Kinnaman Memorial Scholarship • 669
NFMC Gretchen E. Van Roy Music Education Scholarship • 674
Paraprofessional Teacher Preparation Grant • 1713
Phi Delta Kappa (PDK) Educational Foundation Scholarship Program • 2029
Pi Lambda Theta Student Support Scholarships • 686
Presbyterian Church USA Student Opportunity Scholarships • 2031
Robert E. Thunen Memorial Scholarships • 1097
Ruth Abernathy Presidential Scholarship • 1103
Ruth Lutes Bachmann Scholarship • 1775
Sandra Jo Hornick Scholarship • 2040
Sioux Falls Area Retired Teachers Scholarship • 1790
Student CTA (SCTA) Scholarship in Honor of L. Gordon Bittle • 2051
Teacher Education Scholarship Fund • 720
Teacher Loan-For-Service Program • 1825
Teacher Scholarship Program • 1826
Terrel H. Bell Education Scholarship • 1835
William A. Crawford Minority Teacher Scholarship • 1906
Workforce Shortage Student Assistance Grant Program • 1923

EDUCATION -- ELEMENTARY EDUCATION AND TEACHING
Bill Kane Scholarship, Undergraduate • 827
Early Childhood Educators Scholarship • 1348
Scholarships in Mathematics Education • 1782
Sister Mary Petronia Van Straten Scholarship for Pre-Service Teachers • 1792
Teacher Loan Program • 1824
Teacher Scholarship Program • 1826
Winifred R. Reynolds Educational Scholarship • 1913

EDUCATION -- JUNIOR HIGH / INTERMEDIATE / MIDDLE SCHOOL EDUCATION AND TEACHING
Bill Kane Scholarship, Undergraduate • 827
Math and Science Teaching Incentive Scholarships • 1581
Scholarships in Mathematics Education • 1782
Sister Mary Petronia Van Straten Scholarship for Pre-Service Teachers • 1792
Teacher Scholarship Program • 1826

EDUCATION -- SECONDARY EDUCATION AND TEACHING
Bill Kane Scholarship, Undergraduate • 827
Math and Science Teaching Incentive Scholarships • 1581
Scholarships in Mathematics Education • 1782
Sister Mary Petronia Van Straten Scholarship for Pre-Service Teachers • 1792
Teacher Loan Program • 1824

ELECTRICAL, ELECTRONICS AND COMMUNICATIONS ENGINEERING
See: ENGINEERING

EMERGENCY MEDICAL TECHNOLOGY / TECHNICIAN
See: HEALTH PROFESSIONS AND RELATED CLINICAL SCIENCES

ENGINEERING
A.T. Anderson Memorial Scholarship • 2079
ACEC Colorado Scholarship Program • 1184
ACEC Scholarship • 1185
Ada I. Pressman Memorial Scholarship • 2084
Admiral Grace Murray Hopper Memorial Scholarships • 2085
AFCEA Ralph W. Shrader Diversity Scholarships • 761
American Council of Engineering Companies of New Jersey Member Organization Scholarship • 1207
Anne Maureen Whitney Barrow Memorial Scholarship • 2100
ASABE Foundation Engineering Scholarship • 799
ASNE Scholarship Program • 810
Association of Cuban Engineers Scholarship Foundation Scholarships • 2106
Astronaut Scholarship • 816
Auxiliary Legacy Scholarship • 819
AWAF Scholarships • 1233
B.J. Harrod Scholarships • 2107
B.K. Krenzer Reentry Scholarship • 2108
BAFTX Undergraduate Award • 1235
Battery Division Student Research Award • 825
BMO Capital Markets Lime Connect Equity Through Education Scholarship • 2286
BMW/SAE Engineering Scholarship • 829
Boeing Company STEM Scholarship • 1246
Brown Hudner Navy Scholarship • 68
Burlington Northern Santa Fe (BNSF) Foundation Scholarship • 2111
Chevron Corporate Scholars Program • 2121
Choose Ohio First Scholarship • 1293
Computational Science Graduate Fellowship • 845
CRA All-Access Scholarship • 2128
Cummins Scholarship • 849
Davidson Fellows Scholarships • 110
Dellums SMART Scholarship • 856
Desk and Derrick Educational Trust • 858
Development Fund for Black Students in Science and Technology • 2130
Dorothy M. and Earl S. Hoffman Award • 863
Dr. Ivy M. Parker Memorial Scholarship • 2133
Edith Nourse Rogers STEM Scholarship • 134
Edward D. Hendrickson/SAE Engineering Scholarship • 872
Engineering Foundation of Wisconsin Scholarship • 1363
Engineers Foundation of Ohio General Fund Scholarship • 1364
F.W. Beich Beichley Scholarship • 885
Florida Engineers in Construction Scholarship • 1378
Fred M. Young, Sr./SAE Engineering Scholarship • 895
Future Leader Scholarship • 898
Garland Duncan Scholarships • 901
Gary Wagner, K3OMI, Scholarship • 903
GEM MS Engineering Fellowship Program • 2147
GeneTex Scholarship Program • 907
Graduate Research Award (GRA) • 916
Graduate Research Fellowship Program • 917
Heinlein Society Scholarship Program • 433
Hertz Foundation's Graduate Fellowship Award • 932
High Technology Scholar/Intern Tuition Waiver • 1440
HSC Foundation Scholarship • 2165
Hubertus W.V. Wellems Scholarship for Male Students • 2167
Institute of Electrical and Electronics Engineers Life Members' Fellowship in Electrical History • 941
Jill S. Tietjen P.E. Scholarship • 951
John and Elsa Gracik Scholarships • 953
John J. McKetta Scholarship • 956
Joseph P. and Helen T. Cribbins Scholarship • 195
Kansas Agricultural Aviation Association Scholarship • 1508
Kathryn D. Sullivan Earth and Marine Science Fellowship • 1518
Kenneth Andrew Roe Scholarship • 969
LabRoots Scholarship • 970
Lambeth Family Scholarship • 1525
Lillian Moller Gilbreth Memorial Scholarship • 2187
Lockheed Martin STEM Scholarship Program • 982
Lockheed Martin Vocational Scholarship Program • 641
Lucy Kasparian Aharonian Scholarship • 2189
MAES Scholarship Program • 2192
Maple Flooring Manufacturers Association Scholarship • 645
Mary Gunther Memorial Scholarship • 2198
Mary V. Munger Scholarship • 994
Mas Family Scholarships • 2200
Maureen L. and Howard N. Blitman, P.E., Scholarship • 2201
Meredith Thoms Memorial Scholarship • 1001
Michigan Engineering Scholarships • 1594
Mikkelson Foundation Scholarship • 1600
MSPE Kenneth B. Fishbeck, P.E., Memorial Grant • 1628
NDSEG Fellowship Program • 1039
Nellie Yeoh Whetten Award • 1041
Northrop Grumman Scholarship • 1681
Olay Face the Stem Gap Scholarship • 2229

The Ultimate Scholarship Book 2026
Field of Study Index

Olive Lynn Salembier Memorial Reentry Scholarship • 2230
Paul and Ellen Ruckes Scholarship • 2318
Payzer Scholarship • 1063
PixelPlex Bi-Annual STEM Scholarship • 1072
Plan NH Scholarship and Fellowship Program • 1737
R&D Systems Scholarship Program • 1081
Raymond Davis Scholarship • 1085
RBC Wealth Management Colorado Scholarship • 1748
RevPart STEM Scholarship • 1089
Ridgeline International Community Scholarship • 1094
Robert E. Thunen Memorial Scholarships • 1097
Russell and Sigurd Varian Award • 1102
Samsung@First Scholars • 1777
Science Ambassador Scholarship • 1108
SHPE Scholarship Program • 2248
SMART Scholarship • 1114
SMART Scholarship • 1115
Society of American Military Engineers, Albuquerque Post Scholarship • 1797
Society of Plastics Engineers (SPE) Foundation Scholarships • 1120
Society of Vacuum Coaters Foundation Scholarship • 1121
Stantec Equity and Diversity Scholarship • 2251
Steinman Scholarship • 1126
STEM Scholarship • 2252
STEM Scholarship Program • 1127
Stokes Educational Scholarship Program • 311
Student Award Program of FSD • 2325
Student Cash Grant Program • 1131
Study.com Scholarship for Women in STEM • 2256
Susan Miszkowicz Memorial Scholarship • 1136
SWE Past Presidents Scholarship • 2259
T. Eugene Young Montana's Promise Scholarship • 1822
Tau Beta Pi/Society of Automotive Engineers Engineering Scholarship • 1137
TE Connectivity African Heritage Scholarship • 2262
Tech High School Alumni Association/W.O. Cheney Merit Scholarship • 1828
Thomas M. Stetson Scholarship • 1144
TMC/SAE Donald D. Dawson Technical Scholarship • 1148
U.S. Western Digital STEM Scholarship • 346
Undergraduate Engineering Scholarships • 1157
Unitil Scholarship Fund • 1865
Vernon T. Swain, P.E./Robert E. Chute, P.E. Scholarship • 1875
VMSD Scholarship • 502
West Virginia Engineering, Science and Technology Scholarship • 1900
Women In Defense WID Scholar • 2276
Women in STEM Award • 1922
Women in STEM Scholarship/BHW Scholarship • 1172
Yanmar/SAE Scholarship • 1175
YASME Foundation Scholarship • 739
You Can t Label People, but You Can Label Products Essay and Label Design Scholarship • 505

ENGINEERING -- AEROSPACE, AERONAUTICAL AND ASTRONAUTICAL ENGINEERING
AFCEA ROTC Scholarships • 23
Amelia Earhart Fellowships • 779
Brill Family Scholarship • 830
David Alan Quick Scholarship • 853
Ellison Onizuka Memorial Scholarship Fund • 1361
General James H. Doolittle Scholarship • 906
Honeywell International Inc. Scholarships • 2163
International Gas Turbine Institute Scholarship • 942
Judith Resnik Memorial Scholarship • 2177
Vertical Flight Foundation Technical Scholarships • 1165

ENGINEERING -- AGRICULTURAL / BIOLOGICAL ENGINEERING AND BIOENGINEERING
Iowa Pork Foundation Scholarship • 1474
William J. Adams, Jr. and Marijane E. Adams Scholarship • 1170

ENGINEERING -- BIOMEDICAL / MEDICAL ENGINEERING
Brill Family Scholarship • 830
Dr. Bart Kamen Memorial FIRST Scholarship • 865
Intellia Therapeutics - UNCF Scholarship • 2169
Jackson Laboratory Scholarship • 949

ENGINEERING -- CHEMICAL ENGINEERING
ACEC New York Scholarship Program • 752
AISES Intel Scholarship • 2095
American Chemical Society Scholars Program • 2098
Donald F. and Mildred Topp Othmer Scholarships • 861
Honeywell International Inc. Scholarships • 2163
Minority Scholarship Awards for College Students • 2207
Minority Scholarship Awards for Incoming College Freshmen • 2208
National Association for Surface Finishing Scholarships • 1021
National Foundation Scholarships • 662
NYWEA Major Environmental Career Scholarship • 1686
Oliver Moghissi Memorial Scholarship • 1055
Rubber Division Undergraduate Scholarship • 1101
Steel Intern Scholarships • 1125
Student Poster Session Awards • 1132

ENGINEERING -- CIVIL ENGINEERING
ACEC New York Scholarship Program • 752
ACI Scholarship • 753
ACI Student Fellowship Program • 754
AGC Education and Research Foundation Undergraduate Scholarship • 762
AGC of Massachusetts Scholarships • 1189
AIST Ronald E. Lincoln Memorial Scholarship • 770
AIST William E. Schwabe Memorial Scholarship • 772
American Water Scholarship • 781
ASDSO Senior Undergraduate Scholarship • 801
Associated General Contractors of Connecticut Scholarships • 1229
Associated General Contractors of Minnesota Scholarships • 1230
Ben W. Fortson, Jr., Scholarship • 1237
Bryant L. Bench Carollo Engineers Inc. Scholarship • 831
Connecticut Building Congress Scholarships • 1313
Ed and Charlotte Rodgers Scholarships • 1350
Elizabeth McLean Memorial Scholarship • 875
IBTTA Foundation Scholarship Program • 937
J.R. Popalisky Scholarship • 1482
Mackinac Scholarship • 1555
NAPA Research and Education Foundation Scholarship • 1020
NYWEA Major Environmental Career Scholarship • 1686
Pulte Group Build Your Future Scholarship Program • 1080
Samuel Fletcher Tapman ASCE Student Chapter/Club Scholarship • 1106
SmithGroup J.E.D.I. Scholarship • 1116
Trent R. Dames and William W. Moore Fellowship • 1153

ENGINEERING -- COMPUTER ENGINEERING, GENERAL
AISES Intel Scholarship • 2095
Amazon Future Engineer Scholarship • 777
Generation Google Scholarship • 2149
Honeywell International Inc. Scholarships • 2163
Michigan Council of Women in Technology University Scholarship • 1593
PG&E Better Together STEM Scholarship Program • 1734
Student Poster Session Awards • 1132

ENGINEERING -- ELECTRICAL, ELECTRONICS AND COMMUNICATIONS ENGINEERING
ACEC New York Scholarship Program • 752
Amazon Future Engineer Scholarship • 777
Association of Federal Communications Consulting Engineers Scholarships • 812
Charles Clarke Cordle Memorial Scholarship • 555
Charles N. Fisher Memorial Scholarship • 556
Dr. James L. Lawson Memorial Scholarship • 570
Edmond A. Metzger Scholarship • 575
Fred R. McDaniel Memorial Scholarship • 583
Honeywell International Inc. Scholarships • 2163
Irving W. Cook, WA0CGS, Scholarship • 1479
L. Phil and Alice J. Wicker Scholarship • 631
National Foundation Scholarships • 662
Paul and Helen L. Grauer Scholarship • 681
PG&E Better Together STEM Scholarship Program • 1734
PHD Scholarship • 685
RMEL Foundation Scholarships • 1095
SmithGroup J.E.D.I. Scholarship • 1116
Steel Intern Scholarships • 1125

ENGINEERING -- ENGINEERING SCIENCE
ASNT Fellowship • 811
Corrosion Division Morris Cohen Graduate Student Award • 846

Engineering Undergraduate Scholarship • 881
John L. Imhoff Scholarship • 957
New Face of Tech Scholarship Program • 1043
Robert B. Oliver ASNT Scholarship • 1096
SPIE Optics and Photonics Education Scholarship • 1122
Trent R. Dames and William W. Moore Fellowship • 1153

ENGINEERING -- ENVIRONMENTAL / ENVIRONMENTAL HEALTH ENGINEERING
ACEC New York Scholarship Program • 752
American Water Scholarship • 781
Bryant L. Bench Carollo Engineers Inc. Scholarship • 831
Delaware Solid Waste Authority John P. Pat Healy Scholarship • 1327
J.R. Popalisky Scholarship • 1482
Larson Aquatic Research Support (LARS) • 973
N.G. Kaul Memorial Scholarship • 1018
National Association for Surface Finishing Scholarships • 1021
National Environmental Health Association Graduate Scholarship • 1024
National Foundation Scholarships • 662
NEHA/AAS/APU Scholarship Awards • 1040
NYWEA Major Environmental Career Scholarship • 1686
PG&E Better Together STEM Scholarship Program • 1734
Steel Intern Scholarships • 1125
Trent R. Dames and William W. Moore Fellowship • 1153

ENGINEERING -- INDUSTRIAL ENGINEERING
A.O. Putnam Memorial Scholarship • 741
C.B. Gambrell Undergraduate Scholarship • 833
Dwight D. Gardner Scholarship • 869
Gilbreth Memorial Fellowship • 911
IISE Council of Fellows Undergraduate Scholarship • 938
John S.W. Fargher, Jr. Scholarship • 960
Lisa Zaken Award For Excellence • 981
Marvin Mundel Memorial Scholarship • 992
National Foundation Scholarships • 662
PG&E Better Together STEM Scholarship Program • 1734
Society of Manufacturing Engineers Directors Scholarship • 1119
Steel Intern Scholarships • 1125
United Parcel Service Scholarship for Female Students • 1162
United Parcel Service Scholarship for Minority Students • 2272

ENGINEERING -- MATERIALS ENGINEERING
AISI/AIST Foundation Premier Scholarship • 768
AIST Benjamin F. Fairless Scholarship (AIME) • 769
AIST Ronald E. Lincoln Memorial Scholarship • 770
AIST Smith Graduate Scholarship • 771
AIST William E. Schwabe Memorial Scholarship • 772
AIST Willy Korf Memorial Fund • 773

American Innovations Corrosion Scholarship • 780
AMPP Academic Scholarship • 782
ASNT Fellowship • 811
Gordon Rankin Corrosion Engineering Scholarship • 915
Honeywell International Inc. Scholarships • 2163
Lewis C. Hoffman Scholarship • 978
Melvin J. Schiff Fellowship Fund • 998
Michael Kidger Memorial Scholarship • 1004
MTI Bert Krisher Memorial Scholarship • 1014
National Association for Surface Finishing Scholarships • 1021
National Foundation Scholarships • 662
PPG Protective and Marine Coatings Academic Scholarship • 1075
Society of Manufacturing Engineers Directors Scholarship • 1119
Williams Companies Academic Scholarship • 1171

ENGINEERING -- MECHANICAL ENGINEERING
ACEC New York Scholarship Program • 752
AISES Intel Scholarship • 2095
AIST Ronald E. Lincoln Memorial Scholarship • 770
AIST William E. Schwabe Memorial Scholarship • 772
Amazon Future Engineer Scholarship • 777
ASME Auxiliary Lucy and Charles W. E. Clarke Scholarship • 808
ASME Foundation Scholarships • 809
Frank and Dorothy Miller ASME Auxiliary Scholarships • 894
Honeywell International Inc. Scholarships • 2163
International Gas Turbine Institute Scholarship • 942
Melvin R. Green Scholarships • 999
Myrtle and Earl Walker Scholarship • 1017
National Association for Surface Finishing Scholarships • 1021
National Foundation Scholarships • 662
NNM American Society of Mechanical Engineers Scholarship • 1666
PG&E Better Together STEM Scholarship Program • 1734
Ralph K. Hillquist Honorary SAE Scholarship • 1083
Rubber Division Undergraduate Scholarship • 1101
SmithGroup J.E.D.I. Scholarship • 1116
Society of Manufacturing Engineers Directors Scholarship • 1119
Steel Intern Scholarships • 1125

ENGINEERING -- METALLURGICAL ENGINEERING
AIST Benjamin F. Fairless Scholarship (AIME) • 769
AIST Ronald E. Lincoln Memorial Scholarship • 770
AIST William E. Schwabe Memorial Scholarship • 772
AIST Willy Korf Memorial Fund • 773

National Association for Surface Finishing Scholarships • 1021
Robert B. Oliver ASNT Scholarship • 1096

ENGINEERING -- MINING AND MINERAL ENGINEERING
ACAA Educational Foundation Scholarship Program • 748
John S. Marshall Memorial Scholarship • 959

ENGINEERING -- NAVAL ARCHITECTURE AND MARINE ENGINEERING
Mandell and Lester Rosenblatt Undergraduate Scholarship • 989
Robert N. and Helen H. Herbert Undergraduate Scholarship • 1098

ENGINEERING -- NUCLEAR ENGINEERING
ANS Incoming Freshman Scholarships • 792
Operations and Power Division Scholarship • 1056

ENGINEERING -- POLYMER / PLASTICS ENGINEERING
Composites Division/Harold Giles Scholarship • 844
Injection Molding Division Scholarship • 940
Plastics Pioneers Association Scholarships • 1073
Polymer Modifiers and Additives Division Scholarships • 1074
Richard Goolsby Scholarship Fund • 1759
Salvatore J. Monte Thermoplastic Materials and Foams Division Scholarship • 1105
Ted and Ruth Neward Scholarship • 1139
Thermoplastic Elastomers Special Interest Group Scholarship • 1142
Thomas E. Powers/Detroit Section Scholarship • 1143

ENGLISH LANGUAGE AND LITERATURE
ACES Scholarships • 387
Bill Gove Scholarship • 399
Cavett Robert Scholarship • 405
Davidson Fellows Scholarships • 110
Heinlein Society Scholarship Program • 433
Huntington Fellowships • 606
Huntington-British Academy Fellowships for Study in Great Britain • 607
ILA Jeanne S. Chall Research Fellowship • 441
Iowa Scholarship for the Arts • 1475
Julianne Malveaux Scholarship • 2178
Minnesota Academic Excellence Scholarship • 1604
NCTA and AWMF Scholarship • 2224
Oratorical Contest Scholarship • 1706
PenSPRA Scholarship • 1733
Playwright Discovery Award • 475
Ruth Lilly and Dorothy Sargent Rosenberg Poetry Fellowship Program • 481

ENTOMOLOGY
See: BIOLOGICAL AND BIOMEDICAL SCIENCES

ENTREPRENEURSHIP / ENTREPRENEURIAL STUDIES
See: BUSINESS, MANAGEMENT AND MARKETING

The Ultimate Scholarship Book 2026
Field of Study Index

ENVIRONMENTAL / ENVIRONMENTAL HEALTH ENGINEERING
See: ENGINEERING

ENVIRONMENTAL DESIGN / ARCHITECTURE
See: ARCHITECTURE AND RELATED SERVICES

ENVIRONMENTAL SCIENCE
See: NATURAL RESOURCES AND CONSERVATION

EQUESTRIAN / EQUINE STUDIES
See: AGRICULTURE AND RELATED SCIENCES

EUROPEAN HISTORY
See: HISTORY

EUROPEAN STUDIES / CIVILIZATION
See: AREA, ETHNIC, CULTURAL AND GENDER STUDIES

FAMILY AND CONSUMER SCIENCES / HUMAN SCIENCES
- Arc of Washington State Trust Fund Stipend Award • 1221
- Association of Food and Drug Officials Scholarship Award • 813
- IFSEA Worthy Goal Scholarship • 609
- Texas Association FCCLA Regional Scholarship • 1837

FAMILY AND CONSUMER SCIENCES / HUMAN SCIENCES -- CHILD DEVELOPMENT
- Arc of Washington State Trust Fund Stipend Award • 1221
- Scholars for Excellence in Child Care • 1780
- Winifred R. Reynolds Educational Scholarship • 1913

FAMILY AND CONSUMER SCIENCES / HUMAN SCIENCES -- FOODS, NUTRITION AND RELATED SERVICES
- Phyllis V. Roberts Scholarship • 1735
- Undergraduate Scholarships • 1159

FAMILY PRACTICE NURSE / NURSE PRACTITIONER
See: HEALTH PROFESSIONS AND RELATED CLINICAL SCIENCES

FASHION / APPAREL DESIGN
See: VISUAL AND PERFORMING ARTS

FINANCE, GENERAL
See: BUSINESS, MANAGEMENT AND MARKETING

FINE / STUDIO ARTS, GENERAL
See: VISUAL AND PERFORMING ARTS

FINNISH AND RELATED LANGUAGES, LITERATURES AND LINGUISTICS
See: FOREIGN LANGUAGES, LITERATURES AND LINGUISTICS

FIRE PROTECTION
See: SECURITY AND PROTECTIVE SERVICES

FISHING AND FISHERIES SCIENCES AND MANAGEMENT
See: NATURAL RESOURCES AND CONSERVATION

FOOD SCIENCE AND TECHNOLOGY
See: AGRICULTURE AND RELATED SCIENCES

FOODS, NUTRITION AND RELATED SERVICES
See: FAMILY AND CONSUMER SCIENCES / HUMAN SCIENCES

FOREIGN LANGUAGES, LITERATURES AND LINGUISTICS
- Fellowships for Regular Program in Greece • 423
- Finlandia Foundation National Student Scholarships Program • 426
- Language Grants • 451
- Minnesota Academic Excellence Scholarship • 1604
- Nadia Christensen Prize • 461
- Student Translation Award • 490
- Translation Prize Competition • 495
- Fellowships for Regular Program in Greece • 423

FOREIGN LANGUAGES, LITERATURES AND LINGUISTICS -- JAPANESE LANGUAGE AND LITERATURE
- Bridging Scholarships for Study Abroad in Japan • 400
- Language Grants • 451

FOREIGN LANGUAGES, LITERATURES AND LINGUISTICS -- LATIN LANGUAGE AND LITERATURE
- ACL/NJCL National Latin Examination Scholarships • 389
- Fellowships for Regular Program in Greece • 423
- National Junior Classical League (NJCL) Scholarships • 463

FOREIGN LANGUAGES, LITERATURES AND LINGUISTICS -- MODERN GREEK LANGUAGE AND LITERATURE
- ACL/NJCL National Greek Examination Scholarship • 388
- Fellowships for Regular Program in Greece • 423
- National Junior Classical League (NJCL) Scholarships • 463

FORENSIC SCIENCE AND TECHNOLOGY
See: SECURITY AND PROTECTIVE SERVICES

FORESTRY
See: NATURAL RESOURCES AND CONSERVATION

FRENCH LANGUAGE AND LITERATURE
See: FOREIGN LANGUAGES, LITERATURES AND LINGUISTICS

FRENCH STUDIES
See: AREA, ETHNIC, CULTURAL AND GENDER STUDIES

FUNERAL SERVICE AND MORTUARY SCIENCE, GENERAL
See: PERSONAL AND CULINARY SERVICES

GENETICS, GENERAL
See: BIOLOGICAL AND BIOMEDICAL SCIENCES

GEOGRAPHY
See: SOCIAL SCIENCES

GEOLOGICAL AND EARTH SCIENCES / GEOSCIENCES
See: PHYSICAL SCIENCES

GERMAN LANGUAGE AND LITERATURE
See: FOREIGN LANGUAGES, LITERATURES AND LINGUISTICS

GERMAN STUDIES
See: AREA, ETHNIC, CULTURAL AND GENDER STUDIES

GRAPHIC DESIGN
See: VISUAL AND PERFORMING ARTS

HEALTH AND MEDICAL ADMINISTRATIVE SERVICES
See: HEALTH PROFESSIONS AND RELATED CLINICAL SCIENCES

HEALTH AND PHYSICAL EDUCATION, GENERAL
See: PARKS, RECREATION, LEISURE AND FITNESS STUDIES

HEALTH PROFESSIONS AND RELATED CLINICAL SCIENCES
- AAMA Student Essay Competition • 746
- Advanced Practice Healthcare Scholarship Program • 1186
- Allied Healthcare Scholarship Program • 1202
- Alpha Mu Tau Fraternity Undergraduate Scholarships • 776
- Associate Degree Nursing Scholarship Program • 1228
- Avacare Medical Scholarship • 820
- Bachelor of Science Nursing Scholarship Program • 1234
- Boeing Company STEM Scholarship • 1246
- Brown Hudner Navy Scholarship • 68
- Burlington Northern Santa Fe (BNSF) Foundation Scholarship • 2111
- California Health Sciences Scholarships • 1265
- Campus Safety Health and Environmental Management Association Scholarship • 834
- Carole J. Streeter, KB9JBR, Scholarship • 553
- CHCI United Health Foundation Scholar-Intern Program • 2119
- EmPOWERED Scholars Program • 878
- Fellowship Award • 889
- Florence Young Memorial Scholarship • 2141
- Health Professions Pre-Graduate Scholarship Program • 2154
- Health Professions Preparatory Scholarship Program • 2155
- Ida M. Pope Memorial Scholarship • 2168
- International Student Scholarship • 943
- Jimmy A. Young Memorial Education Recognition Award • 952
- Maine Health Professionals Loan Program • 1558
- Maple Flooring Manufacturers Association Scholarship • 645
- Migrant Health Scholarships • 1007
- Minority Fellowship Program • 1008
- NAHN Scholarship • 2213
- National Hispanic Health Professional Student Scholarship • 2218

NBRC/AMP Gareth B. Gish, MS, RRT Memorial and William F. Miller, MD Postgraduate Education Recognition Awards • 1033
NBRC/AMP William W. Burgin, Jr. MD and Robert M. Lawrence, MD Education Recognition Award • 1034
NCPA Foundation Presidential Scholarship • 1036
NFMC Dorothy Dann Bullock Music Therapy Award and the NFMC Ruth B. Robertson Music Ted Brickley/Bernice Shickora Scholarship • 1831
Therapy Award • 1045
Novus Biologicals Scholarship Program • 1048
Oliver Joel and Ellen Pell Denny Healthcare Scholarship Fund • 1702
Pennsylvania Targeted Industry Program • 1732
Presbyterian Church USA Student Opportunity Scholarships • 2031
RevPart STEM Scholarship • 1089
Robanna Fund • 1762
Ruth Abernathy Presidential Scholarship • 1103
SNMTS Paul Cole Scholarship • 1117
STEM Scholarship • 2252
Student Research Fellowship Awards • 1133
Tocris Scholarship • 1152
UNCF Healthcare Workforce Diversity Program Certification • 2271

HEALTH PROFESSIONS AND RELATED CLINICAL SCIENCES -- ATHLETIC TRAINING / TRAINER

Maple Flooring Manufacturers Association Scholarship • 645
Mark Ando and Ito Family Scholarship • 2197
Michael Moody Fitness Scholarship • 1005

HEALTH PROFESSIONS AND RELATED CLINICAL SCIENCES -- CHIROPRACTIC

ChiroHealthUSA Foxworth Family Scholarship • 840
Chiropractic Education Assistance Scholarship • 1292
Cora Aguda Manayan Fund • 1314
Dr. Hans and Clara Zimmerman Foundation Health Scholarships • 1342
Dr. William S. Boyd Scholarship • 1344

HEALTH PROFESSIONS AND RELATED CLINICAL SCIENCES -- CLINICAL / MEDICAL LABORATORY SCIENCE AND ALLIED PROFESSIONS

Alpha Mu Tau Fraternity Undergraduate Scholarships • 776
Diversity Advocacy Council Scholarship • 2132
Foundation for Surgical Technology Scholarships • 892

HEALTH PROFESSIONS AND RELATED CLINICAL SCIENCES -- COMMUNICATION DISORDERS, GENERAL

Graduate Student Scholarship • 920
Minority Student Scholarship • 1009
New Century Scholars Doctoral Scholarship • 1042
Sertoma Communicative Disorders Scholarship • 1111
Student with a Disability Scholarship • 716

HEALTH PROFESSIONS AND RELATED CLINICAL SCIENCES -- DENTAL SUPPORT SERVICES AND ALLIED PROFESSIONS

1Dental Scholarship • 11
ADEA/Crest Oral-B Scholarships for Dental Hygiene Students Pursuing Academic Careers • 755
ADEA/MouthWatch Patti DiGangi Scholarship for Dental Hygiene Innovation • 757
ADEA/Sigma Phi Alpha Linda Devore Scholarship • 759
ADHA Institute Scholarship Program • 760
AMT Student Scholarship • 787
Colgate Bright Smiles, Bright Futures Minority Scholarships • 841
Cora Aguda Manayan Fund • 1314
Crest Oral-B Laboratories Dental Hygiene Scholarships • 848
Dr. Esther Wilkins Scholarship • 866
Dr. Hans and Clara Zimmerman Foundation Health Scholarships • 1342
Irene Woodall Graduate Scholarship • 947
John Dawe Dental Education Fund • 1501
Karla Girts Memorial Community Outreach Scholarship • 968
Sigma Phi Alpha Undergraduate Scholarship • 1112

HEALTH PROFESSIONS AND RELATED CLINICAL SCIENCES -- DENTISTRY

1Dental Scholarship • 11
ADEA/Haleon Preventive Dentistry Scholarships • 756
ADEA/MouthWatch Predoctoral Dental Student Scholarship for Innovation • 758
Cora Aguda Manayan Fund • 1314
Dr. Hans and Clara Zimmerman Foundation Health Scholarships • 1342
Health Professions Pre-Graduate Scholarship Program • 2154
Irene Woodall Graduate Scholarship • 947
John Dawe Dental Education Fund • 1501
Michael Moody Fitness Scholarship • 1005
NHSC Scholarship • 1046

HEALTH PROFESSIONS AND RELATED CLINICAL SCIENCES -- DIETETICS / DIETITIAN

Academy of Nutrition and Dietetics Foundation Student Scholarship • 751
Sister Helen Marie Pellicer Scholarship • 1791

HEALTH PROFESSIONS AND RELATED CLINICAL SCIENCES -- FAMILY PRACTICE NURSE / NURSE PRACTITIONER

AMT Student Scholarship • 787
Annual NBNA Scholarships • 789
Cora Aguda Manayan Fund • 1314
Dr. Hans and Clara Zimmerman Foundation Health Scholarships • 1342
Margaret A. Pemberton Scholarship • 1563
Margaret A. Stafford Nursing Scholarship • 1564
MARILN Professional Scholarship Award • 1565
NHSC Scholarship • 1046
Nurse Corps Scholarship Program • 1052
Nursing Education Scholarship Program • 1682

Predoctoral Research Fellowships • 1077
Spillman-Bischoff Scholarship • 1806
Stephanie Carroll Memorial Scholarship • 1128
Tuition Reduction for Non-Resident Nursing Students • 1858

HEALTH PROFESSIONS AND RELATED CLINICAL SCIENCES -- HEALTH AND MEDICAL ADMINISTRATIVE SERVICES

AHIMA Foundation Merit Scholarships • 765
Harry J. Harwick Scholarship • 927
HIMSS Foundation Scholarship • 933
Leaders Scholarship • 975
Richard J. Stull Student Essay Competition in Healthcare Management • 1090
Richard L. Davis, FACMPE - Managers Scholarship • 1092
Richard L. Davis, FACMPE/Barbara B. Watson, FACMPE - National Scholarship • 1093

HEALTH PROFESSIONS AND RELATED CLINICAL SCIENCES -- LICENSED PRACTICAL / VOCATIONAL NURSE TRAINING

AMT Student Scholarship • 787
Annual NBNA Scholarships • 789
Cora Aguda Manayan Fund • 1314
Dr. Hans and Clara Zimmerman Foundation Health Scholarships • 1342
Kansas Nursing Service Scholarship • 1512
Margaret A. Pemberton Scholarship • 1563
MARILN Professional Scholarship Award • 1565
Nursing Education Scholarship Program • 1682
Nursing Student Loan • 1685
Predoctoral Research Fellowships • 1077
Spillman-Bischoff Scholarship • 1806
Stephanie Carroll Memorial Scholarship • 1128
Tuition Reduction for Non-Resident Nursing Students • 1858
Vocational Nurse Scholarship • 1887

HEALTH PROFESSIONS AND RELATED CLINICAL SCIENCES -- MEDICINE AND PRE-MEDICINE STUDIES

AGBU US Graduate Scholarship • 2089
Annual University Scholarship • 790
Cora Aguda Manayan Fund • 1314
Dr. and Mrs. Arthur F. Sullivan Fund • 1339
Dr. Bart Kamen Memorial FIRST Scholarship • 865
Dr. Hans and Clara Zimmerman Foundation Health Scholarships • 1342
Health Professions Pre-Graduate Scholarship Program • 2154
John D. and Virginia Riesch Scholarship • 1500
Margaret A. Haines Telephony Scholarship • 2008
Medical Loan-For-Service Program • 1586
Medical Student Research Scholarship • 996
NHSC Scholarship • 1046
Resident Research Scholarship • 1087
Student Award Program of FSD • 2325
Visiting Medical Student Scholar • 1167
William and Charlotte Cadbury Award • 2275

The Ultimate Scholarship Book 2026
Field of Study Index

HEALTH PROFESSIONS AND RELATED CLINICAL SCIENCES -- MUSIC THERAPY / THERAPIST
- Music Committee Scholarship • 1630
- NFMC Gretchen E. Van Roy Music Education Scholarship • 674

HEALTH PROFESSIONS AND RELATED CLINICAL SCIENCES -- NURSE / NURSING ASSISTANT / AIDE AND PATIENT CARE ASSISTANT
- Albert E. and Florence W. Newton Nursing Scholarship • 1196
- AMT Student Scholarship • 787
- Annual NBNA Scholarships • 789
- Cora Aguda Manayan Fund • 1314
- Dr. Hans and Clara Zimmerman Foundation Health Scholarships • 1342
- Margaret A. Stafford Nursing Scholarship • 1564
- Nursing Education Scholarship Program • 1682
- Predoctoral Research Fellowships • 1077
- Spillman-Bischoff Scholarship • 1806
- Stephanie Carroll Memorial Scholarship • 1128
- Tuition Reduction for Non-Resident Nursing Students • 1858

HEALTH PROFESSIONS AND RELATED CLINICAL SCIENCES -- NURSING ADMINISTRATION
- H.M. Muffly Memorial Scholarship • 1420
- Nightingale Awards of Pennsylvania Scholarship • 1659
- Nursing Incentive Scholarship Fund • 1683
- South Carolina Nurses Foundation Nurses Care Scholarship • 1802
- Stephanie Carroll Memorial Scholarship • 1128

HEALTH PROFESSIONS AND RELATED CLINICAL SCIENCES -- NURSING SCIENCE
- H.M. Muffly Memorial Scholarship • 1420
- Margaret A. Pemberton Scholarship • 1563
- Margaret A. Stafford Nursing Scholarship • 1564
- MARILN Professional Scholarship Award • 1565
- Michael Moody Fitness Scholarship • 1005
- Nightingale Awards of Pennsylvania Scholarship • 1659
- South Carolina Nurses Foundation Nurses Care Scholarship • 1802
- Stephanie Carroll Memorial Scholarship • 1128

HEALTH PROFESSIONS AND RELATED CLINICAL SCIENCES -- NURSING/ REGISTERED NURSE
- A.T. Anderson Memorial Scholarship • 2079
- Albert E. and Florence W. Newton Nursing Scholarship • 1196
- AMT Student Scholarship • 787
- Annual NBNA Scholarships • 789
- Annual University Scholarship • 790
- Army Nurse Corps Association Scholarships • 52
- Cora Aguda Manayan Fund • 1314
- Dr. Hans and Clara Zimmerman Foundation Health Scholarships • 1342
- H.M. Muffly Memorial Scholarship • 1420
- Harriet Hayes Austin Memorial Scholarship for Nursing • 1421
- Jack E. Barger, Sr. Memorial Nursing Scholarship • 1483
- John D. and Virginia Riesch Scholarship • 1500
- Kansas Nursing Service Scholarship • 1512
- Laurene Ann Opdyke Nursing Scholarship • 1527
- Licensed Vocational Nurse to Associate Degree Nursing Scholarship • 1538
- Margaret A. Pemberton Scholarship • 1563
- Margaret A. Stafford Nursing Scholarship • 1564
- MARILN Professional Scholarship Award • 1565
- McLean Scholarship for Nursing and Physician Assistant Majors • 1584
- Naomi Brack Student Scholarship • 1019
- Nightingale Awards of Pennsylvania Scholarship • 1659
- NROTC Nurse Corps Scholarship • 259
- Nurse Candidate Program • 1051
- Nurse Corps Scholarship Program • 1052
- Nursing Education Scholarship Program • 1682
- Nursing Incentive Scholarship Fund • 1683
- Nursing Loan-For-Service Program • 1684
- Nursing Student Loan • 1685
- Phoebe Pember Memorial Scholarship • 1069
- Predoctoral Research Fellowships • 1077
- Ruth Lutes Bachmann Scholarship • 1775
- South Carolina Nurses Foundation Nurses Care Scholarship • 1802
- Spillman-Bischoff Scholarship • 1806
- Stephanie Carroll Memorial Scholarship • 1128
- Tuition Reduction for Non-Resident Nursing Students • 1858
- Workforce Shortage Student Assistance Grant Program • 1923

HEALTH PROFESSIONS AND RELATED CLINICAL SCIENCES -- OCCUPATIONAL THERAPY / THERAPIST
- AMBUCS Scholars • 778
- Kappa Delta Phi • 966
- Laura N. Dowsett Fund • 1526
- Texas Occupational Therapy Association Scholarships • 1845

HEALTH PROFESSIONS AND RELATED CLINICAL SCIENCES -- OSTEOPATHIC MEDICINE / OSTEOPATHY
- Kansas Osteopathic Medical Service Scholarship • 1514
- Welch Scholars Grant • 1169

HEALTH PROFESSIONS AND RELATED CLINICAL SCIENCES -- PHARMACY
- Annual University Scholarship • 790
- Cora Aguda Manayan Fund • 1314
- Dr. Hans and Clara Zimmerman Foundation Health Scholarships • 1342
- Equity in Pharmacy Scholarship • 882
- Predoctoral Research Fellowships • 1077

HEALTH PROFESSIONS AND RELATED CLINICAL SCIENCES -- PHARMACY TECHNICIAN / ASSISTANT
- Cora Aguda Manayan Fund • 1314
- Dr. Hans and Clara Zimmerman Foundation Health Scholarships • 1342
- Equity in Pharmacy Scholarship • 882
- Predoctoral Research Fellowships • 1077

HEALTH PROFESSIONS AND RELATED CLINICAL SCIENCES -- PHYSICAL THERAPY / THERAPIST
- AMBUCS Scholars • 778
- Cora Aguda Manayan Fund • 1314
- Dr. Hans and Clara Zimmerman Foundation Health Scholarships • 1342
- Linda Craig Memorial Scholarship Presented by St. Vincent Sports Performance • 1542
- Maple Flooring Manufacturers Association Scholarship • 645
- Michael Moody Fitness Scholarship • 1005
- Minority Scholarship Award for Physical Therapy Students • 2206
- Paulina L. Sorg Scholarship • 1722
- William A. Crawford Minority Teacher Scholarship • 1906
- Workforce Shortage Student Assistance Grant Program • 1923

HEALTH PROFESSIONS AND RELATED CLINICAL SCIENCES -- PHYSICIAN ASSISTANT
- AMT Student Scholarship • 787
- Annual NBNA Scholarships • 789
- Cora Aguda Manayan Fund • 1314
- Dr. Hans and Clara Zimmerman Foundation Health Scholarships • 1342
- Iowa Physician Assistant Society Scholarship • 1473
- McLean Scholarship for Nursing and Physician Assistant Majors • 1584
- Nathaniel Alston Student Achievement Award • 1636
- NCAPA Endowment Annual Student Grants • 1035
- New York State Society of Physician Assistants Scholarship • 1655
- NHSC Scholarship • 1046
- Nursing Education Scholarship Program • 1682
- Predoctoral Research Fellowships • 1077
- Tuition Reduction for Non-Resident Nursing Students • 1858
- Veterans Caucus Scholarship • 362

HEALTH PROFESSIONS AND RELATED CLINICAL SCIENCES -- VETERINARY MEDICINE
- Allan Eldin and Agnes Sutorik Geiger Scholarship Fund • 1200
- Dairy Student Recognition Program • 850
- Margaret A. Haines Telephony Scholarship • 2008

HEATING, AIR CONDITIONING, VENTILATION AND REFRIGERATION MAINTENANCE TECHNOLOGY / TECHNICIAN
See: *MECHANIC AND REPAIR TECHNOLOGIES / TECHNICIANS*

HEAVY EQUIPMENT MAINTENANCE TECHNOLOGY / TECHNICIAN
See: *MECHANIC AND REPAIR TECHNOLOGIES / TECHNICIANS*

HIGHER EDUCATION / HIGHER EDUCATION ADMINISTRATION
See: *EDUCATION*

HISTORIC PRESERVATION AND CONSERVATION
See: MULTI / INTERDISCIPLINARY STUDIES

HISTORY
BSA Research Fellowship • 548
Fellowship in Aerospace History • 890
Junior Fellowships • 450
William G. Saletic Scholarship • 1910

HISTORY -- AMERICAN HISTORY
Huntington Fellowships • 606
Huntington-British Academy Fellowships for Study in Great Britain • 607

HISTORY -- EUROPEAN HISTORY
Huntington Fellowships • 606
Huntington-British Academy Fellowships for Study in Great Britain • 607

HOSPITALITY ADMINISTRATION / MANAGEMENT, GENERAL
See: BUSINESS, MANAGEMENT AND MARKETING

HUMANITIES / HUMANISTIC STUDIES
See: LIBERAL ARTS AND SCIENCES, GENERAL STUDIES AND HUMANITIES

INDUSTRIAL DESIGN
See: VISUAL AND PERFORMING ARTS

INDUSTRIAL ENGINEERING
See: ENGINEERING

INFORMATION TECHNOLOGY
See: COMPUTER AND INFORMATION SCIENCES

INTERIOR ARCHITECTURE
See: ARCHITECTURE AND RELATED SERVICES

INTERIOR DESIGN
See: VISUAL AND PERFORMING ARTS

INTERNATIONAL BUSINESS / TRADE / COMMERCE
See: BUSINESS, MANAGEMENT AND MARKETING

INTERNATIONAL RELATIONS AND AFFAIRS
See: SOCIAL SCIENCES

ITALIAN STUDIES
See: AREA, ETHNIC, CULTURAL AND GENDER STUDIES

JAPANESE LANGUAGE AND LITERATURE
See: FOREIGN LANGUAGES, LITERATURES AND LINGUISTICS

JAPANESE STUDIES
See: AREA, ETHNIC, CULTURAL AND GENDER STUDIES

JOURNALISM
See: COMMUNICATION AND JOURNALISM

JUNIOR HIGH / INTERMEDIATE / MIDDLE SCHOOL EDUCATION AND TEACHING
See: EDUCATION

KOREAN LANGUAGE AND LITERATURE
See: FOREIGN LANGUAGES, LITERATURES AND LINGUISTICS

LANDSCAPE ARCHITECTURE
See: ARCHITECTURE AND RELATED SERVICES

LANDSCAPING AND GROUNDSKEEPING
See: AGRICULTURE AND RELATED SCIENCES

LATIN AMERICAN STUDIES
See: AREA, ETHNIC, CULTURAL AND GENDER STUDIES

LATIN LANGUAGE AND LITERATURE
See: FOREIGN LANGUAGES, LITERATURES AND LINGUISTICS

LEGAL PROFESSIONS AND LAW STUDIES
ABF Summer Undergraduate Research Fellowship Program • 511
AGBU US Graduate Scholarship • 2089
Ally Financial Law Scholars • 2097
American Bar Association Law Student Writing Competition • 527
Bick Bickson Scholarship Fund • 1240
Earl Warren Scholarship • 572
Emily M. Hewitt and Stephen K. Stocking Memorial Scholarship • 1362
Florence Young Memorial Scholarship • 2141
George H. Nofer Scholarship for Law and Public Policy • 2296
Giles Sutherland Rich Memorial Scholarship • 592
Honorable William Conner Writing Competition • 603
ISF Policy Scholarship Program • 1992
Japanese American Citizens League Law Scholarships • 2174
Legal Opportunity Scholarship Fund • 637
MALDEF Law School Scholarship • 2193
MCCA Lloyd M. Johnson, Jr. Scholarship Program • 2202
National Foundation Scholarships • 662
NCRA A to Z Scholarship • 667
NCRA CASE Student Scholarship • 668
Otto M. Stanfield Legal Scholarship • 679
Presidential Scholarships • 687
Reiff Law Firm Legal Scholarship • 696
Richard D. Wiegers Scholarship • 1757
Sutliff and Stout Law School Scholarship • 718
Women In Defense WID Scholar • 2276

LIBERAL ARTS AND SCIENCES, GENERAL STUDIES AND HUMANITIES
ACLS Fellowships • 514
ACOR-CAORC Fellowship • 515
Community Scholarship Fund • 1310
Huntington-British Academy Fellowships for Study in Great Britain • 607
Institute of Electrical and Electronics Engineers Life Members' Fellowship in Electrical History • 941
ISF Policy Scholarship Program • 1992

LIBRARY SCIENCE
Beverly Murphy MLA Scholarship for Underrepresented Students • 541
BSA Research Fellowship • 548
Gwendolyn S. Cruzat MLA Scholarship • 597

LICENSED PRACTICAL / VOCATIONAL NURSE TRAINING
See: HEALTH PROFESSIONS AND RELATED CLINICAL SCIENCES

MACHINE TOOL TECHNOLOGY / MACHINIST
See: PRECISION PRODUCTION

MANAGEMENT INFORMATION SYSTEMS, GENERAL
See: BUSINESS, MANAGEMENT AND MARKETING

MARINE BIOLOGY AND BIOLOGICAL OCEANOGRAPHY
See: BIOLOGICAL AND BIOMEDICAL SCIENCES

MARKETING / MARKETING MANAGEMENT, GENERAL
See: BUSINESS, MANAGEMENT AND MARKETING

MASS COMMUNICATION / MEDIA STUDIES
See: COMMUNICATION AND JOURNALISM

MATERIALS ENGINEERING
See: ENGINEERING

MATHEMATICS AND STATISTICS
A.T. Anderson Memorial Scholarship • 2079
AFCEA Ralph W. Shrader Diversity Scholarships • 761
AFCEA ROTC Scholarships • 23
Alice T. Schafer Mathematics Prize • 774
AMS Senior Named Scholarships • 786
Astronaut Scholarship • 816
BAFTX Undergraduate Award • 1235
Boeing Company STEM Scholarship • 1246
Brown Hudner Navy Scholarship • 68
Burlington Northern Santa Fe (BNSF) Foundation Scholarship • 2111
Chevron Corporate Scholars Program • 2121
Collegiate Inventors Competition • 842
Computational Science Graduate Fellowship • 845
CRA All-Access Scholarship • 2128
Davidson Fellows Scholarships • 110
Dellums SMART Scholarship • 856
Edith Nourse Rogers STEM Scholarship • 134
Frank and Brennie Morgan Prize for Outstanding Research in Mathematics by an Undergraduate Student • 893
GeneTex Scholarship Program • 907
Gertrude Cox Scholarship For Women In Statistics • 910
Heinlein Society Scholarship Program • 433
HSC Foundation Scholarship • 2165
LabRoots Scholarship • 970
Lambeth Family Scholarship • 1525
Learner Education Women in Mathematics Scholarship • 976
Lockheed Martin STEM Scholarship Program • 982
Lucy Kasparian Aharonian Scholarship • 2189
Mikkelson Foundation Scholarship • 1600
Minnesota Academic Excellence Scholarship • 1604
NDSEG Fellowship Program • 1039
Northrop Grumman Scholarship • 1681
Olay Face the Stem Gap Scholarship • 2229
Payzer Scholarship • 1063

The Ultimate Scholarship Book 2026
Field of Study Index

PixelPlex Bi-Annual STEM Scholarship • 1072
RBC Wealth Management Colorado Scholarship • 1748
RevPart STEM Scholarship • 1089
Ridgeline International Community Scholarship • 1094
Samsung@First Scholars • 1777
Science Ambassador Scholarship • 1108
SHPE Scholarship Program • 2248
Shuichi, Katsu and Itsuyo Suga Scholarship • 1789
SMART Scholarship • 1114
SMART Scholarship • 1115
Society of American Military Engineers, Albuquerque Post Scholarship • 1797
Stantec Equity and Diversity Scholarship • 2251
STEM Scholarship • 2252
STEM Scholarship Program • 1127
Student Award Program of FSD • 2325
Study.com Scholarship for Women in STEM • 2256
T. Eugene Young Montana's Promise Scholarship • 1822
TE Connectivity African Heritage Scholarship • 2262
U.S. Western Digital STEM Scholarship • 346
Unitil Scholarship Fund • 1865
Women in STEM Award • 1922
Women in STEM Scholarship • 378
Women in STEM Scholarship/BHW Scholarship • 1172

MATHEMATICS AND STATISTICS -- MATHEMATICS, GENERAL
BMO Capital Markets Lime Connect Equity Through Education Scholarship • 2286
Choose Ohio First Scholarship • 1293
Hubertus W.V. Wellems Scholarship for Male Students • 2167
Nebraska Actuaries Club Scholarship • 1640
New Face of Tech Scholarship Program • 1043
Tech High School Alumni Association/W.O. Cheney Merit Scholarship • 1828

MATHEMATICS AND STATISTICS -- STATISTICS, GENERAL
BMO Capital Markets Lime Connect Equity Through Education Scholarship • 2286
Nebraska Actuaries Club Scholarship • 1640

MECHANIC AND REPAIR TECHNOLOGIES / TECHNICIANS
California - Hawaii Elks Association Vocational Grants • 550
CDM Constructors Inc. Workforce Development Scholarship • 1281
DEWALT Trades Scholarship • 566
Educational Foundation Scholarship • 576
John and Anne Clifton Scholarship • 1499
Lockheed Martin Vocational Scholarship Program • 641
Louis B. Russell Scholarship • 1550
Maple Flooring Manufacturers Association Scholarship • 645
MCEC Technical Scholarship • 1583
Medallion Fund • 1585
Shell Associate Scholarship Program • 708
Texas Elks State Association Vocational Grant Program • 1841
TOPS Tech Award • 1851

MECHANIC AND REPAIR TECHNOLOGIES / TECHNICIANS -- AUTOMOBILE / AUTOMOTIVE MECHANICS TECHNOLOGY / TECHNICIAN
DEWALT Trades Scholarship • 566
IAD Foundation Scholarships • 1453

MECHANIC AND REPAIR TECHNOLOGIES / TECHNICIANS -- HEATING, AIR CONDITIONING, VENTILATION AND REFRIGERATION MAINTENANCE TECHNOLOGY / TECHNICIAN
ASHRAE Society Scholarship Program • 806
Clifford H. Ted Rees Jr. Scholarship • 560
DEWALT Trades Scholarship • 566
Duane M. Hanson Scholarship • 867
EGIA Foundation Scholarship Program • 577
Frank M. Coda Scholarship • 582
Henry Adams Scholarship • 930
Reuben Trane Scholarship • 1088

MECHANICAL ENGINEERING
See: ENGINEERING

MEDICINE AND PRE-MEDICINE STUDIES
See: HEALTH PROFESSIONS AND RELATED CLINICAL SCIENCES

MERCHANDISING AND BUYING OPERATIONS
See: BUSINESS, MANAGEMENT AND MARKETING

METALLURGICAL ENGINEERING
See: ENGINEERING

MICROBIOLOGICAL SCIENCES AND IMMUNOLOGY
See: BIOLOGICAL AND BIOMEDICAL SCIENCES

MILITARY TECHNOLOGIES
AOC Scholarships • 794
Women In Defense WID Scholar • 2276

MINING AND MINERAL ENGINEERING
See: ENGINEERING

MODERN GREEK LANGUAGE AND LITERATURE
See: FOREIGN LANGUAGES, LITERATURES AND LINGUISTICS

MULTI / INTERDISCIPLINARY STUDIES

MULTI / INTERDISCIPLINARY STUDIES -- HISTORIC PRESERVATION AND CONSERVATION
Plan NH Scholarship and Fellowship Program • 1737

MUSIC THERAPY / THERAPIST
See: HEALTH PROFESSIONS AND RELATED CLINICAL SCIENCES

MUSIC, GENERAL
See: VISUAL AND PERFORMING ARTS

MUSICOLOGY AND ETHNOMUSICOLOGY
See: VISUAL AND PERFORMING ARTS

NATURAL RESOURCES AND CONSERVATION
ASF Olin Fellowships • 803
Campus Safety Health and Environmental Management Association Scholarship • 834
Emily M. Hewitt and Stephen K. Stocking Memorial Scholarship • 1362
Future Leader Scholarship • 898
Hutton Junior Fisheries Biology Program • 936
Maple Flooring Manufacturers Association Scholarship • 645
Minnesota Division Izaak Walton League Scholarship • 1605
National Garden Clubs Scholarship • 1026
Novus Biologicals Scholarship Program • 1048
Phyllis V. Roberts Scholarship • 1735
Rockefeller State Wildlife Scholarship • 1767
T. Eugene Young Montana's Promise Scholarship • 1822
Truman D. Picard Scholarship • 2269
USDA/1890 National Scholars Program • 1163
Women's Wildlife Management/Conservation Scholarship • 1174
YASME Foundation Scholarship • 739

NATURAL RESOURCES AND CONSERVATION -- ENVIRONMENTAL SCIENCE
Byers Scholarship • 1254
Dairy Student Recognition Program • 850
Delaware Solid Waste Authority John P. Pat Healy Scholarship • 1327
E.H. Marth Food Protection and Food Science Scholarship • 1346
ERC Eco Scholarship Fund • 1366
Grossman Scholarship • 1414
J.R. Popalisky Scholarship • 1482
Karen Ann Shopis-Fox Memorial Scholarship • 1517
Larson Aquatic Research Support (LARS) • 973
National Foundation Scholarships • 662
NOAA Educational Partnership Program Undergraduate Scholarships • 2227
PG&E Better Together STEM Scholarship Program • 1734
Plan NH Scholarship and Fellowship Program • 1737
Society of Exploration Geophysicists (SEG) Scholarship • 1118
Ted Brickley/Bernice Shickora Scholarship • 1831
Thaddeus Colson and Isabelle Saalwaechter Fitzpatrick Memorial Scholarship • 1848

NATURAL RESOURCES AND CONSERVATION -- FORESTRY
John Mabry Forestry Scholarship and Paul Webster Forestry Scholarship • 958
Mabel Mayforth Scholarship • 1554
Oregon Farm Bureau Memorial Scholarships • 1708
Phyllis V. Roberts Scholarship • 1735

Field of Study Index

NATURAL RESOURCES AND CONSERVATION -- NATURAL RESOURCES MANAGEMENT AND POLICY
Grossman Scholarship • 1414
Plan NH Scholarship and Fellowship Program • 1737

NAVAL ARCHITECTURE AND MARINE ENGINEERING
See: ENGINEERING

NON-PROFIT / PUBLIC / ORGANIZATIONAL MANAGEMENT
See: BUSINESS, MANAGEMENT AND MARKETING

NUCLEAR ENGINEERING
See: ENGINEERING

NURSE / NURSING
See: HEALTH PROFESSIONS AND RELATED CLINICAL SCIENCES

OCCUPATIONAL HEALTH AND INDUSTRIAL HYGIENE
See: HEALTH PROFESSIONS AND RELATED CLINICAL SCIENCES

OCCUPATIONAL THERAPY / THERAPIST
See: HEALTH PROFESSIONS AND RELATED CLINICAL SCIENCES

OPERATIONS MANAGEMENT AND SUPERVISION
See: BUSINESS, MANAGEMENT AND MARKETING

OPTOMETRY
See: HEALTH PROFESSIONS AND RELATED CLINICAL SCIENCES

OSTEOPATHIC MEDICINE / OSTEOPATHY
See: HEALTH PROFESSIONS AND RELATED CLINICAL SCIENCES

PARKS, RECREATION, LEISURE AND FITNESS STUDIES
Challenge Scholarship • 79
Emily M. Hewitt and Stephen K. Stocking Memorial Scholarship • 1362
GNC Nutritional Research Grant • 160
Graduate Research Grant - Master and Doctoral • 164
High School Scholarship • 173
Jean Lee/Jeff Marvin Collegiate Scholarships • 1492
Joe Perdue Scholarship • 622
Maple Flooring Manufacturers Association Scholarship • 645
Mary Benevento/CTAHPERD Scholarship • 1570
Michael Moody Fitness Scholarship • 1005
Minority Scholarship • 2205
Ruth Abernathy Presidential Scholarship • 1103
Women's Scholarship • 1173

PARKS, RECREATION, LEISURE AND FITNESS STUDIES -- SPORT AND FITNESS ADMINISTRATION / MANAGEMENT
Michael Moody Fitness Scholarship • 1005
Roller Skating Foundation Scholarship, Current College Student Category • 701

PERSONAL AND CULINARY SERVICES
California - Hawaii Elks Association Vocational Grants • 550
Challenge Scholarship • 79
GNC Nutritional Research Grant • 160
Graduate Research Grant - Master and Doctoral • 164
High School Scholarship • 173
IFSEA Worthy Goal Scholarship • 609
John and Anne Clifton Scholarship • 1499
Medallion Fund • 1585
Minority Scholarship • 2205

PERSONAL AND CULINARY SERVICES -- COOKING AND RELATED CULINARY ARTS, GENERAL
American Culinary Federation Scholarships • 528
GoFoodservice Scholarship • 593
Good Eats Scholarship Fund • 1404
James Beard Foundation Scholarship • 617
John Schwartz Scholarship • 1503

PERSONAL AND CULINARY SERVICES -- FUNERAL SERVICE AND MORTUARY SCIENCE, GENERAL
Dennis Schoepp Memorial Scholarship • 1329
Memorial Classic Golf Tournament Scholarship • 650
National Scholarship Program • 665
Shipley Rose Buckner Memorial Scholarship • 1786
Tennessee Funeral Directors Association Memorial Scholarship • 1832
Wallace S. and Wilma K. Laughlin Foundation Trust Scholarships • 1889

PHARMACY
See: HEALTH PROFESSIONS AND RELATED CLINICAL SCIENCES

PHARMACY TECHNICIAN / ASSISTANT
See: HEALTH PROFESSIONS AND RELATED CLINICAL SCIENCES

PHILOSOPHY AND RELIGIOUS STUDIES
Presbyterian Church USA Student Opportunity Scholarships • 2031

PHILOSOPHY AND RELIGIOUS STUDIES -- CHRISTIAN STUDIES
Mary E. Bivins Religious Scholarship • 2011

PHOTOGRAPHY
See: VISUAL AND PERFORMING ARTS

PHOTOJOURNALISM
See: COMMUNICATION AND JOURNALISM

PHYSICAL SCIENCES
ACOR-CAORC Fellowship • 515
AFCEA Ralph W. Shrader Diversity Scholarships • 761
AFCEA ROTC Scholarships • 23
AMS Graduate Fellowship in the History of Science • 783
AMS Graduate Fellowships • 784
AMS Minority Scholarship • 785
AMS Senior Named Scholarships • 786
ASNE Scholarship Program • 810
Astronaut Scholarship • 816
BAFTX Undergraduate Award • 1235
Battery Division Student Research Award • 825
Boeing Company STEM Scholarship • 1246
Brown Hudner Navy Scholarship • 68
Burlington Northern Santa Fe (BNSF) Foundation Scholarship • 2111
Collegiate Inventors Competition • 842
Computational Science Graduate Fellowship • 845
CRA All-Access Scholarship • 2128
Davidson Fellows Scholarships • 110
Father James B. Macelwane Annual Award in Meteorology • 887
Fellowship Award • 889
Freshman Undergraduate Scholarship • 896
GeneTex Scholarship Program • 907
Gladys Anderson Emerson Scholarship • 913
Gorgas Scholarship Competition • 1405
Graduate Research Fellowship Program • 917
Heinlein Society Scholarship Program • 433
Hertz Foundation's Graduate Fellowship Award • 932
HSC Foundation Scholarship • 2165
Ida M. Pope Memorial Scholarship • 2168
Institute of Electrical and Electronics Engineers Life Members' Fellowship in Electrical History • 941
John J. McKetta Scholarship • 956
LabRoots Scholarship • 970
Lambeth Family Scholarship • 1525
Lockheed Martin STEM Scholarship Program • 982
MAES Scholarship Program • 2192
Mikkelson Foundation Scholarship • 1600
Minnesota Academic Excellence Scholarship • 1604
NDSEG Fellowship Program • 1039
Novus Biologicals Scholarship Program • 1048
Olay Face the Stem Gap Scholarship • 2229
Paul and Ellen Ruckes Scholarship • 2318
Payzer Scholarship • 1063
PixelPlex Bi-Annual STEM Scholarship • 1072
R&D Systems Scholarship Program • 1081
RBC Wealth Management Colorado Scholarship • 1748
RevPart STEM Scholarship • 1089
Ridgeline International Community Scholarship • 1094
Samsung@First Scholars • 1777
SMART Scholarship • 1114
Society of American Military Engineers, Albuquerque Post Scholarship • 1797
Stantec Equity and Diversity Scholarship • 2251
STEM Scholarship • 2252
STEM Scholarship Program • 1127
Student Award Program of FSD • 2325
T. Eugene Young Montana's Promise Scholarship • 1822
TE Connectivity African Heritage Scholarship • 2262
Tech High School Alumni Association/W.O. Cheney Merit Scholarship • 1828
U.S. Western Digital STEM Scholarship • 346
Unitil Scholarship Fund • 1865
West Virginia Engineering, Science and Technology Scholarship • 1900

The Ultimate Scholarship Book 2026
Field of Study Index

William James and Dorothy Bading Lanquist Fund • 1911
Women in STEM Scholarship • 378
Women in STEM Scholarship/BHW Scholarship • 1172
YASME Foundation Scholarship • 739

PHYSICAL SCIENCES -- CHEMISTRY
AACT National Candy Technologists John Kitt Memorial Scholarship Program • 743
AISES Intel Scholarship • 2095
American Chemical Society Scholars Program • 2098
Choose Ohio First Scholarship • 1293
Hubertus W.V. Wellems Scholarship for Male Students • 2167
Intellia Therapeutics - UNCF Scholarship • 2169
Kathryn D. Sullivan Earth and Marine Science Fellowship • 1518
National Association for Surface Finishing Scholarships • 1021
National Foundation Scholarships • 662
Rubber Division Undergraduate Scholarship • 1101
Thermo Fisher Scientific Antibody Scholarship • 1141
Thomas E. Powers/Detroit Section Scholarship • 1143
Undergraduate Award for Excellence in Chemistry • 1156

PHYSICAL SCIENCES -- GEOLOGICAL AND EARTH SCIENCES / GEOSCIENCES
Graduate Student Research Grants • 919
Kathryn D. Sullivan Earth and Marine Science Fellowship • 1518
Leo Bourassa Scholarship • 1535
Marliave Fund • 990
NYWEA Major Environmental Career Scholarship • 1686
Society of Exploration Geophysicists (SEG) Scholarship • 1118
Tilford Field Studies Scholarship • 1146
Trent R. Dames and William W. Moore Fellowship • 1153
Undergraduate Student Research Grants: South-Central Section • 1160
Worthy Women's Professional Studies Scholarship • 2278

PHYSICAL SCIENCES -- PHYSICS, GENERAL
AISES Intel Scholarship • 2095
BMO Capital Markets Lime Connect Equity Through Education Scholarship • 2286
Choose Ohio First Scholarship • 1293
Herbert Levy Memorial Scholarship • 931
Hubertus W.V. Wellems Scholarship for Male Students • 2167
Kathryn D. Sullivan Earth and Marine Science Fellowship • 1518
NOAA Educational Partnership Program Undergraduate Scholarships • 2227
Northrop Grumman Scholarship • 1681
Peggy Dixon Two-Year Scholarship • 1064
Rubber Division Undergraduate Scholarship • 1101
Shuichi, Katsu and Itsuyo Suga Scholarship • 1789

Society of Exploration Geophysicists (SEG) Scholarship • 1118
Society of Vacuum Coaters Foundation Scholarship • 1121
SPS Future Teacher Scholarship • 711
SPS Leadership Scholarships • 1124
Thomas E. Powers/Detroit Section Scholarship • 1143

PHYSICAL THERAPY / THERAPIST
See: HEALTH PROFESSIONS AND RELATED CLINICAL SCIENCES

PHYSICIAN ASSISTANT
See: HEALTH PROFESSIONS AND RELATED CLINICAL SCIENCES

PHYSICS, GENERAL
See: PHYSICAL SCIENCES

PLANT SCIENCES
See: AGRICULTURE AND RELATED SCIENCES

PODIATRIC MEDICINE / PODIATRY
See: HEALTH PROFESSIONS AND RELATED CLINICAL SCIENCES

POLISH STUDIES
See: AREA, ETHNIC, CULTURAL AND GENDER STUDIES

POLITICAL SCIENCE AND GOVERNMENT, GENERAL
See: SOCIAL SCIENCES

POLYMER / PLASTICS ENGINEERING
See: ENGINEERING

PRECISION PRODUCTION
California - Hawaii Elks Association Vocational Grants • 550
DEWALT Trades Scholarship • 566
FFTA Scholarship Competition • 425
JFLF Awards Programs • 620
Johanna Drew Cluney Fund • 1497
John and Anne Clifton Scholarship • 1499
Lockheed Martin Vocational Scholarship Program • 641
Maple Flooring Manufacturers Association Scholarship • 645
MCEC Technical Scholarship • 1583
Medallion Fund • 1585
Texas Elks State Association Vocational Grant Program • 1841
TLMI Two/Four Year College and Vocational Degree Program Scholarship • 723

PRECISION PRODUCTION -- MACHINE TOOL TECHNOLOGY / MACHINIST
DEWALT Trades Scholarship • 566
Edward L. Simeth Scholarships • 1358
Maple Flooring Manufacturers Association Scholarship • 645
NADCA Indiana Chapter 25 Scholarship • 1634
Shell Associate Scholarship Program • 708

PSYCHOLOGY
APF Dr. Christine Blasey Ford Grant • 530
APF/COGDOP Graduate Student Scholarships • 531
APF/Division 54 Lizette Peterson-Homer Injury Prevention Grant • 532

David H. and Beverly A. Barlow Grant • 564
Future Counselors of America Scholarship • 587
Predoctoral Research Fellowships • 1077
Sharon Stephens Brehm Undergraduate Psychology Scholarships • 706
TOPSS Competition for High School Psychology Students • 725

PUBLIC ADMINISTRATION AND SOCIAL SERVICE PROFESSIONS
ABF Summer Undergraduate Research Fellowship Program • 511
AGBU US Graduate Scholarship • 2089
George H. Nofer Scholarship for Law and Public Policy • 2296
Graduate Scholarship Program • 595
Harry S. Truman Research Grant • 600
Henry A. Zuberano Scholarship • 1431
IBTTA Foundation Scholarship Program • 937
Ida M. Pope Memorial Scholarship • 2168
Julianne Malveaux Scholarship • 2178
National Academic Scholarships • 661
Presbyterian Church USA Student Opportunity Scholarships • 2031
Robert R. Robinson Memorial Scholarship • 1764
Workforce Shortage Student Assistance Grant Program • 1923

PUBLIC RELATIONS / IMAGE MANAGEMENT
See: COMMUNICATION AND JOURNALISM

REAL ESTATE
See: BUSINESS, MANAGEMENT AND MARKETING

RESTAURANT / FOOD SERVICES MANAGEMENT
See: BUSINESS, MANAGEMENT AND MARKETING

SALES, DISTRIBUTION AND MARKETING OPERATIONS, GENERAL
See: BUSINESS, MANAGEMENT AND MARKETING

SCANDINAVIAN LANGUAGES, LITERATURES AND LINGUISTICS
See: FOREIGN LANGUAGES, LITERATURES AND LINGUISTICS

SECONDARY EDUCATION AND TEACHING
See: EDUCATION

SECURITY AND PROTECTIVE SERVICES
Lockheed Martin Vocational Scholarship Program • 641
UMSA Foundation Scholarship Program • 1864
Women In Defense WID Scholar • 2276

SECURITY AND PROTECTIVE SERVICES -- CRIMINAL JUSTICE / POLICE SCIENCE
ACJA/Lambda Alpha Epsilon Scholarship • 19
Gene Carte Student Paper Competition • 152
Jonathan Jasper Wright Award • 194
PG&E Better Together STEM Scholarship Program • 1734
Ritchie-Jennings Memorial Scholarship • 699
Ruth D. Peterson Fellowship for Racial and Ethnic Diversity • 2245
Student Paper Competition • 316

Virginia Sheriffs' Institute Scholarship • 1885
William L. Hastie Award • 376

SECURITY AND PROTECTIVE SERVICES -- FIRE PROTECTION
Charles W. Riley Fire and Emergency Medical Services Scholarship Program • 1289
SmithGroup J.E.D.I. Scholarship • 1116

SOCIAL SCIENCES
ACOR-CAORC Fellowship • 515
ARIT Fellowships for Research in Turkey • 533
Byron Hanke Fellowship • 549
Community Scholarship Fund • 1310
Davidson Fellows Scholarships • 110
Gamma Theta Upsilon-Geographical Honor Society Scholarships • 589
Harry S. Truman Research Grant • 600
Herbert Hoover Research Travel Grant Award • 602
IACI/NUIG Visiting Fellowship in Irish Studies • 436
ISF Policy Scholarship Program • 1992
John Kelly Labor Studies Scholarship Fund • 1997
Joseph S. Rumbaugh Historical Oration Contest • 626
Julianne Malveaux Scholarship • 2178
Junior Fellowships • 627
Kenneth W. Payne Student Prize • 2179
Lou Hochberg Awards • 643
Minnesota Academic Excellence Scholarship • 1604
Moody Research Grant • 657
National Academic Scholarships • 661
Presbyterian Church USA Student Opportunity Scholarships • 2031
Women in United Methodist History Writing Award • 2075

SOCIAL SCIENCES -- CRIMINOLOGY
ACJA/Lambda Alpha Epsilon Scholarship • 19
Gene Carte Student Paper Competition • 152
Jonathan Jasper Wright Award • 194
Ruth D. Peterson Fellowship for Racial and Ethnic Diversity • 2245
Student Paper Competition • 316
William L. Hastie Award • 376

SOCIAL SCIENCES -- ECONOMICS, GENERAL
Byron Hanke Fellowship • 549
CRA All-Access Scholarship • 2128
National Foundation Scholarships • 662
Nebraska Actuaries Club Scholarship • 1640
Prize in International Insolvency Studies • 688
Risk Management Association Foundation Scholarship • 698
Women In Defense WID Scholar • 2276

SOCIAL SCIENCES -- GEOGRAPHY
AAGS - NSPS Scholarships • 744
Darrel Hess Community College Geography Scholarship • 563
NOAA Educational Partnership Program Undergraduate Scholarships • 2227
Oklahoma Society of Land Surveyors Scholarships • 1696
Pennsylvania Land Surveyors' Foundation Scholarship • 1726
USGIF Scholarship Program • 731

SOCIAL SCIENCES -- INTERNATIONAL RELATIONS AND AFFAIRS
AGBU US Graduate Scholarship • 2089
Don Riebhoff Memorial Scholarship • 568
Henry A. Zuberano Scholarship • 1431
Louisiana Memorial Scholarship • 1552
WIIT Charitable Trust Scholarship • 735
Women In Defense WID Scholar • 2276

SOCIAL SCIENCES -- POLITICAL SCIENCE AND GOVERNMENT, GENERAL
Ally Financial Public Policy Scholars • 525
Byron Hanke Fellowship • 549
Graduate Scholarship Program • 595
Henry A. Zuberano Scholarship • 1431
Ruth Segal Scholarship • 704
William G. Saletic Scholarship • 1910
Women In Defense WID Scholar • 2276

SOCIAL SCIENCES -- SOCIOLOGY
Byron Hanke Fellowship • 549
Minority Fellowship Program • 655

SOCIAL WORK
See: PUBLIC ADMINISTRATION AND SOCIAL SERVICE PROFESSIONS

SOCIOLOGY
See: SOCIAL SCIENCES

SPANISH AND IBERIAN STUDIES
See: AREA, ETHNIC, CULTURAL AND GENDER STUDIES

SPECIAL EDUCATION AND TEACHING, GENERAL
See: EDUCATION

SPORT AND FITNESS ADMINISTRATION / MANAGEMENT
See: PARKS, RECREATION, LEISURE AND FITNESS STUDIES

STATISTICS, GENERAL
See: MATHEMATICS AND STATISTICS

TECHNOLOGY EDUCATION / INDUSTRIAL ARTS
HSC Foundation Scholarship • 2165
Maple Flooring Manufacturers Association Scholarship • 645
National Foundation Scholarships • 662
Red Boucher Scholarship • 1751

THEOLOGY AND RELIGIOUS VOCATIONS
Allan Jerome Burry Scholarship • 1935
Mary E. Bivins Religious Scholarship • 2011
Religious Studies Scholarship • 2242
UCC Seminarian Scholarship • 2059

TOURISM AND TRAVEL SERVICES MANAGEMENT
See: BUSINESS, MANAGEMENT AND MARKETING

TRANSPORTATION AND MATERIALS MOVING
Academic Merit Scholarships • 512
Associated General Contractors of Minnesota Scholarships • 1230
E.J. Sierleja Memorial Fellowship • 871
Lockheed Martin Vocational Scholarship Program • 641
Maple Flooring Manufacturers Association Scholarship • 645
Material Handling Education Foundation • 647
National Foundation Scholarships • 662

TRANSPORTATION AND MATERIALS MOVING -- AIRLINE / COMMERCIAL / PROFESSIONAL PILOT AND FLIGHT CREW
Eugene S. Kropf Scholarship • 883
H.P. Bud Milligan Aviation Scholarship • 924
Joseph Frasca Excellence in Aviation Scholarship • 964

TRANSPORTATION AND MATERIALS MOVING -- AVIATION / AIRWAY MANAGEMENT AND OPERATIONS
Eugene S. Kropf Scholarship • 883
Gabriel A. Hartl Scholarship • 899
H.P. Bud Milligan Aviation Scholarship • 924
Joseph Frasca Excellence in Aviation Scholarship • 964
Kansas Agricultural Aviation Association Scholarship • 1508

TRUCK AND BUS DRIVER / COMMERCIAL VEHICLE OPERATION
See: TRANSPORTATION AND MATERIALS MOVING

TURF AND TURFGRASS MANAGEMENT
See: AGRICULTURE AND RELATED SCIENCES

URBAN STUDIES / AFFAIRS
See: SOCIAL SCIENCES

VETERINARY MEDICINE
See: HEALTH PROFESSIONS AND RELATED CLINICAL SCIENCES

VISUAL AND PERFORMING ARTS
Against The Grain Artistic Scholarship • 2088
AGL Over the Rainbow Scholarship • 391
AIGA Worldstudio Scholarships • 392
ASCAP Foundation Morton Gould Young Composer Awards • 397
AWAF Scholarships • 1233
Bill Gove Scholarship • 399
Cavett Robert Scholarship • 405
Community Scholarship Fund • 1310
Davidson Fellows Scholarships • 110
Dorian De Long Arts and Music Scholarship • 1335
Educational Theatre Association Board of Directors Scholarship • 419
Great Khalid Performing Arts Scholarship • 431
Iowa Scholarship for the Arts • 1475
Leo H. Grether Memorial Scholarship • 1536
Luce/ACLS Dissertation Fellowships in American Art • 457
Optimist International Oratorical Contest • 678
P. Buckley Moss Endowed Scholarship • 2317
Playwright Discovery Award • 475
State of the Arts Scholarship • 485
You Can t Label People, but You Can Label Products Essay and Label Design Scholarship • 505

The Ultimate Scholarship Book 2026
Field of Study Index

VISUAL AND PERFORMING ARTS -- ART HISTORY, CRITICISM AND CONSERVATION
- Helen C. Evans Scholarship • 929
- Huntington Fellowships • 606
- Huntington-British Academy Fellowships for Study in Great Britain • 607

VISUAL AND PERFORMING ARTS -- DANCE, GENERAL
- Career Transition for Dancers Undergraduate Studies Scholarship • 403
- Jaime Guttenberg Dance Scholarship • 445
- Ruth Abernathy Presidential Scholarship • 1103

VISUAL AND PERFORMING ARTS -- DESIGN AND VISUAL COMMUNICATIONS, GENERAL
- PAVE Student Design Competition • 683
- Student Design Competition • 489
- Vectorworks Design Scholarship • 499

VISUAL AND PERFORMING ARTS -- DRAMA AND DRAMATICS / THEATRE ARTS, GENERAL
- Dr. Kenny D. Hasija Scholarship • 417
- Educational Theatre Association Board of Directors Scholarship • 419
- Performing Arts Scholarship • 2236

VISUAL AND PERFORMING ARTS -- FASHION / APPAREL DESIGN
- Marian A. Smith Costume Award • 458
- Vectorworks Design Scholarship • 499

VISUAL AND PERFORMING ARTS -- FINE / STUDIO ARTS, GENERAL
- AIGA Worldstudio Scholarships • 392
- Cynthia and Alan Baran Fine Arts and Music Scholarship Fund • 1320
- Esther Kanagawa Memorial Art Scholarship • 1367
- Lois Livingston McMillen Memorial Fund • 1546
- Minnesota Academic Excellence Scholarship • 1604
- Predoctoral Fellowship Program • 1076
- Ritchie M. Gregory Fund • 1760
- Senior Fellowship Program • 484
- Visiting Senior Fellowship Program • 501

VISUAL AND PERFORMING ARTS -- GRAPHIC DESIGN
- AIGA Worldstudio Scholarships • 392
- American Institute of Graphic Arts (AIGA) Honolulu Chapter Scholarship Fund • 1209
- CardsDirect Future Designer Scholarship • 401
- LAGRANT Scholarship Program • 2182
- PenSPRA Scholarship • 1733
- Student Design Competition • 489
- TLMI Two/Four Year College and Vocational Degree Program Scholarship • 723
- Vectorworks Design Scholarship • 499

VISUAL AND PERFORMING ARTS -- INDUSTRIAL DESIGN
- IDSA Undergraduate and Graduate Scholarships • 438
- John L. Imhoff Scholarship • 957
- National Foundation Scholarships • 662
- PAVE Student Design Competition • 683
- Student Design Competition • 489
- Vectorworks Design Scholarship • 499

VISUAL AND PERFORMING ARTS -- INTERIOR DESIGN
- IFDA Leaders Commemorative Scholarship • 439
- IFDA Student Member Scholarship • 440
- Joel Polsky Academic Achievement Award • 446
- Legacy Scholarship for Undergraduates • 453
- Part-Time Student Scholarship • 472
- PAVE Student Design Competition • 683
- Predoctoral Fellowship Program • 1076
- Ruth Clark Furniture Design Scholarship • 480
- SmithGroup J.E.D.I. Scholarship • 1116
- Tricia LeVangie Green/Sustainable Design Scholarship • 496
- Vectorworks Design Scholarship • 499
- Vercille Voss IFDA Graduate Student Scholarship • 500
- VMSD Scholarship • 502

VISUAL AND PERFORMING ARTS -- MUSIC PERFORMANCE, GENERAL
- AMCA Music Scholarship • 394
- Cynthia and Alan Baran Fine Arts and Music Scholarship Fund • 1320
- Dr. Robert Hawkins Memorial Scholarship • 571
- Music Committee Scholarship • 1630
- NFMC Gretchen E. Van Roy Music Education Scholarship • 674

VISUAL AND PERFORMING ARTS -- MUSIC THEORY AND COMPOSITION
- Cynthia and Alan Baran Fine Arts and Music Scholarship Fund • 1320
- Dr. Robert Hawkins Memorial Scholarship • 571
- Leiber and Stoller Scholarship for Songwriters • 454
- Music Committee Scholarship • 1630
- NFMC Gretchen E. Van Roy Music Education Scholarship • 674

VISUAL AND PERFORMING ARTS -- MUSIC, GENERAL
- AMCA Music Scholarship • 394
- Cynthia and Alan Baran Fine Arts and Music Scholarship Fund • 1320
- Doris and Clarence Glick Classical Music Scholarship • 1336
- Dr. Robert Hawkins Memorial Scholarship • 571
- Music Committee Scholarship • 1630
- NFMC Gretchen E. Van Roy Music Education Scholarship • 674
- Presbyterian Church USA Student Opportunity Scholarships • 2031
- Women Band Directors International College Scholarships • 503

VISUAL AND PERFORMING ARTS -- MUSICOLOGY AND ETHNOMUSICOLOGY
- Music Committee Scholarship • 1630
- NFMC Gretchen E. Van Roy Music Education Scholarship • 674

VOCATIONAL REHABILITATION COUNSELING / COUNSELOR
See: HEALTH PROFESSIONS AND RELATED CLINICAL SCIENCES

VOICE AND OPERA
See: VISUAL AND PERFORMING ARTS

WELDING TECHNOLOGY / WELDER
See: PRECISION PRODUCTION

WILDLIFE AND WILDLANDS SCIENCE AND MANAGEMENT
See: NATURAL RESOURCES AND CONSERVATION

WOODWORKING, GENERAL
See: PRECISION PRODUCTION

ZOOLOGY / ANIMAL BIOLOGY
See: BIOLOGICAL AND BIOMEDICAL SCIENCES

CAREER INDEX

This index organizes the scholarships by common career fields. If you cannot find your specific career listed simply look at the scholarships under the closest matching career area.

In addition to this index be sure to use the Major Index since many scholarships are targeted to fields of study but do not have specific career requirements.

ACADEMIA
Henry Belin du Pont Dissertation Fellowship • 601
Herbert Hoover Research Travel Grant Award • 602
Humane Studies Fellowship: Flexible Support for PhD Students • 175
Humane Studies Fellowship: Publication Accelerator Grants • 605
Language Grants • 451
Robert E. Thunen Memorial Scholarships • 1097

RELATED CAREER (EDUCATION / TEACHING)
Antonio Cirino Memorial Scholarship • 1220
Burlington Northern Santa Fe (BNSF) Foundation Scholarship • 2111
Carroll C. Hall Memorial Scholarship • 1950
Collaborative Teachers Tuition Waiver • 1299
Community Scholarship Fund • 1310
Educator Support Scholarship • 1356
First-Year Teacher Scholarships • 1376
FTEE Scholarship: Undergraduate Major in Technology and Engineering Education • 585
Golden Apple Scholars of Illinois (Illinois Scholars Program) • 1402
Incentive Program for Aspiring Teachers • 1463
Inspired to Teach • 1468
International Technology Engineering Educators Association Scholarship - FTEE/Undergraduate • 614
Leadership for Diversity Scholarship • 1530
Learning and Leadership Grants • 635
Litherland/ITEEA Scholarship • 640
Maley/FTEE Teacher Professional Development Scholarship • 644
Martin Luther King, Jr. Memorial Scholarship • 2010
NACA Mid Atlantic Graduate Student Scholarship • 658
NACA Northern Plains Regional Student Leadership Scholarship • 1632
Office Supply Scholarship • 470
Ohio Classical Conference Scholarship for Prospective Latin Teachers • 1687
Pennsylvania Business Education Association Scholarship • 1724
Robert G. Porter Scholars Program for Members • 2037
Rudolph Dillman Memorial Scholarship • 2320
Shields-Gillespie Scholarship • 709
Student Success Grants • 715
Teacher of the Year Award • 721
Teacher Shortage Employment Incentive Program • 1827

Truman Scholar • 342
United Commercial Travelers of America (UCT) Scholarship Program • 726

ACCOUNTING / FINANCE / BANKING
Goldberg-Miller Public Finance Scholarship • 594
IMA Memorial Education Fund Scholarship • 610
John W. Rogers Memorial Scholarship • 1504
Language Grants • 451
National Academic Scholarships • 661
Stuart Cameron and Margaret McLeod Memorial Scholarship • 714
Texas Fifth-Year Accounting Student Scholarship Program • 1842

ADVERTISING / PR
Language Grants • 451
Media Fellows Program • 649
PRSA-Hawai'i/Roy Leffingwell Public Relations Scholarship • 1738

RELATED CAREER (BUSINESS AND MANAGEMENT)
Betsy Plank/PRSSA Scholarship • 540
Burlington Northern Santa Fe (BNSF) Foundation Scholarship • 2111
Executive Women International Scholarship Program • 578
Joe Perdue Scholarship • 622
Lawrence G. Foster Award for Excellence in Public Relations • 634
Nebraska Academy of Sciences High School Scholarships • 1639
Steven J. Finkel Service Excellence Scholarship • 713

RELATED CAREER (MARKETING)
Creative Sole Scholarship • 2129
Harry A. Applegate Scholarship • 599

RELATED CAREER (MEDIA / RADIO / TELEVISION / INTERNET)
BEA National Scholarships in Broadcasting • 537
Carole Simpson Scholarship • 554
Congressional Black Caucus Spouses Visual Arts Scholarship • 2127
Ed Bradley Scholarship • 574
Idaho State Broadcasters Association Scholarships • 1455
John Bayliss Radio Scholarship • 623
Lou and Carole Prato Sports Reporting Scholarship • 642
Massachusetts Student Broadcaster Scholarship • 1578
Tony Coelho Media Scholarship • 2327
Upper Midwest Chapter Scholarships • 1867
Wisconsin Broadcasters Association Foundation Student Scholarship Program • 1916
Youth Scholarship • 740

AGRICULTURE / FARMING
Ag Day Essay Contest • 25
ASEV Scholarships • 802
ASF Olin Fellowships • 803
Carville M. Akehurst Memorial Scholarship • 836
Clair A. Hill Scholarship • 1296
John W. Rogers Memorial Scholarship • 1504
Montana CattleWomen Scholarship • 1624
NDPRB Undergraduate Scholarship Program • 1037

New York State Association of Agricultural Fairs/New York State Showpeople's Association Scholarships • 1654
NPFDA Scholarships • 1050
Ranelius Scholarship Program • 1743
Richard Jensen Scholarship • 1091
Schlutz Family Beef Breeding Scholarship • 1778

RELATED CAREER (FORESTRY / FISHING / WILDLIFE)
Arkansas Game and Fish Commission Conservation Scholarship • 1225
Gloria Barron Wilderness Society Scholarship • 914
National Garden Clubs Scholarship • 1026
Nebraska Academy of Sciences High School Scholarships • 1639

RELATED CAREER (ENVIRONMENTAL SCIENCE)
Barry M. Goldwater Scholarship and Excellence in Education Program • 824
Carroll C. Hall Memorial Scholarship • 1950
Morris K. Udall Scholarship • 2211

ARCHEOLOGISTS
Harrell Family Fellowship • 598
Jennifer C. Groot Fellowship • 619

RELATED CAREER (SCIENTIST)
ANS Graduate Scholarship • 791
ANS Undergraduate Scholarship • 793
ASABE Foundation Engineering Scholarship • 799
ASF Olin Fellowships • 803
Barry M. Goldwater Scholarship and Excellence in Education Program • 824
Battery Division Student Research Award • 825
Burlington Northern Santa Fe (BNSF) Foundation Scholarship • 2111
Carroll C. Hall Memorial Scholarship • 1950
Fellowship Award • 889
Gaige Fund Award • 900
Industrial Electrochemistry and Electrochemical Engineering Student Achievement Award • 939
John and Muriel Landis Scholarship • 954
John J. McKetta Scholarship • 956
Language Grants • 451
National Space Club Keynote Scholar • 1029
Nebraska Academy of Sciences High School Scholarships • 1639
Raney Fund Award • 1084
The Industrial Electrochemistry and Electrochemical Engineering Division H. H. Dow Memorial Student Achievement Award • 1140

RELATED CAREER (ACADEMIA)
Henry Belin du Pont Dissertation Fellowship • 601
Herbert Hoover Research Travel Grant Award • 602
Humane Studies Fellowship: Flexible Support for PhD Students • 175
Humane Studies Fellowship: Publication Accelerator Grants • 605
Robert E. Thunen Memorial Scholarships • 1097

RELATED CAREER (GEOLOGISTS)
C. Bertrand and Marian Othmer Schultz Collegiate Scholarship • 1255

The Ultimate Scholarship Book 2026
Career Index

Gloria Barron Wilderness Society Scholarship • 914

ARCHITECTURE / DESIGN
Congressional Black Caucus Spouses Visual Arts Scholarship • 2127
Creative Sole Scholarship • 2129
National Garden Clubs Scholarship • 1026
Robert E. Thunen Memorial Scholarships • 1097
Sir John Soane's Museum Foundation Traveling Grant • 1113

RELATED CAREER (LANDSCAPE ARCHITECTS)
Carville M. Akehurst Memorial Scholarship • 836

ARTIST
Creative Sole Scholarship • 2129
John F. and Anna Lee Stacey Scholarship Fund for Art Education • 447
Office Supply Scholarship • 470
Sir John Soane's Museum Foundation Traveling Grant • 1113
Stanfield and D'Orlando Art Scholarship • 2048

RELATED CAREER (PHOTOGRAPHER)
Bob East Scholarship • 543
College Photographer of the Year • 561
Congressional Black Caucus Spouses Visual Arts Scholarship • 2127
X Society Awards Scholarship • 2280

RELATED CAREER (PERFORMING ARTS)
CBC Spouses Performing Arts Scholarship • 2117

RELATED CAREER (ENTERTAINMENT INDUSTRY)
Career Center • 402
Steven J. Finkel Service Excellence Scholarship • 713
Tony Coelho Media Scholarship • 2327

RELATED CAREER (FASHION / APPAREL)
Aritzia Scholarship • 2102
Fashion Scholarship Fund Scholarships • 421
James J. Burns and C.A. Haynes Textile Scholarship • 1489

RELATED CAREER (MUSICIANS / MUSIC)
ASCAP Foundation Morton Gould Young Composer Awards • 397
John Lennon Scholarship Competition • 448
National Vocal Competition for Young Opera Singers • 465
NFMC Hinda Honigman Award for the Blind • 2314
Sara Tucker Study Grant • 482

ASTRONOMERS
Barry M. Goldwater Scholarship and Excellence in Education Program • 824
GBT Student Observing Support (SOS) Program • 904
Graduate Summer Student Research Assistantship • 921
Undergraduate Summer Student Research Assistantship • 1161

RELATED CAREER (AVIATION / AEROSPACE / SPACE)
AIAA Foundation Undergraduate Scholarship Program • 767
Aviation Distributors and Manufacturers Association Scholarship Program • 821
Aviation Insurance Association Education Foundation Scholarship • 822
Daedalian Foundation Scholarship Program • 108
Dan L. Meisinger Sr. Memorial Learn to Fly Scholarship • 851
David Arver Memorial Scholarship • 854
Dutch and Ginger Arver Scholarship • 868
Full-Time Employee Student Scholarship • 897
Garmin Scholarship • 902
John R. Lillard VAOC Scholarship • 1502
Johnny Davis Memorial Scholarship • 963
Language Grants • 451
Lawrence C. Fortier Memorial Scholarship • 974
Lee Tarbox Memorial Scholarship • 977
Mid-Continent Instruments and Avionics Scholarship • 1006
National Aviation Explorer Scholarships • 1022
Pioneers of Flight • 1071
Tuskegee Airmen Scholarship Foundation Scholarships • 1154
Tweet Coleman Aviation Scholarship • 1861
UAA Janice K. Barden Aviation Scholarship • 1155

RELATED CAREER (PHYSICISTS)
ANS Graduate Scholarship • 791
ANS Undergraduate Scholarship • 793
C. Bertrand and Marian Othmer Schultz Collegiate Scholarship • 1255
Carroll C. Hall Memorial Scholarship • 1950
John and Muriel Landis Scholarship • 954

RELATED CAREER (SCIENTIST)
ASABE Foundation Engineering Scholarship • 799
ASF Olin Fellowships • 803
Battery Division Student Research Award • 825
Burlington Northern Santa Fe (BNSF) Foundation Scholarship • 2111
Fellowship Award • 889
Gaige Fund Award • 900
Industrial Electrochemistry and Electrochemical Engineering Student Achievement Award • 939
John J. McKetta Scholarship • 956
National Space Club Keynote Scholar • 1029
Nebraska Academy of Sciences High School Scholarships • 1639
Raney Fund Award • 1084
The Industrial Electrochemistry and Electrochemical Engineering Division H. H. Dow Memorial Student Achievement Award • 1140

ATHLETES AND SPORTS
Challenge Scholarship • 79
Ethnic Minority and Women's Enhancement Scholarship • 140
GNC Nutritional Research Grant • 160
Graduate Research Grant - Master and Doctoral • 164
High School Scholarship • 173
Minority Scholarship • 2205
NATA Scholarship • 233
Women's Scholarship • 1173

RELATED CAREER (PHYSICAL THERAPISTS)
Allied Healthcare Scholarship Program • 1202
Health Careers Scholarship • 928

RELATED CAREER (MARKETING)
Betsy Plank/PRSSA Scholarship • 540
Creative Sole Scholarship • 2129
Harry A. Applegate Scholarship • 599
Language Grants • 451
Lawrence G. Foster Award for Excellence in Public Relations • 634
Media Fellows Program • 649

RELATED CAREER (ENTERTAINMENT INDUSTRY)
Career Center • 402
Steven J. Finkel Service Excellence Scholarship • 713
Tony Coelho Media Scholarship • 2327

AUTOMOTIVE INDUSTRY
Automotive Hall of Fame Scholarships • 818
NIADA Scholarship • 2024
Specialty Equipment Market Association (SEMA) Memorial Scholarship • 710
University of the Aftermarket Foundation Scholarship • 730

RELATED CAREER (TRANSPORTATION AND TRUCKING)
Allied Van Lines Scholarship • 524
Helene M. Overly Memorial Graduate Scholarship • 2156
Molitoris Leadership Scholarship for Undergraduates • 2210
North American Van Lines Logistics Scholarship • 675
Ohio Section Scholarships • 1688
RV Learning Center Scholarship Program • 1104
Sharon D. Banks Memorial Undergraduate Scholarship • 2247
WTS Minnesota Chapter Scholarships • 1925

RELATED CAREER (MECHANICS)
Language Grants • 451

RELATED CAREER (METAL WORK / MACHINIST / WELDING)
AFS Twin City Memorial Scholarship • 1187
AFS Wisconsin Past President Scholarship • 1188

AVIATION / AEROSPACE / SPACE
AIAA Foundation Undergraduate Scholarship Program • 767
Aviation Distributors and Manufacturers Association Scholarship Program • 821
Aviation Insurance Association Education Foundation Scholarship • 822
Daedalian Foundation Scholarship Program • 108
Dan L. Meisinger Sr. Memorial Learn to Fly Scholarship • 851
David Arver Memorial Scholarship • 854
Dutch and Ginger Arver Scholarship • 868
Full-Time Employee Student Scholarship • 897
Garmin Scholarship • 902
John R. Lillard VAOC Scholarship • 1502
Johnny Davis Memorial Scholarship • 963
Language Grants • 451
Lawrence C. Fortier Memorial Scholarship • 974
Lee Tarbox Memorial Scholarship • 977
Mid-Continent Instruments and Avionics Scholarship • 1006
National Aviation Explorer Scholarships • 1022
Pioneers of Flight • 1071

Tuskegee Airmen Scholarship Foundation Scholarships • 1154
Tweet Coleman Aviation Scholarship • 1861
UAA Janice K. Barden Aviation Scholarship • 1155

Related Career (Defense / Military)
CIA Undergraduate Scholarship Program • 85

Related Career (Engineering)
ANS Graduate Scholarship • 791
ANS Undergraduate Scholarship • 793
ASABE Foundation Engineering Scholarship • 799
ASHRAE Engineering Technology Scholarships • 805
Barry M. Goldwater Scholarship and Excellence in Education Program • 824
Battery Division Student Research Award • 825
Burlington Northern Santa Fe (BNSF) Foundation Scholarship • 2111
Clair A. Hill Scholarship • 1296
DEED Funding Opportunities • 855
Desk and Derrick Educational Trust • 858
Dorothy M. and Earl S. Hoffman Award • 863
E. Noel Luddy Scholarship • 870
F.W. Beich Beichley Scholarship • 885
FTEE Scholarship: Undergraduate Major in Technology and Engineering Education • 585
Graduate Research Award (GRA) • 916
Industrial Electrochemistry and Electrochemical Engineering Student Achievement Award • 939
International Technology Engineering Educators Association Scholarship - FTEE/Undergraduate • 614
John and Muriel Landis Scholarship • 954
John J. McKetta Scholarship • 956
Kenneth Andrew Roe Scholarship • 969
Litherland/ITEEA Scholarship • 640
Maley/FTEE Teacher Professional Development Scholarship • 644
National Space Club Keynote Scholar • 1029
Nellie Yeoh Whetten Award • 1041
Ohio Section Scholarships • 1688
P.O. Pistilli Undergraduate Scholarship for Advancement in Computer Science and Electrical Engineering • 2233
Robert E. Thunen Memorial Scholarships • 1097
Russell and Sigurd Varian Award • 1102
SEE Education Foundation Scholarships • 1110
The Industrial Electrochemistry and Electrochemical Engineering Division H. H. Dow Memorial Student Achievement Award • 1140
Thomas M. Stetson Scholarship • 1144

Biologists
ASABE Foundation Engineering Scholarship • 799
ASF Olin Fellowships • 803
Barry M. Goldwater Scholarship and Excellence in Education Program • 824
C. Bertrand and Marian Othmer Schultz Collegiate Scholarship • 1255
Carroll C. Hall Memorial Scholarship • 1950
Gaige Fund Award • 900
National Garden Clubs Scholarship • 1026
Nebraska Academy of Sciences High School Scholarships • 1639
Paul A. Stewart Grants • 1061
Raney Fund Award • 1084
Student Research Scholarships • 1134

Related Career (Forestry / Fishing / Wildlife)
Arkansas Game and Fish Commission Conservation Scholarship • 1225
Clair A. Hill Scholarship • 1296
Gloria Barron Wilderness Society Scholarship • 914

Related Career (Environmental Science)
Morris K. Udall Scholarship • 2211

Related Career (Biomedical Sciences / Biotechnology)
NIH Undergraduate Scholarship Program • 1047

Related Career (Veterinarian)
Fellowship Award • 889

Related Career (Scientist)
ANS Graduate Scholarship • 791
ANS Undergraduate Scholarship • 793
Battery Division Student Research Award • 825
Burlington Northern Santa Fe (BNSF) Foundation Scholarship • 2111
Industrial Electrochemistry and Electrochemical Engineering Student Achievement Award • 939
John and Muriel Landis Scholarship • 954
John J. McKetta Scholarship • 956
Language Grants • 451
National Space Club Keynote Scholar • 1029
The Industrial Electrochemistry and Electrochemical Engineering Division H. H. Dow Memorial Student Achievement Award • 1140

Biomedical Sciences / Biotechnology
Barry M. Goldwater Scholarship and Excellence in Education Program • 824
Carroll C. Hall Memorial Scholarship • 1950
NIH Undergraduate Scholarship Program • 1047

Related Career (Biologists)
ASABE Foundation Engineering Scholarship • 799
ASF Olin Fellowships • 803
C. Bertrand and Marian Othmer Schultz Collegiate Scholarship • 1255
Gaige Fund Award • 900
National Garden Clubs Scholarship • 1026
Nebraska Academy of Sciences High School Scholarships • 1639
Paul A. Stewart Grants • 1061
Raney Fund Award • 1084
Student Research Scholarships • 1134

Related Career (Doctor (Medicine))
Advanced Practice Healthcare Scholarship Program • 1186
Alice W. Rooke Scholarship • 775
Allied Healthcare Scholarship Program • 1202
Associate Degree Nursing Scholarship Program • 1228
Bachelor of Science Nursing Scholarship Program • 1234
Burlington Northern Santa Fe (BNSF) Foundation Scholarship • 2111
Dr. Ralph E. White Graduating Senior Scholarship • 1343
Fellowship Award • 889
Foundation for Surgical Technology Medical Mission Scholarship • 891
Health Careers Scholarship • 928
Irene and Daisy MacGregor Memorial Scholarship • 946
Language Grants • 451
Loan Assistance Repayment Program Primary Care Services • 1545
Medical Student Training in Aging Research (MSTAR) Program • 997
Minority Fellowship Program • 1008
Morris K. Udall Scholarship • 2211
NAHN Scholarship • 2213
TOPSS Competition for High School Psychology Students • 725
Washington Health Corps • 1892

Business and Management
Betsy Plank/PRSSA Scholarship • 540
Burlington Northern Santa Fe (BNSF) Foundation Scholarship • 2111
Executive Women International Scholarship Program • 578
Joe Perdue Scholarship • 622
Language Grants • 451
Lawrence G. Foster Award for Excellence in Public Relations • 634
Media Fellows Program • 649
Nebraska Academy of Sciences High School Scholarships • 1639
Steven J. Finkel Service Excellence Scholarship • 713

Related Career (Marketing)
Creative Sole Scholarship • 2129
Harry A. Applegate Scholarship • 599

Related Career (Accounting / Finance / Banking)
Goldberg-Miller Public Finance Scholarship • 594
IMA Memorial Education Fund Scholarship • 610
John W. Rogers Memorial Scholarship • 1504
National Academic Scholarships • 661
Stuart Cameron and Margaret McLeod Memorial Scholarship • 714
Texas Fifth-Year Accounting Student Scholarship Program • 1842

Related Career (Advertising / PR)
PRSA-Hawai'i/Roy Leffingwell Public Relations Scholarship • 1738

Related Career (Entrepreneur)
Office Supply Scholarship • 470

Chemists
Barry M. Goldwater Scholarship and Excellence in Education Program • 824
C. Bertrand and Marian Othmer Schultz Collegiate Scholarship • 1255
Carroll C. Hall Memorial Scholarship • 1950
John J. McKetta Scholarship • 956

Related Career (Scientist)
ANS Graduate Scholarship • 791
ANS Undergraduate Scholarship • 793

The Ultimate Scholarship Book 2026
Career Index

ASABE Foundation Engineering Scholarship • 799
ASF Olin Fellowships • 803
Battery Division Student Research Award • 825
Burlington Northern Santa Fe (BNSF) Foundation Scholarship • 2111
Fellowship Award • 889
Gaige Fund Award • 900
Industrial Electrochemistry and Electrochemical Engineering Student Achievement Award • 939
John and Muriel Landis Scholarship • 954
Language Grants • 451
National Space Club Keynote Scholar • 1029
Nebraska Academy of Sciences High School Scholarships • 1639
Raney Fund Award • 1084
The Industrial Electrochemistry and Electrochemical Engineering Division H. H. Dow Memorial Student Achievement Award • 1140

Related Career (Biomedical Sciences / Biotechnology)
NIH Undergraduate Scholarship Program • 1047

Computer Hardware Engineers
Language Grants • 451
Soliant's Sunrise Scholarship • 305

Related Career (Computers / Information Technology)
Achievers in Technology Program • 2082
National Academic Scholarships • 661
National Space Club Keynote Scholar • 1029
P.O. Pistilli Undergraduate Scholarship for Advancement in Computer Science and Electrical Engineering • 2233
VIP Women in Technology Scholarship • 1166
WomenIn Scholarship • 2277

Related Career (Engineering)
AIAA Foundation Undergraduate Scholarship Program • 767
ANS Graduate Scholarship • 791
ANS Undergraduate Scholarship • 793
ASABE Foundation Engineering Scholarship • 799
ASHRAE Engineering Technology Scholarships • 805
Barry M. Goldwater Scholarship and Excellence in Education Program • 824
Battery Division Student Research Award • 825
Burlington Northern Santa Fe (BNSF) Foundation Scholarship • 2111
Clair A. Hill Scholarship • 1296
DEED Funding Opportunities • 855
Desk and Derrick Educational Trust • 858
Dorothy M. and Earl S. Hoffman Award • 863
E. Noel Luddy Scholarship • 870
F.W. Beich Beichley Scholarship • 885
FTEE Scholarship: Undergraduate Major in Technology and Engineering Education • 585
Graduate Research Award (GRA) • 916
Industrial Electrochemistry and Electrochemical Engineering Student Achievement Award • 939
International Technology Engineering Educators Association Scholarship - FTEE/Undergraduate • 614
John and Muriel Landis Scholarship • 954
John J. McKetta Scholarship • 956
Kenneth Andrew Roe Scholarship • 969
Litherland/ITEEA Scholarship • 640
Maley/FTEE Teacher Professional Development Scholarship • 644
Nellie Yeoh Whetten Award • 1041
Ohio Section Scholarships • 1688
Robert E. Thunen Memorial Scholarships • 1097
Russell and Sigurd Varian Award • 1102
SEE Education Foundation Scholarships • 1110
The Industrial Electrochemistry and Electrochemical Engineering Division H. H. Dow Memorial Student Achievement Award • 1140
Thomas M. Stetson Scholarship • 1144

Computer Programmers
Achievers in Technology Program • 2082
Language Grants • 451
Soliant's Sunrise Scholarship • 305
WomenIn Scholarship • 2277

Related Career (Computers / Information Technology)
National Academic Scholarships • 661
National Space Club Keynote Scholar • 1029
P.O. Pistilli Undergraduate Scholarship for Advancement in Computer Science and Electrical Engineering • 2233
VIP Women in Technology Scholarship • 1166

Computers / Information Technology
Achievers in Technology Program • 2082
Language Grants • 451
National Academic Scholarships • 661
National Space Club Keynote Scholar • 1029
P.O. Pistilli Undergraduate Scholarship for Advancement in Computer Science and Electrical Engineering • 2233
Soliant's Sunrise Scholarship • 305
VIP Women in Technology Scholarship • 1166
WomenIn Scholarship • 2277

Construction / Civil Engineering
AGC Graduate Scholarships • 763
AGC Undergraduate Scholarships • 764
ASTM International Katherine and Bryant Mather Scholarship • 815
Geneva Rock Scholarship • 908
Independence Excavating, A DiGeronimo Company Scholarship • 1464
NAWIC Founders' Undergraduate Scholarship • 1032
NPCA Educational Foundation Scholarships • 1049
Ohio Section Scholarships • 1688
Shook Construction Harry F. Gaeke Memorial Scholarship • 1788

Related Career (Metal Work / Machinist / Welding)
AFS Twin City Memorial Scholarship • 1187
AFS Wisconsin Past President Scholarship • 1188

Cosmetologist
Beauty Changes Lives Foundation Scholarships • 538
Great Scholarship Program • 596
Joe Francis Haircare Scholarship Program • 621

Related Career (Personal Service Industry)
Challenge Scholarship • 79
GNC Nutritional Research Grant • 160
Graduate Research Grant - Master and Doctoral • 164
High School Scholarship • 173
Minority Scholarship • 2205

Culinary Arts / Food Service
California Restaurant Association Educational Foundation General Scholarship • 1269
Feeding Tomorrow General Education Scholarships/Freshman Scholarships • 888
IFEC Scholarships Award • 608

Related Career (Hospitality / Travel)
American Express Scholarship Competition • 529
Ecolab Scholarship Competition • 573
HospitalityMaine Scholarship • 1448
Incoming Freshman Scholarship • 612
New York State Association of Agricultural Fairs/New York State Showpeople's Association Scholarships • 1654
Steven J. Finkel Service Excellence Scholarship • 713

Related Career (Personal Service Industry)
Challenge Scholarship • 79
GNC Nutritional Research Grant • 160
Graduate Research Grant - Master and Doctoral • 164
High School Scholarship • 173
Minority Scholarship • 2205

Defense / Military
CIA Undergraduate Scholarship Program • 85

Dentists
Fellowship Award • 889
Health Careers Scholarship • 928
Morris K. Udall Scholarship • 2211
Washington Health Corps • 1892

Doctor (Medicine)
Advanced Practice Healthcare Scholarship Program • 1186
Alice W. Rooke Scholarship • 775
Allied Healthcare Scholarship Program • 1202
Associate Degree Nursing Scholarship Program • 1228
Bachelor of Science Nursing Scholarship Program • 1234
Burlington Northern Santa Fe (BNSF) Foundation Scholarship • 2111
Dr. Ralph E. White Graduating Senior Scholarship • 1343
Fellowship Award • 889
Foundation for Surgical Technology Medical Mission Scholarship • 891
Health Careers Scholarship • 928
Irene and Daisy MacGregor Memorial Scholarship • 946
Language Grants • 451
Loan Assistance Repayment Program Primary Care Services • 1545
Medical Student Training in Aging Research (MSTAR) Program • 997

Minority Fellowship Program • 1008
Morris K. Udall Scholarship • 2211
NAHN Scholarship • 2213
NIH Undergraduate Scholarship Program • 1047
TOPSS Competition for High School Psychology Students • 725
Washington Health Corps • 1892

Related Career (Nursing / PA (Medicine))
Academic Education Award • 750
AORN Foundation Scholarship Program • 795
BSN Scholarship • 832
Dorothy Budnek Memorial Scholarship • 862
Eight and Forty Lung and Respiratory Nursing Scholarship Fund • 873
ENA Foundation Undergraduate Scholarship • 879
Karen O'Neil Memorial Scholarship • 967
National Student Nurses' Association Scholarship • 1030
Senator Patricia K. McGee Nursing Faculty Scholarship • 1783

Related Career (Medical Researcher / Tech)
AUA Foundation Research Scholars Program • 817
Elekta Radiation Therapy Scholarship • 874

Related Career (Biologists)
ASABE Foundation Engineering Scholarship • 799
ASF Olin Fellowships • 803
Barry M. Goldwater Scholarship and Excellence in Education Program • 824
C. Bertrand and Marian Othmer Schultz Collegiate Scholarship • 1255
Carroll C. Hall Memorial Scholarship • 1950
Gaige Fund Award • 900
National Garden Clubs Scholarship • 1026
Nebraska Academy of Sciences High School Scholarships • 1639
Paul A. Stewart Grants • 1061
Raney Fund Award • 1084
Student Research Scholarships • 1134

Education / Teaching
Antonio Cirino Memorial Scholarship • 1220
Burlington Northern Santa Fe (BNSF) Foundation Scholarship • 2111
Carroll C. Hall Memorial Scholarship • 1950
Collaborative Teachers Tuition Waiver • 1299
Community Scholarship Fund • 1310
Educator Support Scholarship • 1356
First-Year Teacher Scholarships • 1376
FTEE Scholarship: Undergraduate Major in Technology and Engineering Education • 585
Golden Apple Scholars of Illinois (Illinois Scholars Program) • 1402
Incentive Program for Aspiring Teachers • 1463
Inspired to Teach • 1468
International Technology Engineering Educators Association Scholarship - FTEE/Undergraduate • 614
Language Grants • 451
Leadership for Diversity Scholarship • 1530
Learning and Leadership Grants • 635
Litherland/ITEEA Scholarship • 640
Maley/FTEE Teacher Professional Development Scholarship • 644
Martin Luther King, Jr. Memorial Scholarship • 2010
NACA Mid Atlantic Graduate Student Scholarship • 658
NACA Northern Plains Regional Student Leadership Scholarship • 1632
Office Supply Scholarship • 470
Ohio Classical Conference Scholarship for Prospective Latin Teachers • 1687
Pennsylvania Business Education Association Scholarship • 1724
Robert E. Thunen Memorial Scholarships • 1097
Robert G. Porter Scholars Program for Members • 2037
Rudolph Dillman Memorial Scholarship • 2320
Shields-Gillespie Scholarship • 709
Student Success Grants • 715
Teacher of the Year Award • 721
Teacher Shortage Employment Incentive Program • 1827
Truman Scholar • 342
United Commercial Travelers of America (UCT) Scholarship Program • 726

Related Career (Academia)
Henry Belin du Pont Dissertation Fellowship • 601
Herbert Hoover Research Travel Grant Award • 602
Humane Studies Fellowship: Flexible Support for PhD Students • 175
Humane Studies Fellowship: Publication Accelerator Grants • 605

Related Career (Social Services)
Allied Healthcare Scholarship Program • 1202
Aritzia Scholarship • 2102

Electrician
Complete Water Solutions Scholarship • 843

Engineering
AIAA Foundation Undergraduate Scholarship Program • 767
ANS Graduate Scholarship • 791
ANS Undergraduate Scholarship • 793
ASABE Foundation Engineering Scholarship • 799
ASHRAE Engineering Technology Scholarships • 805
Barry M. Goldwater Scholarship and Excellence in Education Program • 824
Battery Division Student Research Award • 825
Burlington Northern Santa Fe (BNSF) Foundation Scholarship • 2111
Clair A. Hill Scholarship • 1296
DEED Funding Opportunities • 855
Desk and Derrick Educational Trust • 858
Dorothy M. and Earl S. Hoffman Award • 863
E. Noel Luddy Scholarship • 870
F.W. Beich Beichley Scholarship • 885
FTEE Scholarship: Undergraduate Major in Technology and Engineering Education • 585
Graduate Research Award (GRA) • 916
Industrial Electrochemistry and Electrochemical Engineering Student Achievement Award • 939
International Technology Engineering Educators Association Scholarship - FTEE/Undergraduate • 614
John and Muriel Landis Scholarship • 954
John J. McKetta Scholarship • 956
Kenneth Andrew Roe Scholarship • 969
Language Grants • 451
Litherland/ITEEA Scholarship • 640
Maley/FTEE Teacher Professional Development Scholarship • 644
National Space Club Keynote Scholar • 1029
Nellie Yeoh Whetten Award • 1041
Ohio Section Scholarships • 1688
P.O. Pistilli Undergraduate Scholarship for Advancement in Computer Science and Electrical Engineering • 2233
Robert E. Thunen Memorial Scholarships • 1097
Russell and Sigurd Varian Award • 1102
SEE Education Foundation Scholarships • 1110
The Industrial Electrochemistry and Electrochemical Engineering Division H. H. Dow Memorial Student Achievement Award • 1140
Thomas M. Stetson Scholarship • 1144

Related Career (Computers / Information Technology)
Achievers in Technology Program • 2082
National Academic Scholarships • 661
Soliant's Sunrise Scholarship • 305
VIP Women in Technology Scholarship • 1166
WomenIn Scholarship • 2277

Entertainment Industry
Career Center • 402
Steven J. Finkel Service Excellence Scholarship • 713
Tony Coelho Media Scholarship • 2327

Related Career (Performing Arts)
CBC Spouses Performing Arts Scholarship • 2117

Related Career (Media / Radio / Television / Internet)
BEA National Scholarships in Broadcasting • 537
Carole Simpson Scholarship • 554
Congressional Black Caucus Spouses Visual Arts Scholarship • 2127
Ed Bradley Scholarship • 574
Idaho State Broadcasters Association Scholarships • 1455
John Bayliss Radio Scholarship • 623
Lou and Carole Prato Sports Reporting Scholarship • 642
Massachusetts Student Broadcaster Scholarship • 1578
Upper Midwest Chapter Scholarships • 1867
Wisconsin Broadcasters Association Foundation Student Scholarship Program • 1916
Youth Scholarship • 740

Entrepreneur
Harry A. Applegate Scholarship • 599
Office Supply Scholarship • 470

Related Career (Business and Management)
Betsy Plank/PRSSA Scholarship • 540
Burlington Northern Santa Fe (BNSF) Foundation Scholarship • 2111

The Ultimate Scholarship Book 2026
Career Index

Executive Women International Scholarship Program • 578
Joe Perdue Scholarship • 622
Language Grants • 451
Lawrence G. Foster Award for Excellence in Public Relations • 634
Media Fellows Program • 649
Nebraska Academy of Sciences High School Scholarships • 1639
Steven J. Finkel Service Excellence Scholarship • 713

ENVIRONMENTAL SCIENCE
Barry M. Goldwater Scholarship and Excellence in Education Program • 824
Carroll C. Hall Memorial Scholarship • 1950
Clair A. Hill Scholarship • 1296
Gloria Barron Wilderness Society Scholarship • 914
Morris K. Udall Scholarship • 2211
Nebraska Academy of Sciences High School Scholarships • 1639

RELATED CAREER (BIOLOGISTS)
ASABE Foundation Engineering Scholarship • 799
ASF Olin Fellowships • 803
C. Bertrand and Marian Othmer Schultz Collegiate Scholarship • 1255
Gaige Fund Award • 900
National Garden Clubs Scholarship • 1026
Paul A. Stewart Grants • 1061
Raney Fund Award • 1084
Student Research Scholarships • 1134

RELATED CAREER (FORESTRY / FISHING / WILDLIFE)
Arkansas Game and Fish Commission Conservation Scholarship • 1225

FASHION / APPAREL
Aritzia Scholarship • 2102
Congressional Black Caucus Spouses Visual Arts Scholarship • 2127
Fashion Scholarship Fund Scholarships • 421
James J. Burns and C.A. Haynes Textile Scholarship • 1489
X Society Awards Scholarship • 2280

RELATED CAREER (GRAPHIC DESIGNERS)
Print and Graphics Scholarship • 478
Stanfield and D'Orlando Art Scholarship • 2048

FORESTRY / FISHING / WILDLIFE
Arkansas Game and Fish Commission Conservation Scholarship • 1225
ASF Olin Fellowships • 803
Clair A. Hill Scholarship • 1296
Gloria Barron Wilderness Society Scholarship • 914
National Garden Clubs Scholarship • 1026
Nebraska Academy of Sciences High School Scholarships • 1639

RELATED CAREER (ENVIRONMENTAL SCIENCE)
Barry M. Goldwater Scholarship and Excellence in Education Program • 824
Carroll C. Hall Memorial Scholarship • 1950
Morris K. Udall Scholarship • 2211

RELATED CAREER (VETERINARIAN)
Fellowship Award • 889

GEOLOGISTS
C. Bertrand and Marian Othmer Schultz Collegiate Scholarship • 1255
Carroll C. Hall Memorial Scholarship • 1950
Gloria Barron Wilderness Society Scholarship • 914
Nebraska Academy of Sciences High School Scholarships • 1639

RELATED CAREER (SCIENTIST)
ANS Graduate Scholarship • 791
ANS Undergraduate Scholarship • 793
ASABE Foundation Engineering Scholarship • 799
ASF Olin Fellowships • 803
Barry M. Goldwater Scholarship and Excellence in Education Program • 824
Battery Division Student Research Award • 825
Burlington Northern Santa Fe (BNSF) Foundation Scholarship • 2111
Fellowship Award • 889
Gaige Fund Award • 900
Industrial Electrochemistry and Electrochemical Engineering Student Achievement Award • 939
John and Muriel Landis Scholarship • 954
John J. McKetta Scholarship • 956
Language Grants • 451
National Space Club Keynote Scholar • 1029
Raney Fund Award • 1084
The Industrial Electrochemistry and Electrochemical Engineering Division H. H. Dow Memorial Student Achievement Award • 1140

RELATED CAREER (ARCHEOLOGISTS)
Harrell Family Fellowship • 598
Jennifer C. Groot Fellowship • 619

RELATED CAREER (PHYSICISTS)
AIAA Foundation Undergraduate Scholarship Program • 767

GOVERNMENT / PUBLIC ADMINISTRATION
Boren Scholarships • 546
CIA Undergraduate Scholarship Program • 85
Fellowship on Women and Public Policy • 1373
Goldberg-Miller Public Finance Scholarship • 594
James H. Dunn, Jr. Memorial Fellowship • 1488
Language Grants • 451
Morris K. Udall Scholarship • 2211
Nancy McManus Washington Internship Scholarships • 660
National Washington Crossing Foundation Scholarship • 666
Truman Scholar • 342
University of California Public Policy and International Affairs Junior Summer Institute • 728
University of California Public Policy and International Affairs Law Fellowship • 729
Wisconsin Women in Government Undergraduate Scholarship • 1921

GRAPHIC DESIGNERS
Congressional Black Caucus Spouses Visual Arts Scholarship • 2127
Print and Graphics Scholarship • 478
Stanfield and D'Orlando Art Scholarship • 2048
X Society Awards Scholarship • 2280

RELATED CAREER (ADVERTISING / PR)
Language Grants • 451
Media Fellows Program • 649
PRSA-Hawai'i/Roy Leffingwell Public Relations Scholarship • 1738

RELATED CAREER (MEDIA / RADIO / TELEVISION / INTERNET)
BEA National Scholarships in Broadcasting • 537
Carole Simpson Scholarship • 554
Ed Bradley Scholarship • 574
Idaho State Broadcasters Association Scholarships • 1455
John Bayliss Radio Scholarship • 623
Lou and Carole Prato Sports Reporting Scholarship • 642
Massachusetts Student Broadcaster Scholarship • 1578
Tony Coelho Media Scholarship • 2327
Upper Midwest Chapter Scholarships • 1867
Wisconsin Broadcasters Association Foundation Student Scholarship Program • 1916
Youth Scholarship • 740

RELATED CAREER (ENTERTAINMENT INDUSTRY)
Career Center • 402
Steven J. Finkel Service Excellence Scholarship • 713

HOSPITALITY / TRAVEL
American Express Scholarship Competition • 529
Ecolab Scholarship Competition • 573
HospitalityMaine Scholarship • 1448
IFEC Scholarships Award • 608
Incoming Freshman Scholarship • 612
New York State Association of Agricultural Fairs/New York State Showpeople's Association Scholarships • 1654
Steven J. Finkel Service Excellence Scholarship • 713

HVAC / TECHNICIANS
Complete Water Solutions Scholarship • 843
IAPMO Essay Scholarship Contest • 177

INTERIOR DESIGNERS
Congressional Black Caucus Spouses Visual Arts Scholarship • 2127
Sir John Soane's Museum Foundation Traveling Grant • 1113

RELATED CAREER (LANDSCAPE ARCHITECTS)
Carville M. Akehurst Memorial Scholarship • 836

RELATED CAREER (ARCHITECTURE / DESIGN)
Creative Sole Scholarship • 2129
National Garden Clubs Scholarship • 1026
Robert E. Thunen Memorial Scholarships • 1097

JOURNALISM
BEA National Scholarships in Broadcasting • 537
Bob East Scholarship • 543
Bob Eddy Scholarship Program • 1244
Bohdan Kolinsky Memorial Sports Journalism Scholarship • 1248

Carole Simpson Scholarship • 554
College Photographer of the Year • 561
Creative Sole Scholarship • 2129
Ed Bradley Scholarship • 574
Iowa Newspaper Association Scholarships • 1470
Lou and Carole Prato Sports Reporting Scholarship • 642
Marshall E. McCullough Scholarship • 991
National Press Club Scholarship for Journalism Diversity • 664
Overseas Press Club Foundation Scholarships/Fellowships • 680
RTNDA President's Scholarship • 703
Vincent Chin Scholarship • 733
X Society Awards Scholarship • 2280

Related Career (Writer)
Disney Entertainment Writing Program • 413
Humane Studies Fellowship: Flexible Support for PhD Students • 175
Playwright Discovery Award • 475
Taylor/Blakeslee University Fellowships • 492

Related Career (Media / Radio / Television / Internet)
Congressional Black Caucus Spouses Visual Arts Scholarship • 2127
Idaho State Broadcasters Association Scholarships • 1455
John Bayliss Radio Scholarship • 623
Massachusetts Student Broadcaster Scholarship • 1578
Tony Coelho Media Scholarship • 2327
Upper Midwest Chapter Scholarships • 1867
Wisconsin Broadcasters Association Foundation Student Scholarship Program • 1916
Youth Scholarship • 740

Landscape Architects
Carville M. Akehurst Memorial Scholarship • 836

Related Career (Architecture / Design)
Congressional Black Caucus Spouses Visual Arts Scholarship • 2127
Creative Sole Scholarship • 2129
National Garden Clubs Scholarship • 1026
Robert E. Thunen Memorial Scholarships • 1097
Sir John Soane's Museum Foundation Traveling Grant • 1113

Legal
AALL Educational Scholarships • 510
American Bar Association Law Day Art Contest • 40
George A. Strait Minority Scholarship • 591
LexisNexis / John R. Johnson Memorial Scholarship Endowment • 638
LimNexus Scholarship • 639
Mary Church Terrell Award • 215
University of California Public Policy and International Affairs Law Fellowship • 729

Related Career (Police / Fire / Law Enforcement)
Language Grants • 451
Sheryl A. Horak Memorial Scholarship • 301
Vermont Sheriffs' Association Scholarship • 1874

Library Sciences
AALL Educational Scholarships • 510
Begun Scholarship • 539
Bound to Stay Bound Books Scholarship • 547
CLA Scholarship For BIPOC Students in Memory of Edna Yelland • 559
Frederic G. Melcher Scholarship • 584
George A. Strait Minority Scholarship • 591
Leadership for Diversity Scholarship • 1530
LexisNexis / John R. Johnson Memorial Scholarship Endowment • 638

Manufacturing / Operations
AFS Wisconsin Past President Scholarship • 1188
Giuliano Mazzetti Scholarship • 912
Robert E. Thunen Memorial Scholarships • 1097

Related Career (Business and Management)
Betsy Plank/PRSSA Scholarship • 540
Burlington Northern Santa Fe (BNSF) Foundation Scholarship • 2111
Executive Women International Scholarship Program • 578
Joe Perdue Scholarship • 622
Language Grants • 451
Lawrence G. Foster Award for Excellence in Public Relations • 634
Media Fellows Program • 649
Nebraska Academy of Sciences High School Scholarships • 1639
Steven J. Finkel Service Excellence Scholarship • 713

Marketing
Betsy Plank/PRSSA Scholarship • 540
Creative Sole Scholarship • 2129
Harry A. Applegate Scholarship • 599
Language Grants • 451
Lawrence G. Foster Award for Excellence in Public Relations • 634
Media Fellows Program • 649

Related Career (Advertising / PR)
PRSA-Hawai'i/Roy Leffingwell Public Relations Scholarship • 1738

Related Career (Business and Management)
Burlington Northern Santa Fe (BNSF) Foundation Scholarship • 2111
Executive Women International Scholarship Program • 578
Joe Perdue Scholarship • 622
Nebraska Academy of Sciences High School Scholarships • 1639
Steven J. Finkel Service Excellence Scholarship • 713

Mathematicians
Barry M. Goldwater Scholarship and Excellence in Education Program • 824
Biographies of Contemporary Women in Mathematics Essay Contest • 828
Burlington Northern Santa Fe (BNSF) Foundation Scholarship • 2111
National Space Club Keynote Scholar • 1029

Related Career (Academia)
Henry Belin du Pont Dissertation Fellowship • 601
Herbert Hoover Research Travel Grant Award • 602
Humane Studies Fellowship: Flexible Support for PhD Students • 175
Humane Studies Fellowship: Publication Accelerator Grants • 605
Language Grants • 451
Robert E. Thunen Memorial Scholarships • 1097

Related Career (Physicists)
AIAA Foundation Undergraduate Scholarship Program • 767
ANS Graduate Scholarship • 791
ANS Undergraduate Scholarship • 793
C. Bertrand and Marian Othmer Schultz Collegiate Scholarship • 1255
Carroll C. Hall Memorial Scholarship • 1950
John and Muriel Landis Scholarship • 954

Related Career (Accounting / Finance / Banking)
Goldberg-Miller Public Finance Scholarship • 594
IMA Memorial Education Fund Scholarship • 610
John W. Rogers Memorial Scholarship • 1504
National Academic Scholarships • 661
Stuart Cameron and Margaret McLeod Memorial Scholarship • 714
Texas Fifth-Year Accounting Student Scholarship Program • 1842

Mechanics
Language Grants • 451

Related Career (Transportation and Trucking)
Allied Van Lines Scholarship • 524
Helene M. Overly Memorial Graduate Scholarship • 2156
Molitoris Leadership Scholarship for Undergraduates • 2210
North American Van Lines Logistics Scholarship • 675
Ohio Section Scholarships • 1688
RV Learning Center Scholarship Program • 1104
Sharon D. Banks Memorial Undergraduate Scholarship • 2247
WTS Minnesota Chapter Scholarships • 1925

Related Career (Aviation / Aerospace / Space)
AIAA Foundation Undergraduate Scholarship Program • 767
Aviation Distributors and Manufacturers Association Scholarship Program • 821
Aviation Insurance Association Education Foundation Scholarship • 822
Daedalian Foundation Scholarship Program • 108
Dan L. Meisinger Sr. Memorial Learn to Fly Scholarship • 851
David Arver Memorial Scholarship • 854
Dutch and Ginger Arver Scholarship • 868
Full-Time Employee Student Scholarship • 897
Garmin Scholarship • 902

The Ultimate Scholarship Book 2026
Career Index

John R. Lillard VAOC Scholarship • 1502
Johnny Davis Memorial Scholarship • 963
Lawrence C. Fortier Memorial Scholarship • 974
Lee Tarbox Memorial Scholarship • 977
Mid-Continent Instruments and Avionics Scholarship • 1006
National Aviation Explorer Scholarships • 1022
Pioneers of Flight • 1071
Tuskegee Airmen Scholarship Foundation Scholarships • 1154
Tweet Coleman Aviation Scholarship • 1861
UAA Janice K. Barden Aviation Scholarship • 1155

Related Career (Metal Work / Machinist / Welding)
AFS Twin City Memorial Scholarship • 1187
AFS Wisconsin Past President Scholarship • 1188

Related Career (Manufacturing / Operations)
Giuliano Mazzetti Scholarship • 912
Robert E. Thunen Memorial Scholarships • 1097

Media / Radio / Television / Internet
BEA National Scholarships in Broadcasting • 537
Carole Simpson Scholarship • 554
Congressional Black Caucus Spouses Visual Arts Scholarship • 2127
Ed Bradley Scholarship • 574
Idaho State Broadcasters Association Scholarships • 1455
John Bayliss Radio Scholarship • 623
Lou and Carole Prato Sports Reporting Scholarship • 642
Massachusetts Student Broadcaster Scholarship • 1578
Tony Coelho Media Scholarship • 2327
Upper Midwest Chapter Scholarships • 1867
Wisconsin Broadcasters Association Foundation Student Scholarship Program • 1916
Youth Scholarship • 740

Related Career (Entertainment Industry)
Career Center • 402
Steven J. Finkel Service Excellence Scholarship • 713

Related Career (Advertising / PR)
Language Grants • 451
Media Fellows Program • 649
PRSA-Hawai'i/Roy Leffingwell Public Relations Scholarship • 1738

Related Career (Performing Arts)
CBC Spouses Performing Arts Scholarship • 2117

Medical Researcher / Tech
AUA Foundation Research Scholars Program • 817
Elekta Radiation Therapy Scholarship • 874

Related Career (Nursing / PA (Medicine))
Academic Education Award • 750
AORN Foundation Scholarship Program • 795
BSN Scholarship • 832
Dorothy Budnek Memorial Scholarship • 862
Dr. Ralph E. White Graduating Senior Scholarship • 1343
Eight and Forty Lung and Respiratory Nursing Scholarship Fund • 873
ENA Foundation Undergraduate Scholarship • 879
Karen O'Neil Memorial Scholarship • 967
Morris K. Udall Scholarship • 2211
National Student Nurses' Association Scholarship • 1030
Senator Patricia K. McGee Nursing Faculty Scholarship • 1783
Washington Health Corps • 1892

Related Career (Sports Medicine / Training)
NATA Scholarship • 233

Related Career (Physical Therapists)
Allied Healthcare Scholarship Program • 1202
Challenge Scholarship • 79
GNC Nutritional Research Grant • 160
Graduate Research Grant - Master and Doctoral • 164
Health Careers Scholarship • 928
High School Scholarship • 173
Minority Scholarship • 2205

Metal Work / Machinist / Welding
AFS Twin City Memorial Scholarship • 1187
AFS Wisconsin Past President Scholarship • 1188

Musicians / Music
ASCAP Foundation Morton Gould Young Composer Awards • 397
Creative Sole Scholarship • 2129
John Lennon Scholarship Competition • 448
National Vocal Competition for Young Opera Singers • 465
NFMC Hinda Honigman Award for the Blind • 2314
Sara Tucker Study Grant • 482
Steven J. Finkel Service Excellence Scholarship • 713
X Society Awards Scholarship • 2280

Related Career (Performing Arts)
CBC Spouses Performing Arts Scholarship • 2117

Related Career (Entertainment Industry)
Career Center • 402
Tony Coelho Media Scholarship • 2327

Non-Profit / Volunteer
Truman Scholar • 342

Related Career (Education / Teaching)
Antonio Cirino Memorial Scholarship • 1220
Burlington Northern Santa Fe (BNSF) Foundation Scholarship • 2111
Carroll C. Hall Memorial Scholarship • 1950
Collaborative Teachers Tuition Waiver • 1299
Community Scholarship Fund • 1310
Educator Support Scholarship • 1356
First-Year Teacher Scholarships • 1376
FTEE Scholarship: Undergraduate Major in Technology and Engineering Education • 585
Golden Apple Scholars of Illinois (Illinois Scholars Program) • 1402
Incentive Program for Aspiring Teachers • 1463
Inspired to Teach • 1468
International Technology Engineering Educators Association Scholarship - FTEE/Undergraduate • 614
Language Grants • 451
Leadership for Diversity Scholarship • 1530
Learning and Leadership Grants • 635
Litherland/ITEEA Scholarship • 640
Maley/FTEE Teacher Professional Development Scholarship • 644
Martin Luther King, Jr. Memorial Scholarship • 2010
NACA Mid Atlantic Graduate Student Scholarship • 658
NACA Northern Plains Regional Student Leadership Scholarship • 1632
Office Supply Scholarship • 470
Ohio Classical Conference Scholarship for Prospective Latin Teachers • 1687
Pennsylvania Business Education Association Scholarship • 1724
Robert E. Thunen Memorial Scholarships • 1097
Robert G. Porter Scholars Program for Members • 2037
Rudolph Dillman Memorial Scholarship • 2320
Shields-Gillespie Scholarship • 709
Student Success Grants • 715
Teacher of the Year Award • 721
Teacher Shortage Employment Incentive Program • 1827
United Commercial Travelers of America (UCT) Scholarship Program • 726

Related Career (Social Services)
Allied Healthcare Scholarship Program • 1202
Aritzia Scholarship • 2102

Related Career (Government / Public Administration)
Boren Scholarships • 546
CIA Undergraduate Scholarship Program • 85
Fellowship on Women and Public Policy • 1373
Goldberg-Miller Public Finance Scholarship • 594
James H. Dunn, Jr. Memorial Fellowship • 1488
Morris K. Udall Scholarship • 2211
Nancy McManus Washington Internship Scholarships • 660
National Washington Crossing Foundation Scholarship • 666
University of California Public Policy and International Affairs Junior Summer Institute • 728
University of California Public Policy and International Affairs Law Fellowship • 729
Wisconsin Women in Government Undergraduate Scholarship • 1921

Nuclear Engineers
ANS Graduate Scholarship • 791
ANS Undergraduate Scholarship • 793
John and Muriel Landis Scholarship • 954
Language Grants • 451

Related Career (Engineering)
AIAA Foundation Undergraduate Scholarship Program • 767
ASABE Foundation Engineering Scholarship • 799
ASHRAE Engineering Technology Scholarships • 805

The Ultimate Scholarship Book 2026
Career Index

Barry M. Goldwater Scholarship and Excellence in Education Program • 824
Battery Division Student Research Award • 825
Burlington Northern Santa Fe (BNSF) Foundation Scholarship • 2111
Clair A. Hill Scholarship • 1296
DEED Funding Opportunities • 855
Desk and Derrick Educational Trust • 858
Dorothy M. and Earl S. Hoffman Award • 863
E. Noel Luddy Scholarship • 870
F.W. Beich Beichley Scholarship • 885
FTEE Scholarship: Undergraduate Major in Technology and Engineering Education • 585
Graduate Research Award (GRA) • 916
Industrial Electrochemistry and Electrochemical Engineering Student Achievement Award • 939
International Technology Engineering Educators Association Scholarship - FTEE/Undergraduate • 614
John J. McKetta Scholarship • 956
Kenneth Andrew Roe Scholarship • 969
Litherland/ITEEA Scholarship • 640
Maley/FTEE Teacher Professional Development Scholarship • 644
National Space Club Keynote Scholar • 1029
Nellie Yeoh Whetten Award • 1041
Ohio Section Scholarships • 1688
P.O. Pistilli Undergraduate Scholarship for Advancement in Computer Science and Electrical Engineering • 2233
Robert E. Thunen Memorial Scholarships • 1097
Russell and Sigurd Varian Award • 1102
SEE Education Foundation Scholarships • 1110
The Industrial Electrochemistry and Electrochemical Engineering Division H. H. Dow Memorial Student Achievement Award • 1140
Thomas M. Stetson Scholarship • 1144

Nursing / PA (Medicine)
Academic Education Award • 750
AORN Foundation Scholarship Program • 795
BSN Scholarship • 832
Dorothy Budnek Memorial Scholarship • 862
Dr. Ralph E. White Graduating Senior Scholarship • 1343
Eight and Forty Lung and Respiratory Nursing Scholarship Fund • 873
ENA Foundation Undergraduate Scholarship • 879
Karen O'Neil Memorial Scholarship • 967
Morris K. Udall Scholarship • 2211
National Student Nurses' Association Scholarship • 1030
Senator Patricia K. McGee Nursing Faculty Scholarship • 1783
Washington Health Corps • 1892

Related Career (Medical Researcher / Tech)
AUA Foundation Research Scholars Program • 817
Elekta Radiation Therapy Scholarship • 874

Performing Arts
CBC Spouses Performing Arts Scholarship • 2117

Related Career (Entertainment Industry)
Career Center • 402
Steven J. Finkel Service Excellence Scholarship • 713
Tony Coelho Media Scholarship • 2327

Related Career (Musicians / Music)
ASCAP Foundation Morton Gould Young Composer Awards • 397
Creative Sole Scholarship • 2129
John Lennon Scholarship Competition • 448
National Vocal Competition for Young Opera Singers • 465
NFMC Hinda Honigman Award for the Blind • 2314
Sara Tucker Study Grant • 482
X Society Awards Scholarship • 2280

Related Career (Artist)
John F. and Anna Lee Stacey Scholarship Fund for Art Education • 447
Office Supply Scholarship • 470
Sir John Soane's Museum Foundation Traveling Grant • 1113
Stanfield and D'Orlando Art Scholarship • 2048

Related Career (Media / Radio / Television / Internet)
BEA National Scholarships in Broadcasting • 537
Carole Simpson Scholarship • 554
Congressional Black Caucus Spouses Visual Arts Scholarship • 2127
Ed Bradley Scholarship • 574
Idaho State Broadcasters Association Scholarships • 1455
John Bayliss Radio Scholarship • 623
Lou and Carole Prato Sports Reporting Scholarship • 642
Massachusetts Student Broadcaster Scholarship • 1578
Upper Midwest Chapter Scholarships • 1867
Wisconsin Broadcasters Association Foundation Student Scholarship Program • 1916
Youth Scholarship • 740

Personal Service Industry
Challenge Scholarship • 79
GNC Nutritional Research Grant • 160
Graduate Research Grant - Master and Doctoral • 164
High School Scholarship • 173
Minority Scholarship • 2205

Related Career (Cosmetologist)
Beauty Changes Lives Foundation Scholarships • 538
Great Scholarship Program • 596
Joe Francis Haircare Scholarship Program • 621

Related Career (Culinary Arts / Food Service)
California Restaurant Association Educational Foundation General Scholarship • 1269
Feeding Tomorrow General Education Scholarships/Freshman Scholarships • 888
IFEC Scholarships Award • 608

Pharmacists
Allied Healthcare Scholarship Program • 1202
Health Careers Scholarship • 928
Language Grants • 451
NCPA Foundation Presidential Scholarship • 1036
Washington Health Corps • 1892

Related Career (Medical Researcher / Tech)
AUA Foundation Research Scholars Program • 817
Elekta Radiation Therapy Scholarship • 874

Photographer
Bob East Scholarship • 543
College Photographer of the Year • 561
Congressional Black Caucus Spouses Visual Arts Scholarship • 2127
Stanfield and D'Orlando Art Scholarship • 2048
X Society Awards Scholarship • 2280

Related Career (Artist)
Creative Sole Scholarship • 2129
John F. and Anna Lee Stacey Scholarship Fund for Art Education • 447
Office Supply Scholarship • 470
Sir John Soane's Museum Foundation Traveling Grant • 1113

Related Career (Graphic Designers)
Print and Graphics Scholarship • 478

Related Career (Media / Radio / Television / Internet)
BEA National Scholarships in Broadcasting • 537
Carole Simpson Scholarship • 554
Ed Bradley Scholarship • 574
Idaho State Broadcasters Association Scholarships • 1455
John Bayliss Radio Scholarship • 623
Lou and Carole Prato Sports Reporting Scholarship • 642
Massachusetts Student Broadcaster Scholarship • 1578
Tony Coelho Media Scholarship • 2327
Upper Midwest Chapter Scholarships • 1867
Wisconsin Broadcasters Association Foundation Student Scholarship Program • 1916
Youth Scholarship • 740

Physical Therapists
Allied Healthcare Scholarship Program • 1202
Challenge Scholarship • 79
GNC Nutritional Research Grant • 160
Graduate Research Grant - Master and Doctoral • 164
Health Careers Scholarship • 928
High School Scholarship • 173
Minority Scholarship • 2205

Related Career (Sports Medicine / Training)
NATA Scholarship • 233

Related Career (Nursing / PA (Medicine))
Academic Education Award • 750
AORN Foundation Scholarship Program • 795
BSN Scholarship • 832
Dorothy Budnek Memorial Scholarship • 862

The Ultimate Scholarship Book 2026
Career Index

Dr. Ralph E. White Graduating Senior Scholarship • 1343
Eight and Forty Lung and Respiratory Nursing Scholarship Fund • 873
ENA Foundation Undergraduate Scholarship • 879
Karen O'Neil Memorial Scholarship • 967
Morris K. Udall Scholarship • 2211
National Student Nurses' Association Scholarship • 1030
Senator Patricia K. McGee Nursing Faculty Scholarship • 1783
Washington Health Corps • 1892

Related Career (Medical Researcher / Tech)
AUA Foundation Research Scholars Program • 817
Elekta Radiation Therapy Scholarship • 874

Related Career (Doctor (Medicine))
Advanced Practice Healthcare Scholarship Program • 1186
Alice W. Rooke Scholarship • 775
Associate Degree Nursing Scholarship Program • 1228
Bachelor of Science Nursing Scholarship Program • 1234
Burlington Northern Santa Fe (BNSF) Foundation Scholarship • 2111
Fellowship Award • 889
Foundation for Surgical Technology Medical Mission Scholarship • 891
Irene and Daisy MacGregor Memorial Scholarship • 946
Language Grants • 451
Loan Assistance Repayment Program Primary Care Services • 1545
Medical Student Training in Aging Research (MSTAR) Program • 997
Minority Fellowship Program • 1008
NAHN Scholarship • 2213
NIH Undergraduate Scholarship Program • 1047
TOPSS Competition for High School Psychology Students • 725

Physicists
AIAA Foundation Undergraduate Scholarship Program • 767
ANS Graduate Scholarship • 791
ANS Undergraduate Scholarship • 793
Barry M. Goldwater Scholarship and Excellence in Education Program • 824
C. Bertrand and Marian Othmer Schultz Collegiate Scholarship • 1255
Carroll C. Hall Memorial Scholarship • 1950
John and Muriel Landis Scholarship • 954
Language Grants • 451

Related Career (Academia)
Henry Belin du Pont Dissertation Fellowship • 601
Herbert Hoover Research Travel Grant Award • 602
Humane Studies Fellowship: Flexible Support for PhD Students • 175
Humane Studies Fellowship: Publication Accelerator Grants • 605
Robert E. Thunen Memorial Scholarships • 1097

Related Career (Mathematicians)
Biographies of Contemporary Women in Mathematics Essay Contest • 828
Burlington Northern Santa Fe (BNSF) Foundation Scholarship • 2111
National Space Club Keynote Scholar • 1029

Plumber
Complete Water Solutions Scholarship • 843
IAPMO Essay Scholarship Contest • 177

Police / Fire / Law Enforcement
Language Grants • 451
Sheryl A. Horak Memorial Scholarship • 301
Vermont Sheriffs' Association Scholarship • 1874

Related Career (Defense / Military)
CIA Undergraduate Scholarship Program • 85

Psychiatrists
Aritzia Scholarship • 2102

Related Career (Doctor (Medicine))
Advanced Practice Healthcare Scholarship Program • 1186
Alice W. Rooke Scholarship • 775
Allied Healthcare Scholarship Program • 1202
Associate Degree Nursing Scholarship Program • 1228
Bachelor of Science Nursing Scholarship Program • 1234
Burlington Northern Santa Fe (BNSF) Foundation Scholarship • 2111
Dr. Ralph E. White Graduating Senior Scholarship • 1343
Fellowship Award • 889
Foundation for Surgical Technology Medical Mission Scholarship • 891
Health Careers Scholarship • 928
Irene and Daisy MacGregor Memorial Scholarship • 946
Language Grants • 451
Loan Assistance Repayment Program Primary Care Services • 1545
Medical Student Training in Aging Research (MSTAR) Program • 997
Minority Fellowship Program • 1008
Morris K. Udall Scholarship • 2211
NAHN Scholarship • 2213
NIH Undergraduate Scholarship Program • 1047
TOPSS Competition for High School Psychology Students • 725
Washington Health Corps • 1892

Real Estate
AIERF College Scholarship • 521
AIERF Graduate Scholarship • 522
International Facility Management Association Foundation Scholarship Program • 613
Minorities and Women Educational Scholarship • 654

Related Career (Entrepreneur)
Harry A. Applegate Scholarship • 599
Office Supply Scholarship • 470

Retail
Aritzia Scholarship • 2102

Scientist
ANS Graduate Scholarship • 791
ANS Undergraduate Scholarship • 793
ASABE Foundation Engineering Scholarship • 799
ASF Olin Fellowships • 803
Barry M. Goldwater Scholarship and Excellence in Education Program • 824
Battery Division Student Research Award • 825
Burlington Northern Santa Fe (BNSF) Foundation Scholarship • 2111
Carroll C. Hall Memorial Scholarship • 1950
Fellowship Award • 889
Gaige Fund Award • 900
Industrial Electrochemistry and Electrochemical Engineering Student Achievement Award • 939
John and Muriel Landis Scholarship • 954
John J. McKetta Scholarship • 956
Language Grants • 451
National Space Club Keynote Scholar • 1029
Nebraska Academy of Sciences High School Scholarships • 1639
Raney Fund Award • 1084
The Industrial Electrochemistry and Electrochemical Engineering Division H. H. Dow Memorial Student Achievement Award • 1140

Social Services
Allied Healthcare Scholarship Program • 1202
Aritzia Scholarship • 2102
Language Grants • 451

Related Career (Non-Profit / Volunteer)
Truman Scholar • 342

Sports Medicine / Training
NATA Scholarship • 233

Related Career (Athletes and Sports)
Challenge Scholarship • 79
Ethnic Minority and Women's Enhancement Scholarship • 140
GNC Nutritional Research Grant • 160
Graduate Research Grant - Master and Doctoral • 164
High School Scholarship • 173
Minority Scholarship • 2205
Women's Scholarship • 1173

Related Career (Nursing / PA (Medicine))
Academic Education Award • 750
AORN Foundation Scholarship Program • 795
BSN Scholarship • 832
Dorothy Budnek Memorial Scholarship • 862
Dr. Ralph E. White Graduating Senior Scholarship • 1343
Eight and Forty Lung and Respiratory Nursing Scholarship Fund • 873
ENA Foundation Undergraduate Scholarship • 879
Karen O'Neil Memorial Scholarship • 967
Morris K. Udall Scholarship • 2211
National Student Nurses' Association Scholarship • 1030
Senator Patricia K. McGee Nursing Faculty Scholarship • 1783
Washington Health Corps • 1892

Related Career (Medical Researcher / Tech)
AUA Foundation Research Scholars Program • 817
Elekta Radiation Therapy Scholarship • 874

Related Career (Doctor (Medicine))
Advanced Practice Healthcare Scholarship Program • 1186
Alice W. Rooke Scholarship • 775
Allied Healthcare Scholarship Program • 1202
Associate Degree Nursing Scholarship Program • 1228
Bachelor of Science Nursing Scholarship Program • 1234
Burlington Northern Santa Fe (BNSF) Foundation Scholarship • 2111
Fellowship Award • 889
Foundation for Surgical Technology Medical Mission Scholarship • 891
Health Careers Scholarship • 928
Irene and Daisy MacGregor Memorial Scholarship • 946
Language Grants • 451
Loan Assistance Repayment Program Primary Care Services • 1545
Medical Student Training in Aging Research (MSTAR) Program • 997
Minority Fellowship Program • 1008
NAHN Scholarship • 2213
NIH Undergraduate Scholarship Program • 1047
TOPSS Competition for High School Psychology Students • 725

Transportation and Trucking
Allied Van Lines Scholarship • 524
Helene M. Overly Memorial Graduate Scholarship • 2156
Molitoris Leadership Scholarship for Undergraduates • 2210
North American Van Lines Logistics Scholarship • 675
Ohio Section Scholarships • 1688
RV Learning Center Scholarship Program • 1104
Sharon D. Banks Memorial Undergraduate Scholarship • 2247
WTS Minnesota Chapter Scholarships • 1925

Veterinarian
Fellowship Award • 889

Related Career (Forestry / Fishing / Wildlife)
Arkansas Game and Fish Commission Conservation Scholarship • 1225
ASF Olin Fellowships • 803
Clair A. Hill Scholarship • 1296
Gloria Barron Wilderness Society Scholarship • 914
National Garden Clubs Scholarship • 1026
Nebraska Academy of Sciences High School Scholarships • 1639

Related Career (Medical Researcher / Tech)
AUA Foundation Research Scholars Program • 817
Elekta Radiation Therapy Scholarship • 874

Writer
Disney Entertainment Writing Program • 413
Humane Studies Fellowship: Flexible Support for PhD Students • 175
Playwright Discovery Award • 475
Taylor/Blakeslee University Fellowships • 492

Related Career (Journalism)
BEA National Scholarships in Broadcasting • 537
Bob East Scholarship • 543
Bob Eddy Scholarship Program • 1244
Bohdan Kolinsky Memorial Sports Journalism Scholarship • 1248
Carole Simpson Scholarship • 554
College Photographer of the Year • 561
Creative Sole Scholarship • 2129
Ed Bradley Scholarship • 574
Iowa Newspaper Association Scholarships • 1470
Lou and Carole Prato Sports Reporting Scholarship • 642
Marshall E. McCullough Scholarship • 991
National Press Club Scholarship for Journalism Diversity • 664
Overseas Press Club Foundation Scholarships/Fellowships • 680
RTNDA President's Scholarship • 703
Vincent Chin Scholarship • 733
X Society Awards Scholarship • 2280

Related Career (Media / Radio / Television / Internet)
Congressional Black Caucus Spouses Visual Arts Scholarship • 2127
Idaho State Broadcasters Association Scholarships • 1455
John Bayliss Radio Scholarship • 623
Massachusetts Student Broadcaster Scholarship • 1578
Tony Coelho Media Scholarship • 2327
Upper Midwest Chapter Scholarships • 1867
Wisconsin Broadcasters Association Foundation Student Scholarship Program • 1916
Youth Scholarship • 740

Related Career (Entertainment Industry)
Career Center • 402
Steven J. Finkel Service Excellence Scholarship • 713

INTERESTS / HOBBIES INDEX

This index lists awards that are geared toward students who are active in specific pastimes and hobbies.

Amateur Radio
ARRL Foundation General Fund Scholarship • 534
Bill, W2ONV and Ann Salerno Memorial Scholarship • 542
Carole J. Streeter, KB9JBR, Scholarship • 553
Central Arizona DX Association Scholarship • 1282
Challenge Met Scholarship • 2290
Charles Clarke Cordle Memorial Scholarship • 555
Charles N. Fisher Memorial Scholarship • 556
Dayton Amateur Radio Association Scholarship • 565
Don Riebhoff Memorial Scholarship • 568
Dr. James L. Lawson Memorial Scholarship • 570
Edmond A. Metzger Scholarship • 575
Fred R. McDaniel Memorial Scholarship • 583
Gary Wagner, K3OMI, Scholarship • 903
IRARC Memorial, Joseph P. Rubino, WA4MMD, Scholarship • 615
Irving W. Cook, WA0CGS, Scholarship • 1479
K2TEO Martin J. Green, Sr. Memorial Scholarship • 628
L. Phil and Alice J. Wicker Scholarship • 631
L.B. Cebik, W4RNL and Jean Cebik, N4TZP Memorial Scholarship • 632
Louisiana Memorial Scholarship • 1552
Mary Lou Brown Scholarship • 646
Mississippi Scholarship • 1616
New England FEMARA Scholarship • 672
Paul and Helen L. Grauer Scholarship • 681
PHD Scholarship • 685
Ray, N0RP and Katie, W0KTE Pautz Scholarship • 694
Richard W. Bendicksen, N7ZL, Memorial Scholarship • 697
Six Meter Club of Chicago Scholarship • 1793
Tom and Judith Comstock Scholarship • 724
YASME Foundation Scholarship • 739

Animals
Arizona National Livestock Show Scholarship • 1224
ASHA Youth Scholarships • 804
Federal Junior Duck Stamp Program and Scholarship Competition • 422
Future Without Speciesism Cash Award • 150
George Montgomery/NRA Youth Wildlife Art Contest • 154
Junior Showmanship Scholarship Program • 965
Marshall E. McCullough Scholarship • 991
Rover Sitter Scholarship • 285
Scholars Helping Collars Scholarship • 293
Waggle Human-Pet Bond Scholarship Opportunity • 368

Art / Design
Adobe Design Circle Scholarships • 390
Agota M. Bardos Award • 26
Antonio Cirino Memorial Scholarship • 1220

The Ultimate Scholarship Book 2026
Interests / Hobbies Index

Archibald Rutledge Scholarship Program • 1222
Doodle for Google • 416
Expressions Challenge by Walgreens • 420
Federal Junior Duck Stamp Program and Scholarship Competition • 422
Fellowships for Regular Program in Greece • 423
Frame My Future Scholarship Contest • 427
George Montgomery/NRA Youth Wildlife Art Contest • 154
Herblock Award for Editorial Cartoon • 435
Illustrators of the Future • 442
Mary Bowman Arts in Activism Award • 459
New York Life Award • 466
Ocean Awareness Contest • 469
Pacific Academy Foundation Scholarship • 264
Poster Contest for High School Students • 476
Pretty Photoshop Actions Bi-annual Scholarship • 1079
Wyland National Art Challenge • 504
Young American Creative Patriotic Art Contest • 506
Zicklin Contracting Restoration Awareness Scholarship • 508

ASTRONOMY
National Young Astronomer Award • 1031

BAND
ASCAP Foundation Morton Gould Young Composer Awards • 397
Glenn Miller Scholarship Competition • 430
Stillman Kelley/Thelma Byrum Awards • 487
Women Band Directors International College Scholarships • 503

BUSINESS
Caples Student Campaign of the Year Award • 551
Corporate Culture Scholarship • 98
Foreclosure Scholarship Program • 147
Fund for American Studies Internships • 586
Harry A. Applegate Scholarship • 599
James A. Turner, Jr. Memorial Scholarship • 616
Microsoft Office Specialist World Championship • 652

CAREER PLANNING
CareerFitter Scholarship • 74
Clubs of America Scholarship Award for Career Success • 87

CARS / TRUCKS
Automotive Hall of Fame Scholarships • 818
CJ Pony Parts Scholarship Video Contest • 86

CHOIR
Glenn Miller Scholarship Competition • 430
Stillman Kelley/Thelma Byrum Awards • 487

CIVIL RIGHTS
AU Student Contest • 56
Davis-Putter Scholarship Fund • 111
DoSomething Monthly Scholarships • 127
Kemper Human Rights Education Foundation • 199
Medgar Evers Award • 218
Religious Liberty Essay Scholarship Contest • 2033

COMMUNITY SERVICE / PUBLIC SERVICE
Abacus Life Scholarship • 18
AbbVie Immunology Scholarship • 2282
Agota M. Bardos Award • 26
Alpha Kappa Alpha Financial Need Scholars • 38
Americorps National Civilian Community Corps • 44
Americorps Vista • 45
Boettcher Foundation Scholarship • 1247
Bonner Scholars Program • 65
Burger King Scholars Program • 70
Denes I. Bardos Award • 117
DoSomething Monthly Scholarships • 127
Equitable Excellence Scholarship • 139
Foundation for Surgical Technology Medical Mission Scholarship • 891
GE-Reagan Foundation Scholarship Program • 151
Gloria Barron Prize for Young Heroes • 158
H.P. Bud Milligan Aviation Scholarship • 924
Imagine America High School Scholarship Program • 611
Jackie Robinson Foundation Scholarship Program • 2170
James M. and Virginia M. Smyth Scholarship • 188
LA Tutors Innovation in Education Scholarship • 202
Margaret McNamara Education Grants • 2195
Navin Narayan College Scholarship • 245
Newman Civic Fellow Awards • 254
Pedro Zamora Young Leaders Scholarship • 267
Pilot International Scholarship • 269
Pilot Pen G2 Overachievers Student Grant • 270
Prudential Emerging Visionaries • 274
Rhode Island Foundation Association of Former Legislators Scholarship • 1754
Samuel Huntington Public Service Award • 289
Sodexo Stephen J. Brady STOP Hunger Scholarship • 304
Spirit of Giving Scholarship • 308
Stamps Scholars • 309
Stanley O. McNaughton Community Service Award • 1807
Student Video Contest • 317
Tracking Foundation Scholars Scholarship Program • 2266
United States Hispanic Leadership Institute Denny's Hungry for Education • 351
Urban Fellows Program • 352
Voyager Scholarship, The Obama-Chesky Scholarship for Public Service • 364
White House Fellows Program • 374
Young Women in Public Affairs Award • 2281

COMPUTERS
NCWIT Award for Aspirations in Computing • 2225
Outstanding Undergraduate Researchers Award Program • 1057
Regeneron Science Talent Search • 1086

DANCE
Princess Grace Awards • 477
Thelma A. Robinson Award in Ballet • 494

EAGLE SCOUT
Eagle Scout of the Year • 1347
Emmett J. Doerr Memorial Scout Scholarship • 1966
National Eagle Scout Association Scholarship • 2017
NESA Hall/McElwain Merit Scholarships • 2022
NESA Lawrence S. and Mabel Cooke Scholarship • 2023
Rebecca Palmer Eagle Scout Scholarship Endowment • 2032

ECONOMICS
BMTX Financial Empowerment Scholarship • 63

EDUCATION
Barbizon's College Tuition Scholarship • 59
P.E.O. Program for Continuing Education • 2232
Student View Scholarship • 318

ENTREPRENEURSHIP
Be the Boss Scholarship • 60
Harry A. Applegate Scholarship • 599

ENVIRONMENT
Apprentice Ecologist Initiative Youth Scholarship Program • 798
Eco-Warrior Scholarship • 133
Emily M. Hewitt and Stephen K. Stocking Memorial Scholarship • 1362
Federal Junior Duck Stamp Program and Scholarship Competition • 422
George Montgomery/NRA Youth Wildlife Art Contest • 154
Industrial Metal Service Scholarship • 183
Student Video Contest • 317

FILM / TV / RADIO
Children in Need Scholarship • 406
College Television Awards • 409
ConnectHER Film Festival • 410
Hedy Lamarr Achievement Award for Emerging Leaders in Entertainment Technology • 432
Indiana Broadcasters Association College Scholarships • 1465
Julianne Malveaux Scholarship • 2178
Ocean Awareness Contest • 469
Princess Grace Awards • 477
Scholastic Art and Writing Portfolio Award • 483
Stossel in the Classroom Video Contest • 313
Student Academy Awards Competition • 488
StudentCam Competition • 319
Unboxing Your Life Video Scholarship • 348
Young Filmmakers Contest • 507

GAMES / MARBLES
National Marbles Tournament Scholarship • 236
Play! Pokemon Scholarship • 271

GARDENING / HERBS
Douglas Dockery Thomas Fellowship in Garden History and Design • 864
Spring Meadow Proven Winners Scholarship • 1123
Timothy S. and Palmer W. Bigelow, Jr. Scholarship • 1147
Usrey Family Scholarship • 1164

HEALTH
Mental Health Importance Scholarship • 1000
Student Video Contest • 317
Tampax Flow It Forward Scholarship • 2261

HISTORY
AMS Graduate Fellowship in the History of Science • 783

Interests / Hobbies Index

FMAA Scholarship Program • 144
George S. and Stella M. Knight Essay Contest • 155
Joseph S. Rumbaugh Historical Oration Contest • 626
National History Day Contest • 663
Student Video Contest • 317

Languages
Congress Bundestag Youth Exchange Program • 95
Fellowships for Regular Program in Greece • 423
Fellowships/Grants to Study in Scandinavia • 424
National Latin Exam Scholarship • 464
Student Translation Award • 490
Translation Prize Competition • 495

LGBT Rights
DoSomething Monthly Scholarships • 127

Literature
Fellowships for Regular Program in Greece • 423
Scholastic Art and Writing Portfolio Award • 483

Mathematics
Frank and Brennie Morgan Prize for Outstanding Research in Mathematics by an Undergraduate Student • 893
MIT THINK Scholarship Program • 1010
Modeling the Future Challenge • 1011
Moody's Mega Math Challenge • 1013
Paradigm Challenge • 1058
Regeneron Science Talent Search • 1086
USMA Metric Scholarship Award • 360

Military
Army ROTC Four-Year Scholarship Program • 54
NROTC Scholarship Program • 260
Voice of Democracy Audio Essay Contests • 363

Music Composition
Agota M. Bardos Award • 26
Archibald Rutledge Scholarship Program • 1222
ASCAP Foundation Morton Gould Young Composer Awards • 397
Dolly Parton Songwriters Award • 415
Herb Alpert Young Jazz Composer Awards • 434
John Lennon Scholarship Competition • 448
NFMC Lynn Freeman Olson Composition Awards • 467
Stillman Kelley/Thelma Byrum Awards • 487

Music Performance
Agota M. Bardos Award • 26
AMCA Music Scholarship • 394
Archibald Rutledge Scholarship Program • 1222
ASCAP Foundation Morton Gould Young Composer Awards • 397
Glenn Miller Scholarship Competition • 430
International Trumpet Guild Conference Scholarship • 443
Jack Kent Cooke Young Artist Award • 444
Julius and Esther Stulberg International String Competition • 449
Lotte Lenya Competition • 456
NFMC Wendell Irish Viola Award • 468
Ocean Awareness Contest • 469
Stillman Kelley/Thelma Byrum Awards • 487
Women Band Directors International College Scholarships • 503

Newspaper / Journalism
Bob Stevens Memorial Scholarship • 1245
Dorothy D. Greer Journalist of the Year Scholarship Competition • 1337
Fund for American Studies Internships • 586
Georgia Press Educational Foundation Scholarships • 1398
Julianne Malveaux Scholarship • 2178
Overseas Press Club Foundation Scholarships/Fellowships • 680
Scholastic Art and Writing Portfolio Award • 483
Virginia High School League Charles E. Savedge Journalism Scholarship • 1883

Outdoors / Camping
Bodie McDowell Scholarship • 545
Chick and Sophie Major Memorial Duck Calling Contest • 1290
Federal Junior Duck Stamp Program and Scholarship Competition • 422
George Montgomery/NRA Youth Wildlife Art Contest • 154

Performing Arts / Drama / Theater
Archibald Rutledge Scholarship Program • 1222
Expressions Challenge by Walgreens • 420
Future Theatre Educator Scholarship • 428
Georgia Thespians Achievement Scholarships • 1399
NFMC Wendell Irish Viola Award • 468
Ocean Awareness Contest • 469
Optimist International Oratorical Contest • 678
Playwright Discovery Award • 475
Princess Grace Awards • 477

Photography
Alexia Foundation Student Grants • 393
Federal Junior Duck Stamp Program and Scholarship Competition • 422

Piano
Stillman Kelley/Thelma Byrum Awards • 487

Playwriting
Clauder Competition Prize • 408

Poetry
Expressions Challenge by Walgreens • 420

Politics / Government
Alpha Kappa Alpha Financial Need Scholars • 38
AU Student Contest • 56
Coolidge Scholarship • 97
Council on International Educational Exchange (CIEE) Scholarships • 411
Davis-Putter Scholarship Fund • 111
DoSomething Monthly Scholarships • 127
Foreclosure Scholarship Program • 147
Fund for American Studies Internships • 586
Herblock Award for Editorial Cartoon • 435
Humane Studies Fellowship: Graduate Sabbatical Grants • 176
Julianne Malveaux Scholarship • 2178
Nancy McManus Washington Internship Scholarships • 660
Newman Civic Fellow Awards • 254
Project Vote Smart National Internship Program • 689
Raftelis Leadership Scholarships • 692
Religious Liberty Essay Scholarship Contest • 2033
Student Video Contest • 317
Voice of Democracy Audio Essay Contests • 363
Young Women in Public Affairs Award • 2281

Science
EngineerGirl Essay Contest • 880
ExploraVision National Science Competition • 884
MIT THINK Scholarship Program • 1010
Paradigm Challenge • 1058
Regeneron Science Talent Search • 1086
ScienceSaves Video Scholarship Contest • 1109
SPS Future Teacher Scholarship • 711
Taylor/Blakeslee University Fellowships • 492

Science Fiction / SciFi
Starfleet Scholarships • 2050

Sculpture
Laura Ziegler Scholarship • 452

Singing / Voice
Stillman Kelley/Thelma Byrum Awards • 487
We The Future Contest • 372

Social Justice / Activism
Alpha Kappa Alpha Financial Need Scholars • 38

Speech / Debate
Bill Gove Scholarship • 399
Cavett Robert Scholarship • 405
Joseph S. Rumbaugh Historical Oration Contest • 626
Optimist International Oratorical Contest • 678
Religious Liberty Essay Scholarship Contest • 2033
We The Future Contest • 372

Sports
CIF Scholar-Athlete of the Year • 1295
Fields of Learning Scholarship • 1374
Lou and Carole Prato Sports Reporting Scholarship • 642
NABF Scholarship Program • 231
NCAA Postgraduate Scholarship • 253
Pacific Academy Foundation Scholarship • 264
Paul Flaherty Athletic Scholarship • 1721

String Instrument
Stillman Kelley/Thelma Byrum Awards • 487

Student Government
Alpha Kappa Alpha Financial Need Scholars • 38
Newman Civic Fellow Awards • 254
United States Senate Youth Program • 727

Study Abroad
AIFS Green Ambassador Scholarship • 28
Boren Scholarships • 546
Bright!Tax Global Scholar Initiative • 67
Congress Bundestag Youth Exchange Program • 95
Council on International Educational Exchange (CIEE) Scholarships • 411
Diversity Achievement Scholarship • 414
Gilman International Scholarship • 429
Global Citizen Scholarship • 157
Hispanic Serving Institutions Scholarship • 2161
Historically Black College and University Scholarship • 2162
ICWA Fellowship Program • 437

The Ultimate Scholarship Book 2026
Special Circumstances Index

John S. Linakis Scholarship • 192
Mildred Towle Scholarship - Study Abroad • 1601
Minority Serving Institution Grants • 2209
Russel R. Taylor Foundation Scholarship • 287
Sir Cyril Taylor Legacy Scholarship • 302
Study Abroad Europe Scholarship • 491

Teaching
Bonner Scholars Program • 65
Newman Civic Fellow Awards • 254
Pi Lambda Theta Student Support Scholarships • 686
SPS Future Teacher Scholarship • 711

Technology
ExploraVision National Science Competition • 884
Hedy Lamarr Achievement Award for Emerging Leaders in Entertainment Technology • 432
MIT THINK Scholarship Program • 1010
NCWIT Award for Aspirations in Computing • 2225
Paradigm Challenge • 1058
Regeneron Science Talent Search • 1086

Ukulele
Stillman Kelley/Thelma Byrum Awards • 487
Ukulele Festival Hawaii's College Scholarship Program • 497

Writing
1 for 2 Education Foundation Scholarship • 9
ACES Education Fund Scholarship • 386
Adult Learner Scholarship from Study.com • 21
Amy Lowell Poetry Travelling Scholarship • 395
Anthem Essay Contest • 396
Archibald Rutledge Scholarship Program • 1222
Atlas Shrugged Essay Contest • 398
AU Student Contest • 56
Corporate Office Interiors Scholarship Contest • 99
Courage to Grow Scholarship • 100
Crossword Hobbyist Crossword Scholarship • 105
Delta Theta Chi Sorority National Memorial Scholarship • 116
Eon Essay Contest • 138
Expressions Challenge by Walgreens • 420
Gentlemen Showcase • 2150
GMR Transcription Academic Scholarship • 159
Go City Education Scholarship • 161
International College Counselors Scholarship • 184
IWSH Essay Scholarship • 948
Jane Austen Society of North America Essay Contest • 189
Jeannette Rankin National Scholar Grant • 2176
Julianne Malveaux Scholarship • 2178
Kemper Human Rights Education Foundation • 199
Maison Law California Scholarship • 1561
Mary Bowman Arts in Activism Award • 459
National High School Poetry Contest/Easterday Poetry Award • 462
New York Life Award • 466
Nicholas Virgilio Haiku and Senryu Contest • 257
Ocean Awareness Contest • 469
Oleg Fastovsky Outstanding Citizenship Scholarship • 263
Playwright Discovery Award • 475
Prize in Ethics Essay Contest • 479
Project Yellow Light/Hunter Garner Scholarship • 273
Pulse of Perseverance Scholarship • 275
RealtyHop Scholarship • 278
Religious Liberty Essay Scholarship Contest • 2033
RentHop's College and University Scholarship • 279
Rubincam Youth Writing Competition • 286
Sahara Hope Scholarship For Women Empowered To Change The World • 2246
Scholastic Art and Writing Portfolio Award • 483
Shawn Carter Foundation Scholarship • 707
Sloane Stephens Doc and Glo Scholarship • 303
Steps For Change Scholarship • 310
Stossel in the Classroom Essay Contest • 312
Study.com Community College Student Scholarship • 321
Study.com Scholarship for Nontraditional Students • 327
Tattoo Journal Ink Scholarship • 335
Ted and Holly Rollins Scholarship • 1138
The Fountainhead Essay Contest • 493
Thiel Fellowship Grant • 338
Think For Yourself College Scholarship Essay Contest • 339
Truth Change Maker Awards • 343
We The Future Contest • 372
Zicklin Contracting Restoration Awareness Scholarship • 508

Yearbook
Dorothy D. Greer Journalist of the Year Scholarship Competition • 1337
Virginia High School League Charles E. Savedge Journalism Scholarship • 1883

Youth Ministry
Champions for Christ Scholarship • 1953

SPECIAL CIRCUMSTANCES

This index lists a variety of special circumstances that are used as eligibility limits for these scholarships.

AVID
Dell Scholars Program • 115

Cancer, sibling of survivor or someone with cancer
Cancer Fighter Scholarship • 2288
Northwestern Mutual Foundation Childhood Cancer Sibling Scholarship • 2315

Doctoral degree recipient
ACLS Fellowships • 514
Huntington Fellowships • 606
Visiting Senior Fellowship Program • 501

First generation college student
Douvas Memorial Scholarship • 1338
Education Accessibility Scholarship • 135
First Generation Matching Grant Program • 1375
First in the Family Scholarship • 1971
Hamilton Award • 168
OCA/UPS Gold Mountain Scholarship • 2228
Patty and Melvin Alperin First Generation Scholarship • 1719
Stantec Equity and Diversity Scholarship • 2251
U.S. Western Digital STEM Scholarship • 346

Foster care
BrandSource Scholarship • 2110
California Chafee Grant for Foster Youth • 2113
Casey Family Scholarship • 2114
Department of Children and Families (DCF) Foster Child Tuition Waiver and Fee Assistance Program • 1330
Educational Training Voucher Programs for Foster Youth • 1355
Foster Child Grant Program • 1383
Illinois Department of Children and Family Services Scholarship Program • 1461
National Foster Parent Association (NFPA) Youth Scholarship • 2216
Oklahoma Youth with Promise Scholarship Fund • 1700
Tuition Waiver for Foster Care Recipients • 1859
Victoria S. and Bradley L. Geist Foundation • 1878
Washington State Governors' Scholarship for Foster Youth • 1896

Gay / lesbian
Aritzia Scholarship • 2102
BIPOC Scholarship • 2109
Edie Windsor Coding Scholarship • 2136
Gamma Mu Scholarships Program • 2145
George Choy Memorial/Gay Asian Pacific Alliance (GAPA) Scholarship • 2151
Kenneth W. Payne Student Prize • 2179
Laurel Hester Memorial Scholarship • 2184
LEAGUE Foundation Scholarship • 2185
LGBTQ+ Student Scholarship from Study.com • 2186
New York Ramblers Scholarship • 2226
Pega Scholars Program • 2235
Point Community College Scholarship • 2238

Point Flagship Scholarship • 2239
SpeakOUT's LGBTQ+ Scholarship • 2249
Stantec Equity and Diversity Scholarship • 2251
Traub-Dicker Rainbow Scholarship • 2267

GEAR UP
Dell Scholars Program • 115

HISPANIC SERVING INSTITUTIONS
Hispanic Serving Institutions Scholarship • 2161

HISTORICALLY BLACK COLLEGES AND UNIVERSITIES
Chevron Corporate Scholars Program • 2121
HBCU NREI Scholarship • 2153
Historically Black College and University Scholarship • 2162
James M. and Erma T. Freemont Foundation Scholarship Program • 2171
Meritage Homes Scholarship • 2204

HOMESCHOOLED
Craig Dickinson Memorial Scholarship • 102
Homeschoolers' Support Association Scholarship • 1445
KEM Electric Cooperative Scholarships for Students Attending High School Outside the Service Area • 1519
Mason Lighthouse Scholarship • 217
Sandra Hancock Scholarship • 290
State of the Arts Scholarship • 485
Study.com College Scholarship for Homeschool Students • 320

IMMIGRANT / RESIDENT ALIEN
Agota M. Bardos Award • 26
Denes I. Bardos Award • 117
Paul and Daisy Soros Fellowships for New Americans • 265
TheDream.US Scholarship • 2263

INTERNATIONAL STUDENT
International Student Scholarship • 943
P.E.O. International Peace Scholarship • 2231
Women in STEM Scholarship • 378

ONLINE EDUCATION
Study.com Online Graduate Degree Scholarship • 322
Study.com Online Undergraduate Degree Scholarship • 323

PARENT
Education Support Award • 2139
Study.com Scholarship for Moms • 2255

PARENT DECEASED
Frontline Families Scholarship • 2143
Life Lessons Scholarship Program • 204
Pinnacol Foundation Scholarship Program • 1736

PARENT DISABLED FROM WORK-RELATED INJURY
Pinnacol Foundation Scholarship Program • 1736

PARENT EMPLOYED BY A COLLEGE
Tuition Exchange Scholarships • 2058

PARENT EMPLOYED IN RETAIL
F. Koehnen Ltd. Scholarship Fund • 1371

PARENT IS A FIREFIGHTER
America's 911 Foundation Scholarship • 39
Study.com Scholarship for Children of First Responders • 324

PARENT IS A FIREFIGHTER KILLED IN THE LINE OF DUTY
California Law Enforcement Personnel Dependents Grant Program • 1266
W. H. Howie McClennan Scholarship • 366

PARENT IS A LAW ENFORCEMENT OFFICER
America's 911 Foundation Scholarship • 39
Study.com Scholarship for Children of First Responders • 324

PARENT IS A LAW ENFORCEMENT OFFICER DISABLED IN LINE OF DUTY
California Law Enforcement Personnel Dependents Grant Program • 1266
NACOP Scholarship • 232

PARENT IS A LAW ENFORCEMENT OFFICER KILLED IN LINE OF DUTY
Arkansas Service Memorial Scholarship Endowment • 1226
California Law Enforcement Personnel Dependents Grant Program • 1266
John F. Duffy Scholarship/Grant Program • 190

RETURNING TO COLLEGE AFTER A BREAK
Arizona BPW Foundation Annual Scholarships • 1223
B.K. Krenzer Reentry Scholarship • 2108
Boomer Benefits Scholarship • 66
Non-Traditional Student Scholarship • 2025
P.E.O. Program for Continuing Education • 2232
Women on Par Scholarship • 380

SEPTEMBER 11 VICTIM
Families of Freedom Scholarship Fund • 142
New Jersey World Trade Center Scholarship • 1649
World Trade Center Memorial Scholarship • 1924

SINGLE PARENT
Ford Opportunity Program • 1382
Frances L. Macartney Porter Fund • 1387
Gump and Ayers Scholarship • 1415
James Anderson Logan Jr. and Betty Ann McFarland Logan Scholarship Fund • 1486
Live Your Dream Awards Program • 2188
One Family Scholars Program • 1703
Striving Solo Parent Scholarship • 2253
Study.com Single Parent Scholarship • 2257

SPOUSE LAW ENFORCEMENT OFFICER KILLED IN LINE OF DUTY
California Law Enforcement Personnel Dependents Grant Program • 1266
John F. Duffy Scholarship/Grant Program • 190

SPOUSE OF FIREFIGHTER KILLED IN THE LINE OF DUTY
California Law Enforcement Personnel Dependents Grant Program • 1266

SUBSTANCE ABUSE, OVERCAME
Ho'omaka Hou - A New Beginning Fund • 1444

TALL
Tall Club International Scholarship • 2052

TRANSGENDER
Aritzia Scholarship • 2102
BIPOC Scholarship • 2109
Edie Windsor Coding Scholarship • 2136
Kenneth W. Payne Student Prize • 2179
Laurel Hester Memorial Scholarship • 2184
LEAGUE Foundation Scholarship • 2185
LGBTQ+ Student Scholarship from Study.com • 2186
New York Ramblers Scholarship • 2226
Pega Scholars Program • 2235
SpeakOUT's LGBTQ+ Scholarship • 2249

UPWARD BOUND
Dell Scholars Program • 115

VEGETARIAN
VRG Scholarship • 365

VOCATIONAL, TECHNICAL OR TRADE SCHOOL
Certificate, License or Other Industry-Recognized Credential • 1283
Horatio Alger Career and Technical Scholarship • 604

The Ultimate Scholarship Book 2026
State of Residence Index

STATE OF RESIDENCE INDEX

This index lists awards that are restricted to students who are residents of the state or territory or who are planning to study in the state or territory.

ALABAMA
- Alabama Student Assistance Program • 1193
- Charles Clarke Cordle Memorial Scholarship • 555
- Crumley Roberts Next Step Scholarship • 1317
- Curwen-Guidry-Blackburn Scholarship Fund • 107
- Dixie Boys Baseball Scholarship Program • 120
- Dixie Youth Scholarship Program • 122
- Ed and Charlotte Rodgers Scholarships • 1350
- Educational Training Voucher Programs for Foster Youth • 1355
- Family District 1 Scholarships • 1372
- Gorgas Scholarship Competition • 1405
- Jimmy Rane Foundation Scholarships • 1494
- Linly Heflin Scholarship • 1543
- NACA South Student Leadership Scholarships • 1633
- Northrop Grumman Scholarship • 1681
- Smith Scholarship Program • 1796

ALASKA
- Alaska Education Grant • 1194
- Alaska Performance Scholarship • 1195
- Arc of Washington State Trust Fund Stipend Award • 1221
- Atsuhiko Tateuchi Memorial Scholarship • 1232
- JJ Klein Scholarship Fund • 1495
- Liam Hood Scholarship Fund • 1537
- Lori Rhett Memorial Scholarship • 1547
- Mary Lou Brown Scholarship • 646
- MGMA Western Section Scholarship • 1003
- Red Boucher Scholarship • 1751
- Richard D. Johnson Memorial Post-Secondary Scholarship • 1756

ARIZONA
- Alisa's Angels Scholarship • 1198
- Arizona BPW Foundation Annual Scholarships • 1223
- Arizona National Livestock Show Scholarship • 1224
- Burlington Northern Santa Fe (BNSF) Foundation Scholarship • 2111
- Central Arizona DX Association Scholarship • 1282
- Charles N. Fisher Memorial Scholarship • 556
- Educational Training Voucher Programs for Foster Youth • 1355
- Kappa Delta Phi • 966
- MGMA Western Section Scholarship • 1003
- Shari Simon Greenberg Community Scholarship • 300

ARKANSAS
- Academic Challenge Scholarship • 1179
- American Legion Department of Arkansas High School Oratorical Scholarship Program • 1214
- Arkansas Game and Fish Commission Conservation Scholarship • 1225
- Arkansas Service Memorial Scholarship Endowment • 1226
- Burlington Northern Santa Fe (BNSF) Foundation Scholarship • 2111
- Curwen-Guidry-Blackburn Scholarship Fund • 107
- Dixie Boys Baseball Scholarship Program • 120
- Dixie Youth Scholarship Program • 122
- Fred R. McDaniel Memorial Scholarship • 583
- Governor's Distinguished Scholarship • 1408
- Jimmy Rane Foundation Scholarships • 1494
- Markley Scholarship • 211
- MFA Foundation Scholarships • 1590
- R. Preston Woodruff, Jr. Scholarships • 1740

CALIFORNIA
- ACEC Scholarship • 1185
- Advanced Practice Healthcare Scholarship Program • 1186
- Allied Healthcare Scholarship Program • 1202
- Alyssa McCroskey Memorial Scholarship • 1205
- American Legion Auxiliary, Department of California Educational Assistance General $1,000 Scholarships • 1211
- American Legion Auxiliary, Department of California Educational Assistance General $2,000 Scholarships • 1212
- American Legion Auxiliary, Department of California Educational Assistance General $500 Scholarships • 1213
- Associate Degree Nursing Scholarship Program • 1228
- Atsuhiko Tateuchi Memorial Scholarship • 1232
- AWAF Scholarships • 1233
- Bachelor of Science Nursing Scholarship Program • 1234
- Begun Scholarship • 539
- Betty Bacon Memorial Scholarship • 1239
- Burlington Northern Santa Fe (BNSF) Foundation Scholarship • 2111
- Cal Grant A • 1256
- Cal Grant B • 1257
- Cal Grant C • 1258
- Cal Grant Entitlement Award • 1259
- California - Hawaii Elks Association Vocational Grants • 550
- California - Hawaii Elks Major Project Undergraduate Scholarship Program for Students with Disabilities • 1260
- California Chafee Grant for Foster Youth • 2113
- California Fee Waiver Program for Children of Veterans • 1261
- California Fee Waiver Program for Dependents of Deceased or Disabled National Guard Members • 1262
- California Fee Waiver Program for Recipients of the Medal of Honor and Their Children • 1263
- California Freethought Day High School Essay Scholarship • 1264
- California Health Sciences Scholarships • 1265
- California Law Enforcement Personnel Dependents Grant Program • 1266
- California Masonic Foundation Scholarship • 1267
- California Oratorical Contest • 1268
- California Restaurant Association Educational Foundation General Scholarship • 1269
- California State PTA Volunteer Service Scholarship • 1270
- CAPED Excellence Scholarship • 1272
- CAPPS Memorial Scholarship Program • 1273
- Cathay Bank Foundation Scholarship • 1279
- CDM Constructors Inc. Workforce Development Scholarship • 1281
- Charles N. Fisher Memorial Scholarship • 556
- CIF Scholar-Athlete of the Year • 1295
- CLA Scholarship For BIPOC Students in Memory of Edna Yelland • 559
- Clair A. Hill Scholarship • 1296
- CTA Cesar E. Chavez and Dolores Huerta Education Award Program • 1318
- Dick Griffiths Memorial Scholarship • 1332
- Dr. Ralph E. White Graduating Senior Scholarship • 1343
- Emily M. Hewitt and Stephen K. Stocking Memorial Scholarship • 1362
- ERC Eco Scholarship Fund • 1366
- Friends of the California State Fair Scholarship Program • 1388
- George Choy Memorial/Gay Asian Pacific Alliance (GAPA) Scholarship • 2151
- Incight Scholarship • 2301
- Jack Hughes Education Scholarship • 1485
- Jackson Laboratory Scholarship • 949
- John F. Duffy Scholarship/Grant Program • 190
- Kappa Delta Phi • 966
- Leadership for Diversity Scholarship • 1530
- LEAF Scholarships • 1531
- Licensed Vocational Nurse to Associate Degree Nursing Scholarship • 1538
- Luso-American Education Foundation General Youth Scholarship • 1553
- Mark Ando and Ito Family Scholarship • 2197
- Mary Keith Duff Memorial Scholarship • 1572
- MGMA Western Section Scholarship • 1003
- New York Life Award • 466
- Northrop Grumman Scholarship • 1681
- Past Department Presidents' Junior Scholarship Award • 1718
- PG&E Better Together STEM Scholarship Program • 1734
- Roshan Rahbari Scholarship Fund • 1772
- Samsung@First Scholars • 1777
- Shari Simon Greenberg Community Scholarship • 300
- Sons of Italy Grand Lodge of California Italian Language Study Grant • 1798
- Sons of Italy Grand Lodge of College Scholarship • 1799
- Steve Fasteau Past Presidents' Scholarship • 1816
- Susan Bunch Memorial Scholarship • 1818
- Usrey Family Scholarship • 1164
- Vocational Nurse Scholarship • 1887
- Werks Mobile Scholarship • 1899

COLORADO
- ACEC Colorado Scholarship Program • 1184
- Boettcher Foundation Scholarship • 1247
- Burlington Northern Santa Fe (BNSF) Foundation Scholarship • 2111
- CESDA Diversity Scholarship • 1284
- CollegeInvest 529 Scholarship Program • 1301
- Colorado Council Volunteerism and Community Service Scholarship • 1303

Colorado Masons Benevolent Fund Scholarships • 1304
Colorado Oratorical Contest • 1305
Colorado Student Grant • 1306
Colorado Women's Education Foundation • 1307
Daniels Scholarship Program • 1322
Dorian De Long Arts and Music Scholarship • 1335
Dorothy D. Greer Journalist of the Year Scholarship Competition • 1337
Educational Training Voucher Programs for Foster Youth • 1355
Greenhouse Scholars Scholarship • 1413
Grossman Scholarship • 1414
H.M. Muffly Memorial Scholarship • 1420
Henry Sachs Foundation Scholarship • 1432
MGMA Western Section Scholarship • 1003
Mikkelson Foundation Scholarship • 1600
Northrop Grumman Scholarship • 1681
Pinnacol Foundation Scholarship Program • 1736
RBC Wealth Management Colorado Scholarship • 1748
Winifred R. Reynolds Educational Scholarship • 1913

CONNECTICUT
American Legion - Connecticut Oratorical Contest • 1210
Associated General Contractors of Connecticut Scholarships • 1229
Big Y Scholarship Programs • 1241
Bob Eddy Scholarship Program • 1244
Bohdan Kolinsky Memorial Sports Journalism Scholarship • 1248
Charles Dubose Scholarship • 1286
Clauder Competition Prize • 408
Connecticut Building Congress Scholarships • 1313
CTAHPERD Gibson-Laemel Scholarship • 1319
Dr. and Mrs. Arthur F. Sullivan Fund • 1339
Dr. James L. Lawson Memorial Scholarship • 570
FMC Skaters Scholarship • 145
Jackson Laboratory Scholarship • 949
Karen Ann Shopis-Fox Memorial Scholarship • 1517
Lois Livingston McMillen Memorial Fund • 1546
Mary Benevento/CTAHPERD Scholarship • 1570
Milton Fisher Scholarship for Innovation and Creativity • 1603
New England FEMARA Scholarship • 672
New England Regional Student Program • 1645
New York Women in Communications Foundation Scholarships • 1658
Roberta B. Willis Scholarship - Need and Merit-Based Award • 1765
Roberta B. Willis Scholarship - Need-Based Award • 1766
SGT Felix M. Del Greco, Jr. Memorial Scholarship • 1785
SpeakOUT's LGBTQ+ Scholarship • 2249
Stephen Phillips Memorial Scholarship Fund • 1814
Timothy S. and Palmer W. Bigelow, Jr. Scholarship • 1147
Young Christian Leaders Scholarship • 2076

DC
DC Tuition Assistance Grant Program • 1324
District of Columbia Tuition Assistance Grant • 1333
Educational Training Voucher Programs for Foster Youth • 1355
Margaret A. Pemberton Scholarship • 1563
NACA Mid Atlantic Graduate Student Scholarship • 658
St. Andrew's Society of Washington, DC Scholarship • 2250

DELAWARE
Better Business Bureau of Delaware Foundation Student Ethics Scholarship • 1238
Career Based Scholarship • 1275
Charles L. Hebner Memorial Scholarship • 1287
Delaware Educational Benefits for Children of Deceased Veterans and Others • 1325
Delaware Scholarship Incentive Program • 1326
Delaware Solid Waste Authority John P. Pat Healy Scholarship • 1327
Educator Support Scholarship • 1356
Henry Belin du Pont Dissertation Fellowship • 601
Jimmy Rane Foundation Scholarships • 1494
Lou Manzione Scholarship • 206
Margaret A. Stafford Nursing Scholarship • 1564
NACA Mid Atlantic Graduate Student Scholarship • 658
St. Andrew's Society of Washington, DC Scholarship • 2250

FLORIDA
Access to Better Learning and Education Grant Program • 1183
American Legion Department of Florida General Scholarship • 1215
CDM Constructors Inc. Workforce Development Scholarship • 1281
Curwen-Guidry-Blackburn Scholarship Fund • 107
Dixie Boys Baseball Scholarship Program • 120
Dixie Youth Scholarship Program • 122
Family District 1 Scholarships • 1372
First Generation Matching Grant Program • 1375
Florida Bright Futures Scholarship Program • 1377
Florida Engineers in Construction Scholarship • 1378
Florida Governor's Black History Month Essay Contest • 1379
Florida Oratorical Contest • 1380
Florida Student Assistance Grant Program • 1381
IRARC Memorial, Joseph P. Rubino, WA4MMD, Scholarship • 615
James S. Davis Memorial Scholarship • 1490
Jimmy Rane Foundation Scholarships • 1494
Jose Marti Scholarship Challenge Grant • 1505
Kappa Delta Phi • 966
Lloyd F. Hutt Scholarship • 1544
NACA South Student Leadership Scholarships • 1633
Northrop Grumman Scholarship • 1681
Rosewood Family Scholarship Program • 1771
Roy W. Likins Scholarship • 1773
Shari Simon Greenberg Community Scholarship • 300
Sister Helen Marie Pellicer Scholarship • 1791
Southern Scholarship Foundation Scholarship • 1805
Werks Mobile Scholarship • 1899
William L. Boyd, IV, Effective Access to Student Education Program • 1912

GEORGIA
Ben W. Fortson, Jr., Scholarship • 1237
Charles Clarke Cordle Memorial Scholarship • 555
Curwen-Guidry-Blackburn Scholarship Fund • 107
Dixie Boys Baseball Scholarship Program • 120
Dixie Youth Scholarship Program • 122
Family District 1 Scholarships • 1372
Georgia HOPE GED Grant • 1395
Georgia HOPE Grant • 1396
Georgia Oratorical Contest • 1397
Georgia Press Educational Foundation Scholarships • 1398
Georgia Thespians Achievement Scholarships • 1399
Georgia Tuition Equalization Grant • 1400
Greenhouse Scholars Scholarship • 1413
HOPE Scholarship Program • 1447
James M. and Virginia M. Smyth Scholarship • 188
Jimmy Rane Foundation Scholarships • 1494
Judge William F. Cooper Scholarship • 1506
NACA South Student Leadership Scholarships • 1633
Nancy Penn Lyons Scholarship Fund • 1635
Spillman-Bischoff Scholarship • 1806
Tech High School Alumni Association/W.O. Cheney Merit Scholarship • 1828
Zell Miller Scholarship • 1929

HAWAII
Allan Eldin and Agnes Sutorik Geiger Scholarship Fund • 1200
Alma White - Delta Kappa Gamma Scholarship • 1204
Ambassador Minerva Jean Falcon Hawaii Scholarship • 1206
American Institute of Graphic Arts (AIGA) Honolulu Chapter Scholarship Fund • 1209
Atsuhiko Tateuchi Memorial Scholarship • 1232
Ben and Vicky Cayetano Scholarship Fund • 1236
Bick Bickson Scholarship Fund • 1240
Blossom Kalama Evans Memorial Scholarship Fund • 1242
Booz Allen Hawaii Scholarship Fund • 1249
California - Hawaii Elks Association Vocational Grants • 550
California - Hawaii Elks Major Project Undergraduate Scholarship Program for Students with Disabilities • 1260
Candon, Todd and Seabolt Scholarship Fund • 1271
Clem Judd, Jr., Memorial Scholarship • 1298
Community Scholarship Fund • 1310
Cora Aguda Manayan Fund • 1314
Doris and Clarence Glick Classical Music Scholarship • 1336
Dr. Edison and Sallie Miyawaki Scholarship Fund • 1340
Dr. Hans and Clara Zimmerman Foundation Education Scholarship • 1341

The Ultimate Scholarship Book 2026
State of Residence Index

Dr. Hans and Clara Zimmerman Foundation Health Scholarships • 1342
Duke Award Scholarship • 1345
Edward Payson and Bernice Piilani Irwin Scholarship • 1359
Eizo and Toyo Sakumoto Trust Scholarship • 1360
Ellison Onizuka Memorial Scholarship Fund • 1361
Esther Kanagawa Memorial Art Scholarship • 1367
F. Koehnen Ltd. Scholarship Fund • 1371
George Mason Business Scholarship Fund • 1394
Good Eats Scholarship Fund • 1404
Hawaii Community Foundation Scholarships • 1425
Hawaii High School Athletic Association Hall of Honor • 1426
Hawaii Pizza Hut Scholarship Fund • 1427
Hawaii Rotary Youth Foundation Scholarship • 1428
Hawaii Society of Certified Public Accountants Scholarship Fund • 1429
Henry A. Zuberano Scholarship • 1431
Hideko and Zenzo Matsuyama Scholarship Fund • 1438
Ho'omaka Hou - A New Beginning Fund • 1444
Johanna Drew Cluney Fund • 1497
John and Anne Clifton Scholarship • 1499
John Dawe Dental Education Fund • 1501
Laura N. Dowsett Fund • 1526
Mamoru and Aiko Takitani Foundation Scholarship • 1562
Marion Maccarrell Scott Scholarship • 1566
Mark Ando and Ito Family Scholarship • 2197
MGMA Western Section Scholarship • 1003
Mildred Towle Scholarship - Study Abroad • 1601
Mildred Towle Scholarship for African-Americans • 1602
Pauahi Foundation Public Scholarships • 1720
Paulina L. Sorg Scholarship • 1722
PRSA-Hawai'i/Roy Leffingwell Public Relations Scholarship • 1738
R.W. Bob Holden Scholarship • 1741
Raymond F. Cain Scholarship Fund • 1745
Ritchie M. Gregory Fund • 1760
Robanna Fund • 1762
Rosemary and Nellie Ebrie Fund • 1770
Shirley McKown Scholarship Fund • 1787
Shuichi, Katsu and Itsuyo Suga Scholarship • 1789
State of Hawai'i B Plus Scholarship • 1811
Tongan Cultural Society Scholarship • 1849
Tweet Coleman Aviation Scholarship • 1861
Ukulele Festival Hawaii's College Scholarship Program • 497
Victoria S. and Bradley L. Geist Foundation • 1878
William James and Dorothy Bading Lanquist Fund • 1911

IDAHO
Arc of Washington State Trust Fund Stipend Award • 1221
GEAR UP Idaho Scholarship 3 • 1391
Governor's Cup Scholarship • 1407
Idaho State Broadcasters Association Scholarships • 1455
Lori Rhett Memorial Scholarship • 1547
Mary Lou Brown Scholarship • 646
MGMA Western Section Scholarship • 1003

ILLINOIS
American Legion Department of Illinois Scholarship • 1216
Burlington Northern Santa Fe (BNSF) Foundation Scholarship • 2111
Cathay Bank Foundation Scholarship • 1279
Community Banker Association of Illinois Annual Eagle Scout Scholarship • 1250
Essay Scholarship Program • 1309
Dan L. Meisinger Sr. Memorial Learn to Fly Scholarship • 851
Edmond A. Metzger Scholarship • 575
Golden Apple Scholars of Illinois (Illinois Scholars Program) • 1402
Greenhouse Scholars Scholarship • 1413
Illinois AMVETS Ladies Auxiliary Memorial Scholarship • 1456
Illinois AMVETS Ladies Auxiliary Worchid Scholarship • 1457
Illinois AMVETS Sad Sacks Nursing Scholarship • 1458
Illinois AMVETS Service Foundation Scholarship • 1459
Illinois Association for Health, Physical Education, Recreation and Dance Scholarships • 1460
Illinois Department of Children and Family Services Scholarship Program • 1461
Illinois Veteran Grant Program • 1462
Iowa Student Loan Midwest Senior Scholarship • 185
James H. Dunn, Jr. Memorial Fellowship • 1488
James M. and Virginia M. Smyth Scholarship • 188
Mellinger Scholarships • 1588
MGMA Midwest Section Scholarship • 1002
Michael Curry Summer Internship Program • 1591
Monetary Award Program (MAP) • 1623
Northrop Grumman Scholarship • 1681
Nursing Education Scholarship Program • 1682
Our First Amendment Freedoms Art and Essay Contest • 1710
Richard D. Wiegers Scholarship • 1757
Scholarships in Mathematics Education • 1782
Six Meter Club of Chicago Scholarship • 1793
Township Officials of Illinois Scholarship-Undergraduate Scholarship • 1853
Werks Mobile Scholarship • 1899

INDIANA
Anthony Munoz Scholarship Fund • 1219
David E. Simon Scholarship • 1323
Edmond A. Metzger Scholarship • 575
Indiana Broadcasters Association College Scholarships • 1465
Indiana Golf Foundation Scholarship • 1466
Indiana Oratorical Contest • 1467
Jean Lee/Jeff Marvin Collegiate Scholarships • 1492
Kappa Delta Phi • 966
Lilly Endowment Community Scholarship Program • 1540
Linda Craig Memorial Scholarship Presented by St. Vincent Sports Performance • 1542
Louis B. Russell Scholarship • 1550
Mexican Scholarship Fund • 1589
MGMA Midwest Section Scholarship • 1002
Mitch Daniels Early Graduation Scholarship • 1621
NADCA Indiana Chapter 25 Scholarship • 1634
Our First Amendment Freedoms Art and Essay Contest • 1710
Shari Simon Greenberg Community Scholarship • 300
Shook Construction Harry F. Gaeke Memorial Scholarship • 1788
Twenty-first Century Scholars Program • 1862
William A. Crawford Minority Teacher Scholarship • 1906

IOWA
AFS Twin City Memorial Scholarship • 1187
All Iowa Opportunity Scholarship • 1199
Ann Griffel Scholarship • 1218
Association of Information Technology Professionals (AITP) Scholarships • 814
Burlington Northern Santa Fe (BNSF) Foundation Scholarship • 2111
Byers Scholarship • 1254
Future Ready Iowa Grant • 1389
Future Ready Iowa Last-Dollar Scholarship • 1390
H.L. Taylor Scholarship Program • 1419
Herbert Hoover Uncommon Student Award • 1434
Herman Sani Scholarship • 1436
IAD Foundation Scholarships • 1453
ICCA Scholarships • 1454
Iowa 4-H College Scholarships • 1469
Iowa Newspaper Association Scholarships • 1470
Iowa Oratorical Contest • 1471
Iowa PGA Foundation Charlie Burkart Scholarship • 1472
Iowa Physician Assistant Society Scholarship • 1473
Iowa Pork Foundation Scholarship • 1474
Iowa Scholarship for the Arts • 1475
Iowa Thespian Chapter Board Senior Scholarships • 1476
Iowa Tuition Grants • 1477
Iowa Vocational-Technical Tuition Grants • 1478
ISAA Scholarship Program • 1480
James B. Morris Scholarship • 1487
Jimmy Rane Foundation Scholarships • 1494
Kappa Delta Phi • 966
Kibbie Grant (Iowa Skilled Workforce Shortage Tuition Grant) • 1522
Leo H. Grether Memorial Scholarship • 1536
Masonic Scholarship Program • 1574
Masonry Institute of Iowa Foundation Scholarship Program • 1575
MCEC Technical Scholarship • 1583
Mellinger Scholarships • 1588
MFA Foundation Scholarships • 1590
MGMA Midwest Section Scholarship • 1002
Paul and Helen L. Grauer Scholarship • 681
PHD Scholarship • 685
Ray, N0RP and Katie, W0KTE Pautz Scholarship • 694
Robert D. Blue Scholarship • 1763
Russ Brannen/KENT FEEDS Memorial Beef Scholarship • 1774
Schlutz Family Beef Breeding Scholarship • 1778
UMSA Foundation Scholarship Program • 1864
Upper Midwest Chapter Scholarships • 1867
Winner's Circle Scholarships • 1914

The Ultimate Scholarship Book 2026
State of Residence Index

Kansas
Albert M. Lappin Scholarship • 1197
Association of Information Technology Professionals (AITP) Scholarships • 814
Burlington Northern Santa Fe (BNSF) Foundation Scholarship • 2111
Charles W. and Annette Hill Scholarship • 1288
Dan L. Meisinger Sr. Memorial Learn to Fly Scholarship • 851
Harriet Hayes Austin Memorial Scholarship for Nursing • 1421
Hugh A. Smith Scholarship Fund • 1452
Irving W. Cook, WA0CGS, Scholarship • 1479
Jimmy Rane Foundation Scholarships • 1494
KAB Broadcast Scholarship Program • 1507
Kansas Agricultural Aviation Association Scholarship • 1508
Kansas Career Technical Workforce Grant • 1509
Kansas Comprehensive Grants • 1510
Kansas Ethnic Minority Scholarship • 1511
Kansas Nursing Service Scholarship • 1512
Kansas Oratorical Contest • 1513
Kansas Osteopathic Medical Service Scholarship • 1514
Kansas State Scholarship • 1515
Kansas Teacher Service Scholarship • 1516
MFA Foundation Scholarships • 1590
Midwest Student Exchange Program • 1599
Music Committee Scholarship • 1630
Paul and Helen L. Grauer Scholarship • 681
Paul Flaherty Athletic Scholarship • 1721
PHD Scholarship • 685
Ray, N0RP and Katie, W0KTE Pautz Scholarship • 694
Rosedale Post 346 Scholarship • 1769
Shari Simon Greenberg Community Scholarship • 300
Ted and Nora Anderson Scholarships • 1830

Kentucky
Anthony Munoz Scholarship Fund • 1219
Business and Professional Women of Kentucky Foundation Grant • 1252
College Access Program • 1300
Curwen-Guidry-Blackburn Scholarship Fund • 107
Educational Excellence Scholarship • 1353
Exemption from Tuition Fees for Dependents of Kentucky Veterans • 1370
Harry Barfield KBA Scholarship Program • 1423
Jimmy Rane Foundation Scholarships • 1494
Kappa Delta Phi • 966
Kentucky Tuition Grant • 1520
Kentucky Veterans Tuition Waiver Program • 1521
Nursing Incentive Scholarship Fund • 1683
Shook Construction Harry F. Gaeke Memorial Scholarship • 1788
Teacher Scholarship Program • 1826
Thaddeus Colson and Isabelle Saalwaechter Fitzpatrick Memorial Scholarship • 1848
Zagunis Student Leader Scholarship • 1928

Louisiana
Burlington Northern Santa Fe (BNSF) Foundation Scholarship • 2111
Curwen-Guidry-Blackburn Scholarship Fund • 107
Dixie Boys Baseball Scholarship Program • 120
Dixie Youth Scholarship Program • 122
Dr. William S. Boyd Scholarship • 1344
Fred R. McDaniel Memorial Scholarship • 583
Honors Award • 1446
Jimmy Rane Foundation Scholarships • 1494
Louisiana Go Grant • 1551
Louisiana Memorial Scholarship • 1552
Markley Scholarship • 211
Opportunity Award • 1704
Rockefeller State Wildlife Scholarship • 1767
TOPS Performance Award • 1850
TOPS Tech Award • 1851

Maine
Business and Professional Women/Maine Continuing Education Scholarship • 1253
Career Advancement Scholarship • 1274
Children and Youth Scholarships • 1291
Clauder Competition Prize • 408
Daniel E. Lambert Memorial Scholarship • 1321
Dr. James L. Lawson Memorial Scholarship • 570
Early College for ME • 1349
Educators for Maine Program • 1357
FMC Skaters Scholarship • 145
HospitalityMaine Scholarship • 1448
Jackson Laboratory Scholarship • 949
James V. Day Scholarship • 1491
Lemieux-Lovejoy Youth Scholarship • 1534
Maine Community Foundation Scholarship Program • 1556
Maine Demolay and Pine Tree Youth Foundation Scholarships • 1557
Maine Health Professionals Loan Program • 1558
Maine State Society Foundation Scholarship • 1559
Maine Veterans Dependents Educational Benefits • 1560
Mitchell Scholarship • 1622
New England FEMARA Scholarship • 672
New England Regional Student Program • 1645
SpeakOUT's LGBTQ+ Scholarship • 2249
State of Maine Grant Program • 1812
Stephen Phillips Memorial Scholarship Fund • 1814
Timothy S. and Palmer W. Bigelow, Jr. Scholarship • 1147
Unitil Scholarship Fund • 1865
Vernon T. Swain, P.E./Robert E. Chute, P.E. Scholarship • 1875

Maryland
Carville M. Akehurst Memorial Scholarship • 836
Cathay Bank Foundation Scholarship • 1279
Charles W. Riley Fire and Emergency Medical Services Scholarship Program • 1289
Delegate Scholarship • 1328
Educational Training Voucher Programs for Foster Youth • 1355
Gary Wagner, K3OMI, Scholarship • 903
Howard P. Rawlings Educational Assistance (EA) Grant • 1450
Howard P. Rawlings Guaranteed Access (GA) Grant • 1451
Jack F. Tolbert Memorial Student Grant Program • 1484
Jimmy Rane Foundation Scholarships • 1494
NACA Mid Atlantic Graduate Student Scholarship • 658
Northrop Grumman Scholarship • 1681
Part-Time Grant • 1714
Senatorial Scholarship • 1784
St. Andrew's Society of Washington, DC Scholarship • 2250
Tuition Reduction for Non-Resident Nursing Students • 1858
Tuition Waiver for Foster Care Recipients • 1859
Workforce Shortage Student Assistance Grant Program • 1923

Massachusetts
AGC of Massachusetts Scholarships • 1189
Agnes M. Lindsay Scholarship • 1191
Big Y Scholarship Programs • 1241
Cash Grant Program • 1277
Categorical Tuition Waiver • 1278
Cathay Bank Foundation Scholarship • 1279
Christian A. Herter Memorial Scholarship Program • 1294
Clauder Competition Prize • 408
Collaborative Teachers Tuition Waiver • 1299
Department of Children and Families (DCF) Foster Child Tuition Waiver and Fee Assistance Program • 1330
Dr. James L. Lawson Memorial Scholarship • 570
Early Childhood Educators Scholarship • 1348
FMC Skaters Scholarship • 145
Foster Child Grant Program • 1383
Gilbert Matching Student Grant • 1401
Graduate Tuition Waiver • 1410
High Technology Scholar/Intern Tuition Waiver • 1440
Incentive Program for Aspiring Teachers • 1463
John and Abigail Adams Scholarship • 1498
MARILN Professional Scholarship Award • 1565
Massachusetts Community Colleges Access Grant • 1576
Massachusetts Part-Time Grant • 1577
Massachusetts Student Broadcaster Scholarship • 1578
MASSGrant • 1579
MEFA UPlan Prepaid Tuition Waiver Program • 1587
Need Based Tuition Waiver Program • 1643
New England FEMARA Scholarship • 672
New England Regional Student Program • 1645
One Family Scholars Program • 1703
Paraprofessional Teacher Preparation Grant • 1713
SpeakOUT's LGBTQ+ Scholarship • 2249
Stanley Z. Koplik Certificate of Mastery Tuition Waiver Program • 1808
Stephen Phillips Memorial Scholarship Fund • 1814
Timothy S. and Palmer W. Bigelow, Jr. Scholarship • 1147
Unitil Scholarship Fund • 1865
Valedictorian Program Tuition Waiver • 1871

Michigan
CCCAM Scholarships • 1280
CEW+ Scholarships • 1285

The Ultimate Scholarship Book 2026
State of Residence Index

Guy M. Wilson Scholarship • 1416
Independence Excavating, A DiGeronimo Company Scholarship • 1464
Julius and Esther Stulberg International String Competition • 449
Leaders Advancing and Helping Communities Scholarship • 1529
Lloyd F. Hutt Scholarship • 1544
Mackinac Scholarship • 1555
Marvin L. Zuidema Scholarship Award • 1568
MGMA Midwest Section Scholarship • 1002
Michigan Competitive Scholarship • 1592
Michigan Council of Women in Technology University Scholarship • 1593
Michigan Engineering Scholarships • 1594
Michigan Oratorical Contest • 1595
Michigan Tuition Grant • 1596
Michigan Tuition Incentive Program • 1597
MSPE Kenneth B. Fishbeck, P.E., Memorial Grant • 1628
Raymond J. Faust Scholarship • 1746
Robert R. Robinson Memorial Scholarship • 1764
Rosa L. Parks Scholarships • 1768
William D. and Jewell Brewer Scholarship • 1909
Zagunis Student Leader Scholarship • 1928

MINNESOTA
AFS Twin City Memorial Scholarship • 1187
Alliss Opportunity Grant Program for Adults Returning to College • 1203
Associated General Contractors of Minnesota Scholarships • 1230
Burlington Northern Santa Fe (BNSF) Foundation Scholarship • 2111
Iowa Student Loan Midwest Senior Scholarship • 185
MGMA Midwest Section Scholarship • 1002
Midwest Student Exchange Program • 1599
Minnesota Academic Excellence Scholarship • 1604
Minnesota Division Izaak Walton League Scholarship • 1605
Minnesota Hockey Scholarship • 1606
Minnesota Indian Scholarship Program • 1607
Minnesota Masonic Charities Vocational Scholarship • 1608
Minnesota Oratorical Contest • 1609
Minnesota State Grant • 1610
MSAA Scholarship Program • 1627
Our First Amendment Freedoms Art and Essay Contest • 1710
Page Education Foundation Grants • 1711
Ranelius Scholarship Program • 1743
UMSA Foundation Scholarship Program • 1864
Upper Midwest Chapter Scholarships • 1867
WTS Minnesota Chapter Scholarships • 1925

MISSISSIPPI
Curwen-Guidry-Blackburn Scholarship Fund • 107
Dixie Boys Baseball Scholarship Program • 120
Dixie Youth Scholarship Program • 122
Family District 1 Scholarships • 1372
Fred R. McDaniel Memorial Scholarship • 583
Higher Education Legislative Plan (HELP) • 1443
James M. and Virginia M. Smyth Scholarship • 188
Jimmy Rane Foundation Scholarships • 1494

Mississippi Association of Broadcasters Scholarship Program • 1614
Mississippi Eminent Scholars Grant (MESG) • 1615
Mississippi Scholarship • 1616
Mississippi Tuition Assistance Grant (MTAG) • 1617
NACA South Student Leadership Scholarships • 1633
Nissan Scholarship • 1660

MISSOURI
Association of Information Technology Professionals (AITP) Scholarships • 814
Burlington Northern Santa Fe (BNSF) Foundation Scholarship • 2111
Dan L. Meisinger Sr. Memorial Learn to Fly Scholarship • 851
Educational Training Voucher Programs for Foster Youth • 1355
Higher Education Academic Scholarship Program (Bright Flight) • 1441
Iowa Student Loan Midwest Senior Scholarship • 185
J.R. Popalisky Scholarship • 1482
James M. and Virginia M. Smyth Scholarship • 188
Jimmy Rane Foundation Scholarships • 1494
Kappa Delta Phi • 966
MFA Foundation Scholarships • 1590
Midwest Student Exchange Program • 1599
Missouri 4-H Foundation Scholarships • 1618
Missouri Oratorical Contest • 1619
Missouri State Thespian Scholarships • 1620
Paul and Helen L. Grauer Scholarship • 681
PHD Scholarship • 685
Ray, N0RP and Katie, W0KTE Pautz Scholarship • 694
Ruth Lutes Bachmann Scholarship • 1775

MONTANA
Burlington Northern Santa Fe (BNSF) Foundation Scholarship • 2111
Dennis Schoepp Memorial Scholarship • 1329
Lori Rhett Memorial Scholarship • 1547
Mary Lou Brown Scholarship • 646
MGMA Western Section Scholarship • 1003
Montana CattleWomen Scholarship • 1624
Montana University System Honor Scholarship • 1625
Reach Higher Montana Scholarships • 1750
T. Eugene Young Montana's Promise Scholarship • 1822
Treacy Foundation Scholarship • 1854
William and Sara Jenne' Scholarship • 1908

NEBRASKA
Access College Early Scholarship • 1182
Association of Information Technology Professionals (AITP) Scholarships • 814
Burlington Northern Santa Fe (BNSF) Foundation Scholarship • 2111
C. Bertrand and Marian Othmer Schultz Collegiate Scholarship • 1255
Iowa Student Loan Midwest Senior Scholarship • 185
Jimmy Rane Foundation Scholarships • 1494
MGMA Midwest Section Scholarship • 1002
Midwest Student Exchange Program • 1599

NDVA Waiver of Tuition • 1638
Nebraska Academy of Sciences High School Scholarships • 1639
Nebraska Actuaries Club Scholarship • 1640
Nebraska Elks Association Vocational Scholarship • 1641
Norman and Ruth Good Educational Endowment • 1667
Oratorical Contest Scholarship • 1706
Paul and Helen L. Grauer Scholarship • 681
PHD Scholarship • 685
Ray, N0RP and Katie, W0KTE Pautz Scholarship • 694
Smith Diversity Scholarship • 1795
Susan Thompson Buffett Foundation Scholarship Program • 1820
Wallace S. and Wilma K. Laughlin Foundation Trust Scholarships • 1889

NEVADA
Burlington Northern Santa Fe (BNSF) Foundation Scholarship • 2111
Cathay Bank Foundation Scholarship • 1279
Governor Guinn Millennium Scholarship Program • 1406
Jack Hughes Education Scholarship • 1485
Mark Ando and Ito Family Scholarship • 2197
MGMA Western Section Scholarship • 1003
Nevada Women's Fund Scholarships • 1644
New York Life Award • 466
Sons of Italy Grand Lodge of California Italian Language Study Grant • 1798
Sons of Italy Grand Lodge of College Scholarship • 1799

NEW HAMPSHIRE
Certificate, License or Other Industry-Recognized Credential • 1283
Clauder Competition Prize • 408
Dr. James L. Lawson Memorial Scholarship • 570
FMC Skaters Scholarship • 145
Four-year or Bachelor's Degree Program • 1384
Harry Alan Gregg Foundation Grants • 1422
Mary Eileen Dixey Scholarship • 1571
Master's, Ph.D. or Other Advanced Degree Program • 1580
Medallion Fund • 1585
New England FEMARA Scholarship • 672
New England Regional Student Program • 1645
New Hampshire Charitable Foundation Statewide Student Aid Program • 1646
Plan NH Scholarship and Fellowship Program • 1737
SpeakOUT's LGBTQ+ Scholarship • 2249
Stephen Phillips Memorial Scholarship Fund • 1814
Timothy S. and Palmer W. Bigelow, Jr. Scholarship • 1147
Two-year or Associate Degree Program • 1863
Unitil Scholarship Fund • 1865

NEW JERSEY
American Council of Engineering Companies of New Jersey Member Organization Scholarship • 1207
Bob Stevens Memorial Scholarship • 1245
Cathay Bank Foundation Scholarship • 1279

Clanseer and Anna Johnson Scholarships • 1297
Educational Opportunity Fund (EOF) Grant • 1354
Herb It Forward Scholarship • 1433
Jimmy Rane Foundation Scholarships • 1494
Lou Manzione Scholarship • 206
NACA Mid Atlantic Graduate Student Scholarship • 658
New Jersey Oratorical Contest • 1647
New Jersey State Elks Special Children's Committee Scholarship • 1648
New Jersey World Trade Center Scholarship • 1649
New York Life Award • 466
New York Women in Communications Foundation Scholarships • 1658
NJ Student Tuition Assistance Reward Scholarship (STARS) • 1661
NJ Student Tuition Assistance Reward Scholarship II • 1662
NJCDCA Scholarship • 1663
NJSCA High School Scholarship • 1664
Part-Time Tuition Aid Grant • 1717
Safety Essay Contest • 1776
St. Andrew's Society of Washington, DC Scholarship • 2250
Ted Brickley/Bernice Shickora Scholarship • 1831
Tuition Aid Grant • 1855
Urban Scholars Award • 1868
Young Christian Leaders Scholarship • 2076

New Mexico
Allan Johnston Memorial Scholarship • 1201
Burlington Northern Santa Fe (BNSF) Foundation Scholarship • 2111
Competitive Scholarships • 1311
Daniels Scholarship Program • 1322
Four-Year Undergraduate Scholarships • 1385
Fred R. McDaniel Memorial Scholarship • 583
Legislative Lottery Scholarships • 1533
Los Alamos Employees' Scholarship • 1548
Markley Scholarship • 211
Medical Loan-For-Service Program • 1586
MGMA Western Section Scholarship • 1003
New Mexico Scholars • 1650
NMASBO High School Scholarships • 1665
NNM American Society of Mechanical Engineers Scholarship • 1666
Nursing Loan-For-Service Program • 1684
Rae Lee Siporin Award • 1742
Society of American Military Engineers, Albuquerque Post Scholarship • 1797
Student Incentive Grants • 1817
Sussman-Miller Educational Assistance Award • 1821
Teacher Loan-For-Service Program • 1825
Vietnam Veterans' Scholarship • 1879
William and Gertrude Fradkin Memorial Scholarship • 1907

New York
Aid for Part-Time Study • 1192
Cathay Bank Foundation Scholarship • 1279
Dr. James L. Lawson Memorial Scholarship • 570
Educational Award/Graduating High School Female • 1352
Fellowship on Women and Public Policy • 1373
Greenhouse Scholars Scholarship • 1413
Jimmy Rane Foundation Scholarships • 1494
Mary Ann K. Murtha Memorial Scholarship • 1569
Math and Science Teaching Incentive Scholarships • 1581
NACA Mid Atlantic Graduate Student Scholarship • 658
New York Legion Auxiliary Department Scholarship • 1651
New York Legion Auxiliary District Scholarships • 1652
New York Oratorical Contest • 1653
New York State Association of Agricultural Fairs/New York State Showpeople's Association Scholarships • 1654
New York State Society of Physician Assistants Scholarship • 1655
New York State USBC Scholarships • 1656
New York State USBC Spirit Awards • 1657
New York Women in Communications Foundation Scholarships • 1658
Northrop Grumman Scholarship • 1681
NYWEA Major Environmental Career Scholarship • 1686
Part-Time TAP Program • 1716
Raymond T. Wellington, Jr. Memorial Scholarship • 1747
Scholarships for Academic Excellence • 1781
Senator Patricia K. McGee Nursing Faculty Scholarship • 1783
Tuition Assistance Program (TAP) • 1856
Veterans Tuition Awards • 1876
Werks Mobile Scholarship • 1899
World Trade Center Memorial Scholarship • 1924
Young Christian Leaders Scholarship • 2076

North Carolina
Crumley Roberts Next Step Scholarship • 1317
Dixie Boys Baseball Scholarship Program • 120
Dixie Youth Scholarship Program • 122
Educational Training Voucher Programs for Foster Youth • 1355
Epsilon Sigma Alpha • 1365
Gary Wagner, K3OMI, Scholarship • 903
Golden LEAF Scholars Program - Two-Year Colleges • 1403
Greenhouse Scholars Scholarship • 1413
Jimmy Rane Foundation Scholarships • 1494
L. Phil and Alice J. Wicker Scholarship • 631
NACA South Student Leadership Scholarships • 1633
NCAPA Endowment Annual Student Grants • 1035
NCRA Scholarship • 1637
North Carolina 4-H Development Fund Scholarships • 1669
North Carolina Community College Grant • 1670
North Carolina Education Lottery Scholarship • 1671
North Carolina Oratorical Contest • 1672
Oliver Joel and Ellen Pell Denny Healthcare Scholarship Fund • 1702
R. Flake Shaw Scholarship • 1739
Richard Goolsby Scholarship Fund • 1759
St. Andrew's Society of Washington, DC Scholarship • 2250

North Dakota
Association of Information Technology Professionals (AITP) Scholarships • 814
Burlington Northern Santa Fe (BNSF) Foundation Scholarship • 2111
Hattie Tedrow Memorial Fund Scholarship • 1424
KEM Electric Cooperative Scholarships for Students Attending High School Outside the Service Area • 1519
MGMA Midwest Section Scholarship • 1002
Midwest Student Exchange Program • 1599
North Dakota Career Builders Scholarship • 1673
North Dakota Dollars for Scholars • 1674
North Dakota Jaycee JCI Senate Scholarship • 1675
North Dakota Scholars Program • 1676
North Dakota Scholarship • 1677
North Dakota School Counseling Association • 1678
North Dakota State Student Incentive Grant • 1679
Our First Amendment Freedoms Art and Essay Contest • 1710
UMSA Foundation Scholarship Program • 1864
Upper Midwest Chapter Scholarships • 1867

Ohio
AGC of Ohio Scholarships • 1190
Anthony Munoz Scholarship Fund • 1219
Choose Ohio First Scholarship • 1293
Educational Training Voucher Programs for Foster Youth • 1355
Engineers Foundation of Ohio General Fund Scholarship • 1364
Fields of Learning Scholarship • 1374
Independence Excavating, A DiGeronimo Company Scholarship • 1464
Jimmy Rane Foundation Scholarships • 1494
Kappa Delta Phi • 966
Kokosing Construction Co. Scholarship • 1524
Lila M. Van Sweringen Student Scholarship • 1539
MGMA Midwest Section Scholarship • 1002
Midwest Student Exchange Program • 1599
Minority Scholarship • 1611
New York Life Award • 466
Northrop Grumman Scholarship • 1681
Ohio Classical Conference Scholarship for Prospective Latin Teachers • 1687
Ohio Section Scholarships • 1688
Ohio State Association/AOTF Scholarships • 1689
Ohio Turfgrass Foundation Scholarships • 1690
Shari Simon Greenberg Community Scholarship • 300
Shook Construction Harry F. Gaeke Memorial Scholarship • 1788
Tuttle Construction Inc. Tiny Rauch Scholarship • 1860
University Journalism Scholarships • 1866
Zagunis Student Leader Scholarship • 1928

Oklahoma
Academic Scholars Program • 1181
Burlington Northern Santa Fe (BNSF) Foundation Scholarship • 2111
Chiropractic Education Assistance Scholarship • 1292

Communities Foundation of Oklahoma Scholarships • 1308
Frances Koop Parsons/AT&T Pioneers Memorial Scholarship • 1386
Fred R. McDaniel Memorial Scholarship • 583
George and Donna Nigh Public Service Scholarship • 1393
GPB Art Harris Scholarship • 1409
H. W. Almen/West OKC Rotary Scholarship • 1418
High School Senior Essay Contest • 1439
Inspired to Teach • 1468
James Anderson Logan Jr. and Betty Ann McFarland Logan Scholarship Fund • 1486
James M. and Virginia M. Smyth Scholarship • 188
Jimmie L. Dean Scholarship • 1493
Jimmy Rane Foundation Scholarships • 1494
Laurene Ann Opdyke Nursing Scholarship • 1527
Markley Scholarship • 211
May T. Henry Scholarship Fund • 1582
MFA Foundation Scholarships • 1590
Oklahoma Association of Broadcasters Scholarship • 1691
Oklahoma Foundation for Excellence Academic All-State Scholarships • 1692
Oklahoma Hall of Fame Scholarship • 1693
Oklahoma Rural Rehabilitation Corporation Scholarships • 1694
Oklahoma Schools Insurance Group (OSIG) Scholarship • 1695
Oklahoma Society of Land Surveyors Scholarships • 1696
Oklahoma State Fair Inc. Scholarship Program • 1697
Oklahoma Tuition Aid Grant Program (OTAG) • 1698
Oklahoma Tuition Equalization Grant Program (OTEG) • 1699
Oklahoma Youth with Promise Scholarship Fund • 1700
Oklahoma's Promise • 1701
OROS Scholarship • 1709
Reach Higher Finish Line Scholarship • 1749
Regional University Baccalaureate Scholarship • 1752
Scholars for Excellence in Child Care • 1780
Teacher Shortage Employment Incentive Program • 1827
Tom and Judith Comstock Scholarship • 724

Oregon
Arc of Washington State Trust Fund Stipend Award • 1221
Atsuhiko Tateuchi Memorial Scholarship • 1232
Burlington Northern Santa Fe (BNSF) Foundation Scholarship • 2111
Confederation of Oregon School Administrators Scholarships • 1312
COSA Youth Development Program Scholarships • 1315
Ford Opportunity Program • 1382
Incight Scholarship • 2301
Lori Rhett Memorial Scholarship • 1547
Mary Lou Brown Scholarship • 646
MGMA Western Section Scholarship • 1003
Oregon Army National Guard • 1707

Oregon Farm Bureau Memorial Scholarships • 1708
Retail Chapter Award II and III • 1753

Pennsylvania
Herb It Forward Scholarship • 1433
Hermine Solt Student Scholarship • 1437
Independence Excavating, A DiGeronimo Company Scholarship • 1464
Jack E. Barger, Sr. Memorial Nursing Scholarship • 1483
Jimmy Rane Foundation Scholarships • 1494
Lou Manzione Scholarship • 206
McLean Scholarship for Nursing and Physician Assistant Majors • 1584
NACA Mid Atlantic Graduate Student Scholarship • 658
Nathaniel Alston Student Achievement Award • 1636
New York Women in Communications Foundation Scholarships • 1658
Nightingale Awards of Pennsylvania Scholarship • 1659
Pennsylvania American Legion Essay Contest • 1723
Pennsylvania Business Education Association Scholarship • 1724
Pennsylvania Educational Gratuity Program • 1725
Pennsylvania Land Surveyors' Foundation Scholarship • 1726
Pennsylvania Masonic Youth Foundation Scholarships • 1727
Pennsylvania Oratorical Contest • 1728
Pennsylvania Society of Tax and Accounting Professionals Scholarships • 1729
Pennsylvania State Bowling Association Scholarship Program • 1730
Pennsylvania State Grant Program • 1731
Pennsylvania Targeted Industry Program • 1732
PenSPRA Scholarship • 1733
Road to Safety Scholarship Contest • 1761
Shari Simon Greenberg Community Scholarship • 300
St. Andrew's Society of Washington, DC Scholarship • 2250
You've Got a Friend in Pennsylvania Scholarship • 1927
Zagunis Student Leader Scholarship • 1928

Puerto Rico
NACA South Student Leadership Scholarships • 1633

Rhode Island
Albert E. and Florence W. Newton Nursing Scholarship • 1196
Antonio Cirino Memorial Scholarship • 1220
Clauder Competition Prize • 408
Dr. James L. Lawson Memorial Scholarship • 570
FMC Skaters Scholarship • 145
Frances L. Macartney Porter Fund • 1387
James J. Burns and C.A. Haynes Textile Scholarship • 1489
Lily and Catello Sorrentino Memorial Scholarship • 1541
MARILN Professional Scholarship Award • 1565
New England FEMARA Scholarship • 672
New England Regional Student Program • 1645

Patty and Melvin Alperin First Generation Scholarship • 1719
Rhode Island Foundation Association of Former Legislators Scholarship • 1754
Rhode Island Promise Scholarship • 1755
SpeakOUT's LGBTQ+ Scholarship • 2249
Stephen Phillips Memorial Scholarship Fund • 1814
Timothy S. and Palmer W. Bigelow, Jr. Scholarship • 1147

South Carolina
Archibald Rutledge Scholarship Program • 1222
Crumley Roberts Next Step Scholarship • 1317
Dixie Boys Baseball Scholarship Program • 120
Dixie Youth Scholarship Program • 122
Family District 1 Scholarships • 1372
Jimmy Rane Foundation Scholarships • 1494
Kathryn D. Sullivan Earth and Marine Science Fellowship • 1518
Kittie M. Fairey Educational Fund Scholarships • 1523
L. Phil and Alice J. Wicker Scholarship • 631
Legislative for Future Excellence (LIFE) Scholarship Program • 1532
Lottery Tuition Assistance Program • 1549
NACA South Student Leadership Scholarships • 1633
Palmetto Fellows Scholarship Program • 1712
South Carolina Farm Bureau Foundation Scholarships • 1800
South Carolina Hope Scholarship • 1801
South Carolina Nurses Foundation Nurses Care Scholarship • 1802
South Carolina Tuition Grants Program • 1803
State Need-based Grants • 1810
Willa S. Bellamy Scholarship • 1904

South Dakota
Association of Information Technology Professionals (AITP) Scholarships • 814
Burlington Northern Santa Fe (BNSF) Foundation Scholarship • 2111
Iowa Student Loan Midwest Senior Scholarship • 185
Joe Foss, An American Hero Scholarship • 1496
Marlin R. Scarborough Memorial Scholarship • 1567
MGMA Midwest Section Scholarship • 1002
Our First Amendment Freedoms Art and Essay Contest • 1710
Sioux Falls Area Retired Teachers Scholarship • 1790
South Dakota Free Tuition for Veterans and Others Who Performed War Service • 1804
UMSA Foundation Scholarship Program • 1864
Upper Midwest Chapter Scholarships • 1867

Tennessee
Aspire Award • 1227
Curwen-Guidry-Blackburn Scholarship Fund • 107
Cynthia and Alan Baran Fine Arts and Music Scholarship Fund • 1320
Dixie Boys Baseball Scholarship Program • 120
Dixie Youth Scholarship Program • 122
Family District 1 Scholarships • 1372
Gary Wagner, K3OMI, Scholarship • 903

General Assembly Merit Scholarship • 1392
Helping Heroes Grant • 1430
James M. and Virginia M. Smyth Scholarship • 188
Jimmy Rane Foundation Scholarships • 1494
Minority Teaching Fellows Program • 1612
NACA South Student Leadership Scholarships • 1633
Ned McWherter Scholars Program • 1642
New York Life Award • 466
Shipley Rose Buckner Memorial Scholarship • 1786
Tennessee Funeral Directors Association Memorial Scholarship • 1832
Tennessee HOPE Lottery Scholarship • 1833
Tennessee Student Assistance Awards • 1834

Texas
A.D. Osherman Scholarship Fund • 1178
BAFTX Undergraduate Award • 1235
Bob C. Powers Scholarship • 1243
Burlington Northern Santa Fe (BNSF) Foundation Scholarship • 2111
Career Colleges and Schools of Texas Scholarship Program • 1276
Cathay Bank Foundation Scholarship • 1279
CDM Constructors Inc. Workforce Development Scholarship • 1281
Collegiate Scholarship • 1302
Courageous Heart Scholarship • 1316
Curwen-Guidry-Blackburn Scholarship Fund • 107
Dixie Boys Baseball Scholarship Program • 120
Dixie Youth Scholarship Program • 122
Don't Mess with Texas Scholarship • 1334
Exemption for Highest Ranking High School Graduate • 1368
Exemption for Texas Veterans (Hazelwood Exemption) • 1369
First-Year Teacher Scholarships • 1376
Fred R. McDaniel Memorial Scholarship • 583
H-E-B Scholarships for UIL Participants • 1417
Herman J. Smith Scholarship • 1435
Houston Livestock Show and Rodeo Scholarships • 1449
Ivomec Generations of Excellence Internship and Scholarship Program • 1481
James M. and Virginia M. Smyth Scholarship • 188
Jimmy Rane Foundation Scholarships • 1494
Markley Scholarship • 211
Mary E. Bivins Religious Scholarship • 2011
Moody Scholar Program • 1626
Murray Watson Jr. Scholarship • 1629
New York Life Award • 466
North Texas State Fair Association Scholarship • 1680
Ray Anthony Peacock Scholarship • 1744
Shari Simon Greenberg Community Scholarship • 300
Susan Howard Community Service Award • 1819
Technical Certification Scholarship • 1829
Texas 4-H Opportunity Scholarship Program - Baccalaureate Scholarships • 1836
Texas Association FCCLA Regional Scholarship • 1837
Texas Broadcast Education Foundation Scholarships • 1838
Texas Elks State Association Four-Year Scholarship Program • 1839
Texas Elks State Association Teenager of the Year Scholarship • 1840
Texas Elks State Association Vocational Grant Program • 1841
Texas Fifth-Year Accounting Student Scholarship Program • 1842
Texas History Essay Scholarship • 1843
Texas International Fishing Tournament Inc. Scholarship • 1844
Texas Occupational Therapy Association Scholarships • 1845
Texas Oratorical Contest • 1846
Texas Public Educational Grant • 1847
Tom and Judith Comstock Scholarship • 724
Towards EXcellence, Access and Success (TEXAS) Grant Program • 1852
Tuition Equalization Grant Program • 1857
Werks Mobile Scholarship • 1899
Women in STEM Award • 1922

Utah
Burlington Northern Santa Fe (BNSF) Foundation Scholarship • 2111
Daniels Scholarship Program • 1322
Gump and Ayers Scholarship • 1415
MGMA Western Section Scholarship • 1003
Northrop Grumman Scholarship • 1681
Sterling Scholar Awards of Utah • 1815
Terrel H. Bell Education Scholarship • 1835
Utah Association of Independent Insurance Agents Scholarship • 1869
Utah Young Humanitarian Award • 1870

Vermont
Clauder Competition Prize • 408
Dr. James L. Lawson Memorial Scholarship • 570
FMC Skaters Scholarship • 145
Mabel Mayforth Scholarship • 1554
New England FEMARA Scholarship • 672
New England Regional Student Program • 1645
Part-Time Grants • 1715
SpeakOUT's LGBTQ+ Scholarship • 2249
Stephen Phillips Memorial Scholarship Fund • 1814
Timothy S. and Palmer W. Bigelow, Jr. Scholarship • 1147
Vermont Incentive Grants • 1872
Vermont Oratorical Contest • 1873
Vermont Sheriffs' Association Scholarship • 1874

Virginia
Carville M. Akehurst Memorial Scholarship • 836
Dianne E. H. Wilcox Scholarship Fund • 1331
Dixie Boys Baseball Scholarship Program • 120
Dixie Youth Scholarship Program • 122
Gary Wagner, K3OMI, Scholarship • 903
Granville P. Meade Scholarship • 1411
Jimmy Rane Foundation Scholarships • 1494
John R. Lillard VAOC Scholarship • 1502
L. Phil and Alice J. Wicker Scholarship • 631
Leo Bourassa Scholarship • 1535
Mary Macon McGuire Scholarship • 1573
Middle School Essay Contest • 1598
NACA South Student Leadership Scholarships • 1633
Northrop Grumman Scholarship • 1681
Phyllis V. Roberts Scholarship • 1735
St. Andrew's Society of Washington, DC Scholarship • 2250
VHSL Achievement Award • 1877
Virginia Commonwealth Award • 1880
Virginia Daughters of the American Revolution Scholarships • 1881
Virginia Guaranteed Assistance Program • 1882
Virginia High School League Charles E. Savedge Journalism Scholarship • 1883
Virginia Part-Time Assistance Program • 1884
Virginia Sheriffs' Institute Scholarship • 1885
Virginia Tuition Assistance Grant Program • 1886
Werks Mobile Scholarship • 1899

Washington
American Indian Endowed Scholarship • 1208
Arc of Washington State Trust Fund Stipend Award • 1221
ASWA Seattle Chapter Scholarship • 1231
Atsuhiko Tateuchi Memorial Scholarship • 1232
Boeing Company STEM Scholarship • 1246
Burlington Northern Santa Fe (BNSF) Foundation Scholarship • 2111
Cathay Bank Foundation Scholarship • 1279
Edmund F. Maxwell Foundation Scholarship • 1351
Homeschoolers' Support Association Scholarship • 1445
Incight Scholarship • 2301
John Schwartz Scholarship • 1503
Lambeth Family Scholarship • 1525
Lori Rhett Memorial Scholarship • 1547
Mary Lou Brown Scholarship • 646
MGMA Western Section Scholarship • 1003
Opportunity Grant • 1705
Richard E. Bangert Business Award • 1758
Shari Simon Greenberg Community Scholarship • 300
Smart Choices Scholarship Program • 1794
Stanley O. McNaughton Community Service Award • 1807
State Work Study • 1813
Washington BPW Foundation Mature Woman Educational Scholarship • 1890
Washington College Grant • 1891
Washington Oratorical Contest • 1893
Washington State Auto Dealers Association Bright Future Scholarship • 1894
Washington State College Bound Scholarship • 1895
Washington State Governors' Scholarship for Foster Youth • 1896
Washington State PTA Scholarship • 1897
Washington Women In Need • 1898
William G. Saletic Scholarship • 1910

West Virginia
Carville M. Akehurst Memorial Scholarship • 836
Gary Wagner, K3OMI, Scholarship • 903
Greater Kanawha Valley Foundation Scholarship Program • 1412
Higher Education Adult Part-Time Student (HEAPS) Grant Program • 1442
Independence Excavating, A DiGeronimo Company Scholarship • 1464

The Ultimate Scholarship Book 2026
Athletics Index

Jimmy Rane Foundation Scholarships • 1494
L. Phil and Alice J. Wicker Scholarship • 631
Lawrence C. Yeardley Scholarship • 1528
Norman S. and Betty M. Fitzhugh Fund • 1668
St. Andrew's Society of Washington, DC Scholarship • 2250
W.P. Black Scholarship Fund • 1888
West Virginia Engineering, Science and Technology Scholarship • 1900
West Virginia Higher Education Grant • 1901
West Virginia PROMISE Scholarship • 1902
West Virginia PTA Scholarship • 1903
Willard H. Erwin, Jr. Scholarship • 1905
Zagunis Student Leader Scholarship • 1928

WISCONSIN
Academic Excellence Scholarship • 1180
AFS Twin City Memorial Scholarship • 1187
AFS Wisconsin Past President Scholarship • 1188
Americanism and Government Scholarship Program • 1217
Burlington Northern Santa Fe (BNSF) Foundation Scholarship • 2111
E.H. Marth Food Protection and Food Science Scholarship • 1346
Eagle Scout of the Year • 1347
Edmond A. Metzger Scholarship • 575
Edward L. Simeth Scholarships • 1358
Engineering Foundation of Wisconsin Scholarship • 1363
Iowa Student Loan Midwest Senior Scholarship • 185
John D. and Virginia Riesch Scholarship • 1500
MGMA Midwest Section Scholarship • 1002
Minority Undergraduate Retention Grant • 1613
NACA Northern Plains Regional Student Leadership Scholarship • 1632
Nursing Student Loan • 1685
Our First Amendment Freedoms Art and Essay Contest • 1710
Schneider-Emanuel American Legion Scholarship • 1779
Sister Mary Petronia Van Straten Scholarship for Pre-Service Teachers • 1792
Talent Incentive Program Grant • 1823
Teacher Loan Program • 1824
UMSA Foundation Scholarship Program • 1864
Upper Midwest Chapter Scholarships • 1867
Wisconsin Amusement and Music Operators Scholarships • 1915
Wisconsin Broadcasters Association Foundation Student Scholarship Program • 1916
Wisconsin Higher Education Grant • 1917
Wisconsin National Guard Tuition Grant • 1918
Wisconsin Oratorical Scholarship Program • 1919
Wisconsin Veterans Education Reimbursement Grants • 1920
Wisconsin Women in Government Undergraduate Scholarship • 1921
Xello High School Scholarship • 1926

WYOMING
Burlington Northern Santa Fe (BNSF) Foundation Scholarship • 2111
Daniels Scholarship Program • 1322
Douvas Memorial Scholarship • 1338
MGMA Western Section Scholarship • 1003

ATHLETICS INDEX

Athletics-related scholarships may be based on ability or participation in a sport.

AAU Karate Scholarship • 16
AAUS Student Scholarships • 17
AHHS Foundation Scholarship • 27
All-American Scholars (Cheerleading) • 36
All-American Scholars (Football) • 37
American Legion Baseball Scholarship • 41
Ann Griffel Scholarship • 1218
Banana George Blair Ambassador Scholarship • 58
Big Al Wagner Western Region Scholarship • 62
Carolyn Hines Memorial Scholarship Program • 75
CCA Christian Cheer Nationals • 78
CCCAM Scholarships • 1280
Collegiate Championship Award Program • 93
CPI Highest Point Hunt Seat Rider • 101
Curt Greene Memorial Scholarship • 106
Dinah Shore Scholarship • 119
Dixie Boys Baseball Scholarship Program • 120
Dixie Softball Scholarships • 121
Dixie Youth Scholarship Program • 122
Dizzy Dean Scholarship • 123
Dr. James Earl Kennamer Scholarship • 128
Duke Award Scholarship • 1345
Dwight F. Davis Memorial Scholarship • 129
Dwight Mosley Scholarship Award • 130
Educational Award/Graduating High School Female • 1352
Eve Kraft Education and College Scholarship • 141
FMC Skaters Scholarship • 145
Goldie Bateson Scholarship • 2152
H. U. Lee Scholarship • 166
HD Hogan Rodeo Scholarship • 170
Heisman High School Scholarship • 171
Helen Gee Chin Scholarship Foundation Scholarship • 172
Herman Sani Scholarship • 1436
ICCA Scholarships • 1454
IEA Founders College Scholarship Awards • 178
IEA Zone Specific Scholarships • 179
Ike Foundation Scholarship • 180
Indiana Golf Foundation Scholarship • 1466
Individual Scholarship Program • 182
Iowa PGA Foundation Charlie Burkart Scholarship • 1472
ISAA Scholarship Program • 1480
ISIA Education Foundation Scholarship • 186
Jack Hughes Education Scholarship • 1485
John J. Smith Graduate School Scholarship • 191
Justin Dignam Memorial Scholarship • 197
Kevin Higgins College Scholarship • 200
Lou Manzione Scholarship • 206
Marian Wood Baird College Scholarship • 208
Marilynn Smith Scholarship • 2196
Marsh Scholarship Fund • 212
Memorial Fund Scholarships • 219
Metro Youth Football Association Scholarship • 222
Minnesota Hockey Scholarship • 1606
MSAA Scholarship Program • 1627
NABF Scholarship Program • 231

National Gymnastics Foundation Men's Scholarship • 2217
National Intercollegiate Rodeo Foundation Scholarship • 235
National Sportsmanship Award • 240
National Table Tennis Scholarship • 241
NCAA Division II Degree Completion Award Program • 252
NCAA Postgraduate Scholarship • 253
NCRA Scholarship • 1637
New York Ramblers Scholarship • 2226
New York State USBC Scholarships • 1656
New York State USBC Spirit Awards • 1657
NFAA Scholarship Program • 256
NJCDCA Scholarship • 1663
NSCA Scholarship • 261
Paul Flaherty Athletic Scholarship • 1721
Pennsylvania State Bowling Association Scholarship Program • 1730
PGA WORKS John and Tamara Lundgren Scholars Program • 268
Phyllis G. Meekins Scholarship • 2237
Pony Alumni Scholarship • 272
Race Entry Student Scholarship • 276
Rawhide Scholarship • 277
Richard Avila Scholarship • 282
Roller Skating Foundation Scholarship, Current College Student Category • 701
Roller Skating Foundation Scholarship, High School Student Category • 283
Rosalind P. Walter College Scholarship • 284
SASS Scholarship Foundation Scholarships • 292
Scholastic Honors Team • 297
Scott Hamilton Skaters Education Fund • 298
Smart Choices Scholarship Program • 1794
Southern Region/Elmer Stailing Scholarship • 307
Sweet Karen Alumni Scholarship • 332
Tampa Bay Buccaneers Foundation Girls in Football Scholarship • 334
Texas International Fishing Tournament Inc. Scholarship • 1844
Tim Olson Memorial Scholarship • 340
Trapshooting Hall of Fame College Scholarships • 341
U.S. Lacrosse Native American Scholarships • 2270
USA Roller Sports Scholarship Fund • 353
USA Water Ski and Wake Sports Foundation Scholarships • 354
USAR Scholarship • 355
Wade Trophy • 367
Walter Byers Graduate Scholarship • 369
WBCA Coaches' All-America • 371
William J. Goaziou Scholarship • 375
Women Divers Hall of Fame Scholarships and Grants • 377
Women's Western Golf Foundation Scholarship • 383
Zale Parry Scholarship • 385

MILITARY RELATED INDEX

Most of the awards in this index require that you have a parent, grandparent or spouse who has served in the military. There are also awards if you want to enter the armed services or if you have served.

100th Infantry Battalion Memorial Scholarship Fund • 10
1st Marine Division Association Scholarship • 12
25th Infantry Division Association Educational Scholarship • 13
AFCEA ROTC Scholarships • 23
Air Force ROTC ASCP • 29
Air Force ROTC High School Scholarship Program • 30
Air Force ROTC In-College Program • 31
Air Force ROTC Professional Officer Course-Early Release Program • 32
Air Force ROTC SOAR Program • 33
Airmen Memorial Foundation Scholarship Program • 34
Albert M. Lappin Scholarship • 1197
American Legion Auxiliary, Department of California Educational Assistance General $1,000 Scholarships • 1211
American Legion Auxiliary, Department of California Educational Assistance General $2,000 Scholarships • 1212
American Legion Auxiliary, Department of California Educational Assistance General $500 Scholarships • 1213
American Legion Department of Illinois Scholarship • 1216
American Legion Legacy Scholarships • 42
AMVETS Children/Grandchildren Scholarships • 46
AMVETS National Scholarships for Veterans • 47
Anchor Scholarship Foundation Scholarship • 48
Armed Services YMCA Annual Essay Contest • 49
Army Emergency Relief's MG James Ursano Scholarship Program • 50
Army Engineer Memorial Awards • 51
Army Nurse Corps Association Scholarships • 52
Army ROTC Advanced Course • 53
Army ROTC Four-Year Scholarship Program • 54
Army ROTC Green To Gold Scholarship Program • 55
Arthur M. and Berdena King Eagle Scout Contest • 1943
Brown Hudner Navy Scholarship • 68
California Fee Waiver Program for Children of Veterans • 1261
California Fee Waiver Program for Dependents of Deceased or Disabled National Guard Members • 1262
California Fee Waiver Program for Recipients of the Medal of Honor and Their Children • 1263
Categorical Tuition Waiver • 1278
Charles W. and Annette Hill Scholarship • 1288
Chief Master Sergeants of the Air Force Scholarships • 80
Chief Petty Officer Scholarship Fund • 81
Children of Warriors National Presidents' Scholarship • 82
Coast Guard College Student Pre-Commissioning Initiative • 88
Coast Guard Foundation Scholarship Fund • 89
Congressional Medal of Honor Society Scholarships • 96
Daniel E. Lambert Memorial Scholarship • 1321
Daughters of the Cincinnati Scholarship • 109
Delaware Educational Benefits for Children of Deceased Veterans and Others • 1325
Dolphin Scholarships • 125
Edith Nourse Rogers STEM Scholarship • 134
EOD Warrior Foundation Scholarship • 137
Exemption for Texas Veterans (Hazelwood Exemption) • 1369
Exemption from Tuition Fees for Dependents of Kentucky Veterans • 1370
First Cavalry Division Foundation Scholarship • 143
Folds of Honor Higher Education Scholarship • 146
General Henry H. Arnold Education Grant Program • 153
Google SVA Scholarship • 163
Guy M. Wilson Scholarship • 1416
H and P Veterans Helping Veterans Scholarship • 165
Hanscom Air Force Base Spouses' Club Scholarship • 169
Hattie Tedrow Memorial Fund Scholarship • 1424
Helping Heroes Grant • 1430
Hugh A. Smith Scholarship Fund • 1452
Illinois AMVETS Ladies Auxiliary Memorial Scholarship • 1456
Illinois AMVETS Ladies Auxiliary Worchid Scholarship • 1457
Illinois AMVETS Sad Sacks Nursing Scholarship • 1458
Illinois AMVETS Service Foundation Scholarship • 1459
Illinois Veteran Grant Program • 1462
Jack E. Barger, Sr. Memorial Nursing Scholarship • 1483
James V. Day Scholarship • 1491
Jon C. Ladda Memorial Foundation Scholarship • 193
Joseph P. and Helen T. Cribbins Scholarship • 195
Judith Haupt Member's Child Scholarship • 196
Kathern F. Gruber Scholarship Program • 198
Kentucky Veterans Tuition Waiver Program • 1521
La Fra Scholarship • 201
Leadership Essay Contest • 203
Maine Veterans Dependents Educational Benefits • 1560
Marine Corps League Scholarships • 209
Marine Corps Scholarship Foundation Scholarship • 210
Mary Ann K. Murtha Memorial Scholarship • 1569
Mary Paolozzi Member's Scholarship • 216
Memorial Scholarship Fund • 220
Mike and Gail Donley Spouse Scholarship • 223
Military Award Program (MAP) • 224
Military Family Support Trust Scholarships • 225
Montgomery GI Bill - Active Duty • 227
Montgomery GI Bill - Selected Reserve • 228
Montgomery GI Bill Tuition Assistance Top-Up • 229
Naval Enlisted Reserve Association Scholarships • 242
Naval Intelligence Essay Contest • 244
Navy College Fund • 246
Navy Supply Corps Foundation Scholarship • 247
Navy-Marine Corps ROTC College Program • 248
Navy-Marine Corps ROTC Four-Year Scholarships • 249
Navy/Marine Corps/Coast Guard (NMCCG) Enlisted Dependent Spouse Scholarship • 251
NDVA Waiver of Tuition • 1638
New York Legion Auxiliary Department Scholarship • 1651
New York Legion Auxiliary District Scholarships • 1652
Next Gen Scholars Award • 255
Non Commissioned Officers Association Scholarships • 258
NROTC Nurse Corps Scholarship • 259
NROTC Scholarship Program • 260
Oregon Army National Guard • 1707
Past Department Presidents' Junior Scholarship Award • 1718
Pauline Langkamp Memorial Scholarship • 266
Pennsylvania Educational Gratuity Program • 1725
Phoebe Pember Memorial Scholarship • 1069
Raymond T. Wellington, Jr. Memorial Scholarship • 1747
Rosedale Post 346 Scholarship • 1769
Schneider-Emanuel American Legion Scholarship • 1779
Scholarships for Military Children • 295
Seabee Memorial Scholarship • 299
SGT Felix M. Del Greco, Jr. Memorial Scholarship • 1785
South Dakota Free Tuition for Veterans and Others Who Performed War Service • 1804
Study.com Scholarship for Military Members and Veterans • 325
Study.com Scholarship for Military Spouses and Children • 326
Subic Bay-Cubi Point Scholarship • 329
Supplemental Education Grant (SEG) • 331
Tailhook Educational Foundation Scholarship • 333
Ted and Nora Anderson Scholarships • 1830
UDT-SEAL Scholarship • 347
United Daughters of the Confederacy Scholarships • 350
VA Essay Scholarship • 361
Veterans Caucus Scholarship • 362
Veterans Tuition Awards • 1876
Vietnam Veterans' Scholarship • 1879
Wells Fargo Veterans Scholarship Program • 373
William D. and Jewell Brewer Scholarship • 1909
Wisconsin National Guard Tuition Grant • 1918
Wisconsin Veterans Education Reimbursement Grants • 1920
Women Marines Association Scholarship Program • 379
Women's Army Corps Veterans Association Scholarship • 381

Ethnicity / Race Index

Women's Overseas Service League Scholarships for Women • 382

ETHNICITY AND RACE INDEX

This index lists awards for members of minority and non-minority ethnic groups.

AFRICAN-AMERICAN

Achievers in Technology Program • 2082
Actuarial Diversity Scholarship • 2083
Afro-Academic, Cultural, Technological and Scientific Olympics (ACT-SO) • 2087
Agnes Jones Jackson Scholarship • 2090
AICPA Fellowship for Minority Doctoral Students • 2093
AICPA Scholarship for Minority Accounting Students • 2094
Ally Financial Law Scholars • 2097
Ally Financial Public Policy Scholars • 525
American Chemical Society Scholars Program • 2098
AMS Minority Scholarship • 785
Annual NBNA Scholarships • 789
Beverly Murphy MLA Scholarship for Underrepresented Students • 541
BIPOC Scholarship • 2109
California Health Sciences Scholarships • 1265
Carole Simpson Scholarship • 554
CBC Spouses Essay Contest • 2116
CBC Spouses Performing Arts Scholarship • 2117
CBCF Reducing the Financial Barrier Scholarship • 2118
CESDA Diversity Scholarship • 1284
Chairman's Award • 1952
Chevron Corporate Scholars Program • 2121
CLA Scholarship For BIPOC Students in Memory of Edna Yelland • 559
Clanseer and Anna Johnson Scholarships • 1297
Completing the Dream Scholarship • 94
Congressional Black Caucus Spouses Education Scholarship • 2126
Congressional Black Caucus Spouses Visual Arts Scholarship • 2127
Creative Sole Scholarship • 2129
Development Fund for Black Students in Science and Technology • 2130
Diversity Achievement Scholarship • 414
Diversity Advocacy Council Scholarship • 2132
Dr. Kenny D. Hasija Scholarship • 417
Ed Bradley Scholarship • 574
EDSA Diversity Scholarships • 2137
Gates Scholarship • 2146
GEM MS Engineering Fellowship Program • 2147
Generation Google Scholarship • 2149
George A. Strait Minority Scholarship • 591
HBCU NREI Scholarship • 2153
Henry Sachs Foundation Scholarship • 1432
Holly A. Cornell Scholarship • 934
Hubertus W.V. Wellems Scholarship for Male Students • 2167
Intellia Therapeutics - UNCF Scholarship • 2169
Jackie Robinson Foundation Scholarship Program • 2170
James B. Morris Scholarship • 1487
Jimmy A. Young Memorial Education Recognition Award • 952
Jonathan Jasper Wright Award • 194
Julianne Malveaux Scholarship • 2178
Kansas Ethnic Minority Scholarship • 1511
LAGRANT Scholarship Program • 2182
Leadership for Diversity Scholarship • 1530
Legal Opportunity Scholarship Fund • 637
Louis B. Russell Scholarship • 1550
Marcus Garvey Scholarship • 2194
Martin Luther King, Jr. Memorial Scholarship • 2010
Mary Church Terrell Award • 215
Maureen L. and Howard N. Blitman, P.E., Scholarship • 2201
MBA Fellowship • 648
MCCA Lloyd M. Johnson, Jr. Scholarship Program • 2202
Medgar Evers Award • 218
Meritage Homes Scholarship • 2204
Mildred Towle Scholarship for African-Americans • 1602
Minorities and Women Educational Scholarship • 654
Minority Fellowship Program • 655
Minority Scholarship • 2205
Minority Scholarship Award for Physical Therapy Students • 2206
Minority Scholarship Awards for College Students • 2207
Minority Scholarship Awards for Incoming College Freshmen • 2208
Minority Serving Institution Grants • 2209
Minority Student Scholarship • 1009
Minority Undergraduate Retention Grant • 1613
Mutual of Omaha Actuarial Scholarship for Minority Students • 2212
National Association of Black Accountants National Scholarship Program • 2215
National Scholarship • 2220
NOAA Educational Partnership Program Undergraduate Scholarships • 2227
Olay Face the Stem Gap Scholarship • 2229
P.O. Pistilli Undergraduate Scholarship for Advancement in Computer Science and Electrical Engineering • 2233
Pega Scholars Program • 2235
Phyllis G. Meekins Scholarship • 2237
PRSA Diversity Multicultural Scholarship • 2241
Ron Brown Scholar Program • 2244
Rosewood Family Scholarship Program • 1771
Ruth D. Peterson Fellowship for Racial and Ethnic Diversity • 2245
Smith Diversity Scholarship • 1795
Study.com Scholarship for Black Students • 2254
Tampax Flow It Forward Scholarship • 2261
TE Connectivity African Heritage Scholarship • 2262
Thurgood Marshall College Scholarship Fund • 2264
Tracking Foundation Multi-Year Scholarship Program • 2265
Tracking Foundation Scholars Scholarship Program • 2266
U.S. Western Digital STEM Scholarship • 346
UNCF Healthcare Workforce Diversity Program Certification • 2271
United Parcel Service Scholarship for Minority Students • 2272

Ethnicity / Race Index

William A. Crawford Minority Teacher Scholarship • 1906
William and Charlotte Cadbury Award • 2275
William L. Hastie Award • 376
Write Your Future Scholarship • 2279
X Society Awards Scholarship • 2280

Armenian
AGBU US Graduate Scholarship • 2089
Agnes Missirian Scholarship • 2091
ARS Undergraduate Scholarship • 2103
ASA Scholarships • 2104
Diocese of the Armenian Church of America (Eastern) Scholarships • 1963
Helen C. Evans Scholarship • 929
Lucy Kasparian Aharonian Scholarship • 2189
Performing Arts Scholarship • 2236
Religious Studies Scholarship • 2242
Richard R. Tufenkian Memorial Scholarship • 2243

Asian
Against The Grain Artistic Scholarship • 2088
AICPA Scholarship for Minority Accounting Students • 2094
APIA Scholarship Program • 2101
Asian and Pacific Islander American Scholarships • 2105
Atsuhiko Tateuchi Memorial Scholarship • 1232
Beverly Murphy MLA Scholarship for Underrepresented Students • 541
California Health Sciences Scholarships • 1265
Carole Simpson Scholarship • 554
CLA Scholarship For BIPOC Students in Memory of Edna Yelland • 559
Completing the Dream Scholarship • 94
Diversity Achievement Scholarship • 414
Diversity Advocacy Council Scholarship • 2132
Ed Bradley Scholarship • 574
EDSA Diversity Scholarships • 2137
George A. Strait Minority Scholarship • 591
George Choy Memorial/Gay Asian Pacific Alliance (GAPA) Scholarship • 2151
Holly A. Cornell Scholarship • 934
Hsiao Memorial Social Sciences Scholarship • 2166
Jackie Robinson Foundation Scholarship Program • 2170
James B. Morris Scholarship • 1487
Japanese American Citizens League Entering Freshman Awards • 2172
Japanese American Citizens League Graduate Awards • 2173
Japanese American Citizens League Law Scholarships • 2174
Japanese American Citizens League Undergraduate Awards • 2175
Jimmy A. Young Memorial Education Recognition Award • 952
Kansas Ethnic Minority Scholarship • 1511
Korean Ancestry Grant • 2181
LAGRANT Scholarship Program • 2182
Leadership for Diversity Scholarship • 1530
Legal Opportunity Scholarship Fund • 637
Louis B. Russell Scholarship • 1550
Mark Ando and Ito Family Scholarship • 2197

Martin Luther King, Jr. Memorial Scholarship • 2010
Mary Quan Moy Ing Memorial Scholarship • 2199
MCCA Lloyd M. Johnson, Jr. Scholarship Program • 2202
Minorities and Women Educational Scholarship • 654
Minority Fellowship Program • 655
Minority Scholarship • 2205
Minority Serving Institution Grants • 2209
Minority Student Scholarship • 1009
Mutual of Omaha Actuarial Scholarship for Minority Students • 2212
NOAA Educational Partnership Program Undergraduate Scholarships • 2227
OCA/UPS Gold Mountain Scholarship • 2228
Pega Scholars Program • 2235
Phyllis G. Meekins Scholarship • 2237
PRSA Diversity Multicultural Scholarship • 2241
Rosewood Family Scholarship Program • 1771
Ruth D. Peterson Fellowship for Racial and Ethnic Diversity • 2245
Smith Diversity Scholarship • 1795
United Parcel Service Scholarship for Minority Students • 2272
UPS Hallmark Scholarship • 2274
William and Charlotte Cadbury Award • 2275

Caribbean
EDSA Diversity Scholarships • 2137
Jimmy A. Young Memorial Education Recognition Award • 952
Leadership for Diversity Scholarship • 1530
Minority Scholarship • 2205

Central American
CESDA Diversity Scholarship • 1284
Completing the Dream Scholarship • 94
Diversity Achievement Scholarship • 414
EDSA Diversity Scholarships • 2137
George A. Strait Minority Scholarship • 591
Jackie Robinson Foundation Scholarship Program • 2170
Jimmy A. Young Memorial Education Recognition Award • 952
Jose Marti Scholarship Challenge Grant • 1505
Leadership for Diversity Scholarship • 1530
Minority Scholarship • 2205
Minority Serving Institution Grants • 2209

Chinese
Asian and Pacific Islander American Scholarships • 2105
Atsuhiko Tateuchi Memorial Scholarship • 1232
Completing the Dream Scholarship • 94
Diversity Achievement Scholarship • 414
EDSA Diversity Scholarships • 2137
George A. Strait Minority Scholarship • 591
Jackie Robinson Foundation Scholarship Program • 2170
Jimmy A. Young Memorial Education Recognition Award • 952
Leadership for Diversity Scholarship • 1530
Legal Opportunity Scholarship Fund • 637
Minority Fellowship Program • 655
Minority Scholarship • 2205
Minority Serving Institution Grants • 2209

OCA/UPS Gold Mountain Scholarship • 2228
UPS Hallmark Scholarship • 2274

Cuban
Completing the Dream Scholarship • 94
EDSA Diversity Scholarships • 2137
George A. Strait Minority Scholarship • 591
Mas Family Scholarships • 2200
Minority Serving Institution Grants • 2209

Eskimo
A.T. Anderson Memorial Scholarship • 2079
Adolph Van Pelt Scholarship • 2086
Completing the Dream Scholarship • 94
Diversity Achievement Scholarship • 414
EDSA Diversity Scholarships • 2137
Foundation Scholarships • 2142
GEM MS Engineering Fellowship Program • 2147
George A. Strait Minority Scholarship • 591
Health Professions Pre-Graduate Scholarship Program • 2154
Health Professions Preparatory Scholarship Program • 2155
Jackie Robinson Foundation Scholarship Program • 2170
Jimmy A. Young Memorial Education Recognition Award • 952
Leadership for Diversity Scholarship • 1530
Legal Opportunity Scholarship Fund • 637
Louis B. Russell Scholarship • 1550
Minority Fellowship Program • 655
Minority Scholarship Award for Physical Therapy Students • 2206
Minority Scholarship Awards for College Students • 2207
Minority Scholarship Awards for Incoming College Freshmen • 2208
Minority Serving Institution Grants • 2209
Mutual of Omaha Actuarial Scholarship for Minority Students • 2212
NOAA Educational Partnership Program Undergraduate Scholarships • 2227
Phyllis G. Meekins Scholarship • 2237
PRSA Diversity Multicultural Scholarship • 2241
Rosewood Family Scholarship Program • 1771
Smith Diversity Scholarship • 1795
United Parcel Service Scholarship for Minority Students • 2272
William and Charlotte Cadbury Award • 2275

Filipino
Ambassador Minerva Jean Falcon Hawaii Scholarship • 1206
Asian and Pacific Islander American Scholarships • 2105
Atsuhiko Tateuchi Memorial Scholarship • 1232
CLA Scholarship For BIPOC Students in Memory of Edna Yelland • 559
Completing the Dream Scholarship • 94
Cora Aguda Manayan Fund • 1314
Diversity Achievement Scholarship • 414
EDSA Diversity Scholarships • 2137
Generation Google Scholarship • 2149
George A. Strait Minority Scholarship • 591
Jackie Robinson Foundation Scholarship Program • 2170
Jimmy A. Young Memorial Education Recognition Award • 952

The Ultimate Scholarship Book 2026
Ethnicity / Race Index

Leadership for Diversity Scholarship • 1530
Minority Fellowship Program • 655
Minority Scholarship • 2205
Minority Serving Institution Grants • 2209
OCA/UPS Gold Mountain Scholarship • 2228
UPS Hallmark Scholarship • 2274

Greek
AHEPA Educational Foundation National Scholarship Program • 2092
Family District 1 Scholarships • 1372
National and Chapter Scholarships • 2214

Hawaiian
A.T. Anderson Memorial Scholarship • 2079
AISES Intel Scholarship • 2095
Asian and Pacific Islander American Scholarships • 2105
Atsuhiko Tateuchi Memorial Scholarship • 1232
Blossom Kalama Evans Memorial Scholarship Fund • 1242
California Health Sciences Scholarships • 1265
Clem Judd, Jr., Memorial Scholarship • 1298
Completing the Dream Scholarship • 94
Diversity Achievement Scholarship • 414
EDSA Diversity Scholarships • 2137
Generation Google Scholarship • 2149
Ida M. Pope Memorial Scholarship • 2168
Jackie Robinson Foundation Scholarship Program • 2170
Jimmy A. Young Memorial Education Recognition Award • 952
Leadership for Diversity Scholarship • 1530
Louis B. Russell Scholarship • 1550
Minorities and Women Educational Scholarship • 654
Minority Fellowship Program • 655
Minority Scholarship Award for Physical Therapy Students • 2206
Minority Serving Institution Grants • 2209
OCA/UPS Gold Mountain Scholarship • 2228
Pega Scholars Program • 2235
UPS Hallmark Scholarship • 2274
William and Charlotte Cadbury Award • 2275

Hispanic / Latino
Actuarial Diversity Scholarship • 2083
AICPA Fellowship for Minority Doctoral Students • 2093
AICPA Scholarship for Minority Accounting Students • 2094
American Chemical Society Scholars Program • 2098
AMS Minority Scholarship • 785
Association of Cuban Engineers Scholarship Foundation Scholarships • 2106
Beverly Murphy MLA Scholarship for Underrepresented Students • 541
BIPOC Scholarship • 2109
Cafe Bustelo El Cafe Del Futuro Scholarship • 2112
California Health Sciences Scholarships • 1265
Carole Simpson Scholarship • 554
CHCI United Health Foundation Scholar-Intern Program • 2119
CLA Scholarship For BIPOC Students in Memory of Edna Yelland • 559
Colgate-Palmolive Make the U Educational Grant • 2124
Completing the Dream Scholarship • 94
Diversity Achievement Scholarship • 414
Diversity Advocacy Council Scholarship • 2132
Dr. Juan Andrade, Jr. Scholarship • 2134
Ed Bradley Scholarship • 574
EDSA Diversity Scholarships • 2137
Gates Scholarship • 2146
GEM MS Engineering Fellowship Program • 2147
Generation Google Scholarship • 2149
George A. Strait Minority Scholarship • 591
Hispanic Heritage Youth Awards • 2159
Hispanic Scholarship Fund • 2160
Holly A. Cornell Scholarship • 934
HSC Foundation Scholarship • 2165
Intellia Therapeutics - UNCF Scholarship • 2169
Jackie Robinson Foundation Scholarship Program • 2170
James B. Morris Scholarship • 1487
Jimmy A. Young Memorial Education Recognition Award • 952
Jose Marti Scholarship Challenge Grant • 1505
Kansas Ethnic Minority Scholarship • 1511
LAGRANT Scholarship Program • 2182
Leadership for Diversity Scholarship • 1530
Legal Opportunity Scholarship Fund • 637
Louis B. Russell Scholarship • 1550
LULAC General Awards • 2190
LULAC Honors Awards • 2191
MAES Scholarship Program • 2192
MALDEF Law School Scholarship • 2193
Martin Luther King, Jr. Memorial Scholarship • 2010
Maureen L. and Howard N. Blitman, P.E., Scholarship • 2201
MBA Fellowship • 648
MCCA Lloyd M. Johnson, Jr. Scholarship Program • 2202
Minorities and Women Educational Scholarship • 654
Minority Fellowship Program • 655
Minority Scholarship • 2205
Minority Scholarship Award for Physical Therapy Students • 2206
Minority Scholarship Awards for College Students • 2207
Minority Scholarship Awards for Incoming College Freshmen • 2208
Minority Serving Institution Grants • 2209
Minority Student Scholarship • 1009
Minority Undergraduate Retention Grant • 1613
Mutual of Omaha Actuarial Scholarship for Minority Students • 2212
NAHN Scholarship • 2213
National Association of Black Accountants National Scholarship Program • 2215
National Hispanic Health Professional Student Scholarship • 2218
NOAA Educational Partnership Program Undergraduate Scholarships • 2227
Olay Face the Stem Gap Scholarship • 2229
P.O. Pistilli Undergraduate Scholarship for Advancement in Computer Science and Electrical Engineering • 2233
Pega Scholars Program • 2235
Phyllis G. Meekins Scholarship • 2237
Prospanica Foundation Scholarships • 690
PRSA Diversity Multicultural Scholarship • 2241
Rosewood Family Scholarship Program • 1771
Ruth D. Peterson Fellowship for Racial and Ethnic Diversity • 2245
SHPE Scholarship Program • 2248
Smith Diversity Scholarship • 1795
STEM Scholarship • 2252
U.S. Western Digital STEM Scholarship • 346
United Parcel Service Scholarship for Minority Students • 2272
William A. Crawford Minority Teacher Scholarship • 1906
William and Charlotte Cadbury Award • 2275

Italian
Henry Salvatori Scholarship • 2157
National Italian American Foundation Scholarship • 2219
Sons of Italy Grand Lodge of California Italian Language Study Grant • 1798
Sons of Italy Grand Lodge of College Scholarship • 1799

Japanese
Abe and Esther Hagiwara Student Aid Award • 2081
Asian and Pacific Islander American Scholarships • 2105
Atsuhiko Tateuchi Memorial Scholarship • 1232
Completing the Dream Scholarship • 94
Diversity Achievement Scholarship • 414
EDSA Diversity Scholarships • 2137
Eizo and Toyo Sakumoto Trust Scholarship • 1360
George A. Strait Minority Scholarship • 591
Jackie Robinson Foundation Scholarship Program • 2170
Japanese American Citizens League Entering Freshman Awards • 2172
Japanese American Citizens League Graduate Awards • 2173
Japanese American Citizens League Law Scholarships • 2174
Japanese American Citizens League Undergraduate Awards • 2175
Jimmy A. Young Memorial Education Recognition Award • 952
Leadership for Diversity Scholarship • 1530
Legal Opportunity Scholarship Fund • 637
Minority Fellowship Program • 655
Minority Scholarship • 2205
Minority Serving Institution Grants • 2209
OCA/UPS Gold Mountain Scholarship • 2228
UPS Hallmark Scholarship • 2274

Korean
Asian and Pacific Islander American Scholarships • 2105
Atsuhiko Tateuchi Memorial Scholarship • 1232
Completing the Dream Scholarship • 94
Diversity Achievement Scholarship • 414
EDSA Diversity Scholarships • 2137
George A. Strait Minority Scholarship • 591
Jackie Robinson Foundation Scholarship Program • 2170
Jimmy A. Young Memorial Education Recognition Award • 952

The Ultimate Scholarship Book 2026
Ethnicity / Race Index

Leadership for Diversity Scholarship • 1530
Legal Opportunity Scholarship Fund • 637
Minority Fellowship Program • 655
Minority Scholarship • 2205
Minority Serving Institution Grants • 2209
OCA/UPS Gold Mountain Scholarship • 2228
UPS Hallmark Scholarship • 2274

Lithuanian
Knights of Lithuania Scholarship Program • 2180

Mexican
CESDA Diversity Scholarship • 1284
CLA Scholarship For BIPOC Students in Memory of Edna Yelland • 559
Completing the Dream Scholarship • 94
Diversity Achievement Scholarship • 414
EDSA Diversity Scholarships • 2137
George A. Strait Minority Scholarship • 591
Jackie Robinson Foundation Scholarship Program • 2170
Jimmy A. Young Memorial Education Recognition Award • 952
Jose Marti Scholarship Challenge Grant • 1505
Leadership for Diversity Scholarship • 1530
Legal Opportunity Scholarship Fund • 637
Mexican Scholarship Fund • 1589
Minority Fellowship Program • 655
Minority Scholarship • 2205
Minority Serving Institution Grants • 2209

Middle Eastern
Completing the Dream Scholarship • 94
Dr. Jack G. Shaheen Media Scholarship • 569

Mongolian
Jimmy A. Young Memorial Education Recognition Award • 952
Leadership for Diversity Scholarship • 1530

Native American
A.T. Anderson Memorial Scholarship • 2079
Actuarial Diversity Scholarship • 2083
Adolph Van Pelt Scholarship • 2086
AICPA Fellowship for Minority Doctoral Students • 2093
AICPA Scholarship for Minority Accounting Students • 2094
AISES Intel Scholarship • 2095
Allogan Slagle Memorial Scholarship • 2096
American Chemical Society Scholars Program • 2098
American Indian Endowed Scholarship • 1208
American Indian Services Scholarship • 2099
AMS Minority Scholarship • 785
Beverly Murphy MLA Scholarship for Underrepresented Students • 541
BIPOC Scholarship • 2109
Burlington Northern Santa Fe (BNSF) Foundation Scholarship • 2111
California Health Sciences Scholarships • 1265
Carole Simpson Scholarship • 554
Catching the Dream Native American Scholarship Fund • 2115
CESDA Diversity Scholarship • 1284
Cherokee Nation/Tribal Council At-Large Scholarship • 2120
Chief Manuelito Scholarship Program • 2122

Citizen Potawatomi Nation Tribal Scholarship • 2123
CLA Scholarship For BIPOC Students in Memory of Edna Yelland • 559
Completing the Dream Scholarship • 94
Diversity Achievement Scholarship • 414
Diversity Advocacy Council Scholarship • 2132
Dr. Kenny D. Hasija Scholarship • 417
Ed Bradley Scholarship • 574
EDSA Diversity Scholarships • 2137
Florence Young Memorial Scholarship • 2141
Full Circle Scholarship • 2144
Gates Scholarship • 2146
GEM MS Engineering Fellowship Program • 2147
Generation Google Scholarship • 2149
George A. Strait Minority Scholarship • 591
Health Professions Pre-Graduate Scholarship Program • 2154
Health Professions Preparatory Scholarship Program • 2155
Holly A. Cornell Scholarship • 934
Hopi Scholarship Program • 2164
Intellia Therapeutics - UNCF Scholarship • 2169
Jackie Robinson Foundation Scholarship Program • 2170
James B. Morris Scholarship • 1487
Jimmy A. Young Memorial Education Recognition Award • 952
Kansas Ethnic Minority Scholarship • 1511
LAGRANT Scholarship Program • 2182
Leadership for Diversity Scholarship • 1530
Legal Opportunity Scholarship Fund • 637
Louis B. Russell Scholarship • 1550
Martin Luther King, Jr. Memorial Scholarship • 2010
Maureen L. and Howard N. Blitman, P.E., Scholarship • 2201
MBA Fellowship • 648
MCCA Lloyd M. Johnson, Jr. Scholarship Program • 2202
Minnesota Indian Scholarship Program • 1607
Minorities and Women Educational Scholarship • 654
Minority Fellowship Program • 655
Minority Scholarship • 2205
Minority Scholarship Award for Physical Therapy Students • 2206
Minority Scholarship Awards for College Students • 2207
Minority Scholarship Awards for Incoming College Freshmen • 2208
Minority Serving Institution Grants • 2209
Minority Student Scholarship • 1009
Minority Undergraduate Retention Grant • 1613
Morris K. Udall Scholarship • 2211
Mutual of Omaha Actuarial Scholarship for Minority Students • 2212
National Association of Black Accountants National Scholarship Program • 2215
Native American Education Grant • 2221
Native American Scholarship • 2222
NativeVision Scholarships • 2223
NOAA Educational Partnership Program Undergraduate Scholarships • 2227
Olay Face the Stem Gap Scholarship • 2229

P.O. Pistilli Undergraduate Scholarship for Advancement in Computer Science and Electrical Engineering • 2233
Paumanauke Native American Indian Scholarship • 2234
Pega Scholars Program • 2235
Phyllis G. Meekins Scholarship • 2237
PRSA Diversity Multicultural Scholarship • 2241
Rosewood Family Scholarship Program • 1771
Ruth D. Peterson Fellowship for Racial and Ethnic Diversity • 2245
Smith Diversity Scholarship • 1795
Tribal College and University (TCU) Scholarships • 2268
Truman D. Picard Scholarship • 2269
U.S. Lacrosse Native American Scholarships • 2270
U.S. Western Digital STEM Scholarship • 346
United Parcel Service Scholarship for Minority Students • 2272
William and Charlotte Cadbury Award • 2275

Nigerian
Completing the Dream Scholarship • 94

Pacific Islander
A.T. Anderson Memorial Scholarship • 2079
Against The Grain Artistic Scholarship • 2088
APIA Scholarship Program • 2101
Asian and Pacific Islander American Scholarships • 2105
Atsuhiko Tateuchi Memorial Scholarship • 1232
Beverly Murphy MLA Scholarship for Underrepresented Students • 541
BIPOC Scholarship • 2109
California Health Sciences Scholarships • 1265
Carole Simpson Scholarship • 554
CLA Scholarship For BIPOC Students in Memory of Edna Yelland • 559
Completing the Dream Scholarship • 94
Diversity Achievement Scholarship • 414
Diversity Advocacy Council Scholarship • 2132
Ed Bradley Scholarship • 574
EDSA Diversity Scholarships • 2137
Gates Scholarship • 2146
Generation Google Scholarship • 2149
George A. Strait Minority Scholarship • 591
George Choy Memorial/Gay Asian Pacific Alliance (GAPA) Scholarship • 2151
Hsiao Memorial Social Sciences Scholarship • 2166
Jackie Robinson Foundation Scholarship Program • 2170
James B. Morris Scholarship • 1487
Jimmy A. Young Memorial Education Recognition Award • 952
Kansas Ethnic Minority Scholarship • 1511
LAGRANT Scholarship Program • 2182
Leadership for Diversity Scholarship • 1530
Legal Opportunity Scholarship Fund • 637
Louis B. Russell Scholarship • 1550
Martin Luther King, Jr. Memorial Scholarship • 2010
MCCA Lloyd M. Johnson, Jr. Scholarship Program • 2202
Minorities and Women Educational Scholarship • 654
Minority Fellowship Program • 655

613

The Ultimate Scholarship Book 2026
Religion Index

Minority Scholarship Award for Physical Therapy Students • 2206
Minority Scholarship Awards for College Students • 2207
Minority Serving Institution Grants • 2209
Minority Student Scholarship • 1009
Mutual of Omaha Actuarial Scholarship for Minority Students • 2212
OCA/UPS Gold Mountain Scholarship • 2228
Olay Face the Stem Gap Scholarship • 2229
Pega Scholars Program • 2235
Phyllis G. Meekins Scholarship • 2237
PRSA Diversity Multicultural Scholarship • 2241
Rosewood Family Scholarship Program • 1771
Smith Diversity Scholarship • 1795
Tongan Cultural Society Scholarship • 1849
United Parcel Service Scholarship for Minority Students • 2272
UPS Hallmark Scholarship • 2274
William and Charlotte Cadbury Award • 2275

Polish
Drs. James and Wanda Trefil Science Scholarship • 2135
Education Scholarship • 2138
Polish National Alliance Scholarship • 2240

Portuguese
Luso-American Education Foundation General Youth Scholarship • 1553

Puerto Rican
Completing the Dream Scholarship • 94
Jose Marti Scholarship Challenge Grant • 1505
Leadership for Diversity Scholarship • 1530
Minority Fellowship Program • 655
Minority Scholarship • 2205
Minority Serving Institution Grants • 2209

Samoan
Asian and Pacific Islander American Scholarships • 2105
Atsuhiko Tateuchi Memorial Scholarship • 1232
Completing the Dream Scholarship • 94
Diversity Achievement Scholarship • 414
EDSA Diversity Scholarships • 2137
George A. Strait Minority Scholarship • 591
Jackie Robinson Foundation Scholarship Program • 2170
Leadership for Diversity Scholarship • 1530
Legal Opportunity Scholarship Fund • 637
Minority Fellowship Program • 655
Minority Serving Institution Grants • 2209
UPS Hallmark Scholarship • 2274

Scottish
St. Andrew's Society of Washington, DC Scholarship • 2250

Southeast Asian
Asian and Pacific Islander American Scholarships • 2105
Atsuhiko Tateuchi Memorial Scholarship • 1232
CLA Scholarship For BIPOC Students in Memory of Edna Yelland • 559
Completing the Dream Scholarship • 94
Diversity Achievement Scholarship • 414
EDSA Diversity Scholarships • 2137
Jackie Robinson Foundation Scholarship Program • 2170

Jimmy A. Young Memorial Education Recognition Award • 952
Leadership for Diversity Scholarship • 1530
Louis B. Russell Scholarship • 1550
Minority Fellowship Program • 655
Minority Scholarship • 2205
Minority Serving Institution Grants • 2209
Minority Undergraduate Retention Grant • 1613
OCA/UPS Gold Mountain Scholarship • 2228
Upakar Foundation Indian American Community College Scholarship • 2273
UPS Hallmark Scholarship • 2274

Spanish
Jose Marti Scholarship Challenge Grant • 1505
Minority Scholarship • 2205

Swiss
Medicus Student Exchange • 2203

Taiwanese
Taiwanese American Scholarship Fund • 2260

Welsh
Sarah Josephine Langstaff Memorial Scholarship • 291

RELIGION INDEX

This index lists awards from various churches and religious organizations.

Allan Jerome Burry Scholarship • 1935
Catholic United Financial College Tuition Scholarship • 1951
CCA Christian Cheer Nationals • 78
Champions for Christ Scholarship • 1953
Diller Teen Tikkun Olam Awards • 1962
Education Scholarship • 2138
Emmett J. Doerr Memorial Scout Scholarship • 1966
Fadel Educational Foundation Annual Award Program • 1968
Helen B. and Lewis E. Goldstein Scholarship Fund • 1985
ISF Policy Scholarship Program • 1992
Islamic Society of North America Scholarships • 1993
Moris J. and Betty Kaplun Essay Contest • 2014
National Presbyterian College Scholarship • 2020
Native American Education Grant • 2221
Opportunity Scholarships for Lutheran Laywomen • 2027
Otto M. Stanfield Legal Scholarship • 679
Presbyterian Church USA Student Opportunity Scholarships • 2031
Rev. Dr. Karen Layman Gift of Hope Scholarship • 2034
Stanfield and D'Orlando Art Scholarship • 2048
Student Activist Awards • 315
UCC Seminarian Scholarship • 2059
Undergraduate Scholarships • 2063
United Methodist General Scholarship • 2066
Women in United Methodist History Writing Award • 2075
Young Christian Leaders Scholarship • 2076

DISABILITY INDEX

This index lists awards for students with physical, hearing, vision, mental and learning disabilities. It also includes awards for students who have been afflicted with certain illnesses.

AbbVie Immunology Scholarship • 2282
Alyssa McCroskey Memorial Scholarship • 1205
American Council of the Blind Scholarships • 2283
Anne Ford Scholarship Program • 2284
Baer Reintegration Scholarship • 2285
Betty Bacon Memorial Scholarship • 1239
BMO Capital Markets Lime Connect Equity Through Education Scholarship • 2286
Boomer Esiason Foundation General Academic Scholarship • 2287
California - Hawaii Elks Major Project Undergraduate Scholarship Program for Students with Disabilities • 1260
Cancer for College Scholarships • 2289
CAPED Excellence Scholarship • 1272
Challenge Met Scholarship • 2290
Dick Griffiths Memorial Scholarship • 1332
Duane Buckley Memorial Scholarship • 2291
Dyslexia/Auditory Processing Disorder Scholarship • 2292
Elizabeth Nash Foundation Scholarship Program • 2293
Eric Dostie Memorial College Scholarship • 2294
Fred Scheigert Scholarships • 2295
George H. Nofer Scholarship for Law and Public Policy • 2296
Graeme Clark Scholarship • 2297
Guthrie-Koch PKU Scholarship • 2298
Harry Alan Gregg Foundation Grants • 1422
Help America Hear Scholarship • 2299
HIV-Positive Scholarship • 2300
Incight Scholarship • 2301
Jaime Guttenberg All Abilities Scholarship • 2302
Kevin Child Scholarship • 2303
Lighthouse Guild Scholarships • 2304
Lime Connect Pathways Scholarship for High School Seniors with Disabilities • 2305
Little People of America Scholarships • 2306
Marion Huber Learning Through Listening Awards • 2307
Mary P. Oenslanger Scholastic Achievement Awards • 2308
Michael A. Hunter Memorial Scholarship Fund • 2309
Millie Brother Scholarship • 2310
National Collegiate Cancer Foundation Scholarship • 2311
National Federation of the Blind Scholarship • 2312
National Scholarship Competition for Disabled College Students • 2313
New Jersey State Elks Special Children's Committee Scholarship • 1648
NFMC Hinda Honigman Award for the Blind • 2314
Optimist International Communications Contest • 2316
P. Buckley Moss Endowed Scholarship • 2317
Paul and Ellen Ruckes Scholarship • 2318
Pega Scholars Program • 2235
RAREis Scholarship • 2319
Rudolph Dillman Memorial Scholarship • 2320
Salix Gastrointestinal Health Scholars Award • 2321
Scholarships for Survivors • 2322
Sertoma Scholarship for Students Who Are Hard of Hearing or Deaf • 2323
Soozie Courter Hemophilia Scholarship Program • 2324
Steve Fasteau Past Presidents' Scholarship • 1816
Student Award Program of FSD • 2325
Student with a Disability Scholarship • 716
Susan Bunch Memorial Scholarship • 1818
Susanna and Lucy DeLaurentis Charitable Foundation Memorial Scholarships • 2326
Tony Coelho Media Scholarship • 2327
TPA Scholarship Trust for the Hearing Impaired • 2328
UCB Family Epilepsy Scholarship Program • 2329
Vitality Medical's Student Disability Scholarship • 2330
Wells Fargo Scholarship Program for People with Disabilities • 2331
William and Dorothy Ferrell Scholarship • 2332

MEMBERSHIP INDEX

If you or your parents are members of any of the groups in this index, you may qualify for a scholarship.

Air Line Pilots Association, International
ALPA Scholarship Program • 1936
Alpha Chi
Gaston/Nolle Scholarships • 1976
Alpha Kappa Alpha Educational Advancement Foundation Inc.
Alpha Kappa Alpha Financial Need Scholars • 38
Educational Advancement Foundation Merit Scholarship • 136
Youth Partners Accessing Capital • 2078
Alpha Kappa Psi Foundation
Alpha Kappa Psi Scholarships • 526
American Association of Airport Executives
AAAE Foundation Scholarship • 742
American Association of State Troopers (AAST) Inc.
American Association of State Troopers (AAST) Scholarship • 1937
American Criminal Justice Association
ACJA/Lambda Alpha Epsilon Scholarship • 19
Student Paper Competition • 316
American Culinary Federation
American Culinary Federation Scholarships • 528
Ray and Gertrude Marshall Scholarship • 693
American Dental Hygienists' Association (ADHA) Institute for Oral Health
ADHA Institute Scholarship Program • 760
Colgate Bright Smiles, Bright Futures Minority Scholarships • 841
Crest Oral-B Laboratories Dental Hygiene Scholarships • 848
Dr. Esther Wilkins Scholarship • 866
Irene Woodall Graduate Scholarship • 947
Karla Girts Memorial Community Outreach Scholarship • 968
Sigma Phi Alpha Undergraduate Scholarship • 1112
American Federation of State, County and Municipal Employees (AFSCME), AFL-CIO
AFSCME Family Scholarship • 1934
American Federation of Teachers
Robert G. Porter Post-Secondary Scholarships • 2036
Robert G. Porter Scholars Program for Members • 2037
American Foreign Service Association (AFSA)
AFSA Financial Aid Scholarships • 1932
AFSA National Essay Contest • 24
AFSA/AAFSW Merit Awards • 1933
American Health Information Management Association (AHIMA) Foundation
AHIMA Foundation Merit Scholarships • 765
American Holistic Nurses Association
Charlotte McGuire Scholarship • 839
American Jersey Cattle Association
Cedarcrest Farms Scholarship • 837
American Legion
American Legion Eagle Scout of the Year • 1938
Eight and Forty Lung and Respiratory Nursing Scholarship Fund • 873
National Oratorical Contest • 238

The Ultimate Scholarship Book 2026
Membership Index

American Legion Auxiliary
Children of Warriors National Presidents' Scholarship • 82
Junior Member Loyalty Scholarship • 2001
Non-Traditional Student Scholarship • 2025
Spirit of Youth Scholarship for Junior Members • 2047

American Legion Auxiliary, Department of California
American Legion Auxiliary, Department of California Educational Assistance General $1,000 Scholarships • 1211
American Legion Auxiliary, Department of California Educational Assistance General $2,000 Scholarships • 1212
American Legion Auxiliary, Department of California Educational Assistance General $500 Scholarships • 1213
Past Department Presidents' Junior Scholarship Award • 1718

American Legion, Department of Florida
American Legion Department of Florida General Scholarship • 1215
Florida Oratorical Contest • 1380

American Legion, Department of Illinois
Eagle Scout Scholarship • 1250

American Occupational Therapy Foundation
Kappa Delta Phi • 966
Mary Eileen Dixey Scholarship • 1571
Ohio State Association/AOTF Scholarships • 1689
Texas Occupational Therapy Association Scholarships • 1845

American Ornithologists' Union
AOS Student and Postdoctoral Research Awards • 796

American Quarter Horse Foundation
Adrianna Andreini Scholarship • 1931
AQHF General Scholarship • 1940
AQHF Youth Scholarship • 1941
Boon San Kitty Scholarship • 1948
Margaret A. Haines Telephony Scholarship • 2008
Shawn Maree Vaillant Memorial Scholarship • 2043

American Radio Relay League Foundation
ARRL Foundation General Fund Scholarship • 534
Bill, W2ONV and Ann Salerno Memorial Scholarship • 542
Carole J. Streeter, KB9JBR, Scholarship • 553
Central Arizona DX Association Scholarship • 1282
Challenge Met Scholarship • 2290
Charles Clarke Cordle Memorial Scholarship • 555
Charles N. Fisher Memorial Scholarship • 556
Dayton Amateur Radio Association Scholarship • 565
Don Riebhoff Memorial Scholarship • 568
Dr. James L. Lawson Memorial Scholarship • 570
Edmond A. Metzger Scholarship • 575
Fred R. McDaniel Memorial Scholarship • 583
Gary Wagner, K3OMI, Scholarship • 903
IRARC Memorial, Joseph P. Rubino, WA4MMD, Scholarship • 615
Irving W. Cook, WA0CGS, Scholarship • 1479
K2TEO Martin J. Green, Sr. Memorial Scholarship • 628

L. Phil and Alice J. Wicker Scholarship • 631
L.B. Cebik, W4RNL and Jean Cebik, N4TZP Memorial Scholarship • 632
Louisiana Memorial Scholarship • 1552
Mary Lou Brown Scholarship • 646
Mississippi Scholarship • 1616
New England FEMARA Scholarship • 672
Paul and Helen L. Grauer Scholarship • 681
PHD Scholarship • 685
Ray, N0RP and Katie, W0KTE Pautz Scholarship • 694
Richard W. Bendicksen, N7ZL, Memorial Scholarship • 697
Six Meter Club of Chicago Scholarship • 1793
Tom and Judith Comstock Scholarship • 724
YASME Foundation Scholarship • 739
You've Got a Friend in Pennsylvania Scholarship • 1927

American Red Cross Youth
Navin Narayan College Scholarship • 245

American Society of Civil Engineers (ASCE)
Samuel Fletcher Tapman ASCE Student Chapter/Club Scholarship • 1106
Trent R. Dames and William W. Moore Fellowship • 1153

American Society of Civil Engineers-Michigan Section
Mackinac Scholarship • 1555
Marvin L. Zuidema Scholarship Award • 1568

American Society of Mechanical Engineers (ASME)
ASME Auxiliary Lucy and Charles W. E. Clarke Scholarship • 808
ASME Foundation Scholarships • 809
F.W. Beich Beichley Scholarship • 885
Frank and Dorothy Miller ASME Auxiliary Scholarships • 894
Garland Duncan Scholarships • 901
International Gas Turbine Institute Scholarship • 942
John and Elsa Gracik Scholarships • 953
Kenneth Andrew Roe Scholarship • 969
Melvin R. Green Scholarships • 999
Old Guard Oral Presentation Competition • 1054

American Society of Radiologic Technologists Foundation (ASRT)
Elekta Radiation Therapy Scholarship • 874

AMVETS National Headquarters
AMVETS Children/Grandchildren Scholarships • 46
AMVETS National Scholarships for Veterans • 47

AMVETS National Ladies Auxiliary Headquarters
AMVETS National Ladies Auxiliary Scholarship • 1939

Angus Foundation
Angus Foundation Scholarships • 788

Appaloosa Horse Club
Appaloosa Youth Association Art Contest • 797
Larry Williams Photography and AYA Photo Contest • 972
Youth Program • 1177

ARA Scholarship Foundation Inc.
ARA Scholarship • 1942

ASME International Petroleum Technology Institute
Petroleum Division College Scholarships • 1067

Association for Women in Sports Media
AWSM Internship and Scholarship • 1946

Association of Flight Attendants
Association of Flight Attendants Annual Scholarship • 1944

Association of Government Accountants (AGA)
National Academic Scholarships • 661

Association of Perioperative Registered Nurses
AORN Foundation Scholarship Program • 795

Assured Life Association
Assured Life Association National Scholarship • 1945

Babe Ruth League Inc.
Babe Ruth League Scholarships • 57

Bakery Confectionary Tobacco Workers and Grain Millers (BCTGM) International Union
David B. Durkee Memorial Scholarship Program • 1959

Big Y
Big Y Scholarship Programs • 1241

Bob Warnicke Memorial Scholarship Fund
Bob Warnicke Scholarship • 64

Boys and Girls Clubs of America
Boys and Girls Clubs of America National Youth of the Year Award • 1949

California Teachers Association (CTA)
CTA Cesar E. Chavez and Dolores Huerta Education Award Program • 1318
Martin Luther King, Jr. Memorial Scholarship • 2010
Student CTA (SCTA) Scholarship in Honor of L. Gordon Bittle • 2051

Catholic United Financial
Catholic United Financial College Tuition Scholarship • 1951

Circle K International
Kiwanis Children's Fund Scholarship • 2002

Citizens' Scholarship Foundation of America
Dollars for Scholars Scholarship • 124

Civitan
Shropshire Scholarship • 2045

Communications Workers of America
CWA Joe Beirne Foundation Scholarship • 1958

Conference of Minority Transportation Officials
Conference of Minority Transportation Officials (COMTO) National Scholarship • 2125

Connecticut Association of Health, Physical Education, Recreation and Dance
CTAHPERD Gibson-Laemel Scholarship • 1319
Mary Benevento/CTAHPERD Scholarship • 1570

Costume Society of America (CSA)
Stella Blum Research Grant • 486

DECA Inc.
Harry A. Applegate Scholarship • 599

Delta Gamma Foundation
Delta Gamma Foundation Scholarship • 1960

Delta Phi Epsilon Educational Foundation
Delta Phi Epsilon Educational Foundation Scholarship • 1961

Delta Sigma Pi
Undergraduate Scholarship • 2062

DeMolay Foundation
Frank S. Land Scholarships • 1975

Dixie Boys Baseball
Dixie Boys Baseball Scholarship Program • 120

Dixie Youth Baseball Inc.
Dixie Youth Scholarship Program • 122

EAA Aviation Center
David Alan Quick Scholarship • 853

H.P. Bud Milligan Aviation Scholarship • 924
Payzer Scholarship • 1063
Educational Theatre Association
Christopher L. Hunt Scholarship • 407
Dr. Kenny D. Hasija Scholarship • 417
Educational Theatre Association Board of Directors Scholarship • 419
Future Theatre Educator Scholarship • 428
Michael J. Peitz Leadership Scholarship • 460
Elks National Foundation Headquarters
Emergency Educational Fund Grants • 1965
Legacy Award • 2004
Most Valuable Student Scholarships • 230
Explorers Learning for Life
Capt. James J. Regan Scholarship • 72
James E. Breining Scholarship Award • 1995
National Aviation Explorer Scholarships • 1022
Sheryl A. Horak Memorial Scholarship • 301
Family, Career and Community Leaders of America - Texas Association
Texas Association FCCLA Regional Scholarship • 1837
Federal Employee Education and Assistance Fund
FEEA Scholarship Program • 1970
Fleet Reserve Association (FRA)
Americanism Essay Contest • 43
Fleet Reserve Association Scholarship • 1972
Stanley A. Doran Memorial Scholarship • 2049
Fraternal Order of Eagles
Fraternal Order of Eagles Memorial Foundation • 148
General Society of Mayflower Descendants
General Society of Mayflower Descendants (GSMD) Scholarship • 2148
Geological Society of America Foundation (GSAF)
Roy J. Shlemon Awards • 1100
Golden Key International Honour Society
Golden Key Graduate Scholar Award • 1980
Golden Key Outstanding Member Award • 1981
Golden Key Undergraduate Achievement Award • 1982
Golden Key Undergraduate Achievement Scholarship • 1983
Golf Course Superintendents Association of America
GCSAA Legacy Awards • 1977
GCSAA Scholars Competition • 905
Honor Society of Phi Kappa Phi
Literacy Grants • 2006
Phi Kappa Phi Fellowship • 2030
Illinois Association for Health, Physical Education, Recreation and Dance
Illinois Association for Health, Physical Education, Recreation and Dance Scholarships • 1460
Indiana Golf Association
David E. Simon Scholarship • 1323
Indiana Golf Foundation Scholarship • 1466
Institute of Industrial and Systems Engineers
A.O. Putnam Memorial Scholarship • 741
C.B. Gambrell Undergraduate Scholarship • 833
Dwight D. Gardner Scholarship • 869
E.J. Sierleja Memorial Fellowship • 871
Gilbreth Memorial Fellowship • 911
Harold and Inge Marcus Scholarship • 925
IISE Council of Fellows Undergraduate Scholarship • 938
John L. Imhoff Scholarship • 957
John S.W. Fargher, Jr. Scholarship • 960

Lisa Zaken Award For Excellence • 981
Marvin Mundel Memorial Scholarship • 992
Presidents Scholarship of the Institute of Industrial Engineers • 1078
United Parcel Service Scholarship for Female Students • 1162
United Parcel Service Scholarship for Minority Students • 2272
International Alliance of Theatrical Stage Employees, Artists and Allied Crafts of the U.S.
Richard F. Walsh, Alfred W. DiTolla, Harold P. Spivak Foundation Award • 2035
International Association of Machinists and Aerospace Workers
IAM Scholarship • 1989
International Chemical Workers Union Council/UFCW
Walter L. Mitchell Memorial Scholarship Awards • 2070
International Flight Services Association (IFSA)
IFSA Foundation Scholarship Award • 1990
International Scholarship and Tuition Services Inc.
Glass, Molders, Pottery, Plastics and Allied Workers Memorial Scholarship Fund • 1979
International Union of Electronic, Electrical, Salaried, Machine and Furniture Workers-Communications Workers of America
James B. Carey Scholarship • 1994
Iowa 4-H Foundation
Iowa 4-H College Scholarships • 1469
Iowa Foundation for Agricultural Advancement
Russ Brannen/KENT FEEDS Memorial Beef Scholarship • 1774
Schlutz Family Beef Breeding Scholarship • 1778
Winner's Circle Scholarships • 1914
Iowa Thespian Chapter
Iowa Thespian Chapter Board Senior Scholarships • 1476
IUPAT International Office
S. Frank Bud Raftery Scholarship • 2038
Japanese American Citizens League (JACL)
Abe and Esther Hagiwara Student Aid Award • 2081
Japanese American Citizens League Entering Freshman Awards • 2172
Japanese American Citizens League Graduate Awards • 2173
Japanese American Citizens League Law Scholarships • 2174
Japanese American Citizens League Undergraduate Awards • 2175
Kyutaro and Yasuo Abiko Memorial Scholarship • 2003
Jewish War Veterans of the USA
Bernard Rotberg Memorial Scholarship Fund • 1947
Kappa Delta Pi Educational Foundation
Sandra Jo Hornick Scholarship • 2040
Knights of Columbus
Fourth Degree Pro Deo and Pro Patria Scholarships • 1974
John W. McDevitt (Fourth Degree) Scholarship Fund • 1999
Ladies Auxiliary of the Fleet Reserve Association
La Fra Scholarship • 201
Sam Rose Memorial Scholarship • 2039
Maids of Athena
Maids of Athena Scholarships • 2007

Medical Group Management Association
Harry J. Harwick Scholarship • 927
Leaders Scholarship • 975
MGMA Midwest Section Scholarship • 1002
MGMA Western Section Scholarship • 1003
Richard L. Davis, FACMPE - Managers Scholarship • 1092
Richard L. Davis, FACMPE/Barbara B. Watson, FACMPE - National Scholarship • 1093
Minerals, Metals and Materials Society
Light Metals Division Scholarship • 980
Materials Processing and Manufacturing Division Scholarship • 995
Structural Materials Division Scholarship • 1130
TMS Best Paper Contest • 1149
TMS Technical Division Student Poster Contest • 1150
TMS/International Symposium On Superalloys Scholarships • 1151
Missouri 4-H Foundation
Missouri 4-H Foundation Scholarships • 1618
Missouri State Thespians
Missouri State Thespian Scholarships • 1620
Modern Woodmen of America
Modern Woodmen of America Scholarship • 2013
Mortar Board National Foundation
Mortar Board National Foundation Fellowship • 2015
Mu Alpha Theta Scholarship Committee
Mary Rhein Memorial Scholarship • 993
National 4-H Council
4-H Youth in Action • 1930
National Association of Black Journalists
Larry Whiteside Scholarship • 2183
National Association of Blacks in Criminal Justice
Chairman's Award • 1952
Jonathan Jasper Wright Award • 194
Mary Church Terrell Award • 215
Medgar Evers Award • 218
Owens-Bell Award • 2028
William L. Hastie Award • 376
National Association of Letter Carriers
William C. Doherty Scholarship Fund • 2073
National Cattlemen's Foundation
Beef Industry Scholarship • 826
National Education Association
NEA-Retired Jack Kinnaman Memorial Scholarship • 669
National Exchange Club
Youth of the Year Award • 2077
National Federation of Music Clubs (Coral Gables, FL)
Thelma A. Robinson Award in Ballet • 494
National Federation of Music Clubs (FL)
NFMC Gretchen E. Van Roy Music Education Scholarship • 674
National FFA Organization
CNH Industrial Aftermarket Solutions Scholarship • 1956
Elmer J. and Hester Jane Johnson Memorial FFA Scholarship • 876
Farm Credit Services of America Collegiate Scholarship • 1969
FarmAid FFA Scholarship • 886
Ford Motor Company Fund and Ford Trucks Built Ford Tough - FFA Scholarship Program • 1973
Grow Ag Leaders Scholarship • 923
Hoard's Dairyman FFA Scholarship • 1987

617

The Ultimate Scholarship Book 2026
Membership Index

National FFA Alumni and Supporters Agricultural
Education Scholarship • 1025
National FFA Combined Scholarship • 2018
Tractor Supply Company Endowment • 2055

National Honor Society
National Honor Society Scholarship • 2019

National Independent Automobile Dealers Association
NIADA Scholarship • 2024

National Propane Gas Foundation
National Propane Gas Foundation • 2021

National Scholastic Surfing Association
National Scholarship Program • 239

National Society Daughters of the American Revolution
Alice W. Rooke Scholarship • 775
Irene and Daisy MacGregor Memorial Scholarship • 946
Lillian and Arthur Dunn Scholarship • 2005

National Society of Collegiate Scholars (NSCS)
Community College Transition Award • 1957
First in the Family Scholarship • 1971
Induction Recognition Award • 1991
NSCS Grad School Award • 2026

National Society of Professional Surveyors (NSPS/AAGS)
AAGS - NSPS Scholarships • 744
AAGS Joseph F. Dracup Scholarship Award • 745
Lowell Loving Undergraduate Scholarship • 986
Nettie Dracup Memorial Scholarship • 671
Schonstedt Scholarship in Surveying • 1107

National Society, Sons of the American Revolution
Arthur M. and Berdena King Eagle Scout Contest • 1943
George S. and Stella M. Knight Essay Contest • 155
Joseph S. Rumbaugh Historical Oration Contest • 626

Naval Helicopter Association
Naval Helicopter Association Scholarship • 243

NEA Foundation
Learning and Leadership Grants • 635
Student Success Grants • 715

New England Water Works Association
Elson T. Killam Memorial Scholarship • 877
Francis X. Crowley Scholarship • 581

North Carolina 4-H Youth Development
North Carolina 4-H Development Fund Scholarships • 1669

North Texas Fair and Rodeo
Bob C. Powers Scholarship • 1243
North Texas State Fair Association Scholarship • 1680

Office and Professional Employees International Union
Howard Coughlin Memorial Scholarship Fund • 1988
John Kelly Labor Studies Scholarship Fund • 1997

Phi Sigma Kappa International Headquarters
Terrill Graduate Fellowship • 2054
Wenderoth Undergraduate Scholarship • 2072

Phi Theta Kappa Honor Society
Guistwhite Scholarships • 1984
Hites Transfer Scholarship • 1986

Phi Upsilon Omicron Inc.
Margaret Jerome Sampson Scholarship • 2009
Nell Bryant Robinson Scholarship • 670

Physician Assistant Foundation
Physician Assistant Foundation Scholarship • 1070

Pi Sigma Alpha
Nancy McManus Washington Internship Scholarships • 660

Quill and Scroll Society
Quill and Scroll Student Scholarships • 691

Rhode Island Foundation
Albert E. and Florence W. Newton Nursing Scholarship • 1196
Antonio Cirino Memorial Scholarship • 1220
Frances L. Macartney Porter Fund • 1387
James J. Burns and C.A. Haynes Textile Scholarship • 1489
Lily and Catello Sorrentino Memorial Scholarship • 1541
Patty and Melvin Alperin First Generation Scholarship • 1719
Rhode Island Foundation Association of Former Legislators Scholarship • 1754

School Nutrition Association
Nancy Curry Scholarship • 659
Schwan's Food Service Scholarship • 705

Screen Actors Guild - American Federation of Television and Radio Artists
George Heller Memorial Scholarship Fund of the SAG-AFTRA Foundation • 1978

Screen Actors Guild Foundation
John L. Dales Scholarship Fund • 1998

Seafarers International Union of North America
Charlie Logan Scholarship Program for Dependents • 1955

SEANC Scholarship Foundation
State Employees Association of North Carolina (SEANC) Scholarships • 1809

Service Employees International Union
Service Employees International Union Scholarships • 2041

Shape America
Bill Kane Scholarship, Undergraduate • 827
Ruth Abernathy Presidential Scholarship • 1103

Shasta Head Start Child Development Inc.
Shasta Head Start Alumni Scholarship • 2042

Sheet Metal Workers' International Association
Sheet Metal Workers' International Scholarship Fund • 2044

Sigma Alpha Epsilon (SAE)
Jones-Laurence Award for Scholastic Achievement • 2000
Warren Poslusny Award for Outstanding Achievement • 2071

Sigma Alpha Iota Philanthropies
Undergraduate Scholarships • 498

Sigma Phi Epsilon Fraternity (National)
Sigma Phi Epsilon Balanced Man Scholarship • 2046

Society for Technical Communication
Distinguished Service Award for Students • 567

Society of Automotive Engineers International
BMW/SAE Engineering Scholarship • 829
Edward D. Hendrickson/SAE Engineering Scholarship • 872
Fred M. Young, Sr./SAE Engineering Scholarship • 895
Long-Term Member Sponsored Scholarship • 984
Ralph K. Hillquist Honorary SAE Scholarship • 1083
Tau Beta Pi/Society of Automotive Engineers Engineering Scholarship • 1137
TMC/SAE Donald D. Dawson Technical Scholarship • 1148
Yanmar/SAE Scholarship • 1175

Society of Naval Architects and Marine Engineers (SNAME)
David A. O Neil Scholarship • 852
John V. Wehausen Graduate Scholarship • 961
Mandell and Lester Rosenblatt Undergraduate Scholarship • 989
Robert N. and Helen H. Herbert Undergraduate Scholarship • 1098

Sons of Union Veterans of the Civil War
Sons of Union Veterans of the Civil War Scholarships • 306

South Carolina Farm Bureau Foundation
South Carolina Farm Bureau Foundation Scholarships • 1800

Southern Bowling Congress
Curwen-Guidry-Blackburn Scholarship Fund • 107

SPIE, The International Society for Optical Engineering
SPIE Optics and Photonics Education Scholarship • 1122

Tau Beta Pi Association
Tau Beta Pi Scholarships • 2053

Tau Kappa Epsilon Educational Foundation
Carroll C. Hall Memorial Scholarship • 1950
Charles R. Walgreen Jr. Leadership Award • 1954
Donald A. and John R. Fisher Memorial Scholarship • 1964
Eugene C. Beach Memorial Scholarship • 1967

Texas 4-H Youth Development Foundation
Collegiate Scholarship • 1302
Courageous Heart Scholarship • 1316
Technical Certification Scholarship • 1829
Texas 4-H Opportunity Scholarship Program - Baccalaureate Scholarships • 1836

Transport Worker Union of America, AFL-CIO
Michael J. Quill Scholarship Fund • 2012

Tri Delta
Tri Delta Undergraduate Scholarship • 2056

Triangle Education Foundation
James Rust Scholarship • 1996
Mortin Scholarship • 2016

Truckload Carriers Association
Truckload Carriers Association Scholarship Fund • 2057

U.S. Coast Guard Chief Petty Officers Association
Captain Caliendo College Assistance Fund • 73

U.S. Navy Naval Reserve Officers Training Corps (NROTC)
Navy-Marine Corps ROTC College Program • 248
Navy-Marine Corps ROTC Four-Year Scholarships • 249
Navy-Marine Corps ROTC Two-Year Scholarships • 250
NROTC Nurse Corps Scholarship • 259

Ukrainian Fraternal Association
Eugene and Elinor Kotur Scholarship Trust Fund • 2140

Union Plus
Union Plus Scholarship • 2064

United Agribusiness League
United Agribusiness League and United Agricultural Benefit Trust Scholarships • 2065

United Food and Commercial Workers Union
   UFCW Scholarship Program • 2060
United Mine Workers of America/BCOA T.E.F.
   UMWA-Lorin E. Kerr Scholarships • 2061
United States Bowling Congress
   Earl Anthony Memorial Scholarships • 132
   Gift for Life Scholarships • 156
   USBC Alberta E. Crowe Star of Tomorrow • 356
   USBC Annual Zeb Scholarship • 357
   USBC Chuck Hall Star of Tomorrow • 358
   USBC Youth Ambassador of the Year • 359
United Transportation Union Insurance Association
   United Transportation Union Scholarships • 2067
Utility Workers Union of America
   Utility Workers Union of America Scholarships • 2068
Veterans of Foreign Wars
   Patriot's Pen Youth Essay Contest • 473
   VFW Scout of the Year Scholarship • 2069
   Voice of Democracy Audio Essay Contests • 363
Virginia High School League
   VHSL Achievement Award • 1877
   Virginia High School League Charles E. Savedge Journalism Scholarship • 1883
Wisconsin Amusement and Music Operators
   Wisconsin Amusement and Music Operators Scholarships • 1915
Women in Aviation International
   Women in Aviation International Scholarship • 2074

INDEX BY SPONSOR

1 FOR 2 EDUCATION FOUNDATION
1 for 2 Education Foundation Scholarship • 9

1,000 DREAMS FUND
New Face of Tech Scholarship Program • 1043

1DENTAL.COM
1Dental Scholarship • 11

1ST MARINE DIVISION ASSOCIATION INC.
1st Marine Division Association Scholarship • 12

25TH INFANTRY DIVISION ASSOCIATION (TIDA)
25th Infantry Division Association Educational Scholarship • 13

A PLACE FOR ROVER INC.
Rover Sitter Scholarship • 285

AAU NATIONAL HEADQUARTERS
AAU Karate Scholarship • 16

ABACUS LIFE
Abacus Life Scholarship • 18

ABBVIE IMMUNOLOGY SCHOLARSHIP
AbbVie Immunology Scholarship • 2282

ACADEMY OF INTERACTIVE ARTS AND SCIENCES (AIAS)
WomenIn Scholarship • 2277

ACADEMY OF MOTION PICTURE ARTS AND SCIENCES
Student Academy Awards Competition • 488

ACADEMY OF NUTRITION AND DIETETICS
Academy of Nutrition and Dietetics Foundation Student Scholarship • 751

ACADEMY OF TELEVISION ARTS AND SCIENCES FOUNDATION
College Television Awards • 409

ACADEMY OF UNDERWATER ARTS AND SCIENCES
Zale Parry Scholarship • 385

ACCEPTANCE INSURANCE COMPANY
Heisman High School Scholarship • 171

ACCOUNTING AND FINANCIAL WOMEN'S ALLIANCE
Accounting and Financial Women's Alliance Foundation Scholarship • 513

ACES: THE SOCIETY FOR EDITING
ACES Education Fund Scholarship • 386
ACES Scholarships • 387

ACTORS FUND – CAREER TRANSITION FOR DANCERS
Career Transition for Dancers Undergraduate Studies Scholarship • 403

ACTUARIAL FOUNDATION
Actuarial Diversity Scholarship • 2083
Modeling the Future Challenge • 1011

ADOBE
Adobe Design Circle Scholarships • 390

AGAINST THE GRAIN
Against The Grain Artistic Scholarship • 2088

AGL OVER THE RAINBOW FOUNDATION
AGL Over the Rainbow Scholarship • 391

AGRICULTURE COUNCIL OF AMERICA
Ag Day Essay Contest • 25

AIGA, THE PROFESSIONAL ASSOCIATION FOR DESIGN
AIGA Worldstudio Scholarships • 392

AIR FORCE AID SOCIETY INC.
General Henry H. Arnold Education Grant Program • 153

AIR FORCE ASSOCIATION
Mike and Gail Donley Spouse Scholarship • 223

AIR FORCE RESERVE OFFICER TRAINING CORPS
Air Force ROTC ASCP • 29
Air Force ROTC High School Scholarship Program • 30
Air Force ROTC In-College Program • 31
Air Force ROTC Professional Officer Course-Early Release Program • 32
Air Force ROTC SOAR Program • 33

AIR FORCE SERGEANTS ASSOCIATION
Airmen Memorial Foundation Scholarship Program • 34
Chief Master Sergeants of the Air Force Scholarships • 80

AIR LINE PILOTS ASSOCIATION, INTERNATIONAL
ALPA Scholarship Program • 1936

AIR TRAFFIC CONTROL ASSOCIATION
Full-Time Employee Student Scholarship • 897
Gabriel A. Hartl Scholarship • 899
Lawrence C. Fortier Memorial Scholarship • 974

AIR-CONDITIONING, HEATING AND REFRIGERATION INSTITUTE
Clifford H. Ted Rees Jr. Scholarship • 560

AIRCRAFT ELECTRONICS ASSOCIATION
David Arver Memorial Scholarship • 854
Dutch and Ginger Arver Scholarship • 868
Garmin Scholarship • 902
Johnny Davis Memorial Scholarship • 963
Lee Tarbox Memorial Scholarship • 977
Mid-Continent Instruments and Avionics Scholarship • 1006

AKASH KURUVILLA MEMORIAL SCHOLARSHIP FUND INC.
Akash Kuruvilla Memorial Scholarship • 35

ALABAMA JUNIOR ACADEMY OF SCIENCE
Gorgas Scholarship Competition • 1405

ALABAMA ROAD BUILDERS ASSOCIATION INC.
Ed and Charlotte Rodgers Scholarships • 1350

ALASKA COMMISSION ON POSTSECONDARY EDUCATION
Alaska Education Grant • 1194
Alaska Performance Scholarship • 1195

ALASKA COMMUNITY FOUNDATION
JJ Klein Scholarship Fund • 1495
Liam Hood Scholarship Fund • 1537
Red Boucher Scholarship • 1751

ALBUQUERQUE COMMUNITY FOUNDATION (ACF)
Sussman-Miller Educational Assistance Award • 1821

ALEXANDER GRAHAM BELL ASSOCIATION FOR THE DEAF AND HARD OF HEARING
George H. Nofer Scholarship for Law and Public Policy • 2296

The Ultimate Scholarship Book 2026
Sponsor Index

ALEXANDER HAMILTON SCHOLARS
Hamilton Award • 168

ALEXIA FOUNDATION
Alexia Foundation Student Grants • 393

ALICE L. HALTOM EDUCATIONAL FUND
Alice L. Haltom Educational Fund Scholarship • 523

ALISA'S ANGELS FOUNDATION
Alisa's Angels Scholarship • 1198

ALLIANCE FOR WOMEN IN MEDIA
NCTA and AWMF Scholarship • 2224

ALLIED VAN LINES
Allied Van Lines Scholarship • 524

ALPHA CHI
Gaston/Nolle Scholarships • 1976

ALPHA KAPPA ALPHA EDUCATIONAL ADVANCEMENT FOUNDATION INC.
Alpha Kappa Alpha Financial Need Scholars • 38
Educational Advancement Foundation Merit Scholarship • 136
Youth Partners Accessing Capital • 2078

ALPHA KAPPA PSI FOUNDATION
Alpha Kappa Psi Scholarships • 526

AMAZON FUTURE ENGINEER SCHOLARSHIP
Amazon Future Engineer Scholarship • 777

AMBUCS
AMBUCS Scholars • 778

AMERICA'S 911 FOUNDATION INC.
America's 911 Foundation Scholarship • 39

AMERICAN ACADEMY OF NEUROLOGY
Medical Student Research Scholarship • 996
Resident Research Scholarship • 1087
Visiting Medical Student Scholar • 1167

AMERICAN ACADEMY OF UNDERWATER SCIENCES
AAUS Student Scholarships • 17

AMERICAN ASSOCIATION FOR RESPIRATORY CARE
Jimmy A. Young Memorial Education Recognition Award • 952
NBRC/AMP Gareth B. Gish, MS, RRT Memorial and William F. Miller, MD Postgraduate Education Recognition Awards • 1033
NBRC/AMP William W. Burgin, Jr. MD and Robert M. Lawrence, MD Education Recognition Award • 1034

AMERICAN ASSOCIATION OF AIRPORT EXECUTIVES
AAAE Foundation Scholarship • 742

AMERICAN ASSOCIATION OF LAW LIBRARIES
AALL Educational Scholarships • 510
George A. Strait Minority Scholarship • 591
LexisNexis / John R. Johnson Memorial Scholarship Endowment • 638

AMERICAN ASSOCIATION OF MEDICAL ASSISTANTS
AAMA Student Essay Competition • 746

AMERICAN ASSOCIATION OF OCCUPATIONAL HEALTH NURSES (AAOHN) FOUNDATION
Academic Education Award • 750

AMERICAN ASSOCIATION OF PEOPLE WITH DISABILITIES (AAPD)
Tony Coelho Media Scholarship • 2327

AMERICAN ASSOCIATION OF STATE TROOPERS (AAST) INC.
American Association of State Troopers (AAST) Scholarship • 1937

AMERICAN ASSOCIATION OF TEACHERS OF JAPANESE
Bridging Scholarships for Study Abroad in Japan • 400

AMERICAN ASSOCIATION OF UNIVERSITY WOMEN (AAUW) EDUCATIONAL FOUNDATION
AAUW Educational Foundation Career Development Grants • 2080

AMERICAN ASSOCIATION OF UNIVERSITY WOMEN – HONOLULU BRANCH
Tweet Coleman Aviation Scholarship • 1861

AMERICAN BAPTIST CHURCHES USA
Undergraduate Scholarships • 2063

AMERICAN BAR ASSOCIATION
American Bar Association Law Day Art Contest • 40
American Bar Association Law Student Writing Competition • 527
Legal Opportunity Scholarship Fund • 637

AMERICAN BAR FOUNDATION
ABF Summer Undergraduate Research Fellowship Program • 511

AMERICAN BOARD OF FUNERAL SERVICE EDUCATION
National Scholarship Program • 665

AMERICAN BUS ASSOCIATION (ABA)
Academic Merit Scholarships • 512

AMERICAN CENTER OF ORIENTAL RESEARCH (ACOR)
ACOR-CAORC Fellowship • 515
Harrell Family Fellowship • 598
Jennifer C. Groot Fellowship • 619

AMERICAN CERAMIC SOCIETY
Lewis C. Hoffman Scholarship • 978

AMERICAN CHEMICAL SOCIETY
American Chemical Society Scholars Program • 2098
Rubber Division Undergraduate Scholarship • 1101

AMERICAN CLASSICAL LEAGUE
ACL/NJCL National Greek Examination Scholarship • 388
ACL/NJCL National Latin Examination Scholarships • 389

AMERICAN COAL ASH ASSOCIATION (ACAA)
ACAA Educational Foundation Scholarship Program • 748

AMERICAN COLLEGE OF HEALTHCARE EXECUTIVES
Richard J. Stull Student Essay Competition in Healthcare Management • 1090

AMERICAN CONCRETE INSTITUTE
ACI Scholarship • 753
ACI Student Fellowship Program • 754

AMERICAN COUNCIL OF ENGINEERING COMPANIES CALIFORNIA (ACEC)
ACEC Scholarship • 1185

AMERICAN COUNCIL OF ENGINEERING COMPANIES OF COLORADO
ACEC Colorado Scholarship Program • 1184

AMERICAN COUNCIL OF ENGINEERING COMPANIES OF NEW JERSEY
American Council of Engineering Companies of New Jersey Member Organization Scholarship • 1207

AMERICAN COUNCIL OF ENGINEERING COMPANIES OF NEW YORK
ACEC New York Scholarship Program • 752

AMERICAN COUNCIL OF LEARNED SOCIETIES (ACLS)
ACLS Fellowships • 514
Luce/ACLS Dissertation Fellowships in American Art • 457

AMERICAN COUNCIL OF THE BLIND
American Council of the Blind Scholarships • 2283
Duane Buckley Memorial Scholarship • 2291

AMERICAN CRIMINAL JUSTICE ASSOCIATION
ACJA/Lambda Alpha Epsilon Scholarship • 19
Student Paper Competition • 316

AMERICAN CULINARY FEDERATION
American Culinary Federation Scholarships • 528
Ray and Gertrude Marshall Scholarship • 693

AMERICAN DENTAL EDUCATION ASSOCIATION
ADEA/Crest Oral-B Scholarships for Dental Hygiene Students Pursuing Academic Careers • 755
ADEA/Haleon Preventive Dentistry Scholarships • 756
ADEA/MouthWatch Patti DiGangi Scholarship for Dental Hygiene Innovation • 757
ADEA/MouthWatch Predoctoral Dental Student Scholarship for Innovation • 758
ADEA/Sigma Phi Alpha Linda Devore Scholarship • 759

AMERICAN DENTAL HYGIENISTS' ASSOCIATION (ADHA) INSTITUTE FOR ORAL HEALTH
ADHA Institute Scholarship Program • 760
Colgate Bright Smiles, Bright Futures Minority Scholarships • 841
Crest Oral-B Laboratories Dental Hygiene Scholarships • 848
Dr. Esther Wilkins Scholarship • 866
Irene Woodall Graduate Scholarship • 947
Karla Girts Memorial Community Outreach Scholarship • 968
Sigma Phi Alpha Undergraduate Scholarship • 1112

AMERICAN EPILEPSY SOCIETY
Predoctoral Research Fellowships • 1077

AMERICAN FEDERATION FOR AGING RESEARCH (AFAR)
Medical Student Training in Aging Research (MSTAR) Program • 997

AMERICAN FEDERATION OF STATE, COUNTY AND MUNICIPAL EMPLOYEES (AFSCME), AFL-CIO
AFSCME Family Scholarship • 1934

The Ultimate Scholarship Book 2026
Sponsor Index

AMERICAN FEDERATION OF TEACHERS
- Robert G. Porter Post-Secondary Scholarships • 2036
- Robert G. Porter Scholars Program for Members • 2037

AMERICAN FISHERIES SOCIETY (AFS)
- Hutton Junior Fisheries Biology Program • 936

AMERICAN FLORAL ENDOWMENT
- Harold Bettinger Scholarship • 926

AMERICAN FOREIGN SERVICE ASSOCIATION (AFSA)
- AFSA Financial Aid Scholarships • 1932
- AFSA National Essay Contest • 24
- AFSA/AAFSW Merit Awards • 1933

AMERICAN FOUNDATION FOR THE BLIND SCHOLARSHIP COMMITTEE
- Paul and Ellen Ruckes Scholarship • 2318
- Rudolph Dillman Memorial Scholarship • 2320

AMERICAN FOUNDATION FOR UROLOGIC DISEASE INC.
- AUA Foundation Research Scholars Program • 817

AMERICAN GROUND WATER TRUST
- Baroid Scholarship • 823
- Thomas M. Stetson Scholarship • 1144

AMERICAN HACKNEY HORSE SOCIETY
- AHHS Foundation Scholarship • 27

AMERICAN HEALTH INFORMATION MANAGEMENT ASSOCIATION (AHIMA) FOUNDATION
- AHIMA Foundation Merit Scholarships • 765

AMERICAN HEART ASSOCIATION
- EmPOWERED Scholars Program • 878

AMERICAN HELLENIC EDUCATION PROGRESSIVE ASSOCIATION
- AHEPA Educational Foundation National Scholarship Program • 2092
- Family District 1 Scholarships • 1372
- National and Chapter Scholarships • 2214

AMERICAN HISTORICAL ASSOCIATION
- Fellowship in Aerospace History • 890
- Wesley-Logan Prize • 734

AMERICAN HOLISTIC NURSES ASSOCIATION
- Charlotte McGuire Scholarship • 839

AMERICAN HOTEL AND LODGING EDUCATIONAL FOUNDATION (AHLEF)
- American Express Scholarship Competition • 529
- Ecolab Scholarship Competition • 573
- Incoming Freshman Scholarship • 612

AMERICAN INDIAN COLLEGE FUND
- Full Circle Scholarship • 2144
- Tribal College and University (TCU) Scholarships • 2268

AMERICAN INDIAN SCIENCE AND ENGINEERING SOCIETY
- A.T. Anderson Memorial Scholarship • 2079
- AISES Intel Scholarship • 2095
- Burlington Northern Santa Fe (BNSF) Foundation Scholarship • 2111

AMERICAN INDIAN SERVICES
- American Indian Services Scholarship • 2099

AMERICAN INSTITUTE FOR CONTEMPORARY GERMAN STUDIES - (AICGS)
- DAAD/AICGS Research Fellowship Program • 412

AMERICAN INSTITUTE FOR FOREIGN STUDY
- AIFS Green Ambassador Scholarship • 28
- Diversity Achievement Scholarship • 414
- Hispanic Serving Institutions Scholarship • 2161
- Historically Black College and University Scholarship • 2162
- John S. Linakis Scholarship • 192
- Russel R. Taylor Foundation Scholarship • 287
- Sir Cyril Taylor Legacy Scholarship • 302

AMERICAN INSTITUTE OF AERONAUTICS AND ASTRONAUTICS
- AIAA Foundation Undergraduate Scholarship Program • 767

AMERICAN INSTITUTE OF ARCHITECTS
- Payette Sho-Ping Chin Memorial Academic Scholarship • 1062

AMERICAN INSTITUTE OF CERTIFIED PUBLIC ACCOUNTANTS
- AICPA Fellowship for Minority Doctoral Students • 2093
- AICPA Foundation Scholarship for Future CPAs • 518
- AICPA Foundation Two-year Transfer Scholarship • 519
- AICPA John L. Carey Scholarship • 520
- AICPA Scholarship for Minority Accounting Students • 2094
- AWSCPA Scholarship • 536
- William (Bill) Ezzell Scholarship • 736

AMERICAN INSTITUTE OF CHEMICAL ENGINEERS - (AIChE)
- Donald F. and Mildred Topp Othmer Scholarships • 861
- John J. McKetta Scholarship • 956
- Minority Scholarship Awards for College Students • 2207
- Minority Scholarship Awards for Incoming College Freshmen • 2208

AMERICAN INSTITUTE OF INDIAN STUDIES
- Junior Fellowships • 627

AMERICAN INSTITUTE OF MINING, METALLURGICAL AND PETROLEUM ENGINEERS (AIME)
- John S. Marshall Memorial Scholarship • 959

AMERICAN INSTITUTE OF WINE AND FOOD - PACIFIC NORTHWEST CHAPTER
- John Schwartz Scholarship • 1503

AMERICAN JERSEY CATTLE ASSOCIATION
- Cedarcrest Farms Scholarship • 837

AMERICAN KENNEL CLUB
- Junior Showmanship Scholarship Program • 965

AMERICAN LEGION
- American Legion Eagle Scout of the Year • 1938
- American Legion Legacy Scholarships • 42
- Eight and Forty Lung and Respiratory Nursing Scholarship Fund • 873
- National Oratorical Contest • 238

AMERICAN LEGION AUXILIARY
- Children of Warriors National Presidents' Scholarship • 82
- Junior Member Loyalty Scholarship • 2001
- Non-Traditional Student Scholarship • 2025
- Spirit of Youth Scholarship for Junior Members • 2047

AMERICAN LEGION AUXILIARY, DEPARTMENT OF CALIFORNIA
- American Legion Auxiliary, Department of California Educational Assistance General $1,000 Scholarships • 1211
- American Legion Auxiliary, Department of California Educational Assistance General $2,000 Scholarships • 1212
- American Legion Auxiliary, Department of California Educational Assistance General $500 Scholarships • 1213
- Past Department Presidents' Junior Scholarship Award • 1718

AMERICAN LEGION AUXILIARY, DEPARTMENT OF NEW YORK
- Mary Ann K. Murtha Memorial Scholarship • 1569
- New York Legion Auxiliary Department Scholarship • 1651
- New York Legion Auxiliary District Scholarships • 1652
- Raymond T. Wellington, Jr. Memorial Scholarship • 1747

AMERICAN LEGION BASEBALL
- American Legion Baseball Scholarship • 41

AMERICAN LEGION, DEPARTMENT OF ALASKA
- Richard D. Johnson Memorial Post-Secondary Scholarship • 1756

AMERICAN LEGION, DEPARTMENT OF ARKANSAS
- American Legion Department of Arkansas High School Oratorical Scholarship Program • 1214

AMERICAN LEGION, DEPARTMENT OF CALIFORNIA
- California Oratorical Contest • 1268

AMERICAN LEGION, DEPARTMENT OF COLORADO
- Colorado Oratorical Contest • 1305

AMERICAN LEGION, DEPARTMENT OF CONNECTICUT
- American Legion - Connecticut Oratorical Contest • 1210

AMERICAN LEGION, DEPARTMENT OF FLORIDA
- American Legion Department of Florida General Scholarship • 1215
- Florida Oratorical Contest • 1380

AMERICAN LEGION, DEPARTMENT OF GEORGIA
- Georgia Oratorical Contest • 1397

AMERICAN LEGION, DEPARTMENT OF ILLINOIS
- American Legion Department of Illinois Scholarship • 1216
- Eagle Scout Scholarship • 1250

AMERICAN LEGION, DEPARTMENT OF INDIANA
- Indiana Oratorical Contest • 1467

AMERICAN LEGION, DEPARTMENT OF IOWA
- Iowa Oratorical Contest • 1471

The Ultimate Scholarship Book 2026
Sponsor Index

AMERICAN LEGION, DEPARTMENT OF KANSAS
Albert M. Lappin Scholarship • 1197
Charles W. and Annette Hill Scholarship • 1288
Hugh A. Smith Scholarship Fund • 1452
Kansas Oratorical Contest • 1513
Music Committee Scholarship • 1630
Paul Flaherty Athletic Scholarship • 1721
Rosedale Post 346 Scholarship • 1769
Ted and Nora Anderson Scholarships • 1830

AMERICAN LEGION, DEPARTMENT OF MAINE
Children and Youth Scholarships • 1291
Daniel E. Lambert Memorial Scholarship • 1321
James V. Day Scholarship • 1491

AMERICAN LEGION, DEPARTMENT OF MICHIGAN
Guy M. Wilson Scholarship • 1416
Michigan Oratorical Contest • 1595
William D. and Jewell Brewer Scholarship • 1909

AMERICAN LEGION, DEPARTMENT OF MINNESOTA
Minnesota Oratorical Contest • 1609

AMERICAN LEGION, DEPARTMENT OF MISSOURI
Missouri Oratorical Contest • 1619

AMERICAN LEGION, DEPARTMENT OF NEBRASKA
Oratorical Contest Scholarship • 1706

AMERICAN LEGION, DEPARTMENT OF NEW JERSEY
New Jersey Oratorical Contest • 1647
Safety Essay Contest • 1776

AMERICAN LEGION, DEPARTMENT OF NEW YORK
New York Oratorical Contest • 1653

AMERICAN LEGION, DEPARTMENT OF NORTH CAROLINA
North Carolina Oratorical Contest • 1672

AMERICAN LEGION, DEPARTMENT OF NORTH DAKOTA
Hattie Tedrow Memorial Fund Scholarship • 1424

AMERICAN LEGION, DEPARTMENT OF PENNSYLVANIA
Pennsylvania American Legion Essay Contest • 1723
Pennsylvania Oratorical Contest • 1728

AMERICAN LEGION, DEPARTMENT OF TEXAS
Texas Oratorical Contest • 1846

AMERICAN LEGION, DEPARTMENT OF VERMONT
Vermont Oratorical Contest • 1873

AMERICAN LEGION, DEPARTMENT OF VIRGINIA
Middle School Essay Contest • 1598

AMERICAN LEGION, DEPARTMENT OF WASHINGTON
Washington Oratorical Contest • 1893

AMERICAN LEGION, DEPARTMENT OF WISCONSIN
Americanism and Government Scholarship Program • 1217
Eagle Scout of the Year • 1347
Schneider-Emanuel American Legion Scholarship • 1779
Wisconsin Oratorical Scholarship Program • 1919

AMERICAN MATHEMATICAL SOCIETY AND MATHEMATICAL ASSOCIATION OF AMERICA
Frank and Brennie Morgan Prize for Outstanding Research in Mathematics by an Undergraduate Student • 893

AMERICAN MEDICAL TECHNOLOGISTS
AMT Student Scholarship • 787

AMERICAN METEOROLOGICAL SOCIETY
AMS Graduate Fellowship in the History of Science • 783
AMS Graduate Fellowships • 784
AMS Minority Scholarship • 785
AMS Senior Named Scholarships • 786
Father James B. Macelwane Annual Award in Meteorology • 887
Freshman Undergraduate Scholarship • 896

AMERICAN MONTESSORI SOCIETY
Teacher Education Scholarship Fund • 720

AMERICAN NUCLEAR SOCIETY
ANS Graduate Scholarship • 791
ANS Incoming Freshman Scholarships • 792
ANS Undergraduate Scholarship • 793
John and Muriel Landis Scholarship • 954
Operations and Power Division Scholarship • 1056

AMERICAN NURSES ASSOCIATION (ANA)
Minority Fellowship Program • 1008

AMERICAN OCCUPATIONAL THERAPY FOUNDATION
Kappa Delta Phi • 966
Mary Eileen Dixey Scholarship • 1571
Ohio State Association/AOTF Scholarships • 1689
Texas Occupational Therapy Association Scholarships • 1845

AMERICAN ORFF-SCHULWERK ASSOCIATION (AOSA)
Shields-Gillespie Scholarship • 709

AMERICAN ORNITHOLOGISTS' UNION
AOS Student and Postdoctoral Research Awards • 796

AMERICAN OSTEOPATHIC FOUNDATION (AOF)
Welch Scholars Grant • 1169

AMERICAN PHYSICAL THERAPY ASSOCIATION
Minority Scholarship Award for Physical Therapy Students • 2206

AMERICAN PHYSIOLOGICAL SOCIETY
Summer Undergraduate Research Fellowships • 1135

AMERICAN PSYCHOLOGICAL ASSOCIATION
APF/COGDOP Graduate Student Scholarships • 531
APF Dr. Christine Blasey Ford Grant • 530
APF/Division 54 Lizette Peterson-Homer Injury Prevention Grant • 532
David H. and Beverly A. Barlow Grant • 564
Sharon Stephens Brehm Undergraduate Psychology Scholarships • 706
TOPSS Competition for High School Psychology Students • 725

AMERICAN QUARTER HORSE FOUNDATION
Adrianna Andreini Scholarship • 1931
AQHF General Scholarship • 1940
AQHF Youth Scholarship • 1941
Boon San Kitty Scholarship • 1948
Margaret A. Haines Telephony Scholarship • 2008
Shawn Maree Vaillant Memorial Scholarship • 2043

AMERICAN RADIO RELAY LEAGUE FOUNDATION
ARRL Foundation General Fund Scholarship • 534
Bill, W2ONV and Ann Salerno Memorial Scholarship • 542
Carole J. Streeter, KB9JBR, Scholarship • 553
Central Arizona DX Association Scholarship • 1282
Challenge Met Scholarship • 2290
Charles Clarke Cordle Memorial Scholarship • 555
Charles N. Fisher Memorial Scholarship • 556
Dayton Amateur Radio Association Scholarship • 565
Don Riebhoff Memorial Scholarship • 568
Dr. James L. Lawson Memorial Scholarship • 570
Edmond A. Metzger Scholarship • 575
Fred R. McDaniel Memorial Scholarship • 583
Gary Wagner, K3OMI, Scholarship • 903
IRARC Memorial, Joseph P. Rubino, WA4MMD, Scholarship • 615
Irving W. Cook, WA0CGS, Scholarship • 1479
K2TEO Martin J. Green, Sr. Memorial Scholarship • 628
L. Phil and Alice J. Wicker Scholarship • 631
L.B. Cebik, W4RNL and Jean Cebik, N4TZP Memorial Scholarship • 632
Louisiana Memorial Scholarship • 1552
Mary Lou Brown Scholarship • 646
Mississippi Scholarship • 1616
New England FEMARA Scholarship • 672
Paul and Helen L. Grauer Scholarship • 681
PHD Scholarship • 685
Ray, N0RP and Katie, W0KTE Pautz Scholarship • 694
Richard W. Bendicksen, N7ZL, Memorial Scholarship • 697
Six Meter Club of Chicago Scholarship • 1793
Tom and Judith Comstock Scholarship • 724
YASME Foundation Scholarship • 739
You've Got a Friend in Pennsylvania Scholarship • 1927

AMERICAN RED CROSS YOUTH
Navin Narayan College Scholarship • 245

AMERICAN RESEARCH INSTITUTE IN TURKEY (ARIT)
ARIT Fellowships for Research in Turkey • 533

AMERICAN SADDLEBRED HORSE ASSOCIATION FOUNDATION
ASHA Youth Scholarships • 804

AMERICAN SCHOOL OF CLASSICAL STUDIES AT ATHENS
Fellowships for Regular Program in Greece • 423

AMERICAN SOCIETY FOR CLINICAL LABORATORY SCIENCE
Alpha Mu Tau Fraternity Undergraduate Scholarships • 776
Diversity Advocacy Council Scholarship • 2132

AMERICAN SOCIETY FOR ENGINEERING EDUCATION
SMART Scholarship • 1114

AMERICAN SOCIETY FOR ENOLOGY AND VITICULTURE
ASEV Scholarships • 802

AMERICAN SOCIETY FOR NONDESTRUCTIVE TESTING
ASNT Fellowship • 811
Engineering Undergraduate Scholarship • 881
Robert B. Oliver ASNT Scholarship • 1096

AMERICAN SOCIETY OF AGRICULTURAL AND BIOLOGICAL ENGINEERS FOUNDATION
ASABE Foundation Engineering Scholarship • 799
William J. Adams, Jr. and Marijane E. Adams Scholarship • 1170

AMERICAN SOCIETY OF CERTIFIED ENGINEERING TECHNICIANS (ASCET)
Student Cash Grant Program • 1131

AMERICAN SOCIETY OF CIVIL ENGINEERS (ASCE)
Samuel Fletcher Tapman ASCE Student Chapter/Club Scholarship • 1106
Trent R. Dames and William W. Moore Fellowship • 1153

AMERICAN SOCIETY OF CIVIL ENGINEERS–MICHIGAN SECTION
Mackinac Scholarship • 1555
Marvin L. Zuidema Scholarship Award • 1568

AMERICAN SOCIETY OF CRIMINOLOGY
Ruth D. Peterson Fellowship for Racial and Ethnic Diversity • 2245

AMERICAN SOCIETY OF CRIMINOLOGY GENE CARTE STUDENT PAPER COMPETITION
Gene Carte Student Paper Competition • 152

AMERICAN SOCIETY OF HEATING, REFRIGERATING AND AIR-CONDITIONING ENGINEERS (ASHRAE)
ASHRAE Engineering Technology Scholarships • 805
ASHRAE Society Scholarship Program • 806
Duane M. Hanson Scholarship • 867
Frank M. Coda Scholarship • 582
Henry Adams Scholarship • 930
Reuben Trane Scholarship • 1088
Undergraduate Engineering Scholarships • 1157

AMERICAN SOCIETY OF HUMAN GENETICS
DNA Day Essay Contest • 860

AMERICAN SOCIETY OF ICHTHYOLOGISTS AND HERPETOLOGISTS
Gaige Fund Award • 900
Raney Fund Award • 1084

AMERICAN SOCIETY OF INTERIOR DESIGNERS (ASID) EDUCATIONAL FOUNDATION INC.
Joel Polsky Academic Achievement Award • 446
Legacy Scholarship for Undergraduates • 453

AMERICAN SOCIETY OF LANDSCAPE ARCHITECTS
Karen Ann Shopis-Fox Memorial Scholarship • 1517

AMERICAN SOCIETY OF MECHANICAL ENGINEERS (ASME)
ASME Auxiliary Lucy and Charles W. E. Clarke Scholarship • 808
ASME Foundation Scholarships • 809
F.W. Beich Beichley Scholarship • 885
Frank and Dorothy Miller ASME Auxiliary Scholarships • 894
Garland Duncan Scholarships • 901
International Gas Turbine Institute Scholarship • 942
John and Elsa Gracik Scholarships • 953
Kenneth Andrew Roe Scholarship • 969
Melvin R. Green Scholarships • 999
Old Guard Oral Presentation Competition • 1054

AMERICAN SOCIETY OF NAVAL ENGINEERS
ASNE Scholarship Program • 810

AMERICAN SOCIETY OF RADIOLOGIC TECHNOLOGISTS FOUNDATION (ASRT)
Elekta Radiation Therapy Scholarship • 874

AMERICAN SOCIETY OF WOMEN ACCOUNTANTS - SEATTLE CHAPTER
ASWA Seattle Chapter Scholarship • 1231

AMERICAN SOCIOLOGICAL ASSOCIATION MINORITY FELLOWSHIP PROGRAM
Minority Fellowship Program • 655

AMERICAN SPEECH-LANGUAGE-HEARING FOUNDATION
Graduate Student Scholarship • 920
International Student Scholarship • 943
Minority Student Scholarship • 1009
New Century Scholars Doctoral Scholarship • 1042
Student with a Disability Scholarship • 716

AMERICAN STATISTICAL ASSOCIATION
Gertrude Cox Scholarship For Women In Statistics • 910

AMERICAN TRANSLATORS ASSOCIATION
Student Translation Award • 490

AMERICAN VACUUM SOCIETY
Dorothy M. and Earl S. Hoffman Award • 863
Graduate Research Award (GRA) • 916
Nellie Yeoh Whetten Award • 1041
Russell and Sigurd Varian Award • 1102

AMERICAN WATER WORKS ASSOCIATION
Abel Wolman Fellowship • 747
Academic Achievement Award • 749
American Water Scholarship • 781
Bryant L. Bench Carollo Engineers Inc. Scholarship • 831
Holly A. Cornell Scholarship • 934
Larson Aquatic Research Support (LARS) • 973
Thomas R. Camp Scholarship • 1145

AMERICAN WATER WORKS ASSOCIATION – FLORIDA SECTION
Roy W. Likins Scholarship • 1773

AMERICAN WATER WORKS ASSOCIATION – MICHIGAN SECTION
Raymond J. Faust Scholarship • 1746

AMERICAN WATER WORKS ASSOCIATION – MISSOURI SECTION
J.R. Popalisky Scholarship • 1482

AMERICAN WATER WORKS ASSOCIATION – NEW YORK SECTION
Walter B. Sinnott Scholarship • 1168

AMERICAN WELDING SOCIETY FOUNDATION
James A. Turner, Jr. Memorial Scholarship • 616

AMERICAN-ARAB ANTI-DISCRIMINATION COMMITTEE
Dr. Jack G. Shaheen Media Scholarship • 569

AMERICAN-SCANDINAVIAN FOUNDATION
Fellowships/Grants to Study in Scandinavia • 424
Nadia Christensen Prize • 461
Translation Prize Competition • 495

AMERICANS UNITED FOR SEPARATION OF CHURCH AND STATE
AU Student Contest • 56

AMERICORPS
Americorps National Civilian Community Corps • 44
Americorps Vista • 45

AMVETS NATIONAL HEADQUARTERS
AMVETS Children/Grandchildren Scholarships • 46
AMVETS National Scholarships for Veterans • 47

AMVETS NATIONAL LADIES AUXILIARY HEADQUARTERS
AMVETS National Ladies Auxiliary Scholarship • 1939

ANCHOR SCHOLARSHIP FOUNDATION
Anchor Scholarship Foundation Scholarship • 48

ANGUS FOUNDATION
Angus Foundation Scholarships • 788

ANTHONY MUÑOZ FOUNDATION
Anthony Muñoz Scholarship Fund • 1219

ANTI-DEFAMATION LEAGUE MIDWEST
Our First Amendment Freedoms Art and Essay Contest • 1710

ANTIBODIES-ONLINE INC.
Annual University Scholarship • 790

APIA SCHOLARS
APIA Scholarship Program • 2101

APPALACHIAN STUDIES ASSOCIATION
Carl A. Ross Student Paper Award • 404

APPALOOSA HORSE CLUB
Appaloosa Youth Association Art Contest • 797
Larry Williams Photography and AYA Photo Contest • 972
Youth Program • 1177

APPRAISAL INSTITUTE EDUCATION TRUST
AIERF College Scholarship • 521
AIERF Graduate Scholarship • 522
Minorities and Women Educational Scholarship • 654

ARA SCHOLARSHIP FOUNDATION INC.
ARA Scholarship • 1942

ARC OF WASHINGTON STATE
Arc of Washington State Trust Fund Stipend Award • 1221

ARIZONA BUSINESS AND PROFESSIONAL WOMEN'S FOUNDATION
Arizona BPW Foundation Annual Scholarships • 1223

ARIZONA NATIONAL LIVESTOCK SHOW
Arizona National Livestock Show Scholarship • 1224

The Ultimate Scholarship Book 2026
Sponsor Index

ARKANSAS COMMUNITY FOUNDATION
Arkansas Service Memorial Scholarship Endowment • 1226

ARKANSAS DEPARTMENT OF HIGHER EDUCATION
Academic Challenge Scholarship • 1179
Governor's Distinguished Scholarship • 1408

ARKANSAS GAME AND FISH COMMISSION
Arkansas Game and Fish Commission Conservation Scholarship • 1225

ARKANSAS STUDENT LOAN AUTHORITY
R. Preston Woodruff, Jr. Scholarships • 1740

ARMED FORCES COMMUNICATIONS AND ELECTRONICS ASSOCIATION (AFCEA)
AFCEA Ralph W. Shrader Diversity Scholarships • 761
AFCEA ROTC Scholarships • 23

ARMED SERVICES YMCA
Armed Services YMCA Annual Essay Contest • 49

ARMENIAN EDUCATIONAL FOUNDATION INC.
Richard R. Tufenkian Memorial Scholarship • 2243

ARMENIAN GENERAL BENEVOLENT UNION (AGBU)
AGBU US Graduate Scholarship • 2089
Helen C. Evans Scholarship • 929
Performing Arts Scholarship • 2236
Religious Studies Scholarship • 2242

ARMENIAN INTERNATIONAL WOMEN'S ASSOCIATION
Agnes Missirian Scholarship • 2091
Lucy Kasparian Aharonian Scholarship • 2189

ARMENIAN RELIEF SOCIETY OF EASTERN USA (ARS)
ARS Undergraduate Scholarship • 2103

ARMENIAN STUDENTS' ASSOCIATION OF AMERICA
ASA Scholarships • 2104

ARMY EMERGENCY RELIEF (AER)
Army Emergency Relief's MG James Ursano Scholarship Program • 50

ARMY ENGINEER SPOUSES' CLUB
Army Engineer Memorial Awards • 51

ARMY HEADQUARTERS
Army ROTC Four-Year Scholarship Program • 54
Army ROTC Green To Gold Scholarship Program • 55

ARMY NURSE CORPS ASSOCIATION (ANCA)
Army Nurse Corps Association Scholarships • 52

ASCAP FOUNDATION
ASCAP Foundation Morton Gould Young Composer Awards • 397
Herb Alpert Young Jazz Composer Awards • 434
Leiber and Stoller Scholarship for Songwriters • 454

ASIAN AMERICAN JOURNALISTS ASSOCIATION
Mary Quan Moy Ing Memorial Scholarship • 2199
Vincent Chin Scholarship • 733

ASIAN AND PACIFIC ISLANDER AMERICAN SCHOLARSHIP FUND
Asian and Pacific Islander American Scholarships • 2105

ASIAN PACIFIC COMMUNITY FUND
Cathay Bank Foundation Scholarship • 1279
Hsiao Memorial Social Sciences Scholarship • 2166

ASL MARKETING
Caples Student Campaign of the Year Award • 551

ASME INTERNATIONAL PETROLEUM TECHNOLOGY INSTITUTE
Petroleum Division College Scholarships • 1067

ASSOCIATED GENERAL CONTRACTORS (AGC) EDUCATION AND RESEARCH FOUNDATION
AGC Education and Research Foundation Undergraduate Scholarship • 762

ASSOCIATED GENERAL CONTRACTORS OF AMERICA
AGC Graduate Scholarships • 763
AGC Undergraduate Scholarships • 764

ASSOCIATED GENERAL CONTRACTORS OF MASSACHUSETTS
AGC of Massachusetts Scholarships • 1189

ASSOCIATED GENERAL CONTRACTORS OF MINNESOTA
Associated General Contractors of Minnesota Scholarships • 1230

ASSOCIATED GENERAL CONTRACTORS OF OHIO
AGC of Ohio Scholarships • 1190
Independence Excavating, A DiGeronimo Company Scholarship • 1464
Kokosing Construction Co. Scholarship • 1524
Shook Construction Harry F. Gaeke Memorial Scholarship • 1788
Tuttle Construction Inc. Tiny Rauch Scholarship • 1860

ASSOCIATED MALE CHORUSES OF AMERICA
AMCA Music Scholarship • 394

ASSOCIATION FOR EDUCATION AND REHABILITATION OF THE BLIND AND VISUALLY IMPAIRED
William and Dorothy Ferrell Scholarship • 2332

ASSOCIATION FOR IRON AND STEEL TECHNOLOGY (AIST)
AISI/AIST Foundation Premier Scholarship • 768
AIST Benjamin F. Fairless Scholarship (AIME) • 769
AIST Ronald E. Lincoln Memorial Scholarship • 770
AIST Smith Graduate Scholarship • 771
AIST William E. Schwabe Memorial Scholarship • 772
AIST Willy Korf Memorial Fund • 773
Steel Intern Scholarships • 1125

ASSOCIATION FOR LIBRARY SERVICE TO CHILDREN
Bound to Stay Bound Books Scholarship • 547
Frederic G. Melcher Scholarship • 584

ASSOCIATION FOR QUEER ANTHROPOLOGY (AQA)
Kenneth W. Payne Student Prize • 2179

ASSOCIATION FOR RADIOLOGIC AND IMAGING NURSING
Dorothy Budnek Memorial Scholarship • 862

ASSOCIATION FOR WOMEN IN ARCHITECTURE FOUNDATION
AWAF Scholarships • 1233

ASSOCIATION FOR WOMEN IN MATHEMATICS
Alice T. Schafer Mathematics Prize • 774
Biographies of Contemporary Women in Mathematics Essay Contest • 828

ASSOCIATION FOR WOMEN IN SPORTS MEDIA
AWSM Internship and Scholarship • 1946

ASSOCIATION OF AMERICAN GEOGRAPHERS (AAG) HESS SCHOLARSHIP
Darrel Hess Community College Geography Scholarship • 563

ASSOCIATION OF CALIFORNIA WATER AGENCIES
Clair A. Hill Scholarship • 1296

ASSOCIATION OF CERTIFIED FRAUD EXAMINERS
Ritchie-Jennings Memorial Scholarship • 699

ASSOCIATION OF COLLEGIATE SCHOOLS OF ARCHITECTURE
ASCA/AISC Student Design Competition • 800

ASSOCIATION OF CUBAN-AMERICAN ENGINEERS SCHOLARSHIP FOUNDATION
Association of Cuban Engineers Scholarship Foundation Scholarships • 2106

ASSOCIATION OF ENGINEERING GEOLOGISTS FOUNDATION
Marliave Fund • 990
Tilford Field Studies Scholarship • 1146

ASSOCIATION OF FEDERAL COMMUNICATIONS CONSULTING ENGINEERS
Association of Federal Communications Consulting Engineers Scholarships • 812
E. Noel Luddy Scholarship • 870

ASSOCIATION OF FLIGHT ATTENDANTS
Association of Flight Attendants Annual Scholarship • 1944

ASSOCIATION OF FOOD AND DRUG OFFICIALS
Association of Food and Drug Officials Scholarship Award • 813

ASSOCIATION OF GOVERNMENT ACCOUNTANTS (AGA)
National Academic Scholarships • 661

ASSOCIATION OF INDEPENDENT COLLEGES AND UNIVERSITIES OF PENNSYLVANIA
McLean Scholarship for Nursing and Physician Assistant Majors • 1584

ASSOCIATION OF INFORMATION TECHNOLOGY PROFESSIONALS (AITP) SCHOLARSHIPS
Association of Information Technology Professionals (AITP) Scholarships • 814

ASSOCIATION OF OLD CROWS
AOC Scholarships • 794

ASSOCIATION OF PERIOPERATIVE REGISTERED NURSES
AORN Foundation Scholarship Program • 795

ASSOCIATION OF REHABILITATION NURSES
BSN Scholarship • 832

ASSOCIATION OF STATE DAM SAFETY OFFICIALS
ASDSO Senior Undergraduate Scholarship • 801

ASSOCIATION OF STATE FLOODPLAIN MANAGERS FOUNDATION (ASFPM)
Future Leader Scholarship • 898

ASSOCIATION OF SURGICAL TECHNOLOGISTS
Foundation for Surgical Technology Medical Mission Scholarship • 891
Foundation for Surgical Technology Scholarships • 892

ASSOCIATION OF THE UNITED STATES ARMY
Joseph P. and Helen T. Cribbins Scholarship • 195

ASSOCIATION ON AMERICAN INDIAN AFFAIRS
Adolph Van Pelt Scholarship • 2086
Allogan Slagle Memorial Scholarship • 2096
Florence Young Memorial Scholarship • 2141

ASSURED LIFE ASSOCIATION
Assured Life Association National Scholarship • 1945

ASTM INTERNATIONAL
ASTM International Katherine and Bryant Mather Scholarship • 815

ASTRONAUT SCHOLARSHIP FOUNDATION
Astronaut Scholarship • 816

ASTRONOMICAL LEAGUE
National Young Astronomer Award • 1031

ATLANTIC AMATEUR HOCKEY ASSOCIATION
Lou Manzione Scholarship • 206

ATLANTIC SALMON FEDERATION
ASF Olin Fellowships • 803

AUTOMOTIVE HALL OF FAME
Automotive Hall of Fame Scholarships • 818

AVACARE MEDICAL
Avacare Medical Scholarship • 820

AVIATION DISTRIBUTORS AND MANUFACTURERS ASSOCIATION
Aviation Distributors and Manufacturers Association Scholarship Program • 821

AVIATION INSURANCE ASSOCIATION
Aviation Insurance Association Education Foundation Scholarship • 822

AYN RAND INSTITUTE
Anthem Essay Contest • 396
Atlas Shrugged Essay Contest • 398
The Fountainhead Essay Contest • 493

BABE RUTH LEAGUE INC.
Babe Ruth League Scholarships • 57

BAER REINTEGRATION SCHOLARSHIP
Baer Reintegration Scholarship • 2285

BAKERY CONFECTIONARY TOBACCO WORKERS AND GRAIN MILLERS (BCTGM) INTERNATIONAL UNION
David B. Durkee Memorial Scholarship Program • 1959

BAPTIST JOINT COMMITTEE FOR RELIGIOUS LIBERTY (BJC)
Religious Liberty Essay Scholarship Contest • 2033

BARBIZON INTERNATIONAL
Barbizon's College Tuition Scholarship • 59

BARDOS FOUNDATION
Agota M. Bardos Award • 26
Denes I. Bardos Award • 117

BARRON PRIZE
Gloria Barron Prize for Young Heroes • 158

BARRY M. GOLDWATER SCHOLARSHIP AND EXCELLENCE IN EDUCATION FOUNDATION
Barry M. Goldwater Scholarship and Excellence in Education Program • 824

BAT CONSERVATION INTERNATIONAL
Student Research Scholarships • 1134

BEAUTY CHANGES LIVES
Beauty Changes Lives Foundation Scholarships • 538

BETTER BUSINESS BUREAU (BBB) OF DELAWARE EDUCATION FOUNDATION
Better Business Bureau of Delaware Foundation Student Ethics Scholarship • 1238

BEYOND THE BOROUGHS
Beyond the Boroughs Scholarship • 61

BHW GROUP
Women in STEM Scholarship/BHW Scholarship • 1172

BIBLIOGRAPHICAL SOCIETY OF AMERICA
BSA Research Fellowship • 548

BIG Y
Big Y Scholarship Programs • 1241

BLACK NURSES ASSOCIATION OF GREATER WASHINGTON, DC AREA INC.
Margaret A. Pemberton Scholarship • 1563

BLAKEMORE FOUNDATION
Language Grants • 451

BLINDED VETERANS ASSOCIATION (BVA)
Kathern F. Gruber Scholarship Program • 198

BM TECHNOLOGIES INC.
BMTX Financial Empowerment Scholarship • 63

BMI FOUNDATION INC.
Dolly Parton Songwriters Award • 415
John Lennon Scholarship Competition • 448

BOB WARNICKE MEMORIAL SCHOLARSHIP FUND
Bob Warnicke Scholarship • 64

BOETTCHER FOUNDATION
Boettcher Foundation Scholarship • 1247

BOLD.ORG SLOANE STEPHENS DOC & GLO SCHOLARSHIP
Sloane Stephens Doc and Glo Scholarship • 303

BONNER FOUNDATION
Bonner Scholars Program • 65

BOOMER BENEFITS
Boomer Benefits Scholarship • 66

BOOMER ESIASON FOUNDATION
Boomer Esiason Foundation General Academic Scholarship • 2287

BOW SEAT
Ocean Awareness Contest • 469

BOYS AND GIRLS CLUBS OF AMERICA
Boys and Girls Clubs of America National Youth of the Year Award • 1949

BRAZOS EDUCATION LENDING
Murray Watson Jr. Scholarship • 1629

BRIGHT!TAX
Bright!Tax Global Scholar Initiative • 67

BRITISH AMERICAN FOUNDATION OF TEXAS
BAFTX Undergraduate Award • 1235
Susan Howard Community Service Award • 1819
Women in STEM Award • 1922

BROADCAST EDUCATION ASSOCIATION
BEA National Scholarships in Broadcasting • 537

BRONX BROTHERS
Children in Need Scholarship • 406

BROWN HUDNER NAVY SCHOLARSHIP FOUNDATION
Brown Hudner Navy Scholarship • 68

BULKOFFICESUPPLY.COM
Office Supply Scholarship • 470

BUREAU OF VETERANS' SERVICES
Maine Veterans Dependents Educational Benefits • 1560

BURGER KING SCHOLARS PROGRAM
Burger King Scholars Program • 70

C-SPAN
StudentCam Competition • 319

CALAVERAS BIG TREES ASSOCIATION
Emily M. Hewitt and Stephen K. Stocking Memorial Scholarship • 1362

CALIFORNIA ASSOCIATION FOR POSTSECONDARY EDUCATION AND DISABILITY
CAPED Excellence Scholarship • 1272
Steve Fasteau Past Presidents' Scholarship • 1816

CALIFORNIA ASSOCIATION OF PRIVATE POSTSECONDARY SCHOOLS
CAPPS Memorial Scholarship Program • 1273

CALIFORNIA ASSOCIATION ON POSTSECONDARY EDUCATION AND DISABILITY (CAPED)
Alyssa McCroskey Memorial Scholarship • 1205
Betty Bacon Memorial Scholarship • 1239
Dick Griffiths Memorial Scholarship • 1332
Susan Bunch Memorial Scholarship • 1818

CALIFORNIA DEPARTMENT OF VETERANS AFFAIRS
California Fee Waiver Program for Children of Veterans • 1261
California Fee Waiver Program for Dependents of Deceased or Disabled National Guard Members • 1262
California Fee Waiver Program for Recipients of the Medal of Honor and Their Children • 1263

CALIFORNIA FREETHOUGHT DAY
California Freethought Day High School Essay Scholarship • 1264

CALIFORNIA INTERSCHOLASTIC FEDERATION (CIF)
CIF Scholar-Athlete of the Year • 1295

CALIFORNIA LANDSCAPE CONTRACTORS ASSOCIATION
LEAF Scholarships • 1531

The Ultimate Scholarship Book 2026
Sponsor Index

CALIFORNIA LIBRARY ASSOCIATION
Begun Scholarship • 539
CLA Scholarship For BIPOC Students in Memory of Edna Yelland • 559

CALIFORNIA MASONIC FOUNDATION
California Masonic Foundation Scholarship • 1267

CALIFORNIA NEVADA RACQUETBALL ASSOCIATION
Jack Hughes Education Scholarship • 1485

CALIFORNIA PEACE OFFICERS' MEMORIAL FOUNDATION
John F. Duffy Scholarship/Grant Program • 190

CALIFORNIA RESTAURANT ASSOCIATION
California Restaurant Association Educational Foundation General Scholarship • 1269

CALIFORNIA SCHOOL LIBRARY ASSOCIATION
Leadership for Diversity Scholarship • 1530

CALIFORNIA STATE FAIR
Friends of the California State Fair Scholarship Program • 1388

CALIFORNIA STATE PTA
California State PTA Volunteer Service Scholarship • 1270
Dr. Ralph E. White Graduating Senior Scholarship • 1343

CALIFORNIA STUDENT AID COMMISSION
Cal Grant A • 1256
Cal Grant B • 1257
Cal Grant C • 1258
Cal Grant Entitlement Award • 1259
California Chafee Grant for Foster Youth • 2113
California Law Enforcement Personnel Dependents Grant Program • 1266

CALIFORNIA TEACHERS ASSOCIATION (CTA)
CTA Cesar E. Chavez and Dolores Huerta Education Award Program • 1318
Martin Luther King, Jr. Memorial Scholarship • 2010
Student CTA (SCTA) Scholarship in Honor of L. Gordon Bittle • 2051

CALIFORNIA-HAWAII ELKS ASSOCIATION
California - Hawaii Elks Association Vocational Grants • 550
California - Hawaii Elks Major Project Undergraduate Scholarship Program for Students with Disabilities • 1260

CALVIN COOLIDGE MEMORIAL FOUNDATION INC.
Coolidge Scholarship • 97

CAMPUS COMPACT
Newman Civic Fellow Awards • 254

CAMPUS SAFETY HEALTH AND ENVIRONMENTAL MANAGEMENT ASSOCIATION (CSHEMA)
Campus Safety Health and Environmental Management Association Scholarship • 834

CANCER FOR COLLEGE
Cancer for College Scholarships • 2289

CAP CHARITABLE FOUNDATION
Ron Brown Scholar Program • 2244

CARDRATES.COM
CardRates.com Financial Futures Scholarship • 552

CARDS AGAINST HUMANITY
Science Ambassador Scholarship • 1108

CARDSDIRECT
CardsDirect Future Designer Scholarship • 401

CAREER COLLEGES AND SCHOOLS OF TEXAS
Career Colleges and Schools of Texas Scholarship Program • 1276

CAREERFITTER.COM
CareerFitter Scholarship • 74

CARSON SCHOLARS FUND
Carson Scholars • 76

CASEY FAMILY
Casey Family Scholarship • 2114

CASHTELLIGENT
Cashtelligent Financial Literacy Scholarship • 77

CATCHING THE DREAM
Catching the Dream Native American Scholarship Fund • 2115

CATHOLIC UNITED FINANCIAL
Catholic United Financial College Tuition Scholarship • 1951

CDM CONSTRUCTORS INC. WORKFORCE DEVELOPMENT SCHOLARSHIP
CDM Constructors Inc. Workforce Development Scholarship • 1281

CENTER FOR SCHOLARSHIP ADMINISTRATION
Judge William F. Cooper Scholarship • 1506
Kittie M. Fairey Educational Fund Scholarships • 1523

CENTER FOR THE EDUCATION OF WOMEN+
CEW+ Scholarships • 1285

CENTER FOR WOMEN IN GOVERNMENT AND CIVIL SOCIETY
Fellowship on Women and Public Policy • 1373

CENTRAL INDIANA COMMUNITY FOUNDATION
Mexican Scholarship Fund • 1589

CENTRAL INTELLIGENCE AGENCY
CIA Undergraduate Scholarship Program • 85
Graduate Scholarship Program • 595

CHAMPIONS FOR CHRIST FOUNDATION
Champions for Christ Scholarship • 1953

CHARLES BABBAGE INSTITUTE
Adelle and Erwin Tomash Fellowship in the History of Information Processing • 516

CHARLES RIVER ASSOCIATES
CRA All-Access Scholarship • 2128

CHEROKEE NATION
Cherokee Nation/Tribal Council At-Large Scholarship • 2120

CHIEF PETTY OFFICER SCHOLARSHIP FUND
Chief Petty Officer Scholarship Fund • 81

CHILDREN OF DEAF ADULTS, INTERNATIONAL
Millie Brother Scholarship • 2310

CHINESE AMERICAN CITIZENS ALLIANCE
Chinese American Citizens Alliance Essay Contest • 83

CHIROHEALTHUSA
ChiroHealthUSA Foxworth Family Scholarship • 840

CHIROPRACTIC ASSOCIATION OF LOUISIANA
Dr. William S. Boyd Scholarship • 1344

CHOATE, HALL AND STEWART
Amy Lowell Poetry Travelling Scholarship • 395

CHRISTIAN CHEERLEADERS OF AMERICA
CCA Christian Cheer Nationals • 78

CHRISTOPHERS
Christophers Video Contest for College Students • 84
Poster Contest for High School Students • 476

CHURCH HILL CLASSICS
Frame My Future Scholarship Contest • 427

CIRCLE K INTERNATIONAL
Kiwanis Children's Fund Scholarship • 2002

CIRI FOUNDATION
Foundation Scholarships • 2142

CITIZEN POTAWATOMI NATION
Citizen Potawatomi Nation Tribal Scholarship • 2123

CITIZENS' SCHOLARSHIP FOUNDATION OF AMERICA
Dollars for Scholars Scholarship • 124

CIVILIAN MARKSMANSHIP PROGRAM
Carolyn Hines Memorial Scholarship Program • 75

CIVITAN
Shropshire Scholarship • 2045

CJ PONY PARTS
CJ Pony Parts Scholarship Video Contest • 86

CLUB FOUNDATION
Joe Perdue Scholarship • 622

CLUBS OF AMERICA
Clubs of America Scholarship Award for Career Success • 87

COALITION OF OREGON SCHOOL ADMINISTRATORS
Confederation of Oregon School Administrators Scholarships • 1312
COSA Youth Development Program Scholarships • 1315

COAST GUARD FOUNDATION
Coast Guard Foundation Scholarship Fund • 89

COAST GUARD MUTUAL ASSISTANCE (CGMA)
Supplemental Education Grant (SEG) • 331

COCA-COLA SCHOLARS FOUNDATION
Coca-Cola Community College Academic Team • 90
Coca-Cola Scholars Program • 91

COCHLEAR AMERICAS
Graeme Clark Scholarship • 2297

COLEOPTERISTS SOCIETY
Jean Theodore Lacordaire Prize • 950
Youth Incentive Award • 1176

COLLEGE FOUNDATION OF NORTH CAROLINA
Epsilon Sigma Alpha • 1365
Golden LEAF Scholars Program - Two-Year Colleges • 1403
North Carolina Community College Grant • 1670
North Carolina Education Lottery Scholarship • 1671

COLLEGE IS POWER
C.I.P. Scholarship • 71

COLLEGE JUMPSTART SCHOLARSHIP FUND
$1,000 College JumpStart Gratitude Scholarship • 2
$1,000 College JumpStart Love of Learning Scholarship • 3
$1,000 College JumpStart Pay It Forward Scholarship • 4
$1,000 College JumpStart Show Grit Scholarship • 5

COLLEGE PREPARATORY INVITATIONAL
CPI Highest Point Hunt Seat Rider • 101

COLLEGE SUCCESS FOUNDATION
Washington State Governors' Scholarship for Foster Youth • 1896

COLORADO COUNCIL VOLUNTEERISM AND COMMUNITY SERVICE
Colorado Council Volunteerism and Community Service Scholarship • 1303

COLORADO DEPARTMENT OF HIGHER EDUCATION
CollegeInvest 529 Scholarship Program • 1301
Colorado Student Grant • 1306

COLORADO EDUCATIONAL SERVICES AND DEVELOPMENT ASSOCIATION
CESDA Diversity Scholarship • 1284

COLORADO MASONS BENEVOLENT FUND ASSOCIATION
Colorado Masons Benevolent Fund Scholarships • 1304

COLORADO NURSES FOUNDATION
H.M. Muffly Memorial Scholarship • 1420

COLORADO STUDENT MEDIA ASSOCIATION
Dorothy D. Greer Journalist of the Year Scholarship Competition • 1337

COLORADO WOMEN'S EDUCATION FOUNDATION
Colorado Women's Education Foundation • 1307

COMMERCIAL REAL ESTATE WOMEN (CREW) NETWORK
CREW Network Foundation Scholarship • 562

COMMUNICATIONS WORKERS OF AMERICA
CWA Joe Beirne Foundation Scholarship • 1958

COMMUNITIES FOUNDATION OF OKLAHOMA
Communities Foundation of Oklahoma Scholarships • 1308

COMMUNITIES FOUNDATION OF TEXAS
General James H. Doolittle Scholarship • 906

COMMUNITY BANKER ASSOCIATION OF ILLINOIS
Community Banker Association of Illinois Annual Essay Scholarship Program • 1309

COMMUNITY FOUNDATION FOR GREATER ATLANTA INC.
James M. and Virginia M. Smyth Scholarship • 188
Nancy Penn Lyons Scholarship Fund • 1635
Tech High School Alumni Association/W.O. Cheney Merit Scholarship • 1828

COMMUNITY FOUNDATION OF LOUISVILLE
Thaddeus Colson and Isabelle Saalwaechter Fitzpatrick Memorial Scholarship • 1848

COMMUNITY FOUNDATION OF MIDDLE TENNESSEE
Cynthia and Alan Baran Fine Arts and Music Scholarship Fund • 1320

COMMUNITY FOUNDATION OF NEW JERSEY
Clanseer and Anna Johnson Scholarships • 1297

COMMUNITY FOUNDATION SERVING WESTERN VIRGINIA
Dianne E. H. Wilcox Scholarship Fund • 1331

COMPETITIVE CHEER COACHES ASSOCIATION OF MICHIGAN
CCCAM Scholarships • 1280

COMPLETE WATER SOLUTIONS
Complete Water Solutions Scholarship • 843

COMPUTING RESEARCH ASSOCIATION
Outstanding Undergraduate Researchers Award Program • 1057

CONFERENCE OF MINORITY TRANSPORTATION OFFICIALS
Conference of Minority Transportation Officials (COMTO) National Scholarship • 2125

CONGRESS BUNDESTAG YOUTH EXCHANGE PROGRAM
Congress Bundestag Youth Exchange Program • 95

CONGRESSIONAL BLACK CAUCUS FOUNDATION
Ally Financial Law Scholars • 2097
Ally Financial Public Policy Scholars • 525
CBC Spouses Essay Contest • 2116
CBC Spouses Performing Arts Scholarship • 2117
CBCF Reducing the Financial Barrier Scholarship • 2118
Congressional Black Caucus Spouses Education Scholarship • 2126
Congressional Black Caucus Spouses Visual Arts Scholarship • 2127
HBCU NREI Scholarship • 2153
Tracking Foundation Multi-Year Scholarship Program • 2265
Tracking Foundation Scholars Scholarship Program • 2266

CONGRESSIONAL HISPANIC CAUCUS INSTITUTE INC.
CHCI United Health Foundation Scholar-Intern Program • 2119

CONGRESSIONAL MEDAL OF HONOR SOCIETY
Congressional Medal of Honor Society Scholarships • 96

CONNECTICUT ARCHITECTURE FOUNDATION
Charles Dubose Scholarship • 1286

CONNECTICUT ASSOCIATION OF HEALTH, PHYSICAL EDUCATION, RECREATION AND DANCE
CTAHPERD Gibson-Laemel Scholarship • 1319
Mary Benevento/CTAHPERD Scholarship • 1570

CONNECTICUT BUILDING CONGRESS SCHOLARSHIP FUND INC.
Connecticut Building Congress Scholarships • 1313

CONNECTICUT COMMUNITY FOUNDATION CENTER FOR PHILANTHROPY
Dr. and Mrs. Arthur F. Sullivan Fund • 1339
Lois Livingston McMillen Memorial Fund • 1546

CONNECTICUT CONSTRUCTION INDUSTRIES ASSOCIATION
Associated General Contractors of Connecticut Scholarships • 1229

CONNECTICUT NATIONAL GUARD FOUNDATION INC.
SGT Felix M. Del Greco, Jr. Memorial Scholarship • 1785

CONNECTICUT OFFICE OF HIGHER EDUCATION
Roberta B. Willis Scholarship - Need and Merit-Based Award • 1765
Roberta B. Willis Scholarship - Need-Based Award • 1766

CONNECTICUT SOCIETY OF PROFESSIONAL JOURNALISTS
Bob Eddy Scholarship Program • 1244

CONNECTICUT SPORTS WRITERS ALLIANCE
Bohdan Kolinsky Memorial Sports Journalism Scholarship • 1248

CONNECTICUT TRIAL FIRM LLC
Education Accessibility Scholarship • 135

CONSTITUTING AMERICA
We The Future Contest • 372

CORPORATE OFFICE INTERIORS
Corporate Office Interiors Scholarship Contest • 99

COSMOFORGE
Sahara Hope Scholarship For Women Empowered To Change The World • 2246

COSTUME SOCIETY OF AMERICA (CSA)
Stella Blum Research Grant • 486

COUNCIL FOR THE ADVANCEMENT OF SCIENCE WRITING (CASW)
Taylor/Blakeslee University Fellowships • 492

COUNCIL OF CITIZENS WITH LOW VISION INTERNATIONAL
Fred Scheigert Scholarships • 2295

COUNCIL ON INTERNATIONAL EDUCATIONAL EXCHANGE
Council on International Educational Exchange (CIEE) Scholarships • 411
Minority Serving Institution Grants • 2209

COURAGE TO GROW SCHOLARSHIP
Courage to Grow Scholarship • 100

CREATIVE BIOLABS
Creative Biolabs Scholarship • 847

CROHN'S AND COLITIS FOUNDATION OF AMERICA INC.
Student Research Fellowship Awards • 1133

CROSSWORD HOBBYIST
Crossword Hobbyist Crossword Scholarship • 105

CRUMLEY ROBERTS, ATTORNEYS AT LAW
Crumley Roberts Next Step Scholarship • 1317

The Ultimate Scholarship Book 2026
Sponsor Index

DAEDALIAN FOUNDATION
Daedalian Foundation Scholarship Program • 108

DAMON RUNYON CANCER RESEARCH FOUNDATION
Fellowship Award • 889

DANIEL R. BACALIS P.C.
Striving Solo Parent Scholarship • 2253

DANIELS FUND
Daniels Scholarship Program • 1322

DATINGADVICE.COM
Future Counselors of America Scholarship • 587

DAUGHTERS OF THE BRITISH EMPIRE IN THE USA
Sarah Josephine Langstaff Memorial Scholarship • 291

DAUGHTERS OF THE CINCINNATI
Daughters of the Cincinnati Scholarship • 109

DAVIDSON INSTITUTE FOR TALENT DEVELOPMENT
Davidson Fellows Scholarships • 110

DAVIS-PUTTER SCHOLARSHIP FUND
Davis-Putter Scholarship Fund • 111

DC TUITION ASSISTANCE GRANT OFFICE
District of Columbia Tuition Assistance Grant • 1333

DECA INC.
Harry A. Applegate Scholarship • 599

DEFENSE COMMISSARY AGENCY (DECA)
Scholarships for Military Children • 295

DEG: THE DIGITAL ENTERTAINMENT GROUP
Hedy Lamarr Achievement Award for Emerging Leaders in Entertainment Technology • 432

DELAWARE COMMUNITY FOUNDATION
Margaret A. Stafford Nursing Scholarship • 1564

DELAWARE DEPARTMENT OF EDUCATION - SCHOOL SUPPORTS
Career Based Scholarship • 1275
Charles L. Hebner Memorial Scholarship • 1287
Delaware Educational Benefits for Children of Deceased Veterans and Others • 1325
Delaware Scholarship Incentive Program • 1326
Educator Support Scholarship • 1356

DELAWARE SOLID WASTE AUTHORITY
Delaware Solid Waste Authority John P. Pat Healy Scholarship • 1327

DELETE CYBERBULLYING
Delete Cyberbullying Beyond School Walls Scholarship • 112
Delete Cyberbullying Mental Health Awareness Scholarship • 113
Delete Cyberbullying Social Media Scholarship • 114

DELTA GAMMA FOUNDATION
Delta Gamma Foundation Scholarship • 1960

DELTA PHI EPSILON EDUCATIONAL FOUNDATION
Delta Phi Epsilon Educational Foundation Scholarship • 1961

DELTA SIGMA PI
Undergraduate Scholarship • 2062

DELTA THETA CHI SORORITY
Delta Theta Chi Sorority National Memorial Scholarship • 116

DEMOLAY FOUNDATION
Frank S. Land Scholarships • 1975

DEMONSTRATION OF ENERGY AND EFFICIENCY DEVELOPMENTS (DEED)
DEED Funding Opportunities • 855

DENVER FOUNDATION
RBC Wealth Management Colorado Scholarship • 1748
Winifred R. Reynolds Educational Scholarship • 1913

DEPARTMENT OF DEFENSE SCHOLARSHIP-FOR-SERVICE PROGRAM
Dellums SMART Scholarship • 856
SMART Scholarship • 1115

DEPARTMENT OF DEFENSE, AMERICAN SOCIETY FOR ENGINEERING EDUCATION
NDSEG Fellowship Program • 1039

DEPARTMENT OF ENERGY
Computational Science Graduate Fellowship • 845

DEPARTMENT OF HEALTH CARE ACCESS AND INFORMATION (HCAI)
Advanced Practice Healthcare Scholarship Program • 1186
Allied Healthcare Scholarship Program • 1202
Associate Degree Nursing Scholarship Program • 1228
Bachelor of Science Nursing Scholarship Program • 1234

DEPARTMENT OF VETERANS AFFAIRS
Montgomery GI Bill - Active Duty • 227
Montgomery GI Bill - Selected Reserve • 228
Montgomery GI Bill Tuition Assistance Top-Up • 229

DESERET NEWS-KSL BROADCAST GROUP STERLING SCHOLAR
Sterling Scholar Awards of Utah • 1815

DESIGN AUTOMATION CONFERENCE/ASSOCIATION FOR COMPUTING MACHINERY
P.O. Pistilli Undergraduate Scholarship for Advancement in Computer Science and Electrical Engineering • 2233

DESK AND DERRICK EDUCATIONAL TRUST
Desk and Derrick Educational Trust • 858

DEVELOPMENT FUND FOR BLACK STUDENTS IN SCIENCE AND TECHNOLOGY
Development Fund for Black Students in Science and Technology • 2130

DIGITAL RESPONSIBILITY
Digital Privacy Scholarship • 118
Don't Text and Drive Scholarship • 126
E-waste Scholarship • 131
Technology Addiction Awareness Scholarship • 336

DIOCESE OF THE ARMENIAN CHURCH OF AMERICA (EASTERN)
Diocese of the Armenian Church of America (Eastern) Scholarships • 1963

DISABLEDPERSON INC.
National Scholarship Competition for Disabled College Students • 2313

DISNEY/ABC TELEVISION GROUP
Disney Entertainment Writing Program • 413

DISTINGUISHED YOUNG WOMEN
Distinguished Young Women Scholarship Program • 2131

DIXIE BOYS BASEBALL
Dixie Boys Baseball Scholarship Program • 120

DIXIE SOFTBALL INC.
Dixie Softball Scholarships • 121

DIXIE YOUTH BASEBALL INC.
Dixie Youth Scholarship Program • 122

DIZZY DEAN BASEBALL INC.
Dizzy Dean Scholarship • 123

DMVEDU.ORG
In the Driver's Seat • 181

DO SOMETHING (SCHOLARSHIPS)
DoSomething Monthly Scholarships • 127

DOLPHIN SCHOLARSHIP FOUNDATION
Dolphin Scholarships • 125

DON'T MESS WITH TEXAS
Don't Mess with Texas Scholarship • 1334

DUMBARTON OAKS
Dumbarton Oaks Fellowships • 418
Junior Fellowships • 450

EAA AVIATION CENTER
David Alan Quick Scholarship • 853
H.P. Bud Milligan Aviation Scholarship • 924
Payzer Scholarship • 1063

EARLY COLLEGE FOR ME
Early College for ME • 1349

EASTERN SURFING ASSOCIATION
Marsh Scholarship Fund • 212

EDMUND F. MAXWELL FOUNDATION
Edmund F. Maxwell Foundation Scholarship • 1351

EDUCATIONAL FOUNDATION FOR WOMEN IN ACCOUNTING
Laurels Fund Scholarship • 633

EDUCATIONAL OFFICE PROFESSIONALS OF OHIO
Lila M. Van Sweringen Student Scholarship • 1539

EDUCATIONAL THEATRE ASSOCIATION
Christopher L. Hunt Scholarship • 407
Dr. Kenny D. Hasija Scholarship • 417
Educational Theatre Association Board of Directors Scholarship • 419
Future Theatre Educator Scholarship • 428
Michael J. Peitz Leadership Scholarship • 460

EDWARD ARTHUR MELLINGER EDUCATIONAL FOUNDATION INC.
Mellinger Scholarships • 1588

EF EDUCATIONAL TOURS
Global Citizen Scholarship • 157

EGIA FOUNDATION
EGIA Foundation Scholarship Program • 577

ELECTROCHEMICAL SOCIETY
Battery Division Student Research Award • 825
Corrosion Division Morris Cohen Graduate Student Award • 846
Industrial Electrochemistry and Electrochemical Engineering Student Achievement Award • 939
Student Poster Session Awards • 1132
The Industrial Electrochemistry and Electrochemical Engineering Division H. H. Dow Memorial Student Achievement Award • 1140

ELIE WIESEL FOUNDATION FOR HUMANITY
Prize in Ethics Essay Contest • 479

ELIZABETH NASH FOUNDATION
Elizabeth Nash Foundation Scholarship Program • 2293

ELKS NATIONAL FOUNDATION HEADQUARTERS
Emergency Educational Fund Grants • 1965
Legacy Award • 2004
Most Valuable Student Scholarships • 230

EMERGENCY NURSES ASSOCIATION
ENA Foundation Undergraduate Scholarship • 879
Karen O'Neil Memorial Scholarship • 967

ENGINEERS FOUNDATION OF OHIO
Engineers Foundation of Ohio General Fund Scholarship • 1364

ENTERTAINMENT COMMUNITY FUND FORMERLY THE ACTORS FUND
Career Center • 402

ENVIRONMENTAL RESEARCH CENTER
ERC Eco Scholarship Fund • 1366

EOD WARRIOR FOUNDATION
EOD Warrior Foundation Scholarship • 137

EON ESSAY CONTEST LLC
Eon Essay Contest • 138

EQUITABLE HOLDINGS INC.
Equitable Excellence Scholarship • 139

EXECUTIVE WOMEN INTERNATIONAL (EWI)
Adult Students in Scholastic Transition (ASIST) • 517
Executive Women International Scholarship Program • 578

EXPLORAVISION
ExploraVision National Science Competition • 884

EXPLORERS LEARNING FOR LIFE
Capt. James J. Regan Scholarship • 72
James E. Breining Scholarship Award • 1995
National Aviation Explorer Scholarships • 1022
Sheryl A. Horak Memorial Scholarship • 301

EXPRESSIONS CHALLENGE BY WALGREENS
Expressions Challenge by Walgreens • 420

FACILITY MANAGEMENT CORPORATION (FMC) ICE SPORTS
FMC Skaters Scholarship • 145

FADEL EDUCATIONAL FOUNDATION
Fadel Educational Foundation Annual Award Program • 1968

FAMILIES OF FREEDOM c/o SCHOLARSHIP AMERICA
Families of Freedom Scholarship Fund • 142

FAMILY, CAREER AND COMMUNITY LEADERS OF AMERICA – TEXAS ASSOCIATION
Texas Association FCCLA Regional Scholarship • 1837

FANNIE AND JOHN HERTZ FOUNDATION
Hertz Foundation's Graduate Fellowship Award • 932

FAR WEST ATHLETIC TRAINERS' ASSOCIATION/DISTRICT 8
Mark Ando and Ito Family Scholarship • 2197

FASHION SCHOLARSHIP FUND
Fashion Scholarship Fund Scholarships • 421

FEDERAL CIRCUIT BAR ASSOCIATION
Giles Sutherland Rich Memorial Scholarship • 592

FEDERAL EMPLOYEE EDUCATION AND ASSISTANCE FUND
FEEA Scholarship Program • 1970

FEDERATED GARDEN CLUBS OF VERMONT INC.
Mabel Mayforth Scholarship • 1554

FIELDS OF LEARNING
Fields of Learning Scholarship • 1374

FINANCE AUTHORITY OF MAINE
Educators for Maine Program • 1357
Maine Health Professionals Loan Program • 1558

FINLANDIA FOUNDATION
Finlandia Foundation National Student Scholarships Program • 426

FLAG MANUFACTURERS ASSOCIATION OF AMERICA
FMAA Scholarship Program • 144

FLEET RESERVE ASSOCIATION (FRA)
Americanism Essay Contest • 43
Fleet Reserve Association Scholarship • 1972
Stanley A. Doran Memorial Scholarship • 2049

FLEXOGRAPHIC TECHNICAL ASSOCIATION
FFTA Scholarship Competition • 425

FLORIDA ACADEMY OF NUTRITION AND DIETETICS FOUNDATION
Sister Helen Marie Pellicer Scholarship • 1791

FLORIDA DEPARTMENT OF EDUCATION
Access to Better Learning and Education Grant Program • 1183
First Generation Matching Grant Program • 1375
Florida Bright Futures Scholarship Program • 1377
Florida Student Assistance Grant Program • 1381
Jose Marti Scholarship Challenge Grant • 1505
Rosewood Family Scholarship Program • 1771
William L. Boyd, IV, Effective Access to Student Education Program • 1912

FLORIDA ENGINEERING SOCIETY
Florida Engineers in Construction Scholarship • 1378

FOLDS OF HONOR
Folds of Honor Higher Education Scholarship • 146

FOR INSPIRATION AND RECOGNITION OF SCIENCE AND TECHNOLOGY (FIRST)
Dr. Bart Kamen Memorial FIRST Scholarship • 865

FORD FAMILY FOUNDATION SCHOLARSHIP OFFICE
Ford Opportunity Program • 1382

FORECLOSURE.COM
Foreclosure Scholarship Program • 147

FOSTER CARE TO SUCCESS
Educational Training Voucher Programs for Foster Youth • 1355

FOSTER LOVE–TOGETHER WE RISE
BrandSource Scholarship • 2110

FOUNDATION FOR COMMUNITY ASSOCIATION RESEARCH
Byron Hanke Fellowship • 549

FOUNDATION FOR FINANCIAL SERVICE PROFESSIONALS (FSP)
Paul S. Mills Scholarships • 682

FOUNDATION FOR OUTDOOR ADVERTISING RESEARCH AND EDUCATION (FOARE)
FOARE Scholarship Program • 580
Ruth Segal Scholarship • 704
Vern and Elaine Clark Outdoor Advertising Industry • 732

FOUNDATION FOR SCIENCE AND DISABILITY
Student Award Program of FSD • 2325

FOUNDATION FOR THE CAROLINAS
Richard Goolsby Scholarship Fund • 1759

FOUNDATION OF THE FIRST CAVALRY DIVISION ASSOCIATION
First Cavalry Division Foundation Scholarship • 143

FOUNDRY EDUCATIONAL FOUNDATION
AFS Twin City Memorial Scholarship • 1187
AFS Wisconsin Past President Scholarship • 1188
NADCA Indiana Chapter 25 Scholarship • 1634

FRATERNAL ORDER OF EAGLES
Fraternal Order of Eagles Memorial Foundation • 148

FREEDOM FROM RELIGION FOUNDATION
Student Activist Awards • 315

FROM THE TOP
Jack Kent Cooke Young Artist Award • 444

FRONTLINE FAMILIES SCHOLARSHIP PROGRAM
Frontline Families Scholarship • 2143

FUND FOR AMERICAN STUDIES
Fund for American Studies Internships • 586

FUNERAL SERVICE FOUNDATION
Dennis Schoepp Memorial Scholarship • 1329
Memorial Classic Golf Tournament Scholarship • 650
Shipley Rose Buckner Memorial Scholarship • 1786

FUTURAMA FOUNDATION
Business and Professional Women/Maine Continuing Education Scholarship • 1253

The Ultimate Scholarship Book 2026
Sponsor Index

Career Advancement Scholarship • 1274
Lemieux-Lovejoy Youth Scholarship • 1534

FUTURE READY IOWA
Future Ready Iowa Grant • 1389
Future Ready Iowa Last-Dollar Scholarship • 1390

GALLERY COLLECTION
Create-a-Greeting-Card Scholarship • 104

GAMMA MU FOUNDATION
Gamma Mu Scholarships Program • 2145

GAMMA THETA UPSILON
Gamma Theta Upsilon-Geographical Honor Society Scholarships • 589

GARDEN CLUB OF AMERICA
Loy McCandless Marks Scholarship in Tropical Horticulture • 987

GARDEN STATE SCHOLASTIC PRESS FOUNDATION
Bob Stevens Memorial Scholarship • 1245

GATES FOUNDATION
Gates Scholarship • 2146

GEMM LEARNING
Dyslexia/Auditory Processing Disorder Scholarship • 2292

GEN AND KELLY TANABE SCHOLARSHIP PROGRAM
$1,000 GK Tanabe Student Scholarship • 6

GENERAL COMMISSION ON ARCHIVES AND HISTORY, THE UNITED METHODIST CHURCH
Women in United Methodist History Writing Award • 2075

GENERAL FEDERATION OF WOMEN'S CLUBS OF VIRGINIA
Mary Macon McGuire Scholarship • 1573
Phyllis V. Roberts Scholarship • 1735

GENERAL SOCIETY OF MAYFLOWER DESCENDANTS
General Society of Mayflower Descendants (GSMD) Scholarship • 2148

GENETEX INC.
GeneTex Scholarship Program • 907

GENEVA ROCK
Geneva Rock Scholarship • 908

GEOLOGICAL SOCIETY OF AMERICA FOUNDATION (GSAF)
Graduate Student Research Grants • 919
Roy J. Shlemon Awards • 1100
Undergraduate Student Research Grants: South-Central Section • 1160

GEORGIA ASSOCIATION FOR NURSING EDUCATION INC.
Spillman-Bischoff Scholarship • 1806

GEORGIA PRESS EDUCATIONAL FOUNDATION INC.
Georgia Press Educational Foundation Scholarships • 1398

GEORGIA STUDENT FINANCE COMMISSION
Georgia HOPE GED Grant • 1395
Georgia HOPE Grant • 1396
Georgia Tuition Equalization Grant • 1400
HOPE Scholarship Program • 1447
Zell Miller Scholarship • 1929

GEORGIA THESPIANS
Georgia Thespians Achievement Scholarships • 1399

GERMAN MARSHALL FUND OF THE UNITED STATES
Marshall Memorial Fellowship • 213

GLENN MILLER BIRTHPLACE SOCIETY
Glenn Miller Scholarship Competition • 430

GLOBAL AUTOMOTIVE AFTERMARKET SYMPOSIUM INC.
University of the Aftermarket Foundation Scholarship • 730

GMR TRANSCRIPTION SERVICES
GMR Transcription Academic Scholarship • 159

GO CITY
Go City Education Scholarship • 161

GOFOODSERVICE
GoFoodservice Scholarship • 593

GOLDEN APPLE FOUNDATION
Golden Apple Scholars of Illinois (Illinois Scholars Program) • 1402

GOLDEN DOOR SCHOLARS
Golden Door Scholars • 162

GOLDEN KEY INTERNATIONAL HONOUR SOCIETY
Golden Key Graduate Scholar Award • 1980
Golden Key Outstanding Member Award • 1981
Golden Key Undergraduate Achievement Award • 1982
Golden Key Undergraduate Achievement Scholarship • 1983

GOLDMAN SACHS
MBA Fellowship • 648

GOLF COURSE SUPERINTENDENTS ASSOCIATION OF AMERICA
GCSAA Legacy Awards • 1977
GCSAA Scholars Competition • 905

GOODRX
Equity in Pharmacy Scholarship • 882

GOOGLE DOODLE FOR GOOGLE
Doodle for Google • 416

GOOGLE INC.
Generation Google Scholarship • 2149

GOSKILLS
Be the Boss Scholarship • 60

GOVERNMENT FINANCE OFFICERS ASSOCIATION
Goldberg-Miller Public Finance Scholarship • 594

GOVERNMENT FINANCE OFFICERS ASSOCIATION OF SOUTH CAROLINA
Willa S. Bellamy Scholarship • 1904

GOVERNMENT OF THE DISTRICT OF COLUMBIA
DC Tuition Assistance Grant Program • 1324

GOVERNOR'S OFFICE OF THE STATE OF ILLINOIS DUNN FELLOWSHIP
James H. Dunn, Jr. Memorial Fellowship • 1488

GOVERNOR'S OFFICE OF THE STATE OF ILLINOIS MICHAEL CURRY SUMMER INTERNSHIP PROGRAM
Michael Curry Summer Internship Program • 1591

GRAND LODGE OF IOWA, A.F. AND A.M.
Masonic Scholarship Program • 1574
MCEC Technical Scholarship • 1583

GRAND LODGE OF MISSOURI: ANCIENT, FREE AND ACCEPTED MASONS
Ruth Lutes Bachmann Scholarship • 1775

GREAT CLIPS
Great Scholarship Program • 596

GREAT KHALID FOUNDATION
Great Khalid Performing Arts Scholarship • 431

GREAT MINDS IN STEM (HENAAC)
California Health Sciences Scholarships • 1265
STEM Scholarship • 2252

GREAT PLAINS BANK
GPB Art Harris Scholarship • 1409

GREATER HOUSTON COMMUNITY FOUNDATION
A.D. Osherman Scholarship Fund • 1178

GREATER KANAWHA VALLEY FOUNDATION
Greater Kanawha Valley Foundation Scholarship Program • 1412
Lawrence C. Yeardley Scholarship • 1528
Norman S. and Betty M. Fitzhugh Fund • 1668
W.P. Black Scholarship Fund • 1888
Willard H. Erwin, Jr. Scholarship • 1905

GREENHOUSE SCHOLARS
Greenhouse Scholars Scholarship • 1413

H.U. LEE MEMORIAL FOUNDATION
H. U. Lee Scholarship • 166

HAGAN SCHOLARSHIP FOUNDATION
Hagan Scholarship • 167

HAGLEY MUSEUM AND LIBRARY
Henry Belin du Pont Dissertation Fellowship • 601

HAIKU SOCIETY OF AMERICA
Nicholas Virgilio Haiku and Senryu Contest • 257

HANSCOM OFFICERS' SPOUSES' CLUB
Hanscom Air Force Base Spouses' Club Scholarship • 169

HARNESS HORSE YOUTH FOUNDATION
Curt Greene Memorial Scholarship • 106
Sweet Karen Alumni Scholarship • 332

HARRY ALAN GREGG FOUNDATION GRANTS
Harry Alan Gregg Foundation Grants • 1422

HARRY S. TRUMAN LIBRARY INSTITUTE FOR NATIONAL AND INTERNATIONAL AFFAIRS
Harry S. Truman Research Grant • 600

HARVARD COLLEGE SOCIAL INNOVATION COLLABORATIVE (SIC)
ConnectHER Film Festival • 410

HAWAII COMMUNITY FOUNDATION – SCHOLARSHIPS
100th Infantry Battalion Memorial Scholarship Fund • 10
Allan Eldin and Agnes Sutorik Geiger Scholarship Fund • 1200
Alma White - Delta Kappa Gamma Scholarship • 1204
Ambassador Minerva Jean Falcon Hawaii Scholarship • 1206

American Institute of Graphic Arts (AIGA) Honolulu Chapter Scholarship Fund • 1209
Ben and Vicky Cayetano Scholarship Fund • 1236
Bick Bickson Scholarship Fund • 1240
Blossom Kalama Evans Memorial Scholarship Fund • 1242
Booz Allen Hawaii Scholarship Fund • 1249
Candon, Todd and Seabolt Scholarship Fund • 1271
Community Scholarship Fund • 1310
Cora Aguda Manayan Fund • 1314
Doris and Clarence Glick Classical Music Scholarship • 1336
Dr. Edison and Sallie Miyawaki Scholarship Fund • 1340
Dr. Hans and Clara Zimmerman Foundation Education Scholarship • 1341
Dr. Hans and Clara Zimmerman Foundation Health Scholarships • 1342
Edward Payson and Bernice Piilani Irwin Scholarship • 1359
Eizo and Toyo Sakumoto Trust Scholarship • 1360
Ellison Onizuka Memorial Scholarship Fund • 1361
Esther Kanagawa Memorial Art Scholarship • 1367
F. Koehnen Ltd. Scholarship Fund • 1371
George Mason Business Scholarship Fund • 1394
Good Eats Scholarship Fund • 1404
Hawaii Community Foundation Scholarships • 1425
Hawaii Pizza Hut Scholarship Fund • 1427
Hawaii Society of Certified Public Accountants Scholarship Fund • 1429
Henry A. Zuberano Scholarship • 1431
Hideko and Zenzo Matsuyama Scholarship Fund • 1438
Ho'omaka Hou - A New Beginning Fund • 1444
Ida M. Pope Memorial Scholarship • 2168
Johanna Drew Cluney Fund • 1497
John and Anne Clifton Scholarship • 1499
John Dawe Dental Education Fund • 1501
Laura N. Dowsett Fund • 1526
Marion Maccarrell Scott Scholarship • 1566
Mildred Towle Scholarship - Study Abroad • 1601
Mildred Towle Scholarship for African-Americans • 1602
Paulina L. Sorg Scholarship • 1722
PRSA-Hawai'i/Roy Leffingwell Public Relations Scholarship • 1738
Raymond F. Cain Scholarship Fund • 1745
Ritchie M. Gregory Fund • 1760
Robanna Fund • 1762
Rosemary and Nellie Ebrie Fund • 1770
Shirley McKown Scholarship Fund • 1787
Shuichi, Katsu and Itsuyo Suga Scholarship • 1789
Tongan Cultural Society Scholarship • 1849
Victoria S. and Bradley L. Geist Foundation • 1878
William James and Dorothy Bading Lanquist Fund • 1911

HAWAII HIGH SCHOOL ATHLETIC ASSOCIATION
Hawaii High School Athletic Association Hall of Honor • 1426

HAWAII HOTEL INDUSTRY FOUNDATION
R.W. Bob Holden Scholarship • 1741

HAWAII LODGING AND TOURISM ASSOCIATION
Clem Judd, Jr., Memorial Scholarship • 1298

HAWAII ROTARY YOUTH FOUNDATION
Hawaii Rotary Youth Foundation Scholarship • 1428

HD HOGAN MEMORIAL RODEO SCHOLARSHIP FUND
HD Hogan Rodeo Scholarship • 170

HEALTH PROFESSIONS EDUCATION FOUNDATION
Licensed Vocational Nurse to Associate Degree Nursing Scholarship • 1538
Vocational Nurse Scholarship • 1887

HEALTH RESOURCES AND SERVICES ADMINISTRATION (HRSA)
Nurse Corps Scholarship Program • 1052

HEALTHCARE INFORMATION AND MANAGEMENT SYSTEMS SOCIETY
HIMSS Foundation Scholarship • 933

HEINLEIN SOCIETY
Heinlein Society Scholarship Program • 433

HELEN DILLER FAMILY FOUNDATION
Diller Teen Tikkun Olam Awards • 1962

HELEN GEE CHIN SCHOLARSHIP FOUNDATION
Helen Gee Chin Scholarship Foundation Scholarship • 172

HELP AMERICA HEAR INC.
Help America Hear Scholarship • 2299

HENKEL CONSUMER ADHESIVES
Stuck at Prom Scholarship • 314

HENRY SACHS FOUNDATION
Henry Sachs Foundation Scholarship • 1432

HERB IT FORWARD FOUNDATION
Herb It Forward Scholarship • 1433

HEYSUNDAY
Eco-Warrior Scholarship • 133

HILL & PONTON
H and P Veterans Helping Veterans Scholarship • 165

HISPANIC ASSOCIATION OF COLLEGES AND UNIVERSITIES (HACU)
Cafe Bustelo El Cafe Del Futuro Scholarship • 2112

HISPANIC HERITAGE AWARDS FOUNDATION
Hispanic Heritage Youth Awards • 2159

HISPANIC HERITAGE FOUNDATION COLGATE-PALMOLIVE HAZ LA U
Colgate-Palmolive Make the U Educational Grant • 2124

HISPANIC SCHOLARSHIP CONSORTIUM
HSC Foundation Scholarship • 2165

HISPANIC SCHOLARSHIP FUND (HSF)
Hispanic Scholarship Fund • 2160

HOME DEPOT FOUNDATION
Path to Pro Scholarship • 1060

HOME EDUCATION RECOGNITION ORGANIZATION INC. (HERO)
Craig Dickinson Memorial Scholarship • 102
Mason Lighthouse Scholarship • 217
Sandra Hancock Scholarship • 290
State of the Arts Scholarship • 485

HONOR SOCIETY OF PHI KAPPA PHI
Literacy Grants • 2006
Phi Kappa Phi Fellowship • 2030

HOOVER PRESIDENTIAL FOUNDATION
Herbert Hoover Research Travel Grant Award • 602
Herbert Hoover Uncommon Student Award • 1434

HOPI TRIBE GRANTS AND SCHOLARSHIP PROGRAM
Hopi Scholarship Program • 2164

HORATIO ALGER ASSOCIATION
Horatio Alger Career and Technical Scholarship • 604
Horatio Alger National Scholarship Program • 174

HORIZONS FOUNDATION
George Choy Memorial/Gay Asian Pacific Alliance (GAPA) Scholarship • 2151

HORTICULTURAL RESEARCH INSTITUTE
Carville M. Akehurst Memorial Scholarship • 836
Spring Meadow Proven Winners Scholarship • 1123
Timothy S. and Palmer W. Bigelow, Jr. Scholarship • 1147
Usrey Family Scholarship • 1164

HOSPITALITYMAINE
HospitalityMaine Scholarship • 1448

HOUSE OF BLUES MUSIC FORWARD FOUNDATION
Steven J. Finkel Service Excellence Scholarship • 713

HOUSTON LIVESTOCK SHOW AND RODEO
Houston Livestock Show and Rodeo Scholarships • 1449

HOUZZ INC.
Houzz Women in Architecture • 935

HUNTINGTON LIBRARY, ART COLLECTIONS AND BOTANICAL GARDENS
Huntington Fellowships • 606
Huntington-British Academy Fellowships for Study in Great Britain • 607

ICE SKATING INSTITUTE OF AMERICA (ISIA) EDUCATION FOUNDATION
ISIA Education Foundation Scholarship • 186

IDAHO STATE BOARD OF EDUCATION
GEAR UP Idaho Scholarship 3 • 1391
Governor's Cup Scholarship • 1407

IDAHO STATE BROADCASTERS ASSOCIATION
Idaho State Broadcasters Association Scholarships • 1455

IKE FOUNDATION
Ike Foundation Scholarship • 180

ILLINOIS AMVETS SERVICE FOUNDATION
Illinois AMVETS Ladies Auxiliary Memorial Scholarship • 1456

The Ultimate Scholarship Book 2026
Sponsor Index

Illinois AMVETS Ladies Auxiliary Worchid Scholarship • 1457
Illinois AMVETS Sad Sacks Nursing Scholarship • 1458
Illinois AMVETS Service Foundation Scholarship • 1459

ILLINOIS ASSOCIATION FOR HEALTH, PHYSICAL EDUCATION, RECREATION AND DANCE
Illinois Association for Health, Physical Education, Recreation and Dance Scholarships • 1460

ILLINOIS COUNCIL OF TEACHERS OF MATHEMATICS
Scholarships in Mathematics Education • 1782

ILLINOIS DEPARTMENT OF CHILDREN AND FAMILY SERVICES
Illinois Department of Children and Family Services Scholarship Program • 1461

ILLINOIS DEPARTMENT OF PUBLIC HEALTH
Monetary Award Program (MAP) • 1623

ILLINOIS REAL ESTATE EDUCATIONAL FOUNDATION
Richard D. Wiegers Scholarship • 1757

ILLINOIS STUDENT ASSISTANCE COMMISSION
Illinois Veteran Grant Program • 1462
Nursing Education Scholarship Program • 1682

IMAGINE AMERICA FOUNDATION
Adult Skills Education Award • 22
Imagine America High School Scholarship Program • 611
Military Award Program (MAP) • 224

IMEG
STEM Scholarship Program • 1127

IMPACT TEEN DRIVERS
Create Real Impact Contest • 103

INCIGHT EDUCATION
Incight Scholarship • 2301

INDEPENDENT COLLEGES OF INDIANA
Lilly Endowment Community Scholarship Program • 1540

INDEPENDENT COLLEGES OF WASHINGTON
Boeing Company STEM Scholarship • 1246
Richard E. Bangert Business Award • 1758
Stanley O. McNaughton Community Service Award • 1807
William G. Saletic Scholarship • 1910

INDIAN HEALTH SERVICE
Health Professions Pre-Graduate Scholarship Program • 2154
Health Professions Preparatory Scholarship Program • 2155

INDIANA ASSOCIATION FOR HEALTH, PHYSICAL EDUCATION, RECREATION AND DANCE
Jean Lee/Jeff Marvin Collegiate Scholarships • 1492

INDIANA BROADCASTERS ASSOCIATION
Indiana Broadcasters Association College Scholarships • 1465

INDIANA COMMISSION FOR HIGHER EDUCATION
Mitch Daniels Early Graduation Scholarship • 1621
Twenty-first Century Scholars Program • 1862
William A. Crawford Minority Teacher Scholarship • 1906

INDIANA GOLF ASSOCIATION
David E. Simon Scholarship • 1323
Indiana Golf Foundation Scholarship • 1466

INDIANA STATE TEACHERS ASSOCIATION
Louis B. Russell Scholarship • 1550

INDUSTRIAL DESIGNERS SOCIETY OF AMERICA
IDSA Undergraduate and Graduate Scholarships • 438

INDUSTRIAL METAL SERVICE
Industrial Metal Service Scholarship • 183

INSTITUTE FOR HUMANE STUDIES AT GEORGE MASON UNIVERSITY
Humane Studies Fellowship: Flexible Support for PhD Students • 175
Humane Studies Fellowship: Graduate Sabbatical Grants • 176
Humane Studies Fellowship: Publication Accelerator Grants • 605

INSTITUTE OF CURRENT WORLD AFFAIRS
ICWA Fellowship Program • 437

INSTITUTE OF ELECTRICAL AND ELECTRONICS ENGINEERS (IEEE)
Institute of Electrical and Electronics Engineers Life Members' Fellowship in Electrical History • 941

INSTITUTE OF FOOD TECHNOLOGISTS (IFT)
Feeding Tomorrow General Education Scholarships/Freshman Scholarships • 888
Graduate Scholarships • 918
Undergraduate Scholarships • 1159

INSTITUTE OF INDUSTRIAL AND SYSTEMS ENGINEERS
A.O. Putnam Memorial Scholarship • 741
C.B. Gambrell Undergraduate Scholarship • 833
Dwight D. Gardner Scholarship • 869
E.J. Sierleja Memorial Fellowship • 871
Gilbreth Memorial Fellowship • 911
Harold and Inge Marcus Scholarship • 925
IISE Council of Fellows Undergraduate Scholarship • 938
John L. Imhoff Scholarship • 957
John S.W. Fargher, Jr. Scholarship • 960
Lisa Zaken Award For Excellence • 981
Marvin Mundel Memorial Scholarship • 992
Presidents Scholarship of the Institute of Industrial Engineers • 1078
United Parcel Service Scholarship for Female Students • 1162
United Parcel Service Scholarship for Minority Students • 2272

INSTITUTE OF INTERNATIONAL EDUCATION GILMAN SCHOLARSHIP PROGRAM
Gilman International Scholarship • 429

INSTITUTE OF MANAGEMENT ACCOUNTANTS (IMA)
IMA Memorial Education Fund Scholarship • 610
Stuart Cameron and Margaret McLeod Memorial Scholarship • 714

INSTITUTE OF SCRAP RECYCLING INDUSTRIES
National Foundation Scholarships • 662

INSTITUTE OF TRANSPORTATION ENGINEERS – OHIO SECTION
Ohio Section Scholarships • 1688

INTERNATIONAL ALLIANCE OF THEATRICAL STAGE EMPLOYEES, ARTISTS AND ALLIED CRAFTS OF THE U.S.
Richard F. Walsh, Alfred W. DiTolla, Harold P. Spivak Foundation Award • 2035

INTERNATIONAL ASSOCIATION OF FIRE FIGHTERS
W. H. Howie McClennan Scholarship • 366

INTERNATIONAL ASSOCIATION OF MACHINISTS AND AEROSPACE WORKERS
IAM Scholarship • 1989

INTERNATIONAL ASSOCIATION OF PLUMBING AND MECHANICAL OFFICIALS (IAPMO)
IAPMO Essay Scholarship Contest • 177

INTERNATIONAL BRIDGE, TUNNEL AND TURNPIKE ASSOCIATION FOUNDATION
IBTTA Foundation Scholarship Program • 937

INTERNATIONAL CENTRE FOR DIFFRACTION DATA
Ludo Frevel Crystallography Scholarships • 988

INTERNATIONAL CHEMICAL WORKERS UNION COUNCIL/UFCW
Walter L. Mitchell Memorial Scholarship Awards • 2070

INTERNATIONAL COLLEGE COUNSELORS
International College Counselors Scholarship • 184

INTERNATIONAL FACILITY MANAGEMENT ASSOCIATION
International Facility Management Association Foundation Scholarship Program • 613

INTERNATIONAL FLIGHT SERVICES ASSOCIATION (IFSA)
IFSA Foundation Scholarship Award • 1990

INTERNATIONAL FOOD SERVICE EXECUTIVES ASSOCIATION
IFSEA Worthy Goal Scholarship • 609

INTERNATIONAL FOODSERVICE EDITORIAL COUNCIL (IFEC)
IFEC Scholarships Award • 608

INTERNATIONAL FURNISHINGS AND DESIGN ASSOCIATION (IFDA)
IFDA Leaders Commemorative Scholarship • 439
IFDA Student Member Scholarship • 440
Part-Time Student Scholarship • 472
Ruth Clark Furniture Design Scholarship • 480
Tricia LeVangie Green/Sustainable Design Scholarship • 496
Vercille Voss IFDA Graduate Student Scholarship • 500

INTERNATIONAL HOUSEWARES ASSOCIATION
Student Design Competition • 489

INTERNATIONAL INSOLVENCY INSTITUTE
Prize in International Insolvency Studies • 688

INTERNATIONAL LITERACY ASSOCIATION
ILA Jeanne S. Chall Research Fellowship • 441

INTERNATIONAL ORDER OF THE KING'S DAUGHTERS AND SONS
Health Careers Scholarship • 928
Native American Scholarship • 2222

INTERNATIONAL SCHOLARSHIP AND TUITION SERVICES INC.
Glass, Molders, Pottery, Plastics and Allied Workers Memorial Scholarship Fund • 1979

INTERNATIONAL SOCIETY OF AUTOMATION
Educational Foundation Scholarship • 576

INTERNATIONAL SOCIETY OF EXPLOSIVES ENGINEERS
SEE Education Foundation Scholarships • 1110

INTERNATIONAL SURFING ASSOCIATION
Individual Scholarship Program • 182

INTERNATIONAL TECHNOLOGY AND ENGINEERING EDUCATORS ASSOCIATION
FTEE Scholarship: Undergraduate Major in Technology and Engineering Education • 585
International Technology Engineering Educators Association Scholarship - FTEE/Undergraduate • 614
Litherland/ITEEA Scholarship • 640
Maley/FTEE Teacher Professional Development Scholarship • 644

INTERNATIONAL TRUMPET GUILD
International Trumpet Guild Conference Scholarship • 443

INTERNATIONAL UNION OF ELECTRONIC, ELECTRICAL, SALARIED, MACHINE AND FURNITURE WORKERS-COMMUNICATIONS WORKERS OF AMERICA
James B. Carey Scholarship • 1994

INTERNATIONAL WATER, SANITATION AND HYGIENE FOUNDATION
IWSH Essay Scholarship • 948

INTERNATIONAL WOMEN'S FISHING ASSOCIATION
International Women's Fishing Association Scholarship • 944

INTERSCHOLASTIC EQUESTRIAN ASSOCIATION
IEA Founders College Scholarship Awards • 178
IEA Zone Specific Scholarships • 179
National Sportsmanship Award • 240

INTERTECH FOUNDATION
Intertech Foundation STEM Scholarship • 945

INTERTRIBAL TIMBER COUNCIL
Truman D. Picard Scholarship • 2269

INVESTOR'S PODCAST
Corporate Culture Scholarship • 98

IOTA SIGMA PI (ISP) ND
Gladys Anderson Emerson Scholarship • 913
Undergraduate Award for Excellence in Chemistry • 1156

IOWA 4-H FOUNDATION
Iowa 4-H College Scholarships • 1469

IOWA ARTS COUNCIL
Iowa Scholarship for the Arts • 1475

IOWA AUTOMOBILE DEALERS FOUNDATION FOR EDUCATION
IAD Foundation Scholarships • 1453

IOWA CHEERLEADING COACHES' ASSOCIATION
ICCA Scholarships • 1454

IOWA COLLEGE STUDENT AID COMMISSION
All Iowa Opportunity Scholarship • 1199
Iowa Tuition Grants • 1477
Iowa Vocational-Technical Tuition Grants • 1478
Kibbie Grant (Iowa Skilled Workforce Shortage Tuition Grant) • 1522

IOWA FOUNDATION FOR AGRICULTURAL ADVANCEMENT
Russ Brannen/KENT FEEDS Memorial Beef Scholarship • 1774
Schlutz Family Beef Breeding Scholarship • 1778
Winner's Circle Scholarships • 1914

IOWA GOLF ASSOCIATION
Ann Griffel Scholarship • 1218
Herman Sani Scholarship • 1436

IOWA HIGH SCHOOL MUSIC ASSOCIATION
Leo H. Grether Memorial Scholarship • 1536

IOWA NEWSPAPER ASSOCIATION
Iowa Newspaper Association Scholarships • 1470

IOWA PGA FOUNDATION
Iowa PGA Foundation Charlie Burkart Scholarship • 1472

IOWA PHYSICIAN ASSISTANT SOCIETY
Iowa Physician Assistant Society Scholarship • 1473

IOWA PORK PRODUCERS ASSOCIATION
Iowa Pork Foundation Scholarship • 1474

IOWA PTA
H.L. Taylor Scholarship Program • 1419

IOWA STATE ARCHERY ASSOCIATION
ISAA Scholarship Program • 1480

IOWA STUDENT LOAN EDUCATION LENDING
Iowa Student Loan Midwest Senior Scholarship • 185

IOWA THESPIAN CHAPTER
Iowa Thespian Chapter Board Senior Scholarships • 1476

IRISH-AMERICAN CULTURAL INSTITUTE (IACI)
IACI/NUIG Visiting Fellowship in Irish Studies • 436

ISLAMIC SCHOLARSHIP FUND
ISF Policy Scholarship Program • 1992

ISLAMIC SOCIETY OF NORTH AMERICA
Islamic Society of North America Scholarships • 1993

IUPAT INTERNATIONAL OFFICE
S. Frank Bud Raftery Scholarship • 2038

IZAAK WALTON LEAGUE OF AMERICA-MINNESOTA DIVISION
Minnesota Division Izaak Walton League Scholarship • 1605

JACK KENT COOKE FOUNDATION
Jack Kent Cooke Foundation College Scholarship Program • 187
Undergraduate Transfer Scholarship • 349
Young Scholars Program • 384

JACKIE ROBINSON FOUNDATION
Jackie Robinson Foundation Scholarship Program • 2170

JACKSON LABORATORY
Jackson Laboratory Scholarship • 949

JAMES B. MORRIS SCHOLARSHIP FUND
James B. Morris Scholarship • 1487

JAMES BEARD FOUNDATION SCHOLARSHIP PROGRAM/ISTS
James Beard Foundation Scholarship • 617

JAMES F. LINCOLN ARC WELDING FOUNDATION
JFLF Awards Programs • 620

JAMES M. AND ERMA T. FREEMONT FOUNDATION
James M. and Erma T. Freemont Foundation Scholarship Program • 2171

JANE AUSTEN SOCIETY OF NORTH AMERICA
Jane Austen Society of North America Essay Contest • 189

JAPANESE AMERICAN CITIZENS LEAGUE (JACL)
Abe and Esther Hagiwara Student Aid Award • 2081
Japanese American Citizens League Entering Freshman Awards • 2172
Japanese American Citizens League Graduate Awards • 2173
Japanese American Citizens League Law Scholarships • 2174
Japanese American Citizens League Undergraduate Awards • 2175
Kyutaro and Yasuo Abiko Memorial Scholarship • 2003

JEANNETTE RANKIN FOUNDATION
Jeannette Rankin National Scholar Grant • 2176

JEFFERSON COUNTY EDUCATION ASSOCIATION
Dorian De Long Arts and Music Scholarship • 1335

JEWISH COMMUNITY FEDERATION AND ENDOWMENT FUND
Helen B. and Lewis E. Goldstein Scholarship Fund • 1985

JEWISH WAR VETERANS OF THE USA
Bernard Rotberg Memorial Scholarship Fund • 1947

JIMMIE L. DEAN SCHOLARSHIP FOUNDATION INC.
Jimmie L. Dean Scholarship • 1493

JIMMY RANE FOUNDATION
Jimmy Rane Foundation Scholarships • 1494

JOE FRANCIS HAIRCARE SCHOLARSHIP FOUNDATION
Joe Francis Haircare Scholarship Program • 621

JOHN BAYLISS BROADCAST FOUNDATION
John Bayliss Radio Scholarship • 623

JOHN F. AND ANNA LEE STACEY SCHOLARSHIP FUND
John F. and Anna Lee Stacey Scholarship Fund for Art Education • 447

JOHN F. KENNEDY CENTER FOR THE PERFORMING ARTS
Playwright Discovery Award • 475

The Ultimate Scholarship Book 2026
Sponsor Index

JOHN F. KENNEDY LIBRARY FOUNDATION
John F. Kennedy Profile in Courage Essay Contest • 625

JOHN PHILIP SOUSA FOUNDATION
Dr. Robert Hawkins Memorial Scholarship • 571

JON C. LADDA MEMORIAL FOUNDATION
Jon C. Ladda Memorial Foundation Scholarship • 193

JORGE MAS CANOSA FREEDOM FOUNDATION
Mas Family Scholarships • 2200

JOURNALISM EDUCATION ASSOCIATION FUTURE TEACHER SCHOLARSHIP
Future Journalism Teacher Scholarship • 588

JULIUS AND ESTHER STULBERG COMPETITION INC.
Julius and Esther Stulberg International String Competition • 449

KANSAS AGRICULTURAL AVIATION ASSOCIATION
Kansas Agricultural Aviation Association Scholarship • 1508

KANSAS ASSOCIATION OF BROADCASTERS
KAB Broadcast Scholarship Program • 1507

KANSAS BOARD OF REGENTS
Kansas Career Technical Workforce Grant • 1509
Kansas Comprehensive Grants • 1510
Kansas Ethnic Minority Scholarship • 1511
Kansas Nursing Service Scholarship • 1512
Kansas Osteopathic Medical Service Scholarship • 1514
Kansas State Scholarship • 1515
Kansas Teacher Service Scholarship • 1516

KAPLUN FOUNDATION
Moris J. and Betty Kaplun Essay Contest • 2014

KAPPA DELTA PI EDUCATIONAL FOUNDATION
Sandra Jo Hornick Scholarship • 2040

KE ALI'I PAUAHI FOUNDATION
Pauahi Foundation Public Scholarships • 1720

KEEP IOWA BEAUTIFUL
Byers Scholarship • 1254

KEM ELECTRIC
KEM Electric Cooperative Scholarships for Students Attending High School Outside the Service Area • 1519

KEMPER HUMAN RIGHTS EDUCATION FOUNDATION
Kemper Human Rights Education Foundation • 199

KENTUCKY BOARD OF NURSING
Nursing Incentive Scholarship Fund • 1683

KENTUCKY BROADCASTERS ASSOCIATION
Harry Barfield KBA Scholarship Program • 1423

KENTUCKY DEPARTMENT OF VETERANS AFFAIRS
Exemption from Tuition Fees for Dependents of Kentucky Veterans • 1370
Kentucky Veterans Tuition Waiver Program • 1521

KENTUCKY FEDERATION OF BUSINESS AND PROFESSIONAL WOMEN
Business and Professional Women of Kentucky Foundation Grant • 1252

KENTUCKY HIGHER EDUCATION ASSISTANCE AUTHORITY (KHEAA)
College Access Program • 1300
Educational Excellence Scholarship • 1353
Kentucky Tuition Grant • 1520
Teacher Scholarship Program • 1826

KIDGER OPTICS ASSOCIATES
Michael Kidger Memorial Scholarship • 1004

KNIGHTS OF COLUMBUS
Fourth Degree Pro Deo and Pro Patria Scholarships • 1974
John W. McDevitt (Fourth Degree) Scholarship Fund • 1999

KNIGHTS OF LITHUANIA SCHOLARSHIP PROGRAM
Knights of Lithuania Scholarship Program • 2180

KOSCIUSZKO FOUNDATION
Drs. James and Wanda Trefil Science Scholarship • 2135

KURT WEILL FOUNDATION FOR MUSIC
Lotte Lenya Competition • 456

L. RON HUBBARD'S WRITERS OF THE FUTURE CONTEST
Illustrators of the Future • 442

LA TUTORS
LA Tutors Innovation in Education Scholarship • 202

LABROOTS
LabRoots Scholarship • 970

LADIES AUXILIARY OF THE FLEET RESERVE ASSOCIATION
La Fra Scholarship • 201
Sam Rose Memorial Scholarship • 2039

LADIES AUXILIARY VFW
Young American Creative Patriotic Art Contest • 506

LADIES PROFESSIONAL GOLF ASSOCIATION
Dinah Shore Scholarship • 119
Goldie Bateson Scholarship • 2152
Marilynn Smith Scholarship • 2196
Phyllis G. Meekins Scholarship • 2237

LAGRANT FOUNDATION
LAGRANT Scholarship Program • 2182

LAKE MICHIGAN CREDIT UNION
Lloyd F. Hutt Scholarship • 1544

LANDSCAPE ARCHITECTURE FOUNDATION
ASLA Council of Fellows Scholarships • 807
Douglas Dockery Thomas Fellowship in Garden History and Design • 864
EDSA Diversity Scholarships • 2137
Landscape Forms Scholarship in Memory of Peter Lindsay Schaudt, FASLA • 971
Rain Bird Intelligent Use of Water Scholarship • 1082
Steven G. King Play Environments Scholarship • 1129

LEADERS ADVANCING AND HELPING COMMUNITIES
Leaders Advancing and Helping Communities Scholarship • 1529

LEAGUE FOUNDATION
Laurel Hester Memorial Scholarship • 2184
LEAGUE Foundation Scholarship • 2185

LEAGUE OF UNITED LATIN AMERICAN CITIZENS
LULAC General Awards • 2190
LULAC Honors Awards • 2191
LULAC National Scholastic Achievement Awards • 207

LEARNER
Learner Education Women in Mathematics Scholarship • 976

LEARNING ALLY
Marion Huber Learning Through Listening Awards • 2307
Mary P. Oenslanger Scholastic Achievement Awards • 2308

LESBIANS WHO TECH
Edie Windsor Coding Scholarship • 2136

LET GROW
Think For Yourself College Scholarship Essay Contest • 339

LIFE AND HEALTH INSURANCE FOUNDATION FOR EDUCATION
Life Lessons Scholarship Program • 204

LIGHTHOUSE GUILD
Lighthouse Guild Scholarships • 2304

LIME CONNECT
BMO Capital Markets Lime Connect Equity Through Education Scholarship • 2286
Lime Connect Pathways Scholarship for High School Seniors with Disabilities • 2305

LINCOLN COMMUNITY FOUNDATION
Norman and Ruth Good Educational Endowment • 1667

LINCOLN FORUM
Platt Family Scholarship Prize Essay Contest • 474

LINLY HEFLIN UNIT
Linly Heflin Scholarship • 1543

LIONS CLUB INTERNATIONAL
Lions International Peace Poster Contest • 455

LITTLE PEOPLE OF AMERICA
Little People of America Scholarships • 2306

LIVE POETS SOCIETY
National High School Poetry Contest/Easterday Poetry Award • 462

LOCKHEED MARTIN STEM SCHOLARSHIP PROGRAM
Lockheed Martin STEM Scholarship Program • 982

LOCKHEED MARTIN VOCATIONAL SCHOLARSHIP PROGRAM
Lockheed Martin Vocational Scholarship Program • 641

LOREN L. ZACHARY SOCIETY FOR THE PERFORMING ARTS
National Vocal Competition for Young Opera Singers • 465

Los Alamos National Laboratory Foundation
Allan Johnston Memorial Scholarship • 1201
Four-Year Undergraduate Scholarships • 1385
Los Alamos Employees' Scholarship • 1548
NNM American Society of Mechanical Engineers Scholarship • 1666
Rae Lee Siporin Award • 1742
William and Gertrude Fradkin Memorial Scholarship • 1907

Louisiana Office of Student Financial Assistance
Honors Award • 1446
Louisiana Go Grant • 1551
Opportunity Award • 1704
Rockefeller State Wildlife Scholarship • 1767
TOPS Performance Award • 1850
TOPS Tech Award • 1851

LPGA Amateur Golf Association
Women on Par Scholarship • 380

Luso-American Education Foundation
Luso-American Education Foundation General Youth Scholarship • 1553

Lutheran Family Services of Nebraska
Smith Diversity Scholarship • 1795

Lyndon B. Johnson Foundation
Moody Research Grant • 657

Maids of Athena
Maids of Athena Scholarships • 2007

Maine Community Foundation
Maine Community Foundation Scholarship Program • 1556

Maine Demolay and Pine Tree Youth Foundation
Maine Demolay and Pine Tree Youth Foundation Scholarships • 1557

Maine Education Assistance Division
State of Maine Grant Program • 1812

Maine Society of Professional Engineers
Vernon T. Swain, P.E./Robert E. Chute, P.E. Scholarship • 1875

Maine State Society Foundation of Washington, DC
Maine State Society Foundation Scholarship • 1559

Maison Law Personal Injury Lawyer
Maison Law California Scholarship • 1561

Malcolm Frierson Foundation
Marcus Garvey Scholarship • 2194

Mamoru and Aiko Takitani Foundation
Mamoru and Aiko Takitani Foundation Scholarship • 1562

Maple Flooring Manufacturers Association
Maple Flooring Manufacturers Association Scholarship • 645

Margaret McNamara Memorial Fund
Margaret McNamara Education Grants • 2195

Marine Corps League
Marine Corps League Scholarships • 209

Marine Corps Scholarship Foundation
Marine Corps Scholarship Foundation Scholarship • 210

Marine Technology Society
Charles H. Bussmann Undergraduate Scholarship • 838
John C. Bajus Scholarship • 955
MTS Student Scholarship for Two-Year, Technical, Engineering and Community College Students • 1015
MTS Student Scholarship for Undergraduate Students • 1016
Paros-Digiquartz Scholarship • 1059

Marshall Aid Commemoration Commission
Marshall Scholar • 214

Mary E. Bivins Foundation
Mary E. Bivins Religious Scholarship • 2011

Maryland Criminal Defense Group
Oleg Fastovsky Outstanding Citizenship Scholarship • 263

Maryland Higher Education Commission
Charles W. Riley Fire and Emergency Medical Services Scholarship Program • 1289
Delegate Scholarship • 1328
Howard P. Rawlings Educational Assistance (EA) Grant • 1450
Howard P. Rawlings Guaranteed Access (GA) Grant • 1451
Jack F. Tolbert Memorial Student Grant Program • 1484
Loan Assistance Repayment Program Primary Care Services • 1545
Part-Time Grant • 1714
Senatorial Scholarship • 1784
Tuition Reduction for Non-Resident Nursing Students • 1858
Tuition Waiver for Foster Care Recipients • 1859
Workforce Shortage Student Assistance Grant Program • 1923

Masonic Charity Foundation of Oklahoma
High School Senior Essay Contest • 1439

Masonry Institute of Iowa
Masonry Institute of Iowa Foundation Scholarship Program • 1575

Massachusetts Broadcasters Association
Massachusetts Student Broadcaster Scholarship • 1578

Massachusetts Community Colleges
Massachusetts Community Colleges Access Grant • 1576

Massachusetts Department of Higher Education
Agnes M. Lindsay Scholarship • 1191
Cash Grant Program • 1277
Categorical Tuition Waiver • 1278
Christian A. Herter Memorial Scholarship Program • 1294
Collaborative Teachers Tuition Waiver • 1299
Department of Children and Families (DCF) Foster Child Tuition Waiver and Fee Assistance Program • 1330
Early Childhood Educators Scholarship • 1348
Foster Child Grant Program • 1383
Gilbert Matching Student Grant • 1401
Graduate Tuition Waiver • 1410
High Technology Scholar/Intern Tuition Waiver • 1440
Incentive Program for Aspiring Teachers • 1463
John and Abigail Adams Scholarship • 1498
Massachusetts Part-Time Grant • 1577
MASSGrant • 1579
Need Based Tuition Waiver Program • 1643
Paraprofessional Teacher Preparation Grant • 1713
Stanley Z. Koplik Certificate of Mastery Tuition Waiver Program • 1808
Valedictorian Program Tuition Waiver • 1871

Massachusetts Educational Financing Authority
MEFA UPlan Prepaid Tuition Waiver Program • 1587

Massachusetts/Rhode Island League for Nursing
MARILN Professional Scholarship Award • 1565

Material Handling Industry
Material Handling Education Foundation • 647

Medical Group Management Association
Harry J. Harwick Scholarship • 927
Leaders Scholarship • 975
MGMA Midwest Section Scholarship • 1002
MGMA Western Section Scholarship • 1003
Richard L. Davis, FACMPE - Managers Scholarship • 1092
Richard L. Davis, FACMPE/Barbara B. Watson, FACMPE - National Scholarship • 1093

Medical Library Association
Beverly Murphy MLA Scholarship for Underrepresented Students • 541
Gwendolyn S. Cruzat MLA Scholarship • 597

Mensa Education and Research Foundation
Mensa Foundation Scholarship Program • 221

Merchants Exchange of Portland Scholarship Fund
Merchants Exchange of Portland Scholarship • 651

Metro Youth Football Association
Metro Youth Football Association Scholarship • 222

Metzger Wickersham Injury Lawyers
Road to Safety Scholarship Contest • 1761

Mexican American Legal Defense and Educational Fund
MALDEF Law School Scholarship • 2193

MFA Incorporated
MFA Foundation Scholarships • 1590

Michael and Susan Dell Foundation
Dell Scholars Program • 115

Michael Moody Fitness
Michael Moody Fitness Scholarship • 1005

Michigan Council of Women in Technology Foundation
Michigan Council of Women in Technology University Scholarship • 1593

The Ultimate Scholarship Book 2026
Sponsor Index

MICHIGAN DEPARTMENT OF TREASURY
Michigan Tuition Incentive Program • 1597

MICHIGAN SOCIETY OF PROFESSIONAL ENGINEERS
Michigan Engineering Scholarships • 1594
MSPE Kenneth B. Fishbeck, P.E., Memorial Grant • 1628

MICHIGAN STUDENT AID
Michigan Competitive Scholarship • 1592
Michigan Tuition Grant • 1596

MICHIGAN TOWNSHIPS ASSOCIATION
Robert R. Robinson Memorial Scholarship • 1764

MICROSOFT OFFICE
Microsoft Office Specialist World Championship • 652

MIDWESTERN HIGHER EDUCATION COMPACT
Midwest Student Exchange Program • 1599

MIKE MOLINO RV LEARNING CENTER
RV Learning Center Scholarship Program • 1104

MIKKELSON FOUNDATION
Mikkelson Foundation Scholarship • 1600

MILITARY FAMILY SUPPORT TRUST
Military Family Support Trust Scholarships • 225

MILTON FISHER SCHOLARSHIP FOR INNOVATION AND CREATIVITY
Milton Fisher Scholarship for Innovation and Creativity • 1603

MINERALS, METALS AND MATERIALS SOCIETY
Light Metals Division Scholarship • 980
Materials Processing and Manufacturing Division Scholarship • 995
Structural Materials Division Scholarship • 1130
TMS Best Paper Contest • 1149
TMS Technical Division Student Poster Contest • 1150
TMS/International Symposium On Superalloys Scholarships • 1151

MINNESOTA HOCKEY
Minnesota Hockey Scholarship • 1606

MINNESOTA MASONIC CHARITIES
Minnesota Masonic Charities Vocational Scholarship • 1608

MINNESOTA OFFICE OF HIGHER EDUCATION SERVICES
Alliss Opportunity Grant Program for Adults Returning to College • 1203
Minnesota Academic Excellence Scholarship • 1604
Minnesota Indian Scholarship Program • 1607
Minnesota State Grant • 1610

MINNESOTA STATE ARCHERY ASSOCIATION
MSAA Scholarship Program • 1627

MINNESOTA TURKEY GROWERS ASSOCIATION
Ranelius Scholarship Program • 1743

MINORITY CORPORATE COUNSEL ASSOCIATION (MCCA)
MCCA Lloyd M. Johnson, Jr. Scholarship Program • 2202

MISSISSIPPI ASSOCIATION OF BROADCASTERS
Mississippi Association of Broadcasters Scholarship Program • 1614

MISSISSIPPI OFFICE OF STUDENT FINANCIAL AID
Higher Education Legislative Plan (HELP) • 1443
Mississippi Eminent Scholars Grant (MESG) • 1615
Mississippi Tuition Assistance Grant (MTAG) • 1617

MISSOURI 4-H FOUNDATION
Missouri 4-H Foundation Scholarships • 1618

MISSOURI BANKERS FOUNDATION
John W. Rogers Memorial Scholarship • 1504

MISSOURI STATE THESPIANS
Missouri State Thespian Scholarships • 1620

MISSOURI STUDENT ASSISTANCE RESOURCE SERVICES (MOSTARS)
Higher Education Academic Scholarship Program (Bright Flight) • 1441

MIT TECH FAIR
MIT THINK Scholarship Program • 1010

MITCHELL INSTITUTE
Mitchell Scholarship • 1622

MODERN WOODMEN OF AMERICA
Modern Woodmen of America Scholarship • 2013

MOMETRIX TEST PREPARATION
Mometrix College Scholarship • 226

MONTANA CATTLEWOMEN INC.
Montana CattleWomen Scholarship • 1624

MONTANA COMMUNITY FOUNDATION
Builders Exchange of Billings Scholarship • 1251
T. Eugene Young Montana's Promise Scholarship • 1822

MONTANA STATE ELKS ASSOCIATION
William and Sara Jenne' Scholarship • 1908

MONTANA UNIVERSITY SYSTEM
Montana University System Honor Scholarship • 1625

MOODY FOUNDATION
Moody Scholar Program • 1626

MOOLAHSPOT
$1,000 Moolahspot Scholarship • 7

MORRIS K. UDALL FOUNDATION
Morris K. Udall Scholarship • 2211

MORTAR BOARD NATIONAL FOUNDATION
Mortar Board National Foundation Fellowship • 2015

MPOWER FINANCING
Women in STEM Scholarship • 378

MU ALPHA THETA SCHOLARSHIP COMMITTEE
Mary Rhein Memorial Scholarship • 993

MUTUAL OF OMAHA
Mutual of Omaha Actuarial Scholarship for Minority Students • 2212

MY ACTION PLAN FOR COLLEGE
My Action Plan for College Young Scholars Initiative • 1631

NAACP ACT-SO ACHIEVEMENT PROGRAM
Afro-Academic, Cultural, Technological and Scientific Olympics (ACT-SO) • 2087

NAACP LEGAL DEFENSE AND EDUCATIONAL FUND
Earl Warren Scholarship • 572

NAACP LEGAL DEFENSE AND EDUCATIONAL FUND INC.
Herbert Lehman Education Fund Scholarship • 2158

NADONA/LTC
Stephanie Carroll Memorial Scholarship • 1128

NATIONAL 4-H COUNCIL
4-H Youth in Action • 1930

NATIONAL ACADEMY OF ENGINEERING
EngineerGirl Essay Contest • 880

NATIONAL ACADEMY OF TELEVISION ARTS AND SCIENCES-UPPER MIDWEST FOUNDATION
Upper Midwest Chapter Scholarships • 1867

NATIONAL AIDS MEMORIAL
Mary Bowman Arts in Activism Award • 459
Pedro Zamora Young Leaders Scholarship • 267

NATIONAL AIR TRANSPORTATION FOUNDATION
Dan L. Meisinger Sr. Memorial Learn to Fly Scholarship • 851
Pioneers of Flight • 1071

NATIONAL ALLIANCE OF INDEPENDENT CROP CONSULTANTS
Richard Jensen Scholarship • 1091

NATIONAL AMATEUR BASEBALL FEDERATION
NABF Scholarship Program • 231

NATIONAL ASIAN PACIFIC AMERICAN BAR ASSOCIATION LAW FOUNDATION
LimNexus Scholarship • 639
Presidential Scholarships • 687

NATIONAL ASPHALT PAVEMENT ASSOCIATION
NAPA Research and Education Foundation Scholarship • 1020

NATIONAL ASSOCIATION FOR CAMPUS ACTIVITIES
Lori Rhett Memorial Scholarship • 1547
Markley Scholarship • 211
NACA Mid Atlantic Graduate Student Scholarship • 658
NACA Northern Plains Regional Student Leadership Scholarship • 1632
NACA South Student Leadership Scholarships • 1633
Scholarships for Student Leaders • 296
Zagunis Student Leader Scholarship • 1928

NATIONAL ASSOCIATION FOR SURFACE FINISHING
National Association for Surface Finishing Scholarships • 1021

NATIONAL ASSOCIATION FOR THE ADVANCEMENT OF COLORED PEOPLE
Agnes Jones Jackson Scholarship • 2090
Creative Sole Scholarship • 2129
Hubertus W.V. Wellems Scholarship for Male Students • 2167
Write Your Future Scholarship • 2279
X Society Awards Scholarship • 2280

NATIONAL ASSOCIATION OF BLACK ACCOUNTANTS
National Association of Black Accountants National Scholarship Program • 2215

NATIONAL ASSOCIATION OF BLACK JOURNALISTS
Larry Whiteside Scholarship • 2183

NATIONAL ASSOCIATION OF BLACKS IN CRIMINAL JUSTICE
Chairman's Award • 1952
Jonathan Jasper Wright Award • 194
Mary Church Terrell Award • 215
Medgar Evers Award • 218
Owens-Bell Award • 2028
William L. Hastie Award • 376

NATIONAL ASSOCIATION OF CHIEFS OF POLICE
NACOP Scholarship • 232

NATIONAL ASSOCIATION OF CORROSION ENGINEERS (NACE) INTERNATIONAL FOUNDATION
American Innovations Corrosion Scholarship • 780
AMPP Academic Scholarship • 782
Gordon Rankin Corrosion Engineering Scholarship • 915
Melvin J. Schiff Fellowship Fund • 998
MTI Bert Krisher Memorial Scholarship • 1014
Oliver Moghissi Memorial Scholarship • 1055
PPG Protective and Marine Coatings Academic Scholarship • 1075
Williams Companies Academic Scholarship • 1171

NATIONAL ASSOCIATION OF HISPANIC NURSES
NAHN Scholarship • 2213

NATIONAL ASSOCIATION OF LETTER CARRIERS
William C. Doherty Scholarship Fund • 2073

NATIONAL ASSOCIATION OF NEGRO BUSINESS AND PROFESSIONAL WOMEN'S CLUBS INC.
Julianne Malveaux Scholarship • 2178
National Scholarship • 2220

NATIONAL ASSOCIATION OF WOMEN IN CONSTRUCTION
NAWIC Founders' Undergraduate Scholarship • 1032
Undergraduate Scholarship and Construction Trades Scholarship • 1158

NATIONAL ATHLETIC TRAINERS' ASSOCIATION
NATA Scholarship • 233

NATIONAL BLACK NURSES ASSOCIATION
Annual NBNA Scholarships • 789

NATIONAL BUSINESS AVIATION ASSOCIATION
UAA Janice K. Barden Aviation Scholarship • 1155

NATIONAL CATHOLIC COMMITTEE ON SCOUTING
Emmett J. Doerr Memorial Scout Scholarship • 1966

NATIONAL CATTLEMEN'S FOUNDATION
Beef Industry Scholarship • 826

NATIONAL CENTER FOR FARMWORKER HEALTH INC.
Migrant Health Scholarships • 1007

NATIONAL CENTER FOR LEARNING DISABILITIES
Anne Ford Scholarship Program • 2284

NATIONAL CENTER FOR WOMEN AND INFORMATION TECHNOLOGY (NCWIT)
NCWIT Award for Aspirations in Computing • 2225

NATIONAL COLLEGE TABLE TENNIS ASSOCIATION
National Table Tennis Scholarship • 241

NATIONAL COLLEGIATE ATHLETIC ASSOCIATION
Ethnic Minority and Women's Enhancement Scholarship • 140
NCAA Division II Degree Completion Award Program • 252
NCAA Postgraduate Scholarship • 253
Walter Byers Graduate Scholarship • 369

NATIONAL COLLEGIATE CANCER FOUNDATION
National Collegiate Cancer Foundation Scholarship • 2311

NATIONAL COMMUNITY PHARMACISTS ASSOCIATION
NCPA Foundation Presidential Scholarship • 1036

NATIONAL COURT REPORTERS ASSOCIATION
NCRA A to Z Scholarship • 667
NCRA CASE Student Scholarship • 668

NATIONAL DAIRY PROMOTION AND RESEARCH BOARD
NDPRB Undergraduate Scholarship Program • 1037

NATIONAL DAIRY SHRINE
Dairy Student Recognition Program • 850
DMI Milk Marketing Scholarship • 859
Marshall E. McCullough Scholarship • 991
National Dairy Shrine/Iager Dairy Scholarship • 1023
NDS / Klussendorf / McKown Scholarships • 1038

NATIONAL EAGLE SCOUT ASSOCIATION, SCOUTING AMERICA
National Eagle Scout Association Scholarship • 2017
NESA Hall/McElwain Merit Scholarships • 2022
NESA Lawrence S. and Mabel Cooke Scholarship • 2023
Rebecca Palmer Eagle Scout Scholarship Endowment • 2032

NATIONAL EDUCATION ASSOCIATION
NEA-Retired Jack Kinnaman Memorial Scholarship • 669

NATIONAL ENVIRONMENTAL HEALTH ASSOCIATION AND THE AMERICAN ACADEMY OF SANITARIANS
National Environmental Health Association Graduate Scholarship • 1024
NEHA/AAS/APU Scholarship Awards • 1040

NATIONAL EXCHANGE CLUB
Youth of the Year Award • 2077

NATIONAL FEDERATION OF MUSIC CLUBS (AR)
NFMC Wendell Irish Viola Award • 468

NATIONAL FEDERATION OF MUSIC CLUBS (CORAL GABLES, FL)
Thelma A. Robinson Award in Ballet • 494

NATIONAL FEDERATION OF MUSIC CLUBS (NC)
NFMC Hinda Honigman Award for the Blind • 2314

NATIONAL FEDERATION OF MUSIC CLUBS (FL)
NFMC Gretchen E. Van Roy Music Education Scholarship • 674

NATIONAL FEDERATION OF MUSIC CLUBS BULLOCK AND ROBERTSON AWARDS
NFMC Dorothy Dann Bullock Music Therapy Award and the NFMC Ruth B. Robertson Music Therapy Award • 1045

NATIONAL FEDERATION OF MUSIC CLUBS OLSON AWARDS
NFMC Lynn Freeman Olson Composition Awards • 467

NATIONAL FEDERATION OF MUSIC CLUBS STILLMAN-KELLEY AWARD
Stillman Kelley/Thelma Byrum Awards • 487

NATIONAL FEDERATION OF THE BLIND
National Federation of the Blind Scholarship • 2312

NATIONAL FFA ORGANIZATION
CNH Industrial Aftermarket Solutions Scholarship • 1956
Elmer J. and Hester Jane Johnson Memorial FFA Scholarship • 876
Farm Credit Services of America Collegiate Scholarship • 1969
FarmAid FFA Scholarship • 886
Ford Motor Company Fund and Ford Trucks Built Ford Tough - FFA Scholarship Program • 1973
Grow Ag Leaders Scholarship • 923
Hoard's Dairyman FFA Scholarship • 1987
National FFA Alumni and Supporters Agricultural Education Scholarship • 1025
National FFA Combined Scholarship • 2018
Tractor Supply Company Endowment • 2055

NATIONAL FIELD ARCHERY ASSOCIATION
NFAA Scholarship Program • 256

NATIONAL FOLIAGE FOUNDATION
James S. Davis Memorial Scholarship • 1490
National Horticulture Foundation General Scholarships • 1027

NATIONAL FOSTER PARENT ASSOCIATION (NFPA)
National Foster Parent Association (NFPA) Youth Scholarship • 2216

NATIONAL GALLERY OF ART
Predoctoral Fellowship Program • 1076
Senior Fellowship Program • 484
Visiting Senior Fellowship Program • 501

NATIONAL GARDEN CLUBS INC.
National Garden Clubs Scholarship • 1026

NATIONAL GEM CONSORTIUM
GEM MS Engineering Fellowship Program • 2147

NATIONAL GENEALOGICAL SOCIETY
Rubincam Youth Writing Competition • 286

NATIONAL GROCERS ASSOCIATION
Asparagus Club, Thomas K. Zaucha Scholarship • 535
Bob Richardson Legacy Scholarship • 544
Charlie and Becky Bray Legacy Scholarship • 557
FMS Solutions Holdings LLC Legacy Scholarship • 579

The Ultimate Scholarship Book 2026
Sponsor Index

Kimberly-Clark Corporation Legacy Scholarship • 629
Mondelez International Legacy Scholarship • 656
Peter and Jody Larkin Legacy Scholarship • 684
Roger Collins Leadership Scholarship • 700
Women Grocers of America (WGA) Mary Macey Scholarship • 738

NATIONAL HEMOPHILIA FOUNDATION
Kevin Child Scholarship • 2303

NATIONAL HISPANIC HEALTH FOUNDATION
National Hispanic Health Professional Student Scholarship • 2218

NATIONAL HISTORY DAY
National History Day Contest • 663

NATIONAL HONOR SOCIETY
National Honor Society Scholarship • 2019

NATIONAL HOUSING ENDOWMENT
Herman J. Smith Scholarship • 1435
Pulte Group Build Your Future Scholarship Program • 1080

NATIONAL INDEPENDENT AUTOMOBILE DEALERS ASSOCIATION
NIADA Scholarship • 2024

NATIONAL INSTITUTE FOR LABOR RELATIONS RESEARCH (NILRR)
William B. Ruggles Right to Work Scholarship • 737

NATIONAL INTERCOLLEGIATE RODEO ASSOCIATION
John J. Smith Graduate School Scholarship • 191
National Intercollegiate Rodeo Foundation Scholarship • 235
Rawhide Scholarship • 277

NATIONAL INVENTORS HALL OF FAME
Collegiate Inventors Competition • 842

NATIONAL ITALIAN AMERICAN FOUNDATION
National Italian American Foundation Scholarship • 2219

NATIONAL JUNIOR CLASSICAL LEAGUE
National Junior Classical League (NJCL) Scholarships • 463

NATIONAL LATIN EXAM
National Latin Exam Scholarship • 464

NATIONAL MARBLES TOURNAMENT
National Marbles Tournament Scholarship • 236

NATIONAL MEDICAL FELLOWSHIPS INC.
William and Charlotte Cadbury Award • 2275

NATIONAL MERIT SCHOLARSHIP CORPORATION
National Merit Scholarship Program and National Achievement Scholarship Program • 237

NATIONAL PARENT VOLUNTEER ASSOCIATION
A+A Altruism + All Good Deeds Scholarship • 14
Aaliyah Lee Scholarship • 15
Act of Kindness Scholarship • 20
Building Bridges Scholarship • 69

NATIONAL PKU NEWS
Guthrie-Koch PKU Scholarship • 2298

NATIONAL PORK PRODUCERS COUNCIL
Lois Britt Pork Industry Memorial Scholarship Program • 983

NATIONAL POTATO COUNCIL
National Potato Council Scholarship • 1028

NATIONAL POULTRY AND FOOD DISTRIBUTORS ASSOCIATION
NPFDA Scholarships • 1050

NATIONAL PRECAST CONCRETE ASSOCIATION (NPCA)
NPCA Educational Foundation Scholarships • 1049

NATIONAL PRESS CLUB
National Press Club Scholarship for Journalism Diversity • 664

NATIONAL PRESS PHOTOGRAPHERS ASSOCIATION
Kit C. King Graduate Scholarship Fund • 630

NATIONAL PRESS PHOTOGRAPHERS FOUNDATION
Bob East Scholarship • 543
College Photographer of the Year • 561
NPPF Still and Multimedia Scholarship • 676
NPPF Television News Scholarship • 677
Reid Blackburn Scholarship • 695

NATIONAL PROPANE GAS FOUNDATION
National Propane Gas Foundation • 2021

NATIONAL RADIO ASTRONOMY OBSERVATORY (NRAO)
GBT Student Observing Support (SOS) Program • 904
Graduate Summer Student Research Assistantship • 921
Undergraduate Summer Student Research Assistantship • 1161

NATIONAL RESTAURANT ASSOCIATION EDUCATIONAL FOUNDATION
A.J. Grisanti Memorial Scholarship • 509

NATIONAL RIFLE ASSOCIATION
George Montgomery/NRA Youth Wildlife Art Contest • 154
Women's Wildlife Management/Conservation Scholarship • 1174

NATIONAL ROOFING FOUNDATION (NRF)
Roofing Industry Scholarship - Melvin Kruger Endowed Scholarship • 1099

NATIONAL SCHOLASTIC SURFING ASSOCIATION
National Scholarship Program • 239

NATIONAL SCIENCE FOUNDATION
Graduate Research Fellowship Program • 917

NATIONAL SCULPTURE SOCIETY
Laura Ziegler Scholarship • 452

NATIONAL SECURITY AGENCY (NSA)
Stokes Educational Scholarship Program • 311

NATIONAL SECURITY EDUCATION PROGRAM INITIATIVE, ADMINISTERED BY INSTITUTE OF INTERNATIONAL EDUCATION
Boren Scholarships • 546

NATIONAL SOCIETY DAUGHTERS OF THE AMERICAN REVOLUTION
Alice W. Rooke Scholarship • 775
Irene and Daisy MacGregor Memorial Scholarship • 946
Lillian and Arthur Dunn Scholarship • 2005

NATIONAL SOCIETY OF COLLEGIATE SCHOLARS (NSCS)
Community College Transition Award • 1957
First in the Family Scholarship • 1971
Induction Recognition Award • 1991
NSCS Grad School Award • 2026

NATIONAL SOCIETY OF PROFESSIONAL ENGINEERS
Auxiliary Legacy Scholarship • 819
Maureen L. and Howard N. Blitman, P.E., Scholarship • 2201
Steinman Scholarship • 1126

NATIONAL SOCIETY OF PROFESSIONAL SURVEYORS (NSPS/AAGS)
AAGS - NSPS Scholarships • 744
AAGS Joseph F. Dracup Scholarship Award • 745
Lowell Loving Undergraduate Scholarship • 986
Nettie Dracup Memorial Scholarship • 671
Schonstedt Scholarship in Surveying • 1107

NATIONAL SOCIETY, SONS OF THE AMERICAN REVOLUTION
Arthur M. and Berdena King Eagle Scout Contest • 1943
George S. and Stella M. Knight Essay Contest • 155
Joseph S. Rumbaugh Historical Oration Contest • 626

NATIONAL SPACE CLUB
National Space Club Keynote Scholar • 1029

NATIONAL SPEAKERS ASSOCIATION
Bill Gove Scholarship • 399
Cavett Robert Scholarship • 405

NATIONAL SPORTING CLAYS ASSOCIATION
NSCA Scholarship • 261

NATIONAL STRENGTH AND CONDITIONING ASSOCIATION (NSCA) FOUNDATION
Challenge Scholarship • 79
GNC Nutritional Research Grant • 160
Graduate Research Grant - Master and Doctoral • 164
High School Scholarship • 173
Minority Scholarship • 2205
Women's Scholarship • 1173

NATIONAL STUDENT NURSES' ASSOCIATION
National Student Nurses' Association Scholarship • 1030

NATIONAL WILD TURKEY FEDERATION (NWTF)
Dr. James Earl Kennamer Scholarship • 128

NATIVEVISION
NativeVision Scholarships • 2223

NAVAL ENLISTED RESERVE ASSOCIATION
Naval Enlisted Reserve Association Scholarships • 242

NAVAL HELICOPTER ASSOCIATION
Naval Helicopter Association Scholarship • 243

NAVAL SERVICE TRAINING COMMAND OFFICER DEVELOPMENT
NROTC Scholarship Program • 260

NAVAL SPECIAL WARFARE FOUNDATION
UDT-SEAL Scholarship • 347

Sponsor Index

NAVY EXCHANGE
Next Gen Scholars Award • 255

NAVY LEAGUE FOUNDATION
Subic Bay-Cubi Point Scholarship • 329

NAVY MEDICINE PROFESSIONAL DEVELOPMENT CENTER
Nurse Candidate Program • 1051

NAVY SUPPLY CORPS FOUNDATION INC.
Navy Supply Corps Foundation Scholarship • 247

NAVY WIVES CLUBS OF AMERICA (NWCA)
Judith Haupt Member's Child Scholarship • 196
Mary Paolozzi Member's Scholarship • 216
Navy/Marine Corps/Coast Guard (NMCCG) Enlisted Dependent Spouse Scholarship • 251
Pauline Langkamp Memorial Scholarship • 266

NEA FOUNDATION
Learning and Leadership Grants • 635
Student Success Grants • 715

NEBRASKA ACADEMY OF SCIENCES INC.
C. Bertrand and Marian Othmer Schultz Collegiate Scholarship • 1255
Nebraska Academy of Sciences High School Scholarships • 1639

NEBRASKA ACTUARIES CLUB
Nebraska Actuaries Club Scholarship • 1640

NEBRASKA COORDINATING COMMISSION FOR POSTSECONDARY EDUCATION
Access College Early Scholarship • 1182

NEBRASKA DEPARTMENT OF VETERANS' AFFAIRS
NDVA Waiver of Tuition • 1638

NEBRASKA FUNERAL DIRECTORS ASSOCIATION
Wallace S. and Wilma K. Laughlin Foundation Trust Scholarships • 1889

NEBRASKA STATE ELKS ASSOCIATION
Nebraska Elks Association Vocational Scholarship • 1641

NEMETSCHEK VECTORWORKS
Vectorworks Design Scholarship • 499

NETWORK OF ENLIGHTENED WOMEN
Gentlemen Showcase • 2150

NETWORK OF THE HOSPITALITY INDUSTRY
Green Voice Design Competition • 922

NEVADA OFFICE OF THE STATE TREASURER
Governor Guinn Millennium Scholarship Program • 1406

NEVADA WOMEN'S FUND
Nevada Women's Fund Scholarships • 1644

NEW ENGLAND BOARD OF HIGHER EDUCATION
New England Regional Student Program • 1645

NEW ENGLAND WATER WORKS ASSOCIATION
Elson T. Killam Memorial Scholarship • 877
Francis X. Crowley Scholarship • 581

NEW HAMPSHIRE CHARITABLE FOUNDATION
Certificate, License or Other Industry-Recognized Credential • 1283
Four-year or Bachelor's Degree Program • 1384
Master's, Ph.D. or Other Advanced Degree Program • 1580
Medallion Fund • 1585
New Hampshire Charitable Foundation Statewide Student Aid Program • 1646
Two-year or Associate Degree Program • 1863

NEW JERSEY CHAPTER OF THE AMERICAN SOCIETY OF SAFETY ENGINEERS
Ted Brickley/Bernice Shickora Scholarship • 1831

NEW JERSEY CHEERLEADING AND DANCE COACHES ASSOCIATION
NJCDCA Scholarship • 1663

NEW JERSEY COMMISSION ON HIGHER EDUCATION
Educational Opportunity Fund (EOF) Grant • 1354

NEW JERSEY HIGHER EDUCATION STUDENT ASSISTANCE AUTHORITY
New Jersey World Trade Center Scholarship • 1649
NJ Student Tuition Assistance Reward Scholarship (STARS) • 1661
NJ Student Tuition Assistance Reward Scholarship II • 1662
Part-Time Tuition Aid Grant • 1717
Tuition Aid Grant • 1855
Urban Scholars Award • 1868

NEW JERSEY SCHOOL COUNSELOR ASSOCIATION INC.
NJSCA High School Scholarship • 1664

NEW JERSEY STATE ELKS
New Jersey State Elks Special Children's Committee Scholarship • 1648

NEW MEXICO ASSOCIATION OF SCHOOL BUSINESS OFFICIALS
NMASBO High School Scholarships • 1665

NEW MEXICO ENGINEERING FOUNDATION
Society of American Military Engineers, Albuquerque Post Scholarship • 1797

NEW MEXICO HIGHER EDUCATION DEPARTMENT
Competitive Scholarships • 1311
Legislative Lottery Scholarships • 1533
Medical Loan-For-Service Program • 1586
New Mexico Scholars • 1650
Nursing Loan-For-Service Program • 1684
Student Incentive Grants • 1817
Teacher Loan-For-Service Program • 1825
Vietnam Veterans' Scholarship • 1879

NEW YORK CITY DEPARTMENT OF PERSONNEL
Urban Fellows Program • 352

NEW YORK INTELLECTUAL PROPERTY ASSOCIATION (NYIPLA)
Honorable William Conner Writing Competition • 603

NEW YORK RAMBLERS SOCCER CLUB
New York Ramblers Scholarship • 2226

NEW YORK STATE ASSOCIATION OF AGRICULTURAL FAIRS
New York State Association of Agricultural Fairs/New York State Showpeople's Association Scholarships • 1654

NEW YORK STATE HIGHER EDUCATION SERVICES CORPORATION (HESC)
Aid for Part-Time Study • 1192
Math and Science Teaching Incentive Scholarships • 1581
Part-Time TAP Program • 1716
Scholarships for Academic Excellence • 1781
Senator Patricia K. McGee Nursing Faculty Scholarship • 1783
Tuition Assistance Program (TAP) • 1856
Veterans Tuition Awards • 1876
World Trade Center Memorial Scholarship • 1924

NEW YORK STATE SOCIETY OF PHYSICIAN ASSISTANTS
New York State Society of Physician Assistants Scholarship • 1655

NEW YORK STATE USBC
New York State USBC Scholarships • 1656
New York State USBC Spirit Awards • 1657

NEW YORK STATE WOMEN'S 600 CLUB
Educational Award/Graduating High School Female • 1352

NEW YORK WATER ENVIRONMENT ASSOCIATION INC.
N.G. Kaul Memorial Scholarship • 1018
NYWEA Major Environmental Career Scholarship • 1686

NEW YORK WOMEN IN COMMUNICATIONS FOUNDATION
New York Women in Communications Foundation Scholarships • 1658

NEXT SWELL
Next Swell Scholarship • 1044

NICODEMUS WILDERNESS PROJECT
Apprentice Ecologist Initiative Youth Scholarship Program • 798

NIGHTINGALE AWARDS OF PENNSYLVANIA
Nightingale Awards of Pennsylvania Scholarship • 1659

NISSAN NORTH AMERICA
Nissan Scholarship • 1660

NOAA EDUCATIONAL PARTNERSHIP PROGRAM – OFFICE OF EDUCATION
NOAA Educational Partnership Program Undergraduate Scholarships • 2227

NON COMMISSIONED OFFICERS ASSOCIATION
Non Commissioned Officers Association Scholarships • 258

NORTH AMERICAN VAN LINES
North American Van Lines Logistics Scholarship • 675

NORTH CAROLINA 4-H YOUTH DEVELOPMENT
North Carolina 4-H Development Fund Scholarships • 1669

NORTH CAROLINA ACADEMY OF PHYSICIAN ASSISTANTS
NCAPA Endowment Annual Student Grants • 1035

NORTH CAROLINA FARM BUREAU
R. Flake Shaw Scholarship • 1739

The Ultimate Scholarship Book 2026
Sponsor Index

North Carolina Racquetball Association (NCRA)
NCRA Scholarship • 1637

North Dakota Department of Public Instruction
North Dakota Scholarship • 1677

North Dakota Dollars for Scholars
North Dakota Dollars for Scholars • 1674

North Dakota Jaycee JCI Senate
North Dakota Jaycee JCI Senate Scholarship • 1675

North Dakota School Counselor Association
North Dakota School Counseling Association • 1678

North Dakota University System
North Dakota Scholars Program • 1676
North Dakota State Student Incentive Grant • 1679

North Dakota University System Career Builders Scholarship
North Dakota Career Builders Scholarship • 1673

North Texas Fair and Rodeo
Bob C. Powers Scholarship • 1243
North Texas State Fair Association Scholarship • 1680

Northwestern Mutual Foundation Childhood Cancer Sibling Scholarship
Northwestern Mutual Foundation Childhood Cancer Sibling Scholarship • 2315

Novus Biologicals LLC
Novus Biologicals Scholarship Program • 1048

NuFACTOR
Eric Dostie Memorial College Scholarship • 2294

Nursing Foundation of Pennsylvania
Jack E. Barger, Sr. Memorial Nursing Scholarship • 1483

OCA (formerly Organization of Chinese Americans)
OCA/UPS Gold Mountain Scholarship • 2228

Odenza Vacations
Odenza Marketing Group Scholarship • 262

Office and Professional Employees International Union
Howard Coughlin Memorial Scholarship Fund • 1988
John Kelly Labor Studies Scholarship Fund • 1997

Office of Intramural Training and Education
NIH Undergraduate Scholarship Program • 1047

Office of Navajo Nation Scholarship and Financial Assistance
Chief Manuelito Scholarship Program • 2122

Ohio Classical Conference
Ohio Classical Conference Scholarship for Prospective Latin Teachers • 1687

Ohio Department of Higher Education
Choose Ohio First Scholarship • 1293

Ohio News Media Foundation
Minority Scholarship • 1611
University Journalism Scholarships • 1866

Ohio Turfgrass Foundation
Ohio Turfgrass Foundation Scholarships • 1690

Oklahoma Association of Broadcasters
Oklahoma Association of Broadcasters Scholarship • 1691

Oklahoma City Community Foundation
H. W. Almen/West OKC Rotary Scholarship • 1418
James Anderson Logan Jr. and Betty Ann McFarland Logan Scholarship Fund • 1486
Laurene Ann Opdyke Nursing Scholarship • 1527
Oklahoma Youth with Promise Scholarship Fund • 1700

Oklahoma Foundation for Excellence
Oklahoma Foundation for Excellence Academic All-State Scholarships • 1692

Oklahoma Hall of Fame
Oklahoma Hall of Fame Scholarship • 1693

Oklahoma Rural Rehabilitation Corporation
Oklahoma Rural Rehabilitation Corporation Scholarships • 1694

Oklahoma Schools Insurance Group (OSIG)
Oklahoma Schools Insurance Group (OSIG) Scholarship • 1695

Oklahoma Society of Land Surveyors
Oklahoma Society of Land Surveyors Scholarships • 1696

Oklahoma State Fair
Oklahoma State Fair Inc. Scholarship Program • 1697

Oklahoma State Regents for Higher Education
Academic Scholars Program • 1181
Chiropractic Education Assistance Scholarship • 1292
Frances Koop Parsons/AT&T Pioneers Memorial Scholarship • 1386
George and Donna Nigh Public Service Scholarship • 1393
Inspired to Teach • 1468
Oklahoma's Promise • 1701
Oklahoma Tuition Aid Grant Program (OTAG) • 1698
Oklahoma Tuition Equalization Grant Program (OTEG) • 1699
Reach Higher Finish Line Scholarship • 1749
Regional University Baccalaureate Scholarship • 1752
Scholars for Excellence in Child Care • 1780
Teacher Shortage Employment Incentive Program • 1827

Olay Face the Stem
Olay Face the Stem Gap Scholarship • 2229

One Earth Film Festival
Young Filmmakers Contest • 507

One Family Inc.
One Family Scholars Program • 1703

Optimist International
Optimist International Communications Contest • 2316
Optimist International Essay Contest • 471
Optimist International Oratorical Contest • 678

Orange County Community Foundation
Michael A. Hunter Memorial Scholarship Fund • 2309

Orange Ribbons for Jaime
Jaime Guttenberg All Abilities Scholarship • 2302
Jaime Guttenberg Dance Scholarship • 445

Order of United Commercial Travelers of America
United Commercial Travelers of America (UCT) Scholarship Program • 726

Order Sons of Italy in America (OSIA)
Henry Salvatori Scholarship • 2157

Order Sons of Italy in America, Grand Lodge of California
Sons of Italy Grand Lodge of California Italian Language Study Grant • 1798
Sons of Italy Grand Lodge of College Scholarship • 1799

Oregon Army National Guard
Oregon Army National Guard • 1707

Oregon Association of Nurseries
Nurseries Foundation Award • 1053
Retail Chapter Award II and III • 1753

Oregon Farm Bureau
Oregon Farm Bureau Memorial Scholarships • 1708

Organization for Associate Degree Nursing National Office
Naomi Brack Student Scholarship • 1019

Organization of Rural Oklahoma Schools
OROS Scholarship • 1709

Orgone Biophysical Research Laboratory
Lou Hochberg Awards • 643

Outdoor Writers Association of America
Bodie McDowell Scholarship • 545

Outrigger Duke Kahanamoku Foundation
Duke Award Scholarship • 1345

Overseas Press Club Foundation
Overseas Press Club Foundation Scholarships/Fellowships • 680

P. Buckley Moss Foundation for Children's Education
P. Buckley Moss Endowed Scholarship • 2317

P.E.O. International
P.E.O. International Peace Scholarship • 2231
P.E.O. Program for Continuing Education • 2232

Pacers Foundation
Linda Craig Memorial Scholarship Presented by St. Vincent Sports Performance • 1542

Pacific Academy Foundation
Pacific Academy Foundation Scholarship • 264

Page Education Foundation
Page Education Foundation Grants • 1711

Patient Advocate Foundation
Scholarships for Survivors • 2322

Patsy Takemoto Mink Education Foundation
Education Support Award • 2139

Paul and Daisy Soros
Paul and Daisy Soros Fellowships for New Americans • 265

Paumanauke Native American Festival Inc.
Paumanauke Native American Indian Scholarship • 2234

Pega Scholars Program
Pega Scholars Program • 2235

Pennsylvania Association of Educational Office Professionals (PAEOP)
Hermine Solt Student Scholarship • 1437

Pennsylvania Business Education Association
Pennsylvania Business Education Association Scholarship • 1724

Pennsylvania Department of Military and Veterans Affairs
Pennsylvania Educational Gratuity Program • 1725

Pennsylvania Higher Education Assistance Agency (PHEAA)
Pennsylvania State Grant Program • 1731
Pennsylvania Targeted Industry Program • 1732

Pennsylvania Masonic Youth Foundation
Pennsylvania Masonic Youth Foundation Scholarships • 1727

Pennsylvania School Public Relations Association
PenSPRA Scholarship • 1733

Pennsylvania Society of Land Surveyors
Pennsylvania Land Surveyors' Foundation Scholarship • 1726

Pennsylvania Society of Physician Assistants
Nathaniel Alston Student Achievement Award • 1636

Pennsylvania Society of Tax and Accounting Professionals
Pennsylvania Society of Tax and Accounting Professionals Scholarships • 1729

Pennsylvania State Bowling Association
Pennsylvania State Bowling Association Scholarship Program • 1730

People for the Ethical Treatment of Animals (PETA)
Future Without Speciesism Cash Award • 150

Perennial Plant Association
Perennial Plant Association Scholarship • 1065

Perfect Plants
Perfect Plants Nursery Scholarship • 1066

Pet Lifestyle and You (P.L.A.Y.)
Scholars Helping Collars Scholarship • 293

Pettable
Mental Health Importance Scholarship • 1000

Pfizer
Soozie Courter Hemophilia Scholarship Program • 2324

PG&E Better Together STEM Scholarship Program, Scholarship America
PG&E Better Together STEM Scholarship Program • 1734

PGA Works Golf Management University Scholarship Program
PGA WORKS John and Tamara Lundgren Scholars Program • 268

PHCC Educational Foundation
Delta Faucet Company Scholarships • 857
PHCC Educational Foundation Scholarship • 1068

Phi Delta Kappa International
Phi Delta Kappa (PDK) Educational Foundation Scholarship Program • 2029

Phi Sigma Kappa International Headquarters
Terrill Graduate Fellowship • 2054
Wenderoth Undergraduate Scholarship • 2072

Phi Theta Kappa Honor Society
Guistwhite Scholarships • 1984
Hites Transfer Scholarship • 1986

Phi Upsilon Omicron Inc.
Margaret Jerome Sampson Scholarship • 2009
Nell Bryant Robinson Scholarship • 670

Physician Assistant Foundation
Physician Assistant Foundation Scholarship • 1070

Pi Lambda Theta Scholarships
Pi Lambda Theta Student Support Scholarships • 686

Pi Sigma Alpha
Nancy McManus Washington Internship Scholarships • 660

Pilot International Foundation
Pilot International Scholarship • 269

Pilot Pen
Pilot Pen G2 Overachievers Student Grant • 270

Pinnacol Foundation
Pinnacol Foundation Scholarship Program • 1736

PixelPlex
PixelPlex Bi-Annual STEM Scholarship • 1072

Plan New Hampshire
Plan NH Scholarship and Fellowship Program • 1737

Planning and Visual Education Partnership (PAVE)
PAVE Student Design Competition • 683
VMSD Scholarship • 502

Poetry Magazine
Ruth Lilly and Dorothy Sargent Rosenberg Poetry Fellowship Program • 481

Point Foundation
BIPOC Scholarship • 2109
Point Community College Scholarship • 2238
Point Flagship Scholarship • 2239

Pokemon Company International
Play! Pokemon Scholarship • 271

Polish National Alliance
Polish National Alliance Scholarship • 2240

Polish Roman Catholic Union of America
Education Scholarship • 2138

Pony Baseball/Softball
Pony Alumni Scholarship • 272

Pop Warner Little Scholars Inc.
All-American Scholars (Cheerleading) • 36
All-American Scholars (Football) • 37

Portland Stage Company
Clauder Competition Prize • 408

Presbyterian Church (USA)
National Presbyterian College Scholarship • 2020
Native American Education Grant • 2221
Presbyterian Church USA Student Opportunity Scholarships • 2031

Pretty Photoshop Actions
Pretty Photoshop Actions Bi-annual Scholarship • 1079

Princess Grace Awards
Princess Grace Awards • 477

Print and Graphics Scholarship Foundation
Print and Graphics Scholarship • 478

Project Paradigm
Paradigm Challenge • 1058

Project Vote Smart
Project Vote Smart National Internship Program • 689

Project Yellow Light
Project Yellow Light/Hunter Garner Scholarship • 273

Prospanica
Prospanica Foundation Scholarships • 690

Prudential Financial and Ashoka
Prudential Emerging Visionaries • 274

Public Relations Student Society of America
Betsy Plank/PRSSA Scholarship • 540
Chester Burger Scholarship for Excellence in Public Relations • 558
Gary Yoshimura Scholarship • 590
John D. Graham Scholarship • 624
Lawrence G. Foster Award for Excellence in Public Relations • 634
PRSA Diversity Multicultural Scholarship • 2241
Ron Culp Scholarship for Mentorship • 702
Stephen D. Pisinski Memorial Scholarship • 712

Pulse of Perseverance
Pulse of Perseverance Scholarship • 275

QuestBridge
College Prep Scholarship for High School Juniors • 92
National College Match Program • 234

The Ultimate Scholarship Book 2026
Sponsor Index

QUILL AND SCROLL SOCIETY
Quill and Scroll Student Scholarships • 691

R&D SYSTEMS INC.
R&D Systems Scholarship Program • 1081

R2C SCHOLARSHIP PROGRAM
Return 2 College Scholarship • 280

RACE ENTRY LLC
Race Entry Student Scholarship • 276

RADIO TELEVISION DIGITAL NEWS ASSOCIATION
Carole Simpson Scholarship • 554
Ed Bradley Scholarship • 574
Lee Thornton Scholarship • 636
Lou and Carole Prato Sports Reporting Scholarship • 642
RTNDA President's Scholarship • 703

RAFTELIS
Raftelis Leadership Scholarships • 692

RAILWAY TIE ASSOCIATION
John Mabry Forestry Scholarship and Paul Webster Forestry Scholarship • 958

RAREIS SCHOLARSHIP FUND
RAREis Scholarship • 2319

RAY A. PEACOCK FOUNDATION
Ray Anthony Peacock Scholarship • 1744

REACH HIGHER MONTANA
Reach Higher Montana Scholarships • 1750

REALTYHOP
RealtyHop Scholarship • 278

REGENERON SCIENCE TALENT SEARCH
Regeneron Science Talent Search • 1086

REIFF LAW FIRM
Reiff Law Firm Legal Scholarship • 696

RENTHOP
RentHop's College and University Scholarship • 279

REVPART
RevPart STEM Scholarship • 1089

RHODE ISLAND FOUNDATION
Albert E. and Florence W. Newton Nursing Scholarship • 1196
Antonio Cirino Memorial Scholarship • 1220
Frances L. Macartney Porter Fund • 1387
James J. Burns and C.A. Haynes Textile Scholarship • 1489
Lily and Catello Sorrentino Memorial Scholarship • 1541
Patty and Melvin Alperin First Generation Scholarship • 1719
Rhode Island Foundation Association of Former Legislators Scholarship • 1754

RHODE ISLAND OFFICE OF THE POSTSECONDARY COMMISSIONER
Rhode Island Promise Scholarship • 1755

RHODES SCHOLARSHIP TRUST
Rhodes Scholar • 281

RICHARD TUCKER MUSIC FOUNDATION
Sara Tucker Study Grant • 482

RIDGELINE INTERNATIONAL
Ridgeline International Community Scholarship • 1094

RISK MANAGEMENT ASSOCIATION FOUNDATION SCHOLARSHIP PROGRAM
Risk Management Association Foundation Scholarship • 698

ROBERT D. BLUE SCHOLARSHIP
Robert D. Blue Scholarship • 1763

ROCKY MOUNTAIN ELECTRICAL LEAGUE
RMEL Foundation Scholarships • 1095

ROLLER SKATING FOUNDATION
Roller Skating Foundation Scholarship, Current College Student Category • 701
Roller Skating Foundation Scholarship, High School Student Category • 283

RONALD REAGAN PRESIDENTIAL FOUNDATION
GE-Reagan Foundation Scholarship Program • 151

ROSA L. PARKS SCHOLARSHIP FOUNDATION
Rosa L. Parks Scholarships • 1768

SALIX PHARMACEUTICALS
Salix Gastrointestinal Health Scholars Award • 2321

SALLIE MAE
Completing the Dream Scholarship • 94
Sallie Mae Bridging the Dream Scholarship • 288

SAMUEL HUNTINGTON FUND
Samuel Huntington Public Service Award • 289

SANKOFATECH
Achievers in Technology Program • 2082

SCHOLARSHIP AMERICA DREAM AWARD
Scholarship America Dream Award • 294

SCHOLARSHIP DETECTIVE
$1,000 Scholarship Detective Launch Scholarship • 8

SCHOLASTIC ART AND WRITING AWARDS
Herblock Award for Editorial Cartoon • 435
New York Life Award • 466
Scholastic Art and Writing Portfolio Award • 483

SCHOOL NUTRITION ASSOCIATION
Nancy Curry Scholarship • 659
Schwan's Food Service Scholarship • 705

SCIENCESAVES
ScienceSaves Video Scholarship Contest • 1109

SCREEN ACTORS GUILD – AMERICAN FEDERATION OF TELEVISION AND RADIO ARTISTS
George Heller Memorial Scholarship Fund of the SAG-AFTRA Foundation • 1978
John L. Dales Scholarship Fund • 1998

SEABEE MEMORIAL SCHOLARSHIP ASSOCIATION
Seabee Memorial Scholarship • 299

SEAFARERS INTERNATIONAL UNION OF NORTH AMERICA
Charlie Logan Scholarship Program for Dependents • 1955

SEANC SCHOLARSHIP FOUNDATION
State Employees Association of North Carolina (SEANC) Scholarships • 1809

SEATTLE FOUNDATION
Atsuhiko Tateuchi Memorial Scholarship • 1232
Lambeth Family Scholarship • 1525

SERTOMA INC.
Sertoma Communicative Disorders Scholarship • 1111
Sertoma Scholarship for Students Who Are Hard of Hearing or Deaf • 2323

SERVICE EMPLOYEES INTERNATIONAL UNION
Service Employees International Union Scholarships • 2041

SHAPE AMERICA
Bill Kane Scholarship, Undergraduate • 827
Ruth Abernathy Presidential Scholarship • 1103

SHASTA HEAD START CHILD DEVELOPMENT INC.
Shasta Head Start Alumni Scholarship • 2042

SHAWN CARTER FOUNDATION
Shawn Carter Foundation Scholarship • 707

SHEET METAL WORKERS' INTERNATIONAL ASSOCIATION
Sheet Metal Workers' International Scholarship Fund • 2044

SHELL
Shell Associate Scholarship Program • 708

SIGMA ALPHA EPSILON (SAE)
Jones-Laurence Award for Scholastic Achievement • 2000
Warren Poslusny Award for Outstanding Achievement • 2071

SIGMA ALPHA IOTA PHILANTHROPIES
Undergraduate Scholarships • 498

SIGMA PHI EPSILON FRATERNITY (NATIONAL)
Sigma Phi Epsilon Balanced Man Scholarship • 2046

SILICON VALLEY COMMUNITY FOUNDATION
Roshan Rahbari Scholarship Fund • 1772
Samsung@First Scholars • 1777

SIMON YOUTH FOUNDATION
Shari Simon Greenberg Community Scholarship • 300

SINGLE ACTION SHOOTING SOCIETY (SASS)
SASS Scholarship Foundation Scholarships • 292

SIOUX FALLS AREA COMMUNITY FOUNDATION
Joe Foss, An American Hero Scholarship • 1496
Sioux Falls Area Retired Teachers Scholarship • 1790

SIR JOHN SOANE'S MUSEUM FOUNDATION
AIA/Architects Foundation Diversity Advancement Scholarship • 766
Sir John Soane's Museum Foundation Traveling Grant • 1113

SMITH SCHOLARSHIP FOUNDATION
Smith Scholarship Program • 1796

SMITHGROUP
SmithGroup J.E.D.I. Scholarship • 1116

Society for Chartered Property and Casualty Underwriters (CPCU)
NextGen Scholarship • 673

Society for Imaging Science and Technology
Raymond Davis Scholarship • 1085

Society for Industrial and Applied Mathematics/SIAM
Moody's Mega Math Challenge • 1013

Society for Integrative and Comparative Biology
Libbie H. Hyman Memorial Scholarship • 979

Society for Technical Communication
Distinguished Service Award for Students • 567

Society of Automotive Engineers International
BMW/SAE Engineering Scholarship • 829
Edward D. Hendrickson/SAE Engineering Scholarship • 872
Fred M. Young, Sr./SAE Engineering Scholarship • 895
Long-Term Member Sponsored Scholarship • 984
Ralph K. Hillquist Honorary SAE Scholarship • 1083
Tau Beta Pi/Society of Automotive Engineers Engineering Scholarship • 1137
TMC/SAE Donald D. Dawson Technical Scholarship • 1148
Yanmar/SAE Scholarship • 1175

Society of Broadcast Engineers
Youth Scholarship • 740

Society of Exploration Geophysicists
Society of Exploration Geophysicists (SEG) Scholarship • 1118

Society of Hispanic Professional Engineers
SHPE Scholarship Program • 2248

Society of Industrial and Office REALTORS (SIOR) Foundation
Mildred C. Hanson SIOR Memorial Scholarship • 653

Society of Manufacturing Engineers Education Foundation
Giuliano Mazzetti Scholarship • 912
Myrtle and Earl Walker Scholarship • 1017
Society of Manufacturing Engineers Directors Scholarship • 1119

Society of Mexican American Engineers and Scientists Inc. (MAES)
MAES Scholarship Program • 2192

Society of Naval Architects and Marine Engineers (SNAME)
David A. O Neil Scholarship • 852
John V. Wehausen Graduate Scholarship • 961
Mandell and Lester Rosenblatt Undergraduate Scholarship • 989
Robert N. and Helen H. Herbert Undergraduate Scholarship • 1098

Society of Nuclear Medicine and Molecular Imaging
SNMTS Paul Cole Scholarship • 1117

Society of Physics Students
Herbert Levy Memorial Scholarship • 931
Peggy Dixon Two-Year Scholarship • 1064
SPS Future Teacher Scholarship • 711
SPS Leadership Scholarships • 1124

Society of Plastics Engineers
Composites Division/Harold Giles Scholarship • 844
Injection Molding Division Scholarship • 940
Plastics Pioneers Association Scholarships • 1073
Polymer Modifiers and Additives Division Scholarships • 1074
Salvatore J. Monte Thermoplastic Materials and Foams Division Scholarship • 1105
Society of Plastics Engineers (SPE) Foundation Scholarships • 1120
Ted and Ruth Neward Scholarship • 1139
Thermoplastic Elastomers Special Interest Group Scholarship • 1142
Thomas E. Powers/Detroit Section Scholarship • 1143

Society of Vacuum Coaters Foundation
Society of Vacuum Coaters Foundation Scholarship • 1121

Society of Women Engineers
Ada I. Pressman Memorial Scholarship • 2084
Admiral Grace Murray Hopper Memorial Scholarships • 2085
Anne Maureen Whitney Barrow Memorial Scholarship • 2100
B.J. Harrod Scholarships • 2107
B.K. Krenzer Reentry Scholarship • 2108
Brill Family Scholarship • 830
Cummins Scholarship • 849
Dr. Ivy M. Parker Memorial Scholarship • 2133
Elizabeth McLean Memorial Scholarship • 875
Honeywell International Inc. Scholarships • 2163
Jill S. Tietjen P.E. Scholarship • 951
Judith Resnik Memorial Scholarship • 2177
Lillian Moller Gilbreth Memorial Scholarship • 2187
Mary Gunther Memorial Scholarship • 2198
Mary V. Munger Scholarship • 994
Meredith Thoms Memorial Scholarship • 1001
Meritage Homes Scholarship • 2204
Northrop Grumman Scholarship • 1681
Olive Lynn Salembier Memorial Reentry Scholarship • 2230
Susan Miszkowicz Memorial Scholarship • 1136
SWE Past Presidents Scholarship • 2259

Sodexo Foundation
Sodexo Stephen J. Brady STOP Hunger Scholarship • 304

Soliant Consulting
Soliant's Sunrise Scholarship • 305

Sons of the Republic of Texas
Texas History Essay Scholarship • 1843

Sons of Union Veterans of the Civil War
Sons of Union Veterans of the Civil War Scholarships • 306

Soroptimist International of the Americas
Live Your Dream Awards Program • 2188

South Carolina Commission on Higher Education
Legislative for Future Excellence (LIFE) Scholarship Program • 1532
Lottery Tuition Assistance Program • 1549
Palmetto Fellows Scholarship Program • 1712
South Carolina Hope Scholarship • 1801
State Need-based Grants • 1810

South Carolina Farm Bureau Foundation
South Carolina Farm Bureau Foundation Scholarships • 1800

South Carolina Nurses Foundation Inc.
South Carolina Nurses Foundation Nurses Care Scholarship • 1802

South Carolina Space Grant Consortium
Kathryn D. Sullivan Earth and Marine Science Fellowship • 1518

South Carolina State Department of Education
Archibald Rutledge Scholarship Program • 1222

South Carolina Tuition Grants Commission
South Carolina Tuition Grants Program • 1803

South Dakota Board of Regents
Marlin R. Scarborough Memorial Scholarship • 1567
South Dakota Free Tuition for Veterans and Others Who Performed War Service • 1804

Southeastern Theatre Conference Inc.
Marian A. Smith Costume Award • 458

Southern Bowling Congress
Curwen-Guidry-Blackburn Scholarship Fund • 107

Southern Scholarship Foundation
Southern Scholarship Foundation Scholarship • 1805

SpeakOUT
SpeakOUT's LGBTQ+ Scholarship • 2249

Specialty Equipment Market Association
Specialty Equipment Market Association (SEMA) Memorial Scholarship • 710

SPIE, The International Society for Optical Engineering
SPIE Optics and Photonics Education Scholarship • 1122

Sports in Action
H-E-B Scholarships for UIL Participants • 1417

St. Andrew's Society of Washington, DC
St. Andrew's Society of Washington, DC Scholarship • 2250

Stamps Family Charitable Foundation Inc.
Stamps Scholars • 309

Stanley Black and Decker
DEWALT Trades Scholarship • 566

Stantec
Stantec Equity and Diversity Scholarship • 2251

STARFLEET Scholarship Program
Starfleet Scholarships • 2050

The Ultimate Scholarship Book 2026
Sponsor Index

STATE COUNCIL OF HIGHER EDUCATION FOR VIRGINIA
Virginia Commonwealth Award • 1880
Virginia Guaranteed Assistance Program • 1882
Virginia Part-Time Assistance Program • 1884
Virginia Tuition Assistance Grant Program • 1886

STATE OF ALABAMA COMMISSION ON HIGHER EDUCATION
Alabama Student Assistance Program • 1193

STATE OF WISCONSIN HIGHER EDUCATIONAL AIDS BOARD
Academic Excellence Scholarship • 1180
Minority Undergraduate Retention Grant • 1613
Nursing Student Loan • 1685
Talent Incentive Program Grant • 1823
Teacher Loan Program • 1824
Wisconsin Higher Education Grant • 1917

STDCHECK.COM
HIV-Positive Scholarship • 2300

STEPHEN PHILLIPS MEMORIAL SCHOLARSHIP FUND
Stephen Phillips Memorial Scholarship Fund • 1814

STONEWALL COMMUNITY FOUNDATION
Aritzia Scholarship • 2102
Traub-Dicker Rainbow Scholarship • 2267

STOSSEL IN THE CLASSROOM
Stossel in the Classroom Essay Contest • 312
Stossel in the Classroom Video Contest • 313

STRIDE BANK
May T. Henry Scholarship Fund • 1582

STTARK
Unboxing Your Life Video Scholarship • 348
You Can t Label People, but You Can Label Products Essay and Label Design Scholarship • 505

STUDENT INSIGHTS
Student View Scholarship • 318

STUDENT MOVER AGAINST CANCER (SMAC)
Cancer Fighter Scholarship • 2288

STUDENT VETERANS OF AMERICA
Google SVA Scholarship • 163

STUDY ABOARD EUROPE
Study Abroad Europe Scholarship • 491

STUDY.COM
Adult Learner Scholarship from Study.com • 21
LGBTQ+ Student Scholarship from Study.com • 2186
Study.com College Scholarship for Homeschool Students • 320
Study.com Community College Student Scholarship • 321
Study.com Online Graduate Degree Scholarship • 322
Study.com Online Undergraduate Degree Scholarship • 323
Study.com Scholarship for Black Students • 2254
Study.com Scholarship for Business Students • 717
Study.com Scholarship for Children of First Responders • 324
Study.com Scholarship for Military Members and Veterans • 325
Study.com Scholarship for Military Spouses and Children • 326
Study.com Scholarship for Moms • 2255
Study.com Scholarship for Nontraditional Students • 327
Study.com Scholarship for Transfer Students • 328
Study.com Scholarship for Women in STEM • 2256
Study.com Single Parent Scholarship • 2257

STUTTGART ARKANSAS CHAMBER OF COMMERCE
Chick and Sophie Major Memorial Duck Calling Contest • 1290

SUNFLOWER INITIATIVE
Sunflower Initiative Scholarship • 2258

SUPERCOLLEGE.COM
SuperCollege Scholarship • 330

SURVEYING AND MAPPING SOCIETY OF GEORGIA
Ben W. Fortson, Jr., Scholarship • 1237

SUSAN THOMPSON BUFFETT FOUNDATION
Susan Thompson Buffett Foundation Scholarship Program • 1820

SUSANNA DELAURENTIS CHARITABLE FOUNDATION
Susanna and Lucy DeLaurentis Charitable Foundation Memorial Scholarships • 2326

SUTLIFF & STOUT LAW SCHOOL SCHOLARSHIP
Sutliff and Stout Law School Scholarship • 718

SWISS BENEVOLENT SOCIETY OF NEW YORK
Medicus Student Exchange • 2203

TACO BELL FOUNDATION
Live Mas Scholarship • 205

TAG AND LABEL MANUFACTURERS INSTITUTE INC.
TLMI Two/Four Year College and Vocational Degree Program Scholarship • 723

TAILHOOK ASSOCIATION
Tailhook Educational Foundation Scholarship • 333

TAIWANESE AMERICAN SCHOLARSHIP FUND
Taiwanese American Scholarship Fund • 2260

TALL CLUBS INTERNATIONAL FOUNDATION INC.
Tall Club International Scholarship • 2052

TAMPA BAY BUCCANEERS FOUNDATION
Tampa Bay Buccaneers Foundation Girls in Football Scholarship • 334

TATTOO-JOURNAL.COM
Tattoo Journal Ink Scholarship • 335

TAU BETA PI ASSOCIATION
Tau Beta Pi Scholarships • 2053

TAU KAPPA EPSILON EDUCATIONAL FOUNDATION
Carroll C. Hall Memorial Scholarship • 1950
Charles R. Walgreen Jr. Leadership Award • 1954
Donald A. and John R. Fisher Memorial Scholarship • 1964
Eugene C. Beach Memorial Scholarship • 1967

TE CONNECTIVITY AFRICAN HERITAGE SCHOLARSHIP
TE Connectivity African Heritage Scholarship • 2262

TEACHERS OF ACCOUNTING AT TWO-YEAR COLLEGES
TACTYC Accounting Scholarship • 719

TED ROLLINS
Ted and Holly Rollins Scholarship • 1138

TELLURIDE ASSOCIATION
Telluride Association Summer Seminars (TASS) • 337

TENNESSEE FUNERAL DIRECTORS ASSOCIATION
Tennessee Funeral Directors Association Memorial Scholarship • 1832

TENNESSEE STUDENT ASSISTANCE CORPORATION
Aspire Award • 1227
General Assembly Merit Scholarship • 1392
Helping Heroes Grant • 1430
Minority Teaching Fellows Program • 1612
Ned McWherter Scholars Program • 1642
Tennessee HOPE Lottery Scholarship • 1833
Tennessee Student Assistance Awards • 1834

TEWAARATON FOUNDATION
U.S. Lacrosse Native American Scholarships • 2270

TEXAS 4-H YOUTH DEVELOPMENT FOUNDATION
Collegiate Scholarship • 1302
Courageous Heart Scholarship • 1316
Technical Certification Scholarship • 1829
Texas 4-H Opportunity Scholarship Program - Baccalaureate Scholarships • 1836

TEXAS ASSOCIATION OF BROADCASTERS
Texas Broadcast Education Foundation Scholarships • 1838

TEXAS CATTLEWOMEN
Ivomec Generations of Excellence Internship and Scholarship Program • 1481

TEXAS ELKS STATE ASSOCIATION (TESA)
Texas Elks State Association Four-Year Scholarship Program • 1839
Texas Elks State Association Teenager of the Year Scholarship • 1840
Texas Elks State Association Vocational Grant Program • 1841

TEXAS HIGHER EDUCATION COORDINATING BOARD
Exemption for Highest Ranking High School Graduate • 1368
Exemption for Texas Veterans (Hazelwood Exemption) • 1369
Texas Fifth-Year Accounting Student Scholarship Program • 1842
Texas Public Educational Grant • 1847
Towards EXcellence, Access and Success (TEXAS) Grant Program • 1852
Tuition Equalization Grant Program • 1857

TEXAS INTERNATIONAL FISHING TOURNAMENT
Texas International Fishing Tournament Inc. Scholarship • 1844

TEXAS RETIRED TEACHERS FOUNDATION
First-Year Teacher Scholarships • 1376

THEDREAM.US
TheDream.US Scholarship • 2263

THERMO FISHER SCIENTIFIC
Thermo Fisher Scientific Antibody Scholarship • 1141

THIEL FELLOWSHIP
Thiel Fellowship Grant • 338

THIRD MARINE DIVISION ASSOCIATION
Memorial Scholarship Fund • 220

THOMAS J. WATSON FELLOWSHIP
Watson Travel Fellowship • 370

THUNEN SCHOLARSHIP COMMITTEE
Robert E. Thunen Memorial Scholarships • 1097

THURGOOD MARSHALL SCHOLARSHIP FUND
Thurgood Marshall College Scholarship Fund • 2264

TIMOTHY S.Y. LAM FOUNDATION
Timothy S.Y. Lam Foundation Education Scholarships • 722

TOCRIS BIOSCIENCE
Tocris Scholarship • 1152

TOOL, DIE AND MACHINING ASSOCIATION OF WISCONSIN
Edward L. Simeth Scholarships • 1358

TOPEKA COMMUNITY FOUNDATION
Harriet Hayes Austin Memorial Scholarship for Nursing • 1421

TOWNSHIP OFFICIALS OF ILLINOIS
Township Officials of Illinois Scholarship-Undergraduate Scholarship • 1853

TPA SCHOLARSHIP TRUST FOR THE DEAF AND NEAR DEAF
TPA Scholarship Trust for the Hearing Impaired • 2328

TRANSPORT WORKER UNION OF AMERICA, AFL-CIO
Michael J. Quill Scholarship Fund • 2012

TRAPSHOOTING HALL OF FAME
Trapshooting Hall of Fame College Scholarships • 341

TRAVIS CREDIT UNION
Mary Keith Duff Memorial Scholarship • 1572

TREACY FOUNDATION
Treacy Foundation Scholarship • 1854

TREE RESEARCH AND EDUCATION ENDOWMENT FUND
John Wright Memorial Scholarship • 962

TRI DELTA
Tri Delta Undergraduate Scholarship • 2056

TRIANGLE EDUCATION FOUNDATION
James Rust Scholarship • 1996
Mortin Scholarship • 2016

TRUCKLOAD CARRIERS ASSOCIATION
Truckload Carriers Association Scholarship Fund • 2057

TRUMAN SCHOLARSHIP FOUNDATION
Truman Scholar • 342

TRUTH INITIATIVE
Truth Change Maker Awards • 343

TUITION EXCHANGE
Tuition Exchange Scholarships • 2058

TUSKEGEE AIRMEN SCHOLARSHIP FOUNDATION
Tuskegee Airmen Scholarship Foundation Scholarships • 1154

U.S. ARMY
Army ROTC Advanced Course • 53

U.S. BANK
U.S. Bank Scholarship Program • 344

U.S. COAST GUARD
Coast Guard College Student Pre-Commissioning Initiative • 88

U.S. COAST GUARD CHIEF PETTY OFFICERS ASSOCIATION
Captain Caliendo College Assistance Fund • 73

U.S. DEPARTMENT OF AGRICULTURE
USDA/1890 National Scholars Program • 1163

U.S. DEPARTMENT OF HEALTH AND HUMAN SERVICES
NHSC Scholarship • 1046

U.S. DEPARTMENT OF STATE
Fulbright Grants • 149

U.S. FIGURE SKATING
Collegiate Championship Award Program • 93
Memorial Fund Scholarships • 219
Scholastic Honors Team • 297
Scott Hamilton Skaters Education Fund • 298

U.S. FISH AND WILDLIFE SERVICE HEADQUARTERS
Federal Junior Duck Stamp Program and Scholarship Competition • 422

U.S. METRIC ASSOCIATION
USMA Metric Scholarship Award • 360

U.S. NAVY NAVAL RESERVE OFFICERS TRAINING CORPS (NROTC)
Navy-Marine Corps ROTC College Program • 248
Navy-Marine Corps ROTC Four-Year Scholarships • 249
Navy-Marine Corps ROTC Two-Year Scholarships • 250
NROTC Nurse Corps Scholarship • 259

U.S. NAVY PERSONNEL
Navy College Fund • 246

U.S. PAN ASIAN AMERICAN CHAMBER OF COMMERCE
UPS Hallmark Scholarship • 2274

U.S. WESTERN DIGITAL STEM SCHOLARSHIP
U.S. Western Digital STEM Scholarship • 346

UCB FAMILY EPILEPSY SCHOLARSHIP PROGRAM
UCB Family Epilepsy Scholarship Program • 2329

UKRAINIAN FRATERNAL ASSOCIATION
Eugene and Elinor Kotur Scholarship Trust Fund • 2140

UKULELE FESTIVAL HAWAII
Ukulele Festival Hawaii's College Scholarship Program • 497

UNION PLUS
Union Plus Scholarship • 2064

UNITARIAN UNIVERSALIST ASSOCIATION
Otto M. Stanfield Legal Scholarship • 679
Stanfield and D'Orlando Art Scholarship • 2048

UNITED AGRIBUSINESS LEAGUE
United Agribusiness League and United Agricultural Benefit Trust Scholarships • 2065

UNITED CHURCH OF CHRIST
UCC Seminarian Scholarship • 2059

UNITED DAUGHTERS OF THE CONFEDERACY
Phoebe Pember Memorial Scholarship • 1069
United Daughters of the Confederacy Scholarships • 350

UNITED FOOD AND COMMERCIAL WORKERS UNION
UFCW Scholarship Program • 2060

UNITED METHODIST CHURCH
Allan Jerome Burry Scholarship • 1935
Rev. Dr. Karen Layman Gift of Hope Scholarship • 2034
United Methodist General Scholarship • 2066

UNITED MINE WORKERS OF AMERICA/BCOA T.E.F.
UMWA-Lorin E. Kerr Scholarships • 2061

UNITED NEGRO COLLEGE FUND (UNCF)
Chevron Corporate Scholars Program • 2121
Intellia Therapeutics - UNCF Scholarship • 2169
Tampax Flow It Forward Scholarship • 2261
UNCF Healthcare Workforce Diversity Program Certification • 2271

UNITED STATES BOWLING CONGRESS
Earl Anthony Memorial Scholarships • 132
Gift for Life Scholarships • 156
USBC Alberta E. Crowe Star of Tomorrow • 356
USBC Annual Zeb Scholarship • 357
USBC Chuck Hall Star of Tomorrow • 358
USBC Youth Ambassador of the Year • 359

UNITED STATES DEPARTMENT OF VETERANS AFFAIRS
Edith Nourse Rogers STEM Scholarship • 134

UNITED STATES GEOSPATIAL INTELLIGENCE FOUNDATION (USGIF)
USGIF Scholarship Program • 731

UNITED STATES HISPANIC LEADERSHIP INSTITUTE
Dr. Juan Andrade, Jr. Scholarship • 2134
United States Hispanic Leadership Institute Denny's Hungry for Education • 351

UNITED STATES NAVAL INSTITUTE (USNI)
Leadership Essay Contest • 203
Naval Intelligence Essay Contest • 244

UNITED STATES TENNIS ASSOCIATION FOUNDATION
Dwight F. Davis Memorial Scholarship • 129
Dwight Mosley Scholarship Award • 130
Eve Kraft Education and College Scholarship • 141
Marian Wood Baird College Scholarship • 208
Rosalind P. Walter College Scholarship • 284

UNITED TRANSPORTATION UNION INSURANCE ASSOCIATION
United Transportation Union Scholarships • 2067

UNITIL
Unitil Scholarship Fund • 1865

UNIVERSITY AVIATION ASSOCIATION (UAA)
Eugene S. Kropf Scholarship • 883
Joseph Frasca Excellence in Aviation Scholarship • 964

UNIVERSITY OF CALIFORNIA AT BERKELEY
University of California Public Policy and International Affairs Junior Summer Institute • 728

The Ultimate Scholarship Book 2026
Sponsor Index

University of California Public Policy and International Affairs Law Fellowship • 729

UNIVERSITY OF HAWAII – OFFICE OF STUDENT AFFAIRS
State of Hawai`i B Plus Scholarship • 1811

UPAKAR FOUNDATION
Upakar Foundation Indian American Community College Scholarship • 2273

UPPER MIDWEST SECURITY ALLIANCE (UMSA)
UMSA Foundation Scholarship Program • 1864

US JCI SENATE FOUNDATION
U.S. JCI Senate Scholarship Grants • 345

US RUGBY FOUNDATION
Kevin Higgins College Scholarship • 200

US YOUTH SOCCER
William J. Goaziou Scholarship • 375

USA GYMNASTICS
National Gymnastics Foundation Men's Scholarship • 2217

USA RACQUETBALL
USAR Scholarship • 355

USA ROLLER SPORTS
USA Roller Sports Scholarship Fund • 353

USA WATER POLO INC.
Justin Dignam Memorial Scholarship • 197

USA WATER SKI AND WAKE SPORTS FOUNDATION
Banana George Blair Ambassador Scholarship • 58
Big Al Wagner Western Region Scholarship • 62
Richard Avila Scholarship • 282
Southern Region/Elmer Stailing Scholarship • 307
Tim Olson Memorial Scholarship • 340
USA Water Ski and Wake Sports Foundation Scholarships • 354

UTAH ASSOCIATION OF INDEPENDENT INSURANCE AGENTS
Utah Association of Independent Insurance Agents Scholarship • 1869

UTAH STATE CHAPTER P.E.O.
Gump and Ayers Scholarship • 1415

UTAH SYSTEM OF HIGHER EDUCATION
Terrel H. Bell Education Scholarship • 1835

UTILITY WORKERS UNION OF AMERICA
Utility Workers Union of America Scholarships • 2068

VA MORTGAGE CENTER
VA Essay Scholarship • 361

VEGETARIAN RESOURCE GROUP
VRG Scholarship • 365

VERIFIED SCHOLARSHIPS
$1,000 All Star Verified Scholarship • 1

VERMONT STUDENT ASSISTANCE CORPORATION
Part-Time Grants • 1715
Vermont Incentive Grants • 1872
Vermont Sheriffs' Association Scholarship • 1874

VERTICAL FLIGHT FOUNDATION
Vertical Flight Foundation Technical Scholarships • 1165

VETERANS CAUCUS OF THE AMERICAN ACADEMY OF PHYSICIAN ASSISTANTS
Veterans Caucus Scholarship • 362

VETERANS OF FOREIGN WARS
Patriot's Pen Youth Essay Contest • 473
VFW Scout of the Year Scholarship • 2069
Voice of Democracy Audio Essay Contests • 363

VETERANS OF FOREIGN WARS TEACHER OF THE YEAR AWARD
Teacher of the Year Award • 721

VIRGINIA DAUGHTERS OF THE AMERICAN REVOLUTION
Virginia Daughters of the American Revolution Scholarships • 1881

VIRGINIA DEPARTMENT OF AVIATION
John R. Lillard VAOC Scholarship • 1502

VIRGINIA DEPARTMENT OF EDUCATION
Granville P. Meade Scholarship • 1411

VIRGINIA HIGH SCHOOL LEAGUE
VHSL Achievement Award • 1877
Virginia High School League Charles E. Savedge Journalism Scholarship • 1883

VIRGINIA LAKES AND WATERSHEDS ASSOCIATION
Leo Bourassa Scholarship • 1535

VIRGINIA SHERIFFS' INSTITUTE
Virginia Sheriffs' Institute Scholarship • 1885

VISIONARY INTEGRATION PROFESSIONALS
VIP Women in Technology Scholarship • 1166

VITALITY MEDICAL
Vitality Medical's Student Disability Scholarship • 2330

VOLUNTEER FLORIDA
Florida Governor's Black History Month Essay Contest • 1379

VOLUNTEERS FOR OUTDOOR COLORADO
Grossman Scholarship • 1414

VOYAGER SCHOLARSHIP, THE OBAMA-CHESKY SCHOLARSHIP FOR PUBLIC SERVICE
Voyager Scholarship, The Obama-Chesky Scholarship for Public Service • 364

WAFP SCHOLARSHIP COMMITTEE
E.H. Marth Food Protection and Food Science Scholarship • 1346

WAGGLE
Waggle Human-Pet Bond Scholarship Opportunity • 368

WARRELL CORP
AACT National Candy Technologists John Kitt Memorial Scholarship Program • 743

WASHINGTON BUSINESS AND PROFESSIONAL WOMEN'S FOUNDATION
Washington BPW Foundation Mature Woman Educational Scholarship • 1890

WASHINGTON CROSSING FOUNDATION
National Washington Crossing Foundation Scholarship • 666

WASHINGTON HOMESCHOOL ORGANIZATION
Homeschoolers' Support Association Scholarship • 1445

WASHINGTON INTERSCHOLASTIC ACTIVITIES ASSOCIATION (WIAA)
Smart Choices Scholarship Program • 1794

WASHINGTON MEDIA SCHOLARS FOUNDATION
Media Fellows Program • 649

WASHINGTON STATE AUTO DEALERS ASSOCIATION (WSADA) SCHOLARSHIP PROGRAM
Washington State Auto Dealers Association Bright Future Scholarship • 1894

WASHINGTON STATE BOARD FOR COMMUNITY AND TECHNICAL COLLEGES
Opportunity Grant • 1705

WASHINGTON STATE PTA
Washington State PTA Scholarship • 1897

WASHINGTON STUDENT ACHIEVEMENT COUNCIL
American Indian Endowed Scholarship • 1208
State Work Study • 1813
Washington College Grant • 1891
Washington Health Corps • 1892
Washington State College Bound Scholarship • 1895

WASHINGTON WOMEN IN NEED
Washington Women In Need • 1898

WEALTH BY HEALTH STEPS FOR CHANGE FOUNDATION
Steps For Change Scholarship • 310

WELLS FARGO SCHOLARSHIP PROGRAM FOR PEOPLE WITH DISABILITIES, SCHOLARSHIP AMERICA
Wells Fargo Scholarship Program for People with Disabilities • 2331

WELLS FARGO VETERANS SCHOLARSHIP PROGRAM, SCHOLARSHIP AMERICA
Wells Fargo Veterans Scholarship Program • 373

WELSH PONY AND COB SOCIETY
Mollie Butler Memorial Scholarship • 1012

WERKS MOBILE
Werks Mobile Scholarship • 1899

WEST VIRGINIA HIGHER EDUCATION POLICY COMMISSION
Higher Education Adult Part-Time Student (HEAPS) Grant Program • 1442
West Virginia Engineering, Science and Technology Scholarship • 1900
West Virginia Higher Education Grant • 1901
West Virginia PROMISE Scholarship • 1902

WEST VIRGINIA PTA
West Virginia PTA Scholarship • 1903

WHITE HOUSE
White House Fellows Program • 374

WILDERNESS SOCIETY
Gloria Barron Wilderness Society Scholarship • 914

WILLIAM ORR DINGWALL FOUNDATION
Korean Ancestry Grant • 2181

WILLIAM RANDOLPH HEARST FOUNDATION
United States Senate Youth Program • 727

WILSON ORNITHOLOGICAL SOCIETY
George A. Hall / Harold F. Mayfield Grant • 909
Louis Agassiz Fuertes Award • 985
Paul A. Stewart Grants • 1061

WINE COUNTRY GIFT BASKETS
Spirit of Giving Scholarship • 308

WINFIELD SOLUTIONS LLC
Careers in Agriculture Scholarship Program • 835

WINSTON-SALEM FOUNDATION
Oliver Joel and Ellen Pell Denny Healthcare Scholarship Fund • 1702

WISCONSIN AMUSEMENT AND MUSIC OPERATORS
Wisconsin Amusement and Music Operators Scholarships • 1915

WISCONSIN BROADCASTERS ASSOCIATION
Wisconsin Broadcasters Association Foundation Student Scholarship Program • 1916

WISCONSIN DEPARTMENT OF MILITARY AFFAIRS
Wisconsin National Guard Tuition Grant • 1918

WISCONSIN DEPARTMENT OF VETERANS AFFAIRS
Wisconsin Veterans Education Reimbursement Grants • 1920

WISCONSIN MATHEMATICS COUNCIL INC.
Sister Mary Petronia Van Straten Scholarship for Pre-Service Teachers • 1792

WISCONSIN MEDICAL SOCIETY FOUNDATION
John D. and Virginia Riesch Scholarship • 1500

WISCONSIN SCHOOL COUNSELOR ASSOCIATION
Xello High School Scholarship • 1926

WISCONSIN SOCIETY OF PROFESSIONAL ENGINEERS
Engineering Foundation of Wisconsin Scholarship • 1363

WISCONSIN WOMEN IN GOVERNMENT INC.
Wisconsin Women in Government Undergraduate Scholarship • 1921

WOMEN BAND DIRECTORS INTERNATIONAL
Women Band Directors International College Scholarships • 503

WOMEN DIVERS HALL OF FAME
Women Divers Hall of Fame Scholarships and Grants • 377

WOMEN IN AVIATION INTERNATIONAL
Women in Aviation International Scholarship • 2074

WOMEN IN DEFENSE
Women In Defense WID Scholar • 2276

WOMEN IN INTERNATIONAL TRADE CHARITABLE TRUST
WIIT Charitable Trust Scholarship • 735

WOMEN MARINES ASSOCIATION
Women Marines Association Scholarship Program • 379

WOMEN OF THE EVANGELICAL LUTHERAN CHURCH IN AMERICA
Opportunity Scholarships for Lutheran Laywomen • 2027

WOMEN'S ARMY CORPS VETERANS ASSOCIATION
Women's Army Corps Veterans Association Scholarship • 381

WOMEN'S BASKETBALL COACHES ASSOCIATION
Wade Trophy • 367
WBCA Coaches' All-America • 371

WOMEN'S OVERSEAS SERVICE LEAGUE
Women's Overseas Service League Scholarships for Women • 382

WOMEN'S TRANSPORTATION SEMINAR (WTS) - MINNESOTA CHAPTER
WTS Minnesota Chapter Scholarships • 1925

WOMEN'S TRANSPORTATION SEMINAR (WTS) INTERNATIONAL
Helene M. Overly Memorial Graduate Scholarship • 2156
Molitoris Leadership Scholarship for Undergraduates • 2210
Sharon D. Banks Memorial Undergraduate Scholarship • 2247

WOMEN'S WESTERN GOLF FOUNDATION
Women's Western Golf Foundation Scholarship • 383

WORLD OF 7 BILLION
Student Video Contest • 317

WORTHY
Worthy Women's Professional Studies Scholarship • 2278

WYLAND FOUNDATION
Wyland National Art Challenge • 504

WYOMING DEPARTMENT OF EDUCATION
Douvas Memorial Scholarship • 1338

YOUNG CHRISTIAN LEADERS
Young Christian Leaders Scholarship • 2076

YOUTHLINC
Utah Young Humanitarian Award • 1870

ZICKLIN CONTRACTING
Zicklin Contracting Restoration Awareness Scholarship • 508

ZONTA INTERNATIONAL
Amelia Earhart Fellowships • 779
Jane M. Klausman Women in Business Scholarship Fund • 618
Young Women in Public Affairs Award • 2281

The Ultimate Scholarship Book 2026
Scholarship Name Index

SCHOLARSHIP NAME INDEX

$1,000 All Star Verified Scholarship • 1
$1,000 College JumpStart Gratitude Scholarship • 2
$1,000 College JumpStart Love of Learning Scholarship • 3
$1,000 College JumpStart Pay It Forward Scholarship • 4
$1,000 College JumpStart Show Grit Scholarship • 5
$1,000 GK Tanabe Student Scholarship • 6
$1,000 Moolahspot Scholarship • 7
$1,000 Scholarship Detective Launch Scholarship • 8
1 for 2 Education Foundation Scholarship • 9
100th Infantry Battalion Memorial Scholarship Fund • 10
1Dental Scholarship • 11
1st Marine Division Association Scholarship • 12
25th Infantry Division Association Educational Scholarship • 13
4-H Youth in Action • 1930
A+A Altruism + All Good Deeds Scholarship • 14
A.D. Osherman Scholarship Fund • 1178
A.J. Grisanti Memorial Scholarship • 509
A.O. Putnam Memorial Scholarship • 741
A.T. Anderson Memorial Scholarship • 2079
AAAE Foundation Scholarship • 742
AACT National Candy Technologists John Kitt Memorial Scholarship Program • 743
AAGS - NSPS Scholarships • 744
AAGS Joseph F. Dracup Scholarship Award • 745
Aaliyah Lee Scholarship • 15
AALL Educational Scholarships • 510
AAMA Student Essay Competition • 746
AAU Karate Scholarship • 16
AAUS Student Scholarships • 17
AAUW Educational Foundation Career Development Grants • 2080
Abacus Life Scholarship • 18
AbbVie Immunology Scholarship • 2282
Abe and Esther Hagiwara Student Aid Award • 2081
Abel Wolman Fellowship • 747
ABF Summer Undergraduate Research Fellowship Program • 511
ACAA Educational Foundation Scholarship Program • 748
Academic Achievement Award • 749
Academic Challenge Scholarship • 1179
Academic Education Award • 750
Academic Excellence Scholarship • 1180
Academic Merit Scholarships • 512
Academic Scholars Program • 1181
Academy of Nutrition and Dietetics Foundation Student Scholarship • 751
Access College Early Scholarship • 1182
Access to Better Learning and Education Grant Program • 1183
Accounting and Financial Women's Alliance Foundation Scholarship • 513
ACEC Colorado Scholarship Program • 1184
ACEC New York Scholarship Program • 752
ACEC Scholarship • 1185
ACES Education Fund Scholarship • 386

The Ultimate Scholarship Book 2026
Scholarship Name Index

ACES Scholarships • 387
Achievers in Technology Program • 2082
ACI Scholarship • 753
ACI Student Fellowship Program • 754
ACJA/Lambda Alpha Epsilon Scholarship • 19
ACL/NJCL National Greek Examination Scholarship • 388
ACL/NJCL National Latin Examination Scholarships • 389
ACLS Fellowships • 514
ACOR-CAORC Fellowship • 515
Act of Kindness Scholarship • 20
Actuarial Diversity Scholarship • 2083
Ada I. Pressman Memorial Scholarship • 2084
ADEA/Crest Oral-B Scholarships for Dental Hygiene Students Pursuing Academic Careers • 755
ADEA/Haleon Preventive Dentistry Scholarships • 756
ADEA/MouthWatch Patti DiGangi Scholarship for Dental Hygiene Innovation • 757
ADEA/MouthWatch Predoctoral Dental Student Scholarship for Innovation • 758
ADEA/Sigma Phi Alpha Linda Devore Scholarship • 759
Adelle and Erwin Tomash Fellowship in the History of Information Processing • 516
ADHA Institute Scholarship Program • 760
Admiral Grace Murray Hopper Memorial Scholarships • 2085
Adobe Design Circle Scholarships • 390
Adolph Van Pelt Scholarship • 2086
Adrianna Andreini Scholarship • 1931
Adult Learner Scholarship from Study.com • 21
Adult Skills Education Award • 22
Adult Students in Scholastic Transition (ASIST) • 517
Advanced Practice Healthcare Scholarship Program • 1186
AFCEA Ralph W. Shrader Diversity Scholarships • 761
AFCEA ROTC Scholarships • 23
Afro-Academic, Cultural, Technological and Scientific Olympics (ACT-SO) • 2087
AFS Twin City Memorial Scholarship • 1187
AFS Wisconsin Past President Scholarship • 1188
AFSA Financial Aid Scholarships • 1932
AFSA National Essay Contest • 24
AFSA/AAFSW Merit Awards • 1933
AFSCME Family Scholarship • 1934
Ag Day Essay Contest • 25
Against The Grain Artistic Scholarship • 2088
AGBU US Graduate Scholarship • 2089
AGC Education and Research Foundation Undergraduate Scholarship • 762
AGC Graduate Scholarships • 763
AGC of Massachusetts Scholarships • 1189
AGC of Ohio Scholarships • 1190
AGC Undergraduate Scholarships • 764
AGL Over the Rainbow Scholarship • 391
Agnes Jones Jackson Scholarship • 2090
Agnes M. Lindsay Scholarship • 1191
Agnes Missirian Scholarship • 2091
Agota M. Bardos Award • 26
AHEPA Educational Foundation National Scholarship Program • 2092
AHHS Foundation Scholarship • 27

AHIMA Foundation Merit Scholarships • 765
AIA/Architects Foundation Diversity Advancement Scholarship • 766
AIAA Foundation Undergraduate Scholarship Program • 767
AICPA Fellowship for Minority Doctoral Students • 2093
AICPA Foundation Scholarship for Future CPAs • 518
AICPA Foundation Two-year Transfer Scholarship • 519
AICPA John L. Carey Scholarship • 520
AICPA Scholarship for Minority Accounting Students • 2094
Aid for Part-Time Study • 1192
AIERF College Scholarship • 521
AIERF Graduate Scholarship • 522
AIFS Green Ambassador Scholarship • 28
AIGA Worldstudio Scholarships • 392
Air Force ROTC ASCP • 29
Air Force ROTC High School Scholarship Program • 30
Air Force ROTC In-College Program • 31
Air Force ROTC Professional Officer Course-Early Release Program • 32
Air Force ROTC SOAR Program • 33
Airmen Memorial Foundation Scholarship Program • 34
AISES Intel Scholarship • 2095
AISI/AIST Foundation Premier Scholarship • 768
AIST Benjamin F. Fairless Scholarship (AIME) • 769
AIST Ronald E. Lincoln Memorial Scholarship • 770
AIST Smith Graduate Scholarship • 771
AIST William E. Schwabe Memorial Scholarship • 772
AIST Willy Korf Memorial Fund • 773
Akash Kuruvilla Memorial Scholarship • 35
Alabama Student Assistance Program • 1193
Alaska Education Grant • 1194
Alaska Performance Scholarship • 1195
Albert E. and Florence W. Newton Nursing Scholarship • 1196
Albert M. Lappin Scholarship • 1197
Alexia Foundation Student Grants • 393
Alice L. Haltom Educational Fund Scholarship • 523
Alice T. Schafer Mathematics Prize • 774
Alice W. Rooke Scholarship • 775
Alisa's Angels Scholarship • 1198
All Iowa Opportunity Scholarship • 1199
All-American Scholars (Cheerleading) • 36
All-American Scholars (Football) • 37
Allan Eldin and Agnes Sutorik Geiger Scholarship Fund • 1200
Allan Jerome Burry Scholarship • 1935
Allan Johnston Memorial Scholarship • 1201
Allied Healthcare Scholarship Program • 1202
Allied Van Lines Scholarship • 524
Alliss Opportunity Grant Program for Adults Returning to College • 1203
Allogan Slagle Memorial Scholarship • 2096
Ally Financial Law Scholars • 2097
Ally Financial Public Policy Scholars • 525

Alma White - Delta Kappa Gamma Scholarship • 1204
ALPA Scholarship Program • 1936
Alpha Kappa Alpha Financial Need Scholars • 38
Alpha Kappa Psi Scholarships • 526
Alpha Mu Tau Fraternity Undergraduate Scholarships • 776
Alyssa McCroskey Memorial Scholarship • 1205
Amazon Future Engineer Scholarship • 777
Ambassador Minerva Jean Falcon Hawaii Scholarship • 1206
AMBUCS Scholars • 778
AMCA Music Scholarship • 394
Amelia Earhart Fellowships • 779
America's 911 Foundation Scholarship • 39
American Association of State Troopers (AAST) Scholarship • 1937
American Bar Association Law Day Art Contest • 40
American Bar Association Law Student Writing Competition • 527
American Chemical Society Scholars Program • 2098
American Council of Engineering Companies of New Jersey Member Organization Scholarship • 1207
American Council of the Blind Scholarships • 2283
American Culinary Federation Scholarships • 528
American Express Scholarship Competition • 529
American Indian Endowed Scholarship • 1208
American Indian Services Scholarship • 2099
American Innovations Corrosion Scholarship • 780
American Institute of Graphic Arts (AIGA) Honolulu Chapter Scholarship Fund • 1209
American Legion - Connecticut Oratorical Contest • 1210
American Legion Auxiliary, Department of California Educational Assistance General $1,000 Scholarships • 1211
American Legion Auxiliary, Department of California Educational Assistance General $2,000 Scholarships • 1212
American Legion Auxiliary, Department of California Educational Assistance General $500 Scholarships • 1213
American Legion Baseball Scholarship • 41
American Legion Department of Arkansas High School Oratorical Scholarship Program • 1214
American Legion Department of Florida General Scholarship • 1215
American Legion Department of Illinois Scholarship • 1216
American Legion Eagle Scout of the Year • 1938
American Legion Legacy Scholarships • 42
American Water Scholarship • 781
Americanism and Government Scholarship Program • 1217
Americanism Essay Contest • 43
Americorps National Civilian Community Corps • 44
Americorps Vista • 45
AMPP Academic Scholarship • 782
AMS Graduate Fellowship in the History of Science • 783

648

AMS Graduate Fellowships • 784
AMS Minority Scholarship • 785
AMS Senior Named Scholarships • 786
AMT Student Scholarship • 787
AMVETS Children/Grandchildren Scholarships • 46
AMVETS National Ladies Auxiliary Scholarship • 1939
AMVETS National Scholarships for Veterans • 47
Amy Lowell Poetry Travelling Scholarship • 395
Anchor Scholarship Foundation Scholarship • 48
Angus Foundation Scholarships • 788
Ann Griffel Scholarship • 1218
Anne Ford Scholarship Program • 2284
Anne Maureen Whitney Barrow Memorial Scholarship • 2100
Annual NBNA Scholarships • 789
Annual University Scholarship • 790
ANS Graduate Scholarship • 791
ANS Incoming Freshman Scholarships • 792
ANS Undergraduate Scholarship • 793
Anthem Essay Contest • 396
Anthony Munoz Scholarship Fund • 1219
Antonio Cirino Memorial Scholarship • 1220
AOC Scholarships • 794
AORN Foundation Scholarship Program • 795
AOS Student and Postdoctoral Research Awards • 796
APF Dr. Christine Blasey Ford Grant • 530
APF/COGDOP Graduate Student Scholarships • 531
APF/Division 54 Lizette Peterson-Homer Injury Prevention Grant • 532
APIA Scholarship Program • 2101
Appaloosa Youth Association Art Contest • 797
Apprentice Ecologist Initiative Youth Scholarship Program • 798
AQHF General Scholarship • 1940
AQHF Youth Scholarship • 1941
ARA Scholarship • 1942
Arc of Washington State Trust Fund Stipend Award • 1221
Archibald Rutledge Scholarship Program • 1222
ARIT Fellowships for Research in Turkey • 533
Aritzia Scholarship • 2102
Arizona BPW Foundation Annual Scholarships • 1223
Arizona National Livestock Show Scholarship • 1224
Arkansas Game and Fish Commission Conservation Scholarship • 1225
Arkansas Service Memorial Scholarship Endowment • 1226
Armed Services YMCA Annual Essay Contest • 49
Army Emergency Relief's MG James Ursano Scholarship Program • 50
Army Engineer Memorial Awards • 51
Army Nurse Corps Association Scholarships • 52
Army ROTC Advanced Course • 53
Army ROTC Four-Year Scholarship Program • 54
Army ROTC Green To Gold Scholarship Program • 55
ARRL Foundation General Fund Scholarship • 534
ARS Undergraduate Scholarship • 2103

Arthur M. and Berdena King Eagle Scout Contest • 1943
ASA Scholarships • 2104
ASABE Foundation Engineering Scholarship • 799
ASCA/AISC Student Design Competition • 800
ASCAP Foundation Morton Gould Young Composer Awards • 397
ASDSO Senior Undergraduate Scholarship • 801
ASEV Scholarships • 802
ASF Olin Fellowships • 803
ASHA Youth Scholarships • 804
ASHRAE Engineering Technology Scholarships • 805
ASHRAE Society Scholarship Program • 806
Asian and Pacific Islander American Scholarships • 2105
ASLA Council of Fellows Scholarships • 807
ASME Auxiliary Lucy and Charles W. E. Clarke Scholarship • 808
ASME Foundation Scholarships • 809
ASNE Scholarship Program • 810
ASNT Fellowship • 811
Asparagus Club, Thomas K. Zaucha Scholarship • 535
Aspire Award • 1227
Associate Degree Nursing Scholarship Program • 1228
Associated General Contractors of Connecticut Scholarships • 1229
Associated General Contractors of Minnesota Scholarships • 1230
Association of Cuban Engineers Scholarship Foundation Scholarships • 2106
Association of Federal Communications Consulting Engineers Scholarships • 812
Association of Flight Attendants Annual Scholarship • 1944
Association of Food and Drug Officials Scholarship Award • 813
Association of Information Technology Professionals (AITP) Scholarships • 814
Assured Life Association National Scholarship • 1945
ASTM International Katherine and Bryant Mather Scholarship • 815
Astronaut Scholarship • 816
ASWA Seattle Chapter Scholarship • 1231
Atlas Shrugged Essay Contest • 398
Atsuhiko Tateuchi Memorial Scholarship • 1232
AU Student Contest • 56
AUA Foundation Research Scholars Program • 817
Automotive Hall of Fame Scholarships • 818
Auxiliary Legacy Scholarship • 819
Avacare Medical Scholarship • 820
Aviation Distributors and Manufacturers Association Scholarship Program • 821
Aviation Insurance Association Education Foundation Scholarship • 822
AWAF Scholarships • 1233
AWSCPA Scholarship • 536
AWSM Internship and Scholarship • 1946
B.J. Harrod Scholarships • 2107
B.K. Krenzer Reentry Scholarship • 2108
Babe Ruth League Scholarships • 57

Bachelor of Science Nursing Scholarship Program • 1234
Baer Reintegration Scholarship • 2285
BAFTX Undergraduate Award • 1235
Banana George Blair Ambassador Scholarship • 58
Barbizon's College Tuition Scholarship • 59
Baroid Scholarship • 823
Barry M. Goldwater Scholarship and Excellence in Education Program • 824
Battery Division Student Research Award • 825
Be the Boss Scholarship • 60
BEA National Scholarships in Broadcasting • 537
Beauty Changes Lives Foundation Scholarships • 538
Beef Industry Scholarship • 826
Begun Scholarship • 539
Ben and Vicky Cayetano Scholarship Fund • 1236
Ben W. Fortson, Jr., Scholarship • 1237
Bernard Rotberg Memorial Scholarship Fund • 1947
Betsy Plank/PRSSA Scholarship • 540
Better Business Bureau of Delaware Foundation Student Ethics Scholarship • 1238
Betty Bacon Memorial Scholarship • 1239
Beverly Murphy MLA Scholarship for Underrepresented Students • 541
Beyond the Boroughs Scholarship • 61
Bick Bickson Scholarship Fund • 1240
Big Al Wagner Western Region Scholarship • 62
Big Y Scholarship Programs • 1241
Bill Gove Scholarship • 399
Bill Kane Scholarship, Undergraduate • 827
Bill, W2ONV and Ann Salerno Memorial Scholarship • 542
Biographies of Contemporary Women in Mathematics Essay Contest • 828
BIPOC Scholarship • 2109
Blossom Kalama Evans Memorial Scholarship Fund • 1242
BMO Capital Markets Lime Connect Equity Through Education Scholarship • 2286
BMTX Financial Empowerment Scholarship • 63
BMW/SAE Engineering Scholarship • 829
Bob C. Powers Scholarship • 1243
Bob East Scholarship • 543
Bob Eddy Scholarship Program • 1244
Bob Richardson Legacy Scholarship • 544
Bob Stevens Memorial Scholarship • 1245
Bob Warnicke Scholarship • 64
Bodie McDowell Scholarship • 545
Boeing Company STEM Scholarship • 1246
Boettcher Foundation Scholarship • 1247
Bohdan Kolinsky Memorial Sports Journalism Scholarship • 1248
Bonner Scholars Program • 65
Boomer Benefits Scholarship • 66
Boomer Esiason Foundation General Academic Scholarship • 2287
Boon San Kitty Scholarship • 1948
Booz Allen Hawaii Scholarship Fund • 1249
Boren Scholarships • 546
Bound to Stay Bound Books Scholarship • 547
Boys and Girls Clubs of America National Youth of the Year Award • 1949
BrandSource Scholarship • 2110

The Ultimate Scholarship Book 2026
Scholarship Name Index

Bridging Scholarships for Study Abroad in Japan • 400
Bright!Tax Global Scholar Initiative • 67
Brill Family Scholarship • 830
Brown Hudner Navy Scholarship • 68
Bryant L. Bench Carollo Engineers Inc. Scholarship • 831
BSA Research Fellowship • 548
BSN Scholarship • 832
Builders Exchange of Billings Scholarship • 1251
Building Bridges Scholarship • 69
Burger King Scholars Program • 70
Burlington Northern Santa Fe (BNSF) Foundation Scholarship • 2111
Business and Professional Women of Kentucky Foundation Grant • 1252
Business and Professional Women/Maine Continuing Education Scholarship • 1253
Byers Scholarship • 1254
Byron Hanke Fellowship • 549
C. Bertrand and Marian Othmer Schultz Collegiate Scholarship • 1255
C.B. Gambrell Undergraduate Scholarship • 833
C.I.P. Scholarship • 71
Cafe Bustelo El Cafe Del Futuro Scholarship • 2112
Cal Grant A • 1256
Cal Grant B • 1257
Cal Grant C • 1258
Cal Grant Entitlement Award • 1259
California - Hawaii Elks Association Vocational Grants • 550
California - Hawaii Elks Major Project Undergraduate Scholarship Program for Students with Disabilities • 1260
California Chafee Grant for Foster Youth • 2113
California Fee Waiver Program for Children of Veterans • 1261
California Fee Waiver Program for Dependents of Deceased or Disabled National Guard Members • 1262
California Fee Waiver Program for Recipients of the Medal of Honor and Their Children • 1263
California Freethought Day High School Essay Scholarship • 1264
California Health Sciences Scholarships • 1265
California Law Enforcement Personnel Dependents Grant Program • 1266
California Masonic Foundation Scholarship • 1267
California Oratorical Contest • 1268
California Restaurant Association Educational Foundation General Scholarship • 1269
California State PTA Volunteer Service Scholarship • 1270
Campus Safety Health and Environmental Management Association Scholarship • 834
Cancer Fighter Scholarship • 2288
Cancer for College Scholarships • 2289
Candon, Todd and Seabolt Scholarship Fund • 1271
CAPED Excellence Scholarship • 1272
Caples Student Campaign of the Year Award • 551
CAPPS Memorial Scholarship Program • 1273
Capt. James J. Regan Scholarship • 72
Captain Caliendo College Assistance Fund • 73

CardRates.com Financial Futures Scholarship • 552
CardsDirect Future Designer Scholarship • 401
Career Advancement Scholarship • 1274
Career Based Scholarship • 1275
Career Center • 402
Career Colleges and Schools of Texas Scholarship Program • 1276
Career Transition for Dancers Undergraduate Studies Scholarship • 403
CareerFitter Scholarship • 74
Careers in Agriculture Scholarship Program • 835
Carl A. Ross Student Paper Award • 404
Carole J. Streeter, KB9JBR, Scholarship • 553
Carole Simpson Scholarship • 554
Carolyn Hines Memorial Scholarship Program • 75
Carroll C. Hall Memorial Scholarship • 1950
Carson Scholars • 76
Carville M. Akehurst Memorial Scholarship • 836
Casey Family Scholarship • 2114
Cash Grant Program • 1277
Cashtelligent Financial Literacy Scholarship • 77
Catching the Dream Native American Scholarship Fund • 2115
Categorical Tuition Waiver • 1278
Cathay Bank Foundation Scholarship • 1279
Catholic United Financial College Tuition Scholarship • 1951
Cavett Robert Scholarship • 405
CBC Spouses Essay Contest • 2116
CBC Spouses Performing Arts Scholarship • 2117
CBCF Reducing the Financial Barrier Scholarship • 2118
CCA Christian Cheer Nationals • 78
CCCAM Scholarships • 1280
CDM Constructors Inc. Workforce Development Scholarship • 1281
Cedarcrest Farms Scholarship • 837
Central Arizona DX Association Scholarship • 1282
Certificate, License or Other Industry-Recognized Credential • 1283
CESDA Diversity Scholarship • 1284
CEW+ Scholarships • 1285
Chairman's Award • 1952
Challenge Met Scholarship • 2290
Challenge Scholarship • 79
Champions for Christ Scholarship • 1953
Charles Clarke Cordle Memorial Scholarship • 555
Charles Dubose Scholarship • 1286
Charles H. Bussmann Undergraduate Scholarship • 838
Charles L. Hebner Memorial Scholarship • 1287
Charles N. Fisher Memorial Scholarship • 556
Charles R. Walgreen Jr. Leadership Award • 1954
Charles W. and Annette Hill Scholarship • 1288
Charles W. Riley Fire and Emergency Medical Services Scholarship Program • 1289
Charlie and Becky Bray Legacy Scholarship • 557
Charlie Logan Scholarship Program for Dependents • 1955
Charlotte McGuire Scholarship • 839
CHCI United Health Foundation Scholar-Intern Program • 2119

Cherokee Nation/Tribal Council At-Large Scholarship • 2120
Chester Burger Scholarship for Excellence in Public Relations • 558
Chevron Corporate Scholars Program • 2121
Chick and Sophie Major Memorial Duck Calling Contest • 1290
Chief Manuelito Scholarship Program • 2122
Chief Master Sergeants of the Air Force Scholarships • 80
Chief Petty Officer Scholarship Fund • 81
Children and Youth Scholarships • 1291
Children in Need Scholarship • 406
Children of Warriors National Presidents' Scholarship • 82
Chinese American Citizens Alliance Essay Contest • 83
ChiroHealthUSA Foxworth Family Scholarship • 840
Chiropractic Education Assistance Scholarship • 1292
Choose Ohio First Scholarship • 1293
Christian A. Herter Memorial Scholarship Program • 1294
Christopher L. Hunt Scholarship • 407
Christophers Video Contest for College Students • 84
CIA Undergraduate Scholarship Program • 85
CIF Scholar-Athlete of the Year • 1295
Citizen Potawatomi Nation Tribal Scholarship • 2123
CJ Pony Parts Scholarship Video Contest • 86
CLA Scholarship For BIPOC Students in Memory of Edna Yelland • 559
Clair A. Hill Scholarship • 1296
Clanseer and Anna Johnson Scholarships • 1297
Clauder Competition Prize • 408
Clem Judd, Jr., Memorial Scholarship • 1298
Clifford H. Ted Rees Jr. Scholarship • 560
Clubs of America Scholarship Award for Career Success • 87
CNH Industrial Aftermarket Solutions Scholarship • 1956
Coast Guard College Student Pre-Commissioning Initiative • 88
Coast Guard Foundation Scholarship Fund • 89
Coca-Cola Community College Academic Team • 90
Coca-Cola Scholars Program • 91
Colgate Bright Smiles, Bright Futures Minority Scholarships • 841
Colgate-Palmolive Make the U Educational Grant • 2124
Collaborative Teachers Tuition Waiver • 1299
College Access Program • 1300
College Photographer of the Year • 561
College Prep Scholarship for High School Juniors • 92
College Television Awards • 409
CollegeInvest 529 Scholarship Program • 1301
Collegiate Championship Award Program • 93
Collegiate Inventors Competition • 842
Collegiate Scholarship • 1302
Colorado Council Volunteerism and Community Service Scholarship • 1303

The Ultimate Scholarship Book 2026
Scholarship Name Index

Colorado Masons Benevolent Fund Scholarships • 1304
Colorado Oratorical Contest • 1305
Colorado Student Grant • 1306
Colorado Women's Education Foundation • 1307
Communities Foundation of Oklahoma Scholarships • 1308
Community Banker Association of Illinois Annual Essay Scholarship Program • 1309
Community College Transition Award • 1957
Community Scholarship Fund • 1310
Competitive Scholarships • 1311
Complete Water Solutions Scholarship • 843
Completing the Dream Scholarship • 94
Composites Division/Harold Giles Scholarship • 844
Computational Science Graduate Fellowship • 845
Confederation of Oregon School Administrators Scholarships • 1312
Conference of Minority Transportation Officials (COMTO) National Scholarship • 2125
Congress Bundestag Youth Exchange Program • 95
Congressional Black Caucus Spouses Education Scholarship • 2126
Congressional Black Caucus Spouses Visual Arts Scholarship • 2127
Congressional Medal of Honor Society Scholarships • 96
ConnectHER Film Festival • 410
Connecticut Building Congress Scholarships • 1313
Coolidge Scholarship • 97
Cora Aguda Manayan Fund • 1314
Corporate Culture Scholarship • 98
Corporate Office Interiors Scholarship Contest • 99
Corrosion Division Morris Cohen Graduate Student Award • 846
COSA Youth Development Program Scholarships • 1315
Council on International Educational Exchange (CIEE) Scholarships • 411
Courage to Grow Scholarship • 100
Courageous Heart Scholarship • 1316
CPI Highest Point Hunt Seat Rider • 101
CRA All-Access Scholarship • 2128
Craig Dickinson Memorial Scholarship • 102
Create Real Impact Contest • 103
Create-a-Greeting-Card Scholarship • 104
Creative Biolabs Scholarship • 847
Creative Sole Scholarship • 2129
Crest Oral-B Laboratories Dental Hygiene Scholarships • 848
CREW Network Foundation Scholarship • 562
Crossword Hobbyist Crossword Scholarship • 105
Crumley Roberts Next Step Scholarship • 1317
CTA Cesar E. Chavez and Dolores Huerta Education Award Program • 1318
CTAHPERD Gibson-Laemel Scholarship • 1319
Cummins Scholarship • 849
Curt Greene Memorial Scholarship • 106
Curwen-Guidry-Blackburn Scholarship Fund • 107
CWA Joe Beirne Foundation Scholarship • 1958
Cynthia and Alan Baran Fine Arts and Music Scholarship Fund • 1320

DAAD/AICGS Research Fellowship Program • 412
Daedalian Foundation Scholarship Program • 108
Dairy Student Recognition Program • 850
Dan L. Meisinger Sr. Memorial Learn to Fly Scholarship • 851
Daniel E. Lambert Memorial Scholarship • 1321
Daniels Scholarship Program • 1322
Darrel Hess Community College Geography Scholarship • 563
Daughters of the Cincinnati Scholarship • 109
David A. O Neil Scholarship • 852
David Alan Quick Scholarship • 853
David Arver Memorial Scholarship • 854
David B. Durkee Memorial Scholarship Program • 1959
David E. Simon Scholarship • 1323
David H. and Beverly A. Barlow Grant • 564
Davidson Fellows Scholarships • 110
Davis-Putter Scholarship Fund • 111
Dayton Amateur Radio Association Scholarship • 565
DC Tuition Assistance Grant Program • 1324
DEED Funding Opportunities • 855
Delaware Educational Benefits for Children of Deceased Veterans and Others • 1325
Delaware Scholarship Incentive Program • 1326
Delaware Solid Waste Authority John P. Pat Healy Scholarship • 1327
Delegate Scholarship • 1328
Delete Cyberbullying Beyond School Walls Scholarship • 112
Delete Cyberbullying Mental Health Awareness Scholarship • 113
Delete Cyberbullying Social Media Scholarship • 114
Dell Scholars Program • 115
Dellums SMART Scholarship • 856
Delta Faucet Company Scholarships • 857
Delta Gamma Foundation Scholarship • 1960
Delta Phi Epsilon Educational Foundation Scholarship • 1961
Delta Theta Chi Sorority National Memorial Scholarship • 116
Denes I. Bardos Award • 117
Dennis Schoepp Memorial Scholarship • 1329
Department of Children and Families (DCF) Foster Child Tuition Waiver and Fee Assistance Program • 1330
Desk and Derrick Educational Trust • 858
Development Fund for Black Students in Science and Technology • 2130
DEWALT Trades Scholarship • 566
Dianne E. H. Wilcox Scholarship Fund • 1331
Dick Griffiths Memorial Scholarship • 1332
Digital Privacy Scholarship • 118
Diller Teen Tikkun Olam Awards • 1962
Dinah Shore Scholarship • 119
Diocese of the Armenian Church of America (Eastern) Scholarships • 1963
Disney Entertainment Writing Program • 413
Distinguished Service Award for Students • 567
Distinguished Young Women Scholarship Program • 2131
District of Columbia Tuition Assistance Grant • 1333

Diversity Achievement Scholarship • 414
Diversity Advocacy Council Scholarship • 2132
Dixie Boys Baseball Scholarship Program • 120
Dixie Softball Scholarships • 121
Dixie Youth Scholarship Program • 122
Dizzy Dean Scholarship • 123
DMI Milk Marketing Scholarship • 859
DNA Day Essay Contest • 860
Dollars for Scholars Scholarship • 124
Dolly Parton Songwriters Award • 415
Dolphin Scholarships • 125
Don Riebhoff Memorial Scholarship • 568
Don't Mess with Texas Scholarship • 1334
Don't Text and Drive Scholarship • 126
Donald A. and John R. Fisher Memorial Scholarship • 1964
Donald F. and Mildred Topp Othmer Scholarships • 861
Doodle for Google • 416
Dorian De Long Arts and Music Scholarship • 1335
Doris and Clarence Glick Classical Music Scholarship • 1336
Dorothy Budnek Memorial Scholarship • 862
Dorothy D. Greer Journalist of the Year Scholarship Competition • 1337
Dorothy M. and Earl S. Hoffman Award • 863
DoSomething Monthly Scholarships • 127
Douglas Dockery Thomas Fellowship in Garden History and Design • 864
Douvas Memorial Scholarship • 1338
Dr. and Mrs. Arthur F. Sullivan Fund • 1339
Dr. Bart Kamen Memorial FIRST Scholarship • 865
Dr. Edison and Sallie Miyawaki Scholarship Fund • 1340
Dr. Esther Wilkins Scholarship • 866
Dr. Hans and Clara Zimmerman Foundation Education Scholarship • 1341
Dr. Hans and Clara Zimmerman Foundation Health Scholarships • 1342
Dr. Ivy M. Parker Memorial Scholarship • 2133
Dr. Jack G. Shaheen Media Scholarship • 569
Dr. James Earl Kennamer Scholarship • 128
Dr. James L. Lawson Memorial Scholarship • 570
Dr. Juan Andrade, Jr. Scholarship • 2134
Dr. Kenny D. Hasija Scholarship • 417
Dr. Ralph E. White Graduating Senior Scholarship • 1343
Dr. Robert Hawkins Memorial Scholarship • 571
Dr. William S. Boyd Scholarship • 1344
Drs. James and Wanda Trefil Science Scholarship • 2135
Duane Buckley Memorial Scholarship • 2291
Duane M. Hanson Scholarship • 867
Duke Award Scholarship • 1345
Dumbarton Oaks Fellowships • 418
Dutch and Ginger Arver Scholarship • 868
Dwight D. Gardner Scholarship • 869
Dwight F. Davis Memorial Scholarship • 129
Dwight Mosley Scholarship Award • 130
Dyslexia/Auditory Processing Disorder Scholarship • 2292
Eagle Scout Scholarship • 1250
E-waste Scholarship • 131

The Ultimate Scholarship Book 2026
Scholarship Name Index

E. Noel Luddy Scholarship • 870
E.H. Marth Food Protection and Food Science Scholarship • 1346
E.J. Sierleja Memorial Fellowship • 871
Eagle Scout of the Year • 1347
Earl Anthony Memorial Scholarships • 132
Earl Warren Scholarship • 572
Early Childhood Educators Scholarship • 1348
Early College for ME • 1349
Eco-Warrior Scholarship • 133
Ecolab Scholarship Competition • 573
Ed and Charlotte Rodgers Scholarships • 1350
Ed Bradley Scholarship • 574
Edie Windsor Coding Scholarship • 2136
Edith Nourse Rogers STEM Scholarship • 134
Edmond A. Metzger Scholarship • 575
Edmund F. Maxwell Foundation Scholarship • 1351
EDSA Diversity Scholarships • 2137
Education Accessibility Scholarship • 135
Education Scholarship • 2138
Education Support Award • 2139
Educational Advancement Foundation Merit Scholarship • 136
Educational Award/Graduating High School Female • 1352
Educational Excellence Scholarship • 1353
Educational Foundation Scholarship • 576
Educational Opportunity Fund (EOF) Grant • 1354
Educational Theatre Association Board of Directors Scholarship • 419
Educational Training Voucher Programs for Foster Youth • 1355
Educator Support Scholarship • 1356
Educators for Maine Program • 1357
Edward D. Hendrickson/SAE Engineering Scholarship • 872
Edward L. Simeth Scholarships • 1358
Edward Payson and Bernice Piilani Irwin Scholarship • 1359
EGIA Foundation Scholarship Program • 577
Eight and Forty Lung and Respiratory Nursing Scholarship Fund • 873
Eizo and Toyo Sakumoto Trust Scholarship • 1360
Elekta Radiation Therapy Scholarship • 874
Elizabeth McLean Memorial Scholarship • 875
Elizabeth Nash Foundation Scholarship Program • 2293
Ellison Onizuka Memorial Scholarship Fund • 1361
Elmer J. and Hester Jane Johnson Memorial FFA Scholarship • 876
Elson T. Killam Memorial Scholarship • 877
Emergency Educational Fund Grants • 1965
Emily M. Hewitt and Stephen K. Stocking Memorial Scholarship • 1362
Emmett J. Doerr Memorial Scout Scholarship • 1966
EmPOWERED Scholars Program • 878
ENA Foundation Undergraduate Scholarship • 879
EngineerGirl Essay Contest • 880
Engineering Foundation of Wisconsin Scholarship • 1363
Engineering Undergraduate Scholarship • 881

Engineers Foundation of Ohio General Fund Scholarship • 1364
EOD Warrior Foundation Scholarship • 137
Eon Essay Contest • 138
Epsilon Sigma Alpha • 1365
Equitable Excellence Scholarship • 139
Equity in Pharmacy Scholarship • 882
ERC Eco Scholarship Fund • 1366
Eric Dostie Memorial College Scholarship • 2294
Esther Kanagawa Memorial Art Scholarship • 1367
Ethnic Minority and Women's Enhancement Scholarship • 140
Eugene and Elinor Kotur Scholarship Trust Fund • 2140
Eugene C. Beach Memorial Scholarship • 1967
Eugene S. Kropf Scholarship • 883
Eve Kraft Education and College Scholarship • 141
Executive Women International Scholarship Program • 578
Exemption for Highest Ranking High School Graduate • 1368
Exemption for Texas Veterans (Hazelwood Exemption) • 1369
Exemption from Tuition Fees for Dependents of Kentucky Veterans • 1370
ExploraVision National Science Competition • 884
Expressions Challenge by Walgreens • 420
F. Koehnen Ltd. Scholarship Fund • 1371
F.W. Beich Beichley Scholarship • 885
Fadel Educational Foundation Annual Award Program • 1968
Families of Freedom Scholarship Fund • 142
Family District 1 Scholarships • 1372
Farm Credit Services of America Collegiate Scholarship • 1969
FarmAid FFA Scholarship • 886
Fashion Scholarship Fund Scholarships • 421
Father James B. Macelwane Annual Award in Meteorology • 887
Federal Junior Duck Stamp Program and Scholarship Competition • 422
FEEA Scholarship Program • 1970
Feeding Tomorrow General Education Scholarships/Freshman Scholarships • 888
Fellowship Award • 889
Fellowship in Aerospace History • 890
Fellowship on Women and Public Policy • 1373
Fellowships for Regular Program in Greece • 423
Fellowships/Grants to Study in Scandinavia • 424
FFTA Scholarship Competition • 425
Fields of Learning Scholarship • 1374
Finlandia Foundation National Student Scholarships Program • 426
First Cavalry Division Foundation Scholarship • 143
First Generation Matching Grant Program • 1375
First in the Family Scholarship • 1971
First-Year Teacher Scholarships • 1376
Fleet Reserve Association Scholarship • 1972
Florence Young Memorial Scholarship • 2141
Florida Bright Futures Scholarship Program • 1377
Florida Engineers in Construction Scholarship • 1378
Florida Governor's Black History Month Essay Contest • 1379

Florida Oratorical Contest • 1380
Florida Student Assistance Grant Program • 1381
FMAA Scholarship Program • 144
FMC Skaters Scholarship • 145
FMS Solutions Holdings LLC Legacy Scholarship • 579
FOARE Scholarship Program • 580
Folds of Honor Higher Education Scholarship • 146
Ford Motor Company Fund and Ford Trucks Built Ford Tough - FFA Scholarship Program • 1973
Ford Opportunity Program • 1382
Foreclosure Scholarship Program • 147
Foster Child Grant Program • 1383
Foundation for Surgical Technology Medical Mission Scholarship • 891
Foundation for Surgical Technology Scholarships • 892
Foundation Scholarships • 2142
Four-year or Bachelor's Degree Program • 1384
Four-Year Undergraduate Scholarships • 1385
Fourth Degree Pro Deo and Pro Patria Scholarships • 1974
Frame My Future Scholarship Contest • 427
Frances Koop Parsons/AT&T Pioneers Memorial Scholarship • 1386
Frances L. Macartney Porter Fund • 1387
Francis X. Crowley Scholarship • 581
Frank and Brennie Morgan Prize for Outstanding Research in Mathematics by an Undergraduate Student • 893
Frank and Dorothy Miller ASME Auxiliary Scholarships • 894
Frank M. Coda Scholarship • 582
Frank S. Land Scholarships • 1975
Fraternal Order of Eagles Memorial Foundation • 148
Fred M. Young, Sr./SAE Engineering Scholarship • 895
Fred R. McDaniel Memorial Scholarship • 583
Fred Scheigert Scholarships • 2295
Frederic G. Melcher Scholarship • 584
Freshman Undergraduate Scholarship • 896
Friends of the California State Fair Scholarship Program • 1388
Frontline Families Scholarship • 2143
FTEE Scholarship: Undergraduate Major in Technology and Engineering Education • 585
Fulbright Grants • 149
Full Circle Scholarship • 2144
Full-Time Employee Student Scholarship • 897
Fund for American Studies Internships • 586
Future Counselors of America Scholarship • 587
Future Journalism Teacher Scholarship • 588
Future Leader Scholarship • 898
Future Ready Iowa Grant • 1389
Future Ready Iowa Last-Dollar Scholarship • 1390
Future Theatre Educator Scholarship • 428
Future Without Speciesism Cash Award • 150
Gabriel A. Hartl Scholarship • 899
Gaige Fund Award • 900
Gamma Mu Scholarships Program • 2145
Gamma Theta Upsilon-Geographical Honor Society Scholarships • 589
Garland Duncan Scholarships • 901

Garmin Scholarship • 902
Gary Wagner, K3OMI, Scholarship • 903
Gary Yoshimura Scholarship • 590
Gaston/Nolle Scholarships • 1976
Gates Scholarship • 2146
GBT Student Observing Support (SOS) Program • 904
GCSAA Legacy Awards • 1977
GCSAA Scholars Competition • 905
GE-Reagan Foundation Scholarship Program • 151
GEAR UP Idaho Scholarship 3 • 1391
GEM MS Engineering Fellowship Program • 2147
Gene Carte Student Paper Competition • 152
General Assembly Merit Scholarship • 1392
General Henry H. Arnold Education Grant Program • 153
General James H. Doolittle Scholarship • 906
General Society of Mayflower Descendants (GSMD) Scholarship • 2148
Generation Google Scholarship • 2149
GeneTex Scholarship Program • 907
Geneva Rock Scholarship • 908
Gentlemen Showcase • 2150
George A. Hall / Harold F. Mayfield Grant • 909
George A. Strait Minority Scholarship • 591
George and Donna Nigh Public Service Scholarship • 1393
George Choy Memorial/Gay Asian Pacific Alliance (GAPA) Scholarship • 2151
George H. Nofer Scholarship for Law and Public Policy • 2296
George Heller Memorial Scholarship Fund of the SAG-AFTRA Foundation • 1978
George Mason Business Scholarship Fund • 1394
George Montgomery/NRA Youth Wildlife Art Contest • 154
George S. and Stella M. Knight Essay Contest • 155
Georgia HOPE GED Grant • 1395
Georgia HOPE Grant • 1396
Georgia Oratorical Contest • 1397
Georgia Press Educational Foundation Scholarships • 1398
Georgia Thespians Achievement Scholarships • 1399
Georgia Tuition Equalization Grant • 1400
Gertrude Cox Scholarship For Women In Statistics • 910
Gift for Life Scholarships • 156
Gilbert Matching Student Grant • 1401
Gilbreth Memorial Fellowship • 911
Giles Sutherland Rich Memorial Scholarship • 592
Gilman International Scholarship • 429
Giuliano Mazzetti Scholarship • 912
Gladys Anderson Emerson Scholarship • 913
Glass, Molders, Pottery, Plastics and Allied Workers Memorial Scholarship Fund • 1979
Glenn Miller Scholarship Competition • 430
Global Citizen Scholarship • 157
Gloria Barron Prize for Young Heroes • 158
Gloria Barron Wilderness Society Scholarship • 914
GMR Transcription Academic Scholarship • 159
GNC Nutritional Research Grant • 160

Go City Education Scholarship • 161
GoFoodservice Scholarship • 593
Goldberg-Miller Public Finance Scholarship • 594
Golden Apple Scholars of Illinois (Illinois Scholars Program) • 1402
Golden Door Scholars • 162
Golden Key Graduate Scholar Award • 1980
Golden Key Outstanding Member Award • 1981
Golden Key Undergraduate Achievement Award • 1982
Golden Key Undergraduate Achievement Scholarship • 1983
Golden LEAF Scholars Program - Two-Year Colleges • 1403
Goldie Bateson Scholarship • 2152
Good Eats Scholarship Fund • 1404
Google SVA Scholarship • 163
Gordon Rankin Corrosion Engineering Scholarship • 915
Gorgas Scholarship Competition • 1405
Governor Guinn Millennium Scholarship Program • 1406
Governor's Cup Scholarship • 1407
Governor's Distinguished Scholarship • 1408
GPB Art Harris Scholarship • 1409
Graduate Research Award (GRA) • 916
Graduate Research Fellowship Program • 917
Graduate Research Grant - Master and Doctoral • 164
Graduate Scholarship Program • 595
Graduate Scholarships • 918
Graduate Student Research Grants • 919
Graduate Student Scholarship • 920
Graduate Summer Student Research Assistantship • 921
Graduate Tuition Waiver • 1410
Graeme Clark Scholarship • 2297
Granville P. Meade Scholarship • 1411
Great Khalid Performing Arts Scholarship • 431
Great Scholarship Program • 596
Greater Kanawha Valley Foundation Scholarship Program • 1412
Green Voice Design Competition • 922
Greenhouse Scholars Scholarship • 1413
Grossman Scholarship • 1414
Grow Ag Leaders Scholarship • 923
Guistwhite Scholarships • 1984
Gump and Ayers Scholarship • 1415
Guthrie-Koch PKU Scholarship • 2298
Guy M. Wilson Scholarship • 1416
Gwendolyn S. Cruzat MLA Scholarship • 597
H and P Veterans Helping Veterans Scholarship • 165
H-E-B Scholarships for UIL Participants • 1417
H. U. Lee Scholarship • 166
H. W. Almen/West OKC Rotary Scholarship • 1418
H.L. Taylor Scholarship Program • 1419
H.M. Muffly Memorial Scholarship • 1420
H.P. Bud Milligan Aviation Scholarship • 924
Hagan Scholarship • 167
Hamilton Award • 168
Hanscom Air Force Base Spouses' Club Scholarship • 169
Harold and Inge Marcus Scholarship • 925
Harold Bettinger Scholarship • 926

Harrell Family Fellowship • 598
Harriet Hayes Austin Memorial Scholarship for Nursing • 1421
Harry A. Applegate Scholarship • 599
Harry Alan Gregg Foundation Grants • 1422
Harry Barfield KBA Scholarship Program • 1423
Harry J. Harwick Scholarship • 927
Harry S. Truman Research Grant • 600
Hattie Tedrow Memorial Fund Scholarship • 1424
Hawaii Community Foundation Scholarships • 1425
Hawaii High School Athletic Association Hall of Honor • 1426
Hawaii Pizza Hut Scholarship Fund • 1427
Hawaii Rotary Youth Foundation Scholarship • 1428
Hawaii Society of Certified Public Accountants Scholarship Fund • 1429
HBCU NREI Scholarship • 2153
HD Hogan Rodeo Scholarship • 170
Health Careers Scholarship • 928
Health Professions Pre-Graduate Scholarship Program • 2154
Health Professions Preparatory Scholarship Program • 2155
Hedy Lamarr Achievement Award for Emerging Leaders in Entertainment Technology • 432
Heinlein Society Scholarship Program • 433
Heisman High School Scholarship • 171
Helen B. and Lewis E. Goldstein Scholarship Fund • 1985
Helen C. Evans Scholarship • 929
Helen Gee Chin Scholarship Foundation Scholarship • 172
Helene M. Overly Memorial Graduate Scholarship • 2156
Help America Hear Scholarship • 2299
Helping Heroes Grant • 1430
Henry A. Zuberano Scholarship • 1431
Henry Adams Scholarship • 930
Henry Belin du Pont Dissertation Fellowship • 601
Henry Sachs Foundation Scholarship • 1432
Henry Salvatori Scholarship • 2157
Herb Alpert Young Jazz Composer Awards • 434
Herb It Forward Scholarship • 1433
Herbert Hoover Research Travel Grant Award • 602
Herbert Hoover Uncommon Student Award • 1434
Herbert Lehman Education Fund Scholarship • 2158
Herbert Levy Memorial Scholarship • 931
Herblock Award for Editorial Cartoon • 435
Herman J. Smith Scholarship • 1435
Herman Sani Scholarship • 1436
Hermine Solt Student Scholarship • 1437
Hertz Foundation's Graduate Fellowship Award • 932
Hideko and Zenzo Matsuyama Scholarship Fund • 1438
High School Scholarship • 173
High School Senior Essay Contest • 1439
High Technology Scholar/Intern Tuition Waiver • 1440
Higher Education Academic Scholarship Program (Bright Flight) • 1441

The Ultimate Scholarship Book 2026
Scholarship Name Index

Higher Education Adult Part-Time Student (HEAPS) Grant Program • 1442
Higher Education Legislative Plan (HELP) • 1443
HIMSS Foundation Scholarship • 933
Hispanic Heritage Youth Awards • 2159
Hispanic Scholarship Fund • 2160
Hispanic Serving Institutions Scholarship • 2161
Historically Black College and University Scholarship • 2162
Hites Transfer Scholarship • 1986
HIV-Positive Scholarship • 2300
Ho'omaka Hou - A New Beginning Fund • 1444
Hoard's Dairyman FFA Scholarship • 1987
Holly A. Cornell Scholarship • 934
Homeschoolers' Support Association Scholarship • 1445
Honeywell International Inc. Scholarships • 2163
Honorable William Conner Writing Competition • 603
Honors Award • 1446
HOPE Scholarship Program • 1447
Hopi Scholarship Program • 2164
Horatio Alger Career and Technical Scholarship • 604
Horatio Alger National Scholarship Program • 174
HospitalityMaine Scholarship • 1448
Houston Livestock Show and Rodeo Scholarships • 1449
Houzz Women in Architecture • 935
Howard Coughlin Memorial Scholarship Fund • 1988
Howard P. Rawlings Educational Assistance (EA) Grant • 1450
Howard P. Rawlings Guaranteed Access (GA) Grant • 1451
HSC Foundation Scholarship • 2165
Hsiao Memorial Social Sciences Scholarship • 2166
Hubertus W.V. Wellems Scholarship for Male Students • 2167
Hugh A. Smith Scholarship Fund • 1452
Humane Studies Fellowship: Flexible Support for PhD Students • 175
Humane Studies Fellowship: Graduate Sabbatical Grants • 176
Humane Studies Fellowship: Publication Accelerator Grants • 605
Huntington Fellowships • 606
Huntington-British Academy Fellowships for Study in Great Britain • 607
Hutton Junior Fisheries Biology Program • 936
IACI/NUIG Visiting Fellowship in Irish Studies • 436
IAD Foundation Scholarships • 1453
IAM Scholarship • 1989
IAPMO Essay Scholarship Contest • 177
IBTTA Foundation Scholarship Program • 937
ICCA Scholarships • 1454
ICWA Fellowship Program • 437
Ida M. Pope Memorial Scholarship • 2168
Idaho State Broadcasters Association Scholarships • 1455
IDSA Undergraduate and Graduate Scholarships • 438
IEA Founders College Scholarship Awards • 178
IEA Zone Specific Scholarships • 179

IFDA Leaders Commemorative Scholarship • 439
IFDA Student Member Scholarship • 440
IFEC Scholarships Award • 608
IFSA Foundation Scholarship Award • 1990
IFSEA Worthy Goal Scholarship • 609
IISE Council of Fellows Undergraduate Scholarship • 938
Ike Foundation Scholarship • 180
ILA Jeanne S. Chall Research Fellowship • 441
Illinois AMVETS Ladies Auxiliary Memorial Scholarship • 1456
Illinois AMVETS Ladies Auxiliary Worchid Scholarship • 1457
Illinois AMVETS Sad Sacks Nursing Scholarship • 1458
Illinois AMVETS Service Foundation Scholarship • 1459
Illinois Association for Health, Physical Education, Recreation and Dance Scholarships • 1460
Illinois Department of Children and Family Services Scholarship Program • 1461
Illinois Veteran Grant Program • 1462
Illustrators of the Future • 442
IMA Memorial Education Fund Scholarship • 610
Imagine America High School Scholarship Program • 611
In the Driver's Seat • 181
Incentive Program for Aspiring Teachers • 1463
Incight Scholarship • 2301
Incoming Freshman Scholarship • 612
Independence Excavating, A DiGeronimo Company Scholarship • 1464
Indiana Broadcasters Association College Scholarships • 1465
Indiana Golf Foundation Scholarship • 1466
Indiana Oratorical Contest • 1467
Individual Scholarship Program • 182
Induction Recognition Award • 1991
Industrial Electrochemistry and Electrochemical Engineering Division H. H. Dow Memorial Student Achievement Award • 1140
Industrial Electrochemistry and Electrochemical Engineering Student Achievement Award • 939
Industrial Metal Service Scholarship • 183
Injection Molding Division Scholarship • 940
Inspired to Teach • 1468
Institute of Electrical and Electronics Engineers Life Members' Fellowship in Electrical History • 941
Intellia Therapeutics - UNCF Scholarship • 2169
International College Counselors Scholarship • 184
International Facility Management Association Foundation Scholarship Program • 613
International Gas Turbine Institute Scholarship • 942
International Student Scholarship • 943
International Technology Engineering Educators Association Scholarship - FTEE/Undergraduate • 614
International Trumpet Guild Conference Scholarship • 443
International Women's Fishing Association Scholarship • 944
Intertech Foundation STEM Scholarship • 945
Iowa 4-H College Scholarships • 1469

Iowa Newspaper Association Scholarships • 1470
Iowa Oratorical Contest • 1471
Iowa PGA Foundation Charlie Burkart Scholarship • 1472
Iowa Physician Assistant Society Scholarship • 1473
Iowa Pork Foundation Scholarship • 1474
Iowa Scholarship for the Arts • 1475
Iowa Student Loan Midwest Senior Scholarship • 185
Iowa Thespian Chapter Board Senior Scholarships • 1476
Iowa Tuition Grants • 1477
Iowa Vocational-Technical Tuition Grants • 1478
IRARC Memorial, Joseph P. Rubino, WA4MMD, Scholarship • 615
Irene and Daisy MacGregor Memorial Scholarship • 946
Irene Woodall Graduate Scholarship • 947
Irving W. Cook, WA0CGS, Scholarship • 1479
ISAA Scholarship Program • 1480
ISF Policy Scholarship Program • 1992
ISIA Education Foundation Scholarship • 186
Islamic Society of North America Scholarships • 1993
Ivomec Generations of Excellence Internship and Scholarship Program • 1481
IWSH Essay Scholarship • 948
J.R. Popalisky Scholarship • 1482
Jack E. Barger, Sr. Memorial Nursing Scholarship • 1483
Jack F. Tolbert Memorial Student Grant Program • 1484
Jack Hughes Education Scholarship • 1485
Jack Kent Cooke Foundation College Scholarship Program • 187
Jack Kent Cooke Young Artist Award • 444
Jackie Robinson Foundation Scholarship Program • 2170
Jackson Laboratory Scholarship • 949
Jaime Guttenberg All Abilities Scholarship • 2302
Jaime Guttenberg Dance Scholarship • 445
James A. Turner, Jr. Memorial Scholarship • 616
James Anderson Logan Jr. and Betty Ann McFarland Logan Scholarship Fund • 1486
James B. Carey Scholarship • 1994
James B. Morris Scholarship • 1487
James Beard Foundation Scholarship • 617
James E. Breining Scholarship Award • 1995
James H. Dunn, Jr. Memorial Fellowship • 1488
James J. Burns and C.A. Haynes Textile Scholarship • 1489
James M. and Erma T. Freemont Foundation Scholarship Program • 2171
James M. and Virginia M. Smyth Scholarship • 188
James Rust Scholarship • 1996
James S. Davis Memorial Scholarship • 1490
James V. Day Scholarship • 1491
Jane Austen Society of North America Essay Contest • 189
Jane M. Klausman Women in Business Scholarship Fund • 618
Japanese American Citizens League Entering Freshman Awards • 2172
Japanese American Citizens League Graduate Awards • 2173

Scholarship Name Index

Japanese American Citizens League Law Scholarships • 2174
Japanese American Citizens League Undergraduate Awards • 2175
Jean Lee/Jeff Marvin Collegiate Scholarships • 1492
Jean Theodore Lacordaire Prize • 950
Jeannette Rankin National Scholar Grant • 2176
Jennifer C. Groot Fellowship • 619
JFLF Awards Programs • 620
Jill S. Tietjen P.E. Scholarship • 951
Jimmie L. Dean Scholarship • 1493
Jimmy A. Young Memorial Education Recognition Award • 952
Jimmy Rane Foundation Scholarships • 1494
JJ Klein Scholarship Fund • 1495
Joe Foss, An American Hero Scholarship • 1496
Joe Francis Haircare Scholarship Program • 621
Joe Perdue Scholarship • 622
Joel Polsky Academic Achievement Award • 446
Johanna Drew Cluney Fund • 1497
John and Abigail Adams Scholarship • 1498
John and Anne Clifton Scholarship • 1499
John and Elsa Gracik Scholarships • 953
John and Muriel Landis Scholarship • 954
John Bayliss Radio Scholarship • 623
John C. Bajus Scholarship • 955
John D. and Virginia Riesch Scholarship • 1500
John D. Graham Scholarship • 624
John Dawe Dental Education Fund • 1501
John F. and Anna Lee Stacey Scholarship Fund for Art Education • 447
John F. Duffy Scholarship/Grant Program • 190
John F. Kennedy Profile in Courage Essay Contest • 625
John J. McKetta Scholarship • 956
John J. Smith Graduate School Scholarship • 191
John Kelly Labor Studies Scholarship Fund • 1997
John L. Dales Scholarship Fund • 1998
John L. Imhoff Scholarship • 957
John Lennon Scholarship Competition • 448
John Mabry Forestry Scholarship and Paul Webster Forestry Scholarship • 958
John R. Lillard VAOC Scholarship • 1502
John S. Linakis Scholarship • 192
John S. Marshall Memorial Scholarship • 959
John S.W. Fargher, Jr. Scholarship • 960
John Schwartz Scholarship • 1503
John V. Wehausen Graduate Scholarship • 961
John W. McDevitt (Fourth Degree) Scholarship Fund • 1999
John W. Rogers Memorial Scholarship • 1504
John Wright Memorial Scholarship • 962
Johnny Davis Memorial Scholarship • 963
Jon C. Ladda Memorial Foundation Scholarship • 193
Jonathan Jasper Wright Award • 194
Jones-Laurence Award for Scholastic Achievement • 2000
Jose Marti Scholarship Challenge Grant • 1505
Joseph Frasca Excellence in Aviation Scholarship • 964
Joseph P. and Helen T. Cribbins Scholarship • 195
Joseph S. Rumbaugh Historical Oration Contest • 626

Judge William F. Cooper Scholarship • 1506
Judith Haupt Member's Child Scholarship • 196
Judith Resnik Memorial Scholarship • 2177
Julianne Malveaux Scholarship • 2178
Julius and Esther Stulberg International String Competition • 449
Junior Fellowships • 627
Junior Fellowships • 450
Junior Member Loyalty Scholarship • 2001
Junior Showmanship Scholarship Program • 965
Justin Dignam Memorial Scholarship • 197
K2TEO Martin J. Green, Sr. Memorial Scholarship • 628
KAB Broadcast Scholarship Program • 1507
Kansas Agricultural Aviation Association Scholarship • 1508
Kansas Career Technical Workforce Grant • 1509
Kansas Comprehensive Grants • 1510
Kansas Ethnic Minority Scholarship • 1511
Kansas Nursing Service Scholarship • 1512
Kansas Oratorical Contest • 1513
Kansas Osteopathic Medical Service Scholarship • 1514
Kansas State Scholarship • 1515
Kansas Teacher Service Scholarship • 1516
Kappa Delta Phi • 966
Karen Ann Shopis-Fox Memorial Scholarship • 1517
Karen O'Neil Memorial Scholarship • 967
Karla Girts Memorial Community Outreach Scholarship • 968
Kathern F. Gruber Scholarship Program • 198
Kathryn D. Sullivan Earth and Marine Science Fellowship • 1518
KEM Electric Cooperative Scholarships for Students Attending High School Outside the Service Area • 1519
Kemper Human Rights Education Foundation • 199
Kenneth Andrew Roe Scholarship • 969
Kenneth W. Payne Student Prize • 2179
Kentucky Tuition Grant • 1520
Kentucky Veterans Tuition Waiver Program • 1521
Kevin Child Scholarship • 2303
Kevin Higgins College Scholarship • 200
Kibbie Grant (Iowa Skilled Workforce Shortage Tuition Grant) • 1522
Kimberly-Clark Corporation Legacy Scholarship • 629
Kit C. King Graduate Scholarship Fund • 630
Kittie M. Fairey Educational Fund Scholarships • 1523
Kiwanis Children's Fund Scholarship • 2002
Knights of Lithuania Scholarship Program • 2180
Kokosing Construction Co. Scholarship • 1524
Korean Ancestry Grant • 2181
Kyutaro and Yasuo Abiko Memorial Scholarship • 2003
L. Phil and Alice J. Wicker Scholarship • 631
L.B. Cebik, W4RNL and Jean Cebik, N4TZP Memorial Scholarship • 632
La Fra Scholarship • 201
LA Tutors Innovation in Education Scholarship • 202
LabRoots Scholarship • 970

LAGRANT Scholarship Program • 2182
Lambeth Family Scholarship • 1525
Landscape Forms Scholarship in Memory of Peter Lindsay Schaudt, FASLA • 971
Language Grants • 451
Larry Whiteside Scholarship • 2183
Larry Williams Photography and AYA Photo Contest • 972
Larson Aquatic Research Support (LARS) • 973
Laura N. Dowsett Fund • 1526
Laura Ziegler Scholarship • 452
Laurel Hester Memorial Scholarship • 2184
Laurels Fund Scholarship • 633
Laurene Ann Opdyke Nursing Scholarship • 1527
Lawrence C. Fortier Memorial Scholarship • 974
Lawrence C. Yeardley Scholarship • 1528
Lawrence G. Foster Award for Excellence in Public Relations • 634
Leaders Advancing and Helping Communities Scholarship • 1529
Leaders Scholarship • 975
Leadership Essay Contest • 203
Leadership for Diversity Scholarship • 1530
LEAF Scholarships • 1531
LEAGUE Foundation Scholarship • 2185
Learner Education Women in Mathematics Scholarship • 976
Learning and Leadership Grants • 635
Lee Tarbox Memorial Scholarship • 977
Lee Thornton Scholarship • 636
Legacy Award • 2004
Legacy Scholarship for Undergraduates • 453
Legal Opportunity Scholarship Fund • 637
Legislative for Future Excellence (LIFE) Scholarship Program • 1532
Legislative Lottery Scholarships • 1533
Leiber and Stoller Scholarship for Songwriters • 454
Lemieux-Lovejoy Youth Scholarship • 1534
Leo Bourassa Scholarship • 1535
Leo H. Grether Memorial Scholarship • 1536
Lewis C. Hoffman Scholarship • 978
LexisNexis / John R. Johnson Memorial Scholarship Endowment • 638
LGBTQ+ Student Scholarship from Study.com • 2186
Liam Hood Scholarship Fund • 1537
Libbie H. Hyman Memorial Scholarship • 979
Licensed Vocational Nurse to Associate Degree Nursing Scholarship • 1538
Life Lessons Scholarship Program • 204
Light Metals Division Scholarship • 980
Lighthouse Guild Scholarships • 2304
Lila M. Van Sweringen Student Scholarship • 1539
Lillian and Arthur Dunn Scholarship • 2005
Lillian Moller Gilbreth Memorial Scholarship • 2187
Lilly Endowment Community Scholarship Program • 1540
Lily and Catello Sorrentino Memorial Scholarship • 1541
Lime Connect Pathways Scholarship for High School Seniors with Disabilities • 2305
LimNexus Scholarship • 639
Linda Craig Memorial Scholarship Presented by St. Vincent Sports Performance • 1542

Linly Heflin Scholarship • 1543
Lions International Peace Poster Contest • 455
Lisa Zaken Award For Excellence • 981
Literacy Grants • 2006
Litherland/ITEEA Scholarship • 640
Little People of America Scholarships • 2306
Live Mas Scholarship • 205
Live Your Dream Awards Program • 2188
Lloyd F. Hutt Scholarship • 1544
Loan Assistance Repayment Program Primary Care Services • 1545
Lockheed Martin STEM Scholarship Program • 982
Lockheed Martin Vocational Scholarship Program • 641
Lois Britt Pork Industry Memorial Scholarship Program • 983
Lois Livingston McMillen Memorial Fund • 1546
Long-Term Member Sponsored Scholarship • 984
Lori Rhett Memorial Scholarship • 1547
Los Alamos Employees' Scholarship • 1548
Lotte Lenya Competition • 456
Lottery Tuition Assistance Program • 1549
Lou and Carole Prato Sports Reporting Scholarship • 642
Lou Hochberg Awards • 643
Lou Manzione Scholarship • 206
Louis Agassiz Fuertes Award • 985
Louis B. Russell Scholarship • 1550
Louisiana Go Grant • 1551
Louisiana Memorial Scholarship • 1552
Lowell Loving Undergraduate Scholarship • 986
Loy McCandless Marks Scholarship in Tropical Horticulture • 987
Luce/ACLS Dissertation Fellowships in American Art • 457
Lucy Kasparian Aharonian Scholarship • 2189
Ludo Frevel Crystallography Scholarships • 988
LULAC General Awards • 2190
LULAC Honors Awards • 2191
LULAC National Scholastic Achievement Awards • 207
Luso-American Education Foundation General Youth Scholarship • 1553
Mabel Mayforth Scholarship • 1554
Mackinac Scholarship • 1555
MAES Scholarship Program • 2192
Maids of Athena Scholarships • 2007
Maine Community Foundation Scholarship Program • 1556
Maine Demolay and Pine Tree Youth Foundation Scholarships • 1557
Maine Health Professionals Loan Program • 1558
Maine State Society Foundation Scholarship • 1559
Maine Veterans Dependents Educational Benefits • 1560
Maison Law California Scholarship • 1561
MALDEF Law School Scholarship • 2193
Maley/FTEE Teacher Professional Development Scholarship • 644
Mamoru and Aiko Takitani Foundation Scholarship • 1562
Mandell and Lester Rosenblatt Undergraduate Scholarship • 989

Maple Flooring Manufacturers Association Scholarship • 645
Marcus Garvey Scholarship • 2194
Margaret A. Haines Telephony Scholarship • 2008
Margaret A. Pemberton Scholarship • 1563
Margaret A. Stafford Nursing Scholarship • 1564
Margaret Jerome Sampson Scholarship • 2009
Margaret McNamara Education Grants • 2195
Marian A. Smith Costume Award • 458
Marian Wood Baird College Scholarship • 208
MARILN Professional Scholarship Award • 1565
Marilynn Smith Scholarship • 2196
Marine Corps League Scholarships • 209
Marine Corps Scholarship Foundation Scholarship • 210
Marion Huber Learning Through Listening Awards • 2307
Marion Maccarrell Scott Scholarship • 1566
Mark Ando and Ito Family Scholarship • 2197
Markley Scholarship • 211
Marliave Fund • 990
Marlin R. Scarborough Memorial Scholarship • 1567
Marsh Scholarship Fund • 212
Marshall E. McCullough Scholarship • 991
Marshall Memorial Fellowship • 213
Marshall Scholar • 214
Martin Luther King, Jr. Memorial Scholarship • 2010
Marvin L. Zuidema Scholarship Award • 1568
Marvin Mundel Memorial Scholarship • 992
Mary Ann K. Murtha Memorial Scholarship • 1569
Mary Benevento/CTAHPERD Scholarship • 1570
Mary Bowman Arts in Activism Award • 459
Mary Church Terrell Award • 215
Mary E. Bivins Religious Scholarship • 2011
Mary Eileen Dixey Scholarship • 1571
Mary Gunther Memorial Scholarship • 2198
Mary Keith Duff Memorial Scholarship • 1572
Mary Lou Brown Scholarship • 646
Mary Macon McGuire Scholarship • 1573
Mary P. Oenslanger Scholastic Achievement Awards • 2308
Mary Paolozzi Member's Scholarship • 216
Mary Quan Moy Ing Memorial Scholarship • 2199
Mary Rhein Memorial Scholarship • 993
Mary V. Munger Scholarship • 994
Mas Family Scholarships • 2200
Mason Lighthouse Scholarship • 217
Masonic Scholarship Program • 1574
Masonry Institute of Iowa Foundation Scholarship Program • 1575
Massachusetts Community Colleges Access Grant • 1576
Massachusetts Part-Time Grant • 1577
Massachusetts Student Broadcaster Scholarship • 1578
MASSGrant • 1579
Master's, Ph.D. or Other Advanced Degree Program • 1580
Material Handling Education Foundation • 647
Materials Processing and Manufacturing Division Scholarship • 995

Math and Science Teaching Incentive Scholarships • 1581
Maureen L. and Howard N. Blitman, P.E., Scholarship • 2201
May T. Henry Scholarship Fund • 1582
MBA Fellowship • 648
MCCA Lloyd M. Johnson, Jr. Scholarship Program • 2202
MCEC Technical Scholarship • 1583
McLean Scholarship for Nursing and Physician Assistant Majors • 1584
Medallion Fund • 1585
Medgar Evers Award • 218
Media Fellows Program • 649
Medical Loan-For-Service Program • 1586
Medical Student Research Scholarship • 996
Medical Student Training in Aging Research (MSTAR) Program • 997
Medicus Student Exchange • 2203
MEFA UPlan Prepaid Tuition Waiver Program • 1587
Mellinger Scholarships • 1588
Melvin J. Schiff Fellowship Fund • 998
Melvin R. Green Scholarships • 999
Memorial Classic Golf Tournament Scholarship • 650
Memorial Fund Scholarships • 219
Memorial Scholarship Fund • 220
Mensa Foundation Scholarship Program • 221
Mental Health Importance Scholarship • 1000
Merchants Exchange of Portland Scholarship • 651
Meredith Thoms Memorial Scholarship • 1001
Meritage Homes Scholarship • 2204
Metro Youth Football Association Scholarship • 222
Mexican Scholarship Fund • 1589
MFA Foundation Scholarships • 1590
MGMA Midwest Section Scholarship • 1002
MGMA Western Section Scholarship • 1003
Michael A. Hunter Memorial Scholarship Fund • 2309
Michael Curry Summer Internship Program • 1591
Michael J. Peitz Leadership Scholarship • 460
Michael J. Quill Scholarship Fund • 2012
Michael Kidger Memorial Scholarship • 1004
Michael Moody Fitness Scholarship • 1005
Michigan Competitive Scholarship • 1592
Michigan Council of Women in Technology University Scholarship • 1593
Michigan Engineering Scholarships • 1594
Michigan Oratorical Contest • 1595
Michigan Tuition Grant • 1596
Michigan Tuition Incentive Program • 1597
Microsoft Office Specialist World Championship • 652
Mid-Continent Instruments and Avionics Scholarship • 1006
Middle School Essay Contest • 1598
Midwest Student Exchange Program • 1599
Migrant Health Scholarships • 1007
Mike and Gail Donley Spouse Scholarship • 223
Mikkelson Foundation Scholarship • 1600
Mildred C. Hanson SIOR Memorial Scholarship • 653
Mildred Towle Scholarship - Study Abroad • 1601

Mildred Towle Scholarship for African-Americans • 1602
Military Award Program (MAP) • 224
Military Family Support Trust Scholarships • 225
Millie Brother Scholarship • 2310
Milton Fisher Scholarship for Innovation and Creativity • 1603
Minnesota Academic Excellence Scholarship • 1604
Minnesota Division Izaak Walton League Scholarship • 1605
Minnesota Hockey Scholarship • 1606
Minnesota Indian Scholarship Program • 1607
Minnesota Masonic Charities Vocational Scholarship • 1608
Minnesota Oratorical Contest • 1609
Minnesota State Grant • 1610
Minorities and Women Educational Scholarship • 654
Minority Fellowship Program • 1008
Minority Fellowship Program • 655
Minority Scholarship • 1611
Minority Scholarship • 2205
Minority Scholarship Award for Physical Therapy Students • 2206
Minority Scholarship Awards for College Students • 2207
Minority Scholarship Awards for Incoming College Freshmen • 2208
Minority Serving Institution Grants • 2209
Minority Student Scholarship • 1009
Minority Teaching Fellows Program • 1612
Minority Undergraduate Retention Grant • 1613
Mississippi Association of Broadcasters Scholarship Program • 1614
Mississippi Eminent Scholars Grant (MESG) • 1615
Mississippi Scholarship • 1616
Mississippi Tuition Assistance Grant (MTAG) • 1617
Missouri 4-H Foundation Scholarships • 1618
Missouri Oratorical Contest • 1619
Missouri State Thespian Scholarships • 1620
MIT THINK Scholarship Program • 1010
Mitch Daniels Early Graduation Scholarship • 1621
Mitchell Scholarship • 1622
Modeling the Future Challenge • 1011
Modern Woodmen of America Scholarship • 2013
Molitoris Leadership Scholarship for Undergraduates • 2210
Mollie Butler Memorial Scholarship • 1012
Mometrix College Scholarship • 226
Mondelez International Legacy Scholarship • 656
Monetary Award Program (MAP) • 1623
Montana CattleWomen Scholarship • 1624
Montana University System Honor Scholarship • 1625
Montgomery GI Bill - Active Duty • 227
Montgomery GI Bill - Selected Reserve • 228
Montgomery GI Bill Tuition Assistance Top-Up • 229
Moody Research Grant • 657
Moody Scholar Program • 1626
Moody's Mega Math Challenge • 1013

Moris J. and Betty Kaplun Essay Contest • 2014
Morris K. Udall Scholarship • 2211
Mortar Board National Foundation Fellowship • 2015
Mortin Scholarship • 2016
Most Valuable Student Scholarships • 230
MSAA Scholarship Program • 1627
MSPE Kenneth B. Fishbeck, P.E., Memorial Grant • 1628
MTI Bert Krisher Memorial Scholarship • 1014
MTS Student Scholarship for Two-Year, Technical, Engineering and Community College Students • 1015
MTS Student Scholarship for Undergraduate Students • 1016
Murray Watson Jr. Scholarship • 1629
Music Committee Scholarship • 1630
Mutual of Omaha Actuarial Scholarship for Minority Students • 2212
My Action Plan for College Young Scholars Initiative • 1631
Myrtle and Earl Walker Scholarship • 1017
N.G. Kaul Memorial Scholarship • 1018
NABF Scholarship Program • 231
NACA Mid Atlantic Graduate Student Scholarship • 658
NACA Northern Plains Regional Student Leadership Scholarship • 1632
NACA South Student Leadership Scholarships • 1633
NACOP Scholarship • 232
NADCA Indiana Chapter 25 Scholarship • 1634
Nadia Christensen Prize • 461
NAHN Scholarship • 2213
Nancy Curry Scholarship • 659
Nancy McManus Washington Internship Scholarships • 660
Nancy Penn Lyons Scholarship Fund • 1635
Naomi Brack Student Scholarship • 1019
NAPA Research and Education Foundation Scholarship • 1020
NATA Scholarship • 233
Nathaniel Alston Student Achievement Award • 1636
National Academic Scholarships • 661
National and Chapter Scholarships • 2214
National Association for Surface Finishing Scholarships • 1021
National Association of Black Accountants National Scholarship Program • 2215
National Aviation Explorer Scholarships • 1022
National College Match Program • 234
National Collegiate Cancer Foundation Scholarship • 2311
National Dairy Shrine/Iager Dairy Scholarship • 1023
National Eagle Scout Association Scholarship • 2017
National Environmental Health Association Graduate Scholarship • 1024
National Federation of the Blind Scholarship • 2312
National FFA Alumni and Supporters Agricultural Education Scholarship • 1025
National FFA Combined Scholarship • 2018

National Foster Parent Association (NFPA) Youth Scholarship • 2216
National Foundation Scholarships • 662
National Garden Clubs Scholarship • 1026
National Gymnastics Foundation Men's Scholarship • 2217
National High School Poetry Contest/Easterday Poetry Award • 462
National Hispanic Health Professional Student Scholarship • 2218
National History Day Contest • 663
National Honor Society Scholarship • 2019
National Horticulture Foundation General Scholarships • 1027
National Intercollegiate Rodeo Foundation Scholarship • 235
National Italian American Foundation Scholarship • 2219
National Junior Classical League (NJCL) Scholarships • 463
National Latin Exam Scholarship • 464
National Marbles Tournament Scholarship • 236
National Merit Scholarship Program and National Achievement Scholarship Program • 237
National Oratorical Contest • 238
National Potato Council Scholarship • 1028
National Presbyterian College Scholarship • 2020
National Press Club Scholarship for Journalism Diversity • 664
National Propane Gas Foundation • 2021
National Scholarship • 2220
National Scholarship Competition for Disabled College Students • 2313
National Scholarship Program • 239
National Scholarship Program • 665
National Space Club Keynote Scholar • 1029
National Sportsmanship Award • 240
National Student Nurses' Association Scholarship • 1030
National Table Tennis Scholarship • 241
National Vocal Competition for Young Opera Singers • 465
National Washington Crossing Foundation Scholarship • 666
National Young Astronomer Award • 1031
Native American Education Grant • 2221
Native American Scholarship • 2222
NativeVision Scholarships • 2223
Naval Enlisted Reserve Association Scholarships • 242
Naval Helicopter Association Scholarship • 243
Naval Intelligence Essay Contest • 244
Navin Narayan College Scholarship • 245
Navy College Fund • 246
Navy Supply Corps Foundation Scholarship • 247
Navy-Marine Corps ROTC College Program • 248
Navy-Marine Corps ROTC Four-Year Scholarships • 249
Navy-Marine Corps ROTC Two-Year Scholarships • 250
Navy/Marine Corps/Coast Guard (NMCCG) Enlisted Dependent Spouse Scholarship • 251
NAWIC Founders' Undergraduate Scholarship • 1032

The Ultimate Scholarship Book 2026
Scholarship Name Index

NBRC/AMP Gareth B. Gish, MS, RRT Memorial and William F. Miller, MD Postgraduate Education Recognition Awards • 1033
NBRC/AMP William W. Burgin, Jr. MD and Robert M. Lawrence, MD Education Recognition Award • 1034
NCAA Division II Degree Completion Award Program • 252
NCAA Postgraduate Scholarship • 253
NCAPA Endowment Annual Student Grants • 1035
NCPA Foundation Presidential Scholarship • 1036
NCRA A to Z Scholarship • 667
NCRA CASE Student Scholarship • 668
NCRA Scholarship • 1637
NCTA and AWMF Scholarship • 2224
NCWIT Award for Aspirations in Computing • 2225
NDPRB Undergraduate Scholarship Program • 1037
NDS / Klussendorf / McKown Scholarships • 1038
NDSEG Fellowship Program • 1039
NDVA Waiver of Tuition • 1638
NEA-Retired Jack Kinnaman Memorial Scholarship • 669
Nebraska Academy of Sciences High School Scholarships • 1639
Nebraska Actuaries Club Scholarship • 1640
Nebraska Elks Association Vocational Scholarship • 1641
Ned McWherter Scholars Program • 1642
Need Based Tuition Waiver Program • 1643
NEHA/AAS/APU Scholarship Awards • 1040
Nell Bryant Robinson Scholarship • 670
Nellie Yeoh Whetten Award • 1041
NESA Hall/McElwain Merit Scholarships • 2022
NESA Lawrence S. and Mabel Cooke Scholarship • 2023
Nettie Dracup Memorial Scholarship • 671
Nevada Women's Fund Scholarships • 1644
New Century Scholars Doctoral Scholarship • 1042
New England FEMARA Scholarship • 672
New England Regional Student Program • 1645
New Face of Tech Scholarship Program • 1043
New Hampshire Charitable Foundation Statewide Student Aid Program • 1646
New Jersey Oratorical Contest • 1647
New Jersey State Elks Special Children's Committee Scholarship • 1648
New Jersey World Trade Center Scholarship • 1649
New Mexico Scholars • 1650
New York Legion Auxiliary Department Scholarship • 1651
New York Legion Auxiliary District Scholarships • 1652
New York Life Award • 466
New York Oratorical Contest • 1653
New York Ramblers Scholarship • 2226
New York State Association of Agricultural Fairs/ New York State Showpeople's Association Scholarships • 1654
New York State Society of Physician Assistants Scholarship • 1655

New York State USBC Scholarships • 1656
New York State USBC Spirit Awards • 1657
New York Women in Communications Foundation Scholarships • 1658
Newman Civic Fellow Awards • 254
Next Gen Scholars Award • 255
Next Swell Scholarship • 1044
NextGen Scholarship • 673
NFAA Scholarship Program • 256
NFMC Dorothy Dann Bullock Music Therapy Award and the NFMC Ruth B. Robertson Music Therapy Award • 1045
NFMC Gretchen E. Van Roy Music Education Scholarship • 674
NFMC Hinda Honigman Award for the Blind • 2314
NFMC Lynn Freeman Olson Composition Awards • 467
NFMC Wendell Irish Viola Award • 468
NHSC Scholarship • 1046
NIADA Scholarship • 2024
Nicholas Virgilio Haiku and Senryu Contest • 257
Nightingale Awards of Pennsylvania Scholarship • 1659
NIH Undergraduate Scholarship Program • 1047
Nissan Scholarship • 1660
NJ Student Tuition Assistance Reward Scholarship (STARS) • 1661
NJ Student Tuition Assistance Reward Scholarship II • 1662
NJCDCA Scholarship • 1663
NJSCA High School Scholarship • 1664
NMASBO High School Scholarships • 1665
NNM American Society of Mechanical Engineers Scholarship • 1666
NOAA Educational Partnership Program Undergraduate Scholarships • 2227
Non Commissioned Officers Association Scholarships • 258
Non-Traditional Student Scholarship • 2025
Norman and Ruth Good Educational Endowment • 1667
Norman S. and Betty M. Fitzhugh Fund • 1668
North American Van Lines Logistics Scholarship • 675
North Carolina 4-H Development Fund Scholarships • 1669
North Carolina Community College Grant • 1670
North Carolina Education Lottery Scholarship • 1671
North Carolina Oratorical Contest • 1672
North Dakota Career Builders Scholarship • 1673
North Dakota Dollars for Scholars • 1674
North Dakota Jaycee JCI Senate Scholarship • 1675
North Dakota Scholars Program • 1676
North Dakota Scholarship • 1677
North Dakota School Counseling Association • 1678
North Dakota State Student Incentive Grant • 1679
North Texas State Fair Association Scholarship • 1680
Northrop Grumman Scholarship • 1681
Northwestern Mutual Foundation Childhood Cancer Sibling Scholarship • 2315

Novus Biologicals Scholarship Program • 1048
NPCA Educational Foundation Scholarships • 1049
NPFDA Scholarships • 1050
NPPF Still and Multimedia Scholarship • 676
NPPF Television News Scholarship • 677
NROTC Nurse Corps Scholarship • 259
NROTC Scholarship Program • 260
NSCA Scholarship • 261
NSCS Grad School Award • 2026
Nurse Candidate Program • 1051
Nurse Corps Scholarship Program • 1052
Nurseries Foundation Award • 1053
Nursing Education Scholarship Program • 1682
Nursing Incentive Scholarship Fund • 1683
Nursing Loan-For-Service Program • 1684
Nursing Student Loan • 1685
NYWEA Major Environmental Career Scholarship • 1686
OCA/UPS Gold Mountain Scholarship • 2228
Ocean Awareness Contest • 469
Odenza Marketing Group Scholarship • 262
Office Supply Scholarship • 470
Ohio Classical Conference Scholarship for Prospective Latin Teachers • 1687
Ohio Section Scholarships • 1688
Ohio State Association/AOTF Scholarships • 1689
Ohio Turfgrass Foundation Scholarships • 1690
Oklahoma Association of Broadcasters Scholarship • 1691
Oklahoma Foundation for Excellence Academic All-State Scholarships • 1692
Oklahoma Hall of Fame Scholarship • 1693
Oklahoma Rural Rehabilitation Corporation Scholarships • 1694
Oklahoma Schools Insurance Group (OSIG) Scholarship • 1695
Oklahoma Society of Land Surveyors Scholarships • 1696
Oklahoma State Fair Inc. Scholarship Program • 1697
Oklahoma Tuition Aid Grant Program (OTAG) • 1698
Oklahoma Tuition Equalization Grant Program (OTEG) • 1699
Oklahoma Youth with Promise Scholarship Fund • 1700
Oklahoma's Promise • 1701
Olay Face the Stem Gap Scholarship • 2229
Old Guard Oral Presentation Competition • 1054
Oleg Fastovsky Outstanding Citizenship Scholarship • 263
Olive Lynn Salembier Memorial Reentry Scholarship • 2230
Oliver Joel and Ellen Pell Denny Healthcare Scholarship Fund • 1702
Oliver Moghissi Memorial Scholarship • 1055
One Family Scholars Program • 1703
Operations and Power Division Scholarship • 1056
Opportunity Award • 1704
Opportunity Grant • 1705
Opportunity Scholarships for Lutheran Laywomen • 2027
Optimist International Communications Contest • 2316

Optimist International Essay Contest • 471
Optimist International Oratorical Contest • 678
Oratorical Contest Scholarship • 1706
Oregon Army National Guard • 1707
Oregon Farm Bureau Memorial Scholarships • 1708
OROS Scholarship • 1709
Otto M. Stanfield Legal Scholarship • 679
Our First Amendment Freedoms Art and Essay Contest • 1710
Outstanding Undergraduate Researchers Award Program • 1057
Overseas Press Club Foundation Scholarships/Fellowships • 680
Owens-Bell Award • 2028
P. Buckley Moss Endowed Scholarship • 2317
P.E.O. International Peace Scholarship • 2231
P.E.O. Program for Continuing Education • 2232
P.O. Pistilli Undergraduate Scholarship for Advancement in Computer Science and Electrical Engineering • 2233
Pacific Academy Foundation Scholarship • 264
Page Education Foundation Grants • 1711
Palmetto Fellows Scholarship Program • 1712
Paradigm Challenge • 1058
Paraprofessional Teacher Preparation Grant • 1713
Paros-Digiquartz Scholarship • 1059
Part-Time Grant • 1714
Part-Time Grants • 1715
Part-Time Student Scholarship • 472
Part-Time TAP Program • 1716
Part-Time Tuition Aid Grant • 1717
Past Department Presidents' Junior Scholarship Award • 1718
Path to Pro Scholarship • 1060
Patriot's Pen Youth Essay Contest • 473
Patty and Melvin Alperin First Generation Scholarship • 1719
Pauahi Foundation Public Scholarships • 1720
Paul A. Stewart Grants • 1061
Paul and Daisy Soros Fellowships for New Americans • 265
Paul and Ellen Ruckes Scholarship • 2318
Paul and Helen L. Grauer Scholarship • 681
Paul Flaherty Athletic Scholarship • 1721
Paul S. Mills Scholarships • 682
Paulina L. Sorg Scholarship • 1722
Pauline Langkamp Memorial Scholarship • 266
Paumanauke Native American Indian Scholarship • 2234
PAVE Student Design Competition • 683
Payette Sho-Ping Chin Memorial Academic Scholarship • 1062
Payzer Scholarship • 1063
Pedro Zamora Young Leaders Scholarship • 267
Pega Scholars Program • 2235
Peggy Dixon Two-Year Scholarship • 1064
Pennsylvania American Legion Essay Contest • 1723
Pennsylvania Business Education Association Scholarship • 1724
Pennsylvania Educational Gratuity Program • 1725
Pennsylvania Land Surveyors' Foundation Scholarship • 1726
Pennsylvania Masonic Youth Foundation Scholarships • 1727

Pennsylvania Oratorical Contest • 1728
Pennsylvania Society of Tax and Accounting Professionals Scholarships • 1729
Pennsylvania State Bowling Association Scholarship Program • 1730
Pennsylvania State Grant Program • 1731
Pennsylvania Targeted Industry Program • 1732
PenSPRA Scholarship • 1733
Perennial Plant Association Scholarship • 1065
Perfect Plants Nursery Scholarship • 1066
Performing Arts Scholarship • 2236
Peter and Jody Larkin Legacy Scholarship • 684
Petroleum Division College Scholarships • 1067
PG&E Better Together STEM Scholarship Program • 1734
PGA WORKS John and Tamara Lundgren Scholars Program • 268
PHCC Educational Foundation Scholarship • 1068
PHD Scholarship • 685
Phi Delta Kappa (PDK) Educational Foundation Scholarship Program • 2029
Phi Kappa Phi Fellowship • 2030
Phoebe Pember Memorial Scholarship • 1069
Phyllis G. Meekins Scholarship • 2237
Phyllis V. Roberts Scholarship • 1735
Physician Assistant Foundation Scholarship • 1070
Pi Lambda Theta Student Support Scholarships • 686
Pilot International Scholarship • 269
Pilot Pen G2 Overachievers Student Grant • 270
Pinnacol Foundation Scholarship Program • 1736
Pioneers of Flight • 1071
PixelPlex Bi-Annual STEM Scholarship • 1072
Plan NH Scholarship and Fellowship Program • 1737
Plastics Pioneers Association Scholarships • 1073
Platt Family Scholarship Prize Essay Contest • 474
Play! Pokemon Scholarship • 271
Playwright Discovery Award • 475
Point Community College Scholarship • 2238
Point Flagship Scholarship • 2239
Polish National Alliance Scholarship • 2240
Polymer Modifiers and Additives Division Scholarships • 1074
Pony Alumni Scholarship • 272
Poster Contest for High School Students • 476
PPG Protective and Marine Coatings Academic Scholarship • 1075
Predoctoral Fellowship Program • 1076
Predoctoral Research Fellowships • 1077
Presbyterian Church USA Student Opportunity Scholarships • 2031
Presidential Scholarships • 687
Presidents Scholarship of the Institute of Industrial Engineers • 1078
Pretty Photoshop Actions Bi-annual Scholarship • 1079
Princess Grace Awards • 477
Print and Graphics Scholarship • 478
Prize in Ethics Essay Contest • 479
Prize in International Insolvency Studies • 688
Project Vote Smart National Internship Program • 689
Project Yellow Light/Hunter Garner Scholarship • 273

Prospanica Foundation Scholarships • 690
PRSA Diversity Multicultural Scholarship • 2241
PRSA-Hawai'i/Roy Leffingwell Public Relations Scholarship • 1738
Prudential Emerging Visionaries • 274
Pulse of Perseverance Scholarship • 275
Pulte Group Build Your Future Scholarship Program • 1080
Quill and Scroll Student Scholarships • 691
R&D Systems Scholarship Program • 1081
R. Flake Shaw Scholarship • 1739
R. Preston Woodruff, Jr. Scholarships • 1740
R.W. Bob Holden Scholarship • 1741
Race Entry Student Scholarship • 276
Rae Lee Siporin Award • 1742
Raftelis Leadership Scholarships • 692
Rain Bird Intelligent Use of Water Scholarship • 1082
Ralph K. Hillquist Honorary SAE Scholarship • 1083
Ranelius Scholarship Program • 1743
Raney Fund Award • 1084
RAREis Scholarship • 2319
Rawhide Scholarship • 277
Ray and Gertrude Marshall Scholarship • 693
Ray Anthony Peacock Scholarship • 1744
Ray, N0RP and Katie, W0KTE Pautz Scholarship • 694
Raymond Davis Scholarship • 1085
Raymond F. Cain Scholarship Fund • 1745
Raymond J. Faust Scholarship • 1746
Raymond T. Wellington, Jr. Memorial Scholarship • 1747
RBC Wealth Management Colorado Scholarship • 1748
Reach Higher Finish Line Scholarship • 1749
Reach Higher Montana Scholarships • 1750
RealtyHop Scholarship • 278
Rebecca Palmer Eagle Scout Scholarship Endowment • 2032
Red Boucher Scholarship • 1751
Regeneron Science Talent Search • 1086
Regional University Baccalaureate Scholarship • 1752
Reid Blackburn Scholarship • 695
Reiff Law Firm Legal Scholarship • 696
Religious Liberty Essay Scholarship Contest • 2033
Religious Studies Scholarship • 2242
RentHop's College and University Scholarship • 279
Resident Research Scholarship • 1087
Retail Chapter Award II and III • 1753
Return 2 College Scholarship • 280
Reuben Trane Scholarship • 1088
Rev. Dr. Karen Layman Gift of Hope Scholarship • 2034
RevPart STEM Scholarship • 1089
Rhode Island Foundation Association of Former Legislators Scholarship • 1754
Rhode Island Promise Scholarship • 1755
Rhodes Scholar • 281
Richard Avila Scholarship • 282
Richard D. Johnson Memorial Post-Secondary Scholarship • 1756
Richard D. Wiegers Scholarship • 1757

The Ultimate Scholarship Book 2026
Scholarship Name Index

Richard E. Bangert Business Award • 1758
Richard F. Walsh, Alfred W. DiTolla, Harold P. Spivak Foundation Award • 2035
Richard Goolsby Scholarship Fund • 1759
Richard J. Stull Student Essay Competition in Healthcare Management • 1090
Richard Jensen Scholarship • 1091
Richard L. Davis, FACMPE - Managers Scholarship • 1092
Richard L. Davis, FACMPE/Barbara B. Watson, FACMPE - National Scholarship • 1093
Richard R. Tufenkian Memorial Scholarship • 2243
Richard W. Bendicksen, N7ZL, Memorial Scholarship • 697
Ridgeline International Community Scholarship • 1094
Risk Management Association Foundation Scholarship • 698
Ritchie M. Gregory Fund • 1760
Ritchie-Jennings Memorial Scholarship • 699
RMEL Foundation Scholarships • 1095
Road to Safety Scholarship Contest • 1761
Robanna Fund • 1762
Robert B. Oliver ASNT Scholarship • 1096
Robert D. Blue Scholarship • 1763
Robert E. Thunen Memorial Scholarships • 1097
Robert G. Porter Post-Secondary Scholarships • 2036
Robert G. Porter Scholars Program for Members • 2037
Robert N. and Helen H. Herbert Undergraduate Scholarship • 1098
Robert R. Robinson Memorial Scholarship • 1764
Roberta B. Willis Scholarship - Need and Merit-Based Award • 1765
Roberta B. Willis Scholarship - Need-Based Award • 1766
Rockefeller State Wildlife Scholarship • 1767
Roger Collins Leadership Scholarship • 700
Roller Skating Foundation Scholarship, Current College Student Category • 701
Roller Skating Foundation Scholarship, High School Student Category • 283
Ron Brown Scholar Program • 2244
Ron Culp Scholarship for Mentorship • 702
Roofing Industry Scholarship - Melvin Kruger Endowed Scholarship • 1099
Rosa L. Parks Scholarships • 1768
Rosalind P. Walter College Scholarship • 284
Rosedale Post 346 Scholarship • 1769
Rosemary and Nellie Ebrie Fund • 1770
Rosewood Family Scholarship Program • 1771
Roshan Rahbari Scholarship Fund • 1772
Rover Sitter Scholarship • 285
Roy J. Shlemon Awards • 1100
Roy W. Likins Scholarship • 1773
RTNDA President's Scholarship • 703
Rubber Division Undergraduate Scholarship • 1101
Rubincam Youth Writing Competition • 286
Rudolph Dillman Memorial Scholarship • 2320
Russ Brannen/KENT FEEDS Memorial Beef Scholarship • 1774
Russel R. Taylor Foundation Scholarship • 287
Russell and Sigurd Varian Award • 1102

Ruth Abernathy Presidential Scholarship • 1103
Ruth Clark Furniture Design Scholarship • 480
Ruth D. Peterson Fellowship for Racial and Ethnic Diversity • 2245
Ruth Lilly and Dorothy Sargent Rosenberg Poetry Fellowship Program • 481
Ruth Lutes Bachmann Scholarship • 1775
Ruth Segal Scholarship • 704
RV Learning Center Scholarship Program • 1104
S. Frank Bud Raftery Scholarship • 2038
Safety Essay Contest • 1776
Sahara Hope Scholarship For Women Empowered To Change The World • 2246
Salix Gastrointestinal Health Scholars Award • 2321
Sallie Mae Bridging the Dream Scholarship • 288
Salvatore J. Monte Thermoplastic Materials and Foams Division Scholarship • 1105
Sam Rose Memorial Scholarship • 2039
Samsung@First Scholars • 1777
Samuel Fletcher Tapman ASCE Student Chapter/Club Scholarship • 1106
Samuel Huntington Public Service Award • 289
Sandra Hancock Scholarship • 290
Sandra Jo Hornick Scholarship • 2040
Sara Tucker Study Grant • 482
Sarah Josephine Langstaff Memorial Scholarship • 291
SASS Scholarship Foundation Scholarships • 292
Schlutz Family Beef Breeding Scholarship • 1778
Schneider-Emanuel American Legion Scholarship • 1779
Scholars for Excellence in Child Care • 1780
Scholars Helping Collars Scholarship • 293
Scholarship America Dream Award • 294
Scholarships for Academic Excellence • 1781
Scholarships for Military Children • 295
Scholarships for Student Leaders • 296
Scholarships for Survivors • 2322
Scholarships in Mathematics Education • 1782
Scholastic Art and Writing Portfolio Award • 483
Scholastic Honors Team • 297
Schonstedt Scholarship in Surveying • 1107
Schwan's Food Service Scholarship • 705
Science Ambassador Scholarship • 1108
ScienceSaves Video Scholarship Contest • 1109
Scott Hamilton Skaters Education Fund • 298
Seabee Memorial Scholarship • 299
SEE Education Foundation Scholarships • 1110
Senator Patricia K. McGee Nursing Faculty Scholarship • 1783
Senatorial Scholarship • 1784
Senior Fellowship Program • 484
Sertoma Communicative Disorders Scholarship • 1111
Sertoma Scholarship for Students Who Are Hard of Hearing or Deaf • 2323
Service Employees International Union Scholarships • 2041
SGT Felix M. Del Greco, Jr. Memorial Scholarship • 1785
Shari Simon Greenberg Community Scholarship • 300
Sharon D. Banks Memorial Undergraduate Scholarship • 2247

Sharon Stephens Brehm Undergraduate Psychology Scholarships • 706
Shasta Head Start Alumni Scholarship • 2042
Shawn Carter Foundation Scholarship • 707
Shawn Maree Vaillant Memorial Scholarship • 2043
Sheet Metal Workers' International Scholarship Fund • 2044
Shell Associate Scholarship Program • 708
Sheryl A. Horak Memorial Scholarship • 301
Shields-Gillespie Scholarship • 709
Shipley Rose Buckner Memorial Scholarship • 1786
Shirley McKown Scholarship Fund • 1787
Shook Construction Harry F. Gaeke Memorial Scholarship • 1788
SHPE Scholarship Program • 2248
Shropshire Scholarship • 2045
Shuichi, Katsu and Itsuyo Suga Scholarship • 1789
Sigma Phi Alpha Undergraduate Scholarship • 1112
Sigma Phi Epsilon Balanced Man Scholarship • 2046
Sioux Falls Area Retired Teachers Scholarship • 1790
Sir Cyril Taylor Legacy Scholarship • 302
Sir John Soane's Museum Foundation Traveling Grant • 1113
Sister Helen Marie Pellicer Scholarship • 1791
Sister Mary Petronia Van Straten Scholarship for Pre-Service Teachers • 1792
Six Meter Club of Chicago Scholarship • 1793
Sloane Stephens Doc and Glo Scholarship • 303
Smart Choices Scholarship Program • 1794
SMART Scholarship • 1114
SMART Scholarship • 1115
Smith Diversity Scholarship • 1795
Smith Scholarship Program • 1796
SmithGroup J.E.D.I. Scholarship • 1116
SNMTS Paul Cole Scholarship • 1117
Society of American Military Engineers, Albuquerque Post Scholarship • 1797
Society of Exploration Geophysicists (SEG) Scholarship • 1118
Society of Manufacturing Engineers Directors Scholarship • 1119
Society of Plastics Engineers (SPE) Foundation Scholarships • 1120
Society of Vacuum Coaters Foundation Scholarship • 1121
Sodexo Stephen J. Brady STOP Hunger Scholarship • 304
Soliant's Sunrise Scholarship • 305
Sons of Italy Grand Lodge of California Italian Language Study Grant • 1798
Sons of Italy Grand Lodge of College Scholarship • 1799
Sons of Union Veterans of the Civil War Scholarships • 306
Soozie Courter Hemophilia Scholarship Program • 2324
South Carolina Farm Bureau Foundation Scholarships • 1800
South Carolina Hope Scholarship • 1801
South Carolina Nurses Foundation Nurses Care Scholarship • 1802

South Carolina Tuition Grants Program • 1803
South Dakota Free Tuition for Veterans and Others Who Performed War Service • 1804
Southern Region/Elmer Stailing Scholarship • 307
Southern Scholarship Foundation Scholarship • 1805
SpeakOUT's LGBTQ+ Scholarship • 2249
Specialty Equipment Market Association (SEMA) Memorial Scholarship • 710
SPIE Optics and Photonics Education Scholarship • 1122
Spillman-Bischoff Scholarship • 1806
Spirit of Giving Scholarship • 308
Spirit of Youth Scholarship for Junior Members • 2047
Spring Meadow Proven Winners Scholarship • 1123
SPS Future Teacher Scholarship • 711
SPS Leadership Scholarships • 1124
St. Andrew's Society of Washington, DC Scholarship • 2250
Stamps Scholars • 309
Stanfield and D'Orlando Art Scholarship • 2048
Stanley A. Doran Memorial Scholarship • 2049
Stanley O. McNaughton Community Service Award • 1807
Stanley Z. Koplik Certificate of Mastery Tuition Waiver Program • 1808
Stantec Equity and Diversity Scholarship • 2251
Starfleet Scholarships • 2050
State Employees Association of North Carolina (SEANC) Scholarships • 1809
State Need-based Grants • 1810
State of Hawai`i B Plus Scholarship • 1811
State of Maine Grant Program • 1812
State of the Arts Scholarship • 485
State Work Study • 1813
Steel Intern Scholarships • 1125
Steinman Scholarship • 1126
Stella Blum Research Grant • 486
STEM Scholarship • 2252
STEM Scholarship Program • 1127
Stephanie Carroll Memorial Scholarship • 1128
Stephen D. Pisinski Memorial Scholarship • 712
Stephen Phillips Memorial Scholarship Fund • 1814
Steps For Change Scholarship • 310
Sterling Scholar Awards of Utah • 1815
Steve Fasteau Past Presidents' Scholarship • 1816
Steven G. King Play Environments Scholarship • 1129
Steven J. Finkel Service Excellence Scholarship • 713
Stillman Kelley/Thelma Byrum Awards • 487
Stokes Educational Scholarship Program • 311
Stossel in the Classroom Essay Contest • 312
Stossel in the Classroom Video Contest • 313
Striving Solo Parent Scholarship • 2253
Structural Materials Division Scholarship • 1130
Stuart Cameron and Margaret McLeod Memorial Scholarship • 714
Stuck at Prom Scholarship • 314
Student Academy Awards Competition • 488
Student Activist Awards • 315
Student Award Program of FSD • 2325
Student Cash Grant Program • 1131

Student CTA (SCTA) Scholarship in Honor of L. Gordon Bittle • 2051
Student Design Competition • 489
Student Incentive Grants • 1817
Student Paper Competition • 316
Student Poster Session Awards • 1132
Student Research Fellowship Awards • 1133
Student Research Scholarships • 1134
Student Success Grants • 715
Student Translation Award • 490
Student Video Contest • 317
Student View Scholarship • 318
Student with a Disability Scholarship • 716
StudentCam Competition • 319
Study Abroad Europe Scholarship • 491
Study.com College Scholarship for Homeschool Students • 320
Study.com Community College Student Scholarship • 321
Study.com Online Graduate Degree Scholarship • 322
Study.com Online Undergraduate Degree Scholarship • 323
Study.com Scholarship for Black Students • 2254
Study.com Scholarship for Business Students • 717
Study.com Scholarship for Children of First Responders • 324
Study.com Scholarship for Military Members and Veterans • 325
Study.com Scholarship for Military Spouses and Children • 326
Study.com Scholarship for Moms • 2255
Study.com Scholarship for Nontraditional Students • 327
Study.com Scholarship for Transfer Students • 328
Study.com Scholarship for Women in STEM • 2256
Study.com Single Parent Scholarship • 2257
Subic Bay-Cubi Point Scholarship • 329
Summer Undergraduate Research Fellowships • 1135
Sunflower Initiative Scholarship • 2258
SuperCollege Scholarship • 330
Supplemental Education Grant (SEG) • 331
Susan Bunch Memorial Scholarship • 1818
Susan Howard Community Service Award • 1819
Susan Miszkowicz Memorial Scholarship • 1136
Susan Thompson Buffett Foundation Scholarship Program • 1820
Susanna and Lucy DeLaurentis Charitable Foundation Memorial Scholarships • 2326
Sussman-Miller Educational Assistance Award • 1821
Sutliff and Stout Law School Scholarship • 718
SWE Past Presidents Scholarship • 2259
Sweet Karen Alumni Scholarship • 332
T. Eugene Young Montana's Promise Scholarship • 1822
TACTYC Accounting Scholarship • 719
Tailhook Educational Foundation Scholarship • 333
Taiwanese American Scholarship Fund • 2260
Talent Incentive Program Grant • 1823
Tall Club International Scholarship • 2052
Tampa Bay Buccaneers Foundation Girls in Football Scholarship • 334

Tampax Flow It Forward Scholarship • 2261
Tattoo Journal Ink Scholarship • 335
Tau Beta Pi Scholarships • 2053
Tau Beta Pi/Society of Automotive Engineers Engineering Scholarship • 1137
Taylor/Blakeslee University Fellowships • 492
TE Connectivity African Heritage Scholarship • 2262
Teacher Education Scholarship Fund • 720
Teacher Loan Program • 1824
Teacher Loan-For-Service Program • 1825
Teacher of the Year Award • 721
Teacher Scholarship Program • 1826
Teacher Shortage Employment Incentive Program • 1827
Tech High School Alumni Association/W.O. Cheney Merit Scholarship • 1828
Technical Certification Scholarship • 1829
Technology Addiction Awareness Scholarship • 336
Ted and Holly Rollins Scholarship • 1138
Ted and Nora Anderson Scholarships • 1830
Ted and Ruth Neward Scholarship • 1139
Ted Brickley/Bernice Shickora Scholarship • 1831
Telluride Association Summer Seminars (TASS) • 337
Tennessee Funeral Directors Association Memorial Scholarship • 1832
Tennessee HOPE Lottery Scholarship • 1833
Tennessee Student Assistance Awards • 1834
Terrel H. Bell Education Scholarship • 1835
Terrill Graduate Fellowship • 2054
Texas 4-H Opportunity Scholarship Program - Baccalaureate Scholarships • 1836
Texas Association FCCLA Regional Scholarship • 1837
Texas Broadcast Education Foundation Scholarships • 1838
Texas Elks State Association Four-Year Scholarship Program • 1839
Texas Elks State Association Teenager of the Year Scholarship • 1840
Texas Elks State Association Vocational Grant Program • 1841
Texas Fifth-Year Accounting Student Scholarship Program • 1842
Texas History Essay Scholarship • 1843
Texas International Fishing Tournament Inc. Scholarship • 1844
Texas Occupational Therapy Association Scholarships • 1845
Texas Oratorical Contest • 1846
Texas Public Educational Grant • 1847
Thaddeus Colson and Isabelle Saalwaechter Fitzpatrick Memorial Scholarship • 1848
The Fountainhead Essay Contest • 493
TheDream.US Scholarship • 2263
Thelma A. Robinson Award in Ballet • 494
Thermo Fisher Scientific Antibody Scholarship • 1141
Thermoplastic Elastomers Special Interest Group Scholarship • 1142
Thiel Fellowship Grant • 338
Think For Yourself College Scholarship Essay Contest • 339

The Ultimate Scholarship Book 2026
Scholarship Name Index

Thomas E. Powers/Detroit Section Scholarship • 1143
Thomas M. Stetson Scholarship • 1144
Thomas R. Camp Scholarship • 1145
Thurgood Marshall College Scholarship Fund • 2264
Tilford Field Studies Scholarship • 1146
Tim Olson Memorial Scholarship • 340
Timothy S. and Palmer W. Bigelow, Jr. Scholarship • 1147
Timothy S.Y. Lam Foundation Education Scholarships • 722
TLMI Two/Four Year College and Vocational Degree Program Scholarship • 723
TMC/SAE Donald D. Dawson Technical Scholarship • 1148
TMS Best Paper Contest • 1149
TMS Technical Division Student Poster Contest • 1150
TMS/International Symposium On Superalloys Scholarships • 1151
Tocris Scholarship • 1152
Tom and Judith Comstock Scholarship • 724
Tongan Cultural Society Scholarship • 1849
Tony Coelho Media Scholarship • 2327
TOPS Performance Award • 1850
TOPS Tech Award • 1851
TOPSS Competition for High School Psychology Students • 725
Towards EXcellence, Access and Success (TEXAS) Grant Program • 1852
Township Officials of Illinois Scholarship-Undergraduate Scholarship • 1853
TPA Scholarship Trust for the Hearing Impaired • 2328
Tracking Foundation Multi-Year Scholarship Program • 2265
Tracking Foundation Scholars Scholarship Program • 2266
Tractor Supply Company Endowment • 2055
Translation Prize Competition • 495
Trapshooting Hall of Fame College Scholarships • 341
Traub-Dicker Rainbow Scholarship • 2267
Treacy Foundation Scholarship • 1854
Trent R. Dames and William W. Moore Fellowship • 1153
Tri Delta Undergraduate Scholarship • 2056
Tribal College and University (TCU) Scholarships • 2268
Tricia LeVangie Green/Sustainable Design Scholarship • 496
Truckload Carriers Association Scholarship Fund • 2057
Truman D. Picard Scholarship • 2269
Truman Scholar • 342
Truth Change Maker Awards • 343
Tuition Aid Grant • 1855
Tuition Assistance Program (TAP) • 1856
Tuition Equalization Grant Program • 1857
Tuition Exchange Scholarships • 2058
Tuition Reduction for Non-Resident Nursing Students • 1858
Tuition Waiver for Foster Care Recipients • 1859
Tuskegee Airmen Scholarship Foundation Scholarships • 1154

Tuttle Construction Inc. Tiny Rauch Scholarship • 1860
Tweet Coleman Aviation Scholarship • 1861
Twenty-first Century Scholars Program • 1862
Two-year or Associate Degree Program • 1863
U.S. Bank Scholarship Program • 344
U.S. JCI Senate Scholarship Grants • 345
U.S. Lacrosse Native American Scholarships • 2270
U.S. Western Digital STEM Scholarship • 346
UAA Janice K. Barden Aviation Scholarship • 1155
UCB Family Epilepsy Scholarship Program • 2329
UCC Seminarian Scholarship • 2059
UDT-SEAL Scholarship • 347
UFCW Scholarship Program • 2060
Ukulele Festival Hawaii's College Scholarship Program • 497
UMSA Foundation Scholarship Program • 1864
UMWA-Lorin E. Kerr Scholarships • 2061
Unboxing Your Life Video Scholarship • 348
UNCF Healthcare Workforce Diversity Program Certification • 2271
Undergraduate Award for Excellence in Chemistry • 1156
Undergraduate Engineering Scholarships • 1157
Undergraduate Scholarship • 2062
Undergraduate Scholarship and Construction Trades Scholarship • 1158
Undergraduate Scholarships • 498
Undergraduate Scholarships • 1159
Undergraduate Scholarships • 2063
Undergraduate Student Research Grants: South-Central Section • 1160
Undergraduate Summer Student Research Assistantship • 1161
Undergraduate Transfer Scholarship • 349
Union Plus Scholarship • 2064
United Agribusiness League and United Agricultural Benefit Trust Scholarships • 2065
United Commercial Travelers of America (UCT) Scholarship Program • 726
United Daughters of the Confederacy Scholarships • 350
United Methodist General Scholarship • 2066
United Parcel Service Scholarship for Female Students • 1162
United Parcel Service Scholarship for Minority Students • 2272
United States Hispanic Leadership Institute Denny's Hungry for Education • 351
United States Senate Youth Program • 727
United Transportation Union Scholarships • 2067
Unitil Scholarship Fund • 1865
University Journalism Scholarships • 1866
University of California Public Policy and International Affairs Junior Summer Institute • 728
University of California Public Policy and International Affairs Law Fellowship • 729
University of the Aftermarket Foundation Scholarship • 730
Upakar Foundation Indian American Community College Scholarship • 2273
Upper Midwest Chapter Scholarships • 1867
UPS Hallmark Scholarship • 2274
Urban Fellows Program • 352
Urban Scholars Award • 1868

USA Roller Sports Scholarship Fund • 353
USA Water Ski and Wake Sports Foundation Scholarships • 354
USAR Scholarship • 355
USBC Alberta E. Crowe Star of Tomorrow • 356
USBC Annual Zeb Scholarship • 357
USBC Chuck Hall Star of Tomorrow • 358
USBC Youth Ambassador of the Year • 359
USDA/1890 National Scholars Program • 1163
USGIF Scholarship Program • 731
USMA Metric Scholarship Award • 360
Usrey Family Scholarship • 1164
Utah Association of Independent Insurance Agents Scholarship • 1869
Utah Young Humanitarian Award • 1870
Utility Workers Union of America Scholarships • 2068
VA Essay Scholarship • 361
Valedictorian Program Tuition Waiver • 1871
Vectorworks Design Scholarship • 499
Vercille Voss IFDA Graduate Student Scholarship • 500
Vermont Incentive Grants • 1872
Vermont Oratorical Contest • 1873
Vermont Sheriffs' Association Scholarship • 1874
Vern and Elaine Clark Outdoor Advertising Industry • 732
Vernon T. Swain, P.E./Robert E. Chute, P.E. Scholarship • 1875
Vertical Flight Foundation Technical Scholarships • 1165
Veterans Caucus Scholarship • 362
Veterans Tuition Awards • 1876
VFW Scout of the Year Scholarship • 2069
VHSL Achievement Award • 1877
Victoria S. and Bradley L. Geist Foundation • 1878
Vietnam Veterans' Scholarship • 1879
Vincent Chin Scholarship • 733
VIP Women in Technology Scholarship • 1166
Virginia Commonwealth Award • 1880
Virginia Daughters of the American Revolution Scholarships • 1881
Virginia Guaranteed Assistance Program • 1882
Virginia High School League Charles E. Savedge Journalism Scholarship • 1883
Virginia Part-Time Assistance Program • 1884
Virginia Sheriffs' Institute Scholarship • 1885
Virginia Tuition Assistance Grant Program • 1886
Visiting Medical Student Scholar • 1167
Visiting Senior Fellowship Program • 501
Vitality Medical's Student Disability Scholarship • 2330
VMSD Scholarship • 502
Vocational Nurse Scholarship • 1887
Voice of Democracy Audio Essay Contests • 363
Voyager Scholarship, The Obama-Chesky Scholarship for Public Service • 364
VRG Scholarship • 365
W. H. Howie McClennan Scholarship • 366
W.P. Black Scholarship Fund • 1888
Wade Trophy • 367
Waggle Human-Pet Bond Scholarship Opportunity • 368
Wallace S. and Wilma K. Laughlin Foundation Trust Scholarships • 1889
Walter B. Sinnott Scholarship • 1168

Walter Byers Graduate Scholarship • 369
Walter L. Mitchell Memorial Scholarship Awards • 2070
Warren Poslusny Award for Outstanding Achievement • 2071
Washington BPW Foundation Mature Woman Educational Scholarship • 1890
Washington College Grant • 1891
Washington Health Corps • 1892
Washington Oratorical Contest • 1893
Washington State Auto Dealers Association Bright Future Scholarship • 1894
Washington State College Bound Scholarship • 1895
Washington State Governors' Scholarship for Foster Youth • 1896
Washington State PTA Scholarship • 1897
Washington Women In Need • 1898
Watson Travel Fellowship • 370
WBCA Coaches' All-America • 371
We The Future Contest • 372
Welch Scholars Grant • 1169
Wells Fargo Scholarship Program for People with Disabilities • 2331
Wells Fargo Veterans Scholarship Program • 373
Wenderoth Undergraduate Scholarship • 2072
Werks Mobile Scholarship • 1899
Wesley-Logan Prize • 734
West Virginia Engineering, Science and Technology Scholarship • 1900
West Virginia Higher Education Grant • 1901
West Virginia PROMISE Scholarship • 1902
West Virginia PTA Scholarship • 1903
White House Fellows Program • 374
WIIT Charitable Trust Scholarship • 735
Willa S. Bellamy Scholarship • 1904
Willard H. Erwin, Jr. Scholarship • 1905
William (Bill) Ezzell Scholarship • 736
William A. Crawford Minority Teacher Scholarship • 1906
William and Charlotte Cadbury Award • 2275
William and Dorothy Ferrell Scholarship • 2332
William and Gertrude Fradkin Memorial Scholarship • 1907
William and Sara Jenne' Scholarship • 1908
William B. Ruggles Right to Work Scholarship • 737
William C. Doherty Scholarship Fund • 2073
William D. and Jewell Brewer Scholarship • 1909
William G. Saletic Scholarship • 1910
William J. Adams, Jr. and Marijane E. Adams Scholarship • 1170
William J. Goaziou Scholarship • 375
William James and Dorothy Bading Lanquist Fund • 1911
William L. Boyd, IV, Effective Access to Student Education Program • 1912
William L. Hastie Award • 376
Williams Companies Academic Scholarship • 1171
Winifred R. Reynolds Educational Scholarship • 1913
Winner's Circle Scholarships • 1914
Wisconsin Amusement and Music Operators Scholarships • 1915

Wisconsin Broadcasters Association Foundation Student Scholarship Program • 1916
Wisconsin Higher Education Grant • 1917
Wisconsin National Guard Tuition Grant • 1918
Wisconsin Oratorical Scholarship Program • 1919
Wisconsin Veterans Education Reimbursement Grants • 1920
Wisconsin Women in Government Undergraduate Scholarship • 1921
Women Band Directors International College Scholarships • 503
Women Divers Hall of Fame Scholarships and Grants • 377
Women Grocers of America (WGA) Mary Macey Scholarship • 738
Women in Aviation International Scholarship • 2074
Women In Defense WID Scholar • 2276
Women in STEM Award • 1922
Women in STEM Scholarship • 378
Women in STEM Scholarship/BHW Scholarship • 1172
Women in United Methodist History Writing Award • 2075
Women Marines Association Scholarship Program • 379
Women on Par Scholarship • 380
Women's Army Corps Veterans Association Scholarship • 381
Women's Overseas Service League Scholarships for Women • 382
Women's Scholarship • 1173
Women's Western Golf Foundation Scholarship • 383
Women's Wildlife Management/Conservation Scholarship • 1174
WomenIn Scholarship • 2277
Workforce Shortage Student Assistance Grant Program • 1923
World Trade Center Memorial Scholarship • 1924
Worthy Women's Professional Studies Scholarship • 2278
Write Your Future Scholarship • 2279
WTS Minnesota Chapter Scholarships • 1925
Wyland National Art Challenge • 504
X Society Awards Scholarship • 2280
Xello High School Scholarship • 1926
Yanmar/SAE Scholarship • 1175
YASME Foundation Scholarship • 739
You Can t Label People, but You Can Label Products Essay and Label Design Scholarship • 505
You've Got a Friend in Pennsylvania Scholarship • 1927
Young American Creative Patriotic Art Contest • 506
Young Christian Leaders Scholarship • 2076
Young Filmmakers Contest • 507
Young Scholars Program • 384
Young Women in Public Affairs Award • 2281
Youth Incentive Award • 1176
Youth of the Year Award • 2077
Youth Partners Accessing Capital • 2078
Youth Program • 1177
Youth Scholarship • 740
Zagunis Student Leader Scholarship • 1928
Zale Parry Scholarship • 385

Zell Miller Scholarship • 1929
Zicklin Contracting Restoration Awareness Scholarship • 508

The Ultimate Scholarship Book 2026
Books by SuperCollege

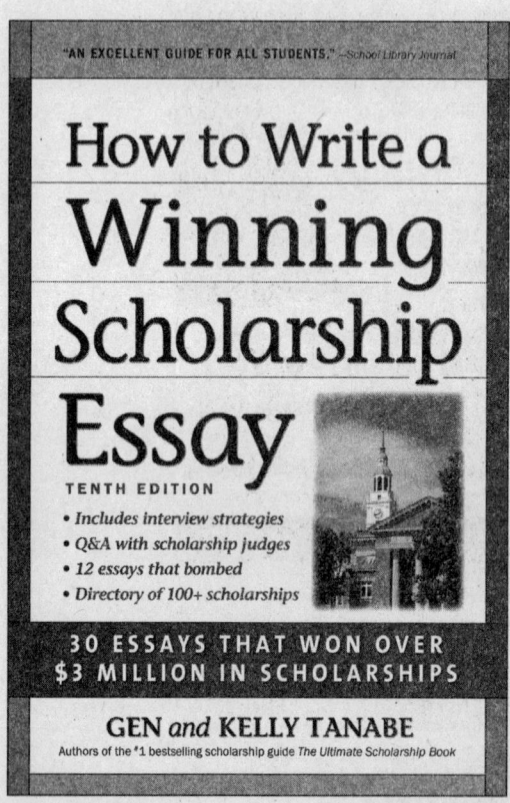

YOU WIN OR LOSE A SCHOLARSHIP WITH YOUR ESSAY AND INTERVIEW. LEARN TO ACE BOTH!

- Complete instructions on crafting a powerful scholarship essay
- 30 money-winning essays that won $3 million in scholarships
- Scholarship judges reveal what separates winners from runner-ups
- 12 essays that bombed and how to avoid these mistakes
- Master the interview with sample questions and answers

ISBN: 978-1-61760-189-7

$19.99

The Ultimate Scholarship Book 2026
Books by SuperCollege

GET THE MONEY YOU NEED TO PAY FOR COLLEGE!

- Insider tips from top scholarship winners and judges
- Secrets to writing applications and essays that win
- Where to find the best scholarships
- Techniques for maximizing your financial aid package

ISBN13: 978-1-61760-187-3

$21.99

LEARN HOW TO GET INTO THE COLLEGE OF YOUR DREAMS

- A complete, step-by-step guide to acing college applications, essays, interviews and more
- How to get free cash for college
- Tips for 9th-12th graders
- How to raise your SAT and ACT scores
- Secrets to writing an irresistible essay
- How to create a stunning application
- Tips for mastering the interview
- Proven methods for parents to give your student an edge

ISBN: 978-1-61760-188-0

$19.99

The Ultimate Scholarship Book 2026
Books by SuperCollege

WRITE THE COLLEGE ADMISSION ESSAY THAT GETS YOU IN!

- 50 successful college essays—learn from the best
- Admission officers reveal exactly what colleges want to see in your admission essays
- 25 essay mistakes to avoid
- Complete instructions on crafting a powerful essay
- How to recycle your essay to save time
- Write the essay that will get you into your dream college

ISBN13: 978-1-61760-182-8

$14.99

The Ultimate Scholarship Book 2026
Books by SuperCollege

EVERY CONCEIVABLE WAY TO PAY FOR COLLEGE

- Where to find the best scholarships
- Pay in-state tuition even if you're an out-of-state student
- Jump-start your college savings
- Get your share of the $257 billion in financial aid available
- Have your state pay for your college education
- Get your student loans forgiven
- And much, much more!

ISBN: 978-1-61760-192-7

$21.99

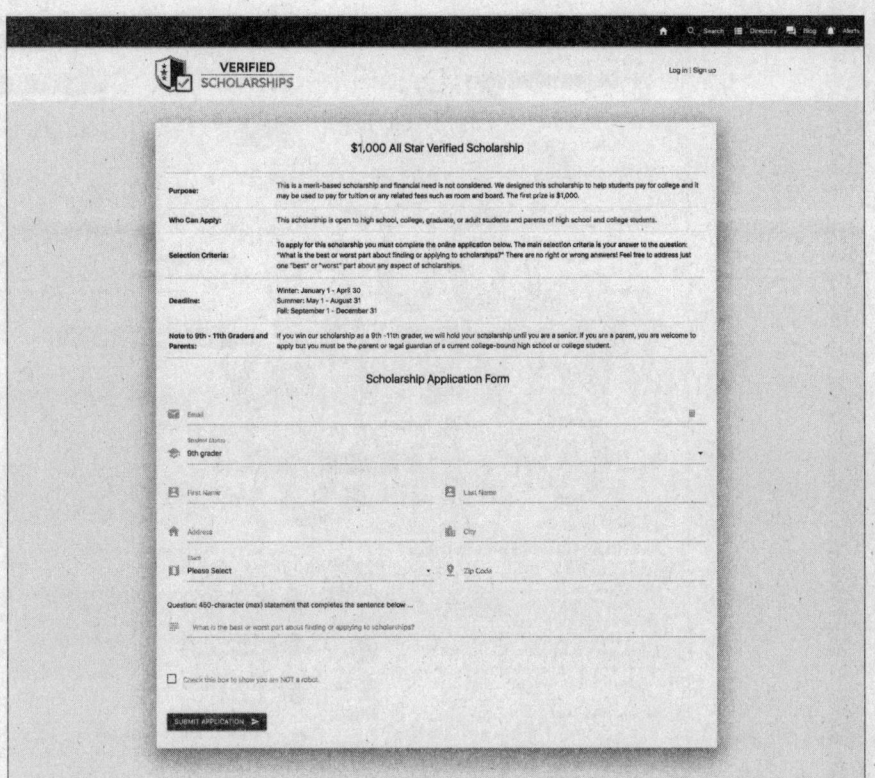

APPLY FOR THE ALL STAR VERIFIED SCHOLARSHIP

The All Star Verified Scholarship assists students with tuition or room and board. The merit-based scholarship is open to 9th-12th grade high school, college or graduate students including adult learners.

Visit **www.verifiedscholarships.com/scholarship-program** to apply.

The Ultimate Scholarship Book 2026
Books by SuperCollege

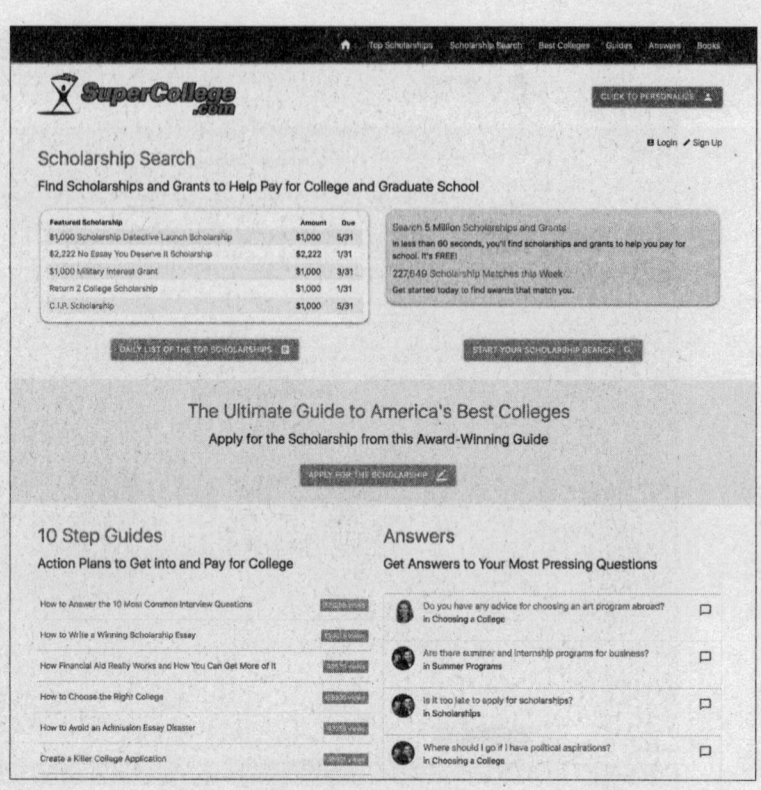

GET MORE TOOLS AND RESOURCES AT SUPERCOLLEGE.COM

Visit **www.supercollege.com** for more free resources on college admission, scholarships and financial aid. And, apply for the SuperCollege Scholarship.

The Ultimate Scholarship Book 2026
Books by SuperCollege

APPLY FOR THE GEN AND KELLY TANABE SCHOLARSHIP

The Gen and Kelly Tanabe Scholarship is a merit-based program that helps students fulfill their dreams of a higher education. The program is open to 9th-12th grade high school, college, or graduate students including adult learners. Visit **www.gkscholarship.com** to apply.

ABOUT THE AUTHORS

Harvard graduates and husband and wife team Gen and Kelly Tanabe are the founders of SuperCollege and award-winning authors of 14 books including: *Get Free Cash for College, 1001 Ways to Pay for College, How to Write a Winning Scholarship Essay, The Ultimate Guide to America's Best Colleges, Get into Any College, Accepted! 50 Successful College Admission Essays, 501 Ways for Adult Students to Pay for College* and *Accepted! 50 Successful Business School Admission Essays*.

Together, Gen and Kelly were accepted to every school to which they applied, including all the Ivy League colleges and won over $100,000 in merit-based scholarships. They were able to graduate from Harvard debt-free.

Gen and Kelly give workshops across the country and write the nationally syndicated "Ask the SuperCollege Experts" column. They have made hundreds of appearances on television and radio and have served as expert sources for *USA Today*, the *New York Times*, *U.S. News & World Report*, *New York Daily News*, *San Jose Mercury News*, *Chronicle of Higher Education*, *CNN* and *Seventeen*.

Gen grew up in Waialua, Hawaii. A graduate of Waialua High School, he was the first student from his school to be accepted at Harvard, where he graduated magna cum laude with a degree in both History and East Asian Studies.

Kelly attended Whitney High School, a nationally ranked public high school in her hometown of Cerritos, California. She graduated magna cum laude from Harvard with a degree in Sociology.

The Tanabes approach financial aid from a practical, hands-on point of view. Drawing on the collective knowledge and experiences of students, they provide real strategies students can use to pay for their education.

Gen and Kelly live in Belmont, California with their sons Zane and Kane.